D0842267

The Creeds of Christendom

The Creeds of Christendom

With a History and Critical Notes

Three Volumes ~ **Sixth Edition**

Edited by
Philip Schaff

Revised by
David S. Schaff

Volume II
The Greek and Latin Creeds

With Translations

Baker Books

A Division of Baker Book House Co
Grand Rapids, Michigan 49516

First reprinted 1983 from the 1931 edition
published by Harper and Row

Reprinted 2007 by
Baker Books
a division of Baker Publishing Group
P.O. Box 6287, Grand Rapids, MI 49516-6287

ISBN-13: 978-0-8010-8232-0
ISBN: 0-8010-8232-3
Three Volume Set

Printed in the United States of America

NOTE.

In the present edition I have added, at the close of this volume, an important document — namely, the Encyclical Letter of Pope Leo XIII., on the Christian constitution and government of States. It is closely connected with the famous Syllabus of his predecessor, Pius IX. (vol. II. pp. 213–233), and sets forth more fully the papal or mediæval theory of the relation between Church and State.

PHILIP SCHAFF.

NEW YORK, *December*, 1889.

TABLE OF CONTENTS.

(Vol. II.)

THE CREEDS OF THE GREEK AND LATIN CHURCHES.

I. SCRIPTURE CONFESSIONS.

	PAGE
Introductory	3
THE CONFESSION OF NATHANAEL	4
THE CONFESSION OF PETER	4
THE CONFESSION OF THOMAS	5
THE BAPTISMAL FORMULA	5
THE CONFESSION OF THE EUNUCH	6
ONE GOD AND ONE LORD	6
THE MYSTERY OF GODLINESS	6
THE ELEMENTARY ARTICLES	7
OTHER ALLUSIONS TO CREEDS	7

II. ANTE-NICENE AND NICENE RULES OF FAITH AND BAPTISMAL CREEDS.

Introductory Remarks	11
IGNATIUS, OF ANTIOCH. A.D. 107	11
IRENÆUS, OF GAUL. A.D. 180	12
First Formula	13
Second Formula	15
Third Formula	16
TERTULLIAN, OF NORTH AFRICA. A.D. 200	16
First Formula	17
Second Formula	17
Third Formula	19

                                                        PAGE
CYPRIAN, OF CARTHAGE.   A.D. 250 20
NOVATIAN, OF ROME.   A.D. 250 21
ORIGEN, OF ALEXANDRIA.   A.D. 230 21
GREGORY THAUMATURGUS, OF NEO-CÆSAREA.   A.D. 270 24
LUCIAN, OF ANTIOCH.   A.D. 300 25
THE PRIVATE CREED OF ARIUS.   A.D. 328 28
EUSEBIUS, OF CÆSAREA IN PALESTINE.   A.D. 325 29
CYRIL, OF JERUSALEM.   A.D. 350 31
    Longer Formula 31
    Shorter Formula 32
EPIPHANIUS, OF CYPRUS.   A.D. 374 32
    First Formula 33
    Second Formula 35
THE APOSTOLICAL CONSTITUTIONS.   A.D. 350 39
COMPARATIVE TABLE of the Ante-Nicene Rules of Faith as related to
    the Apostles' Creed and the Nicene Creed 40

III. ŒCUMENICAL CREEDS.

1. THE APOSTLES' CREED 45
    The Received Form (Eighth Century) 45
    The Old Roman Form (Fourth Century) 47
    The Forms of Aquileja, Rufinus, Fortunatus (Fourth and Fifth
        Centuries) 49
    An Old Italian Form (Fourth Century) 50
    COMPARATIVE TABLE showing the Origin and Gradual Growth
        of the Apostles' Creed 52
2. THE NICENE CREED, A.D. 325 and 381 57
    The Received Text of the Eastern Church, A.D. 381 57
    The Received Text of the Western Church 58
    The Old Nicene Symbol of 325 60
    Other Oriental Creeds of the Nicene Age 61
3. THE CREED OF CHALCEDON, A.D. 451 62
4. THE ATHANASIAN CREED 66
5. THE CREED OF THE SIXTH ŒCUMENICAL COUNCIL AGAINST THE
    MONOTHELITES, A.D. 680 72
    Remarks on the Dogmatic Legislation of the other Œcumen-
        ical Councils 73

IV. ROMAN CREEDS.

PAGE

1. The Canons and Dogmatic Decrees of the Council of Trent, A.D. 1563 77
2. The Profession of the Tridentine Faith, A.D. 1564 . . . 207
3. The Decree of Pope Pius IX. on the Immaculate Conception of the Blessed Virgin Mary, A.D. 1854 211
4. Papal Syllabus of the Principal Errors of Our Time, A.D. 1864 213
5. The Dogmatic Decrees of the Vatican Council concerning the Catholic Faith and the Church of Christ (the Infallibility of the Pope), A.D. 1870 234

V. GREEK AND RUSSIAN CREEDS.

1. The Orthodox Confession of the Eastern Church, A.D. 1643 275
2. The Confession of Dositheus, or the Eighteen Decrees of the Synod of Jerusalem, A.D. 1672 401
3. The Longer Catechism of the Russian Church, prepared by Philaret, Revised and Approved by the Most Holy Synod, A.D. 1839 445

VI. OLD CATHOLIC UNION CREEDS.

1. The Fourteen Theses of the Old Catholic Union Conference with Greeks and Anglicans, A.D. 1874 545
2. The Old Catholic Agreement on the Filioque Controversy, A.D. 1875 552
Appendix I.: Encyclical Letter of Pope Leo XIII., *Immortale Dei*, concerning the Christian Constitution of States. Nov. 1, 1885 . 555
Appendix II.: Fac-similes of the Oldest MSS. of the Athanasian Creed and the Apostles' Creed 601
Appendix III.: Boniface VIII.'s bull, *Unam sanctam*, 1302 605
Appendix IV.: Leo XIII.'s bull, *Apostolicae curae* on Anglican Orders, 1896 608
Appendix V.: Leo XIII., 1899, and Pius X., 1907–10, on 'Americanism' and 'Modernism' 610
Appendix VI.: Pius X.'s oath against 'Modernism,' 1910 613
Appendix VII.: Pius XI.'s bull, *Mortalium* on Church Union, 1928 . . . 616

CONFESSIONES ECCLESIÆ APOSTOLICÆ.

SCRIPTURE CONFESSIONS.

CONFESSIONES ECCLESIÆ APOSTOLICÆ.

SCRIPTURE CONFESSIONS.

	PAGE
INTRODUCTORY	3
THE CONFESSION OF NATHANAEL	4
THE CONFESSION OF PETER	4
THE CONFESSION OF THOMAS	5
THE BAPTISMAL FORMULA	5
THE CONFESSION OF THE EUNUCH	6
ONE GOD AND ONE LORD	6
THE MYSTERY OF GODLINESS	6
THE ELEMENTARY ARTICLES	7
OTHER ALLUSIONS TO CREEDS	7

CONFESSIONES ECCLESIÆ APOSTOLICÆ.

SCRIPTURE CONFESSIONS.

The Bible is the Word of God to man; the Creed is man's answer to God. The Bible reveals the truth in the popular form of life and fact; the Creed states the truth in the logical form of doctrine. The Bible is to be believed and obeyed; the Creed is to be professed and taught. Hence we find few traces of creeds in the Bible.

In the Old Testament the fundamental doctrine of Monotheism is placed as a command at the head of the Decalogue, Exod. xx. 2, 3, and put in the form of a dogma, Deut. vi. 4:

שְׁמַע יִשְׂרָאֵל יְהוָֹה אֱלֹהֵינוּ יְהוָֹה אֶחָד	Hear, O Israel: Jehovah our Elohim, Jehovah is one [The Lord our God, the Lord is one].

These words form the beginning of what is termed *Shama* (*Hear*), and are repeated in the daily morning and evening services of the Jews. They are the Creed of the Jews, in distinction from the Gentiles or idolaters.

The sentence does not mean, 'Jehovah is our God, Jehovah alone' (and no other God), but it means either 'Jehovah, our God, Jehovah is one,'[1] or, 'Jehovah, our God, is one Jehovah.'[2] In either case it is an affirmation of the unity of God, and this is made the basis of the fundamental moral precept which follows (ver. 5): 'And thou shalt love the Lord thy God with all thine heart, and with all thy soul, and with all thy might.' Hence our Lord, Mark iv. 29, quotes these two passages together as 'the first of all the commandments.'

Similar assertions of the unity of God are found in Deut. iv. 35, 39 ('Jehovah is the God; there is none else beside him'); 2 Sam. vii. 22; xxii. 32; 1 Kings viii. 60; 1 Chron. xvii. 20; Psa. xviii. 31 ('Who is God save Jehovah? or who is a rock save our God?'); Psa. lxxxvi. 10 ('Thou art God alone'); Isa. xliii. 10–12; xliv. 6, 8; xlv. 22; Joel ii. 27; Zech. xiv. 9.

The New Testament confirms this doctrine repeatedly: Mark xii. 29; John xvii. 3 ('Thee, the only true God'); 1 Cor. viii. 4 ('There is none other God but one'); Gal. iii. 20; 1 Tim. ii. 5.

But while the New Testament presupposes the unity of the Godhead, it makes the Divinity and Messiahship of Jesus of Nazareth the centre of the Christian religion in its distinctive fundamental creed. The following are the passages which furnished the nucleus for the ancient rules of faith and baptismal creeds.

---

[1] So Oehler (*Theologie des A. Test.* Vol. I. p. 159), and others: 'Our Elohim' is in apposition to the first Jehovah, and אֶחָד is predicate to the second Jehovah.

[2] So our English Version, Keil, and others, who take 'Jehovah, our Elohim' as the subject, and 'one Jehovah' as the predicate, of the sentence. The Mohammedans have borrowed their monotheistic watchword from the Jews, with a heretical addition—'There is no God but Allah; *and Mohammed is his prophet*,'

The Confession of Nathanael (Bartholomew).

JOHN i. 50 (49).

Ἀπεκρίθη Ναθαναὴλ καὶ λέγει αὐτῷ·	Nathanael answered and saith unto him,
Ῥαββὶ, σὺ εἶ ὁ υἰὸς τοῦ θεοῦ, σὺ εἶ ὁ βασιλεὺς τοῦ Ἰσραήλ.	Rabbi, Thou art the Son of God, Thou art the King of Israel.

NOTE.—'King of Israel' is a designation of the Messiah, and an anticipation of the Confession of Peter. Nathanael reasons from the divine character of Christ as revealed in his supernatural knowledge of the heart, to his Messiahship, and returns the commendation, 'Behold an Israelite indeed without guile,' by the acknowledgment, 'Thou art the King of Israel,' and hence my King. The term 'Son of God' was also a designation of the Messiah in his divine nature, derived from Psa. ii. 5, 12 (comp. Isa. ix. 6), and is so used by Peter, Matt. xvi. 16 ; by the disciples in the ship, Matt. xiv. 33 ; by Martha, John xi. 27 ; and by the high-priest, Matt. xxvi. 63. The Apostles, before the pentecostal illumination, had no clear insight into the full meaning of the expression; but their faith, based upon the Old Testament and the personal knowledge of our Lord, contained the living germ of the full knowledge.

The Confession of Peter.

MATT. xvi. 16.

Ἀποκριθεὶς δὲ Σίμων Πέτρος εἶπεν· Σὺ εἶ ὁ Χριστὸς, ὁ υἱὸς τοῦ θεοῦ τοῦ ζῶντος.	And Simon Peter, answering, said, Thou art the Christ [the Messiah], the Son of the living God.

NOTE.—This is the fundamental Christian Confession, and the rock on which the Church is built. See Schaff's Annotations to Lange on *Matthew*, pp. 293-295.

JOHN vi. 68.

Κύριε, πρὸς τίνα ἀπελευσόμεθα ; ῥήματα ζωῆς αἰωνίου ἔχεις· καὶ ἡμεῖς πεπιστεύκαμεν, καὶ ἐγνώκαμεν ὅτι	Lord, to whom shall we go? Thou hast words of life eternal, and we have believed and known that
Σὺ εἶ ὁ ἅγιος τοῦ θεοῦ.	Thou art the Holy One of God.

NOTE.—This is the true reading, instead of the received text: '*Thou art the Christ, the Son of the living God*' (σὺ εἶ ὁ Χριστὸς, ὁ υἱὸς τοῦ θεοῦ τοῦ ζῶντος), which is conformed to Matt. xvi. 16. It is equivalent to *Thou art the Messiah*, and coincides with the testimony of the demoniacs (Mark i. 26), who with ghost-like intuition perceived the supernatural character of Jesus. This Confession of Peter belongs to an earlier period than the one recorded by Matthew. See Lange, *Com. on John*, pp. 234 sq. (Am. ed.).

The Confession of Thomas.

JOHN xx. 28.

Ἀπεκρίθη Θωμᾶς καὶ εἶπεν αὐτῷ·	Thomas answered and said unto him,
Ὁ κύριος μοῦ καὶ ὁ θεός μου.	MY LORD AND MY GOD!

NOTE.—This is the strongest apostolic Confession of Faith in the Lordship and Divinity of Christ, an echo of the beginning of the fourth Gospel (i. 1, 'the Word was God'), and an anticipation of its close (xx. 31, 'that ye may believe that Jesus is the Christ, the Son of God, and that believing ye may have life in his name'). For the words are undoubtedly addressed to Christ, as is evident from the preceding 'to him,' and from the appellation, 'My Lord;'[1] and not an exclamation of astonishment addressed to God.[2] For in the latter case Thomas would utter a profanity unrebuked by the Lord. The words indicate a triumph of faith over doubt. Thomas was not an unbeliever—he was not a doubter from indifference to the truth (as Pontius Pilate), still less from hostility to the truth, but from love of truth. He was an honest and earnest inquirer; his heart was anxious and ready to believe, but his understanding demanded evidence, which he embraced with joy as soon as it was presented. He represents the principle, *intellectus precedit fidem*, which is not entirely inconsistent with the other, *fides precedit intellectum*. He was a rationalist in the best sense of the term, animated and controlled by a love of truth. Blessed are those that seek the truth, for they shall find it. This kind of skepticism, or spirit of inquiry rather, is a stimulating and propelling force in the Church, and is necessary to the progress of theological science and historical and philosophical research. To such skepticism the words of the poet may be applied:

> 'There lives more faith in honest doubt,
> Believe me, than in half the creeds:
> He fought his doubts, and gathered strength,
> To find a stronger faith his own.'

And yet there is a higher faith, which believes without seeing (ver. 29; 1 Pet. i. 8; 2 Cor. v. 7), which holds fast to the invisible as seeing him (Heb. xi. 27), which goes to Christ as the child to his mother's breast, as heart to heart, as love to love, with undoubting, implicit, unbounded trust and confidence.

The Baptismal Formula.

MATT. xxviii. 19.

Μαθητεύσατε πάντα τὰ ἔθνη, βαπτί-ζοντες αὐτοὺς	Disciple [make disciples of] all the nations, baptizing them
εἰς τὸ ὄνομα τοῦ πατρὸς	INTO THE NAME OF THE FATHER,
καὶ τοῦ υἱοῦ	AND OF THE SON,
καὶ τοῦ ἁγίου πνεύματος,	AND OF THE HOLY GHOST;

---

[1] The Greek nominative with the article is used for the vocative, as in Matt. xi. 26, where God is addressed in prayer, ὁ πατήρ; xxvii. 29, χαῖρε ὁ βασιλεύς; in Mark xv. 34, ὁ θεός μου, ὁ θεός μου, εἰς τί ἐγκατέλιπές με; in Luke viii. 54, and in many other passages.

[2] Theodore of Mopsuestia: '*Quasi pro miraculo facto Deum collaudat.*' He is followed by Socinians and Rationalists.

διδάσκοντες αὐτοὺς τηρεῖν πάντα ὅσα ἐνετειλάμην ὑμῖν.	teaching them to observe all things whatsoever I have commanded you.

Note.—For an explanation of the Baptismal Formula, which is the basis of the old Trinitarian creeds, and for the various renderings of εἰς (*into, to, in, with reference to*), see Schaff and Lange, *Com. on Matt.* pp. 556–558.

The Confession of the Eunuch.

Acts viii. 37.

Πιστεύω τὸν υἱὸν τοῦ Θεοῦ εἶναι τὸν Ἰησοῦν Χριστόν.	I believe that JESUS CHRIST IS THE SON OF GOD.

Note.—This confession of the Ethiopian Eunuch before his baptism by Philip the Deacon, together with the preceding words of Philip, 'If thou believest with all thine heart, thou mayest' [be baptized], according to the received text (with sundry variations), is not contained in the best Uncial MSS., and is given up by critical editors (Griesbach, Lachmann, Tischendorf, Tregelles, Alford, Westcott and Hort), as an interpolation made to suit the baptismal service of the Church; but it is found even in Irenæus and Cyprian, and tends to prove the apostolical origin of a baptismal confession of faith in Christ as the Son of God.

One God and One Lord.

1 Cor. viii. 6.

Εἷς Θεὸς ὁ Πατήρ, ἐξ οὗ τὰ πάντα, καὶ ἡμεῖς εἰς αὐτόν· καὶ εἷς κύριος Ἰησοῦς Χριστὸς, δι' οὗ τὰ πάντα, καὶ ἡμεῖς δι' αὐτοῦ.	There is ONE GOD THE FATHER, of whom are all things, and we unto [for] him; and ONE LORD JESUS CHRIST, by whom *are* all things, and we by him.

The Mystery of Godliness.

1 Tim. iii. 16.

Ὁμολογουμένως μέγα ἐστίν τὸ τῆς εὐσεβείας μυστήριον· Ὃς [Θεὸς] ἐφανερώθη ἐν σαρκί, ἐδικαιώθη ἐν πνεύματι, ὤφθη ἀγγέλοις, ἐκηρύχθη ἐν ἔθνεσιν, ἐπιστεύθη ἐν κόσμῳ, ἀνελήφθη ἐν δόξῃ.	Confessedly great is the mystery of godliness: 'Who [God] was manifested in the flesh, justified in the Spirit, seen of angels, preached among the Gentiles, believed on in the world, received up in glory.'

NOTE.—The relative OC (ὅς, *who*) is best sustained by evidence (אAC—though Aleph has been meddled with, and B is wanting), instead of the noun ΘC (ϑεός, *God*, in the text. rec.), or of the neuter gender, ὅ (*which*). See Tischendorf, ed. viii. maj. ii. p. 849, and the long notes of Alford and Wordsworth. The reading ὅς improves the rhythm without changing the sense; for it certainly refers to Christ the God-Man, whether we connect it with μυστήριον (by transition from the mystery to the person of Him who is the sum and substance of the revelation of God), or regard it (in accordance with the parallelism and continuity of the following clauses) as a quotation from a primitive hymn or confession. Wordsworth refers 'who' to the preceding 'living God,' but God as such can not be said to have been 'received in glory.'

The Elementary Articles.

HEB. vi. 1, 2.

Διὸ ἀφέντες τὸν τῆς ἀρχῆς τοῦ Χριστοῦ λόγον, ἐπὶ τὴν τελειό- τητα φερώμεϑα· μὴ πάλιν ϑεμέ- λιον καταβαλλόμενοι	Therefore, leaving the word concerning the beginning of [the] Christ, let us go unto perfection [maturity], not laying again a foundation
μετανοίας ἀπὸ νεκρῶν ἔργων, καὶ πίστεως ἐπὶ ϑεὸν, βαπτισμῶν διδαχῆς,	of repentance from dead works, and of faith in God, of the doctrine of baptisms [washings],
ἐπιϑέσεώς τε χειρῶν, ἀναστάσεώς τε νεκρῶν, καὶ κρίματος αἰωνίου.	and of laying on of hands, and of resurrection of the dead, and of eternal judgment.

NOTE.—Many commentators suppose that the sacred writer here refers to the fundamental and elementary articles of catechetical instruction in the apostolic Church; but the articles mentioned were held by Christians in common with the Jews, and are distinguished from the fullness of Christian knowledge (τελειότης), or 'the strong meat for those who are of full age' (ver. 14). The passage has only a remote bearing on creeds. For details, see the commentaries of Bleek, Tholuck, Delitzsch, Lünemann, Alford, Moll and Kendrick.

Other Allusions to Creeds.

The duty of confessing the faith is taught by our Lord, Matt. x. 32, 33, and by St. Paul, Rom. x. 9, 10.

Allusions to a creed may be found in the following passages:

Acts xvi. 31, where Paul and Silas, in answer to the question of the jailer at Philippi, say: 'BELIEVE ON THE LORD JESUS CHRIST, and thou shalt be saved, and thy house.'

Rom. xii. 6: 'The analogy of faith' (κατὰ τὴν ἀναλογίαν τῆς πίστεως).

1 Cor. xv. 3: 'I delivered unto you among the first things that which I also received, that CHRIST DIED FOR OUR SINS, according to the Scriptures, and that HE WAS BURIED, and that HE ROSE AGAIN the third day, according to the Scriptures,' etc.

2 Tim. i. 13, 14: 'Hold fast THE FORM OF SOUND WORDS [ὑποϑύπωσιν τῶν ὑγιαινόντων λόγων, a sketch or outline of the healing words] which thou hast heard from me, in faith and love, in Christ Jesus. THAT GOOD THING WHICH WAS COMMITTED UNTO THEE [τὴν παρα-

θήκην, or παρακαταθήκην, the deposit] keep, by the Holy Ghost, which dwelleth in us.' Comp. ver. 12, and 1 Tim. vi. 20 (τὴν παραθήκην φύλαξον).

Heb. v. 12: ' Ye have need that one teach you again which be THE FIRST PRINCIPLES OF THE ORACLES OF GOD' (τὰ στοιχεῖα τῆς ἀρχῆς τῶν λογίων τοῦ θεοῦ). Comp. vi. 1, 2.

1 John iv. 2 : ' Hereby know ye the Spirit of God : every spirit that CONFESSETH THAT JESUS CHRIST IS COME IN THE FLESH [ὁμολογεῖ Ἰησοῦν Χριστὸν ἐν σαρκὶ ἐληλυθότα] is of God.'

2 John 10: 'If there come any unto you, and bring not THIS DOCTRINE [ταύτην τὴν διδαχήν, viz., the doctrine of Christ, ver. 9], receive him not into your house.'

Jude 3 : · Exhorting that ye should earnestly contend for THE FAITH WHICH WAS ONCE DELIVERED UNTO THE SAINTS' (τῇ ἅπαξ παραδοθείσῃ τοῖς ἁγίοις πίστει).

REGULÆ FIDEI

ECCLESIÆ ANTE-NICÆNÆ ET NICÆNÆ.

ANTE-NICENE AND NICENE RULES OF FAITH AND BAPTISMAL CREEDS.

REGULÆ FIDEI

ECCLESIÆ ANTE-NICÆNÆ ET NICÆNÆ.

ANTE-NICENE AND NICENE RULES OF FAITH AND BAPTISMAL CREEDS.

	PAGE
INTRODUCTORY REMARKS	11
IGNATIUS, OF ANTIOCH. A.D. 107	11
IRENÆUS, OF GAUL. A.D. 180	12
FIRST FORMULA	13
SECOND FORMULA	15
THIRD FORMULA	16
TERTULLIAN, OF NORTH AFRICA. A.D. 200	16
FIRST FORMULA	17
SECOND FORMULA	17
THIRD FORMULA	19
CYPRIAN, OF CARTHAGE. A.D. 250	20
NOVATIAN, OF ROME. A.D. 250	21
ORIGEN, OF ALEXANDRIA. A.D. 230	22
GREGORY THAUMATURGUS, OF NEO-CÆSAREA. A.D. 270.	24
LUCIAN, OF ANTIOCH. A.D. 300	25
THE PRIVATE CREED OF ARIUS. A.D. 328	28
EUSEBIUS, OF CÆSAREA IN PALESTINE. A.D. 325	29
CYRIL, OF JERSUALEM. A.D. 350	31
LONGER FORMULA	31
SHORTER FORMULA	32
EPIPHANIUS, OF CYPRUS. A.D. 374	33
FIRST FORMULA	33
SECOND FORMULA	35
THE APOSTOLICAL CONSTITUTIONS. A.D. 350	39
COMPARATIVE TABLE OF THE ANTE-NICENE RULES OF FAITH AS RELATED TO THE APOSTLES' CREED AND THE NICENE CREED.	40

REGULÆ FIDEI

ECCLESIÆ ANTE-NICÆNÆ ET NICÆNÆ.

ANTE-NICENE AND NICENE RULES OF FAITH AND BAPTISMAL CREEDS.

INTRODUCTORY REMARKS.

The Rules of Faith and Baptismal Confessions which we find among the ecclesiastical writers of the second and third centuries mark the transition from the Bible to the Œcumenical Creeds. They contain nearly all the articles of the Apostles' and Nicene Creeds, and some are even more full, especially those of the East; for the Greek Church was, at an early period, disturbed by heretical speculations and perversions, and had a greater talent and taste for metaphysical theology than the less learned but more sober, practical, and steady Church of the West. I have included here also some creeds of the fourth century, 'o facilitate the comparison with the Apostles' and the Nicæno-Constantinopolitan symbols. In addition to the valuable collections of HAHN (*Bibliothek der Symbole und Glaubensregeln*, 1842) and HEURTLEY (*Harmonia Symbolica*, 1858, and *De Fide et Symbolo*, 1869), I have examined the more recent works of CASPARI (*Quellen zur Geschichte des Taufsymbols und der Glaubensregel*, 1866-75, 3 vols.), LUMBY (*History of the Creeds*, 1873), SWAINSON (*Literary History of the Nicene and Apostles' Creeds*, 1875), and HORT (*Two Dissertations*, etc., 1876).

IGNATIUS OF ANTIOCH. A.D. 107.

EPISTOLA AD TRALLIANOS, cap. 9.

The following passage is no creed nor part of a creed, but it shows what facts of the gospel history were most prominent in the mind of the famous bishop and martyr IGNATIUS, of Antioch, and the Church of his age, in opposition to the Gnostic heretics, who resolved the birth, death, and resurrection of Christ into an unreal and delusive show or phantom (δόκη-σις, hence *Docetæ*). A similar passage of greater length occurs in the commencement of his letter to the Christians at Smyrna.

The text is from the shorter Greek recension of the seven Epistles, with the chief interpolations of the longer Greek recension added in brackets. The latter mentions also Christ's lonely descent into Hades (καθῆλθεν εἰς ᾅδην μόνος). In the short Syriac Ignatius there is no Epistle to the Trallians. On the Ignatian controversy and literature, see my *Church History*, Vol. I. § 119, pp. 463 sqq.

Κωφώθητε οὖν, ὅταν ὑμῖν χωρὶς Ἰησοῦ Χριστοῦ λαλῇ τις	Be deaf, therefore, when any would speak to you apart from (at variance with) JESUS CHRIST
[τοῦ υἱοῦ τοῦ Θεοῦ],	[the Son of God],
τοῦ ἐκ γένους [γενομένου] Δαβὶδ,	who was descended from the family of David,
τοῦ ἐκ Μαρίας,	born of Mary,
ὃς ἀληθῶς ἐγεννήθη	who truly was born
[καὶ ἐκ θεοῦ καὶ ἐκ παρθένου . . .	[both of God and of the Virgin . . .
ἀληθῶς ἀνέλαβε σῶμα· ὁ Λόγος	truly took a body; for the Word

γὰρ σὰρξ ἐγένετο καὶ ἐπολιτεύ- | became flesh and dwelt among
σατο ἄνευ ἁμαρτίας . . .], | us without sin . . .],

ἔφαγέν τε καὶ ἔπιεν [ἀληθῶς]. | ate and drank [truly],

ἀληθῶς ἐδιώχθη ἐπὶ Ποντίου Πιλά- | truly suffered persecution under
του, | Pontius Pilate,

ἀληθῶς [δὲ, καὶ οὐ δοκήσει] ἐσταυ- | was truly [and not in appearance]
ρώθη καὶ ἀπέθανεν . . . | crucified and died . . .

ὃς καὶ ἀληθῶς ἠγέρθη ἀπὸ νεκρῶν | who was also truly raised from the
[καὶ ἀνέστη διὰ τριῶν ἡμερῶν], | dead [and rose after three days].

ἐγείροντος αὐτὸν τοῦ Πατρὸς αὐ- | his Father raising him up . . .
τοῦ . . .

[καὶ τεσσαράκοντα ἡμέρας συνδια- | [and after having spent forty days
τρίψας τοῖς Ἀποστόλοις, | with the Apostles,

ἀνελήφθη πρὸς τὸν Πατέρα· | was received up to the Father,

καὶ ἐκάθισεν ἐκ δεξιῶν αὐτοῦ, | and sits on his right hand,

περιμένων ἕως ἂν τεθῶσιν οἱ ἐχθροὶ | waiting till his enemies are put
αὐτοῦ ὑπὸ τοὺς πόδας αὐτοῦ]. | under his feet].

IRENÆUS.   A.D. 180.

IRENÆUS was a native of Asia Minor, a pupil of Polycarp of Smyrna (*Adv. Hær.* Lib. III.
cap. 3, § 4; Euseb. *H. E.* v. 20), and through him a grand-pupil of St. John the Apostle.
He was bishop of the church at Lyons (Lugdunum), in the South of France, in 177, wrote
his great work against the Gnostic heresies about 180, while Eleutherus (d. 185) was bishop
of Rome (*Adv. Hær.* Lib. III. cap. 3, § 3), and died about 202.

He was therefore a connecting link between the East and the West, as well as between
post-apostolic and ante-Nicene Christianity, and altogether the most important witness of the
doctrinal status of the Catholic Church at the close of the second century. The ancient
Massilia (Marseilles) was a Greek colony, and the churches of Lyons and Vienne in Gaul
were probably planted by Eastern missionaries, and retained a close connection with the
Eastern churches, as appears from the letter of those churches to their brethren in Asia
Minor after the fierce persecution under Marcus Aurelius, A.D. 177 (see Euseb. *H. E.* v. 1).

Irenæus refutes the heretics of his age by the Scriptures and the apostolic tradition. This
tradition, though different in form from the New Testament, and perhaps older than the
writings of the Apostles, agrees with them, being a summary of their teaching, and is handed
down in all the churches through the hands of the presbyters.[1]   The sum and substance of

---

[1] The essential identity of the Scriptures and the apostolic tradition is asserted by Irenæus
(*Adv. Hær.* Lib. III. cap. 1, § 1): '*Non per alios dispositionem salutis nostræ cognovimus, quam
per eos [apostolos], per quos evangelium pervenit ad nos; quod quidem tunc præconaverunt, postea vero per Dei voluntatem in Scripturis nobis tradiderunt, fundamentum et columnam fidei
nostræ futurum.*' Comp. the fragment of his letter to Florinus, preserved by Eusebius (*H. E.*
v. 20), where he says that the presbyters and Polycarp handed down the teaching of the
Lord as they received it from the eye-witnesses of the Word of Life—in entire accordance
with the Scriptures (πάντα σύμφωνα ταῖς γραφαῖς).

this tradition is the baptismal creed, called by him the κανὼν τῆς ἀληθείας, ἀποστόλων διδαχή, τὸ ἀρχαῖον τῆς ἐκκλησίας σύστημα, γνῶσις ἀληθὴ, traditio veritatis, vera fides, prædicatio ecclesiæ. He does not give the creed in full, but incorporates passages of it in several parts of his work. He gives most of the articles of the Apostles' Creed as it prevailed in the West, but has also several characteristic passages in common with the Nicene Creed (ἕνα . . . σαρκωθέντα ὑπὲρ τῆς ἡμετέρας σωτηρίας . . . τὸ διὰ προφητῶν κεκηρυχός). The ancient liturgies of Gaul likewise have a semi-Oriental character.

First Form.

CONTRA HÆRESES, Lib. I. cap. 10, § 1 (Opera, ed. Stieren, Tom. I. p. 119).

Ἡ μὲν γὰρ ἐκκλησία, καίπερ καθ' ὅλης τῆς οἰκουμένης ἕως περάτων τῆς γῆς διεσπαρμένη, παρὰ δὲ τῶν Ἀποστόλων καὶ τῶν ἐκείνων μαθητῶν παραλαβοῦσα τὴν [πίστιν]	The Church, though scattered through the whole world to the ends of the earth, has received[1] from the Apostles and their disciples the *faith*
εἰς ἕνα Θεὸν, Πατέρα παντοκράτορα,	IN ONE GOD, THE FATHER ALMIGHTY,
τὸν πεποιηκότα τὸν οὐρανὸν, καὶ τὴν γῆν,	*who made the heaven and the earth,*
καὶ τὰς θαλάσσας, καὶ πάντα τὰ ἐν αὐτοῖς, πίστιν·	and the seas, and all that in them is;
καὶ εἰς ἕνα Χριστὸν Ἰησοῦν, τὸν Υἱὸν τοῦ Θεοῦ,	and IN ONE CHRIST JESUS, THE SON OF GOD,
τὸν σαρκωθέντα ὑπὲρ τῆς ἡμετέρας σωτηρίας·	*who became flesh for our salvation;*
καὶ εἰς Πνεῦμα ἅγιον,	and IN THE HOLY GHOST,
τὸ διὰ τῶν προφητῶν κεκηρυχὸς τὰς οἰκονομίας καὶ τὰς ἐλεύσεις [τὴν ἔλευσιν, adventum],	who through the prophets preached the dispensations and the adventr [advent],
καὶ τὴν ἐκ Παρθένου γέννησιν,	and *the birth from the Virgin,*
καὶ τὸ πάθος,	and *the passion,*
καὶ τὴν ἔγερσιν ἐκ νεκρῶν,	and *the resurrection from the dead,*
καὶ τὴν ἔνσαρκον εἰς τοὺς οὐρανοὺς ἀνάληψιν τοῦ ἠγαπημένου Χριστοῦ Ἰησοῦ, τοῦ Κυρίου ἡμῶν,	and the bodily *assumption into heaven* of the beloved Christ Jesus, our Lord,
καὶ τὴν ἐκ τῶν οὐρανῶν ἐν τῇ δόξῃ τοῦ Πατρὸς παρουσίαν αὐτοῦ,	and his *appearing from heaven* in the glory of the Father,

---

[1] Lit. 'yet having received.' In the Greek the creed is part of one sentence, which is resumed in τοῦτο τὸ κήρυγμα παρειληφυῖα καὶ ταύτην τὴν πίστιν . . . ἡ ἐκκλησία . . . ἐπιμελῶς φυλάσσει.

ἐπὶ τὸ ἀνακεφαλαιώσασθαι τὰ πάντα, | to comprehend all things under one head,

καὶ ἀναστῆσαι πᾶσαν σάρκα πάσης ἀνθρωπότητος, | and *to raise up all flesh of all mankind,*

ἵνα Χριστῷ Ἰησοῦ, τῷ Κυρίῳ ἡμῶν, καὶ Θεῷ, καὶ Σωτῆρι, καὶ βασιλεῖ, κατὰ τὴν εὐδοκίαν τοῦ Πατρὸς τοῦ ἀοράτου, πᾶν γόνυ κάμψῃ ἐπουρανίων καὶ ἐπιγείων καὶ καταχθονίων, καὶ πᾶσα γλῶσσα ἐξομολογήσηται αὐτῷ, καὶ κρίσιν δικαίαν ἐν τοῖς πᾶσι ποιήσηται, τὰ μὲν πνευματικὰ τῆς πονηρίας, καὶ ἀγγέλους παραβεβηκότας, καὶ ἐν ἀποστασίᾳ γεγονότας, καὶ τοὺς ἀσεβεῖς, καὶ ἀδίκους καὶ ἀνόμους καὶ βλασφήμους τῶν ἀνθρώπων εἰς τὸ αἰώνιον πῦρ πέμψῃ· τοῖς δὲ δικαίοις, καὶ ὁσίοις, καὶ τὰς ἐντολὰς αὐτοῦ τετηρηκόσι καὶ ἐν τῇ ἀγάπῃ αὐτοῦ διαμεμενηκόσι, τοῖς ἀπ' ἀρχῆς, τοῖς δὲ ἐκ μετανοίας, ζωὴν χαρισάμενος, ἀφθαρσίαν δωρήσηται, καὶ δόξαν αἰωνίαν περιποιήσῃ. | that, according to the good pleasure of the Father invisible, every knee of those that are in heaven and on the earth and under the earth should bow before Christ Jesus, our Lord and God and Saviour and King, and that every tongue should confess to him, and that he *may execute righteous judgment over all:* sending into eternal fire the spiritual powers of wickedness, and the angels who transgressed and apostatized, and the godless and unrighteous and lawless and blasphemous among men, and granting *life* and immortality and *eternal glory* to the righteous and holy, who have both kept the commandments and continued in his love, some from the beginning, some after their conversion.

NOTE.—Irenæus adds to this Creed: 'The Church, having received this preaching and this faith, as before said, though scattered throughout the whole world, zealously preserves it (ἐπιμελῶς φυλάσσει) as one household, ... and unanimously preaches and teaches the same, and hands it down as by one mouth (συμφώνως ταῦτα κηρύσσει καὶ διδάσκει καὶ παραδίδωσιν, ὡς ἓν στόμα κεκτημένη); for although there are different dialects in the world, the power of the tradition is one and the same (ἡ δύναμις τῆς παραδόσεως μία καὶ ἡ αὐτή). And in no other manner have either the churches established in Germany believed and handed down, nor those in Spain, nor among the Celts, nor in the East, nor in Egypt, nor in Libya, nor those established in the middle of the world. But as the sun, God's creature, is one and the same in all the world, so, too, the preaching of the truth shines every where and enlightens all men who wish to come to the knowledge of the truth. And neither will he who is very mighty in language among those who preside over the churches say other than this (for the disciple is not above his Master), nor will he who is weak in the word impair the tradition. For as the faith is one and the same, neither he who is very able to speak on it adds thereto, nor does he who is less mighty diminish therefrom.'

Second Form.

ADV. HÆR. Lib. III. cap. 4, § 1, 2 (*Opera*, Tom. I. p. 437).

Quid autem si neque Apostoli quidem Scripturas reliquissent nobis, nonne oportebat ordinem sequi traditionis, quam tradiderunt iis quibus committebant ecclesias? Cui ordinationi assentiunt multæ gentes barbarorum, eorum qui in Christum credunt, sine charta et atramento scriptam habentes per Spiritum in cordibus suis salutem, et veterem traditionem diligenter custodientes,	If the Apostles had not left to us the Scriptures, would it not be necessary to follow the order of tradition, which those to whom they committed the churches handed down? To this order many nations of barbarians give assent, those who believe in Christ having salvation written in their hearts by the Spirit without paper and ink, and guarding diligently the ancient tradition,
IN UNUM DEUM *credentes,*	*believing* IN ONE GOD,
Fabricatorem cœli et terræ,	*Maker of heaven and earth,*
et omnium quæ in eis sunt,	and all that in them is,
Per CHRISTUM JESUM DEI FILIUM;	Through CHRIST JESUS THE SON OF GOD;
Qui, propter eminentissimam erga figmentum suum dilectionem,	Who, for his astounding love towards his creatures,
eam quæ esset ex Virgine generationem sustinuit,	sustained the *birth of the Virgin,*
ipse per se hominem adunans Deo,	himself uniting his manhood to God,
et passus sub Pontio Pilato,	and *suffered under Pontius Pilate,*
et resurgens,	and *rose again,*
et in claritate receptus.	and *was received in glory,*
in gloria venturus,	*shall come in glory,*
Salvator eorum qui salvantur, et Judex eorum qui judicantur; et mittens in ignem æternum transfiguratores veritatis et	the Saviour of those who are saved, and the *Judge* of those who are judged; and sending into eternal fire the perverters of the truth

contemptores Patris sui et ad- | and the despisers of his Father
ventus ejus. | and his advent.

Third Form.

ADV. HÆR. Lib. IV. cap. 33, § 7 (*Opera*, Tom. I. p. 670).

After remarking that the spiritual man shall judge all those who are beyond the pale of the truth—that is, outside of the Church—and shall be judged by no one, Irenæus goes on to say: 'For to him all things are consistent; he has a full faith (πίστις ὀλόκληρος)—'

Εἰς ἕνα Θεὸν παντοκράτορα, | IN ONE GOD ALMIGHTY,
ἐξ οὗ τὰ πάντα, | from whom are all things;
καὶ εἰς τὸν Υἱὸν τοῦ Θεοῦ, 'Ιη- | and IN THE SON OF GOD, JESUS
σοῦν Χριστὸν, | CHRIST,
τὸν Κύριον ἡμῶν, | *our Lord,*
δι' οὗ τὰ πάντα, | by whom are all things,
καὶ τὰς οἰκονομίας αὐτοῦ, | and in his dispensations,
δι' ὧν ἄνθρωπος ἐγένετο ὁ Υἱὸς τοῦ | through which the Son of God
Θεοῦ· | *became man;*
Πεισμονὴ βεβαία καὶ εἰς τὸ Πνεῦ- | the firm persuasion also IN THE
μα τοῦ Θεοῦ,[1] | SPIRIT OF GOD,
...τὸ τὰς οἰκονομίας Πατρός τε | who furnishes us with a knowledge
καὶ Υἱοῦ σκηνοβατοῦν καθ' ἑκά- | of the truth, and has set forth the
στην γενεὰν ἐν τοῖς ἀνθρώποις, | dispensations of the Father and
καθὼς βούλεται ὁ Πατήρ. | the Son, in virtue of which he
| dwells in every generation of
| men, according to the will of
| the Father.

TERTULLIAN.   A.D. 200.

TERTULLIAN, originally a lawyer, in mature life converted to Christianity, and one of its ablest and most fearless advocates against infidels and heretics, flourished towards the close of the second and the beginning of the third century as presbyter in Northern Africa, till about A.D. 220. He was a rugged and eccentric genius, and joined the Montanist sect, which believed in the advent of the age of the Paraclete in the person of Montanus, the continuance of the gift of prophecy in woman as well as man, and the near approach of the millennium, and which maintained severe discipline and some peculiar customs, in opposition to the more tolerant practice of the Catholic Church. He placed truth (*veritas*) above authority and custom (*vetus consuetudo*). But otherwise he was one of the strongest champions of

---

[1] The Greek original is here defective. The Latin translation reads as follows: '*Sententia firma quæ est in Spiritu Dei, qui præstat agnitionem veritatis, qui dispositiones Patris et Filii exposuit, secundum quas aderat generi humano quemadmodum vult Pater.*'

catholic orthodoxy against the Gnostic heresies, and would allow no change in matters of fundamental doctrine.   He alludes three times to the Creed, and quotes the chief articles with some variations and interwoven with his comments.   In other places he mentions only one or two articles, as the occasion suggested.   See Walch, pp. 7–10 ; Hahn, pp. 68–73 ; Heurtley, pp. 13–17 ; Swainson, pp. 35–40.

First Form.

DE VIRGINIBUS VELANDIS, cap. 1.

Regula quidem fidei una omnino est, sola, immobilis, et irreformabilis, credendi scilicet	The Rule of Faith is altogether one, sole, immovable, and irreformable—namely, to believe
IN UNICUM DEUM OMNIPOTENTEM, *mundi conditorem;*	IN ONE GOD ALMIGHTY, the *Maker of the world;*
et FILIUM EJUS, JESUM CHRISTUM, *natum ex Virgine Maria, crucifixum sub Pontio Pilato, tertia die resuscitatum a mortuis, receptum in cœlis, sedentem nunc ad dexteram Patris, venturum judicare vivos et mortuos, per carnis etiam resurrectionem.*[1]	and HIS SON, JESUS CHRIST, *born of the Virgin Mary, crucified under Pontius Pilate,* on the third day raised again *from the dead,* received in the heavens, sitting now *at the right hand of the Father,* coming to judge the quick and the dead, also through *the resurrection of the flesh.*

Second Form.

ADV. PRAXEAM (*a Patripassian Unitarian*), cap. 2.

Nos vero et semper, et nunc magis, ut instructiores per Paracletum, Deductorem scilicet omnis veritatis,	But we *believe* always, and now more, being better instructed by the Paraclete, the Leader into all truth,

[1] That is : This also belongs to the unchangeable rule of faith, that the Lord will hold general judgment after the dead are raised to life again.   Neander (*Tertull.* p. 303) transposes *etiam* before *per:* 'To judge the dead also through the resurrection.'   To this Tertullian adds : '*Hac lege fidei manente, cætera jam disciplinæ et conversationis admittunt novitatem correctionis, operante scilicet et proficiente usque in finem gratia Dei*' (This law of *faith* remaining, all other matters of *discipline* and conversation admit of the novelty of correction, the grace of God, namely, working and advancing to the end).   The article on the Holy Ghost is here omitted.

UNICUM *quidem* DEUM *credimus:* | ONE GOD:[1]
sub hac tamen dispensatione, quam | but under this dispensation which
œconomiam dicimus, | we call economy,
ut unici Dei sit et FILIUS, | and the SON of the one God,
Sermo ipsius, qui ex ipso pro- | his Word [Logos] who proceeded
cesserit, | from him,
per quem omnia facta sunt, | by whom all things were made,
et sine quo factum est nihil. (John | and without whom nothing was
i. 3.) | made.
Hunc missum a Patre in Virgi- | This was sent from the Father into
nem, | the *Virgin,*
et ex ea natum, | and *was born of her,*
hominem et Deum, Filium homi- | both Man and God, the Son of
nis et Filium Dei, | Man and the *Son of God,*
et cognominatum JESUM CHRISTUM: | and called JESUS CHRIST:
Hunc passum, | He *suffered,*
hunc mortuum et sepultum, | he *died* and *was buried,*
secundum Scripturas; | according to the Scriptures;[2]
et resuscitatum a Patre, | and *raised again* by the Father,
et in cœlos resumptum, | and *taken up into the heavens,*
sedere ad dexteram Patris, | and *sitteth at the right hand of the Father,*
venturum judicare vivos et mor- | he *shall come to judge the quick*
tuos: | *and the dead:*
qui exinde miserit, secundum pro- | He thence did send, according to
missionem suam, a Patre, | his promise, from the Father,
SPIRITUM SANCTUM, *Paracletum,* | the HOLY GHOST, the Paraclete,
Sanctificatorem fidei eorum qui | the Sanctifier of the faith of those
credunt in Patrem et Filium et | who believe in the Father and
Spiritum Sanctum.[3] | the Son and the Holy Ghost.

---

[1] In the Latin the following sentences depend on *credimus.* The English idiom requires more freedom.

[2] This important insertion (the only express recognition of the Scriptures in the Creed) is also found in the Nicene Creed (κατὰ τὰς γραφάς), after the clause *risen on the third day,* but disappeared in the later forms of the Apostles' Creed.

[3] To this Tertullian adds: '*Hanc regulam ab initio Evangelii decucurrisse, etiam ante pri-ores quosque hæreticos, ne dum ante Praxean hesternum, probabit tam ipsa posteritas omnium hæreticorum, quam ipsa novellitas Praxeæ hesterni,*' i. e. 'That this rule has come down from

Third Form.

DE PRÆSCRIPT. HÆRET. cap. 13.

Regula est autem fidei, . . . illa scilicet qua creditur,	The Rule of Faith is, . . . namely, that by which we *believe*
UNUM *omnino* DEUM *esse,*	That there is but ONE GOD,
nec alium præter mundi conditorem,	and no other besides *the Maker of the world,*
qui universa de nihilo produxerit,	who produced the universe out of nothing,
per Verbum suum primo omnium demissum ;	by his Word sent forth first of all ;
id Verbum, FILIUM EJUS *appellatum,*	that this Word, called HIS SON,
in nomine Dei varie visum a patriarchis,	was seen in the name of God in various ways by the patriarchs,
in prophetis semper auditum,	was always heard in the prophets,
postremo delatum, ex Spiritu Patris Dei et virtute, in Virginem Mariam,	at last was sent down, *from the Spirit* and power of God the Father, into the *Virgin Mary,*
carnem factum in utero ejus, et ex ea natum,	*was made flesh* in her womb, and *born of her,*
egisse[1] JESUM CHRISTUM ;	lived (appeared) as JESUS CHRIST ;
exinde prædicasse novam legem	that then he preached the new law
et novam promissionem regni cœlorum ;	and the new promise of the kingdom of heaven ;
virtutes fecisse ;	wrought miracles ;
fixum cruci ;	*was nailed to the cross ;*
tertia die resurrexisse ;	*rose again on the third day ;*
in cœlos ereptum ;	*was caught up to the heavens ;*
sedisse[2] *ad dexteram Patris ;*	and *sat down at the right hand of the Father ;*

---

the beginning of the gospel, even before the earlier heretics, and so of course before the Praxeas of yesterday, is proved both by the lateness of all heretics, and by the novelty of this Praxeas of yesterday.'

[1] Al. *exisse* (Cod. Urs.).

[2] Al. *sedere, sitteth.*

misisse vicariam vim SPIRITUS SANCTI,	sent in his place the power of the HOLY GHOST,
qui credentes agat;	to guide the believers;
venturum cum claritate	he *will come again* with glory
ad sumendos sanctos in vitæ æternæ et promissorum cœlestium fructum,	to take the saints into the enjoyment of *eternal life* and the celestial promises,
et ad profanos adjudicandos igni perpetuo,	and to *judge* the wicked with eternal fire,
facta utriusque partis resuscitatione,	after the resuscitation (resurrection) of both,
cum carnis restitutione.[1]	with the *restitution* (restoration) *of the flesh.*

CYPRIAN, OF CARTHAGE.   A.D. 250.

CYPRIAN, the great bishop and martyr of Carthage, the chief champion of catholic unity against heretics and schismatics, and at the same time of episcopal independence against Rome, during the middle of the third century (died 258), first applies the term *Symbolum* to the baptismal creed, but gives us only scanty fragments of it, in answer to the question whether baptized heretics and schismatics (like the Novatians) should be rebaptized when applying for admission into the Catholic Church. He answers the question in the affirmative, since out of the Catholic Church there is no truth, no sacraments, no salvation (*extra Ecclesiam nulla salus*); and hence if the Novatians used the same terms in their creed as the Catholics, they had not the thing, but a mere sham or empty counterfeit. This opinion on the validity of heretical baptism Cyprian maintained in opposition to Bishop Stephen of Rome.

The first of these fragmentary creeds is contained in his Epistle to Magnus (*Ep.* 69, al. 76), the other in his synodical Epistle to Januarius and other Numidian bishops (*Ep.* 70). Both are in form interrogative, in answer to the question *Credis?* put to the baptismal candidate, and contain the following articles:

Credo in DEUM PATREM,	I believe in GOD THE FATHER,
in FILIUM CHRISTUM,	in his SON CHRIST,
in SPIRITUM SANCTUM.	in the HOLY GHOST.
Credo remissionem peccatorum,	I believe the forgiveness of sins,
et vitam eternam	and eternal life
per sanctam Ecclesiam.	through the holy Church.

---

[1] '*Hæc regula,*' he adds here also, '*a Christo, ut probabitur, instituta nullas habet apud nos quæstiones, nisi quas hæreses inferunt et quæ hæreticos faciunt; cæterum manente forma ejus in suo ordine, quantum libet quæras et tractes et omnem libidinem curiositatis effundas.*'

NOVATIAN, OF ROME. A.D. 250.

NOVATIAN, a presbyter and then a schismatical bishop of Rome, in opposition to Cornelius, from whom he dissented, in the middle of the third century, on a question of discipline concerning the readmission of the lapsed, explains, in his work *De Trinitate s. De Regula Fidei* (*Bibl. PP.* ed. Gallandi, Tom. III. pp. 287 sqq.), the 'rule of truth,' especially the divinity of Christ, in opposition to the heresies of his age, and states:

Regula exigit veritatis, ut primo omnium	The rule of truth demands that, first of all,
credamus in DEUM PATREM *et Dominum omnipotentem,*	we believe in GOD THE FATHER and *Almighty* Lord,
id est, rerum omnium perfectissimum conditorem.	that is, the most perfect *Maker of all things.* . . .
Eadem regula veritatis docet nos credere, post Patrem, etiam in FILIUM DEI, CHRISTUM JESUM, *Dominum Deum nostrum, sed Dei Filium.* . . .	The same rule of truth teaches us to believe, after the Father, also in the SON OF GOD, CHRIST JESUS, our Lord God, but the Son of God. . . .
Sed enim ordo rationis et fidei auctoritas, digestis vocibus et literis Domini, admonet nos, post hæc credere etiam	Moreover, the order of reason and the authority of faith, in due consideration of the words and Scriptures of the Lord, admonishes us, after this, to *believe* also
in SPIRITUM SANCTUM,	in the HOLY GHOST,
olim Ecclesiæ repromissum, sed statutis temporum opportunitatibus redditum.	promised of old to the Church, but granted in the appointed and fitting time.

NOTE.—This rule is little more than the baptismal formula, and represents the Roman creed, which was shorter than the Eastern creeds, since Rome always loved power more than philosophy. and (as Rufinus remarks, *De Symb.* § 3) was less disturbed by heretical speculations than the Greek Church. Novatian, however, takes the knowledge of the whole creed for granted, and hence does not quote it literally and in full. He mentions also incidentally as articles of faith the *holy Church*, the *remission of sins*, and *the resurrection*. Comp. the notes in Hahn, pp. 74, 75.

ORIGEN, OF ALEXANDRIA. ABOUT A.D. 230.

DE PRINCIPIIS, Lib. I. Præf. § 4–6.

ORIGEN (185–254), teacher of the Catechetical School of Alexandria in Egypt, was the greatest divine and one of the noblest characters of his age, equally distinguished for genius,

learning, industry, and enthusiasm for the knowledge of truth. His orthodoxy was questioned by some of his contemporaries, and he was even excommunicated by the Bishop of Alexandria, and condemned as a heretic long after his death by a council of Constantinople, 544. His curious speculations about the pre-existence of souls, the final salvation of all rational beings, etc., arose chiefly from his attempt to harmonize Christianity with Platonism.

In the Introduction to his work, Περὶ ἀρχῶν, *On the Principles* (of the Christian Religion), written before 231 (some date it from 212–215), and preserved to us in the loose and inaccurate Latin translation of Rufinus, Origen gives some fragments of the creed which was used in his day and country. He first remarks that, while all believers in Christ accepted the books of the Old and New Testaments as a full revelation of the divine truth, the diversity of interpretations and opinions demanded a clear and certain rule (*certa linea, manifesta regula*), and that the apostles delivered such articles of faith as they deemed necessary for all, leaving the study of the reasons, the examination of the mode and origin, to the more gifted lovers of wisdom. He then proceeds to give a sketch of these dogmatic teachings of the apostles as follows:

Species eorum, quæ per prædicationem Apostolicam manifeste traduntur, istæ sunt:

Primo, quod UNUS DEUS *est, qui omnia creavit atque composuit quique cum nihil esset, esse fecit universa, Deus a prima creatura et conditione mundi, omnium justorum Deus—Adam, Abel, Seth, Enos, Enoch, Noë, Sem, Abraham, Isaac, Jacob, duodecim Patriarcharum, Moysis et Prophetarum: et quod hic Deus in novissimis diebus, sicut per prophetas suos ante promiserat, misit* DOMINUM NOSTRUM JESUM CHRISTUM, *primo quidem vocaturum Israël, secundo vero etiam gentes post perfidiam populi Israël. Hic Deus justus et bonus, Pater Domini nostri Jesu Christi, Legem et Prophetas et Evangelia ipse dedit, qui et Apostolorum Deus est et Veteris et Novi Testamenti.*

The form of those things which are manifestly delivered by the preaching of the Apostles is this: First, that there is ONE GOD, who created and framed every thing, and who, when nothing was, brought all things into being,—God from the first creation and forming of the world, the God of all the just—Adam, Abel, Seth, Enos, Enoch, Noah, Shem, Abraham, Isaac, Jacob, the twelve Patriarchs, Moses, and the Prophets: and that this God, in the last days, as he had before promised through his Prophets, sent OUR LORD JESUS CHRIST, to all Israel first, and then, after the unbelief of Israel, also to the Gentiles. This just and good God, *the Father of our Lord Jesus Christ,* himself gave the Law and the Prophets and the Gospels, and he also is the God of the Apostles, and of the Old and New Testaments.

Tum deinde, quia JESUS CHRI-STUS *ipse, qui venit, ante omnem creaturam natus ex Patre est. Qui cum in omnium conditione Patri ministrasset (per ipsum enim omnia facta sunt), novissimis temporibus se ipsum exinaniens homo factus incarnatus est, cum Deus esset, et homo factus mansit, quod erat, Deus. Corpus assumsit nostro corpori simile, eo solo differens, quod natum ex Virgine et Spiritu Sancto est. Et quoniam hic Jesus Christus natus et passus est in veritate et non per phantasiam communem hanc mortem sustinuit, vere mortuus; vere enim a mortuis resurrexit et post resurrectionem, conversatus cum discipulis suis, assumtus est.*

Tum deinde honore ac dignitate Patri ac Filio sociatum tradiderunt SPIRITUM SANCTUM.

Then, secondly, that JESUS CHRIST himself, who came, was *born of the Father before all creation.* And when in the formation of all things he had served the Father (for by him all things were made), in these last times, emptying himself, he became *man incarnate,* while he was God, and though made man, remained God as he was before. He took a body like our body, differing in this point only, that it was *born of the Virgin and the Holy Ghost.* And since this Jesus Christ *was born* and *suffered* in truth, and not in appearance, he bore the death common to all men and truly *died;* for he truly *rose from the dead,* and after his resurrection, having conversed with his disciples, he *was taken up.*

They also delivered that the HOLY GHOST was associated in honor and dignity with the Father and the Son.

Origen then goes on to say that 'such questions, as to whether the Holy Spirit was born or unborn (*natus an innatus*), whether he was also to be regarded as a Son of God or not, are left for inquiry and investigation out of the holy Scriptures, according to the best of our ability; but it was most clearly preached in the churches that the Holy Spirit inspired every one of the saints and prophets and apostles, and that there was not one Spirit given to the ancients and another to the Christians.' Then he mentions (§ 5) as part of apostolic preaching (*ecclesiastica prædicatio*) the future resurrection and judgment, the freedom of will (*omnem animam rationabilem esse liberi arbitrii et voluntatis*), the struggle of the soul with the devil and his angels, the inspiration of the Scriptures, and their deeper meaning known only to those to whom the Holy Spirit gives wisdom and understanding.

Throughout this passage Origen makes an important distinction between ecclesiastical preaching and theological science, and confines the former to fundamental facts, while to the latter belongs the investigation of the why and wherefore, and the deeper mysteries.

Gregorius Thaumaturgus, of Neo-Cæsarea.   About A.D. 270.

Gregory, surnamed the Great or Thaumaturgus, i. e., the Wonderworker (from his supposed power of miracles), was a pupil and admirer of Origen (on whom he wrote an eloquent panegyric), and Bishop of Neo-Cæsarea in Pontus (from about 240 to 270), which he changed from a heathen into a Christian city. He took a prominent part in the Synod of Antioch (A.D. 269), which condemned the errors of Paul of Samosata, and issued a lengthy creed.[1] He was held in the highest esteem, as we learn from Basil the Great, his successor in office (De Spiritu Sancto, cap. 29, § 74, where he is compared to the apostles and prophets, and called a 'second Moses'), and from Gregory of Nyssa (Vita Gregorii). The following creed (ἔκθεσις πίστεως κατὰ ἀποκάλυψιν Γρηγορίου ἐπισκόπου Νεοκαισαρείας) was, according to the legend related by Gregory of Nyssa a hundred years later, revealed to him by the Apostle John in a vision, at the request of the Virgin Mary. It is somewhat rhetorical, but more explicit on the doctrine of the Trinity than any other ante-Nicene creed, and approaches in this respect the Symbolum Quicunque. The Greek text in Gallandi, Vet. PP. Bibl. p. 385; in Mansi, Tom. I. p. 1030, and Hahn, p. 97. Hahn gives also two Latin versions, one by Rufinus. Two other creeds ascribed to him are not genuine. An English translation of his writings by S. D. F. Salmond, in the Ante-Nicene Christian Library, Vol. XX. (Edinb. 1871).

Εἷς Θεὸς πατὴρ λόγου ζῶντος, σοφίας ὑφεστώσης καὶ δυνάμεως καὶ χαρακτῆρος ἀϊδίου, τέλειος τελείου γεννήτωρ, πατὴρ υἱοῦ μονογενοῦς.

Εἷς κύριος, μόνος ἐκ μόνου, Θεὸς ἐκ Θεοῦ, χαρακτὴρ καὶ εἰκὼν τῆς Θεότητος, λόγος ἐνεργός, σοφία τῆς τῶν ὅλων συστάσεως περιεκτικὴ καὶ δύναμις τῆς ὅλης κτίσεως ποιητική, υἱὸς ἀληθινὸς ἀληθινοῦ πατρός, ἀόρατος ἀοράτου καὶ ἄφθαρτος ἀφθάρτου καὶ ἀθάνατος ἀθανάτου καὶ ἀΐδιος ἀϊδίου.

Καὶ ἓν πνεῦμα ἅγιον ἐκ Θεοῦ

There is one God, the Father of the living Word, who is the substantive wisdom and eternal power and image of God: the perfect origin (begetter) of the perfect (begotten): the Father of the only-begotten Son.

There is one Lord, one of one (only of the only), God of God, the image and likeness of the Godhead, the mighty Word, the wisdom which comprehends the constitution of all things, and the power which produces all creation; the true Son of the true Father, Invisible of Invisible, and Incorruptible of Incorruptible, and Immortal of Immortal, and Everlasting of Everlasting.

And there is one Holy Ghost,

[1] See the Greek text of the creed of the Antiochean Synod in Hahn, pp. 91–96; an English translation in Swainson, pp. 52–55.

τὴν ὕπαρξιν ἔχον καὶ δι' αὐτοῦ πε-
φηνὸς δηλαδὴ τοῖς ἀνθρώποις, εἰκὼν
τοῦ υἱοῦ τελείου τελεία, ζωὴ ζώντων
αἰτία¹ [πηγὴ ἁγία],² ἁγιότης ἁγια-
σμοῦ χορηγός,³ ἐν ᾧ φανεροῦται θεὸς
ὁ πατὴρ ὁ ἐπὶ πάντων καὶ ἐν πᾶσι,
καὶ θεὸς ὁ υἱὸς ὁ διὰ πάντων, τριὰς
τελεία, δόξῃ καὶ ἀϊδιότητι καὶ βασιλείᾳ μὴ μεριζομένη μηδὲ ἀπαλλο-
τριουμένη.

Οὔτε οὖν κτιστόν τι ἢ δοῦλον ἐν
τῇ τριάδι, οὔτε ἐπείσακτον,⁴ ὡς πρό-
τερον μὲν οὐχ ὑπάρχον, ὕστερον δὲ
ἐπεισελθόν· οὔτε οὖν ἐνέλιπέ ποτε
υἱὸς πατρὶ, οὔτε υἱῷ πνεῦμα, ἀλλὰ
ἄτρεπτος καὶ ἀναλλοίωτος ἡ αὐτὴ
τριὰς ἀεί.

having his existence from God,
and being manifested by the
Son, namely, to men, the perfect
likeness of the perfect Son, Life,
the cause of the living¹ [the sacred fount],² sanctity, the Leader
of sanctification:³ in whom is revealed God the Father, who is over
all things and in all things, and
God the Son, who is through all
things: a perfect Trinity, not divided nor differing in glory and
eternity and sovereignty.

Neither, indeed, is there any
thing created or subservient in the
Trinity, nor introduced,⁴ as though
not there before but coming in
afterwards; nor, indeed, has the
Son ever been without the Father,
nor the Spirit without the Son, but
the Trinity is ever the same, un-
varying and unchangeable.

LUCIAN, OF ANTIOCH. A.D. 300.

From ATHANASIUS, *Epist. de Synodis Arimini et Seleuciæ celebratis*, § 23 (*Opera* ed. Montfauc. Tom. I. Pt. II. p. 735), and Socrates, *Hist. Eccl.* Lib. II. cap. 10.

LUCIANUS was a learned presbyter of Antioch, who died a martyr, A.D. 311, under Maxi-
minus, in Nicomedia. His creed was found after his death, and was, together with three
similar creeds, laid before the Synod of Antioch, held A.D. 341, in the hope that it might be
substituted for the obnoxious Creed of Nicæa. It is also called the *second Antiochean Formula*.
It was translated into Latin by Hilarius Pictav. in his book *De Synodis s. de Fide Orientalium*, § 29. See Socrates, *H. E.* Lib. II. cap. 10 and 18; Sozomen, *H. E.* Lib. III. cap. 5;
VI. 12; Mansi, *Conc.* Tom. II. pp. 1339-1342; Walch, l. c. p. 34; Hahn, l. c. p. 100.

¹ Variations: τελεία ζωὴ ζώντων, *perfecta vita viventium; viventium causa.* See Hahn,
p. 99.
² Omitted in some MSS., and by Hahn.
³ Rufinus: *sanctitas sanctificationis præstatrix.* Another Latin version: *sanctitas et fons
sanctitatis et œdificationis administrator.*
⁴ Latin version: *subintroductum.* Rufinus: *superinductum.*

Πιστεύομεν ἀκολούθως τῇ εὐαγ-
γελικῇ καὶ ἀποστολικῇ παραδόσει
εἰς ἕνα θεὸν πατέρα παντοκράτορα, τὸν τῶν ὅλων δημιουργόν τε
καὶ ποιητὴν καὶ προνοητήν.

Καὶ εἰς ἕνα κύριον Ἰησοῦν
Χριστόν, τὸν υἱὸν αὐτοῦ, τὸν μονογενῆ θεόν,[1] δι' οὗ τὰ πάντα (ἐγένετο),
τὸν γεννηθέντα πρὸ τῶν αἰώνων ἐκ
τοῦ πατρός, θεὸν ἐκ θεοῦ, ὅλον ἐξ
ὅλου [totum ex toto], μόνον ἐκ μόνου
[unum ex uno], τέλειον ἐκ τελείου,
βασιλέα ἐκ βασιλέως, κύριον ἀπὸ
[ἐκ] κυρίου, λόγον ζῶντα, σοφίαν,
ζωήν, φῶς ἀληθινόν, ὁδόν, ἀλήθειαν, ἀνάστασιν, ποιμένα, θύραν,
ἄτρεπτόν τε καὶ ἀναλλοίωτον, τῆς
θεότητος, οὐσίας τε καὶ βουλῆς καὶ
δυνάμεως καὶ δόξης τοῦ πατρὸς ἀπα-
ράλλακτον εἰκόνα, τὸν πρωτότοκον
πάσης κτίσεως, τὸν ὄντα ἐν ἀρχῇ
πρὸς τὸν θεόν, θεὸν λόγον, κατὰ
τὸ εἰρημένον ἐν εὐαγγελίῳ· καὶ θεὸς
ἦν ὁ λόγος, δι' οὗ τὰ πάντα ἐγένετο καὶ ἐν ᾧ τὰ πάντα συνέστηκε·
τὸν ἐπ' ἐσχάτων τῶν ἡμερῶν κατελθόντα ἄνωθεν καὶ γεννηθέντα ἐκ
παρθένου, κατὰ τὰς γραφάς, καὶ
ἄνθρωπον γενόμενον, μεσίτην θεοῦ
καὶ ἀνθρώπων, ἀπόστολόν τε τῆς
πίστεως ἡμῶν, καὶ ἀρχηγὸν ζωῆς,
ὥς φησι· ὅτι καταβέβηκα ἐκ τοῦ
οὐρανοῦ, οὐχ ἵνα ποιῶ τὸ θέλημα

We believe, in accordance with
evangelic and apostolic tradition,
in ONE GOD THE FATHER AL-
MIGHTY, the Maker and Provider
of all things.

And in ONE LORD JESUS CHRIST
his Son, the only-begotten God,
through whom all things were
made, who was begotten of the Father before all ages, God of God,
Whole of Whole, One of One, Perfect of Perfect, King of King, Lord
of Lord, the living Word, Wisdom,
Life, True Light, Way, Truth, Resurrection, Shepherd, Door, unchange-
ble and unalterable, the immutable
likeness of the Godhead, both of the
substance and will and power and
glory of the Father, the first-born of
all creation, who was in the beginning with God, the Divine Logos,
according to what is said in the
gospel: 'And the Word was God,'[2]
through whom all things were made,
and in whom 'all things consist:'[3]
who in the last days came down
from above, and was born of a
Virgin, according to the Scriptures, and became man, the Mediator between God and man, and
the Apostle of our Faith,[4] and the
Prince of life; as he says,[5] 'I have
come down from heaven, not to do

---

[1] I connect μονογενῆ with θεόν, which accords with the reading of some of the oldest MSS.
(the Sinaitic and the Vatican), in John i. 18 (μονογενὴς θεός instead of υἱός). But according
to the usual punctuation adopted by Hahn we must translate, 'his only-begotten Son, God.'

[2] John i. 1.   [3] Col. i. 17.   [4] Heb. iii. 1.   [5] John vi. 38.

τὸ ἐμόν, ἀλλὰ τὸ θέλημα τοῦ πέμ-
ψαντός με· τὸν παθόντα ὑπὲρ
ἡμῶν καὶ ἀναστάντα τῇ τρίτῃ ἡμέρᾳ,
καὶ ἀνελθόντα εἰς οὐρανοὺς καὶ
καθεσθέντα ἐν δεξιᾷ τοῦ πατρος,
καὶ πάλιν ἐρχόμενον μετὰ δόξης
καὶ δυνάμεως κρῖναι ζῶντας καὶ νεκρούς.

Καὶ εἰς τὸ πνεῦμα τὸ ἅγιον,
τὸ εἰς παράκλησιν καὶ ἁγιασμὸν
καὶ τελείωσιν τοῖς πιστεύουσι διδό-
μενον, καθὼς καὶ ὁ κύριος ἡμῶν
Ἰησοῦς Χριστὸς διετάξατο τοῖς μαθηταῖς, λέγων· πορευθέντες μαθητεύσατε πάντα τὰ ἔθνη, βαπτίζοντες
αὐτοὺς εἰς τὸ ὄνομα τοῦ πατρὸς καὶ
τοῦ υἱοῦ καὶ τοῦ ἁγίου πνεύματος·
δηλονότι πατρὸς ἀληθῶς πατρὸς
ὄντος, υἱοῦ δὲ ἀληθῶς υἱοῦ ὄντος,
τοῦ δὲ ἁγίου πνεύματος ἀληθῶς
ἁγίου πνεύματος ὄντος, τῶν ὀνο-
μάτων οὐχ ἁπλῶς οὐδὲ ἀργῶς κει-
μένων, ἀλλὰ σημαινόντων ἀκριβῶς
τὴν οἰκείαν ἑκάστου τῶν ὀνομαζο-
μένων ὑπόστασιν καὶ τάξιν καὶ δό-
ξαν· ὡς εἶναι τῇ μὲν ὑποστάσει
τρία, τῇ δὲ συμφωνίᾳ ἕν.

Ταύτην οὖν ἔχοντες τὴν πίστιν (καὶ
ἐξ ἀρχῆς καὶ μέχρι τέλους ἔχοντες)
ἐνώπιον τοῦ θεοῦ καὶ τοῦ Χριστοῦ
πᾶσαν αἱρετικὴν κακοδοξίαν ἀναθεματίζομεν. Καὶ εἴ τις παρὰ τὴν ὑγιῆ
τῶν γραφῶν ὀρθὴν πίστιν διδάσκει,
λέγων, ἢ χρόνον ἢ καιρὸν ἢ αἰῶνα
ἢ εἶναι ἢ γεγονέναι πρὸ τοῦ γεννη-

mine own will, but the will of him
that sent me:' who suffered for
us, and rose for us the third day,
and ascended into heaven and sitteth on the right hand of the
Father, and again is coming with
glory and power to judge the quick
and the dead.

And in THE HOLY GHOST given
for consolation and sanctification
and perfection to those who believe; as also our Lord Jesus Christ
commanded his disciples, saying,
'Go ye, teach all nations, baptizing
them in the name of the Father,
and of the Son, and of the Holy
Ghost;'[1] clearly of the Father who
is really a Father, and of a Son
who is really a Son, and of the
Holy Ghost who is really a Holy
Ghost; these names being assigned not vaguely nor idly, but
indicating accurately the special
personality, order, and glory of
those named, so that in Personality they are three, but in harmony one.

Having then this faith (from the
beginning and holding it to the end)
before God and Christ we anathematize all heretical false doctrine.
And if any one, contrary to the
right faith of the Scriptures, teaches and says that there has been a
season or time or age before the

---

[1] Matt. xxviii. 19.

θῆναι τὸν υἱόν, ἀνάθεμα ἔστω. Καὶ εἴ τις λέγει τὸν υἱὸν κτίσμα ὡς ἓν τῶν κτισμάτων, ἢ γέννημα ὡς ἓν τῶν γεννημάτων, ἢ ποίημα ὡς ἓν τῶν ποιημάτων, καὶ μὴ ὡς αἱ θεῖαι γραφαὶ παραδέδωκαν τῶν προειρημένων ἕκαστον ἀφ' ἑκάστου, ἢ εἴ τις ἄλλο διδάσκει ἢ εὐαγγελίζεται παρ' ὃ παρελάβομεν, ἀνάθεμα ἔστω.

Ἡμεῖς γὰρ πᾶσι τοῖς ἐκ τῶν θείων γραφῶν παραδεδομένοις ὑπό τε τῶν προφητῶν καὶ ἀποστόλων ἀληθινῶς καὶ ἐμφόβως καὶ πιστεύομεν καὶ ἀκολουθοῦμεν.

Son of God was begotten, let him be accursed. And if any one says that the Son is a creature as one of the creatures, or generated as one of the things generated, or made as one of the things made, and not as the divine Scriptures have handed down each of the forenamed statements; or if a man teaches or preaches any thing else contrary to what we have received, let him be accursed. For we truly and clearly both believe and follow all things from the holy Scriptures that have been transmitted to us by the Prophets and Apostles.

THE PRIVATE CREED OF ARIUS.   A.D. 328.

The preceding Creed of Lucian seems to have already in view the rising heresy of ARIUS, Presbyter of Alexandria (d. 336), which kindled one of the greatest theological controversies, and became the occasion of the Nicene Council and Creed. We insert it, therefore, in this place, between Lucian and Eusebius, to show how far Arius agreed with the Catholic faith of that age. His peculiar tenets, however, which were condemned at Nicæa in 325, are skillfully avoided in this private confession. It is heretical not by what it says, but by what it omits. It was to pave the way for his restoration. It was laid before the Emperor Constantine, at his request, and is reported by Socrates, *Hist. Eccl.* Lib. I. cap. 26, and Sozomen, *Hist. Eccl.* Lib. II. cap. 27 ; see also Mansi, *Conc.* Tom. II. p. 1157, and Hahn, pp. 192 sq.

Πιστεύομεν εἰς ἕνα Θεόν, πατέρα παντοκράτορα·
Καὶ εἰς κύριον Ἰησοῦν Χριστόν, τὸν υἱὸν αὐτοῦ,
τὸν ἐξ αὐτοῦ πρὸ πάντων τῶν αἰώνων γεγεννημένον,
θεὸν λόγον,
δι' οὗ τὰ πάντα ἐγένετο, τά τε ἐν τοῖς οὐρανοῖς καὶ τὰ ἐπὶ τῆς γῆς·

We believe in ONE GOD, the Father Almighty ;
And in THE LORD JESUS CHRIST, his Son,
who was begotten of him before all ages,
the Divine Logos,
through whom all things were made, both those in the heavens and those on the earth :

τὸν κατελϑόντα καὶ σαρκωϑέντα,	who came down and was made flesh;
καὶ παϑόντα,	and suffered;
καὶ ἀναστάντα,	and rose again;
καὶ ἀνελϑόντα εἰς τοὺς οὐρανούς,	and ascended to the heavens;
καὶ πάλιν ἐρχόμενον κρῖναι ζῶντας καὶ νεκρούς.	and shall come again to judge the quick and the dead.
Καὶ εἰς τὸ ἅγιον πνεῦμα.	And in THE HOLY GHOST;
καὶ εἰς σαρκὸς ἀνάστασιν,	and in the resurrection of the flesh;
καὶ εἰς ζωὴν τοῦ μέλλοντος αἰῶνος,	and in the life of the world to come;
καὶ εἰς βασιλείαν οὐρανῶν,	and in a kingdom of heaven;
καὶ εἰς μίαν καϑολικὴν ἐκκλησίαν τοῦ ϑεοῦ, τὴν ἀπὸ περάτων ἕως περάτων.[1]	and in one Catholic Church of God which extends to the ends of the earth.

EUSEBIUS, OF CÆSAREA. A.D. 325.

SOCRATES, *Hist. Eccl.* Lib. I. cap. 8.

EUSEBIUS, Bishop of Cæsarea, in Palestine (d. 340), the Church historian, the friend and eulogist of Constantine I., and a leading member of the Council of Nicæa (325), forms the connecting link between the ante-Nicene and the Nicene Church. In his account of that Council he mentions the following creed, which his church in Cæsarea had received from the bishops of former times in catechizing and at baptism, which he himself had learned from Scripture, believed, and taught, and which he had laid before the Emperor and the Council. It comes very near the Nicene Creed as adopted in 325, and was the basis of it. but the characteristic shibboleth of Nicene orthodoxy, the term *homoousios* or *consubstantial*, is wanting. See *Eusebii Cæsareensis Episcopi de fide Nicænæ exposita*, in Athanasius, *Epistola de decretis Synodi Nicænæ* (*Opera*, Tom. I. Pt. I. pp. 238 sqq., ed. Montfauc.); Socrates, *Hist. Eccl.* Lib. I. cap. 8; Theodoret, *Hist. Eccl.* Lib I. cap. 12.

Πιστεύομεν εἰς ἕνα ϑεόν πατέρα παντοκράτορα,	We believe in ONE GOD THE FATHER Almighty,
τὸν τῶν ἁπάντων ὁρατῶν τε καὶ ἀοράτων ποιητήν·	Maker of all things visible and invisible;
Καὶ εἰς ἕνα κύριον Ἰησοῦν Χριστόν,	And in ONE LORD JESUS CHRIST,
τὸν τοῦ ϑεοῦ λόγον,	the Word of God,

---

[1] The Latin version in Mansi: '*quæ ab una orbis terrarum ora ad alteram usque porrigitur.*'

θεὸν ἐκ θεοῦ,

φῶς ἐκ φωτὸς,

ζωὴν ἐκ ζωῆς,

υἱὸν μονογενῆ,

πρωτότοκον πάσης κτίσεως,

πρὸ πάντων τῶν αἰώνων ἐκ τοῦ θεοῦ πατρὸς γεγεννημένον,

δι' οὗ καὶ ἐγένετο τὰ πάντα·

τὸν διὰ τὴν ἡμετέραν σωτηρίαν σαρκωθέντα καὶ ἐν ἀνθρώποις πολιτευσάμενον,

καὶ παθόντα,

καὶ ἀναστάντα τῇ τρίτῃ ἡμέρᾳ,

καὶ ἀνελθόντα πρὸς τὸν πατέρα,

καὶ ἥξοντα πάλιν ἐν δόξῃ κρῖναι ζῶντας καὶ νεκρούς.

[Πιστεύομεν] καὶ εἰς ἕν πνεῦμα ἅγιον.[1]

Τούτων ἕκαστον εἶναι καὶ ὑπάρχειν πιστεύοντες, πατέρα ἀληθῶς πατέρα καὶ υἱὸν ἀληθῶς υἱὸν καὶ πνεῦμα ἅγιον ἀληθῶς πνεῦμα ἅγιον, καθὼς καὶ ὁ κύριος ἡμῶν ἀποστέλλων εἰς τὸ κήρυγμα τοὺς ἑαυτοῦ μαθητὰς εἶπε· πορευθέντες μαθητεύσατε πάντα τὰ ἔθνη, βαπτίζοντες αὐτοὺς εἰς τὸ ὄνομα τοῦ πατρὸς καὶ τοῦ υἱοῦ καὶ τοῦ ἁγίου πνεύματος.

God of God,

Light of Light,

Life of Life,

the only-begotten Son,

the first-born of every creature,

begotten of God the Father before all ages,

by whom also all things were made;

who for our salvation was made flesh and made his home among men;

and suffered;

and rose on the third day;

and ascended to the Father;

and will come again in glory, to judge the quick and the dead.

[We believe] also in ONE HOLY GHOST.[1]

We believe that each of these is and exists, the Father truly Father, and the Son truly Son, and the Holy Ghost truly Holy Ghost; even as our Lord, when sending forth his disciples to preach, said: 'Go and make disciples of all nations, baptizing them into the name of the Father, and of the Son, and of the Holy Ghost.'

To this creed Eusebius adds: 'And concerning these things we affirm that we so hold and so think, and have of old so held, and will so hold till death, and stand steadfast in this faith, anathematizing all ungodly heresy. We testify before Almighty God and our Lord Jesus Christ that we have thought all this in heart and soul ever since we knew ourselves, and we now so think and speak in truth, being able to show by evidence and to convince you that we in past times so believed and preached accordingly.'

---

[1] Here the Creed of Cæsarea stops. What follows is an explanatory summary or a personal confession of Eusebiu   This difference Hahn seems to have overlooked (p. 47).

CYRIL, OF JERUSALEM. ABOUT A.D. 350.

From his Κατηχήσεις.

CYRIL was elected Bishop of Jerusalem in 350; was expelled by the Arians in 360; reinstated in 361; attended the second œcumenical Council in 381 as an advocate of the Nicene orthodoxy (although for some time he had sided with the semi-Arians); he died in 386. He wrote in 348, while he was presbyter of the Church in Jerusalem, twenty-three Catechetical Lectures (Κατηχήσεις) or Sermons on the baptismal Creed used in Jerusalem, which he asserts to be the faith of the universal Church (*Cat.* XVII. § 3), also 'the holy and apostolic faith' (*Cat.* XVIII. § 32), although Cyril knows nothing of a literal composition by the Apostles. The Lectures were delivered to those who hoped to be baptized on the ensuing Easter eve. The Creed thus explained is not given at length in the manuscripts, since it was not to be written on paper, but to be engraved on the memory, and to serve to the baptized Christian as a viaticum for his journey through life, by which he might test the doctrine of Cyril or any other teacher. He claims for it antiquity and agreement with the Scripture from which it was drawn (*Cat.* V. § 12).

From these Lectures and ancient headings A. Aug. Touttée, the Benedictine editor of the Works of Cyril (Venet. 1763), has compiled the following creed. It closely resembles the Nicene Creed of 325, but, like that of Eusebius, it avoids the ὁμοούσιον. At the same time, it contains most of the additional clauses of the Constantinopolitan Creed of 381.

Comp. the critical edition of Cyril's Lectures by Reischl and Rupp, Munich, 1848–1850; my *Church History*, Vol. III. pp. 924 sqq.; Swainson, l. c. pp. 16 sqq.; Hort, l. c. pp. 84 sqq. The fourth Catechetical Lecture of Cyril, in which he goes over the creed in a summary way, is printed in Heurtley's *De Fide et Symbolo*, pp. 42–60.

Longer Formula.

Πιστεύομεν εἰς ἕνα Θεόν Πατέρα παντοκράτορα,	We believe in ONE GOD THE FATHER Almighty,
ποιητὴν οὐρανοῦ καὶ γῆς, ὁρατῶν τε πάντων καὶ ἀοράτων·	Maker of heaven and earth, and of all things visible and invisible;
Καὶ εἰς ἕνα κύριον Ἰησοῦν Χριστόν,	And in ONE LORD JESUS CHRIST,
τὸν υἱὸν τοῦ Θεοῦ τὸν μονογενῆ,	the only-begotten Son of God,
τὸν ἐκ τοῦ πατρὸς γεννηθέντα, πρὸ πάντων αἰώνων,	begotten of the Father before all ages,
Θεὸν ἀληθινὸν,	very God,
δι' οὗ τὰ πάντα ἐγένετο·	by whom all things were made;
ἐν σαρκὶ παραγενόμενον,[1]	who appeared in the flesh,
καὶ ἐνανθρωπήσαντα	and became man
[ἐκ παρθένου καὶ πνεύματος ἁγίου]·[2]	[of the Virgin and the Holy Ghost];[2]
σταυρωθέντα καὶ ταφέντα,	was crucified and was buried;

---

[1] Ussher, Bull, and Hahn read σαρκωθέντα, *was made flesh.*

[2] The words in brackets are doubtful, and are so considered by Touttée, Hahn, and Swainson.

ἀναστάντα τῇ τρίτῃ ἡμέρᾳ,	rose on the third day;
καὶ ἀνελθόντα εἰς τοὺς οὐρανοὺς	and ascended into heaven,
αἱ καθίσαντα ἐκ δεξιῶν τοῦ πα-	and sitteth on the right hand of
τρὸς,	the Father;
καὶ ἐρχόμενον ἐν δόξῃ,	and will come again in glory,
κρῖναι ζῶντας καὶ νεκρούς·	to judge the quick and the dead;
οὗ τῆς βασιλείας οὐκ ἔσται τέλος.	of whose kingdom there shall be
	no end.
Καὶ εἰς ἓν ἅγιον πνεῦμα,	And in ONE HOLY GHOST,
τὸν παράκλητον,	the Advocate,
τὸ λαλῆσαν ἐν τοῖς προφήταις.	who spake in the Prophets.
Καὶ εἰς ἓν βάπτισμα μετανοίας εἰς	And in one baptism of repentance
ἄφεσιν ἁμαρτιῶν,	for the remission of sins;
καὶ εἰς μίαν ἁγίαν καθολικὴν ἐκκλη-	and in one holy Catholic Church;
σίαν,	
καὶ εἰς σαρκὸς ἀνάστασιν,	and in the resurrection of the flesh,
καὶ εἰς ζωὴν αἰώνιον.	and in life everlasting.

Shorter Formula.

In his *Catechetical Lectures*, XIX. § 9 (ed. Touttée, p. 309), where he gives an account of the baptismal service in the church of Jerusalem, Cyril mentions also a much briefer creed, as follows:

Πιστεύω εἰς τὸν Πατέρα,	I believe in the Father,
καὶ εἰς τὸν Υἱὸν,	and in the Son,
καὶ εἰς τὸ ἅγιον Πνεῦμα,	and in the Holy Ghost,
καὶ εἰς ἓν βάπτισμα μετανοίας.	and in one baptism of repentance.

NOTE.—This is regarded by Touttée, Walch, and Swainson as an independent formula, as the shorter baptismal creed of the church of Jerusalem. On the other hand, Hahn (p. 53) endeavors to show from the context that this form was not properly a baptismal confession, but a preparatory form of consecration (ἡ πρὸς τὸν Χριστὸν σύνταξις) following the formula of renunciation (μετὰ τὴν ἀπόταξιν τοῦ Σατανᾶ). It resembles in brevity the creed of Cyprian (p. 20), and, judging from its simplicity, is much older than the longer form.

Two Creeds of Epiphanius.   A.D. 374.

Ancoratus, cap. 119, 120.

EPIPHANIUS, the learned champion of a narrow and intolerant orthodoxy, was born in Palestine about 310, of Jewish parentage; Bishop of Salamis or Constantia, the capital of the island of Cyprus, 367; died at sea, 403. He has preserved to us two creeds at the close of his work *Ancoratus* (ὁ ἀγκύρωτος, *secured as by an anchor*, the Anchored One), which was written in

373 or 374, at the request of several presbyters in Pamphylia, as an exposition of the Nicene faith of the Holy Trinity, in opposition to the heresies of his age. The creeds are given as brief summaries of the preceding instruction. See Epiphanii *Opera*, ed. Petavius, Tom. II. pp. 122 sqq.; ed. Migne, *Patrol.* Vol. XLIII. pp. 231 sqq.; also Hahn, l. c. pp. 56 sqq.; and Swainson, l. c. pp. 85 sqq. Comp. my *Church History*, Vol. III. pp. 926 sqq.

First Formula.

This is the shorter formula, and is chiefly interesting for its literal agreement with the fuller Nicene Creed as adopted, according to the current opinion, seven years afterwards by the second œcumenical Council (381). At the same time, it retains several clauses from the original Nicene Creed (325), especially · Light of Light, and the concluding anathema against the Arians. Epiphanius introduces this formula by the remark that 'this is the holy faith of the Catholic Church (τὴν ἁγίαν πίστιν τῆς καθολικῆς ἐκκλησίας), as the holy and only Virgin of God [i. e., the pure Church] received it from the holy Apostles and the Lord to keep,' and that 'every person preparing for the holy laver of baptism must learn it as the common mother of us all confesses it, saying, We believe,' etc.

Πιστεύομεν εἰς ἕνα Θεὸν Πατέρα παντοκράτορα,	We believe in ONE GOD THE FATHER Almighty,
ποιητὴν οὐρανοῦ τε καὶ γῆς, ὁρατῶν τε πάντων καὶ ἀοράτων·	Maker of heaven and earth, and of all things visible and invisible;
Καὶ εἰς ἕνα Κύριον Ἰησοῦν Χριστὸν,	And in ONE Lord JESUS CHRIST,
τὸν Υἱὸν τοῦ Θεοῦ τὸν μονογενῆ,	the only-begotten Son of God,
τὸν ἐκ τοῦ Πατρὸς γεννηθέντα πρὸ πάντων τῶν αἰώνων,	begotten of the Father before all worlds,
τουτέστιν ἐκ τῆς οὐσίας τοῦ Πατρὸς,	that is, of the substance of the Father,
φῶς ἐκ φωτὸς,	Light of Light,
Θεὸν ἀληθινὸν ἐκ Θεοῦ ἀληθινοῦ,	very God of very God,
γεννηθέντα, οὐ ποιηθέντα,	begotten, not made,
ὁμοούσιον τῷ Πατρί·	being of one substance (consubstantial) with the Father;
δι' οὗ τὰ πάντα ἐγένετο, τά τε ἐν τοῖς οὐρανοῖς καὶ τὰ ἐν τῇ γῇ·	by whom all things were made, both those in the heavens and those on earth;
τὸν δι' ἡμᾶς τοὺς ἀνθρώπους καὶ διὰ τὴν ἡμετέραν σωτηρίαν κατελθόντα ἐκ τῶν οὐρανῶν,	who for us men, and for our salvation, came down from heaven,

καὶ σαρκωθέντα ἐκ Πνεύματος Ἁγίου καὶ Μαρίας τῆς Παρθένου, καὶ ἐνανθρωπήσαντα·	and was incarnate by the Holy Ghost and the Virgin Mary, and was made man;
σταυρωθέντα τε ὑπὲρ ἡμῶν ἐπὶ Ποντίου Πιλάτου,	He was crucified for us under Pontius Pilate,
καὶ παθόντα, καὶ ταφέντα,	and suffered, and was buried;
καὶ ἀναστάντα τῇ τρίτῃ ἡμέρᾳ, κατὰ τὰς γραφάς·	and the third day He rose again, according to the Scriptures;
καὶ ἀνελθόντα εἰς τοὺς οὐρανοὺς,	and ascended into heaven,
καὶ καθεζόμενον ἐκ δεξιῶν τοῦ Πατρὸς,	and sitteth on the right hand of the Father;
καὶ πάλιν ἐρχόμενον μετὰ δόξης κρῖναι ζῶντας καὶ νεκρούς·	and he shall come again, with glory, to judge the quick and the dead;
οὗ τῆς βασιλείας οὐκ ἔσται τέλος·	of whose kingdom shall be no end;
Καὶ εἰς τὸ Πνεῦμα τὸ Ἅγιον,	And in THE HOLY GHOST,
κύριον, καὶ ζωοποιὸν,	the Lord, and Giver of life,
τὸ ἐκ τοῦ Πατρὸς ἐκπορευόμενον,	who proceedeth from the Father,
τὸ σὺν Πατρὶ καὶ Υἱῷ συμπροσκυνούμενον καὶ συνδοξαζόμενον,	who with the Father and the Son together is worshiped and glorified,
τὸ λαλῆσαν διὰ τῶν προφητῶν·	who spake by the Prophets;
εἰς μίαν ἁγίαν καθολικὴν καὶ ἀποστολικὴν Ἐκκλησίαν·	in one holy Catholic and Apostolic Church;
ὁμολογοῦμεν ἓν βάπτισμα εἰς ἄφεσιν ἁμαρτιῶν·	we acknowledge one baptism for the remission of sins;
προσδοκῶμεν ἀνάστασιν νεκρῶν,	and we look for the resurrection of the dead;
καὶ ζωὴν τοῦ μέλλοντος αἰῶνος.	and the life of the world to come.
Τοὺς δὲ λέγοντας, ἦν ποτὲ ὅτε οὐκ ἦν, καὶ πρὶν γεννηθῆναι οὐκ ἦν, ἢ ὅτι ἐξ οὐκ ὄντων ἐγένετο, ἢ ἐξ ἑτέρας ὑποστάσεως ἢ οὐσίας, φάσκοντας εἶναι ῥευστὸν[1] ἢ ἀλλοιωτὸν τὸν τοῦ Θεοῦ Υἱόν, τούτους ἀναθεματίζει ἡ καθολικὴ καὶ ἀποστολικὴ Ἐκκλησία.	But those who say, 'There was a time when he was not,' and, 'He was not before he was begotten,' or, 'He was made of nothing [of things that are not],' or 'of another substance or essence,' saying that the Son of God is effluent[1] or variable, these the Catholic and Apostolic Church anathematizes.

---

[1] Substituted for κτιστὸν ἢ τρεπτόν, *made or changeable*, in the Nicene Formula of 325.

NOTE.—Epiphanius adds: 'And this faith was delivered from the holy Apostles and in the Church, [in] the holy city, from all the holy bishops (ἀπὸ πάντων ὁμοῦ τῶν ἁγίων ἐπισκό- πων), together more than three hundred and ten in number.' This evidently refers to the Council of Nicæa (which consisted of three hundred and eighteen bishops), and corrects the pre- ceding statement of the apostolic origin of the Nicene Creed, which is true only of the substance, not of the form. But the reference itself is incorrect; for the creed of Epiphanius does not agree with the original Nicene Creed of 325, but word for word with the Nicæno-Constantinopolitan Creed of 381, except that it retains from the former the clauses τουτέστιν ἐκ τῆς οὐσίας τοῦ Πα- τρός, Θεὸν ἐκ Θεοῦ, and the concluding anathema, which was wisely omitted by the Council of Constantinople. It is evident, therefore, that the important clauses which that council added to the original Nicene Creed, especially after the words ' in the Holy Ghost,' existed at least as early as 374, and in part much earlier, since some of them are found also in Cyril (348), and even in the heretical creed of Arius, as well as in the Western creeds of Tertullian and Irenæus. It is questionable whether the Council of Constantinople adopted a new creed differing from that of Nicæa. It appears, indeed, in the seventh canon of the Constantinopolitan Council (in Mansi's Collection, Tom. III. pp. 564 and 565), but it is wanting in the paraphrase from the Arabic (in Mansi), among the canons of Johannes Scholasticus (d. 578), and in the epitome of Symeon Magister, who both give only six canons ; nor is it mentioned by the Church historians Soc- rates, Sozomen, and Theodoret, or by any document before the fourth œcumenical Council of Chalcedon, 451, where the enlarged Nicene Creed was adopted, though not without objection from the Egyptian bishops. It seems, therefore, that the additions to the Nicene Creed, while they *certainly* existed several years before 381, and *may* have been put forward at the Coun- cil of Constantinople, were, nevertheless, not generally received till 451. See Vol. I. p. 25 ; Lumby, l. c. pp. 71–84; Swainson, p. 95 ; Hort, pp. 73 sqq.

Second Formula.

The second formula of Epiphanius is his own production, and is an enlargement or paraphrase of the first, i. e., the Nicene Creed, with several additional clauses against heretical opinions, especially against Apollinarianism (comp. *Ancor*. c. 75–81) and Pneumatomachianism (comp *Ancor*. c. 65–74). He introduces it by the remark : 'Inasmuch as several other heresies, one after another, have appeared in this our generation, that is, in the tenth year of the reign of the Emperors Valentinianus and Valens, and the sixth of Gratianus [i. e., A.D. 374], . . . you as well as we, and all the orthodox bishops—in one word, the whole Catholic Church, especially those who come to holy baptism—make the following confession, in agreement with the faith of those holy fathers above set forth,' etc. The formula was probably intended for converts from the Apollinarian, Pneumatomachian, and Origenistic heresies. As a general baptismal confession it is too long and minute.

Πιστεύομεν εἰς ἕνα Θεὸν Πατέρα παντοκράτορα,	We believe in ONE GOD THE FA- THER Almighty,
πάντων ἀοράτων τε καὶ ὁρατῶν ποιητήν·	Maker of all things, invisible and visible ;
Καὶ εἰς ἕνα Κύριον Ἰησοῦν Χρι- στὸν,	And in ONE Lord JESUS CHRIST,
τὸν Υἱὸν τοῦ Θεοῦ.	the Son of God,
γεννηθέντα ἐκ Θεοῦ Πατρὸς μονο- γενῆ,	the only-begotten Son of God the Father,

τουτέστιν ἐκ τῆς οὐσίας τοῦ Πατρὸς,	that is, of the substance of the Father,
Θεὸν ἐκ Θεοῦ,	God of God,
Φῶς ἐκ Φωτὸς,	Light of Light,
Θεὸν ἀληθινὸν ἐκ Θεοῦ ἀληθινοῦ,	very God of very God,
γεννηθέντα οὐ ποιηθέντα,	begotten, not made,
ὁμοούσιον τῷ Πατρί,	being of one substance with the Father,
δι' οὗ τὰ παντὰ ἐγένετο, τὰ τε ἐν τοῖς οὐρανοῖς καὶ τὰ ἐν τῇ γῇ, ὁρατά τε καὶ ἀόρατα·	by whom all things were made, both those in the heavens and those on earth, things visible and invisible;
τὸν δι' ἡμᾶς τοὺς ἀνθρώπους καὶ διὰ τὴν ἡμετέραν σωτηρίαν κατελθόντα, καὶ σαρκωθέντα,	who for us men, and for our salvation, came down, and was made flesh,
τουτέστι γεννηθέντα τελείως ἐκ τῆς ἁγίας Μαρίας τῆς ἀειπαρθένου διὰ πνεύματος ἁγίου, ἐνανθρωπήσαντα,	that is, begotten perfectly of the holy ever-Virgin Mary by the Holy Ghost, who became man,
τουτέστι τέλειον[1] ἄνθρωπον λαβόντα,	that is, assumed a perfect man,
ψυχὴν καὶ σῶμα καὶ νοῦν καὶ πάντα, εἴ τι ἐστὶν ἄνθρωπος, χωρὶς ἁμαρτίας,	soul and body and mind (spirit), and all that belongs to man, without sin,
οὐκ ἀπὸ σπέρματος ἀνδρὸς, οὐδὲ ἐν ἀνθρώπῳ,	not of the seed of man, nor in a man,
ἀλλ' εἰς ἑαυτὸν σάρκα ἀναπλάσαντα εἰς μίαν ἁγίαν ἑνότητα,	but forming for himself flesh into one holy unity,
οὐ καθάπερ ἐν προφήταις ἐνέπνευσέ τε καὶ ἐλάλησε καὶ ἐνήργησεν,	not, as in the Prophets, where he breathed and spoke and wrought,
ἀλλὰ τελείως ἐνανθρωπήσαντα,	but he became perfectly man,
ὁ γὰρ Λόγος σάρξ ἐγένετο,	for the Word became flesh,

---

[1] τέλειον, as also the preceding τελείως and the following νοῦν, are evidently directed against the Apollinarian heresy, which taught only a partial incarnation, and made the divine Logos take the place of the reasonable soul.

οὐ τροπὴν ὑποστὰς,	not undergoing any change,
οὐδὲ μεταβαλὼν τὴν ἑαυτοῦ θεό-	nor converting his Godhead into
τητα εἰς ἀνθρωπότητα,	Manhood,
εἰς μίαν συνενώσαντα ἑαυτοῦ ἁγίαν	[but] uniting into his own one
τελειότητα τε καὶ θεότητα	holy perfection and Godhead,
(εἷς γὰρ ἐστὶν Κύριος Ἰησοῦς Χρι-	(for there is one Lord Jesus Christ
στὸς καὶ οὐ δύο,	and not two,
ὁ αὐτὸς Θεὸς, ὁ αὐτὸς Κύριος, ὁ	the same God, the same Lord, the
αὐτὸς βασιλεύς)·	same King);
παθόντα δὲ τὸν αὐτὸν ἐν σαρκὶ,	the same suffered in the flesh;
καὶ ἀναστάντα,	and rose again;
καὶ ἀνελθόντα εἰς τοὺς οὐρανοὺς ἐν	and went up into heaven in the
αὐτῷ τῷ σώματι,[1]	same body,
ἐνδόξως καθίσαντα ἐν δεξιᾷ τοῦ Πα-	sat down gloriously at the right
τρός·	hand of the Father;
ἐρχόμενον ἐν αὐτῷ τῷ σώματι ἐν	is coming in the same body in
δόξῃ	glory,
κρῖναι ζῶντας καὶ νεκρούς·	to judge the quick and the dead;
οὗ τῆς βασιλείας οὐκ ἔσται τέ-	of whose kingdom there shall be
λος.	no end.
Καὶ εἰς τὸ Ἅγιον Πνεῦμα πι-	And we believe in the HOLY
στεύομεν,	GHOST,
τὸ λαλῆσαν ἐν νόμῳ,	who spake in the Law,
καὶ κηρῦξαν ἐν τοῖς προφήταις,	and preached in the Prophets,
καὶ καταβὰν ἐπὶ τὸν Ἰορδάνην,	and came down at the Jordan,
λαλοῦν ἐν ἀποστόλοις,	who speaks in Apostles,
οἰκοῦν ἐν ἁγίοις·	dwells in saints;
οὕτως δὲ πιστεύομεν ἐν αὐτῷ,	and thus we believe in Him,
ὅτι ἐστὶ Πνεῦμα ἅγιον,	that there is a Holy Spirit,
Πνεῦμα Θεοῦ,	a Spirit of God,
Πνεῦμα τέλειον,	a perfect Spirit,
Πνεῦμα παράκλητον,	a Paraclete Spirit,
ἄκτιστον,	uncreated,
ἐκ τοῦ Πατρὸς ἐκπορευόμενον,	proceeding from the Father,

---

[1] Probably directed against Origen's view of the spiritual resurrection body.

καὶ ἐκ τοῦ Υἱοῦ λαμβανόμενον[1] καὶ πιστευόμενον.

and received [receiving] from the Son, and believed.

Πιστεύομεν εἰς μίαν καθολικὴν καὶ ἀποστολικὴν ἐκκλησίαν,

We believe in one Catholic and Apostolic Church;

καὶ εἰς ἓν βάπτισμα μετανοίας,

and in one baptism of repentance;

καὶ εἰς ἀνάστασιν νεκρῶν,

and in the resurrection of the dead;

καὶ κρίσιν δικαίαν ψυχῶν καὶ σωμάτων,

and in a righteous judgment of the souls and bodies;

καὶ εἰς βασιλείαν οὐρανῶν,

and in the kingdom of heaven;

καὶ εἰς ζωὴν αἰώνιον.

and in life everlasting.

Τοὺς δὲ λέγοντας, ὅτι ἦν ποτὲ ὅτε οὐκ ἦν ὁ Υἱὸς ἢ τὸ Πνεῦμα τὸ Ἅγιον, ἢ ὅτι ἐξ οὐκ ὄντων ἐγένετο, ἢ ἐξ ἑτέρας ὑποστάσεως ἢ οὐσίας, φάσκοντας εἶναι τρεπτὸν ἢ ἀλλοιωτὸν τὸν τὸν Υἱὸν τοῦ Θεοῦ ἢ τὸ Ἅγιον Πνεῦμα, τούτους ἀναθεματίζει ἡ καθολικὴ καὶ ἡ ἀποστολικὴ ἐκκλησία, ἡ μήτηρ ὑμῶν τε καὶ ἡμῶν. Καὶ παλὶν ἀναθεματίζομεν τοὺς μὴ ὁμολογοῦντας ἀνάστασιν νεκρῶν, καὶ πάσας τὰς αἱρέσεις τὰς μὴ ἐκ ταύτης τῆς ὀρθῆς πίστεως οὔσας.

But those who say, 'There was a time when the Son or the Holy Ghost was not,' or, 'He was made of nothing,' or 'of a different substance or essence,' saying 'the Son of God or the Holy Ghost is changeable or variable,' these the Catholic and Apostolic Church, your and our mother, anathematizes. And again we anathematize those who will not confess the resurrection of the dead, and all the heresies which are not of this, the right faith.

Note.—This creed has a striking resemblance to the 'Interpretation of the [Nicene] Symbol' (Ἑρμηνεία εἰς τὸ σύμβολον), which is ascribed to St. Athanasius, and printed in the first volume of the Benedictine edition of his Works, pp. 1278 sq.; in Migne, Vol. XXVI. p. 1252; and in Caspari, Vol. I. pp. 2 sqq. Formerly overlooked by Walch and Hahn, it has been recently examined by Caspari (Vol. I. pp. 1–72), and conclusively proven to be an abridged modification of the formula of Epiphanius; for the original clauses of this formula agree in spirit and style with Epiphanius and with many passages of his Ancoratus and Panarium. Moreover, Athanasius died May 2, 373 (see Larsow, Die Festbriefe des heil. Athanasius, p. 46), i. e., about a year before the composition of the Ancoratus; and he was generally opposed to anti-heretical creeds beyond that of Nicæa, which he considered to be 'sufficient for the refutation of all impiety.' His Ἔκθεσις πίστεως (Hahn, pp. 175 sq.) is no proof to the contrary, for this is a subjective exposition of his personal faith, and was not intended to be a baptismal confession. Swainson (p. 89), without alluding to the lengthy discussion of Caspari, likewise denies the Athanasian authorship of the Ἑρμηνεία.

The Cappadocian Creed, ascribed to St. Basil, stands between the two Epiphanian Creeds, and is likewise an enlargement of the Nicene Creed with reference to the Apollinarian heresy. See Hort, pp. 120 sqq.

---

[1] The codices read λαμβανόμενον and λαμβάνοντα. Caspari (Vol. I. p. 5) conjectures λαμβάνον with reference to John xvi. 14, ἐκ τοῦ ἐμοῦ λήμψεται, and Ancor. c. 7; Pan. hær. 74, c. 1, where Epiphanius uses λαμβάνον.

THE CREED OF THE APOSTOLICAL CONSTITUTIONS.   ABOUT A.D. 350.

Lib. VII. cap. 41 (ed. Ueltzen, p. 183).

Irenæus, Tertullian, and Novatian give us most of the clauses of the Western or Apostles' Creed in its old Roman form (see next section); while Eusebius, Cyril, and Epiphanius bring us to the very text of the Eastern or Nicene Creed.

The following creed from the *Constitutiones Apostolicæ* (a compilation of several generations) belongs to the Eastern family, and resembles closely the longer formula of Cyril of Jerusalem (p. 31), with some original clauses on the Holy Spirit. It originated probably in Antioch about the middle of the fourth century, though some trace it as far back as 280. It was used as a baptismal confession; hence βαπτίζομαι after πιστεύω, and again before 'The Holy Spirit, that is, the Paraclete, who wrought in all the saints from the beginning of the world, at last was sent to the Apostles from the Father, according to the promise of our Lord and Saviour Jesus Christ, and after the Apostles to all believers in the holy Catholic Church.'

Πιστεύω καὶ βαπτίζομαι εἰς ἕνα ἀγέννητον μόνον ἀληθινὸν Θεὸν παντοκράτορα, τὸν Πατέρα τοῦ Χριστοῦ, κτίστην καὶ δημιουργὸν τῶν ἁπάντων, ἐξ οὗ τὰ πάντα·

Καὶ εἰς τὸν Κύριον Ἰησοῦν τὸν Χριστόν, τὸν μονογενῆ αὐτοῦ Υἱόν, τὸν πρωτότοκον πάσης κτίσεως, τὸν πρὸ αἰώνων εὐδοκίᾳ τοῦ Πατρὸς γεννηθέντα [οὐ κτισθέντα], δι' οὗ τὰ πάντα ἐγένετο τὰ ἐν οὐρανοῖς καὶ ἐπὶ γῆς, ὁρατά τε καὶ ἀόρατα· τὸν ἐπ' ἐσχάτων ἡμερῶν κατελθόντα ἐξ οὐρανῶν, καὶ σάρκα ἀναλαβόντα, καὶ ἐκ τῆς ἁγίας παρθένου Μαρίας γεννηθέντα, καὶ πολιτευσάμενον ὁσίως κατὰ τοὺς νόμους τοῦ Θεοῦ καὶ Πατρὸς αὐτοῦ, καὶ σταυρωθέντα ἐπὶ Ποντίου Πιλάτου, καὶ ἀποθανόντα ὑπὲρ ἡμῶν, καὶ ἀναστάντα ἐκ νεκρῶν μετὰ τὸ παθεῖν τῇ τρίτῃ ἡμέρᾳ, καὶ ἀνελθόντα εἰς τοὺς οὐρανούς, καὶ καθεσθέντα ἐν δεξιᾷ τοῦ Πατρός, καὶ πάλιν ἐρχόμενον ἐπὶ συντελείᾳ τοῦ αἰῶνος μετὰ δόξης, κρῖναι ζῶντας καὶ νεκρούς, οὗ τῆς βασιλείας οὐκ ἔσται τέλος·

Βαπτίζομαι καὶ εἰς τὸ Πνεῦμα τὸ Ἅγιον, τουτέστι τὸν Παράκλητον, τὸ ἐνεργῆσαν ἐν πᾶσιν τοῖς ἀπ' αἰῶνος ἁγίοις, ὕστερον δὲ ἀποσταλὲν καὶ τοῖς ἀποστόλοις παρὰ τοῦ Πατρός, κατὰ τὴν ἐπαγγελίαν τοῦ Σωτῆρος ἡμῶν, Κυρίου Ἰησοῦ Χριστοῦ, καὶ μετὰ τοὺς ἀποστόλους δὲ πᾶσι τοῖς πιστεύουσιν ἐν τῇ ἁγίᾳ καθολικῇ ἐκκλησίᾳ· εἰς σαρκὸς ἀνάστασιν, καὶ εἰς ἄφεσιν ἁμαρτιῶν, καὶ εἰς βασιλείαν οὐρανῶν, καὶ εἰς ζωὴν τοῦ μέλλοντος αἰῶνος.

COMPARATIVE TABLE OF THE ANTE-NICENE RULES OF FAITH,

AS RELATED TO THE APOSTLES' CREED AND THE NICENE CREED.

THE APOSTLES' CREED. (Rome.) About A.D. 340. *Later additions are in italics.*	IRENÆUS. (Gaul.) A.D. 170.	TERTULLIAN. (North Africa.) A.D. 200.	CYPRIAN. (Carthage.) A.D. 250.	NOVATIAN. (Rome.) A.D. 250.	ORIGEN. (Alexandria.) A.D. 230.
I believe	We believe	We believe	I believe	We believe	[We believe in]
1. in GOD THE FATHER Almighty, *Maker of heaven and earth;*	1. in one GOD THE FATHER Almighty, who made heaven and earth, and the sea, and all that in them is;	1. in one GOD, the Creator of the world, who produced all out of nothing ...	1. in GOD THE FATHER;	1. in GOD THE FATHER and Almighty Lord;	1. in ONE GOD, who created and framed every thing ... Who in the last days sent
2. And in JESUS CHRIST, His only Son, our Lord;	2. And in one CHRIST JESUS (our Lord), the Son of God (our Lord);	2. And in the Word, his Son, JESUS CHRIST;	2. in his SON CHRIST;	2. in the Son of God, CHRIST JESUS, our Lord God;	2. Our Lord JESUS CHRIST, born of the Father before all creation ...
3. who was *conceived by the* Holy Ghost, *born of the Virgin Mary;*	3. Who became flesh [of the Virgin] for our salvation;	3. Who through the Spirit and power of God the Father descended into the Virgin Mary, was made flesh in her womb, and born of her;			3. born of the Virgin and the Holy Ghost ... made incarnate while remaining God ...
4. *suffered* under Pontius Pilate, was crucified, *dead,* and buried;	4. and his suffering [under Pontius Pilate];	4. Was fixed on the cross [under Pontius Pilate], was dead and buried;			4. suffered in truth, died;
5. *He descended into Hades;* the third day he rose from the dead;	5. and his rising from the dead;	5. rose again the third day;			5. rose from the dead;
6. He ascended into heaven, and sitteth on the right hand of *God the Father Almighty;*	6. and his bodily assumption into heaven;	6. was taken up into heaven and sitteth at the right hand of God the Father;			6. was taken up ...
7. from thence he shall come to judge the quick and the dead.	7. and his coming from heaven in the glory of the Father to comprehend all things under one head, ... and to execute righteous judgment over all.	7. He will come to judge the quick and the dead.			
8. And *I believe* in THE HOLY GHOST;	8. And in THE HOLY GHOST ...	8. And in THE HOLY GHOST, the Paraclete, the Sanctifier, sent by Christ from the Father.	8. in THE HOLY GHOST;	8. in THE HOLY GHOST (promised of old to the Church, and granted in the appointed and fitting time).	8. THE HOLY GHOST, united in honor and dignity with the Father and the Son.
9. the holy *Catholic* Church; *the communion of saints;*					
10. the forgiveness of sins;			10. {I believe the forgiveness of sins,		
11. the resurrection of the body;	11. And that Christ shall come from heaven to raise up all flesh, ... and to adjudge the impious and unjust ... to eternal fire,	11. And that Christ will, after the restoration of the flesh, receive his saints			
12. *and the life everlasting.*[1]	12. and to give to the just and holy immortality and eternal glory.	12. into the enjoyment of eternal life and the promises of heaven, and judge the wicked with eternal fire.	12. and eternal life through the holy Church.		

CREED.	(Cæsarea.) A.D. 270.	LUCIAN. (Antioch.) A.D. 300.	EUSEBIUS. (Cæsarea, Pal.) A.D. 325.	CYRIL. (Jerusalem.) A.D. 350.	NICENO-CONSTANTINOPOLITAN CREED. A.D. 325 and 381.
I believe 1. in GOD THE FATHER Almighty, *Maker of heaven and earth*;	[We believe in] 1. ONE GOD THE FATHER;	[We believe in] 1. ONE GOD THE FATHER Almighty, Maker and Provider of all things;	We believe 1. in ONE GOD THE FATHER Almighty, Maker of all things visible and invisible;	We believe 1. in ONE GOD THE FATHER Almighty, Maker of heaven, and earth, and of all things visible and invisible;	We [I] believe 1. in ONE GOD THE FATHER Almighty, Maker of *heaven and earth, and of* all things visible and invisible;
2. And in JESUS CHRIST, His only Son, our Lord;	2. one LORD, ... God of God, the image and likeness of the Godhead, ...the Wisdom and Power which produces all creation, the true Son of the true Father ...	2. And it, one LORD JESUS CHRIST his Son, begotten of the Father before all ages, God of God, Wisdom, Light, Light ...	2. And in one LORD JESUS CHRIST, the Word of God, God of God, Light of Light, Life of Life, the only-begotten Son, the first-born of every creature, begotten of God the Father before all ages; by whom all things were made;	2. And in one LORD JESUS CHRIST, the only-begotten Son of God, begotten of the Father before all ages, very God, by whom all things were made;	2. And in one Lord JESUS CHRIST, the *only-begotten* Son of God, begotten of the Father *before all worlds*; [God of God], Light of Light, very God of very God, begotten, not made, being of one substance with the Father (ὁμοούσιον τῷ Πατρί), by whom all things were made;
3. who was *conceived* by the Holy Ghost, born of the Virgin Mary;		3. { who was born of a Virgin, according to the Scriptures, and became man ...	3. who for our salvation was made flesh and lived among men;	3. who was made flesh, and became man;	3. who, for us men, and for our salvation, came down *from heaven*, and was incarnate *by the Holy Ghost and [of, ex] the Virgin Mary*, and was made man;
4. *suffered* under Pontius Pilate, was crucified, *dead*, and buried;		4. who suffered for us;	4. and suffered;	4. was crucified, and was buried;	4. He *was crucified for us under Pontius Pilate, and suffered, and was buried*;
5. *He descended into Hades*; the third day he rose from the dead;		5. and rose for us on the third day;	5. and rose on the third day;	5. rose on the third day;	5. and the third day he rose again, *according to the Scriptures*;
6. He ascended into heaven, and sitteth on the right hand of *God the Father Almighty*;		6. and ascended into heaven, and sitteth on the right hand of God the Father;	6. and ascended into heaven, and sitteth on the right hand of the Father;	6. and ascended into heaven, and sitteth on the right hand of the Father;	6. and ascended into heaven, *and sitteth on the right hand of the Father*;
7. from thence he shall come to judge the quick and the dead.		7. and again is coming with glory and power, to judge the quick and the dead;	7. and will come again with glory, to judge the quick and the dead.	7. and will come again in glory, to judge the quick and the dead; whose kingdom shall have no end;	7. nd he shall come again, *with glory*, to judge the quick and the dead; *whose kingdom shall have no end*;
8. And *I believe* in THE HOLY GHOST;	3. { one HOLY GHOST, ... the minister of sanctification, in whom is revealed God the Father, who is over all things, and through all things, and God the Son, who is through all things — a perfect Trinity, not divided nor differing in glory, eternity, and sovereignty...	8. And in THE HOLY GHOST, given for consolation and sanctification and perfection to those who believe ...	8. We believe also in THE HOLY GHOST.	8. And in one HOLY GHOST, the Advocate, who spake in the Prophets.	8. And [I believe] in THE HOLY GHOST, the Lord, and Giver of life, Who proceedeth from the Father [and the Son, *Filioque*], who with the Father and the Son together is worshipped and glorified, who spake by the Prophets.
9. the holy Catholic Church; *the communion of saints*;				9. { in one baptism of repentance for the remission of sins;	9. And [I believe] in *one holy Catholic and Apostolic Church*.
10. the forgiveness of sins;				10. and in one holy Catholic Church;	10. *we [I] acknowledge one baptism for the remission of sins*;
11. the resurrection of the body;				11. and in the resurrection of the flesh;	11. *and we [I] look for the resurrection of the dead*;
12. *and the life everlasting.*				12. and in life everlasting (ζωὴν αἰώνιον).	12. *and the life of the world to come* (ζωὴν τοῦ μέλλοντος αἰῶνος).

The words in italics in the last column are additions of the second œcumenical Council (381); the words in brackets are Western changes.

SYMBOLA OECUMENICA.

SYMBOLA ŒCUMENICA.

ŒCUMENICAL SYMBOLS.

PAGE

ɪ. SYMBOLUM APOSTOLICUM. THE APOSTLES' CREED.

(a) FORMA RECEPTA. Sixth Century or Later. Latin, Greek, and
English 45

(b) FORMA ROMANA VETUS. SYMBOLUM MARCELLI. SYMBOLUM
AUGUSTINI. Fourth Century 47

(c) FORMA AQUILEJENSIS. RUFINUS. FORTUNATUS. Fourth and
Fifth Centuries 49

(d) FORMA ITALICA VETUS. Fourth Century 50

COMPARATIVE TABLE showing the gradual Formation of the Apos-
tles' Creed 52

II. SYMBOLUM NICÆNO-CONSTANTINOPOLITANUM. THE
NICENE CREED. A.D. 325 and 381.

(a) FORMA RECEPTA ECCLESIÆ ORIENTALIS. A.D. 381. Greek
and Latin 57

(b) FORMA RECEPTA ECCLESIÆ OCCIDENTALIS. Latin and English 58

(c) SYMBOLUM NICÆNUM VETUS. A.D. 325. Greek and Latin 60

APPENDIX. Other Oriental Creeds of the Nicene Age 61

III. SYMBOLUM CHALCEDONENSE. THE CREED OF THE
ŒCUMENICAL COUNCIL OF CHALCEDON. A.D. 451.

Greek, Latin, and English 62

IV. SYMBOLUM ATHANASIANUM. THE ATHANASIAN
CREED.

Latin and English 66

V. SYMBOLUM CONSTANTINOPOLITANUM TERTIUM, AD-
VERSUS MONOTHELETAS. A.D. 680.

THE CREED OF THE SIXTH ŒCUMENICAL COUNCIL, AGAINST THE
MONOTHELITES. Review of the Dogmatic Legislation of the
Seven Œcumenical Councils 72

I. SYMBOLUM APOSTOLICUM. (a) FORMA RECEPTA.[1]

Credo in DEUM PATREM *omnipotentem; Creatorem cœli et terræ.*

Πιστεύω εἰς ΘΕΟΝ ΠΑΤΕΡΑ, παντοκράτορα, ποιητὴν οὐρανοῦ καὶ γῆς.

Et in JESUM CHRISTUM, *Filium ejus unicum, Dominum nostrum; qui conceptus est de Spiritu Sancto, natus ex Maria virgine; passus sub Pontio Pilato, crucifixus, mortuus, et sepultus; descendit ad inferna;*[2] *tertia die resurrexit a mortuis; ascendit ad cœlos; sedet ad dexteram Dei Patris omnipotentis; inde venturus (est) judicare vivos et mortuos.*

Καὶ (εἰς) ᾽ΙΗΣΟΥΝ ΧΡΙΣΤΟΝ, υἱὸν αὐτοῦ τὸν μονογενῆ, τὸν κύριον ἡμῶν, τὸν συλληφθέντα ἐκ πνεύματος ἁγίου, γεννηθέντα ἐκ Μαρίας τῆς παρθένου, παθόντα ἐπὶ Ποντίου Πιλάτου, σταυρωθέντα, θανόντα, καὶ ταφέντα, κατελθόντα εἰς τὰ κατώτατα,[2] τῇ τρίτῃ ἡμέρᾳ ἀναστάντα ἀπὸ τῶν νεκρῶν, ἀνελθόντα εἰς τοὺς οὐρανούς, καθεζόμενον ἐν δεξιᾷ θεοῦ πατρὸς παντοδυνάμου, ἐκεῖθεν ἐρχόμενον κρῖναι ζῶντας καὶ νεκρούς.

Credo in SPIRITUM SANCTUM; *sanctam ecclesiam catholicam; sanctorum communionem; remissionem peccatorum; carnis resurrectionem; vitam æternam. Amen.*

Πιστεύω εἰς τὸ ΠΝΕΥΜΑ ΤΟ ῞ΑΓΙΟΝ, ἁγίαν καθολικὴν ἐκκλησίαν, ἁγίων κοινωνίαν, ἄφεσιν ἁμαρτιῶν, σαρκὸς ἀνάστασιν, ζωὴν αἰώνιον. ᾽Αμήν.

I. THE APOSTLES' CREED. (a) RECEIVED FORM.

I believe in GOD THE FATHER Almighty; Maker of heaven and earth.

And in JESUS CHRIST his only (begotten) Son our Lord; who was conceived by the Holy Ghost, born of the Virgin Mary; suffered under Pontius Pilate, was crucified, dead, and buried; he descended into hell [Hades, spirit-world];[2] the third day he rose from the dead; he ascended into heaven; and sitteth at the right hand of God the Father Almighty; from thence he shall come to judge the quick and the dead.

I believe in the HOLY GHOST; the holy catholic Church; the communion of saints; the forgiveness of sins; the resurrection of the body [flesh];[3] and the life everlasting. Amen.

NOTES.

[1] The Latin and Greek texts of the Apostles' Creed are taken from the *Psalterium Græcum et Romanum*, erroneously ascribed to Pope Gregory the Great, first published from a MS. preserved in the library of Corpus Christi College, Cambridge, by Archbishop Ussher: *De Romanæ Ecclesiæ Symbolo Apostolico vetere*, London, 1647. I used the Geneva edition, 1722, pp. 6, 7. The MS. is written in two parallel columns, the one Latin, the other Greek, but the Greek likewise in Latin characters. The same text is given by Hahn, *Biblioth. der Symb.* p. 10, and Heurtley (in Greek), *Harmonia Symb.* pp. 81–83. The Latin text agrees with the creed of Pirminius (d. 758) in Heurtley, p. 71. Caspari discovered and published four other Greek translations from mediæval MSS. with slight variations, Vol. III. pp. 11 sqq.

[2] *Descendit ad inferna* (other Latin copies: *ad inferos*, to the *inhabitants* of the spirit-world; so also in the Athanasian Symbol), κατελϑόντα εἰς τὰ κατώτατα (other Eastern creeds: εἰς ᾅδου, viz., τόπον, or εἰς τὸν ᾅδην), *he descended into Hades*. This clause was unknown in the older creeds, though believed in the Church, and was transferred into the Roman symbol after the fifth century, probably from that of Aquileia, A.D. 390, where it first appears among Latin creeds, as we learn from Rufinus. In the East it is found before in Arian creeds (about 360). After this we meet it again in the Creed of Venantius Fortunatus, A.D. 590, who had the Creed of Rufinus before him. The words κατώτατα and *inferna*, taken from Eph. iv. 9, correspond here to the Greek ᾅδης, which occurs eleven times in the Greek Testament, viz., Matt. xi. 23; xvi. 18; Luke x. 15; xvi. 23; Acts ii. 27, 31; 1 Cor. xv. 55; Rev. i. 18; vi. 8; xx. 13, 14, and is always incorrectly translated *hell* in the English Version, except in 1 Cor. xv. 55. *Hades* signifies, like the Hebrew *Sheol*, the unseen spirit-world, the abode of all the departed, both the righteous and wicked; while *hell* (probably from the Saxon word *helan*, to *cover*, to *conceal*), at least in modern usage, is a much narrower conception, and signifies the state and place of eternal damnation, like the Hebrew *gehenna*, which occurs twelve times in the Greek Testament, and is so translated in the English Bible, viz., Matt. v. 22, 29, 30; x. 28; xviii. 9; xxiii. 15, 33; Mark ix. 43, 45, 47; Luke xii. 5; James iii. 6. The American editions of the *Book of Common Prayer* leave it optional with the minister to use, in the Creed, *hell*, or *the place of departed spirits;* but it would be much better to restore or popularize the Greek *Hades*. The current translation, *hell*, is apt to mislead, and excludes the important fact—the only one which we *certainly* know of the mysterious *triduum*—that Christ was in *Paradise* in the time between the crucifixion and the resurrection, according to his own declaration to the penitent thief, Luke xxiii. 43. Some connect the descent into Hades with the resurrection in one article; while others, on the contrary, connect it with the preceding article by placing a (,) after buried. It forms rather a separate article, and should be included in (;), as above.

The clause has been explained in three different ways: 1. It is identical with *sepultus* (Rufinus), or means 'continued in the state of death and under the power of death' till the resurrection (Westminster divines). This makes it a useless repetition in figurative language. 2. It signifies the intensity of Christ's sufferings on the cross, where he tasted the pain of hell for sinners (Calvin and the Heidelberg Catechism). This is inconsistent with the order of the clause between death and resurrection. 3. An actual self-manifestation of Christ after the crucifixion to all the departed spirits, Luke xxiii. 43; Acts ii. 27, 31; 1 Pet. iii. 18, 19; iv. 6; comp. Eph. iv. 8,9; Col. ii. 15; Phil. ii. 10; Rev. i. 18. As such the descent is a part of the universality of the scheme of redemption, and forms the transition from the state of humiliation to the state of exaltation. This is the historical explanation, according to the belief of the ancient Church, but leaves much room for speculation concerning the object and effect of the descent.

[3] 'Resurrection of the *body*.' The older English translations of the Creed had the literal rendering *flesh* (*caro*, σάρξ), by which the ancient Church protested against spiritualistic conceptions of the Gnostics. But this may be misunderstood in a grossly materialistic sense, while the resurrection of the *body* is unobjectionable; comp. 1 Cor. xv. 50. According to Heurtley, l. c. p. 147, the change of *flesh* into *body* was first made 1543, in 'The necessary Doctrine and Erudition for any Christian Man,' set forth by Henry VIII.; but in the Interrogative Creed, used at Baptism and at the Visitation of the Sick, *flesh* is retained.

(b) THE OLD ROMAN AND AFRICAN FORM OF THE APOSTLES' CREED.

Forma Romana Vetus. Before A.D. 341.[1]	Symbolum Augustini (354–430). Hippo Regius, Africa (Circ. 400).[2]
Credo in Deum Patrem *omnipotentem.*	*Credo in* Deum Patrem *omnipotentem.*
Et in Jesum Christum, *Filium ejus unicum, Dominum nostrum ;*	*Et in* Jesum Christum, *Filium ejus unigenitum* (*unicum*), *Dominum nostrum ;*
qui natus est de Spiritu Sancto et Maria virgine ;	*qui natus est per Spiritum Sanctum ex virgine Maria ;*
sub Pontio Pilato crucifixus, et sepultus ;	*sub Pontio Pilato crucifixus est, et sepultus ;*
tertia die resurrexit a mortuis ;	*tertio die resurrexit a mortuis ;*
ascendit in cœlum, sedet ad dexteram Patris ;	*ascendit in cœlum, sedet ad dexteram Patris ;*
inde venturus judicare vivos et mortuos.	*inde venturus est judicaturus* (*ad judicandos*) *vivos et mortuos.*
Et in Spiritum Sanctum ;	*Credo et in* Spiritum Sanctum ;
Sanctam Ecclesiam ;	*sanctam ecclesiam ;*
remissionem peccatorum ;	*remissionem peccatorum ;*
carnis resurrectionem.	*carnis resurrectionem* (? *in vitam eternam*).

Professio Fidei Marcelli Ancyrani. Before A.D. 341.[3]	The Roman Form Translated.
Πιστεύω εἰς ΘΕΟΝ [ΠΑΤΕΡΑ], παντοκράτορα·	I believe in God the Father Almighty.
καὶ εἰς ΧΡΙΣΤΟΝ ᾽ΙΗΣΟΥΝ, τὸν υἱὸν αὐτοῦ τὸν μονογενῆ, τὸν κύριον ἡμῶν,	And in Jesus Christ his only-begotten Son our Lord,
τὸν γεννηθέντα ἐκ πνεύματος ἁγίου καὶ Μαρίας τῆς παρθένου,	who was born of the Holy Ghost and the Virgin Mary ;
τὸν ἐπὶ Ποντίου Πιλάτου σταυρωθέντα, καὶ ταφέντα,	crucified under Pontius Pilate, and buried ;

καὶ τῇ τρίτῃ ἡμέρᾳ ἀναστάντα ἐκ τῶν νεκρῶν,

the third day he rose from the dead;

ἀναβάντα εἰς τοὺς οὐρανοὺς, καὶ καθήμενον ἐν δεξιᾷ τοῦ πατρός,

he ascended into heaven, and sitteth at the right hand of the Father;

ὅθεν ἔρχεται κρίνειν ζῶντας καὶ νεκρούς·

from thence he shall come to judge the quick and the dead.

καὶ εἰς τὸ ῞ΑΓΙΟΝ ΠΝΕΥΜΑ,

And in the HOLY GHOST;

ἁγίαν ἐκκλησίαν,

the holy Church;

ἄφεσιν ἁμαρτιῶν,

the forgiveness of sins;

σαρκὸς ἀνάστασιν,

the resurrection of the body;

ζωὴν αἰώνιον.

(the life everlasting).

NOTES.

[1] The Latin text of the old Roman Creed first appears in RUFINUS, *Expositio Symboli Apostolici*, towards the end of the fourth century (compare the Appendix to the *Opp. Cypriani*, ed. John Fell, Oxon. 1682, fol. pp. 17 sqq.), but it must be much older (see note 3 below). The faithful transmission of the Creed in the Church of the City of Rome is testified by Ambrose, *Epistola ad Siricium Pap.*: ʻ*Credatur Symbolo Apostolorum, quod Ecclesia Romana intemeratum semper custodit et servat;*ʼ and by Vigilius of Thapsus, *Contra Entych.* l. IV. c. 1: ʻ*Romæ . . . a temporibus Apostolorum usque ad nunc . . . ita fidelibus Symbolum traditur.*ʼ Compare Hahn, *Bibliothek der Symbole*, pp. 3, 30. 42, 43. On the difference between the old Roman form and the enlarged received text, see Vol. I. pp. 21, 22.

[2] With the early Roman form the Creed of the Church of Hippo Regius, as given in the second column from the genuine expositions of St. AUGUSTINE (*De Fide et Symbolo; De Genesi ad literam; Enchiridion de Fide, Spe et Caritate*), almost literally agrees; so also the Creed of Ambrose, as far as it is quoted in his *Tractatus in Symbolum Apostolorum* (Hahn, p. 16). The close connection of Augustine with the Church of Rome and the Church of Milan (where he was baptized, 387) accounts for the agreement. In his genuine works, however, he never gives the Creed continuously, but, like Rufinus, mixed with the exposition in which it is imbedded, and at times it is difficult to separate it from the writer's own words. See Hahn, pp. 13–15, and especially Heurtley, pp. 32–47. The former adopts the reading *de Spiritu S. et virg. Mar.*; *tertia* die for *tertio;* and omits *in vitam eternam.*

[3] The Greek text is to be found in Epiphanius, *Hæres.* LXXII. *Opp.* ed. Petav. Tom. I. p. 836; ed. Oehler in *Corp. hæreseol.* Tom. II. Pt. III. p. 52. It was inserted in a letter written by MARCELLUS OF ANCYRA to Julius I., Bishop of Rome, about 341 (or 337, as Hahn and Caspari assume), with a view to prove his orthodoxy against the Eusebians, who, under the impeachment of heresy, had previously deposed him. (As regards the chronology, see Zahn, *Marcellus von Ancyra*, Gotha, 1867, p. 68.) It occurs also, in Anglo-Saxon letters, in the Psaltery of King Athelstan (d. 941), to which Ussher first called attention. See a facsimile in Heurtley, p. 80, and the copy and comments in Caspari, Vol. III. pp. 5 sqq. The Greek text of Marcellus differs from the Latin of Rufinus only by the omission of the predicate πατέρα (Father) in the first article (which may be an error of the copyist), and by the addition of the last two words, ζωὴν αἰώνιον (which occur also in the creed of Petrus Chrysologus of Ravenna). It was heretofore regarded as a translation of the Roman Creed, but Caspari, with a vast amount of learning (Vol. III. pp. 28 sqq.), has made it almost certain that it is the original Creed of the Roman Church, in which the Greek language prevailed during the first two centuries. It was probably transplanted to Rome from Asia Minor early in the second century. It is simpler and order than the rules of faith of Tertullian and Irenæus.

(c) THE APOSTLES' CREED, ACCORDING TO RUFINUS AND FORTUNATUS. A.D. 390-570.

ECCLESIA AQUILEJENSIS. CIRC. A.D. 390.[1]	VENANTIUS FORTUNATUS. CIRC. A.D. 570.[2]
Credo in DEO PATRE *omnipotente* [*invisibili et impassibili*].[3]	*Credo in* DEUM PATREM *omnipotentem.*
Et in JESU CHRISTO, *unico Filio ejus, Domino nostro ;*	*Et in* JESUM CHRISTUM, *unicum Filium ;*
qui natus est de Spiritu Sancto ex Maria virgine ;	*qui natus est de Spiritu Sancto ex Maria virgine ;*
crucifixus sub Pontio Pilato, et sepultus ;	*crucifixus sub Pontio Pilato ;*
[*descendit in inferna*] ;[4]	*descendit ad infernum ;*
tertia die resurrexit a mortuis ;	*tertia die resurrexit ;*
ascendit in cœlos ;	*ascendit in cœlum ;*
sedet ad dexteram Patris ;	*sedet ad dexteram Patris ;*
inde venturus est judicare vivos et mortuos.	*judicaturus vivos et mortuos.*
Et in SPIRITU SANCTO ;	*Credo in* SANCTO SPIRITU ;[5]
sanctam ecclesiam ;	*sanctam ecclesiam ;*
remissionem peccatorum ;	*remissionem peccatorum ;*
[*hujus*][6] *carnis resurrectionem.*	*resurrectionem carnis.*

NOTES.

[1] Taken from RUFINUS (d. 410), *Expos. Symboli Apost.* (in Cyprian's *Op.*, ed. Fell, Appendix, pp. 17 sqq.; also in Jerome's Works). Comp. Hahn, *Bibliothek der Symbole*, etc., pp. 30 sqq.; Denzinger, *Enchirid.*, p. 2; and Heurtley, *Harmonia Symb.*, pp. 26 sqq. Hahn and Heurtley add the chief comments of Rufinus. He gives it as the Creed of the Church of Aquileja, where he was baptized ('*illum ordinem sequimur, quem in Aquilejensi ecclesia per lavaori gratiam suscepimus*'). There are, however, two other Creeds used in the churches of the province of Aquileja, of uncertain (possibly of earlier) date, which are more in harmony with the old Roman form, and omit *invisibili et impassibili* in the first article, *hujus* before *carnis* in the last article, and the clause *descendit ad inferna*. They were found and first published by De Rubeis (Venice, 1754), in his *Dissertationes . . . de Liturgicis Ritibus Ecclesiæ Forojuliensis*, pp. 242, 243, 249 ; then by Walch. l. c. p. 54 sq. ; Hahn, p. 39 ; and Heurtley, pp. 30 sqq.

[2] From the *Expositio Symboli* of VENANTIUS HONORIUS CLEMENS FORTUNATUS, an Italian presbyter, afterwards Bishop of Poitiers in France, d. about 600. He follows Rufinus very closely, and evidently made use of his *Exposition*. See Hahn, l. c. p. 33, and Heurtley, pp. 54–56. The Commentary on the Athanasian Creed, which Muratori and Waterland ascribe to the same author, is by an unknown Fortunatus of a later age. See Vol. I. pp. 34–37.

[3] This is the oldest reading, as also *in Jesu Christo*, and *in Spiritu Sancto.* So Vallarsiuʳ (ed. of Jerome), Baluze (the Bened. editor of Cyprian), Walch, and Hahn. Other copies correct the ablative into the accusative: *in Deum Patrem omnipotentem, invisibilem et impassibilem, in Jesum Christum.* So the first printed ed. of 1468, the Bened. ed. of Jerome, Pamelius, Fell, Heurtley. On the article on the Holy Spirit, the majority of authorities agree in reading the ablative, which is confirmed by Fortunatus. The addition of the attributes *invisible and impassible*, which are not found in any other form, have a polemical reference to the heresy of the Patripassians and Sabellians, as Rufinus remarks (§ 5).

[4] Rufinus (§ 18): '*Sciendum sane est quod in Ecclesiæ Romanæ Symbolo non habetur additum "Descendit ad inferna:" sed neque in Orientis Ecclesiis habetur hic sermo: vis tamen verbi eadem videtur esse in eo quod "sepultus" dicitur.*'

[5] Here Venantius adheres to the old Aquileian form, while in the first and second articles he uses the accusative. So also in his Commentaries: '*Ergo una divinitas in trinitate, quia dixit Symbolum; Credo in Deum Patrem, et in Jesum Christum, et in Spiritu Sancto.*' See Hahn, p. 36; Heurtley, p. 55.

[6] The exceptional *hujus* is thus explained by Rufinus (§ 43): '*Ita fit ut unicuique animæ non confusum aut extraneum corpus, sed unum quod habuerat reparetur; ut consequenter possit pro agonibus præsentis vitæ cum anima sua caro vel pudica coronari, vel impudica puniri.*'

(d) AN OLD ITALIAN (PSEUDO-AMBROSIAN) FORM OF THE APOSTLES' CREED. ABOUT A.D. 350.

Credimus in DEUM PATREM *omnipotentem,*	We believe in GOD THE FATHER Almighty,
sæculorum omnium et creaturarum regem et conditorem.	Ruler and Creator of all ages and creatures.
Et in JESUM CHRISTUM, *Filium ejus unicum, Dominum nostrum;*	And in JESUS CHRIST, his only Son, our Lord;
qui natus est de Spiritu Sancto et ex Maria Virgine;	who was born of the Holy Ghost and from the Virgin Mary;
qui sub Pontio Pilato crucifixus et sepultus;	who was crucified under Pontius Pilate, and buried;
tertia die resurrexit a mortuis;	on the third day he rose from the dead;
ascendit in cœlos;	ascended into the heavens;
sedet ad dexteram Dei Patris;	sitteth on the right hand of God the Father;
inde venturus est judicare vivos et mortuos.	from thence he shall come to judge the quick and the dead.
Et in SPIRITUM SANCTUM;	And in the HOLY GHOST;
et sanctam ecclesiam catholicam;	and the holy Catholic Church;
remissionem peccatorum;	the remission of sins;
carnis resurrectionem.	the resurrection of the flesh.

NOTES.

1. This baptismal creed was copied, together with an *Exhortatio sancti Ambrosii ad neo-phytos de Symbolo*, by Dr. Caspari from two MSS. in the Vienna Library, and published in the second volume of his *Quellen zur Geschichte des Taufsymbols*, Vol. II. (1869), pp. 128 sqq. It is inserted in this Exhortation, not in broken fragments, as is usual with ante-Nicene writers, but continuously, with a connecting *itaque* after *credimus* (p. 134). The Exhortation was directed against the heresy of Arianism, and borrows an expression (*Deus de Deo, lumen de lumine*) from the Nicene Creed, but makes no allusion to the Pneumatomachian contro-versy and its settlement in 381. It seems, therefore, to belong to the middle of the fourth century (350–370). Caspari denies the authorship of Ambrose (who was opposed to commit-ting the creed to writing), and is inclined to assign it to Eusebius of Vercelli or Lucifer of Cagliari, in Sardinia, where the symbol may have been in use.

2. The symbol resembles the older Italian forms of Rome, Milan, and Ravenna. With the Roman it omits the articles *descendit ad inferna, communionem sanctorum*, and *vitam æter-nam;* but, unlike the Roman, it has *catholicam* after *ecclesiam*, and the peculiar clause *sæcu-lorum omnium et creaturarum regem et conditorem*. A similar addition occurs in the Symbol of Carthage (*universorum creatorem, regem sæculorum, invisibilem et immortalem*).

3. Other Italian forms of the Western Creed, see in Hahn, pp. 6 sqq.

THE GRADUAL FORMATION OF THE APOSTLES' CREED.

This Table shows the date of the several Articles and the verbal variations of the Apostles' Creed, as far as they can be ascertained, from the earliest rules of faith to the eighth century, or from Irenæus to Pirminius. The first occurrence of any word or phrase of the Creed is marked by small capitals.

ULTIMATE TEXT of the Western CREED. — Pirminius, A.D. 750.	CREDO (I believe):					
	Art. I.			Art. II.		
	In Deum Patrem	Omnipotentem	Creatorem cœli et terræ	Et in Jesum Christum	Filium ejus Unicum	Dominum nostrum
	In God the Father	Almighty	Maker of Heaven and Earth	And in Jesus Christ	His only Son	Our Lord
I. St. Irenæus, A.D. 200.	[Πιστεύω] εἰς ἕνα Θεὸν Πατέρα	παντοκράτορα	τὸν πεποιηκότα τὸν οὐρανὸν καὶ τὴν γῆν, καὶ τὰς θάλασσας καὶ πάντα τὰ ἐν αὐτοῖς	καὶ εἰς ἕνα Χριστὸν Ἰησοῦν	τὸν υἱὸν τοῦ Θεοῦ	(τὸν Κύριον ἡμῶν, δι᾽ οὗ τὰ πάντα)
II. Tertullian, A.D. 220.	In unicum DEUM.	OMNIPOTENTEM	mundi conditorem	JESUM CHRISTUM	FILIUM EJUS	
III. St. Cyprian, A.D. 250.	In Deum PATREM			in Christum	Filium	
IV. Novatian, A.D. 260.	In Deum Patrem	Dominum omnipotentem		in Christum Jesum	Filium Lei	DOMINUM Deum NOSTRUM
V. Marcellus, A.D. 341.	εἰς Θεὸν	παντοκράτορα		εἰς Χριστὸν Ἰησοῦν	τὸν υἱὸν αὐτοῦ τὸν μονογενῆ	τὸν Κύριον ἡμῶν
VI. Rufinus, A.D. 390. Aquileja.	In Deum Patrem	omnipotentem	invisibilem et impassibilem	et in Jesum Christum	UNICUM Filium ejus	Dominum nostrum
VII. Rufinus, Rome, A.D. 390.	In Deum Patrem	omnipotentem		et in Jesum Christum	unicum Filium ejus	Dominum nostrum
VIII. St. Augustine, A.D. 400.	In Deum Patrem	omnipotentem		et in Jesum Christum	unicum Filium ejus also [unigenitum]	Dominum nostrum
IX. St. Nicetas, A.D. 450.	In Deum Patrem	omnipotentem		et in Jesum Christum	Filium ejus	
X. Eusebius Gallus, A.D. 550 (?).	In Deum Patrem	omnipotentem		et in Jesum Christum	Filium ejus	Dominum nostrum
XI. Sacramentarium Gallicanum. A.D. 650.	In Deum Patrem	omnipotentem	CREATOREM CŒLI ET TERRÆ	et in Jesum Christum	Filium ejus unigenitum sempiternum	Dominum nostrum

A blank space indicates that the portion of the Article under which it occurs had not at that time come into general use. The Table is based on J. R. LUMBY's *History of the Creeds* (Cambridge, 1873), p. 182, but contains several additions, especially the chief ante-Nicene rules of faith, viz., that of IRENÆUS, *Adv. hær.* I. 10 (Greek) ; III. 4 (Latin, in parentheses) ; and IV. 33 (Greek, in parentheses) ; and that of TERTULLIAN, *De virg. veland.* c. 1; *Adv. Prax.* c. 2 (in parentheses) ; and *De præscr. hær.* c. 13 (in parentheses).

| CREDO (I believe): | | | | | | | | |
| Art. III. | | | | Art. IV. | | | | |
Qui Conceptus est Who was Conceived	De Spiritu Sancto By the Holy Ghost	Natus Born	Ex Maria Virgine Of the Virgin Mary	Passus Suffered	Sub Pontio Pilato Under Pontius Pilate	Crucifixus Was Crucified	Mortuus Dead	Et Sepultus And Buried
τὸν σαρκω-θέντα ὑπὲρ τῆς ἡμετέρας σωτηρίας (ἄνθρωπος ἐγένετο)		(Generationem)	τὴν ἐκ παρθέ-νου γέν-νησιν (ex Virgine)	καὶ τὸ πάθος	(SUB PONTIO PILATO)			
(missum a Patre in Virginem)	(EX SPIRITU Patris Dei et virtute)	NATUM (carnem factum et ex ea natum)	EX VIRGINE MARĪA	CRUCI-FIXUM (passum)	sub Pontio Pilato		(MOR-TUUM)	(ET SE-PULTUM secundum Scripturas)
	ἐκ πνεύμα-τος ἁγίου	γεννηθέντα	καὶ Μα-ρίας τῆς παρθένου		τὸν ἐπὶ Ποντίου Πιλάτου	σταυρω-θέντα		καὶ ταφέντα
QUI	de Spiritu SANCTO	natus est	ex Maria Virgine		sub Pontio Pilato	cruci-fixus		et sepultus
qui	de Spiritu Sancto	natus est	ex Maria Virgine		sub Pontio Pilato	cruci-fixus		et sepultus
qui	de Spiritu Sancto *also* [per Sp. Sanct.]	natus est	ex Maria Virgine *also* [et]	passus	sub Pontio Pilato	cruci-fixus		et sepultus
qui	ex Spiritu Sancto	natus est	et Virgine Maria	passus	sub Pontio Pilato			
qui CONCEP-TUS EST	de Spiritu Sancto	natus est	ex Maria Virgine				mor-tuus	et sepultus
qui conceptus est	de Spiritu Sancto	natus est	ex Maria Virgine	passus	sub Pontio Pilato	cruci-fixus	mor-tuus	et sepultus

THE GRADUAL FORMATION OF THE APOSTLES' CREED—Continued.

Ultimate Text of the Western Creed. Pirminius, A.D. 750.	CREDO (I believe):								
	Art. V.				Art. VI.				
	Descendit ad Inferna (He descended into Hell)	Tertia die (The third Day)	Resurrexit (He rose again)	A mortuis (From the Dead)	Ascendit ad cœlos (He ascended into Heaven)	Sedet ad dexteram (And sitteth at the right hand)	Dei (Of God)	Patris (The Father)	Omnipotentis (Almighty)
I. St. Irenæus, A.D. 200.		καὶ τὴν ἔγερσιν (et resurgens)		ἐκ νεκρῶν	εἰς τοὺς οὐρανοὺς ἀνάληψιν (et in claritate receptus)				
II. Tertullian, A.D. 220.		TERTIA DIE	resuscitatum (a Patre) (resurrexisse)	E MORTUIS	receptum in cœlis (in cœlos resumptum) (in cœlos ereptum)	SEDENTEM nunc AD DEXTERAM		PATRIS	
III. St. Cyprian, A.D. 250.									
IV. Novatian, A.D. 260.									
V. Marcellus, A.D. 341.		καὶ τῇ τρίτῃ ἡμέρᾳ	ἀναστάντα	ἐκ τῶν νεκρῶν	ἀναβάντα ἐς τοὺς οὐρανοὺς	καὶ καθήμενον ἐν δεξιᾷ		τοῦ πατρὸς	
VI. Rufinus, A.D. 390. Aquileja.	DESCENDIT in INFERNA	tertia die	RESURREXIT	A mortuis	ASCENDIT in CŒLOS	SEDET ad dexteram		Patris	
VII. Rufinus, Rome, A.D. 390.		tertia die	resurrexit	a mortuis	ascendit in cœlos	sedet ad dexteram		Patris	
VIII. St. Augustine, A.D. 400.		tertio die	resurrexit	a mortuis	ascendit in cœlos	sedet ad dexteram		Patris	
IX. St. Nicetas, A.D. 450.		tertio die	resurrexit	vivus a mortuis	ascendit in cœlos	sedet ad dexteram		Patris	
X. Eusebius Gallus, A.D. 550 (?).		tertia die	resurrexit	a mortuis	ascendit AD cœlos	sedet ad dexteram	DEI	Patris	OMNIPOTENTIS
XI. Sacramentarium Gallicanum, A.D. 650.	Descendit AD Inferna	tertia die	resurrexit	a mortuis	ascendit ad cœlos	sedet ad dexteram	Dei	Patris	omnipotentis

Art. VII.	Art. VIII.	Art. IX.			Art. X.	Art. XI.	Art. XII.
CREDO (I believe):							
Inde venturus est judicare vivos et mortuos *From thence he shall come to judge the quick and the dead*	In Spiritum Sanctum *In the Holy Ghost*	Sanctam Ecclesiam *The Holy Catholic Church*	Catholicam	Sanctorum Communionem *The Communion of Saints*	Remissionem peccatorum *The Forgiveness of Sins*	Carnis Resurrectionem *The Resurrection of the Body*	Vitam Æternam *And the Life Everlasting*
τὴν ἐκ τῶν οὐρανῶν ἐν τῇ δόξῃ τοῦ πατρὸς παρουσίαν αὐτοῦ ἐπὶ τὸ ἀνακεφαλαιώσασθαι τὰ πάντα (in gloria venturus)	καὶ εἰς πνεῦμα ἅγιον						ἀφθαρσίαν καὶ δόξαν αἰωνίαν
VENTURUM JUDICARE VIVOS ET MORTUOS (venturum cum claritate)	(SPIRITUM SANCTUM, Paracletum, Sanctificatorem fidei eorum qui credunt in Patrem et Filium et Spiritum Sanctum)					per CARNIS etiam RESURRECTIONEM (cum carnis restitutione)	(ad sumendos sanc. in vitæ æter. et promiss. cœles. fructum et ad profanos adjud. igni perpetuo)
	IN Spiritum Sanctum	per SANCTAM ECCLESIAM			REMISSIONEM PECCATORUM		VITAM ÆTERNAM
	in Spiritum Sanctum						
ὅθεν ἔρχεται κρίνειν ζῶντας καὶ νεκρούς	καὶ εἰς τὸ ἅγιον Πνεῦμα	ἁγίαν ἐκκλησίαν			ἄφεσιν ἁμαρτιῶν	σαρκὸς ἀνάστασιν	ζωὴν αἰώνιον
INDE VENTURUS EST judicare vivos et mortuos	et in Spiritu Sancto	Sanctam Ecclesiam			remissionem peccatorum	hujus carnis resurrectionem	
inde venturus est judicare vivos et mortuos	et in Spiritu Sancto	Sanctam Ecclesiam			remissionem peccatorum	carnis resurrectionem	
inde ventu...us est judicare vivos et mortuos	et in Spiritum Sanctum	Sanctam Ecclesiam			remissionem peccatorum	carnis resurrectionem	vitam æternam
inde venturus est judicare vivos et mortuos	et in Spiritum Sanctum	Sanctam Ecclesiam	CATHOLICAM		remissionem peccatorum	carnis hujus resurrectionem	vitam æternam
inde venturus est judicare vivos et mortuos	et in Spiritum Sanctum	Sanctam Ecclesiam	Catholicam	SANCTORUM COMMUNIONEM	remissionem peccatorum	carnis resurrectionem	vitam æternam
inde venturus est judicare vivos et mortuos	et in Spiritum Sanctum	Sanctam Ecclesiam	Catholicam	sanctorum communionem	remissionem peccatorum	carnis resurrectionem	vitam æternam

II. SYMBOLUM NICÆNO-CONSTANTINOPOLITANUM.

THE NICÆNO-CONSTANTINOPOLITAN CREED.

(a) *Forma Recepta Ecclesiæ Orientalis.* A.D. 381.

THE RECEIVED TEXT OF THE GREEK CHURCH.[1]

LATIN VERSION OF DIONYSIUS EXIGUUS.[2]

Πιστεύομεν εἰς ἕνα ΘΕΟΝ ΠΑΤΕΡΑ παντοκράτορα, ποιητὴν οὐρανοῦ καὶ γῆς, ὁρατῶν τε πάντων καὶ ἀοράτων.

Καὶ εἰς ἕνα κύριον ἸΗΣΟΥΝ ΧΡΙΣΤΟΝ, τὸν υἱὸν τοῦ θεοῦ τὸν μονογενῆ, τὸν ἐκ τοῦ πατρὸς γεννηθέντα πρὸ πάντων τῶν αἰώνων, φῶς ἐκ φωτός, θεὸν ἀληθινὸν ἐκ θεοῦ ἀληθινοῦ, γεννηθέντα, οὐ ποιηθέντα, ὁμοούσιον τῷ πατρί· δι' οὗ τὰ πάντα ἐγένετο· τὸν δι' ἡμᾶς τοὺς ἀνθρώπους καὶ διὰ τὴν ἡμετέραν σωτηρίαν κατελθόντα ἐκ τῶν οὐρανῶν καὶ σαρκωθέντα ἐκ πνεύματος ἁγίου καὶ Μαρίας τῆς παρθένου καὶ ἐνανθρωπήσαντα, σταυρωθέντα τε ὑπὲρ ἡμῶν ἐπὶ Ποντίου Πιλάτου, καὶ παθόντα καὶ ταφέντα, καὶ ἀναστάντα τῇ τρίτῃ ἡμέρᾳ κατὰ τὰς γραφάς, καὶ ἀνελθόντα εἰς τοὺς οὐρανούς, καὶ καθεζόμενον ἐκ δεξιῶν τοῦ πατρός, καὶ πάλιν ἐρχόμενον μετὰ δόξης κρῖναι ζῶντας καὶ νεκρούς· οὗ τῆς βασιλείας οὐκ ἔσται τέλος.

Καὶ εἰς τὸ ΠΝΕΥΜΑ ΤΟ ʽΑΓΙΟΝ, τὸ κύριον, (καὶ) τὸ ζωοποιόν,[1] τὸ ἐκ τοῦ πατρὸς ἐκπορευόμενον, τὸ σὺν

Credimus in unum DEUM PATREM *omnipotentem; factorem cœli et terræ, visibilium omnium et invisibilium.*

Et in unum Dominum JESUM CHRISTUM, *Filium Dei [unigenitum], natum ex Patre ante omnia sæcula [Lumen de Lumine], Deum verum de Deo vero, natum [genitum], non factum, consubstantialem Patri; per quem omnia facta sunt; qui propter nos homines et [propter] salutem nostram descendit de cœlis et incarnatus est de Spiritu Sancto ex Maria virgine et humanatus [homo factus] est; et crucifixus est pro nobis sub Pontio Pilato [passus] et sepultus est; et resurrexit tertia die [secundum scripturas]; ascendit in cœlum [cœlos], sedet ad dexteram Patris; iterum venturus, cum gloria, judicare vivos et mortuos; cujus regni non erit finis.*

Et in SPIRITUM SANCTUM, *Dominum et vivificantem [vivificatorem], ex Patre procedentem, cum Patre*

---

[1] Mansi gives three readings : τὸ κυρ. τὸ ζωοπ., τὸ κυρ. καὶ ζωοπ., and τὸ κυρ. καὶ τὸ ζωοπ. See the critical note of Dr. Hort, p. 81.

πατρὶ καὶ υἱῷ σὺν προσκυνούμενον καὶ
συνδοξαζόμενον, τὸ λαλῆσαν διὰ τῶν
προφητῶν· εἰς μίαν, ἁγίαν, καθολικὴν καὶ ἀποστολικὴν ἐκκλησίαν· ὁμολογοῦμεν ἓν βάπτισμα εἰς ἄφεσιν
ἁμαρτιῶν· προσδοκῶμεν ἀνάστασιν
νεκρῶν, καὶ ζωὴν τοῦ μέλλοντος αἰώ-
νος. Ἀμήν.

et Filio adorandum et conglorifi-
candum, qui locutus est per sanctos
prophetas. Et unam, sanctam, catholicam et apostolicam ecclesiam.
Confitemur unum baptisma in remissionem peccatorum. Expecta-
mus resurrectionem mortuorum et
vitam futuri sœculi. Amen.

NOTES.

[1] See the *History*, pp. 24 sqq. The Greek text is found in the Acts of the First Council of Constantinople in MANSI, *Conc.* Tom. III. p. 565, and twice in the Acts of the Council of Chalcedon, Act. II. Tom. VI. p. 957, and Act. V. Tom. VII. p. 111; also in the Acts of the Third Constantinop. Counc., Act. XVIII. Tom. XI. p. 633. See HAHN, p. 111, and HORT, pp. 73 sqq.

[2] The Latin text is chiefly from the *Canones Concilii Constantinop. ex interpr.* DIONYSII EXIG. in MANSI, Tom. III. p. 567 sq. For the different readings, see WALCH, pp. 94–103, and HAHN, pp. 112–116, who compared with it the translations in the *Codex Canonum et Constitutorum Eccl. Rom.* in *Opp.* LEONIS MAGNI, ed. Quesnel, Tom. II. p. 56; in the *Sacramentarium Gelasianum*, as given by Muratori, *Liturg. Rom. vet.* Tom. I. p. 541, and Assemani, *Codex liturg. univ.* Tom. I. p. 11; the old transl. of the *Canones Conc. Const.* by Isidorus Mercator in Mansi, Tom. III. p. 574; *Acta Conc. Toletani*, of the year 589, given by Mansi, Tom. IX. pp. 977 sqq.; ETHERII ET BEATI *Adv. Elipandum*, Lib. I. in *Bibl. P. P. Lugd.* Tom. XIII. p. 363; *Acta Concilii Chalced. Act. II.* in *Mansi*, Tom. VI. p. 958, and *Act. V.* in *Mansi*, Tom. VII. p. 111; *Codex Reg. Armamentarii Paris.*, published by Ferd. Flor. Fleck, in his *Anecdota* (Leipz. 1837), pp. 347 sqq. All the early and authentic Latin editions omit the *Filioque*, like the Greek, except Assemani's (a convert to Romanism), who inserts, on his own authority, καὶ τοῦ υἱοῦ. A Syriac version is given by CASPARI, l. c. Vol. I. p. 103.

(b) Forma Recepta Ecclesiæ Occidentalis.

THE RECEIVED TEXT OF THE ROMAN CATHOLIC CHURCH.[1]	THE RECEIVED TEXT OF THE PROTESTANT CHURCHES.[2]
Credo in unum DEUM PATREM *omnipotentem; factorem cœli et terræ, visibilium omnium et invisibilium.*	I believe in one GOD THE FATHER Almighty; Maker of heaven and earth, and of all things visible and invisible.
Et in unum Dominum JESUM CHRISTUM, *Filium Dei unigenitum, et ex Patre natum ante omnia sæcula* [*Deum de Deo*], *Lumen de Lumine, Deum verum de Deo vero, genitum, non factum, consubstantialem Patri; per quem*	And in one Lord JESUS CHRIST, the only-begotten Son of God, begotten of the Father before all worlds [God of God], Light of Light, very God of very God, begotten, not made, being of one substance [essence] with the Father;

omnia facta sunt; qui propter nos homines et propter nostram salutem descendit de cœlis, et incarnatus est de Spiritu Sancto ex Maria virgine, et homo factus est; crucifixus etiam pro nobis sub Pontio Pilato, passus et sepultus est; et resurrexit tertia die, secundum Scripturas; et ascendit in cœlum, sedet ad dexteram Patris; et iterum venturus est, cum gloria, judicare vivos et mortuos; cujus regni non erit finis.

by whom all things were made; who, for us men and for our salvation, came down from heaven, and was incarnate by the Holy Ghost of the Virgin Mary, and was made man; and was crucified also for us under Pontius Pilate; he suffered and was buried; and the third day he rose again, according to the Scriptures; and ascended into heaven, and sitteth on the right hand of the Father; and he shall come again, with glory, to judge both the quick and the dead; whose kingdom shall have no end.

Et in SPIRITUM SANCTUM, *Dominum et vivificantem, qui ex Patre [Filioque] procedit; qui cum Patre et Filio simul adoratur et conglorificatur; qui locutus est per Prophetas. Et unam, sanctam, catholicam et apostolicam ecclesiam. Confiteor unum baptisma in remissionem peccatorum; et expecto resurrectionem mortuorum, et vitam venturi seculi. Amen.*

And [I believe] in the Holy Ghost, the Lord and Giver of Life; who proceedeth from the Father [and the Son]; who with the Father and the Son together is worshiped and glorified; who spake by the Prophets. And [I believe] one Holy Catholic and Apostolic Church. I acknowledge one Baptism for the remission of sins; and I look for the resurrection of the dead, and the life of the world to come. Amen.

[The Western additions, of which the *Filioque* is the most important, are inclosed in brackets. Compare Vol. I. pp. 26-28.]

NOTES.

[1] The Latin text is from the *Canons and Decrees of the Council of Trent*, third session, held Feb. 4, 1546, when the Nicene Creed was solemnly professed by this Synod as the '*symbolum fidei, quo sancta Romana ecclesia utitur, tanquam principium illud, in quo omnes, qui fidem Christi profitentur, necessario conveniunt, ac fundamentum firmum et unicum, contra quod portæ inferi nunquam prævalebunt.*' The same text is incorporated in the *Profession of the Tridentine Faith.* The punctuation varies in different editions.

[2] From the Anglican Book of Common Prayer, with which the text in other Protestant liturgies agrees, with slight variations. The Lutheran symbols substitute, in the article on the Church, the term *christliche (Christian)* for *Catholic.* Luther did the same in his German version of the Apostles' Creed; unwisely leaving the Romanists to monopolize the name *Catholic.*

(c) *Symbolum Nicænum.* A.D. 325.

THE ORIGINAL FORM OF THE NI-
CENE CREED, AS ADOPTED AT NI-
CÆA, 325.¹

Πιστεύομεν εἰς ἕνα ΘΕΟΝ ΠΑΤΕ-
ΡΑ παντοκράτορα, πάντων ὁρατῶν
τε καὶ ἀοράτων ποιητήν.

Καὶ εἰς ἕνα κύριον ΊΗΣΟΥΝ
ΧΡΙΣΤΟΝ, τὸν υἱὸν τοῦ ϑεοῦ, γεννηϑέντα ἐκ τοῦ πατρὸς μονογενῆ,
τουτέστιν ἐκ τῆς οὐσίας τοῦ πατρός,
ϑεὸν ἐκ ϑεοῦ, φῶς ἐκ φωτός, ϑεὸν
ἀληϑινὸν ἐκ ϑεοῦ ἀληϑινοῦ, γεννηϑέντα, οὐ ποιηϑέντα, ὁμοούσιον τῷ
πατρί· δι' οὗ τὰ πάντα ἐγένετο, τά τε
ἐν τῷ οὐρανῷ καὶ τὰ ἐπὶ τῆς γῆς·
τὸν δι' ἡμᾶς τοὺς ἀνϑρώπους καὶ διὰ
τὴν ἡμετέραν σωτηρίαν κατελϑόντα
καὶ σαρκωϑέντα καὶ ἐνανϑρωπήσαντα,
παϑόντα, καὶ ἀναστάντα τῇ τρίτῃ ἡμέρᾳ, καὶ ἀνελϑόντα εἰς τοὺς οὐρανούς,
καὶ ἐρχόμενον κρῖναι ζῶντας καὶ
νεκρούς.

Καὶ εἰς τὸ ΆΓΙΟΝ ΠΝΕΥΜΑ.

Τοὺς δὲ λέγοντας, ὅτι ἦν ποτε ὅτε
οὐκ ἦν, καὶ πρὶν γεννηϑῆναι οὐκ ἦν,
καὶ ὅτι ἐξ οὐκ ὄντων ἐγένετο, ἢ ἐξ
ἑτέρας ὑποστάσεως ἢ οὐσίας φάσκοντας εἶναι, [ἢ κτιστόν,] τρεπτὸν
ἢ ἀλλοιωτὸν τὸν υἱὸν τοῦ ϑεοῦ, [τού-
τους] ἀναϑεματίζει ἡ καϑολικὴ [καὶ
ἀποστολικὴ] ἐκκλησία.³

THE LATIN VERSION OF HILARIUS
PICTAVIENSIS, BETWEEN 356 AND
361.²

Credimus in unum DEUM PA-
TREM *omnipotentem, omnium visibilium et invisibilium factorem.*

Et in unum Dominum nostrum
JESUM CHRISTUM, *Filium Dei, natum ex Patre unigenitum, hoc est,
de substantia Patris, Deum ex
Deo, Lumen ex Lumine, Deum verum de Deo vero, natum, non factum, unius substantiæ cum Patre, quod Græci dicunt homoou-
sion; per quem omnia facta sunt,
quæ in cœlo et in terra; qui [prop-
ter nos homines et] propter nostram salutem descendit, incarnatus
est et homo factus est, et passus est;
et resurrexit tertia die, et ascendit
in cœlos; venturus judicare vivos
et mortuos.*

Et in SPIRITUM SANCTUM.

Eos autem qui dicunt : ' *erat,
quando non erat,*' *et* ' *antequam
nasceretur, non erat,*' *et* ' *quod de
non exstantibus factus est,*' *vel* ' *ex
alia substantia*' *aut* ' *essentia,*' *dicentes* [' *creatum,*' *aut*] ' *conver-
tibilem et demutabilem Filium
Dei,*' *hos anathematizat catholica*
[*et apostolica*] *ecclesia.*²

[See the English version both of the original and the enlarged Creed in Vol. I. pp. 28, 29.]

NOTES.

[1] The Greek text after EUSEBIUS, in his *Epist. ad Cæsareenses* (as preserved by Athanasius), and the *Acts of the Council of Chalcedon*, which indorsed both the original and the enlarged form of the Nicene Creed. See Vol. I. p. 28, note 3. The variations are carefully given by WALCH, pp. 87 sqq., and HAHN, pp. 105–107. For a Syriac version, see CASPARI, Vol. I. p. 100. Dr. HORT (*Dissertations*, p. 54) ingeniously but artificially connects μονογενῆ with Θεόν (τοῦτ' ἐστὶν ἐκ τῆς οὐσίας τοῦ πατρός being parenthetical), and thus derives from the Nicene Creed a traditional support for the famous reading μονογενὴς Θεός instead of the received text μονογενὴς υἱός, John i. 18.

[2] The Latin form from HILARIUS (Bishop of Poitiers, called the Athanasius of the West; died 368): *De Synodis sive de fide Orientalium*, § 84, *Opp.* ed. Constant. Veron. Tom. II. p. 510, and *Fragm. II. ex opere historico*, § 27, l. c. p. 643. WALCH (pp. 80–92) gives also other Latin versions from Lucifer, Rufinus, Leo M., Marius Mercator, etc., and HAHN (pp. 108–110) notes the principal variations.

[3] The received text, as sanctioned by the Fourth, or previously by the Second Œcumenical Council, omits the words τοῦτ' ἐστὶν ἐκ τῆς οὐσίας τοῦ πατρός and Θεὸν ἐκ Θεοῦ, and the concluding anathema, but adds the important clauses after the Holy Spirit.

APPENDIX.

OTHER ORIENTAL CREEDS OF THE NICENE AGE.

With the Nicene Creed should be compared several similar Greek forms of the fourth century (see above, pp. 24–40, and Hahn, pp. 42–59), especially the following:

(1.) The Creed of CÆSAREA, which EUSEBIUS read at Nicæa, 325, as his own baptismal creed. It omits Θεὸν ἀληθινόν and ὁμοούσιον, but otherwise agrees nearly with the first Nicene Creed till πνεῦμα ἅγιον, and is the basis of it.

(2.) The Creed of JERUSALEM, which CYRIL of Jerusalem taught in his Catechetical Lectures before 350. It likewise omits ὁμοούσιον, but has after ἅγιον πνεῦμα the articles: 'In (εἰς repeated) one baptism for the remission of sins, and in one holy catholic Church, and in the resurrection of the flesh, and in the life everlasting;' resembling in this conclusion more the later Constantinopolitan Creed, of which it seems to be the chief basis.

(3.) Two Creeds of EPIPHANIUS, a longer and a shorter one, recorded in his *Ancoratus* about 374. Both contain the whole Nicene Creed, with the concluding anathema (enlarged in one formula), and at the same time almost literally the additional articles after 'the Holy Ghost,' which were incorporated in the Nicene Creed by the Synod of Constantinople; showing that these were current in the Churches before 381.

(4.) The Creed of ARIUS, which he delivered to the Emperor Constantine (328), and which is recorded by Socrates and Sozomenus (also in Mansi, Tom. II. p. 1157; Walch, p. 47; Hahn, p. 192; and Denzinger, p. 8). It shrewdly omits the obnoxious words condemned by the Council of Nicæa, confesses Christ as Θεὸν λόγον, δι' οὗ τὰ πάντα ἐγένετο, and adds after ἅγιον πνεῦμα the articles: καὶ εἰς σαρκὸς ἀνάστασιν, καὶ εἰς ζωὴν τοῦ μέλλοντος αἰῶνος, καὶ εἰς βασιλείαν οὐρανῶν, καὶ εἰς μίαν καθολικὴν ἐκκλησίαν τοῦ Θεοῦ, τὴν ἀπὸ περάτων ἕως περάτων.

III. SYMBOLUM CHALCEDONENSE.

The Symbol of Chalcedon.

Oct. 22d, 451.

Ἑπόμενοι τοίνυν τοῖς ἁγίοις πατράσιν ἕνα καὶ τὸν αὐτὸν ὁμολογεῖν υἱὸν τὸν κύριον ἡμῶν Ἰησοῦν Χριστὸν συμφώνως ἅπαντες ἐκδιδάσκομεν, τέλειον τὸν αὐτὸν ἐν ϑεότητι καὶ τέλειον τὸν αὐτὸν ἐν ἀνϑρωπότητι, ϑεὸν ἀληϑῶς καὶ ἄνϑρωπον ἀληϑῶς τὸν αὐτὸν, ἐκ ψυχῆς λογικῆς[1] καὶ σώματος, ὁμοούσιον[2] τῷ πατρὶ κατὰ τὴν ϑεότητα, καὶ ὁμοούσιον[2] τὸν αὐτὸν ἡμῖν κατὰ τὴν ἀνϑρωπότητα, κατὰ πάντα ὅμοιον ἡμῖν χωρὶς ἁμαρτίας· πρὸ αἰώνων μὲν ἐκ τοῦ πατρὸς γεννηϑέντα κατὰ τὴν ϑεότητα, ἐπ' ἐσχάτων δὲ τῶν ἡμερῶν τὸν αὐτὸν δι' ἡμᾶς καὶ διὰ τὴν ἡμετέραν σωτηρίαν ἐκ Μαρίας τῆς παρϑένου τῆς ϑεοτόκου κατὰ τὴν ἀνϑρωπότητα,[3] ἕνα καὶ τὸν αὐτὸν Χριστόν, υἱόν, κύριον, μονογενῆ, ἐκ δύο φύσεων [ἐν δύο φύσεσιν],[4] ἀσυγχύτως, ἀτρέπτως,[5] ἀδιαιρέτως, ἀχωρίστως[6] γνωριζόμενον· οὐδαμοῦ τῆς τῶν φύσεων διαφορᾶς ἀνῃρημένης διὰ τὴν ἕνωσιν, σωζομένης δὲ μᾶλλον τῆς ἰδιότητος ἑκατέρας φύσεως καὶ εἰς ἓν πρόσωπον καὶ μίαν ὑπόστασιν συντρεχούσης, οὐκ εἰς δύο πρόσωπα μεριζόμενον ἢ διαιρούμενον, ἀλλ' ἕνα καὶ τὸν αὐτὸν υἱὸν καὶ μονογενῆ, ϑεὸν λόγον, κύριον Ἰησοῦν

We, then, following the holy Fathers, all with one consent, teach men to confess one and the same Son, our Lord Jesus Christ, the same perfect in Godhead and also perfect in manhood; truly God and truly man, of a reasonable [rational] soul[1] and body; consubstantial [coessential][2] with the Father according to the Godhead, and consubstantial with us according to the Manhood; in all things like unto us, without sin; begotten before all ages of the Father according to the Godhead, and in these latter days, for us and for our salvation, born of the Virgin Mary, the Mother of God, according to the Manhood;[3] one and the same Christ, Son, Lord, Onlybegotten, to be acknowledged in two natures,[4] *inconfusedly, unchangeably,[5] indivisibly, inseparably;*[6] the distinction of natures being by no means taken away by the union, but rather the property of each nature being preserved, and concurring in one Person and one Subsistence, not parted or divided into two persons, but one and the same Son, and only begotten, God the Word, the Lord Jesus Christ, as

Χριστόν· καθάπερ ἄνωθεν οἱ προφῆ-ται περὶ αὐτοῦ καὶ αὐτὸς ἡμᾶς ὁ κύ-ριος Ἰησοῦς Χριστὸς ἐξεπαίδευσε καὶ τὸ τῶν πατέρων ἡμῖν καραδίδωκε σύμβολον.	the prophets from the beginning [have declared] concerning him, and the Lord Jesus Christ himself has taught us, and the Creed of the holy Fathers has handed down to us.

SYMBOLUM CHALCEDONENSE. VERSIO LATINA.

Sequentes igitur sanctos patres, unum eundemque confiteri FILIUM *et* DOMINUM NOSTRUM JESUM CHRISTUM *consonanter omnes docemus, eundem perfectum in deitate et eundem perfectum in humanitate; Deum verum et hominem verum eundem ex anima rationali et corpore; consubstantialem Patri secundum deitatem, consubstantialem nobis eundem secundum humanitatem; 'per omnia nobis similem, absque peccato'* (Heb. iv.): *ante secula quidem de Patre genitum secundum deitatem; in novissimis autem diebus eundem propter nos et propter nostram salutem ex Maria virgine, Dei genitrice secundum humanitatem; unum eundemque Christum, Filium, Dominum, unigenitum, in duabus naturis* INCONFUSE, IMMUTABILITER, INDIVISE, INSEPERABILITER *agnoscendum: nusquam sublata differentia naturarum propter unitionem, magisque salva proprietate utriusque naturæ, et in unam personam atque subsistentiam concurrente: non in duas personas partitum aut divisum, sed unum eundemque Filium et unigenitum, Deum verbum, Dominum Jesum Christum; sicut ante prophetæ de eo et ipse nos Jesus Christus erudivit et patrum nobis symbolum tradidit.*

NOTES.

The Greek text, together with the Latin version, is taken from the ὅρος τῆς ἐν Χαλκηδόνι τετάρτης Συνόδου, Act. V. in MANSI, *Conc.* Tom. VII. p.115. We have inserted ἐν δύο φύσεσιν (see note 4). There are several other Latin versions which Mansi gives, Tom. VII. pp. 115 and 751–758, with the various readings. See also Hahn, l. c. pp. 117 sqq.

The Creed is preceded in the acts of the Council by an express confirmation of the Nicene Creed in both forms, 'the Creed of the three hundred and eighteen holy Fathers of Nicæa,' and 'the Creed of the hundred and fifty holy Fathers who were assembled at Constantinople.' The Fathers of Chalcedon declare that 'this wise and saving Creed [of Nicæa] would be sufficient for the full acknowledgment and confirmation of the true religion; for it teaches completely the perfect doctrine concerning the Father, the Son, and the Holy Spirit, and fully explains the Incarnation of the Lord to those who receive it faithfully.' The addition of a new Creed is justified by the subsequent Christological heresies (Apollinarianism, Nestorianism, and Eutychianism). After stating it, the Synod solemnly prohibits, on pain of 'deposi-

tion and excommunication, the setting forth of any other Creed for those 'who are desirous of turning to the acknowledgment of the truth from Heathenism and Judaism.'

¹ Against Apollinaris, who denied that Christ had a ψυχὴ λογικὴ, *anima rationalis*, or νοῦς, πνεῦμα, and who reduced the Incarnation to the assumption of a human body (σῶμα) with an animal soul (ψυχὴ ἄλογος), inhabited by the Divine Logos. But the rational spirit of man requires salvation as much as the body.

² Ὁμοούσιος, *consubstantialis* (al. *coessentialis*), is used in both clauses, though with a shade of difference. Christ's *homoousia* with the Father implies numerical unity, or identity of essence (God being one in being, or *monoousios*); Christ's *homoousia* with men means only generic unity, or equality of nature.

³ The predicate Θεοτόκος, the *Bringer-forth of God, Dei genitrix* (al. *quæ Deum peperit*, or even *divini numinis creatrix*), is directed against Nestorius, and was meant originally not so much to exalt the Virgin Mary, as to assert the true divinity of Christ and the realness of the Incarnation. Basil of Seleucia: Θεὸν σαρκωθέντα τεκοῦσα Θεοτόκος ὀνομάζεται. It is immediately after qualified by the phrase κατὰ τὴν ἀνθρωπότητα (*secundum humanitatem*), in distinction from κατὰ τὴν θεότητα (*secundum deitatem*). This is a very important limitation, and necessary to guard against Mariolatry, and the heathenish, blasphemous, and contradictory notion that the uncreated, eternal God can be born in time. Mary was the mother not merely of the human *nature* of Jesus of Nazareth, but of the theanthropic *person* of Jesus Christ; yet not of his eternal Godhead (the λόγος ἄσαρκος), but of his incarnate person, or the Logos united to humanity (the λόγος ἔνσαρκος). In like manner, the subject of the Passion was the theanthropic *person;* yet not according to his divine nature, which in itself is incapable of suffering, but according to his human nature, which was the organ of suffering. There is no doubt, however, that the unscriptural terms Θεοτόκος, *Dei genitrix, Deipara, mater Dei,* which remind one of the heathen mothers of gods, have greatly promoted Mariolatry, which aided in the defeat of Nestorius at the Council of Ephesus, 431. It is safer to adhere to the New Testament designation of Mary as μήτηρ Ἰησοῦ, or μήτηρ τοῦ Κυρίου (Luke i. 43).

⁴ Ἐν δύο φύσεσιν, and all the Latin translations, *in duabus naturis* (only the Roman editors in the margin read *ex d. n.*), are directed against Eutyches. The present Greek text reads, it is true, ἐκ δύο φύσεων, *from* two natures; but this signifies, and, according to the connection, can only signify, essentially the same thing; though, separately taken, it admits also of an Eutychian and Monophysite interpretation, namely, that Christ has arisen from the confluence of two natures, and since the act of the Incarnation, or unition of both, has only *one* nature. Understood in that sense, Dioscurus at the Council was very willing to accept the formula ἐκ δύο φύσεων. But for this very reason the Orientals, and also the Roman delegates, protested with one voice against ἐκ, and insisted upon another formula with ἐν, which was adopted. Baur (*Gesch. der Lehre v. d. Dreieinigkeit*, I. p. 820 sq.) and Dorner (*Gesch. d. Lehre v. d. Person Christi*, II. p. 129) assert that ἐκ is the accurate and original expression, and is a concession to Monophysitism; that it also agrees better (?) with the verb γνωρίζειν (to recognize by certain tokens); but that it was from the very beginning changed by the Occidentals into ἐν. But, with Gieseler, Neander (iv. 988), Hefele (*Conciliengesch.* II. 451 sq.), Beck (*Dogmengeschichte*, p. 251), and Hahn (l. c. p. 118, note 6), we prefer the view that ἐν δύο φύσεσιν was the original reading of the symbol, and that it was afterwards altered in the interest of Monophysitism. This is proved by the whole course of the proceedings at the fifth session of the Council of Chalcedon, where the expression ἐκ δύο φύσεων was protested against, and is confirmed by the testimony of the Abbot Euthymius, a contemporary, and by that of Severus, Evagrius, and Leontius of Byzantium, as well as by the Latin translations. Severus, the Monophysite Patriarch of Antioch since 513, charges the Fathers of Chalcedon with the inexcusable crime of having taught ἐν δύο φύσεσιν ἀδιαιρέτοις γνωρίζεσθαι τὸν χριστόν (see Mansi, *Conc.* VII. p. 839). Evagrius (*H. E.* II. c. 5) maintains that both formulas amount to essentially the same thing, and reciprocally condition each other. Dorner also affirms the same. His words are: 'The Latin formula has "to acknowledge Christ as Son *in* two natures;" the Greek has "to recognize Christ as Son *from* two natures," which is plainly the

same thought. The Latin formula is only a free but essentially faithful translation, only that its coloring expresses somewhat more definitely still Christ's subsisting in two natures, and is therefore more literally conformable to the Roman type of doctrine' (l. c. II. 129). From my *Church History*, Vol. III. p. 745 sq.

⁵ ἀσυγχύτως, *inconfuse*, and ἀτρέπτως, *immutabiliter* (*without confusion, without conversion or change*), are directed against Eutychianism, which mixes and confounds the human and the divine natures in Christ (σύγχυσις), and teaches an absorption of the former into the latter; hence the phrases 'God is born; God suffered; God was crucified; God died.' The Monophysites (so called after the Council of Chalcedon) rejected the Eutychian theory of an absorption, but nevertheless taught only one composite nature of Christ (μία φύσις σύνθετος), making his humanity a mere accident of the immutable divine substance, and using the liturgical shibboleth 'God has been crucified' (without a qualifying 'according to the human nature,' or 'the flesh,' as the Θεοτόκος is qualified in the Symbol of Chalcedon). Hence they were also called *Theopaschites*. They divided into several sects and parties on subtle and idle questions, especially the question whether Christ's body *before* the resurrection was corruptible or incorruptible (hence the Phthartolaters, from φθαρτός and λάτρης, and Aphthartodocetæ).

⁶ ἀδιαιρέτως, *indivise*, ἀχωρίστως, *inseparabiliter* (*without division, without separation*), both in opposition to Nestorianism, which so emphasized the duality of natures, and the continued distinction between the human and the divine in Christ, as to lose sight of the unity of person, and to substitute for a real Incarnation a mere conjunction (συνάφεια), a moral union or intimate friendship between the Divine Logos and the man Jesus. Hence, also, the opposition to the term Θεοτόκος, with which the Nestorian controversy began.

With the Symbol of Chalcedon should be compared the semi-symbolical *Epistola dogmatica* of Pope Leo I. to the Patriarch Flavian of Constantinople, which contains a lengthy and masterly exposition of the orthodox Christology against the heresy of Eutyches, and was read and approved by the Council of Chalcedon, as the voice of Peter speaking through 'the Archbishop of old Rome.' It is dated June 13, 449, and is found in the works of Leo M. (*Ep.* 24 in Quesnel's ed., *Ep.* 28 in the ed. Ballerini), in Mansi, *Conc.* Tom. V. pp. 1366–90 (Latin and Greek, with the different readings), Hardouin, *Conc.* Tom. II. pp. 290–300 (also Latin and Greek, but without the variations), Hefele, *Conciliengeschichte*, Vol. II. pp. 335–346 (German and Latin), partly also in Denzinger, *Enchir.* p. 43.

IV. SYMBOLUM QUICUNQUE.

THE ATHANASIAN CREED.

THE LATIN ORIGINAL.	OLD TRANSLATION REVISED.

THE LATIN ORIGINAL.

1. *Quicunque vult salvus esse: ante omnia opus est, ut teneat catholicam fidem.*

2. *Quam nisi quisque integram inviolatamque servaverit: absque dubio in æternum peribit.*

3. *Fides autem catholica hæc est: ut unum Deum in Trinitate, et Trinitatem in Unitate veneremur;*

4. *Neque confundentes personas: neque substantiam separantes.*

5. *Alia est enim persona Patris: alia Filii: alia Spiritus Sancti.*

6. *Sed Patris et Filii et Spiritus Sancti una est divinitas: æqualis gloria, coæterna majestas.*

7. *Qualis Pater: talis Filius: talis [et] Spiritus Sanctus.*

8. *Increatus Pater: increatus Filius: increatus [et] Spiritus Sanctus.*

9. *Immensus Pater: immensus Filius: immensus [et] Spiritus Sanctus.*

OLD TRANSLATION REVISED.

1. Whosoever will be saved: before all things it is necessary that he hold the Catholic Faith:

2. Which Faith except every one do keep whole and undefiled: without doubt he shall perish everlastingly.

3. And the Catholic Faith is this: That we worship one God in Trinity, and Trinity in Unity;

4. Neither confounding the Persons: nor dividing the Substance [Essence].

5. For there is one Person of the Father: another of the Son: and another of the Holy Ghost.

6. But the Godhead of the Father, of the Son, and of the Holy Ghost, is all one: the Glory equal, the Majesty coeternal.

7. Such as the Father is: such is the Son: and such is the Holy Ghost.

8. The Father uncreate [uncreated]: the Son uncreate [uncreated]: and the Holy Ghost uncreate [uncreated].

9. The Father incomprehensible [unlimited]: the Son incomprehensible [unlimited]: and the Holy Ghost incomprehensible [unlimited, or infinite].

10. *Æternus Pater: æternus Filius: æternus* [*et*] *Spiritus Sanctus.*

11. *Et tamen non tres æterni: sed unus æternus.*

12. *Sicut non tres increati: nec tres immensi: sed unus increatus: et unus immensus.*

13. *Similiter omnipotens Pater: omnipotens Filius: omnipotens* [*et*] *Spiritus Sanctus.*

14. *Et tamen non tres omnipotentes: sed unus omnipotens.*

15. *Ita deus Pater: deus Filius: deus* [*et*] *Spiritus Sanctus.*

16. *Et tamen non tres dii: sed unus est Deus.*

17. *Ita dominus Pater: dominus Filius: dominus* [*et*] *Spiritus Sanctus.*

18. *Et tamen non tres domini: sed unus* [*est*] *Dominus.*

19. *Quia sicut singulatim unamquamque personam Deum ac Dominum confiteri, christiana veritate compellimur:*

20. *Ita tres deos, aut* [*tres*] *dominos dicere, catholica religione prohibemur.*

21. *Pater a nullo est factus: nec creatus, nec genitus.*

22. *Filius a Patre solo est: non factus, nec creatus: sed genitus.*

10. The Father eternal: the Son eternal: and the Holy Ghost eternal.

11. And yet they are not three eternals: but one eternal.

12. As also there are not three uncreated: nor three incomprehensibles [infinites], but one uncreated: and one incomprehensible [infinite].

13. So likewise the Father is Almighty: the Son Almighty: and the Holy Ghost Almighty.

14. And yet they are not three Almighties: but one Almighty.

15. So the Father is God: the Son is God: and the Holy Ghost is God.

16. And yet they are not three Gods: but one God.

17. So likewise the Father is Lord: the Son Lord: and the Holy Ghost Lord.

18. And yet not three Lords: but one Lord.

19. For like as we are compelled by the Christian verity: to acknowledge every Person by himself to be God and Lord:

20. So are we forbidden by the Catholic Religion: to say, There be [are] three Gods, or three Lords.

21. The Father is made of none: neither created, nor begotten.

22. The Son is of the Father alone: not made, nor created: but begotten.

23. *Spiritus Sanctus a Patre et Filio: non factus, nec creatus, nec genitus: sed procedens.*

24. *Unus ergo Pater, non tres patres: unus Filius, non tres filii: unus Spiritus Sanctus, non tres spiritus sancti.*

25. *Et in hac Trinitate nihil prius, aut posterius: nihil majus, aut minus.*

26. *Sed totæ tres personæ coæternæ sibi sunt, et coæquales.*

27. *Ita, ut per omnia, sicut jam supra dictum est: et Unitas in Trinitate, et Trinitas in Unitate, venerenda sit.*

28. *Qui vult ergo salvus esse, ita de Trinitate sentiat.*

————

29. *Sed necessarium est ad æternam salutem: ut incarnationem quoque Domini nostri Jesu Christi fideliter credat.*

30. *Est ergo fides recta, ut credamus et confiteamur: quod Dominus noster Jesus Christus Dei Filius, Deus [pariter] et homo est;*

31. *Deus [est] ex substantia Patris, ante secula genitus: et homo ex substantia matris, in seculo natus.*

23. The Holy Ghost is of the Father and of the Son: neither made, nor created, nor begotten: but proceeding.

24. So there is one Father, not three Fathers: one Son, not three Sons: one Holy Ghost, not three Holy Ghosts.

25. And in this Trinity none is afore, or after another: none is greater, or less than another [there is nothing before, or after: nothing greater or less].

26. But the whole three Persons are coeternal, and coequal.

27. So that in all things, as aforesaid: the Unity in Trinity, and the Trinity in Unity, is to be worshiped.

28. He therefore that will be saved, must [let him] thus think of the Trinity.

————

29. Furthermore it is necessary to everlasting salvation: that he also believe rightly [faithfully] the Incarnation of our Lord Jesus Christ.

30. For the right Faith is, that we believe and confess: that our Lord Jesus Christ, the Son of God, is God and Man;

31. God, of the Substance [Essence] of the Father; begotten before the worlds: and Man, of the Substance [Essence] of his Mother, born in the world.

32. *Perfectus Deus: perfectus homo, ex anima rationali et humana carne subsistens.*

33. *Aequalis Patri secundum divinitatem: minor Patre secundum humanitatem.*

34. *Qui licet Deus sit et homo; non duo tamen, sed unus est Christus.*

35. *Unus autem, non conversione divinitatis in carnem: sed assumptione humanitatis in Deum.*

36. *Unus omnino; non confusione substantiæ: sed unitate personæ.*

37. *Nam sicut anima rationalis et caro unus est homo: ita Deus et homo unus est Christus.*

38. *Qui passus est pro nostra salute: descendit ad inferos: tertia die resurrexit a mortuis.*

39. *Ascendit ad [in] cœlos: sedet ad dexteram [Dei] Patris [omnipotentis].*

40. *Inde venturus [est] judicare vivos et mortuos.*

41. *Ad cujus adventum omnes homines resurgere habent cum corporibus suis;*

42. *Et reddituri sunt de factis propriis rationem.*

32. Perfect God: and perfect Man, of a reasonable soul and human flesh subsisting.

33. Equal to the Father, as touching his Godhead: and inferior to the Father as touching his Manhood.

34. Who although he be [is] God and Man; yet he is not two, but one Christ.

35. One; not by conversion of the Godhead into flesh: but by taking [assumption] of the Manhood into God.

36. One altogether; not by confusion of Substance [Essence]: but by unity of Person.

37. For as the reasonable soul and flesh is one man: so God and Man is one Christ;

38. Who suffered for our salvation: descended into hell [Hades, spirit-world]: rose again the third day from the dead.

39. He ascended into heaven, he sitteth on the right hand of the Father God [God the Father] Almighty.

40. From whence [thence] he shall come to judge the quick and the dead.

41. At whose coming all men shall rise again with their bodies;

42. And shall give account for their own works.

43. *Et qui bona egerunt, ibunt in vitam œternam: qui vero mala, in ignem œternum.*

43. And they that have done good shall go into life everlasting: and they that have done evil, into everlasting fire.

44. *Hœc est fides catholica: quam nisi quisque fideliter firmiterque crediderit, salvus esse non poterit.*

44. This is the Catholic Faith: which except a man believe faithfully [truly and firmly], he can not be saved.

NOTES.

[1] The LATIN text of the oldest known MS. in the Utrecht Psalter has been reproduced by Sir Thomas Duffus Hardy in his Report (London, 1873), and in the fac-simile ed. of the Utrecht Psalter (1875). It agrees nearly altogether with the text given above, but has a number of inaccuracies. I have compared also the texts of Waterland (*Works*, Vol. III. pp. 221 sqq.), Usher (*De Romanœ Eccles. Symbolo Apost. vetere*, 1647, Genev. ed. 1722, pp. 13–15), Montfaucon (in his ed. of *Athanasius*, Tom. II. pp. 719 sqq.), Hahn (pp. 122–125), Lumby (p. 259), and Swainson (p. 204). The numbering of verses differs: Waterland, Montfaucon, and the English Book of Common Prayer have only 40 verses by combining 19 and 20, 25 and 26, 39 and 40, 41 and 42; Walch and others make 44, the Roman Breviary 42. In my *Church Hist.* Vol. III. pp. 690–695, I have given the parallel passages from the fathers.

[2] There is no authorized *Greek* text of the Athanasian Creed, since it was never adopted in the Oriental Church. There are several translations, which differ considerably. Usher gives a Greek version with many interpolations. Caspari (Vol. III. pp. 263–267) published for the first time two other Greek versions from MSS. in the Venetian Library of St. Mark and the Ambrosian Library of Milan.

[3] The English translation is that of the sixteenth century (1548), as found in the English editions of the *Book of Common Prayer*, and still in use in the public service of the Church of England. My emendations are inclosed in brackets. The punctuation is adjusted to the liturgical use of this Creed.

Ver. 1.—Some copies read *opus habet* for *opus est*. Usher: τὴν ὀρθόδοξον πίστιν, *orthodoxam fidem*. The MS. in the Utrecht Psalter begins with a grammatical blunder: 'Incipit fides catholicam.'

Ver. 2.—On the damnatory clause, which is twice repeated, ver. 28 and ver. 44, see the *Introduction*, pp. 39, 41. Some MSS. read *inviolabilemque;* some omit *absque dubio*.

Ver. 3.—Usher: *Orthodoxa* for *catholica*. Compare on this verse Gregory Naz., *Orat.* xxiii.: μονάδα ἐν τριάδι, καὶ τριάδα ἐν μονάδι προσκυνουμένην.

Ver. 4.—*Person* in the sense of *persona*, πρόσωπον (also ὑπόστασις in the post-Nicene use of the term), i. e., *character*, *face*, *manifestation*, *subsistence*. It must not be confounded with *essence* or *being* (*essentia, substantia, natura*, οὐσία, φύσις). God is one in essence, three in persons (*Deus est trinus, h. e. in essentia unus, tres habet subsistendi modos*). In modern philosophical usage the term *person* means a separate and distinct rational individual. But the tripersonality of God is not a numerical or essential trinity of three beings (like Abraham, Isaac, and Jacob), for this would be tritheism; nor is it, on the other hand, merely a threefold aspect and mode of manifestation, in the Sabellian or Swedenborgian sense;[1] but it is a real, objective, and eternal, though ineffable, distinction in the one Divine being, with a corresponding threefold revelation of this being in the works of creation, redemption, and sanctification.

---

[1] Swedenborg was willing to adopt the Athanasian Creed if a trinity of (the one Divine) *person* was substituted for a trinity of *persons*. According to him, the Father is the Essential Divinity, the Son the Divine Humanity, the Holy Spirit the Divine Proceeding or Operation.

Hence the distinction between the immanent, intrinsic (or ontological) trinity and the extrinsic (or œconomical) trinity; in other words, between the trinity of essence and the trinity of manifestation.

Ver. 4.—The Latin *substantia* (that which stands under) and *essentia* correspond to the Greek οὐσία, as distinct from πρόσωπον. But in modern English, *substance* is used mostly in the sense of matter, body, or the most important part, summary. Hence *essence* or *being* is preferable. *Hypostasis* (ὑπόστασις, foundation, groundwork, *substratum, substantia*) was originally used in the same sense as οὐσία, but afterwards it became identical with *prosopon, persona*.

Ver. 6.—Usher reads after *divinitas: 'Unum robur, una potestas, unum regnum'* (an interpolation of the Greeks).

Ver. 9.—*Incomprehensible* is a false translation, unless it be taken in the unusual sense, 'not to be comprehended within any bounds.' The Anglican translator of 1548 perhaps followed a Greek copy (of 1533) which renders *immensus* by ἀκατάληπτος. But other Greek copies read ἄπειρος or ἄμετρος instead. Usher's Greek text has παντοκράτωρ, *omnipotent*. The Latin *immensus* means, what can not be circumscribed or limited by any boundaries, what is illocal, omnipresent. Fortunatus explains the word: '*Non est mensurabilis in sua natura, quia illocalis est, incircumscriptus, ubique totus, ubique præsens, ubique potens.*' The author of the Athanasian Creed glories in the clear revelation and statement of the mystery of the Trinity rather than in the mystery itself. The Utrecht Psalter reads *immensus*.

Ver. 20.—Waterland omits *tres* before *Dominos.* Usher reads for *prohibemur: 'Non comprobamus, sed omnino prohibemus.'*

Ver. 21.—Usher: *sed ingenitus* for *nec genitus.*

Ver. 23.—The Greek translation and the Latin text in Usher omit *et Filio*, which is contrary to the Greek doctrine of the single procession. Most Greek copies read only ἀπὸ τοῦ πατρός.

Ver. 25.—Usher: *nullus primus aut postremus, nullus major aut minor*, οὐδεὶς πρῶτος ἢ ἔσχατος, οὐδεὶς μέγας ἢ μικρός.

Ver. 29.—*Fideliter* is variously rendered in the Greek copies by ὀρθῶς, πιστῶς, βεβαίως.

Ver. 30.—Utrecht Psalter reads *quia* for *quod*, and omits *pariter.*

Ver. 31.—Usher's Greek text inserts here a long interpolation, which is not at all in keeping with the sententious character of the symbol.

Ver. 32.—Another long interpolation in Usher.

Ver. 38.—After *passus est* a Greek version adds the anti-patripassian clause: ἀπαθοῦς τῆς θεότητος μενούσης, *impassibili manente divinitate.*

Ver. 38.—Some MSS. read *ad infernos* or *ad inferna.* Usher's enlarged Greek copy omits the clause, and reads ταφεὶς καὶ ἀναστάς. The Utrecht Psalter reads *et qui* for *qui vero.*

Ver. 43.—Usher: εἰς αἰωνίους κολάσεις, *ad cruciatus eternos.*

Ver. 44.—The Greek copies read either πιστῶς alone, or πιστῶς τε καὶ βεβαίως, or ἐκ πίστεως βεβαίως πιστεύσῃ.

Vol. II.—F

V. SYMBOLUM CONSTANTINOPOLITANUM TERTIUM, ADVERSUS MONOTHELETAS, A.D. 680.

THE CREED OF THE SIXTH ŒCUMENICAL COUNCIL, AGAINST THE MONOTHELITES.

Review of the Dogmatic Legislation of the Seven Œcumenical Councils

The NICÆNO-CONSTANTINOPOLITAN Creed, and the Creed of CHALCEDON, both of which we have given in full, embrace the sum and substance of the dogmatic legislation of the œcumenical Councils of the undivided ancient or Græco-Latin Church. All the rest is merely explanatory and supplementary, or disputed.

The SIXTH ŒCUMENICAL (or THIRD CONSTANTINOPOLITAN) COUNCIL (also called *Conc. Trullanum I.*), held A.D. 680, in consequence of the *Monothelite* or *One-Will* Controversy (633–680), enlarged the Creed of Chalcedon, notwithstanding the solemn prohibition of the Council of Chalcedon (see p. 16), by adding a ὅρος, or dogmatic definition to the effect that Jesus Christ had *two* distinct and inseparable *wills* (θελήματα), as well as two natures, a *human* will and a *divine* will, working in harmony, the human in subordination to the divine; the will being regarded as an attribute of nature rather than person. See Actio XVIII. in Mansi, *Conc.*, Tom. XI. pp. 637 sqq. After quoting the Symbol of Chalcedon down to the words παραδέδωκε σύμβολον (see p. 15), the Synod goes on, without interruption, as follows:

Καὶ δύο φυσικὰς θελήσεις ἤτοι θελήματα ἐν αὐτῷ ['Ιησ. Χριστῷ] καὶ δύο φυσικὰς ἐνεργείας ἀδιαιρέτως, ἀτρέπτως, ἀμερίστως, ἀσυγχύτως, κατὰ τὴν τῶν ἁγίων πατέρων διδασκαλίαν ὡσαύτως κηρύττομεν· καὶ δύο μὲν φυσικὰ θελήματα οὐχ' ὑπεναντία, μὴ γένοιτο, καθὼς οἱ ἀσεβεῖς ἔφησαν αἱρετικοί, ἀλλ' ἑπόμενον τὸ ἀνθρώπινον αὐτοῦ θέλημα, καὶ μὴ ἀντιπίπτον ἢ ἀντιπαλαῖον, μᾶλλον μὲν οὖν καὶ ὑποτασσόμενον τῷ θείῳ αὐτοῦ καὶ πανσθενεῖ θελήματι· ἔδει γὰρ τὸ τῆς σαρκὸς θέλημα κινηθῆναι, ὑποταγῆναι δὲ τῷ θελήματι τῷ θεϊκῷ κατὰ τὸν πάνσοφον 'Αθανάσιον.	Et duas naturales voluntates in eo [Jesu Christo], et duas naturales operationes indivise, inconvertibiliter, inseparabiliter, inconfuse secundum sanctorum patrum doctrinam adæque prædicamus; et duas naturales voluntates non contrarias, absit, juxta quod impii asseruerunt hæretici, sed sequentem ejus humanam voluntatem, et non resistentem vel reluctantem, sed potius et subjectam divinæ ejus atque omnipotenti voluntati. Oportebat enim carnis voluntatem moveri, subjici vero voluntati divinæ, juxta sapientissimum Athanasium.

Then follow quotations from John vi. 38, Gregory Nazianzen, Pope Leo (*Ep. ad Flavianum*, c. 4), Cyril of Alexandria, and a repetition of the Ephesian and Chalcedonian prohibition to set forth any new symbol of faith on pain of excommunication. Pope Agatho, by a dogmatic

epistle, exercised a controlling influence over this Council similar to the one of Pope Leo I. over the Council of Chalcedon. On the other hand, the Council emphatically condemned Pope Honorius as a Monothelite heretic. Monothelitism continued among the Maronites on Mount Lebanon.

The THIRD ŒCUMENICAL COUNCIL, held at EPHESUS, A.D. 431, and the FIFTH ŒCUMENICAL COUNCIL, held at CONSTANTINOPLE, A.D. 553 (hence also called the SECOND CONSTANTINOPOLITAN C.), issued no new Creed, but simply reaffirmed the previous Creeds and condemned certain heresies.

The Council of Ephesus condemned 'the impious and profane doctrines' of Nestorius in two of its six canons (can. 1 and 4), and indorsed the twelve anathemas of Cyril of Alexandria hurled against Nestorius, which are purely negative, and need not be inserted here.[1] The same Synod sanctioned also the letters of Cyril and of Cœlestinus of Rome to Nestorius, and incidentally (in can. 1 and 4) condemned *Pelagianism* in the person of *Cœlestius*, the chief pupil of Pelagius, on the supposition that he sympathized with Nestorius; but the Pelagian doctrines are not stated.

The Fifth Œcumenical Council, of 164 Bishops, occasioned by the protracted and tedious Monophysite controversies (which grew out of the Council of Chalcedon), confessed the Nicene Creed as explained and enlarged by the Councils of Constantinople, Ephesus, and Chalcedon, indorsed the dogmatic edicts of Emperor Justinian, and condemned the three Chapters (τρία κεφάλεια), that is, some writings of three departed divines of the Antiochian school, Theodore of Mopsuestia (the teacher of Nestorius), Theodoret of Cyros, and Ibas of Edessa (friends of Nestorius). The last two, however, had been declared orthodox by the Council of Chalcedon. The Fifth Œcumenical Council had a leaning towards Monophysitism, but the Sixth Œcumenical Council reacted again in favor of the dyophysitism of the Council of Chalcedon, and supplemented it by teaching the dyotheletism of Christ.[2]

The SEVENTH (and last strictly) ŒCUMENICAL COUNCIL, held, under the Empress Irene, at Nicæa, A.D. 787, and hence also called the SECOND NICENE COUNCIL, condemned the Iconoclasts, and sanctioned the ecclesiastical use and limited worship of sacred images.[3] But this decision is recognized only by Greeks and Romans, while Protestants regard it as a relapse into a refined form of idolatry, condemned by the Second Commandment and the primitive Christian Church. It became a fruitful source of superstition, but stimulated also the development of Christian art.

---

[1] See the *Anathematismi Cyrilli* in Mansi, *Conc.* Tom. IV. p. 1082 and Tom. V. pp. 85 sqq. (Greek and Latin, with the ἀνατροπή of Theodoret, and the ἀπολογία of Cyril), also in Denzinger's *Enchiridion*, pp. 27–31, and Gieseler's *Church History*, Vol. I. pp. 349 sqq. (Am. ed., only the Greek text). The ambitious, violent, and overbearing Cyril, who controlled the Synod, misrepresented his rival Patriarch of Constantinople, and leaned towards the opposite heresy of Eutychianism. Compare the refutation of Theodoret in Mansi, Tom. V. pp. 87 sqq., and my *Church History*, Vol. III. pp. 722–729. The Œcumenical Council of 431 was saved by its orthodoxy, otherwise it would have shared the disgrace of the infamous Robber Synod (σύνοδος λῃστρική, *latrocinium Ephesinum*), held at Ephesus a few years later (449) under the lead of Dioscurus (Cyril's successor), where passion, intrigue, and uncharitableness ruled supreme. Gregory of Nazianzum, who himself presided over the Second Œcumenical Council, drew a sad picture of the unchristian spirit which disgraced the synodical assemblies of his day. But the Third Œcumenical Council stands morally as well as doctrinally far below its two predecessors.

[2] The Greek Acts of the Fifth Council, with the exception of the fourteen anathemas on the three Chapters, are lost; but a Latin translation, concerning whose genuineness and completeness there has been much controversy, is preserved. See Mansi, *Conc.* Tom. IX. pp. 163 sqq., especially pp. 538–582. Denzinger gives the *Canones XIV. de tribus capitulis* (*Enchir.* pp. 58–73), and also the fifteen Canons against the errors of Origen (pp. 73–80), but the latter belong to an earlier Constantinopolitan Synod, held A.D. 544. On the Three Chapter Controversy, see my *Church History*, Vol. III. pp. 768 sqq., and more fully, Hefele, *Conciliengeschichte*, Vol. II. pp. 775–899.

[3] The ἀσπασμὸς καὶ τιμητικὴ προσκύνησις, *osculum et honoraria adoratio*, but not ἀληθινὴ λατρεία ἡ πρέπει μόνῃ τῇ θείᾳ φύσει, *vera latria, quæ solam divinam naturam decet.* See the decree in Mansi, *Conc.* Tom. XIII. p. 378 sq. Also in Denzinger, *Enchir.* pp. 104, 105.

SYMBOLA ROMANA.

SYMBOLA ROMANA.

ROMAN SYMBOLS.

PAGE

I. CANONES ET DECRETA DOGMATICA CONCILII TRI-
DENTINI.
THE CANONS AND DOGMATIC DECREES OF THE COUNCIL OF
TRENT. A.D. 1563 77

II. PROFESSIO FIDEI TRIDENTINÆ.
THE PROFESSION OF THE TRIDENTINE FAITH. A.D. 1564 207

III. DECRETUM PII IX. DE IMMACULATA CONCEPTIONE
B. VIRGINIS MARIÆ.
THE DECREE OF POPE PIUS IX. ON THE IMMACULATE CONCEP-
TION OF THE BLESSED VIRGIN MARY. A.D. 1854 211

IV. SYLLABUS ERRORUM NOSTRÆ ÆTATIS.
PAPAL SYLLABUS OF THE PRINCIPAL ERRORS OF OUR TIME.
A.D. 1864 ....:. 213

V. DECRETA DOGMATICA CONCILII VATICANI DE FIDE
CATHOLICA ET DE ECCLESIA CHRISTI.
THE DOGMATIC DECREES OF THE VATICAN COUNCIL CONCERN-
ING THE CATHOLIC FAITH AND THE CHURCH OF CHRIST
(THE INFALLIBILITY OF THE POPE). A.D. 1870 234

I. CANONES ET DECRETA DOGMATICA CONCILII TRIDENTINI.

THE CANONS AND DOGMATIC DECREES OF THE COUNCIL OF TRENT.

A.D. 1563.

[The Latin text after the editions of LE PLAT, RICHTER, STREITWOLF and KLENER, and SMITS, compared. It is also incorporated in THEINER's Acta genuina SS. Œcum. Concilii Tridentini, 1874, 2 Tom. The English translation by the Rev. J. WATERWORTH (R. C.): The Canons and Decrees of the Sacred and Œcumenical Council of Trent, London, 1848. The Scripture quotations are conformed to the Vulgate, and are printed in italics. The decrees of the Council on the reformation of discipline are foreign to this collection, and have been omitted also in Denzinger's Enchiridion. On the Council of Trent, see Vol. I. § 24, pp. 90–96.]

SESSIO TERTIA,

celebrata die IV. Februarii 1546.

DECRETUM DE SYMBOLO FIDEI.

In nomine sanctæ et individuæ Trinitatis, Patris, et Filii, et Spiritus sancti.

Hæc sacrosancta, œcumenica, et generalis tridentina synodus, in Spiritu sancto legitime congregata, in ea præsidentibus eisdem tribus apostolicæ sedis legatis, magnitudinem rerum tractandarum considerans, præsertim earum, quæ duobus illis capitibus, de extirpandis hæresibus, et moribus reformandis, continentur, quorum causa præcipue est congregata; agnoscens autem cum apostolo, non esse sibi colluctationem adversus carnem et sanguinem, sed adversus spirituales nequitias in cælestibus, cum eodem omnes et singulos in pri-

THIRD SESSION,

held February 4, 1546.

DECREE TOUCHING THE SYMBOL OF FAITH.

In the name of the Holy and Undivided Trinity, Father, and Son, and Holy Ghost.

This sacred and holy, œcumenical, and general Synod of Trent,— lawfully assembled in the Holy Ghost, the same three legates of the Apostolic See presiding therein,—considering the magnitude of the matters to be treated of, especially of those comprised under the two heads, of the extirpating of heresies, and the reforming of manners, for the sake of which chiefly it is assembled, and recognizing with the apostles, that its *wrestling is not against flesh and blood, but against the spirits of wickedness in the high places*,[1] exhorts, with the same apostle, all and each, above all

---

[1] Ephes. vi. 12.

mis hortatur, ut confortentur in Domino, et in potentia virtutis eius, in omnibus sumentes scutum fidei, in quo possint omnia tela nequissimi ignea extinguere, atque galeam spei salutis accipiant cum gladio spiritus quod est verbum Dei. Itaque, ut hæc pia eius sollicitudo principium et progressum suum per Dei gratiam habeat, ante omnia statuit et decernit præmittendam esse confessionem fidei, patrum exempla in hoc secuta, qui sacratioribus conciliis hoc scutum contra omnes hæreses in principio suarum actionum apponere consuevere: quo solo aliquando et infideles ad fidem traxerunt, hæreticos expugnarunt, et fideles confirmarunt. Quare symbolum fidei, quo sancta romana ecclesia utitur, tanquam principium illud, in quo omnes, qui fidem Christi profitentur, necessario conveniunt, ac fundamentum firmum et unicum, contra quod portæ inferi nunquam prævalebunt, totidem verbis, quibus in omnibus ecclesiis legitur, experimendum esse censuit; quod quidem eiusmodi est:

things, to be *strengthened in the Lord, and in the might of his power,* in all things taking the shield of faith, wherewith they may be able to extinguish all the fiery darts of the most wicked one, and to take the helmet of salvation, with the sword of the Spirit, which is the word of God.[1] Wherefore, that this its pious solicitude may begin and proceed by the grace of God, it ordains and decrees that, before all other things, a confession of faith is to be set forth; following herein the examples of the Fathers, who have been wont, in the most sacred councils, at the beginning of the Actions thereof, to oppose this shield against heresies; and with this alone, at times, have they drawn the unbelieving to the faith, overthrown heretics, and confirmed the faithful. For which cause, this Council has thought good, that the Symbol of faith which the holy Roman Church makes use of,—as being that principle wherein all who profess the faith of Christ necessarily agree, and that firm and alone foundation *against which the gates of hell shall never prevail,*[2]—be expressed in the very same words in which it is read in all the churches. Which Symbol is as follows:

---

[1] Ephes. vi. 16, 17. [2] Matt. xvi. 18.

Credo in unum Deum Patrem omnipoten-tem, factorem cœli et terræ, visibilium om-nium et invisibilium; et in unum Dominum Iesum Christum, Filium Dei unigenitum, et ex Patre natum ante omnia sæcula; Deum de Deo, lumen de lumine, Deum verum de Deo vero; genitum, non factum, consub-stantialem Patri, per quem omnia facta sunt: qui propter nos homines et propter nostram salutem descendit de cœlis, et in-carnatus est de Spiritu Sancto ex Maria virgine, et homo factus est: crucifixus etiam pro nobis sub Pontio Pilato, passus, et se-pultus est: et resurrexit tertia die secun-dum Scripturas, et ascendit in cœlum, sedet ad dexteram Patris, et iterum venturus est cum gloria iudicare vivos et mortuos; cuius regni non erit finis: et in Spiritum Sanc-tum, Dominum et vivificantem, qui ex Patre Filioque procedit; qui cum Patre et Filio simul adoratur et conglorificatur; qui lo-cutus est per prophetas: et unam sanctam catholicam et apostolicam ecclesiam. Con-fiteor unum baptisma in remissionem pec-catorum: et expecto resurrectionem mortu-orum et vitam venturi sæculi. Amen.

I believe in one God, the Father Almighty, Maker of heaven and earth, of all things visi-ble and invisible; and in one Lord Jesus Christ, the only-begotten Son of God, and born of the Father before all ages; God of God, light of light, true God of true God; begotten, not made, consubstantial with the Father, by whom all things were made: who for us men, and for our salvation, came down from the heavens, and was incarnate by the Holy Ghost of the Virgin Mary, and was made man: crucified also for us under Pontius Pilate, he suffered and was buried; and he rose again on the third day, according to the Scriptures; and he ascend-ed into heaven, sitteth at the right hand of the Father; and again he will come with glory to judge the living and the dead; of whose king-dom there shall be no end: and in the Holy Ghost, the Lord, and the giver of life, who pro-ceedeth from the Father and the Son; who with the Father and the Son together is adored and glorified; who spoke by the prophets: and one holy Catholic and Apostolic Church. I con-fess one baptism for the remission of sins; and I look for the resurrection of the dead, and the life of the world to come. Amen.

SESSIO QUARTA,
celebrata die VIII. Aprilis, 1546.

DECRETUM DE CANONICIS SCRIPTU-RIS.

Sacrosancta, œcumenica, et ge-neralis tridentina synodus, in Spiritu Sancto legitime congre-gata, præsidentibus in ea eisdem tribus apostolicæ sedis legatis, hoc sibi perpetuo ante oculos proponens, ut, sublatis erroribus, puritas ipsa evangelii in eccle-sia conservetur; quod promis-

FOURTH SESSION,
held April 8, 1546.

DECREE CONCERNING THE CANONICAL SCRIPTURES.

The sacred and holy, œcumen-ical, and general Synod of Trent,— lawfully assembled in the Holy Ghost, the same three legates of the Apostolic See presiding therein,— keeping this always in view, that, errors being removed, the purity itself of the Gospel be preserved in the Church: which (Gospel), be-

sum ante per prophetas in Scrip-
turis sanctis, Dominus noster Ie-
sus Christus, Dei Filius, proprio
ore primum promulgavit, de-
inde per suos apostolos, tanquam
fontem omnis et salutaris veri-
tatis et morum disciplinæ, omni
creaturæ prædicari iussit; per-
spiciensque hanc veritatem et
disciplinam contineri in libris
scriptis et sine scripto tradition-
ibus, quæ ab ipsius Christi ore
ab apostolis acceptæ, aut ab ip-
sis apostolis, Spiritu Sancto dic-
tante, quasi per manus traditæ,
ad nos usque pervenerunt: or-
thodoxorum patrum exempla se-
cuta, omnes libros tam Veteris
quam Novi Testamenti, cum utri-
usque unus Deus sit auctor, nec-
non traditiones ipsas, tum ad
fidem, tum ad mores pertinen-
tes, tanquam vel oretenus a Chris-
to vel a Spiritu Sancto dictatas,
et continua successione in ecclesia
catholica conservatas, pari pie-
tatis affectu ac reverentia susci-
pit et veneratur.

Sacrorum vero librorum indi-
cem huic decreto adscribendum
censuit, ne cui dubitatio suboriri
possit, quinam sint, qui ab ipsa
synodo suscipiuntur. Sunt vero

fore promised through the prophets
in the holy Scriptures, our Lord Jesus Christ, the Son of God, first promulgated with His own mouth, and
then commanded to be preached by
His Apostles to very creature, as
the fountain of all, both saving
truth, and moral discipline; and seeing clearly that this truth and discipline are contained in the written
books, and the unwritten traditions
which, received by the Apostles
from the mouth of Christ himself,
or from the Apostles themselves,
the Holy Ghost dictating, have
come down even unto us, transmitted as it were from hand to hand:
[the Synod] following the examples of the orthodox Fathers, receives and venerates with an equal
affection of piety and reverence, all
the books both of the Old and of
the New Testament—seeing that
one God is the author of both—as
also the said traditions, as well those
appertaining to faith as to morals,
as having been dictated, either by
Christ's own word of mouth, or by
the Holy Ghost, and preserved in
the Catholic Church by a continuous succession.

And it has thought it meet that
a list of the sacred books be inserted in this decree, lest a doubt may
arise in any one's mind, which are
the books that are received by this

infrascripti. Testamenti veteris, quinque Moysis, id est, Genesis, Exodus, Leviticus, Numeri, Deuteronomium; Iosuæ, Iudicum, Ruth, quatuor Regum, duo Paralipomenon, Esdræ primus et secundus, qui dicitur Nehemias, Tobias, Iudith, Esther, Iob, Psalterium davidicum centum quinquaginta psalmorum, Parabolæ, Ecclesiastes, Canticum canticorum, Sapientia, Ecclesiasticus, Isaias, Ieremias cum Baruch, Ezechiel, Daniel, duodecim prophetæ minores, id est: Osea, Ioel, Amos, Abdias, Ionas, Michæas, Nahum, Habacuc, Sophonias, Aggæus, Zacharias, Malachias, duo Machabæorum, primus et secundus. Testamenti novi: quatuor evangelia, secundum Mathæum, Marcum, Lucam, et Ioannem; actus apostolorum a Luca evangelista conscripti; quatuordecim epistolæ Pauli apostoli, ad Romanos, duæ ad Corinthios, ad Galatas, ad Ephesios, ad Philippenses, ad Colossenses, duæ ad Thessalonicenses, duæ ad Timotheum, ad Titum, ad Philemonem, ad Hebræos; Petri apostoli duæ, Ioannis apostoli tres, Iacobi apostoli una, Iudæ apostoli una, et apocalypsis Ioannis apostoli.

Synod. They are as set down here below: of the Old Testament: the five books of Moses, to wit, Genesis, Exodus, Leviticus, Numbers, Deuteronomy; Josue, Judges, Ruth, four books of Kings, two of Paralipomenon, the first book of Esdras, and the second which is entitled Nehemias; Tobias, Judith, Esther, Job, the Davidical Psalter, consisting of a hundred and fifty psalms; the Proverbs, Ecclesiastes, the Canticle of Canticles, Wisdom, Ecclesiasticus, Isaias, Jeremias, with Baruch; Ezechiel, Daniel; the twelve minor prophets, to wit, Osee, Joel, Amos, Abdias, Jonas, Micheas, Nahum, Habacuc, Sophonias, Aggæus, Zacharias, Malachias; two books of the Machabees, the first and the second. Of the New Testament: the four Gospels, according to Matthew, Mark, Luke, and John; the Acts of the Apostles written by Luke the Evangelist; fourteen epistles of Paul the apostle, (one) to the Romans, two to the Corinthians, (one) to the Galatians, to the Ephesians, to the Philippians, to the Colossians, two to the Thessalonians, two to Timothy, (one) to Titus, to Philemon, to the Hebrews; two of Peter the apostle, three of John the apostle, one of the apostle James, one of Jude the apostle, and the Apocalypse of John the apostle.

Si quis autem libros ipsos integros cum omnibus suis partibus, prout in ecclesia catholica legi consueverunt, et in veteri Vulgata Latina editione habentur, pro sacris, et canonicis non susceperit, et traditiones prœdictas sciens et prudens contempserit, anathema sit. Omnes itaque intelligant, quo ordine et via ipsa synodus, post jactum fidei confessionis fundamentum, sit progressura, et quibus potissimum testimoniis ac prœsidiis in confirmandis dogmatibus et instaurandis in ecclesia moribus sit usura.

But if any one receive not, as sacred and canonical, the said books entire with all their parts, as they have been used to be read in the Catholic Church, and as they are contained in the old Latin vulgate edition; and knowingly and deliberately contemn the traditions aforesaid; let him be anathema. Let all, therefore, understand, in what order, and in what manner, the said Synod, after having laid the foundation of the Confession of faith, will proceed, and what testimonies and authorities it will mainly use in confirming dogmas, and in restoring morals in the Church.

DECRETUM DE EDITIONE, ET USU SACRORUM LIBRORUM.

DECREE CONCERNING THE EDITION, AND THE USE, OF THE SACRED BOOKS.

Insuper eadem sacrosancta synodus considerans, non parum utilitatis accedere posse ecclesiœ Dei, si ex omnibus Latinis editionibus, quœ circumferuntur, sacrorum librorum, quœnam pro authentica habenda sit, innotescat; statuit et declarat, ut hœc ipsa vetus et vulgata editio, quœ longo tot sœculorum usu in ipsa ecclesia probata est, in publicis lectionibus, disputationibus, prœdicationibus et expositionibus pro authentica habeatur; et ut nemo illam rejicere quovis prœtextu audeat vel prœsumat.

Moreover, the same sacred and holy Synod,—considering that no small utility may accrue to the Church of God, if it be made known which out of all the Latin editions, now in circulation, of the sacred books, is to be held as authentic,—ordains and declares, that the said old and vulgate edition, which, by the lengthened usage of so many ages, has been approved of in the Church, be, in public lectures, disputations, sermons, and expositions, held as authentic; and that no one is to dare, or presume to reject it under any pretext whatever.

Præterea, ad coercenda petulantia ingenia, decernit, ut nemo, suæ prudentiæ innixus, in rebus fidei, et morum ad ædificationem doctrinæ christianæ pertinentium, sacram scripturam ad suos sensus contorquens, contra eum sensum, quem tenuit et tenet sancta mater ecclesia, cuius est judicare de vero sensu, et interpretatione scripturarum sanctarum, aut etiam contra unanimem consensum patrum ipsam scripturam sacram interpretari audeat, etiamsi hujusmodi interpretationes nullo unquam tempore in lucem edendæ forent. Qui contravenerint, per ordinarios declarentur, et pœnis a jure statutis puniantur.

Furthermore, in order to restrain petulant spirits, it decrees, that no one, relying on his own skill, shall,—in matters of faith, and of morals pertaining to the edification of Christian doctrine,—wresting the sacred Scripture to his own senses, presume to interpret the said sacred Scripture contrary to that sense which holy mother Church,—whose it is to judge of the true sense and intrepretation of the holy Scriptures,—hath held and doth hold; or even contrary to the unanimous consent of the Fathers; even though such interpretations were never [intended] to be at any time published. Contraveners shall be made known by their Ordinaries, and be punished with the penalties by law established.

Sessio Quinta,
celebrata die XVII. Junii, 1546.

DECRETUM DE PECCATO ORIGINALI.

Ut fides nostra catholica, sine qua impossibile est placere Deo, purgatis erroribus, in sua sinceritate integra et illibata permaneat ; et ne populus christianus omni vento doctrinæ circumferatur ; cum serpens ille antiquus, humani generis perpetuus hostis,

Fifth Session,
held June 17, 1546.

DECREE CONCERNING ORIGINAL SIN.

That our Catholic *faith, without which it is impossible to please God,*[1] may, errors being purged away, continue in its own perfect and spotless integrity, and that the Christian people may not *be carried about with every wind of doctrine ;*[2] whereas that old serpent, the per-

---

[1] Heb. xi. 6.　　　　[2] Ephes. iv. 14.

inter plurima mala, quibus eccle-sia Dei his nostris temporibus perturbatur, etiam de peccato originali ejusque remedio non solum nova, sed vetera etiam dis-sidia excitaverit: sacrosancta œcu-menica et generalis Tridentina synodus, in Spiritu Sancto legi-time congregata, præsidentibus in ea eisdem tribus apostolicæ sedis legatis, jam ad revocandos er-rantes et nutantes confirmandos accedere volens, sacrarum scrip-turarum et sanctorum patrum ac probatissimorum conciliorum testimonia et ipsius ecclesiæ ju-dicium et consensum secuta, hæc de ipso peccato originali statuit, fatetur ac declarat.

petual enemy of mankind, amongst the very many evils with which the Church of God is in these our times troubled, has also stirred up not only new, but even old, dissensions touching original sin, and the rem-edy thereof; the sacred and holy, œcumenical and general Synod of Trent,—lawfully assembled in the Holy Ghost, the three same legates of the Apostolic See presiding there-in,—wishing now to come to the re-claiming of the erring, and the con-firming of the wavering,—follow-ing the testimonies of the sacred Scriptures, of the holy Fathers, of the most approved councils, and the judgment and consent of the Church itself, ordains, confesses, and de-clares these things touching the said original sin:

1. *Si quis non confitetur, pri-mum hominem Adam, cum man-datum Dei in paradiso fuisset transgressus, statim sanctitatem et justitiam, in qua constitutus fuerat, amisisse incurrisseque per offensam prævaricationis hu-jusmodi iram et indignationem Dei, atque ideo mortem, quam antea illi comminatus fuerat Deus, et cum morte captivitatem sub ejus potestate, qui mortis deinde habuit imperium, hoc est, diaboli, totumque Adam, per il-*

1. If any one does not confess that the first man, Adam, when he had transgressed the commandment of God in Paradise, immediately lost the holiness and justice wherein he had been constituted; and that he incurred, through the offense of that prevarication, the wrath and in-dignation of God, and consequently death, with which God had previ-ously threatened him, and, together with death, captivity under his pow-er who thenceforth *had the empire of death, that is to say, the devil*,[1]

---

[1] Heb. ii. 14.

lam prævaricationis offensam, se- and that the entire Adam, through
cundum corpus et animam in that offense of prevarication, was
deterius commutatum fuisse; changed, in body and soul, for the
anathema sit. worse; let him be anathema.

2. *Si quis Adæ prævarication-* 2. If any one asserts, that the
em sibi soli, et non eius propagini prevarication of Adam injured him-
asserit nocuisse; et acceptam a self alone, and not his posterity; and
Deo sanctitatem et justitiam, that the holiness and justice, re-
quam perdidit, sibi soli et non ceived of God, which he lost, he lost
nobis etiam eum perdidisse; aut for himself alone, and not for us
inquinatum illum per inobedi- also; or that he, being defiled by the
entiæ peccatum, mortem et pœ- sin of disobedience, has only trans-
nas corporis tantum in omne fused death and pains of the body
genus humanum transfudisse, into the whole human race, but not
non autem et peccatum, quod sin also, which is the death of the
mors est animæ; anathema sit: soul; let him be anathema:—where-
cum contradicat apostolo di- as he contradicts the apostle who
centi: Per unum hominem pec- says: *By one man sin entered into*
catum intravit in mundum et *the world, and by sin death, and so*
per peccatum mors, et ita in *death passed upon all men, in whom*
omnes homines mors pertransiit, *all have sinned.*[1]
in quo omnes peccaverunt.

3. *Si quis hoc Adæ peccatum,* 3. If any one asserts, that this
quod origine unum est et pro- sin of Adam,—which in its origin
pagatione, non imitatione trans- is one, and being transfused into all
fusum omnibus, inest unicui- by propagation, not by imitation, is
que proprium, vel per humanæ in each one as his own,—is taken
naturæ vires, vel per aliud re- away either by the powers of hu-
medium asserit tolli, quam per man nature, or by any other reme-
meritum unius mediatoris Do- dy than the merit of the *one medi-*
mini nostri Iesu Christi, qui *ator, our Lord Jesus Christ,*[2] *who*
nos Deo reconciliavit in sanguine *hath reconciled us to God in his own*
suo, factus nobis justitia, sanc- *blood, being made unto us justice,*
tificatio et redemptio; aut ne- *sanctification, and redemption;*[3]

---

[1] Rom. v. 12.   [2] 1 Tim. ii. 5.   [3] 1 Cor. i. 30.

gat ipsum Christi Iesu meritum per baptismi sacramentum in forma ecclesiæ rite collatum, tam adultis quam parvulis applicari ; anathema sit : quia non est aliud nomen sub cœlo datum hominibus, in quo oporteat nos salvos fieri. Unde illa vox : Ecce agnus Dei ; ecce qui tollit peccata mundi ; et illa : Quicumque baptizati estis, Christum induistis.

4. Si quis parvulos recentes ab uteris matrum baptizandos negat, etiam si fuerint a baptizatis parentibus orti ; aut dicit in remissionem quidem peccatorum eos baptizari, sed nihil ex Adam trahere originalis peccati, quod regenerationis lavacro necesse sit expiari ad vitam æternam consequendam ; unde fit consequens, ut in eis forma baptismatis in remissionem peccatorum non vera, sed falsa intelligatur ; anathema sit ; quoniam non aliter intelligendum est id, quod dixit apostolus : Per unum hominem peccatum intravit in mundum, et per peccatum mors, et ita in omnes homines mors pertransiit, in quo omnes peccaverunt, nisi quemadmodum ec-

or if he denies that the said merit of Jesus Christ is applied, both to adults and to infants, by the sacrament of baptism rightly administered in the form of the Church; let him be anathema : *For there is no other name under heaven given to men, whereby we must be saved.*[1] Whence that voice : *Behold the lamb of God, behold him who taketh away the sins of the world ;*[2] and that other : *As many as have been baptized, have put on Christ.*[3]

4. If any one denies, that infants, newly born from their mothers' wombs, even though they be sprung from baptized parents, are to be baptized ; or says that they are *baptized* indeed *for the remission of sins,*[4] but that they derive nothing of original sin from Adam, which has need of being expiated by the laver of regeneration for obtaining life everlasting, — whence it follows as a consequence, that in them the form of baptism, *for the remission of sins,* is understood to be not true, but false,—let him be anathema. For that which the apostle has said, *By one man sin entered into the world, and by sin death, and so death passed upon all men, in whom all have sinned,*[5] is not to be understood otherwise

---

[1] Acts iv. 2.　　　[3] Gal. iii. 27.　　　[5] Rom. v. 12.
[2] John i. 29.　　　[4] Acts ii. 38.

clesia catholica ubique diffusa semper intellexit. Propter hanc enim regulam fidei ex traditione apostolorum etiam parvuli, qui nihil peccatorum in semetipsis adhuc committere potuerunt, ideo in remissionem peccatorum veraciter baptizantur, ut in eis regeneratione mundetur, quod generatione contraxerunt. Nisi enim quis renatus fuerit ex aqua et Spiritu Sancto, non potest introire in regnum Dei.

5. *Si quis per Iesu Christi Domini nostri gratiam, quæ in baptismate confertur, reatum originalis peccati remitti negat; aut etiam asserit non tolli totum id quod veram et propriam peccati rationem habet; sed illud dicit tantum radi, aut non imputari; anathema sit. In re natis enim nihil odit Deus; quia nihil est damnationis iis, qui vere consepulti sunt cum Christo per baptisma in mortem; qui non secundum carnem ambulant, sed veterem hominem exuentes, et novum, qui secundum Deum creatus est, induentes, innocentes, immaculati, puri, innoxii, ac Deo dilecti effecti sunt, heredes quidem Dei, coheredes autem*

than as the Catholic Church spread every where hath always understood it. For, by reason of this rule of faith, from a tradition of the apostles, even infants, who could not as yet commit any sin of themselves, are for this cause truly *baptized for the remission of sins,* that in them that may be cleansed away by regeneration, which they have contracted by generation. *For, unless a man be born again of water and the Holy Ghost, he can not enter into the kingdom of God.*[1]

5. If any one denies, that, by the grace of our Lord Jesus Christ, which is conferred in baptism, the guilt of original sin is remitted; or even asserts that the whole of that which has the true and proper nature of sin is not taken away; but says that it is only rased, or not imputed; let him be anathema. For, in those who are *born again,* there is nothing that God hates; because, *There is no condemnation to those who are truly buried together with Christ by baptism into death;*[2] *who walk not according to the flesh,* but, *putting off the old man, and putting on the new who is created according to God,*[3] are made innocent, immaculate, pure, harmless, and beloved of God, *heirs*

---

[1] John iii. 5.   [2] Rom. viii. 1; vi. 4.   [3] Ephes. iv. 22, 24.

Christi; ita ut nihil prorsus eos ab ingressu cœli remoretur. Manere autem in baptizatis concupiscentiam vel fomitem, hæc sancta synodus fatetur et sentit: quæ cum ad agonem relicta sit, nocere non consentientibus, sed viriliter per Christi Iesu gratiam repugnantibus non valet: quinimmo qui legitime certaverit, coronabitur. Hanc concupiscentiam, quam aliquando apostolus peccatum appellat, sancta synodus declarat, ecclesiam catholicam nunquam intellexisse peccatum appellari, quod vere et proprie in renatis peccatum sit, sed quia ex peccato est et ad peccatum inclinat. Si quis autem contrarium senserit, anathema sit.

Declarat tamen hæc ipsa sancta synodus, non esse suæ intentionis comprehendere in hoc decreto, ubi de peccato originali agitur, beatam et immaculatam virginem Mariam, Dei genitricem; sed observandas esse constitutiones felicis recordationis Sixti papæ IV. sub pœnis in eis constitutionibus contentis, quas innovat.[4]

indeed of God, but joint heirs with Christ;[1] so that there is nothing whatever to retard their entrance into heaven. But this holy synod confesses and is sensible, that in the baptized there remains concupiscence, or an incentive (to sin); which, whereas it is left for our exercise, can not injure those who consent not, but resist manfully by the grace of Jesus Christ; yea, he who shall have *striven lawfully shall be crowned.*[2] This concupiscence, which the apostle sometimes calls sin,[3] the holy Synod declares that the Catholic Church has never understood it to be called sin, as being truly and properly sin in those *born again,* but because it is of sin, and inclines to sin. And if any one is of a contrary sentiment, let him be anathema.

This same holy Synod doth nevertheless declare, that it is not its intention to include in this decree, where original sin is treated of, the blessed and immaculate Virgin Mary, the mother of God; but that the constitutions of Pope Sixtus IV., of happy memory, are to be observed, under the pains contained in the said constitutions, which it renews.

---

[1] Rom. viii. 17.   [2] 2 Tim. ii. 5.   [3] Rom. vi. 12; vii. 8.

[4] [This indirect exemption of the *immaculata Virgo Maria* from original sin is a very near approach to the positive definition of the *immaculata conceptio Virginis Mariæ* in 1854.—P. S.]

SESSIO SEXTA,
celebrata die XIII. Januarii 1547.

DECRETUM DE JUSTIFICATIONE.

CAPUT I.

De naturæ et legis ad justificandos homines imbecillitate.

Primum declarat sancta synodus, ad justificationis doctrinam probe et sincere intelligendam oportere, ut unusquisque agnoscat et fateatur, quod cum omnes homines in prævaricatione Adæ innocentiam perdidissent; facti immundi et ut apostolus inquit, natura filii iræ, quemadmodum in decreto de peccato originali exposuit, usque adeo servi erant peccati et sub potestate diaboli ac mortis, ut non modo gentes per vim naturæ, sed ne Iudæi quidem per ipsam etiam litteram legis Moysi, inde liberari aut surgere possent; tametsi in eis liberum arbitrium minime extinctum esset, viribus licet attenuatum et inclinatum.

CAPUT II.

De dispensatione et mysterio Adventus Christi.

Quo factum est, ut cœlestis Pater, Pater misericordiarum, et Deus totius consolationis,

SIXTH SESSION,
held January 13, 1547.

DECREE ON JUSTIFICATION.

CHAPTER I.

On the Inability of Nature and of the Law to justify Man.

The holy Synod declares first, that, for the correct and sound understanding of the doctrine of Justification, it is necessary that each one recognize and confess, that, whereas all men had lost their innocence in the prevarication of Adam,—having become unclean,[1] and, as the apostle says, *by nature children of wrath*,[2] as (this Synod) has set forth in the decree on original sin,—they were so far *the servants of sin*,[3] and under the power of the devil and of death, that not the Gentiles only by the force of nature, but not even the Jews by the very letter itself of the law of Moses, were able to be liberated, or to arise, therefrom; although freewill, attenuated as it was in its powers, and bent down, was by no means extinguished in them.

CHAPTER II.

On the Dispensation and Mystery of Christ's Advent.

Whence it came to pass, that the heavenly Father, *the Father of mercies, and the God of all comfort*,[4]

---

[1] Isa. lxiv. 6.   [2] Ephes. ii. 3.   [3] Rom. vi. 17, 20.   [4] 2 Cor. i. 3.

Christum Iesum, Filium suum, et ante legem et legis tempore multis sanctis patribus declaratum ac promissum, cum venit beata illa plenitudo temporis, ad homines miserit, ut et Iudæos, qui sub lege erant, redimeret, et gentes, quæ non sectabantur justitiam, justitiam apprehenderent, atque omnes adoptionem filiorum reciperent. Hunc proposuit Deus propitiatorem per fidem in sanguine ipsius pro peccatis nostris, non solum autem pro nostris, sed etiam pro totius mundi.

when that blessed *fullness of the time was come*,[1] sent unto men, Jesus Christ, *his own Son*—who had been, both before the Law, and during the time of the Law, to many of the holy fathers announced and promised—*that he might both redeem the Jews who were under the Law*,[2] and that *the Gentiles, who followed not after justice*, might attain to justice,[3] and that all men might receive the adoption of sons. Him God hath *proposed* as a propitiator, *through faith in his blood*,[4] *for our sins, and not for our sins only, but also for those of the whole world.*[5]

CAPUT III.

Qui per Christum justificantur.

Verum, etsi ille pro omnibus mortuus est, non omnes tamen mortis ejus beneficium recipiunt; sed ii dumtaxat, quibus meritum passionis ejus communicatur. Nam, sicut re vera homines, nisi ex semine Adæ propagati nascerentur, non nascerentur injusti; cum ea propagatione, per ipsum dum concipiuntur, propriam injustitiam contrahant: ita, nisi in Christo renascerentur, nunquam justificarentur; cum ea renascentia per meritum passionis ejus gratia,

CHAPTER III.

Who are justified through Christ.

But, though *He died for all*,[6] yet do not all receive the benefit of his death, but those only unto whom the merit of his passion is communicated. For as in truth men, if they were not born propagated of the seed of Adam, would not be born unjust,—seeing that, by that propagation, they contract through him, when they are conceived, injustice as their own,—so, if they were not born again in Christ, they never would be justified; seeing that, in that new birth, there is bestowed upon them, through the

---

[1] Gal. iv. 4.　　[3] Rom. ix. 30.　　[5] 1 John ii. 2.
[2] Gal. v. 4.　　[4] Rom. iii. 25.　　[6] 2 Cor. v. 15.

qua justi fiunt, illis tribuatur. Pro hoc beneficio apostolus gratias nos semper agere hortatur Patri, qui dignos nos fecit in partem sortis sanctorum in lumine, et eripuit de potestate tenebrarum, transtulitque in regnum Filii dilectionis suæ, in quo habemus redemptionem et remissionem peccatorum.

merit of his passion, the grace whereby they are made just. For this benefit the apostle exhorts us, evermore *to give thanks to the Father, who hath made us worthy to be partakers of the lot of the saints in light, and hath delivered us from the power of darkness, and hath translated us into the Kingdom of the Son of his love, in whom we have redemption, and remission of sins.*[1]

Caput IV.

Insinuatur descriptio justificationis impii, et modus ejus in statu gratiæ.

Chapter IV.

A description is introduced of the Justification of the impious, and of the manner thereof in the state of grace.

Quibus verbis justificationis impii descriptio insinuatur, ut sit translatio ab eo statu, in quo homo nascitur filius primi Adæ, in statum gratiæ, et adoptionis filiorum Dei per secundum Adam Iesum Christum, salvatorem nostrum: quæ quidem translatio post evangelium promulgatum, sine lavacro regenerationis, aut ejus voto, fieri non potest; sicut scriptum est: Nisi quis renatus fuerit ex aqua et Spiritu Sancto, non potest introire in regnum Dei.

By which words, a description of the Justification of the impious is indicated,—as being a translation, from that state wherein man is born a child of the first Adam, to the state of grace, and of *the adoption of the sons of God,*[2] through the second Adam, Jesus Christ, our Saviour. And this translation, since the promulgation of the Gospel, can not be effected, without the laver of regeneration, or the desire thereof, as it is written: *unless a man be born again of water and the Holy Ghost, he can not enter into the Kingdom of God.*[3]

---

[1] Coloss. i. 12–14.   [2] Rom. viii. 15, 16, 23.   [3] John iii. 5.

Caput V.

De necessitate præparationis ad justification-
em in adultis, et unde sit.

Declarat præterea, ipsius justi-
ficationis exordium in adultis a
Dei per Christum Iesum præve-
niente gratia sumendum esse, hoc
est, ab ejus vocatione, qua, nullis
eorum existentibus meritis, vo-
cantur; ut, qui per peccata a
Deo aversi erant, per ejus exci-
tantem atque adjuvantem gra-
tiam ad convertendum se ad suam
ipsorum justificationem, eidem
gratiæ libere assentiendo et co-
operando, disponantur: ita ut,
tangente Deo cor hominis per
Spiritus Sancti illuminationem,
neque homo ipse nihil omnino
agat, inspirationem illam reci-
piens, quippe qui illam et abji-
·cere potest, neque tamen sine gra-
tia Dei movere se ad justitiam
coram illo libera sua voluntate
possit. Unde in sacris litteris
cum dicitur: Convertimini ad
me, et ego convertar ad vos: li-
bertatis nostræ admonemur. Cum
respondemus: Converte nos, Do-
mine, ad te, et convertemur: Dei
nos gratia præveniri confitemur.

Chapter V.

On the necessity, in adults, of preparation
for Justification, and whence it proceeds.

The Synod furthermore declares,
that, in adults, the beginning of the
said Justification is to be derived
from the prevenient grace of God,
through Jesus Christ, that is to say,
from his vocation, whereby, without any merits existing on their
parts, they are called; that so they,
who by sins were alienated from
God, may be disposed through his
quickening and assisting grace, to
convert themselves to their own
justification, by freely assenting to
and co-operating with that said
grace: in such sort that, while God
touches the heart of man by the illumination of the Holy Ghost, neither is man himself utterly inactive
while he receives that inspiration,
forasmuch as he is also able to reject it; yet is he not able, by his
own free will, without the grace of
God, to move himself unto justice
in his sight. Whence, when it is
said in the sacred writings: *Turn*
ye to me, and I will turn to you,[1]
we are admonished of our liberty;
and when we answer: *Convert us,*
O Lord, to thee, and we shall be
converted,[2] we confess that we are
prevented (anticipated) by the grace
of God.

---

[1] Zach. i. 3.   [2] Lam. v. 21.

CAPUT VI.

Modus præparationis.

Disponuntur autem ad ipsam justitiam, dum excitati divina gratia et adjuti, fidem ex auditu concipientes, libere moventur in Deum, credentes vera esse, quæ divinitus revelata et promissa sunt; atque illud in primis, a Deo justificari impium per gratiam ejus), per redemptionem, quæ est in Christo Iesu: et, dum peccatores se esse intelligentes, a divinæ justitiæ timore, quo utiliter concutiuntur, ad considerandam Dei misericordiam se convertendo, in spem eriguntur, fidentes Deum sibi propter Christum propitium fore; illumque, tamquam omnis justitiæ fontem diligere incipiunt; ac propterea moventur adversus peccata per odium aliquod et detestationem, hoc est, per eam pœnitentiam, quam ante baptismum agi oportet: denique dum proponunt suscipere baptismum, inchoare novam vitam, et servare divina mandata. De hac dispositione scriptum est: Accedentem ad Deum oportet credere, quia est, et quod inquirentibus se remunerator sit: et, Confide, fili, remittuntur tibi peccata tua; et: Ti-

CHAPTER VI.

The manner of Preparation.

Now they [adults] are disposed unto the said justice, when, excited and assisted by divine grace, conceiving *faith by hearing,*[1] they are freely moved towards God, believing those things to be true which God has revealed and promised— and this especially, that God justifies the impious *by his grace, through the redemption that is in Christ Jesus;*[2] and when, understanding themselves to be sinners, they, by turning themselves, from the fear of divine justice whereby they are profitably agitated, to consider the mercy of God, are raised unto hope, confiding that God will be propitious to them for Christ's sake; and they begin to love him as the fountain of all justice; and are therefore moved against sins by a certain hatred and detestation, to wit, by that penitence which must be performed before baptism: lastly, when they purpose to receive baptism, to begin a new life, and to *keep the commandments* of God. Concerning this disposition it is written: *He that cometh to God, must believe that he is, and is a rewarder to them that seek him;*[3] and, *Be of good faith, son, thy sins*

---

[1] Rom. x. 17.   [2] Rom. iii. 24.   [3] Heb. xi. 6.

*mor Domini expellit peccatum;
et : Pœnitentiam agite, et baptizetur unusquisque vestrum in nomine Iesu Christi, in remissionem peccatorum vestrorum, et ac-
cipietis donum Spiritus Sancti;
et : Euntes ergo docete omnes
gentes, baptizantes eos in nomine
Patris, et Filii et Spiritus Sancti,
docentes eos servare quœcumque
mandavi vobis; denique : Prœ-
parate corda vestra Domino.*

are forgiven thee;[1] and, *The fear
of the Lord driveth out sin;*[2] and,
*Do penance, and be baptized every
one of you in the name of Jesus
Christ, for the remission of your
sins, and you shall receive the gift
of the Holy Ghost;*[3] and, *Going,
therefore, teach ye all nations, baptizing them in the name of the
Father, and of the Son, and of the
Holy Ghost;*[4] finally, *Prepare your
hearts unto the Lord.*[5]

Caput VII.

Quid sit justificatio impii, et quœ ejus causœ.

Chapter VII.

*What the Justification of the impious is, and
what are the causes thereof.*

*Hanc dispositionem, seu prœ-
parationem justificatio ipsa consequitur, quœ non est sola peccatorum remissio, sed et sanctifica-
tio et renovatio interioris hominis per voluntariam susceptionem
gratiœ et donorum, unde homo
ex injusto fit justus, et ex inimi-
co amicus, ut sit heres secundum
spem vitœ œternœ.*

This disposition, or preparation,
is followed by Justification itself,
which is not remission of sins merely, but also the sanctification and
renewal of the inward man, through
the voluntary reception of the grace,
and of the gifts, whereby man of
unjust becomes just, and of an enemy a friend, that so he may be *an
heir according to hope of life everlasting.*[6]

*Hujus justificationis causœ
sunt, finalis quidem : gloria Dei
et Christi, ac vita œterna; effi-
ciens vero : misericors Deus, qui
gratuito abluit, et sanctificat si-
gnans, et ungens Spiritu promissionis Sancto, qui est pignus*

Of this Justification the causes are
these : the final cause indeed is the
glory of God and of Jesus Christ,
and life everlasting; while the efficient cause is a merciful God who
washes and sanctifies[7] gratuitously,
signing, and anointing with the

---

[1] Matt. ii. 5.   [3] Acts ii. 38.   [5] 1 Kings vii. 3.   [7] 1 Cor. vi. 11.
[2] Eccles. i. 27.   [4] Matt. xxviii. 19.   [6] Titus iii. 7.

hereditatis nostræ; meritoria au-
tem : dilectissimus unigenitus su-
us, Dominus noster Iesus Chris-
tus, qui cum essemus inimici,
propter nimiam caritatem, qua
dilexit nos, sua sanctissima pas-
sione in ligno crucis nobis
justificationem meruit, et pro
nobis Deo Patri satisfecit ; in-
strumentalis item : sacramentum
baptismi, quod est sacramen-
tum fidei, sine qua nulli um-
quam contigit justificatio ; de-
mum unica formalis causa est
justitia Dei ; non qua ipse jus-
tus est, sed qua nos justos facit ;
qua videlicet ab eo donati, reno-
vamur spiritu mentis nostræ, et
non modo reputamur, sed vere
justi nominamur et sumus, jus-
titiam in nobis recipientes, unus-
quisque suam secundum mensu-
ram, quam Spiritus Sanctus par-
titur singulis prout vult et se-
cundum propriam cujusque dis-
positionem et cooperationem.
Quamquam enim nemo possit
esse justus, nisi cui merita pas-
sionis Domini nostri Iesu Chris-
ti communicantur : id tamen in
hac impii justificatione fit, dum
ejusdem sanctissimæ passionis
merito per Spiritum Sanctum
caritas Dei diffunditur in cor-

holy *Spirit of promise, who is the*
pledge of our inheritance;[1] but the
meritorious cause is his most beloved only-begotten, our Lord Jesus
Christ, who, when we were enemies,
for the exceeding charity where-
with he loved us,[2] merited Justification for us by his most holy Passion
on the wood of the cross, and made
satisfaction for us unto God the
Father; the instrumental cause is
the sacrament of baptism, which is
the sacrament of faith, without
which [faith] no man was ever justified;[3] lastly, the alone formal cause
is the justice of God, not that whereby he himself is just, but that
whereby he maketh us just, that, to
wit, with which *we,* being endowed
by him, *are renewed in the spirit*
of our mind,[4] and we are not only
reputed, but are truly called, and
are just, receiving justice within us,
each one according to his own measure, *which the Holy Ghost distrib-*
utes to every one as he wills,[5] and
according to each one's proper disposition and co-operation. For, although no one can be just, but he
to whom the merits of the Passion
of our Lord Jesus Christ are communicated, yet is this done in the
said justification of the impious,
when by the merit of that same

---

[1] Ephes. i. 13, 14. [3] Heb. xi. [5] 1 Cor. xii. 2.
[2] Ephes. ii. 4. [4] Ephes. iv. 23.

dibus eorum, qui justificantur, atque ipsis inhæret: unde in ipsa justificatione cum remissione peccatorum hæc omnia simul infusa accipit homo per Iesum Christum, cui inseritur, fidem, spem et caritatem: nam fides, nisi ad eam spes accedat, et caritas, neque unit perfecte cum Christo, neque corporis ejus vivum membrum efficit: qua ratione verissime dicitur, fidem sine operibus mortuam, et otiosam esse: et in Christo Iesu neque circumcisionem aliquid valere neque præputium, sed fidem, quæ per caritatem operatur. Hanc fidem ante baptismi sacramentum ex apostolorum traditione catechumeni ab ecclesia petunt, cum petunt fidem, vitam æternam præstantem: quam sine spe et caritate præstare fides non potest: unde et statim verbum Christi audiunt: Si vis ad vitam ingredi, serva mandata.

Itaque veram et Christianam justitiam accipientes, eam ceu primam stolam pro illa, quam Adam sua inobedienta sibi et nobis per-

most holy Passion, *the charity of God is poured forth,* by the Holy Spirit, *in the hearts*[1] of those that are justified, and is inherent therein: whence, man, through Jesus Christ, in whom he is ingrafted, receives, in the said justification, together with the remission of sins, all these [gifts] infused at once, faith, hope, and charity. For faith, unless hope and charity be added thereto, neither unites man perfectly with Christ, nor makes him a living member of his body. For which reason it is most truly said, that *Faith without works is dead* and profitless;[2] and, *In Christ Jesus neither circumcision availeth any thing nor uncircumcision, but faith which worketh by charity.*[3] This faith, Catechumens beg of the Church—agreeably to a tradition of the apostles—previously to the sacrament of Baptism; when they beg for the faith which bestows life everlasting, which, without hope and charity, faith can not bestow: whence also do they immediately hear that word of Christ: *If thou wilt enter into life, keep the commandments.*[4] Wherefore, when receiving true and Christian justice, they are bidden, immediately on being born again, to preserve it pure and spot

---

[1] Rom. v. 5.
[2] James ii. 20.

[3] Gal. v. 6.
[4] Matt. xix. 17.

didit, per Christum Iesum illis donatum, candidam et immaculatam jubentur statim renati conservare, ut eam perferant ante tribunal Domini nostri Iesu Christi, et habeant vitam æternam.

less, as *the first robe*[1] given them through Jesus Christ in lieu of that which Adam, by his disobedience, lost for himself and for us, that so they may bear it before the judgment-seat of our Lord Jesus Christ, and may have life eternal.

CAPUT VIII.

Quomodo intelligatur, impium per fidem et gratis justificari.

CHAPTER VIII.

In what manner it is to be understood, that the impious is justified by faith, and gratuitously.

Cum vero Apostolus dicit, justificari hominem per fidem et gratis, ea verba in eo sensu intelligenda sunt, quem perpetuus ecclesiæ catholicæ consensus tenuit et expressit : ut scilicet per fidem ideo justificari dicamur, quia fides est humanæ salutis initium, fundamentum et radix omnis justificationis, sine qua impossibile est placere Deo et ad filiorum ejus consortium pervenire : gratis autem justificari ideo dicamur, quia nihil eorum, quæ justificationem præcedunt, sive fides sive opera, ipsam justificationis gratiam promeretur : si enim gratia est, jam non ex operibus : alioquin, ut idem apostolus inquit, gratia jam non est gratia.

And whereas the Apostle saith, that man is *justified by faith* and *freely,*[2] those words are to be understood in that sense which the perpetual consent of the Catholic Church hath held and expressed; to wit, that we are therefore said to be *justified by faith,* because faith is the beginning of human salvation, the foundation, and the root of all Justification; *without which it is impossible to please God,*[3] and to come unto the fellowship of his sons: but we are therefore said to be justified *freely,* because that none of those things which precede j u s t i f i c a t i o n— whether faith or works—merit the grace itself of justification. For, *if it be a grace, it is not now by works,* otherwise, as the same Apostle says, *grace is no more grace.*[4]

---

[1] Luke xv. 22.
[2] Rom. iii. 4.
[3] Heb. xi. 6.
[4] Rom. xi. 6.

CAPUT IX.	CHAPTER IX.
Contra inanem hœreticorum fiduciam.	*Against the vain confidence of heretics.*

Quamvis autem necessarium sit credere, neque remitti, neque remissa unquam fuisse peccata, nisi gratis divina misericordia propter Christum : nemini tamen fiduciam, et certitudinem remissionis peccatorum suorum jactanti, et in ea sola quiescenti, peccata dimitti, vel dimissa esse dicendum est, cum apud hœreticos et schismaticos possit esse, imo nostra tempestate sit, et magna contra ecclesiam catholicam contentione prœdicetur vana hœc et ab omni pietate remota fiducia. Sed neque illud asserendum est, oportere eos, qui vere justificati sunt, absque ulla omnino dubitatione apud semetipsos statuere, se esse justificatos, neminemque a peccatis absolvi ac justificari, nisi eum, qui certo credat se absolutum et justificatum esse; atque hac sola fide absolutionem et justificationem perfici, quasi qui hoc non credit, de Dei promissis, deque mortis et resurrectionis Christi efficacia dubitet. Nam, sicut nemo pius de Dei misericordia, de Christi merito deque sacramentorum virtute et efficacia dubitare debet: sic quilibet, dum se ipsum suamque propriam infirmitatem et

But, although it is necessary to believe that sins neither are remitted, nor ever were remitted save gratuitously by the mercy of God for Christ's sake ; yet is it not to be said, that sins are forgiven, or have been forgiven, to any one who boasts of his confidence and certainty of the remission of his sins, and rests on that alone ; seeing that it may exist, yea does in our day exist, amongst heretics and schismatics ; and with great vehemence is this vain confidence, and one alien from all godliness, preached up in opposition to the Catholic Church. But neither is this to be asserted— that they who are truly justified must needs, without any doubting whatever, settle within themselves that they are justified, and that no one is absolved from sins and justified, but he that believes for certain that he is absolved and justified ; and that absolution and justification are effected by this faith alone : as though whoso has not this belief, doubts of the promises of God, and of the efficacy of the death and resurrection of Christ. For even as no pious person ought to doubt of the mercy of God, of the merit of Christ, and of the virtue and efficacy of the sacraments, even so

indispositionem respicit, de sua gratia formidare et timere potest; cum nullus scire valeat certitudine fidei, cui non potest subesse falsum, se gratiam Dei esse consecutum.

each one, when he regards himself, and his own weakness and indisposition, may have fear and apprehension touching his own grace; seeing that no one can know with a certainty of faith, which can not be subject to error, that he has obtained the grace of God.

CAPUT X.

De acceptæ justificationis incremento.

CHAPTER X.

On the increase of Justification received.

Sic ergo justificati, et amici Dei ac domestici facti, euntes de virtute in virtutem, renovantur, ut apostolus inquit, de die in diem, hoc est, mortificando membra carnis suæ, et exhibendo ea arma justitiæ in sanctificationem: per observationem mandatorum Dei et ecclesiæ, in ipsa justitia per Christi gratiam accepta, cooperante fide bonis operibus, crescunt atque magis justificantur, sicut scriptum est: Qui justus est, justificetur adhuc; et iterum: Ne verearis usque ad mortem justificari; et rursus: Videtis, quoniam ex operibus justificatur homo, et non ex fide tantum. Hoc vero justitiæ incrementum petit sancta ecclesia, cum orat: Da

Having, therefore, been thus justified, and made the friends and *domestics of God,*[1] advancing *from virtue to virtue,*[2] they are *renewed,* as the Apostle says, *day by day;*[3] that is, *by mortifying the members* of their own flesh,[4] and *by presenting them as instruments of justice unto sanctification,*[5] they, through the observance of the commandments of God and of the Church, faith co-operating with good works, increase in that justice which they have received through the grace of Christ, and are still further justified, as it is written: *He that is just, let him be justified still;*[6] and again, *Be not afraid to be justified even to death;*[7] and also, *Do you see that by works a man is justified, and not by faith only.*[8]   And this in-

---

[1] Ephes. ii. 19.
[2] Psa. lxxxiii. 8.
[3] 2 Cor. iv. 16.
[4] Coloss. iii. 5.
[5] Rom. vi. 13, 19.
[6] Apoc. xxii. 11.
[7] Eccles. xviii. 22.
[8] James ii. 24.

nobis Domine fidei, spei, et caritatis augmentum.

crease of justification holy Church begs, when she prays, 'Give unto us, O Lord, increase of faith, hope, and charity.'

CAPUT XI.

De observatione mandatorum, deque illius necessitate et possibilitate.

Nemo autem, quantumvis justificatus, liberum se esse ab observatione mandatorum putare debet ; nemo temeraria illa et a patribus sub anathemate prohibita voce uti, Dei præcepta homini justificato ad observandum esse impossibilia. Nam Deus impossibilia non jubet, sed jubendo monet et facere quod possis, et petere quod non possis, et adjuvat, ut possis. Cujus mandata gravia non sunt, cujus jugum suave est et onus leve. Qui enim sunt filii Dei, Christum diligunt ; qui autem diligunt eum, ut ipsemet testatur, servant sermones ejus, quod utique cum divino auxilio præstare possunt. Licet enim in hac mortali vita quantumvis sancti et justi in levia saltem et quotidiana, quæ etiam venialia dicuntur, peccata quandoque cadant, non propterea desinunt esse justi ; nam justorum illa vox est et humilis et verax : Di-

CHAPTER XI.

On keeping the Commandments, and on the necessity and possibility thereof.

But no one, how much soever justified, ought to think himself exempt from the observance of the commandments; no one ought to make use of that rash saying, one prohibited by the Fathers under an anathema,—that the observance of the commandments of God is impossible for one that is justified. For God commands not impossibilities, but, by commanding, both admonishes thee to do what thou art able, and to pray for what thou art not able (to do), and aids thee that thou mayest be able; *whose commandments are not heary;*[1] *whose yoke is sweet and whose burthen light.*[2] For, whoso are the sons of God, love Christ; but *they who love him, keep his commandments,*[3] as himself testifies; which, assuredly, with the divine help, they can do. For, although, during this mortal life, men, how holy and just soever, at times fall into at least light and daily sins, which are also called venial, not therefore do they cease to

---

[1] 1 John v. 3.   [2] Matt. xi. 30.   [3] John xiv. 15.

mitte nobis debita nostra. Quo fit, ut justi ipsi eo magis se obligatos ad ambulandum in via justitiæ sentire debeant, quo liberati jam a peccato, servi autem facti Deo, sobrie, juste et pie viventes proficere possint per Christum Iesum, per quem accessum habuerunt in gratiam istam. Deus namque sua gratia semel justificatos non deserit, nisi ab eis prius deseratur. Itaque nemo sibi in sola fide blandiri debet, putans fide sola se heredem esse constitutum, hereditatemque consecuturum, etiam si Christo non compatiatur, ut et conglorificetur. Nam et Christus ipse, ut inquit apostolus, cum esset filius Dei, didicit ex iis, quæ passus est, obedientiam, et consummatus factus est omnibus obtemperantibus sibi causa salutis æternæ. Propterea apostolus ipse monet justificatos, dicens: Nescitis, quod ii, qui in stadio currunt, omnes quidem currunt, sed unus accipit bravium? Sic currite, ut comprehendatis. Ego igitur sic curro, non quasi in incertum, sic pugno, non quasi aërem verberans, sed castigo corpus meum, et in servitutem redigo, ne forte,

be just. For that cry of the just, *Forgive us our trespasses*, is both humble and true. And for this cause, the just themselves ought to feel themselves the more obliged to walk in the way of justice, in that, being already *freed from sins, but made servants of God*,[1] they are able, *living soberly, justly, and godly*,[2] to proceed onwards *through Jesus Christ, by whom they have had access unto this grace*.[3] For God forsakes not those who have been once justified by his grace, unless he be first forsaken by them. Wherefore, no one ought to flatter himself up with faith alone, fancying that by faith alone he is made an heir, and will obtain the inheritance, even though *he suffer* not *with Christ, that so he may be also glorified with him*.[4] For even Christ himself, as the Apostle saith, *Whereas he was the son of God, learned obedience by the things which he suffered, and being consummated, he became, to all who obey him, the cause of eternal salvation*.[5] For which cause the same Apostle admonishes the justified, saying: *Know you not that they that run in the race, all run indeed, but one receiveth the prize? So run that you may obtain. I therefore so*

[1] Rom. vi. 18.
[2] Titus ii. 12.
[3] Rom. v. 2.
[4] Rom. viii. 17.
[5] Heb. v. 8, 9.

cum aliis prædicaverim, ipse re-
probus efficiar. Item princeps
apostolorum Petrus: Satagite,
ut per bona opera certam vestram vocationem et electionem
faciatis. Hæc enim facientes,
non peccabitis aliquando. Unde
constat eos orthodoxæ religionis
doctrinæ adversari, qui dicunt,
justum in omni bono opere saltem venialiter peccare, aut, quod
intolerabilius est, pœnas æternas
mereri, atque etiam eos, qui statuunt, in omnibus operibus justos peccare, si in illis suam ipsorum socordiam excitando, et
sese ad currendum in stadio co-
hortando, cum hoc, ut in primis
glorificetur Deus, mercedem quoque intuentur æternam; cum
scriptum sit: Inclinavi cor meum ad faciendas justificationes
tuas propter retributionem; et
de Mose dicat apostolus, quod
respiciebat in remunerationem.

run, not as at an uncertainty: I so
fight, not as one beating the air,
but I chastise my body, and bring
it into subjection; lest, perhaps,
when I have preached to others, I
myself should become a cast-away.[1]
So also the prince of the Apostles,
Peter: Labor the more that by good
works you may make sure your calling and election. For doing those
things, you shall not sin at any
time. From which it is plain, that
those are opposed to the orthodox
doctrine of religion, who assert that
the just man sins, venially at least,
in every good work; or, which is
yet more insupportable, that he
merits eternal punishments; as also
those who state, that the just sin in
all their works, if, in those works,
they, together with this aim principally that God may be glorified,
have in view also the eternal reward, in order to excite their sloth,
and to encourage themselves to run
in the course: whereas it is written,
I have inclined my heart to do all
thy justifications for the reward:[3]
and, concerning Moses, the Apostle
saith, that he looked unto the reward.[4]

---

[1] 1 Cor. ix. 24, 26, 27.
[2] 2 Peter i. 10.

[3] Psa. cxviii. 112.
[4] Heb. xi. 26.

CAPUT XII.

Prædestinationis temerariam præsumptionem cavendam esse.

Nemo quoque, quamdiu in hac mortalitate vivitur, de arcano divinæ prædestinationis mysterio usque adeo præsumere debet, ut certo statuat, se omnino esse in numero prædestinatorum, quasi verum esset, quod justificatus aut amplius peccare non possit, aut, si peccaverit, certam sibi resipiscentiam promittere debeat. Nam, nisi ex speciali revelatione, sciri non potest, quos Deus sibi elegerit.

CAPUT XIII.

De perseverantiæ munere.

Similiter de perseverantiæ munere, de quo scriptum est : Qui perseveraverit usque in finem, hic salvus erit ; quod quidem aliunde haberi non potest, nisi ab eo, qui potens est eum, qui stat, statuere, ut perseveranter stet, et eum, qui cadit, restituere : nemo sibi certi aliquid absoluta certitudine polliceatur, tametsi in Dei auxilio firmissimam spem collocare et reponere omnes debent. Deus enim, nisi ipsi illius gratiæ defuerint, sicut cœpit opus bonum, ita perficiet, ope-

CHAPTER XII.

That a rash presumptuousness in the matter of Predestination is to be avoided.

No one, moreover, so long as he is in this mortal life, ought so far to presume as regards the secret mystery of divine predestination, as to determine for certain that he is assuredly in the number of the predestinate ; as if it were true, that he that is justified, either can not sin any more, or, if he do sin, that he ought to promise himself an assured repentance ; for except by special revelation, it can not be known whom God hath chosen unto himself.

CHAPTER XIII.

On the gift of Perseverance.

So also as regards the gift of perseverance, of which it is written, *He that shall persevere to the end, he shall be saved ;*[1]—which gift can not be derived from any other but Him, who is able to establish him who standeth[2] that he stand perseveringly, and to restore him who falleth :—let no one herein promise himself any thing as certain with an absolute certainty ; though all ought to place and repose a most firm hope in God's help. For God, unless men be themselves wanting in his grace, *as he has begun the*

---

[1] Matt. xxiv. 13.   [2] Rom. xiv. 4.

rans velle et perficere. Verum-
tamen, qui se existimant stare,
videant ne cadant et cum timore,
ac tremore salutem suam ope-
rentur in laboribus, in vigiliis,
in eleemosynis, in orationibus et
oblaticnibus, in jejuniis et casti-
tate ; formidare enim debent, sci-
entes qucd in spem gloriæ, et
nondum in gloriam renati sunt,
de pugna, quæ superest cum
carne, cum mundo, cum diabo-
lo ; in qua victores esse non
possunt, nisi cum Dei gratia
apostolo obtemperent, dicenti :
Debitores sumus non carni, ut
secundum carnem vivamus; si
enim secundum carnem vixeritis,
moriemini ; si autem spiritu
facta carnis mortificaveritis, vi-
vetis.

good work, so will he perfect it,
working (in them) *to will and to*
accomplish.[1] Nevertheless, let those
who *think themselves to stand, take*
heed lest they fall,[2] and, *with fear*
and trembling work out their sal-
vation,[3] in labors, in watchings, in
almsdeeds, in prayers and oblations,
in fastings and chastity : for, knowing that *they are born again unto a*
hope of glory,[4] but not as yet unto
glory, they ought to fear for the
combat which yet remains with the
flesh, with the world, with the devil,
wherein they can not be victorious,
unless they be with God's grace,
obedient to the Apostle, who says :
We are debtors, not to the flesh, to
live according to the flesh ; for if
you live according to the flesh, you
shall die ; but if by the spirit you
mortify the deeds of the flesh, you
shall live.[5]

CAPUT XIV.

De lapsis, et eorum reparatione.

Qui vero ab accepta justifica-
tionis gratia per peccatum exci-
derunt, rursus justificari pote-
runt, cum, excitante Deo, per
pænitentiæ sacramentum merito
Christi amissam gratiam recu-
perare procuraverint ; hic enim
justificationis modus est lapsi

CHAPTER XIV.

On the fallen, and their restoration.

As regards those who, by sin, have
fallen from the received grace of
Justification, they may be again
justified, when, God exciting them,
through the sacrament of Penance
they shall have attained to the recovery, by the merit of Christ, of
the grace lost : for this manner of

---

[1] Phil. i. 6 ; ii. 13.   [3] Phil. ii. 12.   [5] Rom. viii. 12, 13.
[2] 1 Cor. x. 12.   [4] 1 Peter i. 3.

reparatio, quam secundam post naufragium deperditæ gratiæ tabulam sancti patres apte nuncuparunt; etenim pro iis, qui post baptismum in peccata labuntur, Christus Iesus sacramentum instituit pœnitentiæ, cum dixit: Accipite Spiritum Sanctum: quorum remiseritis peccata, remittuntur eis; et quorum retinueritis, retenta sunt. Unde docendum est, Christiani hominis pœnitentiam post lapsum multo aliam esse a baptismali, eaque contineri non modo cessationem a peccatis, et eorum detestationem, aut cor contritum et humiliatum, verum etiam eorundem sacramentalem confessionem saltem in voto et suo tempore faciendam, et sacerdotalem absolutionem; itemque satisfactionem per jejunia, eleemosynas, orationes et alia pia spiritualis vitæ exercitia; non quidem pro pœna æterna, quæ vel sacramento, vel sacramenti voto una cum culpa remittitur; sed pro pœna temporali, quæ, ut sacræ litteræ docent, non tota semper, ut in baptismo fit, dimittitur illis, qui gratiæ Dei, quam acceperunt, ingrati, Spiritum Sanctum contristaverunt, et templum Dei violare non sunt veriti. De qua

Justification is of the fallen the reparation: which the holy Fathers have aptly called a second plank after the shipwreck of grace lost. For, on behalf of those who fall into sins after baptism, Christ Jesus instituted the sacrament of Pen, ance, when he said, *Receive ye the Holy Ghost, whose sins you shall forgive, they are forgiven them, and whose sins you shall retain, they are retained.*[1] Whence it is to be taught, that the penitence of a Christian, after his fall, is very different from that at (his) baptism; and that therein are included not only a cessation from sins, and a detestation thereof, or, *a contrite and humble heart,*[2] but also the sacramental confession of the said sins, —at least in desire, and to be made in its season,—and sacerdotal absolution; and likewise satisfaction by fasts, alms, prayers, and the other pious exercises of a spiritual life; not indeed for the eternal punishment,—which is, together with the guilt, remitted, either by the sacrament, or by the desire of the sacrament,—but for the temporal punishment, which, as the sacred writings teach, is not always wholly remitted, as is done in baptism, to those who, ungrateful to the grace of God which they have received,

[1] John xx. 22, 23.   [2] Psa. l. 19.

pœnitentia scriptum est : Me-mor esto, unde excideris, age pœ-nitentiam, et prima opera fac. Et iterum : Quœ secundum De-um tristitia est, pœnitentiam in salutem stabilem operatur. Et rursus : Pœnitentiam agite, et facite fructus dignos pœniten-tiœ.

have *grieved the Holy Spirit,*[1] and have not feared *to violate the tem-ple of God.*[2] Concerning which penitence it is written: *Be mindful whence thou art fallen; do penance, and do the first works.*[3] And again: *The sorrow that is according to God worketh penance steadfast unto salvation.*[4] And again: *Do penance,* and *bring forth fruits worthy of penance.*[5]

CAPUT XV.

Quolibet mortali peccato amitti gratiam, sed non fidem.

CHAPTER XV.

That, by every mortal sin, grace is lost, but not faith.

Adversus etiam hominum quo-rundam callida ingenia, qui per dulces sermones et benedictiones seducunt corda innocentium, as-serendum est, non modo infi-delitate, per quam et ipsa fides amittitur, sed etiam quocumque alio mortali peccato, quamvis non amittatur fides, acceptam justificationis gratiam amitti; divinœ legis doctrinam defen-dendo, quœ a regno Dei non so-lum infideles excludit, sed et fide-les quoque, fornicarios, adulte-ros, molles, masculorum concu-bitores, fures, avaros, ebriosos, maledicos, rapaces, ceterosque om-nes, qui letalia committunt pec-cata, a quibus cum divinœ gra-

In opposition also to the subtle wits of certain men, who, *by pleas-ing speeches and good words, seduce the hearts of the innocent,*[6] it is to be maintained, that the received grace of Justification is lost, not only by infidelity whereby even faith itself is lost, but also by any other mortal sin whatever, though faith be not lost; thus defending the doctrine of the divine law, which excludes from the kingdom of God not only the unbelieving, but the faithful also [who are] *fornicators, adulterers, effeminate, liers with mankind, thieves, covet-ous, drunkards, railers, extortion-ers,*[7] and all others who commit deadly sins; from which, with the

---

[1] Ephes. iv. 30.   [3] Apoc. ii. 5.   [5] Matt. iii. 2.   [7] 1 Cor. vi. 9, 10.
[2] 1 Cor. iii. 17.   [4] 2 Cor. vii. 10.   [6] Rom. xvi. 18.

tiœ adiumento abstinere possunt, et pro quibus a Christi gratia separantur.

help of divine grace, they can refrain, and on account of which they are separated from the grace of Christ.

CAPUT XVI.

De fructu justificationis, hoc est, de merito bonorum operum, deque ipsius meriti ratione.

CHAPTER XVI.

On the fruit of Justification, that is, on the merit of good works, and on the nature of that merit.

Hac igitur ratione justificatis hominibus, sive acceptam gratiam perpetuo conservaverint, sive amissam recuperaverint, proponenda sunt apostoli verba: Abundate in omni opere bono, scientes, quod labor vester non est inanis in Domino ; non enim injustus est Deus, ut obliviscatur operis vestri et dilectionis, quam ostendistis in nomine ipsius ; et : Nolite amittere confidentiam vestram, quœ magnam habet remunerationem. Atque ideo bene operantibus usque in finem, et in Deo sperantibus proponenda est vita œterna, et tanquam gratia filiis Dei per Christum Iesum misericorditer promissa, et tanquam merces ex ipsius Dei promissione bonis ipsorum operibus et meritis fideliter reddenda. Hœc est enim illa corona justitiœ, quam post suum certamen et cursum repositam sibi esse aiebat apostolus, a justo

Before men, therefore, who have been justified in this manner,—whether they have preserved uninterruptedly the grace received, or whether they have recovered it when lost,—are to be set the words of the Apostle: *Abound in every good work, knowing that your labor is not in vain in the Lord ;*[1] *for God is not unjust, that he should forget your work, and the love which you have shown in his name ;*[2] and, *do not lose your confidence, which hath a great reward.*[3] And, for this cause, life eternal is to be proposed to those working well *unto the end,*[4] and hoping in God, both as a grace mercifully promised to the sons of God through Jesus Christ, and as a reward which is according to the promise of God himself, to be faithfully rendered to their good works and merits. For this is that *crown of justice* which the Apostle declared was, after his *fight* and *course, laid up*

[1] 1 Cor. xv. 58.
[2] Heb. vi. 10.

[3] Heb. x. 35.
[4] Matt. x. 22.

judice sibi reddendam; non so-
lum autem sibi, sed et omnibus,
qui diligunt adventum ejus : cum
enim ille ipse Christus Iesus,
tanquam caput in membra et
tanquam vitis in palmites, in
ipsos justificatos jugiter virtu-
tem influat, quæ virtus bona
eorum opera semper antecedit
et comitatur et subsequitur, et
sine qua nullo pacto Deo grata,
et meritoria esse possent: nihil
ipsis justificatis amplius deesse
credendum est, quo minus plene
illis quidem operibus, quæ in
Deo sunt facta, divinæ legi pro
hujus vitæ statu satisfecisse, et
vitam æternam suo etiam tem-
pore (si tamen in gratia deces-
serint), consequendam, vere pro-
meruisse censeantur, cum Chris-
tus, Salvator noster, dicat: Si
quis biberit ex aqua, quam ego
dabo ei, non sitiet in æternum,
sed fiet in eo fons aquæ salien-
tis in vitam æternam

Ita neque propria nostra jus-
titia, tanquam ex nobis pro-
pria statuitur, neque ignora-
tur aut repudiatur justitia Dei;
quæ enim justitia nostra dici-
tur, quia per eam nobis inhæ-
rentem justificamur, illa eadem

for him, to be rendered to him by
the just Judge, and not only to him,
but also to all that love his coming.[1]
For, whereas Jesus Christ himself
continually infuses his virtue into
the said justified,—as the head into
the members, and the vine into the
branches,—and this virtue always
precedes and accompanies and follows their good works, which without it could not in any wise be
pleasing and meritorious before
God,—we must believe that nothing further is wanting to the justified, to prevent their being accounted to have, by those very works
which have been done in God, fully
satisfied the divine law according to
the state of this life, and to have truly merited eternal life, to be obtained also in its (due) time, if so be, however, that they depart in grace : seeing that Christ, our Saviour, saith :
If any one shall drink of the wa-
ter that I will give him, he shall
not thirst forever; but it shall
become in him a fountain of water
springing up unto life everlasting.[2]
Thus, neither is our own justice *es-*
tablished as our own as from ourselves;[3] nor is the justice of God ig-
nored or repudiated: for that justice
which is called ours, because that we
are justified from its being inherent
in us, that same is (the justice) of

---

[1] 2 Tim. iv. 8.   [2] John iv. 13, 14.   [3] Rom. x. 3.

Dei est, quia a Deo nobis infunditur per Christi meritum. Neque vero illud omittendum est, quod licet bonis operibus in sacris litteris usque adeo tribuatur, ut etiam qui uni ex minimis suis potum aquæ frigidæ dederit, promittat Christus eum non esse sua mercede cariturum, et apostolus testetur, id quod in præsenti est momentaneum et leve tribulationis nostræ, supra modum in sublimitate æternum gloriæ pondus operari in nobis: absit tamen, ut Christianus homo in se ipso vel confidat vel glorietur, et non in Domino, cujus tanta est erga omnes homines bonitas, ut eorum velit esse merita, quæ sunt ipsius dona. Et quia in multis offendimus omnes, unusquisque, sicut misericordiam et bonitatem, ita severitatem et judicium ante oculos habere debet, neque se ipsum aliquis, etiam si nihil sibi conscius fuerit, judicare; quoniam omnis hominum vita non humano judicio examinanda et judicanda est, sed Dei, qui illuminabit abscondita tenebrarum, et manifestabit consilia cordium: et tunc laus erit unicuique a Deo, qui, ut scrip-

God, because that it is infused into us of God, through the merit of Christ. Neither is this to be omitted,—that although, in the sacred writings, so much is attributed to good works, that Christ promises, that even *he that shall give a drink of cold water to one of his least ones, shall not lose his reward;*[1] and the Apostle testifies that, *That which is at present momentary and light of our tribulation, worketh for us above measure exceedingly an eternal weight of glory;*[2] nevertheless God forbid that a Christian should either trust or glory in himself, and not in the Lord, whose bounty towards all men is so great, that he will have the things which are his own gifts be their merits. And forasmuch as *in many things we all offend,*[3] each one ought to have before his eyes, as well the severity and judgment, as the mercy and goodness (of God); neither ought any one *to judge himself, even though he be not conscious to himself of any thing;*[4] because the whole life of man is to be examined and judged, not by the judgment of man, but of God, *who will bring to light the hidden things of darkness, and will make manifest the counsels of the hearts, and then shall every man*

---

[1] Matt. x. 42.
[2] 2 Cor. iv. 17.
[3] James iii. 2.
[4] 1 Cor. iv. 3, 4.

tum est, reddet unicuique opera sua.

Post hanc catholicam de justificatione doctrinam, quam nisi quisque fideliter firmiterque receperit, justificari non poterit, placuit sanctæ synodo hos canones subjungere, ut omnes sciant, non solum quid tenere et sequi, sed etiam quid vitare et fugere debeant.

DE JUSTIFICATIONE.

Canon I.—*Si quis dixerit, hominem suis operibus, quæ vel per humanæ naturæ vires, vel per legis doctrinam fiant, absque divina per Iesum Christum gratia posse justificari coram Deo: anathema sit.*

Canon II.—*Si quis dixerit, ad hoc solum divinam gratiam per Christum Iesum dari, ut facilius homo juste vivere, ac vitam æternam promereri possit; quasi per liberum arbitrium sine gratia utrumque, sed ægre tamen et difficulter possit : anathema sit.*

Canon III.—*Si quis dixerit, sine præveniente Spiritus Sancti inspiratione atque ejus adjutorio hominem credere, sperare, diligere, aut pœnitere posse, sicut*

have praise from God,[1] *who, as it is written, will render to every man according to his works.*[2]

After this Catholic doctrine on Justification, which whoso receiveth not faithfully and firmly can not be justified, it hath seemed good to the holy Synod to subjoin these canons, that all may know not only what they ought to hold and follow, but also what to avoid and shun.

ON JUSTIFICATION.

Canon I.—If any one saith, that man may be justified before God by his own works, whether done through the teaching of human nature, or that of the law, without the grace of God through Jesus Christ: let him be anathema.

Canon II.—If any one saith, that the grace of God, through Jesus Christ, is given only for this, that man may be able more easily to live justly, and to merit eternal life, as if, by free-will without grace, he were able to do both, though hardly indeed and with difficulty : let him be anathema.

Canon III.—If any one saith, that without the prevenient inspiration of the Holy Ghost, and without his help, man can believe, hope, love, or be penitent as he

---

[1] 1 Cor. iv. 5.   [2] Matt. xvi. 27.

oportet, ut ei justificationis gratia conferatur : anathema sit.

CANON IV.—*Si quis dixerit, liberum hominis arbitrium a Deo motum et excitatum nihil cooperari assentiendo Deo excitanti atque vocanti, quo ad obtinendam justificationis gratiam se disponat ac præparet; neque posse dissentire, si velit, sed veluti inanime quoddam nihil omnino agere, mereque passive se habere: anathema sit.*

CANON V.—*Si quis liberum hominis arbitrium post Adæ peccatum amissum et extinctum esse dixerit, aut rem esse de solo titulo, imo titulum sine re, figmentum denique a Satana invectum in ecclesiam : anathema sit.*

CANON VI.—*Si quis dixerit, non esse in potestate hominis, vias suas malas facere, sed mala opera ita, ut bona, Deum operari, non permissive solum, sed etiam proprie et per se, adeo ut sit proprium ejus opus non minus proditio Iudæ, quam vocatio Pauli: anathema sit.*

CANON VII.—*Si quis dixerit, opera omnia, quæ ante justificationem fiunt, quacumque ratione*

ought, so that the grace of Justification may be bestowed upon him: let him be anathema.

CANON IV.—If any one saith, that man's free-will moved and excited by God, by assenting to God exciting and calling, nowise cooperates towards disposing and preparing itself for obtaining the grace of Justification; that it cannot refuse its consent, if it would, but that, as something inanimate, it does nothing whatever and is merely passive: let him be anathema.

CANON V.—If any one saith, that, since Adam's sin, the free-will of man is lost and extinguished; or, that it is a thing with only a name, yea a name without a reality, a figment, in fine, introduced into the Church by Satan: let him be anathema.

CANON VI.—If any one saith, that it is not in man's power to make his ways evil, but that the works that are evil God worketh as well as those that are good, not permissively only, but properly, and of himself, in such wise that the treason of Judas is no less his own proper work than the vocation of Paul: let him be anathema.

CANON VII.—If any one saith, that all works done before Justification, in whatsoever way they be

facta sint, vere esse peccata, vel odium Dei mereri, aut, quanto vehementius quis nititur se disponere ad gratiam, tanto eum gravius peccare: anathema sit.

CANON VIII.—*Si quis dixerit, gehennæ metum, per quem ad misericordiam Dei de peccatis dolendo confugimus vel a peccando abstinemus, peccatum esse, aut peccatores peiores facere: anathema sit.*

CANON IX.—*Si quis dixerit, sola fide impium justificari, ita ut intelligat nihil aliud requiri, quod ad justificationis gratiam coconsequendam cooperetur, et nulla ex parte necesse esse, eum suæ voluntatis motu præparari atque disponi: anathema sit.*

CANON X.—*Si quis dixerit, homines sine Christi justitia, per quam nobis meruit, justificari, aut per eam ipsam formaliter justos esse: anathema sit.*

CANON XI.—*Si quis dixerit, homines justificari, vel sola imputatione justitiæ Christi, vel sola peccatorum remissione, exclusa gratia et caritate, quæ in cordibus eorum per Spiritum Sanctum diffundatur atque il-*

done, are truly sins, or merit the hatred of God; or that the more earnestly one strives to dispose himself for grace, the more grievously he sins: let him be anathema.

CANON VIII.—If any one saith, that the fear of hell,—whereby, by grieving for our sins, we flee unto the mercy of God, or refrain from sinning,—is a sin, or makes sinners worse: let him be anathema.

CANON IX.—If any one saith, that by faith alone the impious is justified, in such wise as to mean, that nothing else is required to cooperate in order to the obtaining the grace of Justification, and that it is not in any way necessary, that he be prepared and disposed by the movement of his own will: let him be anathema.

CANON X.—If any one saith, that men are just without the justice of Christ, whereby he merited for us to be justified; or that it is by that justice itself that they are formally just: let him be anathema.

CANON XI.—If any one saith, that men are justified, either by the sole imputation of the justice of Christ, or by the sole remission of sins, to the exclusion of the grace and *the charity which is poured forth in their hearts by the Holy Ghost,*[1]

---

[1] Rom. v. 5.

lis inhœreat; aut etiam gratiam, qua justificamur, esse tantum favorem Dei: anathema sit.

and is inherent in them; or even that the grace, whereby we are justified, is only the favor of God: let him be anathema.

CANON XII.—*Si quis dixerit, fidem justificantem nihil aliud esse, quam fiduciam divinœ misericordiœ peccata remittentis propter Christum; vel eam fiduciam solam esse, qua justificamur: anathema sit.*

CANON XII.—If any one saith, that justifying faith is nothing else but confidence in the divine mercy which remits sins for Christ's sake; or, that this confidence alone is that whereby we are justified: let him be anathema.

CANON XIII.—*Si quis dixerit, omni homini ad remissionem peccatorum assequendam necessarium esse, ut credat certo, et absque ulla hœsitatione propriœ infirmitatis et indispositionis peccata sibi esse remissa: anathema sit.*

CANON XIII.—If any one saith, that it is necessary for every one, for the obtaining the remission of sins, that he believe for certain, and without any wavering arising from his own infirmity and indisposition, that his sins are forgiven him: let him be anathema.

CANON XIV.—*Si quis dixerit, hominem a peccatis absolvi ac justificari ex eo quod se absolvi ac justificari certo credat; aut neminem vero esse justificatum, nisi qui credat se esse justificatum, et hac sola fide absolutionem et justificationem perfici: anathema sit.*

CANON XIV.—If any one saith, that man is truly absolved from his sins and justified, because that he assuredly believed himself absolved and justified; or, that no one is truly justified but he who believes himself justified; and that, by this faith alone, absolution and justification are effected: let him be anathema.

CANON XV.—*Si quis dixerit, hominem renatum et justificatum teneri ex fide ad credendum, se certo esse in numero prœdestinatorum: anathema sit.*

CANON XV.—If any one saith, that a man, who is born again and justified, is bound of faith to believe that he is assuredly in the number of the predestinate: let him be anathema.

CANON XVI.—*Si quis magnum*

CANON XVI.—If any one saith,

illud usque in finem pers-verantiæ donum se certo habiturum absoluta et infallibili certitudine dixerit, nisi hoc ex speciali revelatione didicerit : anathema sit.

CANON XVII.—*Si quis justificationis gratiam non nisi prædestinatis ad vitam contingere dixerit, reliquos vero omnes, qui vocantur, vocari quidem, sed gratiam non accipere, utpote divina potestate prædestinatos ad malum : anathema sit.*

CANON XVIII.—*Si quis dixerit, Dei præcepta homini etiam justificato et sub gratia constituto esse ad observandum impossibilia : anathema sit.*

CANON XIX.—*Si quis dixerit, nihil præceptum esse in evangelio præter fidem, cetera esse indifferentia, neque præcepta, neque prohibita, sed libera ; aut decem præcepta nihil pertinere ad Christianos : anathema sit.*

CANON XX.—*Si quis hominem justificatum et quantumlibet perfectum dixerit non teneri ad observantiam mandatorum Dei et ecclesiæ, sed tantum ad credendum, quasi vero evangelium sit nuda et absoluta promissio vitæ æternæ sine conditione observa-*

that he will for certain, of an absolute and infallible certainty, have that great gift of perseverance unto the end,—unless he have learned this by special revelation : let him be anathema.

CANON XVII.—If any one saith, that the grace of Justification is only attained to by those who are predestined unto life ; but that all others who are called, are called indeed, but receive not grace, as being, by the divine power, predestined unto evil : let him be anathema.

CANON XVIII.—If any one saith, that the commandments of God are, even for one that is justified and constituted in grace, impossible to keep : let him be anathema.

CANON XIX.—If any one saith, that nothing besides faith is commanded in the Gospel ; that other things are indifferent, neither commanded nor prohibited, but free ; or, that the ten commandments nowise appertain to Christians : let him be anathema.

CANON XX.—If any one saith, that the man who is justified and how perfect soever, is not bound to observe the commandments of God and of the Church, but only to believe ; as if indeed the Gospel were a bare and absolute promise of eternal life, without the condition of

tionis mandatorum: anathema sit.

CANON XXI.—*Si quis dixerit, Christum Iesum a Deo hominibus datum fuisse, ut redemptorem, cui fidant, non etiam ut legislatorem, cui obediant: anathema sit.*

CANON XXII.—*Si quis dixerit, justificatum, vel sine speciali auxilio Dei in accepta justitia perseverare posse, vel cum eo non posse: anathema sit.*

CANON XXIII.—*Si quis hominem semel justificatum dixerit amplius peccare non posse, neque gratiam amittere, atque ideo eum qui labitur et peccat, nunquam vere fuisse justificatum; aut contra, posse in tota vita peccata omnia, etiam venialia, vitare, nisi ex speciali Dei privilegio, quemadmodum de beata Virgine tenet ecclesia: anathema sit.*

CANON XXIV.—*Si quis dixerit, justitiam acceptam non conservari, atque etiam non augeri coram Deo per bona opera; sed opera ipsa fructus solummodo et signa esse justificationis adeptæ, non autem ipsius augendæ causam: anathema sit.*

CANON XXV.—*Si quis in quolibet bono opere justum saltem venialiter peccare dixerit, aut,*

observing the commandments: let him be anathema.

CANON XXI.—If any one saith, that Christ Jesus was given of God to men, as a redeemer in whom to trust, and not also as a legislator whom to obey: let him be anathema.

CANON XXII.—If any one saith, that the justified, either is able to persevere, without the special help of God, in the justice received; or that, with that help, he is not able: let him be anathema.

CANON XXIII.—If any one saith, that a man once justified can sin no more, nor lose grace, and that therefore he that falls and sins was never truly justified; or, on the other hand, that he is able, during his whole life, to avoid all sins, even those that are venial,—except by a special privilege from God, as the Church holds in regard of the Blessed Virgin: let him be anathema.

CANON XXIV.—If any one saith, that the justice received is not preserved and also increased before God through good works; but that the said works are merely the fruits and signs of Justification obtained, but not a cause of the increase thereof: let him be anathema.

CANON XXV.—If any one saith, that, in every good work, the just sins venially at least, or—which is

quod intolerabilius est, morta-
liter, atque ideo pœnas œter-
nas mereri; tantumque ob id
non damnari, quia Deus opera
non imputet ad damnationem:
anathema sit.

CANON XXVI.—*Si quis dixe-*
rit, justos non debere pro bonis
operibus, quœ in Deo fuerint
facta, expectare et sperare œter-
nam retributionem a Deo per
ejus misericordiam et Iesu
Christi meritum, si bene agendo
et divina mandata custodiendo
usque in finem perseveraverint:
anathema sit.

CANON XXVII.—*Si quis dixe-*
rit, nullum esse mortale peccatum,
nisi infidelitatis; aut nullo alio,
quantumvis gravi et enormi, prœ-
terquam infidelitatis, peccato, se-
mel acceptam gratiam amitti:
anathema sit.

CANON XXVIII.—*Si quis dixe-*
rit, amissa per peccatum gratia,
simul et fidem semper amitti;
aut fidem, quœ remanet, non esse
veram fidem, licet non sit viva;
aut eum, qui fidem sine caritate
habet, non esse Christianum:
anathema sit.

CANON XXIX.—*Si quis dixerit,*
eum, qui post baptismum lapsus
est, non posse per Dei gratiam
resurgere; aut posse quidem, sed
sola fide amissam justitiam re-

more intolerable still—mortally,
and consequently deserves eternal
punishments; and that for this cause
only he is not damned, that God
does not impute those works unto
damnation: let him be anathema.

CANON XXVI.—If any one saith,
that the just ought not, for their
good works done in God, to expect
and hope for an eternal recompense
from God, through his mercy and
the merit of Jesus Christ, if so be
that they persevere to the end in
well doing and in keeping the divine commandments: let him be
anathema.

CANON XXVII.—If any one
saith, that there is no mortal sin
but that of infidelity; or, that grace
once received is not lost by any other
sin, however grievous and enor-
mous, save by that of infidelity: let
him be anathema.

CANON XXVIII.—If any one
saith, that, grace being lost through
sin, faith also is always lost with it;
or, that the faith which remains,
though it be not a lively faith, is
not a true faith; or, that he who
has faith without charity is not a
Christian: let him be anathema.

CANON XXIX.—If any one saith,
that he who has fallen after baptism is not able by the grace of
God to rise again; or, that he is
able indeed to recover the justice

cuperare sine sacramento pœnitentiœ, prout sancta romana et universalis ecclesia a Christo Domino et ejus apostolis edocta hucusque professa est, servavit et docuit: anathema sit.

CANON XXX.—Si quis post acceptam justificationis gratiam cuilibet peccatori pœnitenti ita culpam remitti et reatum œternœ pœnœ deleri dixerit, ut nullus remaneat reatus pœnœ temporalis exsolvendœ vel in hoc seculo, vel in futuro in purgatorio, antequam ad regna cœlorum aditus patere possit: anathema sit.

CANON XXXI.—Si quis dixerit, justificatum peccare, dum intuitu œternœ mercedis bene operatur: anathema sit.

CANON XXXII.—Si quis dixerit hominis justificati bona opera ita esse dona Dei, ut non sint etiam bona ipsius justificati merita; aut ipsum justificatum bonis operibus, quœ ab eo per Dei gratiam et Iesu Christi meritum, cujus vivum membrum est, fiunt, non vere mereri augmentum gratiœ, vitam œternam, et ipsius vitœ œternœ, si tamen in gratia decesserit, consecutionem,

which he has lost, but by faith alone without the sacrament of Penance, contrary to what the holy Roman and universal Church—instructed by Christ and his Apostles—has hitherto professed, observed, and taught: let him be anathema.

CANON XXX.—If any one saith, that, after the grace of Justification has been received, to every penitent sinner the guilt is remitted, and the debt of eternal punishment is blotted out in such wise that there remains not any debt of temporal punishment to be discharged either in this world, or in the next in Purgatory, before the entrance to the kingdom of heaven can be opened [to him]: let him be anathema.

CANON XXXI.—If any one saith, that the justified sins when he performs good works with a view to an eternal recompense: let him be anathema.

CANON XXXII.—If any one saith, that the good works of one that is justified are in such manner the gifts of God, that they are not also the good merits of him that is justified; or, that the said justified, by the good works which he performs through the grace of God and the merit of Jesus Christ, whose living member he is, does not truly merit increase of grace, eternal life, and the attainment of that eternal

*atque etiam gloriæ augmentum :
anathema sit.*

CANON XXXIII.—*Si quis dixerit, per hanc doctrinam catholicam de justificatione, a sancta
synodo hoc præsenti decreto expressam, aliqua ex parte gloriæ
Dei vel meritis Iesu Christi Domini nostri derogari, et non potius veritatem fidei nostræ, Dei
denique, ac Christi Iesu gloriam
illustrari: anathema sit.*

life,—if so be, however, that he depart in grace,—and also an increase
of glory: let him be anathema.

CANON XXXIII.—If any one
saith, that, by the Catholic doctrine
touching Justification, by this holy
Synod set forth in this present decree, the glory of God, or the merits of our Lord Jesus Christ are in
any way derogated from, and not
rather that the truth of our faith,
and the glory in fine of God and
of Jesus Christ are rendered [more]
illustrious: let him be anathema.

SESSIO SEPTIMA,

celebrata die III. Martii 1547.

DECRETUM DE SACRAMENTIS.

Proœmium.

*Ad consummationem saluta-
ris de justificatione doctrinæ,
quæ in præcedenti proxima sessione uno omnium patrum consensu promulgata fuit; consentaneum visum est de sanctissimis ecclesiæ sacramentis agere,
per quæ omnis vera justitia
vel incipit, vel cœpta augetur,
vel amissa reparatur. Propterea sacrosancta, œcumenica et
generalis Tridentina synodus, in
Spiritu Sancto legitime congregata, præsidentibus in ea eisdem*

SEVENTH SESSION,

held March 3, 1547.

DECREE ON THE SACRAMENTS.

Proëm.

For the completion of the salutary doctrine on Justification, which
was promulgated with the unanimous consent of the Fathers in the
last preceding Session, it hath seemed suitable to treat of the most holy
Sacraments of the Church, through
which all true justice either begins,
or being begun is increased, or being lost is repaired. With this view,
in order to destroy the errors and to
extirpate the heresies which have
appeared in these our days on the
subject of the said most holy sacra-

apostolicæ sedis legatis, ad er-
rores eliminandos et extirpandas
hæreses, quæ circa sanctissima
ipsa sacramenta hac nostra tem-
pestate, tum de damnatis olim
a patribus nostris hæresibus
suscitatæ, tum etiam de novo
adinventæ sunt, quæ Catholicæ
Ecclesiæ puritati et animarum
saluti magnopere officiunt; sanc-
tarum scripturarum doctrinæ,
apostolicis traditionibus atque
aliorum conciliorum et patrum
consensui inhærendo, hos præ-
sentes canones statuendos et de-
cernendos censuit, reliquos, qui
supersunt ad cæpti operis per-
fectionem, deinceps, divino Spi-
ritu adjuvante, editura.

ments,—as well those which have
been revived from the heresies condemned of old by our Fathers, as
also those newly invented, and which
are exceedingly prejudicial to the
purity of the Catholic Church, and
to the salvation of souls,—the sacred and holy, œcumenical and general Synod of Trent, lawfully assembled in the Holy Ghost, the same
legates of the Apostolic See presiding therein, adhering to the doctrine of the holy Scriptures, to the
apostolic traditions, and to the consent of other councils and of the
Fathers, has thought fit that these
present canons be established and
decreed; intending, the divine Spirit aiding, to publish later the remaining canons which are wanting
for the completion of the work
which it has begun.

DE SACRAMENTIS IN GENERE.

ON THE SACRAMENTS IN GENERAL.

CANON I.—*Si quis dixerit, sa-*
cramenta novæ legis non fuisse
omnia a Iesu Christo Domino
nostro instituta; aut esse plura
vel pauciora quam septem, vide-
licet: baptismum, confirmationem,
eucharistiam, pœnitentiam, extre-
mam unctionem, ordinem, et ma-
trimonium; aut etiam aliquod
horum septem non esse vere et pro-
prie sacramentum: anathema sit.

CANON I.—If any one saith, that
the sacraments of the New Law
were not all instituted by Jesus
Christ, our Lord; or, that they are
more, or less, than seven, to wit,
Baptism, Confirmation, the Eucharist, Penance, Extreme Unction, Order, and Matrimony; or
even that any one of these seven
is not truly and properly a sacrament: let him be anathema.

CANON II.—*Si quis dixerit, ea ipsa novæ legis sacramenta a sacramentis antiquæ legis non differre, nisi quia ceremoniæ sunt aliæ et alii ritus externi: anathema sit.*

CANON II.—If any one saith, that these said sacraments of the New Law do not differ from the sacraments of the Old Law, save that the ceremonies are different, and different the outward rites: let him be anathema.

CANON III.—*Si quis dixerit, hæc septem sacramenta ita esse inter se paria, ut nulla ratione aliud sit alio dignius: anathema sit.*

CANON III.—If any one saith, that these seven sacraments are in such wise equal to each other, as that one is not in any way more worthy than another: let him be anathema.

CANON IV.—*Si quis dixerit, sacramenta novæ legis non esse ad salutem necessaria, sed superflua; et sine eis aut eorum voto per solam fidem homines a Deo gratiam justificationis adipisci; licet omnia singulis necessaria non sint: anathema sit.*

CANON IV.—If any one saith, that the sacraments of the New Law are not necessary unto salvation, but superfluous; and that, without them, or without the desire thereof, men obtain of God, through faith alone, the grace of justification;—though all [the sacraments] are not indeed necessary for every individual: let him be anathema.

CANON V.—*Si quis dixerit, hæc sacramenta propter solam fidem nutriendam instituta fuisse: anathema sit.*

CANON V.—If any one saith, that these sacraments were instituted for the sake of nourishing faith alone: let him be anathema.

CANON VI.—*Si quis dixerit, sacramenta novæ legis non continere gratiam, quam significant; aut gratiam ipsam non ponentibus obicem non conferre; quasi signa tantum externa sint acceptæ per fidem gratiæ, vel justitiæ, et notæ quædam Christianæ professionis, quibus apud ho-*

CANON VI.—If any one saith, that the sacraments of the New Law do not contain the grace which they signify; or, that they do not confer that grace on those who do not place an obstacle thereunto; as though they were merely outward signs of grace or justice received through faith, and certain marks of the Chris-

mines discernuntur fideles ab in-fidelibus : anathema sit.

CANON VII.—*Si quis dixerit, non dari gratiam per hujusmodi sacramenta semper et omnibus, quantum est ex parte Dei, etiam si rite ea suscipiant, sed aliquando et aliquibus : anathema sit.*

CANON VIII.—*Si quis dixerit, per ipsa novæ legis sacramenta ex opere operato non conferri gratiam, sed solam fidem divinæ promissionis ad gratiam consequendam sufficere : anathema sit.*

CANON IX.—*Si quis dixerit, in tribus sacramentis, baptismo scilicet, confirmatione et ordine, non imprimi characterem in anima, hoc est signum quoddam spirituale et indelebile, unde ea iterari non possunt : anathema sit.*

CANON X.—*Si quis dixerit, Christianos omnes in verbo, et omnibus sacramentis administrandis habere potestatem : anathema sit.*

CANON XI.—*Si quis dixerit, in ministris, dum sacramenta conficiunt et conferunt, non requiri intentionem saltem faciendi, quod facit ecclesia : anathema sit.*

CANON XII.—*Si quis dixerit,*

tian profession, whereby believers are distinguished amongst men from unbelievers : let him be anathema.

CANON VII.—If any one saith, that grace, as far as God's part is concerned, is not given through the said sacraments, always, and to all men, even though they receive them rightly, but [only] sometimes, and to some persons : let him be anathema.

CANON VIII.—If any one saith, that by the said sacraments of the New Law grace is not conferred through the act performed, but that faith alone in the divine promise suffices for the obtaining of grace : let him be anathema.

CANON IX.—If any one saith, that, in the three sacraments, to wit, Baptism, Confirmation, and Order, there is not imprinted in the soul a character, that is, a certain spiritual and indelible sign, on account of which they can not be repeated : let him be anathema.

CANON X.—If any one saith, that all Christians have power to administer the word, and all the sacraments : let him be anathema.

CANON XI.—If any one saith, that, in ministers, when they effect, and confer the sacraments, there is not required the intention at least of doing what the Church does : let him be anathema.

CANON XII.—If any one saith,

ministrum in peccato mortali existentem, modo omnia essentialia, quæ ad sacramentum conficiendum aut conferendum pertinent, servaverit, non conficere aut conferre sacramentum: anathema sit.

CANON XIII.—*Si quis dixerit, receptos et approbatos Ecclesiæ Catholicæ ritus, in solemni sacramentorum administratione adhiberi consuetos, aut contemni, aut sine peccato a ministris pro libito omitti, aut in novos alios per quemcumque ecclesiarum pastorem mutari posse: anathema sit.*

DE BAPTISMO.

CANON I.—*Si quis dixerit, baptismum Ioannis habuisse eamdem vim cum baptismo Christi: anathema sit.*

CANON II.—*Si quis dixerit, aquam veram et naturalem non esse de necessitate baptismi; atque ideo verba illa Domini nostri Iesu Christi: Nisi quis renatus fuerit ex aqua et Spiritu Sancto; ad metaphoram aliquam detorserit: anathema sit.*

CANON III.—*Si quis dixerit, in Ecclesiæ Romana, quæ omnium ecclesiarum mater est et magistra, non esse veram de baptismi*

that a minister, being in mortal sin, —if so be that he observe all the essentials which belong to the effecting, or conferring of, the sacrament, —neither effects, nor confers the sacrament : let him be anathema.

CANON XIII.—If any one saith, that the received and approved rites of the Catholic Church, wont to be used in the solemn administration of the sacraments, may be contemned, or without sin be omitted at pleasure by the ministers, or be changed, by every pastor of the churches, into other new ones: let him be anathema.

ON BAPTISM.

CANON I.—If any one saith, that the baptism of John had the same force as the baptism of Christ: let him be anathema.

CANON II.—If any one saith, that true and natural water is not of necessity for baptism, and, on that account, wrests, to some sort of metaphor, those words of our Lord Jesus Christ: *Unless a man be born again of water and the Holy Ghost :*[1] let him be anathema.

CANON III.—If any one saith, that in the Roman Church, which is the mother and mistress of all churches, there is not the true doctrine con-

---

[1] John iii. 5.

sacramento doctrinam : anathema sit.

Canon IV.—*Si quis dixerit, baptismum, qui etiam datur ab hæreticis in nomine Patris, et Filii, et Spiritus Sancti, cum intentione faciendi, quod facit ecclesia, non esse verum baptismum : anathema sit.*

Canon V.—*Si quis dixerit, baptismum liberum esse, hoc est, non necessarium ad salutem : anathema sit.*

Canon VI.—*Si quis dixerit, baptizatum non posse, etiam si velit, gratiam amittere, quantumcumque peccet, nisi nolit credere : anathema sit.*

Canon VII.—*Si quis dixerit, baptizatos per baptismum ipsum, solius tantum fidei debitores fieri, non autem universæ legis Christi servandæ : anathema sit.*

Canon VIII.—*Si quis dixerit, baptizatos liberos esse ab omnibus sanctæ ecclesiæ præceptis, quæ vel scripta vel tradita sunt, ita ut ea observare non teneantur, nisi se sua sponte illis submittere voluerint : anathema sit.*

Canon IX.—*Si quis dixerit, ita revocandos esse homines ad*

cerning the sacrament of baptism : let him be anathema.

Canon IV.—If any one saith, that the baptism which is even given by heretics in the name of the Father, and of the Son, and of the Holy Ghost, with the intention of doing what the Church doth, is not true baptism : let him be anathema.

Canon V.—If any one saith, that baptism is free, that is, not necessary unto salvation : let him be anathema.

Canon VI.—If any one saith, that one who has been baptized can not, even if he would, lose grace, let him sin ever so much, unless he will not believe : let him be anathema.

Canon VII.—If any one saith, that the baptized are, by baptism itself, *made debtors* but to faith alone, and not to the observance of *the whole law*[1] of Christ : let him be anathema.

Canon VIII.—If any one saith, that the baptized are freed from all the precepts, whether written or transmitted, of holy Church, in such wise that they are not bound to observe them, unless they have chosen of their own accord to submit themselves thereunto : let him be anathema.

Canon IX.—If any one saith, that the remembrance of the baptism

---

[1] Gal. v. 3.

baptismi suscepti memoriam, ut vota omnia, quæ post baptismum fiunt, vi promissionis in baptismo ipso jam factæ, irrita esse intelligant, quasi per ea et fidei, quam professi sunt, detrahatur et ipsi baptismo: anathema sit.

which they have received is so to be recalled unto men, as that they are to understand that all vows made after baptism are void, in virtue of the promise already made in that baptism; as if, by those vows, they both derogated from that faith which they have professed, and from that baptism itself: let him be anathema.

CANON X.—*Si quis dixerit, peccata omnia, quæ post baptismum fiunt, sola recordatione et fide suscepti baptismi vel dimitti, vel venialia fieri: anathema sit.*

CANON X.—If any one saith, that by the sole remembrance and the faith of the baptism which has been received, all sins committed after baptism are either remitted, or made venial: let him be anathema.

CANON XI.—*Si quis dixerit, verum et rite collatum baptismum iterandum esse illi, qui apud infideles fidem Christi negaverit, cum ad pœnitentiam convertitur: anathema sit.*

CANON XI.—If any one saith, that baptism, which was true and rightly conferred, is to be repeated, for him who has denied the faith of Christ amongst Infidels, when he is converted unto penitence: let him be anathema.

CANON XII.—*Si quis dixerit, neminem esse baptizandum, nisi ea ætate, qua Christus baptizatus est, vel in ipso mortis articulo: anathema sit.*

CANON XII.—If any one saith, that no one is to be baptized save at that age at which Christ was baptized, or in the very article of death: let him be anathema.

CANON XIII.—*Si quis dixerit, parvulos, eo quod actum credendi non habent, suscepto baptismo inter fideles computandos non esse, ac propterea, cum ad annos discretionis pervenerint, esse rebaptizandos; aut præstare, omitti eorum baptisma,*

CANON XIII.—If any one saith, that little children, for that they have not actual faith, are not, after having received baptism, to be reckoned amongst the faithful; and that, for this cause, they are to be rebaptized when they have attained to years of discretion: or, that it is

quam eos non actu proprio credentes, baptizari in sola fide ecclesiæ: anathema sit.

CANON XIV.—*Si quis dixerit, hujusmodi parvulos baptizatos, cum adoleverint, interrogandos esse, an ratum habere velint, quod patrini eorum nomine, dum baptizarentur, polliciti sunt; et, ubi se nolle responderint, suo esse arbitrio relinquendos; nec alia interim pœna ad Christianam vitam cogendos, nisi ut ab Eucharistiæ aliorumque sacramentorum perceptione arceantur, donec resipiscant: anathema sit.*

DE CONFIRMATIONE.

CANON I.—*Si quis dixerit, confirmationem baptizatorum otiosam ceremoniam esse, et non potius verum et proprium sacramentum; aut olim nihil aliud fuisse, quam catechesim quamdam, qua adolescentiæ, proximi fidei suæ rationem coram ecclesia exponebant: anathema sit.*

CANON II.—*Si quis dixerit, injurios esse Spiritui Sancto eos, qui sacro confirmationis chris-*

better that the baptism of such be omitted, than that, while not believing by their own act, they should be baptized in the faith alone of the Church: let him be anathema.

CANON XIV.—If any one saith, that those who have been thus baptized when children, are, when they have grown up, to be asked whether they will ratify what their sponsors promised in their names when they were baptized; and that, in case they answer that they will not, they are to be left to their own will; and are not to be compelled meanwhile to a Christian life by any other penalty, save that they be excluded from the participation of the Eucharist, and of the other sacraments, until they repent: let him be anathema.

ON CONFIRMATION.

CANON I.—If any one saith, that the confirmation of those who have been baptized is an idle ceremony, and not rather a true and proper sacrament; or that of old it was nothing more than a kind of catechism, whereby they who were near adolescence gave an account of their faith in the face of the Church: let him be anathema.

CANON II.—If any one saith, that they who ascribe any virtue to the sacred chrism of confirmation, offer

*mati virtutem aliquam tribu-
unt : anathema sit.*

CANON III.—*Si quis dixerit,
sanctæ confirmationis ordinari-
um ministrum non esse solum
episcopum, sed quemvis simplicem sacerdotem : anathema sit.*

an outrage to the Holy Ghost: let
him be anathema.

CANON III.—If any one saith,
that the ordinary minister of holy
confirmation is not the bishop
alone, but any simple priest soever : let him be anathema.

SESSIO DECIMATERTIA,

celebrata die XI. Octobris 1551.

DECRETUM DE SANCTISSIMO EUCHA-
RISTIÆ SACRAMENTO.

CAPUT I.

*De reali præsentiæ Domini nostri Iesu Christi
in sanctissimo Eucharistiæ sacramento.*

*Principio docet sancta syno-
dus, et aperte ac simpliciter
profitetur, in almo sanctæ Eucharistiæ sacramento, post panis,
et vini consecrationem, Dominum nostrum Iesum Christum,
verum Deum atque hominem,
vere, realiter, ac substantialiter
sub specie illarum rerum sensi-
bilium contineri. Neque enim
hæc inter se pugnant, ut ipse
Salvator noster semper ad dexteram Patris in cœlis assideat
juxta modum existendi naturalem, et ut multis nihilominus
aliis in locis sacramentaliter
præsens sua substantia nobis
adsit, ea existendi ratione, quam
etsi verbis exprimere vix possu-*

THIRTEENTH SESSION,

held October 11, 1551.

DECREE CONCERNING THE MOST HOLY
SACRAMENT OF THE EUCHARIST.

CHAPTER I.

*On the real presence of our Lord Jesus Christ
in the most holy sacrament of the Eucharist.*

In the first place, the holy Synod
teaches, and openly and simply professes, that, in the august sacrament
of the holy Eucharist, after the consecration of the bread and wine, our
Lord Jesus Christ, true God and
man, is truly, really, and substantially contained under the species
of those sensible things. For neither are these things mutually repugnant,—that our Saviour himself always sitteth at the right hand
of the Father in heaven, according
to the natural mode of existing, and
that, nevertheless, he be, in many
other places, sacramentally present
to us in his own substance, by a manner of existing, which, though we
can scarcely express it in words, yet

mus, possibilem tamen esse Deo, cogitatione per fidem illustrata assequi possumus, et constantissime credere debemus : ita enim majores nostri omnes, quotquot in vera Christi ecclesia fuerunt, qui de sanctissimo hoc sacramento disseruerunt, apertissime professi sunt, hoc tam admirabile sacramentum in ultima cœna redemptorem nostrum instituisse, cum post panis vinique benedictionem se suum ipsius corpus illis præbere, ac suum sanguinem, disertis et perspicuis verbis testatus est; quæ verba a sanctis evangelistis commemorata et a divo Paulo postea repetita, cum propriam illam et apertissimam significationem præ se ferant, secundum quam a patribus intellecta sunt; indignissimum sane flagitium est, ea a quibusdam contentiosis et pravis hominibus ad fictitios et imaginarios tropos, quibus veritas carnis et sanguinis Christi negatur, contra universum ecclesiæ sensum detorqueri; quæ, tamquam columna et firmamentum veritatis, hæc ab impiis hominibus excogitata commenta velut satanica detestata est, grato semper et memore animo præstantissimum hoc Christi beneficium agnoscens.

can we, by the understanding illuminated by faith, conceive, and we ought most firmly to believe, to be possible unto God : for thus all our forefathers, as many as were in the true Church of Christ, who have treated of this most holy Sacrament, have most openly professed, that our Redeemer instituted this so admirable a sacrament at the last supper, when, after the blessing of the bread and wine, he testified, in express and clear words, that he gave them his own very body, and his own blood, words which, — recorded by the holy Evangelists, and afterwards repeated by Saint Paul, whereas they carry with them that proper and most manifest meaning in which they were understood by the Fathers,—it is indeed a crime the most unworthy that they should be wrested, by certain contentious and wicked men, to fictitious and imaginary tropes, whereby the verity of the flesh and blood of Christ is denied, contrary to the universal sense of the Church, which, as *the pillar and ground of truth*, has detested, as satanical, these inventions devised by impious men; she recognizing, with a mind ever grateful and unforgetting, the most excellent benefit of Christ.

CAPUT II.	**CHAPTER II.**
De ratione institutionis sanctissimi hujus sacramenti.	*On the reason of the institution of this most holy sacrament.*

Ergo Salvator noster, discessurus ex hoc mundo ad Patrem, sacramentum hoc instituit, in quo divitias divini sui erga homines amoris velut effudit, memoriam faciens mirabilium suorum; et in illius sumptione colere nos sui memoriam præcepit, suamque annunciare mortem, donec ipse ad judicandum mundum veniat. Sumi autem voluit sacramentum hoc, tamquam spiritualem animarum cibum, quo alantur, et confortentur viventes vita illius, qui dixit: Qui manducat me, et ipse vivet propter me: et tamquam antidotum, quo liberemur a culpis quotidianis, et a peccatis mortalibus præservemur. Pignus præterea id esse voluit futuræ nostræ gloriæ, et perpetuæ felicitatis, adeoque symbolum unius illius corporis, cujus ipse caput existit, cuique nos, tamquam membra, arctissima fidei, spei et caritatis connexione adstrictos esse voluit, ut idipsum omnes diceremus, nec essent in nobis schismata.

Wherefore, our Saviour, when about to depart out of this world to the Father, instituted this sacrament, in which he poured forth as it were the riches of his divine love towards men, *making a remembrance of his wonderful works;*[1] and he commanded us, in the participation thereof, to venerate his memory, and to *show forth his death until he come*[2] to judge the world. And he would also that this sacrament should be received as the spiritual food of souls, whereby may be fed and strengthened those who live with his life who said, *He that eateth me, the same also shall live by me;*[3] and as an antidote, whereby we may be freed from daily faults, and be preserved from mortal sins. He would, furthermore, have it be a pledge of our glory to come, and everlasting happiness, and thus be a symbol of that one body whereof he is the head, and to which he would fain have us as members be united by the closest bond of faith, hope, and charity, *that we might all speak the same things, and there might be no schisms amongst us.*[4]

---

[1] Psa. cx. 4.
[2] 1 Cor. xi. 26.
[3] John vi. 58.
[4] 1 Cor. i. 10.

CAPUT III.

De excellentia sanctissimæ Eucharistiæ super reliqua sacramenta.

Commune hoc quidem est sanctissimæ Eucharistiæ cum ceteris sacramentis, symbolum esse rei sacræ, et invisibilis gratiæ formam visibilem; verum illud in ea excellens et singulare reperitur, quod reliqua sacramenta tunc primum sanctificandi vim habent, cum quis illis utitur: at in Eucharistia ipse sanctitatis auctor ante usum est. Nondum enim Eucharistiam de manu Domini apostoli susceperant, cum vere tamen ipse affirmaret corpus suum esse, quod præbebat.

Et semper hæc fides in Ecclesia Dei fuit, statim post consecrationem verum Domini nostri corpus verumque ejus sanguinem sub panis et vini specie una cum ipsius anima et divinitate existere; sed corpus quidem sub specie panis et sanguinem sub vini specie ex vi verborum; ipsum autem corpus sub specie vini, et sanguinem sub specie panis, animamque sub utraque, vi naturalis illius connexionis et concomitantiæ, qua partes Christi Domini, qui jam ex mortuis resurrexit non am-

CHAPTER III.

On the excellency of the most holy Eucharist over the rest of the sacraments.

The most holy Eucharist has indeed this in common with the rest of the sacraments, that it is a symbol of a sacred thing, and is a visible form of an invisible grace; but there is found in the Eucharist this excellent and peculiar thing, that the other sacraments have then first the power of sanctifying when one uses them, whereas in the Eucharist, before being used, there is the Author himself of sanctity. For the apostles had not as yet received the Eucharist from the hand of the Lord, when nevertheless himself affirmed with truth that to be his own body which he presented [to them]. And this faith has ever been in the Church of God, that, immediately after the consecration, the veritable body of our Lord, and his veritable blood, together with his soul and divinity, are under the species of bread and wine; but the body indeed under the species of bread, and the blood under the species of wine, by the force of the words; but the body itself under the species of wine, and the blood under the species of bread, and the soul under both, by the force of that natural connection and concomitancy whereby the parts of Christ

plius moriturus, inter se copulantur, divinitatem porro propter admirabilem illam ejus cum corpore et anima hypostaticam unionem. Quapropter verissimum est, tantumdem sub alterutra specie atque sub utraque contineri : totus enim, et integer Christus sub panis specie et sub quavis ipsius speciei parte, totus item sub vini specie et sub ejus partibus existit.

our Lord, *who hath now risen from the dead, to die no more,*[1] are united together ; and the divinity, furthermore, on account of the admirable hypostatical union thereof with his body and soul. Wherefore it is most true, that as much is contained under either species as under both; for Christ whole and entire is under the species of bread, and under any part whatsoever of that species ; likewise the whole (Christ) is under the species of wine, and under the parts thereof.

CAPUT IV.

De Transsubstantiatione.

CHAPTER IV.

On Transubstantiation.

Quoniam autem Christus, redemptor noster, corpus suum id, quod sub specie panis offerebat, vere esse dixit; ideo persuasum semper in Ecclesia Dei fuit, idque nunc denuo sancta hæc synodus declarat, per consecrationem panis et vini conversionem fieri totius substantiæ panis in substantiam corporis Christi Domini nostri, et totius substantiæ vini in substantiam sanguinis ejus : quæ conversio convenienter et proprie a sancta Catholica Ecclesia Transsubstantiatio est appellata.

And because that Christ, our Redeemer, declared that which he offered under the species of bread to be truly his own body, therefore has it ever been a firm belief in the Church of God, and this holy Synod doth now declare it anew, that, by the consecration of the bread and of the wine, a conversion is made of the whole substance of the bread into the substance of the body of Christ our Lord, and of the whole substance of the wine into the substance of his blood ; which conversion is, by the holy Catholic Church, suitably and properly called Transubstantiation.

---

[1] 1 Cor. vi. 9.

Caput V.

De cultu et veneratione huic sanctissimo sacramento exhibenda.

Nullus itaque dubitandi locus relinquitur, quin omnes Christi fideles pro more in Catholica Ecclesia semper recepto latriæ cultum, qui vero Deo debetur, huic sanctissimo sacramento in veneratione exhibeant: neque enim ideo minus est adorandum, quod fuerit a Christo Domino, ut sumatur, institutum: nam illum eumdem Deum præsentem in eo adesse credimus, quem Pater æternus introducens in orbem terrarum dicit: Et adorent eum omnes angeli Dei; quem magi procidentes adoraverunt; quem denique in Galilæa ab apostolis adoratum fuisse, scriptura testatur.

Declarat præterea sancta synodus, pie et religiose admodum in Dei Ecclesiam inductum fuisse hunc morem, ut singulis annis peculiari quodam et festo die præcelsum hoc et venerabile sacramentum singulari veneratione ac solemniter celebraretur, utque in processionibus reverenter et honorifice illud per vias et loca publica circumferretur. Æquissimum est enim, sa-

Chapter V.

On the cult and veneration to be shown to this most holy sacrament.

Wherefore, there is no room left for doubt, that all the faithful of Christ may, according to the custom ever received in the Catholic Church, render in veneration the worship of latria, which is due to the true God, to this most holy sacrament. For not therefore is it the less to be adored on this account, that it was instituted by Christ, the Lord, in order to be received; for we believe that same God to be present therein, of whom the eternal Father, when introducing him into the world, says: *And let all the angels of God adore him;*[1] whom the Magi, *falling down, adored;*[2] who, in fine, as the Scripture testifies, was adored by the apostles in Galilee.

The holy Synod declares, moreover, that very piously and religiously was this custom introduced into the Church, that this sublime and venerable sacrament be, with special veneration and solemnity, celebrated, every year, on a certain day, and that a festival; and that it be borne reverently and with honor in processions through the streets and public places. For it is most just that there be certain appointed

---

[1] Psa. xcvi. 7. [2] Matt. ii. 11.

cros aliquos statutos esse dies, cum Christiani omnes singulari ac rara quadam significatione gratos et memores testentur animos erga communem Dominum et Redemptorem pro tam ineffabili et plane divino beneficio, quo mortis ejus victoria et triumphus repræsentatur. Ac sic quidem oportuit victricem veritatem de mendacio et hæresi triumphum agere, ut ejus adversarii in conspectu tanti splendoris, et in tanta universæ ecclesiæ lætitia positi, vel debilitati et fracti tabescant, vel pudore affecti et confusi aliquando resipiscant.

holy days, whereon all Christians may, with a special and unusual demonstration, testify that their minds are grateful and thankful to their common Lord and Redeemer for so ineffable and truly divine a benefit, whereby the victory and triumph of his death are represented. And so indeed did it behoove victorious truth to celebrate a triumph over falsehood and heresy, that thus her adversaries, at the sight of so much splendor, and in the midst of so great joy of the universal Church, may either *pine away*[1] weakened and broken ; or, touched with shame and confounded, at length repent.

Caput VI.

De asservando sacræ Eucharistiæ sacramento, et ad infirmos deferendo.

Chapter VI.

On reserving the sacrament of the sacred Eucharist, and bearing it to the sick.

Consuetudo asservandi in sacrario sanctam Eucharistiam adeo antiqua est, ut eam sæculum etiam Nicæni Concilii agnoverit. Porro deferri ipsam sacram Eucharistiam ad infirmos, et in hunc usum diligenter in ecclesiis conservari, præterquam quod cum summa æquitate et ratione conjunctum est, tum multis in conciliis præceptum invenitur et vetustissimo Catholicæ Ecclesiæ more est ob-

The custom of reserving the holy Eucharist in the sacrarium is so ancient, that even the age of the Council of Nicæa recognized that usage. Moreover, as to carrying the sacred Eucharist itself to the sick, and carefully reserving it for this purpose in churches, besides that it is exceedingly conformable to equity and reason, it is also found enjoined in numerous councils, and is a very ancient observance of the Catholic Church.

---

[1] Psa. cxi. 10.

servatum. Quare sancta hæc synodus retinendum omnino salutarem hunc et necessarium morem statuit.

Wherefore, this holy Synod ordains that this salutary and necessary custom is to be by all means retained.

CAPUT VII.

De præparatione, quæ adhibenda est, ut digne quis sacram Eucharistiam percipiat.

CHAPTER VII.

On the preparation to be given that one may worthily receive the sacred Eucharist.

Si non decet ad sacras ullas functiones quempiam accedere nisi sancte, certe, quo magis sanctitas et divinitas cœlestis hujus sacramenti viro Christiano comperta est, eo diligentius cavere ille debet, ne absque magna reverentia et sanctitate ad id percipiendum accedat, præsertim cum illa plena formidinis verba apud apostolum legamus: Qui manducat et bibit indigne, judicium sibi manducat et bibit, non dijudicans corpus Domini. Quare communicare volenti revocandum est in memoriam ejus præceptum: Probet autem seipsum homo. Ecclesiastica autem consuetudo declarat, eam probationem necessariam esse, ut nullus sibi conscius peccati mortalis, quantumvis sibi contritus videatur, absque præmissa sacramentali confessione ad sacram Eucharistiam accedere debeat. Quod a Christianis omnibus, etiam ab iis sacer-

If it is unbeseeming for any one to approach to any of the sacred functions, unless he approach holily; assuredly, the more the holiness and divinity of this heavenly sacrament are understood by a Christian, the more diligently ought he to give heed that he approach not to receive it but with great reverence and holiness, especially as we read in the Apostle those words full of terror: *He that eateth and drinketh unworthily, eateth and drinketh judgment to himself.*[1] Wherefore, he who would communicate, ought to recall to mind the precept of the Apostle: *Let a man prove himself.*[2] Now ecclesiastical usage declares that necessary proof to be, that no one, conscious to himself of mortal sin, how contrite soever he may seem to himself, ought to approach to the sacred Eucharist without previous sacramental confession. This the holy Synod hath decreed is to be invariably observed by all Christians,

---

[1] 1 Cor. xi. 29.   [2] 1 Cor. v. 28.

lotibus, quibus ex officio incubu-
erit celebrare, hæc sancta syno-
dus perpetuo servandum esse de-
crevit, modo non desit illis copia
confessoris. Quod si necessitate
urgente sacerdos absque prævia
confessione celebraverit, quampri-
mum confiteatur.

Caput VIII.

De usu admirabilis hujus sacramenti.

Quoad usum autem recte et
sapienter Patres nostri tres ra-
tiones hoc sanctum sacramen-
tum accipiendi distinxerunt.
Quosdam enim docuerunt sacra-
mentaliter dumtaxat id sumere
ut peccatores; alios tantum spi-
ritualiter, illos nimirum, qui vo-
to propositum illum cœlestem pa-
nem edentes, fide viva, quæ per
dilectionem operatur, fructum
ejus et utilitatem sentiunt; ter-
tios porro sacramentaliter simul
et spiritualiter; hi autem sunt,
qui ita se prius probant et in-
struunt, ut vestem nuptialem in-
duti ad divinam hanc mensam
accedant.

In sacramentali autem sump-
tione semper in Ecclesia Dei
mos fuit, ut laici a sacerdoti-
bus communionem acciperent;
sacerdotes autem celebrantes se-
ipsos communicarent, qui mos,

even by those priests on whom it
may be incumbent by their office to
celebrate, provided the opportunity
of a confessor do not fail them;
but if, in an urgent necessity, a
priest should celebrate without previous confession, let him confess as
soon as possible.

Chapter VIII.

On the use of this admirable sacrament.

Now as to the use of this holy
sacrament, our Fathers have rightly and wisely distinguished three
ways of receiving it. For they have
taught that some receive it sacramentally only, to wit, sinners: others spiritually only, those to wit who
eating in desire that heavenly bread
which is set before them, are, by a
lively *faith which worketh by char-*
ity,[1] made sensible of the fruit and
usefulness thereof: whereas the
third [class] receive it both sacramentally and spiritually, and these
are they who so *prove* and prepare
themselves beforehand, as to approach to this divine table *clothed*
with the wedding garment.[2] Now
as to the reception of the sacrament,
it was always the custom in the
Church of God that laymen should
receive the communion from priests;
but that priests when celebrating
should communicate themselves;

---

[1] Gal. v. 6.   [2] Matt. xxii. 11, 12.

*tamquam ex traditione aposto-
lica descendens, jure ac merito
retineri debet.*

*Demum autem paterno affectu
admonet sancta synodus, hortatur, rogat et obsecrat per
viscera misericordiæ Dei nostri, ut omnes et singuli, qui
Christiano nomine censentur,
in hoc unitatis signo, in hoc
vinculo caritatis, in hoc concordiæ symbolo jam tandem aliquando conveniant et concordent,
memoresque tantæ majestatis, et
tam eximii amoris Iesu Christi,
Domini nostri, qui dilectam animam suam in nostræ salutis pretium et carnem suam nobis dedit
ad manducandum, hæc sacra
mysteria corporis et sanguinis
ejus ea fidei constantia et firmitate ea animi devotione, ea pietate et cultu credant et veneren-
tur, ut panem illum supersub-
stantialem frequenter suscipere
possint, et is vere eis sit animæ
vita et perpetua sanitas mentis,
cujus vigore confortati, ex hujus
miseræ peregrinationis itinere
ad cœlestem patriam pervenire
valeant, eumdem panem angelorum, quem modo sub sacris vela-
minibus edunt, absque ullo velamine manducaturi.*

Quoniam autem non est satis

which custom, as coming down from
an apostolic tradition, ought with
justice and reason to be retained.

And finally this holy Synod, with
true fatherly affection, admonishes,
exhorts, begs, and beseeches, through
the bowels of the mercy of our God,
that all and each of those who bear
the Christian name would now at
length agree and be of one mind in
this sign of unity, in this bond of
charity, in this symbol of concord;
and that, mindful of the so great
majesty, and the so exceeding love
of our Lord Jesus Christ, who gave
his own beloved soul as the price of
our salvation, and gave us his own
flesh to eat, they would believe and
venerate these sacred mysteries of
his body and blood, with such constancy and firmness of faith, with
such devotion of soul, with such
piety and worship, as to be able frequently to receive that supersub-
stantial bread, and that it may be to
them truly the life of the soul and
the perpetual health of their mind;
that being invigorated by the
strength thereof, they may, after
the journeying of this miserable
pilgrimage, be able to arrive at
their heavenly country, there to
eat, without any veil, that same
bread of angels which they now
eat under the sacred veils.

But forasmuch as it is not enough

veritatem dicere, nisi detegantur et refellantur errores: placuit sanctæ synodo hos canones subjungere, ut omnes, jam agnita Catholica doctrina, intelligant quoque, quæ ab illis hæreses caveri, vitarique debeant.

to declare the truth, if errors be not laid bare and repudiated, it hath seemed good to the holy Synod to subjoin these canons, that all,—the Catholic doctrine being already recognized,—may now also understand what are the heresies which they ought to guard against and avoid.

DE SACROSANCTO EUCHARISTIÆ SACRAMENTO.

ON THE MOST HOLY SACRAMENT OF THE EUCHARIST.

Canon I.—*Si quis negaverit, in sanctissimæ Eucharistiæ sacramento contineri vere, realiter et substantialiter corpus et sanguinem una cum anima et divinitate Domini nostri Iesu Christi, ac proinde totum Christum; sed dixerit, tantummodo esse in eo, ut in signo, vel figura, aut virtute: anathema sit.*

Canon I.—If any one denieth, that, in the sacrament of the most holy Eucharist, are contained truly, really, and substantially, the body and blood together with the soul and divinity of our Lord Jesus Christ, and consequently the whole Christ; but saith that he is only therein as in a sign, or in figure, or virtue: let him be anathema.

Canon II.—*Si quis dixerit, in sacrosancto Eucharistiæ sacramento remanere substantiam panis et vini una cum corpore et sanguine Domini nostri Iesu Christi, negaveritque mirabilem illam et singularem conversionem totius substantiæ panis in corpus, et totius substantiæ vini in sanguinem, manentibus dumtaxat speciebus panis et vini; quam quidem conversionem Catholica Ecclesia aptissime*

Canon II.—If any one saith, that, in the sacred and holy sacrament of the Eucharist, the substance of the bread and wine remains conjointly with the body and blood of our Lord Jesus Christ, and denieth that wonderful and singular conversion of the whole substance of the bread into the body, and of the whole substance of the wine into the blood—the species only of the bread and wine remaining—which conversion indeed the Catholic

Transsubstantiationem appellat: | Church most aptly calls Transub-
anathema sit. | stantiation : let him be anathema.

CANON III.—*Si quis negaverit,* | CANON III.—If any one denieth,
in venerabili sacramento Eucha- | that, in the venerable sacrament of
ristiæ sub unaquaque specie, et | the Eucharist, the whole Christ is
sub singulis cujusque speciei par- | contained under each species, and
tibus, separatione facta, totum | under every part of each species,
Christum contineri : anathema | when separated : let him be anath-
sit. | ema.

CANON IV.—*Si quis dixerit,* | CANON IV.—If any one saith, that,
peracta consecratione, in admira- | after the consecration is completed,
bili Eucharistiæ sacramento non | the body and blood of our Lord Je-
esse corpus et sanguinem Do- | sus Christ are not in the admirable
mini nostri Iesu Christi, sed | sacrament of the Eucharist, but [are
tantum in usu, dum sumitur, | there] only during the use, whilst it
non autem ante vel post, et in | is being taken, and not either before
hostiis seu particulis consecra- | or after ; and that, in the hosts, or
tis, quæ post communionem re- | consecrated particles, which are re-
servantur vel supersunt, non re- | served or which remain after com-
manere verum corpus Domini : | munion, the true body of the Lord
anathema sit. | remaineth not: let him be anathema.

CANON V.—*Si quis dixerit, vel* | CANON V.—If any one saith,
præcipuum fructum sanctissimæ | either that the principal fruit of
Eucharistiæ esse remissionem | the most holy Eucharist is the re-
peccatorum, vel ex ea non alios | mission of sins, or that other effects
effectus provenire : anathema | do not result therefrom : let him be
sit. | anathema.

CANON VI.—*Si quis dixerit,* | CANON VI.—If any one saith,
in sancto Eucharistiæ sacramen- | that, in the holy sacrament of the
to Christum, unigenitum Dei | Eucharist, Christ, the only-begotten
Filium, non esse cultu latriæ | Son of God, is not to be adored
etiam externo adorandum, at- | with the worship, even external of
que ideo non festiva peculiari | latria ; and is, consequently, neither
celebritate venerandum, neque in | to be venerated with a special fes-
processionibus secundum lauda- | tive solemnity, nor to be solemnly
bilem et universalem Ecclesiæ | borne about in procession, accord-

sanctœ ritum et consuetudinem solemniter circumgestandum, vel non publice, ut adoretur, populo proponendum, et ejus adoratores esse idololatras: anathema sit.

CANON VII.—*Si quis dixerit, non licere sacram Eucharistiam in sacrario reservari, sed statim post consecrationem adstantibus necessario distribuendam; aut non licere, ut illa ad infirmos honorifice deferatur: anathema sit.*

CANON VIII.—*Si quis dixerit, Christum in Eucharistia exhibitum spiritualiter tantum manducari, et non etiam sacramentaliter ac realiter: anathema sit.*

CANON IX.—*Si quis negaverit, omnes et singulos Christi fideles utriusque sexus, cum ad annos discretionis pervenerint, teneri singulis annis, saltem in paschate, ad communicandum, juxta præceptum sanctæ matris Ecclesiæ: anathema sit.*

CANON X.—*Si quis dixerit, non licere sacerdoti celebranti seipsum communicare: anathema sit.*

CANON XI.—*Si quis dixerit, solam fidem esse sufficientem præparationem ad sumendum sanctissimæ Eucharistiæ sacra-*

ing to the laudable and universal rite and custom of holy Church; or, is not to be proposed publicly to the people to be adored, and that the adorers thereof are idolators: let him be anathema.

CANON VII.—If any one saith, that it is not lawful for the sacred Eucharist to be reserved in the *sacrarium,* but that, immediately after consecration, it must necessarily be distributed amongst those present; or, that it is not lawful that it be carried with honor to the sick: let him be anathema.

CANON VIII.—If any one saith, that Christ, given in the Eucharist, is eaten spiritually only, and not also sacramentally and really: let him be anathema.

CANON IX.—If any one denieth, that all and each of Christ's faithful of both sexes are bound, when they have attained to years of discretion, to communicate every year, at least at Easter, in accordance with the precept of holy Mother Church: let him be anathema.

CANON X.—If any one saith, that it is not lawful for the celebrating priest to communicate himself: let him be anathema.

CANON XI.—If any one saith, that faith alone is a sufficient preparation for receiving the sacrament of the most holy Eucharist: let him

mentum : anathema sit. Et, ne tantum sacramentum indigne, atque ideo in mortem et condemnationem sumatur, statuit atque declarat ipsa sancta synodus illis, quos conscientia peccati mortalis gravat, quantumcumque etiam se contritos existiment, habita copia confessoris, necessario præmittendam esse confessionem sacramentalem. Si quis autem contrarium docere, prædicare, vel pertinaciter asserere, seu etiam publice disputando defendere præsumpserit, eo ipso excommunicatus existat.

be anathema. And for fear lest so great a sacrament may be received unworthily, and so unto death and condemnation, this holy Synod ordains and declares, that sacramental confession, when a confessor may be had, is of necessity to be made beforehand, by those whose conscience is burthened with mortal sin, how contrite even soever they may think themselves. But if any one shall presume to teach, preach, or obstinately to assert, or even in public disputation to defend the contrary, he shall be thereupon excommunicated.

SESSIO DECIMAQUARTA,

celebrata die XXV. Nov. 1551.

DE SANCTISSIMIS PŒNITENTIÆ ET EXTREMÆ UNCTIONIS SACRAMENTIS.

CAPUT I.

De necessitate et institutione Sacramenti Pœnitentiæ.

Si ea in regeneratis omnibus gratitudo erga Deum esset, ut justitiam in baptismo, ipsius beneficio et gratia susceptam constanter tuerentur, non fuisset opus, aliud ab ipso baptismo sacramentum ad peccatorum remissionem esse institutum. Quoniam autem Deus, dives in misericordia, cognovit figmentum nos-

FOURTEENTH SESSION,

held November 25, 1551.

ON THE MOST HOLY SACRAMENTS OF PENANCE AND EXTREME UNCTION.

CHAPTER I.

On the necessity, and on the institution of the Sacrament of Penance.

If such, in all the regenerate, were their gratitude towards God, as that they constantly preserved the justice received in baptism by his bounty and grace, there would not have been need for another sacrament, besides that of baptism itself, to be instituted for the remission of sins. But because God, *rich in mercy, knows our frame,*[1] he hath

---

[1] Psa. cii. 14.

trum, illis etiam vitæ remedium contulit, qui se postea in peccati servitutem et dæmonis potestatem tradidissent, sacramentum videlicet pœnitentiæ, quo lapsis post baptismum beneficium mortis Christi applicatur. Fuit quidem pœnitentia universis hominibus, qui se mortali aliquo peccato inquinassent, quovis tempore ad gratiam et justitiam assequendam necessaria, illis etiam, qui baptismi sacramento ablui petivissent, ut, perversitate abjecta et emendata, tantam Dei offensionem cum peccati odio et pio animi dolore detestarentur; unde propheta ait: Convertimini, et agite pœnitentiam ab omnibus iniquitatibus vestris; et non erit vobis in ruinam iniquitas. Dominus etiam dixit: Nisi pœnitentiam egeritis, omnes similiter peribitis. Et princeps apostolorum Petrus peccatoribus baptismo initiandis pœnitentiam commendans dicebat: Pœnitentiam agite, et baptizetur unusquisque vestrum. Porro nec ante adventum Christi pœnitentia erat sacramentum, nec est post adventum illius cuiquam ante baptismum. Dominus autem sacramentum pœnitentiæ tunc præ-

bestowed a remedy of life even on those who may, after baptism, have delivered themselves up to the servitude of sin and the power of the devil,—the sacrament to wit of Penance, by which the benefit of the death of Christ is applied to those who have fallen after baptism. Penitence was indeed at all times necessary, in order to attain to grace and justice, for all men who had defiled themselves by any mortal sin, even for those who begged to be washed by the sacrament of Baptism; that so, their perverseness renounced and amended, they might, with a hatred of sin and a godly sorrow of mind, detest so great an offense of God. Wherefore the prophet says: *Be converted and do penance for all your iniquities, and iniquity shall not be your ruin.*[1] The Lord also said: *Except you do penance, you shall also likewise perish;*[2] and Peter, the prince of the apostles, recommending penitence to sinners who were about to be initiated by baptism, said: *Do penance, and be baptized every one of you.*[3] Nevertheless, neither before the coming of Christ was penitence a sacrament, nor is it such, since his coming, to any previously to baptism. But the Lord then principally instituted the sacrament

---

[1] Ezek. xviii. 30.   [2] Luke xiii. 5.   [3] Acts ii. 38.

cipue instituit, cum a mortuis excitatus insufflavit in discipulos suos, dicens: Accipite Spiritum Sanctum; quorum remiseritis peccata, remittuntur eis, et quorum retinueritis, retenta sunt. Quo tam insigni facto et verbis tam perspicuis potestatem remittendi et retinendi peccata, ad reconciliandos fideles post baptismum lapsos, apostolis et eorum legitimis successoribus fuisse communicatam, universorum patrum consensus semper intellexit, et Novatianos, remittendi potestatem olim pertinaciter negantes, magna ratione Ecclesia Catholica, tamquam hæreticos, explosit atque condemnavit. Quare verissimum hunc illorum verborum Domini sensum sancta hæc synodus probans et recipiens, damnat eorum commentitias interpretationes, qui verba illa ad potestatem prædicandi verbum Dei et Christi evangelium annuntiandi, contra hujusmodi sacramenti institutionem, falso detorquent.

of penance, when, being raised from the dead, he breathed upon his disciples, saying: *Receive ye the Holy Ghost: whose sins you shall forgive, they are forgiven them, and whose sins you shall retain, they are retained.*[1] By which action so signal, and words so clear, the consent of all the Fathers has ever understood that the power of *forgiving and retaining sins* was communicated to the apostles and their lawful successors, for the reconciling of the faithful who have fallen after baptism. And the Catholic Church with great reason repudiated and condemned as heretics the Novatians, who of old obstinately denied that power of forgiving. Wherefore, this holy Synod, approving of and receiving as most true this meaning of those words of our Lord, condemns the fanciful interpretations of those who, in opposition to the institution of this sacrament, falsely wrest those words to the power of preaching the Word of God, and of announcing the Gospel of Christ.

CAPUT II.

De differentia Sacramenti Pœnitentiæ et Baptismi.

Ceterum hoc sacramentum multis rationibus a baptismo differre

CHAPTER II.

On the difference between the Sacrament of Penance and that of Baptism.

For the rest, this sacrament is clearly seen to be different from

---

[1] John xx. 23.

dignoscitur. Nam præterquam quod materia et forma, quibus sacramenti essentia perficitur, longissime dissidet: constat certe, baptismi ministrum judicem esse non oportere, cum Ecclesia in neminem judicium exerceat, qui non prius in ipsam per baptismi januam fuerit ingressus. Quid enim mihi, inquit apostolus, de iis, qui foris sunt, judicare? Secus est de domesticis fidei, quos Christus dominus lavacro baptismi sui corporis membra semel effecit; nam hos, si se postea crimine aliquo contaminaverint, non jam repetito baptismo ablui, cum id in Ecclesia Catholica nulla ratione liceat, sed ante hoc tribunal tamquam reos sisti voluit, ut per sacerdotum sententiam non semel, sed quoties ab admissis peccatis ad ipsum pœnitentes confugerint, possent liberari. Alius præterea est baptismi, et alius pœnitentiæ fructus; per baptismum enim Christum induentes, nova prorsus in illo efficimur creatura, plenam et integram peccatorum omnium remissionem consequentes: ad quam tamen novitatem, et integritatem per sacramentum pœnitentiæ, sine magnis nostris fle-

baptism in many respects: for besides that it is very widely different indeed in matter and form, which constitute the essence of a sacrament, it is beyond doubt certain that the minister of baptism need not be a judge, seeing that the Church exercises judgment on no one who has not entered therein through the gate of baptism. For, *what have I,* saith the apostle, *to do to judge them that are without?*[1] It is otherwise with those who are of *the household of the faith,* whom Christ our Lord has once, by the laver of baptism, made the members of his own body; for such, if they should afterwards have defiled themselves by any crime, he would no longer have them cleansed by a repetition of baptism—that being nowise lawful in the Catholic Church—but be placed as criminals before this tribunal; that, by the sentence of the priests, they might be freed, not once, but as often as, being penitent, they should, from their sins committed, flee thereunto. Furthermore, one is the fruit of baptism, and another that of penance. For, by baptism *putting on Christ,*[2] we are made therein entirely a new creature, obtaining a full and entire remission of all sins; unto which newness and

---

[1] 1 Cor. v. 12.   [2] Gal. iii. 23.

tibus et laboribus, divina id exigente justitia, pervenire nequaquam possumus, ut merito pœnitentia laboriosus quidam baptismus a sanctis patribus dictus fuerit. Est autem hoc sacramentum pœnitentiæ lapsis post baptismum ad salutem necessarium, ut nondum regeneratis ipse baptismus.

entireness, however, we are no ways able to arrive by the sacrament of Penance, without many tears and great labors on our parts, the divine justice demanding this; so that penance has justly been called by holy Fathers a laborious kind of baptism. And this sacrament of Penance is, for those who have fallen after baptism, necessary unto salvation; as baptism itself is for those who have not as yet been regenerated.

CAPUT III.

De partibus et fructibus hujus sacramenti.

CHAPTER III.

On the parts and on the fruit of this sacrament.

Docet præterea sancta synodus, sacramenti pœnitentiæ formam, in qua præcipue ipsius vis sita est, in illis ministri verbis positam esse: Ego te absolvo, etc. Quibus quidem de Ecclesiæ sanctæ more preces quædam laudabiliter adjunguntur; ad ipsius tamen formæ essentiam nequaquam spectant, neque ad ipsius sacramenti administrationem sunt necessariæ. Sunt autem quasi materia hujus sacramenti ipsius pœnitentis actus, nempe contritio, confessio, et satisfactio. Qui quatenus in pœnitente ad integritatem sacramenti, ad plenamque et perfectam peccatorum remissionem ex Dei institutione requiruntur,

The holy Synod doth furthermore teach, that the form of the sacrament of Penance, wherein its force principally consists, is placed in those words of the minister: *I absolve thee,* etc.; to which words indeed certain prayers are, according to the custom of holy Church, laudably joined, which nevertheless by no means regard the essence of that form, neither are they necessary for the administration of the sacrament itself. But the acts of the penitent himself, to wit, contrition, confession, and satisfaction, are as it were the matter of this sacrament. Which acts, inasmuch as they are, by God's institution, required in the penitent for the integrity of the sacrament, and for the full and per-

hac ratione pœnitentiœ partes dicuntur. Sane vero res et effectus hujus sacramenti, quantum ad ejus vim et efficaciam pertinet, reconciliatio est cum Deo, quam interdum in viris piis, et cum devotione hoc sacramentum percipientibus, conscientiœ pax ac serenitas cum vehementi spiritus consolatione consequi solet. Hœc de partibus et effectu hujus sacramenti sancta synodus tradens, simul eorum sententias damnat, qui pœnitentiœ partes incussos conscientiœ terrores et fidem esse contendunt.

fect remission of sins, are for this reason called the parts of penance. But the thing signified indeed, and the effect of this sacrament, as far as regards its force and efficacy, is reconciliation with God, which sometimes, in persons who are pious and who receive this sacrament with devotion, is. wont to be followed by peace and serenity of conscience, with exceeding consolation of spirit. The holy Synod, whilst delivering these things touching the parts and the effect of this sacrament, condemns at the same time the opinions of those who contend that the terrors which agitate the conscience, and faith, are the parts of penance.

CAPUT IV.
De Contritione.

CHAPTER IV.
On Contrition.

Contritio, quœ primum locum inter dictos pœnitentis actus habet, animi dolor ac detestatio est de peccato commisso, cum proposito non peccandi de cetero. Fuit autem quovis tempore ad impetrandam veniam peccatorum hic contritionis motus necessarius, et in homine post baptismum lapso ita demum prœparat ad remissionem peccatorum, si cum fiducia divinœ misericordiœ et voto prœstandi reliqua conjunctus sit, quœ ad rite suscipiendum

Contrition, which holds the first place amongst the aforesaid acts of the penitent, is a sorrow of mind, and a detestation for sin committed, with the purpose of not sinning for the future. This movement of contrition was at all times necessary for obtaining the pardon of sins; and, in one who has fallen after baptism, it then at length prepares for the remission of sins, when it is united with confidence in the divine mercy, and with the desire of performing the other things which are required for rightly receiving this sac

hoc sacramentum requiruntur. Declarat igitur sancta synodus, hanc contritionem non solum cessationem a peccato et vitæ novæ propositum et inchoationem, sed veteris etiam odium continere, juxta illud : Projicite a vobis omnes iniquitates vestras, in quibus prævaricati estis, et facite vobis cor novum et spiritum novum. Et certe, qui illos sanctorum clamores consideraverit : Tibi soli peccavi, et malum coram te feci ; Laboravi in gemitu meo, lavabo per singulas noctes lectum meum. Recogitabo tibi omnes annos meos in amaritudine animæ meæ ; et alios hujus generis, facile intelliget, eos ex vehementi quodam anteactæ vitæ odio et ingenti peccatorum detestatione manasse. Docet præterea, etsi contritionem hanc aliquando caritate perfectam esse contingat, hominemque Deo reconciliare, priusquam hoc sacramentum actu suscipiatur, ipsam nihilominus reconciliationem ipsi contritioni sine sacramenti voto, quod in illa includitur, non esse adscribendam. Illam vero contritionem imperfectam, quæ attritio dicitur,

rament. Wherefore the holy Synod declares, that this contrition contains not only a cessation from sin, and the purpose and the beginning of a new life, but also a hatred of the old, agreeably to that saying : *Cast away from you all your iniquities, wherein you have transgressed, and make to yourselves a new heart and a new spirit.*[1] And assuredly he who has considered those cries of the saints : *To thee only have I sinned, and have done evil before thee ;*[2] *I have labored in my groaning, every night I will wash my bed ;*[3] *I will recount to thee all my years, in the bitterness of my soul ;*[4] and others of this kind, will easily understand that they flowed from a certain vehement hatred of their past life, and from an exceeding detestation of sins. The Synod teaches moreover, that, although it sometimes happens that this contrition is perfect through charity, and reconciles man with God before this sacrament be actually received, the said reconciliation, nevertheless, is not to be ascribed to that contrition, independently of the desire of the sacrament which is included therein. And as to that imperfect contrition, which is called attrition, because

---

[1] Ezek. xviii. 31.
[2] Psa. l. 6.
[3] Psa. vi. 7.
[4] Isa. xxxviii. 15.

quoniam vel ex turpitudinis peccati consideratione vel ex gehennæ et pœnarum metu communiter concipitur, si voluntatem peccandi excludat cum spe veniæ, declarat non solum non facere hominem hypocritam et magis peccatorem, verum etiam donum Dei esse et Spiritus Sancti impulsum, non adhuc quidem inhabitantis, sed tantum moventis, quo pœnitens adjutus viam sibi ad justitiam parat. Et quamvis sine sacramento pœnitentiæ per se ad justificationem perducere peccatorem nequeat, tamen eum ad Dei gratiam in sacramento pœnitentiæ impetrandam disponit: hoc enim timore utiliter concussi Ninivitæ, ad Ionæ prædicationem, plenam terroribus pœnitentiam egerunt et misericordiam a Domino impetrarunt. Quamobrem falso quidam calumniantur Catholicos scriptores, quasi tradiderint, sacramentum pœnitentiæ absque bono motu suscipientium gratiam conferre, quod numquam Ecclesia Dei docuit, neque sensit; sed et falso docent, contritionem esse extortam et coactam, non liberam et voluntariam.

that it is commonly conceived either from the consideration of the turpitude of sin, or from the fear of hell and of punishment, it declares that if, with the hope of pardon, it exclude the wish to sin, it not only does not make a man a hypocrite, and a greater sinner, but that it is even a gift of God, and an impulse of the Holy Ghost,—who does not indeed as yet dwell in the penitent, but only moves him,—whereby the penitent being assisted prepares a way for himself unto justice. And although this [attrition] can not of itself, without the sacrament of Penance, conduct the sinner to justification, yet does it dispose him to obtain the grace of God in the sacrament of Penance. For, smitten profitably with this fear, the Ninivites, at the preaching of Jonas, did fearful penance, and obtained mercy from the Lord. Wherefore falsely do some calumniate Catholic writers, as if they had maintained that the sacrament of Penance confers grace without any good motion on the part of those who receive it: a thing which the Church of God never taught, or thought; and falsely also do they assert that contrition is extorted and forced, not free and voluntary.

De Confessione.

Ex institutione sacramenti pœnitentiæ jam explicata universa Ecclesia semper intellexit, institutam etiam esse a Domino integram peccatorum confessionem, et omnibus post baptismum lapsis jure divino necessariam existere, quia Dominus noster Iesus Christus, e terris ascensurus ad cœlos, sacerdotes sui ipsius vicarios reliquit, tamquam præsides et judices, ad quos omnia mortalia crimina deferantur, in quæ Christi fideles ceciderint, quo, pro potestate clavium, remissionis aut retentionis peccatorum sententiam pronuncient. Constat enim, sacerdotes judicium hoc incognita causa exercere non potuisse, nec æquitatem quidem illos in pœnis injungendis servare potuisse, si in genere tumtaxat, et non potius in specie, ac sigillatim sua ipsi peccata declarassent. Ex his colligitur, oportere a pœnitentibus omnia peccata mortalia, quorum post diligentem sui discussionem conscientiam habent, in confessione recenseri, etiam si occultissima illa sint et tantum adversus duo ultima decalogi præcepta commissa, quæ nonnunquam ani-

CHAPTER V

On Confession.

From the institution of the sacrament of Penance, as already explained, the universal Church has always understood that the entire confession of sins was also instituted by the Lord, and is of divine right necessary for all who have fallen after baptism; because that our Lord Jesus Christ, when about to ascend from earth to heaven, left priests his own vicars, as presidents and judges, unto whom all the mortal crimes, into which the faithful of Christ may have fallen, should be carried, in order that, in accordance with the power of the keys, they may pronounce the sentence of forgiveness or retention of sins. For it is manifest that priests could not have exercised this judgment without knowledge of the cause; neither indeed could they have observed equity in enjoining punishments, if the said faithful should have declared their sins in general only, and not rather specifically, and one by one. Whence it is gathered that all the mortal sins, of which, after a diligent examination of themselves, they are conscious, must needs be by penitents enumerated in confession, even though those sins be most hidden, and committed only against the two last precepts of the

mum gravius sauciant, et periculosiora sunt iis, quæ in manifesto admittuntur. Nam venialia, quibus a gratia Dei non excludimur et in quæ frequentius labimur, quamquam recte et utiliter citraque omnem præsumptionem in confessione dicantur, quod piorum hominum usus demonstrat, taceri tamen citra culpam multisque aliis remediis expiari possunt. Verum, cum universa mortalia peccata, etiam cogitationis, homines iræ filios et Dei inimicos reddant, necessum est, omnium etiam veniam cum aperta et verecunda confessione, a Deo quærere. Itaque dum omnia, quæ memoriæ occurrunt, peccata Christi fideles confiteri student, procul dubio omnia divinæ misericordiæ ignoscenda exponunt. Qui vero secus faciunt et scienter aliqua retinent, nihil divinæ bonitati per sacerdotem remittendum proponunt. Si enim erubescat ægrotus vulnus medico detegere, quod ignorat, medicina non curat. Colligitur præterea, etiam eas circumstantias in confessione explicandas esse, quæ speciem peccati mutant, quod sine illis peccata ipsa neque a pœni-

decalogue,—sins which sometimes wound the soul more grievously, and are more dangerous, than those which are committed outwardly. For venial sins, whereby we are not excluded from the grace of God, and into which we fall more frequently, although they be rightly and profitably, and without any presumption, declared in confession, as the custom of pious persons demonstrates, yet may they be omitted without guilt, and be expiated by many other remedies. But, whereas all mortal sins, even those of thought, render men *children of wrath*,[1] and enemies of God, it is necessary to seek also for the pardon of them all from God, with an open and modest confession. Wherefore, while the faithful of Christ are careful to confess all the sins which occur to their memory, they without doubt lay them all bare before the mercy of God to be pardoned: whereas they who act otherwise, and knowingly keep back certain sins, such set nothing before the divine bounty to be forgiven through the priest; for if the sick be ashamed to show his wound to the physician, his medical art cures not that which it knows not of. We gather, furthermore, that those circumstances which change the spe-

---

[1] Ephes. ii. 3.

tentibus integre exponantur, nec judicibus innotescant; et fieri nequeat, ut de gravitate criminum recte censere possint et pœnam, quam oportet, pro illis pœnitentibus imponere. Unde alienum a ratione est docere, circumstantias has ab hominibus otiosis excogitatas fuisse, aut unam tantum circumstantiam confitendam esse, nempe peccasse in fratrem. Sed et impium est, confessionem, quæ hac ratione fieri præcipitur, impossibilem dicere, aut carnificinam illam conscientiarum appellare; constat enim, nihil aliud in Ecclesia a pœnitentibus exigi, quam ut, postquam quisque diligentius se excusserit et conscientiæ suæ sinus omnes et latebras exploraverit, ea peccata confiteatur, quibus se Dominum et Deum suum mortaliter offendissi meminerit; reliqua autem peccata, quæ diligenter cogitanti non occurrunt, in universum eadem confessione inclusa esse intelliguntur; pro quibus fideliter cum propheta dicimus: Ab occultis meis munda me, Domine. Ipsa vero hujusmodi confessionis difficultas ac peccata detegendi verecundia gravis quidem vi-

cies of the sin are also to be explained in confession, because that, without them, the sins themselves are neither entirely set forth by the penitents, nor are they known clearly to the judges; and it can not be that they can estimate rightly the grievousness of the crimes, and impose on the penitents the punishment which ought to be inflicted on account of them. Whence it is unreasonable to teach that these circumstances have been invented by idle men; or that one circumstance only is to be confessed, to wit, that one has sinned against a brother. But it is also impious to assert, that confession, enjoined to be made in this manner, is impossible, or to call it a slaughter-house of consciences; for it is certain, that in the Church nothing else is required of penitents, but that, after each has examined himself diligently, and searched all the folds and recesses of his conscience, he confess those sins by which he shall remember that he has mortally offended his Lord and God: whilst the other sins, which do not occur to him after diligent thought, are understood to be included as a whole in that same confession; for which sins we confidently say with the prophet: *From my secret sins cleanse me, O Lord.*[1] Now, the

---

[1] Psa. xviii. 13.

deri posset, nisi tot tantisque commodis et consolationibus levaretur, quæ omnibus digne ad hoc sacramentum accedentibus per absolutionem certissime conferuntur. Ceterum, quoad modum confitendi secreto apud solum sacerdotem, etsi Christus non vetuerit, quin aliquis in vindictam suorum scelerum et sui humiliationem, cum ob aliorum exemplum, tum ob Ecclesiæ offensæ ædificationem delicta sua publice confiteri possit: non est tamen hoc divino præcepto mandatum, nec satis consulte humana aliqua lege præciperetur, ut delicta, præsertim secreta, publica essent confessione aperienda; unde cum a sanctissimis et antiquissimis patribus magno unanimique consensu secreta confessio sacramentalis, qua ab initio Ecclesia sancta usa est et modo etiam utitur, fuerit semper commendata, manifeste refellitur inanis eorum calumnia, qui eam a divino mandato alienam et inventum humanum esse, atque a patribus in concilio lateranensi congregatis initium habuisse, docere non verentur; neque enim per lateranense concilium Ecclesia statuit, ut Christi fideles confiterentur,

very difficulty of a confession like this, and the shame of making known one's sins, might indeed seem a grievous thing, were it not alleviated by the so many and so great advantages and consolations, which are most assuredly bestowed by absolution upon all who worthily approach to this sacrament. For the rest, as to the manner of confessing secretly to a priest alone, although Christ has not forbidden that a person may,—in punishment of his sins, and for his own humiliation, as well for an example to others as for the edification of the Church that has been scandalized, —confess his sins publicly, nevertheless this is not commanded by a divine precept; neither would it be very prudent to enjoin by any human law, that sins, especially such as are secret, should be made known by a public confession. Wherefore, whereas the secret sacramental confession, which was in use from the beginning in holy Church, and is still also in use, has always been commended by the most holy and the most ancient Fathers with a great and unanimous consent, the vain calumny of those is manifestly refuted, who are not ashamed to teach that confession is alien from the divine command, and is a human invention, and that it took its

quod jure divino necessarium et institutum esse intellexerat, sed ut præceptum confessionis, saltem semel in anno, ab omnibus et singulis, cum ad annos discretionis pervenissent, impleretur; unde jam in universa Ecclesia cum ingenti animarum fidelium fructu observatur mos ille salutaris confitendi sacro illo et maxime acceptabili tempore quadragesimæ : quem morem hæc sancta synodus maxime probat et amplectitur, tamquam pium et merito retinendum.

rise from the Fathers assembled in the Council of Lateran : for the Church did not, through the Council of Lateran, ordain that the faithful of Christ should confess,—a thing which it knew to be necessary, and to be instituted of divine right,—but that the precept of confession should be complied with, at least once a year, by all and each, when they have attained to years of discretion. Whence, throughout the whole Church, the salutary custom is, to the great benefit of the souls of the faithful, now observed, of confessing at that most sacred and most acceptable time of Lent,—a custom which this holy Synod most highly approves of and embraces, as pious and worthy of being retained.

Caput VI.

De ministro hujus sacramenti et Absolutione.

Circa ministrum autem hujus sacramenti declarat sancta synodus, falsas esse et a veritate evangelii penitus alienas doctrinas omnes, quæ ad alios quosvis homines, præter episcopos et sacerdotes clavium ministerium perniciose extendunt, putantes verba illa Domini : Quæcumque alligaveritis super terram, erunt alligata et in cælo, et quæcumque solveritis

Chapter VI.

On the ministry of this sacrament, and on Absolution.

But, as regards the minister of this sacrament, the holy Synod declares all those doctrines to be false, and utterly alien from the truth of the Gospel, which perniciously extend the ministry of the keys to any others soever besides bishops and priests ; imagining, contrary to the institution of this sacrament, that those words of our Lord, *Whatsoever you shall bind upon earth, shall be bound also in heaven, and*

super terram, erunt soluta et in cœlo ; et : Quorum remiseritis peccata, remittuntur eis, et quorum retinueritis, retenta sunt : ad omnes Christi fideles, indifferenter et promiscue, contra institutionem hujus sacramenti ita fuisse dicta, ut quivis potestatem habeat remittendi peccata, publica quidem per correptionem, si correptus acquieverit, secreta vero per spontaneam confessionem cuicumque factam. Docet quoque, etiam sacerdotes, qui peccato mortali tenentur, per virtutem Spiritus Sancti in ordinatione collatam, tamquam Christi ministros, functionem remittendi peccata exercere, eosque prave sentire, qui in malis sacerdotibus hanc potestatem non esse contendunt. Quamvis autem absolutio sacerdotis alieni beneficii sit dispensatio, tamen non est solum nudum ministerium vel annuntiandi evangelium, vel declarandi remissa esse peccata ; sed ad instar actus judicialis, quo ab ipso, velut a judice, sententia pronuntiatur. Atque ideo non debet pœnitens adeo sibi de sua ipsius fide blandiri, ut, etiam si nulla illi adsit contritio, aut sacerdoti animus se-

whatsoever you shall loose upon earth shall be loosed also in heaven,[1] and, Whose sins you shall forgive, they are forgiven them, and whose sins you shall retain, they are retained,[2] were in such wise addressed to all the faithful of Christ indifferently and indiscriminately, as that every one has the power of forgiving sins,—public sins to wit by rebuke, provided he that is rebuked shall acquiesce, and secret sins by a voluntary confession made to any individual whatsoever. It also teaches, that even priests, who are in mortal sin, exercise, through the virtue of the Holy Ghost which was bestowed in ordination, the office of forgiving sins, as the ministers of Christ; and that their sentiment is erroneous who contend that this power exists not in bad priests. But although the absolution of the priest is the dispensation of another's bounty, yet is it not a bare ministry only, whether of announcing the Gospel, or of declaring that sins are forgiven, but is after the manner of a judicial act, whereby sentence is pronounced by the priest as by a judge; and therefore the penitent ought not so to confide in his own personal faith as to think that,— even though there be no contrition on his part, or no intention on the

---

[1] Matt. xviii. 18.   [2] John xx. 23.

rio agendi et vere absolvendi desit, putet tamen se propter suam solam fidem vere et coram Deo esse absolutum. Nec enim fides sine pœnitentia remissionem ullam peccatorum præstaret; nec is esset nisi salutis suæ negligentissimus, qui sacerdotem joco se absolventem cognosceret, et non alium serio agentem sedulo requireret.

part of the priest of acting seriously and absolving truly,—he is nevertheless truly and in God's sight absolved, on account of his faith alone. For neither would faith without penance bestow any remission of sins, nor would he be otherwise than most careless of his own salvation, who, knowing that a priest but absolved him in jest, should not carefully seek for another who would act in earnest.

Caput VII.

De casuum reservatione.

Quoniam igitur natura et ratio judicii illud exposcit, ut sententia in subditos dumtaxat feratur, persuasum semper in Ecclesia Dei fuit, et verissimum esse synodus hæc confirmat, nullius momenti absolutionem eam esse debere, quam sacerdos in eum profert, in quem ordinariam aut subdelegatam non habet jurisdictionem. Magnopere vero ad Christiani populi disciplinam pertinere sanctissimis patribus nostris visum est, ut atrociora quædam et graviora crimina non a quibusvis, sed a summis dumtaxat sacerdotibus absolverentur; unde merito Pontifices maximi pro suprema potestate sibi in Ecclesia universa tradita causas aliquas crimi-

Chapter VII.

On the reservation of cases.

Wherefore, since the nature and order of a judgment require this, that sentence be passed only on those subject [to that judicature], it has ever been firmly held in the Church of God, and this Synod ratifies it as a thing most true, that the absolution, which a priest pronounces upon one over whom he has not either an ordinary or a delegated jurisdiction, ought to be of no weight whatever. And it hath seemed to our most holy Fathers to be of great importance to the discipline of the Christian people, that certain more atrocious and more heinous crimes should be absolved, not by all priests, but only by the highest priests; whence the Sovereign Pontiffs, in virtue of the supreme power delivered to them in

num graviores suo potuerunt peculiari judicio reservare. Neque dubitandum esset, quando omnia, quæ a Deo sunt, ordinata sunt, quin hoc idem episcopis omnibus in sua cuique diœcesi, in ædificationem tamen, non in destructionem liceat, pro illis in subditos tradita supra reliquos inferiores sacerdotes auctoritate, præsertim quoad illa, quibus excommunicationis censura annexa est. Hanc autem delictorum reservationem consonum est divinæ auctoritati non tantum in externa politia, sed etiam coram Deo vim habere. Veruntamen pie admodum, ne hac ipsa occasione aliquis pereat, in eadem Ecclesia Dei custoditum semper fuit, ut nulla sit reservatio in articulo mortis; atque ideo omnes sacerdotes quoslibet pœnitentes a quibusvis peccatis et censuris absolvere possunt; extra quem articulum sacerdotes cum nihil possint in casibus reservatis, id unum pœnitentibus persuadere nitantur, ut ad superiores et legitimos judices pro beneficio absolutionis accedant.

the universal Church, were deservedly able to reserve, for their special judgment, certain more grievous cases of crimes. Neither is it to be doubted,—seeing that all things, that are from God, are well ordered,—but that this same may be lawfully done by all bishops, each in his own diocese, unto edification, however, not unto destruction, in virtue of the authority, above [that of] other inferior priests, delivered to them over their subjects, especially as regards those crimes to which the censure of excommunication is annexed. But it is consonant to the divine authority, that this reservation of cases have effect, not merely in external polity, but also in God's sight. Nevertheless, for fear lest any may perish on this account, it has always been very piously observed in the said Church of God, that there be no reservation at the point of death, and that therefore all priests may absolve all penitents whatsoever from every kind of sins and censures whatever : and as, save at that point of death, priests have no power in reserved cases, let this alone be their endeavor, to persuade penitents to repair to superior and lawful judges for the benefit of absolution.

CAPUT VIII.

De Satisfactionis necessitate et fructu.

Demum quoad satisfactionem, quæ ex omnibus pœnitentiæ partibus, quemadmodum a patribus nostris Christiano populo fuit perpetuo tempore commendata, ita una maxime nostra ætate summo pietatis prætextu impugnatur ab iis, qui speciem pietatis habent, virtutem autem ejus abnegarunt: sancta synodus declarat, falsum omnino esse et a verbo Dei alienum, culpam a Domino nunquam remitti, quin universa etiam pœna condonetur. Perspicua enim et illustria in sacris litteris exempla reperiuntur, quibus, præter divinam traditionem, hic error quam manifestissime revincitur. Sane et divinæ justitiæ ratio exigere videtur, ut aliter ab eo in gratiam recipiantur, qui ante baptismum per ignorantiam deliquerint; aliter vero qui semel a peccati et dæmonis servitute liberati, et accepto Spiritus Sancti dono, scientes templum Dei violare et Spiritum Sanctum contristare non formidaverint. Et divinam clementiam decet, ne ita nobis absque ulla

CHAPTER VIII.

On the necessity and on the fruit of Satisfaction.

Finally, as regards satisfaction,—which as it is, of all the parts of penance, that which has been at all times recommended to the Christian people by our Fathers, so is it the one especially which in our age is, under the loftiest pretext of piety, impugned by those who have *an appearance of godliness, but have denied the power thereof*,[1]—the holy Synod declares, that it is wholly false, and alien from the Word of God, that the guilt is never forgiven by the Lord, without the whole punishment also being therewith pardoned. For clear and illustrious examples are found in the sacred writings, whereby, besides by divine tradition, this error is refuted in the plainest manner possible. And truly the nature of divine justice seems to demand, that they, who through ignorance have sinned before baptism, be received into grace in one manner; and in another those who, after having been freed from the servitude of sin and of the devil, and after having received the gift of the Holy Ghost, have not feared, knowingly *to violate the temple of God*,[2] *and to grieve the Holy Spirit*.[3] And it

---

[1] 2 Tim. iii. 5. [2] 1 Cor. iii. 17. [3] Ephes. iv. 30.

satisfactione peccata dimittuntur, ut, occasione accepta, peccata leviora putantes, velut injurii et contumeliosi Spiritui Sancto in graviora labamur, thesaurizantes nobis iram in die iræ. Procul dubio enim magnopere a peccato revocant et quasi fræno quodam cœrcent hæ satisfactoriæ pœnæ, cautioresque et vigilantiores in futurum pœnitentes efficiunt; medentur quoque peccatorum reliquiis et vitiosos habitus male vivendo comparatos contrariis virtutum actionibus tollunt. Neque vero securior ulla via in Ecclesia Dei umquam existimata fuit ad amovendam imminentem a Domino pœnam, quam ut hæc pœnitentiæ opera homines cum vero animi dolore frequentent. Accedit ad hæc, quod, dum satisfaciendo patimur pro peccatis, Christo Iesu, qui pro peccatis nostris satisfecit, ex quo omnis nostra sufficientia est, conformes efficimur, certissimam quoque inde arrham habentes, quod, si compatimur et conglorificabimur. Neque vero ita nostra est satisfactio hæc, quam pro peccatis nostris exsolvimus, ut

beseems the divine clemency, that sins be not in such wise pardoned us without any satisfaction, as that, taking occasion therefrom, thinking sins less grievous, we, offering as it were an insult and an *outrage to the Holy Ghost*,[1] should fall into more grievous sins, *treasuring up wrath against the day of wrath*.[2] For, doubtless, these satisfactory punishments greatly recall from sin, and check as it were with a bridle, and make penitents more cautious and watchful for the future; they are also remedies for the remains of sin, and, by acts of the opposite virtues, they remove the habits acquired by evil living. Neither indeed was there ever in the Church of God any way accounted surer to turn aside the impending chastisement of the Lord, than that men should, with true sorrow of mind, practice these works of penitence. Add to these things, that, whilst we thus, by making satisfaction, suffer for our sins, we are made conformable to Jesus Christ, who satisfied for our sins, from whom all our *sufficiency is;*[3] having also thereby a most sure pledge, that *if we suffer with him, we shall also be glorified with him*.[4] But neither is this satisfaction, which we

---

[1] Heb. x. 29.
[2] Rom. ii. 4.
[3] 2 Cor. iii. 5.
[4] Rom. viii. 17.

non sit per Christum Iesum, nam qui ex nobis, tamquam ex nobis, nihil possumus, eo cooperante, qui nos confortat, omnia possumus. Ita non habet homo, unde glorietur; sed omnis gloriatio nostra in Christo est; in quo vivimus, in quo meremur, in quo satisfacimus, facientes fructus dignos pœnitentiæ, qui ex illo vim habent, ab illo offeruntur Patri, et per illum acceptantur a Patre. Debent ergo sacerdotes Domini, quantum Spiritus et prudentia suggesserit, pro qualitate criminum et pœnitentium facultate, salutares et convenientes satisfactiones injungere; ne, si forte peccatis conniveant et indulgentius cum pœnitentibus agant, levissima quædam opera pro gravissimis delictis injungendo, alienorum peccatorum participes efficiantur. Habeant autem præ oculis, ut satisfactio, quam imponunt, non sit tantum ad novæ vitæ custodiam et infirmitatis medicamentum, sed etiam ad præteritorum peccatorum vindictam et castigationem: nam claves sacerdotum, non ad solvendum dumtaxat, sed et ad ligandum concessas etiam antiqui patres

discharge for our sins, so our own, as not to be through Jesus Christ. For we who can do nothing of ourselves, as of ourselves, can do all things, he co-operating, who strengthens us. Thus, man has not wherein to glory, but all our glorying is in Christ: in whom we live; in whom we merit; in whom we satisfy; *bringing forth fruits worthy of penance,*[1] which from him have their efficacy; by him are offered to the Father; and through him are accepted by the Father. Therefore the priests of the Lord ought, as far as the Spirit and prudence shall suggest, to enjoin salutary and suitable satisfactions, according to the quality of the crimes and the ability of the penitent; lest, if haply they connive at sins, and deal too indulgently with penitents, by enjoining certain very light works for very grievous crimes, they be made partakers of other men's sins. But let them have in view, that the satisfaction, which they impose, be not only for the preservation of a new life and a medicine of infirmity, but also for the avenging and punishing of past sins. For the ancient Fathers likewise both believe and teach, that the keys of the priests were given, not to *loose* only, but also to *bind.*[2] But not therefore

---

[1] Matt. iii. 8.

[2] Matt. xvi. 19; John xx. 23.

et credunt et docent. Nec prop-
terea existimarunt, sacramentum
pœnitentiæ esse forum iræ vel
pœnarum, sicut nemo umquam
Catholicus sensit, ex hujusmodi
nostris satisfactionibus vim me-
riti et satisfactionis Domini nos-
tri Iesu Christi vel obscurari vel
aliqua ex parte imminui; quod
dum novatores intelligere nolunt,
ita optimam pœnitentiam novam
vitam esse docent, ut omnem satis-
factionis vim et usum tollant.

did they imagine that the sacrament
of Penance is a tribunal of wrath or
of punishments; even as no Catholic ever thought, that, by this kind
of satisfaction on our parts, the efficacy of the merit and of the satisfaction of our Lord Jesus Christ is
either obscured or in any way les-
sened : which when the innovators
seek to understand, they in such wise
maintain a new life to be the best
penance, as to take away the entire
efficacy and use of satisfaction.

Caput IX.

De operibus Satisfactionis.

Docet prœterea, tantam esse
divinæ munificentiæ largitatem,
ut non solum pœnis sponte a
nobis pro vindicando peccato
susceptis, aut sacerdotis arbitrio
pro mensura delicti impositis,
sed etiam, quod maximum amo-
ris argumentum est, tempo-
ralibus flagellis a Deo in-
flictis et a nobis patienter to-
leratis apud Deum Patrem
per Christum Iesum satisfacere
valeamus.

Chapter IX.

On works of Satisfaction.

The Synod teaches furthermore,
that so great is the liberality of the
divine munificence, that we are able
through Jesus Christ to make satisfaction to God the Father, not only
by punishments voluntarily undertaken of ourselves for the punishment
of sin, or by those imposed at the discretion of the priest according to the
measure of our delinquency, but
also, which is a very great proof of
love, by the temporal scourges inflicted of God, and borne patiently by us.

DOCTRINA DE SACRAMENTO EXTREMÆ
UNCTIONIS.

ON THE SACRAMENT OF EXTREME
UNCTION.

Visum est autem sanctæ synodo,
prœcedenti doctrinæ de pœnitentia
adjungere ea, quæ sequuntur de sa-

It hath also seemed good to the
holy Synod, to subjoin to the preceding doctrine on Penance, the fol-

cramento extremæ unctionis, quod non modo pœnitentiæ, sed et totius Christianæ vitæ, quæ perpetua pœnitentia esse debet, consummativum existimatum est a Patribus. Primum itaque circa illius institutionem declarat et docet, quod clementissimus Redemptor noster, qui servis suis quovis tempore voluit de salutaribus remediis adversus omnia omnium hostium tela esse prospectum, quemadmodum auxilia maxima in sacramentis aliis præparavit, quibus Christiani conservare se integros, dum viverent, ab omni graviori spiritus incommodo possint: ita extremæ unctionis sacramento finem vitæ, tamquam firmissimo quodam præsidio, munivit. Nam etsi adversarius noster occasiones per omnem vitam quærat et captet, ut devorare animas nostras quoquo modo possit: nullum tamen tempus est, quo vehementius ille omnes suæ versutiæ nervos intendat ad perdendos nos penitus, et a fiducia etiam, si possit, divinæ misericordiæ deturbandos, quam cum impendere nobis exitum vitæ prospicit.

lowing on the sacrament of Extreme Unction, which by the Fathers was regarded as being the completion, not only of penance, but also of the whole Christian life, which ought to be a perpetual penance. First, therefore, as regards its institution, it declares and teaches, that our most gracious Redeemer,—who would have his servants at all times provided with salutary remedies against all the weapons of all their enemies,—as, in the other sacraments, he prepared the greatest aids, whereby, during life, Christians may preserve themselves whole from every more grievous spiritual evil, so did he guard the close of life, by the sacrament of Extreme Unction, as with a most firm defense. For though *our adversary* seeks and seizes opportunities, all our life long, to be able in any way *to devour*[1] our souls; yet is there no time wherein he strains more vehemently all the powers of his craft to ruin us utterly, and, if he can possibly, to make us fall even from trust in the mercy of God, than when he perceives the end of our life to be at hand.

---

[1] 1 Pet. v. 8.

Caput I.

De institutione sacramenti Extremæ Unctionis.

Instituta est autem sacra unctio infirmorum tamquam vere et proprie sacramentum novi testamenti, a Christo Domino nostro apud Marcum quidem insinuatum, per Iacobum autem apostolum ac Domini fratrem, fidelibus commendatum ac promulgatum. Infirmatur, inquit, quis in vobis? inducat presbyteros Ecclesiæ, et orent super eum, ungentes eum oleo in nomine Domini; et oratio fidei salvabit infirmum; et alleviabit eum Dominus; et si in peccatis sit, dimittentur ei. Quibus verbis, ut ex apostolica traditione per manus accepta Ecclesia didicit, docet materiam, formam, proprium ministrum, et effectum hujus salutaris sacramenti. Intellexit enim Ecclesia, materiam esse oleum ab episcopo benedictum; nam unctio aptissime Spiritus Sancti gratiam, qua invisibiliter anima ægrotantis inungitur, repræsentat; formam deinde esse illa verba: Per istam unctionem, etc.

Chapter I.

On the institution of the sacrament of Extreme Unction.

Now, this sacred unction of the sick was instituted by Christ our Lord, as truly and properly a sacrament of the new law, insinuated indeed in Mark, but recommended and promulgated to the faithful by James the Apostle, and brother of the Lord. *Is any man,* he saith, *sick among you? Let him bring in the priests of the Church, and let them pray over him, anointing him with oil in the name of the Lord: and the prayer of faith shall save the sick man; and the Lord shall raise him up; and if he be in sins, they shall be forgiven him.*[1] In which words, as the Church has learned from apostolic tradition, received from hand to hand, he teaches the matter, the form, the proper minister, and the effect of this salutary sacrament. For the Church has understood the matter thereof to be oil blessed by a bishop. For the unction very aptly represents the grace of the Holy Ghost, with which the soul of the sick person is invisibly anointed; and furthermore that those words, "By this unction," etc., are the form.

---

[1] James v. 14, 15.

CAPUT II.

De effectu hujus Sacramenti.

Res porro et effectus hujus sacramenti illis verbis explicatur : Et oratio fidei salvabit infirmum ; et alleviabit eum Dominus ; et si in peccatis sit, dimittentur ei. Res etenim hæc gratia est Spiritus Sancti, cujus unctio delicta, si quæ sint adhuc expianda, ac peccati reliquias abstergit ; et ægroti animam alleviat et confirmat, magnam in eo divinæ misericordiæ fiduciam excitando ; qua infirmus sublevatus et morbi incommoda ac labores levius fert, et tentationibus dæmonis, calcaneo insidiantis, facilius resistit, et sanitatem corporis interdum, ubi saluti animæ expedierit, consequitur.

CHAPTER II.

On the effect of this Sacrament.

Moreover, the thing signified, and the effect of this sacrament, are explained in those words : *And the prayer of faith shall save the sick man, and the Lord shall raise him up, and if he be in sins they shall be forgiven him.* For the thing here signified is the grace of the Holy Ghost ; whose anointing cleanses away sins, if there be any still to be expiated, as also the remains of sins ; *and raises up* and strengthens the soul of the sick person, by exciting in him a great confidence in the divine mercy ; whereby the sick being supported, bears more easily the inconveniences and pains of his sickness ; and more readily resists the temptations of the devil who *lies in wait for his heel ;* [2] and at times obtains bodily health, when expedient for the welfare of the soul.

CAPUT III.

De ministro hujus Sacramenti, et tempore, quo dari debeat.

Jam vero, quod attinet ad præscriptionem eorum, qui et suscipere et ministrare hoc sacramentum debent, haud obscure fuit illud etiam in verbis prædictis traditum. Nam et ostenditur illic, proprios hujus sa-

CHAPTER III.

On the minister of this Sacrament, and on the time when it ought to be administered.

And now as to prescribing who ought to receive, and who to administer this sacrament, this also was not obscurely delivered in the words above cited. For it is there also shown, that the proper ministers of this sacrament are the *Presbyters*

---

[1] Gen. iii. 15.

cramenti ministros esse Eccle-
sia Presbyteros; quo nomine eo
loco, non œtate seniores, aut pri-
mores in populo intelligendi ve-
niunt, sed aut episcopi, aut sa-
cerdotes ab ipsis rite ordinati per
impositionem manuum presbyte-
rii. Declaratur etiam, esse hanc
unctionem infirmis adhibendam,
illis vero præsertim, qui tam pe-
riculose decumbunt, ut in exitu
vitœ constituti videantur; un-
de et sacramentum exeuntium
nuncupatur. Quod si infirmi
post susceptam hanc unctionem
convaluerint, iterum hujus sa-
cramenti subsidio juvari pote-
runt, cum in aliud simile vi-
tœ discrimen inciderint. Quare
nulla ratione audiendi sunt, qui
contra tam apertam et diluci-
dam apostoli Iacobi sententiam
docent, hanc unctionem vel fig-
mentum esse humanum, vel ri-
tum a patribus acceptum, nec
mandatum Dei, nec promissio-
nem gratiœ habentem; et qui
illam jam cessasse asserunt, qua-
si ad gratiam curationum dum-
taxat in primitiva Ecclesia re-
ferenda esset; et qui dicunt,
ritum et usum, quem sancta Ro-
mana Ecclesia in hujus sacra-
menti administratione observat,
Iacobi apostoli sententiœ repug-

of the Church; by which name are
to be understood, in that place, not
the elders by age, or the foremost
in dignity amongst the people, but
either bishops, or priests by bishops
rightly ordained *by the imposition
of the hands of the priesthood.*[1] It
is also declared, that this unction is
to be applied to the sick, but to
those especially who lie in such
danger as to seem to be about to
depart this life: whence also it is
called the sacrament of the departing. And if the sick should, after
having received this unction, recover, they may again be aided by
the succor of this sacrament, when
they fall into another like danger
of death. Wherefore, they are on
no account to be hearkened to, who,
against so manifest and clear a sentence of the Apostle James, teach,
either that this unction is a human
figment or is a rite received from
the Fathers, which neither has a
command from God, nor a promise
of grace : nor those who assert that
it has already ceased, as though it
were only to be referred to the
grace of healing in the primitive
Church; nor those who say that the
rite and usage which the holy Roman Church observes in the administration of this sacrament is repugnant to the sentiment of the Apostle

---

[1] 1 Tim. iv. 14.

nare, atque ideo in alium commutandum esse; et denique, qui hanc extremam unctionem a fidelibus sine peccato contemni posse affirmant. Hæc enim omnia manifestissime pugnant cum perspicuis tanti apostoli verbis. Nec profecto Ecclesia Romana, aliarum omnium mater et magistra, aliud in hac administranda unctione, quantum ad ea, quæ hujus sacramenti substantiam perficiunt, observat, quam quod beatus Iacobus præscripsit. Neque vero tanti sacramenti contemptus absque ingenti scelere et ipsius Spiritus Sancti injuria esse posset.

Hæc sunt, quæ de pœnitentiæ et extremæ unctionis sacramentis sancta hæc æcumenica synodus profitetur et docet atque omnibus Christi fidelibus credenda et tenenda proponit. Sequentes autem canones inviolabiliter servandos esse tradit, et asserentes contrarium perpetuo damnat et anathematizat.

James, and that it is therefore to be changed into some other; nor finally those who affirm that this Extreme Unction may without sin be contemned by the faithful; for all these things are most manifestly at variance with the perspicuous words of so great an apostle. Neither assuredly does the Roman Church, the mother and mistress of all other churches, observe aught in administering this unction,—as regards those things which constitute the substance of this sacrament,—but what blessed James has prescribed. Nor indeed can there be contempt of so great a sacrament without a heinous sin, and an injury to the Holy Ghost himself.

These are the things which this holy œcumenical Synod professes and teaches and proposes to all the faithful of Christ, to be believed and held, touching the sacraments of Penance and Extreme Unction. And it delivers the following canons to be inviolably preserved; and condemns and anathematizes those who assert what is contrary thereto.

DE SANCTISSIMO PŒNITENTIÆ SACRAMENTO.

CANON I.—Si quis dixerit, in Catholica Ecclesia pœnitentiam non esse vere et proprie sacramentum pro fidelibus, quoties

ON THE MOST HOLY SACRAMENT OF PENANCE.

CANON I.—If any one saith, that in the Catholic Church Penance is not truly and properly a sacrament, instituted by Christ our Lord

post baptismum in peccata labuntur, ipsi Deo reconciliandis a Christo Domino nostro institutum: anathema sit.

CANON II.—*Si quis sacramenta confundens, ipsum baptismum pœnitentiæ sacramentum esse dixerit, quasi hæc duo sacramenta distincta non sint, atque ideo pœnitentiam non recte secundam post naufragium tabulam appellari: anathema sit.*

CANON III.—*Si quis dixerit, verba illa Domini Salvatoris: Accipite Spiritum Sanctum; quorum remiseritis peccata, remittuntur eis; et quorum retinueritis, retenta sunt: non esse intelligenda de potestate remittendi et retinendi peccata in sacramento pœnitentiæ, sicut Ecclesia Catholica ab initio semper intellexit; detorserit autem, contra institutionem hujus sacramenti, ad auctoritatem prædicandi evangelium: anathema sit.*

CANON IV.—*Si quis negaverit, ad integram et perfectam peccatorum remissionem requiri tres actus in pœnitente, quasi materiam sacramenti pœnitentiæ, videlicet, contritionem, confessionem, et satisfactionem quæ tres pœnitentiæ*

for reconciling the faithful unto God, as often as they fall into sin after baptism: let him be anathema.

CANON II.—If any one, confounding the sacraments, saith that baptism is itself the sacrament of Penance, as though these two sacraments were not distinct, and that therefore Penance is not rightly called a second plank after shipwreck: let him be anathema.

CANON III.—If any one saith, that those words of the Lord the Saviour, *Receive ye the Holy Ghost, whose sins you shall forgive, they are forgiven them, and whose sins you shall retain, they are retained,*[1] are not to be understood of the power of forgiving and of retaining sins in the sacrament of Penance, as the Catholic Church has always from the beginning understood them; but wrests them, contrary to the institution of this sacrament, to the power of preaching the gospel: let him be anathema.

CANON IV.—If any one denieth, that, for the entire and perfect remission of sins, there are required three acts in the penitent, which are as it were the matter of the sacrament of Penance, to wit, contrition, confession, and satisfaction, which are called the three parts of

---

[1] John xx. 22, 23.

partes dicuntur; aut dixerit, duas tantum esse pœnitentiæ partes, terrores scilicet incussos conscientiæ, agnito peccato, et fidem conceptam ex evangelio vel absolutione, qua credit quis sibi per Christum remissa peccata: anathema sit.

CANON V.—*Si quis dixerit eam contritionem, quæ paratur per discussionem, collectionem et detestationem peccatorum, qua quis recogitat annos suos in amaritudine animæ suæ, ponderando peccatorum suorum gravitatem, multitudinem, fœditatem, amissionem æternæ beatitudinis, et æternæ damnationis incursum, cum proposito melioris vitæ, non esse verum et utilem dolorem, nec præparare ad gratiam, sed facere hominem hypocritam et magis peccatorem; demum, illum esse dolorem coactum et non liberum ac voluntarium: anathema sit.*

CANON VI.—*Si quis negaverit, confessionem sacramentalem vel institutam, vel ad salutem necessariam esse jure divino; aut dixerit, modum secrete confitendi soli sacerdoti, quem Ecclesia Catholica ab initio semper observavit et observat, alienum*

penance; or saith that there are two parts only of penance, to wit, the terrors with which the conscience is smitten upon being convinced of sin, and the faith, generated by the gospel, or by the absolution, whereby one believes that his sins are forgiven him through Christ: let him be anathema.

CANON V.—If any one saith, that the contrition which is acquired by means of the examination, collection, and detestation of sins,— whereby one *thinks over his years in the bitterness of his soul*,[1] by pondering on the grievousness, the multitude, the filthiness of his sins, the loss of eternal blessedness, and the eternal damnation which he has incurred, having therewith the purpose of a better life,—is not a true and profitable sorrow, does not prepare for grace, but makes a man a hypocrite and a greater sinner; in fine, that this [contrition] is a forced and not free and voluntary sorrow: let him be anathema.

CANON VI.—If any one denieth, either that sacramental confession was instituted, or is necessary to salvation, of divine right; or saith, that the manner of confessing secretly to a priest alone, which the Church hath ever observed from the beginning, and doth observe, is alien

---

[1] Isa. xxxviii. 15.

esse ab institutione et mandato Christi, et inventum esse humanum: anathema sit.

CANON VII.—*Si quis dixerit, in sacramento pœnitentiœ ad remissionem peccatorum necessarium non esse jure divino confiteri omnia et singula peccata mortalia, quorum memoria cum debita et diligenti prœmeditatione habeatur, etiam occulta, et quœ sunt contra duo ultima Decalogi prœcepta, et circumstantias, quœ peccati speciem mutant, sed eam confessionem tantum esse utilem ad erudiendum et consolandum pœnitentem, et olim observatam fuisse tantum ad satisfactionem canonicam imponendam; aut dixerit eos, qui omnia peccata confiteri student, nihil relinquere velle divinœ misericordiœ ignoscendum; aut demum, non licere confiteri peccata venialia: anathema sit.*

CANON VIII.—*Si quis dixerit, confessionem omnium peccatorum, qualem Ecclesia servat, esse impossibilem et traditionem humanam a piis abolendam; aut ad eam non teneri omnes et singulos utriusque sexus Christi fideles, juxta magni Concilii Lateranensis constitutionem, semel in anno et*

from the institution and command of Christ, and is a human invention: let him be anathema.

CANON VII.—If any one saith, that, in the sacrament of Penance, it is not necessary, of divine right, for the remission of sins, to confess all and singular the mortal sins which after due and diligent previous meditation are remembered, even those [mortal sins] which are secret, and those which are opposed to the two last commandments of the Decalogue, as also the circumstances which change the species of a sin; but [saith] that such confession is only useful to instruct and console the penitent, and that it was of old only observed in order to impose a canonical satisfaction; or saith that they, who strive to confess all their sins, wish to leave nothing to the divine mercy to pardon; or, finally, that it is not lawful to confess venial sins: let him be anathema.

CANON VIII.—If any one saith, that the confession of all sins, such as it is observed in the Church, is impossible, and is a human tradition to be abolished by the godly; or that all and each of the faithful of Christ, of either sex, are not obliged thereunto once a year, conformably to the constitution of the great Council of Lateran, and that,

ob id suadendum esse Christi fidelibus, ut non confiteantur tempore quadragesimœ: anathema sit.

CANON IX.—*Si quis dixerit, absolutionem sacramentalem sacerdotis, non esse actum judicialem, sed nudum ministerium pronunciandi et declarandi, remissa esse peccata confitenti, modo tantum credat, se esse absolutum; aut sacerdos non serio, sed joco absolvat; aut dixerit, non requiri confessionem pœnitentis, ut sacerdos ipsum absolvere possit: anathema sit.*

CANON X.—*Si quis dixerit, sacerdotes, qui in peccato mortali sunt, potestatem ligandi et solvendi non habere; aut non solos sacerdotes esse ministros absolutionis, sed omnibus et singulis Christi fidelibus esse dictum: Quæcumque ligaveritis super terram, erunt ligata et in cœlo; et quæcumque solveritis super terram, erunt soluta et in cœlo; et: Quorum remiseritis peccata, remittuntur eis; et quorum retinueritis, retenta sunt: quorum verborum virtute quilibet absolvere possit peccata, publica quidem per correptionem dumtaxat, si correptus acquie-*

for this cause, the faithful of Christ are to be persuaded not to confess during Lent: let him be anathema.

CANON IX.—If any one saith, that the sacramental absolution of the priest is not a judicial act, but a bare ministry of pronouncing and declaring sins to be forgiven to him who confesses; provided only he believe himself to be absolved, or [even though] the priest absolve not in earnest, but in joke; or saith, that the confession of the penitent is not required, in order that the priest may be able to absolve him : let him be anathema.

CANON X.—If any one saith, that priests, who are in mortal sin, have not the power of binding and loosing; or, that not priests alone are the ministers of absolution, but that, to all and each of the faithful of Christ is it said: *Whatsoever you shall bind upon earth shall be bound also in heaven; and whatsoever you shall loose upon earth, shall be loosed also in heaven;*[1] *and, whose sins you shall forgive, they are forgiven them; and whose sins you shall retain, they are retained;*[2] by virtue of which words every one is able to absolve from sins, to wit, from public sins by reproof only, provided he who is

---

[1] Matt. xviii. 15. [2] John xx. 23.

verit, secreta vero per spontaneam confessionem : anathema sit.

CANON XI.—*Si quis dixerit, episcopos non habere jus reservandi sibi casus, nisi quoad externam politiam, atque ideo casuum reservationem non prohibere, quo minus sacerdos a reservatis vere absolvat : anathema sit.*

CANON XII.—*Si quis dixerit, totam pœnam simul cum culpa remitti semper a Deo, satisfactionemque pœnitentium non esse aliam quam fidem, qua apprehendunt Christum pro eis satisfecisse : anathema sit.*

CANON XIII.—*Si quis dixerit, pro peccatis, quoad pœnam temporalem, minime Deo pro Christi merita satisfieri pœnis ab eo inflictis et patienter toleratis, vel a sacerdote injunctis, sed neque sponte susceptis, ut jejuniis, orationibus, eleemosynis, vel aliis etiam pietatis operibus, atque ideo optimam pœnitentiam esse tantum novam vitam : anathema sit.*

CANON XIV.—*Si quis dixerit, satisfactiones, quibus pœnitentes per Christum Iesum peccata redimunt, non esse cultus*

reproved yield thereto, and from secret sins by a voluntary confession : let him be anathema.

CANON XI.—If any one saith, that bishops have not the right of reserving cases to themselves, except as regards external polity, and that therefore the reservation of cases hinders not, but that a priest may truly absolve from reserved cases : let him be anathema.

CANON XII.—If any one saith, that God always remits the whole punishment together with the guilt, and that the satisfaction of penitents is no other than the faith whereby they apprehend that Christ has satisfied for them : let him be anathema.

CANON XIII.—If any one saith, that satisfaction for sins, as to their temporal punishment, is. nowise made to God, through the merits of Jesus Christ, by the punishments inflicted by him, and patiently borne, or by those enjoined by the priest, nor even by those voluntarily undertaken, as by fastings, prayers, alms-deeds, or by other works also of piety ; and that, therefore, the best penance is merely a new life : let him be anathema.

CANON XIV.—If any one saith, that the satisfactions, by which penitents redeem their sins through Jesus Christ, are not a worship of

Dei, sed traditiones hominum, doctrinam de gratia, et rerum Dei cultum atque ipsum beneficium mortis Christi obscurantes : anathema sit.

CANON XV.—*Si quis dixerit, claves Ecclesiæ esse datas tantum ad solvendum, non etiam ad ligandum, et propterea sacerdotes, dum imponunt pœnas confitentibus, agere contra finem clavium et contra institutionem Christi; et fictionem esse, quod, virtute clavium sublata pœna æterna, pœna temporalis plerumque exsolvenda remaneat : anathema sit.*

God, but traditions of men, which obscure the doctrine of grace, and the true worship of God, and the benefit itself of the death of Christ: let him be anathema.

CANON XV.—If any one saith, that the keys are given to the Church, only *to loose,* not also *to bind;* and that, therefore, priests act contrary to the purpose of the keys, and contrary to the institution of Christ, when they impose punishments on those who confess; and that it is a fiction, that, after the eternal punishment has, by virtue of the keys, been removed, there remains for the most part a temporal punishment to be discharged : let him be anathema.

DE SACRAMENTO EXTREMÆ UNCTIONIS.

ON THE SACRAMENT OF EXTREME UNCTION.

CANON I.—*Si quis dixerit, extremam unctionem non esse vere et proprie sacramentum a Christo domino nostro institutum et a beato Iacobo apostolo promulgatum; sed ritum tantum acceptum a patribus aut figmentum humanum : anathema sit.*

CANON II.—*Si quis dixerit, sacram infirmorum unctionem non conferre gratiam, nec remittere peccata, nec alleviare infirmos, sed jam cessasse, quasi olim tantum fuerit gratia curationum : anathema sit.*

CANON I.—If any one saith, that Extreme Unction is not truly and properly a sacrament, instituted by Christ our Lord, and promulgated by the blessed Apostle James; but is only a rite received from the Fathers, or a human figment: let him be anathema.

CANON II.—If any one saith, that the sacred unction of the sick does not confer grace, nor remit sin, nor comfort the sick; but that it has already ceased, as though it were of old only the grace of working cures: let him be anathema.

Canon III.—*Si quis dixerit, extremæ unctionis ritum et usum, quem observat sancta Romana Ecclesia, repugnare sententiæ beati Iacobi apostoli, ideoque eum mutandum, posseque a Christianis absque peccato contemni : anathema sit.*

Canon IV.—*Si quis dixerit, Presbyteros Ecclesiæ, quos beatus Iacobus adducendos esse ad infirmum inungendum hortatur, non esse sacerdotes ab episcopo ordinatos, sed ætate seniores in quavis communitate, ob idque proprium extremæ unctionis ministrum non esse solum sacerdotem : anathema sit.*

Canon III.—If any one saith, that the right and usage of Extreme Unction, which the holy Roman Church observes, is repugnant to the sentiment of the blessed Apostle James, and that is therefore to be changed, and may, without sin, be contemned by Christians : let him be anathema.

Canon IV.—If any one saith, that the *Presbyters of the Church*, whom blessed James exhorts to be brought to anoint the sick, are not the priests who have been ordained by a bishop, but the elders in each community, and that for this cause a priest alone is not the proper minister of Extreme Unction : let him be anathema.

Sessio Vigesimaprima,

celebrata die XVI. Iulii 1562.

DOCTRINA DE COMMUNIONE SUB UTRAQUE SPECIE, ET PARVULORUM.

Caput I.

Laicos et clericos non conficientes non adstringi jure divino ad communionem sub utraque specie.

Itaque sancta ipsa synodus, a Spiritu Sancto, qui spiritus est sapientiæ et intellectus, spiritus consilii et pietatis, edocta, atque ipsius Ecclesiæ judicium

Twenty-first Session,

held July 16, 1562.

DOCTRINE CONCERNING THE COMMUNION UNDER BOTH SPECIES, AND OF LITTLE CHILDREN.

Chapter I.

That laymen and clerics, when not sacrificing, are not bound, of divine right, to communion under both species.

Wherefore, this holy Synod,—instructed by the Holy *Spirit*, who is *the spirit of wisdom and of understanding, the spirit of counsel and of godliness*,[1] and following the

---

[1] Isa. xi. 2.

et consuetudinem secuta, declarat, ac docet, nullo divino præcepto laicos et clericos non conficientes, obligari ad Eucharistiæ sacramentum sub utraque specie sumendum ; neque ullo pacto, salva fide, dubitari posse, quin illis alterius speciei communio ad salutem sufficiat : nam, etsi Christus Dominus in ultima cœna venerabile hoc sacramentum in panis, et vini speciebus instituit et apostolis tradidit ; non tamen illa institutio et traditio eo tendunt, ut omnes Christi fideles statuto Domini ad utramque speciem accipiendam adstringantur. Sed neque ex sermone illo, apud Ioannem VI., recte colligitur, utriusque speciei communionem a Domino præceptam esse : utcumque juxta varias sanctorum patrum et doctorum interpretationes intelligatur : namque, qui dixit : Nisi manducaveritis carnem filii hominis et biberitis ejus sanguinem, non habebitis vitam in vobis : dixit quoque : Si quis manducaverit ex hoc pane, vivet in æternum. Et qui dixit : Qui manducat meam carnem, et bibit meum sanguinem, habet vitam æternam : dixit etiam : Panis, quem ego dabo, caro mea est pro mundi

judgment and usage of the Church itself,—declares and teaches, that laymen, and clerics when not consecrating, are not obliged, by any divine precept, to receive the sacrament of the Eucharist under both species; and that neither can it by any means be doubted, without injury to faith, that communion under either species is sufficient for them unto salvation. For, although Christ, the Lord, in the Last Supper, instituted and delivered to the apostles, this venerable sacrament in the species of bread and wine; not therefore do that institution and delivery tend thereunto, that all the faithful of the Church be bound, by the institution of the Lord, to receive both species. But neither is it rightly gathered, from that discourse which is in the sixth of John,—however according to the various interpretations of holy Fathers and Doctors it be understood, —that the communion of both species was enjoined by the Lord; for he who said, *Except you eat the flesh of the Son of man and drink his blood, you shall not have life in you* (v. 54), also said: *He that eateth this bread shall live forever* (v. 59); and he who said, *He that eateth my flesh and drinketh my blood hath everlasting life* (v. 55), also said: *The bread that I will*

vita. Et denique qui dixit : Qui manducat meam carnem et bibit meum sanguinem, in me manet et ego in illo : dixit nihilominus : Qui manducat hunc panem, vivet in æternum.

give is *my flesh for the life of the world* (v. 52) ; and, in fine, he who said, *He that eateth my flesh and drinketh my blood, abideth in me and I in him* (v. 57), said, nevertheless, *He that eateth this bread shall live forever* (v. 59).

CAPUT II.

Ecclesiæ potestas circa dispensationem sacramenti Eucharistiæ.

CHAPTER II.

The power of the Church as regards the dispensation of the Sacrament of the Eucharist.

Præterea declarat, hanc potestatem perpetuo in Ecclesia fuisse, ut in sacramentorum dispensatione, salva illorum substantia, ea statueret vel mutaret, quæ suscipientium utilitati seu ipsorum sacramentorum venerationi, pro rerum, temporum et locorum veritate, magis expedire judicaret. Id autem apostolus non obscure visus est innuisse, cum ait : Sic nos existimet homo, ut ministros Christi et dispensatores mysteriorum Dei ; atque ipsum quidem hac potestate usum esse satis constat cum in multis aliis, tum in hoc ipso sacramento, cum, ordinatis nonnullis circa ejus usum, Cetera, inquit, cum venero, disponam. Quare agnoscens sancta mater Ecclesia hanc suam in administratione sacramentorum auctoritatem, licet ab

It furthermore declares, that this power has ever been in the Church, that, in the dispensation of the sacraments, their substance being untouched, it may ordain, or change, what things soever it may judge most expedient, for the profit of those who receive, or for the veneration of the said sacraments, according to the difference of circumstances, times, and places. And this the Apostle seems not obscurely to have intimated, when he says : *Let a man so account of us, as of the ministers of Christ, and the dispensers of the mysteries of God.*[1] And, indeed, it is sufficiently manifest that he himself exercised this power, as in many other things, so in regard of this very sacrament; when, after having ordained certain things touching the use thereof, he says : *The rest I will set in order when I come.*[2]   Wherefore, holy

---

[1] 1 Cor. iv. 1.   [2] 1 Cor. xi. 34.

initio Christianæ religionis non infrequens utriusque speciei usus fuisset, tamen progressu temporis, latissime jam mutata illa consuetudine, gravibus et justis causis adducta hanc consuetudinem sub altera specie communicandi approbabit, et pro lege habendam decrevit, quam reprobare aut sine ipsius Ecclesiæ auctoritate pro libito mutare non licet.

Mother Church, knowing this her authority in the administration of the sacraments, although the use of both species has, from the beginning of the Christian religion, not been unfrequent, yet, in progress of time, that custom having been already very widely changed, she, induced by weighty and just reasons, has approved of this custom of communicating under one species, and decreed that it was to be held as a law; which it is not lawful to reprobate, or to change at pleasure, without the authority of the Church itself.

CAPUT III.

Totum et integrum Christum ac verum sacramentum sub qualibet specie sumi.

CHAPTER III.

That Christ whole and entire and a true Sacrament are received under either species.

Insuper declarat, quamvis Redemptor noster, ut antea dictum est, in suprema illa cæna hoc sacramentum in duabus speciebus instituerit et apostolis tradiderit, tamen fatendum esse, etiam sub altera tantum specie totum atque integrum Christum verumque sacramentum sumi; ac propterea, quod ad fructum attinet nulla gratia necessaria ad salutem eos defraudari, qui unam speciam solam accipiunt.

It moreover declares, that although, as hath been already said, our Redeemer, in that last supper, instituted, and delivered to the apostles, this sacrament in two species, yet is to be acknowledged, that Christ whole and entire and a true sacrament are received under either species alone; and that therefore, as regards the fruit thereof, they, who receive one species alone are not defrauded of any grace necessary to salvation.

CAPUT IV.

Parvulos non obligari ad communionem sacramentalem.

Denique eadem sancta synodus docet, parvulos usu rationis carentes nulla obligari necessitate ad sacramentalem Eucharistiæ communionem, siquidem, per baptismi lavacrum regenerati et Christo incorporati, adeptam jam filiorum Dei gratiam in illa ætate amittere non possunt. Neque ideo tamen damnanda est antiquitas, si eum morem in quibusdam locis aliquando servavit. Ut enim sanctissimi illi patres sui facti probabilem causam pro illius temporis ratione habuerunt, ita certe eos nulla salutis necessitate id fecisse sine controversia credendum est.

DE COMMUNIONE SUB UTRAQUE SPECIE ET PARVULORUM.

CANON I. — *Si quis dixerit, ex Dei præcepto vel necessitate salutis omnes et singulos Christi fideles utramque speciem sanctissimi Eucharistiæ sacramenti sumere debere : anathema sit.*

CANON II. — *Si quis dixerit, sanctam Ecclesiam Catholicam non jus-*

CHAPTER IV.

That little Children are not bound to sacramental Communion.

Finally, this same holy Synod teaches, that little children, who have not attained to the use of reason, are not by any necessity obliged to the sacramental communion of the Eucharist : forasmuch as, having been regenerated by the laver of baptism, and being incorporated with Christ, they can not, at that age, lose the grace which they have already acquired of being the sons of God. Not therefore, however, is antiquity to be condemned, if, in some places, it, at one time, observed that custom ; for as those most holy Fathers had a probable cause for what they did in respect of their times, so, assuredly, is it to be believed without controversy, that they did this without any necessity thereof unto salvation.

ON COMMUNION UNDER BOTH SPECIES, AND ON THE COMMUNION OF INFANTS.

CANON I.—If any one saith, that, by the precept of God, or by necessity of salvation, all and each of the faithful of Christ ought to receive both species of the most holy sacrament of the Eucharist : let him be anathema.

CANON II.—If any one saith, that the holy Catholic Church was not

tis causis et rationibus adductam fuisse, ut laicos atque etiam clericos non conficientes sub panis tantummodo specie communicaret, aut in eo errasse : anathema sit.

CANON III.—*Si quis negaverit, totum et integrum Christum, omnium gratiarum fontem et auctorem, sub una panis specie sumi, quia, ut quidam falso asserunt, non secundum ipsius Christi institutionem sub utraque specie sumatur : anathema sit.*

CANON IV.—*Si quis dixerit, parvulis, antequam ad annos discretionis pervenerint, necessariam esse Eucharistiæ communionem : anathema sit.*

Duos vero articulos alias propositos nondum tamen excussos, videlicet : an rationes, quibus sancta Catholica Ecclesia adducta fuit, ut communicaret laicos atque etiam non celebrantes sacerdotes, sub una tantum panis specie, ita sint retinendæ, ut nulla ratione calicis usus cuiquam sit permittendus ; et : an, si honestis et Christianæ caritati consentaneis rationibus concedendus alicui vel nationi vel regno calicis usus videatur, sub aliquibus conditionibus concedendus sit, et quænam sint illæ, eadem

induced, by just causes and reasons, to communicate, under the species of bread only, laymen, and also clerics when not consecrating : let him be anathema.

CANON III.—If any one denieth, that Christ whole and entire,—the fountain and author of all graces, —is received under the one species of bread ; because that, as some falsely assert, he is not received, according to the institution of Christ himself, under both species : let him be anathema.

CANON IV.—If any one saith, that the communion of the Eucharist is necessary for little children, before they have arrived at years of discretion : let him be anathema.

As regards, however, those two articles, proposed on another occasion, but which have not as yet been discussed : to wit, whether the reasons by which the holy Catholic Church was led to communicate, under the one species of bread only, laymen, and also priests when not celebrating, are in such wise to be adhered to, as that on no account is the use of the chalice to be allowed to any one soever ; and whether, in case that, for reasons beseeming and consonant with Christian charity, it appears that the use of the chalice is to be granted to any nation or kingdom, it is to be con-

sancta synodus in aliud tempus, oblata sibi quamprimum occasione, examinandos atque definiendos reservat.

ceded under certain conditions; and what are those conditions: this same holy Synod reserves the same to another time,—for the earliest opportunity that shall present itself,—to be examined and defined.

SESSIO VIGESIMASECUNDA,

celebrata die XVII. Sept. 1562.

DOCTRINA DE SACRIFICIO MISSÆ.

TWENTY-SECOND SESSION,

held Sept. 17, 1562.

DOCTRINE ON THE SACRIFICE OF THE MASS.

CAPUT I.

De institutione sacrosancti missæ sacrificii.

CHAPTER I.

On the institution of the most holy Sacrifice of the Mass.

Quoniam sub priori Testamento, teste Apostolo Paulo, propter Levitici sacerdotii imbecillitatem consummatio non erat, oportuit, Deo patre misericordiarum ita ordinante, sacerdotem alium secundum ordinem Melchisedech surgere, Dominum nostrum Iesum Christum, qui posset omnes, quotquot sanctificandi essent, consummare, et ad perfectum adducere. Is igitur Deus et Dominus noster, etsi semel se ipsum in ara crucis, morte intercedente, Deo patri oblaturus erat, ut æternam illic redemptionem operaretur, quia tamen per mortem sacerdotium ejus

Forasmuch as, under the former Testament, according to the testimony of the Apostle Paul, there was no *perfection, because of the weakness of the Levitical priesthood;*[1] there was need, God, the Father of mercies, so ordaining, that *another priest should rise, according to the order of Melchisedech,*[2] our Lord Jesus Christ, who might consummate, and lead to what is perfect, as many as were to be sanctified. He, therefore, our God and Lord, though he was about to offer himself once on the altar of the cross unto God the Father, *by means of his death,* there to operate *an eternal redemption;*[3] nevertheless, because that his priesthood was not

---

[1] Heb. vii. 11, 18.   [2] Heb. v. 10.   [3] Heb. ix. 12.

*extinguendum non erat, in cœ-
na novissima, qua nocte trade-
batur, ut dilectæ sponsæ suæ
Ecclesiæ visibile, sicut hominum
natura exigit, relinqueret sacrificium, quo cruentum illud semel in cruce peragendum re-
præsentaretur, ejusque memoria in finem usque sœculi per-
maneret, atque illius salutaris
virtus in remissionem eorum,
quæ a nobis quotidie committuntur, peccatorum applicare-
tur, sacerdotem secundum ordinem Melchisedech se in æternum constitutum declarans, corpus et sanguinem suum sub
speciebus panis et vini Deo Patri obtulit, ac sub earumdem
rerum symbolis apostolis, quos
tunc Novi Testamenti sacerdotes constituebat, ut sumerent,
tradidit, et eisdem eorumque
in sacerdotio successoribus, ut
offerrent, præcepit per hæc verba: Hoc facite in meam commemorationem: uti semper Catholica Ecclesia intellexit et docuit. Nam celebrato veteri Pascha, quod in memoriam exitus
de Aegypto multitudo filiorum
Israel immolabat, novum instituit Pascha se ipsum ab Ecclesia per sacerdotes sub signis vi-
sibilibus immolandum in me-*

to be extinguished by his death, in
the Last Supper, on the night in
which he was betrayed,—that he
might leave, to his own beloved
Spouse the Church, a visible sacrifice, such as the nature of man requires, whereby that bloody sacrifice, once to be accomplished on the
cross, might be represented, and the
memory thereof remain even unto
the end of the world, and its salutary virtue be applied to the remission of those sins which we daily
commit,—declaring himself constituted *a priest forever, according to
the order of Melchisedech,*[1] he offered up to God the Father his own
body and blood under the species
of bread and wine; and, under the
symbols of those same things, he
delivered [his own body and blood]
to be received by his apostles, whom
he then constituted priests of the
New Testament; and by those
words, *Do this in commemoration
of me,*[2] he commanded them and
their successors in the priesthood
to offer [them]; even as the Catholic Church has always understood
and taught. For, having celebrated
the ancient Passover, which the
multitude of the children of Israel
immolated in memory of their going out of Egypt, he instituted the
new Passover [to wit], himself to

---

[1] Psa. cix. 4. [2] Luke xxii. 19.

moriam transitus sui ex hoc mundo ad Patrem, quando per sui sanguinis effusionem nos redemit eripuitque de potestate tenebrarum, et in regnum suum transtulit. Et hæc quidem illa munda oblatio est, quæ nulla indignitate aut malitia offerentium inquinari potest; quam Dominus per Malachiam nomini suo, quod magnum futurum esset in gentibus, in omni loco mundam offerendam prædixit, et quam non obscure innuit Apostolus Paulus Corinthiis scribens, cum dicit, non posse eos, qui participatione mensæ dæmoniorum polluti sint, mensæ Domini participes fieri, per mensam altare utrobique intelligens. Hæc denique illa est, quæ per varias sacrificiorum, naturæ et legis tempore, similitudines figurabatur; utpote quæ bona omnia, per illa significata, velut illorum omnium consummatio et perfectio complectitur.

be immolated, under visible signs, by the Church through [the ministry of] priests, in memory of his own passage from this world unto the Father, when by the effusion of his own blood he redeemed us, *and delivered us from the power of darkness, and translated us into his kingdom.*[1] And this is indeed that clean oblation, which can not be defiled by any unworthiness, or malice of those that offer [it]; which the Lord foretold by Malachias was to be *offered in every place, clean to his name, which was to be great amongst the Gentiles;*[2] and which the Apostle Paul, writing to the Corinthians, has not obscurely indicated, when he says, that they who are defiled by *the participation of the table of devils, can not be partakers of the table of the Lord;*[3] by *the table*, meaning in both places the altar. This, in fine, is that oblation which was prefigured by various types of sacrifices, during the period of nature, and of the law; inasmuch as it comprises all the good things signified by those sacrifices, as being the consummation and perfection of them all.

---

[1] Col. i. 13.   [2] Mal. i. 11.   [3] 1 Cor. x. 20 sqq.

Caput II.

Sacrificium missæ est propitiatorium, tam pro vivis, quam pro defunctis.

Et quoniam in divino hoc sacrificio, quod in missa peragitur, idem ille Christus continetur et incruente immolatur, qui in ara crucis semel se ipsum cruente obtulit, docet sancta synodus, sacrificium istud vere propitiatorium esse, per ipsumque fieri, ut, si cum vero corde et recta fide, cum metu et reverentia, contriti ac pœnitentes ad Deum accedamus, misericordiam consequamur et gratiam inveniamus in auxilio opportuno. Hujus quippe oblatione placatus Dominus gratiam et donum pœnitentiæ concedens, crimina et peccata etiam ingentia dimittit. Una enim eademque est hostia, idem nunc offerens sacerdotum ministerio, qui se ipsum tunc in cruce obtulit, sola offerendi ratione diversa. Cujus quidem oblationis cruentæ, inquam, fructus per hanc incruentam uberrime percipiuntur, tantum abest, ut illi per hanc quovis modo derogetur. Quare non solum pro fidelium vivorum peccatis, pœnis, satisfactionibus et aliis necessitatibus, sed pro defunctis

Chapter II.

That the Sacrifice of the Mass is propitiatory, both for the living and the dead.

And forasmuch as, in this divine sacrifice which is celebrated in the mass, that same Christ is contained and immolated in an unbloody manner who once offered himself in a bloody manner on the altar of the cross; the holy Synod teaches, that this sacrifice is truly propitiatory, and that by means thereof this is effected, that we obtain mercy, and find grace *in seasonable aid,*[1] if we draw nigh unto God, contrite and penitent, with a sincere heart and upright faith, with fear and reverence. For the Lord, appeased by the oblation thereof, and granting the grace and gift of penitence, forgives even heinous crimes and sins. For the victim is one and the same, the same now offering by the ministry of priests, who then offered himself on the cross, the manner alone of offering being different. The fruits indeed of which oblation, of that bloody one to wit, are received most plentifully through this unbloody one; so far is this [latter] from derogating in any way from that [former oblation]. Wherefore, not only for the sins, punishments, satisfactions, and other necessities of the faithful who are living, but

---

[1] Heb. iv. 6.

in Christo nondum ad plenum purgatis rite juxta apostolorum traditionem offertur.

also for those who are departed in Christ, and who are not as yet fully purified, is it rightly offered, agreeably to a tradition of the apostles.

Caput III.

De missa in honorem sanctorum.

Et quamvis in honorem et memoriam sanctorum nonnullus interdum missas Ecclesia celebrare consueverit, non tamen illis sacrificium offerri docet, sed Deo soli, qui illos coronavit; unde nec sacerdos dicere solet: Offero tibi sacrificium, Petre vel Paule; sed, Deo de illorum victoriis gratias agens, eorum patrocinia implorat, ut ipsi pro nobis intercedere dignentur in cœlis, quorum memoriam facimus in terris.

Chapter III.

On Masses in honor of the Saints.

And although the Church has been accustomed at times to celebrate certain masses in honor and memory of the saints; not therefore, however, doth she teach that sacrifice is offered unto them, but unto God alone, who crowned them; whence neither is the priest wont to say, ' I offer sacrifice to thee, Peter or Paul;' but, giving thanks to God for their victories, he implores their patronage, that they may vouchsafe to intercede for us in heaven, whose memory we celebrate upon earth.

Caput IV.

De canone missæ.

Et cum sancta sancte administrari conveniat, sitque hoc omnium sanctissimum sacrificium, Ecclesia Catholica, ut digne reverenterque offerretur ac perciperetur, sacrum canonem multis ante sæculis instituit, ita ab omni errore purum, ut nihil in eo contineatur, quod non maxime sanctitatem ac pietatem quamdam redoleat, mentesque offerentium in Deum erigat.

Chapter IV.

On the Canon of the Mass.

And whereas it beseemeth that holy things be administered in a holy manner, and of all holy things this sacrifice is the most holy; to the end that it might be worthily and reverently offered and received, the Catholic Church instituted, many years ago, the sacred Canon, so pure from every error, that nothing is contained therein which does not in the highest degree savor of a certain holiness and piety, and raise

Is enim constat cum ex ipsis Domini verbis, tum ex apostolorum traditionibus ac sanctorum quoque pontificum piis institutionibus.

up unto God the minds of those that offer. For it is composed out of the very words of the Lord, the traditions of the Apostles, and the pious institutions also of holy Pontiffs.

CAPUT V.

De missæ ceremoniis et ritibus.

CHAPTER V.

On the solemn ceremonies of the Sacrifice of the Mass.

Cumque natura hominum ea sit, ut non facile queat sine adminiculis exterioribus ad rerum divinarum meditationem sustolli, propterea pia mater Ecclesia ritus quosdam, ut scilicet quædam summissa voce, alia vero elatiore, in missa pronunciarentur, instituit. Cerimonias item adhibuit, ut mysticas benedictiones, lumina, thymiamata, vestes, aliaque id genus multa ex apostolica disciplina et traditione, quo et majestas tanti sacrificii commendaretur, et mentes fidelium per hæc visibilia religionis et pietatis signa ad rerum altissimarum, quæ in hoc sacrificio latent, contemplationem excitarentur.

And whereas such is the nature of man, that, without external helps, he can not easily be raised to the meditation of divine things; therefore has holy Mother Church instituted certain rites, to wit, that certain things be pronounced in the mass in a low, and others in a louder, tone. She has likewise employed ceremonies, such as mystic benedictions, lights, incense, vestments, and many other things of this kind, derived from an apostolical discipline and tradition, whereby both the majesty of so great a sacrifice might be recommended, and the minds of the faithful be excited, by those visible signs of religion and piety, to the contemplation of those most sublime things which are hidden in this sacrifice.

CAPUT VI.

De missa, in qua solus sacerdos communicat.

CHAPTER VI.

On Mass wherein the priest alone communicates.

Optaret quidem sacrosancta synodus, ut in singulis missis

The sacred and holy Synod would fain indeed that, at each mass, the

fideles adstantes non solum spirituali affectu, sed sacramentali etiam Eucharistiæ perceptione communicarent, quod ad eos sanctissimi hujus sacrificii fructus uberior proveniret ; nec tamen, si id non semper fiat, propterea missas illas, in quibus solus sacerdos sacramentaliter communicat, ut privatas et illicitas damnat, sed probat atque adeo commendat, siquidem illæ quoque missæ vere communes censeri debent, partim, quod in eis populus spiritualiter communicet, partim vero, quod a publico Ecclesiæ ministro non pro se tantum, sed pro omnibus fidelibus, qui ad corpus Christi pertinent, celebrentur.

faithful who are present should communicate, not only in spiritual desire, but also by the sacramental participation of the Eucharist, that thereby a more abundant fruit might be derived to them from this most holy sacrifice : but not therefore, if this be not always done, does it condemn, as private and unlawful, but approves of and therefore commends, those masses in which the priest alone communicates sacramentally; since those masses also ought to be considered as truly common; partly because the people communicate spiritually thereat; partly also because they are celebrated by a public minister of the Church, not for himself only, but for all the faithful, who belong to the body of Christ.

CAPUT VII.

De aqua miscenda vino in calice offerendo.

CHAPTER VII.

On the water that is to be mixed with the wine to be offered in the chalice.

Monet deinde sancta synodus, præceptum esse ab Ecclesia sacerdotibus, ut aquam vino in calice offerendo miscerent, tum quod Christum Dominum ita fecisse credatur, tum etiam quia e latere ejus aqua simul cum sanguine exierit, quod sacramentum hac mixtione recolitur, et,

The holy Synod notices, in the next place, that it has been enjoined by the Church on priests, to mix water with the wine that is to be offered in the chalice; as well because it is believed that Christ the Lord did this, as also because from *his side there came out blood and water ;*[1] the memory of which mystery is

---

[1] John xix. 34.

cum aquæ in apocalypsi beati Ioannis populi dicantur, ipsius populi fidelis cum capite Christo unio repræsentatur.

renewed by this commixture; and, whereas in the apocalypse of blessed John *the peoples* are called *waters*,[1] the union of that faithful people with Christ their head is thereby represented.

Caput VIII.

Missa vulgari lingua non celebretur. Ejus mysteria populo explicentur.

Chapter VIII.

On not celebrating the Mass every where in the vulgar tongue; the mysteries of the Mass to be explained to the people.

Etsi missa magnam contineat populi fidelis eruditionem; non tamen expedire visum est patribus, ut vulgari passim lingua celebraretur. Quamobrem, retento ubique cujusque Ecclesiæ antiquo et a sancta Romana Ecclesia, omnium ecclesiarum matre et magistra, probato ritu, ne oves Christi esuriant, neve parvuli panem petant et non sit qui frangat eis, mandat sancta synodus pastoribus et singulis curam animarum gerentibus, ut frequenter inter missarum celebrationem vel per se vel per alios ex iis, quæ in missa leguntur, aliquid exponant; atque inter cetera sanctissimi hujus sacrificii mysterium aliquod declarent, diebus præsertim dominicis et festis.

Although the mass contains great instruction for the faithful people, nevertheless, it has not seemed expedient to the Fathers that it should be every where celebrated in the vulgar tongue. Wherefore, the ancient usage of each Church, and the rite approved of by the holy Roman Church, the mother and mistress of all churches, being in each place retained; and, that the sheep of Christ may not suffer hunger, *nor the little ones ask for bread, and there be none to break it unto them*,[2] the holy Synod charges pastors, and all who have the cure of souls, that they frequently, during the celebration of mass, expound either by themselves, or others, some portion of those things which are read at Mass, and that, amongst the rest, they explain some mystery of this most holy sacrifice, especially on the Lord's days and festivals.

---

[1] Apoc. xvii. 15.

[2] Lam. iv. 4.

Caput IX.

Prolegomenon canonum sequentium.

Quia vero adversus veterem hanc in sacrosancto evangelio, apostolorum traditionibus sanctorumque patrum doctrina fundatam fidem hoc tempore multi disseminati sunt errores, multaque a multis docentur et disputantur; sancta synodus, post multos gravesque his de rebus mature habitos tractatus, unanimi patrum omnium concensu quæ huic purissimæ fidei sacræque doctrinæ adversantur damnare et a sancta Ecclesia eliminare, per subjectos hos canones constituit.

DE SACRIFICIO MISSÆ.

CANON I.—*Si quis dixerit, in missa non offerri Deo verum et proprium sacrificium, aut quod offerri non sit aliud quam nobis Christum ad manducandum dari : anathema sit.*

CANON II.—*Si quis dixerit, illis verbis : Hoc facite in meam commemorationem, Christum non instituisse apostolos sacerdotes, aut non ordinasse, ut ipsi aliique sacerdotes offerrent corpus et sanguinem suum : anathema sit.*

CANON III.— *Si quis dixerit,*

Chapter IX.

Preliminary Remark on the following Canons.

And because that many errors are at this time disseminated and many things are taught and maintained by divers persons, in opposition to this ancient faith, which is based on the sacred Gospel, the traditions of the Apostles, and the doctrine of the holy Fathers; the sacred and holy Synod, after many and grave deliberations maturely had touching these matters, has resolved, with the unanimous consent of all the Fathers, to condemn, and to eliminate from holy Church by means of the canons subjoined, whatsoever is opposed to this most pure faith and sacred doctrine.

ON THE SACRIFICE OF THE MASS.

CANON I.—If any one saith, that in the mass a true and proper sacrifice is not offered to God ; or, that to be offered is nothing else but that Christ is given us to eat : let him be anathema.

CANON II.—If any one saith, that by those words, *Do this for the commemoration of me* (Luke xxii. 19), Christ did not institute the apostles priests; or, did not ordain that they and other priests should offer his own body and blood : let him be anathema.

CANON III.—If any one saith,

missæ sacrificium tantum esse laudis et gratiarum actionis, aut nudam commemorationem sacrificii in cruce peracti, non autem propitiatorium; vel soli prodesse sumenti; neque pro vivis et defunctis pro peccatis, pœnis, satisfactionibus et aliis necessitatibus offerri debere: anathema sit.

CANON IV.—*Si quis dixerit, blasphemiam irrogari sanctissimo Christi sacrificio in cruce peracto per missæ sacrificium, aut illi per hoc derogari: anathema sit.*

CANON V.—*Si quis dixerit, imposturam esse, missas celebrare in honorem sanctorum et pro illorum intercessione apud Deum obtinenda, sicut Ecclesia intendit: anathema sit.*

CANON VI.—*Si quis dixerit, canonem missæ errores continere, ideoque abrogandum esse: anathema sit.*

CANON VII.—*Si quis dixerit, ceremonias, vestes et externa signa, quibus in missarum celebratione Ecclesia Catholica utitur, irritabula impietatis esse magis quam officia pietatis: anathema sit.*

CANON VIII.—*Si quis dixerit, missas, in quibus solus sacer-*

that the sacrifice of the mass is only a sacrifice of praise and of thanksgiving; or, that it is a bare commemoration of the sacrifice consummated on the cross, but not a propitiatory sacrifice; or, that it profits him only who receives; and that it ought not to be offered for the living and the dead for sins, pains, satisfactions, and other necessities: let him be anathema.

CANON IV.—If any one saith, that, by the sacrifice of the mass, a blasphemy is cast upon the most holy sacrifice of Christ consummated on the cross; or, that it is thereby derogated from: let him be anathema.

CANON V.—If any one saith, that it is an imposture to celebrate masses in honor of the saints, and for obtaining their intercession with God, as the Church intends: let him be anathema.

CANON VI.—If any one saith, that the canon of the mass contains errors, and is therefore to be abrogated: let him be anathema.

CANON VII.—If any one saith, that the ceremonies, vestments, and outward signs, which the Catholic Church makes use of in the celebration of masses, are incentives to impiety, rather than offices of piety: let him be anathema.

CANON VIII.—If any one saith, that masses, wherein the priest alone

dos sacramentaliter communicat, illicitas esse ideoque abrogandas : anathema sit.

CANON IX.—*Si quis dixerit, Ecclesiæ Romanæ ritum, quo submissa voce pars canonis et verba consecrationis proferuntur, damnandum esse; aut lingua tantum vulgari missam celebrari debere ; aut aquam non miscendam esse vino in calice offerendo, eo quod sit contra Christi institutionem : anathema sit.*

communicates sacramentally, are unlawful, and are, therefore, to be abrogated : let him be anathema.

CANON IX.—If any one saith, that the rite of the Roman Church, according to which a part of the canon and the words of consecration are pronounced in a low tone, is to be condemned ; or, that the mass ought to be celebrated in the vulgar tongue only ; or, that water ought not to be mixed with the wine that is to be offered in the chalice, for that it is contrary to the institution of Christ: let him be anathema.

SESSIO VIGESIMATERTIA,

celebrata die XV. Iulii 1563.

VERA ET CATHOLICA DOCTRINA DE SACRAMENTO ORDINIS.

CAPUT I.

De institutione sacerdoti novæ legis.

Sacrificium et sacerdotium ita Dei ordinatione conjuncta sunt, ut utrumque in omni lege exstiterit. Cum igitur in Novo Testamento sanctum Eucharistiæ sacrificium visibile ex Domini institutione Catholica Ecclesia acceperit, fateri etiam oportet, in ea novum esse visibile et externum sacerdotium, in quod vetus translatum est. Hoc autem ab eodem Domino

TWENTY-THIRD SESSION,

held July 15, 1563.

THE TRUE AND CATHOLIC DOCTRINE CONCERNING THE SACRAMENT OF ORDER.

CHAPTER I.

On the institution of the Priesthood of the New Law.

Sacrifice and priesthood are, by the ordinance of God, in such wise conjoined, as that both have existed in every law. Whereas, therefore, in the New Testament, the Catholic Church has received, from the institution of Christ, the holy visible sacrifice of the Eucharist; it must needs also be confessed, that there is, in that Church, a new, visible, and external priesthood, into which the old has been *trans-*

Salvatore nostro institutum esse, atque apostolis eorumque successoribus in sacerdotio potestatem traditam consecrandi, offerendi et ministrandi corpus et sanguinem ejus, necnon et peccata dimittendi et retinendi, sacræ litteræ ostendunt et Catholicæ Ecclesiæ traditio semper docuit.

lated.[1] And the sacred Scriptures show, and the tradition of the Catholic Church has always taught, that this priesthood was instituted by the same Lord our Saviour, and that to the Apostles, and their successors in the priesthood, was the power delivered of consecrating, offering, and administering his body and blood, as also of forgiving and of retaining sins.

Caput II.

De septem ordinibus.

Cum autem divina res sit tam sancti sacerdotii ministerium, consentaneum fuit, quo dignius et majori cum veneratione exerceri posset, ut in Ecclesiæ ordinatissima dispositione plures et diversi essent ministrorum ordines, qui sacerdotio ex officio deservirent, ita distributi, ut, qui jam clericali tonsura insigniti essent, per minores ad majores ascenderent. Nam non solum de sacerdotibus, sed et de diaconis sacræ litteræ apertam mentionem faciunt, et quæ maxime in illorum ordinatione attendenda sunt gravissimis verbis docent; et ab ipso Ecclesiæ initio sequentium ordinum nomina, atque uniuscujusque eorum propria ministeria, subdiaconi sci-

Chapter II.

On the Seven Orders.

And whereas the ministry of so holy a priesthood is a divine thing; to the end that it might be exercised in a more worthy manner, and with greater veneration, it was suitable that, in the most well ordered settlement of the Church, there should be several and diverse orders of ministers to minister to the priesthood, by virtue of their office; orders so distributed as that those already marked with the clerical tonsure should ascend through the lesser to the greater orders. For the sacred Scriptures make open mention not only of priests, but also of deacons; and teach, in words the most weighty, what things are especially to be attended to in the Ordination thereof; and, from the very beginning of the Church, the names of the following orders, and

---

[1] Heb. vii. 12.

licet, acolythi, exorcistæ, lectoris et ostiarii in usu fuisse cognoscuntur, quamvis non pari gradu; nam subdiaconatus ad majores ordines a patribus et sacris conciliis refertur, in quibus et de aliis inferioribus frequentissime legimus.

the ministrations proper to each one of them, are known to have been in use; to wit, those of subdeacon, acolyth, exorcist, lector, and doorkeeper; though these were not of equal rank; for the subdeaconship is classed amongst the greater orders by the Fathers and sacred Councils, wherein also we very often read of the other inferior orders.

Caput III.

Ordinem vere esse sacramentum.

Cum Scripturæ testimonio, apostolica traditione et patrum unanimi consensu perspicuum sit, per sacram ordinationem, quæ verbis et signis exterioribus perficitur, gratiam conferri, dubitare nemo debet, ordinem esse vere et proprie unum ex septem sanctæ Ecclesiæ sacramentis. Inquit enim apostolus: Admoneo te, ut resuscites gratiam Dei, quæ est in te, per impositionem manuum mearum. Non enim dedit nobis Deus spiritum timoris, sed virtutis et dilectionis et sobrietatis.

Chapter III.

That Order is truly and properly a Sacrament.

Whereas, by the testimony of Scripture, by Apostolic tradition, and the unanimous consent of the Fathers, it is clear that grace is conferred by sacred ordination, which is performed by words and outward signs, no one ought to doubt that Order is truly and properly one of the seven sacraments of holy Church. For the Apostle says: *I admonish thee that thou stir up the grace of God, which is in thee by the imposition of my hands. For God has not given us the spirit of fear, but of power, and of love, and of sobriety.*[1]

Caput IV.

De ecclesiastica hierarchia et ordinatione.

Quoniam vero in sacramento ordinis, sicut et in baptismo et

Chapter IV.

On the Ecclesiastical hierarchy, and on Ordination.

But, forasmuch as in the sacrament of Order, as also in Baptism

---

[1] 2 Tim. i. 6, 7.

confirmatione, character imprimitur, qui nec deleri nec auferri potest, merito sancta synodus damnat eorum sententiam, qui asserunt Novi Testamenti sacerdotes temporariam tantummodo potestatem habere, et semel rite ordinatos iterum laicos effici posse, si verbi Dei ministerium non exerceant. Quod si quis omnes Christianos promiscue Novi Testamenti sacerdotes esse, aut omnes pari inter se potestate spirituali præditos affirmet, nihil aliud facere videtur, quam ecclesiasticam hierarchiam, quæ est ut castrorum acies ordinata, confundere; perinde ac si contra beati Pauli doctrinam omnes apostoli, omnes prophetæ, omnes evangelistæ, omnes pastores, omnes sint doctores. Proinde sacrosancta synodus declarat, præter ceteros ecclesiasticos gradus episcopos, qui in apostolorum locum successerunt, ad hunc hierarchicum ordinem præcipue pertinere, et positos, sicut idem apostolus ait, a Spiritu Sancto regere Ecclesiam Dei; eosque presbyteris superiores esse, ac sacramentum confirmationis conferre, ministros Ecclesiæ ordinare, atque alia pleraque pe-

and Confirmation, a character is imprinted which can neither be effaced nor taken away, the holy Synod with reason condemns the opinion of those who assert that the priests of the New Testament have only a temporary power; and that those who have once been rightly ordained can again become laymen, if they do not exercise the ministry of the Word of God. And if any one affirm, that all Christians indiscriminately are priests of the New Testament, or that they are all mutually endowed with an equal spiritual power, he clearly does nothing but confound the ecclesiastical hierarchy, which is *as an army set in array ;*[1] as if, contrary to the doctrine of blessed Paul, *all* were *apostles, all prophets, all evangelists, all pastors, all doctors.*[2] Wherefore, the holy Synod declares that, besides the other ecclesiastical degrees, bishops, who have succeeded to the place of the Apostles, principally belong to this hierarchical order; that they are *placed,* as the same apostle says, *by the Holy Ghost, to rule the Church of God ;*[3] that they are superior to priests; administer the sacrament of Confirmation; ordain the ministers of the Church; and that they can perform very many other things; over which

---

[1] Cant. vi. 3.   [2] Ephes. vi. 11, 12.   [3] Acts xx. 28.

ragere ipsos posse, quarum functionum potestatem reliqui inferioris ordinis nullam habent. Docet insuper sacrosancta synodus, in ordinatione episcoporum, sacerdotum et ceterorum ordinum nec populi nec cujusvis sœcularis potestatis et magistratus consensum sive vocationem sive auctoritatem ita requiri, ut sine ea irrita sit ordinatio; quin potius decernit, eos, qui tantummodo a populo aut sœculari potestate ac magistratu vocati et instituti ad hœc ministeria exercenda adscendunt, et qui ea propria temeritate sibi sumunt, omnes non Ecclesiœ ministros sed fures et latrones per ostium non ingressos habendos esse. Hœc sunt, quœ generatim sacrœ synodo visum est Christi fideles de sacramento ordinis docere. His autem contraria certis et propriis canonibus in hunc, qui sequitur, modum damnare constituit, ut omnes adjuvante Christo fidei regula utentes in tot errorum tenebris Catholicam veritatem facilius agnoscere et tenere possint.

functions others of an inferior order have no power. Furthermore, the sacred and holy Synod teaches, that, in the ordination of bishops, priests, and of the other orders, neither the consent, nor vocation, nor authority, whether of the people, or of any civil power or magistrate whatsoever, is required in such wise as that, without this, the ordination is invalid: yea rather doth it decree, that all those who, being only called and instituted by the people, or by the civil power and magistrate, ascend to the exercise of these ministrations, and those who of their own rashness assume them to themselves, are not ministers of the Church, but are to be looked upon as *thieves and robbers, who have not entered by the door.*[1] These are the things which it hath seemed good to the sacred Synod to teach the faithful of Christ, in general terms, touching the sacrament of Order. But it hath resolved to condemn whatsoever things are contrary thereunto, in express and specific canons, in the manner following; in order that all men, with the help of Christ, using the rule of faith, may, in the midst of the darkness of so many errors, more easily be able to recognize and to hold Catholic truth.

---

[1] John x. 1.

DE SACRAMENTO ORDINIS.

CANON I. — *Si quis dixerit, non esse in Novo Testamento sacerdotium visibile et externum, vel non esse potestatem aliquam consecrandi et offerendi verum corpus et sanguinem Domini, et peccata remittendi et retinendi, sed officium tantum et nudum ministerium prædicandi evangelium, vel eos, qui non prædicant, prorsus non esse sacerdotes : anathema sit.*

CANON II. — *Si quis dixerit, præter sacerdotium non esse in Ecclesia Catholica alios ordines et majores et minores, per quos, velut per gradus quosdam, in sacerdotium tendatur : anathema sit.*

CANON III. — *Si quis dixerit, ordinem sive sacram ordinationem non esse vere et proprie sacramentum a Christo Domino institutum, vel esse figmentum quoddam humanum, excogitatum a viris rerum ecclesiasticarum imperitis, aut esse tantum ritum quemdam eligendi ministros verbi Dei et sacramentorum : anathema sit.*

CANON IV. — *Si quis dixerit, per sacram ordinationem non dari Spiritum Sanctum, ac proinde frustra episcopos di-*

ON THE SACRAMENT OF ORDER.

CANON I.—If any one saith, that there is not in the New Testament a visible and external priesthood; or, that there is not any power of consecrating and offering the true body and blood of the Lord, and of forgiving and retaining sins, but only an office and bare ministry of preaching the Gospel; or, that those who do not preach are not priests at all : let him be anathema.

CANON II.—If any one saith, that, besides the priesthood, there are not in the Catholic Church other orders, both greater and minor, by which, as by certain steps, advance is made unto the priesthood : let him be anathema.

CANON III.—If any one saith, that order, or sacred ordination, is not truly and properly a sacrament instituted by Christ the Lord; or, that it is a kind of human figment devised by men unskilled in ecclesiastical matters; or, that it is only a kind of rite for choosing ministers of the Word of God and of the sacraments : let him be anathema.

CANON IV.—If any one saith, that, by sacred ordination, the Holy Ghost is not given; and that vainly therefore do the bishops say,

cere : Accipe Spiritum Sanctum; aut per eam non imprimi characterem; vel eum, qui sacerdos semel fuit, laicum rursus fieri posse: anathema sit.

CANON V.—*Si quis dixerit, sacram unctionem, qua Ecclesia in sancta ordinatione utitur, non tantum non requiri, sed contemnendam et perniciosam esse, similiter et alias ordinis ceremonias: anathema sit.*

CANON VI.'—*Si quis dixerit, in Ecclesia Catholica non esse hierarchiam divina ordinatione institutam, quæ constat ex episcopis, presbyteris et ministris: anathema sit.*

CANON VII.—*Si quis dixerit, episcopos non esse presbyteris superiores, vel non habere potestatem confirmandi et ordinandi, vel eam, quam habent, illis esse cum presbyteris communem, vel ordines ab ipsis collatos sine populi vel potestatis sæcularis consensu aut vocatione irritos esse; aut eos qui nec ab ecclesiastica et canonica potestate rite ordinati, nec missi sunt, sed aliunde veniunt, legitimos esse verbi et sacramentorum ministros: anathema sit.*

CANON VIII.—*Si quis dixerit, episcopos, qui auctoritate Ro-*

Receive ye the Holy Ghost; or, that a character is not imprinted by that ordination ; or, that he who has once been a priest can again become a layman : let him be anathema.

CANON V.—If any one saith, that the sacred unction which the Church uses in holy ordination is not only not required, but is to be despised and is pernicious, as likewise are the other ceremonies of order : let him be anathema.

CANON VI.—If any one saith, that, in the Catholic Church there is not a hierarchy by divine ordination instituted, consisting of bishops, priests, and ministers : let him be anathema.

CANON VII.—If any one saith, that bishops are not superior to priests ; or, that they have not the power of confirming and ordaining ; or, that the power which they possess is common to them and to priests ; or, that orders, conferred by them, without the consent or vocation of the people, or of the secular power, are invalid ; or, that those who have neither been rightly ordained, nor sent, by ecclesiastical and canonical power, but come from elsewhere, are lawful ministers of the Word and of the sacraments : let him be anathema.

CANON VIII.—If any one saith, that the bishops, who are assumed

mani pontificis assumuntur, non esse legitimos et veros episcopos, sed figmentum humanum: anathema sit.

by authority of the Roman Pontiff, are not legitimate and true bishops, but are a human figment: let him be anathema.

SESSIO VIGESIMAQUARTA,
celebrata die XI. Nov. 1563.

TWENTY-FOURTH SESSION,
held Nov. 11, 1563.

DOCTRINA DE SACRAMENTO MATRIMONII.

DOCTRINE ON THE SACRAMENT OF MATRIMONY.

Matrimonii perpetuum indissolubilemque nexum primus humani generis parens divini Spiritus instinctu pronuntiavit, cum dixit: Hoc nunc os ex ossibus meis et caro de carne mea; quamobrem relinquet homo patrem suum et matrem et adhærebit uxori suæ, et erunt duo in carne una.

The first parent of the human race, under the influence of the Divine Spirit, pronounced the bond of matrimony perpetual and indissoluble, when he said: *This now is bone of my bones, and flesh of my flesh. Wherefore a man shall leave father and mother, and shall cleave to his wife, and they shall be two in one flesh.*[1]

Hoc autem vinculo duos tantummodo copulari et conjungi, Christus Dominus apertius docuit, cum postrema illa verba tamquam a Deo prolata referens dixit: Itaque jam non sunt duo, sed una caro; statimque ejusdem nexus firmitatem ab Adamo tanto ante pronuntiatam his verbis confirmavit: Quod ergo Deus conjunxit, homo non separet.

But, that by this bond two only are united and joined together, our Lord taught more plainly, when, rehearsing those last words as having been uttered by God, he said: *Therefore now they are not two, but one flesh;*[2] and straightway confirmed the firmness of that tie, proclaimed so long before by Adam, by these words: *What therefore God hath joined together, let no man put asunder.*[3]

Gratiam vero, quæ naturalem illum amorem perficeret et in-

But the grace which might perfect that natural love, and confirm

---

[1] Gen. ii. 23, 24.   [2] Matt. xix. 6.   [3] Matt. xix. 6.

dissolubilem unitatem confirma-
ret conjugesque sanctificaret, ip-
se Christus, venerabilium sacra-
mentorum institutor atque per-
fector, sua nobis passione pro-
meruit ; quod Paulus Apostolus
innuit, dicens : Viri, diligite uxo-
res vestras, sicut Christus dilexit
Ecclesiam, et seipsum tradidit pro
ea ; mox subjungens : Sacramen-
tum hoc magnum est, ego autem
dico in Christo et in Ecclesia.

Cum igitur matrimonium in
lege evangelica veteribus connu-
biis per Christum gratia præstet,
merito inter novæ legis sacramen-
ta adnumerandum, sancti patres
nostri, concilia, et universalis
Ecclesiæ traditio semper docu-
erunt, adversus quam impii ho-
mines hujus sæculi insanientes
non solum perperam de hoc ve-
nerabili sacramento senserunt,
sed de more suo prætextu evan-
gelii libertatem carnis introdu-
centes, multa ab Ecclesiæ Ca-
tholicæ sensu et ab apostolorum
temporibus probata consuetudine
aliena scripto et verbo asserue-
runt non sine magna Christi
fidelium jactura ; quorum teme-
ritati sancta et universalis sy-
nodus cupiens occurrere, insigni-
ores prædictorum schismaticorum
hæreses et errores, ne plures ad

that indissoluble union, and sanctify the married, Christ himself,
the institutor and perfecter of the
venerable sacraments, merited for
us by his passion ; as the Apostle
Paul intimates, saying, *Husbands*
love your wives, as Christ also
loved the Church, and delivered
himself up for it ; adding shortly
after, *This is a great sacrament,*
but I speak in Christ and in the
Church.[1]

Whereas therefore matrimony,
in the evangelical law, excels in
grace, through Christ, the ancient
marriages, with reason have our
holy Fathers, the Councils, and the
tradition of the universal Church,
always taught, that it is to be numbered amongst the sacraments of
the new law ; against which, impious men of this age raging, have
not only had false notions touching
this venerable sacrament, but, introducing according to their wont,
under the pretext of the Gospel, a
carnal liberty, they have by word
and writing asserted, not without
great injury to the faithful of Christ,
many things alien from the sentiment of the Catholic Church, and
from the usage approved of since the
times of the Apostles ; the holy and
universal Synod, wishing to meet the
rashness of these men, has thought

---

[1] Ephes. v. 25, 32.

se trahat perniciosa eorum con-tagio, exterminandos duxit, hos in ipsos hæreticos eorumque errores decernens anathematismos.

it proper, lest their pernicious con-tagion may draw more after it, that the more remarkable heresies and errors of the above-named schis-matics be exterminated, by decree-ing against the said heretics and their errors the following anathemas.

DE SACRAMENTO MATRIMONII.

ON THE SACRAMENT OF MATRIMONY.

Canon I.— *Si quis dixerit, matrimonium non esse vere et proprie unum ex septem legis evangelicæ sacramentis a Christo Domino institutum, sed ab hominibus in Ecclesia inventum, neque gratiam conferre : anathema sit.*

Canon I.—If any one saith, that matrimony is not truly and properly one of the seven sacraments of the evangelic law, [a sacrament] insti-tuted by Christ the Lord ; but that it has been invented by men in the Church ; and that it does not con-fer grace : let him be anathema.

Canon II.— *Si quis dixerit, licere Christianis plures simul habere uxores, et hoc nulla lege divina esse prohibitum : anathema sit.*

Canon II.—If any one saith, that it is lawful for Christians to have several wives at the same time, and that this is not prohibited by any divine law : let him be anathema.

Canon III.—*Si quis dixerit, eos tantum consanguinitatis et affinitatis gradus, qui Levitico exprimuntur, posse impedire matrimonium contrahendum et dirimere contractum, nec posse Ecclesiam in nonnullis illorum dispensare aut constituere, ut plures impediant et dirimant : anathema sit.*

Canon III.—If any one saith, that those degrees only of consan-guinity and affinity which are set down in Leviticus can hinder mat-rimony from being contracted, and dissolve it when contracted ; and that the Church can not dispense in some of those degrees, or estab-lish that others may hinder and dis-solve it : let him be anathema.

Canon IV.— *Si quis dixerit, Ecclesiam non potuisse consti-tuere impedimenta matrimoni-um dirimentia, vel in iis con-*

Canon IV.—If any one saith, that the Church could not estab-lish impediments dissolving mar-riage ; or, that she has erred in es-

stituendis errasse : anathema sit.

tablishing them : let him be anath ema.

CANON V.—*Si quis dixerit, propter hæresim, aut molestam cohabitationem, aut affectatam absentiam a conjuge, dissolvi posse matrimonii vinculum : anathema sit.*

CANON V.—If any one saith, that on account of heresy, or irksome cohabitation, or the affected absence of one of the parties, the bond of matrimony may be dissolved : let him be anathema.

CANON VI.—*Si quis dixerit, matrimonium ratum non consummatum per solemnem religionis professionem alterius conjugum non dirimi : anathema sit.*

CANON VI.—If any one saith, that matrimony contracted, but not consummated, is not dissolved by the solemn profession of religion by one of the parties : let him be anathema.

CANON VII.—*Si quis dixerit, Ecclesiam errare, cum docuit et docet juxta evangelicam et apostolicam doctrinam, propter adulterium alterius conjugum matrimonii vinculum non posse dissolvi, et utrumque, vel etiam innocentem, qui causam adulterio non dedit, non posse, altero conjuge vivente, aliud matrimonium contrahere, mœcharique eum, qui, dimissa adultera, aliam duxerit, et eam, quæ, dimisso adultero, alii nupserit : anathema sit.*

CANON VII.—If any one saith, that the Church has erred, in that she hath taught, and doth teach, in accordance with the evangelical and apostolical doctrine, that the bond of matrimony can not be dissolved on account of the adultery of one of the married parties ; and that both, or even the innocent one who gave not occasion to the adultery, can not contract another marriage during the lifetime of the other ; and, that he is guilty of adultery, who, having put away the adulteress, shall take another wife, as also she, who, having put away the adulterer, shall take another husband : let him be anathema.

CANON VIII.—*Si quis dixerit, Ecclesiam errare, cum ob multas causas separationem inter conjuges quoad thorum seu*

CANON VIII.—If any one saith, that the Church errs, in that she declares that, for many causes, a separation may take place between

quoad cohabitationem ad certum incertumve tempus fieri posse decernit : anathema sit.

CANON IX.—*Si quis dixerit, clericos in sacris ordinibus constitutos, vel regulares castitatem solemniter professos posse matrimonium contrahere, contractumque validum esse non obstante lege ecclesiastica vel voto; et oppositum nil aliud esse quam damnare matrimonium, posseque omnes contrahere matrimonium, qui non sentiunt se castitatis, etiam si eam voverint, habere donum : anathema sit ; cum Deus id recte petentibus non deneget, nec patiatur nos supra id quod possumus, tentari.*

CANON X.—*Si quis dixerit, statum conjugalem anteponendum esse statui virginitatis vel cœlibatus, et non esse melius ac beatius manere in virginitate aut cœlibatu, quam jungi matrimonio : anathema sit.*

CANON XI.—*Si quis dixerit, prohibitionem solemnitatis nuptiarum certis anni temporibus superstitionem esse tyrannicam ab ethnicorum superstitione pro-*

husband and wife, in regard of bed, or in regard of cohabitation, for a determinate or for an indeterminate period : let him be anathema.

CANON IX.—If any one saith, that clerics constituted in sacred orders, or regulars, who have solemnly professed chastity, are able to contract marriage, and that being contracted it is valid, notwithstanding the ecclesiastical law, or vow ; and that the contrary is nothing else than to condemn marriage ; and, that all who do not feel that they have the gift of chastity, even though they have made a vow thereof, may contract marriage : let him be anathema ; seeing that God refuses not that gift to those who ask for it rightly, neither does *he suffer us to be tempted above that which we are able.*[1]

CANON X.—If any one saith, that the marriage state is to be placed above the state of virginity, or of celibacy, and that it is not better and more blessed to remain in virginity, or in celibacy, than to be united in matrimony : let him be anathema.

CANON XI.—If any one saith, that the prohibition of the solemnization of marriages at certain times of the year is a tyrannical superstition, derived from the superstition of the

[1] 1 Cor. x. 13.

fectam, aut benedictiones et alias ceremonias, quibus Ecclesia in illis utitur, damnaverit: anathema sit.

CANON XII.—*Si quis dixerit, causas matrimoniales non spectare ad judices ecclesiasticos: anathema sit.*

heathen; or condemn the benedictions and other ceremonies which the Church makes use of therein: let him be anathema.

CANON XII.—If any one saith, that matrimonial causes do not belong to ecclesiastical judges: let him be anathema.

SESSIO VIGESIMAQUINTA,

cœpta die III. absoluta die IV. Decembris 1563.

DECRETUM DE PURGATORIO.

Cum Catholica Ecclesia, Spiritu Sancto edocta ex sacris litteris et antiqua patrum traditione, in sacris conciliis et novissime in hac œcumenica synodo docuerit, purgatorium esse, animasque ibi detentas, fidelium suffragiis, potissimum vero acceptabili altaris sacrificio, juvari; præcipit sancta synodus episcopis, ut sanam de purgatorio doctrinam a sanctis patribus et sacris conciliis traditam, a Christi fidelibus credi, teneri, doceri et ubique prædicari diligenter studeant.

Apud rudem vero plebem difficiliores ac subtiliores quæstiones, quæque œdificationem non faci-

TWENTY-FIFTH SESSION,

begun on the third, and terminated on the fourth of December, 1563.

DECREE CONCERNING PURGATORY.

Whereas the Catholic Church, instructed by the Holy Ghost, has, from the Sacred Writings and the ancient tradition of the Fathers, taught, in sacred Councils, and very recently in this œcumenical Synod, that there is a Purgatory, and that the souls there detained are helped by the suffrages of the faithful, but principally by the acceptable sacrifice of the altar,—the holy Synod enjoins on bishops that they diligently endeavor that the sound doctrine concerning Purgatory, transmitted by the holy Fathers and sacred Councils, be believed, maintained, taught, and every where proclaimed by the faithful of Christ. But let the more difficult and subtle questions, and which tend not to edification, and from which for the

unt, et ex quibus plerumque nulla fit pietatis accessio, a populari- bus concionibus secludantur. In- certa item, vel quæ specie falsi laborant, evulgari ac tractari non permittant. Ea vero, quæ ad curiositatem quamdam aut superstitionem spectant, vel tur- pe lucrum sapiunt, tamquam scandala et fidelium offendicula prohibeant.

Curent autem episcopi, ut fide- lium vivorum suffragia, missa- rum scilicet sacrificia, ora- tiones, eleemosynæ, aliaque pie- tatis opera, quæ a fidelibus pro aliis fidelibus defunctis fieri consueverunt, secundum Ecclesiæ instituta pie et devote fiant; et quæ pro illis ex tes- tatorum fundationibus vel alia ratione debentur, non perfunc- torie, sed a sacerdotibus et Ec- clesia ministris et aliis, qui hoc præstare tenentur, diligenter et accurate persolvantur.

most part there is no increase of piety, be excluded from popular discourses before the uneducated multitude. In like manner, such things as are uncertain, or which labor under an appearance of error, let them not allow to be made pub- lic and treated of. While those things which tend to a certain kind of curiosity or supe₁s:ition, or which savor of filthy lucre, let them pro- hibit as scandals and stumbling- blocks of the faithful. But let the bishops take care that the suffrages of the faithful who are living, to wit, the sacrifices of masses, prayers, alms, and other works of piety, which have been wont to be per- formed by the faithful for the other faithful departed, be piously and devoutly performed, in accordance with the institutes of the Church; and that whatsoever is due on their behalf, from the endowments of testators, or in other way, be dis- charged, not in a perfunctory man- ner, but diligently and accurately, by the priests and ministers of the Church, and others who are bound to render this [service].

DE INVOCATIONE, VENERATIONE, ET RELIQUIIS SANCTORUM, ET SACRIS IMAGINIBUS.

ON THE INVOCATION, VENERATION, AND RELICS OF SAINTS, AND ON SACRED IMAGES.

Mandat sancta synodus omni- bus episcopis et ceteris docendi

The holy Synod enjoins on all bishops, and others who sustain the

munus curamque sustinentibus, ut juxta Catholicæ et Apostolicæ Ecclesiæ usum a primævis Christianæ religionis temporibus receptum sanctorumque patrum consensionem et sacrorum conciliorum decreta in primis de sanctorum intercessione, invocatione, reliquiarum honore et legitimo imaginum usu, fideles diligenter instruant, docentes eos, sanctos una cum Christo regnantes orationes suas pro hominibus Deo offerre ; bonum, atque utile esse, suppliciter eos invocare ; et ob beneficia impenetranda a Deo per filium ejus Iesum Christum Dominum nostrum, qui solus noster redemptor et salvator est, ad eorum orationes, opem, auxiliumque confugere ; illos vero, qui negant, sanctos æterna felicitate in cœlo fruentes invocandos esse ; aut qui asserunt, vel illos pro hominibus non orare, vel eorum, ut pro nobis etiam singulis orent, invocationem esse idololatriam, vel pugnare cum verbo Dei, adversarique honori unius mediatoris Dei et hominum Iesu Christi, vel stultum esse, in cœlo regnantibus voce vel mente supplicare, impie sentire.

office and charge of teaching, that, agreeably to the usage of the Catholic and Apostolic Church, received from the primitive times of the Christian religion, and agreeably to the consent of the holy Fathers, and to the decrees of sacred Councils, they especially instruct the faithful diligently concerning the intercession and invocation of saints ; the honor [paid] to relics ; and the legitimate use of images : teaching them, that the saints, who reign together with Christ, offer up their own prayers to God for men ; that it is good and useful suppliantly to invoke them, and to have recourse to their prayers, aid, [and] help for obtaining benefits from God, through his Son, Jesus Christ our Lord, who is our alone Redeemer and Saviour ; but that they think impiously who deny that the saints, who enjoy eternal happiness in heaven, are to be invoked ; or who assert either that they do not pray for men ; or that the invocation of them to pray for each of us even in particular is idolatry ; or that it is repugnant to the Word of God, and is opposed to the honor of the *one mediator of God and men, Christ Jesus ;*[1] or that it is foolish to supplicate, vocally or mentally, those who reign in heaven.

---

[1] 1 Tim. ii. 5.

Sanctorum quoque martyrum et aliorum cum Christo viventium sancta corpora, quæ viva membra fuerunt Christi et templum Spiritus Sancti, ab ipso ad æternam vitam suscitanda et glorificanda, a fidelibus veneranda esse, per quæ multa beneficia a Deo hominibus præstantur; ita ut affirmantes, sanctorum reliquiis venerationem atque honorem non deberi; vel eas aliaque sacra monumenta a fidelibus inutiliter honorari, atque eorum opis impetrandæ causa sanctorum memorias frustra frequentari; omnino damnandos esse, prout jam pridem eos damnavit, et nunc etiam damnat Ecclesia.

Also, that the holy bodies of holy martyrs, and of others now living with Christ,—which bodies were the living members of Christ, and *the temple of the Holy Ghost*,[1] and which are by him to be raised unto eternal life, and to be glorified,—are to be venerated by the faithful; through which [bodies] many benefits are bestowed by God on men; so that they who affirm that veneration and honor are not due to the relics of saints; or that these, and other sacred monuments, are uselessly honored by the faithful; and that the places dedicated to the memories of the saints are in vain visited with the view of obtaining their aid, are wholly to be condemned, as the Church has already long since condemned, and now also condemns them.

Imagines porro Christi, Deiparæ Virginis et aliorum sanctorum in templis præsertim habendas et retinendas, eisque debitum honorem et venerationem impertiendam; non quod credatur inesse aliqua in iis divinitas vel virtus, propter quam sint colendæ, vel quod ab eis sit aliquid petendum, vel quod fiducia in imaginibus sit figenda veluti olim fiebat a gentibus, quæ in idolis spem suam

Moreover, that the images of Christ, of the Virgin Mother of God, and of the other saints, are to be had and retained particularly in temples, and that due honor and veneration are to be given them; not that any divinity, or virtue, is believed to be in them, on account of which they are to be worshipped; or that any thing is to be asked of them; or that trust is to be reposed in images, as was of old done by the Gentiles, who placed their hope

---

[1] 1 Cor. iii. 6.

collocabant ; sed quoniam honos, qui eis exhibetur, refertur ad prototypa, quæ illæ repræsentant, ita ut per imagines, quas osculamur et coram quibus caput aperimus et procumbimus, Christum adoremus, et sanctos, quorum illæ similitudinem gerunt, veneremur : id quod conciliorum præsertim vero secundæ Nicænæ Synodi decretis contra imaginum oppugnatores est sancitum.

Illud vero diligenter doceant episcopi, per historias mysteriorum nostræ redemptionis picturis vel aliis similitudinibus expressas erudiri et confirmari populum in articulis fidei commemorandis et assidue recolendis ; tum vero ex omnibus sacris imaginibus magnum fructum percipi, non solum quia admonetur populus beneficiorum et munerum, quæ a Christo sibi collata sunt, sed etiam quia Dei per sanctos miracula et salutaria exempla oculis fidelium subjiciuntur, ut pro iis Deo gratias agant, ad sanctorumque imitationem vitam moresque suos componant, excitenturque ad adorandum ac diligendum Deum et ad pietatem colendam. Si quis autem his decretis contraria docue-

in idols; but because the honor which is shown them is referred to the prototypes which those images represent; in such wise that by the images which we kiss, and before which we uncover the head, and prostrate ourselves, we adore Christ, and we venerate the saints, whose similitude they bear : as, by the decrees of Councils, and especially of the second Synod of Nicæa, has been defined against the opponents of images.

And the bishops shall carefully teach this,—that, by means of the histories of the mysteries of our Redemption, portrayed by paintings or other representations, the people is instructed, and confirmed in [the habit of] remembering, and continually revolving in mind the articles of faith; as also that great profit is derived from all sacred images, not only because the people are thereby admonished of the benefits and gifts bestowed upon them by Christ, but also because the miracles which God has performed by means of the saints, and their salutary examples, are set before the eyes of the faithful; that so they may give God thanks for those things; may order their own lives and manners in imitation of the saints; and may be excited to adore and love God, and to cultivate piety. But if any one

rit aut senserit : anathema sit.

In has autem sanctas et salutares observationes si qui abusus irrepserint, eos prorsus aboleri sancta synodus vehementer cupit; ita ut nullæ falsi dogmatis imagines et rudibus periculosi erroris occasionem præbentes, statuantur. Quod si aliquando historias et narrationes sacræ scripturæ, cum id indoctæ plebi expediet, exprimi et figurari contigerit, doceatur populus, non propterea divinitatem figurari, quasi corporeis oculis conspici vel coloribus, aut figuris exprimi possit.

Omnis porro superstitio in sanctorum invocatione, reliquiarum veneratione et imaginum sacro usu tollatur, omnis turpis quæstus eliminetur, omnis denique lascivia vitetur; ita ut procaci venustate imagines non pingantur nec ornentur, et sanctorum celebratione ac reliquiarum visitatione homines ad commessationes atque ebrietates non abutantur, quasi festi dies in honorem sanctorum per luxum ac lasciviam agantur.

Postremo, tanta circa hæc di-

shall teach or entertain sentiments contrary to these decrees: let him be anathema.

And if any abuses have crept in amongst these holy and salutary observances, the holy Synod ardently desires that they be utterly abolished; in such wise that no images [suggestive] of false doctrine, and furnishing occasion of dangerous error to the uneducated, be set up. And if at times, when expedient for the unlettered people, it happen that the facts and narratives of sacred Scripture are portrayed and represented, the people shall be taught, that not thereby is the Divinity represented, as though it could be seen by the eyes of the body, or be portrayed by colors or figures.

Moreover, in the invocation of saints, the veneration of relics, and the sacred use of images, every superstition shall be removed, all filthy lucre be abolished; finally, all lasciviousness be avoided; in such wise that figures shall not be painted or adorned with a beauty exciting to lust; nor the celebration of the saints and the visitation of relics be by any perverted into revelings and drunkenness; as if festivals were celebrated to the honor of the saints by luxury and wantonness.

In fine, let so great care and dili-

gentia et cura ab episcopis ad-hibeatur, ut nihil inordinatum aut præpostere et tumultuarie accomodatum, nihil profanum nihilque inhonestum appareat, cum domum Dei deceat sancti-tudo.

Hæc ut fidelius observentur, statuit sancta synodus, nemini licere ullo in loco vel ecclesia, etiam quomodolibet exempta, ul-lam insolitam ponere vel po-nendam curare imaginem, nisi ab episcopo approbata fuerit; nulla etiam admittenda esse no-va miracula, nec novas reli-quias recipiendas, nisi eodem recognoscente et approbante epis-copo, qui, simul atque de iis aliquid compertum habuerit, ad-hibitis in consilium theologis et aliis piis viris, ea faciat, quæ veritati et pietati consen-tanea judicaverit.

Quod si aliquis dubius, aut difficilis abusus sit exstirpan-dus, vel omnino aliqua de iis rebus gravior quæstio in-cidat, episcopus, antequam controversiam dirimat, metro-politani et comprovincialium episcoporum in concilio pro-vinciali sententiam exspectet, ita tamen, ut nihil inconsulto

gence be used herein by bishops, as that there be nothing seen that is disorderly, or that is unbecoming-ly or confusedly arranged, nothing that is profane, nothing indecorous, seeing that *holiness becometh the house of God.*[1]

And that these things may be the more faithfully observed, the holy Synod ordains, that no one be allowed to place, or cause to be placed, any unusual image, in any place or church, howsoever exempt-ed, except that image has been ap-proved of by the bishop; also, that no new miracles are to be acknowl-edged, or new relics recognized, unless the said bishop has taken cognizance and approved thereof; who, as soon as he has obtained some certain information in regard of these matters, shall, after having taken the advice of theologians, and of other pious men, act therein as he shall judge to be consonant with truth and piety. But if any doubt-ful or difficult abuse has to be ex-tirpated; or, in fine, if any more grave question shall arise touching these matters, the bishop, before de-ciding the controversy, shall await the sentence of the metropolitan and of the bishops of the province, in a provincial Council; yet so that nothing new, or that previously has

---

[1] Psa. xcii. 5.

sanctissimo Romano pontifice novum aut in Ecclesia hactenus inusitatum decernatur.

not been usual in the Church, shall be resolved on without having first consulted the most holy Roman Pontiff.

CONTINUATIO SESSIONIS

die IV. Decembris.

DECRETUM DE INDULGENTIIS.

Cum potestas conferendi indulgentias a Christo Ecclesiæ concessa sit, atque hujusmodi potestate divinitus sibi tradita antiquissimis etiam temporibus illa usa fuerit, sacrosancta synodus indulgentiarum usum, Christiano populo maxime salutarem et sacrorum conciliorum auctoritate probatum, in Ecclesia retinendum esse docet et præcipit, eosque anathemate damnat, qui aut inutiles esse asserunt, vel eas concedendi in Ecclesia potestatem esse negant. In his tamen concedendis moderationem juxta veterem et probatam in Ecclesia consuetudinem adhiberi cupit, ne nimia facilitate ecclesiastica disciplina enervetur.

Abusus vero, qui in his irrepserunt, et quorum occasione insigne hoc indulgentiarum nomen ab hæreticis blasphematur, emendatos et cor-

CONTINUATION OF THE SESSION,

on the fourth day of 'December.

DECREE CONCERNING INDULGENCES.

Whereas the power of conferring Indulgences was granted by Christ to the Church, and she has, even in the most ancient times, used the said power delivered unto her of God, the sacred holy Synod teaches and enjoins that the use of Indulgences, for the Christian people most salutary, and approved of by the authority of sacred Councils, is to be retained in the Church; and it condemns with anathema those who either assert that they are useless, or who deny that there is in the Church the power of granting them. In granting them, however, it desires that, in accordance with the ancient and approved custom in the Church, moderation be observed; lest, by excessive facility, ecclesiastical discipline be enervated. And being desirous that the abuses which have crept therein, and by occasion of which this honorable name of Indulgences is blasphemed by heretics, be amended and corrected, it

rectos cupiens, præsenti decreto generaliter statuit, pravos quæstus omnes pro his consequendis, unde plurima in Christiano populo abusuum causa fluxit, omnino abolendos esse.

Ceteros vero, qui ex superstitione, ignorantia, irreverentia, aut aliunde quomodocumque provenerunt, cum ob multiplices locorum et provinciarum, apud quas hi committuntur, corruptelas commode nequeant specialiter prohiberi; mandat omnibus episcopis, ut diligenter quisque hujusmodi abusus Ecclesiæ suæ colligat, eosque in prima synodo provinciali referat; ut, aliorum quoque episcoporum sententia cognita, statim ad summum Romanum pontificem deferantur, cujus auctoritate et prudentia, quod universali Ecclesiæ expediet, statuatur; ut ita sanctarum indulgentiarum munus pie, sancte et incorrupte omnibus fidelibus dispensetur.

ordains generally by this decree, that all evil gains for the obtaining thereof,—whence a most prolific cause of abuses amongst the Christian people has been derived,—be wholly abolished. But as regards the other abuses which have proceeded from superstition, ignorance, irreverence, or from whatsoever other source, since, by reason of the manifold corruptions in the places and provinces where the said abuses are committed, they can not conveniently be specially prohibited, it commands all bishops diligently to collect, each in his own Church, all abuses of this nature, and to report them in the first provincial Synod; that, after having been reviewed by the opinions of the other bishops also, they may forthwith be referred to the Sovereign Roman Pontiff, by whose authority and prudence that which may be expedient for the universal Church will be ordained; that thus the gift of holy Indulgences may be dispensed to all the faithful, piously, holily, and incorruptly.

II. PROFESSIO FIDEI TRIDENTINÆ.

PROFESSION OF THE TRIDENTINE FAITH. A.D. 1564.

[From the bulls of Pope Pius IV., '*Injunctum nobis*,' Nov. 13, 1564, and '*In sacrosancta*,' Dec. 9, 1564 (in the *Bullar. Rom.*, also in Streitwolf and Klener, *Libri Symb. Eccles. Cath.* Tom. II. pp. 315–321). The Latin text of the Creed is given also by Streitwolf and Klener (Tom. I. p. 98, sub tit.: *Forma juramenti professionis fidei*), by Denzinger, and in other collections of Roman Symbols. See Vol. I. § 25, pp. 96–99.]

I. *Ego —— firma fide credo et profiteor omnia et singula, quæ continentur in symbolo fidei, quo sancta Romana Ecclesia utitur, videlicet:*

'*Credo in unum Deum, Patrem omnipotentem,*' etc. [*Symbolum Nicenum.* See p. 27.]

II. *Apostolicas et ecclesiasticas traditiones, reliquasque ejusdem Ecclesiæ observationes et constitutiones firmissime admitto et amplector.*

III. *Item sacram Scripturam juxta eum sensum, quem tenuit et tenet sancta mater Ecclesia, cujus est judicare de vero sensu et interpretatione sacrarum Scripturarum, admitto; nec eam unquam, nisi juxta unanimem consensum patrum accipiam et interpretabor.*

IV. *Profiteor quoque, septem esse vere et proprie sacramenta novæ legis a Jesu Christo Domino nostro instituta, atque ad salutem humani generis, licet non omnia singulis, necessaria: scilicet baptismum, confirmati-*

I. I, ——, with a firm faith believe and profess all and every one of the things contained in that creed which the holy Roman Church makes use of:

'I believe in one God, the Father Almighty,' etc. [The Nicene Creed. See pp. 27 and 98.]

II. I most steadfastly admit and embrace apostolic and ecclesiastic traditions, and all other observances and constitutions of the same Church.

III. I also admit the holy Scriptures, according to that sense which our holy mother Church has held and does hold, to which it belongs to judge of the true sense and interpretation of the Scriptures; neither will I ever take and interpret them otherwise than according to the unanimous consent of the Fathers.

IV. I also profess that there are truly and properly seven sacraments of the new law, instituted by Jesus Christ our Lord, and necessary for the salvation of mankind, though not all for every one, to wit: baptism, con-

onem, eucharistiam, pœnitentiam, extremam unctionem, ordinem et matrimonium; illaque gratiam conferre; et ex his baptismum, confirmationem et ordinem sine sacrilegio reiterare non posse. Receptos quoque et approbatos Ecclesiæ Catholicæ ritus in supradictorum omnium sacramentorum solemni administratione recipio et admitto.

V. *Omnia et singula, quæ de peccato originali et de justificatione in sacrosancta Tridentina synodo definita et declarata fuerunt, amplector et recipio.*

VI. *Profiteor pariter, in missa offerri Deo verum, proprium et propitiatorium sacrificium pro vivis et defunctis; atque in sanctissimo eucharistiæ sacramento esse vere, realiter et substantialiter corpus et sanguinem, una cum anima et divinitate Domini nostri Jesu Christi, fierique conversionem totius substantiæ panis in corpus et totius substantiæ vini in sanguinem; quam conversionem Catholica Ecclesia transsubstantiationem appellat.*

VII. *Fateor etiam, sub altera tantum specie totum atque integrum Christum, verumque sacramentum sumi.*

VIII. *Constanter teneo, pur-*

firmation, the eucharist, penance, extreme unction, holy orders, and matrimony; and that they confer grace; and that of these, baptism, confirmation, and ordination can not be reiterated without sacrilege. I also receive and admit the received and approved ceremonies of the Catholic Church, used in the solemn administration of the aforesaid sacraments.

V. I embrace and receive all and every one of the things which have been defined and declared in the holy Council of Trent concerning original sin and justification.

VI. I profess, likewise, that in the mass there is offered to God a true, proper, and propitiatory sacrifice for the living and the dead; and that in the most holy sacrament of the eucharist there is truly, really, and substantially, the body and blood, together with the soul and divinity of our Lord Jesus Christ; and that there is made a change of the whole essence of the bread into the body, and of the whole essence of the wine into the blood; which change the Catholic Church calls transubstantiation.

VII. I also confess that under either kind alone Christ is received whole and entire, and a true sacrament.

VIII. I firmly hold that there is

gatorium esse, animasque ibi detentas fidelium suffragiis juvari. Similiter et sanctos una cum Christo regnantes venerandos atque invocandos esse, eosque orationes Deo pro nobis offerre, atque eorum reliquias esse venerandas.

IX. Firmissime[1] assero, imagines Christi ac Deiparæ semper Virginis, nec non aliorum sanctorum habendas et retinendas esse, atque eis debitum honorem ac venerationem impertiendam. Indulgentiarum etiam potestatem a Christo in Ecolesia relictam fuisse, illarumque usum Christiano populo maxime salutarem esse affirmo.

X. Sanctam Catholicam et Apostolicam Romanam Ecclesiam omnium ecclesiarum matrem et magistram agnosco, Romano que pontifici, beati Petri apostolorum principis successori ac Jesu Christi vicario veram obedientiam spondeo ac juro.

XI. Cætera item omnia a sacris canonibus et œcumenicis conciliis, ac præcipue a sacrosancta Tridentina synodo tradita, definita et declarata indubitanter recipio atque profiteor; simulque contraria omnia, atque hæreses quascumque ab Ec-

a purgatory, and that the souls therein detained are helped by the suffrages of the faithful. Likewise, that the saints reigning with Christ are to be honored and invoked, and that they offer up prayers to God for us, and that their relics are to be had in veneration.

IX. I most firmly assert that the images of Christ, and of the perpetual Virgin the Mother of God, and also of other saints, ought to be had and retained, and that due honor and veneration are to be given them. I also affirm that the power of indulgences was left by Christ in the Church, and that the use of them is most wholesome to Christian people.

X. I acknowledge the holy Catholic Apostolic Roman Church for the mother and mistress of all churches; and I promise and swear true obedience to the Bishop of Rome, successor to St. Peter, Prince of the Apostles, and Vicar of Jesus Christ.

XI. I likewise undoubtingly receive and profess all other things delivered, defined, and declared by the Sacred Canons and General Councils, and particularly by the holy Council of Trent; and I condemn, reject, and anathematize all things contrary thereto, and all

[1] Bullarium Rom. : firmiter.

clesia damnatas, rejectas et ana-|heresies which the Church has con-
thematizatas ego pariter damno, demned, rejected, and anathema-
rejicio et anathematizo. tized.

XII. *Hanc veram Catholicam* XII. I do, at this present, freely
fidem, extra quam nemo salvus profess and truly hold this true
esse potest, quam in præsenti Catholic faith, without which no
sponte profiteor et veraciter te- one can be saved; and I promise
neo, eundem integram et invio- most constantly to retain and con-
latam[1] *usque ad extremum vitæ* fess the same entire and invio-
spiritum constantissime, Deo ad- late, with God's assistance, to the
juvante, retinere et confiteri, at- end of my life. And I will take
que a meis subditis vel illis, care, as far as in me lies, that
quorum cura ad me in munere it shall be held, taught, and
meo spectabit, teneri, doceri et preached by my subjects, or by
prædicari, quantum in me erit, those the care of whom shall ap-
curaturum. Ita ego idem —— pertain to me in my office. This
spondeo, voveo ac juro. Sic me I promise, vow, and swear—so
Deus adjuvet, et hæc sancta Dei help me God, and these holy Gos-
Evangelia. pels of God.

[NOTE.—As it was promulgated by Pius IX., Jan. 20, 1877—*Acta sedis sanc.* X., 382—
and is now offered to Catholic priests and professors, Pius IV.'s Profession contains in
article XI, after the words *Tridentino synodo*, the clause *et ab oecumenico concilio Vaticano*
(*tradita, definita et declarata*) *praesertim de Romani pontificis primatu ac infallibili magisterio.* The insertion conforms to Pius IX.'s letter to a German bishop, Nov. 6, 1876,
that it is altogether necessary that priests with full and unreserved assent of will accept
the definition of papal infallibility unless they want to abandon the right faith, *pleno et
absoluto intellectus et voluntatis assensu definitionem complectantur, nisi a recta fide aberrare
velint.* In the same letter, Pius wrote that 'nothing could be more absurd than to think
that the Holy Spirit would vouchsafe truths and that, at the same time, it might be
inopportune to teach them.' The Profession is printed with the insertion in Benedict's
Code of Canon Law.—ED.]

III. DECRETUM PII IX. DE IMMACULATA CONCEPTIONE BEATÆ VIRGINIS MARIÆ.

THE DECREE OF POPE PIUS IX. ON THE IMMACULATE CONCEPTION OF THE BLESSED VIRGIN MARY.

[The Latin text from the Bull '*Ineffabilis Deus*,' in which Pope Pius IX. promulgated to the Roman Catholic world the definition of the Immaculate Conception of the Virgin Mary, as read before an assembly of Cardinals and Bishops in St. Peter's, Dec. 8, 1854. See Vol. I. §§ 28 and 29, pp. 108 sqq.]

Postquam nunquam intermisimus, in humilitate et jejunio privatas nostras et publicas Ecclesiæ preces Deo Patri per Filium Ejus offerre, ut Spiritus Sancti virtute mentem nostram dirigere et confirmare dignaretur, implorato universæ cœlestis curiæ præsidio, et advocato cum genitibus Paraclito Spiritu, eoque sic adspirante, ad honorem Sanctæ et Individuæ Trinitatis, ad decus et ornamentum Virginis Deiparæ, ad exaltationem Fidei Catholicæ et Christianæ Religionis augmentum, auctoritate Domini Nostri Jesu Christi, beatorum apostolorum Petri et Pauli ac nostra declaramus, pronunciamus et definimus,

DOCTRINAM, QUÆ TENET, BEATISSIMAM VIRGINEM MARIAM IN PRIMO INSTANTI SUÆ CONCEPTIONIS FUISSE SINGULARI OMNIPOTENTIS DEI GRATIÆ PRIVILEGIO, INTUITU MERITORUM CHRISTI JESU SALVATORIS HUMANI GENERIS, AB OMNI ORIGINALIS

Since we have never ceased in humility and fasting to offer up our prayers and those of the Church to God the Father through his Son, that he might deign to direct and confirm our mind by the power of the Holy Ghost, after imploring the protection of the whole celestial court, and after invoking on our knees the Holy Ghost the Paraclete, under his inspiration WE PRONOUNCE, DECLARE, AND DEFINE, unto the glory of the Holy and Indivisible Trinity, the honor and ornament of the holy Virgin the Mother of God, for the exaltation of the Catholic faith and the increase of the Christian religion, by the authority of our Lord Jesus Christ and the blessed Apostles Peter and Paul, and in our own authority, that THE DOCTRINE WHICH HOLDS THE BLESSED VIRGIN MARY TO HAVE BEEN, FROM THE FIRST INSTANT OF HER CONCEPTION, BY A SINGULAR GRACE AND PRIVILEGE OF ALMIGHTY GOD, IN VIEW OF THE MERITS OF CHRIST JESUS THE SAVIOUR OF MAN-

CULPÆ LABE PRÆSERVATAM IMMU-
NEM, ESSE A DEO REVELATAM, AD-
QUE IDCIRCO AB OMNIBUS FIDELI-
BUS FIRMITER CONSTANTERQUE CRE-
DENDAM.

*Quapropter si qui secus ac a
nobis definitum est, quod Deus
avertat, præsumpserint corde
sentire, ii noverint, ac porro
sciant, se proprio judicio con-
demnatos, nanfragium circa
fi lem passos esse, et ab unitate Ecclesiæ defecisse, ac præterea facto ipso suo semet pœnis a jure statutis subjicere
si quod corde, sentiunt, verbo
aut scripto vel alio quovis ex-
terno modo significare ausi fuerint.*

KIND, PRESERVED FREE FROM ALL
STAIN OF ORIGINAL SIN, WAS REVEALED
BY GOD, AND IS, THEREFORE, TO BE
FIRMLY AND CONSTANTLY BELIEVED
BY ALL THE FAITHFUL. Therefore,
if some should presume to think in
their hearts otherwise than we have
defined (which God forbid), they
shall know and thoroughly understand that they are by their own
judgment condemned, have made
shipwreck concerning the faith, and
fallen away from the unity of the
Church; and, moreover, that they,
by this very act, subject themselves
to the penalties ordained by law,
if, by word or writing, or any other
external means, they dare to signify
what they think in their hearts.

IV. SYLLABUS ERRORUM.

The Papal Syllabus of Errors. A.D. 1864.

[This document, though issued by the sole authority of Pope Pius IX., Dec. 8, 1864, must be regarded now as infallible and irreformable, even without the formal sanction of the Vatican Council. It is purely negative, but indirectly it teaches and enjoins the very opposite of what it condemns as error. See Vol. I. § 20, pp. 128–134.]

Syllabus complectens præcipuos nostræ ætatis Errores qui notantur in Allocutionibus Consistorialibus, in Encyclicis, aliisque Apostolicis Letteris Sanctissimi Domini Nostri Pii Papæ IX.

The Syllabus of the principal errors of our time, which are stigmatized in the Consistorial Allocutions, Encyclicals, and other Apostolical Letters of our Most Holy Lord, Pope Pius IX.

§ I.—PANTHEISMUS, NATURALISMUS ET RATIONALISMUS ABSOLUTUS.

1. *Nullum supremum, sapientissimum, providentissimumque Numen divinum exsistit ab hac rerum universitate distinctum, et Deus idem est ac rerum natura et iccirco immutationibus obnoxius, Deusque reapse fit in homine et mundo, atque omnia Deus sunt et ipsissimam Dei habent substantiam; ac una eademque res est Deus cum mundo, et proinde spiritus cum materia, necessitas cum libertate, verum cum falso, bonum cum malo, et justum cum injusto.*

Alloc. *Maxima quidem* 9 junii 1862.

2. *Neganda est omnis Dei actio in homines et mundum.*

Alloc. *Maxima quidem* 9 junii 1862.

3. *Humana ratio, nullo pror-*

§ I.—PANTHEISM, NATURALISM, AND ABSOLUTE RATIONALISM.

1. There exists no supreme, most wise, and most provident divine being distinct from the universe, and God is none other than nature, and is therefore subject to change. In effect, God is produced in man and in the world, and all things are God, and have the very substance of God. God is therefore one and the same thing with the world, and thence spirit is the same thing with matter, necessity with liberty, true with false, good with evil, justice with injustice.

Allocution *Maxima quidem*, 9th June, 1862.

2. All action of God upon man and the world is to be denied.

Allocution *Maxima quidem*, 9th June, 1862.

3. Human reason, without any

sus Dei respectu habito, unicus est veri et falsi, boni et mali arbiter, sibi ipsi est lex et naturalibus suis viribus ad hominum ac populorum bonum curandum sufficit.

Alloc. *Maxima quidem* 9 junii 1862.

4. *Omnes religionis veritates ex nativa humanæ rationis vi derivant; hinc ratio est princeps norma, qua homo cognotionem omnium cujuscumque generis veritatum assequi possit ac debeat.*

Epist. encycl. *Qui pluribus* 9 novembris 1846.

Epist. encycl. *Singulari quidem* 17 martii 1856.

Alloc. *Maxima quidem* 9 junii 1862.

5. *Divina revelatio est imperfecta et iccirco subjecta continuo et indefinito progressui, qui humanæ rationis progressioni respondeat.*

Epist. encycl. *Qui pluribus* 9 novembris 1846.

Alloc. *Maxima quidem* 9 junii 1862.

6. *Christi fides humanæ refragatur rationi; divinaque revelatio non solum nihil prodest, verum etiam nocet hominis perfectioni.*

Epist. encycl. *Qui pluribus* 9 novembris 1846.

Alloc. *Maxima quidem* 9 junii 1862.

7. *Prophetiæ et miracula in*

---

regard to God, is the sole arbiter of truth and falsehood, of good and evil; it is its own law to itself, and suffices by its natural force to secure the welfare of men and of nations.

Allocution *Maxima quidem*, 9th June, 1862.

4. All the truths of religion are derived from the native strength of human reason; whence reason is the master rule by which man can and ought to arrive at the knowledge of all truths of every kind.

Encyclical Letters, *Qui pluribus*, 9th November, 1846.

Encyclical Letters, *Singulari quidem*, 17th March, 1856.

Allocution *Maxima quidem*, 9th June, 1862.

5. Divine revelation is imperfect, and, therefore, subject to a continual and indefinite progress, which corresponds with the progress of human reason.

Encyclical Letters, *Qui pluribus*, 9th November, 1846.

Allocution *Maxima quidem*, 9th June, 1862.

6. Christian faith contradicts human reason, and divine revelation not only does not benefit, but even injures the perfection of man.

Encyclical Letters, *Qui pluribus*, 9th November, 1846.

Allocution *Maxima quidem*, 9th June, 1862.

7. The prophecies and miracles

Sacris Litteris exposita et narrata sunt poetarum commenta, et Christianæ fidei mysteria philosophicarum investigationum summa ; et utriusque Testamenti libris mythica continentur inventa; ipseque Jesus Christus est mythica fictio.

Epist. encycl. *Qui pluribus* 9 novembris 1846.

Alloc. *Maxima quidem* 9 junii 1862.

set forth and narrated in the Sacred Scriptures are the fictions of poets; and the mysteries of the Christian faith are the result of philosophical investigations. In the books of both Testaments there are contained mythical inventions, and Jesus Christ is himself a mythical fiction.

Encyclical Letters, *Qui pluribus*, 9th November, 1846.

Allocution *Maxima quidem*, 9th June, 1862

II.—RATIONALISMUS MODERATUS.

8. *Quum ratio humana ipsi religioni æquiparetur, iccirco theologicæ disciplinæ perinde ac philosophicæ tractandæ sunt.*

Alloc. *Singulari quadam perfusi* 9 decembris 1854.

§ II.—MODERATE RATIONALISM.

8. As human reason is placed on a level with religion, so theological matters must be treated in the same manner as philosophical ones.

Allocution *Singulari quâdam perfusi*, 9th December, 1854.

9. *Omnia indiscriminatim dogmata religionis Christianæ sunt objectum naturalis scientiæ seu philosophiæ; et humana ratio historice tantum exculta potest ex suis naturalibus viribus et principiis ad veram de omnibus etiam reconditioribus dogmatibus scientiam pervenire, modo hæc dogmata ipsi rationi tamquam objectum proposita fuerint.*

Epist. ad Archiep. Frising. *Gravissimas* 11 decembris 1862.

Epist. ad eumdem *Tuas libenter* 21 decembris 1863.

9. All the dogmas of the Christian religion are, without exception, the object of scientific knowledge or philosophy, and human reason, instructed solely by history, is able, by its own natural strength and principles, to arrive at the true knowledge of even the most abstruse dogmas : provided such dogmas be proposed as subject-matter for human reason.

Letter *ad Archiep. Frising. Gravissimas*, 11th December, 1862.

To the same, *Tuas libenter*, 21st December, 1863.

10. *Quum aliud sit philosophus, aliud philosophia, ille jus*

10. As the philosopher is one thing, and philosophy is another, so

et officium habet se submittendi auctoritati, quam veram ipse probaverit; at philosophia neque potest, neque debet ulli sese submittere auctoritati.

Epist. ad Archiep. Frising. *Gravissimas* 11 decembris 1862.

Epist. ad eumdem *Tuas libenter* 21 decembris 1863.

it is the right and duty of the philosopher to submit to the authority which he shall have recognized as true; but philosophy neither can nor ought to submit to any authority.

Letter *ad Archiep. Frising. Gravissimas,* 11th December, 1862.

To the same, *Tuas libenter,* 21st December, 1863.

11. *Ecclesia non solum non debet in philosophiam unquam animadvertere, verum etiam debet ipsius philosophiæ tolerare errores, eique relinquere ut ipsa se corrigat.*

Epist. ad Archiep. Frising. *Gravissimas* 11 decembris 1862.

11. The Church not only ought never to animadvert upon philosophy, but ought to tolerate the errors of philosophy, leaving to philosophy the care of their correction.

Letter *ad Archiep. Frising. Gravissimas,* 11th December, 1862.

12. *Apostolicæ Sedis, Romanarumque Congregationum decreta liberum scientiæ progressum impediunt.*

Epist. ad Archiep. Frising. *Tuas libenter* 21 decembris 1863.

12. The decrees of the Apostolic See and of the Roman Congregations fetter the free progress of science.

Letter *ad Archiep. Frising. Tuas libenter,* 21st December, 1863.

13. *Methodus et principia, quibus antiqui Doctores scholastici Theologiam excoluerunt, temporum nostrorum necessitatibus scientiarumque progressui minime congruunt.*

Epist. ad Archiep. Frising. *Tuas libenter* 21 decembris 1863.

13. The method and principles by which the old scholastic doctors cultivated theology are no longer suitable to the demands of the age and the progress of science.

Letter *ad Archiep. Frising. Tuas libenter,* 21st December, 1863.

14. *Philosophia tractanda est, nulla supernaturalis revelationis habita ratione.*

Epist. ad Archiep. Frising. *Tuas libenter* 21 decembris 1863.

14. Philosophy must be treated of without any account being taken of supernatural revelation.

Epist. *ad Archiep. Frising. Tuas libenter,* 21st December, 1863.

N. B.—*Cum rationalismi systemate cohæ-*

N. B.—To the rationalistic system belong,

rent maximam partem errores Antonii Günther, qui damnantur in Epist. ad Card. Archiep. Coloniensem Eximiam tuam 15 *junii* 1857, *et in Epist. ad Episc. Wratislaviensem* Dolore haud mediocri 30 *aprilis* 1860.

in great part, the errors of Anthony Günther, condemned in the letter to the Cardinal Archbishop of Cologne, *Eximiam tuam,* June 15, 1857, and in that to the Bishop of Breslau, *Dolore haud mediocri,* April 30, 1860.

§ III. — INDIFFERENTISMUS, LATITUDINARISMUS.

§ III.—INDIFFERENTISM, LATITUDINARIANISM.

15. *Liberum cuique homini est eam amplecti ac profiteri religionem, quam rationis lumine quis ductus veram putaverit.*

Litt. Apost. *Multiplices inter* 10 junii 1851.

Alloc. *Maxima quidem* 9 junii 1862.

15. Every man is free to embrace and profess the religion he shall believe true, guided by the light of reason.

Apostolic Letter, *Multiplices inter,* 10th June, 1851.

Allocution *Maxima quidem,* 9th June, 1862.

16. *Homines in cujusvis religionis cultu viam æternæ salutis reperire æternamque salutem assequi possunt.*

Epist. encycl. *Qui pluribus* 9 novembris 1846.

Alloc. *Ubi primum* 17 decembris 1847.

Epist. encycl. *Singulari quidem* 17 martii 1856.

16. Men may in any religion find the way of eternal salvation, and obtain eternal salvation.

Encyclical Letters, *Qui pluribus,* 9th November, 1846.

Allocution *Ubi primum,* 17th December, 1847.

Encyclical Letters, *Singulari quidem,* 17th March, 1856.

17. *Saltem bene sperandum est de æterna illorum omnium salute, qui in vera Christi Ecclesia nequaquam versantur.*

Alloc. *Singulari quadam* 9 decembris 1854.

Epist. encycl. *Quanto conficiamur* 17 augustii 1863.

17. We may entertain at least a well-founded hope for the eternal salvation of all those who are in no manner in the true Church of Christ.

Allocution *Singulari quâdam,* 9th December, 1854.

Encyclical Letters, *Quanto conficiamur,* 17th August, 1863.

18. *Protestantismus non aliud est quam diversa veræ ejusdem Christianæ religionis forma, in qua æque ac in Ecclesia Ca-*

18. Protestantism is nothing more than another form of the same true Christian religion, in which it is possible to be equally

tholica   Deo   placere   datum est.

Epist. encycl. *Noscitis et Nobiscum* 8 decembris 1849.

pleasing to God as in the Catholic Church.

Encyclical Letters, *Noscitis et Nobiscum,* 8th December, 1849.

§ IV.— SOCIALISMUS, COMMUNISMUS, SOCIETATES CLANDESTINÆ, SOCIETATES BIBLICÆ, SOCIETATES CLERICO-LIBERALES.

§ IV.— SOCIALISM, COMMUNISM, SECRET SOCIETIES, BIBLICAL SOCIETIES, CLERICO-LIBERAL SOCIETIES.

Ejusmodi pestes sæpe gravissimisque verborum formulis reprobantur in Epist. encycl. Qui pluribus 9 *novembr.* 1846; *in Alloc.* Quibus quantisque 20 *april.* 1849; *in Epist. encycl.* Noscitis et Nobiscum 8 *dec.* 1849; *in Alloc.* Singulari quadam 9 *dec.* 1854; *in Epist. encycl.* Quanto conficiamur mœrore 10 *augusti* 1863.

Pests of this description are frequently rebuked in the severest terms in the Encyc. *Qui pluribus,* Nov. 9, 1846; Alloc. *Quibus quantisque,* April 20, 1849; Encyc. *Noscitis et Nobiscum,* Dec. 8, 1849; Alloc. *Singulari quâdam,* Dec. 9, 1854; Encyc. *Quanto conficiamur mœrore,* Aug. 10, 1863.

§ V.— ERRORES DE ECCLESIA EJUSQUE JURIBUS.

§ V.— ERRORS CONCERNING THE CHURCH AND HER RIGHTS.

19. *Ecclesia non est vera perfectaque societas plane libera, nec pollet suis propriis et constantibus juribus sibi a divino suo fundatore collatis, sed civilis potestatis est definire quæ sint Ecclesiæ jura ac limites, intra quos eadem jura exercere queat.*

19. The Church is not a true, and perfect, and entirely free society, nor does she enjoy peculiar and perpetual rights conferred upon her by her Divine Founder, but it appertains to the civil power to define what are the rights and limits with which the Church may exercise authority.

Alloc. *Singulari quadam* 9 decembris 1854.

Alloc. *Multis gravibusque* 17 decembris 1860.

Alloc. *Maxima quidem* 9 junii 1862.

Allocution *Singulari quâdam,* 9th December, 1854.

Allocution *Multis gravibusque,* 17th December, 1860.

Allocution *Maxima quidem,* 9th June, 1862.

20. *Ecclesiastica potestas suam*

20. The ecclesiastical power must

auctoritatem exercere non debet absque civilis gubernii venia et assensu.

Alloc. *Meminit unusquisque* 30 septembris 1861.

not exercise its authority without the permission and assent of the civil government.

Allocution *Meminit unusquisque*, 30th September, 1861.

21. *Ecclesia non habet potestatem dogmatice definiendi, religionem Catholicæ Ecclesiæ esse unice veram religionem.*

Litt. Apost. *Multiplices inter* 10 junii 1851.

21. The Church has not the power of defining dogmatically that the religion of the Catholic Church is the only true religion.

Apostolic Letter, *Multiplices inter*, 10th June, 1851.

22. *Obligatio, qua Catholici magistri et scriptores omnino adstringuntur, coarctatur in iis tantum, quæ ab infallibili Ecclesiæ judicio veluti fidei dogmata ab omnibus credenda proponuntur.*

Epist. ad Archiep. Frising. *Tuas libenter* 21 decembris 1863.

22. The obligation which binds Catholic teachers and authors applies only to those things which are proposed for universal belief as dogmas of the faith, by the infallible judgment of the Church.

Letter *ad Archiep. Frising. Tuas libenter*, 21st December, 1863.

23. *Romani Pontifices et Concilia œcumenica a limitibus suæ potestatis recesserunt, jura principum usurparunt, atque etiam in rebus fidei et morum definiendis errarunt.*

Litt. Apost. *Multiplices inter* 10 junii 1851.

23. The Roman Pontiffs and œcumenical Councils have exceeded the limits of their power, have usurped the rights of princes, and have even committed errors in defining matters of faith and morals.

Apostolic Letter, *Multiplices inter*, 10th June, 1851.

24. *Ecclesia vis inferendæ potestatem non habet, neque potestatem ullam temporalem directam vel indirectam.*

Litt. Apost. *Ad apostolicæ* 22 augusti 1851.

24. The Church has not the power of availing herself of force, or any direct or indirect temporal power.

Apostolic Letter, *Ad apostolicæ*, 22d August, 1851.

25. *Præter potestatem Episcopatui inhærentem, alia est attributa temporalis potestas a ci-*

25. In addition to the authority inherent in the Episcopate, a further and temporal power is granted

vili imperio vel expresse vel tacite concessa, revocanda propterea, cum libuerit, a civili imperio.

Litt. Apost. *Ad apostolicæ* 22 augusti 1851.

26. *Ecclesia non habet nativum ac legitimum jus acquirendi ac possidendi.*

Alloc. *Nunquam fore* 15 decembris 1856.
Epist. encycl. *Incredibili* 17 septembris 1863.

27. *Sacri Ecclesiæ ministri Romanusque Pontifex ab omni rerum temporalium cura ac dominio sunt omnino excludendi.*

Alloc. *Maxima quidem* 9 junii 1862.

28. *Episcopis, sine gubernii venia, fas non est vel ipsas apostolicas litteras promulgare.*

Alloc. *Nunquam fore* 15 decembris 1856.

29. *Gratiæ a Romano Pontifice concessæ existimari debent tamquam irritæ, nisi per gubernium fuerint imploratæ.*

Alloc. *Nunquam fore* 15 decembris 1856.

30. *Ecclesiæ et personarum ecclesiasticarum immunitas a jure civili ortum habuit.*

Litt. Apost. *Multiplices inter* 10 junii 1851.

31. *Ecclesiasticum forum pro temporalibus clericorum causis sive civilibus sive criminalibus omnino de medio tollendum est,*

to it by the civil authority, either expressly or tacitly, which power is on that account also revocable by the civil authority whenever it pleases.

Apostolic Letter, *Ad apostolicæ*, 22d August, 1851.

26. The Church has not the innate and legitimate right of acquisition and possession.

Allocution *Nunquam fore*, 15th Dec., 1856.
Encyclical Letters, *Incredibili*, 17th September, 1863.

27. The ministers of the Church, and the Roman Pontiff, ought to be absolutely excluded from all charge and dominion over temporal affairs.

Allocution *Maxima quidem*, 9th June, 1862.

28. Bishops have not the right of promulgating even their apostolical letters, without the permission of the government.

Allocution *Nunquam fore*, 15th Dec., 1856.

29. Dispensations granted by the Roman Pontiff must be considered null, unless they have been asked for by the civil government.

Allocution *Nunquam fore*, 15th Dec., 1856.

30. The immunity of the Church and of ecclesiastical persons derives its origin from civil law.

Apostolic Letter, *Multiplices inter*, 10th June, 1851.

31. Ecclesiastical courts for temporal causes, of the clergy, whether civil or criminal, ought by all means to be abolished, either without the

etiam inconsulta et reclamante Apostolica Sede.

Alloc. *Acerbissimum* 27 septembris 1852.

Alloc. *Nunquam fore* 15 decembris 1856.

concurrence and against the protest of the Holy See.

Allocution *Acerbissimum*, 27th September, 1852.

Allocution *Nunquam fore*, 15th December, 1856.

32. *Absque ulla naturalis juris et æquitatis violatione potest abrogari personalis immunitas, qua clerici ab onere subeundæ exercendæque militiæ eximuntur; hanc vero abrogationem postulat civilis progressus maxime in societate ad formam liberioris regiminis constituta.*

Epist. ad Epistc. Montisregal. *Singularis Nobisque* 29 septembris 1864.

32. The personal immunity exonerating the clergy from military service may be abolished, without violation either of natural right or of equity. Its abolition is called for by civil progress, especially in a community constituted upon principles of liberal government.

Letter to the Archbishop of Montreal, *Singularis nobisque*, 29th September, 1864.

33. *Non pertinet unice ad ecclesiasticam jurisdictionis potestatem proprio ac nativo jure dirigere theologicarum rerum doctrinam.*

Epist. ad Archiep. Frising. *Tuas libenter* 21 decembris 1863.

33. It does not appertain exclusively to ecclesiastical jurisdiction, by any right, proper and inherent, to direct the teaching of theological subjects.

Letter *ad Archiep. Frising. Tuas libenter*, 21st December, 1863

34. *Doctrina comparantium Romanum Pontificem principi libero et agenti in universa Ecclesia doctrina est quæ medio ævo prævaluit.*

Litt. Apost. *Ad apostolicæ* 22 augusti 1851.

34. The teaching of those who compare the sovereign Pontiff to a free sovereign acting in the universal Church is a doctrine which prevailed in the middle ages.

Apostolic Letter, *Ad apostolicæ*, 22d August, 1851.

35. *Nihil vetat, alicujus concilii generalis sententia aut universorum populorum facto, summum Pontificatum ab Romano Episcopo atque Urbe ad alium*

35. There would be no obstacle to the sentence of a general council, or the act of all the universal peoples, transferring the pontifical sovereignty from the Bishop and

Episcopum aliamque civitatem transferri.

Litt. Apost. *Ad apostolicæ* 22 augusti 1851.

City of Rome to some other bishopric and some other city.

Apostolic Letter, *Ad apostolicæ*, 22d August, 1851.

36. *Nationalis consilii definitio nullam aliam admittit disputationem, civilisque administratio rem ad hosce terminos exigere potest.*

Litt. Apost. *Ad apostolicæ* 22 augusti 1851.

36. The definition of a national council does not admit of any subsequent discussion, and the civil power can regard as settled an affair decided by such national council.

Apostolic Letter, *Ad apostolicæ*, 22d August, 1851.

37. *Institui possunt nationales Ecclesiæ ab auctoritate Romani Pontificis subductæ planeque divisæ.*

Alloc. *Multis gravibusque* 17 decembris 1860.

Alloc. *Jamdudum cernimus* 18 martii 1861.

37. National churches can be established, after being withdrawn and plainly separated from the authority of the Roman Pontiff.

Allocution *Multis gravibusque*, 17th December, 1860.

Allocution *Jamdudum cernimus*, 18th March, 1861.

38. *Divisioni Ecclesiæ in orientalem atque occidentalem nimia Romanorum Pontificum arbitria contulerunt.*

Litt. Apost. *Ad apostolicæ* 22 augusti 1851.

38. Roman Pontiffs have, by their too arbitrary conduct, contributed to the division of the Church into eastern and western.

Apostolic Letter, *Ad apostolicæ*, 22d August, 1851.

§ VI.—ERRORES DE SOCIETATE CIVILI TUM IN SE, TUM IN SUIS AD ECCLESIAM RELATIONIBUS SPECTATA.

§ VI.—ERRORS ABOUT CIVIL SOCIETY, CONSIDERED BOTH IN ITSELF AND IN ITS RELATION TO THE CHURCH.

39. *Reipublicæ status, utpote omnium jurium origo et fons, jure quodam pollet nullis circumscripto limitibus.*

Alloc. *Maxima quidem* 9 junii 1862.

39. The commonwealth is the origin and source of all rights, and possesses rights which are not circumscribed by any limits.

Allocution *Maxima quidem*, 9th June, 1862.

40. *Catholicæ Ecclesia doctrina*

40. The teaching of the Catholic

humanæ societatis bono et commo-dis adversatur.

Epist. encycl. *Qui pluribus* 9 novembris 1846.

Alloc. *Quibus quantisque* 20 aprilis 1849.

Church is opposed to the well-being and interests of society.

Encyclical Letters, *Qui pluribus*, 9th November, 1846.

Allocution *Quibus quantisque*, 20th April, 1849.

---

41. *Civili potestati vel ab in-fideli imperante exercitæ competit potestas indirecta negativa in sacra; eidem proinde competit nedum jus quod vocant* exequatur, *sed etiam jus* appellationis, *quam nuncupant,* ab abusu.

Litt. Apost. *Ad apostolicæ* 22 augusti 1851.

41. The civil power, even when exercised by an unbelieving sovereign, possesses an indirect and negative power over religious affairs. It therefore possesses not only the right called that of *exequatur,* but that of the (so-called) *appellatio ab abusu.*

Apostolic Letter, *Ad apostolicæ,* 22d August. 1851.

42. *In conflictu legum utriusque potestatis jus civile prævalet.*

Litt. Apost. *Ad apostolicæ* 22 augusti 1851.

42. In the case of conflicting laws between the two powers, the civil law ought to prevail.

Apostolic Letter, *Ad apostolicæ,* 22d August, 1851.

43. *Laica potestas auctoritatem habet rescindendi, declarandi ac faciendi irritas solemnes conventiones (vulgo* Concordata) *super usu jurium ad ecclesiasticam immunitatem pertinentium cum Sede Apostolica initas, sine hujus consensu, immo et ea reclamante.*

Alloc. *In Consistoriali* 1 novembris 1850.

Alloc. *Multis gravibusque* 17 decembris 1860.

43. The civil power has a right to break, and to declare and render null, the conventions (commonly called *Concordats*) concluded with the Apostolic See, relative to the use of rights appertaining to the ecclesiastical immunity, without the consent of the Holy See, and even contrary to its protest.

Allocution *In Consistoriali*, 1st Nov., 1850.

Allocution *Multis gravibusque,* 17th December, 1860.

44. *Civilis auctoritas potest se immiscere rebus quæ ad religionem, mores et regimen spiritu-*

44. The civil authority may interfere in matters relating to religion, morality, and spiritual gov-

ale pertinent. Hinc potest de instructionibus judicare, quas Ecclesiæ pastores ad conscientiarum normam pro suo munere edunt, quin etiam potest de divinorum sacramentorum administratione et dispositionibus ad ea suscipienda necessariis decernere.

Alloc. *In Consistoriali* 1 novembris 1850.
Alloc. *Maxima quidem* 9 junii 1862.

ernment. Hence it has control over the instructions for the guidance of consciences issued, conformably with their mission, by the pastors of the Church. Further, it possesses power to decree, in the matter of administering the divine sacraments, as to the dispositions necessary for their reception.

Allocution *In Consistoriali*, 1st Nov., 1850.
Allocution *Maxima quidem*, 9th June, 1862.

45. *Totum scholarum publicarum regimen, in quibus juventus Christianæ alicujus reipublicæ instituitur, episcopalibus dumtaxat seminariis aliqua ratione exceptis, potest ac debet attribui auctoritati civili, et ita quidem attribui, ut nullam alii cuicumque auctoritati recognoscatur jus immiscendi se in disciplina scholarum, in regimine studiorum, in graduum collatione, in dilectu aut approbatione magistrorum.*

Alloc. *In Consistoriali* 1 novembris 1850.
Alloc. *Quibus luctuosissimis* 5 septembris 1851.

45. The entire direction of public schools, in which the youth of Christian states are educated, except (to a certain extent) in the case of episcopal seminaries, may and must appertain to the civil power, and belong to it so far that no other authority whatsoever shall be recognized as having any right to interfere in the discipline of the schools, the arrangement of the studies, the taking of degrees, or the choice and approval of the teachers.

Allocution *In Consistoriali*, 1st Nov., 1850.
Allocution *Quibus luctuosissimis*, 5th September, 1851.

46. *Immo in ipsis clericorum seminariis methodus studiorum adhibenda civili auctoritati subjicitur.*

Alloc. *Nunquam fore* 15 decembris 1856.

46. Much more, even in clerical seminaries, the method of study to be adopted is subject to the civil authority.

Allocution *Nunquam fore*, 15 Dec., 1856.

47. *Postulat optima civilis societatis ratio, ut populares scholæ, quæ patent omnibus cujusque e populo classis pueris, ac publica*

47. The best theory of civil society requires that popular schools open to the children of all classes, and, generally, all public institutes

universim instituta, quæ litteris severioribusque disciplinis tradendis et educationi juventutis curandæ sunt destinata, eximantur ab omni Ecclesiæ auctoritate, moderatrice vi et ingerentia, plenoque civilis ac politicæ auctoritatis arbitrio subjiciantur ad imperantium placita et ad communium ætatis opinionum amussim.

Epist. ad Archiep. Friburg. *Quum non sine* 14 julii 1864.

48. *Catholicis viris probari potest ea juventutis instituendæ ratio, quæ sit a Catholica fide et ab Ecclesiæ potestate sejuncta, quæque rerum dumtaxat naturalium scientiam ac terrenæ socialis vitæ fines tantummodo vel saltem primario spectet.*

Epist. ad Archiep. Friburg. *Quum non sine* 14 julii 1864.

49. *Civilis auctoritas potest impedire quominus sacrorum antistites et fideles populi cum Romano Pontifice libere ac mutuo communicent.*

Alloc. *Maxima quidem* 9 junii 1862.

50. *Laica auctoritaś habet per se jus præsentandi episcopos et potest ab illis exigere, ut ineant diœcesium procurationem, antequam ipsi canonicam a S. Sede institutionem*

intended for instruction in letters and philosophy, and for conducting the education of the young, should be freed from all ecclesiastical authority, government, and interference, and should be fully subject to the civil and political power, in conformity with the will of rulers and the prevalent opinions of the age.

Letter to the Archbishop of Fribourg, *Quum non sine*, 14th July, 1864.

48. This system of instructing youth, which consists in separating it from the Catholic faith and from the power of the Church, and in teaching exclusively, or at least primarily, the knowledge of natural things and the earthly ends of social life alone, may be approved by Catholics.

Letter to the Archbishop of Fribourg, *Quum non sine*, 14th July, 1864.

49. The civil power has the right to prevent ministers of religion, and the faithful, from communicating freely and mutually with each other, and with the Roman Pontiff.

Allocution *Maxima quidem*, 9th June, 1862.

50. The secular authority possesses, as inherent in itself, the right of presenting bishops, and may require of them that they take possession of their dioceses before having received canonical institu-

et apostolicas litteras accipiant.

Alloc. *Nunquam fore* 15 decembris 1856.

51. *Immo laicum gubernium habet jus deponendi ab exercitio pastoralis ministerii episcopos, neque tenetur obedire Romano Pontifici in iis quæ episcopatuum et episcoporum respiciunt institutionem.*

Litt. Apost. *Multiplices inter* 10 junii 1851.

Alloc. *Acerbissimum* 27 septembris 1852.

52. *Gubernium potest suo jure immutare ætatem ab Ecclesia præscriptam pro religiosa tam mulierum quam virorum professione, omnibusque religiosis familiis indicere, ut neminem sine suo permissu ad solemnia vota nuncupanda admittant.*

Alloc. *Nunquam fore* 15 decembris 1856.

53. *Abrogandæ sunt leges quæ ad religiosarum familiarum statum tutandum, earumque jura et officia pertinent; immo potest civile gubernium iis omnibus auxilium præstare, qui a suscepto religiosæ vitæ instituto deficere ac solemnia vota frangere velint; pariterque potest religiosas easdem familias perinde ac collegiatas Ecclesias, et beneficia simplicia etiam juris patronatus penitus extinguere, illorumque bona et reditus*

tion and the apostolic letters from the Holy See.

Allocution *Nunquam fore*, 15th Dec., 1856.

51. And, further, the secular government has the right of deposing bishops from their pastoral functions, and it is not bound to obey the Roman Pontiff in those things which relate to episcopal sees and the institution of bishops.

Apostolic Letter, *Multiplices inter*, 10th June, 1851.

Allocution *Acerbissimum*, 27th Sept., 1852.

52. The government has of itself the right to alter the age prescribed by the Church for the religious profession, both of men and women; and it may enjoin upon all religious establishments to admit no person to take solemn vows without its permission.

Allocution *Nunquam fore*, 15th Dec., 1856.

53. The laws for the protection of religious establishments, and securing their rights and duties, ought to be abolished: nay, more, the civil government may lend its assistance to all who desire to quit the religious life they have undertaken, and break their vows The government may also suppress religious orders, collegiate churches, and simple benefices, even those belonging to private patronage, and submit their goods and revenues to the adminis-

civilis potestatis administrationi et arbitrio subjicere et vindicare.

Alloc. *Acerbissimum* 27 septembris 1852.

Alloc. *Probe memineritis* 22 januarii 1855.

Alloc. *Cum sæpe* 26 julii 1855.

tration and disposal of the civil power.

Allocution *Acerbissimum*, 27th Sept., 1852.

Allocution *Probe memineritis*, 22d Jan., 1855.

Allocution *Cum sæpe*, 26th July, 1855.

54. *Reges et principes non solum ab Ecclesiæ jurisdictione eximuntur, verum etiam in quæstionibus jurisdictionis dirimendis superiores sunt Ecclesia.*

Litt. Apost. *Multiplices inter* 10 junii 1851.

54. Kings and princes are not only exempt from the jurisdiction of the Church, but are superior to the Church, in litigated questions of jurisdiction.

Apostolic Letter, *Multiplices inter*, 10th June, 1851.

55. *Ecclesia a Statu, Statusque ab Ecclesia sejungendus est.*

Alloc. *Acerbissimum* 27 septembris 1852.

55. The Church ought to be separated from the State, and the State from the Church.

Allocution *Acerbissimum*, 27th Sept., 1852.

§ VII.—ERRORES DE ETHICA NATURALI ET CHRISTIANA.

§ VII.—ERRORS CONCERNING NATURAL AND CHRISTIAN ETHICS.

56. *Morum leges divina haud egent sanctione, minimeque opus est ut humanæ leges ad naturæ jus confirmentur aut obligandi vim a Deo accipiant.*

Alloc. *Maxima quidem* 9 junii 1862.

56. Moral laws do not stand in need of the divine sanction, and there is no necessity that human laws should be conformable to the law of nature, and receive their sanction from God.

Allocution *Maxima quidem*, 9th June, 1862.

57. *Philosophicarum rerum morumque scientia, itemque civiles leges possunt et debent a divina et ecclesiastica auctoritate declinare.*

Alloc. *Maxima quidem* 9 junii 1862.

57. Knowledge of philosophical things and morals, and also civil laws, may and must depart from divine and ecclesiastical authority.

Allocution *Maxima quidem*, 9th June, 1862.

58. *Aliæ vires non sunt agnoscendæ nisi illæ quæ in materia positæ sunt, et omnis morum disciplina honestasque collocari*

58. No other forces are to be recognized than those which reside in matter; and all moral teaching and moral excellence ought to be

debet in cumulandis et augendis quovis modo divitiis ac in voluptatibus explendis.

Alloc. *Maxima quidem* 9 junii 1862.
Epist. encycl. *Quanto conficiamur* 10 augusti 1863.

59. *Jus in materiali facto consistit, et omnia hominum officia sunt nomen inane, et omnia humana facta juris vim habent.*

Alloc. *Maxima quidem* 9 junii 1862.

60. *Auctoritas nihil aliud est nisi numeri et materialium virium summa.*

Alloc. *Maxima quidem* 9 junii 1862.

61. *Fortunata facti injustitia nullum juris sanctitati detrimentum affert.*

Alloc. *Jamdudum cernimus* 18 martii 1861.

62. *Proclamandum est et observandum principium quod vocant de* non-interventu.

Alloc. *Novos et ante* 28 septembris 1860.

63. *Legitimis principibus obedientiam detrectare, immo et rebellare licet.*

Epist. encycl. *Qui pluribus* 9 novembris 1846.
Alloc. *Quisque vestrum* 4 octobris 1847.
Epist. encycl. *Noscitis et Nobiscum* 8 decembris 1849.
Litt. Apost. *Cum catholica* 26 martii 1860.

64. *Tum cujusque sanctissimi*

made to consist in the accumulation and increase of riches by every possible means, and in the enjoyment of pleasure.

Allocution *Maxima quidem*, 9th June, 1862.
Encyclical Letters, *Quanto conficiamur*, 10th August, 1863.

59. Right consists in the material fact, and all human duties are but vain words, and all human acts have the force of right.

Allocution *Maxima quidem*, 9th June, 1862.

60. Authority is nothing else but the result of numerical superiority and material force.

Allocution *Maxima quidem*, 9th June, 1862.

61. An unjust act, being successful, inflicts no injury upon the sanctity of right.

Allocution *Jamdudum cernimus*, 18th March, 1861.

62. The principle of *non-intervention*, as it is called, ought to be proclaimed and adhered to.

Allocution *Novos et ante*, 28th Sept., 1860.

63. It is allowable to refuse obedience to legitimate princes: nay, more, to rise in insurrection against them.

Encyclical Letters, *Qui pluribus*, 9th November, 1846.
Allocution *Quisque vestrum*, 4th Oct., 1847.
Encyclical Letters, *Noscitis et Nobiscum*, 8th December, 1849.
Apostolic Letter, *Cum catholica*, 26th March, 1860.

64. The violation of a solemn

*juramenti violatio, tum quœli-
bet scelesta flagitiosaque actio
sempiternœ legi repugnans, non
solum haud est improbanda, verum etiam omnino licita, sum-
misque laudibus efferenda, quando id pro patriœ amore agatur.*

Alloc. *Quibus quantisque* 20 aprilis
1849.

oath, even every wicked and fla-
gitious action repugnant to the
eternal law, is not only not blam-
able, but quite lawful, and worthy of the highest praise, when
done for the love of country.

Allocution *Quibus quantisque*, 20th April,
1849.

§ VIII.—ERRORES DE MATRIMONIO
CHRISTIANO.

§ VIII.—THE ERRORS CONCERNING
CHRISTIAN MARRIAGE.

65. *Nulla ratione ferri potest,
Christum evexisse matrimonium
ad dignitatem sacramenti.*

Litt. Apost. *Ad apostolicœ* 22 augusti
1851.

65. It can not be by any means
tolerated, to maintain that Christ
has raised marriage to the dignity
of a sacrament.

Apostolic Letter, *Ad apostolicœ*, 22d August, 1851.

66. *Matrimonii sacramentum
non est nisi quid contractui acces-
sorium ab eoque separabile, ipsumque sacramentum in una tantum
nuptiali benedictione situm est.*

Litt. Apost. *Ad apostolicœ* 22 augusti
1851.

66. The sacrament of marriage
is only an adjunct of the contract,
and separable from it, and the sacrament itself consists in the nup-
tial benediction alone.

Apostolic Letter, *Ad apostolicœ*, 22d August, 1851.

67. *Jure naturœ matrimonii
vinculum non est indissolubile
et in variis casibus divortium
proprie dictum auctoritate civili sanciri potest.*

Litt. Apost. *Ad apostolicœ* 22 augusti
1851.

Alloc. *Acerbissimum* 27 septembris 1852.

67. By the law of nature, the
marriage tie is not indissoluble,
and in many cases divorce, properly so called, may be pronounced
by the civil authority.

Apostolic Letter, *Ad apostolicœ*, 22d August, 1851.

Allocution *Acerbissimum*, 27th Sept. 1852.

68. *Ecclesia non habet potestatem impedimenta matrimonium
dirimentia inducendi, sed ea potestas civili auctoritati competit,*

68. The Church has not the power
of laying down what are diriment
impediments to marriage. The
civil authority does possess such a

a qua impedimenta existentia tollenda sunt.

Litt. Apost. *Multiplices inter* 10 junii 1851.

power, and can do away with existing impediments to marriage.

Apostolic Letter, *Multiplices inter,* 10th June, 1851.

69. *Ecclesia sequioribus sœculis dirimentia impedimenta inducere cœpit, non jure proprio, sed illo jure usa, quod a civili potestate mutuata erat.*

Litt. Apost. *Ad apostolicæ* 22 augusti 1851.

69. The Church only commenced in later ages to bring in diriment impediments, and then availing herself of a right not her own, but borrowed from the civil power.

Apostolic Letter, *Ad apostolicæ,* 22d August, 1851.

70. *Tridentini canones, qui anathematis censuram illis inferunt, qui facultatem impedimenta dirimentia inducendi Ecclesiæ negare audeant, vel non sunt dogmatici vel de hac mutuata potestate intelligendi sunt.*

Litt. Apost. *Ad apostolicæ* 22 augusti 1851.

70. The canons of the Council of Trent, which pronounce censure of anathema against those who deny to the Church the right of laying down what are diriment impediments, either are not dogmatic, or must be understood as referring only to such borrowed power.

Apostolic Letter, *Ad apostolicæ,* 22d August, 1851.

71. *Tridentini forma sub infirmitatis pœna non obligat, ubi lex civilis aliam formam præstituat, et velit hac nova forma interveniente matrimonium valere.*

Litt. Apost. *Ad apostolicæ* 22 augusti 1851.

71. The form of solemnizing marriage prescribed by the said Council, under penalty of nullity, does not bind in cases where the civil law has appointed another form, and where it decrees that this new form shall effectuate a valid marriage.

Apostolic Letter, *Ad apostolicæ,* 22d August, 1851.

72. *Bonifacius VIII. votum castitatis in ordinatione emissum nuptias nullas reddere primus asseruit.*

Litt. Apost. *Ad apostolicæ* 22 augusti 1851.

72. Boniface VIII. is the first who declared that the vow of chastity pronounced at ordination annuls nuptials.

Apostolic Letter, *Ad apostolicæ,* 22d August, 1851.

73. *Vi contractus mere civilis potest inter Christianos constare veri nominis matrimonium; falsumque est, aut contractum matrimonii inter Christianos semper esse sacramentum, aut nullum esse contractum, si sacramentum excludatur.*

Litt. Apost. *Ad apostolicæ* 22 augusti 1851.

Lettera di S. S. PIO IX. al Re di Sardegna 9 settembre 1852.

Alloc. *Acerbissimum* 27 septembris 1852.

Alloc. *Multis gravibusque* 17 decembris 1860.

73. A merely civil contract may, among Christians, constitute a true marriage; and it is false, either that the marriage contract between Christians is always a sacrament, or that the contract is null if the sacrament be excluded.

Apostolic Letter, *Ad apostolicæ*, 22d August, 1851.

Letter to the King of Sardinia, 9th September, 1852.

Allocution *Acerbissimum*, 27th Sept., 1852.

Allocution *Multis gravibusque*, 17th December, 1860.

74. *Caussæ matrimoniales et sponsalia suapte natura ad forum civile pertinent.*

Litt. Apost. *Ad apostolicæ* 22 augusti 1851.

Alloc. *Acerbissimum* 27 septembris 1852.

74. Matrimonial causes and espousals belong by their very nature to civil jurisdiction.

Apostolic Letter, *Ad apostolicæ*, 22d August, 1851.

Allocution *Acerbissimum*, 27th Sept., 1852.

N. B.—*Huc facere possunt duo alii errores de clericorum cælibatu abolendo et de statu matrimonii statui virginitatis anteferendo. (Confodiuntur, prior in epist. encycl.* Qui pluribus 9 *novembris* 1846, *posterior in litteris apost.* Multiplices inter 10 *junii* 1851.)

N. B.—Two other errors may tend in this direction, those upon the abolition of the celibacy of priests, and the preference due to the state of marriage over that of virginity. These have been proscribed; the first in the Encyclical *Qui pluribus*, Nov. 9, 1846; the second in the Apostolic Letter *Multiplices inter*, June 10th, 1851.

§ IX.—ERRORES DE CIVILI ROMANI PONTIFICIS PRINCIPATU.

§ IX.—ERRORS REGARDING THE CIVIL POWER OF THE SOVEREIGN PONTIFF.

75. *De temporalis regni cum spirituali compatibilitate disputant inter se Christianæ et Catholicæ Ecclesiæ filii.*

Litt. Apost. *Ad apostolicæ* 22 augusti 1851.

75. The children of the Christian and Catholic Church are not agreed upon the compatibility of the temporal with the spiritual power.

Apostolic Letter, *Ad apostolicæ*, 22d August, 1851.

76. *Abrogatio civilis imperii, quo Apostolica Sedes potitur, ad Ecclesiæ libertatem felicitatemque vel maxime conduceret.*

76. The abolition of the temporal power, of which the Apostolic See is possessed, would contribute in the greatest degree to the liberty and prosperity of the Church.

Alloc. *Quibus quantisque* 20 aprilis 849.

Allocution *Quibus quantisque*, 20th April, 1849.

N. B.—*Præter hos errores explicite notatos, alii complures implicite reprobantur, proposita et asserta doctrina, quam Catholici omnes firmissime retinere debeant, de civili Romani Pontificis principatu. (Ejusmodi doctrina luculenter traditur in Alloc.* Quibus quantisque 20 *aprilis* 1849; *in Alloc.* Si semper antea 20 *maii* 1850; *in Litt. apost.* Quum Catholica Ecclesia 26 *martii* 1860; *in Alloc.* Novos 28 *sept.* 1860; *in Alloc.* Jamdudum 18 *martii* 1861; *in Alloc.* Maxima quidem 9 *junii* 1862.

N. B.—Besides these errors, explicitly noted, many others are impliedly rebuked by the proposed and asserted doctrine, which all Catholics are bound most firmly to hold, touching the temporal sovereignty of the Roman Pontiff. These doctrines are clearly stated in the Allocutions *Quibus quantisque*, 20th April, 1849, and *Si semper antea*, 20th May, 1850; Apost. Letter *Quum Catholica Ecclesia*, 26th March, 1860; Allocutions *Novos*, 28th Sept., 1860; *Jamdudum*, 18th March, 1861; and *Maxima quidem*, 9th June, 1862.

§ X. — ERRORES QUI AD LIBERALISMUM HODIERNUM REFERUNTUR.

§ X. — ERRORS HAVING REFERENCE TO MODERN LIBERALISM.

77. *Ætate hac nostra non amplius expedit, religionem Catholicam haberi tamquam unicam Status religionem, ceteris quibuscumque cultibus exclusis.*

78. In the present day, it is no longer expedient that the Catholic religion shall be held as the only religion of the State, to the exclusion of all other modes of worship.

Alloc. *Nemo vestrum* 26 julii 1855.

Allocution *Nemo vestrum*, 26th July, 1855.

78. *Hinc laudabiliter in quibusdam Catholici nominis regionibus lege cautum est, ut hominibus illuc immigrantibus liceat publicum proprii cujusque cultus exercitium habere.*

78. Whence it has been wisely provided by law, in some countries called Catholic, that persons coming to reside therein shall enjoy the public exercise of their own worship.

Alloc. *Acerbissimum* 27 septembris 1852.

Allocution *Acerbissimum*, 27th Sept., 1852.

79. *Enimvero falsum est, civilium cujusque cultus libertatem,*

79. Moreover, it is false that the civil liberty of every mode of wor-

itemque plenam potestatem omnibus attributam quaslibet opiniones cogitationesque palam publiceque manifestandi conducere ad populorum mores animosque facilius corrumpendos ac indifferentismi pestem propogandam.

Alloc. *Nunquam fore* 15 decembris 1856.

80. *Romanus Pontifex potest ac debet cum progressu, cum liberalismo et cum recenti civilitate sese reconciliare et componere.*

Alloc. *Jamdudum cernimus* 18 martii 1861.

ship, and the full power given to all of overtly and publicly manifesting their opinions and their ideas, of all kinds whatsoever, conduce more easily to corrupt the morals and minds of the people, and to the propagation of the pest of indifferentism.

Allocution *Nunquam fore*, 15th Dec., 1856.

80. The Roman Pontiff can and ought to reconcile himself to, and agree with, progress, liberalism, and civilization as lately introduced.

Allocution *Jamdudum cernimus*, 18th March, 1861.

V. DECRETA DOGMATICA CONCILII VATICANI DE FIDE CATHOLICA ET DE ECCLESIA CHRISTI.

THE DOGMATIC DECREES OF THE VATICAN COUNCIL CONCERNING THE CATHOLIC FAITH AND THE CHURCH OF CHRIST. A.D. 1870.

[The Latin text from *Acta et Decreta sacrosancti et œcumenici Concilii Vaticani*, etc., *cum permissione superiorum*, Friburgi Brisgoviæ, 1871, Fasc. II. pp. 170–179, and 181–187. The English translation from Archbishop MANNING: *Petri Privilegium*, London, 1871, Part III. pp. 192–203, and 211–219. On the Vatican Council, see Vol. I. §§ 31–34, pp. 134 sqq.]

CONSTITUTIO DOGMATICA DE FIDE CATHOLICA.

Sessio III. Habita die 24 *Aprilis* 1870.

PIUS EPISCOPUS, SERVUS SERVORUM DEI, SACRO APPROBANTE CONCILIO, AD PERPETUAM REI MEMORIAM.

Dei Filius et generis humani Redemptor, Dominus Noster Jesus Chrisius, ad Patrem cœlestem rediturus, cum Ecclesia sua in terris militante omnibus diebus usque ad consummationem sæculi futurum se esse promisit. Quare dilectæ sponsæ præsto esse, adsistere docenti, operanti benedicere, periclitanti opem ferre nullo unquam tempore destitit. Hæc vero salutaris ejus providentia, cum ex aliis beneficiis innumeris continenter apparuit, tum iis manifestissime comperta est fructibus, qui orbi Christiano e Conciliis œcumenicis, ac nominatim

DOGMATIC CONSTITUTION ON THE CATHOLIC FAITH.

Published in the Third Session, held April 24, 1870.

PIUS, BISHOP, SERVANT OF THE SERVANTS OF GOD, WITH THE APPROVAL OF THE SACRED COUNCIL, FOR PERPETUAL REMEMBRANCE.

Our Lord Jesus Christ, the Son of God, and Redeemer of Mankind, before returning to his heavenly Father, promised that he would be with the Church Militant on earth all days, even to the consummation of the world. Therefore, he has never ceased to be present with his beloved Spouse, to assist her when teaching, to bless her when at work, and to aid her when in danger. And this his salutary providence, which has been constantly displayed by other innumerable benefits, has been most manifestly proved by the abundant good results which Christendom has derived from œcumenical Councils,

e Tridentino, iniquis licet tempo-ribus celebrato, amplissimi pro-venerunt. Hinc enim sanctissi-ma religionis dogmata pressius definita uberiusque exposita, er-rores damnati atque cohibiti; hinc ecclesiastica disciplina re-stituta firmiusque sancita, pro-motum in clero scientiæ et pie-tatis studium, parata adolescen-tibus ad sacram militiam edu-candis collegia, Christiani de-nique populi mores et accu-ratiore fidelium eruditione et frequentiore sacramentorum usu instaurati. Hinc præterea arc-tior membrorum cum visibili Capite communio, universoque corpori Christi mystico additus vigor; hinc religiosæ multipli-catæ familiæ aliaque Christianæ pietatis instituta; hinc ille eti-am assiduus et usque ad san-guinis effusionem constans ardor in Christi regno late per orbem propagando.

Verumtamen hæc aliaque in-signia emolumenta, quæ per ultimam maxime œcumenicam Synodum divina clementia Ec-clesiæ largita est, dum grato, quo par est, animo recolimus, acer-bum compescere haud possumus dolorem ob mala gravissima. inde

and particularly from that of Trent, although it was held in evil times. For, as a consequence, the sacred doctrines of the faith have been de-fined more closely, and set forth more fully, errors have been con-demned and restrained, ecclesiasti-cal discipline has been restored and more firmly secured, the love of learning and of piety has been pro-moted among the clergy, colleges have been established to educate youth for the sacred warfare, and the morals of the Christian world have been renewed by the more ac-curate training of the faithful, and by the more frequent use of the sac-raments. Moreover, there has re-sulted a closer communion of the members with the visible head, an increase of vigor in the whole mys-tical body of Christ, the multipli-cation of religious congregations, and of other institutions of Chris-tian piety, and such ardor in extend-ing the kingdom of Christ through-out the world as constantly endures, even to the sacrifice of life itself.

But while we recall with due thankfulness these and other sig-nal benefits which the divine mercy has bestowed on the Church, especially by the last œcumenical Council, we can not restrain our bitter sorrow for the grave evils, which are prin-

potissimum orta, quod ejusdem sacrosanctæ Synodi apud permultos vel auctoritas contempta, vel sapientissima neglecta fuere decreta.

Nemo enim ignorat, hæreses, quas Tridentini Patres proscripserunt, dum, rejecto divino Ecclesiæ magisterio, res ad religionem spectantes privati cujusvis judicio permitterentur, in sectas paullatim dissolutas esse multiplices, quibus inter se dissentientibus et concertantibus, omnis tandem in Christum fides apud non paucos labefactata est. Itaque ipsa Sacra Biblia, quæ antea Christianæ doctrinæ unicus fons et judex asserebantur, jam non pro divinis haberi, imo mythicis commentis accenseri cœperunt.

Tum nata est et late nimis per orbem vagata illa rationalismi seu naturalismi doctrina, quæ religioni Christianæ utpote supernaturali instituto per omnia adversans, summo studio molitur, ut Christo, qui solus Dominus et Salvator noster est, a mentibus humanis, a vita et moribus populorum excluso, meræ quod vocant rationis vel naturæ regnum stabiliatur. Relicta autem projectaque Christiana religione, negato vero Deo

cipally due to the fact that the authority of that sacred Synod has been contemned, or its wise decrees neglected, by many.

No one is ignorant that the heresies proscribed by the Fathers of Trent, by which the divine magisterium of the Church was rejected, and all matters regarding religion were surrendered to the judgment of each individual, gradually became dissolved into many sects, which disagreed and contended with one another, until at length not a few lost all faith in Christ. Even the Holy Scriptures, which had previously been declared the sole source and judge of Christian doctrine, began to be held no longer as divine, but to be ranked among the fictions of mythology.

Then there arose, and too widely overspread the world, that doctrine of rationalism, or naturalism, which opposes itself in every way to the Christian religion as a supernatural institution, and works with the utmost zeal in order that, after Christ, our sole Lord and Saviour, has been excluded from the minds of men, and from the life and moral acts of nations, the reign of what they call pure reason or nature may be established. And after forsaking and rejecting the Christian religion, and

et Christo ejus, prolapsa tandem est multorum mens in Pantheismi, Materialismi, Atheismi barathrum, ut jam ipsam rationalem naturam, omnemque justi rectique normam negantes, ima humanæ societatis fundamenta diruere connitantur.

Hac porro impietate circumquaque grassante, infeliciter contigit, ut plures etiam e Catholicæ Ecclesiæ filiis a via veræ pietatis aberrarent, in iisque, diminutis paullatim veritatibus, sensus Catholicus attenuaretur. Variis enim ac peregrinis doctrinis abducti, naturam et gratiam, scientiam humanam et fidem divinam perperam commiscentes, genuinum sensum dogmatum, quem tenet ac docet sancta mater Ecclesia, depravare, integritatemque et sinceritatem fidei in periculum adducere comperiuntur.

Quibus omnibus perspectis, fieri qui potest, ut non commoveantur intima Ecclesiæ viscera? Quemadmodum enim Deus vult omnes homines salvos fieri, et ad agnitionem veritatis venire; quemadmodum Christus venit, ut salvum faceret, quod perierat, et filios Dei, qui erant dispersi, congregaret in unum: ita Ecclesia, a Deo populorum

denying the true God and his Christ, the minds of many have sunk into the abyss of Pantheism, Materialism, and Atheism, until, denying rational nature itself, and every sound rule of right, they labor to destroy the deepest foundations of human society.

Unhappily, it has yet further come to pass that, while this impiety prevailed on every side, many even of the children of the Catholic Church have strayed from the path of true piety, and by the gradual diminution of the truths they held, the Catholic sense became weakened in them. For, led away by various and strange doctrines, utterly confusing nature and grace, human science and divine faith, they are found to deprave the true sense of the doctrines which our holy Mother Church holds and teaches, and endanger the integrity and the soundness of the faith.

Considering these things, how can the Church fail to be deeply stirred? For, even as God wills all men to be saved, and to arrive at the knowledge of the truth, even as Christ came to save what had perished, and to gather together the children of God who had been dispersed, so the Church, constituted by God the mother and teacher of nations, knows its own office as debtor to all,

mater et magistra constituta, omnibus debitricem se novit, ac lapsos erigere, labantes sustinere, revertentes amplecti, confirmare bonos et ad meliora provehere parata semper et intenta est. Quapropter nullo tempore a Dei veritate, quæ sanat omnia, testanda et prædicanda quiescere potest, sibi dictum esse non ignorans: Spiritus meus, qui est in te, et verba mea, quæ posui in ore tuo, non recedent de ore tuo amodo et usque in sempiternum.

Nos itaque, inhærentes prædecessorum nostrorum vestigiis, pro supremo nostro Apostolico munere veritatem Catholicam docere ac tueri perversasque doctrinas reprobare nunquam intermissimus. Nunc autem, sedentibus nobiscum et judicantibus universi orbis Episcopis, in hanc œcumenicam Synodum auctoritate nostra in Spiritu Sancto congregatis, innixi Dei verbo scripto et tradito, prout ab Ecclesia Catholica sancte custoditum et genuine expositum accepimus, ex hac Petri Cathedra, in conspectu omnium, salutarem Christi doctrinam profiteri et declarare constituimus, adversis erroribus potestate nobis a Deo tradita proscriptis atque damnatis.

and is ever ready and watchful to raise the fallen, to support those who are falling, to embrace those who return, to confirm the good and to carry them on to better things. Hence, it can never forbear from witnessing to and proclaiming the truth of God, which heals all things, knowing the words addressed to it: 'My Spirit that is in thee, and my words that I have put in thy mouth, shall not depart out of thy mouth, from henceforth and forever.'[1]

We, therefore, following the footsteps of our predecessors, have never ceased, as becomes our supreme Apostolic office, from teaching and defending Catholic truth, and condemning doctrines of error. And now, with the Bishops of the whole world assembled round us, and judging with us, congregated by our authority, and in the Holy Spirit, in this œcumenical Council, we, supported by the Word of God written and handed down as we received it from the Catholic Church, preserved with sacredness and set forth according to truth, have determined to profess and declare the salutary teaching of Christ from this Chair of Peter, and in sight of all, proscribing and condemning, by the power given to us of God, all errors contrary thereto.

---

[1] Isaiah lix. 21.

CAPUT I.	CHAPTER I.
De Deo rerum omnium Creatore.	*Of God, the Creator of all Things.*

Sancta Catholica Apostolica Romana Ecclesia credit et confitetur, unum esse Deum verum et vivum, Creatorem ac Dominum cœli et terræ, omnipotentem, æternum, immensum, incomprehensibilem, intellectu ac voluntate omnique perfectione infinitum; qui cum sit una singularis, simplex omnino et incommutabilis substantia spiritualis, prædicandus est re et essentia a mundo distinctus, in se et ex se beatissimus, et super omnia, quæ præter ipsum sunt et concipi possunt, ineffabiliter excelsus.

The holy Catholic Apostolic Roman Church believes and confesses that there is one true and living God, Creator and Lord of heaven and earth, almighty, eternal, immense, incomprehensible, infinite in intelligence, in will, and in all perfection, who, as being one, sole, absolutely simple and immutable spiritual substance, is to be declared as really and essentially distinct from the world, of supreme beatitude in and from himself, and ineffably exalted above all things which exist, or are conceivable, except himself.

Hic solus verus Deus bonitate sua et omnipotenti virtute non ad augendam suam beatitudinem, nec ad acquirendam, sed ad manifestandam perfectionem suam per bona, quæ creaturis impertitur, liberrimo consilio simul ab initio temporis utramque de nihilo condidit creaturam, spiritualem et corporalem, angelicam videlicet et mundanam, ac deinde humanam quasi communem ex spiritu et corpore constitutam.

This one only true God, of his own goodness and almighty power, not for the increase or acquirement of his own happiness, but to manifest his perfection by the blessings which he bestows on creatures, and with absolute freedom of counsel, created out of nothing, from the very first beginning of time, both the spiritual and the corporeal creature, to wit, the angelical and the mundane, and afterwards the human creature, as partaking, in a sense, of both, consisting of spirit and of body.

Universa vero, quæ condidit, Deus providentia sua tuetur atque gubernat, attingens a fine

God protects and governs by his providence all things which he hath made, 'reaching from end to end

usque ad finem fortiter, et dis-
ponens omnia suaviter. Omnia
enim nuda et aperta sunt oculis
ejus, ea etiam, quæ libera crea-
turarum actione futura sunt.

mightily, and ordering all things
sweetly.'[1] For 'all things are bare
and open to his eyes,'[2] even those
which are yet to be by the free
action of creatures.

CAPUT II.
De Revelatione.

CHAPTER II.
Of Revelation.

Eadem sancta mater Ecclesia
tenet et docet, Deum, rerum om-
nium principium et finem, na-
turali humanæ rationis lumine
e rebus creatis certo cognosci
posse; invisibilia enim ipsius,
a creatura mundi, per ea quæ
facta sunt, intellecta, conspici-
untur: attamen placuisse ejus
sapientiæ et bonitati, alia, eaque
supernaturali via se ipsum ac
æterna voluntatis suæ decreta
humano generi revelare, dicente
Apostolo: Multifariam, multis-
que modis olim Deus loquens
patribus in Prophetis: novis-
sime, diebus istis locutus est no-
bis in Filio.

The same holy Mother Church
holds and teaches that God, the beginning and end of all things, may
be certainly known by the natural
light of human reason, by means of
created things; 'for the invisible
things of him from the creation of
the world are clearly seen, being
understood by the things that are
made,'[3] but that it pleased his wisdom and bounty to reveal himself,
and the eternal decrees of his will,
to mankind by another and a supernatural way: as the Apostle says,
'God, having spoken on divers occasions, and many ways, in times
past, to the Fathers by the Prophets;
last of all, in these days, hath spoken
to us by his Son.'[4]

Huic divinæ revelationi tri-
buendum quidem est, ut ea, quæ
in rebus divinis humanæ ratio-
ni per se impervia non sunt, in
præsenti quoque generis humani
conditione ab omnibus expedite,
firma certitudine et nullo ad-
mixto errore cognosci possint.

It is to be ascribed to this divine
revelation, that such truths among
things divine as of themselves are
not beyond human reason, can,
even in the present condition of
mankind, be known by every one
with facility, with firm assurance,
and with no admixture of error.

---

[1] Wisd. viii. 1.　　　[2] Heb. iv. 13.　　　[3] Rom. i. 20.　　　[4] Heb. i. 1, 2.

Non hac tamen de causa revelatio absolute necessaria dicenda est, sed quia Deus ex infinita bonitate sua ordinavit hominem ad finem supernaturalem, ad participanda scilicet bona divina, quæ humanæ mentis intelligentiam omnino superant; siquidem oculus non vidit, nec auris audivit, nec in cor hominis ascendit, quæ præparavit Deus iis, qui diligunt illum.

Hæc porro supernaturalis revelatio, secundum universalis Ecclesiæ fidem, a sancta Tridentina Synodo declaratam, continetur in libris scriptis et sine scripto traditionibus, quæ ipsius Christi ore ab Apostolis acceptæ, aut ab ipsis Apostolis Spiritu Sancto dictante quasi per manus traditæ, ad nos usque pervenerunt. Qui quidem veteris et Novi Testamenti libri integri cum omnibus suis partibus, prout in ejusdem Concilii decreto recensentur, et in veteri vulgata latina editione habentur. pro sacris et canonicis suscipiendi sunt. Eos vero Ecclesia pro sacris et canonicis habet, non ideo, quod sola humana industria concinnati, sua deinde

This, however, is not the reason why revelation is to be called absolutely necessary; but because God of his infinite goodness has ordained man to a supernatural end, viz., to be a sharer of divine blessings, which utterly exceed the intelligence of the human mind; for 'eye hath not seen, nor ear heard, neither hath it entered into the heart of man, what things God hath prepared for them that love him.'[1]

Further, this supernatural revelation, according to the universal belief of the Church, declared by the sacred Synod of Trent, is contained in the written books and unwritten traditions which have come down to us, having been received by the Apostles from the mouth of Christ himself; or from the Apostles themselves, by the dictation of the Holy Spirit, have been transmitted, as it were, from hand to hand.[2] And these books of the Old and New Testament are to be received as sacred and canonical, in their integrity, with all their parts, as they are enumerated in the decree of the said Council, and are contained in the ancient Latin edition of the Vulgate. These the Church holds to be sacred and

---

[1] 1 Cor. ii. 9.
[2] Canons and Decrees of the Council of Trent, Session the Fourth. Decree concerning the Canonical Scriptures.

auctoritate sint approbati; nec ideo dumtaxat, quod revelationem sine errore contineant, sed propterea, quod Spiritu Sancto inspirante conscripti Deum habent auctorem, atque ut tales ipsi Ecclesiæ traditi sunt.

canonical, not because, having been carefully composed by mere human industry, they were afterwards approved by her authority, nor merely because they contain revelation, with no admixture of error; but because, having been written by the inspiration of the Holy Ghost, they have God for their author, and have been delivered as such to the Church herself.

Quoniam vero, quæ sancta Tridentina Synodus de interpretatione divinæ Scripturæ ad coërcenda petulantia ingenia salubriter decrevit, a quibusdam hominibus prave exponuntur, nos, idem decretum renovantes, hanc illius mentem esse declaramus, ut in rebus fidei et morum, ad ædificationem doctrinæ Christianæ pertinentium, is pro vero sensu sacræ Scripturæ habendus sit, quem tenuit ac tenet sancta mater Ecclesia, cujus est judicare de vero sensu et interpretatione Scripturarum sanctarum; atque ideo nemini licere contra hunc sensum aut etiam contra unanimem consensum Patrum ipsam Scripturam sacram interpretari.

And as the things which the holy Synod of Trent decreed for the good of souls concerning the interpretation of Divine Scripture, in order to curb rebellious spirits, have been wrongly explained by some, we, renewing the said decree, declare this to be their sense, that, in matters of faith and morals, appertaining to the building up of Christian doctrine, that is to be held as the true sense of Holy Scripture which our holy Mother Church hath held and holds, to whom it belongs to judge of the true sense and interpretation of the Holy Scripture; and therefore that it is permitted to no one to interpret the Sacred Scripture contrary to this sense, nor, likewise, contrary to the unanimous consent of the Fathers.

Caput III.
De Fide.

Quum homo a Deo tamquam Creatore et Domino suo totus

Chapter III.
On Faith.

Man being wholly dependent upon God, as upon his Creator and

dependeat, et ratio creata increatæ veritati penitus subjecta sit, plenum revelanti Deo intellectus et voluntatis obsequium fide præstare tenemur. Hanc vero fidem, quæ humanæ salutis initium est, Ecclesia Catholica profitetur, virtutem esse supernaturalem, qua, Dei aspirante et adjuvante gratia, ab eo revelata vera esse credimus, non propter intrinsecam rerum veritatem naturali rationis lumine perspectam, sed propter auctoritatem ipsius Dei revelantis, qui nec falli nec fallere potest. Est enim fides, testante Apostolo, sperandarum substantia rerum, argumentum non apparentium.

Ut nihilominus fidei nostræ obsequium rationi consentaneum esset, voluit Deus cum internis Spiritus Sancti auxiliis externa jungi revelationis suæ argumenta, facta scilicet divina, atque imprimis miracula et prophetias, quæ cum Dei omnipotentiam et infinitam scientiam luculenter commonstrent, divinæ revelationis signa sunt certissima et omnium intelligentiæ accommodata. Quare tum Moyses et Prophetæ, tum ipse ma-

Lord, and created reason being absolutely subject to uncreated truth, we are bound to yield to God, by faith in his revelation, the full obedience of our intelligence and will. And the Catholic Church teaches that this faith, which is the beginning of man's salvation, is a supernatural virtue, whereby, inspired and assisted by the grace of God, we believe that the things which he has revealed are true; not because of the intrinsic truth of the things, viewed by the natural light of reason, but because of the authority of God himself, who reveals them, and who can neither be deceived nor deceive. For faith, as the Apostle testifies, is 'the substance of things hoped for, the conviction of things that appear not.'[1]

Nevertheless, in order that the obedience of our faith might be in harmony with reason, God willed that to the interior help of the Holy Spirit there should be joined exterior proofs of his revelation; to wit, divine facts, and especially miracles and prophecies, which, as they manifestly display the omnipotence and infinite knowledge of God, are most certain proofs of his divine revelation, adapted to the intelligence of all men. Wherefore, both Moses and the Prophets, and,

---

[1] Heb. i. 11.

xime Christus Dominus multa et manifestissima miracula et prophetias ediderunt; et de Apostolis legimus: Illi autem profecti prædicaverunt ubique, Domino cooperante et sermonem confirmante sequentibus signis. Et rursum scriptum est: Habemus firmiorem propheticum sermonem, cui bene facitis attendentes quasi lucernæ lucenti in caliginoso loco.

Licet autem fidei assensus nequaquam sit motus animi cæcus · nemo tamen evangelicæ prædicationi consentire potest, sicut oportet ad salutem consequendam, absque illuminatione et inspiratione Spiritus Sancti, qui dat omnibus suavitatem in consentiendo et credendo veritati. Quare fides ipsa in se, etiamsi per caritatem non operetur, donum Dei est, et actus ejus est opus ad salutem pertinens, quo homo liberam præstat ipsi Deo obedientiam, gratiæ ejus, cui resistere posset, consentiendo et cooperando.

Porro fide divina et Catholica ea omnia credenda sunt, quæ in verbo Dei scripto vel tradito continentur, et ab Eccle-

most especially, Christ our Lord himself, showed forth many and most evident miracles and prophecies; and of the Apostles we read: 'But they going forth preached every where, the Lord working withal, and confirming the word with signs that followed.'[1] And again, it is written: 'We have the more firm prophetical word, whereunto you do well to attend, as to a light shining in a dark place.'[2]

But though the assent of faith is by no means a blind action of the mind, still no man can assent to the Gospel teaching, as is necessary to obtain salvation, without the illumination and inspiration of the Holy Spirit, who gives to all men sweetness in assenting to and believing in the truth.[3] Wherefore, faith itself, even when it does not work by charity, is in itself a gift of God, and the act of faith is a work appertaining to salvation, by which man yields voluntary obedience to God himself, by assenting to and co-operating with his grace, which he is able to resist.

Further, all those things are to be believed with divine and Catholic faith which are contained in the Word of God, written or handed

---

[1] Mark xvi. 20.　　　　[2] 2 Peter i. 19.

[3] Canons of the Second Council of Orange, confirmed by Pope Boniface II., A.D. 529, against the Semipelagians, Canon VII. See Denzinger's *Enchiridion Symbolorum*, p. 53 (Würzburg, 1865).

sia sive solemni judicio sive ordinario et universali magisterio tamquam divinitus revelata credenda proponuntur.

Quoniam vero sine fide impossibile est placere Deo, et ad filiorum ejus consortium pervenire; ideo nemini unquam sine illa contigit justificatio, nec ullus, nisi in ea perseveraverit usque in finem, vitam æternam assequetur. Ut autem officio veram fidem amplectendi, in eaque constanter perseverandi satisfacere possemus, Deus per Filium suum unigenitum Ecclesiam instituit, suæque institutionis manifestis notis instruxit, ut ea tamquam custos et magistra verbi revelati ab omnibus posset agnosci. Ad solam enim Catholicam Ecclesiam ea pertinent omnia, quæ ad evidentem fidei Christianæ credibilitatem tam multa et tam mira divinitus sunt disposita. Quin etiam Ecclesia per se ipsa, ob suam nempe admirabilem propagationem, eximiam sanctitatem et inexhaustam in omnibus bonis fœcunditatem, ob Catholicam unitatem, invictamque stabilitatem, magnum quoddam et perpetuum est motivum credibilitatis et divinæ suæ legationis testimonium irrefragabile.

down, and which the Church, either by a solemn judgment, or by her ordinary and universal magisterium, proposes for belief as having been divinely revealed.

And since, without faith, it is impossible to please God, and to attain to the fellowship of his children, therefore without faith no one has ever attained justification, nor will any one obtain eternal life unless he shall have persevered in faith unto the end. And, that we may be able to satisfy the obligation of embracing the true faith, and of constantly persevering in it, God has instituted the Church through his only-begotten Son, and has bestowed on it manifest notes of that institution, that it may be recognized by all men as the guardian and teacher of the revealed Word; for to the Catholic Church alone belong all those many and admirable tokens which have been divinely established for the evident credibility of the Christian faith. Nay, more, the Church by itself, with its marvelous extension, its eminent holiness, and its inexhaustible fruitfulness in every good thing, with its Catholic unity and its invincible stability, is a great and perpetual motive of credibility, and an irrefutable witness of its own divine mission.

Quo fit, ut ipsa veluti signum levatum in nationes, et ad se invitet, qui nondum crediderunt, et filios suos certiores faciat, firmissimo niti fundamento fidem, quam profitentur. Cui quidem testimonio efficax subsidium accedit ex superna virtute. Etenim benignissimus Dominus et errantes gratia sua excitat, atque adjuvat, ut ad agnitionem veritatis venire possint, et eos, quos de tenebris transtulit in admirabile lumen suum, in hoc eodem lumine ut perseverent, gratia sua confirmat, non deserens, nisi deseratur. Quocirca minime par est conditio eorum, qui per cœleste fidei donum Catholicæ veritati adhæserunt, atque eorum, qui ducti opinionibus humanis, falsam religionem sectantur; illi enim, qui fidem sub Ecclesiæ magisterio susceperunt, nullam unquam habere possunt justam causam mutandi, aut in dubium fidem eamdem revocandi. Quæ cum ita sint, gratias agentes Deo Patri, qui dignos nos fecit in partem sortis sanctorum in lumine, tantam ne negligamus salutem, sed aspicientes in auctorem fidei et consummatorem Jesum, teneamus spei nostræ confessionem indeclinabilem.

And thus, like a standard set up unto the nations,[1] it both invites to itself those who do not yet believe, and assures its children that the faith which they profess rests on the most firm foundation. And its testimony is efficaciously supported by a power from on high. For our most merciful Lord gives his grace to stir up and to aid those who are astray, that they may come to a knowledge of the truth; and to those whom he has brought out of darkness into his own admirable light he gives his grace to strengthen them to persevere in that light, deserting none who desert not him. Therefore there is no parity between the condition of those who have adhered to the Catholic truth by the heavenly gift of faith, and of those who, led by human opinions, follow a false religion; for those who have received the faith under the magisterium of the Church can never have any just cause for changing or doubting that faith. Therefore, giving thanks to God the Father who has made us worthy to be partakers of the lot of the Saints in light, let us not neglect so great salvation, but with our eyes fixed on Jesus, the author and finisher of our faith, let us hold fast the confession of our hope without wavering.[2]

---

[1] Isaiah xi. 12.　　　　[2] Heb. xii. 2, and x. 23.

CAPUT IV.

De Fide et Ratione.

Hoc quoque perpetuus Ecclesiæ Catholicæ consensus tenuit et tenet, duplicem esse ordinem cognitionis, non solum principio, sed objecto etiam distinctum: principio quidem, quia in altero naturali ratione, in altero fide divina cognoscimus; objecto autem, quia præter ea, ad quæ naturalis ratio pertingere potest, credenda nobis proponuntur mysteria in Deo abscondita, quæ, nisi revelata divinitus, innotescere non possunt. Quocirca Apostolus, qui a gentibus Deum per ea, quæ facta sunt, cognitum esse testatur, disserens tamen de gratia et veritate, quæ per Jesum Christum facta est, pronunciat: Loquimur Dei sapientiam in mysterio, quæ abscondita est, quam prædestinavit Deus ante sæcula in gloriam nostram, quam nemo principum hujus sæculi cognovit: nobis autem revelavit Deus per Spiritum suum: Spiritus enim omnia scrutatur, etiam profunda Dei. Et ipse Unigenitus confitetur Patri, quia abscondit hæc a sapientibus et prudentibus, et revelavit ea parvulis.

Ac ratio quidem, fide illustrata,

CHAPTER IV.

On Faith and Reason.

The Catholic Church, with one consent, has also ever held and does hold that there is a twofold order of knowledge distinct both in principle and also in object; in principle, because our knowledge in the one is by natural reason, and in the other by divine faith; in object, because, besides those things to which natural reason can attain, there are proposed to our belief mysteries hidden in God, which, unless divinely revealed, can not be known. Wherefore, the Apostle, who testifies that God is known by the Gentiles through created things, still, when discoursing of the grace and truth which come by Jesus Christ,[1] says: 'We speak the wisdom of God in a mystery, a wisdom which is hidden, which God ordained before the world unto our glory; which none of the princes of this world knew . . . but to us God hath revealed them by his Spirit. For the Spirit searcheth all things, yea, the deep things of God.'[2] And the only-begotten Son himself gives thanks to the Father, because he has hid these things from the wise and prudent, and has revealed them to little ones.[3]

Reason, indeed, enlightened by

---

[1] John i. 17.   [2] 1 Cor. ii. 7–9.   [3] Matt. xi. 25.

cum sedulo, pie et sobrie quæ-
rit, aliquam, Deo dante, myste-
riorum intelligentiam eamque
fructuosissimam assequitur, tum
ex eorum, quæ naturaliter cogno-
scit, analogia, tum e mysterio-
rum ipsorum nexu inter se et
cum fine hominis ultimo; nun-
quam tamen idonea redditur
ad ea perspicienda instar veri-
tatum, quæ proprium ipsius
objectum constituunt. Divina
enim mysteria suapte natura
intellectum creatum sic exce-
dunt, ut etiam revelatione tra-
dita et fide suscepta, ipsius
tamen fidei velamine contecta et
quadam quasi caligine obvoluta
maneant, quamdiu in hac mor-
tali vita peregrinamur a Domi-
no: per fidem enim ambula-
mus, et non per speciem.

Verum etsi fides sit supra
rationem, nulla tamen unquam
inter fidem et rationem vera dis-
sensio esse potest: cum idem
Deus, qui mysteria revelat et
fidem infundit, animo humano
rationis lumen indiderit; Deus
autem negare seipsum non pos-
sit, nec verum vero unquam con-
tradicere. Inanis autem hujus
contradictionis species inde po-
tissimum oritur, quod vel fidei

faith, when it seeks earnestly, pious-ly, and calmly, attains by a gift from God some, and that a very fruitful, understanding of myster-ies; partly from the analogy of those things which it naturally knows, partly from the relations which the mysteries bear to one another and to the last end of man; but reason never becomes capable of apprehending mysteries as it does those truths which constitute its proper object. For the divine mysteries by their own nature so far transcend the created intelli-gence that, even when delivered by revelation and received by faith, they remain covered with the veil of faith itself, and shrouded in a certain degree of darkness, so long as we are pilgrims in this mortal life, not yet with God; 'for we walk by faith and not by sight.'[1]

But although faith is above rea-son, there can never be any real discrepancy between faith and rea-son, since the same God who re-veals mysteries and infuses faith has bestowed the light of reason on the human mind; and God can not deny himself, nor can truth ever contradict truth. The false ap-pearance of such a contradiction is mainly due, either to the dogmas of faith not having been understood

---

[1] 2 Cor. v. 7.

dogmata ad mentem Ecclesiæ intellecta et exposita non fuerint, vel opinionum commenta pro rationis effatis habeantur. Omnem igitur assertionem veritati illuminatæ fidei contrariam omnino falsam esse definimus. Porro Ecclesia, quæ una cum apostolico munere docendi, mandatum accepit fidei depositum custodiendi, jus etiam et officium divinitus habet falsi nominis scientiam proscribendi, ne quis decipiatur per philosophiam et inanem fallaciam. Quapropter omnes Christiani fideles hujusmodi opiniones, quæ fidei doctrinæ contrariæ esse cognoscuntur, maxime si ab Ecclesia reprobatæ fuerint, non solum prohibentur tanquam legitimas scientiæ conclusiones defendere, sed pro erroribus potius, qui fallacem veritatis speciem præ se ferant, habere tenentur omnino.

Neque solum fides et ratio inter se dissidere nunquam possunt, sed opem quoque sibi mutuam ferunt, cum recta ratio fidei fundamenta demonstret, ejusque lumine illustrata rerum divinarum scientiam excolat; fides vero rationem ab erroribus

and expounded according to the mind of the Church, or to the inventions of opinion having been taken for the verdicts of reason. We define, therefore, that every assertion contrary to a truth of enlightened faith is utterly false.[1] Further, the Church, which, together with the Apostolic office of teaching, has received a charge to guard the deposit of faith, derives from God the right and the duty of proscribing false science, lest any should be deceived by philosophy and vain fallacy.[2] Therefore all faithful Christians are not only forbidden to defend, as legitimate conclusions of science, such opinions as are known to be contrary to the doctrines of faith, especially if they have been condemned by the Church, but are altogether bound to account them as errors which put on the fallacious appearance of truth.

And not only can faith and reason never be opposed to one another, but they are of mutual aid one to the other; for right reason demonstrates the foundations of faith, and, enlightened by its light, cultivates the science of things divine; while faith frees and guards

---

[1] From the Bull of Pope Leo X., *Apostolici regiminis*, read in the Eighth Session of the Fifth Lateran Council, A.D. 1513. See Labbe's Councils, Vol. XIX. p. 842 (Venice, 1732).

[2] Coloss. ii. 8.

liberet ac tueatur, eamque mul-
tiplici cognitione instruat. Qua-
propter tantum abest, ut Eccle-
sia humanarum artium et disci-
plinarum culturæ obsistat, ut
hanc multis modis juvet atque
promoveat. Non enim commo-
da ab iis ad hominum vitam
dimanantia aut ignorat aut de-
spicit; fatetur imo, eas, que-
madmodum a Deo, scientiarum
Domino, profectæ sunt, ita si
rite pertractentur, ad Deum, ju-
vante ejus gratia, perducere.
Nec sane ipsa vetat, ne hujus-
modi disciplinæ in suo quæque
ambitu propriis utantur princi-
piis et propria methodo; sed
justam hanc libertatem agno-
scens, id sedulo cavet, ne divinæ
doctrinæ repugnando errores in
se suscipiant, aut fines proprios
transgressæ, ea, quæ sunt fidei,
occupent et perturbent.

Neque enim fidei doctrina,
quam Deus revelavit, velut phi-
losophicum inventum proposita
est humanis ingeniis perficienda,
sed tanquam divinum deposi-
tum Christi Sponsæ tradita, fide-
liter custodienda et infallibiliter
declaranda. Hinc sacrorum quo-
que dogmatum is sensus perpe-
tuo est retinendus, quem semel
declaravit sancta mater Eccle-
sia, nec unquam ab eo sensu,

reason from errors, and furnishes
it with manifold knowledge. So
far, therefore, is the Church from
opposing the cultivation of human
arts and sciences, that it in many
ways helps and promotes it. For
the Church neither ignores nor de-
spises the benefits of human life
which result from the arts and sciences, but confesses that, as they
came from God, the Lord of all
science, so, if they be rightly used,
they lead to God by the help of his
grace. Nor does the Church forbid that each of these sciences in its
sphere should make use of its own
principles and its own method; but,
while recognizing this just liberty,
it stands watchfully on guard, lest
sciences, setting themselves against
the divine teaching, or trans-
gressing their own limits, should
invade and disturb the domain of
faith.

For the doctrine of faith which
God hath revealed has not been
proposed, like a philosophical invention, to be perfected by human
ingenuity, but has been delivered
as a divine deposit to the Spouse
of Christ, to be faithfully kept and
infallibly declared. Hence, also,
that meaning of the sacred dogmas
is perpetually to be retained which
our holy mother the Church has
once declared; nor is that meaning

altioris intelligentiæ specie et nomine, recedendum. Crescat igitur et multum vehementerque proficiat, tam singulorum, quam omnium, tam unius hominis, quam totius Ecclesiæ, ætatem ac sæculorum gradibus, intelligentia, scientia, sapientia; sed in suo dumtaxat genere, in eodem scilicet dogmate, eodem sensu, eademque sententia.

ever to be departed from, under the pretense or pretext of a deeper comprehension of them. Let, then, the intelligence, science, and wisdom of each and all, of individuals and of the whole Church, in all ages and all times, increase and flourish in abundance and vigor; but simply in its own proper kind, that is to say, in one and the same doctrine, one and the same sense, one and the same judgment.[1]

CANONES.

I.

De Deo rerum omnium Creatore.

1. *Si quis unum verum Deum visibilium et invisibilium Creatorem et Dominum negaverit: anathema sit.*

2. *Si quis præter materiam nihil esse affirmare non erubuerit: anathema sit.*

3. *Si quis dixerit, unam eandemque esse Dei et rerum omnium substantiam vel essentiam: anathema sit.*

4. *Si quis dixerit, res finitas, tum corporeas tum spirituales aut saltem spirituales, e divina substantia emanasse; aut divinam essentiam sui manifestatione vel evolutione fieri omnia; aut denique Deum esse ens uni-*

CANONS.

I.

Of God, the Creator of all things.

1. If any one shall deny one true God, Creator and Lord of things visible and invisible: let him be anathema.

2. If any one shall not be ashamed to affirm that, except matter, nothing exists: let him be anathema.

3. If any one shall say that the substance and essence of God and of all things is one and the same: let him be anathema.

4. If any one shall say that finite things, both corporeal and spiritual, or at least spiritual, have emanated from the divine substance; or that the divine essence by the manifestation and evolution of itself becomes all things; or, lastly, that God is

---

[1] Vincent. of Lerins, *Common. n. 28.*

versale seu indefinitum, quod sese determinando constituat rerum universitatem in genera, species et individua distinctam : anathema sit.

5. *Si quis non confiteatur, mundum, resque omnes, quæ in eo continentur, et spirituales et materiales, secundum totam suam substantiam a Deo ex nihilo esse productas ; aut Deum dixerit non voluntate ab omni necessitate libera, sed tam necessario creasse, quam necessario amat seipsum ; aut mundum ad Dei gloriam conditum esse negaverit : anathema sit.*

universal or indefinite being, which by determining itself constitutes the universality of things, distinct according to genera, species, and individuals : let him be anathema.

5. If any one confess not that the world, and all things which are contained in it, both spiritual and material, have been, in their whole substance, produced by God out of nothing ; or shall say that God created, not by his will, free from all necessity, but by a necessity equal to the necessity whereby he loves himself ; or shall deny that the world was made for the glory of God : let him be anathema.

II.

De Revelatione.

1. *Si quis dixerit, Deum unum et verum, Creatorem et Dominum nostrum, per ea, quæ facta sunt, naturali rationis humanæ lumine certo cognosci non posse : anathema sit.*

2. *Si quis dixerit, fieri non posse, aut non expedire ut per revelationem divinam homo de Deo cultuque ei exhibendo edoceatur : anathema sit.*

3. *Si quis dixerit, hominem ad cognitionem et perfectionem, quæ naturalem superet, divinitus evehi non posse, sed ex seipso*

II.

Of Revelation.

1. If any one shall say that the one true God, our Creator and Lord, can not be certainly known by the natural light of human reason through created things : let him be anathema.

2. If any one shall say that it is impossible or inexpedient that man should be taught by divine revelation concerning God and the worship to be paid to him : let him be anathema.

3. If any one shall say that man can not be raised by divine power to a higher than natural knowledge and perfection, but can and ought,

ad omnis tandem veri et boni possessionem jugi profectu pertingere posse et debere : anathema sit.

by a continuous progress, to arrive at length, of himself, to the possession of all that is true and good : let him be anathema.

4. *Si quis sacræ Scripturæ libros integros cum omnibus suis partibus, prout illos sancta Tridentina Synodus recensuit, pro sacris et canonicis non susceperit, aut eos divinitus inspiratos esse negaverit : anathema sit.*

4. If any one shall not receive as sacred and canonical the books of Holy Scripture, entire with all their parts, as the holy Synod of Trent has enumerated them, or shall deny that they have been divinely inspired : let him be anathema.

III.
De Fide.

1. *Si quis dixerit, rationem humanam ita independentem esse, ut fides ei a Deo imperari non possit : anathema sit.*

2. *Si quis dixerit, fidem divinam a naturali de Deo et rebus moralibus scientia non distingui, ac propterea ad fidem divinam non requiri, ut revelata veritas propter auctoritatem Dei revelantis credatur : anathema sit.*

3. *Si quis dixerit, revelationem divinam externis signis credibilem fieri non posse, ideoque sola interna cujusque experientia aut inspiratione privata homines ad fidem moveri debere : anathema sit.*

4. *Si quis dixerit, miracula nulla fieri posse, proindeque omnes de iis narrationes, etiam*

III.
On Faith.

1. If any one shall say that human reason is so independent that faith can not be enjoined upon it by God : let him be anathema.

2. If any one shall say that divine faith is not distinguished from natural knowledge of God and of moral truths, and therefore that it is not requisite for divine faith that revealed truth be believed because of the authority of God, who reveals it : let him be anathema.

3. If any one shall say that divine revelation can not be made credible by outward signs, and therefore that men ought to be moved to faith solely by the internal experience of each, or by private inspiration : let him be anathema.

4. If any one shall say that miracles are impossible, and therefore that all the accounts regarding

in sacra Scriptura contentas, inter fabulas vel mythos ablegandas esse; aut miracula certo cognosci nunquam posse, nec iis divinam religionis Christianæ originem rite probari: anathema sit.

5. *Si quis dixerit, assensum fidei Christianæ non esse liberum, sed argumentis humanæ rationis necessario produci; aut ad solam fidem vivam, quæ per caritatem operatur, gratiam Dei necessariam esse: anathema sit.*

6. *Si quis dixerit, parem esse conditionem fidelium atque eorum, qui ad fidem unice veram nondum pervenerunt, ita ut Catholici justam causam habere possint, fidem, quam sub Ecclesiæ magisterio jam susceperunt, assensu suspenso in dubium vocandi, donec demonstrationem scientificam credibilitatis et veritatis fidei suæ absolverint: anathema sit.*

IV.

De Fide et Ratione.

1. *Si quis dixerit, in revelatione divina nulla vera et proprie dicta mysteria contineri, sed universa fidei dogmata posse per rationem rite excultam e naturalibus principiis intelligi et demonstrari: anathema sit.*

them, even those contained in Holy Scripture, are to be dismissed as fabulous or mythical; or that miracles can never be known with certainty, and that the divine origin of Christianity can not be proved by them: let him be anathema.

5. If any one shall say that the assent of Christian faith is not a free act, but inevitably produced by the arguments of human reason; or that the grace of God is necessary for that living faith only which worketh by charity: let him be anathema.

6. If any one shall say that the condition of the faithful, and of those who have not yet attained to the only true faith, is on a par, so that Catholics may have just cause for doubting, with suspended assent, the faith which they have already received under the magisterium of the Church, until they shall have obtained a scientific demonstration of the credibility and truth of their faith: let him be anathema.

IV.

On Faith and Reason.

1. If any one shall say that in divine revelation there are no mysteries, truly and properly so called, but that all the doctrines of faith can be understood and demonstrated from natural principles, by properly cultivated reason: let him be anathema.

2. *Si quis dixerit, disciplinas humanas ea cum libertate tractandas esse, ut earum assertiones, etsi doctrinæ revelatæ adversentur, tanquam veræ retineri, neque ab Ecclesia proscribi possint: anathema sit.*

3. *Si quis dixerit, fieri posse, ut dogmatibus ab Ecclesia propositis, aliquando secundum progressum scientiæ sensus tribuendus sit alius ab eo, quem intellexit et intelligit Ecclesia: anathema sit.*

Itaque supremi pastoralis Nostri officii debitum exequentes, omnes Christi fideles, maxime vero eos, qui præsunt vel docendi munere funguntur, per viscera Jesu Christi obtestamur, necnon ejusdem Dei et Salvatoris nostri auctoritate jubemus, ut ad hos errores a Sancta Ecclesia arcendos et eliminandos, atque purissimæ fidei lucem pandendam studium et operam conferant.

Quoniam vero satis non est, hæreticam pravitatem devitare, nisi ii quoque errores diligenter fugiantur, qui ad illam plus minusve accedunt; omnes officii monemus, servandi etiam Constitutiones et Decreta, quibus pravæ ejusmodi opiniones, quæ isthic

2. If any one shall say that human sciences are to be so freely treated that their assertions, although opposed to revealed doctrine, are to be held as true, and can not be condemned by the Church: let him be anathema.

3. If any one shall assert it to be possible that sometimes, according to the progress of science, a sense is to be given to doctrines propounded by the Church different from that which the Church has understood and understands: let him be anathema.

Therefore, we, fulfilling the duty of our supreme pastoral office, entreat, by the mercies of Jesus Christ, and, by the authority of the same, our God and Saviour, we command, all the faithful of Christ, and especially those who are set over others, or are charged with the office of instruction, that they earnestly and diligently apply themselves to ward off and eliminate these errors from holy Church, and to spread the light of pure faith.

And since it is not sufficient to shun heretical pravity, unless those errors also be diligently avoided which more or less nearly approach it, we admonish all men of the further duty of observing those constitutions and decrees by which such erroneous opinions as are not here

diserte non enumerantur, ab hac Sancta Sede proscriptæ et prohibitæ sunt.

specifically enumerated, have been proscribed and condemned by this Holy See.

Datum Romæ in publica Sessione in Vaticana Basilica solemniter celebrata, anno Incarnationis Dominicæ millesimo octingentesimo septuagesimo, die vigesima quarta Aprilis. Pontificatus Nostri anno vigesimo quarto.

Given at Rome in public Session solemnly held in the Vatican Basilica in the year of our Lord one thousand eight hundred and seventy, on the twenty-fourth day of April, in the twenty-fourth year of our Pontificate.

Constitutio Dogmatica Prima de Ecclesia Christi.

Edita in Sessione Quarta Sacrosancti Œcumenici Concilii Vaticani.

PIUS EPISCOPUS, SERVUS SERVORUM DEI SACRO APPROBANTE CONCILIO AD PERPETUAM REI MEMORIAM.

Pastor æternus et Episcopus animarum nostrarum, ut salutiferum Redemptionis opus perenne redderet, sanctam ædificare Ecclesiam decrevit, in qua veluti in domo Dei viventis fideles omnes unius fidei et caritatis vinculo continerentur. Quapropter, priusquam clarificaretur, rogavit Patrem non pro Apostolis tantum, sed et pro eis, qui credituri erant per verbum eorum in ipsum, ut omnes unum

First Dogmatic Constitution on the Church of Christ.

Published in the Fourth Session of the holy Œcumenical Council of the Vatican.

PIUS BISHOP, SERVANT OF THE SERVANTS OF GOD, WITH THE APPROVAL OF THE SACRED COUNCIL, FOR AN EVERLASTING REMEMBRANCE.

The eternal Pastor and Bishop of our souls, in order to continue for all time the life-giving work of his Redemption, determined to build up the holy Church, wherein, as in the house of the living God, all who believe might be united in the bond of one faith and one charity. Wherefore, before he entered into his glory, he prayed unto the Father, not for the Apostles only, but for those also who through their preaching should

essent, sicut ipse Filius et Pater unum sunt. Quemadmodum igitur Apostolos, quos sibi de mundo elegerat, misit, sicut ipse missus erat a Patre: ita in Ecclesia sua pastores et doctores usque ad consummationem sœculi esse voluit. Ut vero episcopatus ipse unus et indivisus esset, et per cohœrentes sibi invicem sacerdotes credentium multitudo universa in fidei et communionis unitate conservaretur, beatum Petrum cœteris Apostolis prœponens in ipso instituit perpetuum utriusque unitatis principium ac visibile fundamentum, super cujus fortitudinem œternum exstrueretur templum, et Ecclesiœ cœlo inferenda sublimitas in hujus fidei firmitate consurgeret. Et quoniam portœ inferi ad evertendam, si fieri posset, Ecclesiam, contra ejus fundamentum divinitus positum majori in dies odio undique insurgunt, Nos ad Catholici gregis custodiam, incolumitatem, augmentum, necessarium esse judicamus, sacro approbante Concilio, doctrinam de institutione, perpetuitate, ac

come to believe in him, that all might be one even as he the Son and the Father are one.[1] As then he sent the Apostles whom he had chosen to himself from the world, as he himself had been sent by the Father: so he willed that there should ever be pastors and teachers in his Church to the end of the world. And in order that the Episcopate also might be one and undivided, and that by means of a closely united priesthood the multitude of the faithful might be kept secure in the oneness of faith and communion, he set blessed Peter over the rest of the Apostles, and fixed in him the abiding principle of this twofold unity, and its visible foundation, in the strength of which the everlasting temple should arise, and the Church in the firmness of that faith should lift her majestic front to Heaven.[2] And seeing that the gates of hell, with daily increase of hatred, are gathering their strength on every side to upheave the foundation laid by God's own hand, and so, if that might be, to overthrow the Church: we, therefore, for the preservation, safe-keeping, and increase of the Catholic flock, with

---

[1] John xvii. 21.

[2] From Sermon IV. chap. ii. of St. Leo the Great, A.D. 440, Vol. I. p. 17 of edition of Ballerini, Venice, 1753; read in the eighth lection on the Feast of St. Peter's Chair at Antioch, February 22.

natura sacri Apostolici prima-
tus, in quo totius Ecclesiæ vis
ac soliditas consistit, cunctis
fidelibus credendam et tenen-
dam, secundum antiquam atque
constantem universalis Ecclesiæ
fidem, proponere, atque contra-
rios, dominico gregi adeo perni-
ciosos, errores proscribere et con-
demnare.

the approval of the sacred Council, do judge it to be necessary to
propose to the belief and acceptance of all the faithful, in accordance with the ancient and constant
faith of the universal Church, the
doctrine touching the institution,
perpetuity, and nature of the sacred
Apostolic Primacy, in which is
found the strength and solidity of
the entire Church, and at the same
time to proscribe and condemn the
contrary errors, so hurtful to the
flock of Christ.

CAPUT I.

De Apostolici Primatus in beato Petro institutione.

Docemus itaque et declaramus,
juxta Evangelii testimonia pri-
matum jurisdictionis in univer-
sam Dei Ecclesiam immediate
et directe beato Petro Apostolo
promissum atque collatum a
Christo Domino fuisse. Unum
enim Simonem, cui jam pridem
dixerat : Tu vocaberis Cephas,
postquam ille suam edidit con-
fessionem inquiens : Tu es
Christus, Filius Dei vivi, solem-
nibus his verbis allocutus est
Dominus : Beatus es, Simon
Bar-Jona, quia caro et sanguis
non revelavit tibi, sed Pater
meus, qui in cœlis est : et ego

CHAPTER I.

Of the Institution of the Apostolic Primacy in blessed Peter.

We therefore teach and declare
that, according to the testimony of
the Gospel, the primacy of jurisdiction over the universal Church
of God was immediately and directly promised and given to blessed
Peter the Apostle by Christ the
Lord. For it was to Simon alone,
to whom he had already said: ' Thou
shalt be called Cephas,'[1] that the
Lord after the confession made by
him, saying: ' Thou art the Christ,
the Son of the living God,' addressed
these solemn words: ' Blessed art
thou, Simon Bar-Jona, because flesh
and blood have not revealed it to
thee, but my Father who is in heaven

---

[1] John i. 42.

dico tibi, quia tu es Petrus, et super hanc Petram ædificabo Ecclesiam meam, et portæ inferi non prævalebunt adversus eam : et tibi dabo claves regni cælorum : et quodcumque ligaveris super terram, erit ligatum et in · cælis : et quodcumque solveris super terram, erit solutum et in cælis. Atque uni Simoni Petro contulit Jesus post suam resurrectionem summi pastoris et rectoris jurisdictionem in totum suum ovile dicens : Pasce agnos meos : Pasce oves meas. Huic tam manifestæ sacrarum Scripturarum doctrinæ, ut ab Ecclesia Catholica semper intellecta est, aperte opponuntur pravæ eorum sententiæ, qui, constitutam a Christo Domino in sua Ecclesia regiminis formam pervertentes, negant, solum Petrum præ cæteris Apostolis, sive seorsum singulis sive omnibus simul, vero pro prioque jurisdictionis primatu fuisse a Christo instructum ; aut qui affirmant, eundem primatum non immediate directeque ipsi beato Petro, sed Ecclesiæ, et per hanc illi ut ipsius Ecclesiæ ministro delatum fuisse.

Si quis igitur dixerit, beatum

And I say to thee that thou art Peter ; and upon this rock I will build my Church, and the gates of hell shall not prevail against it. And I will give to thee the keys of the kingdom of heaven. And whatsoever thou shalt bind on earth, it shall be bound also in heaven ; and whatsoever thou shalt loose on earth, it shall be loosed also in heaven.'[1] And it was upon Simon alone that Jesus after his resurrection bestowed the jurisdiction of chief pastor and ruler over all his fold in the words : ' Feed my lambs; feed my sheep.'[2] At open variance with this clear doctrine of Holy Scripture as it has been ever understood by the Catholic Church are the perverse opinions of those who, while they distort the form of government established by Christ the Lord in his Church, deny that Peter in his single person, preferably to all the other Apostles, whether taken separately or together, was endowed by Christ with a true and proper primacy of jurisdiction ; or of those who assert that the same primacy was not bestowed immediately and directly upon blessed Peter himself, but upon the Church, and through the Church on Peter as her minister.

If any one, therefore, shall say

---

[1] Matt. xvi. 16–19. [2] John xxi. 15–17.

Petrum Apostolum non esse a Christo Domino constitutum Apostolorum omnium principem et totius Ecclesiæ militantis visibile caput; vel eundem honoris tantum, non autem veræ propri que jurisdictionis primatum ab eodem Domino nostro Jesu Christo directe et immediate accepisse: anathema sit.

that blessed Peter the Apostle was not appointed the Prince of all the Apostles and the visible Head of the whole Church Militant; or that the same directly and immediately received from the same our Lord Jesus Christ a primacy of honor only, and not of true and proper jurisdiction: let him be anathema.

CAPUT II.

De perpetuitate Primatus beati Petri in Romanis Pontificibus.

Quod autem in beato Apostolo Petro princeps pastorum et pastor magnus ovium Dominus Christus Jesus in perpetuam salutem ac perenne bonum Ecclesiæ instituit, id eodem auctore in Ecclesia, quæ fundata super petram ad fidem sæculorum usque firma stabit, jugiter durare necesse est. Nulli sane dubium, imo sæculis omnibus notum est, quod sanctus beatissimusque Petrus, Apostolorum princeps et caput fideique columna, et Ecclesiæ Catholicæ fundamentum, a Domino nostro Jesu Christo, Salvatore humani generis ac Redemptore, claves regni accepit: qui ad hoc usque tempus et semper in suis successoribus, episcopis sanctæ Romanæ Sedis, ab ipso fun-

CHAPTER II.

On the Perpetuity of the Primacy of blessed Peter in the Roman Pontiffs.

That which the Prince of Shepherds and great Shepherd of the sheep, Jesus Christ our Lord, established in the person of the blessed Apostle Peter to secure the perpetual welfare and lasting good of the Church, must, by the same institution, necessarily remain unceasingly in the Church; which, being founded upon the Rock, will stand firm to the end of the world. For none can doubt, and it is known to all ages, that the holy and blessed Peter, the Prince and Chief of the Apostles, the pillar of the faith and foundation of the Catholic Church, received the keys of the kingdom from our Lord Jesus Christ, the Saviour and Redeemer of mankind, and lives, presides, and judges, to this day and always, in his successors the Bishops of the Holy See of

datæ, ejusque consecratæ san-guine, vivit et præsidet et judicium exercet. Unde quicumque in hac Cathedra Petro succedit, is secundum Christi ipsius institutionem primatum Petri in universam Ecclesiam obtinet. Manet ergo dispositio veritatis, et beatus Petrus, in accepta fortitudine petræ perseverans, suscepta Ecclesiæ gubernacula non reliquit. Hac de causa ad Romanam Ecclesiam propter potentiorem principalitatem necesse semper fuit omnem convenire Ecclesiam, hoc est, eos, qui sunt undique fideles, ut in ea Sede, e qua venerandæ communionis jura in omnes dimanant, tamquam membra in capite consociata, in unam corporis compagem coalescerent.

Rome, which was founded by him, and consecrated by his blood.[1] Whence, whosoever succeeds to Peter in this See, does by the institution of Christ himself obtain the Primacy of Peter over the whole Church. The disposition made by Incarnate Truth therefore remains, and blessed Peter, abiding through the strength of the Rock in the power that he received, has not abandoned the direction of the Church.[2] Wherefore it has at all times been necessary that every particular Church—that is to say, the faithful throughout the world —should agree with the Roman Church, on account of the greater authority of the princedom which this has received; that all being associated in the unity of that See whence the rights of communion spread to all, might grow together as members of one Head in the compact unity of the body.[3]

Si quis ergo dixerit, non esse ex ipsius Christi Domini institutione, seu jure divino, ut beatus Petrus in primatu super universam Ecclesiam habeat per-

If, then, any should deny that it is by the institution of Christ the Lord, or by divine right, that blessed Peter should have a perpetual line of successors in the Primacy over

---

[1] From the Acts (Session Third) of the Third General Council of Ephesus, A.D. 431, Labbe's Councils, Vol. III. p. 1154, Venice edition of 1728. See also letter of St. Peter Chrysologus to Eutyches, in life prefixed to his works, p. 13, Venice, 1750.

[2] From Sermon III. chap. iii. of St. Leo the Great, Vol. I. p. 12.

[3] From St. Irenæus against Heresies, Book III. cap. iii. p. 175, Benedictine edition, Venice, 1734; and Acts of Synod of Aquileja, A.D. 381, Labbe's Councils, Vol. II. p. 1185, Venice, 1728.

petuos successores; aut Roma-
num Pontificem non esse beati
Petri in eodem primatu succes-
sorem: anathema sit.

the universal Church, or that the
Roman Pontiff is the successor of
blessed Peter in this primacy: let
him be anathema.

Caput III.

De vi et ratione Primatus Romani Ponti-
ficis.

Chapter III.

On the Power and Nature of the Primacy of
the Roman Pontiff.

Quapropter apertis innixi sa-
crarum litterarum testimoniis, et
inhærentes tum Prædecessorum
Nostrorum, Romanorum Ponti-
ficum, tum Conciliorum genera-
lium disertis perspicuisque de-
cretis, innovamus œcumenici Con-
cilii Florentini definitionem, qua
credendum ab omnibus Christi
fidelibus est, sanctam Apostoli-
cam Sedem, et Romanum Ponti-
ficem in universum orbem tenere
primatum, et ipsum Pontificem
Romanum successorem esse beati
Petri, principis Apostolorum, et
verum Christi Vicarium, totius-
que Ecclesiæ caput, et omnium
Christianorum patrem ac docto-
rem existere; et ipsi in beato Pe-
tro pascendi, regendi ac guber-
nandi universalem Ecclesiam a
Domino nostro Jesu Christo ple-
nam potestatem traditam esse;
quemadmodum etiam in gestis
œcumenicorum Conciliorum et sa-
cris canonibus continetur.

Wherefore, resting on plain testimonies of the Sacred Writings,
and adhering to the plain and express decrees both of our predecessors, the Roman Pontiffs, and of
the General Councils, we renew
the definition of the œcumenical
Council of Florence, in virtue of
which all the faithful of Christ
must believe that the holy Apostolic See and the Roman Pontiff
possesses the primacy over the
whole world, and that the Roman
Pontiff is the successor of blessed
Peter, Prince of the Apostles, and
is true vicar of Christ, and head
of the whole Church, and father
and teacher of all Christians;
and that full power was given to
him in blessed Peter to rule, feed,
and govern the universal Church
by Jesus Christ our Lord; as is
also contained in the acts of the
General Councils and in the sa
cred Canons.

Docemus proinde et declara-
mus, Ecclesiam Romanam, dis-

Hence we teach and declare that
by the appointment of our Lord the

ponente Domino, super omnes ulias ordinariœ potestatis obtinere principatum, et hanc Romani Pontificis jurisdictionis potestatem, quœ vere episcopalis est, immediatam esse : erga quam cujuscumque ritus et dignitatis pastores atque fideles, tam seorsum singuli quam simul omnes, officio hierarchicœ subordinationis verœque obedientiœ obstringuntur, non solum in rebus, quœ ad fidem et mores, sed etiam in iis, quœ ad disciplinam et regimen Ecclesiœ per totum orbem diffusœ pertinent ; ita ut, custodita cum Romano Pontifice tam communionis, quam ejusdem fidei professionis unitate, Ecclesiœ Christi sit unus grex sub uno summo pastore. Hœc est Catholicœ veritatis doctrina, a qua deviare salvâ fide atque salute nemo potest.

Tantum autem abest, ut hœc Summi Pontificis potestas officiat ordinariœ ac immediatœ illi episcopalis jurisdictionis potestati, qua Episcopi, qui positi a Spiritu Sancto in Apostolorum locum successerunt, tamquam veri pastores assignatos sibi greges, singuli singulos, pascunt et regunt, ut eadem a supremo et

Roman Church possesses a superiority of ordinary power over all other churches, and that this power of jurisdiction of the Roman Pontiff, which is truly episcopal, is immediate ; to which all, of whatever rite and dignity, both pastors and faithful, both individually and collectively, are bound, by their duty of hierarchical subordination and true obedience, to submit not only in matters which belong to faith and morals, but also in those that appertain to the discipline and government of the Church throughout the world, so that the Church of Christ may be one flock under one supreme pastor through the preservation of unity both of communion and of profession of the same faith with the Roman Pontiff. This is the teaching of Catholic truth, from which no one can deviate without loss of faith and of salvation.

But so far is this power of the Supreme Pontiff from being any prejudice to the ordinary and immediate power of episcopal jurisdiction, by which Bishops, who have been set by the Holy Ghost to succeed and hold the place of the Apostles,[1] feed and govern, each his own flock, as true pastors, that this their episcopal authority is really

---

[1] From chap. iv. of Twenty-third Session of Council of Trent. 'Of the Ecclesiastical Hierarchy.'

*universali Pastore asseratur, ro-
boretur ac vindicetur, secundum
illud sancti Gregorii Magni :
Meus honor est honor universalis Ecclesiæ. Meus honor est
fratrum meorum solidus vigor.
Tum ego vere honoratus sum,
cum singulis quibusque honor
debitus non negatur*

*Porro ex suprema illa Roma-
ni Pontificis potestate gubernandi universam Ecclesiam jus eidem esse consequitur, in hujus
sui muneris exercitio libere communicandi cum pastoribus et
gregibus totius Ecclesiæ, ut iidem
ab ipso in via salutis doceri ac
regi possint. Quare damnamus
ac reprobamus illorum sententias, qui hanc supremi capitis
cum pastoribus et gregibus com-
municationem licite impediri
posse dicunt, aut eandem red-
dunt sæculari potestati obnoxi-
am, ita ut contendant, quæ .ab
Apostolica Sede vel ejus auctoritate ad regimen Ecclesiæ con-
stituuntur, vim ac valorem non
habere, nisi potestatis sæcularis
placito confirmentur.*

*Et quoniam divino Apostolici
primatus jure Romanus Pontifex universæ Ecclesiæ præest,*

asserted, strengthened, and protect-
ed by the supreme and universal
Pastor; in accordance with the
words of St. Gregory the Great:
'My honor is the honor of the
whole Church. My honor is the
firm strength of my brethren. 1
am truly honored when the honor
due to each and all is not withheld.[1]

Further, from this supreme power possessed by the Roman Pontiff
of governing the universal Church,
it follows that he has the right of
free communication with the pastors of the whole Church, and with
their flocks, that these may be taught
and ruled by him in the way of salvation. Wherefore we condemn
and reject the opinions of those
who hold that the communication
between this supreme head and
the pastors and their flocks can
lawfully be impeded; or who make
this communication subject to the
will of the secular power, so as to
maintain that whatever is done by
the Apostolic See, or by its authority, for the government of the
Church, can not have force or value
unless it be confirmed by the assent of the secular power.

And since by the divine right
of Apostolic primacy the Roman
Pontiff is placed over the universal

---

[1] From the letters of St. Gregory the Great, Book VIII. 30, Vol. II. p. 919, Benedictine
•dition, Paris, 1705.

docemus etiam et declaramus, eum esse judicem supremum fidelium, et in omnibus causis ad examen ecclesiasticum spectantibus ad ipsius posse judicium recurri; Sedis vero Apostolicæ, cujus auctoritate major non est, judicium a nemine fore retractandum, neque cuiquam de ejus licere judicare judicio. Quare a recto veritatis tramite aberrant, qui affirmant, licere ab judiciis Romanorum Pontificum ad œcumenicum Concilium tamquam ad auctoritatem Romano Pontifice superiorem appellare.

Si quis itaque dixerit, Romanum Pontificem habere tantummodo officium inspectionis vel directionis, non autem plenam et supremam potestatem jurisdictionis in universam Ecclesiam, non solum in rebus, quæ ad fidem et mores, sed etiam in iis, quæ ad disciplinam et regimen Ecclesiæ per totum orbem diffusæ pertinent; aut eum habere tantum potiores partes, non vero totam plenitudinem hujus supremæ potestatis; aut hanc ejus potestatem non esse ordinariam et immediatam sive in om-

Church, we further teach and declare that he is the supreme judge of the faithful,[1] and that in all causes, the decision of which belongs to the Church, recourse may be had to his tribunal,[2] and that none may re-open the judgment of the Apostolic See, than whose authority there is no greater, nor can any lawfully review its judgment.[3] Wherefore they err from the right course who assert that it is lawful to appeal from the judgments of the Roman Pontiffs to an œcumenical Council, as to an authority higher than that of the Roman Pontiff.

If, then, any shall say that the Roman Pontiff has the office merely of inspection or direction, and not full and supreme power of jurisdiction over the universal Church, not only in things which belong to faith and morals, but also in those which relate to the discipline and government of the Church spread throughout the world; or assert that he possesses merely the principal part, and not all the fullness of this supreme power; or that this power which he enjoys is not ordinary and immediate, both over each and all the

[1] From a Brief of Pius VI. *Super soliditate*, of Nov. 28, 1786.
[2] From the Acts of the Fourteenth General Council of Lyons, A.D. 1274 (Labbe's Councils, Vol. XIV. p. 512).
[3] From Letter VIII. of Pope Nicholas I., A.D. 858, to the Emperor Michael (Labbe's Councils, Vol. IX. pp. 1339 and 1570).

nes ac singulas ecclesias, sive in omnes et singulos pastores et fideles : anathema sit.

churches, and over each and all the pastors and the faithful : let him be anathema.

CAPUT IV.

De Romani Pontificis infallibili magisterio.

CHAPTER IV.

Concerning the Infallible Teaching of the Roman Pontiff.

Ipso autem Apostolico primatu, quem Romanus Pontifex, tamquam Petri principis Apostolorum successor, in universam Ecclesiam obtinet, supremam quoque magisterii potestatem comprehendi, hæc Sancta Sedes semper tenuit, perpetuus Ecclesiæ usus comprobat, ipsaque œcumenica Concilia, ea imprimis, in quibus Oriens cum Occidente in fidei caritatisque unionem conveniebat, declaraverunt. Patres enim Concilii Constantinopolitani quarti, majorum vestigiis inhærentes, hanc solemnem ediderunt professionem : Prima salus est, rectæ fidei regulam custodire. Et quia non potest Domini nostri Jesu Christi prætermitti sententia dicentis : Tu es Petrus, et super hanc petram ædificabo Ecclesiam meam, hæc, quæ dicta sunt, rerum probantur effectibus, quia in Sede Apostolica immaculata est semper Catholica reservata religio, et sancta celebrata

Moreover, that the supreme power of teaching is also included in the Apostolic primacy, which the Roman Pontiff, as the successor of Peter, Prince of the Apostles, possesses over the whole Church, this Holy See has always held, the perpetual practice of the Church confirms, and œcumenical Councils also have declared, especially those in which the East with the West met in the union of faith and charity. For the Fathers of the Fourth Council of Constantinople, following in the footsteps of their predecessors, gave forth this solemn profession : The first condition of salvation is to keep the rule of the true faith. And because the sentence of our Lord Jesus Christ can not be passed by, who said : 'Thou art Peter, and upon this rock I will build my Church,'[1] these things which have been said are approved by events, because in the Apostolic See the Catholic religion and her holy and well-known doctrine has always been kept undefiled. De-

---

[1] Matt. xvi. 18.

doctrina. Ab hujus ergo fide et doctrina separari minime cupientes, speramus, ut in una communione, quam Sedes Apostolica prædicat, esse mereamur, in qua est integra et vera Christianæ religionis soliditas. Approbante vero Lugdunensi Concilio secundo, Græci professi sunt: Sanctam Romanam Ecclesiam summum et plenum primatum et principatum super universam Ecclesiam Catholicam obtinere, quem se ab ipso Domino in beato Petro, Apostolorum principe sive vertice, cujus Romanus Pontifex est successor, cum potestatis plenitudine recepisse veraciter et humiliter recognoscit; et sicut præ cæteris tenetur fidei veritatem defendere, sic et, si quæ de fide subortæ fuerint quæstiones, suo debent judicio definiri. Florentinum denique Concilium definivit: Pontificem Romanum, verum Christi Vicarium, totiusque Ecclesiæ caput et omnium Christianorum patrem ac doctorem existere; et ipsi in beato Petro pascendi, regendi ac gubernandi universalem

siring, therefore, not to be in the least degree separated from the faith and doctrine of that See, we hope that we may deserve to be in the one communion, which the Apostolic See preaches, in which is the entire and true solidity of the Christian religion.[1] And, with the approval of the Second Council of Lyons, the Greeks professed that the holy Roman Church enjoys supreme and full primacy and preeminence over the whole Catholic Church, which it truly and humbly acknowledges that it has received with the plenitude of power from our Lord himself in the person of blessed Peter, Prince or Head of the Apostles, whose successor the Roman Pontiff is; and as the Apostolic See is bound before all others to defend the truth of faith, so also, if any questions regarding faith shall arise, they must be defined by its judgment.[2] Finally, the Council of Florence defined:[3] That the Roman Pontiff is the true vicar of Christ, and the head of the whole Church, and the father and teacher of all Christians; and that to him in blessed Peter was delivered by

---

[1] From the Formula of St. Hormisdas, subscribed by the Fathers of the Eighth General Council (Fourth of Constantinople), A.D. 869 (Labbe's Councils, Vol. V. pp. 583, 622).

[2] From the Acts of the Fourteenth General Council (Second of Lyons), A.D. 1274 (Labbe, Vol. XIV. p. 512).

[3] From the Acts of the Seventeenth General Council of Florence, A.D. 1438 (Labbe, Vol. XVIII. p. 526).

Ecclesiam a Domino nostro Jesu Christo plenam potestatem traditam esse.

our Lord Jesus Christ the full power of feeding, ruling, and governing the whole Church.[1]

Huic pastorali muneri ut satisfacerent, Prædecessores Nostri indefessam semper operam dederunt, ut salutaris Christi doctrina apud omnes terræ populos propagaretur, parique cura vigilarunt, ut, ubi recepta esset, sincera et pura conservaretur. Quocirca totius orbis Antistites, nunc singuli, nunc in Synodis congregati, longam ecclesiarum consuetudinem et antiquæ regulæ formam sequentes, ea præsertim pericula, quæ in negotiis fidei emergebant, ad hanc Sedem Apostolicam retulerunt, ut ibi potissimum resarcirentur damna fidei, ubi fides non potest sentire defectum. Romani autem Pontificis, prout temporum et rerum conditio suadebat, nunc convocatis œcumenicis Conciliis aut explorata Ecclesiæ per orbem dispersæ sententia, nunc per Synodos particulares, nunc aliis, quæ divina suppeditabat providentia, adhibitis auxiliis, ea tenenda de-

To satisfy this pastoral duty, our predecessors ever made unwearied efforts that the salutary doctrine of Christ might be propagated among all the nations of the earth, and with equal care watched that it might be preserved genuine and pure where it had been received. Therefore the Bishops of the whole world, now singly, now assembled in Synod, following the long-established custom of churches,[2] and the form of the ancient rule,[3] sent word to this Apostolic See of those dangers especially which sprang up in matters of faith, that there the losses of faith might be most effectually repaired where the faith can not fail.[4] And the Roman Pontiffs, according to the exigencies of times and circumstances, sometimes assembling œcumenical Councils, or asking for the mind of the Church scattered throughout the world, sometimes by particular Synods, sometimes using other helps which Divine Providence supplied, de-

---

[1] John xxi. 15–17.

[2] From a letter of St. Cyril of Alexandria to Pope St. Celestine I., A.D. 422 (Vol. VI. Part II. p. 36, Paris edition of 1638).

[3] From a Rescript of St. Innocent I. to the Council of Milevis, A.D. 402 (Labbe, Vol. III. p. 47).

[4] From a letter of St. Bernard to Pope Innocent II. A.D. 1130 (Epist. 191, Vol. IV. p. 433, Paris edition of 1742).

finiverunt, quæ sacris Scripturis et apostolicis traditionibus consentanea, Deo adjutore, cognoverant. Neque enim Petri successoribus Spiritus Sanctus promissus est, ut eo revelante novam doctrinam patefacerent, sed ut, eo assistente, traditam per Apostolos revelationem seu fidei depositum sancte custodirent et fideliter exponerent. Quorum quidem apostolicam doctrinam omnes venerabiles Patres amplexi et sancti doctores orthodoxi venerati atque secuti sunt; plenissime scientes, hanc sancti Petri Sedem ab omni semper errore illibatam permanere, secundum Domini Salvatoris nostri divinam pollicitationem discipulorum suorum principi factam: Ego rogavi pro te, ut non deficiat fides tua, et tu aliquando conversus confirma fratres tuos.

Hoc igitur veritatis et fidei numquam deficientis charisma Petro ejusque in hac Cathedra successoribus divinitus collatum est, ut excelso suo munere in omnium salutem fungerentur, ut universus Christi grex per eos ab erroris venenosa esca aversus, cœlestis doctrinæ pabulo nutri-

fined as to be held those things which with the help of God they had recognized as conformable with the sacred Scriptures and Apostolic traditions. For the Holy Spirit was not promised to the successors of Peter, that by his revelation they might make known new doctrine; but that by his assistance they might inviolably keep and faithfully expound the revelation or deposit of faith delivered through the Apostles. And, indeed, all the venerable Fathers have embraced, and the holy orthodox doctors have venerated and followed, their Apostolic doctrine; knowing most fully that this See of holy Peter remains ever free from all blemish of error according to the divine promise of the Lord our Saviour made to the Prince of his disciples: 'I have prayed for thee that thy faith fail not, and, when thou art converted, confirm thy brethren.'[1]

This gift, then, of truth and never-failing faith was conferred by heaven upon Peter and his successors in this chair, that they might perform their high office for the salvation of all; that the whole flock of Christ, kept away by them from the poisonous food of error, might be nourished with the pas-

---

[1] Luke xxii. 32. See also the Acts of the Sixth General Council, A.D. 680 (Labbe, Vol. VII. p. 659).

retur, ut, sublata schismatis oc-
casione, Ecclesia tota una con-
servaretur, atque suo fundamen-
to innixa, firma adversus inferi
portas consisteret.

At vero cum hac ipsa ætate,
qua salutifera Apostolici mune-
ris efficacia vel maxime requiri-
tur, non pauci inveniantur, qui
illius auctoritati obtrectant; ne-
cessarium omnino esse censemus,
prærogativam, quam unigenitus
Dei Filius cum summo pasto-
rali officio conjungere dignatus
est, solemniter asserere.

Itaque Nos traditioni a fidei
Christianæ exordio perceptæ fide-
liter inhærendo, ad Dei Salva-
toris nostri gloriam, religionis
Catholicæ exaltationem et Chris-
tianorum populorum salutem,
sacro approbante Concilio, doce-
mus et divinitus revelatum do-
gma esse definimus: Romanum
Pontificem, cum ex Cathedra lo-
quitur, id est, cum omnium
Christianorum pastoris et docto-
ris munere fungens pro supre-
ma sua Apostolica auctoritate
doctrinam de fide vel moribus
ab universa Ecclesia tenendam
definit, per assistentiam divi-
nam, ipsi in beato Petro pro-
missam, ea infallibilitate pol-
lere, qua divinus Redemptor

ture of heavenly doctrine; that the occasion of schism being removed, the whole Church might be kept one, and, resting on its foundation, might stand firm against the gates of hell.

But since in this very age, in which the salutary efficacy of the Apostolic office is most of all required, not a few are found who take away from its authority, we judge it altogether necessary solemnly to assert the prerogative which the only-begotten Son of God vouchsafed to join with the supreme pastoral office.

Therefore faithfully adhering to the tradition received from the beginning of the Christian faith, for the glory of God our Saviour, the exaltation of the Catholic religion, and the salvation of Christian people, the sacred Council approving, we teach and define that it is a dogma divinely revealed: that the Roman Pontiff, when he speaks *ex cathedra*, that is, when in discharge of the office of pastor and doctor of all Christians, by virtue of his supreme Apostolic authority, he defines a doctrine regarding faith or morals to be held by the universal Church, by the divine assistance promised to him in blessed Peter, is possessed of that infallibility with which the divine Re-

Ecclesiam suam in definienda doctrina de fide vel moribus instructam esse voluit; ideoque ejusmodi Romani Pontificis definitiones ex sese, non autem ex consensu Ecclesiæ, irreformabiles esse.

deemer willed that his Church should be endowed for defining doctrine regarding faith or morals; and that therefore such definitions of the Roman Pontiff are irreformable[1] of themselves, and not from the consent of the Church.

Si quis autem huic Nostræ definitioni contradicere, quod Deus avertat, præsumpserit: anathema sit.

But if any one—which may God avert—presume to contradict this our definition: let him be anathema.

Datum Romæ, in publica Sessione in Vaticana Basilica solemniter celebrata, anno Incarnationis Dominicæ millesimo octingentesimo septuagesimo, die decima octava Julii. Pontificatus Nostri anno vigesimo quinto.

Given at Rome in public Session solemnly held in the Vatican Basilica in the year of our Lord one thousand eight hundred and seventy, on the eighteenth day of July, in the twenty-fifth year of our Pontificate.

---

[1] That is, in the words used by Pope Nicholas I., note 13, and in the Synod of Quedlinburg, A.D. 1085, 'It is allowed to none to revise its judgment, and to sit in judgment upon what it has judged' (Labbe, Vol. XII. p. 679).

SYMBOLA GRÆCA ET RUSSICA.

SYMBOLA GRÆCA ET RUSSICA.

GREEK AND RUSSIAN SYMBOLS.

PAGE

I. ORTHODOXA CONFESSIO FIDEI CATHOLICÆ ET APOS-
TOLICÆ ECCLESIÆ ORIENTALIS.
THE ORTHODOX CONFESSION OF THE CATHOLIC AND APOSTOLIC
EASTERN CHURCH.   A.D. 1643..................................... 275

II. DOSITHEI CONFESSIO, SIVE DECRETA XVIII. SYNODI
HIEROSOLYMITANÆ.
THE CONFESSION OF DOSITHEUS, OR THE EIGHTEEN DECREES
OF THE SYNOD OF JERUSALEM.   A.D. 1672..................... 401

III. THE LONGER CATECHISM OF THE RUSSIAN CHURCH,
PREPARED BY PHILARET.   REVISED AND APPROVED
BY THE MOST HOLY SYNOD, A.D. 1839..................... 445

THE ORTHODOX CONFESSION OF THE EASTERN CHURCH. A.D. 1643.

[THE ORTHODOX CONFESSION OF FAITH OF THE CATHOLIC AND APOSTOLIC CHURCH OF THE EAST (also called CATECHISM from its method) was drawn up by Peter Mogilas, Metropolitan of Kieff, the father of Russian theology (d. 1647), or under his direction, and was revised and adopted by the Græco-Russian Synod at Jassy, 1643, signed by the Eastern Patriarchs, and approved again by the Synod of Jerusalem, 1672. It sets forth the faith of the Eastern Church in distinction both from the Latin and Protestant Churches. We print the introduction and doctrinal part in full, but omit Parts II. and III., which contain an exposition of the Lord's Prayer, the Beatitudes, and the Ten Commandments, and belong to Ethics rather than Symbolics. In the division of the Decalogue the Greek Church sides with the Reformed against the Roman and the Lutheran. Comp. *History*, pp. 58 sqq.

The modern Greek text, with the semi-official Latin translation of Panagiota, appeared first at Amsterdam, 1662. It is here reprinted from KIMMEL'S *Monumenta Fidei Ecclesiæ Orientalis*, Pars I. pp. 56-203. On other editions and textual variations, see his Prolegomena, p. lxii.]

'Ορϑόδοξος ὁμολογία τῆς πίστεως τῆς καϑολικῆς καὶ ἀποστολικῆς ἐκκλησίας τῆς ἀνατολικῆς.

Orthodoxa Confessio Fidei Catholicæ et Apostolicæ Ecclesiæ Orientalis.

'Ερώτησις α'.

QUÆSTIO I.

'Ο ἄνθρωπος ὁ χριστιανὸς ὁ ὀρϑόδοξος καὶ καϑολικὸς τί χρεωστεῖ νὰ φυλάττῃ, διὰ νὰ κληρονομήσῃ' τὴν ζωὴν τὴν αἰώνιον ;

'Απόκρισις. Πίστιν ὀρϑὴν καὶ ἔργα καλά. Διατὶ ὁποῖος τὰ δύο ταῦτα κρατεῖ, εἶναι καλὸς χριστιανός, καὶ ἔχει βεβαίαν ἐλπίδα τῆς αἰωνίου σωτηρίας· μαρτυρούσης τῆς ἁγίας Γραφῆς ('Ιακ. β'. κδ'.)· ὁρᾶτε, ὅτι ἐξ ἔργων δικαιοῦται ἄνθρωπος, καὶ οὐκ ἐκ πίστεως μόνον· καὶ ὁ λόγος κατώτερον (στιχ. κϛ'.)· ὥσπερ γὰρ τὸ σῶμα χωρὶς πνεύματος νεκρόν ἐστιν, οὕτω καὶ ἡ πίστις χωρὶς τῶν ἔργων νεκρά ἐστι· καὶ ἀλλαχοῦ ὁ Παῦλος ὁ ϑεῖος λέγει τὸ αὐτό (α'. Τιμ. α'. ιϑ'.)· ἔχων πίστιν καὶ

Quid tenere atque observare Orthodoxus et Catholicus homo Christianus debet, ut æternæ olim vitæ heres fiat ?

RESPONSIO. Rectam fidem et bona opera. Qui enim hæc duo servat, ille bonus Christianus est, certamque æternæ salutis spem habet teste sacra scriptura (Jac. ii. 24): ' Videtis, quod ex operibus justificetur homo non autem ex fide tantum.' Tum paullo post (v. 26): ' Nam quemadmodum corpus sine spiritu mortuum est: ita et fides sine operibus mortua est.' Idem alibi divinus ille Paulus adstruit (1 Tim. i. 19): ' Habens fidem et bonam conscientiam : qua

ἀγαϑὴν συνείδησιν· ἥν τινες ἀπωσά-μενοι περὶ τὴν πίστιν ἐνανάγησαν· καὶ ἀλλαχοῦ (α΄. Τιμ. γ΄. ϑ΄.)· ἔχον-τες τὸ μυστήριον τῆς πίστεως ἐν κα-ϑαρᾷ συνειδήσει.

repulsa nonnulli fidei naufragium fecerunt.' Et alio idem loco (1 Tim. iii. 9): 'Habentes mysterium fidei in pura conscientia.'

Ἐρώτησις β΄.

Διατί χρεωστεῖ ὁ χριστιανὸς νὰ πιστεύῃ πρῶτον, καὶ ὕστερα νὰ κάμῃ τὰ καλὰ ἔργα;

Ἀπ. Ἐπειδὴ εἶναι ἀδύνατον νὰ ἀρέσσῃ τινὰς τοῦ Θεοῦ χωρὶς πίστιν, κατὰ τὸν Παῦλον λέγοντα (Ἐβρ. ια΄. ς΄.)· χωρὶς πίστεως ἀδύνατον εὐαρε-στῆσαι· πιστεῦσαι γὰρ δεῖ τὸν προσ-ερχόμενον τῷ Θεῷ, ὅτι ἔστι, καὶ τοῖς ἐκζητοῦσιν αὐτὸν μισϑαποδότης γίνεται. Διὰ νὰ ἀρέσσῃ λοιπὸν ὁ χριστιανὸς τῷ Θεῷ, καὶ τὰ ἔργα τοῦ νὰ εἶναι εἰς αὐτὸν εὐπρόσδεκτα, πρῶ-τον πρέπει νὰ ἔχῃ πίστιν εἰς τὸν Θεὸν, καὶ δεύτερον νὰ εὐϑήνῃ τὴν ζωὴν τοῦ κατὰ τὴν πίστιν.

QUÆSTIO II.

Quid vero prius credere, tum deinde bona opera efficere debet Christianus?

RESP. Quoniam sine fide nemo Deo placere potest, secundum dic-tum Pauli (Hebr. xi. 6): 'Fieri non potest, ut sine fide quisquam placeat; nam qui ad Deum acce-dit, hunc credere oportet, et esse Deum, et remuneratorem iis esse, qui illum sedulo quærunt.' Ut ac-ceptus igitur Deo homo Christia-nus sit, ut illique grata ejus sint opera; primum fidem in Deum habeat oportet: postmodum ut vi-tam etiam suam ad fidei regulam componat ac conformet.

Ἐρώτησις γ΄.

Τὰ δύο ταῦτα εἰς τί στέκουνται;

Ἀπ. Εἰς τὰς τρεῖς ϑεολογικὰς ἀρετάς· ἤγουν εἰς τὴν πίστιν· εἰς τὴν ἐλπίδα· καὶ εἰς τὴν ἀγάπην· κατὰ τὰς ὁποίας ϑέλομεν μερίσειν καὶ τὰ τρία μέρη τῆς Ὁμολογίας, ὥστε εἰς τὸ πρῶτον νὰ ὁμολογήσω-μεν περὶ τῶν ἄρϑρων τῆς πίστεως, εἰς τὸ δεύτερον περὶ ἐλπίδος, καὶ τῆς

QUÆSTIO III.

Quibus in rebus hæc duo con-sistunt?

RESP. In tribus hisce virtutibus theologicis: in Fide, in Spe, in Caritate, secundum quas etiam tres Confessionis hujus partes distribu-ere nobis animus est: nimirum ut in prima parte concordi concessione de Articulis Fidei agamus; in se-cunda, de Spe et Oratione Domini-

προσευχῆς τῆς Κυριακῆς, καὶ περὶ τῶν μακαρισμῶν, εἰς δὲ τὸ τρίτον, περὶ τῶν θείων ἐντολῶν, ἐν αἷς περιέχεται ἡ πρὸς Θεὸν καὶ τὸν πλησίον ἀγάπη.

ca, et Beatitudinibus Evangelicis: in tertia denique, de Præceptis Divinis, quibus Caritas in Deum et Proximum continetur.

Πρῶτον μέρος

τῆς ὀρθοδόξου ὁμολογίας,

ἐν ᾧ περὶ Πίστεως.

Orthodoxæ Confessionis

PARS PRIMA,

DE FIDE.

Ἐρώτησις δ'.

QUÆSTIO IV.

Τί ἐστὶ Πίστις;

Ἀπ. Πίστις ἐστι (κατὰ τὸν μακάριον Παῦλον Ἑβρ. ιά. ά.) ἐλπιζομένων ὑπόστασις, πραγμάτων ἔλεγχος οὐ βλεπομένων· ἐν ταύτῃ γὰρ ἐμαρτυρήθησαν οἱ πρεσβύτεροι· ἢ οὕτω· πίστις ὀρθόδοξος, καθολική τε καὶ ἀποστολική ἐστι, καρδίᾳ πιστεύειν καὶ στόματι ὁμολογεῖν ἕνα Θεὸν τρισυπόστατον, κατὰ τὴν αὐτοῦ τοῦ Παύλου διδασκαλίαν, λέγοντος· (Ῥωμ. ι. ί.) καρδίᾳ γὰρ πιστεύεται εἰς δικαιοσύνην, στόματι δὲ ὁμολογεῖται εἰς σωτηρίαν. Πρὸς τούτῳ πρέπει νὰ κρατῇ διὰ βέβαιον καὶ ἀναμφίβολον ὁ ὀρθόδοξος χριστιανὸς (ς'. Συνοδ. καν. πβ'.), πῶς ὅλα τὰ ἄρθρα τῆς πίστεως τῆς καθολικῆς καὶ ὀρθοδόξου ἐκκλησίας εἶναι παραδεδομένα ἀπὸ τὸν Κύριον ἡμῶν Ἰησοῦν Χριστὸν μὲ τὸ μέσον τῶν ἀποστόλων του εἰς τὴν ἐκκλησίαν, καὶ αἱ οἰκουμενικαὶ σύνοδοι τὰ ἑρμηνεύουσαν καὶ τὰ ἐδοκίμασαν, καὶ νὰ πιστεύῃ εἰς αὐτὰ καθὼς προστάσ-

Quid est Fides?

RESP. 'Fides (secundum beatum Paulum (Heb. xi. 1) est substantia earum rerum quæ sperantur, earumque quæ non videntur demonstratio; per hanc enim testimonium consecuti sunt seniores.' Aut hunc in modum: Fides Orthodoxa, Catholica et Apostolica est corde credere et ore profiteri unum *Deum*, personis trinum; idque secundum Pauli ipsius doctrinam (Rom. x. 10): 'Corde creditur ad justitiam: ore fit confessio ad salutem.' Ad hæc pro certo atque indubitato tenere debet orthodoxus Christianus (Synod. VI. Can. LXXXII.), omnes fidei Articulos, quos Catholica et Orthodoxa credit Ecclesia, a Domino nostro Jesu Christo per Apostolos Ecclesiæ traditos: atque ab œcumenicis conciliis expositos approbatosque fuisse. Quos et ipse vera fide complecti debet, secundum præ-

σει ὁ Ἀπόστολος, λέγων (β΄. Θεσσ. β΄. ιε΄.)· ἄρα οὖν, ἀδελφοὶ, στήκετε καὶ κρατεῖτε τὰς παραδόσεις, ἃς ἐδιδάχθητε, εἴτε διὰ λόγου εἴτε δι᾽ ἐπιστολῆς ἡμῶν· καὶ ἀλλαχοῦ (α΄. Κορ. ια΄. β΄.)· ἐπαινῶ δὲ ὑμᾶς, ἀδελφοὶ, ὅτι πάντα μου μέμνησθε, καὶ καθὼς παρέδωκα ὑμῖν τὰς παραδόσεις, κατέχετε. Ἀπὸ τὰ ὁποῖα λόγια εἶναι φανερὸν, πῶς τὰ ἄρθρα τῆς πίστεως ἔχοῃσι τὸ κῦρος καὶ τὴν δοκιμασίαν, μέρος ἀπὸ τὴν ἁγίαν γραφὴν, μέρος ἀπὸ τὴν ἐκκλησιαστικὴν, παράδοσιν, καὶ ἀπὸ τὴν διδασκαλίαν τῶν συνόδων καὶ τῶν ἁγίων πατέρων. Τὸ ὁποῖον φανερώνωντας τὸ ὁ ἱερὸς Διονύσιος λέγει (ἐκκλ. Ἱερ. α΄.) οὕτως· οὐσία γὰρ τῆς κατ᾽ ἡμᾶς ἱεραρχίας ἐστὶ τὰ θεοπαράδοτα λόγια· σεπτότατα δὲ λόγια ταῦτα φαμὲν, ὅσα πρὸς τῶν ἐνθέων ἡμῶν ἱεροτελεστῶν ἐν ἁγιογράφοις ἡμῖν καὶ θεολογικαῖς δεδώρηται δέλτοις, καὶ μὴν ὅσα πρὸς τῶν ἱερῶν ἀνδρῶν ἀϋλωτέρᾳ μυήσει, καὶ γείτονι πῶς ἤδη τῆς οὐρανίας ἱεραρχίας ἐκ νοὸς εἰς νοῦν, διὰ μέσου λόγου σωματικοῦ μὲν ἀϋλωτέρου δὲ ὅμως, γραφῆς ἐκτὸς, οἱ καθηγεμόνες ἡμῶν ἐμυήθησαν, ἤγουν πῶς δύο λογίων εἶναι τὰ δόγματα. Ἄλλα παραδίδει ἡ γραφὴ, τὰ ὁποῖα περιέχονται εἰς τὰ θεολογικὰ βιβλία τῆς ἁγίας γραφῆς· καὶ ἄλλα εἶναι δόγματα παραδεδομένα ἐκ στόματος ἀπὸ τοὺς Ἀποστόλους, καὶ τοῦτα ἑρμηνεύθησαν ἀπὸ τὰς συνόδους καὶ

ceptum Apostoli (2 Thess. ii. 15): 'Vos igitur, fratres, perstate traditionesque tenete, quas sive ex sermone nostro sive epistola didicistis.' Rursus alibi (1 Cor. xi. 2): 'Collaudo ego vos, fratres, quod mea omnia memoria tenetis; quodque traditiones, prout illas vobis tradidi, retinetis.' Ex hisce manifestum est, Articulos Fidei auctoritatem approbationemque suam partim sacræ scripturæ partim traditioni Ecclesiasticæ atque doctrinæ Conciliorum sanctorumque Patrum acceptam referre. Quam rem hunc in modum clarius illustrat S. Dionysius (Hierarch. Eccles. cap. i. p. 108, Morell.): 'Quippe essentia Hierarchiæ hujus nostræ tradita divinitus oracula sunt, quorum ea quam maxime venerabilia ducimus, quæcunque a divinis doctoribus nostris (Apostolis) in sacris ac theologicis codicibus nobis data sunt: itemque illa, in quibus a sanctissimis istis hominibus immateriali quadam initiatione, et cœlesti Hierarchiæ jam quodammodo vicina, de mente in mentem facta, ope quidem corporeæ sermocinationis, sed minus tamen materiatæ, nec ullis literis proditæ, præceptores et duces nostri initiati institutique fuere. Scilicet quod gemina ac duplicia Ecclesiæ dogmata sunt: alia literis mandata, quæ divinis sacræ scrip-

τοὺς ἁγίους πατέρας· καὶ εἰς τὰ δύο ταῦτα ἡ πίστις εἶναι τεθεμελιωμένη. Καὶ δὲν εἶναι πρέπον, νὰ στέκεται μόνον φυλαγμένη εἰς τὸ κρυπτὸν τῆς καρδίας, μὰ καὶ μὲ τὸ στόμα νὰ κηρύττεται ἡ αὐτὴ, καὶ νὰ ὁμολογᾶται ἀφόβως καὶ ἀναμφιβόλως· καθὼς καὶ ὁ ἱερὸς Ψάλτης λέγει (Ψαλ. ριϛ'. ί. β'. Κορ. δ'. ιγ'.)· ἐπίστευσα, διὸ ἐλάλησα, καὶ ἡμεῖς πιστεύομεν, διὸ καὶ λαλοῦμεν.

turæ libris comprehensa habentur; alia viva voce ab Apostolis tradita. Atque hæc ipsa sunt, quæ postmo dum a Concilis sanctisque Patribus plenius declarata fuerunt; binisque hisce fundamentis fides superstructa exstat. Quam neutiquam arcanis pectorum claustris duntaxat abstru di oportet: verum etiam confessione oris intrepide atque indubitanter prædicari ac proferri. Quemadmo dum et sacer Psaltes loquitur (Psa. cxvi. 10 et 2 Cor. iv. 13): 'Credidi, propterea et locutus sum. Nos quoque credimus, ideoque etiam loquimur.'

Ἐρώτησις έ.

Πόσα εἶναι τὰ ἄρθρα τῆς καθολικῆς καὶ ὀρθοδόξου πίστεως;

Ἀπ. Τὰ ἄρθρα τῆς ὀρθοδόξου καὶ καθολικῆς πίστεως εἶναι δώδεκα, κατὰ τὸ σύμβολον τῆς ἐν Νικαίᾳ πρώτης συνόδου, καὶ τὴν ἐν Κωνσταντινουπόλει δευτέραν· εἰς ταῖς ὁποίαις οὕτως ἐφανερώθησαν ὅλα, ὅπου συντείνουσι πρὸς τὴν ἡμετέραν πίστιν, ὅπου οὔτε πλειότερα πρέπει νὰ πιστεύωμεν, οὔτε ὀλιγώτερα, οὔτε ἀλλοιῶς παρὰ ὁποῦ ἐγροίκησαν οἱ πατέρες ἐκεῖνοι. Μόνον κάποια ἀπ' αὐτὰ τὰ ἄρθρα εἶναι φανερὰ, καὶ καθ' ἑαυτὰ γνώριμα, καὶ ἄλλα περικρατοῦσι μυστικὰ εἰς ἑαυτὰ, καὶ ἀπ' αὐτὰ νοοῦνται καὶ τὰ ἄλλα.

QUÆSTIO V.

Quot Catholicæ atque Orthodoxæ fidei Articuli sunt?

RESP. Orthodoxæ et Catholicæ fidei Articuli numero duodecim sunt, secundum Symbolum Concilii primi Nicææ, et secundi Constantinopoli habiti. Quibus in Conciliis ita sunt accurate exposita, quæ ad fidem nostram attinent, omnia; ut neque plura neque pauciora a nobis credi oporteat, neque alio sensu intellectuque, quam quo Patres illi intellexerunt. Verumenimvero nonnulli horumce Articulorum clari per seque manifesti sunt, alii quædam occultius complectuntur, unde cetera etiam intelliguntur.

Ἐρώτησις ϛ'.

Ποῖον εἶναι τὸ πρῶτον ἄρθρον τῆς πίστεως;

Ἀπ. (Συνοδ. α'.). Πιστεύω εἰς ἕνα Θεὸν Πατέρα παντοκράτορα, ποιητὴν οὐρανοῦ καὶ γῆς, ὁρατῶν τε πάντων καὶ ἀοράτων.

Ἐρώτησις ζ'.

Εἰς τοῦτο τὸ ἄρθρον τῆς πίστεως τί λογῆς διδασκαλία περικρατεῖται;

Ἀπ. Τοῦτο τὸ ἄρθρον τῆς πίστεως δύο τινα περιέχει, πρῶτον νὰ πιστεύῃ τινὰς καὶ νὰ ὁμολογῇ (Δευτ. ϛ'. δ'.), πῶς εἶναι ἕνας Θεὸς ἐν τριάδι ἁγίᾳ δοξαζόμενος· καὶ πῶς εἰς τὴν θεότητα ἡ ἀρχὴ καὶ ἡ ῥίζα τοῦ Υἱοῦ καὶ τοῦ ἁγίου Πνεύματος εἶναι ὁ Πατήρ· δεύτερον διδάσκει, πῶς αὐτὸς ὁ ἐν τριάδι Θεὸς ἐποίησεν ἐκ τοῦ μὴ ὄντος πάντα τὰ ὁρατὰ καὶ ἀόρατα· καθὼς ὁ Ψαλμῳδὸς μαρτυρῶν λέγει (Ψαλ. λγ'. θ'.)· ὅτι αὐτὸς εἶπε, καὶ ἐγενήθησαν, αὐτὸς ἐνετείλατο καὶ ἐκτίσθησαν.

Ἐρώτησις ή.

Τίνα γνώμην πρέπει νὰ ἔχω περὶ Θεοῦ;

Ἀπ. Πρέπει νὰ πιστεύῃς πώς εἶναι ἕνας Θεὸς ἐν τριάδι ἁγίᾳ, κατὰ τὴν γραφὴν τὴν λέγουσαν (Ἐφ. δ'. ϛ'.)· εἰς Θεὸς καὶ Πατὴρ πάντων, ὁ ἐπὶ πάντων καὶ διὰ πάντων καὶ ἐν πᾶσιν ἡμῖν· ὁ ὁποῖος ὡς ἀγαθὸς

QUÆSTIO VI.

Primus Fidei Articulus quis est?

RESP. (Synod. I.). Credo in unum Deum, Patrem omnipotentem, conditorem cœli et terræ, rerumque visibilium atque invisibilium omnium.

QUÆSTIO VII.

Cujusmodi in hoc Fidei Articulo continetur doctrina?

RESP. Hic Articulus duo quædam complectitur. Prius, ut credat quisque ac confiteatur (Deut. vi. 4), Deum esse unum, in sanctissimâ Trinitate adorandum, et in Divinitate originem et radicem Filii Sanctique Spiritus Patrem esse. Posterius, hunc ipsum trinunum Deum cuncta de nihilo condidisse, visibilia pariter atque invisibilia, teste sacro vate (Psa. xxxiii. 9): 'Ipse dixit, et facta sunt. Ipse jussit, et creata sunt.'

QUÆSTIO VIII.

Quam de Deo habere debeo opinionem?

RESP. Credere debes Deum in sancta Trinitate unum esse, secundum hæc scripturæ verba (Ephes. iv. 6): 'Unus Deus itemque omnium pater: qui super omnes, per omnes, in nobisque omnibus est.'

καὶ ὑπεράγαθος, μὲ ὅλον ὁποῦ εἶναι
καθ᾽ ἑαυτὸν ὑπερτελὴς καὶ δεδοξασ-
μένος, μὲ ὅλον τοῦτο διὰ νὰ μετέχουσι καὶ ἄλλα ὄντα τὴν ἀγαθότητά
του, δοξάζοντα αὐτὸν, ἐποίησεν ἐκ
τοῦ μὴ ὄντος τὸν κόσμον. Μὰ τί
νὰ εἶναι ὁ Θεὸς εἰς τὴν φύσιν του,
τοῦτο εἶναι ἀδύνατον νὰ γνωρισθῇ
ἀπὸ κἂν ἕνα κτίσμα, ὄχι μόνον ὁρατὸν, ἀλλὰ καὶ αὔρατον, ἤγουν καὶ
ἀπ᾽ αὐτοὺς τοὺς ἀγγέλους, διατὶ δὲν
εἶναι οὐδὲ μία σύγκρισις καθόλου
ἀνάμεσον τοῦ κτίστου καὶ κτίσμα-
τος. Καὶ ἐξ ἑπομένου φθάνει μᾶς
πρὸς εὐσέβειαν (καθὼς μαρτυρεῖ ὁ
Ἱεροσολυμ. Κύριλλος Κατηχ. ς΄.),
νὰ ἠξεύρωμεν, πῶς ἔχομεν Θεὸν ἕνα,
Θεὸν ὄντα, καὶ ἀεὶ ὄντα, ὅμοιον καὶ
ταὐτὸν πάντοτε μὲ τὸν ἑαυτόν του·
ἐξω ἀπὸ τὸν ὁποῖον ἄλλος Θεὸς δὲν
εἶναι. Καθὼς λέγει ὁ αὐτὸς Θεὸς
διὰ τοῦ προφήτου (Ἡσ. μδ΄. ζ΄.)·
ἐγὼ (εἰμὶ Θεὸς) πρῶτος, καὶ ἐγὼ
μετὰ ταῦτα, καὶ πλὴν ἐμοῦ οὐκ
ἔστιν Θεός· καὶ ὁ Μωϋσῆς πρὸς τὸν
Ἰσραηλητικὸν λαὸν μετὰ πρυτροπῆς
οὕτω λέγει (Δευτ. ς΄. δ΄.)· ἄκουε
Ἰσραὴλ, Κύριος ὁ Θεὸς ἡμῶν Κύριος εἷς ἐστίν.

Qui ut bonus, immo plus quam
summe bonus, quamvis in semet
ipso longe perfectissimus gloriosis-
simusque esset, quo tamen et alia
Entia, gloriam ipsius celebrando,
bonitatem ejusdem participarent,
totum hunc mundum ex nihilo effinxit. Ceterum quidnam omnino
in natura sua Deus sit, id ipsum
res creata nulla satis assequi ac
percipere potest: non visibilis modo sed ne invisibilis quidem, sive
Angeli ipsimet, quoniam nulla penitus inter creatorem et rem creatam comparatio proportioque intercedit. Sed illud denique nobis
ad pietatem satis esse potest (teste
Cyrillo Hierosolymitano, Catechesi
VI. p. 40, Morell.). Si recte te-
nemus, Deum nos habere, Deum
unum, eumque sempiternum; atque similem semper et eundem si-
bimet ipsi: præterque illum, Deum
exsistere neminem, quemadmodum
idem ille Deus per Prophetam (Jes.
xliv. 7) fatur: 'Ego (sum Deus) primus, et ego postea; et præter me
non est Deus.' In quam sententiam et Moses, cum adhortatione,
ita populum Israëliticum alloqui-
tur (Deut. vi. 4): 'Audi Israël,
Dominus Deus noster, Dominus
unus est.'

Ἐρώτησις Θ΄.

Ἂν ἴσως καὶ ὁ Θεὸς εἶναι ἕνας

QUÆSTIO IX.

Atqui si unus Deus est, necesse

φαίνεται, πῶς νὰ ἦτον ἀνάγκη, νὰ ἦτον καὶ ἕνα πρόσωπον;

Ἀπ. Δὲν εἶναι ἀνάγκη· διατὶ ὁ Θεὸς εἶναι ἕνας εἰς τὴν φύσιν καὶ τὴν οὐσίαν, μὰ τρισυπόστατος, καθὼς εἶναι φανερὸν ἀπὸ τὴν διδασκαλίαν αὐτοῦ τοῦ Σωτῆρος ἡμῶν, ὁποῦ εἶπεν πρὸς τοὺς Ἀποστόλους του (Ματθ. κή. ιθ΄.)· πορευθέντες μαθητεύσατε πάντα τὰ ἔθνη· βαπτίζοντες αὐτοὺς εἰς τὸ ὄνομα τοῦ Πατρὸς, καὶ τοῦ Υἱοῦ, καὶ τοῦ ἁγίου Πνεύματος. Ἀπὸ τὰ ὁποῖα λόγια φανερώνεται, πῶς εἰς τὴν μίαν Θεότητα νὰ εἶναι τρία πρόσωπα, ὁ Πατὴρ, ὁ Υἱὸς, τὸ Πνεῦμα τὸ ἅγιον, Πατὴρ ὁ ὁποῖος πρὸ αἰώνων γεννᾷ τὸν υἱὸν ἀπὸ τὴν ἰδίαν του οὐσίαν, καὶ τὸ ἅγιον Πνεῦμα προΐησιν. Υἱὸς ἐκ Πατρὸς γεννηθεὶς πρὸ αἰώνων ὁμοούσιος αὐτῷ· Πνεῦμα ἅγιον ἀπ᾽ αἰῶνος ἐκπορευόμενον ἐκ Πατρὸς, ὁμοούσιον τῷ Πατρὶ καὶ τῷ υἱῷ· τοῦτο ἑρμηνεύων ὁ θεῖος Δαμασκηνὸς λέγει οὕτως (ἁ. Βιβ. κεφ. ιά.)· ὁ Υἱὸς καὶ τὸ Πνεῦμα τὸ ἅγιον, εἰς μίαν αἰτίαν, τὸν Πατέρα, ἀναφέρονται. Καὶ ἀλλαχοῦ (κεφ. ί.) ὁ αὐτός· ὁ υἱὸς ἐκ τοῦ Πατρὸς ἔστι μὲ τρόπον γεννήσεως· τὸ Πνεῦμα τὸ ἅγιον καὶ αὐτὸ ἐκ τοῦ Πατρὸς εἶναι, μὰ ὄχι μὲ τρόπον γεννήσεως, ἀλλ᾽ ἐκπορεύσεως. Καὶ ὁ θεολόγος Γρηγόριος εἰς τὰ λόγια τοῦ Ἀποστόλου τὰ πρὸς Ῥωμαίους (κεφ. ιά. λς΄.), ὅτι ἐξ αὐτοῦ, καὶ δι᾽ αὐτοῦ, καὶ εἰς αὐτὸν, τὰ πάντα, λέγει

videtur, illum etiam unicam tantumodo personam esse?

Resp. Nihil necesse est. Quippe secundum naturam et essentiam Deus unus est; at personis trinus. Quod ex ipsius Servatoris nostri, ad Apostolos suos loquentis, doctrina satis claret (Matt. xxviii. 19): 'Euntes docete omnes gentes, baptizantes eos in nomine Patris, Filii, et Spiritus Sancti.' Unde patet, in una et eadem Divinitate tres omnino esse personas; Patrem, Filium et Spiritum Sanctum; Patrem, qui ante secula, de propria essentia sua, Filium gignit, ac Spiritum Sanctum emittit; Filium, a Patre ante secula genitum, illique consubstantialem; Spiritum Sanctum, ab omni æternitate de Patre procedentem, Patrique ac Filio coëssentialem. Quam rem hisce verbis exponit divinus Damascenus (Lib. I. c. xi.): Filius, et Spiritus Sanctus ad caussam unam, nempe Patrem, referuntur. Idem alio loco (cap. x.): Filius a Patre per modum generationis exsistit: Spiritus Sanctus itidem a Patre est; at non per modum generationis verum processionis. Porro et Gregorius Theologus, in verba Apostoli ad Romanos (xi. 36): 'Ex illo, et per illum, et in illum omnia;' sic loquitur (de Spiritu

οὕτω· τὸ πρῶτον (ἤγουν τὸ ἐξ αὐτοῦ)
πρέπει νὰ ἀποδώσωμεν εἰς τὸν Πατέρα, τὸ δεύτερον, εἰς τὸν Υἱὸν, καὶ
τὸ τρίτον, εἰς τὸ ἅγιον Πνεῦμα· διὰ
νὰ γνωρισθῇ, πῶς εἶναι τριὰς εἰς
τὴν θεότητα. Καὶ πρὸς τούτοις διατί
ὁμοίως καὶ ἀπαραλάκτως, χωρίς τινος ἐξαιρέσεως, βαπτιζόμεθα εἰς τὸ
ὄνομα τοῦ Πατρὸς, καὶ τοῦ Υἱοῦ, καὶ
τοῦ ἁγίου Πνεύματος; Λοιπὸν ὅ, τι
εἶναι ὁ Πατὴρ εἰς τὴν φύσιν, τὸ αὐτὸ
εἶναι καὶ ὁ Υἱὸς καὶ τὸ ἅγιον Πνεῦμα.
Ἀλλὰ μὴν ὁ Πατὴρ εἶναι Θεὸς κατὰ
φύσιν ἀληθὴς καὶ αἰώνιος, καὶ πάντων ποιητὴς τῶν ὁρατῶν καὶ ἀοράτων, τοιοῦτος λοιπὸν εἶναι καὶ ὁ Υἱὸς
καὶ τὸ ἅγιον Πνεῦμα. Καὶ εἶναι ὁμοούσια ἀλλήλοις, κατὰ τὴν διδασκαλίαν
τοῦ Εὐαγγελιστοῦ Ἰωάννου, ὁποῦ λέγει (α΄. Ἰωαν. ε΄. ζ΄.)· ὅτι τρεῖς εἰσιν
οἱ μαρτυροῦντες ἐν τῷ οὐρανῷ, ὁ Πατὴρ, ὁ Λόγος καὶ τὸ ἅγιον Πνεῦμα·
καὶ οὗτοι οἱ τρεῖς ἕν εἰσιν. Εἰς τὰ
ὁποῖα λόγια τοῦτο μόνον ἐξαιρεῖται,
ὁποῦ ὁ Πατὴρ εἶναι αἴτιος εἰς τὴν
Θεότητα τοῦ Υἱοῦ καὶ τοῦ ἁγίου Πνεύ-
ματος· ταῦτα δὲ τὰ δύο πρόσωπα εἶναι ἐξ ἐκείνου, ἐκεῖνος δὲ ἐξ οὐδενός.
Οὕτως ἐδιδάχθημεν ἀπ᾽ αὐτῆς τῆς αἰωνίου ἀληθείας, τὸν Ἰησοῦν τὸν Σωτῆρα μας, οὕτως ἀπὸ τοὺς ἁγίους ἀπος-
τόλους παρελάβομεν. Καὶ αἱ οἰκουμενικαὶ καὶ τοπικαὶ Σύνοδοι, ὁμοίως
καὶ οἱ διδάσκαλοι τῆς ἐκκλησίας ἀλ-
λοιᾶς λογῆς οὔτε ἐδίδαξαν, οὔτε ἐπα-
ραδώκασιν, ἢ ἐκυρώσασι παρὰ οὕτω·

S. f. 64, Ald. p. 604, Par. adde
p. 431): Primum (nimirum ex
illo), Patri reddemus: secundum
Filio: tertium Spiritui Sancto:
ut inde palam fiat, exsistere re
vera in Divinitate Trinitatem.
Tum præterea quare æquali ratione nullaque differentia aut ex-
ceptione in nomen Patris, Filii et
Spiritus Sancti baptizemur? Quapropter quod secundum naturam
Pater est: id ipsum et Filius et
Spiritus Sanctus est. Atqui Pater natura verus et æternus Deus
est, rerumque omnium, quæ sub
adspectum veniunt aut non veniunt, conditor; talis igitur omnino
tum Filius est, tum Spiritus Sanctus, sibique invicem consubstan-
tiales sunt, docente ita Joanne
Evangelista (1 Joh. v. 7): 'Tres
sunt, qui testificantur in cælo, Pater, Verbum et Spiritus Sanctus:
et hi tres unum sunt.' Unum illud tamen his in verbis singillatim excipiendum, quod in essentia divina Filii Sanctique Spiritus
caussa Pater est, quod ambæque
hac personæ ab illo originem habent: at ipsemet ab nemine. Hunc
in modum ab ipsa æterna Veritate,
Jesu Servatore nostro, edocti sumus: hunc in modum de sanctis
Apostolis accepimus: hunc omnino in modum, et non alium, univer-
sales particularesque Synodi una

καὶ τοῦτο κρατεῖ ὁμοίως ἡ ὀρϑόδοξος ἡμῶν καὶ καϑολικὴ ἐκκλησία.
Διὰ τὴν πίστιν ταύτην οἱ ἅγιοι
μάρτυρες ἔχυσαν τὸ αἷμα των, καὶ
ἀλλάξασι τὴν ζωὴν ταύτην μὲ τὸν
ϑάνατον. Τέτοιας λογῆς καὶ ἡμεῖς
χρεωστοῦμεν νὰ πιστεύωμεν ἐξ ὅλης
μας τῆς καρδίας ἀναμφιβόλως, καὶ
νὰ φυλάττωμεν τὴν πίστιν ταύτην
ἀσφαλῶς καὶ στερεῶς, καὶ δι' αὐτὴν
νὰ ἀποϑνήσκωμεν (ὅταν ἡ χρεία τὸ
καλέσῃ) διὰ τὴν ἐλπίδα τῆς σωτηρίας μας, συνεργούντων καὶ τῶν
ἀγαϑῶν ἡμῶν ἔργων, ὧν τὰς ἀμει-
βὰς ϑέλομεν ἔχειν ἐν οὐρανοῖς αἰωνίους.

cum doctoribus Ecclesiæ docuerunt,
tradiderunt, sanxerunt. Idemque
consimiliter Orthodoxa ac Catholica Ecclesia nostra tenet docetque.
Hanc eandem ob fidem sanguinem
suum sancti Martyres profuderunt,
mortemque cum vita præsente com-
mutarunt. Hoc plane et nos modo,
ex toto corde nostro, sine ulla titu-
batione credere, atque hanc firmam
et inconcussam servare fidem, illiusque caussa, si necesse sit, mortem op-
petere debemus ; ob spem nimirum
æternæ salutis nostræ, adminiculan-
tibus etiam bonis operibus nostris,
quorum præmia fructusque sempi-
ternos in cælo percepturi sumus.

Ἐρώτησις ί.

Ἐπεϑύμουν μὲ φανερώτερον τρόπον νὰ κατανοήσω τὸ μυστήριον τῆς
ἁγίας τριάδος.

'Απ. Μὲ οὐδὲ κἂν μίαν ὁμοιότη-
τα εἶναι δυνατὸν νὰ φανερωϑῇ τελείως τὸ πρᾶγμα τοῦτο, καὶ νὰ πα-
ραστῇ εἰς τὸν νοῦν μας φανερά, μὲ
τίνα τρόπον εἶναι ὁ Θεὸς ἕνας εἰς
τὴν οὐσίαν, καὶ τρεῖς εἰς τὰς ὑποστάσεις. Καὶ πῶς μὲ οὐδεμίαν ὁμοι-
ότητα ἠμπορεῖ νὰ γνωρισϑῇ, τὸ μαρτυρᾷ ὁ αὐτὸς Θεὸς, ὀνομαζόμενος
'Ιεχωβᾶ, διὰ τοῦ προφήτου λέγοντος (Ησ. μς'. ε'.), τίνι με ὁμοιώσατε
καὶ μὲ ἐξισάσετε καὶ ἐπαραβάλετέ με,
καὶ ἐπερωμοιάσετέ με, διὰ νὰ εἶμαι
ὅμοιος μετ' ἐκεῖνον ; ὥστε ὁποῦ οὐ-

QUÆSTIO X.

Vellem sane paullo clarius dis-
tinctiusque isthoc sacræ Trinitatis
mysterium percipere.

RESP. Atqui nulla profecto similitudine fieri potest, ut plene
perfecteque res illustretur ; ut evi-
denterque apud animum nostrum
proponatur, quonam tandem pacto
Deus essentia unus, idemque personis trinus sit. Quod nulla penitus imagine, nullo exemplo, satis
declarari posse, Deus ipsemet, cui
Jehovæ nomen est, per Prophetam testificatur (Jes. xlvi. 5): ' Cui
me adsimilastis ? cui me æquastis ?
et cui comparavistis me, consimi-
lemque fecistis, ut illi similis sim ?'

δένας νοῦς ὄχι μόνον ἀνθρώπινος, ἀλλὰ οὔτε ἀγγελικὸς ἠμπορεῖ νὰ καταλάβῃ, ἢ γλῶσσα νὰ τὸ ἑρμηνεύσῃ. Διὰ τοῦτο πρέπει νὰ εἰποῦμεν μαζὶ μὲ τὸν Ἀπόστολον (β. Κορ. ί. έ.)· λογισμοὺς καθαιροῦντες, καὶ πᾶν ὕψωμα ἐπαιρόμενον κατὰ τῆς γνώσεως τοῦ Θεοῦ, καὶ αἰχμαλωτίζοντες πᾶν νόημα εἰς τὴν ὑπακοὴν τοῦ Χριστοῦ. Πιστεύομεν βεβαίως, ὅτι ὁ Θεὸς καὶ Πατὴρ ὑπάρχων ἀπ᾽ αἰῶνος, καὶ ἐπ᾽ αἰῶνα, καὶ ἔτι ἀπ᾽ οὐδενὸς παραγόμενος γεννᾷ τὸν Υἱὸν καὶ προάγει τὸ Πνεῦμα τὸ ἅγιον. Περὶ οὗ ὁ μέγας Ἀθανάσιος πλατύτερον διδάσκωντας εἰς τὸ σύμβολόν του εἶπε, καὶ οὕτω πιστεύοντες περαιτέρω δὲν ἐρευνοῦμεν. Διατὶ ὁ συζητητὴς καὶ ἐξετακτὴς τῆς θείας μεγαλοπρεπείας κωλύεται ἀπὸ τὴν Γραφὴν τὴν λέγουσαν (Σειρ. γ'. κ'.)· χαλεπώτερά σου μὴ ζήτει, καὶ ἰσχυρότερά σου μὴ ἐξέταζε. Ἄπροσετάγη σοι, ταῦτα διανοοῦ, οὐ γάρ ἔστι σοι χρεία τῶν κρυπτῶν. Ἐν τοῖς περισσοῖς τῶν ἔργων σου μὴ περιεργάζου. Φθάνει μᾶς λοιπὸν τόσον, πῶς ἡ ἁγία Γραφὴ τοῦ παλαιοῦ νόμου προβαλλομένη ἕνα Θεὸν μᾶς ἑρμηνεύει τρία πρόσωπα, λέγουσα (Γεν. ά. κϛ'.)· εἶπε Κύριος ὁ Θεὸς, ποιήσωμεν ἄνθρωπον κατ᾽ εἰκόνα ἡμετέραν καὶ καθ᾽ ὁμοίωσιν· καὶ (Γεν. γ'. κβ'.)· ἰδοὺ Ἀδὰμ γέγονεν ὡς εἷς ἐξ ἡμῶν· καὶ (Γεν. ιά. ζ'.)· δεῦτε καταβάντες αὐτῶν τὰς

Adeo ut nullus intellectus, non modo humanus, sed ne angelicus quidem hoc comprehendere, nulla eloqui valeat lingua. Quamobrem rectissime cum Apostolo dixerimus (2 Cor. x. 5): 'Destruentes ratiocinationes, omnemque celsitudinem, quæ attollitur adversus cognitionem Dei, et captivam ducentes omnem cogitationem in obedientiam Christi.' Firma fide credimus, Deum Patrem, ab æterno, et in æternum reapse exsistentem, eundemque a nullo prorsus oriundum generare Filium, Spiritumque Sanctum producere. Qua de re plenius uberiusque in Symbolo suo magnus Athanasius tractat. Hac fidei simplicitate contenti nihil ulterius exquirimus ac scrutamur. Scrutator enim disputatorque divinæ majestatis vetatur a scriptura dicente (Sirach. iii. 20): 'Difficiliora quam pro tuo captu ne require: et viribus tuis fortiora ne scrutare. Quæ tibi mandata sunt, ea meditare. Non enim indiges iis, quæ occulta sunt. In iis, quæ supervacua tibi sunt, ne curiosus esto.' Hoc igitur nobis satis sit, quod sacra legis antiquæ Scriptura, dum Deum unum proponit, simul nobis trinitatem personarum exponit (Gen. i. 26): 'Dixit Dominus Deus, faciamus hominem ad imaginem nostram et ad similitudinem;' et (cap. iii.

γλώσσας συγχέωμεν ἐκεῖ, ἵνα μὴ
ἀκούσωσιν ἕκαστος τὴν φωνὴν τοῦ
πλησίου· τὸ αὐτὸ καὶ ὁ Προφήτης
λέγων ἐδήλωσεν ('Ησ. ς'. γ'.)· καὶ
ἐκέκραγεν ἕτερος (ἄγγελος) πρὸς τὸν
ἕτερον, καὶ ἔλεγον· "Αγιος, ἅγιος,
ἅγιος, Κύριος Σαββαὼϑ, πλήρης
πᾶσα ἡ γῆ τῆς δόξης αὐτοῦ· καὶ
ὁ Ἱεροψάλτης ἔφηδε (Ψαλ. λβ'. ς'.)·
τῷ λόγῳ Κυρίου οἱ οὐρανοὶ ἐστε-
ρεώϑησαν, καὶ τῷ Πνεύματι τοῦ στόματος αὐτοῦ πᾶσα ἡ δύναμις αὐτῶν·
περὶ οὗ φησὶ πλατύτερον καὶ ἡ ἁγία
Γραφὴ καὶ οἱ διδάσκαλοι τῆς Ἐκκλησίας.

22): 'Ecce Adam ut unus nostrum
jam factus est;' et (cap. xi. 7):
'Age, descendamus et confunda-
mus illic linguas eorum: ut ne alii
aliorum voces exaudiant.' Declarat id ipsum manifeste et Propheta,
qui ait (Jes. vi. 3): 'Et clamabat
alter (Angelus) alteri, dixitque:
Sanctus, sanctus, sanctus Dominus
Zebaoth. Plena est omnis terra gloria illius.' Pariter et sacer Psalmista
(Psa. xxxiii. 6): 'Verbo Domini
cœli firmati sunt, et Spiritu oris
ejus omnis exercitus eorum.' De
quo fusius latiusque sacræ literæ
Doctoresque ecclesiastici agunt.

Ἐρώτησις ιά.

Ποῖα εἶναι τὰ ἰδιώματα τοῦ Θεοῦ;
Ἀπ. Καϑὼς ὁ Θεὸς εἶναι ἀκατάληπτος, ἔτζη καὶ τὰ ἰδιώρατά του
εἶναι ἀκατάληπτα. Μὰ ὅσον ἠμποροῦμεν ἡμεῖς νὰ συνάξωμεν ἀπὸ τὴν
ἁγίαν Γραφὴν καὶ ἀπὸ τοὺς διδασκά-
λους τῆς ἐκκλησίας, τόσον ἔχομεν
ἐξουσίαν, καὶ νὰ νοοῦμεν, καὶ νὰ λέγωμεν. Καὶ διὰ τοῦτο πρέπει νὰ
ἠξεύρωμεν, πῶς τὰ ϑεῖα ἰδιώματα
ἄλλα εἶναι προσωπικὰ καὶ ἄλλα οὐσιώδη.

QUÆSTIO XI.

Quænam Dei Proprietates sunt?
RESP. Quemadmodum Deus ipse
incomprehensibilis est, sic etiam in-
comprehensibiles proprietates illius
sunt. Veruntamen quantum cum
e Scriptura tum Doctoribus ecclesiæ colligere ac conducere poteri-
mus: tantum item fas nobis est, et
animo concipere, et ore proferre.
Scire itaque licet proprietatum Divinarum alias Personales esse alias
Essentiales.

Ἐρώτησις ιβ'.

Ποῖα εἶναι τὰ προσωπικὰ ἰδιώματα τοῦ Θεοῦ;
Ἀπ. Τὰ προσωπικὰ ἰδιώματα εἰς
τὰ ϑεῖα εἶναι ἐκεῖνα, μετὰ ὁποῖα τὰ

QUÆSTIO XII.

Personales Dei proprietates quæ
sunt?
RESP. Proprietates personales in
Divinis illæ sunt, quibus ita ab se

πρόσωπα τῆς ἁγίας τριάδος οὕτω διαιροῦνται πρὸς ἄλληλα, ὥστε ὅπου τὸ ἕνα εἶναι μὴν ἠμπορῇ νὰ εἶναι τὸ ἄλλο· ἤγουν τὸ πρόσωπον τοῦ Πατρὸς· δὲν εἶναι πρόσωπον τοῦ Υἱοῦ, διατὶ ὁ Πατὴρ δὲν εἶναι γεννητὸς ἀπό τινος, μὰ ὁ Υἱὸς εἶναι γεγεννημένος ἀπὸ τὸν Πατέρα κατὰ φύσιν πρὸ τῶν αἰώνων, κατὰ τὴν Γραφὴν τὴν λέγουσαν (Ψαλ. ρί. γ́.)· ἐκ γαστρὸς πρὸ ἑωσφόρου ἐγέννησά σε. Τὸ, Πατὴρ λοιπὸν, καὶ τὸ, Υἱὸς, καὶ τὸ, Πνεῦμα τὸ ἅγιον· τὸ ἀγέννητον, καὶ τὸ γεννητὸν, καὶ τὸ ἐκπορευτὸν διαιρεῖ τὰ πρόσωπα ἐν τοῖς θείοις, μὰ ὄχι τὴν οὐσίαν, ἡ ὁποία ποτὲ δὲν διαιρεῖται εἰς ἑαυτὴν, μόνον χωρίζεται ἀπὸ τὴν κτίσιν. Τὸ δὲ ἕνα καὶ τὸ αὐτὸ πρόσωπον δὲν ἠμπορεῖ νὰ εἶναι γεννητοῦ μαζὶ καὶ ἀγεννήτου. Ὁμοίως πρέπει νὰ γροικοῦμεν καὶ διὰ τὸ Πνεῦμα τὸ ἅγιον, τὸ ὁποῖον ἐκπορεύεται ἀπὸ τὴν οὐσίαν καὶ φύσιν τοῦ Πατρὸς ἀνάρχως εἴτουν αἰωνίως, καὶ εἶναι ὁμοούσιων μὲ τὸν Πατέρα καὶ τὸν Υἱὸν. Μὰ διαιρεῖται ἀπὸ τὸν Πατέρα μὲ τὸ ἰδίωμα τὸ προσωπικὸν, διατὶ ἀπ᾿ ἐκεῖνον ἐκπορεύεται. Καὶ πάλιν ἀπὸ τὸν υἱὸν χωρίζεται, διατὶ δὲν εἶναι ἀπὸ τὸν Πατέρα μὲ τρόπον γεννήσεως, καθὼς εἶναι ὁ Υἱὸς, μὰ μὲ τρόπον ἐκπορεύσεως, ἐκ τοῦ αὐτοῦ Πατρὸς· καὶ εἶναι ὁμοούσιοι ἀλλήλοις καὶ ὁ Υἱὸς καὶ τὸ Πνεῦμα τὸ ἅγιον, διατὶ ἀπὸ τὴν αὐτὴν ἰδίαν φύσιν τοῦ Πατρὸς εἶναι καὶ τὰ δύο τοῦτα πρό-

invicem sanctissimæ Trinitatis personæ distinguuntur, ut quod una est, alia esse nequeat. Scilicet persona Patris haudquaquam Filii persona est, quoniam Pater a nullo genitus est; sed Filius ante ævum omne essentialiter a Patre genitus est; dicente Scriptura (Psa. cx. 3): Ex utero ante luciferum genui te, Pater itaque et Filius et Spiritus Sanctus : et rursus ingenitum et genitum et procedens : hæc sunt, quæ personas divinas discriminant; non vero essentiam, quæ in semet ipsam haud unquam distinguitur : verum a rebus creatis duntaxat secernitur. Iam vero nullo modo una et eadem geniti pariter et ingeniti esse potest persona. Idem de Spiritu Sancto sentiendum est, qui de essentia et natura Patris absque ullo temporali principio hoc est ab æterno procedit, patrique ac Filio consubstantialis est; sed sua personali proprietate, quod a Patre emanat, ab eodem distinguitur. Uti rursus a Filio; quod non ut Filius per modum generationis, verum per modum processionis, ab eodem illo Patre exsistit. Sunt igitur sibi mutuo coëssentiales Filius ac Spiritus Sanctus : quod ab eadem illa Patris natura ambæ hæ personæ sunt. Patri vero omnino consub-

σωπα· καὶ μὲ τὸν Πατέρα εἶναι ὁμοούσια, ἔστωντας καὶ νὰ εἶναι ἀπὸ τὴν
φύσιν του· διὰ τὸ ὁποῖον ὁ Γρηγόριος ὁ θεολόγος (λόγ. κγ'.) λέγει οὕ-
τως· τοῦτο εἶναι κοινὸν εἰς τὸν Υἱὸν
καὶ τὸ Πνεῦμα τὸ ἅγιον, διατὶ καὶ τὸ
ἕνα καὶ τὸ ἄλλο πρόσωπον ἀπὺ τὰ δύο
τοῦτα εἶναι ἀπὸ τὸν Πατέρα· τὸ δὲ
ἰδίωμα τοῦ Πατρὸς εἶναι τοῦτο, ἤγουν
τὸ νὰ εἶναι ἀγέννητος· καὶ τοῦ Υἱοῦ,
τὸ νὰ εἶναι γεννητός· καὶ τοῦ Πνεύματος τοῦ ἁγίου, τὸ νὰ εἶναι ἐκπορευτόν. Ἀκόμι προσωπικὸν ἰδίωμα τοῦ
Υἱοῦ εἶναι καὶ ἡ ἔνσαρκος πᾶσα οἰκο-
νομία, τὴν ὁποίαν δὲν ἀνείληφε μήτε
ὁ Πατὴρ μήτε τὸ Πνεῦμα τὸ ἅγιον.
Τέτοιας λογῆς διδάσκει, νὰ πιστεύωμεν καὶ νὰ ὁμολογοῦμεν, ἡ ἁγία ἐκκλησία ἡ καθολικὴ καὶ ἀποστολικὴ,
ἕνα Θεὸν τῇ φύσει, ἐν τριάδι προσώπων, περὶ οὗ ἀνάγνωθι τὴν πρώτην
ἐν Νικαίᾳ Σύνοδον καὶ τὴν δευτέραν
τὴν ἐν Κωνσταντινουπόλει τὴν οἰ-
κουμενικήν.

stantiales sunt; quandoquidem de
ipsa illius natura ortum ducunt.
Qua de re ita disserit Gregorius
Theologus (Orat. XXIII. εἰς Ἡρω-
va, p. 422): Commune hoc equi-
dem Filio ac Spiritui Sancto est,
quod utraque persona a Patre oritur. Sed illud Patri proprium,
quod genitus est: et Spiritui
Sancto, quod procedit. Præterea
etiam personalis Filii proprietas
universa adsumtæ humanitatis
œconomia est, quam neque Pater
neque Spiritus Sanctus in se sus-
cepit. Hoc pacto unum natura
Deum in trinitate personarum
credere nos et confiteri, Sancta,
Catholica et Apostolica docet Ecclesia. De quo lege primam Synodum Nicænam ac secundam
eamque œcumenicam Constanti-
nopolitanam.

Ἐρώτησις ιγ'.

Ποῖα εἶναι τὰ οὐσιώδη ἰδιώματα
τοῦ Θεοῦ;

Ἀπ. Οὐσιώδη ἰδιώματα τοῦ Θεοῦ
εἶναι ἐκεῖνα, ὅπου ἁρμόζουσιν ὁμοίως
καὶ εἰς τὸν Πατέρα, καὶ εἰς τὸν Υἱὸν,
καὶ εἰς τὸ ἅγιον Πνεῦμα· οἷον τὸ
εἶναι Θεὸν, τὸ εἶναι ἀΐδιον, ἄναρχον,
ἀτελεύτητον, ἀγαθὸν, παντοδύναμον,
ποιητὴν, προνοητὴν, παντεπίσκοπον,
πᾶσι παρόντα, καὶ τὰ πάντα πληροῦν-

QUÆSTIO XIII.

Quænam Essentiales Dei Proprietates sunt?

RESP. Essentiales Dei Proprietates illæ sunt, quæ in Patrem
et Filium et Spiritum Sanctum
æqualiter conveniunt. Nimirum
esse Deum, esse æternum, carere
omni et principio et fine, bonum
esse, omnipotentem, creatorem,
futuri providum, perspectare res

τα· ἀπερίγραπτον, γνώστην πάντων, τῶν τε κρυπτῶν καὶ φανερῶν. Καὶ διὰ νὰ τὸ εἴπῶ συντόμως, ἔξω ἀπ᾽ ἐκεῖνα τὰ προσωπικὰ ἰδιώματα, ὅπου εἴπαμεν, τὸ ἀγέννητον, ἢ τὸ Πατὴρ, καὶ αἰτίαν εἶναι· τὸ γεννητὸν, ἢ τὸ Υἱὸς, καὶ λόγος σεσαρκωμένος, τὸ ἐκπορευτὸν ἢ Πνεῦμα ἅγιον· ὅ, τι πρᾶγμα λέγεται περὶ Θεοῦ, ὅλα εἶναι ἰδιώματα τῆς θείας οὐσίας κοινὰ ὁμοίως καὶ τῶν τριῶν προσώπων χωρίς τινος διαφορᾶς.

Ἐρώτησις ιδ.

Διατί εἰς τὸ πρῶτον ἄρθρον τῆς πίστεως, ἀφήνοντες τὰ ἄλλα ἰδιώματα, ἐβάλασι μόνον τὸ, παντοκράτορα;

Ἀπ. Διατὶ μὲ τὸν λόγον τοῦτον ἑρμηνεύεται ἀκριβέστερον τὸ ἰδίωμα τοῦ Θεοῦ, ἐπειδὴ οὐδένα κτίσμα ἠμπορεῖ νὰ ὀνομασθῇ παντοδύναμον· καὶ τοῦτο διὰ δύο αἰτίας. Πρῶτον διατὶ δὲν ἔχει ἀφ᾽ ἑαυτοῦ τὴν φύσιν του, μὰ ἀπὸ τὸν κτίστην του. Δεύτερον διατὶ δὲν ἠμπορεῖ καὶ ἐκεῖνο νὰ κάμῃ κἂν ἕνα κτίσμα ἀπὸ τὸ μηδαμῆ μηδαμῶς εἶναι. Τὰ ὁποῖα δύο τοῦτα μόνον ἁρμόζουσιν εἰς τὸ παντοδύναμον τοῦ Θεοῦ. Ὅτι δὲ ὁ Θεὸς εἶναι παντοδύναμος, δείκνυσι τοῦτο ὁ αὐτὸς, λέγων ἐν τῇ Ἀποκαλύψει (Κεφ.

cunctas, cunctis præsentem adesse, cunctas implere, infinitum esse et incircumscriptum, omniumque tum occultorum tum manifestorum gnarum. Atque ut paucis rem verbis complectar, præter personales, quas diximus, proprietates: ingenitum esse, sive Patrem, ceterarumque personarum causam: genitum esse, sive Filium, verbumque carne vestitum: atque procedere, sive Spiritum Sanctum esse; quidquid sane de Deo dicitur, id omne proprium naturæ divinæ attributum est: et æqualiter, nulloque prorsus discrimine, tribus commune personis.

QUÆSTIO XIV.

Quamobrem omissis ceteris, unum hoc *Omnipotentiæ* Attributum, in primo Fidei Articulo positum est?

RESP. Quoniam illud Essentiæ Divinæ proprietatem quam accuratissime exprimit. Nulla namque res creata omnipotens appellari duas præcipue ob caussas potest: tum quod nihil a se ipso naturam suam habet, sed a creatore suo: tum quod nihil ex mero nihilo quidquam creatum producere ac creare potest: quæ res duæ soli omnipotentiæ divinæ conveniunt. Quod vero omnipotens Deus est, ipsemet in Apocalypsi demonstrat (i. 8): 'Ego sum Alpha, et ego

α΄. η΄.)· ἐγὼ εἰμὶ τὸ Ἄλφα, καὶ τὸ Ὠμέγα, ἀρχὴ καὶ τέλος· λέγει Κύριος ὁ ὢν, καὶ ὁ ἦν καὶ ὁ ἐρχόμενος, παντοκράτωρ· ὁμοίως λέγει καὶ ὁ Ἀρχάγγελος (Λουκ. α΄. λζ΄.)· ὅτι οὐκ ἀδυνατήσει παρὰ τῷ Θεῷ πᾶν ῥῆμα. Καὶ τούτη ἡ παντοκρατορία καὶ παντοδυναμία τοῦ Θεοῦ εἶναι διωρισμένη ἀπὸ τὴν ἰδίαν θέλησιν καὶ τὴν εὐδοκίαν του, ὥστε δηλαδὴ νὰ μὴν κάμῃ ἐκεῖνον ὅλον, ὅπου ἠμπορεῖ, μὰ ἐκεῖνο μόνον, ὅπου θέλει, ἐκεῖνο καὶ ἠμπυρεῖ, ἐκεῖνο καὶ κάμει. Καθὼς λέγει ὁ ἱερὸς Ψάλτης (Ψαλ. ριέ. γ΄.)· ὁ Θεὸς ἡμῶν ἐν τῷ οὐρανῷ καὶ ἐν τῇ γῇ, πάντα ὅσα ἠθέλησεν ἐποίησεν. Ἠμπόρει νὰ κάμῃ μυριάδας κόσμων, ὡς ἂν τοῦτον, μὰ δὲν ἠθέλησεν. Ἔπειτα πρέπει νὰ γροικᾶται τὸ παντοδύναμον τοῦτο τοῦ Θεοῦ, πῶς εἶναι εἰς τὴν τελειότητα, μακρὰν ἀπὸ πᾶσαν, ἀτελειότητα ἢ ἀδυναμίαν, ὡς δῆλον μὲ παράδειγμα. Ὁ Θεὸς δὲν ἠμπορεῖ νὰ εἶναι κακὸς, ἢ νὰ ἁμάρτῃ ἢ ψεύσασθαι ἑαυτὸν, ἢ ἀρνήσασθαι, ὡς φῆ Παῦλος (β΄. Τιμ. β΄. ιγ΄.· Ἑβρ. ϛ΄. ιη΄.), διατὶ τοῦτο εἶναι ἀτελειότητον πρᾶγμα. Καὶ ἂν ὁ Θεὸς ἤθελεν εἶναι κακὸς, ἢ νὰ ἔσφαλλεν, ἢ νὰ ἠρνεῖτο τὸν ἑαυτὸν του, δὲν ἤθελεν εἶναι παντοδύναμος. Διατὶ τοῦτα ἀφ᾽ ἑαυτοῦ τως εἶναι σημάδια τῶν ἀτελῶν πραγμάτων. Εἶναι λοιπὸν ὁ Θεὸς παντοδύναμος κατὰ τὴν θέλησιν καὶ τελειοτάτην του ἀγαθότητα, καθὼς τὸν ἐξυμνᾷ ὁ μελῳδὸς Προφήτης (Ψαλ. οή.

Omega, principium et finis, ait Dominus, qui est, qui fuit, qui venturus est, omnipotens.' Idem ait et Archangelus Gabriel (Luc. i. 37): 'Quoniam non impossibile erit Deo ullum verbum.' Verum enimvero secreta et distincta universalis hæcce potestas Dei atque omnipotentia a voluntate illius et arbitrio est, ita ut non illud omne efficiat, quod efficere potis est; verum id solum, quod vult, et possit et efficiat; teste sacro cantore (Psa. cxv. 3): 'Deus noster in cœlo et in terra, fecit omnia, quæ voluit.' Ille quidem certe sexcenta mundorum millia æque ac nostrum hunc fabricari potuit at noluit. Porro eadem divina omnipotentia summæ perfectioni conjuncta longisimoque intervallo ab imperfectione ac impotentia omni sejuncta existimanda est: ut hoc patescet exemplo. Deus malus esse non potest, non peccare, non mentiri, aut abnegare semet ipsum, teste Paulo (2 Tim. ii. 13; Heb. vi. 18), quia hæ meræ imperfectiones sunt. Quod si aut improbus Deus foret, aut peccando laberetur, aut se ipse inficiaretur: haudquaquam omnipotens esset. Sunt ista enim per se rerum imperfectarum signa. Est itaque plane omnipotens Deus, ex voluntate ac perfectissima bonitate sua; quemadmodum illum

ιγ΄. ιδ΄.), λέγων· τίς Θεὸς μέγας ὡς
ὁ Θεὸς ἡμῶν; σὺ εἶ ὁ Θεὸς, ὁ ποιῶν
θαυμάσια μόνος· ἐγνώρισας ἐν τοῖς
λαοῖς τὴν δύναμίν σου. Καὶ τέλος
πάντων παντοδύναμος ἢ παντοκράτωρ ὀνομάζεται, διατὶ ὅλα εἶναι εἰς
τὴν δύναμίν του, καὶ τὸν κόσμον
ἐποίησὲ χωρὶς κἂν μίαν δυσκολίαν,
καὶ χωρὶς κἂν ἕνα κόπον, μόνον μὲ
τὴν θέλησίν του.

'Ερώτησις ιέ.

Καὶ ἂν εἶναι ὁ Θεὸς ἀπερίγραπτος
καὶ πανταχοῦ πάρεστι, πῶς λέγεται,
ὅτι ἐν οὐρανοῖς κατοικᾷ, καὶ εἰς ἄλλους τινὰς τόπους τῆς γῆς ἐξαιρετω-
τέρως;

'Απ. Ὄχι ὡς ἂν τάχα ὁ οὐρα-
νὸς ἢ ἡ Σιὼν ἢ ἄλλος τινὰς τόπος
νὰ περιορίζῃ τὴν ἄϋλον καὶ ἀσώμα-
τον θεότητα, διατὶ ὁ Θεὸς δὲν ἔχει
κἂν ἕνα τόπον, μὰ εἶναι τόπος αὐτὸς
ἑαυτοῦ. Μὰ διατὶ ἐνεργεῖ εἰς αὐτοὺς
τοὺς τόπους περισσότερα, καὶ φαί-
νονται φανερώτερα καὶ συνεχέστερον
αἱ ἐνεργείαι του καὶ ἡ χάρις του, διὰ
τοῦτο λέγεται νὰ κατοικᾷ εἰς αὐτούς.
Οἷον εἰς τοὺς οὐρανοὺς (ὡς λέγει ὁ
ἱερὸς Δαμασκηνὸς Βιβ. α΄. κεφ. ις΄.),
ἐν αὐτοῖς γὰρ εἰσιν οἱ ποιοῦντες τὸ
θέλημα αὐτοῦ ἄγγελοι, καὶ ἀεὶ δοξά-
ζοντες αὐτὸν· εἰς τὴν γῆν· ἐν αὐτῇ
γὰρ διὰ σαρκὸς τοῖς ἀνθρώποις συ-

concelebrat Propheta, Psalmorum
auctor (lxxvii. 13, 14): ‘ Ecquis ita
magnus Deus est, ut Deus noster?
Tu es Deus, qui mirabilia solus
efficis. Notam fecisti in populis
potentiam tuam.’ Ad extremum
ideo etiam omnipotens sive rerum
omnium arbiter moderatorque Deus
nuncupatur, quod omnia in potestate et imperio illius sunt, et quod
mundum universum nulla difficul-
tate nullo labore ac molimine, solo
arbitrio suo, architectatus fuit.

QUÆSTIO XV.

Siquidem vero nullo Deus loco
circumscribitur et ubique præsto
est: quo quæso modo in cœlo certisque quibusdam terræ locis potissimum habitare dicitur?

RESP. Minime istuc quidem,
quasi immaterialem et incorpore-
am illam Divinitatem, cœlum fortasse, aut Zijon, aut quicunque
locus alius circumscribat. Nullum enim Deus occupat locum;
sed ipse sibi locus est. Verum
quoniam iis in locis, illustriora
quædam magisque insignia efficit,
ibique opera ipsius et gratiæ vestigia clarius sæpiusque emicant;
ideo illic habitare fertur. Velut
in cœlo (sicut sanctus ait Damascenus Orthod. Fid. Lib. I. cap.
xvi.), quoniam ibi sunt, qui jussa
atque arbitria illius capessunt, il-

νανεστράφη· εἰς τὴν ἁγίαν ἐκκλη-
σίαν· διοτὶ ἐκεῖ μὲ ξεχωριστὸν τρόπον ἡ χάρις του δίδεται εἰς τοὺς
πιστοὺς, καὶ ἡ δόξα του καταγγέλ-
λεται· ὁμοίως καὶ κάθα τύπος, εἰς
τὸν ὁποῖον νὰ φαίνεται μὲ κἂν ἕνα
τρόπον ἡ χάρις τοῦ Θεοῦ, λέγεται
τόπος αὐτοῦ.

Ἐρώτησις ις΄.

Καὶ ἂν λέγῃς, πῶς εἶναι ἰδίωμα
τοῦ Θεοῦ μόνου, τὸ εἰδέναι πάντα,
τὰ κρύφια δηλαδὴ καὶ φανερά, πῶς
καὶ οἱ ἄνθρωποι, οἱ προφῆται, καὶ
οἱ ἄγγελοι τὰ ἠξεύρασι;

Ἀπ. Ὁ Θεὸς ἠξεύρει ἀφ᾽ ἑαυτοῦ
του πάντα τὰ ἀπόκρυφα καὶ τὰ βαθέα τῶν ἀνθρώπων καὶ τῶν ἀγγέ-
λων· ὄχι μόνον ὅταν τὰ λογιάζουσι,
μὰ καὶ πρὸ κτίσεως κόσμου, καθὼς ἡ
Γραφὴ (Σειρ. κγ΄. κθ΄.) λέγει· ὀφθαλμοὶ Κυρίου μυριοπλασίως ἡλίου
φωτεινότεροι, ἐπιβλέποντες πάσας
ὁδοὺς ἀνθρώπων, καὶ κατανοοῦντες
εἰς ἀπόκρυφα μέρη· καὶ ἀλλαχοῦ
(Σειρ. μβ΄. ιθ΄. κ΄.)· ἔγνω ὁ Κύριος
πᾶσαν εἴδησιν, καὶ ἐνέβλεψεν εἰς σημεῖον αἰῶνος, ἀπαγγέλλων τὰ παρε-
ληλυθότα, καὶ ἐπεσόμενα, καὶ ἀπο-
καλύπτων ἴχνη ἀποκρύφων· καὶ ὁ
Ἰωάννης εἰς τὴν Ἀποκάλυψιν (κεφ.
β΄. κγ΄.)· Ἐγὼ εἰμὶ ὁ ἐρευνῶν νε-
φροὺς καὶ καρδίας· καὶ δώσω ὑμῖν
ἑκάστῳ κατὰ τὰ ἔργα ὑμῶν. Μὰ οἱ
ἄγγελοι καὶ οἱ ἄνθρωποι ἂν ἠξεύ-

lumque perpetuo concelebrant An
geli. In terra, quoniam illic in carne cum hominibus versabatur. In
sancta Ecclesia, quoniam illic modo peculiari et gratia ipsius fidelibus datur, et prædicatur gloria.
Similiter et locus quilibet alius, in
quo aliqua gratiæ Dei significatio
ostenditur, locus illius appellatur.

QUÆSTIO XVI.

Quando autem Dei solius hoc
esse adfirmas, nosse omnia, occulta
videlicet et aperta: quo igitur pacto
tum Angeli tum inter mortales Prophetæ eadem cognoverunt?

RESP. Deus per se ipsum abdita
et arcana omnia, profundasque hominum Angelorumque cogitationes
cognoscit: non illo solum momen-
to, quo cogitantur; sed et ante orbem conditum. Sic enim Scriptura (Sirach. xxiii. 29): 'Oculi Domini millies sole lucidiores sunt;
intuentur omnes vias hominum;
partesque abstrusas contemplantur.'
Itemque loco alio (Sirach. xlii. 19,
20): 'Novit Dominus scientiam
omnem, ac intuetur signum seculi. Enunciat præterita et futura;
et vestigia rerum occultarum manifestat.' Et Ioannes in Apocalypsi (ii. 23): 'Ego sum, qui corda
ac renes perscrutor; et dabo cuique
vestrum secundum opera sua.' Si
quando autem Angelis ac homin-

ρουσι κἂν μίαν φορὰν τὰ ἀπόκρυφα μέλλοντα, τὰ ἠξεύρουσιν ἐκ θείας ἀποκαλύψεως, ὡς μαρτυρᾷ ἡ Γραφὴ, λέγουσα (Δαν. β΄. κβ΄.)· ὁ Θεὸς ἀποκαλύπτει βαθέα καὶ ἀπόκρυφα. Καθὼς ἀπεκάλυψεν εἰς τὸν Ἐλισσαῖον ἐκεῖνο, ὁποῦ ὁ δοῦλος του ὁ Γιεζῆ ἐπῆρε κρυφὰ εἰς τὸν δρόμον ἀπὸ τὸν Νεεμὰν (β΄. Βασ. ε΄. κς΄.)· καὶ εἰς τὸν Πέτρον τὸν Ἀπόστολον, περὶ τοῦ Ἀνανίου καὶ Σαπφείρας (Πραξ. ε΄.). Καὶ τοιαύτην ἐπιστήμην εἴχασιν ἀκόμι καὶ ὅλοι οἱ προφῆται.

Ἐρώτησις ιζ΄.

Εἶναι τάχα ἄλλα ἰδιώματα μόνου τοῦ Θεοῦ ἴδια;

Ἀπ. Τὰ ἰδιώματα τοῦ Θεοῦ εἶναι ἀναρίθμητα. Μὰ τοῦτα, ὅπου ἐπροείπαμεν, ὡς ἂν ὠφέλημα πρὸς τὴν σωτηρίαν φθάνουσι νὰ μᾶς, δείξουσι, ποῖαν γνώμην νὰ ἔχωμεν περὶ Θεοῦ. Διὰ τοῦτο ἀφήνωντας ἐσὺ τὰ ἄλλα, πίστευε σταθερῶς καὶ ἀμετακινήτως, πῶς εἶναι ἕνας Θεὸς ἐν τριάδι προσώπων, παντοδύναμος, πανταχοῦ παρὼν καὶ τὰ πάντα εἰδώς· ἀμετάβλητος εἰς τὴν φύσιν καὶ ἀΐδιος.

Ἐρώτησις ιή.

Ἐπειδὴ καὶ εἰς τοῦτο τὸ ἄρθρον βάλλουσι τὸν λόγον τοῦτον, ποιητὴν, τάχα ὁ Θεὸς ὁλωνῶν τῶν πραγμάτων εἶναι ποιητὴς;

Ἀπ. Χωρὶς κἂν μίαν ἀμφιβολίαν

ibus occulta futura prænoscere contingit; utique eadem ex divina patefactione cognoscunt, teste Scriptura (Dan. ii. 22): 'Deus est, qui profunda ac abscondita detegit.' Quomodo Elisæo patefecit, id quod servus illius Gehasi clanculum in via a Naëmane abstulerat (2 Reg. v. 26); pariterque Petro apostolo factum Ananiæ et Sapphiræ (Act. v.). Cujusmodi rerum futurarum præsensione Prophetæ omnes instructi fuerunt.

QUÆSTIO XVII.

Suntne vero et aliæ quædan, Dei solius Proprietates?

Resp. Proprietates divinæ sane innumerabiles sunt; quas tamen ut ad salutem utiles hactenus recensuimus; illæ satis demonstrant nobis, quam de Deo habere conveniat sententiam. Tu itaque, reliquis sepositis, firma immotaque fide crede, unum in trinitate personarum Deum esse, omnipotentem, omnipræsentem, omniscium, natura immutabilem atque sempiternum.

QUÆSTIO XVIII.

Quando autem nomen Creatoris in hoc Articulo positum est, num igitur rerum omnino omnium conditor Deus est?

Resp. Rerum profecto creata-

ὁ Θεὺς εἶναι ποιητὴς πάντων τῶν ὁρατῶν καὶ ἀοράτων κτισμάτων · καὶ προτήτερα ἀπὸ ὅλα ἔκαμε πάσας τὰς δυνάμεις τοῦ οὐρανοῦ ἐκ τοῦ μὴ ὄντος μὲ τὸ νόημά του, ὡς ἂν ὑμνητὰς ἐξαιρέτους τῆς δόξης του. Καὶ ἔκτισε τὸν νοερὸν ἐκεῖνον κόσμον, ὅπου ἐγνωρίσασι καλᾷ τὸν Θεὸν, κατὰ τὴν χάριν τὴν δοθεῖσαν αὐτοῖς, καὶ ὑποτάσσονται ὅλως διόλου εἰς τὴν θέλησίν του. Ἔπειτα ὁ κόσμος οὗτος, ὁ ὁρατὸς καὶ ὑλικὸς, ἐκτίσθηκεν ἀπὸ τὸ μὴ εἶναι ἐκ Θεοῦ. Καὶ ὕστερον ὁ Θεὺς τὸν ἄνθρωπον ἔπλασε, σύνθετον ἀπὸ ἄϋλον καὶ λογικὴν ψυχὴν καὶ ἀπὸ ὑλικὸν σῶμα, διὰ νὰ γνωρισθῇ μὲ τὸν ἕνα σύνθετον ἄνθρωπον, πῶς ὁ ἴδιος τοῦτος εἶναι ὁ ποιητὴς καὶ τῶν δύο κόσμων, τοῦ ἀΰλου καὶ ὑλικοῦ. Καὶ διὰ τὴν ἀφορμὴν τούτην ὁ ἄνθρωπος ὀνομάζεται κόσμος μικρὸς, διατὶ βαστᾷ εἰς τὸν ἑαυτόν του τὸ παράδειγμα ὅλου τοῦ μεγάλου κόσμου (Δαμ. Βιβ. β΄. κεφ. γ΄. ιβ΄.).

Ἐρώτησις ιθ΄.

Ἐπειδὴ καὶ ὁ Θεὸς ἔπλασε πρῶτον τοὺς ἀγγέλους, τίνα γνώμην πρέπει νὰ ἔχωμεν δι᾽ αὐτούς;

Ἀπ. Οἱ ἄγγελοι εἶναι πνεύματα, πλασθέντες ἀπὸ τὸ μὴ εἶναι εἰς τὸ εἶναι ἐκ Θεοῦ, διὰ νὰ ὑμνοῦσι τὸν

rum omnium, tum visibilium, tum invisibilium sine ulla controversia creator Deus est. Atque ante cetera quidem omnia, cælestes omnes Exercitus, ut præcipuos gloriæ majestatisque suæ præcones, sola cogitatione, de nihilo effinxit; mundumque illum intellectualem condidit, qui secundum concessam sibi gratiam Deum pulchre cognoscunt, penitusque ac perpetuo voluntati illius morem gerunt. Tum vero postea aspectabilem atque materiatum hunc orbem item ex nihilo Deus fabricatus est. Ad ultimum denique et hominem fecit, immateriali mentisque compote anima et materiato corpore compositum, ut vel ex uno homine hunc in modum coagmentato constaret, eundem illum Deum, mundi utriusque, immaterialis puta atque materialis, opificem auctoremque esse. Ideoque haud abs re homo pusillus mundus appellatur; quippe qui universi mundi majoris expressam in sese imaginem circumfert (Damasc. ii. 3 et 12).

QUÆSTIO XIX.

Iam quoniam primo loco Angelos creavit Deus, dic quæso quidnam de iis statuendum habemus?

RESP. Angeli sunt Spiritus, ex non ente, in ens verum, ea fini a Deo conformati, ut et ipsum hym-

Θεὸν, καὶ νὰ τοῦ δουλεύουσιν, ἔπει=α
καὶ νὰ διακονοῦσι καὶ εἰς τὸν κόσμον
τοῦτον τῶν ἀνθρώπων, ὁδηγοῦντες
τοὺς εἰς τὴν βασιλείαν τοῦ Θεοῦ.
Δίδονται ἀκόμι εἰς φύλαξιν πόλεων,
βασιλειῶν, χωρῶν, μοναστηρίων, ἐκ-
κλησιῶν καὶ ἀνθρώπων πνευματικῶν
καὶ κοσμικῶν. Τοῦ ὁποίου πράγματος παράδειγμα ἔχομεν εἰς τὰς
πράξεις τῶν Ἀποστόλων, ὁποῦ γράφει (κεφ. ἑ. ιθ´.)· ἄγγελος δὲ Κυρίου
διὰ τῆς νυκτὸς ἤνοιξε τὰς θύρας τῆς
φυλακῆς, ἐξαγαγών τε αὐτοὺς εἶπε·
πορεύεσθε, καὶ σταθέντες λαλεῖτε ἐν
τῷ ἱερῷ τῷ λαῷ πάντα τὰ ῥήματα
τῆς ζωῆς ταύτης· καὶ πάλιν (Πραξ.
ιβ´. ή.)· ἄγγελος Κυρίου ἐπέστη,
καὶ εἶπε τῷ Πέτρῳ, περίζωσαι καὶ
ὑπόδησαι τὰ σανδάλιά σου· περιβα-
λοῦ τὸ ἱμάτιόν σου καὶ ἀκολούθει μοι.
Καὶ μετ᾽ ὀλίγα (στοιχ. ιβ´)· καὶ ὁ Πέτρος γενόμενος ἐν ἑαυτῷ εἶπε, νῦν
οἶδα ἀληθῶς, ὅτι ἐξαπέστειλε Κύριος
τὸν ἄγγελον αὐτοῦ, καὶ ἐξείλετό με
ἐκ χειρὸς Ἡρώδου, καὶ πάσης τῆς
προσδοκίας τοῦ λαοῦ τῶν Ἰουδαίων.
Ὁμοίως φυλάττουσι καὶ τὰ μικρὰ παιδία, κατὰ τὴν διδασκαλίαν τοῦ Σωτῆρος ἡμῶν τὴν λέγουσαν (Ματθ. ιή. ί.)·
λέγω γὰρ ὑμῖν, ὅτι οἱ ἄγγελοι αὐτῶν
ἐν οὐρανοῖς διὰ παντὸς βλέπουσι τὸ
πρόσωπον τοῦ Πατρός μου τοῦ ἐν
οὐρανοῖς. Ἀκόμι προσφέρουσιν εἰς
τὴν θείαν μεγαλειότητα τὰς προσευχὰς καὶ ἐλεημοσύνας μας, καὶ τὰς
λοιπὰς ἀγαθοεργίας· ὄχι διατὶ τάχα

nis suis concelebrent illique appa-
reant: et præterea hoc in orbe suo
ministerio hominibus adsint, illis,
que in regnum Dei viam præeant.
Est illis etiam urbium, regnorum,
regionum, monasteriorum, ecclesiarum, hominumque item, tum religiosorum, tum secularium cura et
tutela commissa. Cujus rei lucu-
lentum in Actibus Apostolicis com-
memoratur exemplum (cap. v. 19).
Angelus autem Domini noctu fores
carceris reclusit, illisque eductis
dixit: 'Ite, et in templo consisten-
tes omnia vitæ hujus verba populo
exponite.' Et rursus (xii. 8): 'Ecce
vero subito adstabat Angelus Domini, dixitque Petro: accinge te
ocius, indue soleas, circumda tibi
pallium et sequere me.' Et mox
(v. 12): 'Verum ut ad se rediit Petrus, dixit: nunc vero plane scio,
emisisse Dominum Angelum suum,
meque eripuisse de manu Herodis,
et de omni exspectatione populi
Iudæorum.' Pari modo parvulorum infantum curam agunt, docente ipso Servatore nostro (Matt.
xviii. 10): 'Dico enim vobis, quod
Angeli illorum in cœlis perpetuo
vultum patris mei, qui in cœlis est,
intuentur.' Iidem preces et eleemosynas nostræ et benefacta reliqua ad divinam majestatem perfe-
runt. Minime istuc quidem, quasi
eleemosynas non animadverteret

ὁ Θεὸς νὰ μὴν θεωρῇ τὰς ἐλεημοσύνας μας, ἢ νὰ μὴ γροικᾷ ταῖς προσευχαῖς μας, μὰ διατὶ ἐκεῖνοι μεσιτεύουσι
διὰ μᾶς. Καὶ εἰς τὸν παλαιὸν νόμον,
πρὶν δοθῇ ὁ νόμος τοῦ Μωϋσέως, ἐδι-
δάσκασι οἱ ἄγγελοι τὸν νόμον, καὶ τὴν
θέλησιν τοῦ Θεοῦ εἰς τοὺς προπάτο-
ράς μας, καὶ τοὺς ἐδείχνασι τὴν ὁδὸν
τῆς σωτηρίας· καθὼς τὸ μαρτυρᾷ ὁ
ἱερὸς Διονύσιος. Καὶ ὕστερον, ἀφ'
οὗ ἐδόθηκεν ὁ νόμος, ἐδιδάσκασιν
ὁδήγωντας) τοὺς εἰς τὸ ἀγαθόν.
Καὶ τοῦτο ἡ Γραφὴ τὸ σημαδεύει λέγουσα, πῶς οἱ ἄγγελοι ἐφαίνοντο εἰς
τοὺς προφήτας, καὶ τοὺς ἐπρολέγασι
τὰ μέλλοντα, ὡς ἂν εἰς τὸν Ἰωσὴφ,
ὁπού ἔδωκεν ὁ ἄγγελος λόγον, νὰ
προσέχῃ ἀπὸ τὴν ἀπόφασιν τοῦ
Ἡρώδου, εἰπών (Ματ. β'. ιγ')· ἐγερ-
θεὶς παράλαβε τὸ παιδίον καὶ τὴν
μητέρα αὐτοῦ, καὶ φεῦγε εἰς Αἴγυπ-
τον, καὶ ἴσθι ἐκεῖ, ἕως ἂν εἴπω σοι,
μέλλει γὰρ Ἡρώδης ζητεῖν τὸ παιδίον, τοῦ ἀπολέσαι αὐτό. Ἀκόμι καὶ
ὅταν ἐφοβεῖτο, νὰ δουλεύῃ τῆς παρθένου (Ματθ. ά. κ'.), ὁ ἄγγελος τοῦ
Κυρίου τὸν ἐθάρρυνε, καὶ τὸν ἐδίδα-
ξεν. Ἀποκαλύπτουσιν ἀκόμι τὰς
θείας ἐνεργείας, καθὼς εἰς τὸν καιρὸν τῆς γεννήσεως Χριστοῦ ἀπεκά-
λυψαν (Λουκ. β'.) εἰς τους ποιμένας,
ὅτι ὁ Χριστὸς ἐγεννήθηκεν εἰς τὴν
Βηθλεέμ. Καὶ μὲ τὸ πρόσταγμα τοῦ
Θεοῦ, παραστέκοντας τοπικῶς κάθα
ἀνθρώπου, μᾶς ἐλευθερώνουσιν ἀπὸ
κάθα κίνδυνον, καὶ διώκουσι τὸν ἐχ-

nostras, aut preces non ipse satis
exaudiret Deus, sed quod illi pro
nobis intercedunt. Et in antiqua
lege, lege Mosaica nondum lata,
legem voluntatemque Dei omnen
majores nostros Angeli edocebant;
eisque rectum salutis iter common-
strabant, teste S. Dionysio (Hierarch. Eccl. iv. p. 26). Postea vero
quam promulgata lex erat, instrue-
bant homines ducebantque ad bonum. Prout ipsa satis Scriptura
arguit, dum et apparuisse Prophetis
Angelos, et futura aperuisse, prodit. Veluti quum Iosephum Angelus præmonuit, caveret sibi a san-
guinario Herodis proposito (Matt.
ii. 13): 'Surge, inquit, acceptoque
puerulo illiusque matre, in Ægyp-
tum effuge; et mane illic, donec
dixero tibi. Certo enim puerulum
ad necem quæsiturus est Herodes.'
Rursus quando idem Virgini fami-
liariter servire verebatur (Matt. i.
20); mox animum illi Angelus
Domini addit, rectiusque edocet.
Horum item indicio divina opera
divulgantur: quemadmodum, na-
scente Christo (Luc. ii.), illum
Bethlehemi jam modo in lucem
editum esse, pastoribus nunciabant.
Illi etiam, mandatu Dei localiter
singulis hominibus præsto adsunt,
et periculis quibuslibet nos eri-
piunt, animarumque nostrarum
hostem propulsant, qui crudelis-

ϑρὸν τῶν ψυχῶν ἡμῶν, ὁποῦ ἀπη-
νῶς τιμωρᾷ τὸν ἄνϑρωπον, ὅταν καταλάβῃ πως ὁ Θεὸς τοῦ ἔδωκεν
ἄδειαν. Καὶ πῶς ὁ ἄγγελος νά μᾶς
φυλάττῃ, τὸ ἔχομεν φανερὸν ἀπὸ
τοῦτο, ὁποῦ λέγει ἡ Γραφὴ, διὰ τὸν
ἐλπίζοντα ἐπὶ Κύριον (Ψαλ. μα΄. ιά.)·
ὅτι τοῖς ἀγγέλοις αὐτοῦ ἐντελεῖται
περὶ σοῦ, τοῦ διαφυλάξαι σε ἐν πάσαις ταῖς ὁδοῖς σου. Ἐπὶ χειρῶν
ἀροῦσί σε, μή ποτε προσκόψῃς πρὸς
λίϑον τὸν πόδα σου.

Ἐρώτησις κ΄.

Εἰς πόσας τάξεις διαιροῦνται οἱ
ἄγγελοι;

Ἀπ. Καϑὼς λέγει ὁ Διονύσιος
(Οὐραν. ἱεραρ. κεφ. ζ΄.), εἰς ἐννέα χο-
ροὺς διαιροῦνται, καὶ οἱ ἐννέα τοῦτοι
εἰς τρεῖς τάξεις. Καὶ εἰς τὴν πρώτην τάξιν εὑρίσκουνται ἐκεῖνοι, ὁποῦ
εἶναι σιμώτερον εἰς τὸν Θεὸν, οἷον
Θρόνοι, Χερουβὶμ, καὶ Σεραφὶμ· εἰς
τὴν δευτέραν τάξιν Ἐξουσίαι, Κυριό-
τητες, καὶ Δυνάμεις· εἰς τὴν τρίτην,
Ἄγγελοι, Ἀρχάγγελοι, Ἀρχαί. Καὶ
οὕτως εἶναι διατεϑειμένοι, ὁποῦ οἱ
κατότεροι ἄγγελοι πέρνουσιν ἀπὸ
τοὺς πλέον ἀπάνω τὴν ἔλλαμψιν
καὶ τὰς ϑείας εὐεργεσίας. Οὗτοι οἱ
ἄγγελοι ἐσταματίσασιν εἰς τὴν χάριν
τοῦ Θεοῦ αἰωνίως ἔστωντας, καὶ νὰ
μὴ συμφωνήσουσι μὲ τὸν Ἑωσφόρον,
νὰ ἐναντιωϑοῦσι του Θεοῦ. Καὶ διὰ
τοῦτο πέρνοντες ταύτην τὴν χάριν
δὲν ἠμποροῦσι ποτὲ νὰ σφάλουσιν,

sime discruciare hominem solet,
quandocunque id sibi divino permissu licere intelligit. Iam quod
sua nos custodia cælestis ille genius
noster sepiat tueaturque, id ex hoc
scripturæ dicto, de eo qui Domino
unice confidit, satis apparet (Psa.
xci. 11): 'Angelis suis de te præ-
cipiet, ut custodiant te in omnibus viis tuis; attollent te manibus, ne ad lapidem pedem tuum
offendas.'

QUÆSTIO XX.

In quot Classes distribuuntur
Angeli?

RESP. Ex sententia Dionysii
(Hier. Cælest. cap. vi. et vii.) in
novem distinguuntur choros, qui
denuo in tres distribuuntur classes.
Prima in classe ævum agitant, qui
Deum propius circumstant: Throni, Cherubim et Seraphim. In
secunda Potestates, Dominationes,
Exercitus (sive etiam Virtutes). In
tertia Angeli, Archangeli, Principatus. Sunt autem eo dispositi ordine, ut inferiores a superioribus
illuminationem ac divina beneficia
accipiant. Hi Angeli in gratia
Dei jugiter permanent. Quippe
quoniam Luciferi ad rebellionem
adversus Deum incitamentis au-
rem non præbuerunt, hanc gratiam
adepti non amplius labi possunt;
non illud quidem certe ulla naturæ

ὄχι ἀπὸ τὴν φύσιν τους, μὰ ἀπὸ τὴν χάριν τοῦ Θεοῦ. Καὶ τοῦτα τὰ σεσημειωμένα φϑάνουσι πρὸς γνῶσιν τῶν ἀγγέλων, καϑ᾽ ὅσον ἀπαιτεῖ ὁ λόγος τῆς παρούσης συντόμου διδασκαλίας τῆς ὀρϑοδόξου. Καὶ γνωρίζοντες ἡμεῖς, πῶς μᾶς βοηϑοῦσι καὶ μεσιτεύουσι δι᾽ ἡμᾶς, εἰς πᾶσαν ϋας προσευχὴν τοὺς ἐπικαλούμεϑα, νὰ παρακαλοῦσι δι᾽ ἡμᾶς τὸν Θεὸν καὶ μάλιστα τὸν ἄγγελον ἐκεῖνον, ὁποῦ εἶναι φύλακάς μας.

suæ præstantia, sed mera Dei gratia. Hæc ita breviter annotata ad notitiam Angelorum in tantum sufficere arbitramur, quantum compendiariæ hujus Orthodoxæ doctrinæ modus exigere videatur. Itaque cognito jam satis, cum opem nobis auxiliumque Angelos ferre, tum sua nos intercessione juvare, merito omnibus in precibus nostris illos obtestamur, ut Deum nobis propitient; illumque ante alios Angelum, qui præses noster custosque est.

Ἐρώτησις κά.

Τίνα γνώμην πρέπει νὰ ἔχωμεν διὰ τοὺς κακοὺς ἀγγέλους;

Ἀκ. Πῶς οἱ πονηροὶ ἄγγελοι ἐπλασϑήκασιν ἀπὸ τὸν Θεὸν καλοί, διατὶ ὅ, τι ἐποίησεν ὁ Θεὸς, καλὸν τὸ ἐποίησε. Μὰ ἐκεῖνοι μὲ τὴν ἰδίαν τους ϑέλησιν ἐγενήκασι κακοὶ, καϑὼς μαρτυρᾷ ὁ Κύριος ἡμῶν, διὰ τὸν ἄρχοντά τους λέγων (Ἰωαν. ή. μδ᾽.)· ἐκεῖνος ἀνϑρωποκτόνος ἦν ἀπ᾽ ἀρχῆς· καὶ ἐν τῇ ἀληϑείᾳ οὐχ ἕστηκεν, ὅτι οὐκ ἔστιν ἀλήϑεια ἐν αὐτῷ· ὅταν λαλῇ τὸ ψεῦδος, ἐκ τῶν ἰδίων λαλεῖ, ὅτι ψεύστης ἐστι, καὶ ὁ πατὴρ αὐτοῦ. Τοῦτοι εἶναι οἱ ἀρχηγοὶ πάσης πονηρίας, βλάσφημοι τῆς ϑείας μεγαλειότητος, ἀπατεῶνες τῶν ἀνϑρωπίνων ψυχῶν, καὶ αὐτοὶ, καὶ τὰ ὄργανά των. Καϑὼς παραδίδωσιν ἡ Γραφὴ λέγουσα (ά. Πετρ. έ. ή.)· νήψατε,

QUÆSTIO XXI.

Poro quid de malis Angelis sentiendum nobis?

RESP. Ipsos quidem bonos omnino a Deo creatos fuisse: quidquid enim fecit Deus, bonum fecit; sed propria voluntate sua improbos evasisse; prout testatur Dominus noster de principe Dæmonum loquens (Ioh. viii. 44): 'Ille homicida fuit ab initio, nec in veritate stetit. Non enim est in illo veritas. Quando mendacium loquitur, de suis loquitur. Nam mendax est, illiusque pater.' Hi impietatis omnis auctores et signiferi divinæque majestatis blasphemi obtrectatores sunt; hi mentium humanarum deceptores; tum ipsimet tum instrumenta ipsorum, tradente Scriptura (1 Pet. v. 8): 'Sobrii

γρηγορήσατε, ὅτι ὁ ἀντίδικος ὑμῶν διάβολος ὡς λέων ὠρυόμενος περιπατεῖ, ζητῶν τίνα καταπίῃ. Μὲ ὅλον τοῦτο, πρέπει νὰ ἠξεύρωμεν, πῶς οἱ δαίμονες δὲν ἠμποροῦσι νὰ μεταχειρισθοῦσι τὴν δύναμίν τους εἰς κᾂν ἕνα ἄνθρωπον ἢ καὶ ἄλλο κτίσμα, χωρὶς νὰ συγχωρήσῃ ὁ Θεός. Καὶ τούτου μάρτυς ἡ Γραφὴ λέγουσα· καὶ παρεκάλουν αὐτὸν οἱ δαίμονες, λέγοντες (Ματθ. ή. λά.)· εἰ ἐκβάλλεις ἡμᾶς, ἐπίτρεψον ἡμῖν ἀπελθεῖν εἰς τὴν ἀγέλην τῶν χοίρων. Καὶ εἶπεν αὐτοῖς· ὑπάγετε. Ἀκόμι καὶ τοῦτο πρέπει καθ᾽ ἕνας νὰ ἠξεύρῃ, πῶς δὲν ἠμποροῦσι νὰ ἀναγκάσουσι τὸν ἄνθρωπον εἰς τὸ νὰ ἁμάρτῃ· μόνον μὲ πειρασμὸν τὸν ἐξαπατοῦσι. Διατὶ ὁ ἄνθρωπος εἶναι αὐτεξούσιος, καὶ εἰς τὸ αὐτεξούσιον μήτε ὁ ἴδιος Θεὸς φέρνει κᾂν μίαν βίαν ἢ ἀνάγκην. Καὶ ἔστωντας νὰ εἶναι κατακεκριμένοι εἰς τὸν αἰῶνα, οὐδέποτε γίνονται δεκτικοὶ τῆς θείας χάριτος, κατὰ τὸ εἰρημένον (Ματθ. κέ. μά.)· πορεύεσθε ἀπ᾽ ἐμοῦ οἱ κατηραμένοι εἰς τὸ πῦρ τὸ αἰώνιον τὸ ἡτοιμασμένον τῷ διαβόλῳ καὶ τοῖς ἀγγέλοις αὐτοῦ.

estote, vigilate. Nam adversarius vester Diabolus tanquam leo rugiens obambulat, quærens quem deglutiat.' Quæ quanquam ita comparata sunt, sciendum tamen, non posse Dæmones vim ac violentiam suam in hominem ullum ullamque rem aliam nisi Deo indulgente exercere, teste Scriptura (Matt. viii. 21): 'Rogabant vero illum Dæmones ac dicebant: siquidem nos expellis, permitte nobis abire in gregem porcorum. Ille vero dixit eis: Ite.' Porro illud etiam cuivis exploratum esse debet, minime in illorum manu positum esse, ut peccare hominem cogant, quem suis duntaxat instigationibus illecebrisque in fraudem et errorem deducunt. Est enim libertate sui arbitrii homo præditus, cui libertati nec Deus ipse vim ullam necessitatemque infert. Ceterum quoniam æternis suppliciis pœnisque multati Dæmones sunt, idcirco nullo unquam tempore divinæ gratiæ misericordiæque participes fieri possunt, ut dictum est (Matt. xxv. 41): 'Discedite a me maledicti in ignem æternum, qui Diabolo angelisque ejus præparatus est.'

Ἐρώτησις κβ'.

Τίνα γνώμην πρέπει νὰ ἔχωμεν διὰ τὴν ἄλλην κτίσιν;

Ἀπ. Πῶς ὁ Θεὸς ἀπὸ τὸ μὴ εἶναι

QUÆSTIO XXII.

De reliquis autem rebus creatis quid statuendum nobis est?

RESP. Hoc nimirum, quod Deus

ἔκαμε τὰ πάντα μὲ τὸ πρόσταγμά του, καὶ εἰς τὸ ὕστερον ἔπλασε τὸν ἄνθρωπον, καὶ τὸν ἔκαμεν αὐθέντην ἀπάνω εἰς ὅλην τὴν κτίσιν, ὁποῦ εἶναι ὑποκάτω τοῦ οὐρανοῦ, λέγωντας (Γεν. ά. κς΄.)· ποιήσωμεν ἄνθρωπον κατ᾽ εἰκόνα ἡμετέραν καὶ καθ᾽ ὁμοίωσιν· καὶ ἀρχέτωσαν τῶν ἰχθύων τῆς θαλάσσης, τῶν πετεινῶν τοῦ οὐρανοῦ, τῶν κτηνῶν, καὶ πάσης τῆς γῆς. Τὸ αὐτὸ λέγει καὶ ὁ ἱερὸς Ψάλτης (Ψαλ. ή. ς΄.)· κατέστησας αὐτὸν ἐπὶ τὰ ἔργα τῶν χειρῶν σου· πάντα ὑπέταξας ὑποκάτω τῶν ποδῶν αὐτοῦ, πρόβατα καὶ βόας ἁπάσας, ἔτι δὲ καὶ τὰ κτήνη τοῦ πεδίου· τὰ πετεινὰ τοῦ οὐρανοῦ, καὶ τοὺς ἰχθύας τῆς θαλάσσης, τὰ διαπορευόμενα τρίβους θαλασσῶν, καὶ ἀνωτέρω· ἠλάττωσας αὐτὸν βραχύ τι παρ᾽ ἀγγέλους, δόξῃ καὶ τιμῇ ἐστεφάνωσας αὐτόν. Μὰ διατὶ δὲν ἐφύλαξεν ὁ ἄνθρωπος τὴν ἐντολὴν τοῦ Θεοῦ εἰς τὸν παράδεισον, ὅταν ἦτον ἀθῶος, μὰ ἀπὸ τὸν ἀπηγορευμένον καρπὸν ἐπίασε καὶ ἔφαγε· διὰ τοῦτο ἐστερήθηκεν ἀπὸ τὴν ἀξίαν του καὶ ἀπὸ τὴν κατάστασιν, ὁποῦ εἶχεν εἰς τὸν καιρὸν τῆς ἀθωότητός του. Καὶ διωχθεὶς ἀπὸ τὸν παράδεισον τοιοῦτος ἔγινεν, ὅ, τι λογῆς τὸν περιγράφει ὁ Προφήτης (Ψαλ. μθ΄. κ΄.) λέγωντας· ἄνθρωπος ἐν τιμῇ ὢν οὐ συνῆκε, παρασυνεβλήθη τοῖς κτήνεσι τοῖς ἀνοήτοις, καὶ ὡμοιώθη αὐτοῖς. Καὶ ἤκουσεν (Γεν. γ΄. ιθ΄.)· ὅτι γῆ εἶ, καὶ εἰς γῆν ἀπελεύσῃ.

verbo jussuque suo cuncta e nihilo fecerit; quodque post reliqua omnia hominem creaverit, illumque herum ac dominum rerum, quæ sub cœlo sunt, omnium constituerit, dicens (Gen. i. 26): 'Faciamus hominem ad imaginem nostram et secundum similitudinem; et dominentur piscibus maris, et volucribus cœli, et jumentis, et orbi terrarum universo.' Idem et sacer Psaltes adstruit (Psa. viii. 6): 'Præfecisti eum operibus manuum tuarum; subjecisti omnia sub pedes illius: oves et boves universas, insuper et pecora campi, volucres cœli, et pisces maris, qui semitas marinas perambulant.' Et paullo antea (v. 5): 'Paullo minorem Angelis fecisti eum, gloria et honore coronasti eum.' Quoniam vero mandatum Dei in Paradiso, quum adhuc in statu innocentiæ homo esset, neglexit de vetitoque fructu carpsit gustavitque; ea re honoribus fortunisque omnibus, queis tempore integritatis suæ ornatus fuerat, subito exutus, beatoque pulsus horto, talis omnino evasit, qualem illum Propheta depingit (Psa. xlix. 20): 'Homo quum in honore esset, non intellexit.' Comparatus est brutis jumentis, iisque similis factus est. Ideoque hanc sententiam audivit (Gen. iii. 10): 'Terra es, et in terram reverteris.'

Ἐρώτησις κγʹ.

Ποία ἦτον ἡ κατάστασις τῆς ἀν-
Θρωπίνης ἀθωότητος, εἴτουν καθα-
ρότητος καὶ ἀναμαρτησίας του ;

Ἀπ. Δύο λογιῶν εἶναι ἡ κατάστασις τῆς ἀκακίας εἴτουν ἀθωότητος
(κατὰ τὸν ἅγιον Βασίλειον εἰς τὴν
ἀρχὴν τῶν Παροιμ.). Ἡ πρώτη
εἶναι μία προαιρετικὴ ἀλλοτρίωσις
ἀπὸ ταῖς ἁμαρτίαις, ἤγουν ὅταν λείπῃ
ὁ ἄνθρωπος μὲ τὴν ἰδίαν του προαίρεσιν ἀπὸ τὰ ἁμαρτήματα, διὰ τὴν
γυμνασίαν, ὁποῦ ἔχει, καὶ μακρὰν
συνήθειαν εἰς τὰ κακά. Ἡ δευτέρα
εἶναι ἡ ἄγνοια καὶ ἡ ἀπειρία τοῦ κακοῦ, ἤγουν ὅταν δὲν γνωρίζῃ, οὔτε
ἐδοκίμασε καθόλου τὸ κακὸν ἢ διὰ
τὴν ἡλικίαν του, ἢ δι' ἄλλαις αἰτίαις.
Καὶ κατὰ τὸν δεύτερον τοῦτον τρόπον
ἦτον εἰς τὸν Ἀδὰμ ἡ ἀθωότης καὶ ἡ
ἀκακία, πρὶν ἁμάρτῃ, κατὰ πᾶσαν τελειότητα καὶ δικαιοσύνην ἔμφυτον, τόσον ἀπὸ τὸ μέρος τῆς διανοίας, ὅσον
καὶ ἀπὸ τὸ μέρος τῆς θελήσεως· εἰς
τὴν διάνοιαν περικλείεται πᾶσα ἐπιστήμη, καὶ εἰς τὴν θέλησιν πᾶσα
χρηστότης καὶ καλοσύνη. Διατὶ
γνωρίζωντας ὁ Ἀδὰμ τὸν Θεὸν κα-
λώτατα (καθ' ὅσον εἰς τὸν καιρὸν
ἐκεῖνον τοῦ ἦτον συγκεχωρημένον,
καὶ καθ' ὅσον ἔπρεπε) μὲ τοῦτο, ὁποῦ
ἐγνώριζε τὸν Θεὸν, ἐγνώριζεν ὅλα τὰ
πράγματα μετ' ἐκεῖνον. Καὶ τούτου
ἔχομεν σημάδια ἀνάμεσα εἰς τὰ ἄλλα,
ὁποῦ ἐφελθήκασιν εἰς τὸν Ἀδὰμ ὅλα

QUÆSTIO XXIII.

Cujusmodi erat status Innocentiæ hominis sive puritatis et a peccando immunitatis?

RESP. Innocentiæ integritatis-
que status duorum generum est
(ex sententia S. Basilii, Homilia
in Principium Proverbiorum pag.
184. Bas.). Prior est voluntaria
quædam a peccato discessio ; nimirum quum homo, cui ex diuturno
vitiorum exercitio ac consuetudine
(nota mala sunt), proprio delibe-
ratoque consilio peccata deserit.
Alter, simplex quædam mali inscientia et imperitia est, quando
mali penitus ignarus quispiam in-
expertusque est ; sive per tenellam
ætatulam suam, sive caussas alias.
Posteriore hoc modo ante lapsum
comparata innocentia Adami inte-
gritasque fuit ; cunjuncta cum
summa absolutaque perfectione ac
justitia insita intellectus pariter
voluntatisque, ita ut in intellectu
scientia omnis includeretur, in voluntate probitas omnis et honestas.
Quando itaque perfectissimo sane
modo (quantum illo temporis habi-
tu concessum ipsi ac decorum erat),
Deum cognoscebat Adamus ; ideo
hoc ipso, quod Deum cognoscebat,
cetera item omnia per ipsum nosci-
tabat. Cujus rei clarum inter alia
indicium habemus, quum ad Ada-

τὰ ζῶα, διὰ νὰ τοὺς δώσῃ ὄνομα.
Καὶ τὰ ὠνόμασε καθ᾽ ἕνα ἀπ᾽ αὐτά.
Τὸ ὁποῖον ἐγεννᾶτο ἀπὸ τὸ νὰ γνωρίζῃ τὴν φύσιν τους, ὄχι ἀπὸ ἄλλην
μάθησιν, μόνον ἀπὸ τὸ νὰ μελετᾷ
καὶ νὰ λογιάζῃ περὶ Θεοῦ, καὶ τὰς
ἐκείνου χριστότητας. Περὶ δὲ τῆς
θελήσεως, αὕτη πάντοτε ὑπετάσσετο
εἰς τὸν λόγον· καλᾷ καὶ πάντοτε νὰ
ἦτον ἐλεύθερα, καὶ ἦτον ἐξουσία εἰς
τὸν ἄνθρωπον νὰ ἁμάρτῃ, ἢ νὰ μὴν
ἁμάρτῃ. Καθὼς λέγεται εἰς τὴν
Γραφήν (Σειρ. ιε΄. ια΄.)· μὴ εἴπῃς, ὅτι
διὰ Κύριον ἀπέστην. Ἃ γὰρ ἐμίσησεν, οὐ ποιήσεις. Μὴ εἴπῃς, ὅτι
αὐτός με ἐπλάνησεν. Οὐ γὰρ χρείαν ἔχει ἀνδρὸς ἁμαρτωλοῦ. Πᾶν
βδέλυγμα ἐμίσησεν ὁ Κύριος, καὶ
οὐκ ἔστιν ἀγαπητὸν τοῖς φοβουμένοις αὐτόν. Αὐτὸς ἐξ ἀρχῆς ἐποίησεν ἄνθρωπον, καὶ ἀφῆκεν αὐτὸν ἐν
χειρὶ διαβουλίου αὐτοῦ. Ἐὰν θέλῃς, συντηρήσεις ἐντολὰς καὶ πίστιν,
ποιῆσαι εὐδοκίας. Παρέθηκέ σοι πῦρ
καὶ ὕδωρ, οὗ ἐὰν θέλῃς ἐκτενεῖς τὴν
χεῖρά σου. Ἔναντι ἀνθρώπων ἡ
ζωὴ καὶ ὁ θάνατος· καὶ ὃ ἐὰν εὐδο-
κήσῃ, δοθήσεται αὐτῷ. Καὶ μετ᾽
ὀλίγα (σιχ. κ΄.)· οὐκ ἐνετείλατο οὐδενὶ ἀσεβεῖν, καὶ οὐκ ἔδωκεν ἄνεσιν
οὐδενὶ ἁμαρτάνειν. Εἰς τοιαύτην
λοιπὸν τῆς ἀθωότητος καὶ ἀναμαρτησίας κατάστασιν ἦτον ὁ ἄνθρωπος
ὅμοιος τοῖς ἀγγέλοις. Μὰ ὡς ἂν
ἔσφαλε μὲ τὴν παράβασιν, παρευθὺς
εἰς τὸν ἴδιον τόπον τοῦ παραδείσου,

mum animantes omnes convenie-
bant, ut iis sua nomina daret, quas
ille etiam singulatim suis appella-
bat nominibus. Inde id autem
fiebat, quod animantis cujusque
naturam ac indolem perspectam
haberet, non parta aliunde instructus scientia, sed ex eo, quod de
Deo illiusque beneficiis secum me-
ditaretur commentareturque. Iam
quod ad voluntatem attinet; illa
rationi perpetuo obtemperabat,
quanquam et tum suam semper
libertatem retineret, et situm plane
in hominis esset potestate, sive peccaret sive non peccaret, sicut in
scriptura dicitur (Sirach. xv. 11):
'Ne dixeris: propter Dominum
defeci; non enim facere debes,
quæ illi odiosa sunt. Ne dixeris:
ipse me in errorem impulit.' Nihil enim illi homine peccatore
opus est. Odit Dominus omnem
abominationem, eademque illum
timentibus haudquaquam accepta
est. Ipse ab initio hominem fecit,
eumque in manu consilii sui dimi-
sit. Si voles, mandata et fidem
servabis; faciendo, quæ illi grata
sunt. Ignem et aquam proposuit
tibi; utrum voles, ad id extendes
manum tuam. Vita et mors coram hominibus est; dabiturque illi,
utrum ipsi placuerit. Et mox (v.
20): 'Nulli impie agere præcepit;
nulli peccandi licentiam tribuit.'

πέρνωντας τὴν κατάστασιν τῆς ἁμαρτίας, ἐγίνηκε θνητός. Οὕτω γὰρ ἡ
ἁγία Γραφὴ παραδίδωσι ('Ρωμ. ϛ'.
κγ'.), λέγουσα· τὰ ὀψώνια τῆς ἁμαρτίας θάνατος. Καὶ τότε παρευθὺς
ἔχασε τὴν τελειότητα τοῦ λόγου καὶ
τῆς γνώσεως· καὶ ἡ θέλησις ἔκλινε
περισσότερον εἰς τὸ κακὸν παρὰ εἰς
τὸ καλόν. Καὶ οὕτως ἡ κατάστασις
τῆς ἀθωότητος καὶ ἀκακίας, ἔστωντας
καὶ νὰ δοκιμάσῃ τὸ κακὸν, ἄλλαξεν
εἰς κατάστασιν ἁμαρτίας, καὶ ὁ τέλειος ἄνθρωπος τόσον ἐταπεινώθη-
κεν, ὥστε νὰ λέγῃ μὲ τόν Δαβὶδ
(Ψαλ. κβ'. ϛ'.)· ἐγὼ δὲ εἰμὶ σκώληξ,
καὶ οὐκ ἄνθρωπος.

Hujusmodi igitur innocentiæ ac
impeccabilitatis in statu simillimus
Angelis homo erat. Simulac vero
per transgressionem præcepti pec-
cavisset, continuo eodem Paradisi
loco, suscepto peccati statu, mortalis evasit, tradente ita Scriptura
(Rom. vi. 23): 'Stipendium peccati mors est.' Mox amissa rationis
et intelligentiæ perfectione, etiam
voluntas in malum, quam in bonum, pronior facta est. Atque hoc
pacto integritatis innocentiæque
status, homine malum jam experto,
in statum peccati transiit, illeque
antea perfectus homo eo humilita-
tis redactus est, ut jam merito cum
Davide dicat (Psa. xxii. 6): 'Ego
vermis sum, non homo.'

Ἐρώτησις κδ'.

Εἶναι τάχα ὅλοι οἱ ἄνθρωποι ὑπο-
κείμενοι εἰς τὴν αὐτὴν ἁμαρτίαν;

Ἀπ. Καθὼς ὅλοι οἱ ἄνθρωποι
ἦσαν εἰς τὴν κατάστασιν τῆς ἀθωότητος εἰς τὸν Ἀδὰμ, τέτοιας λογῆς καὶ
ἀφ' οὗ ἔσφαλεν, ὅλοι ἔσφαλαν εἰς αὐτὸν, καὶ ἔμειναν εἰς τὴν κατάστασιν
τῆς ἁμαρτίας. Διὰ τοῦτο ὄχι μόνον
εἰς τὴν ἁμαρτίαν ὑπόκεινται, μὰ καὶ
εἰς τὴν τιμωρίαν διὰ τὴν ἁμαρτίαν.
Ἡ ὁποία τιμωρία γνωρίζεται μὲ τούτην τὴν ἀπόφασιν τοῦ Θεοῦ (Γεν. β'.
ιζ'.)· ᾗδ' ἂν ἡμέρᾳ φάγητε ἀπ' αὐτοῦ, θανάτῳ ἀποθανεῖσθε. Τὸ αὐτὸ
καὶ ὁ Ἀπόστολος ('Ρωμ. ε'. ιβ'.) ἀνα-

QUÆSTIO XXIV.

Numquid vero eidem omnes homines peccato sunt obnoxii ?

RESP. Quemadmodum homines
omnes durante innocentiæ statu in
Adamo fuerunt; eodem modo, ex
quo lapsus ille fuit, in ipso omnes
collapsi, simul in statu peccati per-
manserunt. Quamobrem non solum peccato, sed ejus caussa, pœna
item tenentur. Quæ pœna hoc
Dei edicto promulgatur (Gen. ii.
17): 'Quacunque die de arbore
ista comederitis, morte moriemini.'
Refert id ipsum et Apostolus (Rom.
v. 12): 'Ut per unum hominem

φέρνωντας λέγει· ὥσπερ δι' ἑνὸς ἀνθρώπου ἡ ἁμαρτία εἰς τὸν κόσμον
εἰσῆλθε, καὶ διὰ τῆς ἁμαρτίας ὁ θάνατος, καὶ οὕτως εἰς πάντας ἀνθρώπους ὁ θάνατος διῆλθεν, ἐφ' ᾧ πάντες ἥμαρτον. Διὰ τὴν ὁποίαν ἀφορμὴν ἀκόμι εἰς τὴν κοιλίαν τῆς μητρός
μας συλλαμβανόμεθα μὲ τὴν ἁμαρτίαν τούτην καὶ γεννώμεθα, καθὼς
λέγει ὁ ἱερὸς Ψάλτης (Ψαλ. νά. ζ'.)·
ἰδοὺ γὰρ ἐν ἀνομίαις συνελήφθην,
καὶ ἐν ἁμαρτίαις ἐκίσσησέ με ἡ μήτηρ
μου. Καὶ καλεῖται τὸ ἁμάρτημα
τοῦτο προπατορικὸν, πρῶτον μὲν διατὶ προτήτερα ἀπ' αὐτὸ ὁ ἄνθρωπος
δὲν ἤθελε μολυνθῇ ἀπὸ κἂν ἕνα ἄλλο
ἁμάρτημα. Καλᾷ καὶ ὁ διάβολος
νὰ ἦτον διεφθαρμένος μὲ τὴν ἁμαρτίαν του, ἀπὸ τοῦ ὁποίου τὴν παρακίνησιν καὶ εἰς τὸν ἄνθρωπον ἐβλάσ-
τησε τὸ λεγόμενον τοῦτο προπατορικὸν ἁμάρτημα, εἰς τὸ ὁποῖον καὶ ὁ
Ἀδὰμ, ὁποῦ τὸ ἔκαμεν, εἶναι ὑποκείμε-
νος, καὶ ἡμεῖς, ὅπου καταβαίνομεν ἀπ'
αὐτόν. Δεύτερον, διατὶ ὁ ἄνθρωπος
δὲν συλλαμβάνεται παρὰ ἐν ἁμαρτίᾳ.

Ἐρώτησις κέ.

Ἐπειδὴ ὁ Θεὸς ἐγνώριζε τὸν
Ἀδὰμ, πῶς ἔμελλε νὰ σφάλῃ, διατί
τὸν ἔπλασε ;

Ἀπ. Ὄχι μόνον διὰ τὴν ἁμαρτίαν
τοῦ Ἀδὰμ, ἀλλὰ καὶ διὰ τὴν κακίαν
τοῦ Ἑωσφόρου, καὶ πρὶν τὸν κάμει,
ἤξευρε καλώτατα· καὶ διὰ κάθα μικρὸν λογισμὸν, καὶ διὰ κάθα κάμωμα,

peccatum in mundum introiit, et
per peccatum mors; quæ hoc
pacto in mortales omnes pervasit,
quod in illo omnes peccaverunt.'
Quapropter etiam in utero materno
mox cum hoc peccato concipimur
nascimurque, teste sacro Psalte
(li. 7): 'Ecce enim in iniquitatibus
conceptus sum, et in peccatis mea
me mater concepit.' Quod peccatum Avitum (sive Originale), appellatur; primum ideo, quod ante
illud nullo dum alio peccato infec-
tus homo fuit. Tametsi jam tum
per lapsum suum corruptus esset
Diabolus; quo etiam instigante,
pullulare in homine hoc ipsum
avitum peccatum cœpit cui et
Adamus, auctor ejusdem effector-
que, obnoxius erat, et nos omnes,
qui ab illo genus ducimus. Deinde, quod nemo mortalium, nisi
cum hac naturæ contagione, concipitur.

QUÆSTIO XXV.

Quando autem lapsurum Ada-
mum norat Deus, quid ita, quæso,
illum condidit?

RESP. Non modo lapsum Adami,
verum et malitiam Luciferi, priusquam utrumque conderet, planis-
sime scivit Deus. Immo et minu-
tissimas quasque cogitationes, ac

τὶ ἔμελλε νὰ λογιάσῃ, καὶ νὰ κάμῃ. Μὲ ὅλον τοῦτο δὲν ἠθέλησεν ὅτι τὸ ἀνθρώπινον ἁμάρτημα ἢ τοῦ διαβόλου ἡ πονηρία νὰ νικήσῃ τὴν θείαν του ἀγαθότητα (Δαμ. Βιβ. β΄. κεφ. κζ΄). Διὰ φανέρωσιν λοιπὸν μεγαλητέρην τῆς ἀγαθότητός του ἔπλασε τὸν ἄγγελον ἐκεῖνον καλὸν, καὶ αὐτὸς μὲ τὴν ἰδίαν του θέλησιν καὶ προαίρεσιν ἐγίνηκε κακός· ὁμοίως καὶ τὸν ἄνθρωπον, ὁποῦ ἔσφαλε μὲ τὴν παρακίνησιν ἐκείνου. Μὲ ὅλον τοῦτο εἰς τὸν ἄνθρωπον ὁ Θεὸς ᾠκονόμησεν, ὥστε μὲ τὴν ἁμαρτίαν ἐκείνου περισσότερον νὰ λάμψῃ ἡ τοῦ Θεοῦ ἀγαθότης· ἐπειδὴ εἶχε νὰ πέμψῃ τὸν μονογενῆ του Υἱὸν εἰς τὴν κοιλάδα ταύτην τῆς γῆς, νὰ πάρῃ σάρκα ἀπὸ τὴν καθαρωτάτην Παρθένον μὲ τὴν συνεργίαν τοῦ ἁγίου Πνεύματος, διὰ νὰ ἐξαγοράσῃ τὸν ἄνθρωπον, καὶ νὰ τὸν ἀναβάσῃ εἰς τὴν βασιλείαν του μὲ μεγαλητέρην δόξαν παρὰ ὁποῦ ἦτον εἰς τὸν παράδεισον, διὰ αἰσχύνην τοῦ διαβόλου. Καὶ διὰ τοῦτο ἡ ἁμαρτία ἐκείνη δὲν ἐμπόδισε τὸν Θεὸν νὰ μὴν πλάσῃ τὸν ἄνθρωπον.

tionesque singulas, quas cogitaturus acturusque aliquando esset. Neque tamen aut peccato hominis, aut improbitate Diaboli, divinam bonitatem suam vinci superarique passus est (Damasc. ii. cap. 27. Adde Dialog. κατὰ Μανιχαίων. p. 542, 556). Itaque ut tanto illustrior illa testatiorque fieret; illum quidem Angelum bonum creabat, qui sua postmodum voluntate ac arbitrio, impius sceleratusque evasit, consimiliter et hominem, Dæmonis instinctu deinde lapsum. Verum enim vero cum homine illum in modum egit Deus, ut per lapsum illius majorem in modum sua effulgeret bonitas; quippe unigenam filium suum in terrestrem hanc vallem demittere poterat, qui carne de Virgine castissima operá Spiritus Sancti adsumta, hominem redimeret; majoreque gloria, quam olim in Paradiso habuerat, exornatum, cum infamia ac dedecore Diaboli, in cœleste regnum suum subveheret. Ideoque nec illud hominis peccatum, ab ipsius creatione Deum deducere atque revocare potuit.

Ἐρώτησις κς΄.

Ἂν ὁ Θεὸς ἐγνώριζε τὰ πάντα πρὶν τὰ κτίσῃ, τάχα καὶ ὅλα τὰ ἐπροώρισεν ὁμοίως καλὰ καὶ κακὰ, νὰ μὴ γίνουνται ἀλλοιῶς, παρὰ καθὼς γίνουνται;

Ἀπ. Ὁ Θεὸς πρὶν τῆς κτίσεως

QUÆSTIO XXVI.

Si norat igitur omnia Deus antequam conderet, an bona ac mala omnia item prædestinavit, ne aliter fiant, quam fiunt.

RESP. Res quidem universas an-

τοῦ κόσμου ὅλα τὰ πράγματα τὰ ἐπρογνώριζε, μὰ μόνα τὰ ἀγαθὰ ἐπροώρισεν (ὡς λέγει ὁ ἱερὸς Δαμασκηνὸς Βιβ. β′. κεφ. λ′.)· διατὶ τὸ νὰ προωρίζῃ τὰ κακὰ, εἶναι ἐναντίον εἰς τὴν θείαν ἀγαθότητα. Κακὸν δὲ νόμιζε μόνον τὴν ἁμαρτίαν· ἐπειδὴ οὐδένα κυρίως κακὸν εὑρίσκεται εἰς τὸν κόσμον, μόνον ἡ ἁμαρτία, ἡ ὁποία εἶναι ἡ παράβασις τοῦ θείου νόμου καὶ τῆς θείας θελήσεως (Δαμ. εἰς τὸ περὶ δύο θελήσεων τοῦ Χριστοῦ.). Τὰ δὲ ἐπίλοιπα, ὅπου ὁ Θεός μᾶς τιμωρᾷ διὰ τὰς ἁμαρτίας μας, οἷον θανατικὰ, πόλεμοι, ἀσθένειαι καὶ τὰ ὅμοια, λέγονται κακὰ ὡς πρὸς ἡμᾶς (Βασίλ. ὁμιλ. Θ′. ὅτι οὐκ αἴτιος τῶν κακῶν ὁ Θεός.), διατὶ μᾶς φέρουσιν ὀδύνας καὶ λύπας, ὅπου ἀποτρεπόμεθα. Μὰ εἰς τὸν Θεὸν δὲν εἶναι κακά· διατὶ ἔχουσι δύναμιν ἀγαθοῦ· ἐπειδὴ, τιμωρῶντας ἡμᾶς μετ᾽ αὐτὰ, μᾶς παρακινᾷ εἰς τὸ ἀγαθόν. Καὶ ὅταν λέγει ἡ Γραφὴ (Ἀμὼς γ′. ϛ′.)· εἰ ἔστι κακία ἐν πόλει, ἣν Κύριος οὐκ ἐποίησεν; ὀνομάζει τὴν δικαίαν παίδευσιν τοῦ Θεοῦ κακίαν. Ἀκόμι ἐκεῖνα μόνον ὁ Θεὸς προορίζει κατὰ τὴν σοφίαν καὶ δικαιοσύνην του, ὁποῦ δὲν στέκουνται εἰς τὴν ἐξουσίαν τὴν ἐδικήν μας νὰ γενοῦσι. Μὰ ἐκεῖνα τὰ ἀγαθὰ, ὅπου στέκουνται εἰς τὴν ἐξουσίαν μας νὰ γενοῦσι, τὰ προγνωρίζει, συντρέχων καὶ αὐτὸς κατὰ τὴν εὐδοκίαν τοῦ μὲ τὴν θέλησίν μας· τὸ ὁποῖον δὲν ἀνελεῖ τὴν φύσιν τοῦ αὐτεξουσίου.

te creationem præscivit Deus, sed bonas duntaxat prædestinavit (uti loquitur S. Damascenus, lib. II. cap. 30): nam illud divinæ bonitati repugnat, ut malas præfiniat. Malum autem non aliud existimandum est, quam peccatum. Nam præter peccatum, quæ divinæ legis voluntatisque transgressio est, si proprie loquimur, nihil in orbe mali reperitur (Idem in : de duabus Christi voluntatibus). At cetera, quibus ob noxias nostras Deus in nos animadvertit, ut pestilentia, bella, morbi, aliaque ejusmodi ; respectu nostri mala dicuntur (Basil. Homil. IX. Deum non esse malorum caussam), quoniam ærumnas nobis atque dolores afferunt, quos fugimus ac aversamur. Ceterum Deo nequaquam mala sunt ; siquidem vim quandam boni habent. Iis enim nos castigans ad bonum excitat. Ideoque quum dicit Scriptura (Amos iii. 6): 'Numquid ullum in civitate malum est, Dominus non fecit? tum justam Dei castigationem malum vocat.' Porro illa duntaxat prædeterminat Deus, secundum sapientiam justitiamque suam, quæ utrum fiant, nec ne, id in nostra potestate situm non est. Verum bona illa, quæ ut fiant, in nostra manu est, præcognoscit ; ita vero, ut simul et ipse, ex propensa voluntate sua, cum nostra voluntate concurrat. Quod naturæ liberi Arbitrii nihil quidquam officit.

Ἐρώτησις κζ'.

Τί εἶναι τὸ αὐτοξούσιον;

Ἀπ. Τὸ αὐτεξούσιον τοῦ ἀνθρώπου εἶναι μία θέλησις ἐλευθέρα καὶ
ἀπολελυμένη. Καὶ γεννᾶται ἀπὸ
τὸν λογαριασμὸν, εἴτουν τὸ λογικὸν,
εἰς τὸ νὰ ἐνεργᾷ τὸ ἀγαθὸν, ἢ τὸ κα-
κόν· ἐπειδὴ τὰ λογικὰ κτίσματα πρέπει νὰ ἔχουσι φύσιν ἐξουσιαστικὴν,
καὶ νὰ τὴν μεταχειρίζουνται ἐλευθέ-
ρως, ὁδηγοῦντος τοῦ λόγου. Καὶ
οὗτος ὁ λόγος, ὅταν ὁ ἄνθρωπος ἦτον
εἰς τὴν κατάστασιν τῆς ἀθωότητος,
ἤγουν πρὶν ἁμάρτῃ, ἦτον ἀδιάφθορος
εἰς τὴν τελειότητά του, καὶ διὰ τὴν
ἁμαρτίαν ἐφθάρη. Μὰ ἡ θέλησις,
καλᾷ καὶ νὰ ἔμεινεν ἄβλαβης, εἰς τὸ
νὰ ἐπιθυμᾷ τὸ καλὸν ἢ τὸ κακὸν·
ἔγινεν μ' ὅλον τοῦτο εἰς κάποιους
πλέον ἐπιρρεπὴς καὶ κλίνει πρὸς τὸ
κακὸν, καὶ εἰς ἄλλους πρὸς τὸ καλόν.
Διὰ τὸ ὁ ὁποῖον μέγας Βασίλειος
(Εἰς τὸν Ἡσ. ιδ'.) λέγει οὕτως· "ἀπὸ
τὴν ἰδίαν του θέλησιν καὶ προαίρεσιν
ὁ καθεὶς ἠμπορεῖ νὰ εἶναι ἢ σπέρμα
ἅγιον, ἢ τὸ ἐναντίον. Ἄκουσον τοῦ
Παύλου λέγοντος (α'. Κορ. δ'. ιε'.)·
ἐν Χριστῷ Ἰησοῦ διὰ τοῦ εὐαγγελίου
ἐγὼ ὑμᾶς ἐγέννησα· καὶ ἐκεῖνα τὰ
λόγια, ὅπου (Ἰωαν. ά. ιβ'.) λέγει·
ὅσοι δὲ ἔλαβον αὐτὸν, ἔδωκεν αὐτοῖς
ἐξουσίαν, τέκνα Θεοῦ γενέσθαι."
Δείχνει ὁ ἅγιος τοῦτος διδάσκαλος,
πῶς, καλᾷ καὶ ἡ ἀνθρωπίνη θέλησις
ἐβλάβη μὲ τὸ προπατορικὸν ἁμάρ-

QUÆSTIO XXVII.

Quid est Arbitrium liberum?

RESP. Liberum hominis Arbitrium est libera et absoluta illius voluntas, orta a ratione sive rationali
anima ad bonum, aut malum effi-
ciendum. Quibus enim in rebus
mens ratioque inest, eas naturam
cum potestate sui arbitrii conjunc-
tam habere, eamque duce ratione
libere exercere oportet. Hæc autem ratio quamdiu in statu innocentiæ homo stetit, hoc est, antequam peccaret, incorrupta et perfecta erat; per lapsum corrupta
fuit. At voluntas, etiamsi quod ad
appetitum boni, aut mali, illæsa
maneret; nihilominus in nonnullis
haud paullo propensior atque ad
malum inclinatior evasit: in aliis
rursus ad bonum. De quo ita loquitur magnus Basilius (in Iesai.
xiv.): 'Per voluntatem quisque
suam arbitriumque, aut semen
sanctum, aut contrarium esse potest.' Audi sodes Paulum dicen-
tem (1 Cor. iv. 15): 'Ego vos in
Christo Iesu per Evangelium genui.' Audi et hæc Scripturæ verba (Ioh. i. 12): 'Quotquot illum
receperunt, iis potestatem dedit, ut
filii Dei fierent.' Quo sane sanctus doctor declarat, quamvis et ipsa
hominis voluntas peccato originis
misere labefactata fuerit; nihilo-

τημα, μ᾽ ὅλον τοῦτο καὶ τῶρα κατὰ τὸν παρόντα καιρὸν εἰς τὴν προαίρεσιν τοῦ καθ᾽ ἑνὸς στέκεται τὸ νὰ εἶναι καλὸς καὶ τέκνον Θεοῦ, ἢ κακὸς καὶ υἱὸς διαβόλου· ὅλον τοῦτο εἶναι εἰς τὸ χέρι καὶ ἐξουσίαν τοῦ ἀνθρώπου. Καὶ εἰς μὲν τὸ καλὸν ἡ θεία χάρις συμβοηθᾷ· ἀλλὰ καὶ ἀπὸ τὸ πακὸν ἡ ἰδία γυρίζει τὸν ἄνθρωπον, χωρὶς νὰ ἀναγκάσῃ τὸ αὐτεξούσιον τοῦ ἀνθρώπου.

minus etiam præsenti hoc tempore in cujusque arbitrio positum esse, ut bonus Deique filius sit, aut e contrario improbus filiusque Diaboli. Hoc omne, inquam, in manu atque potestate hominis situm est, ita tamen, ut in bonum divina gratia homini adjutrix sit, eumque item a malo retrahat; at non ut arbitrium hominis suis ingratiis compellat.

Ἐρώτησις κή.

Ἐπειδὴ καὶ οἱ ἄνθρωποι γενοῦνται εἰς τὴν κατάστασιν τῆς ἁμαρτίας, τάχα μόνον τὸ σῶμα εἶναι ἀπὸ σπέρμα τοῦ Ἀδὰμ, ἢ μαζὶ καὶ ἡ ψυχή;

Ἀπ. Τὸ σῶμα τὸ ἀνθρώπινον ἀπὸ τὸ σπέρμα τοῦ Ἀδὰμ καταβαίνει· μὰ ἡ ψυχὴ γίνεται ἀπὸ τὸν Θεὸν, καθὼς λέγει ἡ Γραφὴ (Ζαχ. ιβ΄. ά.)· ὁ Κύριος ἐκτείνων οὐρανὸν, καὶ θεμελιῶν γῆν, καὶ πλάσσων πνεῦμα ἀνθρώπου ἐν αὐτῷ. Καὶ ἀλλαχοῦ (Ἐκκλ. ιβ΄. ζ΄.)· καὶ ἐπιστρέψῃ ὁ χοῦς ἐπὶ τὴν γῆν, ὡς ἦν· καὶ τὸ πνεῦμα ἐπιστρέψῃ πρὸς τὸν Θεὸν, ὅσ ἔδωκεν αὐτό. Πρὸς τούτοις ἂν ἡ ψυχὴ ἤθελεν εἶναι ἀπὸ τὸ σπέρμα τοῦ ἀνθρώπου, μαζὶ μὲ τὸ κορμὶ ἤθελεν συναποθνήσκειν, καὶ ἤθελε διαλυθῇ εἰς χοῦν. Τοῦ ὁποίου τὸ ἐναντίον βλέπομεν εἰς τὴν Γραφὴν, ἐκεῖ ὅπου ὁ Χριστὸς (Λουκ. κγ΄. μγ΄.), ὁμιλῶντας τοῦ λῃστοῦ εἰς τὸν σταυρὸν, εἶπεν· ἀμὴν λέγω σοι, σήμερον μετ᾽ ἐμοῦ ἔσῃ ἐν τῷ παραδεί-

Quæstio XXVIII.

Siquidem vero in statu peccati nascuntur homines, an igitur corpus solum de semine Adami est an vero etiam anima?

Resp. Corpus humanum ex semine Adami descendit, anima vero a Deo oritur, teste Scriptura (Zach. xii. 1): 'Dominus, qui expandit cœlum, et fundat terram, et. format Spiritum hominis in eo.' Et alibi (Eccles. xii. 7): 'Et redeat pulvis in terram, quemadmodum fuerat, et Spiritus ad Deum revertatur, qui dedit illum.' Super hæc si semine humano procrearetur anima, haud dubie item cum corpore commoreretur solvereturque in pulverem. Atqui contrarium in sacris literis, quo loco cum latrone in cruce colloquitur Christus, adstrui videmus (Luc. xxiii. 43): 'Amen dico tibi, hodie mecum eris in Paradiso.' Quippe corpus latronis in cruce re-

σῳ. Διατὶ τὸ κορμίν του ἔμεινεν εἰς τὸν σταυρὸν, ἡ δὲ ψυχή του ὡς πνεῦμα ἀθάνατον ἐπῆγε ματὶ μὲ τὸν Χριστὸν εἰς τὸν παράδεισον. Μὰ ἂν ἤθελεν εἶναι ἀπὸ τὸ σπέρμα τοῦ ἀνθρώπου, μαζὶ μὲ τὸ κορμὶ ἤθελεν ἀποθάνῃ εἰς τὸν σταυρόν. Ἔπειτα δὲ πῶς ἐθέλασιν ἠμπορέσει νὰ ἀληθεύσουσι τὰ λόγια τοῦ Κυρίου ἡμῶν, ὅπου εἶπεν· οὐκ ἀνέγνωτε τὸ ῥηθὲν ὑμῖν ὑπὸ τοῦ Θεοῦ (Ματθ. κβ'. λα'.) λέγοντος· ἐγώ εἰμι ὁ Θεὸς 'Αβραὰμ, καὶ ὁ Θεὸς 'Ισαὰκ, καὶ ὁ Θεὸς 'Ιακώβ· οὐκ ἔστιν ὁ Θεὸς Θεὸς νεκρῶν ἀλλὰ ζώντων. Τὸ ὁποῖον πρέπει νὰ γροικᾶται ὄχι διὰ τὸ σῶμα, ἀλλὰ διὰ τὴν ψυχήν· διατὶ τὰ σώματα τῶν νεκρῶν εἰς χοῦν ἀνελύθησαν· μὰ ἀληθεύει ὁ λόγος διὰ τὴν ψυχὴν, ἡ ὁποία, ἔστωντας καὶ νὰ εἶναι ζῶσα εἰς κάθα καιρὸν, στέκεται ἔμπροσθεν εἰς τὸν Θεόν. Μὰ ἂν ἤθελεν εἶναι καὶ αὐτὴ ἀπὸ τὸ ἴδιον σπέρμα, ὅπου εἶναι καὶ τὸ κορμὶ, μαζὶ ἐθέλασι συναποθνήσκειν. Καὶ δίδοται ἀπὸ τὸν Θεὸν ἡ ψυχὴ, ἀφ' οὗ ὀργανισθῇ τὸ κορμὶ καὶ γένῃ ἐπιτήδειον εἰς τὴν ὑποδοχήν της· καὶ ὅταν δίδοται εἰς αὐτὸ, χύνεται εἰς ὅλον τὸ κορμὶ, ὡς ἂν τὸ πῦρ εἰς τὸ ἀναμμένον σίδερον. Μὰ μὲ πλέον ἐξαίρετον λόγον εὑρίσκεται εἰς τὴν κεφαλὴν καὶ εἰς τὴν καρδίαν.

Ἐρώτησις κθ'.

Ἐπειδὴ ὁ Θεὸς εἶναι ποιητὴς πάν-

---

manebat, at anima, ut Spiritus immortalis, cum Christo Paradisum ingressa est. Quæ si humano satu genita fuisset, utique etiam suo cum corpore in cruce esset exstincta. Porro, quo alio pacto hisce Domini nostri verbis ratio constare possit, quum dixit (Matt. xxii. 31): 'Annon legistis, quod vobis a Deo dictum fuit: ego sum Deus Abraami, et Deus Isaaci, et Deus Iacobi; at Deus non mortuorum Deus est, verum viventium.' Quæ non de corpore verum de anima exaudienda sunt. Quippe dudum jam defunctorum patrum istorum in pulveres dissipata corpora erant; at de anima vera est oratio, quæ ut omni tempore vivit, ita semper in conspectu Dei adstat. Sin autem eodem illo seminio, unde corporis constructa erat fabrica, conflata anima fuisset; eadem haud dubie involuta ruina cum corpore suo interierat. Inseritur autem a Deo anima corpori, membris suis organisque jam performato, animæque recipiendæ accommodato inserta, continuo per totam ejusdem compagem diffunditur, more ignis, qui se in omnes ferri candentis sinus insinuat. Præcipuum tamen domicilium in capite, atque corde habet.

QUÆSTIO XXIX.

Quoniam vero rerum omnium

ρων, λοιπὸν πρέπει καὶ ὁλωνῶν νὰ προνοᾶται;

'Απ. Οὗτως εἶναι ἡ ἀλήθεια· ἀπὸ μικροῦ ἕως μεγάλου ὅλα τὰ γνωρίζει μὲ ἀκρίβειαν καὶ ὁλωνῶν προνοᾶται, καθ᾽ ἑνὸς ὅσα ἔκαμε· καθὼς ἠμποροῦμεν νὰ τὸ γνωρίσωμεν ἀπὸ τὰ λόγια τοῦ Χριστοῦ, ὅπου (Ματθ. ί. κθ'.) λέγει· οὐχὶ δύο στρουθία ἀσσαρίου πωλεῖται; καὶ ἕν ἐξ αὐτῶν οὐ πεσεῖται ἐπὶ τὴν γῆν ἄνευ τοῦ Πατρὸς ὑμῶν. Ὑμῶν δὲ αἱ τρίχες τῆς κεφαλῆς πᾶσαι ἠριθμημέναι εἰσιν. Ἡ πρόνοια τούτη φανερώνεται καὶ εἰς τὴν παλαιὰν Γραφὴν μὲ τὸ στόμα τὸ Δαβιδικὸν, ὅταν λέγει (Ψαλ. ρμέ. ιέ.)· οἱ ὀφθαλμοὶ πάντων εἰς σὲ ἐλπίζουσι (Κύριε) καὶ σὺ δίδως τὴν τροφὴν αὐτῶν ἐν εὐκαιρίᾳ· ἀνοίγεις σὺ τὴν χεῖρά σου, καὶ ἐμπιπλᾷς πᾶν ζῶον εὐδοκίας.

Ἐρώτησις λ'.

Ταὐτὸ εἶναι τάχα εἰς τὰ Θεῖα, πρόγνωσις, προορισμὸς καὶ πρόνοια;

'Απ. Πρόγνωσις, προορισμὸς καὶ πρόνοια εἶναι διαφορετικαῖς ἐνεργείαις εἰς τὰ Θεῖα· διατὶ ἡ πρόνοια ἀναφέρεται εἰς τὰ κτιστὰ πράγματα, μὰ ἡ πρόγνωσις καὶ ὁ προορισμὸς εἶναι εἰς τὸν Θεὸν, πρὶν παρὰ νὰ γενοῦσιν ὅλα τὰ κτίσματα, καλᾷ καὶ μὲ διαφορετικὸν τρόπον. Ἡ πρόγνωσις εἶναι μία γνῶσις τῶν μελλόντων, χωρὶς περιορισμὸν τῶν εἰδῶν, ἤγουν χωρὶς νὰ διορίζῃ τὶ καὶ τὶ νὰ γένῃ. Ὁ δὲ

---

creator Deus est, decetne igitur illum omnibus itidem providere?

RESP. Ita prorsus: quippe a minimis ad usque maxima accuratissime omnia cognoscit, omniumque, quæ fecit, curam separatim singulatimque habet, ut ex verbis Christi facile intelligi licet (Matt. x. 29): 'Nonne duo passerculi asse uno veneunt? et unus tamen ex iis sine patre vestro in terram non decidet. At capitis vestri pili etiam omnes numerati sunt.' Eadem hæc Providentia in Veteri Testamento ore Davidis luculenter explicatur, quum ait (Psa. cxiv. 15): 'Oculi omnium in te sperant Domine, et tu escam illorum tempore opportuno largiris. Aperis tu manum tuam, et imples omne animal beneplacito.'

QUÆSTIO XXX.

Idemne in divinis valent vocabula Præscientiæ, Prædestinationis atque Providentiæ?

RESP. Præscientia, Prædestinatio et Providentia diversas in divinis habent potestates. Nam Providentia res jam creatas respicit; at Præscientia Prædestinatioque in Deo sunt, priusquam ullæ res creatæ exsistant, quanquam modo quodam distincto. Præscientia enim nuda rerum futurarum cognitio est, sine determinata earundem specificatione, sic nimirum, ut non necessa-

κατὰ πρόγνωσιν προορισμὸς εἶναι διορισμὸς τῶν εἰδῶν· ἤγουν διορίζει καὶ τί μέλλει νὰ γένῃ, μὰ μόνον τὸ καλὸν, καὶ ὄχι τὸ κακόν. Διατὶ ἂν ἐδιώριζε καὶ τὸ κακὸν, ἤθελεν εἶναι ἐναντίος εἰς τὴν φυσικὴν ἀγαθότητα τοῦ Θεοῦ.

Διὰ τοῦτο εὐλόγως ἠμπορούμεν νὰ εἰπούμεν ἀπὸ τὰ καθ' ἡμᾶς, πῶς εἰς τὸν Θεὸν πρῶτον εἶναι εἰς τὴν τάξιν ἡ πρόγνωσις, δεύτερον ὁ προορισμὸς, ἔπειτα μετὰ τὴν κτίσιν ἀκολουθεῖ ἡ πρόνοια τῶν κτισμάτων.

Τὸ ὁποῖον ὁ Ἀπόστολος (Ῥωμ. ή. κθ'.) φανερὰ μᾶς τὸ ἐδίδαξε λέγωντας· ὅτι οὓς προέγνω, τούτους καὶ προώρισεν, οὓς δὲ προώρισε, τούτους καὶ ἐκάλεσε· καὶ οὓς ἐκάλεσε, τούτους καὶ ἐδικαίωσεν· οὓς δὲ ἐδικαίωσε, τούτους καὶ ἐδόξασε.

Καὶ ὁ τοιοῦτος λογισμὸς πρέπει νὰ εἶναι διὰ μόνον τὸν ἄνθρωπον, διατὶ τὰ ἄλλα κτίσματα (ἔξω ἀπὸ τοὺς ἀγγέλους, ὅπου εἶναι εἰς βεβαίαν καὶ ἀκίνδυνον κατάστασιν) δὲν περικρατοῦνται εἰς τὸν προορισμόν· ἐπειδὴ δὲν ἔχουσιν αὐτεξούσιον, καὶ διὰ τοῦτο δὲν εἶναι εἰς αὐτὰ κἂν ἕνα ἁμάρτημα, καὶ ὅ, τι κάμνουσιν, ὅλον ἐκεῖνο τὸ κάμνουσιν ἀπὸ τὴν φύσιν. Καὶ διὰ τοῦτο μήτε τιμωροῦνται μήτε δοξάζονται.

rio definiat, hoccine an illud plane futurum sit. Atqui Prædestinatio Præscientiæ juncta specierum ipsarum determinatio est, quid omnino fieri debeat definiens. Definit autem bonum duntaxat non malum. Nam si malum quoque definiret Prædestinatio, jam essentiali Dei bonitati contraria esset.

Itaque secundum nostrum concipiendi statuendique modum recte atque probabiliter etiam de Deo dici potest: ordine primam Præscientiam esse, secundam Prædestinationem, denique creatis jam rebus earum sequi Providentiam.

Quod perspicue nos docet Apostolus (Rom. viii. 29): ' Quoniam quos præscivit, eos et prædestinavit· quos autem prædestinavit, eosdem etiam vocavit: quos autem prædestinavit, eosdem etiam vocavit, eos item justificavit: quos vero justificavit: eosdem et glorificavit.'

Sed hoc de solo homine cogitandum est. Nam reliquas res creatas (præter Angelos, qui jam in vado salutis extra omnem aleam positi sunt), divina Prædestinatio non complectitur, quippe libertate Arbitrii destitutas, ideoque nec ullis vitiorum maculis adspersas. Quidquid enim faciunt, naturali instinctu faciunt, unde neque supplicio aliquo plectuntur, neque laudis gloriæque præmiis ornantur.

'Ερώτησις λα'.

'Από τουτο τὸ ἄρθρον τῆς πίστεως τί ἄλλο μανθάνομεν περὶ Θεοῦ καὶ τῶν κτισμάτων ;

'Απ. "Ο, τι ἀγαθὸν ἠμπορεῖς νὰ λογιάσῃς, ὅλον τοῦτο ἀπόδος εἰς τὸν Θεὸν, τὸν ἄκρως ἀγαθὸν, ὡς ἂν εἰς αἰτίαν καὶ ἀρχήν. ' Καὶ ὅ, τι κακὸν εἶναι, τοῦτο ἤξευρε πῶς εἶναι ξένον καὶ μακρὰν ἀπ' ἐκεῖνον, ὅχι κατὰ τὸν τόπον, μὰ κατὰ τὴν φύσιν· περὶ δὲ κτίσεως, καθ' ὅσον ἀπ' ἐκεῖνον ἐπλάσθη τὸν ἀγαθὸν, εἶναι καὶ αὐτὴ ἀγαθή· μὰ μὲ τούτην τὴν διαίρεσιν ὅταν ἡ λογικὴ καὶ αὐτεξούσιος κτίσις ἀποστατήσῃ ἀπὸ τὸν Θεὸν, εἶναι κακή· ὅχι διατὶ τέτοιας λογῆς ἐκτίσθηκε· μὰ διὰ τὰ παράλογά της ἔργα. Μὰ ἡ ἄλογος κτίσις, ὅπου δὲν ἔχει αὐτεξούσιον, εἶναι καλὴ μὲ κάθε τρόπον εἰς τὴν φύσιν της.

'Ερώτησις λβ'.

Ποῖον εἶναι τὸ δεύτερον ἄρθρον τῆς πίστεως ;

'Απ. Καὶ εἰς ἕνα Κύριον 'Ιησοῦν Χριστὸν, τὸν Υἱὸν τοῦ Θεοῦ τὸν μονογενῆ, τὸν ἐκ τοῦ Πατρὸς γεννηθέντα πρὸ πάντων τῶν αἰώνων, φῶς ἐκ φωτὸς, Θεὸν ἀληθινὸν ἐκ Θεοῦ ἀληθινοῦ, γεννηθέντα, οὐ ποιηθέντα, ὁμοούσιον τῷ Πατρὶ, δι' οὗ τὰ πάντα ἐγένετο.

QUÆSTIO XXXI.

Numquid aliud est, quod ære Deo rebusque ab eo creatis ex hoc Articulo disci possit ?

RESP. Quidquid boni animo atque cogitatione complecti potes, id omne Deo summe bono, ut caussæ ac principio, adscribe. Contra quidquid malum est, id peregrinum longeque a Deo remotum esse non tam locali quam essentiali distantia, scito. De re creata vero sic habe: Bonam esse, quatenus ab optimo illo creatore producta est; sed cum hoc discrimine, ut mala fiat intellectu et libertate arbitrii prædita res creata, quando a Deo desciscit. Non quod ejusmodi condita fuerit; sed quod per opera rationi dissentanea talis evadat. At irrationabilis, quoniam arbitrii libertate caret, modis omnibus naturæ suæ bona est.

QUÆSTIO XXXII.

Quinam secundus fidei Articulus est ?

RESP. Et in unum Dominum, Iesum Christum, filium Dei unigenitum, ex Patre natum ante omnia secula, lucem de luce, Deum verum de Deo vero, genitum, non factum, consubstantialem Patri, per quem omnia facta sunt.

'Ερώτησις λγ'.

Τί διδάσκει τοὺς ὀρθοδόξους τοῦτο τὸ ἄρθρον τῆς πίστεως ;

'Απ. Δύο πράγματα ἑρμηνεύει ·
πρῶτον, πῶς ὁ Υἱὸς τοῦ Θεοῦ ὁ 'Ιησοῦς Χριστὸς εἶναι Θεὸς ἀΐδιος, γεν-
νημένος ἀπὸ τὴν ἰδίαν φύσιν τοῦ
Πατρὸς, ὁμότιμος καὶ ὁμόδοξος τῷ
Πατρί · ὡς αὐτὸς ('Ιωαν. ιζ'. ἑ.) περὶ
ἑαυτοῦ εἶπε · καὶ νῦν δόξασόν με σύ,
Πάτερ, παρὰ σεαυτῷ τῇ δόξῃ, ᾗ εἶχον
πρὸ τοῦ τὸν κόσμον εἶναι παρὰ σοί.
Δεύτερον εἰς τὸ ἄρθρον τοῦτο ἡ διδασκαλία αὕτη εὑρίσκεται, ἤγουν πῶς
ὁ 'Ιησοῦς Χριστὸς εἶναι ποιητὴς, ὄχι
μόνον τῶν πραγμάτων, ἀλλὰ καὶ αὐτοῦ τοῦ χρόνου καὶ τοῦ αἰῶνος, εἰς
τὸν ὁποῖον τὰ ὄντα ἐγενήκασι · καθὼς εἶπεν ὁ 'Απόστολος ('Εβρ. ά.
β'.) · δι' οὗ καὶ τοὺς αἰῶνας ἐποίησε.
Περὶ δὲ τῶν ὄντων λέγει ὁ 'Ιωάννης
(κεφ. ά. ί.) ὁ εὐαγγελιστής · ὁ κόσμος
δι' αὐτοῦ ἐγένετο, καὶ ὁ κόσμος αὐτὸν
οὐκ ἔγνω.

'Ερώτησις λδ'.

Τὰ δύο λόγια τοῦτα ὅπου εἶναι
βαλλομένα εἰς τὸ ἄρθρον τοῦτο, 'Ιησοῦν, Χριστὸν, τί σημαίνουσιν ;

'Απ. Τὸ 'Ιησοῦς σημαίνει Σωτὴρ,
καθὼς ὁ ἀρχάγγελος ἡρμήνευσε, λέγων (Ματθ. ά. κά.) πρὸς τὸν 'Ιωσήφ ·
τέξεται δὲ Υἱὸν, καὶ καλέσεις τὸ ὄνομα αὐτου 'Ιησοῦν · αὐτὸς γὰρ σώσει
τὸν λαον αὐτοῦ ἀπὸ τῶν ἁμαρτιῶν

QUÆSTIO **XXXIII.**

Quid hic fidei Articulus fideles
docet ?

RESP. Duo potissimum exponit.
Prius, Filium Dei, Iesum Christum,
esse Deum sempiternum, de propria Patris natura natum, honore
ac gloria Patri æqualem, quemadmodum de se ipse dicit (Ioh.
xvii. 5): 'Glorifica nunc me apud
te ipsum Pater illa gloria, quam
apud te habui, priusquam mundus
exsisteret.' Alterum, quod hoc
Articulo docetur, hoc est: Iesum
Christum esse Creatorem non modo rerum ipsarum sed et temporis
et ævi, in quo res ipsæ factæ sunt,
dicente Apostolo (Heb. i. 2): 'Per
quem et secula fecit.' Sed de rebus (permanentibus) ita loquitur
Ioannes Evangelista (i. 10): 'Mundus per ipsum factus est, sed mundus illum non cognovit.'

QUÆSTIO **XXXIV.**

Ecquid sibi volunt duo hæcce
nomina, *Iesus, Christus,* quæ in
hoc Articulo reperiuntur?

RESP. Iesus Salvatorem significat, interprete Archangelo, qui Io-
sepho dixit (Matt. i. 21): 'Pariet
autem filium, et vocabis nomen
ejus Iesum, quoniam salvum ille
populum suum faciet a peccatis

αὐτῶν. Καὶ διὰ τοῦτο μὲ εὔλογον λογαριασμὸν τὸ ὄνομα τοῦτο δὲν ἠμπορεῖ ποτὲ νὰ ἀποδοθῇ κυρίως εἰς τὸν κόσμον τοῦτον ἄλλου τινὸς, παρὰ εἰς τὸν Κύριον ἡμῶν καὶ Σωτῆρα, ὅπου ἐλευθέρωσεν ὅλον τὸ γένος τῶν ἀνθρώπων ἀπὸ τὴν αἰώνιον σκλαβίαν τῶν δαιμόνων. Ὁ δὲ Χριστὸς σημαίνει ἀλειμμένος· διατὶ εἰς τὸν παλαιὸν νόμον οἱ ἀλειμμένοι ὠνομάζουνται Χριστοὶ, ἤγουν οἱ ἱερεῖς, οἱ βασιλεῖς καὶ οἱ προφῆται· εἰς τὰ ὁποῖα τοῦτα τρία ὁ Χριστὸς ἐχρίσθη, ὄχι κατὰ τρόπον κοινὸν, ὡς ἂν τοὺς ἄλλους, μὰ ἐξαιρέτως ἀπὸ ὅλους τοὺς ἄλλους χριστοὺς, ὡς ἀναφέρει περὶ αὐτοῦ ὁ Ψαλμῳδός (Ψαλ. μέ. ή.)· ἠγάπησας δικαιοσύνην, καὶ ἐμίσησας ἀνομίαν, διὰ τοῦτο ἔχρισέ σε ὁ Θεὸς, ὁ Θεός σου ἔλαιον ἀγαλλιάσεως παρὰ τοὺς μετόχους σου. Καὶ τούτη ἡ χρίσις πρέπει νὰ γροικᾶται περὶ τοῦ ἁγίου πνεύματος, ὅτι ἐχρίσθη μὲ τὸ Πνεῦμα τὸ ἅγιον, κατὰ τὸ εἰρημένον διὰ τοῦ προφήτου Ἠσαΐου (κεφ. ξά. ά.)· Πνεῦμα Κυρίου ἐπ᾽ ἐμὲ, οὗ εἵνεκεν ἔχρισέ με, εὐαγγελίσασθαι πτωχοῖς ἀπέσταλκέ με. Τὰ ὁποῖα λόγια ὁ Χριστὸς τὰ ἀνεφέρει εἰς τὸν ἑαυτόν του (Λουκ. δ′. κα′.), λέγων· ὅτι σήμερον πεπλήρωται ἡ Γραφὴ αὕτη ἐν τοῖς ὠσὶν ὑμῶν. Κατὰ τρεῖς δὲ ὑπεροχὰς παὶ ἐξαίρετα μεγαλεῖα ὑπερέχει ὁ Χριστὸς τοὺς μετόχους του. Καὶ ἡ μὲν πρώτη εἶναι ἡ ἱερωσύνη κατὰ τὴν τάξιν Μελχισε-

suis.' Ideoque vere recteque alii in hoc mundo nemini tribui id nominis potest, quam Salvatori et Domino nostro, qui universum genus humanum de æterna Dæmonum servitute liberali caussa manu adseruit. *Christus* Unctum significat, quoniam in Antiqua lege uncti appellantur Christi, Sacerdotes scilicet, Reges et Prophetæ. In quæ tria officia inunctus Christus est: non more rituque communi, ut ceteri, sed præ unctis reliquis omnibus, prorsus singulari, ut de eo narrat Psalmorum auctor (Psa. xlv. 8): 'Amavisti justitiam, et odisti iniquitatem; propterea unxit te Deus, Deus tuus, oleo lætitiæ præ consortibus tuis.' Quæ unctio de Spiritu Sancto intelligenda est. Eo enim secundum hoc Prophetæ Iesaiæ dictum inunctus fuit (lxi. 1): 'Spiritus Domini super me est, ideo unxit me, misitque me ad annunciandum pauperibus Evangelium.' Quæ verba Christus ipse sibi vindicat (Luc. iv. 21): 'Hodie, inquit, impleta est hæc scriptura audientibus vobis.' Triplici vero excellentia eximiaque majestate consortibus suis singulariter antecellit Christus. Prima est Pontificatus secundum ordinem Melchizedeki, de quo ita Apostolus (Heb. v. 10): 'Appellatus a Deo Pontifex maximus secundum ordinem

δἑκ. Περὶ ἧς φησὶν οὕτως ('Εβρ. έ.
ί.` έ 'Απόστολος· προσαγορευθεὶς
ὑπὸ τοῦ Θεοῦ ἀρχιερεὺς κατὰ τὴν
τάξιν Μελχισεδέκ· ὁ αὐτὸς ἀλλαχοῦ
('Εβρ. ϑ'. ιδ'.) καλεῖ τὸν Χριστὸν
ἱεοέα, διότι προσέφερεν ἑαυτὸν τῷ
Θεῷ καὶ Πατρί, καὶ λέγει· ὃς διὰ
Πνεύματος αἰωνίου ἑαυτὸν προσή-
νεγκεν ἄμωμον τῷ Θεῷ· καὶ κατω-
τέρω· ὁ Χριστὸς ἅπαξ προσηνέχϑη
εἰς τὸ πολλῶν ἀνενεγκεῖν ἁμαρτίας.
Ἡ δευτέρα ἐξαίρετος μεγαλειότης καὶ
ὑπεροχὴ εἶναι ἡ βασιλεία του· τὴν
ὁποῖαν ἐφανέρωσεν ὁ 'Αρχάγγελος
Γαβριὴλ, ὅταν ἔδωκε τὰ σωτηριώδη
μηνύματα πρὸς τὴν καϑαρωτάτην
Παρϑένον, λέγων (Λουκ. ά. λβ'.)·
καὶ δώσει αὐτῷ Κύριος ὁ Θεὸς τὸν
ϑρόνον Δαβὶδ τοῦ Πατρὸς αὐτοῦ,
καὶ βασιλεύσει ἐπὶ τὸν οἶκον 'Ιακὼβ
εἰς τοὺς αἰῶνας, καὶ τῆς βασιλείας
αὐτοῦ οὐκ ἔσται τέλος. 'Ακόμι καὶ
οἱ μάγοι εἰς τὸν καιρὸν τῆς γεννή-
σεώς του φέρνοντες τὰ δῶρα ἔδωκαν
μαρτυρίαν τῆς βασιλείας του, λέγοντες (Ματϑ. β'. β'.)· ποῦ ἐστιν ὁ τεχ-
ϑεὶς βασιλεὺς τῶν 'Ιουδαίων; Τὸ
αὐτὸ βεβαιώνει καὶ ὁ τίτλος ('Ιωαν.
ιϑ'. ϑ'.) τῆς τιμωρίας του, εἰς τὸν καιρὸν τοῦ ϑανάτου του· 'Ιησοῦς ὁ Να-
ζαραῖος, ὁ βασιλεὺς τῶν 'Ιουδαίων.
Καὶ διὰ τὴν τρίτην του ὑπεροχὴν ὁ
Μωϋσῆς (Δευτ. ιή. ιή.) ἐπροφήτευσεν
ἐκ Θεοῦ, εἰπών· προφήτην ἔκ τῶν
ἀδελφῶν σου ὡς ἐμὲ ἀναστήσει Κύριος ὁ Θεός σου. Ἡ ὁποία τούτη

Melchizedeki.' Idem alibi (Heb.
ix. 14). Christum sacerdotem vocat, quod semet ipsum Deo et Patri obtulit, dicens : 'Qui per Spiritum æternum obtulit semet ipsum
immaculatum Deo. Et inferius
(v. 28): 'Christus semel oblatus
est, ut multorum peccata tolleret.'
Secunda singularis majestas et excellentia officium Regium illius
est, quod indicavit Gabriel Archangelus, quum salutarem conceptionis nuncium pudicissimæ virgini
attulit (Luc. i. 32): 'Dabit illi
Dominus Deus thronum Davidis,
patris sui, et regnabit super domum Iacobi in æternum, et regni
illius nullus erit finis.' Huc accedit, quod et Magi mox a nativi-
tate dona illi afferentes regii ejus
imperii testificationem dederint
(Matt. ii. 2): 'Ubi est, inquiunt,
recens natus Rex Iudæorum ?'
Idem affirmat et supplicii titulus,
mortis illius tempore propositus
(Ioh. xix. 9): 'Iesus Nazarenus
Rex Iudæorum.' De tertia ipsius
præcellentia jam olim instinctus a
Deo Moses vaticinatus est (Deut.
xviii. 18): 'Dominus Deus tuus ex
fratribus tuis Prophetam, qualis
ego sum, suscitabit.' Quæ illius
majestas satis perspecta atque com-
probata fuit ex sanctissima illius
doctrina, qua et divinitatem suam
luculenter enarravit, et quæ præ-

μεγαλειότης του ἐγνωρίσϑηκε μὲ τὴν ἁγίαν του διδασκαλίαν, μὲ τὴν ὁποῖαν ἡρμήνευσε καὶ τὴν Θεότητά του, καὶ ὅσα ἄλλα ἦσαν ἀρκετὰ πρὸς τὴν ἀν-ϑρωπίνην σωτηρίαν· καϑὼς ὁ ἴδιως εἶπεν (Ἰωαν. ιζ'. κϛ'.)· ἐγνώρισα αὐτοῖς τὸ ὄνομά σου· καὶ ἀνωτέρω (ϛιχ. ή.)· τὰ ῥήματα ἃ δέδωκάς μοι-δέδωκα αὐτοῖς, καὶ αὐτοὶ ἔλαβον καὶ ἔγνωσαν ἀληϑῶς, ὅτι παρὰ σοῦ ἐξῆλ-ϑον, καὶ ἐπίστευσαν, ὅτι σύ με ἀπέσ-τειλας. Τὸ δὲ προφητικὸν ἀξίωμα (ὅπου ἦτον ἡ τρίτη ὑπεροχὴ) τότε ὁ Χριστὸς τὸ ἔδειξεν, ὅταν ἐπρόλεγε τὰ μέλλοντα, ὄχι διά τινος ἀποκαλύψ-εως, μὰ ἀπὸ τὴν ἰδίαν του γνῶσιν, ὡς Θεὸς ἀληϑινὸς καὶ ἄνϑρωπος.

Ἐρώτησις λέ.

Διὰ τίνα αἰτίαν ὁ Υἱὸς τοῦ Θεοῦ ὀνομάζεται μονογενής;

Ἀπ. Ἡ ἁγία Γραφὴ φανερῶς δι-δάσκει, πῶς εἶναι μονογενὴς ὁ Υἱὸς τοῦ Θεοῦ (Ἰωαν. ά. ιδ'.) λέγουσα· ἐϑεασάμεϑα τὴν δόξαν αὐτοῦ, δόξαν ὡς μονογενοῦς παρὰ Πατρός· καὶ κατωτέρω (ϛιχ. ιή.)· Υἱὸς, ὁ ὢν ὁ μο-νογενὴς, εἰς τὸν κόλπον τοῦ Πατρός. Καὶ λέγεται μονογενὴς, διατὶ ἕνας μόνος εἶναι ὁ κατ' οὐσίαν Υἱὸς τοῦ Θεοῦ· οἱ δὲ λοιποὶ, ὅσοι ὀνομάζουνται Υἱοὶ Θεοῦ, ἔχουσιν τὸ ὄνομα τοῦτο κατὰ χάριν καὶ ϑετικῶς, μὰ ὄχι φυσι-κῶς, ὡς πάντες οἱ πιστοὶ καὶ ἐκλεκτοὶ τοῦ Θεοῦ. Καὶ ἡ χάρις τούτη τῆς υἱοϑεσίας διὰ μέσου τοῦ Χριστοῦ χα-

terea ad salutem humanam suffi-cere poterant. Sicut ipse ait (Ioh. xvii. 26): 'Notum illis feci nomen tuum.' Et superius (v. 8): 'Ver-ba, quæ dederas mihi, dedi illis, et ipsi receperunt et revera cog-noverunt, quod a te exivi, et cre-diderunt, quod tu me misisti.' Ce-terum Prophetico hocce munere (quæ tertia præstantia erat) egre-gie tum Christus functus est, quum futura prædixit, non pate-factione aliqua sibi cognita, sed ex propria suaque cognitione, ut qui verus idem Deus ac homo esset.

Quæstio XXXV.

Quamobrem filius Dei vocatur *Unigenitus?*

Resp. Filium Dei unigenam es-se, id manifesto comprobat Scrip-tura (Ioh. i. 14): 'Vidimus gloriam ipsius, ut gloriam unigeniti a Pa-tre.' Et paulo post (v. 18): 'Fi-lius unigenitus, qui est in sinu Patris.' Unigena autem ea re di-citur, quod unus duntaxat natura Dei filius est; reliqui vero, quot-quot Dei filii nuncupantur, per gratiam atque adoptionem, non per naturam id nominis habent; uti fideles omnes et electi Dei. Quæ filialis adoptionis gratia per Christum conceditur, teste Scrip

ρίζεται, ὡς λέγει ('Ιωαν. ά. ιβ'.) ἡ Γραφή· ὅσοι ἔλαβον αὐτὸν, ἔδωκεν αὐτοῖς ἐξουσίαν τέκνα Θεοῦ γενέσθαι.

tura (Ioh. i. 12): 'Quotquot receperunt illum, illis potestatem fecit, ut filii Dei fierent.'

'Ερώτησις λς'.

Τί σημαίνουσι τὰ δύο ταῦτα λόγια, φῶς ἐκ φωτός;

'Α π. Πρὸς τὴν τούτου κατάληψιν πρέπει νὰ ἠξεύρωμεν, πῶς τὸ φῶς εἶναι διττὸν, ἄλλο κτιστὸν καὶ ἄλλο ἄκτιστον. Καὶ διὰ τὸ κτιστὸν φῶς ἡ Γραφὴ (Γεν. ά. γ'.) λέγει· καὶ εἶπεν ὁ Θεὸς, γενηθήτω φῶς, καὶ ἐγένετο φῶς· καὶ εἶδεν ὁ Θεὸς τὸ φῶς ὅτι καλὸν, καὶ διεχώρισεν ὁ Θεὸς ἀνάμεσον τοῦ φωτὸς καὶ ἀνάμεσον τοῦ σκότους. Περὶ δὲ τοῦ ἀκτίστου φωτὸς λέγει ὁ Προφήτης ('Ησ. ξ'. ιθ'.)· καὶ οὐκ ἔσται σοι ἔτι ὁ ἥλιος εἰς φῶς ἡμέρας· οὐδὲ ἀνατολὴ σελήνης φωτιεῖ σου τὴν νύκτα· ἀλλ' ἔσται σοι Κύριος φῶς αἰώνιον, καὶ ὁ Θεὸς δόξα σου. Οὐ γὰρ δύσεται ὁ ἥλιός σοι, καὶ ἡ σελήνη σοι οὐκ ἐκλείψει· ἔσται γάρ σοι Κύριος φῶς αἰώνιον. Καὶ τοῦτο τὸ φῶς εἰς τὸν τόπον τοῦτον γροικᾶται διὰ τὸ ἄκτιστον, καθὼς εἶναι φανερὸν ἀπὸ τὰ λόγια τοῦ παρόντος ἄρθρου, ὅπου λέγει· Θεὸν ἀληθινὸν ἐκ Θεοῦ ἀληθινοῦ, γεννηθέντα, οὐ ποιηθέντα. 'Αλλὰ τὸ κτιστὸν ἐκ τοῦ μηδαμῆ μηδαμῶς ἐκτίσθη, μὰ τὸ γεννητὸν φῶς, εἴτουν ὁ Υἱὸς, εἶναι ἀπὸ τὴν οὐσίαν τοῦ Πατρός· διὰ τὸ ὁποῖον λέγει ὁ 'Απόστολος ('Εβρ. ά. γ'.) οὕτως· ὃς ὢν ἀπαύγασμα τῆς

QUÆSTIO XXXVI.

Quid autem duo hæc verba, *Lucem de luce*, significant?

RESP. Ad hujus rei planiorem intellectum sciendum, geminam esse lucem; alteram creatam, alteram increatam. De creata ita loquitur Scriptura (Gen. i. 3): 'Dixit Deus: fiat lux, et facta est lux.' Et vidit Deus, lucem esse bonam, et distinxit inter lucem et tenebras. At de luce illa increata ita Propheta (Ies. lx. 19): 'Nec amplius sol tibi in lucem diurnam erit, neque exortus lunæ noctem tuam illuminabit; sed Dominus ipse erit tibi lux æterna, et Deus gloria tua. Non enim occidet sol tuus, nec deficiet luna tua: nam Dominus tibi lux æterna erit.' Atque hæc ipsa lux utpote increata hoc loco intelligitur, ut ex verbis in hoc Articulo mox sequentibus dilucide patet: Deum verum de Deo vero; genitum, non factum. Etenim lux creata, de puro puto nihilo producta fuit: at genita lux sive filius de essentia Patris emersit. Unde dicit Apostolus (Heb. i. 3): 'Qui quum sit splendor gloriæ, et expressa imago substantiæ illius, et ferat omnia verbo poten-

δόξης, καὶ χαρακτὴρ τῆς ὑποστάσεως αὐτοῦ, φέρων τε τὰ πάντα τῷ ῥήματι τῆς δυνάμεως αὐτοῦ, δι᾽ ἑαυτοῦ καθαρισμὸν ποιησάμενος τῶν ἁμαρτιῶν ἡμῶν, ἐκάθισεν ἐν δεξιᾷ τῆς μεγαλοσύνης ἐν ὑψηλοῖς. Ὁμοίως καὶ αὐτὸς περὶ ἑαυτοῦ (Ἰωαν. ἡ ιβ΄.) λέγει· ἐγὼ εἰμὶ τὸ φῶς τοῦ κόσμου, ὁ ἀκολουθῶν ἐμοὶ οὐ μὴ περιπατήσει ἐν τῇ σκοτίᾳ, ἀλλ᾽ ἕξει τὸ φῶς τῆς ζωῆς. Λέγεται δὲ φ ῶ ς ἐ κ φ ω τ ὸ ς, ὅτι πᾶσαν τὴν οὐσίαν τοῦ Πατρὸς ἔχει εἰς ἑαυτὸν, καθὼς ὅταν ἕνα φῶς ἀπὸ ἄλλο ἀνάπτεται, ὅλην τὴν ἐκείνου φύσιν ἔχει. Ἀκόμι τὰ λόγια τοῦτα, ὁποῦ εὑρίσκουνται εἰς τὸ παρὸν ἄρθρον, δι᾽ οὗ τὰ πάντα ἐγένετο, πρέπει νὰ γροικοῦνται, πῶς καθὼς ὁμοίως εἶναι ὁμοούσιος μὲ τὸν Θεὸν καὶ Πατέρα, οὕτως ὁμοίως εἶναι καὶ ποιητής· καὶ ὄχι, δι᾽ αὐτοῦ, ὡς διά τινος ὑπηρέτου, ἢ ὀργάνου· ὡς φησὶν (Ἰωαν. ά. έ.) ἡ Γραφή· ἐν τῷ κόσμῳ ἦν, καὶ ὁ κόσμος δι᾽ αὐτοῦ ἐγένετο, τοῦτ᾽ ἐστιν, ἐξ αὐτοῦ.

Ἐρώτησις λζ΄.

Πῶς εἶναι τὸ τρίτον ἄρθρον τῆς Πίστεως;

Ἀπ. Τὸν δι᾽ ἡμᾶς τοὺς ἀνθρώπους καὶ διὰ τὴν ἡμετέραν σωτηρίαν κατελθόντα ἐκ τῶν οὐρανῶν, καὶ σαρκωθέντα ἐκ Πνεύματος ἁγίου καὶ Μαρίας τῆς Παρθένου, καὶ ἐνανθρωπήσαντα.

tiæ suæ, per semet ipsum purgatione peccatorum nostrorum facta, consedit in dextra majestatis in excelsis.᾽ Eodem modo ipse de se ipso loquitur (Ioh. viii. 12): ‘Ego lux mundi sum, qui me sequitur, in tenebris non ambulabit, sed habebit lumen vitæ.᾽ Dicitur vero lux de luce, quod totam Patris essentiam in se ipso habet. Quemadmodum quum lux una de alia accenditur, totam illius naturam accipit. Iam verba, quæ in hoc eodem Articulo adduntur: *per quem omnia facta sunt*, hoc sensu sunt accipienda, quod, quemadmodum ejusdem naturæ æqualiter Deo Patri consors est, item ex æquo creator sit; non vero sic per ipsum, quasi per famulum aut instrumentum, docente Scriptura (Ioh. i. 10): ‘In mundo fuit, et per ipsum mundus factus est, hoc est, ab ipso.᾽

QUÆSTIO XXXVII.

Tertius fidei Articulus quomodo se habet?

RESP. *Qui propter nos homines et propter salutem nostram descendit de cœlo, et incarnatus est ex Spiritu Sancto et Maria Virgine, et homo factus est.*

Ἐρώτησις λή.

Τί διδάσκει τὸ ἄρθρον τοῦτο τῆς Πίστεως;

Ἀπ. Τέσσερα πράγματα διδάσκει. Πρῶτον πῶς ὁ Υἱὸς τοῦ Θεοῦ διὰ τὴν σωτηρίαν μας ἐκατέβηκεν ἀπὸ τοὺς οὐρανοὺς κατὰ τὴν ὑπόσχεσίν του εἰς τὴν γαστέρα τῆς καθαρωτάτης Παρθένου Μαρίας, καθὼς ὁ αὐτὸς λέγει (Ἰωαν. γ΄. ιγ΄.) περὶ ἑαυτοῦ· οὐδεὶς ἀναβέβηκεν εἰς τὸν οὐρανὸν, εἰ μὴ ὁ ἐκ τοῦ οὐρανοῦ καταβὰς, ὁ Υἱὸς τοῦ ἀνθρώπου. Καὶ κατέβη ἀπὸ τὸν οὐρανὸν, ὄχι διὰ νὰ ἀλλάξῃ τόπον· διατὶ ἔστωντας καὶ νὰ εἶναι Θεὸς πανταχοῦ εὑρίσκεται, καὶ ὅλα τὰ πράγματα πληροῖ· μὰ διατὶ οὕτως ἤρεσσεν εἰς τὴν μεγαλειότητά του, νὰ ταπεινώσῃ τὸν ἑαυτόν του, πέρνωντας τὴν ἀνθρωπότητα. Δεύτερον διδάσκει τὸ ἄρθρον τοῦτο, πῶς ὁ Κύριος ἡμῶν Ἰησοῦς Χριστὸς ἐπῆρεν ἀληθινὴν ἀνθρωπότητα, καὶ ὄχι φαινομένην ἢ φαντασιώδη. Καὶ τότε τὸ σῶμά του ἐπλάσθηκεν εἰς τὴν κοιλίαν τῆς μακαριωτάτης παρθένου, ὅταν ἐκείνη πρὸς τὸν Ἄγγελον ἀπεκρίθη καὶ (Λουκ. ά. λή.) εἶπεν· ἰδοὺ ἡ δούλη Κυρίου, γένοιτό μοι κατὰ τὸ ῥῆμά σου· τότε παρευθὺς ἄνθρωπος τέλειος ἐγίνηκε μὲ ὅλα του τὰ μέρη καὶ μὲ ψυχὴν λογικήν· ἐσμιμένα μὲ τὴν θεότητα (Δαμ. γ΄. ά.). Καὶ κατὰ τὴν μίαν καὶ τὴν αὐτὴν ὑπόστασιν ἦτον Θεὸς ἀληθινὸς καὶ ἄνθρωπος

QUÆSTIO XXXVIII.

Quidnam hic Articulus docet?

RESP. Res quatuor. Primo, filium Dei nostræ salutis caussa de cœlo, ut olim pollicitus fuerat, in uterum purissimæ virginis Mariæ descendisse; quemadmodum de semet ipso loquitur (Ioh. iii. 13): 'Nemo adscendit in cœlum, nisi qui de cœlo descendit, filius hominis.' De cœlo autem descendit, non ut locum mutaret, quippe qui ut verus Deus ubique locorum adest, resque omnes implet, sed quoniam sic majestati illius placuit, humiliare semet ipsum, adsumta humanitate. Secundo docet hic Articulus, dominum nostrum Iesum Christum induisse veram non apparentem quampiam aut imaginariam humanitatem. Nempe illo temporis articulo in utero beatissimæ virginis corpus illius formabatur, quo ipsa Angelo respondens (Luc. i. 38): 'Ecce me, inquit, ancillam Domini, fiat mihi secundum verbum tuum.' Tum illico perfectus homo membris omnibus animaque rationali, junctim cum divinitate, exstitit (Damascen. iii. 1). Et in una eademque persona verus Deus verusque homo erat. Sed et illibata virgo mox Deipara agnita ac comperta fuit,

ἀληθινός· καὶ ἡ ἀμόλυντος Παρθένος θεοτόκος ἐγνωρίζετο· καθὼς ἡ
Ἐλισάβετ εἶπε (Λουκ. ά. μγ΄.) πρὸς
αὐτήν· καὶ πόθεν μοι τοῦτο, ἵνα
ἔλθῃ ἡ μήτηρ τοῦ Κυρίου μου πρός
με; Ἀκόμι εἶναι ἀναγκαῖον καὶ τοῦτο νὰ ἠξεύρωμεν, πῶς οὔτε ἡ θεότης
ἄλλαξεν εἰς τὴν ἀνθρωπότητα, μήτε
ἡ ἀνθρωπότης εἰς τὴν θεότητα· μὰ
κάθα μία φύσις ἔμεινε τελεία, εἰς μίαν
ὑπόστασιν, μὲ ὅλα τὰ ἰδιώματα της·
ἔξω ἀπὸ τὴν ἁμαρτίαν, ὅσον πρὸς
τὴν ἀνθρωπότητα.

quemadmodum ipsi Elisabeta dixit
(Luc. i. 43): 'Unde vero istuc mihi, quod mater Domini mei ad me
venit?' Ad hæc illud etiam scitu
nobis necessarium est, quod neque
divinitas in humanitatem conversa
sit, neque humanitas in divinitatem; sed manserit natura utraque
absoluta, cum proprietatibus suis
omnibus, in persona una; peccato
tamen, quod ad humanitatem attinet, excepto.

Ἐρώτησις λθ΄.

Τί διδάσκει τρίτον τοῦτο τὸ ἄρθρον
τῆς Πίστεως;

Ἀπ. Πῶς τοῦ Χριστοῦ ἡ ἐνανθρώπησις ἐγίνηκε μὲ τὴν συνεργίαν
τοῦ ἁγίου Πνεύματος· ὥστε καθὼς ἡ
Παρθένος πρὶν τῆς συλλήψεως (Ἡσ.
ζ΄. ιδ΄.) ἦτον Παρθένος, οὕτω καὶ εἰς
τὴν σύλληψιν καὶ ὕστερα ἀπὸ τὴν
σύλληψιν ἔμεινε παρθένος, καὶ εἰς
αὐτὸν τὸν τόκον· διατὶ ἀπ' αὐτὴν
ἐγεννήθηκε, φυλάξας ἀλώβητον τῆς
παρθενίας της τὴν σφραγίδα· ὥστε
καὶ ὕστερα ἀπὸ τὴν γέννησιν εἰς αἰῶνας ἀτελευτήτους εἶναι παρθένος.

QUÆSTIO XXXIX.

Quodnam tertium est eorum,
quæ hoc Articulo docentur?

RESP. Incarnationem Christi
opera Spiritus Sancti factam fuisse,
adeo ut, quemadmodum beata virgo
ante conceptionem virgo erat (Ies.
vii. 14); ita etiam in conceptu, post
conceptum, itemque in partu ipso
virgo permanserit. Sic enim de
Genetricis alvo editus est Christus,
ut intactum penitus inviolatumque
virginitatis illius signaculum con-
servarit, ipsaque post partum in
secula interminata virgo maneret.

Ἐρώτησις μ΄.

Τί ἄλλο περιέχεται εἰς τὸ ἄρθρον
τοῦτο;

Ἀπ. Διὰ τὴν πάναγνον παρθένον
τὴν θεοτόκον Μαρίαν, τὴν ὁποίαν
ἔστωντας καὶ νὰ ἀξιωθῇ νὰ πληρώσῃ

QUÆSTIO XL.

Quid præterea in hoc Articulo
continetur?

RESP. De castissima virgine atque deipara Maria, quam, quoniam
digna habita fuit, quæ tantum im-

τόσον μυστήριον, ἔχουσι χρέος ὅλοι οἱ ὀρθόδοξοι, νὰ τὴν δοξάζουσι πρεπούμενα, καὶ νὰ τὴν εὐλαβοῦνται, ὡς μητέρα τοῦ Κυρίου ἡμῶν Ἰησοῦ Χριστοῦ, ἢ μᾶλλον εἰπεῖν, ὡς θεοτόκον. Διὰ τοῦτο ἡ ἐκκλησία χαιρετισμόν της ἔκαμε, συνθεμένον ἀπὸ τὰ λόγια τοῦ Ἀρχαγγέλου καὶ τῆς ἁγίας Ἐλισάβετ, βάνωντας καὶ αὐτὴ ἀνάμεσα κάποια ὀλίγα εἰς τὸν τρόπον τοῦτον· Θεοτόκε παρθένε, χαῖρε κεχαριτωμένη Μαρία, ὁ Κύριος μετὰ σοῦ· εὐλογημένη σὺ ἐν γυναιξὶ, καὶ εὐλογημένος ὁ καρπὸς τῆς κοιλίας σου, ὅτι Σωτῆρα ἔτεκες τῶν ψυχῶν ἡμῶν.

Ἐρώτησις μά.

Πῶς πρέπει νὰ γροικοῦμεν διὰ τὸν χαιρετισμὸν τοῦτον;

Ἀπ. Πρῶτον πρέπει τοῦτο νὰ πιστεύῃς, πῶς ὁ χαιρετισμὸς οὗτος ἔχει τὴν ἀρχὴν καὶ τὴν ῥίζαν του ἀπ᾽ αὐτὸν τὸν Θεόν· καὶ ἐφέλθηκεν εἰς τὴν γῆν, ἐπὶ τοὺς ἀνθρώπους διὰ τοῦ Ἀρχαγγέλου, διατὶ ὁ Ἀρχάγγελος δὲν ἤθελεν ἀποκοτήσειν, νὰ τὸν εἰπῇ, ἂν ὁ Θεὸς δὲν τὸν ἤθελε προστάξειν. Τὰ δὲ λόγια ὁποῦ εἶπεν ἡ ἁγία Ἐλισάβετ, τὰ ἔλεγεν ἐκ Πνεύματος ἁγίου· τὸ ὁποῖον εἶναι φανερὸν, διατὶ (Λουκ. ά. μά.) λέγει ὁ Εὐαγγελιστής· καὶ ἐπλήσθη Πνεύματος ἁγίου ἡ Ἐλισάβετ, καὶ ἀνεφώνησε φωνῇ μεγάλῃ καὶ εἶπεν· εὐλογημένη σὺ ἐν γυναιξὶ, καὶ εὐλογημένος ὁ καρπὸς τῆς κοιλίας σου. Τὰ δὲ λόγια ὅπου ἐπρόσθεσεν

pleret mysterium, Orthodoxi omnes, ut fas piumque est, jure ac merito collaudare venerarique debent; velut matrem Domini nostri *Iesu Christi*, vel potius, ut Dei genetricem. Quam etiam ob caussam Ecclesia salutationem illius ex verbis Archangeli et S. Elisabetæ, quibus et paucula quædam sua adjecit, hunc in modum concinnavit: O Deipara Virgo, ave Maria, gratia plena, Dominus tecum. Benedicta tu in mulieribus, et benedictus fructus ventris tui, quoniam Salvatorem animarum nostrarum peperisti.

QUÆSTIO XLI.

Quid nobis de hac salutatione censendum?

RESP. Primum illud credas oportet, salutationem istam originem et radicem suam Deo ipsi debere; sed ad homines in terra degentes per Gabrielem Archangelum delatam esse, qui illam alioqui neutiquam proferre atque usurpare ausurus erat, nisi a Deo ipsi mandata fuisset: rursus, quæ Elisabeta protulit verba, ea Spiritus Sancti afflatu protulisse, satis ex narratione Evangelistæ liquet (Luc. i. 41): 'Et repleta est Spiritu Sancto Elisabeta, altaque inclamans voce dixit: benedicta tu in mulieribus, et benedictus fructus ventris tui.' Sed et illa verba, quæ Ecclesia adjecit,

ἡ ἐκκλησία, καὶ αὐτὰ ἐκ Πνεύματος
ἁγίου εἶναι· καὶ αὐτὴ ἡ ἐκκλησία μὲ
τὴν ἐξουσίαν, ὅπου ἔχει, προστάσσει,
νὰ δοξάζωμεν πολλὰ συνεχῶς τὴν
παρθένον μὲ τὸν χαιρετισμὸν τοῦτον
εἰς τὸν καιρὸν τῆς προσευχῆς.

'Ερώτησις μβ'.

Τί διδασκαλία εὑρίσκεται εἰς τὸν
χαιρετισμὸν τοῦτον;

'Απ. Εἰς τὸν χαιρετισμὸν τοῦτον
εὑρίσκεται ἡ ἀνάμνησις τῆς ἐνανθρω-
πήσεως τοῦ Υἱοῦ τοῦ Θεοῦ καὶ τῶν
αὐτοῦ εὐεργεσιῶν, ὅπου μᾶς ἔδωκε
μετ' αὐτήν. 'Ακόμι παραδίδοται καὶ
ἡ τοιαύτη διδασκαλία (Δαμ. γ'. κεφ.
ά. καὶ β'.), ἤγουν πῶς ὁ λόγος τοῦ
Θεοῦ ὁ ἄναρχος ἐξ οὐρανοῦ καταβὰς
δὲν ἐβάστα σάρκα μὲ τὸν ἑαυτόν του,
μὰ εἰς τὴν κοιλίαν τῆς παναγίας
Παρθένου, ἀπὸ τὰ καθαρώτατά της
αἵματα τὴν ἐπῆρε, τοῦ ἁγίου Πνεύματος συνεργοῦντος, καὶ ἀπ' αὐτὴν
ἐγεννήθηκεν, ὡς ἀπὸ γνησίαν του
μητέρα. Οὕτω βεβαίως καὶ ἀληθῶς
πρέπει νὰ πιστεύωμεν. Τοὺς δὲ λέγοντας (Κυριλ. 'Ιερ. Κατ. ιγ'.), πῶς
ἐκατάβασεν ἀπὸ τὸν οὐρανὸν τὴν
σάρκα ὅπου ἐφόρεσε, καὶ τὴν ἐπέρασεν
ἀπὸ τὴν ἁγίαν Παρθένον, ὡς ἂν ἀπὸ
σωληνάρι, ἡ ἐκκλησία τοὺς ἔκρινεν αἱρετικοὺς, καὶ τοὺς κατέκρινεν. 'Ακόμι
εἰς τὸν ἴδιον χαιρετισμὸν εἶναι καὶ
τούτη ἡ διδασκαλία, ὅπου μᾶς διδάσκει νὰ τὴν ὀνομάζωμεν Θεοτόκον
κατὰ τὴν ἀνθρωπότητα· καὶ ἀπ' αὐ-

ex Spiritu Sancto sunt. Eadem
Ecclesia pro suo jure atque auctoritate, inter orandum, crebro multumque hac ipsa salutatione B.
Virginem coli a nobis celebrari-
que jussit.

QUÆSTIO XLII.

Quid doctrinæ in hac salutatione
inest?

RESP. In hac salutatione continetur commemoratio assumtæ a
filio Dei humanitatis, eorumque illius beneficiorum, quæ per humanitatem suam in nos contulit. Tum
hæc etiam in ea proponitur doctrina (Damasc. III. cap. I. et II.), quod
nimirum, dum cœlo æternum illud
et principii expers Dei verbum de-
scenderet, nullam secum carnem
attulerit; verum illam in sanctissimæ virginis utero de purissimis
sanguinis illius guttis opera Spiritus Sancti assumserit, itaque de illa,
ut de genuina matre sua, natus fuerit. Quod firme vereque ita nobis
credendum est. Ceterum qui Servatorem cœlo descendentem jam carnem gestavisse affirmant, eamque
sic per S. virginem tanquam per
canaliculam quampiam traduxisse
(apud Cyrillum Hieros. Catech.
XIII.); eos Ecclesia pro hæreticis
habet damnatque. Porro et hæc
doctrina salutatione ista comprehen-
ditur, qua docemur nuncupare B

τὴν ἐγεννήθηκεν ὁ Χριστὸς, Θεὸς
τέλειος καὶ ἄνθρωπος τέλειος. Ἔτι
δὲ εὑρίσκεται καὶ τοιαύτη διδασκαλία
εἰς τὸν χαιρετισμὸν τοῦτον, εἰς τὸν
λόγον, ὅπου ὀνομάζει τὴν Παρθένον
κεχαριτωμένην, πῶς αὐτὴ εἶναι
μέτοχος τῆς θείας χάριτος, περισσότερον παρὰ κἂν ἕνα ἄλλο κτίσμα·
διατὶ εἶναι μήτηρ Θεοῦ· καὶ διὰ τοῦτο ἡ ἐκκλησία τὴν ὑψώνει ὑπὲρ τὰ
Χερουβὶμ καὶ Σεραφίμ· καὶ τῶρα
αὐτὴ ὑπεραίρει πάσας τὰς χορείας
τῶν ἀγγέλων, ἱσταμένη ἐκ δεξιῶν τοῦ
Υἱοῦ της, ἐν πάσῃ τιμῇ καὶ δόξῃ· κα-
θῶς ὁ Ψαλμῳδὸς (Ψαλ. μδʹ. θʹ.) λέ-
γει· παρέστη ἡ βασίλισσα ἐκ δεξιῶν
σου, ἐν ἱματισμῷ διαχρύσῳ περιβε-
βλημένη, πεποικιλμένη. Τὸν χαιρετισμὸν τοῦτον καθ᾽ ἕνας ἀπὸ τοὺς
ὀρθοδόξους χριστιανοὺς πρέπει μετ᾽
εὐλαβείας νὰ τὸν λέγῃ, ζητῶντας τὴν
μεσιτείαν τῆς Παρθένου· πολλὰ γὰρ
ἰσχύει δέησις μητρὸς πρὸς εὐμένειαν
Υἱοῦ. Καὶ ὁποῖος θέλει νὰ εἶναι
πρὸς αὐτὴν εὐλαβὴς, ἂς διαβάζῃ τὸν
ἀκάθιστον ὕμνον, καὶ τὰς παρακλή-
σεις, καὶ τοὺς λοιποὺς ὕμνους τῆς
ἐκκλησίας τοὺς πρὸς δόξαν αὐτῆς
συντεθέντας.

'Ερώτησις μγʹ.

Ποῖον εἶναι τὸ τέταρτον ἄρθρον
τῆς πίστεως;
Ἀπ. Σταυρωθέντα ὑπὲρ
ἡμῶν ἐπὶ Ποντίου Πιλάτου
καὶ παθόντα καὶ ταφέντα.

virginem Deiparam secundum humanam Christi naturam, natumque
ex ea Christum Deum pariter hominemque perfectum fuisse. Super
hæc salutatio ista, dum virginem
gratia plenam vocat, docet, eandem,
eo quod mater Dei est, largius multo
atque abundantius divinæ gratiæ
participem factam esse, quam aliam
quamcunque rem creatam; eaque
re illam ecclesia super Cherubim et
Seraphim merito extollit. Nunc
enim illa omnes Angelorum choros
longe supergressa ad dextram filii
sui omni cum honore atque gloria
adstat, dicente Davide (Psa. xlv. 9):
' Adstat regina ad dextram tuam, in
veste auro distincta, amicta versico-
loribus.' Debet autem orthodoxus
Christianus quilibet salutationem
hanc summa cum reverentia recitare
virginisque intercessionem implorare. Plurimum enim matris ad
pietatem filii valet oratio. Ceterum
qui devotus virginis cultor esse velit, ille hymnum ἀκάθιστον dictum
(quod stantibus, non vero sedentibus
canatur), recitabit et supplicationes
et ceteros ecclesiæ hymnos, in honorem Deiparæ compositos.

QUÆSTIO XLIII.

Quartus fidei Articulus quis
est?
RESP. *Qui pro nobis crucifixus
est sub Pontio Pilato, passus et
sepultus.*

Ἐρώτησις μδ'.

Τί διδάσκει τὸ ἄρθρον τοῦτο;

Ἀπ. Ἔξ πράγματα διδάσκει· πρῶτον πῶς κατ' ἐκείνην τὴν ἀληθινὴν ἀνθρωπότητα, ὅπου ἐπῆρεν ἀπὸ τὴν παρθένον Μαρίαν ὁ Λόγος, κατ' ἐκείνην ἔπαθεν εἰς τὸν σταυρὸν ἀπάνω δι' ἡμᾶς, κυρίως καὶ ἀληθῶς· καὶ ἀπέθανεν ἀληθῶς· τὸ ὁποῖον τοῦτο εἶναι φανερὸν ἀπὸ τὴν ἁγίαν Γραφὴν, ὅπου (Λουκ. κγ'. μς'.) λέγει· καὶ φωνήσας φωνῇ μεγάλῃ ὁ Ἰησοῦς εἶπε· Πάτερ, εἰς χεῖρας σου παρατίθημι τὸ πνεῦμά μου· καὶ ταῦτα εἰπὼν, ἐξέπνευσε· Καὶ τὸ τίμιόν του αἷμα ἀληθῶς δι' ἡμᾶς ἐξέχεε, καὶ μετ' αὐτὸ μᾶς ἐξηγόρασεν· ὡς λέγει (Ἐφ. ά. ἑ. καὶ ζ'.) ὁ Ἀπόστολος· προορίσας ἡμᾶς εἰς υἱοθεσίαν διὰ Ἰησοῦ Χριστοῦ, ἐν τῷ ἔχομεν τὴν ἀπολύτρωσιν διὰ τοῦ αἵματος αὐτοῦ, τὴν ἄφεσιν τῶν παραπτωμάτων, κατὰ τὸν πλοῦτον τῆς χάριτος αὐτοῦ.

Ἐρώτησις μέ.

Ποῖον εἶναι τὸ δεύτερον, ὅπου περιέχει τὸ ἄρθρον τοῦτο;

Ἀπ. Πῶς ἀναμαρτήτως ἔπαθε διὰ τὰς ἡμῶν ἁμαρτίας· καθὼς λέγει ὁ Ἀπόστολος Πέτρος (ά. ἐπιστ. ά. ιή.)· εἰδότες ὅτι οὐ φθαρτοῖς ἀργυρίῳ ἢ χρυσίῳ ἐλυτρώθητε ἐκ τῆς ματαίας ὑμῶν ἀναστροφῆς πατροπαραδότου, ἀλλὰ τιμίῳ αἵματι, ὡς ἀμνοῦ ἀμώμου καὶ ἀσπίλου Χριστοῦ. Ἀκόμι καὶ ὁ

QUÆSTIO XLIV.

Quid hic docet Articulus?

RESP. Sex admodum res docet. Primo, quod secundum veram illam humanitatem, quam de Maria virgine verbum sustulit, etiam in cruce nostra caussa vere et proprie passum fuerit vereque mortem oppetierit, quod ex sacro codice manifestum est (Luc. xxiii. 46): 'Exclamans autem voce magna Iesus dicit: Pater in manus tuas depono spiritum meum; eoque dicto exspiravit.' Quod pretiosum sanguinem suum pro nobis vere profuderit eoque nos redemerit, teste Apostolo (Eph. i. 5 et 7: 'Qui praedestinavit nos in adoptionem filialem per Iesum Christum, in quo habemus redemtionem per sanguinem ipsius, remissionem peccatorum, secundum divitias gratiae ipsius.'

QUÆSTIO XLV.

Secundum hoc Articulo contentum, quid est?

RESP. Christum sine ullo peccato peccatorum nostrorum pœnas luisse, teste Petro Apostolo (1 Pet. i. 18): 'Cum sciatis vos non caducis rebus, auro argentoque, redemtos esse a vana vestra vivendi ratione per majores tradita sed pretioso sanguine Christi, velut agni immaculati et in-

βαπτιστὴς Ἰωάννης μαρτυρᾷ, πῶς ἔστωντας καὶ νὰ εἶναι ἀθῶος ὁ Ἰησοῦς καὶ ἀναμάρτητος ἔπαθε διὰ τὰς ἁμαρτίας μας· διὸ (Ἰωαν. ά. κθ´.) λέγει· ἴδε ὁ ἀμνὸς τοῦ Θεοῦ, ὁ αἴρωι τὴν ἁμαρτίαν τοῦ κόσμου· Καὶ ἔπαϑ θελητικῶς· καϑὼς ὁ ἴδιος (Ἰωαν ί. ιή.) λέγει· ἐξουσίαν ἔχω θεῖναι τὴ. ψυχήν μου, καὶ ἐξουσίαν ἔχω πάλιι λαβεῖν αὐτήν.

contaminati.' Similiter et Ioannes Baptista testatur, Iesum, qui insons omnino et ab omni peccati contagione intactus esset, nostra ob peccata supplicium pertulisse; ita enim ille (Ioh. i. 29): 'Ecce agnus Dei, qui tollit peccata mundi.' Pertulit vero sua plane sponte atque voluntate, quemadmodum ipse dicit (Ioh. x. 18): 'Potestatem habeo ponendi animam meam, habeo item potestatem recipiendi eam.'

Ἐρώτησις μς´.

Τί διδάσκει τρίτον τοῦτο τὸ ἄρθρον;

Ἀπ. Πῶς ὁ Χριστὸς ἔπαθεν εἰς τὸν σταυρὸν κατὰ τὴν σάρκα, καὶ ὄχι κατὰ τὴν θεότητα· διατὶ ἡ θεότης δὲν ἔπασχε, μήτε ἐκαρφώνετο εἰς τὸν σταυρὸν, μήτε ἐμτυσμοὺς ἢ κολαφισμοὺς ἐδέχετο, μήτε ἀπέθνησκε· καὶ ὅσον πῶς μὲ μόνην τὴν σάρκα ἔπασχεν, ὁ Ἀπόστολος (Κολ. ά. κβ´.) τὸ φανερώνει λέγωντας· νυνὶ δὲ ἀποκατήλλαξεν ἐν τῷ σώματι τῆς σαρκὸς αὐτοῦ διὰ τοῦ θανάτου, παραστῆσαι ἡμᾶς ἁγίους καὶ ἀμώμους, καὶ ἀνεγκλήτους κατενώπιον αὐτοῦ. Ἀλλὰ μὴν ἡ θεότης ὡς ἂν ἔλαβε τὴν ἀνθρωπότητα, ποτὲ δὲν ἐχωρίσθηκεν ἀπ᾽ αὐτήν· οὔτε (Δαμασκ. ὁμιλ. εἰς τὸ ά. σάββ. ἅγιον ut 70), εἰς τὸν καιρὸν τοῦ πάθους ἢ τοῦ θανάτου εἰς τὸν σταυρὸν, οὔτε μετὰ τὸν θάνατον· καλᾷ καὶ ἡ ψυχὴ νὰ ἐχωρίσθηκεν ἀπὸ

QUÆSTIO XLVI.

Quidnam tertium iste docet Articulus?

RESP. Christum in cruce secundum carnem non vero secundum divinitatem passum fuisse. Nihil enim perpessa fuit Divinitas: non illa cruci affixa fuit: non consputationibus, non alapis os præbuit: non vitam amisit. Quod autem carne sola cruciatus fuit, id manifeste docet Apostolus (Coloss. i. 22): 'Nunc autem reconciliavit in corpore carnis suæ per mortem; ut sisteret nos sanctos et inculpatos et irreprehensibiles coram se ipso.' Ceterum ex quo humanitatem semel assumserat divinitas, nunquam ab ea separata fuit: non tempore passionis mortisque in cruce: non etiam a morte: quamquam enim disjuncta a corpore anima esset; divinitas tamen nec a corpore nec

τὸ κορμί· μὰ ἡ θεότης οὔτε ἀπὸ τὸ κορμὶ οὔτε ἀπὸ τὴν ψυχὴν ποτὲ ἐχωρίσθηκε. Διὰ τοῦτο καὶ εἰς καιρὸν τοῦ θανάτου ἡ ὑπόστασις τοῦ Χριστοῦ ἦτον μία καὶ ἡ αὐτή.

'Ερώτησις μζ'.

Τί διδάσκει τέταρτον τὸ ἄρθρον τοῦτο;

'Aπ. Πῶς ὁ θάνατος τοῦ Χριστοῦ νὰ ἦτον μὲ διαφορώτερον τρόπον παρὰ ὅπου ἦτον τῶν ἄλλων ὅλων ἀνθρώπων, διὰ ταῖς ἀφορμαῖς τούταις· πρῶτον διὰ τὸ βάρος τῶν ἁμαρτιῶν μας, καθὼς λέγει ὁ Προφήτης ('Ησ. νγ'. δ'.) περὶ αὐτοῦ· οὗτος τὰς ἁμαρτίας ἡμῶν φέρει, καὶ περὶ ἡμῶν ὀδυνᾶται· καὶ ἡμεῖς ἐλογισάμεθα, αὐτὸν εἶναι ἐν πόνῳ καὶ ἐν πληγῇ ὑπὸ Θεοῦ καὶ ἐν κακώσει· αὐτὸς δὲ ἐτραυματίσθη διὰ τὰς ἁμαρτίας ἡμῶν, καὶ μεμαλάκισται διὰ τὰς ἀνομίας ἡμῶν. Καὶ ἄλλος Προφήτης (Θρῆν. ά. ιβ'.) ὡς ἐκ προσώπου τοῦ Χριστοῦ· οἱ πρὸς ὑμᾶς πάντες παραπορευόμενοι ὁδὸν, ἐπιστρέψατε, καὶ ἴδετε, εἰ ἔστιν ἄλγος κατὰ τὸ ἄλγος μου, ὃ ἐγενήθη μοι. Δεύτερον, διατὶ εἰς τὸν σταυρὸν ἀπάνω ἐπλήρου τὴν ἱερωσύνην, ἑαυτὸν προσενέγκας τῷ Θεῷ καὶ Πατρὶ εἰς ἀπολύτρωσιν τοῦ γένους τῶν ἀνθρώπων· ὡς φησὶν ὁ 'Απόστολος (ά. Τιμ. β'. ς'.) περὶ αὐτοῦ· ὁ δοὺς ἑαυτὸν ἀντίλυτρον ὑπὲρ πάντων. Καὶ ἀλλαχοῦ ('Εφεσ. έ. β'.)· ὁ Χριστὸς ἠγάπησεν

ab anima unquam secessit: unde ipsa etiam in morte una eademque Christi erat persona (Damascen. Homilia in sanctum Sabbatum, p. 292, Pantin.).

Quæstio XLVII.

Quartum in hoc Articulo, quid est?

Resp. Quod mors Christi præstantiore magisque fructuoso quodam modo quam mortes reliquorum hominum omnium, contigit. Has præcipue ob caussas: Primum, ob gravissimam scelerum nostrorum sarcinam, ut de eo ait Propheta (Ies. liii. 4): 'Hic peccata nostra fert, et pro nobis dolore affligitur. Nos existimabamus, illum dolore et plagis et afflictionibus a Deo affici: sed ille ob peccata nostra sauciatus est, et ob iniquitates nostras languore correctus est.' Et Propheta alius, tanquam ex persona Christi (Ier. Thr. i. 12): 'Numquid non ad vos attinet, vos omnes qui iter facitis? revertimini ac videte, si est dolor, ut dolor meus, qui mihi accidit.' Deinde, quod in cruce Pontificium munus suum adimplevit, offerendo semet ipsum Deo et Patri in redemtionem generis humani. Sicut de illo loquitur Apostolus (1 Tim. ii. 6): 'Qui dedit se ipsum pretium redemtionis pro omnibus.' Et alibi (Ephes. v. 2):

ἡμᾶς, καὶ παρέδωκεν ἑαυτὸν ὑπὲρ ἡμῶν προσφορὰν, καὶ θυσίαν τῷ θεῷ εἰς ὀσμὴν εὐωδίας. Καὶ εἰς ἄλλον τόπον ('Ρωμ. ἑ. ἡ.)· ἔτι ἁμαρτωλῶν ὄντων ἡμῶν, κατὰ καιρὸν Χριστὸς ὑπὲρ ἡμῶν ἀπέθανεν. Ἐκεῖ ἀκόμι εἰς τὸν σταυρὸν ἐτελείωνε τὴν μεσιτείαν ἀνάμεσον Θεοῦ καὶ ἀνθρώπων· καθὼς ὁ αὐτὸς Ἀπόστολος λέγει (Κολ. ά. κ́.) περὶ αὐτοῦ· καὶ δι' αὐτοῦ ἀποκαταλλάξαι τὰ πάντα εἰς αὐτὸν· εἰρηνοποιήσας διὰ τοῦ αἵματος τοῦ σταυροῦ αὐτοῦ· καὶ ἀλλαχοῦ (Κολ. β΄. ιδ΄.)· ἐξαλείψας τὸ καθ' ἡμῶν χειρόγραφον τοῖς δόγμασιν, ὃ ἦν ὑπεναντίον ἡμῖν, καὶ αὐτὸ ἦρεν ἐκ τοῦ μέσου, προσηλώσας αὐτὸ τῷ σταυρῷ.

'Christus dilexit nos, et se oblationem pro nobis ac victimam Deo tradidit in odorem suaviter fragrantem.' Et alio loco (Rom. v. 8): 'Cum adhuc inimici Dei essemus, Christus pro nobis mortuus est.' Tum quod ibidem in cruce, susceptam inter Deum atque homines conciliationem absolvit, quemadmodum idem de illo loquitur Apostolus (Col. i. 20): 'Et per illum reconciliare sibi omnia, pace facta per sanguinem crucis illius.' Et alibi (c. ii. 14): 'Delebat, quod contra nos erat, chirographum in decretis, quod adversum nobis erat: et cruci illud affixum de medio sustulit.'

Ἐρώτησις μή.

Τί διδάσκει πέμπτον τὸ ἄρθρον τοῦτο;

Ἀπ. Περὶ τῆς ταφῆς τοῦ Κυρίου ἡμῶν Ἰησοῦ Χριστοῦ· πῶς καταπῶς ἔπαθε κυρίως καὶ ἀληθῶς εἰς τὸν σταυρὸν ἀπάνω· οὕτως καὶ ἀπέθανεν ἀληθῶς καὶ ἀληθῶς ἐτάφη εἰς τόπον ἐπίσημον. Καὶ τοῦτο ἔγινεν ὄχι χωρὶς αἰτίαν, μὰ διὰ νὰ μὴν ὑποπτεύεται τινὰς ὕστερον περὶ τῆς ἀληθοῦς αὐτοῦ ἐκ νεκρῶν ἀναστάσεως. Διατὶ ἂν ἤθελε ταφῇ εἰς κἂν ἕνα τόπον ἀπόκρυφον, καὶ καθὼς τὸ λέγουσιν, ἐν παραβύστῳ, ἐθέλασιν ἔχειν ἀφορμὴν οἱ Ἰουδαῖοι, νὰ διασύρουσι τὸν Χριστόν. Πρὸς μεγαλήτερην λοιπὸν

Quæstio XLVIII.

Quodnam quintum est, quod hic docet Articulus?

Resp. De sepultura Domini nostri Iesu Christi. Quod quemadmodum proprie vereque in crucem actus ultimos pertulit cruciatus: ita revera etiam mortuus, locoque celebri sepultus fuit. Id quod neutiquam sine caussa factum; verum ut ne deinde quisquam de vera Christi e mortuis resurrectione addubitaret. Quippe si loco quodam obscuro et abstruso, quod ajunt, angulo, sepultus fuisset: caussam haud inopportunam calumniis suis oppugnandi Christi reperissent Iu-

πίστωσιν καὶ δόξαν τῆς ἐνδόξου τοῦ Χριστοῦ ἀναστάσεως ἐπαρακινηθήκασιν οἱ Ἰουδαῖοι, καὶ ἦλθασι πρὸς Πιλάτον (Ματθ. κζ΄. ξδ΄.) λέγοντες· κέλευσον ἀσφαλισθῆναι τὸν τάφον ἕως τῆς τρίτης ἡμέρας· καὶ αὐτὸς τοὺς ἀπεκρίθη· ἔχετε κουστωδίαν, ὑπάγετε, ἀσφαλίσασθε ὡς οἴδατε. Οἱ δὲ πορευθέντες ἠσφαλίσαντο τὸν τάφον, σφραγίσαντες τὸν λίθον, μετὰ τῆς κουστωδίας. Ἡ ὁποία κουστωδία τῶν Ἰουδαίων φανερώτατα ἐμαρτύρησε, πῶς ὁ Χριστὸς ἀνέστη ἀπὸ τοὺς νεκρούς· διατὶ εἰς τὸν καιρὸν ἐκεῖνον αὐτοὶ ἐφοβήθησαν, ὡς λέγει (Ματθ. κή. β΄.) ἡ Γραφή· καὶ ἰδοὺ σεισμὸς ἐγένετο μέγας· ἄγγελος γὰρ Κυρίου καταβὰς ἐξ οὐρανοῦ προσελθὼν ἀπεκύλισε τὸν λίθον ἀπὸ τῆς θύρας, κάθετο ἐπάνω αὐτοῦ. Ἀπὸ δὲ τοῦ φόβου αὐτοῦ ἐσείσθησαν οἱ τηροῦντες, καὶ ἐγένοντο ὡσεὶ νεκροί. Οἵτινες ὕστερον ἐλθόντες εἰς τὴν πόλιν ἀπήγγειλαν τοῖς Ἀρχιερεῦσιν ἅπαντα τὰ γενόμενα· καὶ διὰ τοῦτο ἠναγκάζοντο νὰ εἰποῦσι καὶ ἐκεῖνα τὰ λόγια, ὅπου εἶπεν ὁ ἄγγελος Κυρίου (στιχ. έ.) εἰς τὰς γυναῖκας· οἶδα ὅτι Ἰησοῦν τὸν ἐσταυρωμένον ζητεῖτε· οὐκ ἔστιν ὧδε· ἠγέρθη γὰρ καθὼς εἶπε· δεῦτε, ἴδετε τὸν τόπον, ὅπου ἔκειτο ὁ Κύριος· καὶ ταχὺ πορευθεῖσαι εἴπατε τοῖς μαθηταῖς αὐτοῦ, ὅτι ἠγέρθη ἀπὸ τῶν νεκρῶν. Διὰ τούτην λοιπὸν τὴν ἀφορμὴν ὁ τάφος οὗ Κυρίου εἶναι ὀνομαστὸς, διὰ νὰ

dæi. Quocirca ad majorem gloriosæ Christi resurrectionis fidem ac gloriam, quodam quasi instinctu commoti, ad Pilatum adeunt ajuntque (Matt. xxvii. 64): 'Iube accurate asservari sepulcrum in diem tertium.' Quibus ille respondit: habetis custodiam, ite, asservate prout poteritis. Illi vero abeuntes asservabant sepulcrum, obsignato saxo atque apposita custodia. Quod Iudæorum custodia manifestissimum resurrectionis Christi perhibuit testimonium, quippe quæ eo ipso temporis articulo magno pavore percellebatur, teste Scriptura (Matt. xxviii. 2): 'Ecce autem ingens terræ motus exstitit. Nam Angelus Domini de cœlo descendens, accedens saxum ab ostio devolvit, in eoque consedit; cujus terrore conturbati custodes velut mortui facti sunt.' Qui postea (versu 11) in urbem ingressi Pontificibus summis, quæ evenerant omnia, renunciarunt. Unde ea etiam proferre coacti sunt verba, quæ Angelus mulieribus dixerat (vers. 5): 'Scio Iesum vos, qui crucifixus erat, quærere. Ille vero hic non est. Iam enim, sicut prædixerat, surrexit. Venite, videte locum, in quo situs fuit Dominus, et cito euntes, enumerate discipulis illius, ipsum a mortuis resurrexisse.' Hanc igitur ob caussam sepulcrum Domini cele-

εἶναι πιστὸν εἰς ὅλους, πῶς οἱ μαθηταί του δὲν τὸν ἔκλεψαν, μήτε εἰς ἀπόκρυφον τόπον τὸν ἔθαψαν, ὡς οἱ διεστραμμένοι Ἰουδαῖοι διεφήμισαν, δίδοντες χρήματα εἰς τοὺς στρατιώτας. Μὰ τὴν ὑποψίαν τούτην τὴν ἔκβαλε τὸ μνῆμα, εἰς τὸ ὁποῖον ἐκείτετο· ἡ σφραγὶς τοῦ λίθου μετὰ τῆς κουστωδίας τῶν Ἰουδαίων· ὁμοίως καὶ ὁ Ἰωσὴφ καὶ ὁ Νικόδημος, οἱ ὁποῖοι ἦσαν ἔντιμοι ἀνάμεσα εἰς τοὺς Ἰουδαίους· ἀκόμι ἡ συνδόνα, μὲ τὴν ὁποῖαν ἐτυλίξασι τὸ νενεκρωμένον σῶμα τοῦ Κυρίου ἡμῶν, καὶ τὸ σουδάριον, ὅπου ἦτον εἰς τὴν κεφαλήν του καὶ ἔμεινεν εἰς τὸν τάφον διπλωμένον (Ἰωαν. κ΄. ζ΄.) ἀναστάντος αὐτοῦ. Ταῦτα πάντα φανερώνουσι, πῶς δὲν ἐκλέφθηκεν ἀπὸ τοὺς μαθητάς του τὸ σῶμα, ἀλλὰ ἀνέστη. Μὲ τὴν διδασκαλίαν τούτην πρέπει καὶ τοῦτο νὰ νοῆται, πῶς κατὰ τὴν προφητείαν ἦτον ἀνάγκη, νὰ εἶναι τὸ μνημεῖον του ἔντιμον, καθὼς ἦτον, καὶ εἶναι μέχρι τῆς σήμερον· φησὶ γὰρ ὁ Προφήτης (Ἡσ. ιά. ι.)· καὶ ἔσται ἡ ἀνάπαυσις αὐτοῦ τιμή. Καὶ εἰς αὐτὸ ὁποῖος ἐν πίστει καὶ ἀγάπῃ τῇ εἰς Χριστὸν ὑπαγένει, μεγάλην ἄφεσιν τῶν ἁμαρτιῶν ἀποκτᾶται, δι᾽ αὐτοῦ πρὸς Χριστὸν προσερχόμενος.

bre fuit, quo liquidum omnibus fieret, non furto illum suorum discipulorum subductum, locoque quodam abstruso conditum fuisse. Cujusmodi rumusculos perversi Iudæi sparsere, militibus multo ære corruptis. Sed inanem suspiciunculam facile refellebant tum monumentum illud, in quo conditus fuerat Dominus, tum signatura saxi Iudæorumque excubiæ, Iosephus item, et Nicodemus, viri inter suos clari honoratique, ad hæc pretiosa illa sindon, qua involutum exanimum Domini corpus fuerat, et sudarium capitis velamen, quod postquam resurrexerat, in sepulcro complicatum remansit (Ioh. xx. 7). Quæ omnia satis evincunt, non surreptum furto discipulorum corpus illius fuisse, sed reapse revixisse. Ad quam doctrinam illud etiam animadversu dignum est: nimirum, ut secundum sacra vaticinia necesse erat honoratum Christi conditorium esse, ita etiam fuisse, itemque hodie esse. Sic enim Propheta (Ies. xi. 10): 'et erit requies illius honos.' Quod sepulcrum quisquis in fide et amore Christi visit: ille multam criminum suorum remissionem consequitur, dum per illud ad Christum ipsum animo accedit.

Ἐρώτησις μθ΄.

Ἀνάμεσα εἰς τὰ εἰρημένα ἐπεθύμουν νὰ ἔμαθα περὶ τῆς ψυχῆς τοῦ

QUÆSTIO XLIX.

Inter hæc quæ modo dicta fuere, suborta mihi cupido noscendi, quo-

Χριστοῦ, εἰς ποῖον τόπον νὰ εὑρίσκετο ὕστερα ἀπὸ τὸν θάνατόν του πρὶν τῆς ἀναστάσεως;

Ἀπ. Ἡ ψυχὴ (Δαμ. ὁμιλ. εἰς τὸ ἅγιον σάββατον.) τοῦ Χριστοῦ, ἔστωντας καὶ νὰ χωρισθῇ ἀπὸ τὸ σῶμα, ἦτον πάντοτε ἐσμιμένη μὲ τὴν θεότητα, καὶ μὲ τὴν θεότητα ἐκατέβηκεν εἰς τὸν ᾅδην· καλᾷ καὶ εἰς τὸν τόπον τοῦτον νὰ μὴν ἔχωμεν κἂν μίαν ἐνθύμησιν δι᾽ αὐτό. Μόνον τὸ ἔχομεν βέβαιον ἀπὸ ὅλους τοὺς ἐκκλησιαστικοὺς ὕμνους, ὅπου πραγματεύονται δι᾽ αὐτό· πῶς ὁ Χριστὸς νὰ ἐκατέβηκεν εἰς τὸν ᾅδην μὲ τὴν ψυχὴν καὶ μὲ τὴν θεότητα· καὶ πλέον χοριστᾷ μὲ τὸ τροπάριον ἐκεῖνο τῆς ἐκκλησίας, ὅπου λέγει· "ἐν τάφῳ σωματικῶς, ἐν ᾅδου δὲ μετὰ ψυχῆς ὡς Θεὸς, ἐν παραδείσῳ δὲ μετὰ λῃστοῦ, καὶ ἐν θρόνῳ ὑπῆρχες, Χριστὲ, μετὰ Πατρὸς καὶ Πνεύματος πάντα πληρῶν ὁ ἀπερίγραπτος." Καὶ ἀπὸ τὸν ᾅδην ἐλύτρωσε τὰς ψυχὰς τῶν ἁγίων προπατόρων καὶ τὰς ἔβαλεν εἰς τὸν παράδεισον· μαζὶ μὲ τοὺς ὁποίους συνεισήγαγε καὶ τὸν λῃστὴν, ὅπου ἐπίστευσεν ἐν τῷ σταυρῷ εἰς αὐτόν.

Ἐρώτησις ν΄.

Τί εἶναι τὸ ἕκτον, ὅπου πραγματεύεται καὶ διδάσκει τὸ ἄρθρον τοῦτο;

Ἀπ. Διατὶ τὸ ἄρθρον τοῦτο κάμει ἐνθύμησιν τοῦ σταυροῦ τοῦ Χριστοῦ, εἰς τὸ ὁποῖον ἀπάνω ἀπέθανεν ὁ Χριστὸς, καὶ ἔσωσε μᾶς· δίδει ἀφορ-

nam sane loco anima Christi post excessum e corpore ante resurrectionem egerit?

RESP. (Ex Damasc. in sanctum sabbatum, loc. cit. sup. pag. 113). Anima Christi, quamquam corpore suo tum exsoluta, usque tamen juncta manebat divinitati, quacum etiam ad inferos descendit, tametsi nihil hoc (hujus Articuli) loco de isto negotio innuitur. Sed certum illud tamen contestatumque ex tot ecclesiæ hymnis, qui de eo agunt, habemus, quod nimirum simul anima et divinitate sua ad inferos descendit Christus. Inprimis autem rem sigillatim exprimit hoc Ecclesiæ Troparium: Tu corpore in sepulcro: tu anima apud inferos, ut Deus: tu in Paradiso cum latrone: itemque in throno gloriæ cum Patre ac Spiritu, *Christe*, fuisti, qui cuncta imples, ipse incircumscriptus. Simul ereptas orco sanctorum Patrum animas Paradiso intulit, quibuscum etiam latronem, qui in cruce pendens in ipsum crediderat, introduxit.

QUÆSTIO L.

Quodnam sextum est, quod hic tractat docetque articulus?

RESP. Quoniam mentionem crucis Christi, in qua Christus mortuus est nosque in salutem vindicavit, hic facit articulus: eo et nobis an-

μὴν διὰ τοῦτο, νὰ ἐνθυμούμεν καὶ ἡμεῖς τοῦ σταυροῦ· διὰ τὸν ὁποῖον τέτοιας λογῆς ὁμιλεῖ (Γαλ. ς'. ιδ'.) ὁ Ἀπόστολος Παῦλος· ἐμοὶ δὲ μὴ γένοιτο καυχᾶσθαι, εἰ μὴ ἐν τῷ σταυρῷ τοῦ Κυρίου ἡμῶν Ἰησοῦ Χριστοῦ, δι' οὗ ἐμοὶ κόσμος ἐσταύρωται, κἀγὼ τῷ κόσμῳ. Καὶ ἀλλαχοῦ (ά. Κορ. ά. ιή.)· ὁ λόγος γὰρ τοῦ σταυροῦ τοῖς μὲν ἀπολλυμένοις μωρία ἐστὶ, τοῖς δὲ σωζομένοις εἴτουν ἡμῖν δύναμις Θεοῦ ἐστιν. Ὥστε λοιπὸν διὰ μεγάλαις ἀφορμαῖς πρέπει νὰ τιμᾶται ἀπὸ ἡμᾶς ὁ σταυρός· ὡς ἂν σημεῖον τοῦ Χριστοῦ, εἰς τὸν ὁποῖον ἐδόθηκε δύναμις, διατὶ ἐχύθηκεν εἰς αὐτὸν τὸ αἷμα τοῦ Υἱοῦ τοῦ Θεοῦ, καὶ εἰς αὐτὸν ἀπέθανε, νὰ διώκῃ τὰ πονηρὰ πνεύματα. Διὰ τοῦτο ὁ ἅγιος Κύριλλος ὁ Ἱεροσολύμων (Κατ. ιγ'.) λέγει οὕτως· ὅταν μὲ τὸ σημεῖον τοῦ τιμίου σταυροῦ σημειώνωμεν τοὺς ἑαυτούς μας, τότε ὁ διάβολος, κατανοῶντας πῶς ὁ Χριστὸς ὁ Κύριος εἰς αὐτὸν ἐκαρφώθηκε διὰ τὴν σωτηρίαν τὴν ἐδικήν μας καὶ διὰ τὴν ἐξολόθρευσιν τῆς δαιμονικῆς δυνάμεως, δὲν ἠμπορεῖ νὰ στέκεται παρὼν, μήτε νὰ ὑποφέρῃ τὴν δύναμιν τοῦ σταυροῦ· μὰ φεύγει ἀπὸ μᾶς καὶ πλέον δὲν πειράζει, καὶ μάλιστα διατὶ τότε ἔχομεν συνήθειαν, νὰ ἐπικαλούμεθα τὸ ὄνομα τοῦ Χριστοῦ. Διὰ τοῦτο χρεωστοῦμεν νὰ κάμνωμεν τὸν σταυρόν μας πολλὰ συχνιᾶ, διατὶ συχνιᾶ γροικοῦμεν καὶ τοὺς πειρασμοὺς τοῦ δαίμονος· τοὺς ὁποίους μὲ ἄλ-

sam de cruce commentandi offert, de qua hunc in modum Paulus Apostolus disserit (Gal. vi. 14): 'Absit a me ut gloriari velim, nisi in cruce Domini nostri Iesu Christi, per quam mihi mundus crucifixus est, et ego mundo.' Et alio loco (1 Cor. i. 18): 'Sermo crucis iis, qui pereunt, stultitia est: at nobis, qui salutem consequimur, potentia Dei est.' Multis igitur magnisque de causis venerabilis nobis crux erit, ut peculiare quoddam signum Christi, cui virtus mirifica fugandi dæmonum impressa est; siquidem effuso in illam sanguine filii Dei, qui et animam in ea efflabat, imbuta fuit. Qua de re ita dicit S. Cyrillus, Episcopus Hierosolymitanus (Catechesi XIII.): Quando venerabilis crucis signo nosmet ipsos signamus, tum Diabolus recogitans secum, Christum Dominum propter salutem nostram potentiæque diabolicæ exstirpationem cruci clavis suffixum fuisse, diutius præsens esse crucisque sufferre vim nequit; sed fugit a nobis, nec ulterius nos pertentat, maxime quoniam simul sanctissimum Servatoris Christi invocare nomen solemus. Est igitur necesse, ut crucis signum in nobis sæpe frequentemus, quoniam nimis frequentes dæmonis persentiscimus tentationes, quas haud alio profligare modo

λον τρόπον δὲν ἠμποροῦμεν νὰ διώ-
κωμεν, παρὰ μὲ τὸν ζωοποιὸν σταυρὸν καὶ μὲ τὴν ἐπίκλησιν τοῦ ὀνόματος τοῦ Ἰησοῦ Χριστοῦ. Καὶ ὄχι
μόνον τοὺς διώκομεν ἀπὸ ἡμᾶς, ἀλλὰ
καὶ ἀπὸ ὅλα τὰ ἄλλα μας πράγματα,
ἤγουν ἀπὸ φαγητὰ, πιοτὰ, σκεύη καὶ
τὰ λοιπά. Διὰ τοῦτο ὁ αὐτὸς Κύριλλος (εἰς τὸ αὐτό) διδάσκει λέγων·
κάμνε τὸ σημεῖον τοῦ τιμίου σταυροῦ
τρώγωντας, πίνωντας, καθήμενος,
ἱστάμενος, ὁμιλῶντας, ἢ καὶ περιπα-
τῶντας· καὶ μὴν ἀρχίζῃς κᾂν μίαν
σου δουλείαν, παρὰ νὰ κάμῃς τὸ σημεῖον, τοῦ τιμίου σταυροῦ, εἰς τὸ ὀσ-
πήτιον, εἰς τὸν δρόμον, ἡμέραν καὶ
νύκτα, καὶ εἰς κάθα τόπον.

'Ερώτησις να.

Πῶς χρεωστοῦμεν νὰ σημειωνώ-
μεσθαν μὲ τὸ σημεῖον τοῦ τιμίου καὶ
ζωοποιοῦ σταυροῦ;

'Απ. Μὲ τὴν δεξιὰν χεῖρα πρέπει
νὰ κάμῃς τὸν σταυρὸν βάνωντας εἰς
τὸ μέτοπόν σου τὰ τρία μεγάλα δάκ-
τυλα· καὶ νὰ λέγῃς· εἰς τὸ ὄνομα
τοῦ Πατρός. Καὶ τότε καταβάζεις
τὸ χέρι εἰς τὸν θώρακα μὲ τὸ ἴδιον
σχῆμα καὶ λέγεις· καὶ τοῦ Υἱοῦ. Καὶ
ἀπ' ἐκεῖ εἰς τὸν δεξιὸν βραχίονα λέ-
γωντας· καὶ τοῦ ἁγίου Πνεύματος,
παγένωντας ἕως εἰς τὸν ἀριστερόν.
Καὶ ἀφ' οὗ σημειώσῃς τὸν ἑαυτόν
σου μὲ τὸ ἅγιον τοῦτο σημεῖον τοῦ
σταυροῦ, πρέπει νὰ τελειώσῃς μὲ τὸν
λόγον τοῦτον· ἀμήν. Ἤ καὶ ὅταν

possumus, quam signo vivificæ crucis et seria invocatione nominis
Iesu Christi. Quo modo non solum a nobis ipsis insultus dæmonum arcemus; sed a reliquis etiam
omnibus rebus nostris, ut ab escu-
lentis potulentisque, a vasis, aliisque quibuslibet. Quapropter ita
idem ille Cyrillus docet (loco eodem): Fac venerabilis crucis signum, dum edis bibisque, dum sedes, aut stas; dum loqueris, aut
ambulas. Nullam cœptabis rem,
nullum opus, nisi facto prius venerabilis crucis signo, domi, in via,
diu noctuque omnibusque in locis.

QUÆSTIO LI.

Quo ritu signum venerabilis et
vivificæ crucis in nobis formare
debemus?

RESP. Crucem hoc modo dextra
manu formabis. Primum tribus
majusculis digitis frontem tanges
dicesque: In nomine Patris. Tum
manum, eodem gestu conforma-
tum, in pectus deduces addesque:
et Filii. Hinc in brachium (sive
potius humerum) dextrum tradu-
cens manum dices: et Spiritus
Sancti, simul ductum manus in
humerum sinistrum usque contin-
uabis. Atque ubi sacro hocce
crucis signaculo temet signasti,
claudes verbo: Amen. Potes eti-

κάμῃς τὸν σταυρόν σου, ἠμπορεῖς νὰ | am in cruce formando hæc adhi-
λέγῃς· Κύριε Ἰησοῦ Χριστὲ, Υἱὲ τοῦ | bere verba: Domine Iesu Christe,
Θεοῦ, ἐλέησόν με τὸν ἁμαρτωλὸν, | fili Dei, miserere mei peccatoris.
ἀμήν. | Amen.

Ἐρώτησις νβ΄. | QUÆSTIO LII.

Ποῖον εἶναι τὸ πέμπτον ἄρθρον | Quintus Fidei Articulus, quis
τῆς πίστεως; | est?

Ἀπ. Καὶ ἀναστάντα τῇ τρίτῃ | RESP. *Qui resurrexit die tertio*
ἡμέρᾳ κατὰ τὰς γραφάς. | *secundum Scripturas.*

Ἐρώτησις νγ΄. | QUÆSTIO LIII.

Τί διδασκαλίαν μᾶς διδάσκει τὸ | Quam doctrinam iste nos fidei
ἄρθρον τοῦτο τῆς πίστεως; | Articulus docet?

Ἀπ. Δύο πράγματα διδάσκει, | RESP. Duo docet. Alterum,
πρῶτον πῶς ὁ Κύριος ἡμῶν Ἰησοῦς | Dominum nostrum Iesum Chris-
Χριστὸς μὲ τὴν δύναμιν τῆς θεότητός | tum suæ divinitatis viribus in vi-
του ἠγέρθη (Λουκ. κδ΄. ζ΄.) ἀπὸ τῶν | tam rediisse (Luc. xxiv. 7), prout
νεκρῶν· καθὼς εἶναι γεγραμμένον | de illo perscriptum erat in Pro-
περὶ αὐτοῦ εἰς τοὺς Προφήτας καὶ εἰς | phetis et Psalmis. Alterum, re-
τοὺς Ψαλμούς· δεύτερον, πῶς ἀνεσ- | surrexisse ipsum in eodem illo
τάθηκε μὲ τὸ ἴδιον σῶμα, ὅπου ἐγεν- | corpore suo, quicum natus mortu-
νήθη καὶ ἀπέθανε. | usque fuerat.

Ἐρώτησις νδ΄. | QUÆSTIO LIV.

Κατὰ τίνας γραφὰς ὁ Χριστὸς | Secundum quas scripturas ita ne-
ἦτον χρεία νὰ πάθῃ, καὶ νὰ ἀποθάνῃ, | cesse erat, tum pati Christum atque
καὶ τὴν τρίτην ἡμέραν νὰ ἀνασταθῇ; | emori, tum die tertio reviviscere?

Ἀπ. Δύο λογίων εἶναι αἱ ἅγιαι | RESP. Duplices sacræ scripturæ
γραφαὶ· κάποιαις τοῦ παλαιοῦ νόμου | sunt, quædam veteris legis, quæ-
καὶ κάποιαις τοῦ νέου. Αἱ πρῶται | dam novæ. Priores Christum ven-
ἐπροείπασι, πῶς ὁ Χριστὸς μέλλει νὰ | turum, modumque ipsum, quo ge-
ἔλθῃ, καὶ μὲ τίνα τρόπον εἶχε νὰ | nus humanum in salutem assertu-
σώσῃ τὸ γένος τῶν ἀνθρώπων, ἤγουν | rus esset, prædixerunt: nimirum
μὲ τὸ νὰ πάθῃ, νὰ λάβῃ θάνατον, καὶ | passurum, moriturum, e mortuisque
νὰ ἀνασταθῇ ἀπὸ τοὺς νεκρούς. Καὶ | resurrecturum. Itaque hæc omnia

κατὰ τὰς γραφὰς ταύτας ὁ Χριστὸς
ἔπρεπε, νὰ τὰ πληρώσῃ ὅλα. Κατὰ
δὲ τὰς γραφὰς τοῦ νέου νόμου ἐβε-
βαιώθηκε, πῶς τὰ ἐπλήρωσε, καὶ πῶς
τέτοιας λογῆς ἦλθε, καθὼς γέγραπται περὶ αὐτοῦ· ὡς ὁ αὐτὸς λέγει
(Μαρκ. ιδ'. κά.) περὶ ἑαυτοῦ· ὁ μὲν
Υἱὸς τοῦ ἀνθρώπου ὑπάγει, καθὼς
γέγραπται περὶ αὐτοῦ. Καὶ ὕστερα
ἀπὸ τὴν ἐκ νεκρῶν αὐτοῦ ἀνάστασιν
ἔλεγε (Λουκ. κδ'. κς'.) πρὸς δύο του
μαθητὰς στρατοκόπους· οὐχὶ ταῦτα
ἔδει παθεῖν τὸν Χριστὸν καὶ εἰσελθεῖν
εἰς τὴν δόξαν αὐτοῦ; καὶ ἀρξάμενος
ἀπὸ Μωσέως καὶ ἀπὸ πάντων τῶν
Προφητῶν, διηρμήνευεν αὐτοῖς ἐν
πάσαις ταῖς γραφαῖς τὰ περὶ ἑαυτοῦ.
Καὶ πῶς πρέπει νὰ ἔχῃ τὸ κῦρος καὶ
τὴν βεβαιότητα ἡ παλαιὰ γραφὴ εἰς
ἡμᾶς, τὸ μαρτυρᾷ λέγων ὁ Ἀπόστολος (β'. Πέτρ. ά. ιθ'.) περὶ αὐτῆς·
ἔχομεν βεβαιότερον τὸν προφητικὸν
λόγον, ᾧ καλῶς ποιεῖτε προσέχοντες,
ὡς λύχνῳ φαίνοντι ἐν αὐχμηρῷ τόπῳ,
ἕως οὗ ἡμέρα διαυγάσῃ, καὶ φωσφό-
ρος ἀνατείλῃ ἐν ταῖς καρδίαις ὑμῶν.
Καὶ πῶς νὰ ἐτελειώθηκεν οὕτως κατὰ τὰς γραφὰς ταύτας, ὅλοι οἱ εὐαγ-
γελισταὶ μᾶς βεβαιώνουσι· καὶ ὁ
Ἀπόστολος (ά. Κορ. ιέ. γ'.) λέγει·
ὅτι Χριστὸς ἀπέθανεν ὑπὲρ τῶν ἁμαρτιῶν ἡμῶν κατὰ τὰς γραφάς· καὶ
ὅτι ἐτάφη, καὶ ὅτι ἐγήγερται τῇ τρίτῃ
ἡμέρᾳ κατὰ τὰς γραφάς· καὶ ὅτι
ὤφθη Κηφᾷ, εἶτα τοῖς δώδεκα. Ἔπειτα ὤφθη ἐπάνω πεντακοσίοις ἀδελ-

secundum istas scripturas adim-
plenda Christo fuere. Rursus ex
novæ legis scripturis, isthæc omnia
Christum implesse, luculenter con-
firmatum est, eaque prorsus ratione
in mundum venisse, quemadmodum
de eo scriptum fuerat. Sicut ipse
de semet ipso affirmat (Marc. xiv.
21): 'Filius quidem hominis vadit,
sicut scriptum est de illo.' Atque
denuo ex inferis in lucem redux,
duobus discipulis iter facientibus,
dixit (Luc. xxiv. 26): 'Nonne hæc
pati Christum oportuit, et intrare in
gloriam suam? et exorsus a Mose et
Prophetis omnibus, interpretabatur
illis, quæ de ipso omnibus in scripturis prædicta essent.' Iam suam
veteri testamento apud nos auctoritatem firmitudinemque sartam tec-
tam constare oportere, illud testificatur Apostolus de ipso dicens (2
Pet. i. 19): 'Habemus firmiorem
sermonem Propheticum, cui recte
ac merito attenditis, veluti lucernæ
lucenti in loco obscuro, donec elu-
cescat dies, et lucifer in cordibus
vestris exoriatur.' Porro quod eodem modo secundum Scripturas
istas hæc perfecta sunt, Evangelistæ omnes nobis confirmant. Confirmat et Apostolus (1 Cor. xv. 3):
'Quod Christus mortuus fuerit pro
peccatis nostris secundum Scripturas: quod sepultus sit, quodque tertio die resurrexerit secundum Scrip-

φοῖς ἐφάπαξ, ἐξ ὧν οἱ πλείους μένου-
σιν ἕως ἄρτι, τινὲς δὲ καὶ ἐκοιμήθη-
σαν. Ἔπειτα ὤφθη Ἰακώβῳ· εἶτα
τοῖς Ἀποστόλοις πᾶσιν. Ἔσχατον
δὲ πάντων ὥσπερ τῷ ἐκτρώματι ὤφθη
κἀμοί. Τὴν τοῦ Χριστοῦ ἀνάστασιν
προετύπου καὶ ὁ Προφήτης Ἰωνᾶς,
τὸν ὁποῖον τύπον ὁ Κύριος ἡμῶν
Ἰησοῦς Χριστὸς τὸν ἀναφέρει πρὸς
τὸν ἑαυτόν του, λέγων (Ματθ. ιβ΄.
λθ΄.) πρὸς τοὺς Ἰουδαίους· γενεὰ
πονηρὰ καὶ μοιχαλὶς σημεῖον ἐπιζη-
τεῖ, καὶ σημεῖον οὐ δοθήσεται αὐτῇ, εἰ
μὴ τὸ σημεῖον Ἰωνᾶ τοῦ Προφήτου.
Ὥσπερ γὰρ ἦν Ἰωνᾶς ἐν τῇ κοιλίᾳ
τοῦ κήτους τρεῖς ἡμέρας καὶ τρεῖς
νύκτας, οὕτως ἔσται ὁ Υἱὸς τοῦ ἀνθρώπου ἐν τῇ ·καρδίᾳ τῆς γῆς τρεῖς
ἡμέρας καὶ τρεῖς νύκτας.

turas; et quod visus sit Cephæ, deinde duodecim (Apostolis), postea
plus quam quingentis fratribus simul, quorum plerique ad hunc usque diem in vita sunt, nonnulli etiam obdormierunt. Deinde visus
est Iacobo, post Apostolis omnibus.
Postremo vero omnium, velut abor-
tivo, visus est et mihi.' Resurrectionem Christi pulchre etiam olim
adumbraverat Ionas Propheta,
quem typum Dominus noster Iesus
Christus ipse sibi accommodat, dum
Iudæis dicit (Matt. xii. 39): 'Natio
prava et adultera signum postulat,
nec aliud illi signum dabitur, quam
Ionæ Prophetæ. Quemadmodum
enim Ionas tribus diebus tribusque
noctibus in ventre ceti fuit: ita
filius hominis tres dies noctesque
in corde terræ erit.'

Ἐρώτησις νέ.

Ποῖον εἶναι τὸ ἕκτον ἄρθρον τῆς
πίστεως;

Ἀπ. Καὶ ἀνελθόντα εἰς τοὺς
οὐρανοὺς, καὶ καθεζόμενον ἐκ
δεξιῶν τοῦ Πατρός.

QUÆSTIO LV.

Sextus fidei Articulus quis est?

RESP. Qui adscendit in cœlos,
sedetque ad dexteram Patris.

Ἐρώτησις νϛ΄.

Τί μᾶς ἑρμηνεύει τὸ ἄρθρον τοῦτο
τῆς πίστεως;

Ἀπ. Τέσσαρα πράγματα διδάσκει
τὸ ἄρθρον τοῦτο· πρῶτον πῶς μὲ τὸ
ἴδιον σῶμα, εἰς τὸ ὁποῖον ἔπαθεν ἀληθῶς, καὶ ἀνέστη ἀπὸ τοὺς νεκροὺς,

QUÆSTIO LVI.

Quidnam iste nobis exponit Articulus?

RESP. Dogmata quattuor. Primum est, Christum illo ipso corpore
suo, in quo crucis supplicium vere
pertulerat, et in quo postea a mor-

μὲ τὸ ἴδιον ἐκεῖνο ἀνέβη εἰς τοὺς οὐρανοὺς, καὶ ἐκάθισεν εἰς τὴν δεξιὰν
τοῦ Πατρὸς μὲ δόξαν καὶ αἶνον.
Δεύτερον, πῶς ὡς ἄνθρωπος μόνος
ἀνέβηκεν εἰς τὸν οὐρανὸν, διατὶ ὡς
Θεὸς πάντοτε ἦτον εἰς τὸν οὐρανὸν,
καὶ εἰς πάντα τόπον. Τρίτον διδάσκει, πῶς τὴν ἀνθρωπότητα, ὅπου
ἐπῆρε μίαν φορὰν ἀπὸ τὴν παρθένον
Μαρίαν, ποτὲ δὲν τὴν ἐξαφῆκε· μὰ
μετ᾽ αὐτὴν πάλιν θέλει ἔλθει νὰ
κρίνῃ· καθὼς οἱ Ἄγγελοι εἶπασιν
(Πραξ. ά. ιά.) εἰς τοὺς Ἀποστόλους·
οὗτος ὁ Ἰησοῦς ὁ ἀναληφθεὶς ἀφ᾽
ὑμῶν εἰς τὸν οὐρανὸν οὕτως ἐλεύσε-
ται, ὃν τρόπον ἐθεάσασθε αὐτὸν πο-
ρευόμενον εἰς τὸν οὐρανόν. Τέταρτον διδάσκει, πῶς ὁ Χριστὸς, εἶναι
μόνον εἰς τὸν οὐρανὸν, καὶ ὄχι εἰς
τὴν γῆν κατὰ τὸν τρόπον τῆς σαρκὸς,
ὅπου ἐφόρεσε, καὶ συνανεστράφηκεν
εἰς τὴν γῆν· μὰ κατὰ τὸν μυστηριώδη
τρόπον, ὅπου εὑρίσκεται εἰς τὴν θείαν εὐχαριστίαν, εἶναι καὶ εἰς τὴν γῆν
ὁ αὐτὸς Υἱὸς τοῦ Θεοῦ, Θεὸς καὶ ἄνθρωπος, κατὰ μετουσίωσιν. Ἔστωντας καὶ ἡ οὐσία τοῦ ἄρτου νὰ μεταβάλλεται εἰς τὴν οὐσίαν τοῦ ἁγίου
σώματος αὐτοῦ· καὶ ἡ οὐσία τοῦ
οἴνου εἰς τὴν οὐσίαν τοῦ τιμίου αἵματος αὐτοῦ· διὰ τὸ ὁποῖον πρέπει νὰ
δοξάζωμεν, καὶ νὰ λατρεύωμεν τὴν
ἁγίαν εὐχαριστίαν ὁμοίως καθὼς καὶ
αὐτὸν τὸν Σωτῆρα μας Ἰησοῦν.

tuis resurrexerat, eodem inquam ipso in cœlum adscendisse, et ad dexteram Patris cum gloria ac laude
consedisse. Secundum, qua homo
est, illum tantummodo in cœlum
adscendisse; namque qua Deus est,
semper in cœlo fuit locisque aliis
omnibus. Tertium est: Christum
humanam naturam, semel ex B.
Virgine assumtam, nunquam postea dimisisse, eademque etiam vestitum olim ad judicium reventu-
rum. Sicuti Angeli Apostolis dicebant (Actor. i. 11): ‘Hic Iesus,
qui a vobis in cœlum receptus est,
ita redibit, quemadmodum eum in
cœlum ire vidistis.’ Quartum quod
docet, hoc est: Christum nunc in
cœlo tantum esse, non vero in terra
eo corporis sui modo, quo olim,
dum his in locis agebat, usus fuerat; verum modo sacramentali,
quo in sacra cœna præsto est, eundem Dei filium, Deum hominemque, etiam in terra adesse, nimirum per Transsubstantiationem.
Quippe substantia panis in substantiam sanctissimi corporis ipsius convertitur; et substantia vini
in substantiam pretiosi sanguinis
ipsius. Quamobrem sanctam Eucharistiam sic venerari adorareque
nos oportet, quemadmodum ipsum
Servatorem nostrum Iesum

Ἐρώτησις νζ'.

Ποῖον εἶναι τὸ ἕβδομον ἄρθρον τῆς πίστεως;

Ἀπ. Καὶ πάλιν ἐρχόμενον μετὰ δόξης κρῖναι ζῶντας καὶ νεκροὺς, οὗ τῆς βασιλείας οὐκ ἔσται τέλος.

Ἐρώτησις νή.

Τί μᾶς διδάσκει τοῦτο τὸ ἄρθρον τῆς πίστεως;

Ἀπ. Τρία πράγματα· πρῶτον πῶς ὁ Χριστὸς μέλλει νὰ στρέψῃ διὰ νὰ κρίνῃ ζῶντας καὶ νεκροὺς, καθὼς ὁ ἴδιος λέγει (Ματθ. κέ. λά.) διὰ λόγου του· ὅταν δὲ ἔλθῃ ὁ Υἱὸς τοῦ ἀνθρώπου ἐν τῇ δόξῃ αὐτοῦ καὶ πάντες οἱ ἅγιοι ἄγγελοι μετ' αὐτοῦ. Καὶ θέλει ἔλθει τόσον γοργὰ (Ματθ. κδ'. κζ'.), ὥσπερ ἡ ἀστραπὴ ἐξέρχεται ἀπὸ ἀνατολῶν, καὶ φαίνεται ἕως δυσμῶν, οὕτως ἔσται καὶ ἡ παρουσία τοῦ Υἱοῦ τοῦ ἀνθρώπου. Περὶ (εἰς τὸ αὐτὸ ςίχῳ λς'.) δὲ τῆς ἡμέρας τῆς παρουσίας ἐκείνης καὶ τῆς ὥρας οὐδεὶς οἶδεν, οὔτε οἱ ἄγγελοι. Μ' ὅλον τοῦτο προτήτερα μέλλει, νὰ γενοῦσι τὰ πράγματα τοῦτα· νὰ κηρυχθῇ τὸ Εὐαγγέλιον (εἰς τὸ αὐτὸ ςίχῳ ιδ'. καὶ κά.) εἰς ὅλα τὰ ἔθνη, νὰ ἔλθῃ ὁ Ἀντίχριστος, νὰ γενοῦσι μεγάλοι πόλεμοι, πεῖναις, θανατικὰ, καὶ ἕτερα ὅμοια· καὶ διὰ νὰ τὰ εἰπῷ συντόμως, μεγάλη πολλὰ θλίψις θέλει γένῃ, κατὰ τὰ λόγια τοῦ Κυρίου λέγοντος·

QUÆSTIO LVII.

Septimus fidei Articulus quis est?

RESP. *Qui iterum venturus est in gloria, iudicatum vivos et mortuos, cuius regni nullus finis erit.*

QUÆSTIO LVIII.

Quid iste nos Articulus docet?

RESP. Tria. Primum est, rediturum Christum, iudicatum vivos ac mortuos. Sicut ipse suis verbis testatur (Matt. xxv. 31): 'Quando venerit filius hominis in gloria sua, et sancti omnes Angeli cum illo.' Venturus autem est usque adeo velociter (Matt. xxiv. 27): 'Ut fulgur, quod exit ab oriente, et apparet ad occasum usque; eiusmodi item erit adventus filii hominis.' 'Atqui (ibidem 36) diem et horam adventus illius nemo novit, ne quidem Angeli.' Prius tamen ut eveniant hæc ipsa, necesse est. Nimirum (vers. 14) ut annuncietur Evangelium omnibus gentibus: ut veniat Antichristus: ut fiant bella horrida ac immania: itemque fames frugumque penuria et pestilentia aliaque consimilia. Atque ut summatim absolvam, multæ antea magnæque afflictiones secundum verbum Domini exsistent (vers. 21):

ἔσται γὰρ τότε θλίψις μεγάλη, οἷα οὐ γέγονεν ἀπ᾽ ἀρχῆς κόσμου ἕως τοῦ νῦν, οὐδ᾽ οὐ μὴ γένηται. Διὰ τὴν κρίσιν ταύτην φανερὰν ὁμιλεῖ λέγων (β΄. Τιμ. δ΄. ά.) ὁ Ἀπόστολος· διαμαρτύρομαι οὖν ἐγὼ ἐνώπιον τοῦ Θεοῦ καὶ τοῦ Κυρίου Ἰησοῦ Χριστοῦ τοῦ μέλλοντος κρίνειν ζῶντας καὶ νεκροὺς κατὰ τὴν ἐπιφάνειαν αὐτοῦ καὶ τὴν βασιλείαν αὐτοῦ.

'Eo tempore magna erit afflictio, cuiusmodi ab origine mundi ad hoc usque tempus nec fuit, nec in posterum futura est.' De hoc iudicio manifeste hunc in modum disserit Apostolus (2 Tim. iv. 1): 'Testificor igitur ego coram Deo et Domino Iesu Christo, qui vivos mortuosque in apparitione sua et regno suo iudicaturus est.'

Ἐρώτησις νθ΄.

Τί διδάσκει δεύτερον τὸ ἄρθρον τοῦτο;

Ἀπ. Πῶς εἰς τὴν τελευταίαν κρίσιν οἱ ἄνθρωποι θέλουσιν ἀποδώσειν λόγον διὰ τοὺς λογισμοὺς, διὰ τὰ λόγια καὶ διὰ τὰ ἔργα· κατὰ τὴν γραφὴν τὴν (Ματθ. ιβ΄. λς΄.) λέγουσαν· λέγω δὲ ὑμῖν, ὅτι πᾶν ῥῆμα ἀργὸν, ὃ ἐὰν λαλήσουσιν οἱ ἄνθρωποι, ἀποδώσουσι περὶ αὐτοῦ λόγον ἐν ἡμέρᾳ κρίσεως· καὶ ὁ Ἀπόστολος (ά. Κορ. δ΄. έ.) λέγει· ὥστε μὴ πρὸ καιροῦ τι κρίνετε, ἕως ἂν ἔλθῃ ὁ Κύριος· ὃς καὶ φωτίσει τὰ κρυπτὰ τοῦ σκότους· καὶ φανερώσει τὰς βουλὰς τῶν καρδιῶν· καὶ τότε ὁ ἔπαινος γενήσεται ἑκάστῳ ἀπὸ τοῦ Θεοῦ.

QUÆSTIO LIX.

Quid secundo loco hic docet Articulus?

RESP. Quod extremo in iudicio cogitationum, dictorum factorumque suorum omnium rationem redituri sunt homines, teste Scriptura (Matt. xii. 36): 'Dico ego vobis, quod de quovis otioso verbo, quod locuti homines fuerint, rationem in die iudicii reddent.' Et Apostolus ait (1 Cor. iv. 5): 'Ne itaque, ne ante tempus quidquam iudicetis, donec venerit Dominus: qui et abscondita tenebrarum illustrabit, et consilia cordium manifestabit, et tunc sua cuique laus a Deo reddetur.'

Ἐρώτησις ξ΄.

Τί διδάσκει τρίτον τοῦτο τὸ ἄρθρον;

Ἀπ. Πῶς εἰς τὴν ἡμέραν ἐκείνην καθ᾽ ἕνας κατὰ τὰ ἔργα του θέλει λάβει τελείαν καὶ αἰωνίαν πληρωμήν·

QUÆSTIO LX.

Quid tertio loco hic Articulus docet?

RESP. Quod illo die unusquisque secundum promerita sua plenam eamque sempiternam accepturus sit

διατὶ κάποιοι θέλουσιν ἀκούσειν τὴν ἀπόφασιν ταύτην (Ματθ. κέ. λδ'.)· δεῦτε οἱ εὐλογημένοι τοῦ Πατρός μου, κληρονομήσατε τὴν ἡτοιμασμένην ὑμῖν βασιλείαν ἀπὸ καταβολῆς κόσμου. Καὶ ἄλλοι ἀκούσουσι τὴν ἀπόφασιν ταύτην (ςιχ. μά.)· πορεύεσθε ἀπ' ἐμοῦ οἱ κατηραμένοι εἰς τὸ πῦρ τὸ αἰώνιον, τὸ ἡτοιμασμένον τῷ διαβόλῳ καὶ τοῖς ἀγγέλοις αὐτοῦ· ὅπου (Μαρ. θ'. μδ'. μή.) ὁ σκώληξ αὐτῶν οὐ τελευτᾷ, καὶ τὸ πῦρ οὐ σβέννυται.

mercedem, quippe alii hanc audient sententiam (Matt. xxv. 34): 'Venite benedicti Patris mei, et hereditario jure possidete præparatum vobis a mundi exordio regnum.' Alii e contrario tristissimum hocce carmen audient (vers. 41): 'Discedite a me maledicti in ignem illum sempiternum, qui Diabolo atque Angelis ejus structus paratusque est;' (Marc. ix. 44): 'ubi vermis eorum non emoritur, et ignis non exstinguitur.'

Ἐρώτησις ξά.

Τάχα τὸν καιρὸν ἐκεῖνον ὅλοι οἱ ἄνθρωποι θέλουσιν ἀποδώσειν λόγον διὰ τὰ ἔργα τους, ἢ ξεχωριστὰ καθ' ἕνας ἀποθνήσκωντας ἀποδίδει τὸν λογαριασμὸν τῆς ξωῆς του, καὶ ἂν εἶναι κριτήριον μερικόν;

Ἀπ. Καθὼς εἰς τὴν ἡμέραν ἐκείνην τῆς τελευταίας κρίσεως δὲν ζητᾶται τινὰς λογαριασμὸς ξεχωρᾷ διὰ τὸν καθ' ἕνα, διατὶ ὅλα τὰ πράγματα εἶναι γνωρισμένα σιμᾶ εἰς τὸν Θεὸν, καθ' ἕνας εἰς τὸν καιρὸν τοῦ θανάτου του γνωρίζει τὰ ἁμαρτήματά του· τέτοιας λογῆς μάλιστα ὕστερα ἀπὸ τὸν θάνατον καθ' ἕνας θέλει γνωρίζει τὴν ἀμοιβὴν τῶν ἔργων του. Διατὶ ἐπειδὴ καὶ τὰ ἔργα του θέλουσιν εἶναι φανερά, λοιπὸν καὶ ἡ ἀπόφασις τοῦ Θεοῦ εἶναι φανερὴ εἰς αὐτόν· καθὼς λέγει ὁ θεολόγος Γρηγό-

QUÆSTIO LXI.

Illo igitur fortasse die universi homines actionum rerumque suarum reddituri rationem sunt, an vero singulatim unusquisque, dum lucis hujus usuram relinquit, vitæ suæ rationem reddit, atque particulare quoddam exercetur judicium? RESP. Quemadmodum illo extremi judicii die ratio de unoquoque singillatim non exigitur; siquidem Deo res simul omnes per se mani-festissimæ sunt, atque ut unusquis que in articulo mortis suæ satis suorum sibi delictorum conscius est: ita eodem prorsus modo post mortem operum suorum remunerationem unusquisque probe novit. Quoniam itaque opera ipsius manifesto patent; patet etiam Dei in illum sententia. Sicuti ait Gregorius Theologus (laudatione funebri

ριος (λόγῳ εἰς Καισάριον τὸν ἀδελ-
φόν)· πείθομαι σοφῶν λόγοις, ὅτι
ψυχὴ πᾶσα καλή τε καὶ θεοφιλὴς,
ἐπειδὰν τοῦ συνδεδεμένου σώματος
ἐνθένδε ἀπαλλαγῇ, εὐθὺς ἐν συναισθήσει καὶ θεωρίᾳ τοῦ μένοντος αὐτὴν
καλοῦ γενομένη (ἅτε τοῦ ἐπισκοτοῦν-
τος ἀνακαθαρθέντος, ἢ ἀποτεθέντος,
ἢ—οὐκ οἶδ᾽ ὅ, τι καὶ λέγειν χρή) θαυ-
μασίαν τινα ἡδονὴν ἥδεται καὶ ἀγάλ-
λεται, καὶ ἵλεως χωρεῖ πρὸς τὸν ἑαυτῆς δεσπότην, ὥσπερ τι δεσμωτήριον
χαλεπὸν τὸν ἐνταῦθα βίον ἀποφυ-
γοῦσα· καὶ τὰς περικειμένας ἀποσει-
σαμένη πέδας· ὑφ᾽ ὧν τὸ τῆς διανοίας πτερὸν καθείλκετο, καὶ οἷον
ἤδη τῇ φαντασίᾳ καρποῦται τὴν
ἀποκειμένην μακαριότητα· μικρὸν δ᾽
ὕστερον καὶ τὸ συγγενὲς σαρκίον
ἀπολαβοῦσα, ᾧ τὰ ἐκεῖθεν συνεφι-
λοσόφησε, παρὰ τῆς καὶ δούσης καὶ
πιστευθείσης γῆς, τρόπον ὃν οἶδεν ὁ
ταῦτα συνδήσας καὶ διαλύσας Θεός·
τούτῳ συγκληρονομεῖ τῆς ἐκεῖθεν
δόξης. Ὁμοίως πρέπει νὰ λογιά-
ζωμεν καὶ διὰ τὰς ψυχὰς τῶν ἁμαρτωλῶν ἐκ τοῦ ἐναντίου· πῶς καὶ
αὐταὶ γροικοῦσι καὶ ἠξεύρουσι τὴν
κόλασιν, ὅπου ταῖς ἀναμένει. Καὶ
καλᾷ καὶ νὰ μὴν ἔχουσι μήτε οἱ δίκαιοι μήτε οἱ ἁμαρτωλοὶ τελείαν τὴν
ἀμοιβὴν τῶν ἔργων τῶν πρὶν τῆς
τελευταίας κρίσεως, διατὶ μὲ ὅλον
τοῦτο δὲν εἶναι ὅλαις εἰς μίαν καὶ
τὴν αὐτὴν κατάστασιν, μήτε εἰς τὸν
αὐτὸν τόπον πέμπονται. Ἀπὸ τοῦ-

fratris sui Cæsarii, p. 56, Bas. 173,
Par.): Ego vero sapientum sermo-
nibus adductus credo, bonam quam-
libet Deoque acceptam animam, ut
e conjugato soluta corpore hinc dis-
cedit, confestim intellectu ac contemplatione boni illius, quod ipsam
manet, fruentem (quippe eo, quod
caliginem antea offundebat, perpur-
gato jam aut deposito, aut — sed
haud scio satis quod usurpem verbum), singulari et mirifica quadam
efferri atque exsultare lætitia hila-
remque admodum ad Dominum
suum properare; dum ita nimirum
ex hac vita tanquam ex ærumnoso
quodam ergastulo aufugit, et cir-
cumjectas excutit pedicas, quibus
gravatæ antea mentis alæ deprime-
bantur; jamque adeo velut imagi-
nando reservatam sibi degustare felicitatem: verum paullo post, ubi
cognatum corpusculum, quocum
olim ætheriam illam vitam religio-
sissime vivebat, de terra, quæ illud
et dederat, et suæ traditum fidei as-
servarat, receperit, modo eo, quem
solus novit, qui ista duo tum colli-
gavit tum dissolvit Deus; tum una
cum illo cœlestis gloriæ hereditatem
cernere. Pari ratione de facinoro-
sorum animis e contrario existimandum, illos videlicet extemplo sensum item intellectumque destinato-
rum sibi cruciatuum hábere. Quamvis vero neque justi neque damnati

το γίνεται φανερὸν, πῶς τὸ τοιοῦτο νὰ μὴ γίνεται πρὶν τῆς τελευταίας κρίσεως χωρὶς κρίσεως μερικῆς· εἶναι λοιπὸν μερικὸν κριτήριον. Καὶ ὅταν λέγωμεν πῶς δὲν ζητᾷ λογαριασμὸν τῆς ζωῆς μας ὁ Θεὸς ἀπὸ ἐμᾶς, τοῦτο νοεῖται πῶς δὲν ἀποδίδοται ὁ λογαριασμὸς τοῦτος κατὰ τὸν ἐδικόν μας τρόπον.

plenam rerum actionumque suarum mercedem ante extremum assequantur judicium : non tamen in uno et eodem omnes statu sunt, nec in unum compelluntur locum. Hinc facile patet, hoc ipsum ante postremum illud judicium sine particulari aliquo judicio non fieri, atque hujuscemodi particulare judicium omnino esse. Quando igitur dicimus, non exigere a nobis Deum vitæ nostræ rationem, tum intelligendum est, non reddi hanc rationem secundum proprium nostrorum judiciorum morem.

Ἐρώτησις ξβ'.

Τάχα αἱ ψυχαὶ τῶν ἁγίων μετὰ θάνατον εἰς τὸν αὐτὸν βαθμὸν εὑρίσκονται;

Ἀπ. Διατὶ αἱ ψυχαὶ δὲν μισεύουσιν ἀπὸ τὸν κόσμον τοῦτον εἰς μίαν καὶ τὴν αὐτὴν χάριν· τέτοιας λογῆς καὶ ὕστερα, ἀφ' οὗ μισεύσουσιν ἀπὸ τὸν κόσμον, δὲν στέκουνται εἰς ἕνα καὶ τὸν αὐτὸν βαθμὸν τῆς μακαριότητος κατὰ τὴν Χριστοῦ διδασκαλίαν, ὅπου (Ἰωαν. ιδ'. β'.) λέγει· ἐν τῇ οἰκίᾳ τοῦ Πατρός μου μοναὶ πολλαί εἰσι· καὶ ἀλλαχοῦ (Λουκ. ζ'. μζ'.)· ἀφέωνται αἱ ἁμαρτίαι αὐτῆς αἱ πολλαί, ὅτι ἠγάπησε πολύ· ᾧ δὲ ὀλίγον ἀφίεται, ὀλίγον ἀγαπᾷ. Ὁμοίως καὶ ὁ Ἀπόστολος (Ῥωμ. ζ'. ς'.) λέγει, ὅτι ἀποδώσει ἑκάστῳ κατὰ τὰ ἔργα αὐτοῦ.

QUÆSTIO LXII.

Numquid vero in eodem beatitudinis gradu, postquam e vita excesserunt, collocatæ Sanctorum animæ sunt ?

RESP. Quoniam animæ non in uno et eodem gratiæ divinæ gradu ex hoc mundo emigrant; pari modo, postquam hinc emigrarunt, non in uno eodemque beatitatis gradu consistunt; Christo ipso his illud docente verbis (Ioh. xiv. 2): 'In domo Patris mei multæ sunt mansiones;' et alibi (Luc. vii. 47): 'Remissa sunt multa illius peccata, quoniam dilexit multum; at parum diligit, cui parum remittitur.' Consimiliter et Apostolus ait (Rom. ii. 6): 'Quod redditurus sit cuique secundum opera sua.'

Ἐρώτησις ξγ'.

Τίνα γνώμην πρέπει νὰ ἔχωμεν δι' ἐκείνους, ὅπου ἀποθνήσκουσιν εἰς τὴν ὀργὴν τοῦ Θεοῦ;

Ἀπ. Πῶς μετὰ τὴν ἐσχάτην κρίσιν ἄλλοι θέλουσιν εἶναι εἰς μεγαλητέρην κόλασιν, καὶ ἄλλοι εἰς μικρὰν, αἰωνίως· κατὰ τὸ εἰρημένον (Λουκ. ιβ'. μζ'.) εἰς τὴν Γραφήν· ἐκεῖνος δὲ ὁ δοῦλος ὁ γνοὺς τὸ θέλημα τοῦ Κυρίου ἑαυτοῦ καὶ μὴ ἑτοιμάσας μηδὲ ποιήσας πρὸς τὸ θέλημα αὐτοῦ δαρήσεται πολλάς. Ὁ δὲ μὴ γνοὺς, ποιήσας δὲ ἄξια πληγῶν, δαρήσεται ὀλίγας.

Ἐρώτησις ξδ'.

Ἀποθνήσκουσι τάχα καὶ ἄνθρωποι, ὅπου νὰ εἶναι ἀνάμεσα τῶν σωζομένων καὶ ἀπολλυμένων;

Ἀπ. Τοιαύτης τάξεως ἄνθρωποι δὲν εὑρίσκονται. Μὰ βέβαια πολλοὶ ἀπὸ τοὺς ἁμαρτωλοὺς ἐλευθερώνουνται ἀπὸ τῶν δεσμῶν τοῦ ᾅδου, ὄχι μὲ μετάνοιαν ἢ ἐξομολόγησιν ἐδικήν τους, καθὼς ἡ Γραφὴ (Ψαλ. ϛ'. ἑ.) λέγει· ἐν γὰρ τῷ ᾅδῃ τίς ἐξομολογήσεταί σοι; καὶ ἀλλαχοῦ (Ψαλ. ριέ. ιζ'.)· οὐχ οἱ νεκροὶ αἰνέσουσί σε, Κύριε, οὐδὲ πάντες οἱ καταβαίνοντες εἰς ᾅδου· ἀλλὰ μὲ τὰς εὐποιίας τῶν ζώντων καὶ προσευχὰς ὑπὲρ αὐτῶν τῆς ἐκκλησίας, καὶ μὲ τὴν ἀναίμακτον μάλιστα θυσίαν, ὅπου καθ' ἡμέραν προσφέρει ἡ ἐκκλησία

QUÆSTIO LXIII.

Quid de iis vero judicandum, qui decedentes in offensa apud Deum sunt?

RESP. Horum alios, ultimo peracto judicio, gravioribus, alios levioribus, sed æternis omnes tormentis cruciatum iri, dicente ita Scriptura (Luc. xii. 47): 'Servus ille, qui novit voluntatem Domini sui, neque tamen præparavit fecitque secundum voluntatem illius, vapulabit multis. Sed qui non cognovit et plagis tamen digna admisit, paucis vapulabit.'

QUÆSTIO LXIV.

Annon et aliqui sic diem suum obeunt, ut beatorum damnatorumque medii sint?

RESP. Hujusmodi homines nulli reperiuntur. At illud probe constat, sceleratos homines non paucos de orci claustris eripi atque liberari, non sua quidem ipsorum pœnitentia sive confessione, quemadmodum Scriptura dicit (Psa. vi. 5): 'Quis enim confiteatur tibi in inferno?' et loco alio (Psa. cxv. 17): 'Non laudabunt te mortui, Domine, neque omnes qui descendunt in infernum,' verum piis superstitum officiis et ecclesiæ pro ipsis deprecationibus, præcipue vero per incruentum (Liturgiæ) sacrificium, quod Ecclesia

διὰ τοὺς ζῶντας καὶ τεθνηκότας κοινῶς ὅλους, καθὼς καὶ ὁ Χριστὸς ἀπέθανε δι᾽ αὐτούς. Καὶ ὅτι δὲν ἐλευθερώνουνται ἀφ᾽ ἑαυτῶν των αἱ τοιαῦται ψυχαὶ, λέγει ὁ Θεοφύλακτος εἰς τὸ κατὰ Λουκᾶν ς΄. κεφ. ἑρμηνεύων τὸν λόγον τοῦ Χριστοῦ, ὅπου εἶπεν, ὅτι ἔχει ἐξουσίαν ἐπὶ τῆς γῆς ἀφιέναι ἁμαρτίας· ὅρα, ὅτι ἐπὶ τῆς γῆς ἀφίενται αἱ ἁμαρτίαι· ἕως οὗ γὰρ ἐσμὲν ἐπὶ τῆς γῆς, δυνάμεθα ἐξαλεῖψαι τὰς ἁμαρτίας ἡμῶν· μεθ᾽ ὃ μέντοι τῆς γῆς ἀπαναστῶμεν, οὐκ ἔτι ἡμεῖς αὐτοὶ δυνάμεθα δι᾽ ἐξομολογήσεως ἐξαλεῖψαι τὰς ἁμαρτίας ἡμῶν· ἀποκέκλεισται γὰρ ἡ θύρα. Καὶ εἰς τὸ κβ΄. τοῦ Ματθαίου ἑρμηνεύων τὸ· δήσαντες αὐτοῦ χεῖρας καὶ πόδας, ἀντὶ τῶν πρακτικῶν τῆς ψυχῆς δυνάμεων, λέγει· ἐν τῷ αἰῶνι μὲν γὰρ τῷ ἐνεστῶτι ἔστι πρᾶξαι καὶ ἐνεργῆσαι τὶ, ἐν δὲ τῷ μέλλοντι δεσμοῦνται πᾶσαι αἱ πρακτικαὶ δυνάμεις τῆς ψυχῆς· καὶ οὐκ ἔστι ποιῆσαι τι ἀγαθὸν εἰς ἀντισήκωσιν τῶν ἁμαρτιῶν. Καὶ εἰς τὸ κέ. τοῦ αὐτοῦ εὐαγγελίου· μεταμελείας γὰρ καὶ ἐργασίας καιρὸς οὐκ ἔστι μετὰ τὴν ἐνθένδε ἀποβίωσιν. ᾽Απὸ τὰ ὁποῖα λόγια γίνεται φανερὸν, πῶς ὕστερα ἀπὸ τὸν θάνατον ἡ ψυχὴ δὲν ἠμπορεῖ νὰ ἐλευθερωθῇ ἢ νὰ μετανοήσῃ· καὶ νὰ κάμῃ τίποτες ἔργον, ὅπου νὰ λυτρωθῇ ἀπὸ τὸν δεσμὸν τοῦ ᾅδου, μόνον αἱ θεῖαι λειτουργίαι, αἱ προσευχαὶ καὶ ἐλεημοσύναι, ὅπου γίνουν-

pro vivis mortuisque omnibus communiter, quemadmodum et Christus pro iis pariter mortuus est, quotidie offert. Ceterum haudquaquam suapte opera animas hujusmodi ex inferis liberari, docet Theophylactus in caput sextum Lucæ, ea Christi verba, quibus potestatem remittendi peccata in terra sibi vindicat, exponens (immo in cap. v. 24, p. 236, Rom.): Observa, inquit, remitti peccata in terra. Quamdiu enim in hac terra commoramur, peccata nostra expungere possumus; at postquam e terra demigravimus, non possumus deinde ipsimet ope confessionis peccata nostra inducere. Jam enim oppessulatæ sunt fores. Et in cap. xx. Matt. enarrans hæc verba (vers. 13): Colligantes manus illius ac pedes; per quæ animæ facultates activæ designantur, ait: In seculo quidem præsenti agere operarique licet; at in futuro vinciuntur omnes activæ facultates animæ, nec tum boni quidpiam efficere possumus in compensationem nostrarum noxiarum. Et in cap. xxv. ejusdem Evangelii (p. 108): Non est pœnitentiæ operationisque tempus post discessum ex hac vita. Quibus ex verbis clarum evadit, ab excessu suo leberari per se animam, pœnitentiamque agere non posse, nihilque ejusmodi moliri, quo infernis eximatur vinculis. Solæ igitur

ται δι᾽ αὐτὴν ἀπὸ τοὺς ζῶντας, ἐκεῖνα τὴν ὠφελοῦσι πολλότατα, καὶ ἀπὸ τὰ δεσμὰ τοῦ ᾅδου τὴν ἐλευθε-ροῦσιν.

sacræ liturgiæ precesque et eleemo-synæ, quæ animæ caussa a vivent-ibus præstantur, illam plurimum adjuvant, atque ex Acheronte redi-munt.

'Ερώτησις ξέ.

QUÆSTIO LXV.

Τίνα γνώμην πρέπει νὰ ἔχωμεν διὰ ταῖς ἐλεημοσύναις καὶ ταῖς ἀγαθοερ-γίαις, ὅπου δίδουνται διὰ τοὺς ἀπο-θαμένους ;

Quid igitur sentiendum de elee-mosynis piisque officiis, quæ in refrigerium mortuorum præstan-tur?

'Απ. Περὶ τούτου ὁ ἴδιος Θεοφύ-λακτος διδάσκει εἰς τὸ ιβ΄. κεφ. ϛιχ. έ. τοῦ Λουκᾶ, ἐξηγῶντας τὸν λόγον τοῦ Χριστοῦ, ὅπου εἶπεν· φοβήθητε τὸν ἐξουσίαν ἔχοντα ἐμβαλεῖν εἰς τὴν γέενναν· γράφει δὲ οὕτως· ‘ὅρα γὰρ, ὅτι οὐκ εἶπε, φοβήθητε τὸν με-τὰ τὸ ἀποκτεῖναι βάλλοντα εἰς τὴν γέενναν, ἀλλ᾽ ἐξουσίαν ἔχοντα βα-λεῖν· οὐ γὰρ πάντως οἱ ἀποθνήσ-κοντες ἁμαρτωλοὶ βάλλονται εἰς τὴν γέενναν· ἀλλ᾽ ἐν τῇ ἐξουσίᾳ κεῖται τοῦτο τοῦ Θεοῦ· ὥστε καὶ τὸ συγ-χωρεῖν. Τοῦτο δὲ λέγω διὰ τὰς ἐπὶ τοῖς κεκοιμημένοις γινομένας προσ-φορὰς καὶ τὰς διαδόσεις · αἳ οὐ μικ-ρὰ συντελοῦσι τοῖς καὶ ἐν ἁμαρ-τίαις βαρείαις ἀποθανοῦσιν. Οὐ πάντως οὖν μετὰ τὸ ἀποκτεῖναι βάλ-λει εἰς τὴν γέενναν· ἀλλ᾽ ἐξουσίαν ἔχει βαλεῖν. Μὴ τοίνυν ἐλλείψω-μεν ἡμεῖς σπουδάζοντες δι᾽ ἐλεημο-συνῶν καὶ πρεσβειῶν ἐξιλεοῦσθαι τὸν ἐξουσίαν μὲν ἔχοντα βαλεῖν, οὐ πάντως δὲ τῇ ἐξουσίᾳ ταύτῃ χρώμε-

RESP. Ea de re idem Theophy-lactus in caput xii. Lucæ exponens verba Christi (vers. 5): ‘ Timete il-lum, qui potestatem conjiciendi in geennam habet;’ ita commentatur: Animadverte, sodes, non dicere, Christum, timete illum, qui post-quam occidit, in geennam conjicit, sed qui potestatem conjiciendi ha-bet. Neque enim omnes omnino, qui in peccatis suis moriuntur, in geennam conjiciuntur. Sed id in Dei situm est manu; sicut et veni-am illis largiri, quod propter pias oblationes erogationesque, quæ dor-mientium bono fiunt, dico; quippe quæ non parum conducunt iis eti-am, qui gravissimis sceleribus con-taminati hinc decesserunt. Itaque non omnino postquam occidit, in geennam sontes projicit Deus; sed projiciendi potestatem habet. Ne igitur cessemus nos etiam atque eti-am adniti, quo eleemosynis et inter-cessionibus nostris illum propitie-

νον, ἀλλὰ καὶ συγχωρεῖν δυνάμε-
νον.' Ἀπὸ τὴν διδασκαλίαν λοιπὸν τῆς ἁγίας Γραφῆς καὶ τοῦ Πατρὸς τούτου τὴν ἐξήγησιν τοῦτο
ἐκβάζωμεν, πῶς πρέπει πάντως νὰ
παρακαλοῦμεν διὰ τοὺς κεκοιμημέ-
νους, καὶ νὰ προσφέρωμεν θυσίας
ἀναιμάκτους, διδόντες ἐλεημοσύνας·
ἐπειδὴ ἐκεῖνοι δὲν ἠμποροῦσι τὰ τοιαῦτα νὰ κάμουσιν διὰ τοὺς ἑαυτούς
τους.

Ἐρώτησις ξς'.

Πῶς πρέπει νὰ γροικοῦμεν διὰ τὸ
πῦρ τὸ καθαρτήριον;

Ἀπ. Οὐδεμία Γραφὴ διαλαμβάνει
περὶ αὐτοῦ, νὰ εὑρίσκεται δηλαδὴ κᾂν
μία πρόσκαιρος κόλασις καθαρτικὴ
τῶν ψυχῶν, ὕστερα ἀπὸ τὸν θάνα-
τον· μάλιστα ἡ γνώμη τοῦ Ὠριγέ-
νους διὰ τοῦτο κατεκρίθη ὑπὸ τῆς
Ἐκκλησίας εἰς τὴν δευτέραν Σύνοδον τὴν ἐν Κωνσταντινουπόλει. Ἔτι
δὲ φανερὸν εἶναι, πῶς ὕστερα ἀπὸ
τὸν θάνατον ἡ ψυχὴ δὲν ἠμπορεῖ νὰ
δεχθῇ κᾂν ἕνα μυστήριον τῆς ἐκκλη-
σίας· καὶ ἂν ἴσως καὶ ἤθελεν εἶναι
δυνατὸν, νὰ πλερώσῃ ἀτή της διὰ τὰ
ἁμαρτήματά της, ἤθελεν ἠμπορεῖ νὰ
δεχθῇ καὶ μέρος ἀπὸ τὸ μυστήριον
τῆς μετανοίας, τὸ ὁποῖον ἔστωντας
καὶ νὰ εἶναι ἔξω ἀπὸ τὴν ὀρθόδοξον
διδασκαλίαν. Ἡ ἐκκλησία μὲ δικαιοσύνην προσφέρει δι' αὐτὰς τὴν ἀναίμακτον θυσίαν, καὶ προσευχὰς πρὸς
Θεὸν πέμπει ὑπὲρ ἀφέσεως τῶν ἁμαρ-

mus, qui hac projiciendi potestate
instructus ea non semper utitur;
sed veniam etiam indulgere potest.
Igitur e doctrina S. Scripturæ Pa-
trisque hujus expositione illud de-
ducimus: oportere omnino a nobis
preces pro defunctis concipi atque
offerri incruenta sacrificia spargi-
que liberali manu eleemosynas; siquidem non possunt pia hujusmodi
opera sua caussa ipsimet præstare.

QUÆSTIO LXVI.

De Purgatorio autem Igne, quid
nobis judicandum?

RESP. Nihil usquam de eo in sacris literis traditur, quod tempora-
ria ulla poena, animorum expurga-
trix, a morte exsistat. Imo vero
eam præcipue ob caussam in secunda Synodo Constantinopolitana ab
Ecclesia Origenis damnata est sententia. Præterea per se satis manifestum est, morte semel obita nullius Sacramenti ecclesiastici participem fieri posse animam. Tum si
fieri fortassean posset, ut admissas
noxias sua satisfactione ipsamet ex-
piaret: haud dubie etiam partem
aliquam sacramenti poenitentiæ accipere eadem posset. Quod quoniam ab orthodoxa doctrina abhorret;
jure meritoque ecclesia manium
istorum caussa sacrificium incruentum offert, precesque ad Deum ab-
legat ad impetrandam eorum ve-

τιῶν αὐτῶν· μὰ ὄχι ἐκεῖνοι νὰ πάσ-
χουσι κᾶν μίαν κόλασιν, καὶ μετ'
αὐτὴν νὰ καθαρίζωνται. Τοὺς δὲ
μύθους τινῶν ἀνθρώπων, ὅπου λέγουσι περὶ ψυχῶν, πῶς, ὅταν μισεύσουσιν ἀμετανόητας ἀπὸ τὸν κόσμον,
κολάζονται εἰς σουβλία, εἰς νερὰ καὶ
λίμναις, ποτὲ δὲν τοὺς ἐδέχθηκεν ἡ
ἐκκλησία.

niam, quæ olim in vita deliquerant;
non vero ut ipsi nonnihil supplicii
sustinentes eo dein perpurgentur.
Ceterum fabulas quorundam hominum, quas de animis comminiscun-
tur: quod videlicet, ubi pœnitentia
non procurati satis expiatique fato
intercipiuntur, discrucientur subu-
lis, aquis, lacubus nostra nunquam
admisit probavitque ecclesia.

Ἐρώτησις ξζ'.

Ποῖος τόπος εἶναι ἰδίᾳ διωρισμένος
εἰς ταῖς ψυχαῖς ἐκείνων, ὅπου ἀποθνήσκουσιν εἰς τὴν χάριν τοῦ Θεοῦ;

Ἀπ. Αἱ ψυχαὶ τῶν ἀνθρώπων ἐκείνων, ὅπου μισεύουσιν ἀπὸ τὸν κόσμον
τοῦτον εὑρισκόμεναι εἰς τὴν χάριν τοῦ
Θεοῦ μὲ μετάνοιαν τῶν ἰδίων ἁμαρτημάτων, ἔχουσι τόπον τὰς χεῖρας
τοῦ Θεοῦ· διατὶ οὕτω λέγει (Σοφ.
γ'. ά.) ἡ ἁγία Γραφή· δικαίων ψυχαὶ
ἐν χειρὶ Θεοῦ, καὶ οὐ μὴ ἄψηται αὐτῶν
βάσανος. Ἀκόμι ὀνομάζεται ὁ τόπος
αὐτῶν παράδεισος· καθὼς ὁ Χριστὸς ὁ Κύριος ἡμῶν (Λουκ. κγ'. μγ'.)
εἶπεν εἰς τὸν σταυρὸν ἀπάνω πρὸς τὸν
λῃστήν· ἀμὴν λέγω σοι, σήμερον μετ'
ἐμοῦ ἔσῃ ἐν τῷ παραδείσῳ. Κράζεται
καὶ κόλπος τοῦ Ἀβραάμ, κατὰ τὸ
(Λουκ. ιϛ'. κβ'.) γεγραμμένον· ἐγένετο δὲ ἀποθανεῖν τὸν πτωχὸν, καὶ ἀπε-
νεχθῆναι αὐτὸν ἀπὸ τῶν ἀγγέλων εἰς
τὸν κόλπον τοῦ Ἀβραάμ. Καὶ βασιλεία τῶν οὐρανῶν, κατὰ τὸν
λόγον τοῦ Κυρίου (Ματθ. ή. ιά.) λέ-

Quæstio LXVII.

Quinam locus peculiariter ani-
mabus eorum destinatus est, qui in
gratia Dei vita concedunt?

Resp. Animæ hominum, quæ
hoc mundo egredientes in gratia
apud Deum sunt criminumque
suorum pœnitentiam egerunt, locum suum *in manibus Dei* habent. Sic enim sacra loquitur
Scriptura (Sap. iii. 1): 'Animæ
justorum in manu Dei sunt, nec
attinget eas cruciatus.' Nuncupatur earum locus etiam *Paradisus*,
quomodo Dominus noster Christus
latroni in cruce dixit (Luc. xxiii.
43): 'Amen dico tibi, hodie mecum eris in Paradiso.' Vocatur et
sinus Abraami, uti scriptum est
(Luc. xvi. 22): 'Contigit autem,
mori pauperem, et deferri ab Angelis in sinum Abraami.' Dicitur etiam *regnum cælorum*, secundum dictum Domini (Matt.
viii. 11): 'Dico vobis, multi ab

γοντος· λέγω δὲ ὑμῖν, ὅτι πολλοὶ ἀπὸ ἀνατολῶν καὶ δυσμῶν ἥξουσι, καὶ ἀνακλιθήσονται μετὰ 'Αβραὰμ καὶ 'Ισαὰκ καὶ 'Ιακὼβ ἐν τῇ βασιλείᾳ τῶν οὐρανῶν. Διὰ τοῦτο ὅποιος ὀνομάσει τὸν τόπον τοῦτον ἕνα ὄνομα ἀπὸ ὅσα εἴπαμεν, δὲν σφάλει· μόνον νὰ γροικᾷ, πῶς εἶναι αἱ ψυχαὶ εἰς τὴν χάριν τοῦ Θεοῦ καὶ εἰς τὴν οὐράνιον βασιλείαν· καὶ, καθὼς οἱ ἐκκλησιαστικοὶ ὕμνοι ψάλλουσιν, εἰς τὸν οὐρανόν.

'Ερώτησις ξή.

Καὶ αἱ ψυχαὶ ἐκεῖναι, ὅπου μισεύουσιν ἀπὸ τὰ κορμία εὑρισκόμεναι εἰς θεϊκὴν ὀργὴν, ποῦ εἶναι;

'Απ. Ὁ τόπος ἐκείνων μὲ διαφορετικὰ ὀνόματα λέγεται. Πρῶτον ὀνομάζεται ᾅδης, εἰς τὸν ὁποῖον ἀπώσθηκεν ὁ διάβολος, ἀπὸ τὸν οὐρανὸν διωχθείς· ὡς λέγει ὁ Προφήτης ('Ησ. ιδ'. ιδ'.)· ἔσομαι ὅμοιος τῷ ὑψίστῳ (εἶπεν ὁ διάβολος)· νῦν δὲ εἰς ᾅδου καταβήσῃ, καὶ εἰς τὰ θεμέλια τῆς γῆς. Δεύτερον λέγεται πῦρ αἰώνιον· λέγει γὰρ (Ματθ. κέ. μά.) ἡ Γραφή. πορεύεσθε ἀπ' ἐμοῦ οἱ κατηραμένοι εἰς τὸ πῦρ τὸ αἰώνιον, τὸ ἡτοιμασμένον τῷ διαβόλῳ καὶ τοῖς ἀγγέλοις αὐτοῦ. 'Ακόμι σκότος ἐξώτερον (εἰς τὸ αὐτὸ λ'.)· καὶ τὸν ἀχρεῖον δοῦλον ἐκβάλλετε εἰς τὸ σκότος τὸ ἐξώτερον· ἐκεῖ ἔσται ὁ κλαυθμὸς καὶ ὁ βρυγμὸς τῶν ὀδόντων. 'Ονομάζεται ἀκόμι καὶ μὲ ἄλλα ὀνόματα. μὰ ὅλα σημαίνουσι,

oriente et occidente venient, et accumbent cum Abraamo, Isaaco et Jacobo in regno cœlorum.' Nihil igitur erraverit, quisquis locum illum aliquo istorum nominum, quæ recensuimus, nominaverit; modo ut recte intelligat, esse animas in gratia Dei et in regno cœlesti et ut hymni ecclesiastici canunt in cœlo.

Quæstio LXVIII.

At ubinam locorum illæ agunt animæ, quæ e corporibus suis exeuntes in offensa apud Deum sunt?

Resp. Variis locus ille designatur nominibus. Primum nuncupatur *Infernus,* in quem exturbatus cœlo Diabolus detrusus est, teste Propheta (Jes. xiv. 14): 'Similis ero Altissimo' (dixit Diabolus). 'Nunc autem in infernum descendes, et in fundamenta terræ.' Secundum est: *Ignis sempiternus;* dicit enim Scriptura (Matt. xxv. 41): 'Discedite a me maledicti in ignem illum sempiternum, qui Diabolo et Angelis illius paratus est.' Etiam *Tenebræ exteriores* (ibidem versu 30): 'Ejicite inutilem istum servum in tenebras exteriores, ubi erit ejulatio et stridor dentium.' Appellatur et aliis vocabulis, sed quæ omnia locum condemnationis iræque divinæ valent, quem in locum

πῶς εἶναι τόπος τῆς κατακρίσεως καὶ
τῆς θείας ὀργῆς· εἰς τὸν ὁποῖον κα-
ταβαίνουσιν αἱ ψυχαὶ ἐκείνων, ὅπου
μισεύουσιν ἀπ᾽ ἐδῶ ὠργισμένοι ἀπὸ
τὸν Θεὸν καὶ ἀπεγνωσμένοι. Μὰ τοῦ-
·ο εἶναι ἄξιον νὰ τὸ ἠξεύρῃ καθ᾽ ἕνας,
πῶς αἱ ψυχαὶ τῶν δικαίων, καλᾷ καὶ
νὰ εἶναι εἰς τοὺς οὐρανοὺς, δὲν ἐπή-
ρασι μὲ ὅλον τοῦτο τέλειον τὸν στέφανον πρὶν τῆς τελευταίας κρίσεως μήτε
αἱ ψυχαὶ τῶν κατακρίτων τελείαν κόλασιν πάσχουσι· μὰ ὕστερα ἀπὸ τὴν
ἐσχάτην κρίσιν θέλουσι πάρειν αἱ
ψυχαὶ μαζὶ μὲ τὰ σώματα τελείως τὸν
·στέφανον τῆς δόξης ἢ τὴν κόλασιν.

animæ eorum descendunt, qui hinc
demigrant invisi offensique Deo ac
damnati. Porro et illud omnibus
tenendum est, animas justorum,
quamquam cœlo jam receptas,
neutiquam tamen ante extremum
judicium plenam perfectamque
gloriæ coronam consequi, neque
rursus animas damnatorum plenam antea ultionem pœnamque
perpeti. Verum post summum
illud atque decretorium judicium
animas una cum corporibus suis
usquequaque aut coronam gloriæ
aut suppliciorum ferre cruciatus.

Ἐρώτησις ξθ'.

• Πῶς εἶναι τὸ ὄγδοον ἄρθρον τῆς
πίστεως ;

Ἀπ. Καὶ εἰς τὸ Πνεῦμα, τὸ
ἅγιον, τὸ κύρον, τὸ ζωοποιὸν,
τὸ ἐκ τοῦ Πατρὸς ἐκπορευόμε-
νον· τὸ σὺν Πατρὶ καὶ Υἱῷ συμ-
προσκυνούμενον, καὶ συνδοξαζόμενον, τὸ λαλῆσαν διὰ τῶν
Προφητῶν.

QUÆSTIO LXIX.

Octavus fidei Articulus quomodo habet ?

RESP. *Et in Spiritum Sanctum,
Dominum et vivificantem, qui ex
Patre procedit, et una cum Patre et Filio adoratur et glorifica-
tur, qui item per Prophetas locutus est.*

Ἐρώτησις ό.

Τί διδάσκει τὸ ἄρθρον τοῦτο τῆς
πίστεως ;

Ἀπ. Τρία πράγματα· πρῶτον
πῶς τὸ Πνεῦμα τὸ ἅγιον εἶναι Θεὸς,
ὁμοούσιος τῷ Πατρὶ καὶ τῷ Υἱῷ,
τὸ ὁποῖον εἶναι φανερὸν ἀπὸ τὰ
λόγια τοῦ Ἀποστόλου (ά. Κορ. ιβ'.
δ'.) λέγοντος· Διαιρέσεις δὲ χαρισ-

QUÆSTIO LXX.

Quid iste docet Articulus ?

RESP. Tria. Primum est: Spiritum Sanctum Deum esse Patri et
Filio consubstantialem, quod ex
verbis Apostoli manifestum est (1
Cor. xii. 4): 'Distinctiones donorum
sunt, sed idem est Spiritus. Et dis-

μάτων εἰσί, τὸ δὲ αὐτὸ Πνεῦμα· καὶ
διαιρέσεις διακονιῶν εἰσί, καὶ ὁ αὐτὸς Κύριος· καὶ διαιρέσεις ἐνεργη-
μάτων εἰσίν, ὁ δὲ αὐτὸς Θεὸς, ὁ
ἐνεργῶν τὰ πάντα ἐν πᾶσι· καὶ
ἀλλαχοῦ (β'. Κορ. ιγ'. ιγ'.)· ἡ χάρις τοῦ Κυρίου ἡμῶν Ἰησοῦ Χριστοῦ, καὶ ἡ ἀγάπη τοῦ Θεοῦ, καὶ ἡ
κοινωνία τοῦ ἁγίου Πνεύματος μετὰ πάντων ὑμῶν. Εἰς τὰ ὁποῖα,
καλᾷ καὶ ποτὲ νὰ προηγῇται τὸ
Πνεῦμα τὸ ἅγιον, καὶ ποτὲ ὁ Υἱὸς,
τοῦτο γίνεται διατὶ εἶναι ὁμοούσια,
καὶ ἰσότιμα, καὶ τὰ τρία πρόσωπα·
μὰ ὄχι νὰ ἔχῃ κᾶν μίαν οὐσίαν ὁ
Υἱὸς ἢ τὸ Πνεῦμα, καθὼς ἔχει ὁ
Πατήρ· ἀμέσως καὶ ὁμοίως εἰς τὸν
Υἱὸν καὶ τὸ Πνεῦμα. Καὶ εἰς τὰς
Πράξεις τῶν Ἀποστόλων τὸ αὐτὸ
ἔδειξεν ὁ Πετρὸς (Πράξ. ἑ. γ'.), λέγων τῷ Ἀνανίᾳ· διατὶ ἐπλήρωσεν
ὁ σατανᾶς τὴν καρδίαν σου, ψεύ-
σασθαί σε τὸ Πνεῦμα τὸ ἅγιον;
καὶ τελειώνωντας τὸν ἴδιον λόγον
προστίθησιν· οὐκ ἐψεύσω ἀνθρώποις ἀλλὰ τῷ Θεῷ. Θεὸς ἄρα τὸ
Πνεῦμα τὸ ἅγιον.

tinctiones ministeriorum sunt, sed
idem est Dominus. Et distinctiones operationum sunt, sed idem est
Deus, qui omnia operatur in omnibus.' Et alibi (2 Cor. xiii. 13):
'Gratia Domini nostri Jesu Christi
et caritas Dei et communio Spiritus
Sancti sit vobiscum omnibus.' Quibus in locis quod alibi primo loco
nominatur Spiritus Sanctus rursus
alibi Filius, id ea re fit, quod tres
Personæ ejusdem substantiæ, hono-
risque æqualis consortes sint; minime vero, quasi essentia a Spiritu
Sancto Filius differat, aut a Filio
Spiritus. Id quod dictu nefas est;
sed quod ejusdem et essentiæ et gloriæ (personæ divinæ), ut jam diximus, consortes sint, et quod proxime
ac pariter in simplicissimo *simul*,
suam a Patre originem Filius Spi-
ritusque habeant, per generationem
Filius, at Spiritus per processionem.
Idem et in Actibus Apostolicis declarat Petrus Ananiam alloquens
cap. v. 3): 'Quare implevit Satanas
cor tuum, ut falleres Spiritum Sanctum?' et mox sermonem illum suum
absolvens addit: 'Non mentitus es
hominibus sed Deo.' Est itaque
omnino Spiritus Sanctus Deus.

Ἐρώτησις οά.

Ποῖον εἶναι τὸ δεύτερον, ὅπου
διδάσκει τὸ ἄρθρον τοῦτο;
Ἀπ. Διδάσκει πῶς τὸ Πνεῦμα τὸ

QUÆSTIO LXXI.

Quodnam secundum est, quod
hoc Articulo docetur?
RESP. Quod Spiritus Sanctus ex

ἅγιον ἐκπορεύεται ἐκ μόνου τοῦ Πατρὸς, ὡς πηγῆς καὶ ἀρχῆς τῆς θεότητος· διὰ τὸ ὁποῖον ὁ αὐτὸς Σωτὴρ μᾶς διδάσκει (Ἰωαν. ιέ. κϛ'.) λέγων· ὅταν ἔλθῃ ὁ Παράκλητος, ὃν ἐγὼ πέμψω ὑμῖν παρὰ τοῦ Πατρὸς, τὸ Πνεῦμα τῆς ἀληθείας, ὃ παρὰ τοῦ Πατρὸς ἐκπορεύεται. Τὴν διδασκαλίαν ταύτην τὴν ἑρμηνεύει ὁ ἱερὸς Ἀθανάσιος εἰς τὸ σύμβολόν του· τὸ Πνεῦμα τὸ ἅγιον ἀπὸ τοῦ Πατρὸς, οὐ πεποιημένον, οὔτε δεδημιουργημένον, οὔτε γεγεννημένον· ἀλλ' ἐκπορευτόν. Ὁ Θεὸς (ὁ αὐτὸς Ἀθανάσ. ἐν ταῖς ἱεραῖς ἐρωτήσεσι. δ'.) καὶ Πατὴρ, αὐτὸς μόνος ἐστὶν αἴτιος τοῖς δυσὶ καὶ ἀγέννητος· ὁ δὲ Υἱὸς ἐκ μόνου τοῦ Πατρὸς αἰτιατὸς, καὶ γεννητύς· καὶ αὐτὸ τὸ Πνεῦμα ἐκ μόνου τοῦ Πατρὸς αἰτιατὸν καὶ ἐκπορευτὸν, διὰ δὲ τοῦ Υἱοῦ ἐν τῷ κόσμῳ ἀποστελλόμενον. Καὶ ὁ θεολόγος Γρηγόριος (λόγ. έ. περὶ θεολογίας) οὕτω φησί· τὸ Πνεῦμα τὸ ἅγιον, ὃ παρὰ τοῦ Πατρὸς ἐκπορεύεται, ὃ καθ' ὅσον μὲν ἐκεῖθεν ἐκπορεύεται, οὐ κτίσμα· καθ' ὅσον δὲ οὐ γεννητὸν, οὐχ Υἱός· καθ' ὅσον δὲ ἀγεννήτου καὶ γεννητοῦ μέσον, Θεός. Περὶ τούτου εἴρηται πλατύτερον εἰς τὸ πρῶτον ἄρθρον· φθάνει λοιπὸν τώρα νὰ κρατοῦμεν βέβαιον καὶ νὰ πιστεύωμεν ἐκεῖνο, ὅπου ὁ Χριστὸς μᾶς ἐδίδαξε, καὶ ἡ ἀνατολικὴ ἐκκλησία ἡ καθολικὴ καὶ ὀρθόδοξος πιστεύει, καὶ ὡμολόγησεν εἰς τὴν δευτέραν οἰκουμενικὴν σύνο-

solo Patre, velut fonte ac origine divinitatis, procedit. Qua de re ita ipse nos Servator noster edocet (Joh. xv. 26): 'Quando venerit Paracletus, quem ego a Patre missurus sum, Spiritus veritatis, qui a Patre procedit.' Eandem doctrinam ita in Symbolo suo explicat S. Athanasius (T. ii. p. 32): Spiritus Sanctus a Patre, non factus, nec creatus, nec genitus, sed procedens est (id. in sacris Quæstionibus IV. T. II. p. 438, conf. Quæst. XV.); Deus et Pater, ipse solus duorum caussa est, et ingenitus. Filius ex solo Patre, ortus sui caussa, editus genitusque est. Ipse etiam Spiritus de solo Patre ut caussa oritur ac procedit; sed per Filium in mundum emittitur. Et Gregorius Theologus hunc in modum loquitur (de Theologia, oratione V. de Spiritu Sancto, Ald. f. 58, Par. p. 597): Spiritus Sanctus, qui a Patre procedit, quatenus illinc procedit, res creata non est; quatenus autem genitus non est, non est Filius; quatenus vero inter ingenitum et genitum medius est, Deus utique est. Verum de hoc negotio uberius jam actum a nobis fuit ad articulum primum. Satis igitur nunc nobis est, ut firma fide teneamus credamusque, quod ipse nos Christus docuit, quod orientalis Catholica et Orthodoxa credit Ecclesia et in secundo œcumeni-

δον, καὶ ἐκύρωσε τὸ σύμβολον χωρὶς τῆς προσθήκης· καὶ ἐκ τοῦ Υἱοῦ. Καὶ ἐναντίον ἐκείνων, ὅπου ἐπροσθέσασι τὸν λόγον τοῦτον καὶ ἐκ τοῦ Υἱοῦ, ἔκαμεν ἐπιτίμησιν, ὄχι μόνον ἡ ἀνατολικὴ ἐκκλησία ἡ ὀρθόδοξος καὶ καθολικὴ, ἀλλὰ καὶ ἡ δυτικὴ τῆς Ῥώμης· τὸ ὁποῖον διαμαρτύρονται δύο πίνακαις ἀργυραῖ, εἰς τὰς ὁποίας ἦτον γεγραμμένον τὸ ἱερὸν σύμβολον τῆς πίστεως Ἑλληνιστὶ εἰς τὴν μίαν καὶ εἰς τὴν ἄλλην Λατινιστὶ, χωρὶς τὴν πρόσθεσιν τούτου τοῦ μέρους καὶ ἐκ τοῦ Υἱοῦ· αἱ ὁποῖαι μὲ πρόσταγμα τοῦ Πάπα Ῥώμης Λέοντος τρίτου ἐκρέμαντο εἰς τὴν ἐκκλησίαν τοῦ ἁγίου Πέτρου, ἐν ἔτει Χριστοῦ ωθʹ. ὡς φησὶ βαρώνιος. Διὰ τοῦτο ὅποιος στέκιται σταθερὸς καὶ βέβαιος εἰς τὴν πίστιν τούτην, ἔχει βεβαίαν ἐλπίδα τῆς σωτηρίας του, διατὶ δὲν παρεκκλίνει καθόλου ἀπὸ τὴν κοινὴν γνώμην τῆς ἐκκλησίας.

Ἐρώτησις οβ΄.

Τί διδάσκει τρίτον τὸ ἄρθρον τοῦτο;

Ἀπ. Διδάσκει πῶς τὸ Πνεῦμα τὸ ἅγιον εἶναι εὑρετὴς τῆς ἁγίας Γραφῆς, τόσον τῆς παλαιᾶς ὅσον καὶ τῆς νέας, καὶ αὐτὸ τὴν ὡμίλησε μὲ τὸ μέσον πολλῶν συνεργῶν. Διὰ τοῦτο καθὼς ἡ Γραφὴ τῆς παλαιᾶς διαθήκης τέτοιας λογῆς καὶ τῆς νέας εἶναι διδασκαλία τοῦ ἁγίου Πνεύματος. Καὶ διὰ τὴν ἀφορμὴν τούτην εἰς ὅλας

co Concilio communiter professa fuit; atque symbolum sine isthac appendicula: *et ex Filio* ratum esse jussit. Immo vero gravi illos censura, qui hæc adjecere verba, non modo orientalis Ecclesia orthodoxa ac Catholica perstrinxit: sed et occidentalis Romana. Quod satis confirmant tabulæ binæ argenteæ, in quarum altera Græce altera Latine sacrum fidei symbolum, non adjecta ista particula, *et ex Filio*, proscriptum erat. Quæ jussu Leonis tertii, Papæ Romani, in æde S Petri fixæ propositæque sunt, anno Christi IOCCCIX, quemadmodum prodit Baronius (A. 809, tmem. 62). Qui itaque constans et firmus in hac fide persistit, is indubiam suæ salutis habet fiduciam, ut qui nihil omnino declinat a communi Ecclesiæ sententia.

QUÆSTIO LXXII.

Quid tertium est, quod in hoc Articulo docetur ?

RESP. Spiritum Sanctum sacræ Scripturæ tam Veteris quam Novæ, genuinum esse auctorem, illamque per manus multorum administrorum ipsum edidisse, eaque re ut Veteris Testamenti Scripturam ita etiam Novi Spiritus Sancti doctrinam esse. Quamobrem quidquid sancti Patres in omnibus uni-

τὰς οἰκουμενικὰς συνόδους καὶ τοπικὰς, τὰς ὀρθοδόξους, ὅπου καὶ ἂν ἐγίνησαν, πίστευε πῶς ὅ, τι ἀποφασίσασιν οἱ ἅγιοι Πατέρες, νὰ εἶναι ἀπὸ τὸ ἅγιον Πνεῦμα· καθὼς εἴπασιν οἱ Ἀπόστολοι (Πράξ ιέ. κή.) εἰς τὴν σύνοδον· ἔδοξε τῷ ἁγίῳ Πνεύματι καὶ ἡμῖν· κατὰ τὸ παράδειγμα τῶν ὁποίων καὶ αἱ λοιπαὶ ἄλλαι ὀρθόδοξοι σύνοδοι ἐσυμπεραίνασι τὰ δόγματά τως μὲ τὸν ὅμοιον τρόπον.

versalibus atque particularibus orthodoxis Conciliis quocunque tandem loco habitis statuerunt: id a Spiritu Sancto profectum esse credas oportet; quemadmodum in Synodo sua ipsimet loquuntur Apostoli (Act xv. 28): 'Visum est Spiritui Sancto ac nobis.' Quorum exemplo cetera item orthodoxa Concilia simili modo decreta sua concluserunt.

Ἐρώτησις ογ´

Πόσα καὶ ποῖα εἶναι τὰ Χαρίσματα τοῦ ἁγίου Πνεύματος;

Ἀπ. Ἑπτὰ, διὰ τὰ ὁποῖα λέγει ἡ Γραφὴ εἰς τὴν Ἀποκάλυψιν (Κεφ. δ´. έ.)· καὶ ἑπτὰ λαμπάδες πυρὸς καιόμεναι ἐνώπιον τοῦ θρόνου· αἱ εἰσὶ τὰ ἑπτὰ πνεύματα τοῦ Θεοῦ. Ταῦτα λοιπὸν τὰ χαρίσματα τοῦ Πνεύματος ἢ μᾶλλον εἰπεῖν αὐτὸ τὸ Πνεῦμα ἦτον εἰς τὸν Χριστὸν πλουσιώτερα καὶ τελειότερα, ἢ κατ᾽ ἄνθρωπον, ὡς λέγει ὁ Προφήτης (Ἠσ. ιά. β´.)· καὶ ἀναπαύσεται ἐπ᾽ αὐτὸν πνεῦμα Κυρίου· πνεῦμα σοφίας καὶ συνέσεως· πνεῦμα βουλῆς καὶ ἰσχύος· πνεῦμα γνώσεως καὶ εὐσεβείας· καὶ ἐμπλήσει αὐτὸν πνεῦμα φόβου Θεοῦ. Τοῦτο βεβαιώνει ὁ εὐαγγελιστὴς Ἰωάννης (Κεφ. ά. ιδ´.) λέγωντας· καὶ ὁ λόγος σὰρξ ἐγένετο καὶ ἐσκήνωσεν ἐν ἡμῖν, καὶ ἐθεασάμεθα τὴν δόξαν αὐτοῦ, δόξαν ὡς μονογενοῦς παρὰ πατρὸς, πλήρης χάριτος καὶ ἀληθείας. Καὶ ἐκ τοῦ

Quæstio LXXIII.

Quot et quænam Spiritus Sancti Charismata sunt?

Resp. Septem. De quibus ita in Apocalypsi sacra Scriptura loquitur (iv. 5): 'Et septem lampades igneæ ardentes coram throno, quæ sunt septem Spiritus Dei.' Hæc igitur Spiritus dona, aut rectius loquendo, ipse Spiritus Sanctus in Christo, quam in ullo alio homine modis omnibus copiosiora atque consummatiora erant, dicente Propheta (Ies. xi. 2): 'Et requiescet super illum Spiritus Domini, Spiritus sapientiæ et intelligentiæ, Spiritus consilii et roboris, Spiritus cognitionis et pietatis, et implebit illum Spiritus timoris Domini.' Quod suo testimonio affirmat Evangelista Ioannes (i. 14): 'Et verbum caro factum est, et habitabat nobiscum et vidimus gloriam illius, ut gloriam unigeniti a Patre, ple-

πληρώματος αὐτοῦ ἡμεῖς πάντες ἐλά-
βομεν· καὶ χάριν ἀντὶ χάριτος· διότι τὸ Πνεῦμα ἦτον εἰς αὐτὸν ὡς
ὁμοούσιον αὐτῷ κατὰ τὴν θεότητα·
καὶ ἔπλησεν αὐτὸν σοφίας καὶ χάρι-
τος· κατὰ τὸ (Λουκ. β'. μ'.) εἰρημέ-
νον· τὸ δὲ παιδίον ηὔξανε καὶ ἐκρα-
ταιοῦτο πνεύματι, πληρούμενον σοφίας, καὶ χάρις Θεοῦ ἦν ἐπ' αὐτό.
Καὶ ταῦτα πάντα πρέπει νὰ γροικοῦνται κατὰ τὴν ἀνθρωπότητα.

Ἐρώτησις οδ'.

Ποῖον εἶναι τὸ πρῶτον χάρισμα
τοῦ ἁγίου Πνεύματος ;

Ἀπ. Τὸ πρῶτον χάρισμα εἶναι ἡ
σοφία· ἤγουν ἡ ἄνωθεν σοφία, διὰ
τὴν ὁποίαν λέγει ὁ Ἀπόστολος (Ἰακ.
γ'. ιζ'.)· ἡ ἄνωθεν σοφία πρῶτον
μὲν ἁγνή ἐστιν, ἔπειτα εἰρηνικὴ, ἐπι-
εικὴς, εὐπειθὴς, μεστὴ ἐλέους καὶ καρ-
πῶν ἀγαθῶν· ἀδιάκριτος καὶ ἀνυπό-
κριτος. Εἰς τὴν σοφίαν τούτην ἐναν-
τιοῦται ἡ σαρκικὴ σοφία κατὰ τὸν
Ἀπόστολον τὸν (β'. Κορ. ά. ιβ'.) λέ-
γοντα· ὅτι ἐν ἁπλότητι καὶ εἰλικρι-
νείᾳ Θεοῦ, οὐκ ἐν σοφίᾳ σαρκικῇ, ἀλλ'
ἐν χάριτι Θεοῦ ἀνεστράφημεν ἐν τῷ
κόσμῳ. Ἐναντίον τῆς ὁποίας σαρ-
κικῆς καὶ κοσμικῆς σοφίας λέγει ὁ
ἴδιος Ἀπόστολος (ά. Κορ. ά. ιθ'.),
ἀναφέρωντας τὴν παλαιὰν Γραφὴν
(Ἡσ. κθ'. ιδ'. καὶ λγ'. ιή.)· ἀπολῶ
τὴν σοφίαν τῶν σοφῶν, καὶ τὴν σύνεσιν τῶν συνετῶν ἀθετήσω· ποῦ

num gratia et veritate' (v. 16), 'et
ex plenitudine ipsius nos omnes
accepimus, et gratiam pro gratia.'
Erat enim in Christo Spiritus Sanctus, ut ipsi secundum divinitatem
consubstantialis, ipsumque sapientia ac gratia replebat, prout dictum
est (Luc. ii. 40) : 'Puer vero adoles-
cebat et corroborabatur Spiritu, et
implebatur sapientia, et gratia Dei
cum illo erat.' Quæ omnia de humanitate Christi exaudienda sunt.

QUÆSTIO LXXIV.

Quodnam primum Spiritus Sancti charisma est ?

RESP. Primum donum est Sapientia. Nimirum superna illa sapientia, de qua ita Apostolus (Iac.
iii. 17): 'Quæ e supernis est sapientia, primum quidem casta est,
deinde pacifica, æqua, obsequens,
plena misericordia ac bonis fructibus, sine disceptatione, sine simulatione.' Huic Sapientiæ contraria carnalis est secundum Apostolum (2 Cor. i. 12): 'Quod in simplicitate et sinceritate Dei, non in
carnali sapientia, sed in gratia
Dei conversati fuimus in mundo.'
Quam carnalem ac mundanam sapientiam ita idem incessit Apostolus (1 Cor. i. 19), antiquam addu-
cens Scripturam (Ies. xxix. 14, et
xxxiii. 18): 'Perdam sapientiam
sapientum, et intelligentiam in·

σοφὸς, ποῦ γραμματεὺς, ποῦ συζητη- τῆς τοῦ αἰῶνος τούτου ; οὐχὶ ἐμώρα- νεν ὁ Θεὸς τὴν σοφίαν τοῦ κόσμου τούτου ;

telligentium rejiciam; ubi sapiens ubi scriba, ubi disputator seculi hujus? nonne infatuavit Deus sa- pientiam mundi hujus?

Ἐρώτησις οέ.

QUÆSTIO LXXV.

Ποῖον εἶναι τὸ δεύτερον χάρισμα τοῦ ἁγίου Πνεύματος ;

Secundum Spiritus Sancti do- num, quodnam est ?

Ἀπ. Τὸ χάρισμα τῆς συνέσεως ἢ κατανοήσεως τῶν ἀποῤῥήτων καὶ τῆς θείας θελήσεως· περὶ τῆς ὁποίας ἡ Γραφὴ διδάσκει ('Εξ. λς'. ά.) λέγου- σα· καὶ πᾶς σοφὸς τῇ διανοίᾳ, ᾧ ἐδόθη σοφία καὶ ἐπιστήμη ἐν αὐτοῖς, συνιέναι ποιεῖν πάντα τὰ ἔργα, τὰ καλὰ τὰ ἅγια καθήκοντα· κατὰ πάν- τα ὅσα συνέταξε Κύριος. Καὶ εἰς τοὺς περὶ τὸν Δανιὴλ (κεφ. ά. ιζ'.)· καὶ ἔδωκεν αὐτοῖς ὁ Θεὸς σύνεσιν καὶ φρόνησιν ἐν πάσῃ γραμματικῇ καὶ σοφίᾳ· καὶ Δανιὴλ συνῆκεν ἐν πασῃ ὁράσει καὶ ἐνυπνίοις. Καὶ ἀλλαχοῦ (Λουκ. κδ'. μέ.)· τότε διήνοιξεν αὐ- τῶν τὸν νοῦν τοῦ συνιέναι τὰς Γρα- φάς. Καὶ ὁ Ἀπόστολος (β'. Τιμ. β'. ζ'.) λέγει· δῴη γάρ σοι Κύριος σύνεσιν ἐν πᾶσιν. Εἰς τὴν σύνεσιν τούτην εἶναι ἀντικειμένη ἡ ἀνοησία καὶ ἀπιστία· διὰ τὴν ὁποίαν λέγει (Λουκ. κδ'. κέ.) ὁ Κύριος· ᾧ ἀνόητοι καὶ βραδεῖς τῇ καρδίᾳ τοῦ πιστεύειν ἐπὶ πᾶσιν οἷς ἐλάλησαν οἱ Προφῆται. Καὶ εἰς ἄλλον τόπον (Γαλ. γ'. γ'.) λέγει ὁ Ἀπόστολος· οὕτως ἀνόητοί ἐστε ; ἐναρξάμενοι Πνεύματι, νῦν σαρκὶ ἐπιτελεῖσθε ;

RESP. Donum Intelligentiæ sive cognitionis arcanorum et occultæ voluntatis divinæ, de qua ita docet Scriptura (Exod. xxxvi. 1): ' Et om- nis sapiens animo, cui data erat sapi- entia et scientia in illis; ut intelli- genter sciret facere omnia opera pul- chra et sancta, modo debito, secun- dum omnia ea, quæ præscripserat Dominus.' Et de sodalibus Danielis (Dan. i. 17): ' Et dedit illis Deus in- telligentiam et prudentiam in omni literatura ac sapientia. Daniel au- tem intellectu omnis visionis et in- somnii instructus erat.' Et alibi (Luc. xxiv. 45): ' Tunc aperuit illis men- tem, ut intelligerent scripturas.' Et Apostolus (2 Tim. ii. 7): ' Det vero tibi Dominus intelligentiam in om- nibus.' Intelligentiæ huic opposita est stultitia et incredulitas, de qua sic ait Dominus (Luc. xxiv. 25): 'O stulti et tardi corde ad credendum iis omnibus, quæ locuti sunt Pro- phetæ.' Et alio loco Apostolus (Gal. iii. 3): ' Adeo stulti estis, ut, quum in Spiritu cœperitis, nunc in carne perficiamini ?

'Ερώτησις ος'.

Ποῖον εἶναι τὸ τρίτον χάρισμα τοῦ ἁγίου Πνεύματος ;

'Απ. Τὸ τρίτον χάρισμα τοῦ ἁγίου Πνεύματος εἶναι ἡ βουλὴ, ἡ ὑποῖα συντρέχει πρὸς τὴν θείαν δόξαν καὶ πρὸς τὴν σωτηρίαν τῆς ἀνθρωπίνης ψυχῆς· καὶ εἶναι συμφωνισμένη μὲ τὴν δικαιοσύνην. Διὰ τὴν ὁποῖαν καὶ ἡ Γραφὴ (Πρᾶξ. κ'. κζ'.) λέγει· οὐ γὰρ ὑπεστειλάμην τοῦ μὴ ἀναγγεῖλαι ὑμῖν πᾶσαν τὴν βουλὴν τοῦ Θεοῦ. Εἰς αὐτὴν εἶναι ἐναντία ἡ βουλὴ τῶν ἀσεβῶν, διὰ τὴν ὁποῖαν λέγει ὁ Ψαλμῳδός (Ψαλ. ά. ά.)· μακάριος ἀνὴρ, ὃς οὐκ ἐπορεύθη ἐν βουλῇ ἀσεβῶν· καὶ ἀλλαχοῦ (Ψαλ. λγ'. ί.)· Κύριος διασκεδάζει βουλὰς ἐθνῶν, ἀθετεῖ δὲ λογισμοὺς λαῶν, καὶ ἀθετεῖ βουλὰς ἀρχόντων.

'Ερώτησις οζ'.

Ποῖον εἶναι τὸ τέταρτον χάρισμα τοῦ ἁγίου Πνεύματος ;

'Απ. Ἡ ἰσχὺς, διατὶ φυλάττοντες πᾶσαν σταθερότητα καὶ ἀνδρείαν εἰς τὴν πίστιν, πρέπει νὰ ἀντιστέκωμεν εἰς ὅλους τοὺς πειρασμούς. Περὶ ταύτης ἡ Γραφὴ (ά. Κορ, ις'. ιγ'.) λέγει· γρηγορεῖτε, στήκετε ἐν τῇ πίστει, ἀνδρίζεσθε, κραταιοῦσθε· καὶ ἀλλαχοῦ ('Εφ. ς'. ιδ'.)· στῆτε οὖν περιζωσάμενοι τὴν ὀσφῦν ὑμῶν ἐν ἀληθεία, καὶ ἐνδυσάμενοι τὸν θώρακα τῆς δικαιοσύνης· καὶ ὑποδυσάμενοι τοὺς

QUÆSTIO LXXVI.

Quodnam tertium Spiritus Sancti donum est?

RESP. Tertium Spiritus Sancti charisma est Consilium, quod gloriæ divinæ animæque humanæ saluti provehendæ servit et cum justitia pulchre consentit. De hujusmodi consilio ita loquitur Scriptura (Actor. xx. 27): 'Non subterfugiebam, quominus annunciarem vobis omne consilium Dei.' Huic consilio consilium impiorum oppositum est, de quo divinus Psalmista (Psa. i. 1): 'Beatus vir, qui non ambulat in consilio impiorum. Et alibi (Psa. xxxiii. 10): 'Dominus dissipat consilia gentium, reprobat cogitationes populorum, et reprobat consilia principum.'

QUÆSTIO LXXVII.

Quartum Spiritus Sancti donum, quodnam est?

RESP. Robur. Quippe tuentes omnem constantiam ac fortitudinem in fide, mascule obsistere debemus quibuslibet tentationibus, de quo robore animi ita Scriptura (1 Cor. xvi. 13): 'Vigilate, persistite in fide, viri estote, corroboramini.' Et alibi (Ephes. vi. 14): 'State igitur lumbis balteo præcinctis in veritate, induti thoracem justitiæ, et calceati pedibus,

πόδας ἐν ἑτοιμασίᾳ τοῦ Εὐαγγελίου τῆς εἰρήνης· ἐπὶ πᾶσιν ἀναλαβόντες τὸν θυρεὸν τῆς πίστεως, ἐν ᾧ δυνήσεσθε πάντα τὰ βέλη τοῦ πονηροῦ τὰ πεπυρωμένα σβέσαι· καὶ τὴν περικεφαλαίαν τοῦ σωτηρίου δέξασθε, καὶ τὴν μάχαιραν τοῦ Πνεύματος, ὅ ἐστι ῥῆμα Θεοῦ. Τὸ ἐναντίον τῆς ἰσχύος εἶναι ὁ φόβος, περὶ οὗ λέγει ὁ Ψαλμῳδός (Ψαλ. ιδ΄. ἑ.)· ἐκεῖ ἐφοβήθησαν φόβον, οὗ οὐκ ἦν φόβος. Καὶ ὁ Κύριος ἡμῶν Ἰησοῦς Χριστὸς μᾶς προστάσσει, νὰ μὴν ἔχωμεν τοιοῦτον φόβον (Λουκ. ιβ΄. δ΄.) λέγων· μὴ φοβεῖσθε ἀπὸ τῶν ἀποκτεινόντων τὸ σῶμα, καὶ μετὰ ταῦτα μὴ ἐχόντων περισσότερόν τι ποιῆσαι.

in præparatione Evangelii pacis. Super omnia adsumite scutum fidei, quo omnia mali illius igniti. jacula exstinguere queatis, et accipite galeam salutis et gladium Spiritus, qui est verbum Dei.' Robori adversatur Timor, de quo vates sacer (Psa. xiv. 5): 'Illic trepidaverunt timore, ubi non erat timor.' Et Dominus noster Iesus Christus timorem nos ejusmodi habere vetat (Luc. xii. 4): 'Ne timeatis eos, qui corpus occidunt, nec deinde amplius quidquam efficere possunt.'

Ἐρώτησις οή.

Ποῖον εἶναι τὸ πέμπτον χάρισμα τοῦ ἁγίου Πνεύματος;

Ἀπ. Ἡ γνῶσις εἶναι τὸ πέμπτον χάρισμα, τὴν ὁποίαν ὁ ἱερὸς Ψάλτης (Ψαλ. ζδ΄. ἰ.) ἑρμηνεύει, λέγων· ὁ παιδεύων ἔθνη, οὐχὶ ἐλέγξει, ὁ διδάσκων ἄνθρωπον γνῶσιν; καὶ ἕτερος Προφήτης (Ἱερ. γ΄. ιέ.) λέγει· καὶ δώσω ὑμῖν ποιμένας κατὰ τὴν καρδίαν μου· καὶ ποιμανοῦσιν ὑμᾶς ποιμαίνοντες μετ' ἐπιστήμης ἤτουν γνώσεως. Τούτη ἡ γνῶσις καὶ ἐπιστήμη πρέπει νὰ ἁπλώνεται εἰς τὸ νὰ γνωρίζῃ τὸ θέλημα τοῦ Θεοῦ, καὶ τοῦ νόμου του. Εἰς αὐτὴν ἐναντιώνεται ἡ ἄγνοια τοῦ νόμου καὶ τῆς θελήσεως τοῦ Θεοῦ· διὰ τὴν ὁποῖαν λέγει ὁ Ψαλμῳδός (Ψαλ. οθ΄. ς΄.)·

QUÆSTIO LXXVIII.

Quodnam quintum Spiritus Sancti charisma est?

RESP. Cognitio. Quam hunc in modum sacer Psaltes exponit (xciv. 10): 'Qui corripit gentes, nonne arguet qui docet hominem cognitionem?' Et Propheta alius (Ier. iii. 15): 'Dabo vobis pastores secundum cor meum, et pascent vos pascentes cum scientia, sive item cognitione.' Quæ cognitio et scientia in id potissimum extendenda atque explicanda est, ut voluntatem legemque Dei cognoscat. Contraria illi est inscientia legis voluntatisque divinæ, de qua auctor Psalmorum ait (Psa. lxxix.

ἔκχεον τὴν ὀργήν σου ἐπὶ τὰ ἔθνη τὰ μὴ γινώσκοντά σε, καὶ ἐπὶ βασιλείας, αἳ τὸ ὄνομά σου οὐκ ἐπεκαλέσαντο.

6): 'Effunde iram tuam in gentes, quæ te non noverunt, et in regna, quæ nomen tuum non invocant.'

Ἐρώτησις οθ´.

Ποῖον εἶναι τὸ ἕκτον χάρισμα τοῦ ἁγίου Πνεύματος;

Ἀπ. Ἡ εὐσέβεια· ἡ ὁποία μὲ τὴν ὀρθὴν πίστιν θεμελιώνεται εἰς τὴν ἐκτενῆ προσευχὴν καὶ εἰς τὰ ἀγαθὰ ἔργα· διὰ τὴν ὁποίαν οὕτω (ά. Τιμ. δ´. ή.) λέγει ὁ Ἀπόστολος· ἡ δὲ εὐσέβεια πρὸς πάντα ὠφέλιμός ἐστιν, ἐπαγγελίαν ἔχουσα ζωῆς τῆς νῦν καὶ τῆς μελλούσης. Καὶ βέβαια εὐσεβεῖς ἐκεῖνοι λέγονται, οἱ ὁποῖοι κάμοντες συνεχεῖς προσευχὰς πρὸς τὸν Θεὸν φεύγουσιν ὅλαις ταῖς ἀσεβείαις καὶ ἁμαρτίαις. Ἡ εὐσέβεια λέγω ἡ μὴ φαινομένη, ἡ ὁποία εἶναι τῶν Φαρισαίων· ἀλλ᾽ ἡ ἀληθινὴ καὶ ἐγκάρδιος· ἵνα μὴ καὶ περὶ αὐτῆς (Ματθ. ιέ. ή.) εἴπει ὁ Κύριος· οὗτος ὁ λαὸς τοῖς χείλεσί με τιμᾷ, ἡ δὲ καρδία αὐτῶν πόῤῥω ἀπέχει ἀπ᾽ ἐμοῦ· καὶ πάλιν (Ματθ. κγ´. κς´.)· Φαρισαῖε τυφλὲ, καθάρισον πρῶτον τὸ ἐντὸς τοῦ ποτηρίου καὶ τῆς παροψίδος, ἵνα γένηται καὶ τὸ ἐκτὸς αὐτῶν καθαρόν.

Qᴜᴀ̨sᴛɪo LXXIX.

Sextum Spiritus Sancti charisma, quodnam est?

Rᴇsᴘ. Pietas. Quæ una cum vera fide in assidua ardentique precatione bonisque operibus fundatur, de qua sic disserit Apostolus (1 Tim. iv. 8): 'Pietas ad omnia utilis est habetque promissionem hujus et venturæ vitæ.' Itaque vere illi pii appellantur, qui perpetuis Deum precibus venerantur omnemque impietatem ac peccati labem vitant. Pietas, inquam, non apparens et adumbrata, qualis olim Pharisæorum erat; sed solida et germana cordique penitus infixa, ne de illa etiam hujusmodi Dominus sententiam ferat (Matt. xv. 8): 'Populus iste labiis me suis honorat, sed cor ipsorum procul a me abest.' Et rursus (Matt. xxiii. 26): 'O cæcule Pharisæe, prius interiora calicis ac patinæ purga; ita etiam exteriora eorum munda erunt.'

Ἐρώτησις π´.

Ποῖον εἶναι τὸ ἕβδομον χάρισμα τοῦ ἁγίου Πνεύνατος;

Ἀπ. Ὁ φόβος τοῦ Θεοῦ, ὁ ὁποῖος πρέπει νὰ εἶναι ὡς ἂν ἐκεῖνος, ὅπου ἔχουσι τὰ παιδία πρὸς τοὺς πατέρας

Qᴜᴀ̨sᴛɪo LXXX.

Septimum Spiritus Sancti donum, quodnam est?

Rᴇsᴘ. Timor Dei. Quem ejusmodi esse oportet, cujusmodi erga parentes liberorum, non qualis erga

τους, καὶ ὄχι ὡς ἂν ἐκεῖνος, ὅπου ἔχουσιν οἱ δοῦλοι πρὸς τοὺς δεσπότας των. Καὶ περὶ τοῦ πρώτου λέγει ὁ Ψαλμῳδός (Ψαλ. λδʹ. θʹ.)· φοβήθητε τὸν Κύριον πάντες οἱ ἅγιοι αὐτοῦ· ὅτι οὐκ ἔστιν ὑστέρημα τοῖς φοβουμένοις αὐτόν. Περὶ δὲ τοῦ δευτέρου λέγει (άʹ. Ἰωάν. θʹ. ιή.) ὁ Ἀπόστολος· φόβος οὐκ ἔστιν ἐν τῇ ἀγάπῃ, ἀλλʼ ἡ τελεία ἀγάπη ἔξω βάλλει τὸν φόβον· ὅτι ὁ φόβος κόλασιν ἔχει· ὁ δὲ φοβούμενος οὐ τετελείωται ἐν τῇ ἀγάπῃ. Μὲ τὸν τρόπον τοῦτον προστάσσει (Ψαλ. κβʹ. κγʹ.) ἡ Γραφή· νὰ φοβούμεθα τὸν Θεὸν ἐξ ἀγάπης, ὅταν λέγει· οἱ φοβούμενοι τὸν Κύριον αἰνέσατε αὐτὸν, ἅπαν τὸ σπέρμα Ἰακὼβ, δοξάσατε αὐτόν· φοβηθήτω δὴ ἀπʼ αὐτοῦ ἅπαν τὸ σπέρμα Ἰσραήλ. Καὶ ὁποῖος μὲ τὸν τοιοῦτον φόβον θέλει φοβᾶσθαι τὸν Θεὸν, ἐκεῖνος φυλάττει τὰς ἐντολάς του κατὰ τὸ (Ἰωαν. ιδʹ. κγʹ.) εἰρημένον· ἐάν τις ἀγαπᾷ με, τὸν λόγον μου τηρήσει.

heros servorum est. De priore illo sic divinus Psalmista (Psa. xxxiv. 10): 'Timete Dominum omnes Sancti ejus; quoniam non est penuria timentibus eum.' De posteriore autem ita Apostolus (1 Ioh. iv. 18): 'Timor non est in caritate, sed perfecta caritas timorem expellit; habet enim cruciatum timor, et qui timet non est perfectus in caritate.' Hoc modo, ut Deum ex amore timeamus, præcipit Scriptura (Psa. xxii. 24): 'Qui timetis Dominum, laudate eum; universum semen Iacobi glorificate eum. Timeat eum omne semen Israëlis.' Qui hujusmodi timore Deum timet, ille præcepta ipsius observat, ut dictum est (Ioh. xiv. 23): 'Si quis diligit me, is sermonem meum servabit.'

Ἐρώτησις παʹ.

Πόσοι καὶ ποῖοι εἶναι οἱ καρποὶ τοῦ ἁγίου Πνεύματος;

Ἀπ. Καρποὺς τοῦ ἁγίου Πνεύματος ἢ σημάδια τῆς θείας χάριτος ὁ Ἀπόστολος Παῦλος ἀπαριθμεῖ ἐννέα λέγων (Γαλ. έ. κβʹ.) οὕτως· ὁ δὲ καρπὸς τοῦ Πνεύματός ἐστιν ἀγάπη, χαρά, εἰρήνη, μακροθυμία, χρηστότης, ἀγαθοσύνη, πίστις, πρᾳότης, ἐγκράτεια. Μὰ πρέπει νὰ πιστεύωμεν, πῶς καὶ αἱ

QUÆSTIO LXXXI.

Quot et quinam sunt fructus Spiritus Sancti?

RESP. Fructus Spiritus Sancti sive signa divinæ gratiæ novem recenset Paulus (Gal. v. 22): 'Fructus vero Spiritus est Caritas, Gaudium, Pax, Lenitas, Benignitas, Bonitas, Fides, Mansuetudo, Continentia.' Verum enim vero ceteræ item virtutes omnes fructus

λοιπαὶ ἀρεταὶ νὰ λέγωνται καρποὶ τοῦ ἁγίου Πνεύματος, ἐπειδὴ ἀπ᾽ αὐτὸ καταβαίνουσι, καὶ αὐτὸ συνεργεῖ εἰς τὸ νὰ τελειώνουνται ἀπὸ τὸν ἄνθρωπον. Διὰ τοῦτο δὲν λέγει ὁ Παῦλος· κατὰ τούτων μόνων οὐκ ἔστι νόμος· ἀλλὰ κατὰ τῶν τοιούτων, ὡς ἂν ὅπου εἶναι, καὶ ἄλλα ὅμοια τούτοις.

Spiritus Sancti habendæ nobis appellandæque sunt, quoniam ab eo descendunt, eoque adjuvante, recte ab hominibus perficiuntur. Ideoque non addit Paulus: Contra has solas non est Lex; sed, contra hujusmodi, eo quod et aliæ his similes sunt.

Ἐρώτησις πβ΄.

Ποῖον εἶναι τὸ ἔννατον ἄρθρον τῆς πίστεως;

Ἀπ. Εἰς μίαν ἁγίαν καθολικὴν καὶ ἀποστολικὴν Ἐκκλησίαν.

Quæstio LXXXII.

Nonus fidei Articulus quis est?

Resp. *In unam sanctam, Catholicam et Apostolicam Ecclesiam.*

Ἐρώτησις πγ΄.

Τί διδάσκει ἡ ἁγία ἐκκλησία εἰς τοῦτο τὸ ἄρθρον τῆς πίστεως;

Ἀπ. Τέσσαρα πράγματα· πρῶτον πῶς ἡ ἐκκλησία εἶναι μία, ἁγία, καθολικὴ καὶ ἀποστολικὴ, κατὰ τὴν·διδασκαλίαν τοῦ Ἀποστόλου (β΄. Κορ. ιά. β΄.) λέγοντος· ἡρμοσάμην ὑμᾶς ἑνὶ ἀνδρὶ παρθένον ἁγνὴν παραστῆσαι τῷ Χριστῷ. Καὶ καθὼς ὁ Χριστὸς εἶναι ἕνας, τέτοιας λογῆς καὶ ἡ νύμφη του εἶναι μία· ὡς δῆλον ἀπὸ τὸ δ΄. κεφαλ. τῆς πρὸς Ἐφεσίους (εἰχ. ἑ.) ἐπιστολῆς, ὅπου λέγει· εἷς Κύριος, μία πίστις, ἐν βάπτισμα, καὶ εἷς Θεὸς καὶ Πατὴρ πάντων.

Quæstio LXXXIII.

Quid docet sancta Ecclesia, in hoc fidei Articulo?

Resp. Res quatuor. Primum: Ecclesiam esse unam, sanctam, Catholicam et Apostolicam, secundum doctrinam Apostoli (2 Cor. xi. 2): 'Despondi vos viro uni, ut virginem castam exhiberem Christo.' Sicuti vero Christus unus est, ita et sponsa illius non nisi una est, ut manifestum est ex capite quarto epistolæ ad Ephesios (v. 5): 'Unus Dominus, una fides, unum baptisma, et unus Deus itemque Pater omnium.'

Ἐρώτησις πδ΄.

Ποῖον εἶναι τὸ δεύτερον, ὅπου διδάσκεται εἰς τὸ ἄρθρον τοῦτο;

Ἀπ. Δεύτερον διδάσκει τὸ ἄρθρον

Quæstio LXXXIV.

Secundum, quod hoc Articulo docetur, quodnam est?

Resp. Hoc nimirum, Catholicam

τοῦτο, πῶς ἡ καθολικὴ ἐκκλησία δὲν πέρνει ὄνομα ἀπὸ κἂν ἕνα τόπον, ἂν εἶναι καὶ ὁ πλέον ἐξαίρετος· διατὶ αἱ τοπικαὶ ἐκκλησίαι εἶναι μερικαὶ· οἷον ἡ Ἐφεσίνη, ἡ ἐν Φιλαδελφείᾳ, ἡ ἐν Λαοδικείᾳ, ἡ ἐν Ἀντιοχείᾳ, ἡ ἐν Ἱεροσολύμοις, ἡ ἐν Ῥώμῃ, ἡ ἐν Ἀλεξανδρείᾳ, καὶ αἱ λοιπαί. Μὰ ἀνάμεσα εἰς τούταις ταῖς ἐκκλησίαις ταῖς μερικαῖς ἐκείνη ὀνομάζεται μήτηρ αὐτῶν, ἡ ὁποία πρώτη ἐπλούτησε τὴν παρουσίαν τοῦ Χριστοῦ, καὶ ἐδέχθηκε τὴν αἰώνιον σωτηρίαν καὶ τὴν ἄφεσιν τῶν ἁμαρτιῶν· καὶ ἀπὸ τὴν ὁποῖαν ἐπῆρεν ἀρχὴν ἡ κήρυξις τοῦ εὐαγγελίου εἰς ὅλον τὸν περίγειον κόσμον, ὡς μαρτυρᾷ ἡ Γραφὴ (Λουκ. κδ΄. μζ΄.) λέγουσα· οὕτως ἔδει παθεῖν τὸν Χριστὸν καὶ ἀναστῆναι ἐκ νεκρῶν τῇ τρίτῃ ἡμέρᾳ, καὶ κηρυχθῆναι ἐπὶ τῷ ὀνόματι αὐτοῦ μετάνοιαν καὶ ἄφεσιν ἁμαρτιῶν εἰς πάντα τὰ ἔθνη, ἀρξάμενον ἀπὸ Ἱερουσαλήμ. Ὑμεῖς δὲ ἐστε μάρτυρες τούτων. Καὶ ἀλλαχοῦ (Πρᾶξ. ά. ή.)· ἔσεσθέ μοι μάρτυρες ἔν τε Ἱερουσαλὴμ καὶ ἐν πάσῃ τῇ Ἰουδαίᾳ καὶ Σαμαρείᾳ καὶ ἕως ἐσχάτου τῆς γῆς. Ἀκόμι ἐκείνη λέγεται πρώτη, ἡ ὁποία ἔλαμψε περισσότερον ἀπὸ ὅλαις ταῖς ἄλλαις ἐκκλησίαις εἰς τὴν διδασκαλίαν, καὶ εἰς τὰ ἤθη· ἔμπροσθεν τῆς ὁποίας οἱ Ἀπόστολοι ἐδίδασι τὸν λογαριασμόν τους, καθὼς μαρτυρᾷ (Πρᾶξ. ιά. β΄) ἡ Γραφὴ, λέγουσα· καὶ ὅτε ἀνέβη Πέτρος εἰς Ἱεροσόλυμα, διεκρίνοντο πρὸς αὐτὸν οἱ

Ecclesiam non uni alicui loco etiam præcipuo et clarissimo nominis sui decus acceptum referre. Quotquot enim certis locis continentur ecclesiæ, particulares sunt, ut Ephesina, ut Philadelphiensis, ut Laodicena, ut Antiochena, ut Hierosolymitana, ut Romana, ut Alexandrina, ut ceteræ item. Verum enim vero inter particulares istas ecclesias illa mater reliquarum dicitur, quæ prima omnium præsentia Christi ornata fuit ac salutem æternam veniamque peccatorum accepit, et ex qua annunciatio Evangelii in totum terrarum orbem primum propagata est, teste ipsa Scriptura (Luc. xxiv. 47): 'Sic pati oportuit Christum et tertio die resurgere a mortuis et prædicari in nomine ejus pœnitentiam ac remissionem peccatorum in omnes gentes, facto initio ab Hierosolymis; vos autem harum rerum testes estis.' Et alibi (Act i. 8): 'Eritis mihi testes, cum Hierosolymis tum in universa Iudæa et Samaria et ad ultimos usque terræ fines.' Solet et illa prima salutari, quæ doctrinæ morumque sanctimonia super reliquas omnes ecclesias clarius effulsit, et coram qua ipsimet Apostoli actionum suarum rationem exposuerunt, prout testatur Scriptura, quæ dicit (Act xi. 2): 'Quum autem adscendisset Hierosolymam Petrus; disceptabant ad-

ἐκ περιτομῆς λέγοντες, ὅτι πρὸς ἄνδρας ἀκροβυστίαν ἔχοντας εἰσῆλθες
καὶ συνέφαγες αὐτοῖς; Εἰς τοὺς ὁποίους ἀπεκρίθη ὁ Πέτρος· ἐγὼ τίς
ἤμην δυνατὸς κωλῦσαι τὸν Θεόν;
ἀκούσαντες δὲ ταῦτα ἡσύχασαν καὶ
ἐδόξαζον τὸν Θεὸν λέγοντες· ἄραγε
καὶ τοῖς ἔθνεσιν ὁ Θεὸς τὴν μετάνοιαν ἔδωκεν εἰς ζωήν. Καὶ κατωτέρω
(στίχῳ κβ'.)· ἠκούσθη ὁ λόγος εἰς τὰ
ὦτα τῆς ἐκκλησίας τῆς ἐν Ἱεροσολύμοις περὶ αὐτῶν· καὶ ἐξαπέστειλαν
Βαρνάβαν διελθεῖν ἕως Ἀντιοχείας.
Καὶ ἀλλαχοῦ (Πρᾶξ. ιέ. β'.)· ἔταξαν
ἀναβαίνειν Παῦλον καὶ Βαρνάβαν
καί τινας ἄλλους ἐξ αὐτῶν πρὸς τοὺς
Ἀποστόλους καὶ πρεσβυτέρους εἰς
Ἱερουσαλὴμ περὶ τοῦ ζητήματος τούτου (στίχῳ κβ'.). Τότε ἔδοξε τοῖς
Ἀποστόλοις καὶ τοῖς πρεσβυτέροις
σὺν ὅλῃ τῇ ἐκκλησίᾳ, ἐκλεξαμένους
ἄνδρας ἐξ αὐτῶν πέμψαι εἰς Ἀντιό-
χειαν σὺν τῷ Παύλῳ καὶ Βαρνάβᾳ,
μετὰ τοιαύτης γραφῆς· ἔδοξε τῷ
ἁγίῳ Πνεύματι καὶ ἡμῖν, μηδὲν πλέον
ἐπιτίθεσθαι ὑμῖν βάρος πλὴν τῶν
ἐπάναγκες τούτων. Ἀκόμι εἰς ἄλλον τόπον (Πρᾶξ, ις'. δ'.) λέγει· ὡς
δὲ διεπορεύοντο τὰς πόλεις, παρεδί-
δουν αὐτοῖς φυλάσσειν τὰ δόγματα τὰ
κεκριμένα ὑπὸ τῶν Ἀποστόλων καὶ
τῶν πρεσβυτέρων τῶν ἐν Ἱερουσαλήμ. Λοιπὸν ἡ ἐν Ἱεροσολύμοις ἐκκλησία εἶναι μήτηρ πασῶν τῶν ἐκκλη-
σιῶν καὶ πρώτη, διατὶ ἀπ' ἐκείνην
ἤρχισε νὰ ἀπλώνεται τὸ Εὐαγγέλιον

versus illum, qui ex circumcisione
erant, dicentes: Atqui ad homines
incircumcisos ingressus es et una
cum illis edisti.' Quibus respon-
debat Petrus (vers. 17): 'Ego vero
quis eram, ut Deum inhibere pos-
sem? quibus illi auditis acquieve-
runt Deumque collaudarunt dicentes: jam itaque et gentibus pœnitentiam ad vitam concessit Deus?'
Et paullo post (vers. 22): 'Pervenit is rumor ad aures ecclesiæ,
quæ Hierosolymis erat, de istis.
Itaque Barnabam miserunt, qui
Antiochiam usque iret.' Et alibi
(Act. xv. 2): 'Statuerunt, ut adscen-
derent Paulus et Barnabas et quidam præterea alii de suis ad Apostolos et seniores Hierosolymam
super hac quæstione' (vers. 22).
'Tum placuit Apostolis et senioribus, una cum tota Ecclesia delectos
ex sese viros Antiochiam mittere
cum Paulo et Barnaba cum literis
hujusmodi' (vers. 28): 'Visum est
Spiritui Sancto et nobis, ne quid
amplius imponeremus vobis oneris
præter hæc necessaria.' Etiam alio
loco (Act. xvi. 4): 'Quum autem
transirent per civitates, servanda
illis tradebant dogmata, quæ decreta erant ab Apostolis et senioribus
qui erant Hierosolymis.' Est itaque haud dubie mater et princeps
Ecclesiarum omnium Ecclesia Hierosolymitana, quoniam ex illa in

εἰς ὅλα τὰ πέρατα, καλᾷ καὶ οἱ βασιλεῖς ὕστερον νὰ ἐδώκασι τὰ πρωτεῖα τῆς τιμῆς εἰς τὴν πρεσβυτέραν καὶ εἰς τὴν νέαν ʽΡώμην διὰ τὸ κράτος τῆς βασιλείας, ὅπου ἦτον εἰς αὐτὰς κατὰ τὸν τρίτον κανόνα τῆς δευτέρας οἰκουμενικῆς Συνόδου τῆς ἐν Κωνσταντινουπόλει. Καὶ αὕτη ἐγίνηκε καθολική· διατὶ ἐδέχθησαν τὴν πίστιν καὶ διδασκαλίαν της ὅλα τὰ ἔθνη.

omnes orbis terminos diffundi cœpit evangelium; quamvis postea imperatores primos dignitatis gradus antiquæ novæque Romæ tribuerint ob majestatem Imperii, quæ iis locis domicilium habebat, secundum canonem tertium secundæ œcumenicæ Synodi Constantinopolitanæ (Adde Chalced. KH. Iustin. Νεαρ. Διαταξ. ρλά., etc.). Eadem ecclesia Hierosolymitana postmodum catholica evasit, fide illius et doctrina ab omnibus gentibus communiter recepta.

Ἐρώτησις πέ.

Τί διδάσκεται τρίτον εἰς τοῦτο τὸ ἄρθρον τῆς πίστεως;

Ἀπ. Πῶς ἄλλο θεμέλιον δὲν εἶναι τῆς ἐκκλησίας παρὰ μόνον ὁ Χριστὸς, κατὰ τὸν Ἀπόστολον (ά Κορ. γ΄. ιά.) τὸν λέγοντα· θεμέλιον γὰρ ἄλλον οὐδεὶς δύναται θεῖναι παρὰ τὸν κείμενον, ὅς ἐστιν Ἰησοῦς ὁ Χριστός. Καὶ ἂν κᾂν μίαν φορὰν λέγονται καὶ οἱ Ἀπόστολοι καὶ οἱ Προφῆται θεμέλια τῆς πίστεως καὶ τῆς ἐκκλησίας, ὡς ἂν ὅταν (Ἀποκ. κά. ιδ΄.) λέγῃ ὁ Ἰωάννης, πῶς ἡ μεγάλη πόλις ἡ Ἱερουσαλὴμ εἶχε τεῖχος εἰς δώδεκα θεμέλια κτισμένον, καὶ ἐν αὐτοῖς ἦσαν ὀνόματα τῶν δώδεκα Ἀποστόλων τοῦ Ἀρνίου· καὶ ὁ Παῦλος (Ἐφ. β΄. κ΄.) λέγει, πῶς εἴμεσθαν ἐποικοδομηθέντες ἐπὶ τῷ θεμελίῳ τῶν Ἀποστόλων καὶ Προφητῶν· τοῦτο πρέπει νὰ γροικᾶται

QUÆSTIO LXXXV.

Tertium, quod in hoc Articulo docetur, quid est?

RESP. Nullum aliud ecclesiæ fundamentum esse, quam Christum solum secundum verba Apostoli (1 Cor. iii. 2): ʽFundamentum aliud nemo jacere potest. præter id, quod jactum est, quod est Iesus Christus.ʼ Quamvis autem semel alicubi Apostoli et Prophetæ fundamenta fidei et Ecclesiæ dicantur, veluti quum Ioannes ait (Apoc. xxi. 14): ʽMagnam urbem Hierosolymam muro super duodecim fundamenta exstructo septam esse, fundamentisque inscripta esse nomina duodecim Apostolorum Agni.ʼ Sed et Paulus affirmat (Eph. ii. 20): ʽNos exædificatos esse super fundamento Apostolorum et Prophetarum.ʼ Id vero

πῶς οἱ Προφῆται καὶ οἱ Ἀπόστολοι
δὲν εἶναι ἁπλῶς καὶ πρώτως θεμέλια
τῆς πίστεως· διατὶ ὁ τοιοῦτος θεμέλιος εἶναι μόνος ὁ Χριστός· μὰ κατά
τι καὶ δεύτερον· καθ᾽ ὅσον ἐκεῖνοι ὡς
ἐγγυτέρω καὶ πλησιέστεροι ἐπῳκοδο-
μήθησαν ἀπάνω εἰς τὴν σωτηριώδη
διδασκαλίαν τοῦ Ἰησοῦ Χριστοῦ τοῦ
Κυρίου ἡμῶν, καὶ ἐφάνησαν πρῶτοι
εἰς τὸ νὰ ἁπλώσουσι τὴν πίστιν τοῦ
Χριστοῦ εἰς ὅλα τὰ πέρατα τῆς οἰκου-
μένης. Διατὶ ὁ Χριστὸς δὲν ἐθεμε-
λίωσε τὴν ἐκκλησίαν του ἀπάνω εἰς
ἀνθρώπους, μὰ ἀπάνω εἰς τὸν ἑαυτόν
του, καὶ ἀπάνω εἰς τὴν θείαν του διδασκαλίαν. Ἀκόμι ἀπὸ τοῦτο τὸ
ἄρθρον διδασκόμεθα, πῶς μόνος ὁ
Χριστὸς εἶναι κεφαλὴ τῆς ἐκκλησίας
κατὰ τὴν διδασκαλίαν τοῦ Ἀποστόλου (Ἐφ. ἑ. κγ΄.) λέγοντος· ὅτι ὁ
ἀνήρ ἐστι κεφαλὴ τῆς γυναικὸς, ὡς
καὶ ὁ Χριστὸς κεφαλὴ τῆς ἐκκλησίας·
καὶ αὐτός ἐστι σωτὴρ τοῦ σώματος.
Καὶ ἀλλαχοῦ (Κολ. ά. ιή.)· αὐτός
ἐστιν ἡ κεφαλὴ τοῦ σώματος τῆς ἐκκλησίας, ὅς ἐστιν ἀρχὴ, πρωτότοκος
ἐκ τῶν νεκρῶν· ἵνα γένηται ἐν πᾶσιν
αὐτὸς πρωτεύων. Διατὶ ἂν λέγωνται
καὶ εἰς τὰς ἐκκλησίας οἱ προϊστάμενοι
αὐτῶν ἀρχιερεῖς κεφαλαὶ αὐτῶν, τοῦτο πρέπει νὰ γροικᾶται πῶς αὐτοὶ
εἶναι τοποτηρηταὶ τοῦ Χριστοῦ εἰς
τὴν ἰδίαν του καθ᾽ ἕνας ἐπαρχίαν, καὶ
κεφαλαὶ μερικαί· κατὰ τὴν Γραφὴν
(Πρᾶξ. κ΄. κή.) τὴν λέγουσαν· προσ-
έχετε ἑαυτοῖς καὶ παντὶ τῷ ποιμνίῳ,

ita accipiendum est, quod Prophetæ et Apostoli non simpliciter et
primario fidei fundamenta sint;
nam ejusmodi fundamentum solus
est Christus: sed secundum quid
et secundarium, quod illi, ut pro-
pinquiores et viciniores, super salutarem Iesu Christi Domini nostri
doctrinam structi sint, primique
omnium fuerint, qui fidem Christi
per totum terrarum orbem propa-
garint. Non enim super mortales
homines, sed super semet ipsum et
divinam doctrinam suam ecclesiam
fundavit Christus. Ad haec item
ex hoc articulo docemur, Christum
solum ecclesiæ suæ caput esse secundum doctrinam Apostoli (Ephes.
v. 23): 'Quoniam vir uxoris caput
est, ut et Christus caput Ecclesiæ,
qui et corpori toti salutem dat.' Et
alibi (Col. i. 18): 'Ipse corporis ecclesiæ caput est, qui principium
est et primogenitus ex mortuis, ut
in omnibus primas ipse teneat.'
Tametsi vero antistites in ecclesiis,
queis præsunt, capita earum dicuntur: sic illud tamen accipiendum, quod ipsi vicarii Christi in
sua quisque provincia et particula-
ria quædam capita sint, dicente
Scriptura (Act. xx. 28): 'Attendite
vobis et toti gregi, in quo vos Spiritus Sanctus posuit episcopos, ad pa-
scendam ecclesiam Dei, quam suo
sibi sanguine acquisivit.' Ita nimi-

ἐν ᾧ ὑμᾶς τὸ Πνεῦμα τὸ ἅγιον ἔθετο
ἐπισκόπους, ποιμαίνειν τὴν ἐκκλησίαν
τοῦ Θεοῦ, ἣν περιεποιήσατο διὰ τοῦ
ἰδίου αἵματος· ὄντος ἀρχιποίμενος
αὐτοῦ Ἰησοῦ Χριστοῦ· ὡς λέγει Πέτρος (ά. Ἐπ. ἑ. δ΄.)· καὶ φανερωθέντος
τοῦ ἀρχιποιμένος κομιεῖσθε τὸν ἀμα-
ράντινον τῆς δόξης στέφανον.

rum, ut Christus ipse pastorum
princeps sit, teste Petro (1 Pet. v.
4): 'Cum apparuerit ille pastorum
princeps, reportabitis coronam gloriæ nunquam marcescentem.'

Ἐρώτησις πς΄.

Τ{· διδάσκεται τέταρτον εἰς τοῦτο
τὸ ἄρθρον τῆς πίστεως;

Ἀπ. Τὸ ἄρθρον τοῦτο διδάσκει
κάθα ὀρθόδοξον, πῶς πρέπει νὰ ὑπο-
τάσσεται εἰς τὴν ἐκκλησίαν κατὰ τὴν
διδασκαλίαν τοῦ Χριστοῦ (Ματθ. ιή.
ιζ΄.) τὴν λέγουσαν· ἐὰν δὲ καὶ τῆς
ἐκκλησίας παρακούσῃ, ἔστω σοι ὥσπερ
ὁ ἐθνικὸς καὶ ὁ τελώνης. Καὶ πρὸς
τούτοις ἡ ἐκκλησία ἔχει τὴν ἐξουσίαν
ταύτην, ὥστε μὲ τὰς συνόδους τὰς
οἰκουμενικὰς νὰ δοκιμάζῃ τὰς Γρα-
φάς· νὰ κρίνῃ Πατριάρχας, Παπά-
δας, Ἐπισκόπους, νὰ τοὺς καθυπο-
βάλλῃ κατὰ τὰ σφάλματά των εἰς
ταῖς κανονικαῖς τιμωρίαις καὶ ἐπιτίμια.
Ἐπειδὴ εἶναι στήλη τῆς ἀληθείας καὶ
θεμέλιος, κατὰ τὸν Ἀπόστολον (ά.
Τιμ. γ΄. ιέ.) λέγοντα· ἵνα εἰδῇς, πῶς
δεῖ ἐν οἴκῳ Θεοῦ ἀναστρέφεσθαι·
ἥτις ἐστιν ἐκκλησία Θεοῦ ζῶντος,
στύλος καὶ ἑδραίωμα τῆς ἀληθείας.

Quæstio LXXXVI.

Quartum, quod hic docet Articulus, quid est?

Resp. Docet unumquemque
Christianum oportere ipsum morem
gerere subjectumque esse ecclesiæ
secundum doctrinam Christi, quæ
ita habet (Matt. xviii. 17): 'Quod
si neque ecclesiæ obtemperet, sit tibi
velut ethnicus ac publicanus.' Ad
hæc ea etiam instructa potestate est
ecclesia, ut per synodos œcumenicas
examinare atque approbare queat
scripturas; cognoscere item ac judicare de actis Patriarcharum, Pontificum, Episcoporum, eosque pro gravitate delicti, multis pœnisque canonicis mulctare: est enim columna
atque fundamentum veritatis, dicente Apostolo (1 Tim. iii. 15): 'Ut sci-
as, quomodo versari oporteat in domo
Dei; quæ est Ecclesia Dei viventis,
columna et firmamentum veritatis.

Ἐρώτησις πζ΄.

Ποῖαι εἶναι αἱ ἐντολαὶ τῆς ἐκκλησίας;

Quæstio LXXXVII.

Quænam sunt Præcepta ecclesiæ?

'Aπ. Αἱ ἐντολαὶ τῆς ἐκκλησίας αἱ μᾶλλον ἐξαίρετ᾽ι εἶναι ἐννέα. Τὸ πρῶτον εἶναι, νὰ προσεύχεται καθ᾽ ἕνας εἰς τὸν Θεὸν μὲ συντριβὴν καὶ κατάνυξιν τῆς καρδίας· καὶ νὰ μυεῖται μὲ ταῖς τελεταῖς τῆς ἐκκλησίας εἰς κάθα κυριακὴν καὶ εἰς ταῖς ἑορτάσιμαις ἡμέραις· ἤγουν ἀκούωνται τὸν ὄρθρον, τὴν λειτουργίαν, τὸν ἑσπερινὸν, καὶ διδαχήν· διατὶ λέγει (Λουκ. ιή. ά.) ἡ Γραφή· δεῖ πάντοτε προσεύχεσθαι, καὶ μὴ ἐκκακεῖν· καὶ ἀλλαχοῦ (Ἐφ. ς'. ιή.)· διὰ πάσης προσευχῆς καὶ δεήσεως προσευχόμενοι ἐν παντὶ καιρῷ ἐν πνεύματι· καὶ εἰς αὐτὸ τοῦτο ἀγρυπνοῦντες ἐν πάσῃ προσκαρτερήσει καὶ δεήσει περὶ πάντων τῶν ἁγίων. Καὶ ἀλλαχοῦ λέγει (ά. Θεσσ. ὲ. ιζ'.) ὁ ἴδιος Παῦλος· ἀδιαλείπτως προσεύχεσθε.

Ἐρώτησις πή.

Ποία εἶναι ἡ δευτέρα ἐντολὴ τῆς ἐκκλησίας;

'Aπ. Ἡ δευτέρα ἐντολὴ εἶναι, νὰ φυλάττῃ ὁ Χριστιανὸς κάθα χρόνον τὰς τέσσαρας διατεταγμέναις νηστείας· πρώτην, τὴν πρὸ τῆς Χριστοῦ γεννήσεως· ἡ ὁποία ἀρχίζει ἀπὸ τὰς ιέ. τοῦ Νοεμβρίου· δευτέραν τὴν μεγάλην τεσσαρακοστήν, τὴν ὁποίαν ὁ Χριστὸς ἔκαμε· καθὼς (Ματθ. δ'. β'.) λέγει ἡ Γραφή· καὶ νηστεύσας ἡμέρας τεσσαράκοντα καὶ νύκτας τεσσαράκοντα ὕστερον ἐπείνασε· τρίτην τῶν ἁγίων Ἀποστόλων, τὴν ὁποίαν ἀρχί-

RESP. Præcepta Ecclesiæ summa et præcipua novem sunt. Primum est, ut Deum quisque cum contritione et compunctione cordis adoret, ut singulis diebus dominicis ac festis solemnibus ecclesiæ sacris rite operetur, hoc est, ut horas matutinas, liturgiam, vesperas, concionem diligenter audiat. Sic enim Scriptura (Luc. xviii. 1): 'Oportet semper precari et non defatigari.' Et alibi (Eph. vi. 18): 'Omni oratione et precatione orantes omni tempore in spiritu: et in hoc ipsum vigilantes cum omni assiduitate et supplicatione pro omnibus sanctis.' Rursus alibi idem ille Paulus (1 Thess. v. 17): 'Orate sine intermissione.'

QUÆSTIO LXXXVIII.

Quodnam secundum Ecclesiæ præceptum est?

RESP. Ut homo Christianus quotannis quatuor statuta Jejunia servet. Primum proximo ante nativitatem Christi tempore, cujus initium a quinto decimo mensis Novembris die ducitur. Secundum, quod magna Quadragesima dicitur, Christo ipsi inedia actum, tradente Scriptura (Matt. iv. 2): 'Et quum jejunasset dies quadraginta noctesque totidem, tandem esuriit.' Tertium sanctorum Apostolorum est,

ζει ἡ ἐκκλησία μετὰ μίαν ἑβδομάδα
τῆς ἑορτῆς τῆς ἁγίας πεντηκοστῆς·
καὶ λέγεται τῶν Ἀποστόλων διὰ τὴν
ἀφορμὴν ταύτην· διατὶ εἰς τὸν καιρὸν
ἐκείνον οἱ Ἀπόστολοι ἐνηστεύασι,
πεμπόμενοι εἰς τὸ κήρυγμα τοῦ Εὐ-
αγγελίου· καθὼς φαίνεται εἰς τὰς
Πράξεις αὐτῶν, ὅπου (κεφ. ιγ΄. γ΄.)
λέγει· τότε νηστεύσαντες καὶ προσευξάμενοι καὶ ἐπιθέντες τὰς χεῖρας
αὐτοῖς ἀπέλυσαν. Ἡ τετάρτη νηστεία
γίνεται πρὸ τῆς ἑορτῆς τῆς κοιμήσεως
τῆς ὑπεραγίας Θεοτόκου καὶ ἀειπαρθένου Μαρίας· ἡ ὁποία ἀρχίζει ἀπὸ
τὴν πρώτην τοῦ Αὐγούστου μηνὸς,
καὶ τελειώνει τῇ ιέ. τοῦ αὐτοῦ μηνός.
Ἀκόμι πρέπει νὰ φυλάττεται καὶ ἡ
νηστεία τῆς τετράδης καὶ τῆς παρασ-
κευῆς· μὰ ὄχι τοῦ Σαββάτου καὶ
τῆς Κυριακῆς, κατὰ τὸν ξς΄. κανόνα
τῶν ἁγίων Ἀποστόλων, ἔξω ἀπὸ τὸ
μέγα σάββατον. Ἀκόμι ἐπαρέδωκεν
ἡ ἐκκλησία νὰ νηστεύωμεν καὶ τῇ ιδ΄.
τοῦ Σεπτεμβρίου μηνὸς κατὰ τὴν
ὕψωσιν τοῦ σταυροῦ· διατὶ κάμνομεν
τὴν ἐνθύμησιν τοῦ πάθους τοῦ Κυρίου
ἡμῶν Ἰησοῦ Χριστοῦ, διαβάζοντες
τὰ Εὐαγγέλια τοῦ πάθους αὐτοῦ.
Καὶ τῇ κθ΄. τοῦ Αὐγούστου, διὰ νὰ
τιμήσωμεν τὴν ἀποτομὴν τοῦ προδρό-
μου μὲ νηστείαν. Ἔξω ἀπὸ τοῦτο
μᾶς ἐπαρέδωκε, νὰ μὴ νηστεύωμεν εἰς
κάποιαις ἡμέραις διατεταγμέναις· ὡς
ἂν εἶναι ἀπὸ τὴν ἡμέραν τῆς γεννήσεως τοῦ Χριστοῦ ἕως τῶν ἁγίων
ἐπιφανίων· κα ὅλη ἡ διακαινήσιμος

quod mox, exacta sacræ Pente-
costes hebdomade, orditur ecclesia.
(Claudit die Petri et Pauli, Junii
xxix.) Apostolorum autem ideo
nuncupatur, quod illo temporis spatio jam ad divulgandum evangelium ituri Apostoli jejunium cele-
braverunt, id quod ex Actis ipsorum
clarum est (Cap. xiii. 3): ‘Ubi jejunassent et Deum comprecati essent,
manus illis imponebant eosque
dimittebant.’ Quartum jejunium
proxime ante diem emortualem
(sive Assumtionis), sanctissimæ Deiparæ, et semper-Virginis Mariæ,
agitur. Initium illi Calendis Sexti-
libus: finis die XV. mensis ejusdem.
Porro quarto etiam sextoque cujusque hebdomadis die jejunia ob-
servari oportet. Sabbato et die
Dominico non item, vetante id ca-
none LXVI. sanctorum Apostolorum; excepto tamen magno Sabbato (quo compositæ sepulcro suo
sacræ Servatoris reliquiæ quievere).
Sed et XIV. Septembris diem, ex-
altationi S. Crucis dedicatum, jejunio coli jussit ecclesia, siquidem eo
die memoriam passionis Dominicæ
recitatis, quæ de ea agunt, evan-
geliis recolimus. Itemque diem
XXIX. Augusti, nimirum ut Ioannis, Christi præcursoris, obtrunca-
tionem religiosa inediâ celebremus.
Ad hæc etiam, ut ne statis quibusdam diebus cibo nos abstinea-

ἑβδομὰς, καὶ ἡ ἑβδομὰς μετὰ τὴν πεντηκοστὴν, καὶ ἡ προφωνήσιμος, καὶ ἡ τυρινή. Τὰ ὁποῖα χρεωστεῖ ::άϑα Χριστιανὸς ὀρϑόδοξος νὰ φυλάττῃ.

mus, eadem tradidit ecclesia. Puta, a die natali Christi usque ad diem sacrorum Epiphaniorum, totaque Paschali atque Pentecostali hebdomade, ut et illa, quæ Dominicam Septuagesimæ præcedit hebdomada (προφωνήσιμον dicunt). Eaque itidem, quæ inter Sexagesimam et Quinquagesimam interest (Græcis τυρινὴ est). Quæ omnia orthodoxus quisque Christianus bona fide custodire debet.

Ἐρώτησις πϑ΄.

Ποία εἶναι ἡ τρίτη ἐντολὴ τῆς ἐκκλησίας;

Ἀπ. Νὰ τιμοῦνται οἱ πνευματικοὶ μὲ τὴν πρεπουμένην εὐλάβειαν, ὡς δοῦλοι τοῦ Θεοῦ καὶ μεσῖται, ὅπου μεσιτεύουσι δι᾽ ἡμᾶς πρὸς τὸν Θεόν· μάλιστα ἐκεῖνοι, ὅπου ἐξομολογοῦσιν, ὡς Πατέρες πνευματικοὶ, καὶ ἀπ᾽ ἐκείνους πρέπει νὰ βουλευώμεϑα περὶ τῆς σωτηρίας ἡμῶν. Διὰ τὸ πρόσταγμα τοῦτο ἡ Γραφὴ (ά. Κορ. δ΄. ά.) ὁμιλεῖ τέτοιας λυγῆς· οὕτως ἡμᾶς λογιζέσϑω ἄνϑρωπος, ὡς ὑπηρέτας Χριστοῦ καὶ οἰκονόμους μυστηρίων Θεοῦ. Καὶ (ά. Θεσσ. έ. ιβ΄.) ἀλλαχοῦ· ἐρωτῶμεν δὲ ὑμᾶς, ἀδελφοὶ, εἰδέναι τοὺς κοπιῶντας ἐν ὑμῖν, καὶ προϊσταμένους ὑμῶν ἐν Κυρίῳ, καὶ νουϑετοῦντας ὑμᾶς, καὶ ἡγεῖσϑαι αὐτοὺς ὑπερεκπερισσοῦ ἐν ἀγάπῃ διὰ τὸ ἔργον αὐτῶν. Καὶ (ά. Κορ. ϑ΄. ιγ΄.) εἰς ἄλλον τόπον· οὐκ οἴδατε ὅτι οἱ τὰ ἱερὰ ἐργαζόμενοι

QUÆSTIO LXXXIX.

Quodnam tertium Ecclesiæ præceptum est?

RESP. Ut homines ecclesiasticos debita colamus observantia, velut ministros Dei ac sequestres, qui pro nobis apud Deum deprecatores se præbent. Inprimisque illos, qui ut Patres spirituales confessiones nostras excipiunt, et quos a nobis in salutis negotio consuli fas est. De quo præcepto ita loquitur Scriptura (1 Cor. iv. 1): 'Sic nos æstimet homo, ut ministros Christi et dispensatores mysteriorum Dei.' Et alibi (1 Thess. v. 12): 'Rogamus vos fratres, ut agnoscatis illo' qui laborant in vobis et præsunt vobis in Domino et commonefaciunt vos, ut eos summo in pretio habeatis, in caritate, propter opus ipsorum.' Et loco alio (1 Cor. ix. 13): 'Nescitis, quod qui sacris ope-

ἐκ τοῦ ἱεροῦ ἐσθίουσι; καὶ οἱ τῷ θυσιαστηρίῳ προσεδρεύοντες τῷ θυσιαστηρίῳ συμμερίζονται; Οὕτω καὶ ὁ
Κύριος διέταξε τοῖς τὸ Εὐαγγέλιον
καταγγέλλουσιν ἐκ τοῦ Εὐαγγελίου
ζῆν. Καὶ (ά. Τιμ. έ. ιζ´.) πάλιν· οἱ
καλῶς προεστῶτες πρεσβύτεροι δι-
πλῆς τιμῆς ἀξιούσθωσαν· μάλιστα
οἱ κοπιῶντες ἐν λόγῳ καὶ διδασκαλίᾳ.
Καὶ οἱ κοσμικοὶ ἄνθρωποι δὲν πρέπει
νὰ ἀνακατώνουνται εἰς τὰ πνευματικὰ
ἔργα, κατὰ τὸν Ἀπόστολον (Γαλ. ς´.
ά.) λέγοντα· ἀδελφοὶ, ἐὰν καὶ προσ-
ληφθῇ ἄνθρωπος ἔν τινι παραπτώ-
ματι, ὑμεῖς οἱ πνευματικοὶ καταρτί-
ζετε τὸν τοιοῦτον ἐν πνεύματι πραό-
τητος.

Ἐρώτησις ϟ´.

Ποία εἶναι ἡ τετάρτη ἐντολὴ τῆς
Ἐκκλησίας;

Ἀπ. Νὰ ἐξομολογούμεθα τὰς ἁμαρτίας μας τέσσαρες φοραῖς τὸν χρόνον
ἔμπροσθεν τοῦ ἱερέως τοῦ νομίμως
καὶ ὀρθοδόξως κεχειροτονημένου· οἱ
δὲ προκόπτοντες εἰς τὴν εὐσέβειαν
καὶ εὐλάβειαν ἃς ἐξομολογοῦνται
κάθα μῆνα· οἱ δὲ ἁπλούστεροι χρεωστοῦσι κἂν ἀπὸ μίαν φορὰν τὸν
χρόνον νὰ κάμουσιν ἐξομολόγησιν
τῶν ἁμαρτιῶν των, καὶ τοῦτο νὰ γίνεται εἰς τὸν καιρὸν τῆς ἁγίας τεσσα-
ρακοστῆς. Εἰς δὲ τοὺς ἀρρώστους
τοῦτο πρέπει, νὰ εἶναι ἡ πρώτη ἔν-
νοια, νὰ καθαρίσουσι τὸ γοργώτερον
τὴν συνείδησίν των μὲ τὴν ἐξομολό-

rantur, ex sanctuario edunt? et
qui altari assidue ministrant, cum
altari participant? sic et Dominus
constituit, ut 'qui Evangelium an-
nuntiant ex Evangelio vivant.' Et
rursus (1 Tim. v. 17): 'Presbyteri,
qui bene praesunt, duplici honore
digni habeantur: maxime, qui laborant in verbo et doctrina.' Nefas vero est profanis et laicis hominibus in munia spiritualia inferre
se atque immiscere, dicente Apostolo (Gal. vi. 1): 'Fratres, si forte
occupatus aliquo lapsu homo fuerit, vos qui spirituales estis instau-
rate hominem ejusmodi in spiritu
lenitatis.'

Quæstio XC.

Quartum Ecclesiæ præceptum
quodnam est?

Resp. Ut quatuor quotannis delicta nostra sacerdoti recte atque
ex ordine creato confiteamur. At
qui in pietate ac religione longius
progressi sunt, singulis mensibus
noxas suas expiant. Simpliciores
minimum semel in anno, videlicet
tempore sanctæ Quadragesimæ,
lustralem peccatorum suorum confessionem edere debent. Morbo
oppressi id ante omnia operam da-
bunt, ut quam primum conscientiæ
suæ maculas earum confessione
coenæque sacræ participatione elu-
ant; prius tamen summa cum re-

γησιν, καὶ νὰ γενοῦσι μέτοχοι τῆς ἁγίας κοινωνίας, πέρνοντες μὲ πᾶσαν εὐλάβειαν προτίμερα τὸ ἅγιον εὐχέλαιον.

verentia rite usurpato sacro chrismate.

Ἐρώτησις ϟά.

Ποία εἶναι ἡ πέμπτη ἐντολὴ τῆς ἐκκλησίας;

Ἀπ. Νὰ μὴ διαβάζουνται τὰ βιβλία τῶν αἱρετικῶν, μήτε νὰ ἀκούεται ἡ βλάσφημος διδασκαλία των ἀπ' ἐκείνους, ὅπου δὲν εἶναι γεγυμνασμένοι εἰς τὴν ἁγίαν Γραφὴν καὶ εἰς ταῖς ἐπιστήμαις· μήτε νὰ διαλέγουνται μετ' αὐτοὺς, μήτε νὰ συναναστρέφουνται· κατὰ τὸν μελῳδὸν Προφήτην τὸν (Ψαλ. ά. ά.) λέγοντα· μακάριος ἀνὴρ, ὃς οὐκ ἐπορεύθη ἐν βουλῇ ἀσεβῶν, καὶ ἐν ὁδῷ ἁμαρτωλῶν οὐκ ἔστη· καὶ ἀλλαχοῦ προστάσσει ἡ Γραφὴ (Τίτ. γ'. ί.) λέγουσα· αἱρετικὸν ἄνθρωπον μετὰ πρώτην καὶ δευτέραν νουθεσίαν παραιτοῦ.

QUÆSTIO XCI.

Quintum Ecclesiæ præceptum quod est?

RESP. Ut ne legantur Hæreticorum libri, neque fando blasphema illorum audiatur doctrina ab iis, qui in divinis ac humanis literis atque disciplinis inexercitati sunt; ne sermones cum ejusmodi hominibus conferant; ne ad familiaritatem eorum sese applicent, monente Propheta cantore (Psa. i. 1): 'Beatus vir, qui non ambulat in consilio impiorum, et in via peccatorum non consistit.' Et alibi præcipit Scriptura (Tit. iii. 10): 'Hæreticum hominem post unam alteramque admonitionem devita.'

Ἐρώτησις ϟβ'.

Ποία εἶναι ἡ ἕκτη ἐντολὴ τῆς ἐκκλησίας;

Ἀπ. Νὰ παρακαλοῦμεν τὸν πανάγαθον Θεὸν διὰ πᾶσαν κατάστασιν τῶν ἀνθρώπων· πρῶτον μὲν διὰ τοὺς πνευματικοὺς, ἤγουν διὰ τὸν παναγιώτατον Πατριάρχην, διὰ τὸν Μητροπολίτην, καὶ Ἐπίσκοπον τῆς ἐπαρχίας καὶ διὰ τὸν κλῆρον ὅλον· ἔπειτα διὰ τὸν βασιλέα, διὰ τὸν ἡγεμόνα, διὰ ὅλην τὴν γερουσίαν, καὶ

QUÆSTIO XCII.

Sextum Ecclesiæ præceptum quodnam est?

RESP. Ut Deum optimum maximumque pro omni hominum ordine ac statu pie veneremur. Primum pro spiritualibus: nimirum pro sanctissimo Patriarcha, pro Metropolita et Episcopo nostræ provinciæ cleroque universo. Tum pro rege, pro præside provinciæ, pro senatu omni et rep., pro exer-

πᾶσαν τὴν πολιτείαν· διὰ τὸ στρατό-
πεδον· ἐξαιρέτως δὲ δι' ἐκείνους,
ὅπου ἀγαθοεργοῦσιν εἰς ταῖς ἐκκλησίαις καὶ φροντίζουσι, νὰ αὐξήσουσι
τὴν πίστιν καθολικὴν καὶ ὀρθόδοξον·
κατὰ τὸν Ἀπόστολον, ὅπου (ά. Τιμ.
β'. ά.) λέγει· παρακαλῶ οὖν πρῶτον
πάντων ποιεῖσθαι δεήσεις, προσευχὰς,
ἐντεύξεις, εὐχαριστίας ὑπὲρ πάντων
ἀνθρώπων, ὑπὲρ βασιλέων καὶ πάντων τῶν ἐν ὑπεροχῇ ὄντων· ἵνα ἤρε-
μον καὶ ἡσύχιον βίον διάγωμεν ἐν
πάσῃ εὐσεβείᾳ καὶ σεμνότητι. Τοῦτο
γὰρ καλὸν καὶ ἀπόδεκτον ἐνώπιον τοῦ
σωτῆρος ἡμῶν Θεοῦ. Ἀκόμι νὰ παρακαλοῦμεν καὶ διὰ τοὺς κεκοιμημέ-
νους, ὅπου ἐμισεύσασιν ἀπὸ τὴν ζωὴν
τούτην μὲ πίστιν ὀρθόδοξον· ἀκόμι
καὶ διὰ τοὺς αἱρετικοὺς καὶ σχισματι-
κοὺς, διὰ νὰ ἐπιστρέψουσιν εἰς τὴν
ὀρθόδοξον πίστιν, πρὶν νὰ μισεύσουσιν ἀπὸ τὴν παροῦσαν ζωήν.

Ἐρώτησις ϟγ'.

Ποία εἶναι ἡ ἑβδόμη ἐντολὴ τῆς
ἐκκλησίας;

Ἀπ. Νὰ φυλάττωνται αἱ νηστεῖαι
ἐκεῖναι καὶ δεήσεις, ὅπου θέλουσι
προστάσσεσθαι ξεχωριστὰ ἀπὸ τὸν
Μητροπολίτην ἢ Ἐπίσκοπον εἰς τὴν
ἐπαρχίαν του, ἀπὸ ὅλους τοὺς ἐπαρ-
χιότας ἀπαρασαλεύτως, ὅπου ταῖς
προστάσσει ἐκεῖνος διὰ κἂν μίαν ἀν-
αγκαίαν ὑπόθεσιν, ἤγουν διὰ νὰ ἐπισ-

citu et legionibus ; sed vero inprimis pro iis orandum, qui bene de
ecclesiis merentur sedulamque na-
vant operam, quo pacto orthodoxæ
ac catholicæ religionis pomœria
terminosque proferant, auctore
Apostolo, qui ait (1 Tim. ii. 1): 'Adhortor igitur ante omnia, ut fiant
deprecationes, orationes, interces-
siones, gratiarumque actiones, pro
omnibus hominibus ; pro regibus,
omnibusque loco eminenti colloca-
tis ; ut quietam ac tranquillam vitam degamus in omni pietate atque
honestate.' Nam bonum hoc est
et acceptum coram Deo Servatore
nostro. Porro et pro iis orandum,
qui jam obdormierunt ; nimirum
qui in orthodoxa fide ex hominum
vita demigrarunt. Denique etiam
pro Hæreticis et Schismaticis, ut
resipiscant atque ad germanam pietatis sanctimoniam ante supremum
vitæ diem sese recipiant.

QUÆSTIO XCIII.

Quodnam septimum Ecclesiæ est
præceptum ?

RESP. Ut probe inviolateque jejunia illa supplicationesque, quæ
seorsum a Metropolita aut Episcopo
in diœcesi sua indicuntur, ab omnibus provinciæ incolis serventur.
Scilicet quando necessaria aliqua
de caussa indicuntur, sive ad expi-
andas justas Numinis violati iras,

τρέψῃ τὴν δικαίαν ὀργὴν τοῦ Θεοῦ τὴν ἐπικειμένην εἰς τὸν λαόν του· καὶ νὰ τὸν λυτρώσῃ ἢ ἀπὸ θανατικὸν, ἢ πεῖναν, ἢ πόλεμον, ἢ ἀβροχίαν, ἢ πολυβροχίαν, ἢ διὰ ἰατρείαν τῶν ἀσθενῶν, ἢ διὰ παρηγορίαν τῶν τεθλιμμένων· καθὼς φαίνεται εἰς τὰς Πράξεις τῶν Ἀποστόλων ὅπου (κεφ. ιβʹ. ϛʹ.) γράφουσιν· ὁ μὲν οὖν Πέτρος ἐτηρεῖτο ἐν τῇ φυλακῇ, προσευχὴ δὲ ἦν ἐκτενὴς γινομένη ὑπὸ τῆς ἐκκλησίας πρὸς τὸν Θεὸν ὑπὲρ αὐτοῦ.

Ἐρώτησις ϟδʹ.

Ποία εἶναι ἡ ὀγδόη ἐντολὴ τῆς ἐκκλησίας;

Ἀπ. Νὰ μὴν ἀποτολμῶσιν οἱ κοσμικοὶ, νὰ πέρνουσι βιαίως τὰ καλὰ καὶ στεκούμενα τῆς ἐκκλησίας, καὶ νὰ τὰ μεταχειρίζουνται εἰς ἰδίαις τως χρείαις. Οἱ δὲ πνευματικοὶ προεστῶτες χρεωστοῦσι νὰ προμηθεύουνται ἀπὸ τὰ καλὰ τῆς ἐκκλησίας τὰ στολίσματα καὶ ὅσα ἄλλα εἶναι ἀναγκαῖα εἰς τὴν ἐκκλησίαν· ἀκόμι τὴν ζωοτροφίαν καὶ ἐνδύματα ἐκείνων, ὅπου ὑπηρετοῦσι τὴν ἐκκλησίαν· καὶ τῶν πτωχῶν, καὶ τῶν ξένων· κατὰ τὴν διδασκαλίαν τῆς Γραφῆς ὅπου (Πράξ. ιά. κθʹ.) λέγει· τῶν δὲ μαθητῶν καθὼς ηὐπορεῖτό τις, ὥρισαν ἕκαστος αὐτῶν εἰς διακονίαν πέμψαι τοῖς κατοικοῦσιν ἐν τῇ Ἰουδαίᾳ ἀδελφοῖς. Ὃ καὶ ἐποίησαν, ἀποστείλαντες πρὸς τοὺς πρεσβυτέρους διὰ χειρὸς Βαρνάβα καὶ Σαύλου. Ἀκόμι δὲν εἶναι δίκαιον

populum suum urgentes, populumque a pestilentia, a fame, a bello, a siccitate, aut pluvia nimia, eripiendum; sive ad sanandos ægrotos consolandosque oppressos, prout apparet ex Actis Apostolorum, ubi scribitur (xii. 6): 'Et Petrus quidem in carcere attinebatur, assiduæ vero pro eo ad Deum ab Ecclesia fiebant preces.'

QUÆSTIO XCIV.

Quodnam octavum Ecclesiæ est præceptum?

RESP. Ut ne profani homines bona nummosque ecclesiæ vi auferre aut ad privatas necessitates suas intervertere ausint. Ceterum ad sacrorum Antistites hæc cura pertinet, ut de bonis ecclesiæ mundum aliaque illi necessaria comparent: ut victum et vestitum iis, qui ecclesiæ ministrant, et egenis et peregrinis suppeditent, docente ita Scriptura (Act. xi. 29): 'Discipuli autem, prout cuique suppetebat, statuerunt in usum fratrum in Iudæa habitantium mittere. Quod etiam fecerunt, mittentes senioribus per Barnabam et Saulum.' Præterea minime æquum est, sive Sæculares, sive Pontifices ipsos, qui in Ecclesia aliqua sacrorum antistites sunt, nummos illius aut

οὔτε εἰς τοὺς κοσμικοὺς, οὔτε εἰς τοὺς ἀρχιερεῖς, ὅπου ἀρχιερατεύουσιν εἰς κᾂν μίαν ἐκκλησίαν, νὰ ἀποξενώνουσι τὰ ἄσπρα ἢ τὰ ἄλλα κινητά της πράγματα, ὅπου τῆς ἔρχονται, ἢ ἀπὸ πρεσβείας τινὸς ἢ δωρεᾶς· καὶ νὰ τὰ μεταχειρίζουνται εἰς ἰδιωτικαῖς τως χρείαις· διὰ νὰ μὴν πάθῃ βίαν καὶ ἀνατροπὴν ἡ γνώμη ἐκείνου, ὅπου τὰ ἔδωκεν.

res mobiles alias sive testamento legatas, sive dono datas, quovis modo intercipere, in propriosque usus suos convertere, ne vim et subversionem pia donantis intentio perpetiatur.

’Ε ρ ώ τ η σ ι ς ϟέ.

Ποία εἶναι ἡ ἐννάτη ἐντολὴ τῆς ἐκκλησίας;

’Α π. Νὰ μὴν γίνουνται γάμοι εἰς ταῖς ἡμέραις, ὅπου κωλύει ἡ ἐκκλησία. ’Ακόμι νὰ μὴν εἶναι παρόντες οἱ ὀρθόδοξοι Χριστιανοὶ εἰς τὰ ἀπηγορευμένα παιγνίδια καὶ θέατρα· μήτε νὰ ἀκολουθοῦσιν εἰς τὰ ἤθη τὰ βάρβαρα, μὰ νὰ ἐγκρατεύωνται ἀπ’ αὐτὰ ὅσον εἶναι δυνατόν.

QUÆSTIO XCV.

Nonum Ecclesiæ præceptum quodnam est?

RESP. Ne solemnia nuptiarum vetitis ecclesiæ diebus celebrentur. Tum ne orthodoxi Christiani in ludis prohibitis theatralibusque spectaculis intersint; nec peregrinos et barbaros consectentur mores; verum ut ab iis quantum potest sibi temperent.

’Ε ρ ώ τ η σ ι ς ϟϛ′.

Διατὶ λέγομεν πῶς πιστεύομεν ε ἰ ς τ ὴ ν ἐ κ κ λ η σ ί α ν, ὅπου εἶναι κτίσμα, ὀφείλοντες εἰς μόνον τὸν Θεὸν πιστεύειν;

’Α π. Διατὶ καλᾷ καὶ ἡ ἐκκλησία νὰ εἶναι κτίσμα, ἀπὸ ἀνθρώπους συστεμένη, ἀλλὰ ἔχει κεφαλὴν αὐτὸν τὸν Χριστὸν τὸν ἀληθινὸν Θεὸν, τὸ Πνεῦμα τὸ ἅγιον, ὅπου τὴν διδάσκει πάνταρ καὶ κάμει τὴν ὡς λέγει (ά. Τιμ. γ′. ιέ.) ὁ ’Απόστολος, νύμφην ἄσπιλον καὶ ἄμωμον τοῦ Χριστοῦ, καὶ στύλον

QUÆSTIO XCVI.

Verum enimvero quo pacto profitemur, nos in ecclesiam, rem creatam, credere; qui in solum Deum credere debemus?

RESP. Nempe quamquam res creata ab hominibusque conflata ecclesia est: habet illa tamen caput Christum ipsum verum Deum; habet Spiritum Sanctum, qui illam perpetuo docet et instruit, eamque efficit, teste Apostolo, sponsam immaculatam et inculpatam Christi

καὶ ἑδραίωμα τῆς ἀληθείας. Καὶ τὰ δόγματα καὶ διδάγματά της δὲν εἶναι ἀνθρώπινα ἀλλὰ θεῖα· διὰ τοῦτο λέγοντες πῶς πιστεύομεν εἰς αὐτὴν, νοοῦμεν πῶς πιστεύομεν εἰς τὰ θεοπαράδοτά της λόγια, καὶ θεόπνευστα δόγματα. Φησὶ γὰρ ἡ Γραφή· ὅτι ὑπὸ Πνεύματος ἁγίου φερόμενοι ἐλάλησαν οἱ ἅγιοι Θεοῦ ἄνθρωποι· καὶ ὁ Παῦλος (ά. Θεσσ. β'. ιγ'.) φησίν· οὐ λόγον ἀνθρώπου ἐδέξασθε, ἀλλὰ, καθὼς ἐστὶν ἀληθῶς, λόγον Θεοῦ. Καὶ ἀπὸ τοῦτο κινοῦμεθα νὰ πιστεύωμεν ὄχι μόνον τὸ ἱερὸν Εὐαγγέλιον, ὅπου ἐκείνη ἐδιάλεξε, περὶ οὗ ὁ Χριστὸς (Μαρκ. ά. ιέ.) διετάξατο εἰπών· πιστεύετε ἐν τῷ Εὐαγγελίῳ, ἀλλὰ καὶ εἰς πάσας τὰς λοιπὰς γραφὰς καὶ συνοδικὰς διατάξεις.

(Ephes. v. 27); et 'columnam atque stabilimentum veritatis' (1 Tim. iii. 15). Sed et dogmata et doctrina illius nequaquam humana verum divina sunt. Quando itaque nos in illam credere profitemur; intelligimus, nos credere in traditas divinitus sacras illius Scripturas et inspirata a Deo dogmata. Ait enim Scriptura (2 Pet. i. 21), actos a Spiritu Sancto locutus fuisse sanctos Dei homines. Similiter et Paulus (1 Thess. ii. 13): 'Non ut sermonem hominum excepistis, sed (sicut revera est) ut sermonem Dei.' Hinc adducimur ad fidem habendam non modo sacro Evangelio ab Ecclesia recepto, de quo Christus ipse præcepit (Marc. i. 15): 'Credite Evangelio; verum etiam reliquis omnibus sacris Scripturis et synodicis decretis.'

Ἐρώτησις ςζʹ.

Ποῖον εἶναι τὸ δέκατον ἄρθρον τῆς πίστεως;

Ἀπ. Ὁμολογῶ ἓν βάπτισμα εἰς ἄφεσιν ἁμαρτιῶν.

QUÆSTIO XCVII.

Decimus fidei Articulus quis est?

RESP. *Confiteor unum baptisma in remissionem peccatorum.*

Ἐρώτησις ςή.

Τί διδάσκει τὸ ἄρθρον τοῦτο τῆς πίστεως;

Ἀπ. Ἐπειδὴ ἐνθυμᾶται τοῦ βαπτίσματος, ὅπου εἶναι τὸ πρῶτον μυστήριον, μας δίδει ἀφορμὴν, νὰ θεωρήσωμεν περὶ τῶν ἑπτὰ μυστηρίων

QUÆSTIO XCVIII.

Quid hic fidei Articulus docet?

RESP. Quandoquidem baptismatis mentionem facit, quod primum ecclesiæ mysterium est: locum nobis opportunum præbet disserendi,

τῆς ἐκκλησίας· τὰ ὁποῖα εἶναι ταῦτα·
τὸ βάπτισμα, τὸ μύρον τοῦ χρίσματος,
ἡ εὐχαριστία, ἡ μετάνοια, ἡ ἱερωσύνη,
ὁ τίμιος γάμος, καὶ τὸ εὐχέλαιον.
Ταῦτα τα ἑπτὰ μυστήρια ἀναβιβά-
ζονται εἰς τὰ ἑπτὰ χαρίσματα τοῦ
ἁγίου Πνεύματος· ἐπειδὴ διὰ μέσου
τῶν μυστηρίων τούτων χύνει τὰς δω-
ρεάς του τὸ Πνεῦμα τὸ ἅγιον εἰς τὰς
ψυχὰς ἐκείνων, ὅπου τὰ μετέχουσι
καθὼς πρέπει, καὶ τὴν χάριν του.
Διὰ τὸ ὁποῖον πρᾶγμα ὁ Πατριάρχης
Ἱερεμίας εἰς πλάτος διαλέγεται εἰς τὸ
βιβλίον, ὅπου ἔγραψε πρὸς τοὺς Λου-
τεράνους, διὰ νὰ ἐπιστρέψουσιν.

de *septem mysteriis* ecclesiæ, quæ
sunt: Baptisma, Unguentum Chrismatis, Eucharistia, Pœnitentia, Sacerdotium, honorabile Conjugium,
et Oleum consecratum (extrema
unctio). Quæ septem sacramenta
septenis Spiritus Sancti donis re-
spondent, quoniam per ea dona
sua ac gratiam animis recte et
legitime utentium Spiritus Sanctus
infundit. Qua de re pluribus egit
Patriarcha Hieremias in libro,
quem convertendis Lutheranis
scripsit.

Ἐρώτησις ϟθ'.

Τί ἐστι μυστήριον;

Ἀπ. Τὸ μυστήριον εἶναι μία τελε-
τὴ, ἡ ὁποία ἀποκάτω[1] εἰς κάποιον εἶδος
ὁρατὸν εἶναι αἰτία, καὶ φέρει εἰς τὴν
ψυχὴν τοῦ πιστοῦ τὴν ἀόρατον χάριν
τοῦ Θεοῦ· διαταχθὲν ὑπὸ τοῦ Κυρίου
ὑμῶν, δι' οὗ ἕκαστος τῶν πιστῶν τὴν
θείαν χάριν λαμβάνει.

Ἐρώτησις ρ'.

Πόσα πράγματα ζητοῦνται εἰς τὸ
μυστήριον;

Ἀπ. Τρία, ὕλη ἁρμόδιος, ὡς
εἶναι τὸ ὕδωρ εἰς τὸ βάπτισμα· ὁ
ἄρτος καὶ ὁ οἶνος εἰς τὴν εὐχαρισ-
τίαν· τὸ ἔλαιον, καὶ τὰ λοιπὰ κατὰ

Quæstio XCIX.

Quid est mysterium sive sacramentum?

Resp. Mysterium est sacra quædam cærimonia, quæ sub specie aliqua visibili causa est, et in animam
hominis fidelis invisibilem Dei gratiam infert: institutum a Domino
nostro, per quem unusquisque fidelium divinam gratiam accipit.

Quæstio C.

Quot res ad Mysterium opus
sunt?

Resp. Tres. *Materia idonea*,
utpote aqua in baptismate; panis
et vinum in eucharistia; oleum et
cetera in suis quæque mysteriis.

---

[1] Or ὑποκάτω.

τὸ μυστήριον. Δεύτερον ὁ ἱερεὺς, ὅπου νὰ εἶναι νομίμως κεχειροτονημένος ἢ ὁ ἐπίσκοπος. Τρίτον ἡ ἐπίκλησις τοῦ ἁγίου Πνεύματος, καὶ τὸ εἶδος τῶν λογίων, μετὰ ὁποῖα ὁ ἱερεὺς ἁγιάζει τὸ μυστήριον τῇ δυνάμει τοῦ ἁγίου Πνεύματος μὲ γνώμην ἀποφασισμένην του νὰ τὸ ἁγιάσῃ.

Secunda, *Sacerdos* legitimis suffragiis ordinatus aut *Episcopus.* Tertia *Invocatio Spiritus Sancti et solemnis verborum formula.* Quibus verbis vi et efficacia Spiritus Sancti mysterium sacerdos rite sanctificat ; accedente fixa et deliberata ejusdem intentione sanctificandi mysterii.

Ἐρώτησις ρά.

Διὰ ποῖον τέλος τὰ μυστήρια διετάχθησαν ;

Ἀπ. Πρῶτον διὰ νὰ εἶναι σημάδια τῶν ἀληθινῶν υἱῶν τοῦ Θεοῦ, ἤγουν τῆς ἐκκλησίας τῆς ὀρθοδόξου, τῆς καθολικῆς καὶ ἀποστολικῆς· διατὶ ὅποιος χρᾶται τὰ μυστήρια τοῦτα καθὼς πρέπει, εἶναι εἰς τὴν ἐκκλησίαν τοῦ Θεοῦ ἀληθινὸν καὶ γνήσιον μέλος της καὶ κατὰ χάριν υἱὸς Θεοῦ. Δεύτερον, διὰ νὰ ἔχωμεν ἀσφαλὲς σημεῖον τῆς εἰς Θεὸν ἡμῶν πίστεως, ἔστωντας καὶ νὰ εἴμεσθαν βέβαιοι μὲ τὴν πίστιν, καὶ μετὰ καλὰ ἔργα, νὰ σωθοῦμεν εἰς τὴν αἰώνιον ζωήν. Τρίτον, διὰ νὰ ἔχωμεν ἰατρικὰ ἀναμφίβολα, νὰ διώχνωμεν ταῖς ἀσθενείαις τῶν ἁμαρτιῶν μας.

QUÆSTIO CI.

Quem in finem instituta sunt mysteria ?

RESP. Primo ut signa atque tesseræ verorum Dei filiorum sive Ecclesiæ orthodoxæ, catholicæ et apostolicæ sint. Nam quisquis, ut oportet, hisce utitur mysteriis, is verum et genuinum ecclesiæ Dei membrum est et secundum gratiam Dei filius. Secundo ut certum nostræ in Deum fiduciæ habeamus pignus. Si videlicet in fide bonisque operibus constanter perseveraverimus, tum vitæ nos ac salutis æternæ compotes omnino fore. Tertio ut explorata atque præsentanea habeamus remedia, quibus infirmitates peccatorum nostrorum depellamus.

Ἐρώτησις ρβ'.

Τί εἶναι τὸ πρῶτον μυστήριον τοῦ βαπτίσματος ;

Ἀπ. Τὸ βάπτισμα εἶναι μία ἔκπλυσις καὶ ἀναίρεσις τοῦ προπατορι-

QUÆSTIO CII.

Quid est primum mysterium sive baptismatis ?

RESP. Baptisma est ablutio quædam et exstirpatio peccati origi-

κοῦ ἁμαρτήματος· διὰ τῆς τρίτης κα-
ταδύσεως εἰς τὸ ὕδωρ, λέγοντος τοῦ
ἱερέως τὰ λόγια τοῦτα· εἰς τὸ ὄνομα
τοῦ Πατρὸς, ἀμήν· καὶ τοῦ Υἱοῦ,
ἀμήν· καὶ τοῦ ἁγίου Πνεύματος,
ἀμήν. ('Ο ἀνάδοχος ὀφείλει προφέ-
ρειν τὸ ἀμήν.) Καὶ μετὰ τὴν ἀνα-
γέννησιν τούτην ἐξ ὕδατος καὶ Πνεύματος γίνεται ἡ διαλλαγὴ τοῦ ἀνθρώπου μὲ τὸν Θεὸν, καὶ συγχωρεῖται ἡ
εἴσοδος εἰς τὴν βασιλείαν τῶν οὐρανῶν, κατὰ τὰ λόγια τοῦ Σωτῆρος
ἡμῶν ('Ιωαν. γ΄. ἑ.), λέγοντος· ἐὰν
μή τις γεννηθῇ ἐξ ὕδατος καὶ Πνεύματος, οὐ δύναται εἰσελθεῖν εἰς τὴν
βασιλείαν τοῦ Θεοῦ. Τοῦτο τὸ μυστήριον μίαν φορὰν λαμβανόμενον δὲν
δίδεται δεύτερον· μόνον ἐκεῖνος ὅπου
βαπτίζει νὰ πιστεύῃ ὀρθοδόξως ἕνα
Θεὸν τρισυπόστατον, καὶ νὰ εἶπεν ἀκριβῶς καὶ ἀπαραλλάκτως τὰ προρρη-
θέντα λόγια· εἰς τὸ ὄνομα τοῦ Πατρὸς, καὶ τοῦ Υἱοῦ, καὶ τοῦ ἁγίου
Πνεύματος ἀμήν, κατὰ τὴν γνώμην τῆς
καθολικῆς καὶ ὀρθοδόξου ἐκκλησίας.

'Ερώτησις ργ΄.

Τί πρέπει νὰ φυλάττεται εἰς τὸ
μυστήριον τοῦτο;

'Απ. Τὸ πρῶτον εἶναι, ὅπου τὸ
βρέφος μὲ τὸν ἀνάδοχόν του (ὁ ὁποῖος πρέπει νὰ εἶναι ὀρθόδοξος) ἔχει
ἀνάγκην, νὰ ἀποταγῇ ἤγουν νὰ ἀρνη-
θῇ τὸν διάβολον καὶ ὅλα του τὰ ἔργα
καὶ τὴν λατρείαν του καὶ πᾶσαν τὴν
πομπήν του. Μὰ ἂν ὁ βαπτιζόμενος

nalis, terna in aquam immersione
facta, pronunciante hæc verba sacerdote: In nomine Patris; Amen;
et Filii; Amen; et Spiritus Sancti; Amen. (Nota: Susceptor sive
pater lustricus respondet: Amen.)
Post hanc ex aqua et Spiritu re-
generationem homo in gratiam
cum Deo reducitur, patetque illi
cœlestis regni aditus secundum
verba Servatoris nostri (Joh. iii.
5): 'Nisi quis ex aqua et Spiritu
genitus fuerit, non potest ingredi
in regnum Dei.' Hoc autem mysterium semel acceptum iterum non
repetitur; modo si is, qui baptizat, orthodoxe in unum Deum
personis trinum credat, et accurate nullaque immutatione prædicta verba: In nomine Patris, et
Filii, et Spiritus Sancti Amen secundum catholicæ et orthodoxæ
Ecclesiæ sententiam proferat.

QUÆSTIO CIII.

Quidnam in hoc Mysterio observandum?

RESP. Primum necesse infantulo
est, per susceptorem suum, qui orthodoxus esse debet, penitus re-
nunciare familiaritati diaboli, illumque cum operibus suis omnibus, cum cultu pompaque omni
repudiare. Quod si baptizandus

θέλει εἶναι νομίμου ἡλικίας, εἶναι
ἀνάγκη, ὅτι αὐτὸς ὁ ἴδιος, αὐτός του
νὰ κάμῃ τὴν ἄρνησιν τοῦ διαβόλου,
ἀποκρινόμενος εἰς τὰς ἐρωτήσεις τοῦ
ἱερέως, καὶ ἐμπτύωντας τὸν διάβολον
καὶ τὰ ἔργα του ὅλα· ἔπειτα νὰ ὁμολογήσῃ τὸ σύμβολον τῆς πίστεως·
καὶ ἂν εἶναι νήπιον, νὰ ὁμολογήσῃ ὁ
ἀνάδοχός του δι᾽ αὐτὸν τὸ σύμβολον
τοῦτο τῆς πίστεως· καὶ νὰ ὑποσχεθῇ
δι᾽ αὐτὸν εἰς τὸν Χριστόν. Ἀκόμι
καὶ τοῦτο πρέπει νὰ φυλάττεται εἰς τὸ
βάπτισμα, νὰ εἶναι εἰλικρινὲς ὕδωρ,
ὄχι μικτὸν μὲ ἄλλο πρᾶγμα οὔτε τεχ-
νητὸν, μήτε ἄλλο ὑγρόν. Καὶ τὸ
διατεταγμένον βάπτισμα δὲν πρέπει
νὰ γίνεται ἀπὸ ἄλλον τινὰ παρὰ ἀπὸ
τὸν νόμιμον ἱερέα· μὰ εἰς καιρὸν τινὸς ἀνάγκης ἠμπορεῖ νὰ τὸ κάμῃ τὸ
μυστήριον τοῦτο καὶ κοσμικὸν πρόσωπον ἀνδρὸς ἢ γυναικὸς, μεταχειριζό-
μενον τὴν πρεπουμένην ὕλην, νερὸν
ἁπλοῦν καὶ φυσικὸν, ἐπιφέρον καὶ τὰ
ῥηθέντα λόγια· εἰς τὸ ὄνομα τοῦ Πατρὸς, καὶ τοῦ Υἱοῦ, καὶ τοῦ ἁγίου
Πνεύματος· κάμωντας καὶ τὴν τρίτην
κατάδυσιν. Καὶ τὸ τοιοῦτον βάπτισμα τόσην δύναμιν ἔχει, ὅπου ἔστωντας
καὶ νὰ μὴ δίδεται δεύτερον, εἶναι ἀναμ-
φίβολος σφραγὶς τῆς σωτηρίας τῆς
αἰωνίου. Καὶ ποῖος νὰ εἶναι ὁ καρπὸς καὶ τὸ κέρδος τοῦ μυστηρίου τούτου, εὔκολα καθ᾽ ἕνας τὸ γνωρίζει.
Διατὶ πρῶτον τὸ μυστήριον τοῦτο σι-
κώνει ὅλα τὰ ἁμαρτήματα· εἰς μὲν τὰ
βρέφη τὸ προπατορικὸν, εἰς δὲ τοὺς

justam ingressus est ætatem, ut
ille ipse, suo ore, repudium diabolo
renunciet, respondendo ad inter-
rogationes sacerdotis, satanamque
et omnia opera illius consputando.
Dein ut symbolum fidei aperte
profiteatur, sin infans est, ut ipsius
nomine idem symbolum sponsor
edat et Christo sacramentum dicat.
Porro illud etiam in baptismate
curandum est, ut aqua pura, nullaque re alia permixta, neque ar-
tificialis, nec alius liquor ullus ad-
hibeatur. Tum legitimum baptisma a nemine alio administrari
oportet, quam ordinario verbi ministro. Veruntamen urgente aliqua
necessitate etiam alius quisque
homo, sive mas sive femina hoc
peragere sacramentum potest, sum-
ta in manus debita materie, aqua
simplici atque naturali, verbisque
solemnibus: In nomine Patris, et
Filii, et Spiritus Sancti, ad trinam
immersionem rite adjectis. Ea
vero baptismatis hujus, etsi non
amplius iterandi, vis et efficacitas
est, ut indubium æternæ salutis
signaculum ac pignus sit. Qui
fructus vero quodve emolumen-
tum hujus mysterii sit, id per
se facile quisque videt. Primum
enim peccata omnia abolet, in infantibus originale, in adultis tum
illud tum voluntarium. Deinde
hominem plane renovat, in eum-

μεγάλους καὶ τὸ προπατορικὸν καὶ τὸ προαιρετικόν. Δεύτερον ὁ ἄνθρωπος ἀνακαινίζεται καὶ ἀποκαθίσταται εἰς τὴν δικαίωσιν ἐκείνην, ὅπου εἶχεν, ὅταν ἦτον ἀθῶος καὶ ἀναμάρτητος· καθὼς μαρτυρᾷ (ά. Κορ. ς'. ιά) ὁ Ἀπόστολος, λέγων· ἀλλὰ ἀπελούσασθε, ἀλλὰ ἡγιάσθητε, ἀλλ' ἐδικαιώθητε ἐν τῷ ὀνόματι τοῦ Κυρίου Ἰησοῦ, καὶ ἐν τῷ Πνεύματι τοῦ Θεοῦ ἡμῶν. Ἔπειτα οἱ βαπτισθέντες γίνουνται μέλη τοῦ σώματος τοῦ Χριστοῦ, καὶ τὸν Κύριον ἡμῶν ἐνδυόμεθα· διατὶ (Γαλ. γ'. κζ'.) λέγει ὁ Ἀπόστολος· ὅσοι εἰς Χριστὸν ἐβαπτίσθητε, Χριστὸν ἐνεδύσασθε.

Ἐρώτησις ρδ'.

Ποῖον εἶναι τὸ δεύτερον μυστήριον εἰς τὴν ἐκκλησίαν τοῦ Χριστοῦ;

Ἀπ. Τὸ δεύτερον μυστήριον εἶναι τὸ μύρον τοῦ χρίσματος· τὸ ὁποῖον ἤρχισεν ἀπὸ τὸν καιρὸν ἐκεῖνον, ὅπου τὸ Πνεῦμα τὸ ἅγιον ἐκατάβηκεν (Πράξ. β'.) εἰς τοὺς Ἀποστόλους, σφραγίζοντας τοὺς μὲ τὴν θείαν του χάριν, διὰ νὰ κηρύττουσι σταθερῶς καὶ ἀδιαλείπτως τὴν πίστιν τοῦ Χριστοῦ. Καὶ τὴν βοήθειαν τούτην χρειάζονται καὶ οἱ βαπτιζόμενοι· καὶ καθὼς πάλαι τὸ Πνεῦμα τὸ ἅγιον ἐκατάβηκεν εἰς τοὺς Ἀποστόλους ἐν εἴδει πυρὸς καὶ ἔχυσεν εἰς αὐτοὺς τὰ χαρίσματά του· τέτοιας λογῆς καὶ τῶρα, ὅταν ὁ ἱερεὺς χρίει τὸν βαπτιζόμενον μὲ τὸ ἅγιον μύρον, χύνουνται ἀπάνω εἰς αὐτὸν τὰ

que justitiæ sanctitatisque restituit locum, quo innocens adhuc intactusque peccato olim steterat, quemadmodum testatur Apostolus (1 Cor. vi. 2): 'Sed abluti estis, sed sanctificati, sed justificati in nomine Domini Iesu et in Spiritu Dei nostri.' Super hæc membra corporis Christi baptizati evadimus, Dominumque nostrum induimus, teste Apostolo (Gal. iii. 27): 'Quotquot in Christum baptizati estis, Christum induistis.'

QUÆSTIO CIV.

Quodnam secundum in Ecclesia Christi Mysterium est?

RESP. Secundum Mysterium unguentum chrismatis (sive confirmationis) est. Quod ab eo tempore initium habuit (Act. ii), quo super Apostolos cœlo devectus consedit Spiritus Sanctus, eosque divina gratia sua obsignavit, quo constanter et sine intermissione fidem Christi prædicarent. Eodem numine auxilioque iis omnino opus est, qui Christianismo initiantur. Rursus, uti tunc temporis visibili ignis specie delapsus Spiritus Sanctus charismata sua Apostolis impertivit: pariter et hodie, quando sacerdos oleo sacro recens baptiza-

χαρίσματα τοῦ ἁγίου Πνεύματος. Τὸ ὁποῖον εἶναι δῆλον ἀπὸ τὰ λόγια, ὅπου χρεωστεῖ ὁ ἱερεὺς νὰ λέγῃ, ὅταν ἐνεργῇ τὸ τοιοῦτο μυστήριον· σφραγὶς δωρεᾶς Πνεύματος ἁγίου, ἀμήν. Ὡς ἂν νὰ ἔλεγε, μὲ τὴν χρίσιν τούτου τοῦ ἁγίου μύρου σφραγίζεσαι καὶ βεβαιώνεσαι εἰς τὰ χαρίσματα τοῦ ἁγίου Πνεύματος, ὅπου πέρνεις εἰς βεβαίωσιν τῆς Χριστιανικῆς σου πίστεως· καὶ τοῦτο συμφωνᾷ μὲ τὰ λόγια τοῦ Ἀποστόλου (β'. Κορ. ά. κά.) λέγοντος· ὁ δὲ βεβαιῶν ἡμᾶς σὺν ὑμῖν εἰς Χριστὸν καὶ χρίσας ἡμᾶς, Θεός· ὁ καὶ σφραγισάμενος ἡμᾶς Θεὸς, καὶ δοὺς τὸν ἀῤῥαβῶνα τοῦ Πνεύματος ἐν ταῖς καρδίαις ἡμῶν. Ἡ χρίσις αὕτη τοῦ μύρου, ἢ μᾶλλον εἰπεῖν, ἡ ἐνέργεια τούτη τῆς χρίσεως, ἐγίνετο εἰς τὸν καιρὸν τῶν Ἀποστόλων διὰ τῆς ἐπιθέσεως τῶν χειρῶν. Διατὶ (Πρᾶξ. ή. ιζ'.) λέγει ἡ Γραφὴ· Τότε ἐπετίθουν τὰς χεῖρας ἐπ' αὐτοὺς, καὶ ἐλάμβανον Πνεῦμα ἅγιον. Ὕστερα ἐγίνετο μὲ τὴν χρίσιν τοῦ μύρου, καθὼς μαρτυρᾷ ὁ ἱερὸς Διονύσιος ὁ Ἀρεοπαγίτης, ὁ μαθητὴς τοῦ μακαρίου Παύλου.

Ἐρώτησις ρέ.

Πόσα πράγματα ζητοῦνται εἰς τοῦτο τὸ μυστήριον;

Ἀπ. Πρῶτον ζητεῖται νὰ γίνεται ἀπὸ τὸν ἀνωτάτω ἐπίσκοπον τὸ μύρον τοῦτο. Δεύτερον, νὰ ἔχῃ τὴν πρεπουμένην του ὕλην, ἤγουν τὸ

tum inungit, desuper idem Spiritus Sancti donis perfunditur. Quod manifeste arguunt verba sacerdoti mysterium hoc peragenti de more pronuncianda: Signaculum muneris Spiritus Sancti, Amen. Quasi si dicat: Inunctione sacri hujus unguenti obsignaris confirmarisque in Spiritus Sancti donis, quæ in confirmationem Christianæ fidei tuæ accipis. Quod cum verbis Apostoli congruit (2 Cor. i. 21): 'Qui confirmat nos vobiscum in Christo, et qui unxit nos Deus, qui etiam obsignavit nos, indiditque arrhabonem Spiritus in cordibus nostris.' Hæc vero unguenti inunctio aut potius hæc unctionis hujus efficientia ævo Apostolorum per impositionem manuum fiebat, dicente ita Scriptura (Act. viii. 17): 'Tunc imponebant illis manus, et accipiebant Spiritum Sanctum.' Postmodum inunctione unguenti fieri cœpit, teste S. Dionysio Areopagita, B. Pauli discipulo (Eccles. Hierarch. cap. ii. et iv.).

QUÆSTIO CV.

Quot ad hoc Mysterium necessariæ res sunt?

RESP. Primum necesse est, ut ab summi loci ordinisque Episcopo hoc consecretur unguentum. Secundo, ut aptam congruentemque

ἔλαιον, τὸ βάλσαμον καὶ τὰ λοιπὰ μυρίσματα. Τρίτον ζητεῖται, ὅτι παρευθὺς μετὰ τὸ βάπτισμα νὰ χρίῃ ὁ ἱερεὺς τὸν βαπτιζόμενον εἰς τὰ διωρισμένα μέλη, ἐπιλέγων τὰ λόγια ἐκεῖνα· σφραγὶς δωρεᾶς Πνεύματος ἁγίου, ἀμήν. Ἀπὸ τὸ μυστήριον τοῦτο γενοῦνται οἱ καρποὶ τοῦτοι. Πρῶτον, διατὶ καθώς με τὸ βάπτισμα ἀναγεννώμεθα· τέτοιας λογῆς, μὲ τὸ ἅγιον μύρον γενόμεθα μέτοχοι τοῦ ἁγίου Πνεύματος, βεβαιωθέντες εἰς τὴν πίστιν τοῦ Κυρίου, καὶ αὐξάνομεν εἰς τὴν θείαν χάριν κατὰ τὸν Ἀπόστολον (Τιτ. γ΄. ἑ.) τὸν λέγοντα, ὅτι ἔσωσεν ἡμᾶς κατὰ τὸν αὐτοῦ ἔλεον διὰ λουτροῦ παλιγγενεσίας καὶ ἀνακαινώσεως Πνεύματος ἁγίου, οὗ ἐξέχεεν ἐφ᾽ ἡμᾶς πλουσίως διὰ Ἰησοῦ Χριστοῦ τοῦ σωτῆρος ἡμῶν. Δεύτερον, διατὶ μὲ τὴν δύναμιν τοῦ ἁγίου Πνεύματος οὕτως εἴμεσθεν βέβαιοι καὶ στερεοὶ, ὁποῦ δὲν ἠμπορεῖ νὰ βλάψῃ καθόλου ὁ νοητὸς ἐχϑρὸς τὴν ψυχήν μας. Τοῦτο τὸ μυστήριον δὲν δίδοται δεύτερον παρὰ εἰς ἐκείνους, ὁποῦ θέλουσιν ἐπιστρέψειν ἀπὸ τὴν ἄρνησιν τοῦ ὀνόματος τοῦ Χριστοῦ.

Ἐρώτησις ρς΄.

Ποῖον εἶναι τὸ τρίτον μυστήριον;

Ἀπ. Ἡ ἁγία εὐχαριστία, ἤγουν τὸ σῶμα καὶ αἷμα τοῦ Κυρίου ἡμῶν Ἰησοῦ Χριστοῦ, ὑποκάτω εἰς τὴν θεωρίαν τοῦ ἄρτου καὶ τοῦ οἴνου, εἰς τὸ

---

sibi materiam habeat; nimirum oleum, balsamum, unguenta cetera. Tertio, ut e vestigio post baptismum, certis definitisque membris, baptizatum sacerdos inungat, cum hac formula: *Signaculum muneris Spiritus Sancti, Amen.* Ex hoc Mysterio hi proveniunt fructus. Primum, velut per Baptisma renascimur: ita per sacrum hocce unguentum Spiritus Sancti participes efficimur, confirmamur in fide Domini atque in gratia divina sensim adolescimus, docente Apostolo (Tit. iii. 5): ' Salvavit nos secundum misericordiam suam, per lavacrum regenerationis et renovationis Spiritus Sancti, quem copiose super nos effudit per Iesum Christum Salvatorem nostrum.' Secundo, quod adjutorio Spiritus Sancti ita confirmamur et corroboramur, ut nihil penitus animæ nostræ spiritualis hostis noster nocere valeat. Denique neque hoc unquam repetitur Mysterium nisi in illis, qui ab nominis Christi ejuratione (ad professionem ejusdem) postliminio redeunt.

QUÆSTIO CVI.

Quodnam tertium est Mysterium?

RESP. Sancta Eucharistia, sive corpus et sanguis Domini nostri Iesu Christi, sub visibili specie panis et vini, in quo vere et proprie,

ὁποῖον εἶναι ἀληθῶς καὶ κυρίως παρὼν, ἤγουν κατὰ τὸ πρᾶγμα, ὁ Ἰησοῦς
Χριστός. Τοῦτο τὸ μυστήριον ὑπερέχει ὅλα τὰ ἄλλα, καὶ μᾶλλον τῶν
ἄλλων ὠφελεῖ εἰς τὴν σωτηρίαν τὴν
ἐδικήν μας. Ἐπειδὴ εἰς τὸ μυστήριον
τοῦτο πᾶσα χάρις καὶ χρηστότης τοῦ
Κυρίου Ἰησοῦ φαινερώνεται εἰς τοὺς
πιστοὺς καὶ παριστάνεται, καθὼς θέλει γένῃ γνώριμον κατωτέρω.

Ἐρώτησις ρζ΄.

Τί πρέπει νὰ φυλάττεται εἰς τὸ μυστήριον τοῦτο;

Ἀπ. Πρῶτον τοῦτο τὸ μυστήριον
οὐδένας ἄλλος ἠμπορεῖ νὰ τὸ κάμῃ,
εἰς ὁποῖαν χρείαν καὶ ἂν τύχῃ, παρὰ
νὰ εἶναι ἱερεὺς νόμιμος. Δεύτερον
πρέπει, νὰ προμηθεύῃ, νὰ εἶναι θυσι-
αστήριον ἐκεῖ, ὁποῦ μέλλει νὰ ἱερουρ-
γήσῃ, ἢ ἀντιμίσιον, χωρὶς τοῦ ὁποίου
καθ᾽ οὐδένα τρόπον ἠμπορεῖ νὰ προσ-
φέρῃ τὴν ἀναίμακτον θυσίαν. Τρίτον
πρέπει, νὰ προσέχῃ, νὰ εἶναι ἡ πρε-
πουμένη ὕλη, ἤγουν ἄρτος σίτινος
ἔνζημος, ὅσον δυνατὸν καθαρός, καὶ
οἶνος ἄμικτος ἀπὸ κάθα λογῆς ἄλλο
ὑγρὸν, καὶ εἰλικρινὴς εἰς ἑαυτόν. Καὶ
εἰς τὴν προσκομιδὴν ἐγχεῖται καὶ ὕδωρ
πρὸς πλήρωσιν τῆς Γραφῆς (Ἰωαν.
ιθ΄. λδ΄.) τῆς λεγούσης, ὅτι εἷς τῶν
στρατιωτῶν λόγχῃ τὴν πλευρὰν αὐτοῦ ἔνυξε, καὶ εὐθὺς ἐξῆλθεν αἷμα καὶ
ὕδωρ. Τέταρτον πρέπει, νὰ ἔχῃ ὁ
ἱερεὺς τοιαύτην γνώμην εἰς τὸν καιρὸν, ὁποῦ ἁγιάζει τὰ δῶρα, πῶς αὐτὴ

hoc est, secundum rem ipsam præsto adest Iesu Christus. Hoc Mysterium inter reliqua omnia unum
præcipue eminet, atque plus ceteris
ad salutem consequendam nobis
confert. Namque in eo gratiæ
benignitatisque Domini Iesu opes
universæ fidelibus monstrantur ex-
hibenturque, ut postea patebit.

Quæstio CVII.

Quid in hoc Mysterio observandum?

Resp. Primum, quod hoc Mysterium nemo homo, nisi legitime
creatus sacerdos, quantacunque urgente necessitate, administrare possit. Secundo providendum sacerdoti, ut, quo loco sacrificium fac-
turus est, altare aut tapes saltem
mensalis consecratus ad manum
sit, absque quo nullo modo integrum est, incruentum offere sacrificium. Tertio curabit, ut in promtu
sit materia debita, sive panis ex
frugibus confectus, fermentatus et
quantum potest purus; et vinum
haud alio humore confusum in
seque purum et sincerum. Affun-
ditur in actu ipso et aqua (calida)
implendæ Scripturæ, quæ dicit (Io.
xix. 34): 'quod quum unus quispiam militis hasta latus Christi
hausisset: sanguis continuo et aqua
profluxerit.' Quarto eo temporis

ἡ οὐσία τοῦ ἄρτου καὶ ἡ οὐσία τοῦ
οἴνου μεταβάλλεται εἰς τὴν οὐσίαν
τοῦ ἀληθινοῦ σώματος καὶ αἵματος
τοῦ Χριστοῦ διὰ τῆς ἐνεργείας τοῦ
ἁγίου Πνεύματος, οὗ τὴν ἐπίκλησιν
κάμει τὴν ὥραν ἐκείνην, διανατεληὼς
τὸ μυστήριον τοῦτο, ἐπευχόμενος καὶ
λέγων· Κατάπεμψον τὸ Πνεῦμά σου
τὸ ἅγιον ἐφ' ἡμᾶς καὶ ἐπὶ τὰ π〟οκεί-
μενα δῶρα ταῦτα· καὶ ποίησον τὸν
μὲν ἄρτον τοῦτον τίμιον σῶμα τοῦ
Χριστοῦ σου, τὸ δὲ ἐν τῷ ποτηρίῳ
τούτῳ τίμιον αἷμα τοῦ Χριστοῦ σου,
μεταβαλὼν τῷ Πνεύματί σου τῷ ἁγίῳ.
Μετὰ γὰρ τὰ ῥήματα ταῦτα ἡ μετουσίωσις παρευθὺς γίνεται, καὶ ἀλλήσει
ὁ ἄρτος εἰς τὸ ἀληθινὸν σῶμα τοῦ
Χριστοῦ, καὶ ὁ οἶνος εἰς τὸ ἀληθινὸν
αἷμα. Ἀπομένονται μόνον τὰ εἴδη
ὑποῦ φαίνουνται, καὶ τοῦτο κατὰ τὴν
θείαν οἰκονομίαν. Πρῶτον μὲν, διὰ
νὰ μὴν βλέπωμεν σῶμα Χριστοῦ, μὰ
νὰ τὸ πιστεύωμεν πῶς εἶναι, διὰ τὰ
λόγια ὑποῦ εἶπεν· τοῦτό ἐστι τὸ σῶμά
μου, καὶ τοῦτό ἐστι τὸ αἷμά μου· πιστεύοντες μᾶλλον εἰς τὰ λόγια καὶ δύναμιν ἐκείνου, παρὰ εἰς ταῖς ἐδικαῖς
μας αἰσθήσεις. Τὸ ὁποῖον προξενεῖ
μακαρισμὸν τῆς πίστεως· μακάριοι
γὰρ (Ἰωαν. κ'. κθ'.) οἱ μὴ ἰδόντες καὶ
πιστεύσαντες. Δεύτερον, διατὶ ἡ φύσις ἡ ἀνθρωπίνη ἀποτρέπεται τὴν
ὠμὴν σαρκοφαγίαν, καὶ ἐπειδὴ ἔμελλε
νὰ πέρνῃ τὴν ἕνωσιν τοῦ Χριστοῦ μὲ
τὴν μετάληψιν τῆς σαρκὸς καὶ αἵματός
του, διὰ νὰ μὴν τὴν ἀποτρέπεται

articulo, quo sacra munera conse-
crat sacerdos, ita omnino secum
statuere debet, quod substantia ipsa
panis et vini in substantiam veri
corporis et sanguinis Christi opera
Spiritus Sancti immutetur, cujus
numen illo interim spatio implorat
his nimirum verbis, ut rite hoc ipse
perficiat mysterium, exoptans: De-
mitte o Deus de cœlo Spiritum
tuum Sanctum, super nos, et super
proposita hæcce dona, et panem
hunc effice pretiosum corpus Christi tui; idque, quod in calice hoc
inest, effice pretiosum sanguinem
Christi tui, transformans ea per
Spiritum tuum Sanctum. Quippe
pronunciatis hisce verbis, confestim
Transsubstantiatio peragitur, muta-
turque panis in verum corpus Christi, vinum in verum ejusdem sanguinem; manentibus tantummodo
per divinam dispositionem speciebus, quæ visu percipiuntur. Primum ut ne ipsummet corpus Christi
oculis nostris cernamus, sed fide
potius credamus, id ipsum esse,
propter Christi ipsius verba: Hoc
est corpus meum; hoc est sanguis
meus; plus videlicet fidei habentes
verbis et potentiæ illius quam nostris ipsorum sensibus. Quæ res
beatitudinis fidei nos compotes facit
(Io. xx. 29): 'Nam beati illi, qui
credunt, etsi non viderunt.' Secundo, quoniam ab esu crudæ carnis

βδελυττόμενος ὁ ἄνθρωπος· ᾠκονόμησεν ἡ πρόνοια τοῦ Θεοῦ, καὶ δίδως
τὴν σάρκα τὴν ἰδίαν καὶ τὸ αἷμά του
εἰς βρῶσιν καὶ πόσιν τοῖς πιστοῖς,
ὑποκάτω εἰς τὸ ἔνδυμα τοῦ ἄρτου καὶ
τοῦ οἴνου. Περὶ τούτου ὁ Γρηγόριος
Νύσσης καὶ ὁ ἱερὸς Δαμασκηνὸς εἰς
πλάτος διαλέγονται. Ἡ δὲ κοινωνία
τοῦ μυστηρίου τούτου πρέπει νὰ γίνεται καὶ κατὰ τὰ δύο εἴδη τοῦ ἄρτου
καὶ τοῦ οἴνου, τόσον ἀπὸ τοὺς πνευματικοὺς, ὅσον καὶ ἀπὸ τοὺς κοσμι-
κούς· ἐπειδὴ ὁ Χριστὸς, δὲν ἐκβά-
ζωντας κἂν ἕνα, οὕτω προσέταξε
(Ἰωαν. ϛ'. νγ'.) λέγων· ἀμὴν ἀμὴν
λέγω ὑμῖν, ἐὰν μὴ φάγητε τὴν σάρκα
τοῦ υἱοῦ τοῦ ἀνθρώπου καὶ πίητε αὐτοῦ τὸ αἷμα, οὐκ ἔχετε ζωὴν αἰώνιον
ἐν ἑαυτοῖς. Ὁ τρώγων μου τὴν σάρκα καὶ πίνων μου τὸ αἷμα, ἐν ἐμοὶ
μένει, κἀγὼ ἐν αὐτῷ. Διατὶ καὶ οἱ
ἅγιοι Ἀπόστολοι κατὰ τὸν τρόπον,
ὅπου τὸ ἐπαραλάβασιν ἀπὸ τὸν Χριστὸν, οὕτω καὶ τὸ ἐπαραδίδασιν εἰς κοινωνίαν κοσμικῶν τε καὶ ἱερωμένων,
καὶ εἰς τὰ δύο εἴδη· καθὼς (ά. Κορ.
ιά. κβ'.) γράφει πρὸς Κορινθίους ὁ
Παῦλος ὁ Ἀπόστολος λέγων· ἐγὼ
γὰρ παρέλαβον ἀπὸ τοῦ Κυρίου, ὁ
καὶ παρέδωκα ὑμῖν, ὅτι ὁ Κύριος Ἰησοῦς Χριστὸς ἐν τῇ νυκτὶ ᾗ παρεδί-
δοτο ἔλαβεν ἄρτον, καὶ εὐχαριστήσας
ἔκλασε καὶ εἶπε· λάβετε, φάγετε, τοῦτό μου ἐστὶ τὸ σῶμα τὸ ὑπὲρ ὑμῶν
κλώμενον· τοῦτο ποιεῖτε εἰς τὴν ἐμὴν
ἀνάμνησιν. Ὡσαύτως καὶ τὸ ποτή-

humana abhorret natura, et tamen
in hoc mysterio per participationem
carnis et sanguinis Christi arctissi-
mam cum illo conjunctionem homo
Christianus initurus erat. Ut ne
igitur participationem istam idem
abominaretur et respueret: famil-
iari rem ratione divina temperavit
providentia, propriamque carnem
et sanguinem suum fidelibus in cibum potumque sub panis et vini in-
volucris tradidit. Qua de re fusius uberiusque disserunt Gregorius
Nyssenus et S. Damascenus. Ceterum communio mysterii hujus secundum utramque speciem, panis
videlicet et vini, tam ab ecclesiasticis quam secularibus hominibus
omnino fieri debet. Ita enim Christus sine ulla cujusquam exclusione
præcepit (Io. vi. 53): 'Amen, amen,
dico vobis, nisi manducaveritis carnem filii hominis et biberitis sanguinem illius, non habebitis vitam
æternam in vobis. Qui carnem
meam edit et sanguinem meum
bibit, is in me manet et ego in illo.'
Quare ad eundem etiam modum
prout a Christo acceperant, ita aliis
hoc mysterium sancti Apostoli peragendum tradiderunt; æquali nimirum tum secularium tum religiosorum usu, et utraque specie. Quemadmodum Corinthiis scribit Paulus
Apostolus (1 Cor. xi. 22): 'Namque
ego a Domino accepi, quod et tra-

ριον μετὰ τὸ δειπνῆσαι, λέγων· τοῦτο τὸ ποτήριον ἡ καινὴ διαθήκη ἐστὶν ἐν τῷ ἐμῷ αἵματι· τοῦτο ποιεῖτε,
ὁσάκις ἂν πίνητε, εἰς τὴν ἐμὴν ἀνάμνησιν. Τὴν τιμὴν, ὅπου πρέπει νὰ
ᾖδῃς εἰς τὰ φρικτὰ ταῦτα μυστήρια,
πρέπει νὰ εἶναι τοιαύτη, ὡς ἐκείνη,
ὅπου δίδεται τοῦ ἰδίου Χριστοῦ (ὡς
ἀνωτέρω εἴρηται)· ὥστε καθὼς δι'
ἐκεῖνον εἶπεν ὁ Πέτρος ἐκ στόματος
πάντων τῶν Ἀποστόλων (Ματθ. ιϛ'.
ιϛ'.)· σὺ εἶ ὁ Χριστὸς, ὁ υἱὸς τοῦ
Θεοῦ, τοῦ ζῶντος· τέτοιας λογῆς
νὰ λέγωμεν καὶ ἡμεῖς, λατρεύοντες
καθ' ἕνας· πιστεύω, Κύριε, καὶ ὁμολογῶ, ὅτι σὺ εἶ ἀληθῶς ὁ Χριστὸς,
ὁ υἱὸς τοῦ Θεοῦ, τοῦ ζῶντος, ὁ ἐλ-
θὼν εἰς τὸν κόσμον ἁμαρτωλοὺς
σῶσαι, ὧν πρῶτος εἰμὶ ἐγὼ. Ἀκόμι
τὸ μυστήριον τοῦτο προσφέρεται θυσία ὑπὲρ πάντων τῶν ὀρθοδόξων
χριστιανῶν ζώντων τε καὶ κεκοιμημένων ἐπ' ἐλπίδι ἀναστάσεως ζωῆς
αἰωνίου· ἡ ὁποία θυσία δὲν θέλει
τελειώσειν ἕως τῆς τελευταίας κρίσεως. Οἱ καρποὶ τοῦ μυστηρίου τούτου εἶναι τοῦτοι· πρῶτον ἡ ἀνάμνησις τοῦ ἀναμαρτήτου πάθους καὶ
τοῦ θανάτου τοῦ Χριστοῦ· κατὰ τὸ
(ἁ. Κορ. ιά. κέ.) εἰρημένον· ὁσάκις
γὰρ ἂν ἐσθίητε τὸν ἄρτον τοῦτον,
καὶ τὸ ποτήριον τοῦτο πίνητε, τὸν
θάνατον τοῦ Κυρίου καταγγέλλετε,
ἄχρις οὗ ἂν ἔλθῃ. Τὸ δεύτερον
κέρδος ὅπου μὲν δίδῃ εἶναι, διατὶ τὸ
μυστήριον τοῦτο γίνεται ἱλασμὸς καὶ

didi vobis: quod Dominus Iesus ea
nocte, qua traditus est, accepit panem, et actis gratiis fregit dixitque:
accipite, edite. Hoc meum est corpus, quod provobis frangitur. Hoc
facite in mei recordationem. Similiter et poculum, postquam cœnav-
erant, dicens: Hoc poculum Novum
Testamentum est, in meo sanguine.
Hoc facite, quotiescunque biberitis
in mei recordationem.' Porro honor,
quem tremendis hisce Mysteriis ex-
hibere convenit, par illi similisque
esse debet, qui Christo ipsi habetur
(sicut supra dictum est. Quæst.
LVI.); ut quemadmodum de eo
Petrus ore ac nomine reliquorum
Apostolorum dixit (Matt. xvi. 16):
'Tu es Christus filius Dei viventis;'
consimili et nos ratione quisque illum sancte venerantes dicamus:
'Credo Domine ac confiteor, revera
esse Christum filium Dei viventis,
qui in mundum venisti, ut salvos
faceres peccatores, quorum ego primus sum.' Offertur etiam sacrificii
vicem hoc mysterium pro orthodoxis Christianis omnibus viventibus
pariter et in spe resurrectionis vitæ
æternæ consopitis. Quod sacrificium usque ad supremum orbis diem
non intermittetur. Fructus hujus
mysterii hi fere sunt. Primum re-
cordatio supplicii, quo ob nullam
plane noxiam suam affectus fuit, et
mortis Christi, quemadmodum dici-

καλοσύνημα πρὸς τὸν Θεὸν διὰ τὰς ἁμαρτίας ἡμῶν, εἴτε ζώντων εἴτε καὶ ἀποθαμένων· διὰ τοῦτο οὐδεμία τῶν ἁγίων λειτουργιῶν γίνεται, ὅπου νὰ μὴν γένοιεν εἰς αὐτὴν ἱκεσίας καὶ δεήσεις πρὸς τὸν Θεὸν ὑπὲρ τῶν ἡμετέρων ἁμαρτημάτων. Τὸ τρίτον διάφορον εἶναι, ὅπου ὅποιος Χριστιανὸς εὑρίσκεται παρὼν συχνᾷ εἰς τὴν θυσίαν ταύτην καὶ νὰ κοινωνᾷ τοῦ μυστηρίου τούτου, ἐλευθερώνεται δι᾽ αὐτοῦ ἀπὸ κάθα πειρασμὸν καὶ κίνδυνον τοῦ διαβόλου· διατὶ δὲν ἀποτολμᾷ ὁ ἐχθρὸς τῆς ψυχῆς, νὰ βλάψῃ ἐκεῖνον, ὁποῦ ἠξεύρει πῶς ἔχει τὸν Χριστὸν μένοντα ἐν αὐτῷ. Ἡ ἑτοιμασία πρὸς τὴν μετάληψιν τῶν φρικτῶν μυστηρίων πρέπει νὰ γίνεται κατὰ τὴν τάξιν τῆς ἐκκλησίας ἡμῶν τῆς ὀρθοδόξου ἤγουν μὲ καθαρὰν ἐξομολόγησιν, νηστείαν τε καὶ κατάνυξιν καὶ διαλλαγὴν τελείαν μὲ ὅλους, καὶ μὲ ἄλλα τούτοις ὅμοια.

tur (1 Cor. xi. 26): 'Quotiescunque enim comederitis panem hunc et biberitis hoc poculum, mortem Domini annunciabitis, donec venerit.' Secundum, quod affert commodum, hoc est, quod hoc mysterium est propitiatio reconciliatioque apud Deum pro peccatis nostris, sive viventium sive mortuorum ; unde nulla etiam sacrarum Liturgiarum celebratur, in qua non fiant supplicationes deprecationesque ad Deum pro peccatis nostris. Tertium, quod Christianus quisque, qui crebro huic sacrificio interest de eoque participat, per illud eximitur quibusvis tentationibus et objectis a Diabolo periculis. Nihil enim iste animæ nostræ hostis nocere illi audet, quem Christum in sese manentem habere animadvertit. Denique *præparatio* hominis ad tremenda hæcce mysteria percipienda secundum præscriptum ordinem orthodoxæ nostræ Ecclesiæ fieri debet. Nimirum per sinceram peccatorum confessionem, per jejunia cordisque compunctionem atque perfectam cum omnibus reconciliationem aliaque his consimilia.

Ἐρώτησις ρή.

Ποῖον εἶναι τὸ τέταρτον μυστήριον ;

Ἀπ. Ἡ ἱερωσύνη, ἡ ὁποία εἶναι δύο λογιῶν, ἄλλη πνευματικὴ καὶ

QUÆSTIO CVIII.

Quodnam quartum est mysterium ?

RESP. Sacerdotium, quod duum est generum, alterum spirituale,

ἄλλη μυστηριώδης. Τῆς πνευματι-
κῆς ἱερωσύνης ὅλοι οἱ Χριστιανοὶ
οἱ ὀρθόδοξοι μετέχουσιν, καθὼς (ά.
Πετρ. β΄. θ΄.) διδάσκει Πέτρος ὁ
Ἀπόστολος, λέγων· ὑμεῖς δὲ γένος
ἐκλεκτὸν, βασίλειον ἱεράτευμα, ἔθνος
ἅγιον, λαὸς εἰς περιποίησιν· καὶ ὁ
Ἰωάννης εἰς τὴν Ἀποκάλυψιν (κεφ. ἐ.
θ΄.)· ἐσφάγης καὶ ἠγόρασας τῷ Θεῷ
ἡμᾶς ἐν τῷ αἵματί σου ἐκ πάσης φυ-
λῆς καὶ γλώσσης καὶ λαοῦ καὶ ἔθ-
νους· καὶ ἐποίησας ἡμᾶς τῷ Θεῷ
ἡμῶν βασιλεῖς καὶ ἱερεῖς. Καὶ κατὰ
τὴν τοιαύτην ἱερωσύνην γίνονται καὶ
προσφοραὶ τοιαῦται· ἤγουν προσευχαὶ, εὐχαριστίαι, νεκρώσεις τοῦ σώματος, παραδόσεις εἰς μαρτύριον διὰ
τὸν Χριστὸν, καὶ ἄλλα ὅμοια· πρὸς
τὰ ὁποῖα παρακινῶντας λέγει (ά. Πετρ.
β΄. ἐ.) ὁ Ἀπόστολος Πέτρος· καὶ αὐτοὶ ὡς λίθοι ζῶντες οἰκοδομεῖσθε,
οἶκος πνευματικὸς, ἱεράτευμα ἅγιον,
ἀνενέγκαι πνευματικὰς θυσίας εὐ-
προσδέκτους τῷ Θεῷ διὰ Ἰησοῦ Χρισ-
τοῦ· καὶ (Ῥωμ. ιβ΄. ά.) ὁ Παῦλος·
παρακαλῶ οὖν ὑμᾶς, ἀδελφοὶ, διὰ τῶν
οἰκτιρμῶν τοῦ Θεοῦ, παραστῆσαι τὰ
σώματα ὑμῶν θυσίαν ζῶσαν, ἁγίαν,
εὐάρεστον τῷ Θεῷ, τὴν λογικὴν λατρείαν ὑμῶν.

Ἐρώτησις ρθ΄.

Πῶς γίνεται ἡ μυστηριώδης Ἱερωσύνη;

Ἀπ. Ἡ ἱερωσύνη, ὁποῦ εἶναι μυσ-

alterum sacramentale. Communione sacerdotii spiritualis orthodoxi omnes Christiani fruuntur, sicut docet Petrus Apostolus (1 Pet.
ii. 9): 'Vos autem genus electum,
regale sacerdotium, gens sancta,
populus in acquisitionem.' Et Ioannes in Apocalypsi (v. 9): 'Occi-
sus es, et redemisti nos Deo in sanguine tuo, ex omni tribu et lingua
et populo et natione et fecisti nos
Deo nostro reges et sacerdotes.'
Atque prout sacerdotium hocce est,
ita ejusdemmodi etiam fiunt oblationes; nimirum preces, gratiarum
actiones, exstirpationes pravarum
corporis cupiditatum affectionum-
que, voluntaria martyrii propter
Christum susceptio ac perpessio
ceteraque hujusmodi. Ad quæ ita
cohortatur Apostolus Petrus (1 Pet.
ii. 5): 'Ipsi quoque veluti vivi lapi-
des ædificemini in domum spiritualem, sacerdotium sanctum, ad of-
ferendum spirituales hostias accep-
tabiles Deo per Iesum Christum.'
Et Paulus (Rom. xii. 1): 'Adhortor
vos fratres per misericordias Dei, ut
præbeatis corpora vestra, hostiam
viventem, sanctam, acceptam Deo,
rationalem cultum vestrum.'

QUÆSTIO CIX.

Quo pacto fit sacramentale sacerdotium?

RESP. Sacerdotium id mysterium

τήριον, διετάχϑη τοῖς ᾿Αποστόλοις
ἀπὸ τὸν Χριστὸν, καὶ διὰ τῆς ἐπιϑέ-
σεως τῶν χειρῶν αὐτῶν μέχρι τῆς
σήμερον γίνεται ἡ χειροτονία· δια-
δεξαμένων τῶν ἐπισκόπων αὐτοὺς
πρὸς διάδοσιν τῶν ϑείων μυστηρίων
καὶ διακονίαν τῆς σωτηρίας τῶν ἀνϑρώπων, καϑὼς (ά Κορ. δ´. ά.) εἶπεν
ὁ ᾿Απόστολος· οὕτως ἡμᾶς λογιζέσϑω ἄνϑρωπος, ὡς ὑπηρέτας Χριστοῦ, καὶ οἰκονόμους μυστηρίων Θεοῦ.
Εἰς τὴν οἰκονομίαν τούτην δύο πράγματα περιέχονται· πρῶτον ἡ δύναμις
καὶ ἡ ἐξουσία τοῦ λύειν τὰς τῶν
ἀνϑρώπων ἁμαρτίας· διατὶ πρὸς αὐτὴν (Ματϑ. ιή. ιή.) εἴρηται· ὅσα ἂν
λύσητε ἐπὶ τῆς γῆς, ἔσται λελυμένον
ἐν τῷ οὐρανῷ. Δεύτερον ἡ ἐξουσία
καὶ ἡ δύναμις τοῦ διδάσκειν, ἡ ὁποία
μετὰ λόγια τοῦτα ἑρμηνεύεται· πο-
ρευϑέντες (Ματϑ. κή. ιϑ´.) οὖν μαϑη-
τεύσατε πάντα τὰ ἔϑνη, βαπτίζοντες
αὐτοὺς εἰς τὸ ὄνομα τοῦ Πατρὸς καὶ
τοῦ Υἱοῦ καὶ τοῦ ἁγίου Πνεύματος.
῾Ο Χριστὸς λοιπὸν ἐξαπέστειλε τοὺς
᾿Αποστόλους εἰς τὸ κήρυγμα· οἱ δὲ
᾿Απόστολοι χειροτονοῦντες ἄλλους
τοὺς ἐπέμπασιν εἰς τὸ αὐτὸ ἔργον·
καϑὼς συνάγεται ἀπὸ τὰ λόγια τοῦ
ἁγίου Λουκᾶ (Πρᾶξ. ή. ιζ´.) λέγον-
τος· τότε ἐπετίϑουν τὰς χεῖρας ἐπ᾽
αὐτοὺς, καὶ ἐλάμβανον Πνεῦμα ἅγιον·
ὁμοίως (κεφ. ιγ´. β´.) ἔστωντας ἐκεῖνοι
νὰ λειτουργοῦσιν, ἤγουν νὰ προσφέ-
ρουσι τὴν ἀναίμακτον ϑυσίαν πρὸς
τὸν Θεὸν καὶ νὰ νηστεύουσιν, εἶπε

est, Apostolis a Christo mandatum
fuit; deinceps per manuum illorum impositionem usque in hodiernum diem ordinatio ejusdem
peragitur, succedentibus in locum
Apostolorum Episcopis ad distribu-
enda divina mysteria salutisque
humanæ obeundum ministerium;
teste Apostolo (1 Cor. iv. 1): 'Ita
nos æstimet homo, ut ministros
Christi, et œconomos mysteriorum
Dei.' Hæc œconomia res præcipue
duas complectitur: una est facultas
ac potestas solvendi delicta hominum; quamobrem sic ad illam dictum fuit (Matt. xviii. 18): 'Quidquid solveritis super terram, id
solutum erit in cœlo.' Altera potestas et facultas docendi est, quæ
his verbis exponitur (Matt. xxviii.
19): 'Euntes docete omnes gentes,
baptizantes eos in nomine Patris et
Filii et Spiritus Sancti.' Emisit
igitur Apostolos ad prædicandum
evangelium Christus. Rursus Apostoli alios postea ad idem opus impositis manibus ordinatos miserunt,
ut ex verbis S. Lucæ colligitur (Act.
viii. 17): 'Tunc imponebant illis
manus, et accipiebant Spiritum
Sanctum.' Similiter (xiii. 2): 'Illis
sacrum officium celebrantibus (h. e.
hostiam incruentam Deo offerenti-
bus), ac jejunantibus dixit Spiritus
Sanctus: segregate mihi Barnabam
et Saulum in id opus, in quod vocavi

τὸ Πνεῦμα τὸ ἅγιον· ἀφορίσατε δή μοι τόν τε Βαρνάβαν καὶ τὸν Σαῦλον εἰς τὸ ἔργον ὃ προσκέκλημαι αὐτούς. Τότε νηστεύσαντες καὶ προσευξάμενοι καὶ ἐπιθέντες τὰς χεῖρας αὐτοῖς ἀπέλυσαν· καὶ (ά.Τιμ. έ. κβ'.) ὁ Παῦλος· χεῖρας ταχέως μηδενὶ ἐπιτίθει. Μὲ τούτην λοιπὸν τὴν χειροτονίαν καὶ τὴν διαδοχὴν τὴν μηδέποτε διακοπεῖσαν ἔχουσιν τὴν δύναμιν τοῦ διδάσκειν τὰ σωτηριώδη δόγματα ἐκεῖνοι, ὅπου εἶναι πεμπόμενοι εἰς τοῦτο τὸ ἔργον. Μὰ ὅσοι δὲν ἐπέμφθησαν οὔτε ἐδιλέχθησαν εἰς αὐτό, δὲν πρέπει καθόλου νὰ τὸ ἐπιχειρίζουνται, κατὰ τὸ εἰρημένον ('Ρωμ. ί. ιέ.) τῷ Παύλῳ· πῶς δὲ κηρύξωσιν, ἐὰν μὴ ἀπυσταλῶσιν;

'Ερώτησις ρί.

Τί πρέπει νὰ θεωρῆται εἰς τοῦτο τὸ μυστήριον;

'Απ. Πρέπει νὰ ἐξετάζουνται τὰ πρόσωπα, ὅπου μέλλουσι νὰ ἀναβοῦσιν εἰς τὸ τοιοῦτον μυστήριον, νὰ ἔχουσι τρία πράγματα· πρῶτον καλὴν καὶ καθαρὰν συνείδησιν, ἀπέχοντες μακρὰν ἀπὸ τὰ ἁμαρτήματα ἐκεῖνα, ὅπου ἐμποδίζουσιν τὴν ἱερωσύνην. Δεύτερον, νὰ ἔχουσιν καὶ ἐπιστήμην καὶ σοφίαν, τόσον εἰς τὴν οἰκονομίαν τῶν θείων μυστηρίων, ὅσον καὶ εἰς τὴν οἰκοδομὴν τοῦ κοινοῦ λαοῦ μὲ ταῖς διδαχαῖς των. Καὶ τρίτον, νὰ ἔχουσι ὅλα των τὰ μέλη γερά, ὁποῦ εἶναι ἀναγκαῖα εἰς τοῦτο.

illos. Quumque jejunassent et orassent et imposuissent eis manus, dimiserunt eos.' Et Paulus (1 Tim. v. 22): 'Manus nemini cito imponas.' Hujusmodi ordinatione nulloque tempore interrupta successione facultatem docendi doctrinam salutis habent, qui ad hoc opus mittuntur. Non missi vero nec ad hoc opus delecti, illi nullo modo manus eidem admovere debent, dicente Paulo (Rom. x. 15): 'Quomodo prædicabunt, nisi mittantur?'

QUÆSTIO CX.

Quid in hoc Mysterio spectandum?

RESP. Probe examinandi explorandique sunt, quotquot ad hoc adscensuri sunt mysterium, ut tribus imprimis rebus instructi veniant. Primum bona mundaque conscientia, adeo ut procul ab iis flagitiis absint, quæ capessendo sacro ordini obstaculo sunt. Secundo scientia atque sapientia exornati sint: tam in dispensandis divinis mysteriis, quam ædificanda et instruenda per conciones suas rudi plebecula. Tertio, ut membris omnibus sanis integrisque utantur, quæ muneri exsequendo necessaria sunt.

Ἐρώτησις ριά.

Πρὶν τῆς ἱερωσύνης εἶναι τάχα ἄλλαις τάξεις, ὅπου δίδονται;

Ἀπ. Ἡ ἱερωσύνη περικρατεῖ εἰς τὴν ἑαυτήν της ὅλους τοὺς βαθμούς· μὲ ὅλον τοῦτο πρέπει κατὰ τὴν τάξιν νὰ δίδονται· οἷον ἀναγνώστης, ψάλτης, λαμπαδάριος, ὑποδιάκονος, διάκονος, διὰ τὰ ὁποῖα πλατύτερον διαλαμβάνουσιν τὰ ἀρχιερευτικὰ εὐχελόγια, λεγόμενα τακτικά. Εἰς τὸν παρόντα τόπον φθάνει μόνον νὰ εἰποῦμεν πρὸς διδασκαλίαν τῆς ὀρθοδόξου ὁμολογίας, πῶς ὁ ἐπίσκοπος πρέπει νὰ φανερώνῃ, εἰς κάθα βαθμὸν ὅπου χειροτονᾷ, τὸ ἔργον ὅπου τοῦ ἐγχειρίζει, ἢ τὴν θείαν ἱερουργίαν, ἢ τὴν Εὐαγγελίου ἀνάγνωσιν, ἢ τοῦ Ἀποστόλου, ἢ νὰ φέρῃ τὰ ἱερὰ σκεύη, ἢ τὸν κόσμον τῆς ἐκκλησίας, διατὶ πᾶσα τάξις ἔχει τὸ ἴδιόν της σημάδιον, μὲ τὸ ὁποῖον καθ᾽ ἕνας διαφέρει ἀπὸ τὸν ἄλλον· καὶ πρέπει ὁ ἐπίσκοπος νὰ τὸ διερμηνεύῃ.

Ἐρώτησις ριβ΄.

Ποῖον εἶναι τὸ πέμπτον μυστήριον;

Ἀπ. Τὸ πέμπτον μυστήριον εἶναι ἡ μετάνοια, ἡ ὁποία εἶναι ἕνας πόνος τῆς καρδίας διὰ τὰ ἁμαρτήματα, ὅπου ἔσφαλεν ὁ ἄνθρωπος, τὰ ὁποῖα κατηγορᾷ ἔμπροσθεν τοῦ ἱερέως μὲ γνώ-

QUÆSTIO CXI.

Aliine etiam Ordines quidam sunt, qui ante sacerdotium conferuntur?

RESP. Sacerdotium ceteros omnes in se continet gradus, qui nihilo secius legitimo ordine conferri debent: ut Lector, Cantor, Lampadarius, Subdiaconus, de quibus latius in Euchologiis Pontificalibus, quæ Tactica nuncupantur, agitur. Satis autem in præsens est, ut ad doctrinam Orthodoxæ hujus Confessionis paucis dicamus, ad officium Episcopi pertinere, ut, in quocunque gradu quempiam constituit, clare et dilucide muneris illius rationes homini exponat, quod ipsi committit; sive divinum Liturgiæ officium sit, sive lectio evangelii, sive Apostolicarum epistolarum, sive ut sacra vasa gestet, sive ut mundum ecclesiæ servet. Est enim cuique ordini peculiare insigne suum, quo singillatim alius ab alio distinguitur, quod explanare debet Episcopus.

QUÆSTIO CXII.

Quodnam quintum et Mysterium?

RESP. Quintum Mysterium Pœnitentia est, quæ vera quædam penitusque infixa tristitia est, ob ea, quæ in se quisquam admisit peccata. Quæ cum firmo animi proposito

μην βεβαίαν, νὰ διορϑώσῃ τὴν ζωήν
του εἰς τὸ μέλλον, καὶ μὲ ἐπιϑυ-
μίαν, νὰ τελειώσῃ ὅ, τι τὸν ἐπιτι-
μήσει ὁ ἱερεὺς ὁ πνευματικός του.
Τοῦτο τὸ μυστήριον ἰσχύει καὶ πέρνει
τὴν δύναμίν του, ὁπόταν ἡ λύσις
τῶν ἁμαρτιῶν γίνεται διὰ τοῦ ἱερέως,
κατὰ τὴν τάξιν καὶ ζυνήϑειαν τῆς
ἐκκλησίας· ὁποῦ παρευϑὺς ὡς ἂν
πάρῃ τὴν συγχώρησίν του, ἀφέωνται τὰ ἁμαρτήματα τὴν ὥραν ἐκείνην
ὅλα ἀπὸ τὸν Θεὸν διὰ τοῦ ἱερέως,
κατὰ τὸν λόγον τοῦ Χριστοῦ, ὁποῦ
(Ἰωαν. κ΄. κγ΄.) εἶπε· λάβετε πνεῦμα
ἅγιον· ἄν τινων ἀφῆτε τὰς ἁμαρτίας,
ἀφίενται αὐτοῖς, ἄν τινων κρατῆτε,
κεκράτηνται.

emendandæ in posterum vitæ suæ,
plenaque voluntate observandi ef-
ficiendique, quidquid mulctæ sup-
pliciique irroget sacerdos, pater
suus spiritualis, illi accusatorie detegit. Hoc Mysterium tum potissimum valet vimque exserit suam
absolutio peccatorum per sacerdotem secundum constitutionem atque
morem ecclesiæ conceditur. Quippe ut delictorum suorum veniam
quispiam consequitur; extemplo
omnia illius peccata a Deo per sacerdotem illi remissa sunt, secundum Christi ipsius verba qui dixit
(Io. xx. 23): 'Accipite Spiritum
Sanctum, si quorum peccata remiseritis, remittuntur illis; si quorum retinueritis, retenta sunt.'

Ἐρώτησις ριγ΄.

Τί πρέπει νὰ ϑεωροῦμεν εἰς τοῦτο
τὸ μυστήριον;

Ἀπ. Πρῶτον πρέπει νὰ προσέχω-
μεν, ὥστε ὁ μετανοῶν νὰ εἶναι χριστιανὸς πίστεως ὀρϑοδόξου καὶ κα-
ϑολικῆς· διατὶ ἡ μετάνοια χωρὶς τὴν
ἀληϑινὴν πίστιν δὲν εἶναι μετάνοια,
οὔτε εἰς τὸν Θεὸν εὐπρόσδεκτος. Δεύτερον, νὰ ἐξετάζωμεν, ὥστε ὁ πνευματικὸς, ὁποῦ δέχεται τοὺς λογισμοὺς τῶν μετανοούντων χριστιανῶν,
νὰ εἶναι ὀρϑόδοξος, διατὶ ὁ αἱρετικὸς
καὶ ὁ ἀποστάτης δὲν ἔχει δύναμιν τοῦ
λύειν τὰς ἁμαρτίας. Τρίτον εἶναι
ἀναγκαῖον νὰ ἔχῃ συντριβὴν καρδίας

QUÆSTIO CXIII.

Quid observandum in hoc Mysterio?

RESP. Primo videndum, ut pœnitens sit Christianus, fidei orthodoxæ
et catholicæ. Namque pœnitentia,
quæ vera destituitur fide, non est
pœnitentia nec Deo accepta. Secundo ut confessionarius, qui confessionem Christianorum resipis-
centium audit et excipit, pariter
orthodoxus sit. Nam hæreticus et
apostata nullam solvendi piacula
potestatem habet. Tertio necesse
est, habere pœnitentem contritionem cordis seriumque de admissis

ὁ μετανοῶν καὶ λύπην διὰ τὰ ἁμαρτήματά του· μετὰ ὁποῖα ἐπαρόξυνε τὸν Θεὸν ἢ ἔβλαψε τὸν πλησίον του· διὰ τὴν ὁποῖαν συντριβὴν λέγει (Ψαλ. νά. ιζ΄.) ὁ Δαβίδ· καρδίαν συντετριμμένην καὶ τεταπεινωμένην ὁ Θεὸς οὐκ ἐξουδενώσει. Εἰς τὴν συντριβὴν τούτην τῆς καρδίας πρέπει νὰ ἀκολουθᾷ καὶ ἡ διὰ στόματος ἐξομολόγησις πάντων τῶν ἁμαρτημάτων καθ᾽ ἕκαστον· διατὶ δὲν ἠμπορεῖ ὁ πνευματικὸς νὰ λύσῃ τίποτες, ἂν δὲν ἠξεύρῃ ποῖα πρέπει νὰ λυθοῦσι, καὶ τί ἐπιτίμιον νὰ δόσῃ. Δι᾽ αὐτὰ ἡ ὁποῖα ἐξομολόγησις εἶναι φανερὴ εἰς τὴν ἁγίαν Γραφὴν, ὁποῦ (Πρᾶξ. ιθ΄. ιή.) λέγει· πολλοί τε τῶν πεπιστευκότων ἤρχοντο ἐξομολογούμενοι, καὶ ἀναγγέλλοντες τὰς πράξεις αὐτῶν. Καὶ (Ἰακ. έ. ις΄.) ἀλλαχοῦ· ἐξομολογεῖσθε ἀλλήλοις τὰ παραπτώματα, καὶ εὔχεσθε ὑπὲρ ἀλλήλων, ὅπως ἰαθῆτε. Καὶ (Μαρκ. ά. έ.) πάλιν· ἐξεπορεύετο πρὸς αὐτὸν πᾶσα ἡ Ἰουδαία χώρα καὶ Ἱεροσολυμῖται, καὶ ἐβαπτίζοντο πάντες ἐν τῷ Ἰορδάνι ποταμῷ ὑπ᾽ αὐτοῦ (τοῦ Ἰωάννου), ἐξομολογούμενοι τὰς ἁμαρτίας αὐτῶν. Ἡ ἐξομολόγησις αὕτη πρέπει νὰ ἔχῃ ταῦτα τὰ ἰδιώματα, νὰ εἶναι ταπεινὴ, εὐλαβὴς, ἀληθινὴ, εἰλικρινὴς, κατηγορητικὴ ἑαυτῆς μετ᾽ ὀδύνης, ὅταν γίνεται. Καὶ τὸ τέταρτον μέρος τῆς μετανοίας πρέπει νὰ εἶναι ὁ κανόνας καὶ τὸ ἐπιτίμιον, ὁποῦ δίδῃ καὶ διορίζῃ ὁ πνευματικὸς, ὡς ἂν εἶναι προσευχαὶ, ἐλεημοσύναι, νηστεῖαι,

noxis dolorem, queis Dei iram lacessivit aut damnum proximo dedit, de qua contritione ait David (Psa. li. 19): 'Cor contritum et humiliatum Deus non despiciet.' Hanc cordis contritionem sequi debet viva voce sigillatim facta omnium peccatorum confessio. Nihil enim solvere pater spiritualis potest, ubi nihil solvendum deprehendit: nec pœnam mulctamque ideo imponere. Cujusmodi confessio in Sacra Scriptura aperte memoratur (Act. xix. 18): 'Multi credentium veniebant, confitentes et renunciantes facta sua.' Et alibi (Iac. v. 16): 'Confitemini invicem alius alii delicta, et orate pro vobis invicem, ut sanemini.' Et rursus (Marc. i. 5): 'Egrediebatur ad illum omnis regio Iudææ et Hierosolymitæ; et baptizabantur omnes ab illo (Ioanne) in Iordane fluvio, confitentes peccata sua.' Confessio ista has habere debet proprietates: ut sit humilis, religiosa, vera, sincera, sui ipsius accusatrix cum dolore gemituque, quando exercetur. Postrema pœnitentiæ pars est canon pœnitentialis et piaculare supplicium, quod definit et imponit Confessionarius. Quod genus preces, eleemosynæ, jejunia, peregrinationes ad loca sacra, religiosæ poplitum inflexiones, et his similia sunt; quæ

ἐπίσκεψις ἁγίων τόπων, αἱ γονυκλι-
σίαι καὶ τὰ ὅμοια, ὁποῦ θέλουσι φα-
νεῖν ἁρμόδια εἰς τὴν κρίσιν τοῦ πνευ-
ματικοῦ. Πλὴν ἐκεῖνος, ὁποῦ μισεύων
ἀπὸ τὴν ἐξομολόγησιν, πρέπει νὰ λογιάζῃ ἐκεῖνα, ὁποῦ εἶπεν (Ψαλ. λγ'.
ιέ.) ὁ Ψαλμῳδός· ἔκκλινον ἀπὸ κακοῦ, καὶ ποίησον ἀγαθόν· καὶ ἐκεῖνα,
ὁποῦ ('Ιωαν. έ. ιδ'.) εἶπεν ὁ Σωτὴρ
ἡμῶν· ἴδε ὑγιὴς γέγονας, μικέτι ἁμάρτανε, ἵνα μὴ χεῖρον τί σοι γένηται· καὶ
('Ιωαν. ή. ιά.) ἄλλοτε· πορεύου, καὶ
μηκέτι ἁμάρτανε. Καλᾷ καὶ νὰ εἶναι
ἀδύνατον εἰς τὸν ἄνθρωπον, νὰ φύγῃ
ὅλως διόλου τὸ ἁμαρτάνειν, μὲ ὅλον
τοῦτο κάθα ὀρθόδοξος εἶναι κρατημέ-
νος ἀπὸ μίαν ἐξομολόγησιν ἕως εἰς
τὴν ἄλλην, νὰ κάμῃ ὅσην διόρθωσιν
ἠμπορεῖ εἰς τὴν ζωήν του, κατὰ τὴν
συνείδησιν ὁποῦ ἔχει.

'Ερώτησις ριδ'.

Ποῖα εἶναι τὰ κέρδη τούτου τοῦ
ιυστηρίου;

'Απ. Τὸ πρῶτον κέρδος εἶναι· δι-
ιτὶ καθὼς μὲ τὴν ἁμαρτίαν χάνομεν
ἀθωότητα ἐκείνην, ὁποῦ ἀποκτήσαμεν
εἰς τὸ ἅγιον βάπτισμα· τέτοιας λογῆς
πάλιν ἐγγίζομεν εἰς αὐτὴν διὰ τῆς
μετανοίας· καὶ καθὼς μὲ τὴν ἁμαρτίαν ὑστερούμεθα τῆς θείας χάριτος·
τέτοιας λογῆς διὰ τῆς μετανοίας ταύτην πάλιν ἀποκτώμεθα. Καὶ καθὼς
διὰ τὴν ἁμαρτίαν ἐρχόμεθα εἰς τὴν
αἰχμαλωσίαν τοῦ διαβόλου· οὕτω διὰ
τῆς μετανοίας ἐλευθερούμεθα ἀπ' αὐ-

nimirum patri spirituali conve-
nientissima videbuntur. Qui ex-
piatus a confessione recedit, merito
illa secum reputabit, quæ ait auctor Psalmorum (xxxiv. 14): 'De-
clina a malo, et fac bonum.' Et
quæ Servator noster dicit (Ioh. v.
14): 'Ecce sanus factus es, ne
posthac pecces, ne quid deterius
tibi contingat.' Et alibi (Ioh. viii.
11): 'Vade, et ne pecces amplius.'
Quamvis vero impossibile homini
sit, ut omnino et in totum peccata
vitet: debet tamen pius quisque
secundum conscientiam, quam habet, ab una confessione ad aliam,
quantam poterit maximam, emen-
dationi vitæ suæ dare operam.

Quæstio CXIV.

Qui fructus hujus mysterii
sunt?

Resp. Primum illud emolumen-
tum est, quod, quemadmodum per
peccatum jacturam facimus ejus
innocentiæ, quam in sacro baptismate acquisivimus: ita rursus
ad illam per pœnitentiam propius
accedimus. Et ut per peccatum
divina excidimus gratia: ita re-
sipiscendo eamdem recuperamus;
atque ut per peccatum in captivitatem diaboli incidimus: ita
per pœnitentiam ab illa liberamur.

τήν. Καὶ καθὼς διὰ τῆς ἁμαρτίας αἰσχύνη καὶ φόβος εἰσέρχεται εἰς τὴν συνείδησίν μας· τέτοιας λογῆς διὰ τῆς μετανοίας ἐπιστρέφει εἰς ἡμᾶς εἰρήνη καὶ θάρρος τοιοῦτον, ὡς ἂν ἔχουσι τὰ τέκνα πρὸς τοὺς πατέρας των.

'Ερώτησις ριέ.

Ποῖον εἶναι τὸ ἔκτον μυστήριον;

'Απ. Ὁ τίμιος γάμος, ὁ ὁποῖος γίνεται πρῶτον μέν με τὴν εἰς ἀλλή-λους συμφωνίαν τοῦ ἀνδρὸς καὶ τῆς γυναικὸς χωρίς τινος ἐμποδίσματος. Ἡ ὁποία συμφωνία δὲν φάνισεν διὰ ἀληθινοῦ γάμου σύββασις, παρὰ ἐκεῖνοι οἱ ἴδιοι νὰ μαρτυρήσωσιν ἀλλήλους των ἔμπροσθεν τοῦ ἱερέως τὴν ὑπόσχεσίν τως, καὶ νὰ δώσουσι χεῖρα, πῶς ὁ ἕνας θέλει φυλάξειν εἰς τὸν ἄλλον πίστιν, τιμὴν, ἀγάπην τοῦ γάμου ἐφ' ὅρου ζωῆς αὐτῶν εἰς κάθα κίνδυνον, δὲν ἐξαφίνωται ὁ ἕνας τὸν ἄλλον· ὕστερον δὲ βε-βαιώνεται. Καὶ εὐλογῆται ἀπὸ τὸν ἱερέα τούτη ἡ συμφωνία καὶ ὑπόσχε-σίς των· καὶ γίνεται τὸ (Ἑβρ. ιγ'. δ'.) γεγραμμένον· τίμιος ὁ γάμος ἐν πᾶσι, καὶ ἡ κοίτη ἀμίαντος.

'Ερώτησις ριϛ'.

Ποῖοι εἶναι τοῦ μυστηρίου τούτου οἱ καρποί;

'Απ. Πρῶτον, ὁποῦ ἄνθρωπος μὲ τὸν γάμον ἐκκλίνει ἀπὸ κάθα κίνδυ-

Denique, ut per peccatum pudor terrorque conscientiam nostram invadunt: ita per poenitentiam redit nobis pax et fiducia ejus-modi, qualem erga parentes suos liberi habent.

QUÆSTIO CXV.

Quodnam sextum est Mysterium?

RESP. Honorabile Conjugium. Quod primo quidem mutuo viri feminæque in se invicem consensu, nullo interveniente legitimo impe-dimento, instituitur; sed ejusmodi consensus non videtur justarum nuptiarum stipulatio conventioque esse, nisi iidem illi sponsalia sua, mutua testificatione, coram sacer-dote, affirment: junctisque dextris fidem dent, quod alter alteri fidem, honorem, amoremque conjugalem, ad finem usque vitæ, quocunque re-rum discrimine, constanter servatu-rus, nec alter alterum deserturus sit. Deinde sancitur consecraturque hæc illorum consensio ac promissio per sacerdotem, fitque illud, quod scrip-tum est (Heb. xiii. 4): 'Honorabile in omnibus conjugium et torus im-pollutus.'

QUÆSTIO CXVI.

Qui fructus ex hoc Mysterio nascuntur?

RESP. Primum, quod homo per nuptias a periculo scortationis ac

νον τῆς πορνείας καὶ ἀκρασίας·
ἐπειδὴ ὁ γάμος ὁ τίμιος διετάχϑηκεν
ἐπὶ τούτου, διὰ νὰ σβήνῃ ἡ τῆς
σαρκὸς ἐπιϑυμία, καϑὼς (ά. Κορ. ζ'.
β'.) λέγει ὁ Παῦλος· διὰ τῆς πορνείας ἕκαστος τὴν ἑαυτοῦ γυναῖκα
ἐχέτω. Δεύτερον διατὶ τιμᾶται ἡ
παιδοποιΐα μὲ τὴν τιμίαν γέννησιν.
Τρίτον, διατὶ εἰς καιροὺς τινὰς ἀσϑενείας, ἢ ὁποῦ νὰ τύχῃ ἄλλου κιν-
δύνου, ὁ ἄνδρας δίδει τὸν ἑαυτόν
του πιστὸν σύντροφον εἰς τὴν γυναῖκα, καὶ ἡ γυναῖκα εἰς τὸν ἄνδρα,
διὰ τὴν μεγάλην ἀγάπην καὶ δεσμὸν
τῆς φιλίας, ὁποῦ γεννᾶται ἀνάμεσόν
των· διὰ τὸ ὁποῖον ἡ Γραφὴ (Γενεσ.
β'. κδ'.) μαρτυρᾷ· ἕνεκεν τούτου κατα-
λείψει ἄνϑρωπος τὸν πατέρα αὐτοῦ
καὶ τὴν μητέρα, καὶ προσκολληϑή-
σεται τῇ ἰδίᾳ γυναικὶ, καὶ ἔσονται οἱ
δύο εἰς σάρκα μίαν.

Ἐρώτησις ριζ'.

Ποῖον εἶναι τὸ ἕβδομον μυστήριον
τῆς Ἐκκλησίας;

Ἀπ. Τὸ εὐχέλαιον, τὸ ὁποῖον
εἶναι διατεταγμένον ἀπὸ τὸν Χριστὸν,
ἐπειδὴ ὅταν ἔπεμπε τοὺς μαϑητάς
(Μαρκ. ς'. ιγ'.) του ἀνὰ δύο, ἤλειφον
ἐλαίῳ πολλοὺς ἀρρώστους, καὶ ἐϑε-
ράπευον· ἔπειτα ὅλη ἡ ἐκκλησία τὸ
ἔλαιον εἶχε συνήϑειαν νὰ τὸ κάμου-
σιν· τὸ ὁποῖον φαίνεται ἀπὸ τὴν
ἐπιστολὴν τοῦ ἁγίου Ἰακώβου (κεφ.
έ. ιδ'.) λέγοντος· ἀσϑενεῖ τις ἐν ὑμῖν,
προσκαλεσάσϑω τοὺς πρεσβυτέρους

incontinentiæ cujusvis deflectit.
Quippe ideo honorabile matrimonium institutum est, ut exstingua-
tur libidinis ardor, docente Paulo
(1 Cor. vii. 2): 'Propter scorta-
tionem unusquisque suam habeat
uxorem.' Secundo, quod merito
in honore habeatur, quæ honesto
satu fit sobolis procreatio. Tertio,
quod si quando morbus incidit aut
aliud quodcunque periculum, tum
fidum sese sodalem maritus uxori,
et uxor invicem marito ob summam caritatem et arctissima mu-
tui ipsorum amoris vincula præbet,
qua de re testimonium perhibet
Scriptura (Gen. ii. 24): 'Idcirco
relinquet homo patrem suum et
matrem, et adhærebit propriæ uxori suæ; eruntque duo illi in carnem unam.'

QUÆSTIO CXVII.

Quodnam septimum Ecclesiæ
mysterium est?

RESP. *Oleum consecratum*, quod
a Christo ipso institutum est. Quando enim discipulos suos, binos et
binos, misit (Marc. vi. 13); 'illi
oleo ægrotos multos ungebant ac
sanabant.' Quod postmodum universa Ecclesia in sollemnem consuetudinem recepit, ut apparet ex
epistola S. Iacobi (cap. v. 14), ubi
ait: 'Si quis vestrum ægrotat,
advocet Presbyteros Ecclesiæ, et

τῆς ἐκκλησίας, καὶ προσευξάσθωσαν
ἐπ᾽ αὐτὸν, ἀλείψαντες αὐτὸν ἐλαίῳ ἐν
τῷ ὀνόματι τοῦ Κυρίου. Καὶ ἡ εὐχὴ
τῆς πίστεως σώσει τὸν κάμνοντα, καὶ
ἐγερεῖ αὐτὸν ὁ Κύριος, κἂν ἁμαρτίας
ᾖ πεποιηκὼς, ἀφεθήσεται αὐτῷ.

orent super eum, ungentes eum
oleo in nomine Domini; et oratio
fidei servabit ægrotum, et excita-
bit eum Dominus; et si peccata
commisit, id illi condonabitur.'

Ἐρώτησις ριή.

Τί πρέπει νὰ βλέπωμεν εἰς τὸ μυστήριον τοῦτο;

Ἀπ. Πρῶτον πρέπει νὰ προσέχω-
μεν, νὰ γίνεται τὸ μυστήριον τοῦτο
ἀπὸ ἱερεῖς μὲ τὰ ἀκόλουθα τοῦ μυστηρίου, καὶ ὄχι ἀπό τινα ἄλλον.
Δεύτερον, νὰ εἶναι τὸ ἔλαιον καθαρὸν
χωρίς τινος ἀρτύματος, καὶ νὰ εἶναι
ὁ ἀσθενὴς ὀρθόδοξος καὶ καθολικῆς
πίστεως, νὰ εἶναι ἐξομολογούμενος τὰ
ἁμαρτήματά του ἔμπροσθεν εἰς τὸν
ἱερέα τὸν πνευματικόν του. Καὶ τρίτον, εἰς τὸν καιρὸν τοῦ χρίσματος νὰ
διαβάζεται ἡ εὐχὴ ἐκείνη, εἰς τὴν
ὁποῖαν ἑρμηνεύεται τοῦ μυστηρίου
τούτου ἡ δύναμις.

Ἐρώτησις ριθ΄.

Ποῖοι εἶναι οἱ καρποὶ τοῦ μυστηρίου τούτου;

Ἀπ. Τὰ διάφορα χαὶ καρποὺς,
ὁποῦ γεννοῦνται ἀπὸ τὸ μυστήριον
τοῦτο, ὁ Ἀπόστολος Ἰάκωβος τοὺς
ἑρμηνεύει, λέγωντας ἄφεσιν ἁμαρτιῶν
ἢ σωτηρίαν ψυχῆς, ἔπειτα ὑγείαν τοῦ
σώματος. Καλᾷ καὶ πάντοτε ἡ θε-
ραπεία τοῦ σώματος νὰ μὴν γίνεται,
ἀλλ᾽ ἡ ἄφεσις τῶν ἁμαρτιῶν τῆς

QUÆSTIO CXVIII.

Quid observandum nobis in hoc
Mysterio?

RESP. Primum ut hoc Mysterium cum omni consequentia sua
per sacerdotes non vero per alium
ullum ministretur. Secundo ut
oleum purum inconditumque sit,
atque ut ægrotus tum orthodoxus
fideique Catholicæ addictus sit,
tum ut paullo antea patri suo
spirituali, quidquid deliquerat, con-
fessus fuerit. Tertio ut interea,
dum unctio peragitur, recitetur
illa oratio, qua Mysterii hujus vis
et efficacia exponitur.

QUÆSTIO CXIX.

Quinam hujus Mysterii fructus
sunt?

RESP. Emolumenta ac fructus
Mysterii hujus enarrat Apostolus Iacobus (loco modo apposito),
nimirum criminum admissorum
gratiam sive salutem animæ atque sanitatem etiam corporis.
Quæ, utut non semper obtine-
atur, certe remissio peccatorum

ψυχῆς πάντοτε εἰς τὸν μετανοοῦντα ἀκολουθῇ.

animæ in pœnitente semper ob tinetur.

Ἐρώτησις ρκ΄.

Ποῖον εἶναι τὸ ἑνδέκατον ἄρθρον τῆς πίστεως;

Ἀπ. Προσδοκῶ ἀνάστασιν νεκρῶν.

QUÆSTIO CXX.

Undecimus fidei Articulus quis est?

RESP. Exspecto resurrectionem mortuorum.

Ἐρώτησις ρκά.

Τί διδάσκει τοῦτο τὸ ἄρθρον τῆς πίστεως;

Ἀπ. Διδάσκει τὴν ἀδιάψευστον ἀνάστασιν τῶν ἀνθρωπίνων σωμάτων, τόσον τῶν ἀγαθῶν ὡς ἂν καὶ τῶν κακῶν, ὁποῦ μέλλει νὰ γένῃ μὲ τὸν θάνατον· κατὰ τὸν λόγον τοῦ Κυρίου, ὁποῦ (Ἰωαν. ἑ. κή.) λέγει· ὅτι πάντες οἱ ἐν τοῖς μνημείοις ἀκούσονται τῆς φωνῆς τοῦ Υἱοῦ τοῦ Θεοῦ καὶ ἐκπορεύσονται, οἱ τὰ ἀγαθὰ ποιήσαντες εἰς ἀνάστασιν ζωῆς, οἱ δὲ τὰ φαῦλα πράξαντες εἰς ἀνάστασιν κρίσεως. Τὰ δὲ σώματα θέλουσιν εἶναι τὰ αὐτὰ, μετὰ ὁποῖα ἔζησαν εἰς τὸν κόσμον τοῦτον, καθὼς (Ἰὼβ. ιθ΄. κέ.) λέγει ὁ Ἰώβ· οἶδα γὰρ, ὅτι ἀέννάος ἐστιν ὁ ἐκλύειν μὲ μέλλων ἐπὶ γῆς· ἀναστήσεται τὸ δέρμα μου τὸ ἀναντλοῦν ταῦτα· παρὰ γὰρ Κύριον ταῦτά μοι συνετελέσθη· ἃ ἐγὼ ἐμαυτῷ συνεπίσταμαι· ἃ ὁ ὀφθαλμός μου ἑώρακε, καὶ οὐκ ἄλλος, πάντα δὲ μοι συντετέλεσται ἐν κόλπῳ. Πλὴν τὸ σῶμα τοῦτο, ὁποῦ λέγομεν ὅτι θέλει εἶναι τὸ αὐτὸ, τότε θέλει εἶναι ἄφ-

QUÆSTIO CXXI.

Quid hic fidei Articulus docet?

RESP. Docet certam minimeque commentitiam corporum humanorum resuscitationem, proborum pariter atque improborum, a morte obita futuram; secundum verbum Domini, qui ait (Ioh. v. 28): 'Omnes, qui in monumentis suis sunt, audient vocem filii Dei et egredientur, qui bona egerunt, in resurrectionem vitæ; qui mala, in resurrectionem judicii.' Eadem autem omnino corpora erunt, quibuscum in hoc mundo vixerant, dicente Iobo (xix. 25): 'Scio ego, æternum esse, qui me exsoluturus est, super terram. Resurget cutis mea, quæ hæc exantlat. Namque a Domino hæc mihi confecta sunt, quorum ego mihi conscius sum, quæ oculus meus vidit, et non alius. Omnia vero mihi in sinu confecta sunt.' Verum corpus hoc, quod idem numero futurum diximus, resuscitatum incorruptibile erit atque im-

θαρτον καὶ ἀθάνατον ἐν τῇ ἀναστάσει, κατὰ τὸ εἰρημένον (ά. Κορ. ιέ.
νά.) τῷ Παύλῳ· πάντες μὲν οὐ κοι-
μηθησόμεθα, πάντες δὲ ἀλλαγησόμεθα ἐν ἀτύμῳ, ἐν ῥιπῇ ὀφθαλμοῦ,
ἐν τῇ ἐσχάτῃ σάλπιγγι. Σαλπίσει
γὰρ, καὶ οἱ νεκροὶ ἐγερθήσονται ἄφθαρτοι καὶ ἡμεῖς ἀλλαγησόμεθα. Δεῖ
γὰρ τὸ φθαρτὸν τοῦτο ἐνδύσασθαι
ἀφθαρσίαν, καὶ τὸ θνητὸν τοῦτο ἐνδύσασθαι ἀθανασίαν. Ἀκόμι καὶ τοῦτο πρέπει νὰ ἠξεύρωμεν, πῶς πᾶσα
ψυχὴ θέλει ἐπιστρέψειν εἰς τὸ ἴδιόν
της σῶμα, καὶ τότε μαζὶ θέλει πάρῃ
τέλειον τὸν αἰώνιον μισθὸν, κατὰ τὰ
ἔργα ὁποῦ ἔπραξεν. Ἀκόμι καὶ τῶν
ἀσεβῶν τὰ σώματα θέλουσιν εἶναι
ἀθάνατα, διατὶ θέλουσι κολάζεσθαι
αἰωνίως.

Ἐρώτησις ρκβ'.

Τί διδάσκει τὸ δεύτερον τοῦτο τὸ
ἄρθρον τῆς πίστεως;

Ἀπ. Διδάσκει κάθα Χριστιανὸν
νὰ ἐνθυμᾶται πάντοτε τέσσαρα πράγ-
ματα· τὸν θάνατον, τὴν τελευταίαν
κρίσιν, τὴν κόλασιν τοῦ ᾅδου, καὶ τὴν
βασιλείαν τῶν οὐρανῶν τὴν αἰώνιον.

Ἐρώτησις ρκγ'.

Τί κέρδος ἔχει ὁ ἄνθρωπος ἀπὸ
τὴν ἐνθύμησιν τῶν τεσσάρων τούτων
πραγμάτων;

Ἀπ. Διατὶ γεννᾶται εἰς αὐτὸν
εὐσέβεια, φύλαξις ἀπὸ τὴν ἁμαρτίαν,
φόβος πρὸς τὸν Θεὸν, φόβος τῆς

mortale, teste Paulo (1 Cor. xv.
51): 'Non omnes quidem dor-
miemus, sed tamen omnes immutabimur, in puncto, in ictu oculi,
cum extrema tuba. Canet enim
tuba et mortui resurgent incorruptibiles, et nos immutabimur.
Oportet enim corruptibile hocce
induere incorruptibilitatem, et
mortale hocce induere immortalitatem.' Præterea et illud sciendum, animas omnes in sua quasque corpora reversuras, et tum
una cum iis perfectam æternamque mercedem actionum operum-
que suorum accepturas; sed et
impiorum corpora immortalia
erunt, quippe æternis discrucianda
suppliciis.

QUÆSTIO CXXII.

Quid secundo loco hic docet
Articulus?

RESP. Docet, Christianum quemvis semper in animo habere hæc
quattuor: mortem, extremum judicium, cruciatus inferorum, regnum
denique cœlorum sempiternum.

QUÆSTIO CXXIII.

Quidnam commodi nanciscetur
homo ex quattuor rerum istarum
recordatione?

RESP. Nimirum quod animo illius
inseritur pietas et fuga peccati et
timor Dei et geennæ infernæ for-

κατὰ τὸν ᾅδην γεέννης, ἀγάπη τῆς
οὐρανίου βασιλείας, καὶ ταῦτα λογι-
ζόμενος πρέπει νὰ ἑτοιμάζεται πρὸς
τὸν θάνατον, ἐνθυμούμενος τὴν τελευταίαν ἡμέραν, νὰ γίνεται ἕτοιμος
εἰς τὸ νὰ ἀποδώσῃ λόγον διὰ τοὺς
λογισμοὺς, διὰ τοὺς λόγους, διὰ τὰς
πράξεις του· ἐνθυμούμενος δὲ τοῦ
ᾅδου νὰ προσέχῃ, νὰ μὴν πέσῃ εἰς
αὐτὸν· ἐνθυμούμενος δὲ τῆς τῶν οὐρανῶν βασιλείας νὰ σπουδάζῃ νὰ
τὴν ἀπολαύσῃ.

mido regnique cœlestis desiderium.
Quæ qui assidue animo volutat,
haud dubie ad suprema sese diligenter componet. Quippe summum illum ac censorium orbis
diem recogitat, ut paratior fiat ad
reddendas rationes cogitationum,
dictorum factorumque omnium.
De inferis cogitat, quo ne illuc in-
cidat caveat. Idem cœleste regnum mente complectitur, ut omni
studio ad illud assequendum con-
tendat.

Ἐρώτησις ρκδ'.

Ποῖον εἶναι τὸ δωδέκατον ἄρθρον
τῆς πίστεως;
Ἀπ. Καὶ ζωὴν τοῦ μέλλον-
τος αἰῶνος.

QUÆSTIO CXXIV.

Duodecimus fidei Articulus quis
est?
RESP. Et vitam venturi seculi.

Ἐρώτησις ρκέ.

Τί διδάσκει ἡ ἁγία ἐκκλησία εἰς
τοῦτο τὸ ἄρθρον τῆς πίστεως;
Ἀπ. Πῶς εἰς τὸν μέλλοντα αἰῶνα
θέλει ἔλθῃ ἡ εὐλογία τοῦ Θεοῦ εἰς
τοὺς ἐκλεκτούς του καὶ ἡ αἰώνιος ζωὴ
μὲ χαραῖς καὶ εὐφροσύναις πνευματι-
καῖς, ὁποῦ ποτὲ δὲν θέλουσιν ἔχειν
τέλος, καθὼς ἡ Γραφὴ (ά. Κορ. β'.
θ'.) μαρτυρᾷ λέγουσα· ἃ ὀφθαλμὸς
οὐκ εἶδε καὶ οὖς οὐκ ἤκουσε καὶ ἐπὶ
καρδίαν ἀνθρώπου οὐκ ἀνέβη, ἃ ἡτοί-
μασεν ὁ Θεὸς τοῖς ἀγαπῶσιν αὐτόν.
Ὡσαύτως καὶ εἰς ἄλλον τόπον (Ῥωμ.
ιδ'. ιζ'.) λέγει· οὐ γάρ ἐστιν ἡ βασιλεία τοῦ Θεοῦ βρῶσις καὶ πόσις,

QUÆSTIO CXXV.

Quid in hoc fidei Articulo sancta docet Ecclesia?
RESP. Quod in seculo futuro
ventura est Dei gratia et benefi-
centia super electos suos, et æterna
vita gaudiis ac lætitiis spiritualibus nullum unquam finem habitu-
ris cumulatissima, teste Scriptura
(1 Cor. ii. 9): 'Quæ oculus non
vidit, nec auris audivit, nec in
cor hominis adscenderunt, quæ
paravit Deus iis, qui ipsum diligunt.' Eodem et alibi modo
(Rom. xiv. 17): 'Non enim est
regnum Dei esca et potus; sed

ἀλλὰ δικαιοσύνη καὶ εἰρήνη καὶ χαρὰ ἐν Πνεύματι ἁγίῳ.

'Ερώτησις ρκστ'.

Ἡ ψυχὴ μόνη τάχα, ἢ καὶ τὸ σῶμα θέλουσιν ἀπολαύσειν μαζὶ τὴν αἰώνιον εὐφροσύνην;

'Απ. Καθὼς ἡ ψυχὴ μὲ τὸ κορμίον μαζὶ τὰ ἀγαθὰ ἐνεργοῦσιν διὰ τὸν αἰώνιον μισθὸν· τέτοιας λογῆς καὶ ἡ ψυχὴ μὲ τὸ κορμίον μαζὶ θέλουσιν ἔχειν τὴν εὐφροσύνην καὶ τὴν ἀγαλλίασιν. Μὰ ὄχι διαιρετῶς· διατὶ δὲν θέλει εἶναι ἄλλη ἡ χαρὰ τῆς ψυχῆς καὶ ἄλλη τοῦ σώματος, ἐπειδὴ τὸ σῶμα θέλει γένει δεδοξασμένον καὶ ὁ ἄνθρωπος εἶναι σύνθετος ἐκ ψυχῆς καὶ σώματος δεδοξασμένου. Τότε θέλει εἶναι ὅμοιος μὲ τοὺς ἀγγέλους κατὰ τὴν Γραφὴν (Ματθ. κβ'. λ'.) τὴν λέγουσαν· ἐν γὰρ τῇ ἀναστάσει οὔτε γαμοῦσιν οὔτε ἐκγαμίζονται, ἀλλ' ὡς ἄγγελοι τοῦ Θεοῦ ἐν οὐρανῷ εἰσίν. Τὸ σῶμα θέλει εἶναι δεδοξασμένον, ἀθάνατον, ἄφθαρτον, ἀνενδεὲς βρώσεως καὶ πόσεως, ὅμοιον πνεύματι κατὰ τὴν Γραφὴν (ά. Κορ. ιέ. νβ'.) τὴν λέγουσαν· οἱ νεκροὶ ἐγερθήσονται ἄφθαρτοι, καὶ ἡμεῖς ἀλλαγησόμεθα· δεῖ γὰρ τὸ φθαρτὸν τοῦτο ἐνδύσασθαι ἀφθαρσίαν, καὶ τὸ θνητὸν τοῦτο ἐνδύσασθαι ἀθανασίαν. Ἡ δὲ χαρὰ καὶ ἡ ἀγαλλίασις δὲν θέλει εἶναι ἄλλη παρὰ ἡ θεωρία τῆς μακαρίας Τριάδος καὶ ὁ πνευματικὸς χορὸς

justitia et pax et gaudium in Spiritu Sancto.'

QUÆSTIO CXXVI.

Solane fortasse an anima an vero etiam corpus simul æternis fruentur gaudiis?

RESP. Quemadmodum anima et corpus sociata opera spe æternæ mercedis bonum efficiunt: ita etiam lætitiam exsultationemque eamdem, communem, non autem separatam et divisam habebunt. Non enim alia animæ lætitia alia corporis erit; siquidem corpus gloria coruscabit; totus vero homo ex anima et corpore glorioso compositus erit. Atque tunc Angelis ipsis similis et æqualis fiet, secundum Scripturam, quæ dicit (Matt. xxii. 30): 'Nam in resurrectione nec ducunt uxores nec ducuntur, sed sunt ut Angeli Dei in cœlo.' Corpus gloriosum erit, immortale, incorruptibile, non cibi, non potus indigum, simile spiritui, dicente ita Scriptura (1 Cor. xv. 52): 'Mortui resurgent incorruptibiles, et nos immutabimur. Oportet enim corruptibile hocce induere incorruptibilitatem et mortale hocce induere immortalitatem.' Ceterum lætitia ista exsultatioque non alia erit, quam contemplatio beatissimæ Trinitatis et chorus spiritualis junctim cum Angelis agitandus, dicente

μαζὶ μὲ τοὺς ἀγγέλους, καθὼς (ά. Κορ. ιγ'. ιβ'.) λέγει ὁ Ἀπόστολος· βλέπομεν γὰρ ἄρτι δι' ἐσόπτρου ἐν αἰνίγματι, τότε δὲ πρόσωπον πρὸς πρόσωπον· ἄρτι γινώσκω ἐκ μέρους, τότε δὲ ἐπιγνώσομαι, καθὼς καὶ ἐπεγνώσθην. Καὶ καλᾷ νὰ εἶπε (Ἐξοδ. λγ'. κ'.) πρὸς τὸν Μωϋσῆν ὁ Κύριος· οὐ μὲ ἴδῃ ἄνθρωπος τὸ πρόσωπόν μου καὶ ζήσεται· ἀλλὰ τοῦτο νοεῖται πρὶν τῆς ἀπολυτρώσεως καὶ διὰ τὸ σῶμα τοῦτο τὸ φθαρτὸν καὶ οὐ δεδοξασμένον καὶ διὰ τὴν παροῦσαν ζωὴν· μὰ μετὰ τὴν ἀπολύτρωσιν ἐν σώματι δεδοξασμένῳ εἰς τὴν μέλλουσαν καὶ αἰώνιον ξωὴν, ὕστερα ἀπὸ τὴν ἡμέραν τῆς τελευταίας κρίσεως θέλει δοθῇ ἀπὸ τὸν Θεὸν φῶς εἰς ἡμᾶς, μὲ τὸ ὁποῖον θέλομεν ἰδεῖν τὸ φῶς τοῦ Θεοῦ, καθὼς (Ψαλ. λς'. θ'.) λέγει ὁ Ψαλμῳδός· ὅτι παρά σοι πηγὴ ζωῆς, ἐν τῷ φωτί σου ὀψόμεθα φῶς. Τὸ ὁποῖον ἔστωντας καὶ νὰ θεωρεῖται, καταπαύει πᾶσαν ἐπιθυμίαν πάσης σοφίας καὶ καλοσύνης· διατὶ εἰς τὴν τοῦ ἄκρου ἀγαθοῦ θεωρίαν ὅλα τὰ ἄλλα ἀγαθὰ περικλείονται, καὶ πάσης εὐφροσύνης εἶναι πλήρωμα ἡ ἐκείνου ἀπόλαυσις κατὰ τὸν αὐτὸν Ψαλμῳδὸν, τὸν λέγοντα (Ψαλ. ιζ'. ιέ.)· χορτασθήσομαι ἐν τῷ ὀφθῆναι τὴν δόξαν σου.

Apostolo (1 Cor. xiii. 12): 'Cernimus nunc per speculum in ænigmate, tunc autem a facie ad faciem. Nunc cognosco ex parte, tunc vero cognoscam pro cognitione, qua instructus fuero.' Quamquam vero Mosi dixit Dominus (Exod. xxxiii. 20): 'Nequaquam faciem meam videre, et vivere homo potest;' sed illud intelligendum est ante summam perfectissimamque istam redemptionem et de corpore hoc corruptibili, necdum gloriæ suæ compote vitaque præsenti; sed post omnimodam istam redemptionem in corpore cœlesti gloria decorato, in futura et æterna vita, post diem extremi judicii indet nobis lucem Deus, qua lucem Dei ipsius contueri queamus, prout canit divinus vates (Psa. xxxvi. 9): 'Apud te est fons vitæ, et in luce tua videbimus lucem.' Quæ lux quoniam adspectu ipso percipietur, desiderium omne omnis sapientiæ atque pulchritudinis sedabit ac compescet. Namque in contemplatione summi boni cetera bona universa continentur, bonique illius fruitio omnis lætitiæ complementum est, secundum eumdem sacrum fidicinem (Psa. xvii. 15): 'Satiabor, quum apparuerit gloria tua.'

II. DOSITHEI CONFESSIO, SIVE DECRETA XVIII. SYNODI HIEROSOLYMITANÆ.

The Confession of Dositheus, or the Eighteen Decrees of the Synod of Jerusalem.

[The Greek original and Latin version are taken from Kimmel's *Monumenta Fidei Ecclesiæ Orientalis*, Pt. I. pp. 425–488, compared with Hardouin's *Acta Conciliorum*, Tom. XI. pp. 233–268. For an account and abridgment of these articles, see Vol. I. pp. 61–67. The Eighteen Decrees of the Synod of Jerusalem are a refutation of the Eighteen Articles of the Confession of Cyril Lucar, which should be compared with them. See Vol. I. § 54, pp. 54–57.]

Δοσίθεος ἐλέῳ Θεοῦ Πατριάρχης Ἱεροσολυμῶν τοῖς ἐρωτῶσι καὶ πυνθανομένοις περὶ τῆς πίστεως καὶ θρησκείας τῶν Γραικῶν ἤτοι τῆς ἀνατολικῆς ἐκκλησίας, πῶς δηλονότι περὶ τῆς ὀρθοδόξου πίστεως φρονεῖ, ἐν ὀνόματι κοινῶς τῶν ὑποκειμένων τῷ καθ᾽ ἡμᾶς ἀποστολικῷ θρόνῳ Χριστιανῶν ἁπάντων καὶ τῶν ἐπιδημούντων τῇ ἁγίᾳ ταύτῃ καὶ μεγάλῃ πόλει Ἱερουσαλὴμ ὀρθοδόξων προσκυνητῶν (οἷς πᾶσα ἐν τοῖς περὶ πίστεως ἡ καθολικὴ ἐκκλησία συνᾴδει) ἐκδίδωσι σύντομον ὁμολογίαν ταύτην εἰς μαρτύριον πρός τε Θεοῦ πρός τε ἀνθρώπων εἰλικρινεῖ συνειδήσει, οὐδεμιᾶς ἄνευ προσποιήσεως.

Ὅρος ά.

Πιστεύομεν εἰς ἕνα Θεὸν ἀληθῆ, παντοκράτορα καὶ ἀόριστον, πατέρα, υἱὸν καὶ ἅγιον πνεῦμα· πατέρα ἀγέννητον, υἱὸν γεννητὸν ἐκ τοῦ πατρὸς πρὸ αἰώνων, ὁμοούσιον αὐτῷ, πνεῦμα ἅγιον ἐν τοῦ πατρὸς ἐκπορευόμενον, πατρὶ καὶ υἱῷ ὁμοούσιον. Ταύτας

Dositheus, miseratione divina Patriarcha Hierosolymitanus, his, qui audire avent, quænam sit Græcorum sive Orientalis Ecclesiæ fides ac professio, quæve circa fidem orthodoxam sententia, nomine Christianorum omnium ad thronum nostrum apostolicum pertinentium nec non et peregrinorum fidelium in hanc sanctam et magnam urbem Hierosolymam pietatis ergo convenientium (quibuscum circa res fidei Orientalis Ecclesia per omnia consentit) compendiosam hancce confessionem in testimonium coram Deo et hominibus ex sincera conscientia atque omni simulatione procul conscribit.

DECRETUM I.

Credimus in unum Deum verum, omnipotentem et immensum, Patrem, Filium et Spiritum Sanctum; Patrem ingenitum, Filium ex Patre ante sæcula genitum, ei consubstantialem, Spiritum Sanctum ex Patre procedentem, Patri Filioque consub-

τὰς τρεῖς ὑποστάσεις ἐν μιᾷ οὐ-σίᾳ παναγίαν τριάδα προσαγορεύ-ομεν ὑπὸ πάσης κτίσεως ἀεὶ εὐλο-γουμένην, δοξαζομένην καὶ προσκυ-νουμένην.

Ὅρος β΄.

Πιστεύομεν τὴν θείαν καὶ ἱερὰν γραφὴν εἶναι θεοδίδακτον, καὶ διὰ τοῦτο ταύτῃ ἀδιστάκτως πιστεύειν ὀφείλομεν, οὐκ ἄλλως μέντοι ἀλλ' ἢ ὡς ἡ καθολικὴ ἐκκλησία ταύτην ἡρμή-νευσε καὶ παρέδωκεν.

Πᾶσα γὰρ αἱρετικῶν βδελυρία δέ-χεται μὲν τὴν θείαν γραφὴν, παρε-ξηγεῖται δ' αὐτὴν μεταφοραῖς καὶ ὁμωνυμίαις καὶ σοφίσμασι σοφίας ἀνθρωπίνης χρωμένη, συγχέουσα τὰ ἀσύγχυτα καὶ παίζουσα ἐν οὐ παι-κτικοῖς. Ἄλλως γὰρ ἂν, ἄλλου ἄλλην ὁσημέραι περὶ αὐτῆς γνώμην ἐσχηκότος, οὐκ ἂν εἴη ἡ καθολικὴ ἐκκλησία Χριστοῦ χάριτι ἕως τῆς σήμερον ἐκκλησία, μίαν γνώμην ἔχου-σα περὶ πίστεως καὶ ἀεὶ ὡσαύτως καὶ ἀπαρασαλεύτως πιστεύουσα· ἀλλ' ἐσχίσθη ἂν εἰς μύρια, καὶ αἱρέσεσιν ὑπέκειτο· καὶ μηδ' ἦν ἡ ἐκκλησία ἁγία στύλη καὶ ἑδραίωμα τῆς ἀλη-θείας, ἄσπιλός τε καὶ ῥυτίδος χω-ρὶς, ἀλλ' ἡ ἐκκλησία πονηρευομέ-νων, ὡς φαίνεται γεγονυῖα ἀναμφι-βόλως ἡ τῶν αἱρετικῶν καὶ μάλιστα τῶν ἀπὸ Καλουίνου, οἳ οὐκ αἰσχύ-νονται παρὰ τῆς ἐκκλησίας μανθά-νειν, ἔπειτα ταύτην πονηρῶς ἀπο-

stantialem. Itaque tres una in es-sentia personas sanctissimam Trini-tatem appellamus, quæ ab omni creatura continuo benedicitur, glo-rificatur et adoratur.

DECRETUM II.

Credimus Sacram Scripturam a Deo traditam, eique propterea, non quidem, ut lubuerit, sed secundum Ecclesiæ Catholicæ traditionem et interpretationem adhibendam esse fidem omni dubitatione majorem. Hanc quidem universa recipit hæ-reticorum colluvies, at sub metapho-ris et æquivocationibus, nec non et humanæ sapientiæ sophismatis per-peram interpretantur; quæ sunt distincta, confundunt, atque in re-bus ab omni joco alienis nugantur. Quippe si alteri atque alteri diebus singulis novus probaretur scripturæ sensus: eadem ipsa per gratiam Christi hactenus Catholica non per-stitisset Ecclesia, unam eamdemque retinens de fide sententiam, illique semper eodem modo et inconcusse adhærens; sed in infinitas foret fac-tiones conscissa ac variis hæretico-rum sectis divisa; nec esset veritatis columna et firmamentum sancta Ec-clesia, immaculataque ac sine ruga, sed congregatio improborum, cujus-modi esse manifestum est conven-tum hæreticorum ac potissimum Calvinistarum, quos quidem non

κρούεσθαι· ὅθεν καὶ τὴν τῆς καθο-
λικῆς ἐκκλησίας μαρτυρίαν οὐχ ἧττον τῆς ἦν κέκτηται ἡ θεία γραφὴ
εἶναι πιστεύομεν.

Ἑνὸς γὰρ καὶ τοῦ αὐτοῦ ἁγίου
πνεύματος ὄντος ἀμφοτέρων δημιουργοῦ, ἴσόν ἐστι πάντως ὑπὸ τῆς
γραφῆς καὶ ὑπὸ τῆς καθολικῆς ἐκκλησίας διδάσκεσθαι. Ἔπειτα ἄνθρωπον μὲν ὄντινα οὖν λαλοῦντα
ἀφ᾽ ἑαυτοῦ ἐνδέχεται ἁμαρτῆσαι καὶ
ἀπατῆσαι καὶ ἀπατηθῆναι· τὴν δὲ
καθολικὴν ἐκκλησίαν ὡς μηδέποτε
λαλήσασαν ἢ λαλοῦσαν ἀφ᾽ ἑαυτῆς
ἀλλ᾽ ἐκ τοῦ πνεύματος τοῦ Θεοῦ,
ὃ καὶ διδάσκαλον ἀδιαλείπτως πλουτεῖ εἰς τὸν αἰῶνα, ἀδύνατον πάντῃ
ἁμαρτῆσαι ἢ ὅλως ἀπατῆσαι καὶ
ἀπατηθῆναι· ἀλλ᾽ ἔστιν ὡσαύτως τῇ
θείᾳ γραφῇ ἀδιάπτωτος καὶ ἀένναον
κῦρος ἔχουσα.

Ὅρος γ΄.

Πιστεύομεν τὸν ἄκρως ἀγαθὸν
θεὸν ἐξ ἀϊδίου οὓς ἐξελέξατο εἰς
δόξαν προορίσαι, οὓς δ᾽ αὖ ἀπεδοκίμασεν εἰς κατάκρισιν παραχωρῆσαι· οὐχ ὅτι δὲ τούτους οὕτως ἠβουλήθη δικαιῶσαι, τούτους δ᾽ ἀναιτίως
παραχωρῆσαι καὶ κατακρῖναι. Ἀνοίκειον γὰρ τοῦτο τῷ πατρὶ τῶν ὅλων
καὶ ἀπροσωπολείπτῃ καὶ θέλοντι πάντας ἀνθρώπους σωθῆναι καὶ εἰς ἐπίγνωσιν ἀληθείας ἐλθεῖν, Θεῷ· ἀλλ᾽
ὅτι τούτους μὲν προεῖδεν καλῶς
τῷ αὐτεξουσίῳ χρησομένους, τούτους

pudet ab Ecclesia discere, ac deinde ipsam flagitiose repudiare. Quamobrem non minorem esse Ecclesiæ Catholicæ auctoritatem credimus, quam Sacræ Scripturæ. Enimvero utriusque auctor quum sit Spiritus Sanctus, perinde est, Catholicam Ecclesiam audieris ac Sacram Scripturam. Deinde, loquentem a se ipso hominem, quisquis ille sit, contingit errare et falli, quin et fallere; Catholicam vero Ecclesiam, utpote a se ipsa nunquam; sed Spiritus Sancti, cujus magisterio ad usque sæculi consummationem absque intermissione eruditur, illustratione aut lucutam aut loquentem errare nequaquam contingere potest, aut omnino fallere ac falli; sed perpetuam habet perinde ac Sacra Scriptura firmitatem et auctoritatem.

DECRETUM III.

Credimus Deum Optimum ab æterno, quos elegit, prædestinasse ad gloriam: quos vero reprobavit, damnationi deputasse: at non sic, ut illos justificare, hos autem sine caussa reprobare voluerit atque damnare. Hoc enim a Deo communi omnium patre prorsus alienum, qui quidem personarum nescit acceptionem, sed vult omnes homines salvos fieri et ad agnitionem veritatis venire. Sed illos quidem prædestinavit, quos arbitrio suo

δὲ κακῶς, προορίσαι ἢ κατακρῖναι. Ἐννοοῦμεν δὲ τὴν χρῆσιν τοῦ αὐτεξουσίου οὕτως, ὥστε τῆς θείας καὶ φωτιστικῆς χάριτος, ἣν καὶ προκαταρκτικὴν προσαγορεύομεν, οἷον φῶς τοῖς ἐν σκότει παρὰ τῆς θείας ἀγαθότητος πᾶσι χορηγουμένης, τοῖς βουλομένοις ὑπεῖξαι ταύτῃ, καὶ γὰρ οὐ τοὺς μὴ θέλοντας ἀλλὰ τοὺς θέλοντας ὠφελεῖ—καὶ συγκατατεθῆναι, ἐν οἷς ἐκείνη ἐντέλλεται, πρὸς σωτηρίαν οὖσιν ἀναγκαιοτάτοις, δωρεῖσθαι ἑπομένως καὶ ἰδικὴν χάριν, ἥτις συνεργοῦσα καὶ ἐνδυναμοῦσα καὶ ἐμμόνους πρὸς τὴν τοῦ θεοῦ ἀγάπην, ταὐτὸν εἰπεῖν, πρὸς ἃ θεὸς θέλει ἡμᾶς ἐργάζεσθαι ἀγαθὰ, ἃ καὶ ἡ προκαταρκτικὴ χάρις προσενετείλατο, ἀποτελοῦσα, δικαιοῖ καὶ προωρισμένους ποιεῖ. Τοῖς δὲ μὴ θέλουσιν ὑπακοῦσαι καὶ συγκατατεθῆναι τῇ χάριτι, καὶ διὰ τοῦτο οὐδ᾽ ἃ θεὸς βούλεται ἡμᾶς ἐργάζεσθαι τηροῦσι καὶ ἐν τοῖς τοῦ σατανᾶ ἐπιτηδεύμασι τὴν ἣν παρὰ θεοῦ εἰλήφασιν αὐτεξουσιότητα εἰς τὸ ἐργάζεσθαι ἑκουσίως τὸ ἀγαθὸν, καταχρωμένοις, γίνεσθαι τὴν παραχώρησιν εἰς ἀΐδιον κατάκρισιν.

Τὸ δὲ λέγειν παμμιάρους αἱρετικοὺς-ὡς κεῖται ἐν τῷδε τῷ κεφαλαίῳ-τὸν θεὸν προορίζειν ἢ κατακρίνειν μηδαμῶς εἰς τὰ ἔργα ἀποβλέποντα τῶν προοριζομένων ἢ κατακρινομένων, βέβηλον καὶ ἀνόσιον οἴδαμεν. Ἐμάχετο γὰρ ἂν οὕτως ἡ γραφὴ πρὸς ἑαυτὴν, διὰ τῶν ἔργων τῷ πιστῷ δι-

bene usuros præscivit : quos vero male, damnavit. Hunc porro liberi arbitrii usum ita intelligimus, ut divina quidem illuminatrix gratia, quam et prævenientem appellamus, ceu lumen in tenebris ab divina bonitate omnibus impendatur; ac postmodum iis, qui obtemperare illi, atque ad ea, quæ tamquam saluti pernecessaria hæc ipsa præcipit, cooperari voluerint — neque enim non volentibus utilis est, sed solum volentibus — peculiaris gratia subministretur, quæ cooperando nobis viresque præbendo atque ad Dei amorem, id est ad ea, quæ vult Deus et præveniens gratia monuit, bona facienda perseverantiam impertiendo, justos nos facit et prædestinatos; iis vero, qui gratiæ consentire et cooperari noluerint ac proinde, quæ a nobis exigit Deus, prætermiserint, suoque arbitrio, quod, ut bonum voluntarie facerent, a Deo acceperunt, ad gerendum satanæ morem abusi sunt in reprobationem cedit et æternam damnationem.

Quod vero scelestissimi ajunt hæretici, ut eodem capite habetur, Deum nullo prorsus respectu ad prædestinatorum reproborumve opera illos prædestinare, hos damnare, abominandum ducimus et sacrilegum. Secum enim ita Scriptura pugnaret, utpote quæ fideli salu-

δάσκουσα τὴν σωτηρίαν καὶ τὸν
θεὸν μόνον αἴτιον ὑποθεμένη κατὰ
μόνην τὴν φωτιστικὴν χάριν, ἣν
μὴ προηγησαμένων ἔργων παρέχει,
δεῖξαι τῷ ἀνθρώπῳ τὴν τῶν θείων
πραγμάτων ἀλήθειαν, καὶ διδάξαι,
ὅπως οὗτος ἐκείνῃ συγκατατεθῇ εἰ
βούλοιτο, καὶ ποιήσει τὸ ἀγαθὸν καὶ
εὐάρεστον, καὶ οὕτω σωτηρίας τυχεῖν.
Οὐκ ἀναιρεῖ τὸ θέλειν, ἢ μὴν θέλειν
ὑπακοῦσαι ἢ μὴ ὑπακοῦσαι αὐτῷ.

Ἀλλὰ καὶ τὸ τὴν θείαν θέλησιν
αἰτίαν εἶναι τῶν κατακρινομένων οὕτως ἁπλῶς καὶ ἀναιτίως, ποίαν οὐκ
ἔχει μανίαν; ποίαν οὐκ ἐπιφέρει κατὰ
τοῦ θεοῦ συκοφαντίαν; καὶ ποίαν εἰς
τὸ ὕψος οὐ λαλεῖ ἀδικίαν καὶ βλασφημίαν; Ἀπείραστον μὲν γὰρ κακῶν τὸ
θεῖον καὶ πάντων ἐξ ἴσου ἔθελον σωτηρίαν, ὡς μὴ ἐχούσης χώραν τῆς
προσωπολημψίας παρ' αὐτῷ οἴδαμεν,
καὶ τοῖς βεβήλοις γενομένοις σκεύεσι διὰ μοχθηρὰν αὐτῶν προαίρεσιν
καὶ ἀμετανόητον καρδίαν, ὡς δίκαιον, παραχωρεῖν τὴν κατάκρισιν ὁμολογοῦμεν. Κολάσεως δ' αἰωνίου,
ὠμότητός τε καὶ ἀσπλαγχνίας καὶ
μισανθρωπίας αἴτιον οὔποτε, οὔποτέ
φαμεν τὸν θεόν, τὴν χαρὰν γίνεσθαι
ἐν οὐρανῷ ἐπὶ ἑνὶ μετανοοῦντι ἁμαρ-
τωλῷ ἀποφηνάμενον. Μὴ γένοιτο,
ἡμᾶς οὕτως ἢ πιστεῦσαι ἢ ἐννοῆσαι,
ἕως ἂν ἑαυτῶν ἐσμέν, ἀναθέματι δὲ αἰω-
νίῳ καθυποβάλλομεν τοὺς τὰ τοιαῦτα
καὶ λέγοντας καὶ φρονοῦντας καὶ χεί-
ρους πάντων ἀπίστων γινώσκομεν.

tem ex operibus statuit, deumque
solum auctorem supponit per solam
illuminatricem gratiam, quam quidem nullis præcedentibus operibus
exhibet rerum divinarum homini
veritatem ostendere, eumque, qui
adsentiatur illi, si voluerit, atque ad
opera bona deoque accepta, quibus
salutem assequatur, incumbat, edo-
cere. Non aufert illi velle: aut
velle obedire, aut non obedire.

Sed et hominum ita simpliciter
ac sine caussa damnatorum auctorem statuere divinam voluntatem,
insania quanta? quæ major Deo
inseratur calumnia? quanta in supremum Numen injuria? quanta
blasphemia? Quippe intentatorem
malorum esse Deum et omnium ex
æquo salutem velle, ceu apud quem
personarum acceptio nulla est, cognoscimus, et his qui pravis voluntatibus ac secundum impœnitens cor
vasa in contumeliam evasere, damnationem juste decerni confitemur.
Æternæ autem punitionis, immani-
tatis, duritiæ et inhumanitatis nusquam, nusquam dicimus auctorem
esse Deum, super uno peccatore
pœnitentiam agente esse in cœlo
gaudium asserentem Absit a nobis
ita credere vel cogitare, quamdiu
nostri compotes sumus: imo vero
talia dicentes ac sentientes anathemati sempiterno subjicimus et cunctis infidelibus pejores agnoscimus.

Ὅρος δ´.

Πιστεύομεν τὸν τρισυπόστατον Θεὸν, τὸν πατέρα, τὸν υἱὸν, καὶ τὸ ἅγιον πνεῦμα ποιητὴν εἶναι ὁρατῶν τε πάντων καὶ ἀοράτων· καὶ ἀόρατα μὲν τὰς ἀγγελικὰς δυνάμεις, ψυχὰς τε λογικὰς καὶ δαίμονας, — εἰ καὶ μὴ τοιούτους τοὺς δαίμονας, ὡς αὐτοὶ προαιρέσει ἰδίᾳ ὕστερον ἐγένοντο, ὁ Θεὸς πεποίηκεν — ὁρατὰ δ᾽ οὐρανὸν καὶ τὰ ὑπ᾽ οὐρανὸν. Ὅτι δὲ φύσει ἀγαθὸς ὁ ποιητὴς, ἐποίησε καλὰ λίαν πάντα ὅσα ἐποίησεν, οὐδὲ δύναταί ποτε κακοῦ ποιητής εἶναι. Εἰ δέ τι κακόν, ταὐτὸν εἰπεῖν, ἁμάρτημα, γινόμενον ἐναντίως τῇ θείᾳ θελήσει, ἐστὶν ἐν τῷ ἀνθρώπῳ ἢ τῷ δαίμονι — ἁπλῶς γὰρ ἐν τῇ φύσει κακὸν οὐκ οἴδαμεν — ἐκεῖνο ἢ τοῦ ἀνθρώπου ἢ τοῦ διαβόλου εἶναι. Κανὼν γάρ ἐστιν ἀληθὴς καὶ ἀδιάπτωτος, κακοῦ τὸν Θεὸν μηδαμῶς εἶναι δημιουργὸν, μήδε μὴν ὅλως δικαίῳ λόγῳ τοῦ Θεοῦ καταψηφίζεσθαι.

Ὅρος ἐ.

Πιστεύομεν πάντα τὰ ὄντα, εἴτε ὁρατὰ εἴτε ἀόρατα ὑπὸ τῆς τοῦ Θεοῦ κυβερνᾶσθαι προνοίας, τὰ δὲ κακὰ, ᾗ κακὰ, προειδέναι μὲν τὸν Θεὸν καὶ παραχωρεῖν, οὐ μὴν καὶ προνοητὴν εἶναι τούτων, ἐπεὶ μηδὲ ποιητήν. Ἤδη γεγενημένα δὲ ἐσθ᾽ ὅτε ἐπευθύνεσθαι πρός τι χρήσιμον ὑπὸ τῆς ἄκρας ἀγαθότητος, οὐ ποιούσης μὲν,

DECRETUM IV.

Credimus Deum in personis trinum, Patrem, Filium et Spiritum Sanctum visibilium ac invisibilium esse conditorem: invisibilium quidem, quæ sunt angelicæ virtutes, animæ rationales et dæmones — quamquam tales Deus dæmones non fecit, quales postea voluntate sua facti sunt, — visibilium autem, quæ sunt cœlum et ea, quæ sub cœlo sunt. Quia vero natura bonus est creator, valde bona fecit quæcunque fecit, nec potest opifex esse malorum. Si quod vero malum, videlicet peccatum, quod contra divinam voluntatem sit, in homine vel dæmone deprehenditur, — simpliciter enim nullum in natura malum agnoscitur;—hoc vel ab homine est, vel a diabolo. Vera quippe juxta ac firmissima est hæc regula, malum nec a Deo usquam fieri, nec absque injuria posse illi ullatenus adscribi.

DECRETUM V.

Credimus res omnes cum visibiles tum invisibiles Dei Providentia gubernari, Deum vero mala ut præsciat et permittat, eorum tamen, qua mala sunt, haudquaquam esse provisorem uti nec opificem. Quæ vero jam patrata sunt, ab summa bonitate in finem utilem quandoque ordinari, non illa faciendo, sed pro

ἐγκεντριζούσης δὲ πρὸς τὸ κρεῖττον ὡς οἷόντε ἐκείνοις. Ἐκθειάζειν δὲ, ἀλλ᾽ οὐκ ἐξετάζειν ὀφείλομεν τὴν θείαν πρόνοιαν ἐν τοῖς ἀπορρήτοις καὶ μηδ᾽ ὅλως ἀποκαλυφθεῖσι κρίμασι. Τὰ μέντοι παρὰ τῇ θείᾳ γραφῇ παραδεδόμενα περὶ αὐτῆς, ὡς συντείνοντα πρὸς ζωὴν αἰώνιον, δεῖν ἡμᾶς εὐγνωμόνως ἀνερευνᾶν καὶ ἑπομένως ταῖς πρώταις περὶ Θεοῦ ἐννοίαις ἀνενδοιάστως ἐκλαμβάνειν.

Ὅρος ς᾽.

Πιστεύομεν τὸν πρῶτον ἄνθρωπον κτισθέντα παρὰ Θεοῦ ἐν παραδείσῳ πεπτωκέναι, ὅτε καὶ παριδὼν τὴν θείαν ἐντολὴν τῇ τοῦ ὄφεως ἀπατηλῇ συμβουλῇ ἐπειθάρχησε· κἀντεῦθεν ἀναβλύσαι τὴν προπατορικὴν ἁμαρτίαν τῇ διαδοχῇ, ὥστε μηδένα κατὰ σάρκα γεννᾶσθαι, ὃς τὸ φορτίον οὐκ ἐπιφέρει τοῦτο καὶ τοὺς καρποὺς αὐτῆς οὐκ αἰσθάνεται ἐν τῷ νῦν αἰῶνι. Καρποὺς δέ φαμεν καὶ φορτίον οὐ τὴν ἁμαρτίαν, οἷον ἀσέβειαν, βλασφημίαν, φόνον, παιδεραστείαν, μοιχείαν, πορνείαν, ἔχθος, καὶ εἴ τι ἕτερον ὑπὸ μοχθηρᾶς προαιρέσεως ἐναντίον τῇ θείᾳ θελήσει γίνεται, οὐχ ὑπὸ φύσεως· πολλοὶ γὰρ τῶν τε προπατόρων καὶ προφητῶν καὶ ἕτεροι μυρίοι ὅσοι τῶν ἐν τῇ σκιᾷ καὶ τῇ ἀληθείᾳ, ὅ τε θεῖος πρόδρομος καὶ κατ᾽ ἐξαίρετον λόγον ἡ τοῦ Θεοῦ Λόγου μήτηρ

modo uniuscujusque ad aliquid melius dirigendo. Hæc porro divinæ decreta providentiæ ejusdemque incomprehensibilia adorare judicia debemus, non investigare. Quamquam et ea, quæ apud Sacram Scripturam nobis de illa tradita sunt, ceu ad vitam æternam conducentia, bona mente perscrutari illaque proinde juxta præstantissimas de deo notiones absque hæsitatione interpretari debemus.

DECRETUM VI.

Credimus primum hominem a Deo creatum in paradiso recidisse, quum neglecto divino præcepto serpentis fraudulento obtemperavit consilio; indeque originale peccatum ceu hæreditarium profluxisse: quatenus carnali propagatione hunc in mundum nemo prodeat, quin hujus et pondus secum afferat, et fructus in hoc sæculo persentiat. Hos porro fructus, hoc pondus nequaquam tale peccatum intelligimus, quale impietatem, blasphemiam, homicidium, sodomiam, adulterium, fornicationem, simultates, et si quid aliud divinæ contrarium voluntati ab voluntate prava, non autem a natura, committitur: quum et Patriarchæ et Prophetæ non pauci alique innumeri non modo sub legis umbra sed etiam sub veritate gratiæ, uti divinus præcursor atque

καὶ ἀειπάρϑενος Μαρία τῶν τοιούτων καὶ τῶν ὁμοίων τούτοις πλημ-
μελημάτων οὐκ ἐπειράϑησαν · ἀλλ'
ἅπιρ ὡς ποινὴν τῷ ἀνϑρώπῳ διὰ τὴν
παράβασιν δέδωκεν ἡ ϑεία δικαιοσύνη, οἷον ἱδρῶτας τῶν πόνων, ϑλί-
ψεις, σωματικὰς ἀσϑενείας, ὠδῖνας
τοῦ τίκτειν καὶ τέως τὸ ζῆν ἐν τῇ
παροικίᾳ ἐπιπόνως, καὶ τελευταῖον
τὸν σωματικὸν ϑάνατον.

imprimis Verbi divini mater ac
semper virgo Maria nullum istorum
aut hujusmodi experti sint peccatorum; at ea dumtaxat, quæ divina
justitia homini ceu pœnam inflixit,
nimirum sudores laborum, ærumnas, corporis infirmitates, dolores in
partu, denique vitam in hac peregri-
natione laboriosam, et quod cumulus
est omnium, mortem corporalem.

Ὅρος ζ'.

Πιστεύομεν τὸν υἱὸν τοῦ Θεοῦ Ἰησοῦν Χριστὸν κένωσιν ὑποστῆναι, τοῦτ'
ἔστιν, ἐν τῇ ἰδίᾳ ὑποστάσει τὴν ἀνϑρω-
πίνην σάρκα προσειληφέναι ἐκ πνεύματος ἁγίου, ἐν τῇ γαστρὶ τῆς ἀειπαρ-
ϑένου Μαρίας συλληφϑέντα καὶ ἐνανϑρωπήσαντα, γεννηϑέντα χωρὶς τοῦ
δοῦναι πόνον ἢ ὠδῖνας τῇ ἰδίᾳ κατὰ
σάρκα μητρὶ ἢ τὴν παρϑενίαν αὐτῆς
διασεῖσαι, παϑόντα, ταφέντα, ἀναστάντα ἐν δόξῃ τῇ τρίτῃ ἡμέρᾳ κατὰ τὰς
γραφὰς, ἀνελϑόντα εἰς τοὺς οὐρανοὺς
καὶ καϑεζόμενον ἐκ δεξιῶν τοῦ Θεοῦ
καὶ πατρὸς, ὃν καὶ προσδοκῶμεν ἐλευ-
σόμενον κρῖναι ζῶντας καὶ νεκρούς.

DECRETUM VII.

Credimus Filium Dei Dominum
nostrum Jesum Christum exinani-
visse semet ipsum, id est, humanam
carnem in propriam assumsisse personam, Mariæ semper virginis in
utero de Spiritu Sancto conceptum
et incarnatum, absque ullo matris
labore aut dolore aut virginitatis
ejus læsione natum, passum, sepultum; huncque die tertia secundum
scripturas gloriosum recurrexisse,
in cœlum adscendisse et a dextris
Dei Patris considere, atque ad vivos
mortuosque judicandos exspecta-
mus adventurum.

Ὅρος ή.

Πιστεύομεν τὸν κύριον ἡμῶν Ἰησοῦν Χριστὸν μόνον μεσίτην γεγονέναι, καὶ δόντα ἑαυτὸν λύτρον περὶ
πάντων τὴν καταλλαγήν διὰ τοῦ
ἰδίου αἵματος πεποιηκέναι ἀνάμεσον
Θεοῦ καὶ ἀνϑρώπων, καὶ αὐτὸν κηδό-
μενον τῶν ἰδίων εἶναι παράκλητον

DECRETUM VIII.

Credimus Dominum nostrum Jesum Christum solum esse mediato-
rem, seque ipsum dedisse pretium
pro omnibus, ac per proprium sanguinem Deum inter et homines fecisse reconciliationem, quin et solli-
citum suorum esse advocatum ac

καὶ ἱλασμὸν περὶ τῶν ἁμαρτιῶν ἡμῶν. Ἐν ταῖς πρὸς αὐτὸν μέντοι ἐντεύξεσι καὶ αἰτήσεσιν εἶναι πρεσβευτὰς τοὺς ἁγίους φαμὲν καὶ πρὸ πάντων τὴν παναχραντον μητέρα αὐτοῦ τοῦ Θεοῦ Λόγου, τούς τε ἁγίους ἀγγέλους, οὓς καὶ προστατοῦντας ἡμῶν οἴδαμεν, ἀποστόλους, προφήτας, μάρτυρας, ὁσίους καὶ πάντας, οὓς ἐκεῖνος ἐδόξασεν ὡς πιστοὺς αὐτοῦ θεράποντας, οἷς συναριθμοῦμεν καὶ τοὺς ἀρχιερεῖς καὶ ἱερεῖς ὡς περισταμένους τῷ θείῳ θυσιαστηρίῳ καὶ τοὺς ἀρετῇ διαφέροντας δικαίους ἄνδρας. Εὔχεσθαι γὰρ ὑπὲρ ἀλλήλων καὶ πολὺ ἰσχύειν τὴν δέησιν τοῦ δικαίου, καὶ μᾶλλον ἀκούειν τὸν Θεὸν τῶν ἁγίων ἤπερ τῶν ἐν ἁμαρτίαις ἐγκαλινδουμένων, ἐκ τῶν ἱερῶν διδασκόμεθα λογίων. Οὐ μόνον δὲ ἔτι ὄντας ἐν τῇ παροικίᾳ τοὺς ἁγίους μεσίτας καὶ πρεσβευτὰς ἡμῶν πρὸς Θεὸν ὁμολογοῦμεν, ἀλλὰ καὶ μετὰ θάνατον μάλιστα, ὅτε καὶ, τῶν ἐσόπτρων λυθέντων, καθαρῶς ἐποπτεύουσι τὴν ἁγίαν τριάδα τὸ ἄπειρον ἐκείνης φῶς τούτων ἐν τῷ νῷ τίθησι τὰ ἡμέτερα. Ὡς γὰρ τοὺς προφήτας ἐν τῷ αἰσθητῷ ὄντας σώματι οὐκ ἀμφιβάλλομεν εἰδέναι τὰ ἐν οὐρανῷ, δι᾽ ὧν τὰ μέλλοντα ἐχρησμῳδότουν· οὕτω καὶ τοὺς ἀγγέλους καὶ τοὺς ὡς ἀγγέλους γεγενημένους ἁγίους εἰδέναι τὰ ἡμέτερα τῷ ἀπείρῳ τοῦ Θεοῦ φωτὶ οὐ διστάζομεν, ἀλλὰ μᾶλλον ἀνενδοιάστως πιστεύομεν καὶ ὁμολογοῦμεν.

pro peccatis nostris propitiationem. Ad deferendas vero apud ipsum orationes ac petitiones nostras intercessores dicimus esse sanctos ac præ omnibus immaculatam ejusdem Verbi divini matrem, nec non et sanctos angelos, quos scimus nobis esse præpositos, Apostolos, Prophetas, Martyres, Sanctos, et quoscunque ceu fideles servos suos glorificavit, in quibus episcopos et sacerdoces, tanquam Dei altare circumstantes, ceterosque homines justos virtutibus eximios numeramus. Enimvero orandum esse pro invicem, multumque valere justi deprecationem, ac Sanctos a Deo audiri magis quam qui in peccatis volutantur, sacris e paginis didicimus. Non solum autem eos, qui in terris agunt, Sanctos nostros apud Deum oratores et mediatores esse profitemur, sed et post mortem maxime, quando sublatis speculis sanctissimam Trinitatem clare contemplantur, cujus et infinito in lumine ea quæ apud nos geruntur agnoscunt. Quemadmodum enim Prophetas sensibile corpus gestantes ea scivisse, quæ in cœlo fiunt, non dubitamus, unde et futura vaticinabantur, ita et angelos et æquatos angelis sanctos in infinito Dei lumine videre nostra non modo non ambigimus, at etiam firmiter credimus et confitemur.

"Ορος θ'.

Πιστεύομεν μηδένα σώζεσθαι ἄνευ πίστεως. Καλοῦμεν δὲ πίστιν τὴν οὖσαν ἐν ἡμῖν ὀρθοτάτην ὑπόληψιν περὶ Θεοῦ καὶ τῶν θείων, ἥτις ἐνεργουμένη διὰ τῆς ἀγάπης, ταὐτὸν εἰπεῖν, διὰ τῶν θείων ἐντολῶν, δικαιοῖ ἡμᾶς παρὰ Χριστοῦ καὶ ταύτης ἄνευ τῷ θεῷ εὐαρεστῆσαι ἀδύνατον.

DECRETUM IX.

Credimus neminem sine fide salvari : fidem autem appellamus certissimam, quæ in nobis est, de Deo rebusque divinis, persuasionem: quæ quidem operans per caritatem, id est, per divinorum mandatorum observationem, justificat nos apud Christum et sine qua nemo potest placere Deo.

"Ορος ι.

Πιστεύομεν τὴν λεγομένην, μᾶλλον δὲ τὴν οὖσαν ἁγίαν καθολικὴν καὶ ἀποστολικὴν ἐκκλησίαν, εἰς ἣν καὶ πιστεύειν δεδιδάγμεθα, πάντας τοὺς ἐν χριστῷ πιστοὺς καθόλου περιέχειν, οἵτινες δηλονότι εἰσέτι καὶ νῦν ἐν τῇ παροικίᾳ ὄντες οὐκ ἔφθασαν ἐν τῇ πατρίδι ἀποδημῆσαι. Μηδαμῶς δὲ συγχέομεν τὴν ἐν τῇ παροικίᾳ ταύτην ἐκκλησίαν τῇ ἐν τῇ πατρίδι, διὰ τὸ εἶναι τυχὸν, ὥς φασί τινες τῶν αἱρετικῶν, καὶ τῶν δύο τὰ μέλη πρόβατα τοῦ ἀρχιποιμένος Θεοῦ καὶ καθαγιάζεσθαι ὑπὸ τοῦ αὐτοῦ ἁγίου πνεύματος· ἄτοπον γὰρ ἅμα καὶ ἀδύνατον, ἐπειδὴ ἡ μὲν ἔτι πυκτεύει καὶ ἐν τῇ ὁδῷ ἐστίν, ἡ δὲ τροπαιοφορεῖ καὶ ἐν τῇ πατρίδι ἀποκατέστη, καὶ τὸ βραβεῖον εἴληφεν. Ἥστινος καθολικῆς ἐκκλησίας ἐπειδὴ θνητὸς ἄνθρωπος καθόλου καὶ ἀΐδιος κεφαλὴ εἶναι οὐ δύναται, αὐτὸς ὁ κύριος ἡμῶν Ἰησοῦς Χριστός ἐστι κεφαλὴ καὶ αὐ-

DECRETUM X.

Credimus eam, quæ vocatur, seu potius quæ vere est Sancta Catholica et Apostolica Ecclesia, in quam et credere docti sumus, omnes prorsus in Christo fideles comprehendere, eos videlicet, qui ad patriam nondum pervenere, sed etiamnum peregrinantur in terris. Nequaquam vero hanc, quæ in via, cum ea, quæ in patria est, ecclesiam confundimus; quod forte, quemadmodum quidam dicunt hæretici, binarum ecclesiarum membra sint oves principis pastorum Dei, et ab eodem Spiritu Sancto sanctificentur. Id enim absurdum ac impossibile, quum altera quidem adhuc in via militet, altera bravium acceperit et in patria collocata triumphet. Hujus autem Catholicæ Ecclesiæ quum universim ac perenniter caput esse mortalis homo non possit, caput est ipse Dominus noster Jesus Christus, et in ejus gubernatione clavum ipse

τὸς τοὺς οἴακας ἔχων ἐν τῇ τῆς ἐκκλησίας κυβερνήσει πηδαλιουχεῖ διὰ τῶν ἁγίων πατέρων. Καὶ διὰ τοῦτο ταῖς κατὰ μέρος ἐκκλησίαις, κυρίως οὔσαις ἐκκλησίαις, καὶ ὑπὸ κυρίως μελῶν συνισταμέναις, ἡγουμένους καὶ ποιμένας καὶ ὅλως οὐκ ἐν καταχρήσει ἀλλὰ κυρίως ἀρχὰς καὶ κεφαλὰς τοὺς ἐπισκόπους ἔθηκε τὸ πνεῦμα τὸ ἅγιον, εἰς τὸν τῆς σωτηρίας ἡμῶν ἀρχηγὸν καὶ τελειωτὴν ἀφορώσας, καὶ εἰς αὐτὸν τὴν ἐνέργειαν τῆς κατὰ τὴν κεφαλὴν χορηγίας ἀναβιβαζούσας δηλονότι.

Ἐπειδὴ δὲ μετὰ τῶν ἄλλων ἀσεβειῶν ἔδοξε καὶ τοῦτο τοῖς Καλουΐνοις, ὅτι τυχόν ταὐτόν ἐστιν ἱερεὺς ἁπλῶς καὶ ἀρχιερεὺς· καὶ δυνατὸν μὴ εἶναι ἀρχιερέα καὶ διά τινων ἱερέων τὴν ἐκκλησίαν κυβερνᾶσθαι, καὶ οὐκ ἀρχιερεὺς ἀλλὰ καὶ ἱερεὺς δύναται χειροτονεῖν ἱερέα, καὶ πλείονας ἱερεῖς χειροτονεῖν ἀρχιερέα· καὶ ταύτης τῆς κακεντρεχίας κοινωνὸν εἶναι μεγαλορρημονοῦσι καὶ τὴν ἀνατολικὴν ἐκκλησίαν, οὗ ἕνεκα καὶ τὸ δέκατον κεφάλαιον συγγέγραπται Κυρίλλῳ, φαμὲν πλατύτερον κατὰ τὴν ἄνωθεν ἐπικρατήσασαν γνώμην τῇ ἀνατολικῇ ἐκκλησίᾳ·

Ὅτι τὸ τοῦ ἐπισκόπου ἀξίωμα οὕτως ἐστὶν ἐν τῇ ἐκκλησίᾳ ἀναγκαῖον, ὥστε χωρὶς αὐτοῦ μὴ δύνασθαι μήτε ἐκκλησίαν μήτε Χριστιανόν τινα ἢ εἶναι ἢ ὅλως λέγεσθαι. Αὐτὸς γὰρ ὡς ἀποστολικὸς διάδοχος τὴν χάριν

tenens hanc sanctorum patrum ministerio gubernat; ac singulis propterea ecclesiis, quæ proprie Ecclesiæ sunt, atque ejus inter membra vere locum obtinent, præpositos ac pastores, qui nequaquam abusive, sed verissime capitum instar illis præsint, episcopos Spiritus Sanctus posuit, qui quidem in auctorem et consummatorem nostræ salutis adspiciant, et ad eum hanc, quam pro ratione capitum impendunt, operam referant.

Quod vero ad impietates ceteras addidere Calvinistæ, non alium esse episcopi quam simplicis sacerdotis gradum posseque absque episcopis ecclesiam esse et a quibusdum sacerdotibus gubernari, item non ab episcopo dumtaxat, sed etiam ab sacerdote posse sacerdotem ordinari; quin et a pluribus sacerdotibus episcopum; atque ejusdem impietatis participem esse deblaterant Orientalem Ecclesiam—qua utique de caussa caput decimum ab Cyrillo conscriptum est—juxta eam, quæ a principio in Orientali Ecclesia obtinuit, sententiam planius dicimus:

Quod ita necessaria est in Ecclesia dignitas episcopalis, ut, ea submota, neque Ecclesia neque Christianus aliquis esse aut dici possit. Quippe apostolorum successor episcopus impositione manuum et

τὴν δοθεῖσαν ἐκείνῳ παρὰ τοῦ κυρίου εἰς τὸ δεσμεῖν τε καὶ λύειν, χειρῶν ἐπιθέσει καὶ ἐπικλήσει τοῦ παναγίου πνεύματος ἀλληλοδιαδόχως λαβὼν, ζῶσά ἐστι εἰκὼν τοῦ Θεοῦ ἐπὶ τῆς γῆς καὶ μετέξει πληρεστάτῃ ἐνεργείας τοῦ τελεταρχικοῦ πνεύματος, πήγη πάντων τῶν μυστηρίων τῆς καθολικῆς ἐκκλησίας, δι' ὧν σωτηρίας ἐπιτυγχάνομεν.

Οὕτω δὲ αὐτοῦ τὸ ἀναγκαῖον ἐννοοῦμεν ἐν τῇ ἐκκλησίᾳ, ὡς ἐν τῷ ἀνθρώπῳ τὴν ἀναπνοὴν καὶ ἐν τῷ κόσμῳ τὸν ἥλιον. Ὅθεν καί τισι κομψῶς πρὸς ἔπαινον τοῦ ἀρχιερατικοῦ ἀξιώματος εἴρηται· ὅ,τι Θεὸς ἐν τῇ οὐρανίῳ τῶν πρωτοτόκων ἐκκλησίᾳ, καὶ ἥλιος ἐν τῷ κόσμῳ, τοῦτο ἕκαστος ἀρχιερεὺς ἐν τῇ κατὰ μέρος ἐκκλησίᾳ, ὡς δι' οὗ τὸ ποίμνιον λαμπρύνεται, θάλπει καὶ ναὸς Θεοῦ γίνεται.

Ὅτι δὲ ἀλληλοδιαδόχως τὸ τῆς ἐπισκοπικῆς μέγα μυστήριον καὶ ἀξίωμα δίδοται μέχρις ἡμῶν, φανερὸν. Ὁ γὰρ κύριος εἰπὼν εἶναι μεθ' ἡμῶν εἰς τὸν αἰῶνα, εἰ καὶ κατ' ἄλλους τρόπους χάριτος καὶ θείων εὐεργετημάτων ἐστὶ μεθ' ἡμῶν, ἀλλ' οὖν κυριωτέρῳ τρόπῳ διὰ τῆς ἐπισκοπικῆς τελεταρχίας οἰκειοῦται ἡμᾶς καὶ σύνεστιν ἡμῖν, καὶ διὰ τῶν ἱερῶν μυστηρίων ἑνοῦται ἡμῖν, ὧν πρωτουργός ἐστι καὶ τελετάρχης διὰ τοῦ πνεύματος ὁ ἐπίσκοπος· καὶ οὐκ ἐᾷ αἱρέσει ὑποπεσεῖν. Καὶ διὰ τοῦτο καὶ Δαμασκηνὸς τετάρτῃ ἐπιστολῇ πρὸς Ἀφρικανοὺς ἔλεγε, τὴν καθόλου ἐκκλησίαν

Sancti Spiritus invocatione datam sibi a Deo ex successione continua ligandi solvendique potestatem quum acceperit; viva Dei imago est in terris et auctoris sacrorum Spiritus operationis participatione plenissima fons omnium Ecclesiæ sacramentorum, quibus ad salutem pervenimus.

Porro quam homini respiratio et sol mundo, tam necessarius in Ecclesia nobis videtur episcopatus. Unde et ad episcopalis dignitatis encomium pulchre nonnulli dixere, quod Deus in cœlesti primogenitorum Ecclesia est et sol in mundo, hoc in sua quemlibet Ecclesia episcopum esse, utpote qui gregem suum illustret, foveat, et Dei templum efficiat.

Transiisse autem successione continua ad nos usque magnum episcopatus sacramentum et dignitatem, manifestum est. Quum enim dixerit dominus, futurum se nobiscum usque ad consummationem sæculi, ut aliis nobiscum sit gratiæ beneficiorumque suorum modis; nullo tamen præstantiori, quam per sacram episcopatus potestatem nobiscum est, in nobis habitat et per sacra mysteria nobis unitur, quorum primus minister est episcopus imo et per Spiritum Sanctum auctor sacrorum constitutus, neque hæresi succumbere nos permittit.

τοῖς ἐπισκόποις γενικῶς ἐπιτετρά-
φθαι, καὶ Κλήμης πρῶτος Ῥωμαίων
ἐπίσκοπος καὶ Εὐόδιος ἐν Ἀντιοχείᾳ
καὶ Μάρκος ἐν Ἀλεξανδρείᾳ Πέτρου
διάδοχοι ὁμολογοῦνται. Καὶ Στά-
χυν ἐν τῷ τῆς Κωνσταντινουπόλεως
θρόνῳ ὁ θεῖος Ἀνδρέας ἀντ' ἐκείνου
καθίστησι, καὶ ἐν τῇ μεγάλῃ ταύτῃ
ἁγίᾳ πόλει Ἱερουσαλὴμ ὁ μὲν κύριος
Ἰάκωβον ποιεῖ, μετὰ δὲ Ἰάκωβον ἕτερος ἐγένετο, καὶ μετ' ἐκεῖνον ἕτερος
ἄχρις ἡμῶν, καὶ διὰ τοῦτο Τερτουλ-
λιανὸς ἐν τῇ πρὸς Παπιανόν ἐπιστολῇ πάντας τοὺς ἐπισκόπους ἀπο-
στολικοὺς διαδόχους καλεῖ. Τούτων
τὴν διαδοχὴν· καὶ τὴν ἀποστολικὴν
ἀξίαν καὶ ἐξουσίαν καὶ Εὐσέβιος ὁ
Παμφίλου μαρτυρεῖ καὶ ἁπλῶς οἱ
πατέρες μαρτυροῦσιν, οὖς περιττὸν
ἐγκαταλέγειν, καὶ ἡ κοινὴ καὶ ἀρχαιοτάτη τῆς καθολικῆς ἐκκλησίας συνήθεια βεβαιοῖ.

Ὅτι δὲ διαφέρει τὸ ἐπισκοπικὸν
ἀξίωμα τοῦ ἁπλῶς ἱερέως, δῆλον.
Ὁ γὰρ ἱερεὺς χειροτονεῖται ὑπὸ τοῦ
ἐπισκόπου, ἐπίσκοπος δὲ οὐ χειροτονεῖται ὑπὸ ἱερέως, ἀλλ' ὑπὸ δύο ἢ
τριῶν ἀρχιερέων, ὡς ὁ ἀποστολικὸς
βούλεται κανών. Καὶ ὁ μὲν ἱερεὺς
ἐκλέγεται ὑπὸ τοῦ ἐπισκόπου, ὁ δὲ
ἀρχιερεὺς οὐκ ἐκλέγεται ὑπὸ τῶν ἱερέων εἴτ' οὖν πρεσβυτέρων, οὔτ' ἐκλέγεται ὑπὸ πολιτικῶν ἀρχόντων, ἀλλ'

Propterea Damascenus quarta ad Africanos epistola dixit, universam Ecclesiam fuisse episcopis genera-liter commissam; et Clementem primum Romæ episcopum, et Evo-dium Antiochiæ et Marcum Alexandriæ Petri successores fuisse, nemo non confitetur. Item et divus Andreas Stachymum throno Constantinopolitano suum in locum suffecit. Item in hac magna civitate sancta Jerusalem Jacobum ipse dominus constituit, Jacobo deinde alter et huic deinceps alter ad nos usque successit. Unde et Tertullianus epistola ad Papianum episcopos omnes apostolorum vocat successores. Horum denique successionem et apostolicam dignitatem juxta ac potestatem Eusebius quoque Pamphili et omnes prorsus patres, quos hic recensere supervacanuum esset, contestantur, et communis ac prima Ecclesiæ Catholicæ vel nascentis consuetudo confirmat.

Superiorem vero esse simplici sacerdotio pontificiam dignitatem, vel inde liquet, quod sacerdotem ordinet episcopus, non vero ab sacerdote sed a duobus tribusve pontificibus juxta apostolorum canones episcopus ordinetur. Et sacerdos quidem eligitur ab episcopo; episcopus vero nequaquam ab sacerdotibus sive presbyteris neque etiam ab sæculi principibus quantacunque

ὑπὸ τῆς συνόδου τῆς ἀνωτάτω ἐκκλησίας τοῦ κλίματος ἐκείνου, ἐν ᾧ κεῖται
ἡ πόλις ἡ δεξομένη τὸν χειροτονηθη-
σόμενον, ἢ τοὐλάχιστον ὑπὸ τῆς συνόδου τῆς ἐπαρχίας ἐκείνης, ἐν ᾧ δεῖ
γίνεσθαι τὸν ἐπίσκοπον. Εἰ δέ ποτε
καὶ ἡ πόλις ἐκλέγοι, ἀλλ᾽ οὐχ ἁπλῶς·
ἡ γὰρ ἐκλογὴ τῇ συνόδῳ ἀναφέρεται,
καὶ εἰ μὲν δόξοι ταύτην κατὰ κανόνας
καλῶς ἔχειν, ὁ ἐκλεχθεὶς προβάλλε-
ται διὰ τῆς χειροθεσίας μὲν τῶν ἐπισκόπων, τῇ ἐπικλήσει δὲ τοῦ παναγίου
πνεύματος· εἰ δὲ μὴ, ὃν βούλεται ἡ
σύνοδος, ἐκεῖνος καὶ προβιβάζεται.
Καὶ ὁ μὲν ἱερεὺς εἰς ἑαυτὸν σώζει
τὴν, ἣν εἴληφεν, ἐξουσίαν καὶ χάριν
τῆς ἱερωσύνης, ὁ ἐπίσκοπος δὲ καὶ
ἑτέροις μεταδίδωσι. Καὶ ὁ μὲν ἤδη
λαβὼν τὸ τῆς ἱερωσύνης ἀξίωμα ὑπὸ
τοῦ ἐπισκόπου, βάπτισμα μόνον τελεῖ
τὸ ἅγιον καὶ εὐχέλαιον, ἱερουργεῖ τὴν
ἀναίμακτον θυσίαν καὶ μεταδίδωσι τῷ
λαῷ τὸ πανάγιον σῶμα καὶ αἷμα τοῦ
κυρίου ἡμῶν Ἰησοῦ Χριστοῦ, χρίει
τοὺς βαπτιζομένους τῷ ἁγίῳ μύρῳ,
στεφανοῖ τοὺς κατὰ νόμον γαμοῦντας
εὐσεβεῖς, εὔχεται ὑπὲρ τῶν ἀσθενῶν
καὶ ὑπὲρ πάσης σωτηρίας καὶ ἀληθείας ἐπιγνώσε ς πάντων ἀνθρώπων,
ἐξαιρέτως δ᾽ ὑπὲρ τῆς τῶν εὐσεβῶν
ζώντων καὶ τεθνεώτων ἀφέσεως καὶ
συγχωρήσεως τῶν ἁμαρτιῶν. Εἰ δὲ
καὶ δοκιμῇ καὶ ἀρετῇ διαφέροι, λαβὼν
ἐξουσίαν παρὰ τοῦ ἐπισκόπου διορ-
θοῖ τοὺς πρὸς αὐτὸν ἐρχομένους εὐσεβεῖς, καὶ εἰς τὴν πρὸς κτῆσιν τῆς

virtute eximiis eligitur, sed ab supremæ Ecclesiæ illius tractus con-
ventu, in quo urbs illa est, cui is,
qui ordinandus est, destinatur, vel
certe ab hujus provinciæ synodo,
in qua opus est episcopum conse-
crari. Sin vero quandoque et civitas elegerit, at non una electum
statuit: etenim ad Synodum defer-
tur electio, quam si canonicam illa
duxerit, impositione manuum episcoporum et Sancti Spiritus invocatione, qui electus est episcopus re-
nuntiatur: sin minus, quemcunque
synodus ipsa voluerit, ille præfici-
tur. Rursum quam sacerdotii potestatem et gratiam sacerdos accepit,
in se ipso conservat, episcopus vero
ceteris impertitur. Et ille quidem
sacerdotali dignitate ab episcopo
initiatus tantummodo baptismum
extremamque administrat unctionem, incruentum offert sacrificium,
et Domini nostri Jesu Christi corpus et sanguinem populo distribuit,
sancto unguento baptizatos ungit,
fideles legitime nubentes coronat,
orat pro infirmis, utque omnes salvi
fiant homines et ad veritatis agnitionem perveniant, deprecatur, præcipue vero pro remissione et venia
peccatorum fidelium tam vivorum
quam defunctorum. Si vero experientia et virtute præstiterit, facta
sibi ab episcopo potestate, venien-
tes ad se fideles emendat, eisque

οὐρανίου βασιλείας ὁδὸν ποδηγετεῖ, καὶ κῆρυξ τοῦ ἱεροῦ προχειρίζεται εὐαγγελίου. Ὁ δὲ ἀρχιερεὺς καὶ τούτων ἁπάντων διάκονός ἐστιν, ἐπείδηπερ αὐτός ἐστιν, ὡς εἴρηται, πηγὴ τῶν θείων μυστηρίων καὶ χαρισμάτων διὰ τοῦ ἁγίου πνεύματος, καὶ τὸ ἅγιον μύρον μονώτατος ἐπιτελεῖ. Καὶ αἱ χειροτονίαι πάντων τῶν ἐν τῇ ἐκκλησίᾳ τάξεων καὶ βαθμῶν τούτου εἰσὶν ἴδιαι· καὶ κατὰ πρῶτον καὶ ὑπέρτερον λόγον οὗτος δεσμεῖ καὶ λύει, καὶ Θεῷ ἡ κρίσις εὐαπόδεκτος, ὡς ὁ κύριος εἴρηκε. Καὶ τὸ ἱερὸν εὐαγγέλιον διδάσκει καὶ τῆς εὐσεβοῦς ὑπερμαχεῖ πίστεως καὶ τοὺς παρακούοντας ὡς ἐθνικοὺς καὶ τελώνας τῆς ἐκκλησίας ἀποδιΐστησι, καὶ τοὺς αἱρετικοὺς ἀφορισμῷ καὶ ἀναθέματι καθυποβάλλει, καὶ τὴν ψυχὴν αὐτοῦ τίθησιν ὑπὲρ τῶν προβάτων. Ἐξ ὧν καταφανές ἐστιν, ἀναντιρρήτως διαφέρειν τὸν ἐπίσκοπον τοῦ ἁπλῶς ἱερέως καὶ πλὴν αὐτοῦ μὴ δυναμένους πάντας τοὺς ἐν τῷ κόσμῳ ἱερεῖς ἐκκλησίαν Θεοῦ ποιμάναι ἢ ὅλως κυβερνῆσαι.

Ἀλλὰ καλῶς λέγεταί τινι τῶν πατέρων, οὐ ῥᾴδιον, αἱρετικὸν ἄνδρα συνετὸν εὑρεῖν. Καταλιπόντες γὰρ οὗτοι τὴν ἐκκλησίαν, ἐγκατελείφθησαν ὑπὸ τοῦ ἁγίου πνεύματος καὶ οὐκ ἔμεινεν ἐν αὐτοῖς σύνεσις οὔτε φῶς ἀλλὰ σκότος καὶ πώρωσις. Εἰ γὰρ μὴ τοιαῦτα πεπόνθασιν, οὐκ ἂν

ad cœlestis regni possessionem viam ostendit atque sancti evangelii prædicator initiatur. Episcopus autem horum omnium et ipse quidem minister est, utpote qui divinorum mysteriorum gratiarumque fons per Spiritum Sanctum, uti jam diximus, exsistat: sed et sanctum unguentum solus ille conficit et omnium officiorum et graduum, qui in Ecclesia sunt, ordinationes ad ipsum attinent, ac primario et sublimiori modo ligat et solvit, sententiam ejus approbante Deo, uti et Dominus spospondit. Insuper sacrum evangelium annunciat, ac pro fide orthodoxa decertat: et audire renuentes ceu ethnicos et publicanos ab Ecclesia ejicit, hæreticosque excommunicationi et anathemati subjicit, ac denique suam pro ovibus animam ponit. E quibus evidenter et invictissime constat, ab sacerdote simplici distingui episcopum, quo deficiente nec omnes, qui in mundo sunt, sacerdotes pascere ecclesiam possunt, nec omnino gubernare.

At enim, ut recte quidam patrum ait, haud ita facile hæreticorum quempiam reperias sapientem. Quum enim ab Ecclesia illi defecerint, ab eis Sanctus etiam Spiritus abscessit et omnis intelligentiæ ac luminis expertes facti tenebris et cœcitate sunt involuti. Id enim

πρὸς τὰ φανερώτατα ἀντιτείναιντο, ἐξ ὧν ἐστὶ καὶ τὸ τῆς ἐπισκοπικῆς μέγα ὄντως μυστήριον ὑπὸ τῆς γραφῆς διδασκόμενον, ὑπό τε πάσης ἐκκλησιαστικῆς ἱστορίας καὶ συγγραφῆς ἁγίων συγγραφόμενόν τε καὶ μαρτυρούμενον, καὶ ὑπὸ τῆς καθολικῆς ἐκκλησίας ἀεὶ γινόμενόν τε καὶ ὁμολογούμενον.

ipsis ni contigisset, haudquaquam rebus ita obniterentur apertissimis, cujusmodi profecto magnum episcopatus sacramentum est, quod Scriptura nobis indicit, quod omnium annalium ecclesiasticorum monumenta et sanctorum Scripta contestantur, quod denique Catholica Ecclesia nunquam non credidit et sine intermissione tenuit.

Ὅρος ιά.

Πιστεύομεν μέλη τῆς καθολικῆς ἐκκλησίας εἶναι πάντας καὶ μόνους τοὺς πιστούς, τοὺς τὴν τοῦ σωτῆρος Χριστοῦ δηλαδὴ ἀμώμητον πίστιν ὑπό τε ἐκείνου τοῦ Χριστοῦ καὶ τῶν ἀποστόλων καὶ τῶν ἁγίων οἰκουμενικῶν συνόδων δειχθεῖσαν, ἀδιστάκτως πρεσβεύοντας, κἂν καί τινες ἐξ αὐτῶν ἁμαρτίαις παντοίαις ὑπεύθυνοι εἶεν. Εἰ γὰρ μὴ ἦν μέλη τῆς ἐκκλησίας οἱ πιστοὶ μὲν, ἁμαρτίαις δὲ συζῶντες, οὐκ ἂν ὑπὸ τῆς ἐκκλησίας ἐκρίνοντο. Νῦν δὲ κρινόμενοι ὑπ' αὐτῆς, εἴς τε μετάνοιαν προσκαλούμενοι καὶ εἰς τὸν τρίβον τῶν σωτηρίων ἐντολῶν ποδηγετούμενοι, κἂν καὶ ἔτι ἁμαρτίαις ῥυπαίνοιντο, μόνον δι' αὐτὸ τοῦτο, ὅτι οὐ πεπτώκασιν εἰς ἀπόγνωσιν καὶ ὅτι τῆς καθολικῆς καὶ εὐσεβοῦς ἀντέχοντες πίστεως μέλη τῆς καθολικῆς ἐκκλησίας εἰσὶ καὶ γινώσκονται.

DECRETUM XI.

Credimus Ecclesiæ Catholicæ membra esse omnes ac solos fideles, eos nimirum, qui Salvatoris Christi fidem, ab ipso quidem Christo et ab Apostolis nec non et ab sanctis synodis œcumenicis traditam, firma mente servant illibatam, quamvis eorum aliqui variis peccatis sint obnoxii. Nisi enim essent Ecclesiæ membra, qui fidem quidem habent, sed in peccatis vivunt, utique non judicarentur ab Ecclesia. Nunc autem, quum et ab Ecclesia judicentur, et ad pœnitentiam incitentur, et in salutarium mandatorum semitam deducantur, etiamsi peccatis sordescant, eo solum, quod in desperationem non sunt prolapsi, sed Catholicam et rectam fidem retinent, Ecclesiæ Catholicæ membra sunt et reputantur.

Ὅρος ιβ'.

Πιστεύομεν ὑπὸ τοῦ ἁγίου πνεύματος διδάσκεσθαι τὴν καθολικὴν
ἐκκλησίαν. Αὐτὸ γάρ ἐστιν ὁ ἀληθὴς παράκλητος, ὃν πέμπει παρὰ τοῦ
πατρὸς ὁ Χριστὸς τοῦ διδάσκειν τὴν
ἀλήθειαν καὶ τὸ σκότος ἀπὸ τῆς τῶν
πιστῶν διανοίας ἀποδιώκειν. Ἡ τοῦ
ἁγίου πνεύματος ὅμως διδαχὴ οὐκ
ἀμέσως ἀλλὰ διὰ τῶν ἁγίων πατέρων
καὶ καθηγεμόνων τῆς καθολικῆς ἐκκλησίας καταγλαΐζει τὴν ἐκκλησίαν,
Ὡς γὰρ ἡ πᾶσα γραφή ἐστί τε καὶ
λέγεται λόγος τοῦ ἁγίου πνεύματος,
οὐχ ὅτι ἀμέσως ὑπ' αὐτοῦ ἐλαλήθη,
ἀλλ' ὅτι ὑπ' αὐτοῦ διὰ τῶν ἀποστόλων καὶ προφητῶν· οὕτω καὶ ἡ ἐκκλησία διδάσκεται μὲν ὑπὸ τοῦ ζωαρχικοῦ
πνεύματος ἀλλὰ διὰ μέσου τῶν ἁγίων
πατέρων καὶ διδασκάλων (ὧν κανὼν
αἱ οἰκουμενικαὶ καὶ ἅγιαι ὡμολόγην-
ται σύνοδοι· οὐ γὰρ τοῦτο παύσομαι
μυριάκις λέγειν), καὶ διὰ τοῦτο οὐ
μόνον πεπείσμεθα, ἀλλὰ καὶ ἀληθὲς
καὶ βέβαιον ἀναμφιβόλως εἶναι ὁμολογοῦμεν, τὴν καθολικὴν ἐκκλησίαν
ἀδύνατον ἁμαρτῆσαι ἢ ὅλως πλανη-
θῆναι ἤ ποτε τὸ ψεῦδός ἀντὶ τῆς
ἀληθείας ἐκλέξαι. Τὸ γὰρ πανάγιον
πνεῦμα ἀείποτε ἐνεργοῦν διὰ τῶν
πιστῶς διακονούντων ἁγίων πατέρων καὶ καθηγεμόνων πάσης ὁποιασ-
οῦν πλάνης τὴν ἐκκλησίαν ἀπαλ-
λαττει.

DECRETUM XII.

Credimus ab Spiritu Sancto doceri Catholicam Ecclesiam. Quippe
verus consolator ipse est, quem ad
docendum fideles veritatem expel-
lendasque eorum e mentibus tenebras Christus a Patre mittit. Porro haudquaquam immediate sed
per sanctos patres et Ecclesiæ Catholicæ præpositos Ecclesiam ipsam doctrina Sancti Spiritus illu-
minat. Quemadmodum enim verbum Sancti Spiritus Sacra Scriptura est et dicitur, non quod ab
ipso immediate sed per Apostolos
et Prophetas fuerit enunciata:
ita et ab vivifico Spiritu docetur
quidem Ecclesia, sed medio sanctorum patrum doctorumque magisterio (quibus sanctæ synodi
œcumenicæ regulæ instar exstitere; quod millies dixero) ac propterea errare aut aliquatenus de-
cipi, aut aliquando pro veritate
mendacium eligere Catholicam
Ecclesiam non posse nedum censemus, at etiam id ipsum ceu verum ac certissimum constanter
profitemur. Etenim per sanctos
patres ac præpositos fideliter ad
ministrantes jugiter operans Spiritus Sanctus omnem quemcunque ab Ecclesia removet er-
rem.

Ὅρος ιγ'.

Πιστεύομεν οὐ διὰ πίστεως ἁπλῶς μόνης δικαιοῦσθαι τὸν ἄνθρωπον ἀλλὰ διὰ πίστεως καὶ ἐνεργουμένης διὰ τῆς ἀγάπης, ταὐτὸν εἰπεῖν, διὰ τῆς πίστεως καὶ τῶν ἔργων. Τὸ δὲ τὴν πίστιν χειρὸς ἔργον ἀποπληροῦσαν ἀντιλαμβάνεσθαι τῆς ἐν Χριστῷ δικαιοσύνης καὶ προσάπτειν ἡμῖν εἰς σωτηρίαν, πόῤῥω πάσης εὐσεβείας γινώσκομεν. Οὕτω γὰρ ἐννοουμένη ἡ πίστις πᾶσιν ἐφαρμοσθείη καὶ, οὐκ ἂν εἴη ὁ μὴ σωζόμενος, ὅπερ ἀντικρὺ ψεῦδός ἐστι. Τοὐναντίον δὲ μᾶλλον πιστεύομεν, ὅτι οὐ τῆς πίστεως ἀναφορικὸν ἀλλὰ τὴν οὖσαν ἐν ἡμῖν πίστιν διὰ τῶν ἔργων δικαιοῦν ἡμᾶς παρὰ Χριστοῦ. Ἐννοοῦμεν δὲ τὰ ἔργα οὐ μάρτυρας τήν ἡμετέραν κλῆσιν ἐπιβεβαιοῦντας, ἀλλὰ καρποὺς καθ' ἑαυτοὺς ὄντας, δι' ὧν ἡ πίστις λαμβάνει τὸ ἔμπρακτον καὶ καθ' ἑαυτὰ ἄξια διὰ τὰς θείας ἐπαγγελίας τοῦ κομίσασθαι ἕκαστον τῶν πιστῶν τὰ διὰ τοῦ σώματος αὐτῷ πεπραγμένα, εἴ τ' ἀγαθὸν εἴτε κακὸν δηλονότι.

Ὅρος ιδ'.

Πιστεύομεν τὸν ἄνθρωπον κατολισθήσαντα τῇ παραβάσει παρασυμβληθῆναι καὶ ὁμοιωθῆναι τοῖς κτήνεσι, τοῦτ' ἔστιν, ἀμαυρωθῆναι καὶ τῆς τελειότητος καὶ ἀπαθείας ἐκπεσεῖν, οὐ μὴν καὶ τῆς ἧς ἔτυχε παρὰ τοῦ

DECRETUM XIII.

Credimus non sola fide simpliciter, sed ea, quæ per caritatem operatur, id est, fide atque operibus hominem justificari. Quod vero fides, quasi manus adimplens munus, justitiam, quæ in Christo est, apprehendat, nobisque applicet ad salutem, ab omni pietate longissime esse censemus. Enimvero sic intellecta fides omnibus conveniret, unde et ad salutem nemo non perveniret; quod aperte falsum est. Imo contrarium credimus, scilicet non fidei correlativum sed ipsam, quæ in nobis est, fidem per opera Christi munere nos justificare. Porro certitudinis vocationis nostræ argumenta esse hujusmodi opera nequaquam intelligimus, sed fructus ex se ipsis, per quos efficax redditur fides, eaque ex divinis promissionibus esse talia dicimus, pro quibus recipere unusquisque fidelium dignus exsistat, prout gessit in corpore suo, sive bonum sive malum.

DECRETUM XIV.

Credimus hominem transgressione lapsum comparatum esse et assimilatum jumentis, id est, debilitatum et a perfectione ac passionum immunitate excidisse, haudquaquam tamen hujus, quam ab

ἄκρως ἀγαϑοῦ Θεοῦ φύσεως καὶ ἐνερ
γείας ἐξεστηκ.΄ναι. Οὕτω γὰρ οὐκ
ἂν ἦν λογικὸς καὶ ἑπομένως οὐδ' ἄν
ϑρωπος· ἀλλ ἔχειν τὴν φύσιν αὐ
τὴν, ἣ ἔκτισται καὶ τὴν τῆς φύσεως
ἐνέργειαν, ἥτις ἐστὶ τὸ αὐτεξούσιον,
ζῶσαν καὶ ἐνεργὸν· ὥστε κατὰ φύσιν
δύνασϑαι αἱρεῖσϑαι μὲν καὶ ἐργάζε
σϑαι τὸ καλὸν, φεύγειν δὲ καί μυσάτ
τεσϑαι τὸ κακόν. Ἄτοπον γὰρ τὸ
τὴν καλὴν παρὰ τοῦ ἄκρως ἀγαϑοῦ
δημιουργηϑεῖσαν φύσιν ἄμοιρον ἀγα
ϑῆς ἐνεργείας ὁμολογεῖν. Τοῦτο γὰρ
κακὴν εἶναι τὴν φύσιν λέγειν ἐστίν·
οὗ τί ἀσεβέστερον; Ἡ γὰρ ἐνέργεια
τῆς φύσεως ἤρτηται, ἡ φύσις δὲ τοῦ
δημιουργοῦ· εἰ καὶ ὁ τρόπος διαφέ
ρει. Ὅτι δὲ δύναται ὁ ἄνϑρωπος
φύσει ἐργάζεσϑαι τὸ ἀγαϑὸν, ὑπαινίτ
τεται μὲν καὶ ὁ κύριος λέγων, καὶ τοὺς
ἐϑνικοὺς ἀγαπᾷν τοὺς ἀγαπῶντας
αὐτούς. Διδάσκεται δὲ σαφέστατα
καὶ ὑπὸ τοῦ Παύλου Ῥωμ. πρώτ.
κεφ. ιϑ'. καὶ ἀλλαχοῦ ῥητῶς, ἐν οἷς
φησὶ, τὰ μὴ νόμον ἔχοντα ἔϑνη φύ
σει τὰ τοῦ νόμου ποιεῖν. Ἐξ ὧν
φανερὸν καὶ τοῦτο, ὅτι δηλαδὴ ἀδύ
νατον, ὅτι ποιήσει ὁ ἄνϑρωπος ἀγα
ϑὸν, ἁμαρτίαν εἶναι. Τὸ γὰρ καλὸν
ἀδύνατον κακὸν εἶναι. Γινόμενον
μέντοι φύσει μόνῃ καὶ ψυχικὸν οὐχὶ
δὲ καὶ πνευματικὸν ποιοῦν τὸν μετερ
χόμενον, οὐ συμβάλλεται πρὸς σω
τηρίαν ἁπλῶς ἄνευ πίστεως, ἀλλ'
οὐδὲ μὴν πρὸς κατάκρισιν· οὐδὲ γὰρ
ἐνδέχεται. τὸ καλὸν, ᾗ τοιοῦτον,

optimo Deo acceperat, naturæ virtutisque naturalis jacturam fecisse.
Alioqui enim rationalis jam non
esset ac proinde nec homo: imo
vero ejusdem et modo credimus
esse naturæ, quam, quum crearetur, accepit, imo et eadem naturali virtute utique viva et efficaci
quæ est facultas liberi arbitrii pollere, ita ut possit naturaliter eligere
et operari bonum ac fugere et
odisse malum. Minus quippe rationi consentaneum videtur, ut naturam bonam ab summo bono conditam cujuscunque operationis bonæ confiteamur expertem. Hoc
enim est, naturam esse malam, dicere; quo quid magis impium? A
natura etenim operatio pendet, et
ab opifice natura, etsi ratione diversa. Posse autem hominem naturaliter operari bonum, innuit vel
ipse dominus, ethnicos redamare dicens eos, a quibus amantur. Sed
et hoc ipsum manifestissime Paulus
edocet ad Romanos (I. 19), et alibi
expressis verbis, ubi ait, gentes, quæ
legem non habent, naturaliter, quæ
legis sunt, facere. Ex quibus et hoc
quoque manifestum est, nimirum
fieri non posse, ut bonum, quod facit homo, sit peccatum. Quippe impossibile est, malum esse quod bonum est. Quod autem fit naturaliter solum, et quod animalem non
vero etiam spiritalem facit auctorem

κακοῦ γενέσθαι αἰτίαν. Ἐν τοῖς ἀναγεννηθεῖσι δὲ, ὑπὸ τῆς χάριτος καὶ μετὰ τῆς χάριτος ἐνεργούμενον τέλειον ἀπεργάζεται καὶ σωτηρίας ἄξιον ποιεῖται τὸν ἐνεργοῦντα.

Ὁ ἄνθρωπος τοιγαροῦν πρὸ τῆς ἀναγεννήσεως δύναται φύσει κλίνειν πρὸς τὸ καλὸν καὶ αἱρεῖσθαι καὶ ἐργάζεσθαι τὸ ἠθικὸν καλὸν. Ἀναγεννηθεὶς δὲ ἵνα ποιῇ τὸ πνευματικὸν καλὸν—σωτηρίας γὰρ ὄντα παραίτια τοῦ πιστοῦ τὰ ἔργα καὶ ὑπὸ χάριτος ὑπερφυοῦς ἐνεργούμενα καὶ πνευματικὰ εἰκότως ὀνομάζεται—ἀνάγκη προηγεῖσθαι καὶ προφθάνειν τὴν χάριν, ὃν τρόπον εἴρητο· ἐν τοῖς περὶ προορισμοῦ· ὥστε μηδὲν δύνασθαι ἐξ ἑαυτοῦ τῆς κατὰ Χριστὸν ζωῆς ἄξιον ἔργον ἐκτελέσαι, ἐξ ἑαυτοῦ μέντοι ἔχειν τὸ θελῆσαι ἢ μὴ θελῆσαι τῇ χάριτι συγκατατεθῆναι.

Ὅρος ιέ.

Πιστεύομεν τὰ εὐαγγελικὰ μυστήρια ἐν τῇ ἐκκλησίᾳ εἶναι, κἀκεῖνα εἶναι ἑπτά. Ἐλάττονα γὰρ ἢ μείζονα ἀριθμὸν μυστηρίων ἐν τῇ ἐκκλησίᾳ οὐκ ἔχομεν· ἐπειδὴ ὁ παρὰ τὸν ἑπτὰ τῶν μυστηρίων ἀριθμὸς αἱρετικῆς φρενοβλαβείας ἐστὶν ἀποκύημα. Ὁ δὲ τῶν ἑπτὰ παρὰ τοῦ ἱεροῦ εὐαγγελίου νομοθετεῖται καὶ συνάγεται, ὡς καὶ τὰ λοιπὰ τῆς

suum, sine fide nihil omnino confert ad salutem, sed nec ad damnationem; neque enim bonum, qua tale, aliquando contingit mali caussam exsistere. In regeneratis vero illud, quod fit sub gratia et cum gratia, perfectum facit et salute dignum præstat operantem.

Potest igitur naturaliter homo nondum regeneratus ad *bonum morale* propendere illudque eligere et operari: ut vero *spirituale bonum* regeneratus operetur nam et spiritualia merito vocantur fidelium opera, quæ caussa salutis exsistunt et ex supernaturali gratia fiunt præire ac prævenire gratiam necesse est, quemadmodum de prædestinatione agentes diximus, ita ut nullum omnino Christianæ vitæ dignum possit ex se ipso opus edere; quamquam ex se ipso habet velle aut nolle assentiri gratiæ.

DECRETUM XV.

Credimus esse in Ecclesia Evangelica Sacramenta, eaque septem. Nec minorem majoremve in Ecclesia Sacramentorum numerum admittimus; siquidem hæreticorum dementiæ fœtus est alius sacramentorum numerus quam septenarius, qui non secus ac cetera Catholicæ fidei dogmata in Evangelio statuitur et ex ipso colligitur.

καθολικῆς πίστεως δόγματα. Αὐτίκα γὰρ ὁ κύριος τὸ μὲν ἅγιον βάπτισμα δια τοῦ· πορευθέντες μαθητεύσατε πάντα τὰ ἔθνη, βαπτίζοντες αὐτοὺς εἰς τὸ ὄνομα τοῦ πατρὸς καὶ τοῦ υἱοῦ καὶ ἁγίου πνεύματος, καὶ τοῦ· ὁ πιστεύσας καὶ βαπτισθεὶς σωθήσεται, ὁ δὲ ἀπιστήσας κατακριθήσεται, παραδέδωκε.

Τὸ δὲ τῆς βεβαιώσεως, ταὐτὸν εἰπεῖν, τοῦ ἁγίου μύρου καὶ ἁγίου χρίσματος, διὰ τοῦ· ὑμεῖς δὲ καθήσατε ἐν τῇ πόλει Ἱερουσαλὴμ, ἕως ἂν ἐνδύσησθε δύναμιν ἐξ ὕψους. Ἣν ἐνεδύσαντο τῇ ἐπιδημίᾳ τοῦ ἁγίου πνεύματος, καὶ ταύτην δηλοῖ τὸ τῆς βεβαιώσεως μυστήριον, περὶ οὗ καὶ Παῦλος δευτέρας πρὸς Κορινθίους κεφαλαίῳ πρώτῳ, καὶ τρανώτερον διὰ τοῦ Ἀρεοπαγίτου Διονυσίου διαλέγεται.

Τὴν δὲ ἱερωσύνην διὰ τοῦ· τοῦτο ποιεῖτε εἰς τὴν ἐμὴν ἀνάμνησιν, καὶ διὰ τοῦ· ὅσα ἂν δήσητε καὶ λύσητε ἐπὶ τῆς γῆς, ἔσται δεδεμένα καὶ λελυμένα ἐν τοῖς οὐρανοῖς.

Τὴν δὲ ἀναίμακτον θυσίαν διὰ τοῦ· λάβετε, φάγετε· τοῦτό ἐστι τὸ σῶμά μου, καὶ· πίετε ἐξ αὐτοῦ πάντες, τοῦτό ἐστι τὸ αἷμά μου τὸ τῆς καινῆς διαθήκης, καὶ τοῦ· ἐὰν μὴ φάγητε τὴν σάρκα τοῦ υἱοῦ τοῦ ἀνθρώπου, οὐκ ἔχετε ζωὴν ἐν ἑαυτοῖς.

Τὸν δὲ γάμον μετὰ τὸ εἰπεῖν τὰ ἐν

Ac primo quidem Baptismi sacramentum Dominus tradidit, quando dixit: Euntes docete omnes gentes, baptizantes eos in nomine patris et filii et Spiritus Sancti; item et quum dixit: Qui crediderit et baptizatus fuerit, salvus erit: qui vero non crediderit, condemnabitur.

Confirmationis vero seu unguenti sacri et sancti chrismatis, quum dixit: Vos autem sedete in civitate Jerusalem, quoadusque induamini virtute ex alto. Hac autem per Sancti Spiritus adventum sunt induti, et hanc declarat confirmationis sacramentum. De quo et Apostolus II. Corinth. cap. I. et apertius per Dionysium Areopagitam disseritur.

Sacramentum Ordinis tradidit, dicens: Hoc facite in meam commemorationem; item et quum dixit: Quæcunque ligaveritis et solveritis super terram, erunt ligata et soluta in cœlis.

Incruentum vero tradidit sacrificium dicens: Accipite et manducate, hoc est corpus meum; et: Bibite ex hoc omnes, hic est sanguis meus Novi Testamenti; item et quum dixit: Nisi manducaveritis carnem filii hominis; non habebitis vitam in vobis.

Sacramentum vero matrimonii

τῇ παλαιᾷ περὶ αὐτοῦ εἰρημένα διὰ
τῆς οἷον ἐπισφραγίσεως τοῦ · οὓς ὁ
Θεὸς συνέζευξεν, ἄνθρωπος μὴ χω-
ριζέτω, ὃν καὶ ὁ θεῖος ἀπόστολος
μέγα ἐπικαλεῖ μυστήριον.

Τὴν δὲ μετάνοιαν, ᾗτινί ἐστι σύμ-
μικτος ἡ μυστηριακὴ ἐξομολόγησις,
διὰ τοῦ · ἄν τινων ἀφῆτε τὰς ἁμαρτίας, ἀφίενται αὐτοῖς · ἄν τινων κρατῆτε, κεκράτηνται, καὶ τοῦ · ἐὰν μὴ
μετανοήσητε, ὡσαύτως ἀπολεῖσθε.

Τὸ δὲ ἅγιον ἔλαιον εἴτ' οὖν εὐχέλαιον λέγεται παρὰ τῷ Μάρκῳ, μαρ-
τυρεῖται δὲ ῥητῶς ὑπὸ τοῦ ἀδελφο-
θέου.
Σύγκειται δὲ τὰ μυστήρια ἐκ τοῦ
φυσικοῦ καὶ ὑπερφυοῦς · οὐκ εἰσὶ δὲ
ψιλὰ σημεῖα τῶν ἐπαγγελιῶν τοῦ
Θεοῦ. Οὕτω γὰρ οὐκ ἂν διενήνοχε
τῆς περιτομῆς, οὗ τί ἀθλιώτερον;
Ὁμολογοῦμεν δ' αὐτὰ εἶναι ὄργανα
δραστικὰ τοῖς μυουμένοις χάριτος ἐξ
ἀνάγκης. Ἀποπτύομεν δὲ ὡς ἀλλό-
τριον τῆς Χριστιανικῆς διδασκαλίας
τὸ τὴν ἀκεραιότητα τῶν μυστηρίων
ἀπαιτεῖν τὴν χρῆσιν τοῦ γηΐνου
πράγματος · ἀντίκειται γὰρ τῷ μυ-
στηρίῳ τῆς προσφορᾶς, ὃ ῥήματι
ὑπαρκτικῷ νομοθετηθὲν καὶ τῇ ἐπικλήσει τοῦ ἁγίου πνεύματος ἁγια-
σθὲν τελειοῦται τῇ ὑπάρξει τοῦ ση-
μαινομένου, τοῦ σώματος δηλαδὴ καὶ

tunc tradidit, quum recensitis velut ejus in obsignationem iis, quæ
de illo in veteri testamento scripta
sunt, ait: Quos Deus conjunxit,
homo non separet. Quin et magnum ab apostolo sacramentum appellatur.

Pœnitentiam, in qua sacramentalis includitur confessio, tunc tradidit, quum dixit: Quorum remiseritis peccata, remittuntur eis; quorum retinueritis, retenta sunt; item
et quum dixit: Nisi pœnitentiam
habueritis; omnes similiter peribitis.

Sanctum denique oleum sive
extrema unctio apud Marcum legitur, et aperto Jacobi fratris domini testimonio comprobatur.

Porro naturali et supernaturali
constant sacramenta: neque nuda
illa sunt divinarum signa promis-
sionum, quippe ita nihil ab circumcisione discreparent; quo quid mi-
serabilius dici possit? Imo vera ea
esse instrumenta his, qui initiantur
illis, gratiam necessario conferen-
tia, confitemur. Quod autem rei
terrenæ usum sacramentorum in-
tegritas necessario exigat, ab doctrina Christiana alienum id omnino existimamus, utpote eucharistiæ
sacramento contrarium, quod ab
substantiali quidem verbo institutum et a sancto spiritu sanctifica-
tum, rei, quam significat, nimirum

αἵματος τοῦ Χριστοῦ. Καὶ προη-
γεῖται ἡ τούτου τελείωσις ἀναγκαίως
τῆς χρήσεως. Εἰ γὰρ πρὸ τῆς χρήσεως μὴ ἦν τέλειον, οὐκ ἂν ὁ κακῶς
χρώμενος κρῖμα ἑαυτῷ ἦσθιε καὶ ἔπι-
νεν· ἐπεὶ ψιλοῦ ἄρτου καὶ οἴνου ἦν
μετεσχηκώς. Νῦν δ᾽ ἀναξίως μετέ-
χων κρῖμα ἑαυτῷ ἐσθίει καὶ πίνει·
ὥστε οὐκ ἐν τῇ χρήσει ἀλλὰ καὶ πρὸ
τῆς χρήσεως ἔχει τὸ τῆς εὐχαριστίας
μυστήριον τὴν τελείωσιν. Ἔτι ἀπορ-
ρίπτομεν ὡς κάθαρμά τι καὶ μίασμα
τὸ· ἐλλιπῶς γὰρ ἐχούσης τῆς πίστεως ζημιοῦται ἡ ὁλοκληρία τοῦ μυστηρίου. Οἱ γὰρ αἱρετικοί, οὓς τὴν
αἵρεσιν ἀποσεισαμένους καὶ προστε-
θέντας τῇ καθολικῇ ἐκκλησίᾳ, δέχεται ἡ ἐκκλησία· καίτοι ἐλλιπῆ ἐσχη-
κότες τὴν πίστιν τέλειον ἔλαβον τὸ
βάπτισμα· ὅθεν τελείαν ὕστερον τὴν
πίστιν κεκτημένοι οὐκ ἀναβαπτί-
ζονται.

Ὅρος ις΄.

Πιστεύομεν τὸ ἅγιον βάπτισμα, τὸ
διαταγὲν μὲν παρὰ τοῦ κυρίου, γινόμενον δὲ ἐν ὀνόματι τῆς ἁγίας τριάδος, εἶναι τῶν ἀναγκαιοτάτων. Χωρὶς γὰρ αὐτοῦ οὐδεὶς δύναται σωθῆναι, ὡς ὁ κύριός φησιν· ὅστις οὐ μὴ
γεννηθῇ ἐξ ὕδατος καὶ πνεύματος, οὐ
μὴ εἰσέλθῃ εἰς τὴν βασιλείαν τῶν
οὐρανῶν. Καὶ διὰ τοῦτό ἐστιν ἀναγκαῖον καὶ τοῖς νηπίοις, ἐπειδὴ κἀκεῖνα

corporis et sanguinis Christi, præsentia perficitur. Et prius quidem
in se necessario perfectum est quam
cedati in usum. Etenim ni com-
pletum esset ante usum, suum
utique non manducaret ac biberet
ille judicium, qui eo male utitur;
quandoquidem nudum panem et
vinum sumeret. Atqui judicium
sibi manducat et bibit, qui sumit
indigne. Eucharistiæ itaque sacramentum nequaquam in usu sed ante
usum suum obtinet complementum.
Deinde et hanc quaque sententiam,
videlicet integritati sacramenti di-
spendium afferre defectum fidei, ut
exitialem et abominandam rejici-
mus. Nam et hæresim abjurantes
fidemque Catholicam amplectentes
hæreticos Ecclesia recipit, qui quamvis fidei defectu laborantes perfectum baptisma receperunt: unde nec
eos denuo baptizat, ubi perfectam
fidem sunt adepti.

DECRETUM XVI.

Credimus sanctum Baptisma, a
Domino quidem institutum et in
nomine sanctæ Trinitatis collatum,
esse summe necessarium. Etenim
sine illo salvari nemo potest juxta
Domini sententiam: Nisi quis renatus fuerit ex aqua et Spiritu
Sancto, non intrabit in regnum cœlorum. Igitur et parvulis necessarium illud est, utpote qui rei quoque

ὑπόκεινται τῇ ἀρχεγόνῳ ἁμαρτίᾳ καὶ χωρὶς τοῦ βαπτίσματος οὐ δύναται τυχεῖν τῆς ἀφέσεως· ὅπερ ὁ κύριος δεικνύων οὐκ ἔφη μερικῶς ἀλλ' ἁπλῶς καὶ καθόλου· ὅστις οὐ μὴ γεννηθῇ, ὃ ταὐτόν ἐστι τῷ· πάντας τοὺς μετὰ τὴν ἔλευσιν τοῦ σωτῆρος Χριστοῦ εἰσελευσομένους ἐν τῇ βασιλείᾳ τῶν οὐρανων δεῖ ἀναγεννηθῆναι. Εἰ δὲ τὰ νήπια ἄνθρωποι, εἴπερ καὶ ταῦτα δεῖται σωτηρίας· δεῖται σωτηρίας, δεῖται καὶ τοῦ βαπτίσματος. Καὶ τὰ μὴ ἀναγεννηθέντα, ὡς μὴ τὴν ἄφεσιν τῆς προπατορικῆς ἁμαρτίας λαβόντα, ὑπόκειται τῇ ἀϊδίῳ τῆς ἁμαρτίας ἀνάγκης ποινῇ, καὶ ἑπομένως οὐ σώζεται χωρὶς τοῦ βαπτίσματος· ὥστε δεῖ ἀναγκαίως καὶ τὰ νήπια βαπτίζεσθαι. Ἔτι τὰ νήπια σώζεται, ὡς λέγεται παρὰ τῷ Ματθαίῳ· ὁ δὲ μὴ βαπτισθεὶς οὐ σώζεται· καὶ τὰ νήπια ἄρα ἀναγκαίως βαπτισθήσονται. Καὶ ἐν ταῖς Πράξεσι λέγεται, ὅτι πᾶσαι αἱ οἰκίαι ἐβαπτίζοντο, ἄρα καὶ τὰ νήπια. Τοῦτο καὶ οἱ πάλαι πατέρες μαρτυροῦσι σαφῶς, ἐν οἷς καὶ Διονύσιος ἐν τῷ περὶ ἐκκλησιαστικῆς ἱεραρχίας. Καὶ Ἰουστῖνος πεντεκοστῷ ἕκτῳ ζητήματι, ὃς λέγει ῥητῶς· ἀξιοῦνται δὲ τῶν διὰ τοῦ βαπτίσματος ἀγαθῶν τῇ πίστει τῶν προσφερόντων αὐτὰ τῷ βαπτίσματι. Καὶ Αὐγουστῖνος παράδοσιν εἶναί φησιν ἀποστολικὴν, τὰ παιδία διὰ τοῦ βαπτίσματος σώζεσθαι· καὶ ἀλλαχοῦσε· ἡ ἐκκλησία

peccati originalis exsistant et sole possint baptismate mundari. Quod docens Dominus nequaquam de quibusdam tantum sed simpliciter et de omnibus dixit: Nisi quis renatus fuerit, etc. Quod item est ac si dixisset, omnes post Christi salvatoris adventum cœlorum regnum ingressuros esse regenerandos. Si autem parvuli homines sunt, siquidem salute indigent, indigent et baptismate; et qui non regenerati decedunt, tamquam qui originalis peccati remissionem non acceperint, simpiternæ peccati pœnæ de necessitate subjiciuntur et consequenter sine baptismo haudquaquam salvantur: quare necesse est, parvulos baptizari. Insuper salutem parvuli consequuntur, ut apud Matthæum dicitur: Non baptizatus autem non salvatur. Ergo necesse est, et parvulos baptizari. Et in Actis dicitur, familias totas fuisse baptizatas; ergo et parvulos. Sed et hoc ipsum Patres antiqui testantur evidenter, in quibus Dionysius de ecclesiastica hierarchia; Justinus quæstione quinquagesima sexta, ubi sic expresse loquitur: Bonorum, quæ per Baptismum adveniunt, digni fiunt fide eorum, a quibus sacros ad fontes offeruntur. Et Augustinus Apostolicam ait esse traditionem, parvulos baptismo salvari. Item alibi: Alienos

τοῖς βρέφεσιν ἑτέρων πόδας ἐντί-
θησιν, ὅπως ἔρχωνται· ἑτέρων παρ-
δίας, ὅπως πιστεύωσιν· ἑτέρων γλῶσ-
σαν, ὅπως ἐπαγγέλλωνται. Καὶ ἀλ-
λαχοῦ· ἡ μήτηρ ἐκκλησία μερικὴν
καρδίαν ἐκείνοις χαρίζεται.

Γίνεται δὲ τὸ βάπτισμα δι᾽ ὕλης
μὲν ὕδατος καθαροῦ καὶ οὐδένος ἑτέρου ὑγροῦ. Ἀποτελεῖται δὲ διὰ μόνου τοῦ ἱερέως, καὶ κατ᾽ ἀνάγκην
ἀπροφάσιστον ἔχει γίνεσθαι καὶ δι᾽
ἑτέρου ἀνθρώπου, πλὴν ὀρθοδόξου
καὶ σκοπὸν ἔχοντος τὸν ἁρμόδιον τῷ
θείῳ βαπτίσματι. Ἀποτελέσματα δὲ
τοῦ βαπτίσματος, συνελόντι φάναι,
πρῶτον ἡ ἄφεσις τοῦ προπατορικοῦ
πλημμελήματος καὶ ὅσων ἄλλων
ἁμαρτιῶν πεπραχὼς ἦν ὁ βάπτι-
σθείς. Δεύτερον ῥύεται ἐκεῖνον τῆς
ἀϊδίου ποινῆς, ᾗτινι ὑπέκειτο, εἴτε διὰ
τὸ ἀρχέγονον ἁμάρτημα εἴτε δι᾽ ἃ
ἰδικῶς ἔπραξε θανασίμως. Τρίτον
δίδωσιν αὐτοῖς τὴν ἀθανασίαν· δικαιοῦν γὰρ αὐτοὺς τῶν προημαρτη-
μένων ναοὺς Θεοῦ ἀποκαθίστησιν.
Οὐκ ἔστι δ᾽ εἰπεῖν, μὴ λύεσθαι διὰ τοῦ
βαπτίσματος πάσας τὰς ὁπωσοῦν
πρὸ τούτου ἁμαρτίας, ἀλλὰ μένειν
μὲν, οὐκ ἰσχύειν δέ. Τοῦτο γὰρ ἀσε-
βείας τῆς ἐσχάτης ἐστὶ γέμον καὶ
ἄρνησις μᾶλλον ἢ ὅλως ὁμολογία
εὐσεβείας· ἀλλ᾽ ὅτι πᾶσα ἁμαρτία
πρὸ τοῦ βαπτίσματος οὖσα, ἢ γεγονυῖα ἀφανίζεται, καὶ ὡς μὴ οὖσά
ποτε ἢ γεγονυῖα λογίζεται. Οἱ
γὰρ τύποι τοῦ βαπτίσματος, πᾶσαι

infantibus pedes Ecclesia tribuit, ut
ad se veniant; aliena corda, ut credant; linguam alienam, ut spon-
deant. Et rùrsum alibi: Cor illis
singulare mater Ecclesia submini-
strat.

Porro baptismi materia aqua pura est seu naturalis et non ullus
alius liquor. Per solum autem sacerdotem perficitur; urgente tamen
inexcusabili necessitate potest et
per alium hominem conferri, modo
sit orthodoxus et convenientem sacro baptismati scopum intendat.
Effectus porro baptismi breviter
recensendi. Primus est originalis
peccati remissio et aliorum, quotquot voluntate propria is qui baptizatur admisit. Secundus ab æternis, quæ sive propter originale sive
propter propria mortalia peccata
manebant hominem, pœnis eximit.
Tertio inmortalitatem baptizatis
impertitur, quippe a peccatis præcedentibus eos emundans in Dei
templa restituit. Neque dicere licet
omnia prorsus, quæ Baptismum
præcessere, peccata, per hunc non
deleri, sed manere quidem at non
imputari. Extremæ etenim id impietatis est et pietatis abnegatio
censenda magis quam confessio.
Imo vero omne, quodcunque peccatum, quod ante baptismum aut
est aut fuit, deletur atque perinde,
ac si nunquam exstitisset, reputatur.

ἑκάτερον καὶ αἱ προμηνύουσαι καὶ τελειοῦσαι ῥήσεις τὸ βάπτισμα τὴν τελείαν ὑπαινίττουσι κάθαρσιν. Τοῦτο αὐτὸ καὶ αὐτὰ τὰ τοῦ βαπτίσματος ὀνόματα περιστῶσιν. Εἰ γὰρ βάπτισμα διὰ πνεύματος καὶ πυρὸς, δῆλον ὅτι καὶ τελεία πᾶσιν ἡ κάθαρσις· τὸ γὰρ πνεῦμα τελείως καθαίρει. Εἰ φῶς, τὸ σκότος ἔλυσεν· εἰ ἀναγέννησις, παρῆλθε τὰ ἀρχαῖα. Τίνα δὲ ταῦτα, εἰ μὴ τὰ ἁμαρτήματα; Εἰ ἀπεκδύεται ὁ βαπτιζόμενος τὸν παλαιὸν ἄνθρωπον, ἄρα καὶ τὴν ἁμαρτίαν. Εἰ ἐνδύεται τὸν Χριστὸν, ἄρα ἀναμαρτητὸς γίνεται ἐνεργείᾳ διὰ τοῦ βαπτίσματος. Μακρὰν γὰρ ἀπὸ ἁμαρτωλῶν ὁ Θεὸς. Τοῦτο καὶ Παῦλος διδάσκει τρανώτερον λέγων· ὥσπερ διὰ τοῦ ἑνὸς ἁμάρτωλοι κατεστάθημεν οἱ πολλοὶ, οὕτω διὰ τοῦ ἑνὸς δίκαιοι. Εἰ δὲ δίκαιοι, ἄρα ἁμαρτίας ἐλεύθεροι. Οὐ γὰρ δύναται, ἐν ταυτῷ εἶναι τὴν ζωὴν καὶ τὸν θάνατον. Εἰ ἀληθῶς ἀπέθανεν ὁ Χριστὸς, ἄρα καὶ ἀληθὴς ἡ διὰ τοῦ πνεύματος ἄφεσις.

Ἐντεῦθεν δὲ δῆλον, πάντα τὰ βαπτισθέντα καὶ κοιμηθέντα βρέφη ἀναμφιβόλως σώζεσθαι, προορισθέντα διὰ τοῦ θανάτου τοῦ Χριστοῦ. Εἰ γὰρ ἐκτὸς πάσης ἦσαν ἁμαρτίας· κοινῆς μὲν, ὅτι ἐλυτρώθησαν τῷ θείῳ λουτρῷ, ἰδικῆς δὲ, ὅτι τὰ βρέφη μὴ ἔχοντα ἐνεργείᾳ προαίρεσιν οὐχ ἁμαρτάνει· ἄρα καὶ σώζεται. Ἐντίθησι δὲ τὸ βάπτισμα καὶ χαρακτῆρα

Etenim baptismi symbola et verba baptismum præsignantia ac perficientia perfectam munditiam designant, idemque et illa, quibus appellatur, vocabula confirmant. Si enim per spiritum et ignem perficitur baptismus, perfectam utique *munditiam* hunc esse, manifestum est, quum perfecte spiritus expurget; si *lumen*, tenebras dissipat; si *regeneratio*, utique vetera desiere; quæ porro vetera, nisi peccata? Veterem hominem, si qui baptizatur, exuit; ergo et peccatum. Christum si induit, igitur per baptismum a peccato mundus actu efficitur; longe enim a peccatoribus Deus. Hoc ipsum vero et apertius Paulus edocet, dicens: Sicut per unum peccatores constituti sumus multi, ita et per unum justi. Porro si justi, igitur et a peccato liberi; neque enim simul esse possunt vita et mors. Si vere mortuus est Christus; vera profecto est et per spiritum condonatio peccati.

Hinc vero compertum, baptizatos parvulos et defunctos omnes dubio procul salutem consequi, per mortem Christi prædestinatos. Quum enim nullius rei sint peccati; non quidem omnibus communis, utpote jam divino lavacro mundati, neque etiam proprii, utpote qui actu electione carentes non peccant, certissime salvantur.

ἀνεξάλειπτον, ὥσπερ καὶ ἡ ἱερωσύνη. Καθὼς γὰρ ἀδύνατον, τὸν
αὐτὸν δὶς ἱερωσύνης τυχεῖν τῆς αὐ-
τῆς· οὕτως ἀδύνατον ἀναβαπτισθῆ-
ναι τὸν ἅπαξ ὀρθῶς βαπτισθέντα,
κἂν καὶ μυρίαις συμβέβηκεν αὐτὸν
ὑποπεσεῖν ἁμαρτίαις, ἢ καὶ αὐτῇ ἐξο-
μομώσει τῆς πίστεως. Θέλων γὰρ
ἐπιστρέψαι πρὸς κύριον ἀναλαμβάνει
τὴν ἣν ἀπώλεσεν υἱοθεσίαν διὰ τοῦ
μυστηρίου τῆς μετανοίας.

"Ορος ιζ'.

Πιστεύομεν τὸ πανάγιον μυστήριον
τῆς ἱερᾶς εὐχαριστίας, ὅπερ ἀνωτέρω
κατὰ τάξιν τέταρτον ἐθέμεθα, ἐκεῖνο
εἶναι, ὅπερ ὁ κύριος παρέδωκε τῇ
νυκτὶ, ᾗ παρεδίδου ἑαυτὸν ὑπὲρ τῆς
τοῦ κόσμου ζωῆς. Λαβὼν γὰρ ἄρτον καὶ εὐλογήσας ἔδωκε τοῖς ἁγίοις
αὐτοῦ μαθηταῖς καὶ ἀποστόλοις εἰ-
πών· λάβετε, φάγετε· τοῦτό ἐστι τὸ
σῶμα μου. Καὶ λαβὼν τὸ ποτήριον
εὐχαριστήσας εἴρηκε· πίετε ἐξ αὐτοῦ
πάντες, τοῦτό ἐστι τὸ αἷμά μου τὸ
ὑπὲρ ὑμῶν ἐκχυνόμενον εἰς ἄφεσιν
ἁμαρτιῶν.

Τούτου ἐν τῇ ἱερουργίᾳ πιστεύομεν
παρεῖναι τὸν κύριον Ἰησοῦν Χριστὸν
οὐ τυπικῶς, οὐδ᾽ εἰκονικῶς, οὐδὲ χάριτι ὑπερβαλλούσῃ, ὡς ἐν τοῖς λοι-
ποῖς μυστηρίοις, οὐδὲ κατὰ μόνην
παρουσίαν, καθώς τινες τῶν πατέρων εἰρήκασι περὶ τοῦ βαπτίσματος,
οὐδὲ κατ᾽ ἀναρτισμὸν, ὥστε ἐνοῦσθαι
τὴν θεότητα τοῦ λόγου τῷ προκειμένῳ

Porro æque ac Ordo Baptismus
characterem imprimit indelebilem:
unde, quemadmodum eodem ordine initiari bis nemo potest; ita
nec recte semel baptizatus iterum
baptizari, ut in mille peccata forte
prolapsus, imo ut a fide etiam apostata. Enimvero converti ad Dominum quisquis voluerit; eam, a
qua exciderat, per Pœnitentiæ sacramentum recuperat adoptionem.

DECRETUM XVII.

Credimus sanctissimum divinæ
Eucharistiæ sacramentum, quod
ordine quartum supra recensuimus,
illud ipsum esse, quod ea nocte,
qua semet ipsum pro mundi vita
tradidit dominus, nobis traditione
reliquit. Panem quippe accipiens
ac benedicens dedit sanctis Discipulis suis et Apostolis, dicens: Accipite, manducate, hoc est corpus
meum. Et accipiens calicem gratias
agens dixit: Bibite ex eo omnes, hic
est sanguis meus, qui pro vobis effun-
detur in remissionem peccatorum.

In hujus itaque celebratione sacramenti Dominum nostrum Jesum Christum credimus esse præsentem, non quidem secundum
figuram aut imaginem neque etiam secundum quamdam ut ceteris
in sacramentis gratiæ excellentiam
neque secundum simplicem, quam
et in baptismo patres nonnulli

τῆς εὐχαριστίας ἄρτῳ ὑποστατικῶς, καθὼς οἱ ἀπὸ Λουθήρου λίαν ἀμαθῶς καὶ ἀθλίως ἐοξάζουσιν· ἀλλ' ἀληθῶς καὶ πραγματικῶς, ὥστε μετὰ τὸν ἁγιασμὸν τοῦ ἄρτου καὶ τοῦ οἴνου μεταβάλλεσθαι, μετουσιοῦσθαι, μεταποιεῖσθαι, μεταῤῥυθμίζεσθαι τὸν μὲν ἄρτον εἰς αὐτὸ τὸ ἀληθὲς τοῦ κυρίου σῶμα, ὅπερ ἐγεννήθη ἐν Βηθλεέμ ἐκ τῆς ἀειπαρθένου, ἐβαπτίσθη ἐν Ἰορδάνῃ, ἔπαθεν, ἐτάφη, ἀνέστη, ἀνελήφθη, κάθηται ἐκ δεξιῶν τοῦ Θεοῦ καὶ πατέρος, μέλλει ἐλθεῖν ἐπὶ τῶν νεφελῶν τοῦ οὐρανοῦ,—τὸν δ' οἶνον μεταποιεῖσθαι καὶ μετουσιοῦσθαι εἰς αὐτὸ τὸ ἀληθὲς τοῦ κυρίου αἷμα, ὅπερ κρεμαμένου ἐπὶ τοῦ σταυροῦ ἐχύθη ὑπὲρ τῆς τοῦ κόσμου ζωῆς.

Ἔτι μετὰ τὸν ἁγιασμὸν τοῦ ἄρτου καὶ τοῦ οἴνου οὐκ ἔτι μένειν τὴν οὐσίαν τοῦ ἄρτου καὶ τοῦ οἴνου, ἀλλ' αὐτὸ τὸ σῶμα καὶ τὸ αἷμα τοῦ κυρίου ἐν τῷ τοῦ ἄρτου καὶ τοῦ οἴνου εἴδει καὶ τύπῳ, ταὐτὸν εἰπεῖν, ὑπὸ τοῖς τοῦ ἄρτου συμβεβηκόσιν.

Ἔτι αὐτὸ τὸ πανακήρατον τοῦ κυρίου σῶμα καὶ αἷμα μεταδίδοσθαι καὶ εἰσδύειν εἰς τὸ στόμα καὶ στόμαχον τῶν μετεχόντων εὐσεβῶν τε καὶ ἀσεβῶν. Πλὴν τοῖς μὲν εὐσεβέσι καὶ ἀξίοις ἄφεσιν ἁμαρτιῶν καὶ ζωὴν αἰώνιον προξενεῖν· τοῖς δὲ ἀσεβέσι καὶ ἀναξίοις κατάκρισιν καὶ κόλασιν αἰώνιον παραχωρεῖν.

commemoravere, præsentiam, neque penes impanationem, qua proposito eucharistiæ pani verbi divinitas substantialiter uniatur, quemadmodum inscite juxta ac misere arbitrantur Lutherani, sed vere realiterque; quatenus panis et vini facta consecratione transmutetur, transsubstantietur, convertatur, transformetur panis quidem in ipsum corpus Domini versum, quod natum est in Bethlehem ex perpetua Virgine, baptizatum in Jordane, passum, sepultum, quod resurrexit, adscendit, sedet a dextris Dei patris, in cœli denique nubibus adventurum,—vinum vero in ipsum Domini sanguinem verum converti ac transsubstantiari, qui ex illo in cruce pendente pro mundi vita defluxit.

Item facta panis et vini consecratione nec panis nec vini manere amplius substantiam credimus, sed ipsum corpus et sanguinem Domini sub panis et vini specie et figura, id est, sub panis accidentibus.

Item et ipsum distribui Domini corpus et sanguinem purissimum inque communicantium sive piorum sive impiorum os ac stomachum introduci: nisi quod remissionem peccatorum vitamque piis ac dignis impertitur æternam, impiis vero ac indignis damnationem pœnamque accersit sempiternam.

Ἔτι τέμνεσθαι μὲν καὶ διαιρεῖσθαι εἴτε χέρσιν εἴτε καὶ ὀδοῦσι τὸ σῶμα καὶ τὸ αἷμα τοῦ κυρίου κατὰ συμβεβηκὸς μέντοι ἤτοι κατὰ τὰ συμβεβηκότα τοῦ ἄρτου καὶ τοῦ οἴνου, καθ' ἃ καὶ ὁρατὰ καὶ ἁπτὰ εἶναι ὁμολογοῦνται, καθ' ἑαυτὰ δὲ μένειν ἄτμητα πάντη καὶ ἀδιαίρετα. Ὅθεν καὶ ἡ καθολικὴ ἐκκλησία φησὶ· Μερίζεται καὶ διαμερίζεται ὁ μελιζόμενος καὶ μὴ διαιρούμενος, ὁ πάντοτε ἐσθιόμενος καὶ οὐδέποτε δαπανώμενος, ἀλλὰ τοὺς μετέχοντας—δηλονότι ἀξίως—ἁγιάζων.

Ἔτι ἐν ἑκάστῳ μέρει καὶ τμήματι ἐλαχίστῳ τοῦ μεταβληθέντος ἄρτου καὶ οἴνου οὐκ εἶναι μέρος τοῦ σώματος καὶ αἵματος τοῦ κυρίου—βλάσφημον γὰρ τοῦτο καὶ ἄθεον—ἀλλ' ὅλον ὁλικῶς τὸν δεσπότην Χριστὸν κατ' οὐσίαν μετὰ ψυχῆς δηλονότι καὶ θεότητος, ἤτοι τέλειον Θεὸν καὶ τέλειον ἄνθρωπον. Ὅθεν καὶ πολλῶν γινομένων ἐν τῇ οἰκουμένῃ μιᾷ καὶ τῇ αὐτῇ ὥρᾳ ἱερουργιῶν, μὴ γίνεσθαι πολλοὺς Χριστοὺς ἢ πολλὰ σώματα Χριστοῦ, ἀλλ' ἕνα καὶ τὸν αὐτὸν Χριστὸν παρεῖναι ἀληθῶς καὶ πραγματικῶς, καὶ ἓν εἶναι αὐτοῦ τὸ σῶμα καὶ τὸ αἷμα ἐν πάσαις ταῖς κατὰ μέρος τῶν πιστῶν ἐκκλησίαις καὶ τοῦτο οὐχ ὅτι τὸ ἐν οὐρανοῖς τοῦ δεσπότου ἐν τοῖς θυσιαστηρίοις κάτεισι σῶμα, ἀλλ' ὅτι ὁ τῆς προθέσεως ἐν πάσαις ταῖς κατὰ μέρος ἐκκλησίαις προκείμενος ἄρτος μεταποιούμενος καὶ με-

Item manibus dentibusve concidi quidem Domini corpus et sanguinem ac dividi; verum per accidens dumtaxat sive penes accidentia panis et vini, per quæ et visibilia ea esse et contrectabilia in confesso est: at insecta prorsus et indivisa secundum se permanere. Unde et Catholica dixit Ecclesia: Conciditur et dividitur, quum membratim concidatur, nequaquam dividitur, semper manducatur, et nunquam consumitur: sed digne accedentes sanctificat.

Item nequaquam sub divisione qualibet ac minima panis et vini transmutati particula esse partem corporis et sanguinis Domini—quippe hoc sine blasphemia et impietate nemo dixerit—sed totum ac integrum Dominum Christum secundum substantiam, animam videlicet suam et divinitatem, id est, Deum perfectum et perfectum hominem. Unde et multæ quum per orbem una et eadem hora celebrantur Missæ, haudquaquam Christi plures plurave Christi sunt corpora, sed unus in omnibus ac singulis fidelium ecclesiis vere ac realiter præsens est ipse Christus, unum et corpus est, et sanguis unus. Atque id quidem, non quod illud, quod in cœlo est, Domini corpus super altaria descendat, sed quod post consecrationem conversus ac

῾ουσιουμ͜νος μετὰ τὸν ἁγιασμὸν γίνεται καί ἐστι ἓν καὶ τὸ αὐτὸ τῇ ἐν
οὐρανοῖς. Ἐν γὰρ τὸ σῶμα τοῦ
κυρίου ἐν πολλοῖς τόποις καὶ οὐ
πολλὰ, καὶ διὰ τοῦτο τὸ μυστήριον
τοῦτο μάλιστά ἐστι καὶ λέγεται θαυ-
μαστὸν καὶ πίστει μόνῃ κατάληπτον,
οὐ σοφίσμασι σοφίας ἀνθρωπίνης,
ἧς τὴν μάταιαν καὶ ἀνόητον ἐν τοῖς
θείοις περιέργειαν ἀποσείεται ἡ εὐσε-
βὴς καὶ θεοπαράδοτος ἡμῶν θρη-
σκεία.

Ἔτι αὐτὸ τὸ σῶμα καὶ αἷμα τοῦ
κυρίου τὸ ἐν τῷ τῆς εὐχαριστίας μυ-
στηρίῳ ὀφείλειν τιμᾶσθαι ὑπερβαλ-
λόντως καὶ προσκυνεῖσθαι λατρευτικῶς. Μία γὰρ ἡ προσκύνησις τῆς
ἁγίας τριάδος καὶ τοῦ σώματος καὶ
αἵματος τοῦ κυρίου.

Ἔτι εἶναι θυσίαν ἀληθῆ καὶ ἱλα-
στικὴν προσφερομένην ὑπὲρ πάντων
τῶν εὐσεβῶν ζώντων καὶ τεθνεώτων
καὶ ὑπὲρ ὠφελείας πάντων, ὡς κεῖται ῥητῶς ἐν ταῖς τοῦ μυστηρίου
προσευχαῖς ὑπὸ τῶν ἀποστόλων
τῇ ἐκκλησίᾳ παραδοθείσαις κατὰ
τὴν πρὸς αὐτοὺς διαταγὴν τοῦ κυρίου.

Ἔτι καὶ πρὸ τῆς χρήσεως εὐθὺς
μετὰ τὸν ἁγιασμὸν καὶ μετὰ τὴν
χρῆσιν τὸ φυλαττόμενον ἐν ταῖς ἱεραῖς θήκαις πρὸς μετάληψιν τῶν
ἀποδημῆσαι μελλόντων ἀληθὲς εἶναι
τοῦ κυρίου σῶμα, καὶ κατὰ μηδὲν
διαφέρον ἑαυτου, ὥστε πρὸ τῆς χρή-

transsubstantiatus, qui singulis ir
ecclesiis offertur, panis propositio
nis fiat et sit illud ipsum corpus,
quod est in cœlo. Quippe multis
in locis non multa sed unum est
corpus Domini; ac vel hinc maxime mirabile est diciturque hujusmodi sacramentum et sola fide com-
prehensibile, non autem humanæ
ratiunculis sapientiæ, cujus quidem
vanam et circa res divinas cœcam
inquisitionem pia atque divinitus
nobis tradita abnuit professio nostra.

Item et honore supremo colen-
dum esse cultuque latriæ adorandum idem Domini corpus et sanguinem, quæ sunt in Sacramento
Eucharistiæ. Quippe sanctissimæ
Trinitatis et corporis sanguinisque
Domini una est adoratio.

Item et verum ac propitiatorium
esse Sacrificium, quod pro fidelibus
omnibus tum vivis tum defunctis
nec non et pro utilitate omnium
offeratur, uti et in hujusce Sacramenti precibus exprimitur, quas
juxta id, quod a Domino mandatum
acceperant, Apostoli Ecclesiæ tra-
didere.

Item ante usum statim a consecratione ac post usum, id quod
sacris in pixibus communioni
moribundorum asservatur, corpus
esse Domini verum et a se ipso
ne vel levissime quidem diver-
sum, quatenus ante usum et post

σεως μετὰ τὸν ἁγιασμὸν, ἐν τῇ χρή- σει καὶ μετὰ τὴν χρῆσιν, εἶναι κατὰ πάντα τὸ ἀληθὲς τοῦ κυρίου σῶμα.

Ἔτι τῇ μετουσίωσις λέξει οὐ τὸν τρόπον πιστεύομεν δηλοῦσθαι, καθ' ὃν ὁ ἄρτος καὶ ὁ οἶνος μετα- ποιοῦνται εἰς τὸ σῶμα καὶ τὸ αἷμα τοῦ κυρίου,—τοῦτο γὰρ ἄληπτον πάντη καὶ ἀδύνατον πλὴν αὐτοῦ τοῦ Θεοῦ, καὶ τοῖς πιστεύουσιν ἀμάθειαν ἅμα καὶ ἀσέβειαν ἐπιφέρει—ἀλλ' ὅτι ὁ ἄρτος καὶ ὁ οἶνος μετὰ τὸν ἁγια- σμὸν οὐ τυπικῶς οὐδ' εἰκονικῶς, οὐ- δὲ χάριτι ὑπερβαλλούσῃ, οὐδὲ τῇ κοινωνίᾳ ἢ τῇ παρουσίᾳ τῆς θεότη- τος μόνης τοῦ μονογενοῦς μεταβάλ- λεται εἰς τὸ σῶμα καὶ αἷμα τοῦ κυ- ρίου, οὐδὲ συμβεβηκός τι τοῦ ἄρτου καὶ τοῦ οἴνου εἰς συμβεβηκός τι τοῦ σώματος καὶ αἵματος τοῦ Χριστοῦ κατά τινα τροπὴν ἢ ἀλλοίωσιν με- ταποιεῖται, ἀλλ' ἀληθῶς καὶ πραγ- ματικῶς καὶ οὐσιωδῶς γίνεται ὁ μὲν ἄρτος αὐτὸ τὸ ἀληθὲς τοῦ κυρίου σῶμα, ὁ δ' οἶνος αὐτὸ τοῦ κυρίου αἷμα, ὡς εἴρηται ἀνωτέρω.

Ἔτι μὴ γίνεσθαι ὑπό τινος ἄλλου τὸ τῆς ἱερᾶς εὐχαριστίας τοῦτο μυ- στήριον, εἰ μὴ μόνον ὑπὸ ἱερέως εὐσε- βοῦς καὶ ὑπὸ εὐσεβοῦς καὶ νομίμου ἐπισκόπου τὴν ἱερωσύνην λαβόντος, καθ' ὃν τρόπον ἡ ἀνατολικὴ ἐκκλη- σία διδάσκει. Αὕτη ἐστὶν ἐν συντό- μῳ ἡ τῆς καθολικῆς ἐκκλησίας καὶ περὶ τοῦ μυστηρίου τούτου δόξα καὶ ἀληθὴς ὁμολογία καὶ ἀρχαιοτάτη

consecrationem in usu ac post usum verum omnino sit corpus Domini.

Præterea verbo *Transsubstan- tionis* modum illum, quo in cor- pus et sanguinem Domini panis et vinum convertuntur, explicari mi- nime credimus,—id enim penitus incomprehensibile præterquam ip- si Deo, et capere se credentibus inscitiæ ac impietatis notam inurit —sed quod panis et vinum, facta consecratione, non per figuram aut per imaginem, non penes super- abundantem gratiam, non per com- munionem aut solius divinitatis unigeniti filii Dei præsentiam in corpus et sanguinem Domini con- vertitur, nec panis aut vini acci- dens aliquod in quoddam corporis et sanguinis accidens aliqua con- versione vel alteratione mutatur, sed vere realiterque ac substantia- liter fit quidem panis ipsum verum Domini corpus, vinum vero ipse san- guis ejus, uti jam ante dictum est.

Denique neminem præter pium Sacerdotem, ab pio utique Episco- po canonice instituto sacerdotii charactere initiatum, juxta Orien- talis Ecclesiæ doctrinam hoc sacro- sanctæ Eucharistiæ credimus posse conficere Sacramentum. Hæc est compendiaria Orientalis Catholicæ Ecclesiæ hoc de sacramento do- ctrina veraque confessio et traditio

παράδοσις, ἣν οὐ δεῖ κολοβοῦσθαι κατ᾽ οὐδένα τρόπον ὑπὸ τῶν εὐσεβεῖν βουλομένων καὶ ἀποσειομένων τοὺς νεωτερισμοὺς καὶ τὰς βεβήλους τῶν αἱρετικῶν κενοφωνίας· ἀλλ᾽ ἀναγκαίως σῶαν καὶ ἀδιάσειστον τηρεῖσθαι τὴν νομοθετηθεῖσαν παράδοσιν. Τοὺς γὰρ παραβαίνοντας ἀποποιεῖται καὶ ἀναθεματίζει ἡ καθολικὴ τοῦ Χριστοῦ ἐκκλησία.

     "Ορος ιή.

Πιστεύομεν τὰς τῶν κεκοιμημένων ψυχὰς εἶναι ἢ ἐν ἀνέσει ἢ ἐν ὀδύνῃ, καθ᾽ ὅ,τι ἕκαστος ἔπραξεν·—χωριζομένας γὰρ ἀπὸ τῶν σωμάτων παραυτίκα ἢ πρὸς εὐφροσύνην ἢ πρὸς λύπην καὶ στεναγμὸν ἐκδημεῖν, ὁμολογουμένης μέντοι μήτε τῆς ἀπολαύσεως μήτε τῆς κατακρίσεως τελείας. Μετὰ γὰρ τὴν κοινὴν ἀνάστασιν, ὅτε ἡ ψυχὴ ἑνωθείη τῷ σώματι, μεθ᾽ οὗ καλῶς ἢ πονηρῶς ἐπολιτεύσατο, ἀπολήψεται ἕκαστος τὸ τέλειον ἢ τῆς ἀπολαύσεως ἢ τῆς κατακρίσεως δηλονότι.

Τοὺς δὲ συμφθαρέντας θανασίμοις πλημμελήμασι καὶ μὴ ἐν ἀπογνώσει ἀποδημήσαντας ἀλλὰ μετανοήσαντας μὲν, ἔτι περιόντας ἐν τῷ μετὰ σώματος βίῳ, μὴ ποιήσαντας· δὲ οὐδοτιοῦν καρπὸν μετανοίας—ἐκχέαι δάκρυα δηλονότι καὶ γονυπετῆσαι ἐν γρηγορήσει προσευχῶν, θλιβῆναι, πτωχοὺς παραμυθῆσαι, καὶ τέως ἐν ἔργοις τὴν πρὸς τὸν Θεὸν καὶ τὸν

---

perantiqua, cui detrahere quid-quam non convenit eos, qui pie sentire cupiunt et novitates horrent ac profana hæreticorum vaniloquia detestantur; sed hanc, quæ jam pridem obtinuit, traditionem integram servent et illibatam. Hanc enim violantes Catholica Christi rejicit ac anathematizat Ecclesia.

     DECRETUM XVIII.

Credimus *defunctorum animas* aut in requie aut in pœnis esse, prout quisque gesserit; quippe separatas a corporibus ad gaudii vel ad tristitiæ gemitusque locum commigrare; nondum tamen eis concessa integra beatitudinis aut damnationis mensura. Etenim generali facta resurrectione, quando anima unietur corpori, quocum aut bene gessit aut male, tunc beatitudinis ac pœnarum perfectam unusquisque vicem recipiet.

Eorum vero, qui peccatis impliciti non in desperatione defuncti sunt, sed quos adhuc superstites pœnituit, at nullum fecerunt pœnitentiæ fructum, lacrimas videlicet effundendo genibus flexis in orationibus vigilando, semet ipsos afflictando, pauperes recreando, suam denique tum in Deum, quum in proximum caritatem

πλησίον ἀγάπην ἐπιδεῖξαι, ἃ καὶ
ἱκανοποίησιν καλῶς ἡ καθολικὴ ἐκκλησία ἀπ᾽ ἀρχῆς ὠνόμασε—τούτων
καὶ αὐτῶν τὰς ψυχὰς ἀπέρχεσθαι εἰς
ᾅδου καὶ ὑπομένειν τῶν ἕνεκα ὧν εἰρ-
γάσαντο ἁμαρτημάτων ποινήν. Εἶναι δ᾽ ἐν συναισθήσει τῆς ἐκεῖθεν
ἀπαλλαγῆς, ἐλευθεροῦσθαι δὲ ὑπὸ
τῆς ἄκρας ἀγαθότητος διὰ τῆς δεήσεως τῶν ἱερέων καὶ εὐποιῶν, ἃ τῶν
ἀποιχομένων ἕνεκα οἱ ἑκάστου συγ-
γενεῖς ἀποτελοῦσι· μεγάλα δυναμέ-
νης μάλιστα τῆς ἀναιμάκτου θυσίας,
ἣν ἰδίως ὑπὲρ τῶν κεκοιμημένων συγγενῶν ἕκαστος καὶ κοινῶς ὑπὲρ πάντων ἡ καθολικὴ καὶ ἀποστολικὴ ὁσημέραι ποιεῖ ἐκκλησία· ἐννοουμένου
μέντοι καὶ τούτου τοῦ μὴ εἰδέναι
ἡμᾶς δηλαδὴ τὸν καιρὸν τῆς ἀπαλλαγῆς. Ὅτι γὰρ γίνεται ἐλευθερία
τῶν τοιούτων, ἀπὸ τῶν δεινῶν καὶ
πρὸ τῆς κοινῆς ἀναστάσεώς τε καὶ
κρίσεως οἴδαμεν καὶ πιστεύομεν·
πότε δὲ, ἀγνοοῦμεν.

Ἐρώτησις ά.

Εἰ δεῖ τὴν θείαν γραφὴν κοινῶς παρὰ πάντων τῶν Χριστιανῶν ἀναγινώσκεσθαι;

Οὔ. Τὴν πᾶσαν γὰρ γραφὴν θεόπνευστον
καὶ ὠφέλιμον οἴδαμεν, καὶ οὕτω τὸ ἀναγκαῖον
ἔχουσαν μεθ᾽ ἑαυτῆς, ὥστε χωρὶς αὐτῆς ἀδύνατον ὁπωσοῦν εὐσεβεῖν. Οὐ μὴν καὶ ὑπὸ πάντων ἀναγινώσκεσθαι ταύτην ἀλλ᾽ ὑπὸ μόνον
τῶν μετὰ τῆς πρεπούσης ἐρεύνης τοῖς βάθεσιν
ἐγκυπτόντων τοῦ πνεύματος καὶ εἰδότων, οἷς
τρόποις ἡ θεία γραφὴ ἐρευνᾶται καὶ διδάσκεται
καὶ ὅλως ἀναγινώσκεται. Τοῖς δὲ μὴ γεγυ-
μνασμένοις καὶ ἀδιαφόρως ἢ μόνον κατὰ τὸ

operibus demonstrando, quæ et
Catholica Ecclesia recte ab initio
satisfactiones appellavit, horum,
inquam, ipsorum animas credimus ad inferos abire ibique justas pro iis, quæ commisere, peccatis pœnas sustinere, at suæ tamen exhinc futuræ liberationis
esse conscias et ab summa bonitate per sacerdotum orationes et
eleemosynas, quas pro defunctis
eorum propinqui faciunt, liberari.
Ad hoc vero potissime valet incruentum Missæ sacrificium, quod
peculiariter singuli pro consangui-
neis defunctis, Catholica vero et
Apostolica Ecclesia quotidie pro
omnibus communiter facit. Porro
liberationis hujusmodi notum nobis
esse tempus nequaquam dicimus;
tales enim solvi quidem pœnis; idque ante resurrectionem et univer-
sale judicium et scimus et credimus;
id vero, quando fiat, ignoramus.

QUÆSTIO I.

Decetne Sacram Scripturam communiter
ab omnibus legi Christianis?

Non decet. Enimvero omnem scripturam
divinitus inspiratam et utilem novimus, et ita
ex se necessariam, ut pie sine illa vivere nul-
latenus quisquam possit. Hanc tamen haudquaquam convenit omnes legere; at eos dumtaxat, qui ad profunda, quæ in illa latent,
Spiritus arcana convenienti discussione in-
cumbunt, quive eam, qua scrutanda, docenda,
legenda est Scriptura Sacra, rationem probe
norunt. Inexercitatis autem et Scripturam

γράμμα ἢ καὶ κατ' ἄλλον τινὰ τρόπον ἀλλό-
τριον τῆς εὐσεβείας τὰ τῆς γραφῆς ἐκλαμβά-
νουσιν, ἡ καθολικὴ ἐκκλησία, διὰ τῆς πείρας τὴν
βλαβὴν ἐγνωκυῖα, οὐ θεμιτὴν τὴν ἀνάγνωσιν
εἶναι ἐντέλλεται. Ὥστε παντὶ εὐσεβεῖ ἐπιτέ-
τραφθαι μὲν ἀκούειν τὰ τῆς γραφῆς, ἵνα πιστεύῃ τῇ καρδίᾳ εἰς δικαιοσύνην, ὁμολογῇ δὲ
τῷ στόματι εἰς σωτηρίαν· ἀναγινώσκειν δὲ ἔνια
τῆς γραφῆς μέρη καὶ μάλιστα τῆς παλαιᾶς
ἀπηγορεύεται τῶν εἰρημένων αἰτίων καὶ τῶν
ὁμοίων τούτοις ἕνεκα. Καί ἐστιν ἴσον παραγ-
γέλλειν τοῖς ἀγυμνάστοις μὴ ἀναγινώσκειν
ὡσαύτως τὴν πᾶσαν ἱερὰν γραφὴν, καὶ τοῖς
βρέφεσιν ἐντέλλεσθαι, μὴ ἅπτεσθαι στερεᾶς
τροφῆς.

Ἐρώτησις β'.

Εἰ σαφής ἐστιν ἡ γραφὴ πᾶσι τοῖς ἀναγινώ-
σκουσι Χριστιανοῖς;

Εἰ σαφὴς ἦν ἡ θεία γραφὴ πᾶσι τοῖς ἀναγι-
νώκουσι Χριστιανοῖς, οὐκ ἂν ὁ κύριος ἐρευνᾷν
ταύτην τοῖς βουλομένοις σωτηρίας τυχεῖν ἐπέ-
τρεπε· καὶ τὸ χάρισμα τῆς διδασκαλίας μα-
ταίως τῷ Παύλῳ ἐλέγετο τεθῆναι ὑπὸ τοῦ Θεοῦ
τῇ ἐκκλησίᾳ· καὶ ὁ Πέτρος οὐκ ἂν περὶ τῶν
τοῦ Παύλου ἐπιστολῶν ἔχειν τινὰ δυσνόητα
ἔλεγε. Δῆλον οὖν, ὡς πολὺ τὸ βάθος ἔχειν
τὴν γραφὴν καὶ τὸ μέγεθος τῶν ἐννοιῶν καὶ
δεῖσθαι ἐπιστημόνων καὶ θείων ἀνδρῶν πρὸς
ἔρευναν καὶ ἀληθῆ κατάληψιν καὶ γνῶσιν ὀρθὴν καὶ συνῳδὸν τῇ πάσῃ γραφῇ καὶ τῷ δη-
μιουργῷ ταύτης ἁγίῳ πνεύματι.

Ὥστε τοῖς ἀναγεννηθεῖσιν, εἰ καὶ γνώριμος
ἡ περὶ τριάδος πίστις καὶ ἡ τοῦ υἱοῦ τοῦ Θεοῦ
ἐνανθρώπησις, τὰ πάθη, ἡ ἀνάστασις, ἡ εἰς
οὐρανοὺς ἄνοδος, ὁ περὶ τῆς παλιγγενεσίας καὶ
κρίσεως λόγος, ὧν εἵνεκα καὶ πολλοὶ θάνατον
ὑπομεῖναι οὐκ ὤκνησαν· οὐκ ἀναγκαῖον δὲ,
μᾶλλον δὲ ἀδύνατον πᾶσιν, εἰδέναι καὶ ἃ τὸ
πνεῦμα τὸ ἅγιον μόνοις τοῖς ἐγγεγυμνασμένοις
ἐπὶ σοφίᾳ καὶ ἁγιότητι φανεροῖ.

Sacram absque discrimine vel penes literam
aut alieno a pietate sensu intelligentibus Ecclesia Catholica utique, per experientiam de
dispendio certa, lectione ejus interdixit. Itaque omnibus quidem fidelibus Sacram audire
Scripturam quatenus corde credant ad justitiam, ore autem confessionem promant ad
salutem, permissum est; aliquos vero scripturæ ac veteris potissimum instrumenti libros legere, prædictis ac consimilibus de
caussis prohibitum. Et vero perinde est,
Sacræ Scripturæ lectione inexercitatos prohibere ac solidiori abstineant cibo infantibus
imperare.

QUÆSTIO II.

Sitne perspicua omnibus legentibus Christianis Scriptura?

Si legentibus omnibus perspicua esset Sacra Scriptura Christianis, nequaquam perscrutari scripturas his, qui salutis desiderio
tenentur, Dominus mandasset; frustra quoque Paulus positam a Deo in Ecclesia docto-
ratus gratiam scripsisset, neque intellectu
difficilia habere Pauli epistolas Petrus dice-
ret. Maximam itaque constat esse scripturæ altitudinem juxta ac sensuum ejus ampli-
tudinem ac doctissimis proinde divinisque
hominibus ad ejus indagationem veramque
intelligentiam ac rectum sensum, Scripturæ
et ejusdem auctori Spiritui Sancto consonum,
opus esse.

Itaque quamvis regeneratis conspicua sit
fides sanctissimæ Trinitatis et incarnatio filii
Dei, ejusdem passio, resurrectio, in cœlos
ascensio, item et regenerationis ac judicii
veritas pro quibus mortem subire multi non
dubitarunt;—haud tamen necesse est imo
impossibile, et ea scire omnes, quæ solis sapientia et sanctitate exercitatis Spiritus Sanctus manifestat.

Ἐρώτησις γ'.

Ἱερὰν γραφὴν ποῖα βιβλία καλεῖς;

Στοιχοῦντες τῷ κανόνι τῆς καθολικῆς ἐκκλησίας ἱερὰν γραφὴν καλοῦμεν ἐκεῖνα πάντα,
ἅπερ ὁ Κύριλλος ὑπὸ τῆς ἐν Λαοδικείᾳ συνόδου
ἐρανισάμενος ἀριθμεῖ καὶ πρὸς τούτοις ἅπερ
ἀσυνέτως καὶ ἀμαθῶς εἴτ' οὖν ἐθελοκακούργως
ἀπόκρυφα κατωνόμασε· τὴν Σοφίαν δηλαδὴ
τοῦ Σολομῶντος, τὴν Ἰουδὴθ, τὸν Τωβίαν, τὴν
Ἱστορίαν τοῦ δράκοντος, τὴν Ἱστορίαν τῆς
Σωσάννης, τοὺς Μακκαβαίους καὶ τὴν Σοφίαν
τοῦ Σειράχ. Ἡμεῖς γὰρ μετὰ τῶν ἄλλων τῆς
θείας γραφῆς γνησίων βιβλίων καὶ ταῦτα γνήσια τῆς γραφῆς μέρη κρίνομεν, ὅτι ἡ παραδό-
σασα ἀρχαία συνήθεια καὶ μάλιστα ἡ καθολικὴ
ἐκκλησία γνήσια εἶναι τὰ ἱερὰ εὐαγγέλια καὶ τ'
ἄλλα τῆς γραφῆς βιβλία καὶ ταῦτα εἶναι τῆς
ἁγίας γραφῆς μέρη ἀναμφιβόλως παρέδωκε,
καὶ τούτων ἡ ἄρνησις ἐκείνων ἐστὶν ἀθέτησις.
Εἰ δέ που δοκεῖ μὴ ἀεὶ πάντα ὑπὸ πάντων
συγκαταριθμεῖσθαι, οὐδὲν ἧττον ὅμως καὶ ταῦτα παρά τε συνόδων καὶ πολλῶν ὅσων τῆς καθολικῆς ἐκκλησίας παλαιοτάτων τε καὶ ἐγκρί-
των θεολόγων ἀριθμεῖται καὶ συγκαταριθμεῖται
τῇ πάσῃ γραφῇ, ἃ πάντα καὶ ἡμεῖς κανονικὰ
βιβλία κρίνομεν, καὶ ταῦτα τὴν ἱερὰν γραφὴν
εἶναι ὁμολογοῦμεν.

Ἐρώτησις δ'.

Περὶ τῶν ἁγίων εἰκόνων καὶ τῆς προσκυνήσεως τῶν ἁγίων πῶς ὀφείλομεν φρονεῖν;

Τῶν ἁγίων ὄντων καὶ ὁμολογουμένων παρὰ
τῆς καθολικῆς ἐκκλησίας πρεσβευτῶν, ὃν τρόπον εἴρηται ἐν τῷ ὀγδόῳ κεφαλαίῳ· καιρὸς εἰπεῖν, ὅτι καὶ τιμῶμεν αὐτοὺς ὡς φίλους Θεοῦ
καὶ ὡς ὑπὲρ ἡμῶν δεομένους τῷ τῶν ὅλων
Θεῷ. Τιμῶμεν δὲ τούτους διττῶς· καθ' ἕνα
μὲν τρόπον τὴν μητέρα τοῦ Θεοῦ Λόγου, ὃν
καὶ ὑπερδουλικόν φαμεν. Εἰ γὰρ καὶ ὡς ἀληθῶς δούλη ἡ Θεοτόκος τοῦ μόνου Θεοῦ, ἀλλὰ
καὶ μήτηρ, ὡς τὸν ἕνα τῆς Τριάδος γεννήσασα
σαρκικῶς, διὸ καὶ ἀσυγκρίτως ὑπερέχειν ὑμνεῖ-
ται πάντων ἀγγέλων τε καὶ ἁγίων, ὅθεν καὶ
ὑπερδουλικὴν αὐτῇ ἀπονέμομεν τὴν προσκύνη-

QUÆSTIO III.

Quosnam libros Sacram Scripturam vocas?

Ecclesiæ Catholicæ regulam sequentes Sacram Scripturam eos omnes appellamus libros, quos ab Laodicena synodo Cyrillus mu-
tuatus recenset, iis insuper additis, quos in-
sipienter, inscite aut magis malitiose vocavit
apocryphos: Sapientiam videlicet Salomonis,
librum Judith, Tobiam, Draconis historiam,
Historiam Susannæ, Machabæos, et Sapientiam Sirach. Hos etenim cum ceteris genui-
nis Sacræ Scripturæ libris ceu germanas ejusdem Scripturæ partes censemus esse nume-
randos. Qnoniam quæ sancta Evangelia ali-
osque Scripturæ libros ut genuinos tradidit
antiqua consuetudo seu magis Ecclesia Catholica; et istos hæc ipsa ceu Sacræ Scripturæ partes procul dubio tradidit; quatenus
istos qui neget et illos recusaverit. Sin vero
ab cunctis haud recenseri omnes fortasse videantur; isti nihilo secius ab synodis nec
non et a multis quum antiquissimis tum no-
minatissimis Catholicæ Ecclesiæ theologis
recensentur et sacras inter scripturas nume-
rantur. Quos omnes et nos judicamus esse
canonicos et Sacram eos esse Scripturam confitemur.

QUÆSTIO IV.

Quid de sanctis imaginibus et cultu sanctorum sentire debemus?

Oratores nostri quum sint et ab Catholica
Ecclesia habeantur sancti, quemadmodum in
octavo capitulo dictum est; dicendi modo
tempus est, eos a nobis ceu Dei amicos no-
strosque apud Deum universorum intercessores honorari. Porro duplicem Sanctis cuī-
tum adhibemus. Alterum quippe verbi divini matri, quem hyperduliam appellamus.
Enimvero Dei et hujus quidem solius ut fa-
mula vere sit et ipsa Deipara; at mater ejus
est, utpote quæ unum e Trinitate in carne
genuit. Quare omnium quum Sanctorum
tum Angelorum longe superior prædicatur;

σιν. Κατὰ δεύτερον δὲ τρόπον, ὃν καὶ δουλι-
κὸν ὀνομάζομεν, προσκυνοῦμεν εἶτ' οὖν τιμῶμεν τοὺς ἁγίους ἀγγέλους, ἀποστόλους, προφήτας, μάρτυρας καὶ ἁπλῶς πάντας τοὺς ἁγίους.

Πρὸς τούτοις προσκυνοῦμεν καὶ τιμῶμεν τὸ
ξύλον τοῦ τιμίου τοῦ ζωοποιοῦ σταυροῦ, ἐν ᾧ
ὁ σωτήρ ἡμῶν τὸ κοσμοσωτήριον εἰργάσατο
πάθος, καὶ τὸν τύπον τοῦ ζωοποιοῦ σταυροῦ,
τὴν ἐν Βηθλεὲμ φάτνην, δι' ἧς τῆς ἀλογίας
ἐρρύσθημεν, τὸν τόπον τοῦ κρανίου, τὸν ζωη-
φόρον τάφον καὶ τὰ λοιπὰ ἅγια προσκυνή-
ματα· τά τε ἱερὰ εὐαγγέλια καὶ τὰ ἱερὰ σκεύη,
δι' ὧν ἡ ἀναίμακτος ἐπιτελεῖται θυσία. Μνή-
μαις τε ἐτησίοις καὶ δημοσίοις ἑορταῖς καὶ
θείοις ἱδρύμασι καὶ ἀναθέμασι τοὺς ἁγίους γε-
γαίρομεν καὶ τιμῶμεν.

Ἔπειτα δὲ καὶ τὴν εἰκόνα τοῦ κυρίου ἡμῶν
Ἰησοῦ Χριστοῦ καὶ τῆς ὑπεραγίας θεοτόκου
καὶ πάντων τῶν ἁγίων προσκυνοῦμεν καὶ τιμῶμεν καὶ ἀσπαζόμεθα, καὶ μὴν καὶ τῶν ἁγίων
ἀγγέλων, ὡς ὤφθησαν ἐνίοις τῶν τε προπατόρων καὶ προφητῶν. Ἱστοροῦμεν δὲ καὶ τὸ
πανάγιον πνεῦμα, ὡς ὤφθη, ἐν εἴδει περι-
στερᾶς.

Εἰ δέ τινες εἰδωλολατρεῖν ἡμᾶς, ἁγίους καὶ
εἰκόνας ἁγίων καὶ τὰ λοιπὰ προσκυνοῦντας,
λέγουσι, μάταιον ἡγούμεθα καὶ ἀδρανές. Ἡμεῖς
γὰρ μόνῳ τῷ ἐν τριάδι Θεῷ λατρεύομεν καὶ
οὐδενὶ ἑτέρῳ· τοὺς δὲ ἁγίους τιμῶμεν διττῶς·
πρῶτον μὲν κατὰ τὴν πρὸς Θεὸν ἀναφοράν,
ἐπειδὴ ἐκείνου ἕνεκα τιμῶμεν αὐτούς, καὶ καθ'
ἑαυτούς, ὅτι ζῶσαί εἰσιν εἰκόνες τοῦ Θεοῦ. Τὸ
δὲ καθ' ἑαυτοὺς διώρισται ὅτι δουλικόν. Τὰς
δὲ ἁγίας εἰκόνας σχετικῶς, ὡς τῆς πρὸς ἐκείνας
τιμῆς ἐπὶ τὰ πρωτότυπα ἀναφερομένης. Ὁ
γὰρ εἰς τὴν εἰκόνα προσκυνῶν διὰ τῆς εἰκόνος
τὸν πρωτότυπον προσκυνεῖ, καὶ ἡ δόξα οὐ μερίζεται, οὐδ' ὅλως σχίζεται τῆς τε εἰκόνος καὶ
τοῦ εἰκονιζομένου, καὶ ἐν ταὐτῷ γίνεται, ὡς ἡ
εἰς τὸν βασιλικὸν πρέσβυν γινομένη.

Ἃ δὲ πρὸς σύστασιν καινοτομίας αὐτῶν
παρὰ τῆς γραφῆς λαμβάνουσιν, οὐχ οὕτως

unde et hyperdulico eam cultu veneramur.
Alterum vero, quem et dulicum vocamus,
sanctis Angelis, Apostolis, Martyribus, omnibus denique Sanctis adhibemus.

Insuper venerandæ ac vivificæ Crucis li-
gnum, in quo pro salute mundi Salvator noster passus est, quin et ejusdem Crucis signum veneramur et adoramus, item et quod
apud Bethleem est præsepe, per quod ab irra-
tionali affectu liberati sumus, item et Calva-
riæ locum, et quod theca fuit vitæ sepulcrum, ceteras denique res sanctas, quas adoramus : sancta videlicet evangelia, nec non et
sacra vasa, in quibus sacrificium incruentum
celebratur. Sed et annuis commemorationi-
bus festisque solemnibus, sacris ædiculis et
anathematis sanctos ornamus et honoramus.

Deinde et Domini nostri Jesu Christi et
sanctissimæ Deiparæ omniumque Sanctorum,
quin et sanctorum Angelorum secundum eam,
qua quibusdam Patriarchis aut Prophetis ap-
paruere, formam, imagines veneramur, adoramus et osculamur. Denique et Spiritum
Sanctum sub ea, qua visus est columbæ specie, repræsentamus.

Eam porro, quam sanctis et eorum imaginibus ceterisque prædictis venerationem adhibemus, idololatriam esse si qui dicunt, stultum
ac inane reputamus. Nos enim soli in Trinitate Deo ac præter ipsum nemini latriæ cultum
impendimus. Sanctos vero duplici modo veneramur, imprimis quidem relative ad Deum ;
quippe propter ipsum illos honoramus, deinde
et in se ipsis, quoniam animatæ Dei imagines
illi sunt. Duliam porro esse qua Sanctos veneramur in se ipsis, supra definitum est, sanctos vero imagines relative ; siquidem, qui exhibetur illis cultus, ad earum prototypa refertur. Quisquis enim colit imaginem, per imaginem colit prototypum, neque aliquantum
dividitur separatûrve imaginis honor et proto-
typi ; sed in eodem positus est, quemadmodum in prorege rex honoratur.

Quæ vero e Scripturis in confirmationem
suæ novitatis assumunt, non sic ipsis favent,

αὐτοῖς βοηθεῖ, ὡς βούλονται, ἀλλὰ μάλιστα ἡμῖν συνῳδὰ φαίνεται. Ἡμεῖς γὰρ τὴν θείαν γραφὴν ἀναγινώσκοντες ἐξετάζομεν καιρὸν καὶ προσωπον, παράδειγμα καὶ αἰτίαν. Ὅθεν καὶ τὸν αὐτὸν Θεόν ποτε μὲν λέγοντα· οὐ ποιήσεις σεαυτῷ εἴδωλον, οὔτε ὁμοίωμα, οὐδὲ προσκυνήσεις, οὐδὲ λατρεύσεις αὐτοῖς, ποτὲ δὲ προστάττοντα, γενέσθαι Χερουβὶμ; Καὶ ἔτι βόας καὶ λέοντας γινώμενα ἐν τῷ ἱερῷ θεωροῦντες οὐ πεισματικῶς τούτων τὴν ἔννοιαν θεωροῦμεν. Ἐν γὰρ τῇ πεισμονῇ οὐκ ἔστι πίστις, ἀλλ', ὡς εἴρηται, καιρὸν καὶ τὰ λοιπὰ θεωροῦντες, τῆς ὀρθῆς περὶ τούτων δόξης ἐπιτυγχάνομεν καὶ τὸ· οὐ ποιήσεις σεαυτῷ εἴδωλον ἢ ὁμοίωμα ταὐτὸν ἡγούμεθα τὸ· οὐ προσκυνήσεις Θεοὺς ἀλλοτρίους, εἴτ' οὖν μὴ εἰδωλολατρήσῃς. Οὕτω γὰρ καὶ ἡ παρὰ τοῦ καιροῦ τῶν ἀποστόλων ἐπικρατήσασα συνήθεια τῇ ἐκκλησίᾳ τοῦ προσκυνεῖσθαι σχετικῶς τὰς ἁγίας εἰκόνας καὶ ἡ μόνῳ τῷ Θεῷ λατρεια διασωθείη καὶ ὁ Θεὸς οὐκ ἐναντίως λέγων ἑαυτῷ φανείη. Εἰ γὰρ ἡ γραφή φησιν· οὐ ποιήσεις οὐδὲ προσκυνήσεις, τίνα τρόπον ὕστερον ὁ Θεὸς τὸ μὲν ποιῆσαι ὁμοιώματα συγκεχώρηκε, τὸ δὲ προσκυνῆσαι οὔ, οὐκ ἔχομεν συνορᾶν. Ὅθεν, περὶ μόνης τῆς εἰδωλολατρείας οὔσης τῆς ἐντολῆς, εὑρίσκομεν καὶ ὄφεις καὶ λέοντας καὶ βόας καὶ Χερουβὶμ γεγονότα καὶ εἴδη εἴτ' οὖν ὁμοιώματα, ἐν οἷς οἱ ἄγγελοι, ἐφαίνοντο προσκυνηθέντα.

Οὓς δὲ προφέρουσι τῶν ἁγίων ὡς λέγοντας, μὴ ἐξὸν προσκυνεῖν τὰς εἰκόνας· ἡμῖν μᾶλλον βοηθεῖν ἐκείνους ἡγούμεθα, ἐπεὶ ἐκεῖνοι ἀγωνιστικῶς διαλεγόμενοι καὶ κατὰ τῶν λατρευτικῶς προσκυνούντων τὰς ἁγίας εἰκόνας καὶ κατὰ τῶν φερόντων εἰς τὰς ἐκκλησίας τὰς εἰκόνας τῶν τεθνηκότων συγγενῶν ἐκείνων ἐφέροντο καὶ ἀναθέματι τοὺς οὕτω ποιοῦντας καθυποβάλλουσιν, οὐ κατὰ τῆς ὀρθῆς προσκυνήσεως τῶν τε ἁγίων καὶ ἁγίων εἰκόνων καὶ τοῦ τιμίου σταυροῦ καὶ τῶν λοιπῶν, ὧν εἴρηται, ὅπου μάλιστα καὶ ἀπὸ τοῦ καιροῦ τῶν ἀποστόλων εἶναι τὰς ἁγίας εἰκόνας ἐν τῇ ἐκκλησίᾳ καὶ προσκυνεῖσθαι παρὰ τῶν πιστῶν πλεῖστοι ὅσοι καὶ ἱστοροῦσι καὶ κηρύττουσι, μεθ' ὧν καὶ μεθ' οὓς ἡ ἁγία οἰκουμενικὴ ἑβδό-

uti autumant, imo nobis maxime concinunt. Nos enim Sacram Scripturam quum legimus, tempus, personam, exemplum, caussam examinamus. Cur nimirum idem ipse Deus modo dicat: Non facies tibi idolum, neque simulacrum, neque adorabis, neque coles illa; modo autem Cherubim fieri præcipiat? Imo et quum sculptos in templo boves leonesque spectamus, haudquaquam pervicaciter de illis judicamus; non enim in pervicavia est fides: sed tempus ceteraque, ut dictum est, considerantes rectam eorum interpretationem assequimur, idemque esse dicimus: *Non facies tibi idolum et simulacrum* ac: *Non adorabis deos alienos*, seu: *Idololatra non eris*. Ita enim et soli Deo latria conservata est et relativi sanctarum imaginum cultus in Ecclesia ab temporibus Apostolorum inducta consuetudo, Deumque nequaquam secum pugnare verbis, commonstratum. Verum enimvero si absolute scriptura dicit: Non facies neque adorabis; qui tandem simulacra facere non autem adorare postea Deus indulsit, prorsus non intelligimus. Quamobrem quum de Idololatria sola prohibitio facta sit et Cherubim et serpentes et leones sculptos fuisse ac honoratos invenimus, et figuræ sive simulacra, inter quæ et Angeli, adorata comparuere.

Quos vero allegant sanctos, adorationem imaginum asserentes illicitam, nostris potius quam illorum favere partibus æstimamus · quandoquidem acerrimis disputationibus suis in eos dumtaxat invehebantur, qui latriæ cultum sacris imaginibus impendebant, quive parentum suorum defunctorum effigies in ecclesiam inferebant, quos et insuper anathemati subjecere; non autem in rectum tum sanctorum tum sacrarum imaginum tum et venerandæ crucis ceterorumque prædictorum cultum; maxime quum ab Apostolorum temporibus decoratam sacris imaginibus ecclesiam eisque adhibitum ab fidelibus cultum quam plurimi tradant et attestentur, quibuscum et quos secuta sancta œcumenica syno-

μη σύνοδος καταισχύνει πᾶσαν αἱρετικῶν βδε-
λυρίαν.

Ἐπειδὴ σαφέστατα μὲν δίδωσιν ἐννοεῖν,
ὅπως δεῖ προσκυνεῖν τὰς ἁγίας εἰκόνας, καὶ
τὰ προειρημένα ἄνωθεν, ἀναθεματίζει δὲ καὶ
ἀφορισμῷ καθυποβάλλει τοὺς ἢ προσκυνοῦντας λατρευτικῶς τὰς εἰκόνας ἢ λέγοντας τοὺς
ὀρθοδόξους εἰδωλολατρεῖν, προσκυνοῦντας τὰς
εἰκόνας. Ἀναθεματίζομεν οὖν καὶ ἡμεῖς μετ'
ἐκείνων τοὺς προσκυνοῦντας ἢ ἅγιον ἢ ἄγγελον ἢ εἰκόνα, ἢ σταυρόν ἢ λείψανον ἁγίον ἢ
ἱερὸν σκεῦος, ἢ εὐαγγέλιον, ἢ ἄλλο τι ὅσα ἐν
τῷ οὐρανῷ ἄνω καὶ ὅσα ἐν τῇ γῇ καὶ ἐν τῇ
θαλάσσῃ λατρευτικῶς καὶ μόνῳ τῷ ἐν τριάδι
Θεῷ τὴν λατρευτικὴν προσκύνησιν ἀπονέμομεν.
Ἀναθεματίζομεν καὶ τοὺς λέγοντας τὴν προσκύνησιν τῶν εἰκόνων εἰκονολατρείαν, ἢ μὴ
προσκυνοῦντας αὐτὰς, καὶ μὴ τιμῶντας τὸν
σταυρὸν καὶ τοὺς ἁγίους, ὡς ἡ ἐκκλησία παρέδωκε.

Καὶ τοὺς ἁγίους καὶ τὰς ἁγίας εἰκόνας
προσκυνοῦμεν, ὃν εἴρηται τρόπον, καὶ ἱστοροῦμεν ταύτας εἰς καλλωπισμὸν τῶν ναῶν, καὶ
ἵν' ὦσι βιβλία τῶν ἀμαθῶν καὶ πρὸς μίμησιν
τῶν ἀρετῶν τῶν ἁγίων καὶ ἀνάμνησιν καὶ
ἔρωτος αὔξησιν καὶ πρὸς ἐγρήγορσιν τοῦ ἐπι-
καλεῖσθαι ἀεὶ τὸν μὲν κύριον, ὡς δεσπότην καὶ
πατέρα, τοὺς δὲ ἁγίους ὡς δούλους μὲν ἐκείνου, βοηθοὺς δὲ καὶ μεσίτας ἡμῶν.

Καὶ ταῦτα μὲν περὶ τῶν κεφαλαίων καὶ ἐρωτήσεων Κυρίλλου. Οἱ δὲ αἱρετικοὶ καὶ τὴν
προσευχὴν τῶν εὐσεβῶν πρὸς τὸν Θεόν κακί-
ζουσιν, ἔπειτα οὐκ οἴδαμεν, ὅπως αὐτὴν μόνων
τῶν μοναχῶν κατηγοροῦσι. Τὴν προσευχὴν
τοίνυν ἡμεῖς ὁμιλίαν μετὰ Θεοῦ καὶ πρεπόντων
ἀγαθῶν αἴτησιν, παρ' οὗ λαβεῖν ἐλπίζομεν,
ἀνάβασίν τε νοῦ πρὸς Θεὸν καὶ εὐσεβῆ πρὸς
Θεὸν ἀπευθυνομένην διάθεσιν, ζήτησιν τῶν
ἀνωτέρω, ψυχῆς ἁγίας βοήθημα, λατρείαν τῷ
Θεῷ κεχαρισμένην, σημεῖον μετανοίας καὶ βε-
βαίας ἐλπίδος οἴδαμεν· γίνεσθαι δὲ ἢ νῷ μόνῳ
ἢ νοΐ καὶ φωνῇ· θεωρεῖσθαι ἐν αὐτῇ θεωρίαν
τῆς ἀγαθότητος καὶ τοῦ ἐλέους τοῦ Θεοῦ, ἀνα-

dus septima omnem hæreticorum impuden-
tiam confundit.

Siquidem manifestissime, qualem sacris
imaginibus adhibere oporteat cultum et ea,
quæ supra dicta sunt, demonstrant; quoscunque vero, quum qui latriæ cultum sacris imaginibus impendunt, tum qui fideles, honorem
imaginibus deferentes, idololatriæ insimulant,
anathematizat et excommunicationi subjicit.
Et nos igitur cum ipsis eos omnes, qui sive
sanctum, sive angelum, sive imaginem, sive
crucem, sive reliquias sanctorum, sive vas aliquod sacrum, sive evangelium, sive quidpiam
aliud ex iis, quæ in cœlo et in terra et in mari
sunt, latriæ cultu venerantur, anathematiza-
mus solique in trinitate Deum cultum hujusmodi ducimus esse tribuendum. Insuper et
cultum imaginum appellantes iconolatriam easque ac crucem et sanctos juxta traditionem
Ecclesiæ adorare et colere recusantes anathe-
matizamus.

Sanctos quippe eo, quo supra diximus, cultu
veneramur nec non et sanctas imagines, quas
ad templorum ornamentum depingimus, ut librorum instar inibi sint et ad virtutum Sanctorum imitationem, memoriam, amoris incrementum, atque ad jugem Dei quidem ceu Domini et Patris, Sanctorum vero ceu servorum
ejus, nostrorum autem adjutorum juxta ac
oratorum obsecrationem rudiores, excitentur.

Atque hæc quidem de Cyrilli capitibus
quæstionibusque dicta sint. Porro fidelium
quoque orationes ad Deum improbant hæretici. Deinde vero quamobrem eam, quæ ab
solis fit monachis, calumnientur nescimus.
Nos igitur orationem ceu cum Deo colloquium
ac convenientium, a quo speramus illa, bonorum postulationem, item adscensum piumque
affectum mentis tendentem in Deum, cœlestium rerum inquisitionem, animæ sanctæ
subsidium, cultum Deo acceptissimum, pœnitentiæ ac firmæ spei signum agnoscimus. Fieri autem vel sola mente, vel mente simul et
voce; Deique bonitatem et misericordiam ac
orantis pariter indignitatem et futuræ ad Deum

ξιότητα τοῦ αἰτοῦντος καὶ εὐχαριστίαν καὶ ἐπαγγελίαν τῆς μελλούσης πρὸς Θεὸν ὑποτάξεως.

Ἔχειν δ' αὐτὴν πίστιν καὶ ἐλπίδα καὶ διαμονὴν καὶ τήρησιν τῶν ἐντολῶν καὶ κατὰ πρῶτον λόγον αἴτησιν τῶν οὐρανίων· πολλοὺς δ' ἔχειν τοὺς καρποὺς, οὓς περιττὸν ἐγκαταλέγειν· γίνεσθαι δὲ συνεχῶς, ἐπιτελεῖσθαι δὲ ὀρθίῳ καὶ γονυκλίτῳ σχήματι. Τοσαύτη δὲ ἥπερ αὐτῆς ὠφέλεια, ὥστε καὶ ψυχῆς τροφὴν καὶ ζωὴν ὁμολογεῖσθαι. Συνάγεται καὶ ταῦτα πάντα ἐκ τῆς θείας γραφῆς, ὥστε εἴ τις τούτων ἀπόδειξιν αἰτεῖ, ὅμοιος ἄφρονι, ἢ τυφλῷ περὶ τοῦ ἡλιακοῦ φωτὸς ὥρᾳ μεσημβρίας καὶ αἰθρίας ἀμφισβητοῦντι.

Οἱ δ' αἱρετικοί, βουλόμενοι μηδὲν ὧν Χριστὸς ἐπέτρεψε ἀπαράθραυστον ἐᾶσαι, καὶ ταύτης καθήψαντο. Αἰσχυνόμενοι δ' οὕτω φανερῶς ἀσεβεῖν τέως μὲν περὶ προσευχῆς, ἁπλῶς μὴ γίνεσθαι οὐ κωλύουσι, ταῖς τῶν μοναχῶν δ' εὐχαῖς ταράττονται· ὅπερ καὶ αὐτὸ ποιοῦσιν, ἵνα τοῖς ἁπλοϊκοῖς μῖσος κατὰ τῶν μοναχῶν θῶσι πρὸς τὸ μὴ ὅλως ἀνέχεσθαι τούτους τυχὸν ὡς βεβήλους καὶ νεωτεριστὰς ὁρᾶν, μὴ ὅτιγε ἀνέχεσθαι τὰ τῆς εὐσεβοῦς καὶ ὀρθοδόξου πίστεως δόγματα διδάσκεσθαι παρ' αὐτῶν. Σοφὸς γὰρ ὁ ἀντίδικος περὶ τὸ κακὸν καὶ ἀγχίνους περὶ τὰ μάταια· ὅθεν καὶ τοῖς ὁπαδοῖς αὐτοῦ—οἷοι οἱ αἱρετικοὶ οὗτοι μάλιστα—οὐκ ἔστι τοσοῦτον κατάθυμον εὐσεβεῖν, ὅσον περισπούδαστον τὸ ἀείποτε ἐκτραχηλιάζειν ἐπὶ βάθει κακῶν καὶ ἐκρήγνυσθαι ἐς τόπους, οὓς οὐκ ἐπισκοπεῖ κύριος.

Ἐρωτητέον οὖν αὐτούς, τίνας φασὶν εἶναι τὰς τῶν μοναχῶν προσευχάς· καὶ εἰ μὲν τοὺς μοναχοὺς φαῖεν ἐξ ἑαυτῶν τινὰ ἀλλόκοτα πεποιηκέναι καὶ ἀπάδοντα τῇ ὀρθοδόξῳ τῶν Χριστιανῶν θρησκείᾳ, καὶ αὐτοὶ ξυντιθέμεθα καὶ τοὺς μοναχοὺς οὐ μόνον οὐ μοναχοὺς ἀλλ' οὐδὲ Χριστιανοὺς φαμεν. Εἰ δὲ οἱ μοναχοὶ διηγοῦνται ἐν ἐκτάσει τὴν δόξαν καὶ τὰ θαυμάσια τοῦ Θεοῦ καὶ συνεχῶς καὶ ἀδιαλείπτως, καὶ ἐν παντὶ καιρῷ τὸ θεῖον, ὡς δυνατὸν ἀνθρώπῳ, ὕμνοις καὶ δοξολογίαις καταγεραίρουσι, πῇ μὲν τὰ τῆς γραφῆς δηλονότι

subjectionis beneficium ac promissionem in illa considerari.

Fidem vero et spem et perseverantiam et mandatorum observationem ac, ut prædiximus, cœlestium cumprimis habere petitionem, quin et fructus id genus quam plurimos, quos frustra recenseamus. Denique sine intermissione fieri, et qua stando, qua genua flectendo peragi. Tanta vero est orationis utilitas, ut animæ cibus et vita merito censeatur. Et hæc quidem omnia sacris ita manifeste colliguntur e Scripturis, ut insipienti aut cœco, meridie ac sereno cœlo de solis lumine dubitanti, similis ille sit, qui probationem eorum exegerit.

Hæretici vero, quum eorum, quæ fidelibus mandavit Christus, nihil relinquere integrum statuerint, et illam canino ore arrosere. Id tamen tam apertæ circa orationem impietatis tandem erubescentes, orare omnino minime prohibent; sed monachorum orationibus commoventur; ea nimirum mente, ut simpliciorum odium in monachus excitent: quatenus eorum ceu profanorum ac novatorum nec adspectum sustineant et Catholicæ atque Apostolicæ fidei ab illis exponi dogmata multo minus patiantur. Prudens enim est in malum diabolus et ad confingendas calumnias ingeniosus. Unde et ejus asseclas—cujusmodi sunt isti maxime, quibus de loquimur, hæretici—non tam pietatis propositum, quam homines ad malorum abyssum detrudendi et ad ea, quæ non visitat dominus, loca rapiendi, movet institutum.

Itaque, quales esse dicant monachorum orationes, interrogandi sunt; et si quidem a se ipsis aliqua aliena vel orthodoxæ Christianorum professioni dissentanea fecisse monachos probaverint; jam adversus monachos cum illis caussam agimus, eosque non modo monachos non esse dicimus, sed neque Christianos. Sin vero gloriam et mirabilia Dei et intenta mente assidue et indesinenter et omni tempore enarrant monachi Deumque pro viribus humanis hymnis et canticis celebrant, nunc quidem Scripturæ verba psallentes, nunc

ψάλλοντες, πῇ δὲ τοὺς ὕμνους ἐκ τῆς γραφῆς συνάγοντες, εἶτ᾽ οὖν συνῳδὰ ἐκείνῃ φθεγγόμενον· ἀποστολικὸν καὶ προφητικὸν, μᾶλλον δὲ κυριακὸν ἔργον αὐτοὺς πληροῦν ὁμολογοῦμεν. Ὅθεν καὶ ἡμεῖς Παρακλητικὴν, Τριώδιον καὶ Μηναῖα ψάλλοντες μηδὲν ἀπᾷδον Χριστιανοῖς ἔργον πληροῦμεν. Πᾶσαι γὰρ αἱ τοιαῦται βίβλοι περὶ ἡνωμένης καὶ διακεκριμένης θεολογίας διαλέγονται καὶ ὕμνοις, πῇ μὲν συνηγμένοις ἐκ τῆς θείας γραφῆς, πῇ δὲ κατὰ τὴν χορηγίαν τοῦ πνεύματος, ἵν᾽ ὦσι τοῖς μέλεσιν αἱ λέξεις κατάλληλοι δι᾽ ἑτέρων λέξεων, τὰ τῆς γραφῆς ᾄδομεν· ἔπειτα ἵν᾽ ὅλως ᾖ κατάδηλον, ὅτι τὰ τῆς γραφῆς ἀεὶ ψάλλομεν, ἐν ἑκάστῳ τῶν ὕμνων λεγομένῳ Τροπαρίῳ στίχον τῆς γραφῆς ἐπιλέγομεν. Εἰ δὲ καὶ Θηκαρᾶ καὶ ἄλλας τοῖς πάλαι πατράσι πονηθείσας εὐχὰς ψάλλομεν καὶ ἀναγινώσκομεν· εἰπάτωσαν οὗτοι, ποῖον ἐκείνων τὸ βλάσφημον καὶ μὴ εὐσεβὲς, καὶ μετ᾽ ἐκείνων τούτους ἀποδιώξομεν.

Εἰ δὲ καὶ μόνον τοῦτό φασι, τὸ συνεχῶς καὶ ἀδιαλείπτως προσεύχεσθαι κακὸν, τί αὐτοῖς καὶ ἡμῖν; Μαχέσθωσαν Χριστῷ—καθάπερ καὶ μάχονται—εἰπόντι τὴν τοῦ ἀδίκου κριτοῦ παραβολὴν, πρὸς τὸ δεῖν συνεχῶς προσεύχεσθαι, καὶ διδάξαντι ἀγρυπνεῖν καὶ εὔχεσθαι, φυγεῖν τὰ θλιβερὰ καὶ σταθῆναι ἔμπροσθεν τοῦ υἱοῦ τοῦ ἀνθρώπου. Μαχέσθωσαν Παύλῳ πρώτης πρὸς Θεσσαλονικεῖς κεφαλαίῳ καὶ ἀλλαχοῦ ἐν πολλοῖς. Ἐῶ λέγειν τοὺς θείους τῆς καθολικῆς ἐκκλησίας καθηγεμόνας ἀπὸ χριστοῦ ἄχρις ἡμῶν· ἀρκεῖ γὰρ αὐτοῖς πρὸς αἰσχύνειν τὸ τύντονον τῆς προσευχῆς τῶν τε προπατόρων, ἀποστόλων καὶ προφητῶν.

Εἰ οὖν τὰ τῶν μοναχῶν ἐστι τὰ τῶν ἀποστόλων καὶ προφητῶν, δὸς δ᾽ εἰπεῖν καὶ τῶν ἁγίων πατέρων καὶ τῶν προπατόρων αὐτοῦ τοῦ Χριστοῦ· δῆλον ὅτι αἱ τῶν μοναχῶν εὐχαὶ καρποί εἰσι τοῦ τῶν χαρισμάτων δοτῆρος ἁγίου πνεύματος. Ἃ δὲ Καλουῖνοι κεκαινοτομήκασιν ἔν τε τοῖς περὶ Θεοῦ καὶ τῶν θείων βλασφημοῦντες καὶ τὴν θείαν γραφὴν παρεξηγούμενοι,

vero hymnos et Scriptura componentes, sive eidem Scripturæ consona loquentes; Apostolicum et Propheticum imo vero dominicum opus eos implere confitemur.

Unde et nos nullum ab Christianis alienum opus facimus, quando Paracleticen, Triodion et Menæa cantamus: quum de conjuncta atque discreta edisserant omnes isti libri theologia. Imo vero per hymnos tum e Scripturæ quidem desumtos, tum spiritus adminiculo donoque aliis vocibus, quæ voces melodiæ coincinant, quæ sunt Scripturæ, decantamus. Deinde sacram semper nos canere Scripturam, hinc prorsus liquet, quod cuilibet hymnorum, modulo versiculum e Scriptura subjungamus. Si vero et Thecaræ aliusve ab antiquis patribus compositas orationes, canimus et legimus; quidnam blasphemiæ, quid impietatis habentur in illis, adversarii nostri demonstrent; et una cum ipsis monachos, ipsa canentes, insequemur.

Sin autem hoc solum, quod semper et sine intermissione oramus, ceu malum quid improbant; quid hanc in nos querelam movent? In Christum magis certamen sumant—quemadmodum et sumunt—qui, sine intermissione orandum esse ut probaret, iniqui judicis parabolam proposuit et ad cavendas tentationes vigilandum esse docuit et orandum standumque coram filio hominis. Sumant et cum Paulo, qui tum primæ ad Thessalonicenses quinto, tum et alibi passim ad continuam orationem adhortatur. Divinos prætermitto a Christo ad nos usque Catholicæ Ecclesiæ præpositos: satis enim superque concors proavorum, Apostolorum et Prophetarum de oratione sententia hæreticos pudore suffundit.

Porro si quæ fecerunt Apostoli, quæ Prophetæ, imo—dicere liceat—et quæ sancti patres atque ipsius Christi progenitores; hæc ipsa faciunt et monachi: utique donorum largitoris Spiritus Sancti fructus esse orationes monachorum manifestum est. Quas vero novitates induxere Calvinistæ, tum circa Deum resque divinas blasphemando, quum Scriptu-

κολοβοῦντες καὶ καθυβρίζοντες· τοῦ διαβόλου
εἰσὶ σοφίσματά τε καὶ ἐφευρήματα.

Ἀλυσιτελὲς δὲ καὶ τὸ· ἀδύνατον τῇ ἐκκλησίᾳ βρωμάτων τινῶν ἀποχὰς καὶ νηστείας
διατάττειν ἄνευ βίας καὶ τυραννίδος. Ἡ γὰρ
ἐκκλησία πρὸς νέκρωσιν τῆς σαρκὸς καὶ ὅλως
τῶν παθῶν, μάλα καλῶς ποιοῦσα, διατάττει
ἐπιμελῶς τὴν προσευχὴν καὶ τὴν νηστείαν, ἧς
ἐρασταὶ καὶ τύποι γεγόνασι οἱ ἅγιοι πάντες,
δι᾽ ὧν—τῇ ἄνωθεν χάριτι καθαιρόμενος ὁ ἀντίδικος ἡμῖν διάβολος σὺν τοῖς στρατεύμασι καὶ
ταῖς δυνάμεσι αὐτοῦ—ῥᾳδίως τελειοῦται ὁ προκείμενος τοῖς εὐσεβέσι δρόμος. Ταῦτα οὖν
σκεπτομένη ἡ ἄσπιλος ἀπανταχοῦ ἐκκλησία οὐ
βιάζει οὐδὲ τυραννεῖ· ἀλλὰ παρακαλεῖ, νου-
θετεῖ, διδάσκει τὰ τῆς γραφῆς καὶ πείθει τῇ
δυνάμει τοῦ πνεύματος.

Προστίθησι δὲ τοῖς εἰρημένοις καί τις ἀνθρω-
πίσκος ὁ ἐν Καρεντονίᾳ προειρημένος, φαμὲν,
Κλαύδιος καὶ ἕτερά τινα καθ᾽ ἡμῶν γελοῖα καὶ
μηδενὸς λόγου ἄξια· ἀλλ᾽ ἡμεῖς καὶ τὰ εἰρημένα αὐτῷ μύθους ἡγούμεθα καὶ τοῦτον αὐτὸν
τερατοποιὸν καὶ πάντη ἀμαθῆ γνωρίζομεν.
Καὶ μετὰ Φώτιον γὰρ μύριοι ὅσοι καὶ γεγόνασι
καὶ εἰσὶν ἐπὶ σοφίᾳ καὶ θεολογίᾳ καὶ ἁγιότητι
παρὰ τῇ ἀνατολικῇ ἐκκλησίᾳ διαφέροντες τῇ
δυνάμει τοῦ πνεύματος.

Γελοιότατον δὲ καὶ τὸ· διὰ τὸ ἔχειν τινὰς τῶν
ἀνατολικῶν ἱερέων τὸν ἅγιον ἄρτον ἐν σκεύεσι
ξυλίνοις, ἔσω που τοῦ ναοῦ, ἔξω τοῦ βήματος
ἔν τινι τῶν κιόνων κρεμάμενον, μὴ ὁμολογεῖν
αὐτοὺς τὴν πραγματικὴν καὶ ἀληθῆ μεταβολὴν
τοῦ ἄρτου εἰς τὸ σῶμα τοῦ κυρίου. Ὅτι μὲν
γὰρ τινες τῶν πτωχῶν ἱερέων ἔχουσι τὸ δεσπο-
τικὸν σῶμα ἐν σκεύεσι ξυλίνοις, οὐκ ἀρνού-
μεθα· καὶ γὰρ ὁ Χριστὸς οὐχ ὑπὸ λίθων καὶ
μαρμάρων τιμᾶται, ἀλλὰ διάνοιαν ὑγιῆ καὶ
καρδίαν καθαρὰν αἰτεῖ παρ᾽ ἡμῶν.

Τοῦτο καὶ Παύλῳ συμβέβηκεν· ἔχομεν γάρ,
φησι, τὸν θησαυρὸν ἐν ὀστρακίνοις σκεύεσιν.
Ὅπου δ᾽ αἱ κατὰ μέρος ἐκκλησίαι δύνανται,
ὥσπερ τυχὸν παρ᾽ ἡμῖν ἐν Ἱεροσολύμοις, ἔνδον

ram Sacram perperam interpretando, decur-
tando et injuriose tractando; diaboli sophis-
mata esse dicimus et inventa.

Neque minus inepte garriunt, non posse
Ecclesiam absque violentia et tyrannide ab
quibusdam cibis abstinentiam et jejunia constituere. Enimvero recte admodum ad carnis et passionum prorsus mortificationem orationem et jejunia, quorum amantes ac exempla exstitere sancti omnes, sollicite præcipit:
quibus, ac cœlestis ope gratiæ dejecto cum
exercitibus et virtutibus suis adversante nobis
diabolo, propositum sibi cursum perquam facile fideles absolvunt. Hunc igitur quum in-
culpata ubique Ecclesia spectat, vim nullam,
nullam adhibet tyrannidem, sed hortatur, sed
admonet, sed ea, quæ Scripturæ sunt, edocet, illaque Sancti Spiritus operante virtute persuadet.

His et nonnulla adversum nos ridicula penitusque contemnenda homuncio quidam apud
Carentonium Claudius nomine, uti diximus,
adjicit. Sed et inter fabulas, quæcunque dixit ille, recensemus, ipsumque circulatorem
ac funditus illiteratum agnoscimus. Etenim
etiam post Photium quam plurimi apud Orientalem Ecclesiam exstiterunt et sunt per virtutem Spiritus Sancti sapientia, theologia et
sanctitate præstantes.

Ineptissimam pariter adversarii nostri pre-
munt argumentationem, quum Orientales
nonnullos sacerdotes realem ac veram panis
in corpus Domini conversionem minime confiteri inde probari contendunt, quod panem
sanctum in aliquo templi loco extra Bema sive
Sanctuarium ligneis inclusum thecis ad aliquam appensum columnam asservant. Neque enim negamus, pauperes quosdam sacerdotes ligneis in vasis Dominicum corpus as-
servare; verum nec lapidibus nec marmori-
bus honoratur Christus; sed mentem sanam
et cor purum a nobis exposcit.

Hoc ipsum et Paulo contigit. Ait enim:
Habemus thesaurum in vasis fictilibus. Ast
singulis in Ecclesiis, quarum per facultates
licet, quemadmodum apud nos Ierosolymis,

τοῦ ἁγίου βήματος ἑκάστου τῶν ναῶν τὸ δ -
σποτικὸν σῶμα τιμᾶται καὶ φωταγωγεῖται ἀείποτε ἑπταφώτῳ κανδήλῳ.

῎Επεισι δέ μοι θαυμάζειν, πῶς τὸ δεσποτι-
κὸν σῶμα παρά τινι ἐκκλησίᾳ ἰδὼν κρεμάμενον
οἱ αἱρετικοὶ ἔξω τοῦ βήματος, διὰ τὸ ἴσως
σεσαθρῶσθαι τοὺς τοίχους τοῦ βήματος ὑπὸ
τῆς παλαιότητος, κἀκ τούτου συμπεραίνουσι
τὰ ἀσύστατα · τὸν δὲ Χριστὸν οὐκ εἶδον ὑπὸ
τὸ ἡμικύκλιον τοῦ ἁγίου βήματος ἱστορούμε-
νον ὡς βρέφος ἔνδον τοῦ δίσκου, ἵνα ἴδω·ιν,
ὅτι, ὡς ἱστοροῦσιν οἱ ἀνατολικοὶ ἔνδον . οὗ
δίσκου οὐ τύπον, οὐ χάριν, οὐκ ἄλλο τι, ἀλλ᾽
αὐτὸν τὸν Χριστὸν, οὕτω καὶ πιστεύουσι, τὸν
ἄρτον τῆς εὐχαριστίας οὐκ ἄλλο τι, ἀλλ᾽ αὐτὸ
γίνεσθαι οὐσιωδῶς τὸ σῶμα τοῦ κυρίου καὶ
οὕτω συμπαραινοῦσι τὸ ἀληθές.

᾿Αλλὰ περὶ μὲν τούτων ἁπάντων εἴρηται
πλατύτερον καὶ σαφέστερον τῇ ὀρθοδόξῳ λε-
γομένῃ τῆς ἀνατολικῆς ἐκκλησίας ὁμολογίᾳ ·
Γεωργίῳ Χίῳ τῷ Κορεσίῳ ἐν τοῖς περὶ μυστηρίων καὶ προορισμοῦ καὶ χάριτος καὶ τοῦ ἐφ᾽
ἡμῖν, καὶ πρεσβείας καὶ προσκυνήσεως ἁγίων
καὶ προσκυνήσεως εἰκόνων, καὶ ἐν τῇ πονηθείσῃ αὐτῷ ἀντιρρήσει κατὰ τῆς ἐν Φλανδρίᾳ
ποτὲ τῶν αἱρετικῶν ἀθεμίτου συνόδου καὶ ἐν ἄλλοις πολλοῖς · Γαβριὴλ Πελοποννησίῳ τῷ μη-
τροπολίτῃ Φιλαδελφίας καὶ Γ .γορίῳ πρωτο-
συγγέλλῳ τῷ Χίῳ ἐν τοῖς περὶ μυστηρίων, ᾿Ιερε-
μίᾳ τῷ ἁγιωτάτῳ πατριάρχῃ Κωνσταντινουπόλεως ἐν τρισὶ δογματικαῖς καὶ συνοδικαῖς πρὸς
τοὺς ἐν Τυβίγγῃ τῆς Γερμανίας Λουθήρους ἐπι-
στολαῖς · ᾿Ιωάννῃ ἱερεῖ καὶ οἰκονόμῳ Κωνσταντινουπόλεως τῷ Ναθαναήλ · Μελετίῳ Συρίγῳ
τῷ Κρητὶ ἐν τῇ πονηθείσῃ αὐτῷ ὀρθοδόξῳ
ἀντιρρήσει κατὰ τῶν κεφαλαίων καὶ ἐρωτήσεων
τοῦ λεγομένου Κυρίλλου · Θεοφάνῃ τῷ πατριάρχῃ ᾿Ιεροσολύμων ἐν τῇ πρὸς ῾Ρωξολάνους
δογματικῇ ἐπιστολῇ, καὶ ἄλλοις μυρίοις. Πρὸ
τούτων δὲ εἴρηται μάλιστα καλῶς Συμεὼν τῷ
Θεσσαλονίκης καὶ πρὸ ἐκείνου πᾶσι τοῖς πατράσι καὶ ταῖς οἰκουμενικαῖς συνόδοις, ἱστορι-
κοῖς τε ἐκκλησιαστικοῖς, καὶ μὴν καὶ τοῖς ἐπὶ
τῶν Χριστιανῶν Ρωμαίων αὐτοκρατόρων συγ-
γράψασι τὰς ἐξωτερικὰς ἱστορίας εἴρηται σπο-

in sacro cujuslibet templi bemate dominicum
corpus honoratur, septemplici lampade coram
illo jugiter ardente.

Mihi vero subit admirari, quomodo ob
collapsos fortassis vetustate sacrarii muros
dominicum corpus extra sacrarium hæretici viderint appensum, unde et absur-
dissima conficiunt; Christum vero non viderint infantis specie in disco sacri bema-
tis fornici depictum. Apertissime enim
utique nossent ac verissime concluderent,
Orientales, ut nequaquam figuram aut gratiam, aut id genus quidpium in disco sed
ipsummet Christum repræsentant, ita et credere, panem eucharisticum nihil aliuu
quam ipsum corpus Domini substantialiter
esse.

Sed et fusius juxta ac luculentius de istis
dictum est in libro, qui Confessio orthodoxa
Ecclesiæ Orientalis inscribitur; item ab
Georgio Chio Coresio in libris de sacramentis, de prædestinatione et gratia, de libero
arbitrio, de invocatione et adoratione sanctorum, de veneratione imaginum, et in confu-
tatione pseudosynodi ab hæreticis in Belgio
habitæ, et in aliis plurimis; item ab Gabri-
ele Peloponnesio Philadelphiæ Metropolita;
item ab Gregorio Chio Protosyncello in libro
de sacramentis, item ab Jeremia sanctissimo Patriarcha Constantinopoleos in tribus
dogmaticis ac synodalibus epistolis ad Lu-
theranos Tubingenses item ab Ioanne Na-
thanaele Presbytero et Œconomo Constantinopoleos; item ab Meletio Syrigo Cretensi
in ea, quam composuit, refutatione orthodoxa capitum et quæstionem Cyrilli, quem
vocant; item ab Theophane Hierosolymorum Patriarcha in dogmatica ad Roxolanos
epistola; item ab aliis innumeris; sed et
ante istos ab Symeone Thessalonicensi de
iisdem egregie scriptum, imo ab omnibus
retro ipsum patribus, synodis œcumenicis et
Annalium ecclesiasticorum scriptoribus, quin
etiam et ab iis, qui sub Christiano-Romanis
principibus degentes res politicas sparsim

ράδην, οἷς ἅπασι τὰ εἰρημένα χωρὶς πάσης
ἀντιλογίας εἴληπται παρὰ τῶν ἀποστόλων, ὧν
αἵ τε διὰ γραφῆς καὶ λόγου παραδόσεις διὰ τῶν
πατέρων ἀφίκοντο μέχρις ἡμῶν.

Συνίστησι δὲ τὰ προειρημένα καὶ ὁ παρὰ
τῶν αἱρετικῶν λόγος. Νεστορίται μὲν γὰρ
μετὰ ἔτη τῆς σωτηρίας υκη΄, Ἀρμήνιοί τε καὶ
Κόπται καὶ Σύροι καὶ ἔτι Αἰθίοπες οἱ ὑπὸ τὸν
ἰσημερινὸν καὶ ἐπέκεινα τούτου κατὰ τὸν χειμε-
ρινὸν τροπικὸν οἰκοῦντες, οὓς καὶ Καμπεσίους
οἱ ἐνταῦθα κοινῶς ὀνομάζουσι, μετὰ ἔτη . . .
τῆς ἐνσάρκου ἐπιδημίας ἀπερράγησαν τῆς καθόλου ἐκκλησίας καὶ · ἕκαστος τούτων ἔχει μόνην τὴν αἵρεσιν, ἣν ἅπαντες ἀπὸ τῶν πρακτικῶν τῶν οἰκουμενικῶν ἴσασι συνόδων. Περὶ
μέντοι τοῦ σκόπου καὶ τοῦ ἀριθμοῦ τῶν ἱερῶν
μυστηρίων καὶ τῶν εἰρημένων ἡμῖν ἀνωτέρω
ἅπαντων—πλὴν τῆς ἰδίας αὐτῶν αἱρέσεως, ὡς
εἴρηται—ὡσαύτως πιστεύουσι τῇ καθολικῇ ἐκκλησίᾳ, ὡς αὐτοῖς ὄμμασιν ὅσαι ὧραι βλέπομεν
καὶ αἰσθῆσαι καὶ λόγῳ μανθάνομεν, ἐνταῦθα
ἐν τῇ ἁγίᾳ πόλει Ἱερουσαλήμ, ἐν ᾗ ἀπὸ πάντων καὶ οἰκοῦσι καὶ πάντοτε ἐπιδημοῦσι πλεῖστοι ὅσοι παρ' αὐτῶν, σοφοί τε, ὅσον τὸ κατ'
αὐτοὺς, καὶ ἰδιῶται.

Σιωπάτωσαν τοίνυν οἱ κενόφωνοι καὶ νεω-
τερισταὶ αἱρετικοὶ καὶ μὴ ἐπιχειρείτωσαν ἔκ τε
τῆς γραφῆς καὶ τῶν πατέρων καθ᾽ ἡμῶν κλέ-
πτοντες ῥησίδιά τινα σεσοφισμένως εἰς σύστασιν τοῦ ψεύδους, ὡς πεποιήκασι πάντες οἱ ἀπ'
αἰῶνος ἀποστάται καὶ αἱρετικοί, καὶ λεγέτωσαν
ἕν ρ᾽ ὄνον, ὅτι προφασιζόμενοι προφάσεις ἐν
α῾ρτίαις προΰρηνται λαλεῖν ἄδικα κατὰ τοῦ
Θεοῦ καὶ βλάσφημα κατὰ τῶν ἁγίων.

Ἐπίλογος.

Ταῦτα ἐκ τῶν πολλῶν ὀλίγα εἰς καθαίρεσιν
τοῦ ψεύδους τῶν ἀντικειμένων, ὅπερ ἐπενόησαν
κατὰ τῆς ἀνατολικῆς ἐκκλησίας, προβαλλόμε-
νοι μέσον τῆς ἐπιφορᾶς τοῦ ψεύδους τὰ ἀσύστατα καὶ ἄθεα κεφάλαια τοῦ λεγομένου Κυρίλλου. Εἴησαν δὲ οὐκ εἰς σημεῖον ἀντιλεγό-
μενον τοῖς ὡς ἀληθῶς ἀδίκως ἡμᾶς διασύρουσιν

sunt prosecuti. Quorum omnia una sententia est ab Apostolis prædicta omnia dima-
nasse, quorum traditiones sive scripto sive
verbo per patres ad nos usque pervenere.

Validissimum porro habemus prædictorum vel ex ipsis hæreticis argumentum.
Etenim Nestoriani post annum salutis
CCCCXXVIII., item Armenii et Cophtæ
et Syri, item Æthiopes, qui sub Æquinoctiali
habitant, et trans illum versus tropicum Ca-
pricorni, quos hujusmodi locorum incolæ vulgo Campesios vocant, post annos ab incar-
natione Domini . . . ab Catholica Ecclesia
recessere, singuli singularem hæresim amplexi, ut ex œcumenicis conciliorum actis
nemo non intelligit. Veruntamen circa scopum numerumque sacramentorum nec non et
circa omnia, quæ supra diximus—præter singularem suam hæresim, ut dictum est—cum
Ecclesia Catholica prorsus consentiunt, uti
per singulas horas ipsis oculis conspicimus, et
sermone atque usu discimus in hac sancta
civitate Hierusalem, in qua ex omnibus enu-
meratis homines tum sapientes apud illos
quum illiterati aut habitant aut peregrinationis ergo commorantur.

Taceant igitur inepti nugatores et novitatum artifices hæretici, et mutilas tum e Scriptura tum ex patribus adversum nos senten-
tiolas, quibus mendacium exstruant, callide
furari ne moliantur, quemadmodum aposta-
tarum et hæreticorum ab initio exstitit consuetudo: atque hoc loquuntur unum, sese
nimirum, excusationes excusantes in peccatis,
injurias in Deum et in sanctos evomere bla-
sphemias instituisse.

EPILOGUS.

Hæc ex multis pauca sufficiant ad ever-
sionem mendacii, quod adversus Orientalem
Ecclesiam excogitaverunt adversarii nostri,
in medium illationis mendacii sui nutantia ac
impia proferentes, dicti Cyrilli capita. Sint
vero hæreticis nos injuste quidem traducenti-
bus in signum non contradictionis sed in

αἱρετικοῖς, ἀλλ' εἰς σημεῖον πιστευόμενον ἤτοι εἰς διόρθωσιν τῶν καινοτομηθέντων αὐτοῖς καὶ ἐπιστροφὴν αὐτῶν πρὸς τὴν καθολικὴν καὶ ἀποστολικὴν ἐκκλησίαν, ἐν ᾗ παλαίποτε καὶ οἱ πρόγονοι αὐτῶν ἦσαν, καὶ ἐν ταῖς κατὰ τῶν αἱρετικῶν συνόδοις, αἷς νῦν αὐτοὶ ἀθετοῦντες καθυβρίζουσι, καὶ ἀγῶσι παρῆσαν. Ἄτοπον γὰρ πεπεῖσθαι αὐτούς, καὶ μάλιστα αὐχοῦντας εἶναι σοφούς, ἀνδράσι φιλαύτοις τε καὶ βεβήλοις καὶ λαλήσασιν οὐκ ἐκ τοῦ πνεύματος τοῦ ἁγίου, ἀλλ' ἐκ τοῦ ἄρχοντος τοῦ ψεύδους, τὴν δ' ἁγίαν καθολικὴν καὶ ἀποστολικὴν ἐκκλησίαν, ἣν περιεποιήσατο ὁ Θεὸς τῷ αἵματι τοῦ υἱοῦ αὐτοῦ ἐγκαταλιπεῖν καὶ ταύτης ἀποσκιρτῆσαι. Ἄλλως γὰρ ἂν αὐτοὺς μὲν τοὺς ἀπορραγέντας τῆς ἐκκλησίας τὰ ἐκεῖσε δικαιωτήρια μετὰ τῶν ἐθνικῶν καὶ τελωνῶν δέξονται· τὴν δὲ καθολικὴν ἐκκλησίαν οὐ παρόψεται ὁ ταύτην ἕως ἄρτι ἀπὸ πάντων τῶν ἐναντίων διατηρῶν κύριος, ᾧ ἡ δόξα καὶ τὸ κράτος εἰς αἰῶνας τῶν αἰώνων. Ἀμήν.

Ἐν ἔτει τῷ σωτηρίῳ αχοβ'· μηνὶ Μαρτίῳ ις'. Ἐν τῇ ἁγίᾳ πόλει Ἱερουσαλήμ.

Δοσίθεος ἐλέῳ Θεοῦ πατριάρχης τῆς ἁγίας Ἱερουσαλὴμ καὶ πάσης Παλαιστίνης ἀποφαίνομαι καὶ ὁμολογῶ, ταύτην εἶναι τὴν πίστιν τῆς ἀνατολικῆς ἐκκλησίας.

signum rerum, quas credimus et in emendationem novitatum, quas invexere: nec non et in conversionem ipsorum ad Catholicam et Apostolicam Ecclesiam, in qua majores eorum olim meruerunt, et ecclesiasticis contra eos synodis, quas nunc respuentes ludibrio habent isti, ac certaminibus interfuerunt. Ab omni quippe ratione longe alienum est, eos, maxime quum se jactent sapientes, hominibus suimet amantibus et execrandis ac nequaquam ex Spiritu Sancto sed ex mendacii principe loquentibus attendisse; sanctam autem Catholicam et Apostolicam Ecclesiam, quam filii sui sanguine Deus acquisivit, deseruisse ab eaque resiliisse. Ceteroquin hos quidem ab Ecclesia separatos inferni supplicia una cum ethnicis et publicanis excipient; Catholicam vero Ecclesiam, qui cunctis ab contrariis eam hucusque protexit, Deus non derelinquet, cui gloria et imperium in sæcula sæculorum. Amen.

Anno salutis cIɔIɔcLxxii. die XVI. Martii. Apud sanctam civitatem Hierosolymam.

Dositheus miseratione divina Patriarcha sanctæ Hierusalem et totius Palæstinæ assero et confiteor, hanc esse fidem Ecclesiæ Orientalis.

Sequuntur in editt. post aliorum et quidem LXVIII. nomina; deinde Dosithei testimonium, quo affirmat, ipsum autographum cum legitimis illis subscriptionibus rerumque serie in magnum Apostolici sui throni codicem relatum esse die XX. Mart. MDCLXXII. Deinceps est Nectarii, Hierosolymorum ante Patriarchæ, nomen, et, post locum sigilli, tum Patriarchæ, XII. Hieroglyphicis notis constantis, tum Imperatoris Orientis cum insignibus Aquilæ bicipitis, ut legere est in tabulis Amst. edit. intersertis, quibus signaturæ ad similitudinem autographi depictæ sunt, Nectarii Monachi de se testimonium; ita ut, si summam facimus, LXXI. viri nomina dederint, inter quos VIII. archiepiscopi, episcopi et metropolitæ. Azarias, Archidiaconus Hierosolymit. non solum suo sed etiam diaconorum nomine subscripsit, item Agapius, Sacerdos et Œconomus Gazæorum. Aderat ex majore Russia Timotheus monachus, confitens, hanc esse fidem et Russicæ et Orientalis Ecclesiæ; assensum etiam nomine subscripto præbuit Apocrisiarius serenissimi Moscoviæ imperatoris Alexii *Josaphat*, Hieromonachus, Archimandrita, sancti sepulchri. Arabicis literis signaverunt in Paris. edit. novem, in Amst. et Bibl. decimus est *Chaleles*, magnus Protonotariuʳ Patriarchæ, qui ei ab epistolis fuit.

III. THE LONGER CATECHISM OF THE ORTHODOX, CATHOLIC, EASTERN CHURCH.

EXAMINED AND APPROVED BY THE MOST HOLY GOVERNING SYNOD, AND PUBLISHED FOR THE USE OF SCHOOLS, AND OF ALL ORTHODOX CHRISTIANS, BY ORDER OF HIS IMPERIAL MAJESTY. (Moscow, at the Synodical Press, 1839.)

[The large Russian Catechism of Philaret, approved by the holy Synod (although omitted by Kimmel in his Collection, and barely mentioned by Gass in his Greek Symbolics), is now the most authoritative doctrinal standard of the orthodox Græco-Russian Church, and has practically superseded the older Catechism, or Orthodox Confession of Mogila. Originally composed in Slavono-Russian, it was by authority translated into several languages. We have before us a Russian edition (Moscow, 1869), a Greek edition (Χριστιανικὴ κατ' ἔκτασιν κατήχησις τι,ς ὀρϑοδόξου, καϑολικι,ς καὶ ἀνατολικι,ς ἐκκλησίας, Odessa, 1848), and a German edition (*Ausführlicher christlicher Katechismus der orthodox-katholischen orientalischen Kirche*, St. Petersburg, 1850).

The English translation here given was prepared by the Rev. R. W. BLACKMORE, B.A., formerly chaplain to the Russia Company in Kronstadt, and published at Aberdeen, 1845, in the work *The Doctrine of the Russian Church*. On comparing it with the authorized Greek and German translations, we found it faithful and idiomatic. The numbering of Questions, and the difference in type of Questions and Answers, are ours. In all other editions we have seen, the Questions are not numbered. As this Catechism has never before appeared in America, we thought it best to give it in full, although the Introduction and the First Part would be sufficient for this collection of doctrinal symbols. Comp. Vol. I. § 19, pp. 68–73.]

INTRODUCTION TO THE ORTHODOX CATECHISM.
PRELIMINARY INSTRUCTION.

1. What is an Orthodox Catechism?

An Orthodox Catechism is an instruction in the orthodox Christian faith, to be taught to every Christian, to enable him to please God and save his own soul.

2. What is the meaning of the word Catechism?

It is a Greek word, signifying *instruction,* or oral teaching, and has been used ever since the Apostles' times to denote that primary *instruction* in the orthodox faith which is needful for every Christian. Luke i. 4; Acts xviii. 25.

3. What is necessary in order to please God and to save one's own soul?

In the first place, a knowledge of the true God, and a right faith in him; in the second place, a life according to faith, and good works.

4. Why is faith necessary in the first place?

Because, as the Word of God testifies, *Without faith it is impossible to please God.* Heb. xi. 6.

5. Why must a life according to faith, and good works, be inseparable from this faith?

Because, as the Word of God testifies, *Faith without works is dead* James ii. 20.

6. What is faith ?

According to the definition of St. Paul, *Faith is the substance of things hoped for, the evidence of things not seen* (Heb. xi. 1); that is, a trust in the unseen as though it were seen, in that which is hoped and waited for as if it were present.

7. What is the difference between knowledge and faith ?

Knowledge has for its object things visible and comprehensible; faith, things which are invisible, and even incomprehensible. Knowledge is founded on experience, on examination of its object; but faith on belief of testimony to truth. Knowledge belongs properly to the intellect, although it may also act on the heart; faith belongs principally to the heart, although it is imparted through the intellect.

8. Why is faith, and not knowledge only, necessary in religious instruction ?

Because the chief object of this instruction is God invisible and incomprehensible, and the wisdom of God hidden in a mystery; consequently, many parts of this learning can not be embraced by knowledge, but may be received by faith.

Faith, says St. Cyril of Jerusalem, *is the eye which enlighteneth every man's conscience; it giveth man knowledge. For,* as the prophet says, *If ye will not believe, ye shall not understand.* Isa. vii. 9; Cyr. Cat. v.

9. Can you illustrate further the necessity of faith ?

St. Cyril thus illustrates it: *It is not only amongst us, who bear the name of Christ, that faith is made so great a thing; but every thing which is done in the world, even by men who are unconnected with the Church, is done by faith. Agriculture is founded on faith; for no one who did not believe that he should gather in the increase of the fruits of the earth would undertake the labor of husbandry. Mariners are guided by faith when they intrust their fate to a slight plank, and prefer the agitation of the unstable waters to the more stable element of the earth. They give themselves up to uncertain expectations, and retain for themselves nothing but faith, to which they trust more than to any anchors.* Cyr. Cat. v.

On Divine Revelation.

10. Whence is the doctrine of the orthodox faith derived ?

From divine revelation.

11. What is meant by the words *divine revelation ?*

That which God himself has revealed to men, in order that they

might rightly and savingly believe in him, and worthily honor him.

12. Has God given such a revelation to all men?

He has given it for all, as being necessary for all alike, and capable of bringing salvation to all; but, since not all men are capable of receiving a revelation immediately from God, he has employed special persons as heralds of his revelation, to deliver it to all who are desirous of receiving it.

13. Why are not all men capable of receiving a revelation immediately from God?

Owing to their sinful impurity, and weakness both in soul and body.

14. Who were the heralds of divine revelation?

Adam, Noah, Abraham, Moses, and other Prophets, received and preached the beginnings of divine revelation; but it was the incarnate Son of God, our Lord Jesus Christ, who brought it to earth in its fullness and perfection, and spread it over all the world by his Disciples and Apostles.

The Apostle Paul says, in the beginning of his Epistle to the Hebrews: *God, who at sundry times, and in divers manners, spake in times past unto the Fathers by the Prophets, hath in these last days spoken unto us by his Son, whom he hath appointed heir of all things, by whom also he made the worlds.*

The same Apostle writes as follows to the Corinthians: *But we speak the wisdom of God in a mystery, even the hidden things which God ordained before the world unto our glory, which none of the princes of this world knew. But God hath revealed them unto us by his Spirit; for the Spirit searcheth all things, yea, the deep things of God.* 1 Cor. ii. 7, 8, 10.

The Evangelist John writes in his Gospel: *No man hath seen God at any time; the only-begotten Son, which is in the bosom of the Father, he hath declared him.* John i. 18.

Jesus Christ himself says: *No man knoweth the Son but the Father; neither knoweth any man the Father save the Son, and he to whomsoever the Son will reveal him.* Matt. xi. 27.

15. Can not man, then, have any knowledge of God without a special revelation from him?

Man may have some knowledge of God by contemplation of those things which he has created; but this knowledge is imperfect and in-

sufficient, and can serve only as a preparation for faith, or as a help to-wards the knowledge of God from his revelation.

For the invisible things of him, from the creation of the world, are clearly seen, being understood by the things that are made, even his eternal power and Godhead. Rom. i. 20.

And he hath made of one blood all nations of men, for to dwell on all the face of the earth; and hath determined the times before appointed, and the bounds of their habitation; that they should seek the Lord, if haply they might feel after him, and find him, though he be not far from every one of us. For in him we live, and move, and have our being. Acts xvii. 26–28.

With regard to faith in God, it is preceded by the idea that God is, which idea we get from the things which have been created. Attentively examining the creation of the world, we perceive that God is wise, powerful, and good; we perceive, also, his invisible properties. By these means we are led to acknowledge him as the Supreme Ruler. Seeing that God is the Creator of the whole world, and we form a part of the world, it follows that God is also our Creator. On this knowledge follows faith, and on faith adoration. (Basil. Magn. Epist. 232.)

On Holy Tradition and Holy Scripture.

16. How is divine revelation spread among men and preserved in the true Church?

By two channels—holy tradition and holy Scripture.

17. What is meant by the name *holy tradition?*

By the name holy tradition is meant the doctrine of the faith, the law of God, the sacraments, and the ritual as handed down by the true believers and worshipers of God by word and example from one to another, and from generation to generation.

18. Is there any sure repository of holy tradition?

All true believers united by the holy tradition of the faith, collectively and successively, by the will of God, compose the Church; and she is the sure repository of holy tradition, or, as St. Paul expresses it, *The Church of the living God, the pillar and ground of the truth.* 1 Tim. iii. 15.

St. Irenæus writes thus: *We ought not to seek among others the truth, which we may have for asking from the Church; for in her, as in a*

rich treasure-house, the Apostles have laid up in its fullness all that pertains to the truth, so that whosoever seeketh may receive from her the food of life. She is the door of life. (Adv. Hæres. lib. iii. c. 4.)

19. What is that which you call *holy Scripture!*

Certain books written by the Spirit of God through men sanctified by God, called Prophets and Apostles. These books are commonly termed the Bible.

20. What does the word *Bible* mean?

It is Greek, and means *the books*. The name signifies that the sacred books deserve attention before all others.

21. Which is the more ancient, holy tradition or holy Scripture?

The most ancient and original instrument for spreading divine revelation is holy tradition. From Adam to Moses there were no sacred books. Our Lord Jesus Christ himself delivered his divine doctrine and ordinances to his Disciples by word and example, but not by writing. The same method was followed by the Apostles also at first, when they spread abroad the faith and established the Church of Christ. The necessity of tradition is further evident from this, that books can be available only to a small part of mankind, but tradition to all.

22. Why, then, was holy Scripture given?

To this end, that divine revelation might be preserved more exactly and unchangeably. In holy Scripture we read the words of the Prophets and Apostles precisely as if we were living with them and listening to them, although the latest of the sacred books were written a thousand and some hundred years before our time.

23. Must we follow holy tradition, even when we possess holy Scripture?

We must follow that tradition which agrees with the divine revelation and with holy Scripture, as is taught us by holy Scripture itself. The Apostle Paul writes: *Therefore, brethren, stand fast, and hold the traditions which ye have been taught, whether by word or our epistle.* 2 Thess. ii. 15.

24. Why is tradition necessary even now?

As a guide to the right understanding of holy Scripture, for the right ministration of the sacraments, and the preservation of sacred rites and ceremonies in the purity of their original institution.

St. Basil the Great says of this as follows: *Of the doctrines and injunctions kept by the Church, some we have from written instruction,*

*but some we have received from apostolical tradition, by succession in
private. Both the former and the latter have one and the same force
for piety, and this will be contradicted by no one who has ever so little
knowledge in the ordinances of the Church; for were we to dare to
reject unwritten customs, as if they had no great importance, we should
insensibly mutilate the Gospel, even in the most essential points, or,
rather, for the teaching of the Apostles leave but an empty name. For
instance, let us mention before all else the very first and commonest act
of Christians, that they who trust in the name of our Lord Jesus Christ
should sign themselves with the sign of the cross—who hath taught
this by writing? To turn to the east in prayer—what Scripture have
we for this? The words of invocation in the change of the Eucharistic bread and of the Cup of blessing—by which of the Saints have
they been left us in writing? for we are not content with those
words which the Apostle or the Gospel records, but both before them
and after them we pronounce others also, which we hold to be of great
force for the sacrament, though we have received them from unwritten
teaching. By what Scripture is it, in like manner, that we bless the
water of baptism, the oil of unction, and the person himself who is
baptized? Is it not by a silent and secret tradition? What more?
The very practice itself of anointing with oil—what written word
have we for it? Whence is the rule of trine immersion? and the rest
of the ceremonies at baptism, the renunciation of Satan and his angels?—from what Scripture are they taken? Are they not all from
this unpublished and private teaching, which our Fathers kept under
a reserve inaccessible to curiosity and profane disquisition, having
been taught as a first principle to guard by silence the sanctity of the
mysteries? for how were it fit to publish in writing the doctrine of
those things, on which the unbaptized may not so much as look?*
(Can. xcvii. De Spir. Sanct. c. xxvii.)

On Holy Scripture in Particular.

25. When were the sacred books written?

At different times: some before the birth of Christ, others after.

26. Have not these two divisions of the sacred books each their own names?

They have. Those written before the birth of Christ are called the
books of the *Old Testament*, while those written after are called the
books of the *New Testament*.

27. What are the *Old* and *New Testaments?*

In other words, the old and new Covenants of God with men.

28. In what consisted the *Old Testament?*

In this, that God promised men a divine Saviour, and prepared them to receive him.

29. How did God prepare men to receive the Saviour?

Through gradual revelations, by prophecies and types.

30. In what consists the *New Testament?*

In this, that God has actually given men a divine Saviour, his own only-begotten Son, Jesus Christ.

31. How many are the books of the Old Testament?

St. Cyril of Jerusalem, St. Athanasius the Great, and St. John Damascene reckon them at *twenty-two*, agreeing therein with the Jews, who so reckon them in the original Hebrew tongue. (Athanas. Ep. xxxix. De Test.; J. Damasc. Theol. lib. iv. c. 17.)

32. Why should we attend to the reckoning of the Hebrews?

Because, as the Apostle Paul says, *unto them were committed the oracles of God;* and the sacred books of the Old Testament have been received from the Hebrew Church of that Testament by the Christian Church of the New. Rom. iii. 2.

33. How do St. Cyril and St. Athanasius enumerate the books of the Old Testament?

As follows: 1, The book of Genesis; 2, Exodus; 3, Leviticus; 4, the book of Numbers; 5, Deuteronomy; 6, the book of Jesus the son of Nun; 7, the book of Judges, and with it, as an appendix, the book of Ruth; 8, the first and second books of Kings, as two parts of one book; 9, the third and fourth books of Kings; 10, the first and second books of Paralipomena; 11, the first book of Esdras, and the second, or, as it is entitled in Greek, the book of Nehemiah; 12, the book of Esther; 13, the book of Job; 14, the Psalms; 15, the Proverbs of Solomon; 16, Ecclesiastes, also by Solomon; 17, the Song of Songs, also by Solomon; 18, the book of the Prophet Isaiah; 19, of Jeremiah; 20, of Ezekiel; 21, of Daniel; 22, of the Twelve Prophets.

34. Why is there no notice taken in this enumeration of the books of the Old Testament of the book of the Wisdom of the son of Sirach, and of certain others?

Because they do not exist in the Hebrew.

35. How are we to regard these last-named books?

Athanasius the Great says that they have been appointed of the

Fathers to be read by proselytes who are preparing for admission into the Church.

36. Is there any division of the books of the Old Testament by which you can give a more distinct account of their contents?

They may be divided into the four following classes:

1. Books *of the Law*, which form the basis of the Old Testament.

2. *Historical* books, which contain principally the history of religion.

3. *Doctrinal*, which contain the doctrine of religion.

4. *Prophetical*, which contain prophecies, or predictions of things future, and especially of Jesus Christ.

37. Which are the books *of the Law?*

The five books written by Moses—Genesis, Exodus, Leviticus, Numbers, and Deuteronomy.

Jesus Christ himself gives to these books the general name of *the Law of Moses.* Luke xxiv. 44.

38. What in particular is contained in the book of Genesis?

The account of the creation of the world and of man, and afterwards the history and ordinances of religion in the first ages of mankind.

39. What is contained in the other four books of Moses?

The history of religion in the time of the Prophet Moses, and the Law given through him from God.

40. Which are the *historical* books of the Old Testament?

The books of Jesus the son of Nun, Judges, Ruth, Kings, Paralipomena, the book of Esdras, and the books of Nehemiah and Esther.

41. Which are the *doctrinal?*

The book of Job, the Psalms, and the books of Solomon.

42. What should we remark in particular of the book of Psalms?

This book, together with the doctrine of religion, contains also allusions to its history, and many prophecies of our Saviour Christ. It is a perfect manual of prayer and praise, and on this account is in continual use in the divine service of the Church.

43. Which books are *prophetical?*

Those of the Prophets—Isaiah, Jeremiah, Ezekiel, Daniel, and the twelve others.

44. How many are the books of the New Testament?

Twenty-seven.

45. Are there among these any which answer to the books of the *Law*, or form the basis of the New Testament?

Yes. The *Gospel*, which consists of the four books of the Evangelists, Matthew, Mark, Luke, and John.

46. What means the word *Gospel?*

It is the same as the Greek work *Evangely*, and means good or joyful tidings.

47. Of what have we good tidings in the books called the Gospel?

Of the Divinity of our Lord Jesus Christ, of his advent and life on earth, of his miracles and saving doctrine, and, finally, of his death upon the cross, his glorious resurrection, and ascension into heaven.

48. Why are these books called the Gospel?

Because man can have no better nor more joyful tidings than these, of a Divine Saviour and everlasting salvation. For the same cause, whenever the Gospel is read in the church, it is prefaced and accompanied by the joyful exclamation, *Glory be to thee, O Lord, glory be to thee.*

49. Are any of the books of the New Testament *historical?*

Yes. One: the book of the *Acts of the holy Apostles.*

50. Of what does it give an account?

Of the descent of the Holy Ghost on the Apostles, and of the extension through them of Christ's Church.

51. What is an *Apostle?*

The word means a *messenger.* It is the name given to those disciples of our Lord Jesus Christ whom he sent to preach the Gospel.

52. Which books of the New Testament are *doctrinal?*

The seven general Epistles: namely, one of the Apostle James, two of Peter, three of John, and one of Jude; and fourteen Epistles of the Apostle Paul: namely, one to the Romans, two to the Corinthians, one to the Galatians, one to the Ephesians, one to the Philippians, one to the Colossians, two to the Thessalonians, two to Timothy, one to Titus, one to Philemon, and one to the Hebrews.

53. Are there also among the books of the New Testament any *prophetical?*

Such is the book of the *Apocalypse.*

54. What means this word *Apocalypse?*

It is Greek, and means *revelation.*

55. What are the contents of this book?

A mystical representation of the future destinies of the Christian Church, and of the whole world.

56. What rules must we observe in reading holy Scripture?

First, we must read it devoutly, as the Word of God, and with prayer to understand it aright; secondly, we must read it with a pure desire of instruction in faith, and incitement to good works; thirdly, we must take and understand it in such sense as agrees with the interpretation of the orthodox Church and the holy Fathers.

57. When the Church proposes the doctrine of Divine Revelation and of holy Scripture to people for the first time, what signs does she offer that it is really the Word of God?

Signs of this are the following:

1. The sublimity of this doctrine, which witnesses that it can not be any invention of man's reason.

2. The purity of this doctrine, which shows that it is from the all-pure mind of God.

3. Prophecies.

4. Miracles.

5. The mighty effect of this doctrine upon the hearts of men, beyond all but divine power.

58. In what way are *prophecies* signs of a true revelation from God?

This may be shown by an example. When the Prophet Isaiah foretold the birth of the Saviour Christ from a virgin, a thing which the natural reason of man could not have so much as imagined, and when, some hundred years after this prophecy, our Lord Jesus Christ was born of the most pure Virgin Mary, it was impossible not to see that the prophecy was the word of the Omniscient, and its fulfillment the work of the Almighty God. Wherefore also the holy Evangelist Matthew, when relating the birth of Christ, brings forward the prophecy of Isaiah: *But all this was done, that it might be fulfilled which was spoken of the Lord by the Prophet, saying: Behold a Virgin shall be with child, and shall bring forth a son, and they shall call his name Emmanuel, which, being interpreted, is, God with us.* Matt. i. 22, 23.

59. What are *miracles?*

Acts which can be done by no power or art of man, but only by the almighty power of God: for example, to raise the dead.

60. How do miracles serve for a sign that the word spoken is from God?

He who does true miracles works by the power of God; consequently he is in favor with God, and partaker of the divine Spirit; but to such it must belong to speak only the pure truth; and so, when such a man speaks in God's name, we are sure that by his mouth there speaketh really the Word of God.

On this account our Lord Jesus Christ himself owns miracles as a powerful testimony to his divine mission: *The works which the Father hath given me to finish, the same works that I do, bear witness of me, that the Father hath sent me.* John v. 36.

61. Whence may we more particularly see the *mighty effect* of the doctrine of Christ?

From this: that twelve Apostles, taken from among poor and unlearned people, of the lowest class, by this doctrine overcame and subdued to Christ the mighty, the wise, and the rich, kings and their kingdoms.

The Composition of the Catechism.

62. What may be a good order for setting forth a catechetical instruction in religion?

For this we may follow the book of the Orthodox Confession, approved by the Eastern Patriarchs, and take as our basis the saying of the Apostle Paul, that the whole energies of a Christian, during this present life, consist in these three: faith, hope, charity. *And now abideth faith, hope, charity; these three.* 1 Cor. xiii. 13.

And so the Christian needs: First, Doctrine on *faith* in God, and on the Sacraments which he reveals; Secondly, Doctrine on *hope* towards God, and on the means of being grounded in it; Thirdly, Doctrine on *love* to God, and all that he commands us to love.

63. What does the Church use as her instrument to introduce us to the doctrine of faith?

The *Creed.*

64. What may we take as a guide for the doctrine of hope?

Our Lord's *Beatitudes* and the *Lord's Prayer.*

65. Where may we find the elements of the doctrine of charity?

In the *Ten Commandments* of the Law of God.

THE FIRST PART OF THE ORTHODOX CATECHISM.

ON FAITH.

ON THE CREED GENERALLY, AND ON ITS ORIGIN.

66. What is the Creed?

The Creed is an exposition, in few but precise words, of that doc trine which all Christians are bound to believe.

67. What are the words of this exposition?

They are as follows:

1. *I believe in one God the Father, Almighty, Maker of heaven and earth, and of all things visible and invisible;*

2. *And in one Lord Jesus Christ, the Son of God, the only-begotten, begotten of the Father before all worlds, Light of light, very God of very God, begotten, not made, of one substance with the Father, by whom all things were made;*

3. *Who for us men, and for our salvation, came down from heaven, and was incarnate of the Holy Ghost, and of the Virgin Mary, and was made man;*

4. *And was crucified for us, under Pontius Pilate, and suffered, and was buried;*

5. *And rose again the third day according to the Scripture;*

6. *And ascended into heaven, and sitteth on the right hand of the Father;*

7. *And he shall come again with glory to judge the quick and the dead, whose kingdom shall have no end.*

8. *And I believe in the Holy Ghost, the Lord, the Giver of life, who proceedeth from the Father, who with the Father and the Son together is worshiped and glorified, who spake by the Prophets.*

9. *I believe one Holy, Catholic, and Apostolic Church.*

10. *I acknowledge one baptism for the remission of sins.*

11. *I look for the resurrection of the dead;*

12. *And the life of the world to come. Amen.*

68. From whom have we this exposition of the faith?

From the Fathers of the first and second œcumenical Councils.

69. What is an *œcumenical Council?*

An assembly of the Pastors and Doctors of the Catholic Church of

Christ, as far as possible, from the whole world, for the confirmation of true doctrine and holy discipline among Christians.

70. How many œcumenical Councils have there been?

Seven: 1, Of Nicæa; 2, Of Constantinople; 3, Of Ephesus; 4, Of Chalcedon; 5, The second of Constantinople; 6, The third of Constantinople; 7, The second of Nicæa.

71. Whence is the rule for assembling Councils?

From the example of the Apostles, who held a Council in Jerusalem. Acts xv.   This is grounded also upon the words of Jesus Christ himself, which give to the decisions of the Church such weight that whosoever disobeys them is left deprived of grace as a heathen.   But the mean, by which the œcumenical Church utters her decisions, is an œcumenical Council.

Tell it unto the Church; but if he neglect to hear the Church, let him be unto thee as a heathen man and a publican.   Matt. xviii. 17.

72. What were the particular occasions for assembling the first and second œcumenical Councils, at which the Creed was defined?

The first was held for the confirmation of the true doctrine respecting the Son of God, against the error of Arius, who thought unworthily of the Son of God; the second for the confirmation of the true doctrine respecting the Holy Ghost, against Macedonius, who thought unworthily of the Holy Ghost.

73. Is it long ago that these Councils were held?

The first was held in the year 325 from the birth of Christ; the second in 381.

ON THE ARTICLES OF THE CREED.

74. What method shall we follow in order the better to understand the œcumenical Creed?

We must notice its division into twelve *articles* or *parts*, and consider each article separately.

75. What is spoken of in each several article of the Creed?

The first article of the Creed speaks of *God* as the prime origin, more particularly of the *first Person of the Holy Trinity*, God the *Father*, and of God as the *Creator* of the world;

The second article, of the *second Person* of the Holy Trinity, Jesus Christ, the Son of God;

The third article, of the *incarnation* of the Son of God;

The fourth article, of the *suffering* and *death* of Jesus Christ;

The fifth article, of the *resurrection* of Jesus Christ;

The sixth article, of the *ascension* of Jesus Christ into heaven;

The seventh article, of the *second coming* of Jesus Christ upon earth;

The eighth article, of the *third Person* of the Holy Trinity, the Holy Ghost;

The ninth article, of the *Church;*

The tenth article, of *Baptism,* under which are implied the other *Sacraments* also;

The eleventh article, of the future *resurrection of the dead;*

The twelfth article, of the *life everlasting.*

On the First Article.

76. What is it to believe in God?

To believe in God is to have a lively belief of his being, his attributes, and works; and to receive with all the heart his revealed Word respecting the salvation of men.

77. Can you show from holy Scripture that faith in God must consist in this?

The Apostle Paul writes: *Without faith it is impossible to please God; for he that cometh to God must believe that he is, and that he is a rewarder of them that diligently seek him.* Heb. xi. 6.

The same Apostle expresses the effect of faith on Christians in the following prayer for them to God: *That he would grant you, according to the riches of his glory, to be strengthened with might by his Spirit in the inner man, that Christ may dwell in your hearts by faith.* Eph. iii. 16, 17.

78. What must be the immediate and constant effect of a hearty faith in God?

The confession of this same faith.

79. What is the confession of the faith?

It is openly to avow that we hold the orthodox faith, and this with such sincerity and firmness that neither seductions, nor threats, nor tortures, nor death itself may be able to make us deny our faith in the true God and in our Lord Jesus Christ.

80. For what is the confession of the faith necessary?

The Apostle Paul witnesses that it is necessary for salvation. *For*

*with the heart man believeth unto righteousness, and with the mouth
confession is made unto salvation.* Rom. x. 10.

81. Why is it necessary to salvation not only to believe, but also to confess the orthodox
faith?

Because if any one, to preserve his temporal life or earthly goods,
shrink from confessing the orthodox faith, he shows thereby that he
has not a true faith in God the Saviour, and the life of happiness to
come.

82. Why is it not said in the Creed simply, *I believe in God,* rather than with the addition,
in one God?

In order to contradict the error of the heathen, who, taking the creature for God, thought there were many gods.

83. What does holy Scripture teach us of the unity of God?

The very words of the Creed on this point are taken from the following passage of the Apostle Paul: *There is none other God but one.
For though there be that are called gods, whether in heaven or on
earth, as there be gods many, and lords many, but to us there is but
one God, the Father, of whom are all things, and we in him; and one
Lord Jesus Christ, by whom are all things, and we by him.* 1 Cor.
viii. 4, 5, 6.

84. Can we know the very essence of God?

No.   It is above all knowledge, not of men only, but of angels.

85. How does holy Scripture speak on this point?

The Apostle Paul says, that God *dwelleth in the light, which no man
can approach unto, whom no man hath seen, nor can see.* 1 Tim.
vi. 16.

86. What idea of the essence and essential attributes of God may be derived from divine
revelation?

That God is a Spirit, eternal, all-good, omniscient, all-just, almighty,
omnipresent, unchangeable, all-sufficing to himself, all-blessed.

87. Show all this from holy Scripture.

Jesus Christ himself has said that *God is a Spirit.*   John iv. 24.

Of the eternity of God David says: *Before the mountains were
brought forth, or ever the earth and the world were made, Thou art
from everlasting and world without end.*   Psalm xc. 2.   In the Apocalypse we read the following doxology to God: *Holy, Holy, Holy,
Lord God Almighty, which was, and is, and is to come.*   Apoc. iv. 8.

The Apostle Paul says that the Gospel was made manifest *according to the commandment of the everlasting God.* Rom. xvi. 26.

Of the goodness of God Jesus Christ himself said: *There is none good but one, that is God.* Matt. xix. 17. The Apostle John says: *God is Love.* 1 John iv. 16. David sings: *The Lord is gracious and merciful, long-suffering, and of great goodness. The Lord is loving unto every man, and his mercies are over all his works.* Psalm cxlv. 8, 9.

Of the omniscience of God the Apostle John says: *God is greater than our heart, and knoweth all things.* 1 John iii. 20. The Apostle Paul exclaims: *O the depth of the riches both of the wisdom and knowledge of God! how unsearchable are his judgments, and his ways past finding out.* Rom. xi. 33.

Of the justice of God David sings: *The righteous Lord loveth righteousness, his countenance will behold the thing that is just.* Psalm xi. 8. The Apostle Paul says that *God will render to every man according to his deeds,* and that *there is no respect of persons with God.* Rom. ii. 6, 11.

Of the almighty power of God the Psalmist says: *He spake, and it was done; he commanded, and it stood fast.* Psalm xxxiii. 9. The archangel says in the Gospel: *With God nothing shall be impossible.* Luke i. 37.

The omnipresence of God David describes thus: *Whither shall I go from thy Spirit? or whither shall I go from thy presence? If I climb up into heaven, thou art there; if I go down to hell, thou art there also. If I take the wings of the morning, and remain in the uttermost parts of the sea, even there shall thy hand lead me, and thy right hand shall hold me. If I say, Peradventure the darkness shall cover me; then shall my night be turned to day. Yea, the darkness is no darkness with thee, but the night is as clear as the day; the darkness and light to thee are both alike.* Psalm cxxxix. 6–11.

The Apostle James says that *With the Father of lights there is no variableness, neither shadow of turning.* James i. 17.

The Apostle Paul writes that *God receiveth not worship of men's hands as though he needed any thing, seeing he giveth to all life, and breath, and all things.* Acts xvii. 25. The same Apostle calls God *The blessed and only potentate, the King of kings and Lord of lords.* 1 Tim. vi. 15.

88. If God is a *Spirit*, how does holy Scripture ascribe to him bodily parts, as *heart*, *eyes*, *ears*, *hands?*

Holy Scripture in this suits itself to the common language of men; but we are to understand such expressions in a higher and spiritual sense. For instance, the heart of God means his *goodness* or love; eyes and ears mean his *omniscience;* hands, his *almighty power*.

89. If God is every where, how do men say that God is *in heaven*, or *in the church?*

God is every where; but in heaven he has a special presence manifested in everlasting glory to the blessed spirits; also in churches he has, through grace and sacraments, a special presence devoutly recognized and felt by believers, and manifested sometimes by extraordinary signs.

Jesus Christ says: *Where two or three are gathered together in my name, there am I in the midst of them.* Matt. xviii. 20.

90. How are we to understand these words of the Creed, *I believe in one God the Father?*

This is to be understood with reference to the mystery of the Holy Trinity; because God is one in substance but trine in persons—the Father, the Son, and the Holy Ghost—a Trinity consubstantial and undivided.

91. How does holy Scripture speak of the Blessed Trinity?

The chief texts on this point in the New Testament are the following: *Go ye therefore and teach all nations, baptizing them in the name of the Father, and of the Son, and of the Holy Ghost.* Matt. xxviii. 19. *There are three that bear record in heaven—the Father, the Word, and the Holy Ghost; and these three are one.* 1 John v. 7.

92. Is the Holy Trinity mentioned in the Old Testament also?

Yes; only not so clearly. For instance: *By the Word of the Lord were the heavens made, and all the hosts of them by the Breath of his mouth.* Psalm xxxiii. 6. *Holy, Holy, Holy is the Lord of Hosts: the whole earth is full of his glory.* Isaiah vi. 3.

93. How is one God in three Persons?

We can not comprehend this inner mystery of the Godhead; but we believe it on the infallible testimony of the Word of God. *The things of God knoweth no man, but the Spirit of God.* 1 Cor. ii. 11.

94. What *difference* is there between the Persons of the Holy Trinity?

God the Father is neither begotten, nor proceeds from any other Person: the Son of God is from all eternity begotten of the Father: the Holy Ghost from all eternity proceeds from the Father.

95. Are the three Hypostases or Persons of the Most Holy Trinity all of equal majesty?

Yes; all of absolutely equal divine majesty. The Father is true God, the Son equally true God, and the Holy Ghost true God; but yet so that in the three Persons there is only one Tri-personal God.

96. Why is God called the *Almighty* (Παντοκράτορα)?

Because he upholds all things by his power and his will.

97. What is expressed by the words of the Creed, *Maker of heaven and earth, and of all things visible and invisible?*

This: that all was made by God, and that nothing can be without God

98. Are not these words taken from holy Scripture?

They are. The book of Genesis begins thus: *In the beginning God created the heaven and the earth.*

The Apostle Paul, speaking of Jesus Christ, the Son of God, says: *By him were all things created, that are in heaven, and that are in earth, visible and invisible, whether they be thrones, or dominions, or principalities, or powers: all things were created by him, and for him.* Coloss. i. 16.

99. What is meant in the Creed by the word *invisible?*

The *invisible* or *spiritual world*, to which belong the *angels.*

100. What are the *angels?*

Incorporeal spirits, having intelligence, will, and power.

101. What means the name *angel?*

It means a *messenger.*

102. Why are they so called?

Because God sends them to announce his will. Thus, for instance, Gabriel was sent to announce to the Most Holy Virgin Mary the conception of the Saviour.

103. Which was created first, the *visible* world or the *invisible?*

The invisible was created before the visible, and the angels before men. (Orthod. Confess. Pt. I. Q. 18.)

104. Can we find any testimony to this in holy Scripture?

In the book of Job God himself speaks of the earth thus: *Who laid the corner-stone thereof? When the stars were* CREATED, *all my angels praised me with a loud voice.* Job xxxviii. 6, 7.

105. Whence is taken the name of *guardian* angels?

From the following words of holy Scripture: *He shall give his angels charge over thee, to guard thee in all thy ways.* Psalm xci. 11.

106. Has each one of us his guardian angels?

Without doubt. Of this we may be assured from the following words of Jesus Christ: *Take heed that ye despise not one of these little ones: for I say unto you, that in heaven their angels do always behold the face of my Father, which is in heaven.* Matt. xviii. 10.

107. Are all angels good and beneficent?

No. There are also evil angels, otherwise called devils.

108. How came they to be evil?

They were created good, but they swerved from their duty of perfect obedience to God, and so fell away from him into self-will, pride, and malice. According to the words of the Apostle Jude, they are *the angels which kept not their first estate, but left their own habitation.* Jude 6.

109. What means the name *devil?*

It means *slanderer* or *deceiver.*

110. Why are the evil angels called devils—that is, slanderers or deceivers?

Because they are ever laying snares for men, seeking to deceive them, and inspire them with false notions and evil wishes.

Of this Jesus Christ, speaking to the unbelieving Jews, says: *Ye are of your father the devil, and the lusts of your father ye will do. He was a murderer from the beginning, and abode not in the truth, because there is no truth in him. When he speaketh a lie, he speaketh of his own, for he is a liar and the father of it.* John viii. 44.

111. What has holy Scripture revealed to us of the creation of the world?

In the beginning God created from nothing the heaven and the earth; and the earth was without form and void. Afterwards God successively produced: on the *first day* of the world, light; on the *second*, the firmament or visible heaven; on the *third*, the gathering together of waters on the earth, the dry land, and what grows thereupon; on the *fourth*, the sun, moon, and stars; on the *fifth*, fishes and birds; on the *sixth*, four-footed creatures living on the earth, and lastly, man With man the creation finished; and on the *seventh* day God rested from all his works. Hence the seventh day was called the *sabbath*, which in the Hebrew tongue means *rest*. Gen. ii. 2.

112. Were the visible creatures created such as we see them now?

No. At the creation every thing was *very good*, that is, pure, beautiful, and harmless.

113. Are we not informed of something particular in the creation of man?

God in the Holy Trinity said : *Let us make man in our own image, and after our likeness.* Gen. i. 26. And God made the body of the first man, *Adam,* from the earth; breathed into his nostrils the breath of life; brought him into Paradise; gave him for food, beside the other fruits of Paradise, the fruit of the tree of life; and lastly, having taken a rib from Adam while he slept, made from it the first woman, *Eve.* Gen. ii. 22.

114. In what consists the *image of God?*

It consists, as explained by the Apostle Paul, *In righteousness and holiness of truth.* Eph. iv. 24.

115. What is the *breath of life?*

The soul, a substance spiritual and immortal.

116. What is *Paradise?*

The word Paradise means a *garden.* It is the name given to the fair and blissful abode of the first man, described in the book of Genesis as like a garden.

117. Was the Paradise in which man first lived material or spiritual?

For the body it was material, a visible and blissful abode; but for the soul it was spiritual, a state of communion by grace with God, and spiritual contemplation of the creatures. (Greg. Theol. Serm. xxxviii. 42; J. Damasc. Theol. lib. ii. cap. 12, § 3.)

118. What was the *tree of life?*

A tree, by feeding on whose fruit man would have been, even in the body, free from disease and death.

119. Why was Eve made *from a rib* of Adam?

To the intent that all mankind might be by origin naturally disposed to love and defend one another.

120. With what design did God create man?

With this, that he should know God, love, and glorify him, and so be happy forever.

121. Has not that will of God, by which man is designed for eternal happiness, its own proper name in theology?

It is called the *predestination* of God.

122. Does God's predestination of man to happiness remain unchanged, seeing that now man is not happy?

It remains unchanged; inasmuch as God, of his foreknowledge and

infinite mercy, hath predestined to open for man, even after his departure from the way of happiness, a new way to happiness, through his
only-begotten Son Jesus Christ.

He hath chosen us, in him, before the foundation of the world, are
the words of the Apostle Paul. Eph. i. 4.

123. How are we to understand the predestination of God, with respect to men in general,
and to each man severally?

God has predestined to give to all men, and has actually given them
preparatory grace, and means sufficient for the attainment of happiness.[1]

124. What is said of this by the Word of God?

For whom he did foreknow, he also did predestinate. Rom. viii. 29.

125. How does the orthodox Church speak on this point?

In the exposition of the faith by the Eastern Patriarchs it is said:
*As he foresaw that some would use well their free will, but others ill,
he accordingly predestined the former to glory, while the latter he condemned.* (Art. iii.)

126. What divine energy with respect to the world, and especially to man, follows immediately upon their creation?

Divine providence.

127. What is divine providence?

Divine providence is the constant energy of the almighty power,
wisdom, and goodness of God, by which he preserves the being and
faculties of his creatures, directs them to good ends, and assists all that
is good; but the evil that springs by departure from good he either
cuts off, or corrects it, and turns it to good results.

128. How does holy Scripture speak of God's providence?

Jesus Christ himself says: *Behold the fowls of the air, for they sow
not, neither do they reap, nor gather into barns; yet your heavenly
Father feedeth them. Are ye not much better than they?* Matt. vi. 26.
From these words is shown at once God's general providence over the
creatures, and his special providence over man.

The whole of the ninety-first Psalm is a description of God's special
and manifold providence over man.

---

[1] The Greek and the German edition have the following addition: 'But those who freely
accept the grace given them, who make good use of the means of grace granted unto them,
and who walk in the appointed path of salvation, God has properly foreordained for salvation.'

ON THE SECOND ARTICLE.

129. How are we to understand the names *Jesus Christ, the Son of God?*

Son of God is the name of the second Person of the Holy Trinity in respect of his Godhead : This same Son of God was called *Jesus*, when he was conceived and born on earth as man ; *Christ* is the name given him by the Prophets, while they were as yet expecting his advent upon earth.

130. What means the name *Jesus?*

Saviour.

131. By whom was the name Jesus first given ?

By the Angel Gabriel.

132. Why was this name given to the Son of God at his conception and birth on earth ?

Because he was conceived and born to *save* men.

133. What means the name *Christ?*

Anointed.

134. Whence came the name *Anointed?*

From the anointing with holy ointment, through which are bestowed the gifts of the Holy Ghost.

135. Is it only Jesus, the Son of God, who is called *Anointed?*

No. *Anointed* was in old time a title of *kings, high-priests*, and *prophets.*

136. Why, then, is Jesus, the Son of God, called *The Anointed?*

Because to his manhood were imparted without measure all the gifts of the Holy Ghost ; and so he possesses in the highest degree the *knowledge* of a prophet, the *holiness* of a high-priest, and the *power* of a king.

137. In what sense is Jesus Christ called *Lord?*

In this sense : that he is *very God ;* for the name *Lord* is one of the names of God.

138. What says holy Scripture of the divinity of Jesus Christ, the Son of God ?

In the beginning was the Word, and the Word was with God, and the Word was God. John i. 1.

139. Why is Jesus Christ called the Son of God, *Only-begotten?*

By this is signified that he only is the Son of God begotten of the substance of God the Father ; and so is *of one substance* with the Father ; and consequently excels, beyond comparison, all holy angels and holy men, who are called sons of God *by grace.* John i. 12.

140. Does holy Scripture call Jesus the *Only-begotten?*

It does. For instance, in the following places of the Evangelist John : *The Word was made flesh, and dwelt among us, and we beheld his glory, the glory as of the Only-begotten of the Father, full of grace and truth.* John i. 14. *No man hath seen God at any time; the Only-begotten Son, which is in the bosom of the Father, he hath declared him.* John i. 18.

141. Why in the Creed is it said further of the Son of God that he is *begotten of the Father?*

By this is expressed that personal property by which he is distinguished from the other Persons of the Holy Trinity.

142. Why is it said that he is begotten *before all worlds?*

That none should think there was ever a time when he was not. In other words, by this is expressed that Jesus Christ is the Son of God from everlasting, even as God the Father is from everlasting.

143. What mean in the Creed the words *Light of light?*

Under the figure of the visible light they in some manner explain the incomprehensible generation of the Son of God from the Father. When we look at the sun, we see light : from this light is generated the light visible every where beneath; but both the one and the other is one light, indivisible, and of one nature. In like manner, God the Father is the everlasting *Light.* 1 John i. 5. Of him is begotten the Son of God, who also is the everlasting Light; but God the Father and God the Son are one and the same everlasting Light, indivisible, and of one divine nature.

144. What force is there in the words of the Creed, *Very God of very God?*

This : that the Son of God is called God in the same proper sense as God the Father.

145. Are not these words from holy Scripture?

Yes. They are taken from the following passage of John the Divine : *We know that the Son of God is come, and hath given us [light and] understanding, that we may know the true God, and be in him that is true, in his Son Jesus Christ. This is the true God and eternal life.* 1 John v. 20.

146. Why is it further added of the Son of God in the Creed that he is *begotten, not made?*

This was added against Arius, who impiously taught that the Son of God was made.

147. What mean the words, *Of one substance with the Father?*

They mean that the Son of God is of one and the same divine substance with God the Father.

148. How does holy Scripture speak of this?

Jesus Christ himself speaks of himself and of God the Father thus: *I and the Father are one.* John x. 30.

149. What is shown by the next words in the Creed, *By whom all things were made?*

This: that God the Father created all things by his Son, as by his eternal Wisdom and his eternal Word.

All things were made by him, and without him was not any thing made which was made. John i. 3.

ON THE THIRD ARTICLE.

150. Of whom is it said in the Creed, that he *came down from heaven?*

Of the Son of God.

151. How came he down from heaven, seeing that as God he is every where?

It is true that he is every where; and so he is always in heaven, and always on earth; but on earth he was before invisible; afterwards he appeared in the flesh. In this sense it is said that he *came down from heaven.*

152. How does holy Scripture speak of this?

I will repeat Jesus Christ's own words: *No man hath ascended up to heaven but he that came down from heaven, even the Son of Man which is in heaven.* John iii. 13.

153. Wherefore did the Son of God come down from heaven?

For *us men, and for our salvation,* as it is said in the Creed.

154. In what sense is it said that the Son of God came down from heaven for *us men?*

In this sense: that he came upon earth not for one nation, nor for some men only, but for *us men* universally.

155. To save men from what did he come upon earth?

From sin, the curse, and death.

156. What is *sin?*

Transgression of the law. *Sin is the transgression of the law.* 1 John iii. 4.

157. Whence is sin in men, seeing that they were created in the image of God, and God can not sin?

From the devil. *He that committeth sin is of the devil; for the devil sinneth from the beginning.* 1 John iii. 8.

158. How did sin pass from the devil to men?

The devil deceived Eve and Adam, and induced them to transgress God's commandment.

159. What commandment?

God commanded Adam in Paradise not to eat of the fruit of the *Tree of the knowledge of good and evil*, and withal told him, that so soon as he ate thereof he should surely die.

160. Why did it bring death to man to eat of the fruit of the *Tree of the knowledge of good and evil?*

Because it involved disobedience to God's will, and so separated man from God and his grace, and alienated him from the life of God.

161. What propriety is there in the name of *the Tree of the knowledge of good and evil?*

Man through this tree came to know by the act itself what good there is in obeying the will of God, and what evil in disobeying it.

162. How could Adam and Eve listen to the devil against the will of God?

God of his goodness, at the creation of man, gave him *a will* naturally disposed to love God, but still *free;* and man used this freedom *for evil.*

163. How did the devil deceive Adam and Eve?

Eve saw in Paradise a serpent, which assured her that if men ate of the fruit of the tree of the knowledge of good and evil, they would know good and evil, and would become as gods. Eve was deceived by this promise, and by the fairness of the fruit, and ate of it. Adam ate after her example.

164. What came of Adam's sin?

The curse, and death.

165. What is the *curse?*

The condemnation of sin by God's just judgment, and the evil which from sin came upon the earth for the punishment of men. God said to Adam, *Cursed is the ground for thy sake.* Gen. iii. 17.

166. What is the *death* which came from the sin of Adam?

It is twofold: *bodily,* when the body loses the soul which quickened it; and *spiritual,* when the soul loses the grace of God, which quickened it with the higher and spiritual life.

167. Can the soul, then, die as well as the body?

It can die, but not so as the body. The body, when it dies, loses sense, and is dissolved; the soul, when it dies by sin, loses spiritual

light, joy, and happiness, but is not dissolved nor annihilated, but remains in a state of darkness, anguish, and suffering.

168. Why did not the first man only die, and not all, as now?

Because all have come of Adam since his infection by sin, and all sin themselves. As from an infected source there naturally flows an infected stream, so from a father infected with sin, and consequently mortal, there naturally proceeds a posterity infected like him with sin, and like him mortal.

169. How is this spoken of in holy Scripture?

By one man sin entered into the world, and death by sin, and so death passed upon all men, for that all have sinned. Rom. v. 12.

170. Had man any benefit from the fruit of the tree of life after he had sinned?

After he had sinned, he could no more eat of it, for he was driven out of Paradise.

171. Had men, then, any hope left of salvation?

When our first parents had confessed before God their sin, God, of his mercy, gave them a hope of salvation.

172. In what consisted this hope?

God promised that the *seed of the woman should bruise the serpent's head.* Gen. iii. 15.

173. What did that mean?

This: that Jesus Christ should overcome the devil who had deceived men, and deliver them from sin, the curse, and death.

174. Why is Jesus Christ called *the seed of the woman?*

Because he was born on earth *without man*, from the Most Holy Virgin Mary.

175. What *benefit* was there in this promise?

This: that from the time of the promise men could *believe* savingly in the Saviour that was to come, even as we now believe in the Saviour that has come.

176. Did people, in fact, in old time believe in the Saviour that was to come?

Some did, but the greater part forgot God's promise of a Saviour.

177. Did not God repeat this promise?

More than once. For instance, he made to Abraham the promise of a Saviour in the following words: *In thy seed shall all the nations of the earth be blessed.* Gen. xxii. 18. The same promise he repeated afterwards to David in the following words: *I will set up thy seed*

after thee, and I will establish his throne forever. 2 Kings vii. 12, 13.

178. What do we understand by the word *incarnation?*

That the Son of God took to himself human flesh without sin, and was made man, without ceasing to be God.

179. Whence is taken the word *incarnation?*

From the words of the Evangelist John: *The Word was made flesh.* John i. 14.

180. Why in the Creed, after it has been said of the Son of God that he *was incarnate,* is it further added that he *was made man?*

To the end that none should imagine that the Son of God took only *flesh* or a body, but should acknowledge in him a *perfect man* consisting of body and soul.

181. Have we for this any testimony of holy Scripture?

The Apostle Paul writes: *There is one Mediator between God and men, the man Christ Jesus.* 1 Tim. ii. 5.

182. And so is there only one nature in Jesus Christ?

No. There are in him, without separation and without confusion, *two natures,* the divine and the human, and answering to these natures two wills.

183. Are there not, therefore, two persons?

No. *One person,* God and man together; in one word, a *God-man.*

184. What says holy Scripture of the incarnation of the Son of God by the Holy Ghost of the Virgin Mary?

The Evangelist Luke relates that when the Virgin Mary had asked the angel, who announced to her the conception of Jesus, *How shall this be, seeing I know not a man?* The angel replied to her: *The Holy Ghost shall come upon thee, and the power of the Highest shall overshadow thee : therefore also that holy thing which shall be born of thee shall be called the Son of God.* Luke i. 34, 35.

185. Who was the Virgin Mary?

A holy virgin of the lineage of Abraham and David, from whose lineage the Saviour, by God's promise, was to come; betrothed to Joseph, a man of the same lineage, in order that he might be her guardian; for she was dedicated to God with a vow of perpetual virginity.

186. Did the Most Holy Mary remain, in fact, ever a virgin?

She remained and remains a virgin before the birth, during the birth,

and after the birth of the Saviour; and therefore is called *ever-virgin*.

187. What other great title is there with which the Orthodox Church honors the Most Holy Virgin Mary?

That of *Mother of God*.

188. Can you show the origin of this title in holy Scripture?

It is taken from the following words of the Prophet Isaiah: *Behold, a virgin shall conceive, and bear a Son, and they shall call his name Immanuel, which, being interpreted, is, God with us.* Isaiah vii. 14; Matt. i. 23.

So, also, the righteous Elisabeth calls the Most Holy Virgin *The Mother of the Lord;* which title is all one with that of Mother of God. *Whence is this to me, that the Mother of my Lord should come to me?* Luke i. 43.

189. In what sense is the Most Holy Virgin called Mother of God?

Although Jesus Christ was born of her not after his Godhead, which is eternal, but after the manhood, still she is rightly called the Mother of God; because he that was born of her was, both in the conception itself and in the birth from her, as he ever is, *very God*.

190. What thoughts should you have of the exalted dignity of the Most Holy Virgin Mary?

As Mother of the Lord she excels in grace and nearness to God, and so also in dignity, every created being; and therefore the Orthodox Church honors her far above the cherubim and seraphim.

191. What is there further to be remarked of the birth of Jesus Christ from the Most Holy Mother of God?

This: that since this birth was perfectly holy and void of sin, it was also without pain; for it was among the penalties of sin that God ordained Eve *in sorrows to bring forth children.* (J. Damasc. Theol. lib. iv. cap. 14, § 6.)

192. What tokens had God's providence prepared, that men might know the Saviour, when he was born to them?

Many exact predictions of various circumstances of his birth and life on earth. For instance, the Prophet Isaiah foretold that the Saviour should be born of a virgin. Isaiah vii. 14. The Prophet Micah foretold that the Saviour should be born in Bethlehem; and this prophecy the Jews understood even before they heard of its ful-

fillment. Matt. ii. 4–6. The Prophet Malachi, after the building of the second temple at Jerusalem, foretold that the coming of the Saviour was drawing nigh, that he should come to this temple, and that before him should be sent a forerunner like unto the Prophet Elias, clearly pointing by this to John the Baptist. Mal. iii. 1; iv. 5. The Prophet Zachariah foretold the triumphal entry of the Saviour into Jerusalem. Zach. ix. 9. The Prophet Isaiah, with wonderful clearness, foretold the sufferings of the Saviour. Isaiah liii. David, in the twenty-second Psalm, described the sufferings of the Saviour on the cross with as great exactness as if he had written at the foot of the cross itself. And Daniel, 490 years before, foretold the appearance of the Saviour, his death on the cross, and the subsequent destruction of the temple and of Jerusalem, and abolition of the Old Testament sacrifices. Dan. ix.

193. Did men, in fact, recognize Jesus Christ as the Saviour at the time that he was born and lived upon earth?

Many did recognize him by various ways. The wise men of the East recognized him by a star, which before his birth appeared in the East. The shepherds of Bethlehem knew of him from angels, who distinctly told them that the Saviour was born in the City of David. Simeon and Anna, by special revelation of the Holy Ghost, knew him when he was brought, forty days after his birth, into the temple. John the Baptist, at the river Jordan, at his baptism, knew him by revelation, by the descent of the Holy Ghost upon him in the form of a dove, and by a voice from heaven from God the Father: *This is my beloved Son, in whom I am well pleased.* Matt. iii. 17. A like voice was heard of him by the Apostles Peter, James, and John, at the time of his transfiguration on the mount: *This is my beloved Son, in whom I am well pleased: hear him.* Mark ix. 7. Besides this, very many recognized him by the excellence of his doctrine, and especially by the miracles which he wrought.

194. What miracles did Jesus Christ work?

People suffering under incurable diseases, and possessed by demons, were healed by him in the twinkling of an eye, by a single word, or by the touch of his hand, and even through their touching his garment. Once with five, at another time with seven loaves he fed in the wilderness several thousand men. He walked on the waters, and by a word

calmed the storm.   He raised the dead : the son of the widow of Nain, the daughter of Jairus, and Lazarus on the fourth day after his death.

195. You said that the Son of God was incarnate for our salvation : in what way did he effect it ?

By his doctrine, his life, his death, and resurrection.

196. What was Christ's doctrine ?

The Gospel of the kingdom of God, or, in other words, the doctrine of salvation and eternal happiness, the same that is now taught in the Orthodox Church.   Mark i. 14, 15.

197. How have we salvation by Christ's doctrine ?

When we receive it with all our heart, and walk according to it. For, as the lying words of the devil, received by our first parents, became in them the seed of sin and death; so, on the contrary, the true Word of Christ, heartily received by Christians, becomes in them the seed of a holy and immortal life.   They are, in the words of the Apostle Peter, *born again, not of corruptible seed, but of incorruptible, by the Word of God, which liveth and abideth forever.* 1 Peter i. 23.

198. How have we salvation by Christ's life ?

When we imitate it.   For he says, *If any one serve me, let him follow me; and where I am, there shall also my servant be.*   John xii. 26.

On the Fourth Article.

199. How came it to pass that Jesus Christ was *crucified*, when his doctrine and works should have moved all to reverence him?

The elders of the Jews and the scribes hated him, because he rebuked their false doctrine and evil lives, and envied him, because the people, which heard him teach and saw his miracles, esteemed him more than them ; and hence they falsely accused him, and condemned him to death.

200. Why is it said that Jesus Christ was crucified *under Pontius Pilate?*

To mark the time when he was crucified.

201. Who was Pontius Pilate?

The Roman governor of Judæa, which had become subject to the Romans.

202. Why is this circumstance worthy of remark ?

Because in it we see the fulfillment of Jacob's prophecy : *The sceptre*

shall not depart from Judah, nor a lawgiver from between his feet, until Shiloh come : and he is the desire of the nations. Gen. xlix. 10.

203. Why is it not only said in the Creed that Jesus Christ was *crucified*, but also added that he *suffered?*

To show that his crucifixion was not only a semblance of suffering and death, as some heretics said, but a real suffering and death.

204. Why is it also mentioned that he was *buried?*

This likewise is to assure us that he really died, and rose again; for his enemies even set a watch at his sepulchre, and sealed it.

205. How could Jesus Christ suffer and die when he was God?

He suffered and died, not in his Godhead, but in his manhood; and this not because he could not avoid it, but because it pleased him to suffer.

He himself had said : *I lay down my life, that I may take it again. No man taketh it from me, but I lay it down of myself. I have power to lay it down, and I have power to take it again.* John x. 17, 18.

206. In what sense is it said that Jesus Christ was *crucified for us?*

In this sense : that he, by his death on the cross, delivered us from *sin*, the *curse*, and *death*.

207. How does holy Scripture speak of this deliverance?

Of deliverance from sin : *In whom we have redemption through his blood, the forgiveness of sins, according to the riches of his grace.* Ephes. i. 7.

Of deliverance from the curse: *Christ has redeemed us from the curse of the law being made a curse for us.* Gal. iii. 13.

Of deliverance from death : *Forasmuch then as the children are partakers of flesh and blood, he also himself likewise took part of the same ; that through death he might destroy him that hath the power of death, that is, the devil; and deliver them who, through fear of death, were all their lifetime subject to bondage.* Heb. ii. 14, 15.

208. How does the death of Jesus Christ upon the cross deliver us from sin, the curse, and death?

That we may the more readily believe this mystery, the Word of God teaches us of it, so much as we may be able to receive, by the comparison of Jesus Christ with Adam. Adam is by nature the head of all mankind, which is one with him by natural descent from him.

Jesus Christ, in whom the Godhead is united with manhood, graciously
made himself the new almighty Head of men, whom he unites to himself through faith. Therefore as in Adam we had fallen under sin, the
curse, and death, so we are delivered from sin, the curse, and death in
Jesus Christ. His voluntary suffering and death on the cross for us,
being of infinite value and merit, as the death of one sinless, God and
man in one person, is both a perfect satisfaction to the justice of God,
which had condemned us for sin to death, and a fund of infinite merit,
which has obtained him the right, without prejudice to justice, to give
us sinners pardon of our sins, and grace to have victory over sin and
death.

*God hath willed to make known to his saints what is the riches of
the glory of this mystery of the Gentiles, which is Christ in you, the
hope of glory.* Col. i. 26, 27.

*For if by one man's offense death reigned by one, much more they
which receive abundance of grace and of the gift of righteousness shall
reign in life by one, Jesus Christ.* Rom. v. 17.

*There is therefore now no condemnation to them which are in
Christ Jesus, who walk not after the flesh, but after the spirit. For
the law of the spirit of life in Christ Jesus hath made me free from
the law of sin and death. For what the law could not do, in that it
was weak through the flesh, God sending his own Son in the likeness
of sinful flesh, and for sin, condemned sin in the flesh; that the righteousness of the law might be fulfilled in us, who walk not after the
flesh, but after the spirit.* Rom. viii. 1–4.

209. Was it for us all, strictly speaking, that Jesus Christ suffered?

For his part, he offered himself as a sacrifice strictly for all, and obtained for all grace and salvation; but this benefits only those of us
who, for their parts, of their own free will, have *fellowship in his sufferings, being made conformable unto his death.* Phil. iii. 10.

210. How can we *have fellowship in the sufferings and death of Jesus Christ?*

We have fellowship in the sufferings and death of Jesus Christ
through a lively and hearty faith, through the Sacraments, in which is
contained and sealed the virtue of his saving sufferings and death,
and, lastly, through the crucifixion of our flesh with its affections and
lusts.

I, says the Apostle, *through the law, am dead to the law, that I may*

live unto God. I am crucified with Christ: nevertheless I live; yet not I, but Christ liveth in me: and the life which I now live in the flesh I live by the faith of the Son of God, who loved me and gave himself for me. Gal. ii. 19, 20.

Know ye not, that as many of us as were baptized into Jesus Christ, were baptized into his death? Rom. vi. 3.

For as often as ye eat this bread, and drink this cup, ye do show the Lord's death till he come. 1 Cor. xi. 26.

They that are Christ's have crucified the flesh with the affections and lusts. Gal. v. 24.

211. How can we *crucify the flesh* with the affections and lusts?

By bridling the affections and lusts, and by doing what is contrary to them. For instance, when anger prompts us to revile an enemy and to do him harm, but we resist the wish, and, remembering how Jesus Christ on the cross prayed for his enemies, pray likewise for ours; we thus crucify the affection of anger.

ON THE FIFTH ARTICLE.

212. What is the first proof and earnest given by Jesus Christ that his sufferings and death have wrought salvation for us men?

This: that he rose again, and so laid the foundation for our like blessed resurrection.

Now is Christ risen from the dead, and become the first-fruits of them that slept. 1 Cor. xv. 20.

213. What should we think of the state in which Jesus Christ was after his death, and before his resurrection?

This is described in the following hymn of the Church: *In the grave as to the flesh, in hades with thy soul, as God, in paradise with the thief, and on the throne wert thou, O Christ, together with the Father and the Spirit, filling all things, thyself uncircumscribed.*

214. What is *hades* or *hell?*

Hades is a Greek word, and means a place *void of light.* In divinity, by this name is understood a spiritual prison, that is, the state of those spirits which are separated by sin from the sight of God's countenance, and from the light and blessedness which it confers. Jude i. 6; Octoich. tom. v.; sticher. ii. 4.

215. Wherefore did Jesus Christ descend into hell?

To the end that he might there also preach his victory over death, and deliver the souls which with faith awaited his coming.

216. Does holy Scripture speak of this?

It is referred to in the following passage: *For Christ also hath once suffered for sins, the just for the unjust, that he may bring us to God, being put to death in the flesh, but quickened in the Spirit; in which also he went and preached unto the spirits in prison.* 1 Pet. iii. 18, 19.

217. What is there for us to remark on the next words of the Creed : *and rose again the third day, according to the Scripture?*

These words were put into the Creed from the following passage in the Epistle to the Corinthians: *For I delivered unto you first of all that which I also received, how that Christ died for our sins, according to the Scripture; and that he was buried, and that he rose again the third day, according to the Scripture.* 1 Cor. xv. 3, 4.

218. What force is there in these words : *according to the Scripture?*

By this is shown that Jesus Christ died and rose again, precisely as had been written of him prophetically in the books of the Old Testament.

219. Where, for instance, is there any thing written of this?

In the fifty-third chapter of the book of the Prophet Isaiah, for instance, the suffering and death of Jesus Christ is imaged forth with many particular traits : as, *He was wounded for our transgressions, he was bruised for our iniquities : the chastisement of our peace was upon him; and with his stripes we are healed.* Isaiah liii. 5.

Of the resurrection of Christ the Apostle Peter quotes the words of the sixteenth Psalm: *For why? thou shalt not leave my soul in hell, neither shalt thou suffer thy holy one to see corruption.* Acts ii. 27.

220. Is this also in the Scripture of the Old Testament, that Jesus Christ should rise again precisely *on the third day?*

A prophetic type of this was set forth in the Prophet Jonah: *And Jonah was in the belly of the fish three days and three nights.* Jonah i. 17.

221. How was it known that Jesus Christ had risen?

The soldiers who watched his sepulchre knew this with terror, because an angel of the Lord rolled away the stone which closed his sepulchre, and at the same time there was a great earthquake. Angels

likewise announced the resurrection of Christ to Mary Magdalene and some others. Jesus Christ himself on the very day of his resurrection appeared to many: as to the women bringing spices, to Peter, to the two disciples going to Emmaus, and, lastly, to all the Apostles in the house, the doors being shut. Afterwards he oftentimes showed himself to them during the space of forty days; and one day he was seen of more than five hundred believers at once. 1 Cor. xv. 6.

222. Why did Jesus Christ after his resurrection show himself to the Apostles during the space of forty days?

During this time he continued to teach them the mysteries of the kingdom of God. Acts i. 3.

On the Sixth Article.

223. Is the statement of our Lord's ascension in the sixth article of the Creed taken from holy Scripture?

It is taken from the following passages of holy Scripture: *He that descended is the same also that ascended up far above all heavens, that he might fill all things.* Eph. iv. 10. *We have such a High-Priest, who is set on the right hand of the throne of the majesty in the heavens.* Heb. viii. 1.

224. Was it in his Godhead or his manhood that Jesus Christ ascended into heaven?

In his manhood. In his Godhead he ever was and is in heaven.

225. How does Jesus Christ *sit at the right hand of God the Father*, seeing that God is every where?

This must be understood spiritually; that is, Jesus Christ has one and the same majesty and glory with God the Father.

On the Seventh Article.

226. How does holy Scripture speak of Christ's coming again?

This Jesus, which is taken up from you into heaven, shall so come in like manner as ye have seen him go into heaven. Acts i. 11. This was said to the Apostles by angels at the very time of our Lord's ascension.

227. How does it speak of his future judgment?

The hour is coming, in which all that are in the graves shall hear the voice of the Son of God, and shall come forth: they that have done good, unto the resurrection of life; and they that have done evil,

unto the resurrection of damnation. John v. 28, 29. These are the words of Christ himself.

228. How does it speak of his kingdom which is to have no end?

He shall be great, and shall be called the Son of the Highest; and the Lord God shall give unto him the throne of his father David; and he shall reign over the house of Jacob forever; and of his kingdom there shall be no end. Luke i. 32, 33. These are the words of the angel to the Mother of God

229. Will the second coming of Christ be like his first?

No; very different. He came to suffer for us in great humility, but he shall come to judge us *in his glory, and all the holy angels with him.* Matt. xxv. 31.

230. Will he judge all men?

Yes. All, without exception.

231. How will he judge them?

The conscience of every man shall be laid open before all, and not only all deeds which he has ever done in his whole life upon earth be revealed, but also all the words he has spoken, and all his secret wishes and thoughts. *The Lord shall come, who will bring to light the hidden things of darkness, and will make manifest the counsels of the heart: and then shall every man have praise of God.* 1 Cor. iv. 5.

232. Will he then condemn us even for evil words or thoughts?

Without doubt he will, unless we efface them by repentance, faith, and amendment of life. *I say unto you, that every idle word that men shall speak, they shall give account thereof in the day of judgment.* Matt. xii. 36.

233. Will Jesus Christ soon come to judgment?

We know not. Therefore we should live so as to be always ready. *The Lord is not slack concerning his promise, as some men count slackness; but is long-suffering to us-ward, not willing that any should perish, but that all should come to repentance. But the day of the Lord will come as a thief in the night.* 2 Pet. iii. 9, 10. *Watch, therefore, for ye know neither the day nor the hour wherein the Son of man cometh.* Matt. xxv. 13.

234. Are there not, however, revealed to us some *signs* of the nearer approach of Christ's coming?

In the Word of God certain signs are revealed, as the decrease of

faith and love among men, the abounding of iniquity and calamities, the preaching of the Gospel to all nations, and the coming of Antichrist. Matt. xxiv.

235. What is *Antichrist?*

An adversary of Christ, who will strive to overthrow Christianity, but instead of doing so shall himself come to a fearful end. 2 Thess. ii. 8.

236. What is Christ's kingdom?

Christ's kingdom is, first, the whole world; secondly, all believers upon earth; thirdly, all the blessed in heaven.

The first is called the kingdom of *nature;* the second, the kingdom of *grace;* the third, the kingdom of *glory.*

237. Which of these is meant when it is said in the Creed that of Christ's kingdom *there shall be no end?*

The kingdom of glory.

On the Eighth Article.

238. In what sense is the Holy Ghost called *the Lord?*

In the same sense as the Son of God, that is, as very God.

239. Is this witnessed by holy Scripture?

It is plain from the words spoken by the Apostle Peter to rebuke Ananias: *Why hath Satan filled thine heart to lie to the Holy Ghost?* and further on, *Thou hast not lied unto men, but unto God.* Acts v. 3, 4.

240. What are we to understand by this, that the Holy Ghost is called *the Giver of life?*

That he, together with God the Father and the Son, giveth life to all creatures, especially spiritual life to men.

Except a man be born of water and of the Spirit, he can not enter into the kingdom of God. John iii. 5.

241. Whence know we that the Holy Ghost *proceedeth from the Father?*

This we know from the following words of Jesus Christ himself: *But when the Comforter is come, whom I will send unto you from the Father, even the Spirit of truth, which proceedeth from the Father, he shall testify of me.* John xv. 26.

242. Does the doctrine of the procession of the Holy Ghost from the Father admit of any change or supplement?

No. First, because the Orthodox Church, in this doctrine, repeats

the very words of Jesus Christ; and his words, without doubt, are an exact and perfect expression of the truth.   Secondly, because the second œcumenical Council, whose chief object was to establish the true doctrine respecting the Holy Ghost, has without doubt sufficiently set forth the same in the Creed; and the Catholic Church has acknowledged this so decidedly, that the third œcumenical Council in its seventh canon forbade the composition of any new Creed.

For this cause John Damascene writes: *Of the Holy Ghost, we both say that he is from the Father, and call him the Spirit of the Father; while we nowise say that he is from the Son, but only call him the Spirit of the Son.*   (Theol. lib. i. c. 11; v. 4.)

243. Whence does it appear that the Holy Ghost is equally *with the Father and the Son,* and, *together* with them, *to be worshiped and glorified?*

It appears from this, that Jesus Christ commanded to *baptize in the name of the Father, and of the Son, and of the Holy Ghost.*   Matt. xxviii. 19.

244. Why is it said in the Creed that the Holy Ghost *spake by the prophets?*

This is said against certain heretics, who taught that the books of the Old Testament were not written by the Holy Ghost.

245. Does holy Scripture witness that the Holy Ghost really spake by the prophets?

The Apostle Peter writes: *For prophecy came not in old time by the will of man; but holy men of God spake as they were moved by the Holy Ghost.*   2 Pet. i. 21.

246. Did not the Holy Ghost speak also by the Apostles?

Certainly he did.   *Unto the prophets,* says also the Apostle Peter, *it was revealed, that not unto themselves, but unto us they did minister the things which are now reported unto you by them that have preached the Gospel unto you by the Holy Ghost sent down from heaven.* Pet. i. 12.

247. Why, then, is there no mention of the Apostles in the Creed?

Because when the Creed was composed none doubted of the inspiration of the Apostles.

248. Was not the Holy Ghost manifested to men in some very special manner?

Yes.   He came down upon the Apostles, in the form of fiery tongues, on the fiftieth day after the resurrection of Jesus Christ.

249. Is the Holy Ghost communicated to men even now likewise?

He is communicated to all true Christians.   *Know ye not that ye*

are the temple of God, and that the Spirit of God dwelleth in you?
1 Cor. iii. 16.

250. How may we be made partakers of the Holy Ghost?

Through fervent prayer, and through the Sacraments.

If ye then, being evil, know how to give good gifts unto your children, how much more shall your heavenly Father give the Holy Spirit to them that ask him?   Luke xi. 13.

But after that the kindness and love of God our Saviour toward man appeared, not by works of righteousness which we have done, but according to his mercy he saved us, by the washing of regeneration, and renewing of the Holy Ghost, which he shed on us abundantly through Jesus Christ our Saviour.   Titus iii. 4–6.

251. What are the chief *gifts of the Holy Ghost?*

The chief and more general are, as reckoned by the Prophet Isaiah, the following seven: the spirit of the fear of God, the spirit of knowledge, the spirit of might, the spirit of counsel, the spirit of understanding, the spirit of wisdom, the spirit of the Lord, or the gift of piety and inspiration in the highest degree.   Isaiah xi. 2.

ON THE NINTH ARTICLE.

252. What is the *Church?*

The Church is a divinely instituted community of men, united by the orthodox faith, the law of God, the hierarchy, and the Sacraments.

253. What is it to *believe in the Church?*

It is piously to honor the true Church of Christ, and to obey her doctrine and commandments, from a conviction that grace ever abides in her, and works, teaches, and governs unto salvation, flowing from her one only everlasting Head, the Lord Jesus Christ.

254. How can the Church, which is visible, be the object of faith, when faith, as the Apostle says, is *the evidence of things not seen?*

First, though the Church be visible, the grace of God, which dwells in her, and in those who are sanctified in her, is not so; and this it is which properly constitutes the object of faith in the Church.

Secondly, the Church, though visible so far as she is upon earth, and contains all Orthodox Christians living upon earth, still is at the same time invisible, so far as she is also partially in heaven, and contains all those that have departed hence in true faith and holiness.

255. On what may we ground the idea that the Church is at once upon earth and in heaven?

On the following words of the Apostle Paul, addressed to Christians: *Ye are come unto Mount Sion, and unto the city of the living God, the heavenly Jerusalem, and to an innumerable company of angels, to the general assembly and Church of the first-born, which are written in heaven, and to God the Judge of all, and to the spirits of just men made perfect, and to Jesus Christ the Mediator of the new covenant.* Heb. xii. 22–24.

256. How are we assured that the grace of God abides in the true Church?

First, by this: that her Head is Jesus Christ, God and man in one person, *full of grace and truth*, who fills his body also, that is, the Church, with like grace and truth. John i. 14, 17.

Secondly, by this: that he has promised his disciples the Holy Ghost to *abide with them forever*, and that, according to this promise, the Holy Ghost appoints the pastors of the Church. John xiv. 16.

The Apostle Paul says of Jesus Christ, that God the Father *gave him to be head over all things to the Church, which is his body.* Eph. i. 22, 23. The same Apostle says to the pastors of the Church: *Take heed therefore unto yourselves, and to all the flock, over which the Holy Ghost hath made you Bishops, to feed the Church of our Lord and God, which he hath purchased with his own blood.* Acts xx. 28.

257. How are we further assured that the grace of God abides in the Church even till now, and shall abide in it to the end of the world?

Of this we are assured by the following sayings of Jesus Christ himself and his Apostle: *I will build my Church, and the gates of hell shall not prevail against it.* Matt. xvi. 18. *I am with you alway, even unto the end of the world. Amen.* Matt. xxviii. 20. *Unto him,* God the Father, *be glory in the Church by Christ Jesus throughout all ages, world without end. Amen.* Eph. iii. 21.

258. Why is the Church *one?*

Because she is one spiritual Body, has one Head, Christ, and is animated by one Spirit of God. *There is one body and one Spirit, even as ye are called in one hope of your calling; one Lord, one faith, one baptism, one God and Father of all.* Eph. iv. 4–6.

259. Are we still more expressly assured that Jesus Christ is the one only Head of the one Church?

The Apostle Paul writes, that for the Church, as *the building of*

God, other foundation can no man lay than that is laid, which is Jesus Christ. 1 Cor. iii. 10, 11. Wherefore the Church, as the Body of Christ, can have no other Head than Jesus Christ.

The Church, being to abide through all generations of time, needs also an ever-abiding head ; and such is Jesus Christ alone.

Wherefore, also, the Apostles take no higher title than that of *ministers of the Church.* Col. i. 24, 25.

260. What duty does the unity of the Church lay on us?

That of *endeavoring to keep the unity of the Spirit in the bond of peace.* Eph. iv. 3.

261. How does it agree with the unity of the Church, that there are many separate and independent churches, as those of Jerusalem, Antioch, Alexandria, Constantinople, Russia ?

These are particular churches, or parts of the one Catholic Church : the separateness of their visible organization does not hinder them from being all spiritually great members of the one body of the Universal Church, from having one Head, Christ, and one spirit of faith and grace. This unity is expressed outwardly by unity of Creed, and by communion in prayer and Sacraments.

262. Is there likewise unity between the Church on earth and the Church in heaven ?

Doubtless there is, both by their common relation to one Head, our Lord Jesus Christ, and by mutual communion with one another.

263. What means of communion has the Church on earth with the Church in heaven ?

The prayer of faith and love. The faithful who belong to the Church militant upon earth, in offering their prayers to God, call at the same time to their aid the saints who belong to the Church in heaven ; and these, standing on the highest steps of approach to God, by their prayers and intercessions purify, strengthen, and offer before God the prayers of the faithful living upon earth, and by the will of God work graciously and beneficently upon them, either by invisible virtue, or by distinct apparitions, and in divers other ways.

264. On what is grounded the rule of the Church upon earth *to invoke in prayer the saints* of the Church in heaven ?

On a holy tradition, the principle of which is to be seen also in holy Scripture. For instance, when the Prophet David cries out in prayer, *O Lord God of Abraham, Isaac, and of Israel our fathers,* he makes mention of saints in aid of his prayer, exactly as now the Orthodox Church calls upon *Christ our true God, by the*

prayers of his most pure Mother and all his saints. See 1 Chron.
xxix. 18.

Cyril of Jerusalem, in his explanation of the divine Liturgy, says:
*We make mention also of those who are before departed, first, of the
Patriarchs, Prophets, Apostles, and Martyrs, that by their entreaties
and intercession God may receive our prayers.* (Cat. Myst. v. c. 9.)

Basil the Great, in his sermon on the day of the Forty Holy Martyrs, says : *Whoever is afflicted has recourse to the Forty, and whoever
is joyful runs to the same ; the one that he may find relief from his
sorrows, the other that he may keep his happiness. Here the pious
wife is to be seen praying for her children ; another asks the return
of her absent husband ; another the restoration of health to the sick.
Yes ; let your petitions be with the Martyrs.*

265. Is there any testimony of holy Scripture to the *mediatory prayer* of the saints in
heaven ?

The Evangelist John, in the Revelation, saw in heaven an angel, to
whom *was given much incense, that he should offer it, by the prayers
of all saints, upon the golden altar which was before the throne ; and
the smoke of the incense ascended up by the prayers of the saints out
of the hands of the angel before God.* Rev. viii. 3, 4.

266. Is there any testimony of holy Scripture to beneficent *apparitions of saints* from
heaven?

The Evangelist St. Matthew relates that after the death of our Lord
Jesus Christ upon the cross, *many bodies of the saints which slept
arose, and came out of the graves, after his resurrection, and went into
the holy city, and appeared unto many.* Matt. xxvii. 52, 53. And since
a miracle so great could not be without some adequate end, we must
suppose that the saints which then arose appeared for this, that they
might announce the descent of Jesus Christ into hell, and his triumphal
resurrection ; and so move men born in the Church of the Old Testament to pass over the more readily into that of the New, then opened.

267. What testimonies are there to confirm us in the belief that *the saints*, after their
departure, *work miracles* through certain earthly means ?

The second (fourth in the Greek) book of Kings testifies that by
touching the bones of the Prophet Elisha a dead man was raised to
life. 2 (4) Kings xiii. 21.

The Apostle Paul not only in his own immediate person wrought

healings and miracles, but the same was done also in his absence by handkerchiefs and aprons taken from his body. Acts xix. 12. By this example we may understand that the saints, even after their deaths, may in like manner work beneficently through earthly means, which have received from them holy virtue.

Gregory the Divine, in his first discourse against Julian, says : *Thou wast not abashed by the sacrifices offered for Christ, nor didst fear the great athletes, John, Peter, Paul, James, Stephen, Luke, Andrew, Thecla, and the rest, who before and after these suffered for the truth ; who withstood both fire and sword, the torturers, and all sufferings present or threatened, as if their bodies were not their own, or they had had no bodies at all. For what? That they might not, so much as by a word, betray their religion. To whom also great honors and triumphs are with just reason awarded : by whom devils are expelled and diseases healed : who appear in visions, and prophecy : whose very bodies, though separate, when touched or reverenced, have like power with their holy souls ; and drops of whose blood, those least tokens of their suffering, like power with their bodies.*

John Damascene writes thus : *The relics of the saints have been given us by our Lord Jesus Christ as salutary springs, from which manifold blessings flow.* And as if in explanation of this, he remarks, that *through the mind their bodies also were inhabited of God.* (Theol. lib. iv. cap. 15, § 3, 4.)

268. Why is the Church *holy?*

Because she is sanctified by Jesus Christ through his passion, through his doctrine, through his prayer, and through the Sacraments. *Christ loved the Church, and gave himself for it ; that he might sanctify it, having cleansed it with the washing of water by the Word, that he might present it to himself a glorious Church, not having spot, or wrinkle, or any such thing, but that it should be holy, and without blemish.* Eph. v. 25–27.

In his prayer to God the Father for believers, Jesus Christ said among other things : *Sanctify them through thy truth : thy Word is truth. And for their sakes I sanctify myself, that they also may be sanctified in truth.* John xvii. 17, 19.

269. How is the Church holy, when she has in her sinners?

Men who sin, but purify themselves by true repentance, hinder not

the Church from being holy; but impenitent sinners, either by the visible act of Church authority, or by the invisible judgment of God, are cut off from the body of the Church; and so she is, in respect of these, also kept holy.

Put away from among yourselves that wicked person. 1 Cor. v. 13. *Nevertheless the foundation of God standeth sure, having this seal: The Lord knoweth them that are his. And, Let every one that nameth the name of Christ depart from iniquity.* 2 Tim. ii. 19.

270. Why is the Church called *Catholic,* or, which is the same thing, *Universal ?*

Because she is not limited to any place, nor time, nor people, but contains true believers of all places, times, and peoples.

The Apostle Paul says that *the Word of the Gospel* is *in all the world ; and bringeth forth fruit* (Coloss. i. 5, 6), and that in the Christian Church *there is neither Greek nor Jew, circumcision nor uncircumcision, barbarian nor Scythian, bond nor free : but Christ is all, and in all.* Coloss. iii. 11. *They which be of faith are blessed with faithful Abraham.* Gal. iii. 9.

271. What great privilege has the Catholic Church?

She alone has the sublime promises *that the gates of hell shall not prevail against her ;* that the Lord shall *be with* her *even to the end of the world;* that in her shall abide *the glory* of God *in Christ Jesus throughout all generations forever;* and consequently that she shall never apostatize from the faith, nor sin against the truth of the faith, or fall into error.

We undoubtingly confess, as . sure truth, that the Catholic Church can not sin, nor err, nor utter falsehood in place of truth ; for the Holy Ghost, ever working through his faithful ministers the fathers and doctors of the Church, preserves her from all error. (Missive of the Eastern Patriarchs on the Orthodox Faith, Art. 12.)

272. If the Catholic Church contains all true believers in the world, must we not acknowledge it to be necessary for salvation that every believer should belong to her?

Exactly so. Since Jesus Christ, in the words of St. Paul, *is the Head of the Church, and he is the Saviour of the Body,* it follows that, to have part in his salvation, we must necessarily be members of his body, that is, of the Catholic Church. Eph. v. 23.

The Apostle Peter writes that *baptism saveth us* after the figure of *the ark of Noah.* All who were saved from the general deluge were

saved only in the ark; so all who obtain everlasting salvation obtain it only in the one Catholic Church.

273. What thoughts and remembrances should we associate with the name of the *Eastern* Church?

In Paradise, planted in the East, was founded the first Church of our parents in innocence; and in the East, after the fall, was laid a new foundation of the Church of the redeemed, in the promise of a Saviour. In the East, in the land of Judæa, our Lord Jesus Christ, having finished the work of our salvation, laid the foundation of his own proper Christian Church: from thence she spread herself over the whole universe; and to this day the orthodox Catholic œcumenical faith, confirmed by the seven œcumenical Councils, is preserved unchanged in its original purity in the ancient Churches of the East, and in such as agree with them, as does by God's grace the Church of Russia.

274. Why is the Church called *Apostolic?*

Because she has from the Apostles, without break or change, both her doctrine and the succession of the gifts of the Holy Ghost, through the laying on of consecrated hands. In the same sense the Church is called also *Orthodox*, or *Rightly-believing*.

Ye are no more strangers and foreigners, but fellow-citizens with the saints, and of the household of God, and are built on the foundation of the Apostles and Prophets, Jesus Christ himself being the chief corner-stone. Eph. ii. 19, 20.

275. What does the Creed teach us, when it calls the Church *Apostolic?*

It teaches us to hold fast the *Apostolical doctrine* and *tradition*, and eschew such doctrine and such teachers as are not warranted by the doctrine of the Apostles.

The Apostle Paul says: *Therefore, brethren, stand fast, and hold the traditions which ye have been taught, whether by word or our epistle.* 2 Thess. ii. 15. *A man that is a heretic after the first and second admonition reject.* Titus iii. 10. *For there are many unruly, vain talkers and deceivers, especially they of the circumcision, whose mouths must be stopped; who subvert whole houses, teaching things which they ought not, for filthy lucre's sake.* Titus i. 10, 11. *But if* thy brother *neglect to hear the Church, let him be to thee as a heathen man and a publican.* Matt. xviii. 17.

276. What ecclesiastical institution is there through which the succession of the Apostolical ministry is preserved?

The ecclesiastical *Hierarchy.*

277. Whence originates the Hierarchy of the Orthodox Christian Church?

From Jesus Christ himself, and from the descent of the Holy Ghost on the Apostles; from which time it is continued, in unbroken succession, through the laying on of hands, in the Sacrament of Orders. *And he gave some, Apostles; and some, Prophets; and some, Evangelists; and some, Pastors and Teachers; for the perfecting of the saints, for the work of the ministry, for the edifying of the Body of Christ.* Eph. iv. 11, 12.

278. What hierarchical authority is there which can extend its sphere of action over the whole Catholic Church?

An œcumenical Council.

279. Under what hierarchical authority are the chief divisions of the Catholic Church?

Under the Orthodox Patriarchs and the Most Holy Synod.

280. Under what ecclesiastical authority are lesser orthodox provinces and cities?

Under Metropolitans, Archbishops, and Bishops.

281. What rank in the Hierarchy is held by the Most Holy Russian Synod?

The same rank with the Most Holy Orthodox Patriarchs. (See the Letters of the M. H. Patriarchs on the institution of the M. H. Synod.)

282. If any one desire to fulfill his duty of obedience to the Church, how may he learn what she requires of her children?

This may be learned from holy Scripture, from the canons of the holy Apostles, the holy œcumenical and provincial Councils, and the holy Fathers, and from the books of Ecclesiastical Rules and Rubrics.

On the Tenth Article.

283. Why does the Creed mention Baptism?

Because faith is sealed by Baptism, and the other Mysteries or Sacraments.

284. What is a *Mystery* or Sacrament?

A Mystery or Sacrament is a holy act, through which *grace*, or, in other words, the saving power of God, works *mysteriously* upon man.

285. How many are the Sacraments?

Seven: 1. Baptism; 2. Unction with Chrism; 3. Communion; 4. Penitence; 5. Orders; 6. Matrimony; 7. Unction with Oil.

286. What virtue is there in each of these Sacraments?

1. In Baptism man is mysteriously born to a spiritual life.

2. In Unction with Chrism he receives a grace of spiritual growth and strength.

3. In the Communion he is spiritually fed.

4. In Penitence he is healed of spiritual diseases, that is, of sin.

5. In Orders he receives grace spiritually to regenerate, feed, and nurture others, by doctrine and Sacraments.

6. In Matrimony he receives a grace sanctifying the married life, and the natural procreation and nurture of children.

7. In Unction with Oil he has medicine even for bodily diseases, in that he is healed of spiritual.

287. But why does not the Creed mention all these Sacraments, instead of mentioning Baptism only?

Because Baptism was the subject of a question, whether some people, as heretics, ought not to be rebaptized; and this required a decision, which so came to be put into the Creed.

On Baptism.

288. What is Baptism?

Baptism is a Sacrament, in which a man who believes, having his body thrice plunged in water in the name of God the Father, the Son, and the Holy Ghost, dies to the carnal life of sin, and is born again of the Holy Ghost to a life spiritual and holy. *Except a man be born of water and of the Spirit, he can not enter into the kingdom of God.* John iii. 5.

289. When and how began Baptism?

First, *John baptized with the baptism of repentance, saying unto the people, that they should believe on him which should come after him, that is, on Christ Jesus.* Acts xix. 4. Afterwards, Jesus Christ, by his own example, sanctified Baptism, when he received it from John. Lastly, after his resurrection, he gave the Apostles this solemn commandment: *Go ye and teach all nations, baptizing them in the name of the Father, and of the Son, and of the Holy Ghost.* Matt. xxviii. 19.

290. What is most essential in the administration of Baptism?

Trine immersion in water, in the name of the Father, and of the Son, and of the Holy Ghost.

291. What is required of him that seeks to be baptized?

Repentance and faith; for which cause, also, before Baptism the*p* recite the Creed. *Repent, and be baptized every one of you in the name of Jesus Christ for the remission of sins, and ye shall receive the gift of the Holy Ghost.* Acts ii. 38. *He that believeth and is baptized shall be saved.* Mark xvi. 16.

292. But why, then, are children baptized?

For the faith of their parents and sponsors, who are also bound to teach them the faith so soon as they are of sufficient age to learn.

293. How can you show from holy Scripture that we ought to baptize infants?

In the time of the Old Testament, infants were circumcised when eight days old; but Baptism in the New Testament takes the place of circumcision; consequently infants should also be baptized.

294. Whence does it appear that *Baptism* takes the place of *circumcision?*

From the following words of the Apostle to believers: *Ye are circumcised with the circumcision made without hands, in putting off the body of the sins of the flesh, by the circumcision of Christ, buried with him in Baptism.* Coloss. ii. 11, 12.

295. Why are there sponsors at Baptism?

In order that they may stand sureties before the Church for the faith of the baptized, and after Baptism may take him in charge, to confirm him in the faith. (See Dion. Areop. on the Eccl. Hier. cap. ii.)

296. Why before baptizing do we use *exorcism?*

To drive away the devil, who since Adam's fall has had access to men, and power over them, as his captives and slaves.

The Apostle Paul says, that all men, without grace, *walk according to the course of this world, according to the prince of the power of the air, the spirit that now worketh in the children of disobedience.* Eph. ii. 2.

297. Wherein lies the force of exorcism?

In the name of Jesus Christ, invoked with prayer and faith. Jesus Christ gave to believers this promise: *In my name shall they cast out devils.* Mark xvi. 17.

298. What force has *the sign of the cross* used on this and other occasions?

What the name of Jesus Christ crucified is when pronounced with faith by motion of the lips, the very same is also the sign of the cross when made with faith by motion of the hand, or represented in any other way.

Cyril of Jerusalem writes: *Let us not be ashamed to confess the Crucified; let us boldly make the sign of the Cross on the forehead, and on every thing; on the bread which we eat; on the cups from which we drink; let us make it. at our going out, and coming in; when we lie down to sleep, and when we rise; when we journey, and when we rest: it is a great safeguard, given to the poor without price, to the weak without labor. For this is the grace of God; a token for the faithful, and a terror for evil spirits.* (Cat. Lect. xiii. 36.)

299. Whence have we the use of the sign of the Cross?

From the very times of the Apostles. (See Dion. Areop. on the Eccl. Hier. cap. ii. and v.; also Tertull. de Coron. cap. iii.; de Resurr. cap. viii.)

300. What means the *white garment* which is put on after Baptism?

The purity of the soul, and of the Christian life.

301. Why do they hang upon the baptized a *Cross?*

As a visible expression and continual remembrance of Christ's command: *If any man will come after me, let him deny himself, and take up his cross, and follow me.* Matt. xvi. 24.

302. What means the *procession* of the baptized round the font with a *light?*

Spiritual joy, joined with spiritual illumination.

303. How is this to be understood, that in the Creed we are made to confess *one* Baptism?

In this sense: that Baptism can not be repeated.

304. Why can not Baptism be repeated?

Baptism is spiritual birth: a man is born but once; therefore he is also baptized but once.

305. What is to be thought of those who sin after Baptism?

That they are more guilty in their sins than the unbaptized, since they had from God special help to do well, and have thrown it away.

For if after they have escaped the pollutions of the world through the knowledge of the Lord and Saviour Jesus Christ, they are again entangled therein and overcome, the latter end is worse with them than the beginning. 2 Peter ii. 20.

305. But is there not any way even for such as have sinned after Baptism to obtain pardon?

There is a way, which is penitence.

On Unction with Chrism.

307. What is *Unction with Chrism?*

Unction with Chrism is a Sacrament, in which the baptized believer, being anointed with holy chrism on certain parts of the body in the name of the Holy Ghost, receives the gifts of the Holy Ghost for growth and strength in spiritual life.

308. Is this Sacrament mentioned in holy Scripture?

The inward grace of this Sacrament is spoken of by the Apostle John, as follows: *But ye have an unction from the Holy One, and ye know all things. And the anointing which ye have received of him abideth in you, and ye need not that any man teach you; but as the same anointing teacheth you of all things, and is truth, and is no lie; and even as it hath taught you, abide therein.* 1 John ii. 20, 27.

In like manner the Apostle Paul also says: *Now he which stablisheth us with you in Christ, and hath anointed us, is God; who hath also sealed us, and given the earnest of the Spirit in our hearts.* 2 Cor. i. 21, 22.

Hence are taken the words pronounced at the Unction: *The seal of the gift of the Holy Ghost.*

309. Is the outward form of Unction with Chrism mentioned in holy Scripture?

It may well be supposed that the words of St. John refer to a visible as well as to an inward unction; but it is more certain that the Apostles, for imparting to the baptized the gifts of the Holy Ghost, used *imposition of hands.* Acts viii. 14, 16. The successors of the Apostles, however, in place of this, introduced unction with chrism, drawing, it may be, their precedent from the unction used in the Old Testament. Exod. xxx. 25; 1 (3 in the Greek) Kings i. 39. (Dion. Areop. de Eccl. Hier. cap. iv.)

310. What is to be remarked of the *holy Chrism?*

This: that its consecration is reserved to the heads of the Hierarchy, as successors of the Apostles, who used the laying on of their own hands to communicate the gifts of the Holy Ghost.

311. What is specially signified by *anointing the forehead?*

The sanctification of the mind, or thoughts.

312. What by anointing the *chest?*

The sanctification of the heart, or desires.

313. What by anointing the *eyes, ears,* and *lips?*

The sanctification of the senses.

314. What by anointing the *hands* and *feet?*

The sanctification of the works and whole walk of the Christian.

ON THE COMMUNION.

315. What is the *Communion?*

The Communion is a Sacrament, in which the believer, under the forms of bread and wine, partakes of the very Body and Blood of Christ, to everlasting life.

316. How was this Sacrament instituted?

Jesus Christ, immediately before his passion, consecrated it for the first time, exhibiting in it by anticipation a lively image of his sufferings for our salvation; and after having administered it to the Apostles, he gave them at the same time a commandment ever after to perpetuate this Sacrament.

317. What is to be noticed of the Sacrament of the Communion in regard to divine service in the Church?

This: that it forms the chief and most essential part of divine service.

318. What is the name of that service in which the Sacrament of the Communion is consecrated?

The Liturgy.

319. What means the word *Liturgy?*

Common service; but the name Liturgy is specially appropriated to that divine service in which the Sacrament of the Communion is consecrated.

320. What is to be noted of the *place* where the Liturgy is celebrated?

It must always be consecrated in a *temple,* the *table* in which, or at least, if there be no such table, the *antimense* on which the Sacrament is consecrated, must have been consecrated by a Bishop.

321. Why is the *temple* called a *church?*

Because the faithful, who compose the Church, meet in it for prayer and Sacraments.

322. Why is the table, on which the Sacrament of the Communion is consecrated, called *the throne?*

Because on it Jesus Christ, as King, is mystically present.

323. What general *order of parts* may be remarked in the Liturgy ?

This : that first the elements are prepared for the Sacrament; secondly, the faithful are prepared for the Sacrament; lastly, the Sacrament itself is consecrated.

324. What is the name for that part of the Liturgy in which the elements are prepared for the Sacrament ?

Proskomidè, προσκομιδή.

325. What is the meaning of the word *Proskomidè?*

Offertory.

326. Why is this name given to the first part of the Liturgy ?

From the custom of the primitive Christians to offer in the Church bread and wine for the celebration of the Sacrament. On the same account this bread is called *prosphora*, which means *oblation.*

327. In what consists the Offertory, as a part of the Liturgy ?

In this : that with mention made of the prophecies and types, and partly also of the events themselves, relating to the birth and suffering of Jesus Christ, a portion is taken from the prosphora for use in the Sacrament, and likewise a portion of wine mixed with water is poured off into the holy chalice, while the celebrator makes commemoration of the whole Church, honors the glorified saints, prays for the living and the departed, especially for the ruling powers, and for those who, of their own faith and zeal, have brought prosphoræ, or oblations.

328. Of what kind should be the *bread* for the Sacrament?

Such as the name itself of bread, the holiness of the Mystery, and the example of Jesus Christ and the Apostles all require; that is, leavened, pure, wheaten bread.

329. What is signified by this, that the *bread* or loaf which is strictly to be used for the Communion is only *one ?*

It signifies, as the Apostle explains, that *we, being many, are one bread, and one body; for we are all partakers of that one bread.* 1 Cor. x. 17.

330. Why is the bread, when prepared for the Communion, called *the Lamb ?*

Because it is the figure of Jesus Christ suffering, as was in the Old Testament *the Paschal Lamb.*

331. What was the Paschal Lamb?

The lamb which the Israelites, by God's command, killed and ate in memory of their deliverance from destruction in Egypt.

332. Why is the *wine* for the Sacrament of the Communion mixed *with water?*

Because the whole of this celebration is ordered so as to figure forth the sufferings of Christ; and when he suffered there flowed from his pierced side *blood and water.*

333. What name has that part of the Liturgy in which the faithful are prepared for the Sacrament?

The ancients called it the *Liturgy of the Catechumens;* because, besides baptized communicants, the catechumens, also, who are preparing for Baptism, and the penitents, who are not admitted to communion, may be present at it.

334. With what does this part of the Liturgy begin?

With the Blessing, or glorification of the Kingdom of the Most Holy Trinity.

335. In what consists this part of the Liturgy?

In prayers, singing, and reading from the books of the Apostles, and from the Gospel.

336. With what does it end?

With the order given to the catechumens to go out and leave the church.

337. What is the name for that part of the Liturgy in which the Sacrament itself is celebrated and consecrated?

The *Liturgy of the Faithful;* because the faithful only, that is, the baptized, have the right to be present at this service.

338. What is the most essential act in this part of the Liturgy?

The utterance of the words which Jesus Christ spake in instituting the Sacrament: *Take, eat; this is my body. Drink ye all of it; for this is my Blood of the New Testament.* Matt. xxvi. 26, 27, 28. And after this the invocation of the Holy Ghost, and the blessing the gifts, that is, the bread and wine which have been offered.

339. Why is this so essential?

Because at the moment of this act the bread and wine are changed, or transubstantiated, into the very Body of Christ, and into the very Blood of Christ.

340. How are we to understand the word *transubstantiation?*

In the exposition of the faith by the Eastern Patriarchs, it is said that the word transubstantiation is not to be taken to define the manner in which the bread and wine are changed into the Body and Blood

of the Lord ; for this none can understand but God; but only thus much is signified, that the bread truly, really, and substantially becomes the very true Body of the Lord, and the wine the very Blood of the Lord. In like manner John Damascene, treating of the Holy and Immaculate Mysteries of the Lord, writes thus: *It is truly that Body, united with Godhead, which had its origin from the Holy Virgin; not as though that Body which ascended came down from heaven, but because the bread and wine themselves are changed into the Body and Blood of God. But if thou seekest after the manner how this is, let it suffice thee to be told that it is by the Holy Ghost; in like manner as, by the same Holy Ghost, the Lord formed flesh to himself, and in himself, from the Mother of God; nor know I aught more than this, that the Word of God is true, powerful, and almighty, but its manner of operation unsearchable.* (J. Damasc. Theol. lib. iv. cap. 13, § 7.)

341. What is required individually of every one who desires to approach the Sacrament of the Communion?

To examine his conscience before God, and to cleanse it from sin by penitence ; for doing which he has helps in fasting and prayer.

Let a man examine himself, and so let him eat of that bread, and drink of that cup; for he that eateth and drinketh unworthily, eateth and drinketh damnation to himself, not discerning the Lord's Body. 1 Cor. xi. 28, 29.

342. What benefit does he receive who communicates in the Body and Blood of Christ?

He is in the closest manner united to Jesus Christ himself, and, in him, is made partaker of everlasting life.

He that eateth my Flesh, and drinketh my Blood, dwelleth in me, and I in him. John vi. 56. *Whoso eateth my Flesh, and drinketh my Blood, hath eternal life.* John vi. 54.

343. Ought we to communicate often in the holy Mysteries?

The primitive Christians communicated every Lord's Day; but now few have such purity of life as to be always prepared to approach so great a Mystery. Our Mother the Church calls on all, who would live religiously, to confess before their ghostly Father, and communicate in the Body and Blood of Christ, four times yearly, or even every month, but requires all, without exception, to receive it at the least once in the year. (See Orthod. Confess. Pt. I. Q. 90.)

344. What part can they have in the divine Liturgy who only hear it without approaching the holy Communion?

They may and should take part in the Liturgy by prayer and faith, and especially by a continual remembrance of our Lord Jesus Christ, who expressly has commanded us to *do this in remembrance of him.* Luke xxii. 19.

345. What should we remember at that time in the Liturgy when they make the Procession with the Gospel?

Jesus Christ appearing to preach the Gospel.   So also while the Gospel is reading, we should have the same attention and reverence as if we saw and heard Jesus Christ himself.

346. What should we remember at that time in the Liturgy when they make the Procession with the gifts from the table of preparation to the altar?

Jesus Christ going to suffer voluntarily, as a victim to the slaughter, while more than twelve legions of angels were ready around to guard him as their King.

The King of kings, and Lord of lords, cometh to be slaughtered. (Hymn for the Liturgy on the Great Sabbath.)

347. What should we remember at the moment of the consecration of the Sacrament, and while the clergy are communicating within the altar?

The mystical supper of Jesus Christ himself with his Apostles; his suffering, death, and burial.

348. What is set forth after this, by the drawing back of the veil, the opening of the royal doors, and the appearance of the holy gifts?

The appearance of Jesus Christ himself after his resurrection.

349. What is figured by the last showing of the holy gifts to the people, after which they are hid from view?

The ascension of Jesus Christ into heaven.

350. Will the use of the Sacrament of the holy Communion continue ever in the true Church of Christ?

Assuredly it will ever continue, even to Christ's coming again, agreeably to the words of the Apostle Paul: *For as oft as ye eat this bread, and drink this cup, ye do show forth the Lord's death till he come* 1 Cor. xi. 26.

On Penitence.

351. What is *Penitence?*

Penitence is a Sacrament, in which he who confesses his sins is, on the outward declaration of pardon by the priest, inwardly loosed from his sins by Jesus Christ himself.

352. What is the origin of this Sacrament?

They who came to John the Baptist, who *preached the baptism of repentance for the remission of sins, confessed their sins.* Mark i. 4, 5. The Apostles were promised by Jesus Christ power to forgive sins, when he said, *Whatsoever ye shall bind on earth, shall be bound in heaven; and whatsoever ye shall loose on earth, shall be loosed in heaven.* Matt. xviii. 18. And after his resurrection he actually gave them this power, saying, *Receive ye the Holy Ghost : whosesoever sins ye remit, they are remitted unto them ; and whosesoever sins ye retain, they are retained.* John xx. 22, 23.

353. What is required of the penitent?

Contrition for his sins, with a full purpose of amendment of life, faith in Jesus Christ, and hope in his mercy.

For godly sorrow worketh repentance to salvation not to be repented of. 2 Cor. vii. 10. *But if the wicked turn from his wickedness, and do that which is lawful and right, he shall live thereby.* Ezek. xxxiii. 19. *To him,* that is to Jesus Christ, *give all the Prophets witness, that through his name whosoever believeth in him shall receive remission of sins.* Acts x. 43.

354. Are there not besides certain preparations and aids to Penitence?

Such are fasting and prayer.

355. Is there not besides these a certain special mean used by holy Church for cleansing and giving peace to the conscience of the penitent?

Such a mean is the *epitimia,* or penance.

356. What is the *epitimia?*

The word means *punishment.* See 2 Cor. ii. 6. Under this name are prescribed to the penitent, according as may be requisite, divers particular exercises of piety, and divers abstinences or privations, serving to efface the unrighteousness of sin, and to subdue sinful habit; as, for instance, fasting beyond what is prescribed for all, or for grievous sins suspension from the holy Communion for a given time.

On Orders.

357. What are *Orders?*

Orders are a Sacrament, in which the Holy Ghost, by the laying on of the Bishop's hands, ordains them that be rightly chosen to minister sacraments, and to feed the flock of Christ.

Let a man so account of us, as of the ministers of Christ, and stewards of the mysteries of God. 1 Cor. iv. 1.

Take heed therefore unto yourselves, and to all the flock, over the which the Holy Ghost hath made you overseers, to feed the Church of God, which he hath purchased with his own blood. Acts xx. 28.

358. What is it to feed the Church?

To instruct the people in faith, piety, and good works.

359. How many necessary *degrees* are there of Orders?

Three: those of *Bishop*, *Priest*, and *Deacon*.

360. What difference is there between them?

The Deacon serves at the Sacraments; the Priest hallows Sacraments in dependence on the Bishop; the Bishop not only hallows the Sacraments himself, but has power also to impart to others, by the laying on of his hands, the gift and grace to hallow them.

Of the Episcopal power the Apostle Paul thus writes to Titus: *For this cause left I thee in Crete, that thou shouldest set in order the things that are wanting, and ordain elders in every city.* Titus i. 5. And to Timothy: *Lay hands suddenly on no man.* 1 Tim. v. 22.

On Matrimony.

361. What is Matrimony?

Matrimony is a Sacrament, in which, on the free promise of the man and woman before the priest and the Church to be true to each other, their conjugal union is blessed to be an image of Christ's union with the Church, and grace is asked for them to live together in godly love and honesty, to the procreation and Christian bringing up of children.

362. Whence does it appear that Matrimony is a Sacrament?

From the following words of the Apostle Paul: *A man shall leave his father and mother, and shall be joined unto his wife, and they two shall be one flesh. This Sacrament is great: but I speak concerning Christ and the Church.* Eph. v. 31, 32.

363. Is it the duty of all to marry?

No. Virginity is better than wedlock, if any have the gift to keep it undefiled.

Of this Jesus Christ has said expressly: *All men can not receive this saying, save they to whom it is given. He that is able to receive it, let him receive it.* Matt. xix. 11, 12.

And the Apostle says: *I say therefore to the unmarried and widows, It is good for them if they abide even as I; but if they can not contain, let them marry. . . . . He that is unmarried careth for the things that belong to the Lord, how he may please the Lord; but he that is married careth for the things that are of the world, how he may please his wife. . . . . He that giveth his virgin in marriage doeth well; but he that giveth her not in marriage doeth better.* 1 Cor. vii. 8, 9, 32, 33, 38.

On Unction with Oil.

364. What is Unction with Oil?

Unction with Oil is a Sacrament, in which, while the body is anointed with oil, God's grace is invoked on the sick, to heal him of spiritual and bodily infirmities.

365. Whence is the origin of this Sacrament?

From the Apostles, who, having received power from Jesus Christ, *anointed with oil many that were sick, and healed them.* Mark vi. 13.

The Apostles left this Sacrament to the priests of the Church, as is evident from the following words of the Apostle James: *Is any sick among you? let him call for the elders of the Church; and let them pray over him, anointing him with oil in the name of the Lord; and the prayer of faith shall save the sick, and the Lord shall raise him up; and if he have committed sins, they shall be forgiven him.* James v. 14, 16.

On the Eleventh Article.

366. What is the *resurrection of the dead*, which, in the words of the Creed, we *look for* or expect?

An act of the almighty power of God, by which all bodies of dead men, being reunited to their souls, shall return to life, and shall thenceforth be spiritual and immortal.

It is sown a natural body, it is raised a spiritual body. 1 Cor. xv. 44. *For this corruptible must put on incorruption, and this mortal must put on immortality.* 1 Cor. xv. 53.

367. How shall the body rise again after it has rotted and perished in the ground?

Since God formed the body from the ground originally, he can equally restore it after it has perished in the ground. The Apostle Paul illustrates this by the analogy of a grain of seed, which rots in the earth, but from which there springs up afterwards a plant, or tree. *That which thou sowest is not quickened except it die.* 1 Cor. xv. 36.

368. Shall all, strictly speaking, rise again?

All, without exception, that have died; but they who at the time of the general resurrection shall be still alive shall have their present gross bodies changed in a moment, so as to become spiritual and immortal.

We shall not all sleep, but we shall all be changed, in a moment, in the twinkling of an eye, at the last trump; for the trumpet shall sound, and the dead shall be raised incorruptible, and we shall be changed. 1 Cor. xv. 51, 52.

369. When shall the resurrection of the dead be?

At the end of this visible world?

370. Shall the world then too come to an end?

Yes; this corruptible world shall come to an end, and shall be transformed into another, incorruptible.

Because the creature itself also shall be delivered from the bondage of corruption into the glorious liberty of the children of God. Rom. viii. 21. *Nevertheless we, according to his promise, look for new heavens and a new earth, wherein dwelleth righteousness.* 2 Peter iii. 13.

371. How shall the world be transformed?

By fire. *The heavens and the earth, which are now, by the same, that is, by God's word, are kept in store, reserved unto fire against the day of judgment and perdition of ungodly men.* 2 Peter iii. 7.

372. In what state are the souls of the dead till the general resurrection?

The souls of the righteous are in light and rest, with a foretaste of eternal happiness; but the souls of the wicked are in a state the reverse of this.

373. Why may we not ascribe to the souls of the righteous perfect happiness immediately after death?

Because it is ordained that the perfect retribution according to works

shall be received by the perfect man after the resurrection of the body and God's last judgment.

The Apostle Paul says : *Henceforth there is laid up for me a crown of righteousness, which the Lord, the righteous Judge, shall give me at that day ; and not to me only, but unto all them also that love his appearing.* 2 Tim. iv. 8. And again : *We must all appear before the judgment-seat of Christ ; that every one may receive the things done in his body, according to that he hath done, whether it be good or bad.* 2 Cor. v. 10.

374. Why do we ascribe to the souls of the righteous a foretaste of bliss before the last judgment ?

On the testimony of Jesus Christ himself, who says in the parable that the righteous Lazarus was immediately after death carried into Abraham's bosom. Luke xvi. 22.

375. Is this foretaste of bliss joined with a sight of Christ's own countenance ?

It is so more especially with the saints, as we are given to understand by the Apostle Paul, who *had a desire to depart, and to be with Christ.* Phil. i. 23.

376. What is to be remarked of such souls as have departed with faith, but without having had time to bring forth fruits worthy of repentance ?

This : that they may be aided towards the attainment of a blessed resurrection by prayers offered in their behalf, especially such as are offered in union with the oblation of the bloodless sacrifice of the Body and Blood of Christ, and by works of mercy done in faith for their memory.

377. On what is this doctrine grounded ?

On the constant tradition of the Catholic Church ; the sources of which may be seen even in the Church of the Old Testament. Judas Maccabæus offered sacrifice for his men that had fallen. 2 Macc. xii. 43. Prayer for the departed has ever formed a fixed part of the divine Liturgy, from the first Liturgy of the Apostle James. St. Cyril of Jerusalem says : *Very great will be the benefit to those souls for which prayer is offered at the moment when the holy and tremendous Sacrifice is lying in view.* (Lect. Myst. v. 9.)

St. Basil the Great, in his prayers for Pentecost, says that the Lord vouchsafes to receive from us propitiatory prayers and sacrifices *for those that are kept in Hades,* and allows us the hope of obtaining for them *peace, relief, and freedom.*

ON THE TWELFTH ARTICLE.

378. What is *the life of the world to come?*

The life that shall be after the resurrection of the dead and the general judgment of Christ.

379. What kind of life shall this be?

For those who believe, who love God, and do what is good, it shall be so happy that we can not now even conceive such happiness. *It doth not yet appear what we shall be.* 1 John iii. 2. *I knew a man in Christ,* says the Apostle Paul, *who was caught up into Paradise, and heard unspeakable words, which it is not lawful for a man to utter.* 2 Cor. xii. 2, 4.

380. Whence shall proceed this so great happiness?

From the contemplation of God in light and glory, and from union with him. *For now we see through a glass darkly, but then face to face: now I know in part, but then shall I know, even as also I am known.* 1 Cor. xiii. 12.

Then shall the righteous shine forth as the sun, in the kingdom of their Father. Matt. xiii. 43. *God shall be all in all.* 1 Cor. xv. 28.

381. Shall the body also share in the happiness of the soul?

Yes; it too will be glorified with the light of God, as Christ's body was at his transfiguration on Mount Tabor.

It is sown in dishonor, it is raised in glory. 1 Cor. xv. 43. *As we have borne the image of the earthy,* that is, of Adam, *we shall also bear the image of the heavenly.* 1 Cor. xv. 49.

382. Will all be equally happy?

No. There will be different degrees of happiness, in proportion as every one shall have here endured the fight of faith, love, and good works. *There is one glory of the sun, and another glory of the moon, and another glory of the stars; for one star differeth from another star in glory. So also is the resurrection of the dead.* 1 Cor. xv. 41, 42.

383. But what will be the lot of unbelievers and transgressors?

They will be given over to everlasting death—that is, to everlasting fire, to everlasting torment, with the devils.

Whosoever was not found written in the book of life was cast into the lake of fire. Rev. xx. 15. And, *That is the second death.* Rev. xx. 14. *Depart from me, ye cursed, into everlasting fire, prepared for the devil and his angels.* Matt. xxv. 41. *And these shall go away into*

everlasting punishment, but the righteous into life eternal. Matt. xxv 46. *It is better for thee to enter into the kingdom of God with one eye, than having two eyes to be cast into hell fire: where their worm dieth not, and the fire is not quenched.* Mark ix. 47, 48.

384. Why will such severity be used with sinners?

Not because God willed them to perish; but they of their own will *perish, because they receive not the love of the truth, that they might be saved.* 2 Thess. ii. 10.

385. Of what benefit will it be to us to meditate on death, on the resurrection, on the last judgment, on everlasting happiness, and on everlasting torment?

These meditations will assist us to abstain from sin, and to wean our affections from earthly things; they will console us for the absence or loss of worldly goods, incite us to keep our souls and bodies pure, to live to God and to eternity, and so to attain everlasting salvation.

THE SECOND PART OF THE ORTHODOX CATECHISM.

ON HOPE.

DEFINITION OF CHRISTIAN HOPE, ITS GROUND, AND THE MEANS THERETO.

386. What is *Christian hope?*

The resting of the heart on God, with the full trust that he ever cares for our salvation, and will give us the happiness he has promised.

387. What is the ground of Christian hope?

The *Lord Jesus Christ is our hope,* or the ground of our hope. 1 Tim. i. 1. *Hope to the end for the grace that is to be brought unto you by the revelation of Jesus Christ.* 1 Peter i. 13.

388. What are the means for attaining to a saving hope?

The means to this are, first, prayer; secondly, the true doctrine of blessedness, and its practical application.

ON PRAYER.

389. Is there any testimony of God's Word to this, that prayer is a mean for attaining to a saving hope?

Jesus Christ himself joins the hope of receiving our desire with prayer: *Whatsoever ye shall ask* of the Father *in my name, that will I do, that the Father may be glorified in the Son.* John xiv. 13.

390. What is *Prayer?*

The lifting up of man's mind and heart to God, manifested by devout words.

391. What should the Christian do when he lifts up his mind and heart to God?

First, he should *glorify* him for his divine perfections; secondly, *give thanks* to him for his mercies; thirdly, *ask* him for what he needs. So there are three chief forms of prayer: *Praise, Thanksgiving,* and *Petition.*

392. Can a man pray without words?

He can: in mind and heart. An example of this may be seen in Moses before the passage through the Red Sea. Exod. xiv. 15.

393. Has not such prayer a name of its own?

It is called *spiritual,* or prayer of the *heart* and *mind,* in one word, *inward* prayer; while, on the other hand, prayer expressed in words, and accompanied by other marks of devotion, is called *oral* or *outward* prayer.

394. Can there be outward prayer without inward?

There can: if any man utter words of prayer without attention or earnestness.

395. Does outward prayer alone suffice to obtain grace?

So far is it from sufficing to obtain grace, that contrariwise it provokes God to anger.

God has himself declared his displeasure at such prayer: *This people draweth nigh unto me with their mouth, and honoreth me with their lips, but their heart is far from me : but in vain do they worship me.* Matt. xv. 8, 9.

396. Does not inward prayer alone suffice without outward?

This question is as if one should ask whether soul alone might not suffice for man without body. It is idle to ask this, seeing that God has been pleased to make man consist of soul and body; likewise idle it is to ask whether inward prayer alone may not suffice without outward. Since we have both soul and body, we ought to *glorify God in our bodies, and in our souls, which are God's :* this being besides natural, *that out of the abundance of the heart the mouth should speak.* Our Lord Jesus Christ was spiritual in the highest degree, but even he expressed his spiritual prayer both by words and by devout gestures of body, sometimes, for instance, lifting up

his eyes to heaven, sometimes kneeling, or falling on his face to the ground. 1 Cor. vi. 20; Matt. xii. 34; John xvii. 1; Luke xxii. 41; Matt. xxvi. 39.

ON THE LORD'S PRAYER.

397. Is there not a prayer which may be termed the common Christian prayer, and pattern of all prayers?

Such is the Lord's Prayer.

398. What is the *Lord's Prayer?*

A prayer which our Lord Jesus Christ taught the Apostles, and which they delivered to all believers.

399. Repeat it.

Our Father, who art in heaven;

1. *Hallowed be thy Name;*
2. *Thy kingdom come;*
3. *Thy will be done, as in heaven, so in earth;*
4. *Give us this day our bread for subsistence;*
5. *And forgive us our debts, as we forgive our debtors;*
6. *And lead us not into temptation;*
7. *But deliver us from evil.*

For thine is the kingdom, the power, and the glory, forever and ever. Amen. Matt. vi. 9–13.

400. In order the better to understand the Lord's Prayer, how may we divide it?

Into the *invocation,* seven *petitions,* and the *doxology.*

ON THE INVOCATION.

401. How dare we call God *Father?*

By faith in Jesus Christ, and by the grace of regeneration.

As many as received him, to them gave he power to become the sons of God, even to them that believe on his name: which were born, not of blood, nor of the will of the flesh, nor of the will of man, but of God. John i. 12, 13.

402. Must we say *Our Father* even when we pray alone?

Certainly we must.

403. Why so?

Because Christian charity requires us to call upon God, and ask good things of him, for all our brethren, no less than for ourselves.

404. Why in the invocation do we say, *Who art in heaven?*

That, entering upon prayer, we may leave every thing earthly and corruptible, and raise our minds and hearts to what is heavenly, everlasting, and divine.

ON THE FIRST PETITION.

405. Is not God's name holy?

Doubtless it is holy in itself. *Holy is his name.* Luke i. 49.

406. How, then, can it yet be hallowed?

It may be hallowed in men; that is, his eternal holiness may be manifested in them.

407. How?

First, when we, having in our thoughts and heart the name of God, so live as his holiness requires, and thus glorify God; secondly, when others also, seeing our good lives, glorify God.

Let your light so shine before men, that they may see your good works, and glorify your Father which is in heaven. Matt. v. 16.

ON THE SECOND PETITION.

408. What is the *kingdom* of God spoken of in the second petition of the Lord's Prayer?

The kingdom of *grace*, which, as St. Paul says, is *righteousness, and peace, and joy in the Holy Ghost.* Rom. xiv. 17.

409. Is not this kingdom come already?

To some it has not yet come in its full sense; while to others it has not yet come at all. inasmuch as *sin still reigns in their mortal bodies, that they should obey it in the lusts thereof.* Rom. vi. 12.

410. How does it come?

Secretly, and inwardly. *The kingdom of God cometh not with observation; for, behold, the kingdom of God is within you.* Luke xvii. 20, 21.

411. May not the Christian ask for something further under the name of God's kingdom?

He may ask for the kingdom of *glory*—that is, for the perfect bliss of the faithful.

Having a desire to depart, and be with Christ. Phil. i. 23.

On the Third Petition.

412. What means the petition, *Thy will be done?*

Hereby we ask of God that all we do, and all that befalls us, may be ordered not as we will, but as pleases him.

413. Why need we ask this?

Because we often err in our wishes; but God unerringly, and incomparably more than we ourselves, wishes for us all that is good, and is ever ready to bestow it, unless he be prevented by our willfulness and obstinacy.

Unto him that is able to do exceeding abundantly above all that we ask or think, according to the power that worketh in us, unto him be glory in the Church. Eph. iii. 20, 21.

414. Why do we ask that God's will be done in earth *as in heaven?*

Because in heaven the holy angels and saints in bliss, all without exception, always, and in all things, do God's will.

On the Fourth Petition.

415. What is *bread for subsistence?* [1]

The bread which we need in order to subsist or live.

416. With what thoughts should we ask of God this bread?

Agreeably with the instruction of our Lord Jesus Christ, we should ask no more than *bread for subsistence;* that is, necessary food, and such clothing and shelter as is likewise necessary for life; but whatever is beyond this, and serves not so much for necessity as for gratification, we should leave to the will of God; and if it be given, return thanks to him; if it be not given, we should be content without it.

417. Why are we directed to ask for bread for subsistence only for *this day?*

That we may not be too anxious about the future, but trust for that to God. *Take therefore no thought for the morrow, for the morrow shall take thought for the things of itself: sufficient unto the day is the evil thereof.* Matt. vi. 34. *For your heavenly Father knoweth that ye have need of all these things.* Matt. vi. 32.

---

[1] [The German edition reads: *Tägliches Brot, daily bread;* the Greek, ὁ ἄρτος ὁ ἐπιούσιος. On the different derivations and interpretations of ἐπιούσιος, see a very learned and able essay by Prof. J. B. LIGHTFOOT, D.D., in an appendix to his work on a *Fresh Revision of the English New Testament*, 1872, Harper's ed. pp. 163-184.—ED.]

418. May we not ask for something further under the name of bread for subsistence?

Since man is made of both a bodily and a spiritual substance, and the substance of the soul far excels that of the body, we may and should seek for the soul also that bread of subsistence without which the inward man must perish of hunger.

(See Cyril. Hier. Lect. Myst. iv. 15 ; Orthod. Confess. Pt. II. Q. 19.)

419. What is the bread of subsistence for the soul?

The Word of God, and the Body and Blood of Christ.

Man shall not live by bread alone, but by every word that proceedeth out of the mouth of God. Matt. iv. 4. *My flesh is meat indeed, and my blood is drink indeed.* John vi. 55.

On the Fifth Petition.

420. What is meant in the Lord's Prayer by *our debts?*

Our sins.

421. Why are our sins called debts?

Because we, having received all from God, ought to render all back to him—that is, subject all to his will and law; which if we do not, we are left debtors to his justice.

422. But who are *our debtors?*

People who have not rendered us that which they owed us by the law of God; as, for instance, have not shown us love, but malice.

423. If God is just, how can we be forgiven our debts?

Through the mediation of Jesus Christ.

For there is one God, and one Mediator between God and man, the man Jesus Christ, who gave himself a ransom for all. 1 Tim. ii. 5, 6.

424. What will be the consequence, if we ask God to forgive us our sins without ourselves forgiving others?

In that case neither shall we be forgiven.

For if ye forgive men their trespasses, your heavenly Father will also forgive you; but if ye forgive not men their trespasses, neither will your Father forgive you your trespasses. Matt. vi. 14, 15.

425. Why will not God forgive us if we do not forgive others?

Because we hereby show ourselves evil, and so alienate from us God's goodness and mercy.

426. What disposition, then, must we have to use aright those words of the Lord's Prayer, *As we forgive our debtors?*

These words absolutely require that when we pray we should bear no malice nor hatred, but be in peace and charity with all men.

Therefore if thou bring thy gift to the altar, and there rememberest that thy brother hath aught against thee, leave there thy gift before the altar, and go thy way: first be reconciled to thy brother, and then come and offer thy gift.   Matt. v. 23, 24.

427. But what am I to do if I can not readily find him who hath aught against me, or if he show himself unwilling to be reconciled?

In such a case it is enough to be reconciled with him in heart, before the eyes of the all-seeing God.

If it be possible, as much as lieth in you, live peaceably with all men.   Rom. xii. 18.

On the Sixth Petition.

428. What is meant in the Lord's Prayer by *temptation?*

Any conjuncture of circumstances in which there is imminent danger of losing the faith, or falling into great sin.

429. Whence come such temptations?

From *our flesh,* from the *world,* or other people, and from the *devil.*

430. What do we ask in these words of the prayer, *Lead us not into temptation?*

First, that God suffer us not to be led into temptation; secondly, that if it be needful for us to be tried and purified through temptation, he give us not up wholly to temptation, nor suffer us to fall.

On the Seventh Petition.

431. What do we ask in these words of the prayer, *Deliver us from evil?*

We ask for deliverance from all evil that can reach us in the *world,* which since the fall *lieth in wickedness* (1 John v. 19): but especially from the evil of sin, and from the evil suggestions and snares of the spirit of evil, which is the devil.

On the Doxology.

432. Why after the Lord's Prayer do we subjoin the *Doxology?*

First, that when we ask mercies for ourselves from our heavenly Father, we may at the same time render him that honor which is his

due; secondly, that by the thought of his everlasting *kingdom, power,* and *glory,* we may be more and more established in the hope that he will give us what we ask, because this is in his power, and makes to his glory.

433. What means the word *Amen?*

It means *verily,* or *so be it.*

434. Why is this word added to the Doxology?

To signify that we offer the prayer in faith, and without doubting, as we are taught to do by the Apostle James. James i. 6.

On the Doctrine of Blessedness.

435. What must we join with prayer in order to be grounded in the hope of salvation and blessedness?

Our own exertions for the attainment of blessedness.

Of this point the Lord himself says: *Why call ye me Lord, Lord, and do not the things which I say?* Luke vi. 46. *Not every one that saith unto me Lord, Lord, shall enter into the kingdom of heaven, but he that doeth the will of my Father which is in heaven.* Matt. vii. 21.

436. What doctrine may we take as our guide in these exertions?

The doctrine of our Lord Jesus Christ, which is briefly set forth in his *Beatitudes,* or sentences on blessedness.

437. How many such sentences are there?

The nine following:

1. *Blessed are the poor in spirit: for theirs is the kingdom of heaven.*

2. *Blessed are they that mourn: for they shall be comforted.*

3. *Blessed are the meek: for they shall inherit the earth.*

4. *Blessed are they which do hunger and thirst after righteousness: for they shall be filled.*

5. *Blessed are the merciful: for they shall obtain mercy.*

6. *Blessed are the pure in heart: for they shall see God.*

7. *Blessed are the peacemakers: for they shall be called the children of God.*

8. *Blessed are they which are persecuted for righteousness' sake: for theirs is the kingdom of heaven.*

9. *Blessed are ye, when men shall revile you, and persecute you, and shall say all manner of evil against you falsely, for my sake.*

Rejoice, and be exceeding glad : for great is your reward in heaven.
Matt. v. 3–12.

438. What is to be observed of all these sentences in order to their right understanding?

This: that the Lord proposed in these sentences a *doctrine* for the attainment of blessedness, as is expressly said in the Gospel: *He opened his mouth, and taught;* but, being meek and lowly of heart, he proposed his doctrine not in the form of commandment, but of blessing, to those who should of their own free will receive and fulfill it. Consequently in each sentence or Beatitude we must consider, first, the doctrine or precept; secondly, the blessing or promise of reward.

ON THE FIRST BEATITUDE.

439. What is the Lord's first precept of blessedness?

They who would be blessed must be *poor in spirit.*

440. What is it to be *poor in spirit?*

It is to have a spiritual conviction that we have nothing of our own, nothing but what God bestows upon us, and that we can do nothing good without God's help and grace, thus counting ourselves as nothing, and in all throwing ourselves upon the mercy of God; in brief, as St. Chrysostom explains it, *spiritual poverty is humility.* (Hom. in Matt. xv.)

441. Can the rich, too, be poor in spirit?

Doubtless they can: if they consider that visible riches are corruptible and soon pass away, and can never compensate for the want of spiritual goods. *What is a man profited, if he gain the whole world, and lose his own soul? or what shall a man give in exchange for his soul?* Matt. xvi. 26.

442. May not bodily poverty serve to the perfection of spiritual?

It may, if the Christian choose it voluntarily, for God's sake. Of this, Jesus Christ himself said to the rich man: *If thou wilt be perfect, go, sell that thou hast, and give to the poor, and thou shalt have treasure in heaven; and come and follow me.* Matt. xix. 21.

443. What does our Lord promise to the poor in spirit?

The kingdom of heaven.

444. How is the kingdom of heaven theirs?

In the present life inwardly, and inchoately,[1] by faith and hope; but

---

[1] [In an incipient degree, in germ. The Greek ed. reads, ἐσωτερικῶς καὶ προκαταρκτικῶς; the German, *innerlich und anfänglich.*—ED.]

in the life to come perfectly, by their being made partakers of everlasting blessedness.

On the Second Beatitude.

445. What is the Lord's second precept for blessedness?

They who would be blessed must *mourn*.

446. What is meant in this precept by the word *mourn?*

Sorrow and contrition of heart, with unfeigned tears, for that we so
imperfectly and unworthily serve the Lord, or even rather deserve his
anger by our sins. *For godly sorrow worketh repentance unto salvation not to be repented of; but the sorrow of this world worketh
death.* 2 Cor. vii. 10.

447. What special promise does the Lord make to mourners?

That they *shall be comforted*.

448. What comfort is here to be understood?

That of grace, consisting in the pardon of sin, and in peace of conscience.

449. Why is this promise added to the precept for mourning?

In order that sorrow for sin may not reach to despair.

On the Third Beatitude.

450. What is the Lord's third precept for blessedness?

They who would be blessed must be *meek*.

451. What is *meekness?*

A quiet disposition of spirit, joined with care neither to offend any
man, nor be offended at any thing one's self.

452. What are the special effects of Christian meekness?

These: that we never murmur against God, nor even against men,
when any thing falls out against our wishes, nor give way to anger, nor
set ourselves up.

453. What is promised by the Lord to the meek?

That they *shall inherit the earth*.

454. How are we to understand this promise?

As regards Christ's followers generally it is a prediction which has
been literally fulfilled; for the ever-meek Christians, instead of being
destroyed by the fury of the heathen, have inherited the universe
which the heathen formerly possessed. But the further sense of this
promise, as regards Christians both generally and individually, is

this, that they shall receive an inheritance, as the Psalmist says, *in the land of the living;* that is, where men live and never die; in other words, that they shall receive everlasting blessedness. See Psalm xxvii. 13.

On the Fourth Beatitude.

455. What is the Lord's fourth precept for blessedness?

They who would be blessed must *hunger and thirst after righteousness.*

456. What is meant here by the word *righteousness?*

Though this word may well stand for every virtue which the Christian ought to desire even as his meat and drink, yet should we here specially understand that righteousness of which, in the book of Daniel, it is said, *An everlasting righteousness shall be brought in;* that is, the justification of guilty man through grace and faith in Jesus Christ. Dan. ix. 24.

The Apostle Paul speaks thus: *The righteousness of God which is by faith of Jesus Christ unto all, and upon all them that believe; for there is no difference: for all have sinned, and come short of the glory of God; being justified freely by his grace through the redemption that is in Christ Jesus, whom God hath set forth to be a propitiation through faith in his blood, to declare his righteousness for the remission of sins that are past.* Rom. iii. 22–25.

457. Who are they that *hunger and thirst after righteousness?*

They who, while they love to do good, yet count not themselves righteous, nor rest on their own good works, but acknowledge themselves sinners and guilty before God; and who, by the wish and prayer of faith, hunger and thirst after the justification of grace through Jesus Christ, as after spiritual meat and drink.

458. What does the Lord promise to them who hunger and thirst after righteousness?

That they *shall be filled.*

459. What is meant here by *being filled?*

As the filling or satisfying of the body produces, first, the cessation of the sense of hunger and thirst; secondly, the strengthening the body by food, so the filling of the soul means, first, the inward peace of the pardoned sinner; secondly, the acquisition of strength to do good, given by justifying grace. The perfect filling, however, of the soul created for the enjoyment of endless good is to follow in the life eter-

nal, according to the words of the Psalmist: *When I awake up after thy likeness, I shall be satisfied with it.* Psalm xvii. 15.

ON THE FIFTH BEATITUDE.

460. What is the Lord's fifth precept for blessedness?

They who would be blessed must be *merciful.*

461. How are we to fulfill this precept?

By works of mercy, corporal and spiritual; for, as St. Chrysostom says, *the forms of mercy are manifold, and this commandment is broad.* (Hom. in Matt. xv.)

462. Which are the *corporal works of mercy?*

1. To feed the hungry.

2. To give drink to the thirsty.

3. To clothe the naked, or such as have not necessary and decent clothing.

4. To visit them that are in prison.

5. To visit the sick, minister to them, and forward their recovery, or aid them to a Christian preparation for death.

6. To show hospitality to strangers.

7. To bury them that have died in poverty.

463. Which are the *spiritual works of mercy?*

1. By exhortation *to convert the sinner from the error of his way.* James v. 20.

2. To instruct the ignorant in truth and virtue.

3. To give our neighbor good and seasonable advice in difficulty, or in any danger of which he is unaware.

4. To pray for others to God.

5. To comfort the afflicted.

6. Not to return the evil which others may have done us.

7. To forgive injuries from our heart.

464. Is it not contrary to the precept of mercy for civil justice to punish criminals?

Not in the least; if this be done as of duty, and with a good intent, that is, in order to correct them, or to preserve the innocent from their crimes.

465. What does the Lord promise to the merciful?

That they *shall obtain mercy.*

466. What mercy is here to be understood?

That of being delivered from everlasting condemnation for sin at God's Judgment.

On the Sixth Beatitude.

467. What is the Lord's sixth precept for blessedness?

They who would be blessed must be *pure in heart.*

468. Is not *purity of heart* the same thing as sincerity?

Sincerity which feigns not any good dispositions foreign to the heart, but shows the really good dispositions of the heart by good deeds, is only the lowest degree of purity of heart. This last a man attains by constant and strict watchfulness over himself, driving away from his heart every unlawful wish and thought, and every affection for earthly things, and ever keeping there the remembrance of God and our Lord Jesus Christ with faith and charity.

469. What does the Lord promise to the pure in heart?

That they *shall see God.*

470. How are we to understand this promise?

The Word of God compares the heart of man to the eye, and ascribes to perfect Christians *enlightened eyes of the heart.* Eph. i. 18. As the eye that is clear can see the light, so the heart that is pure can behold God. But since the sight of God's countenance is the very source of everlasting blessedness, the promise of seeing God is the promise of the highest degree of everlasting blessedness.

On the Seventh Beatitude.

471. What is the Lord's seventh precept for blessedness?

They who would be blessed must be *peace-makers.*

472. How are we to fulfill this commandment?

We must live friendly with all men, and give no occasion for disagreement: if any arise, we must try all possible ways to put a stop to it, even by yielding our own right, unless this be against duty, or hurtful to any other: if others are at enmity, we must do all we can to reconcile them; and if we fail, we must pray to God for their reconciliation.

473. What does the Lord promise to peace-makers?

That they *shall be called the Sons of God.*

474. What is signified by this promise?

The sublimity both of their office and of their reward. Since in what they do they imitate the only-begotten Son of God, who came upon earth to reconcile fallen man with God's justice, they are for this

promised the gracious name of Sons of God, and without doubt a degree of blessedness answering thereto.

On the Eighth Beatitude.

475. What is the Lord's eighth precept for blessedness?

They who would be blessed must be ready *to endure persecution for righteousness' sake,* without betraying it.

476. What qualities are required by this precept?

Love of righteousness, constancy and firmness in virtue, fortitude and patience, when one is subjected to calamity or danger for refusing to betray truth and virtue.

477. What does the Lord promise to those who are persecuted for righteousness' sake?

The *kingdom of heaven,* as if in recompense for what they lose through persecution; in like manner as the same is promised to the poor in spirit, to make up for the feeling of want and privation.

On the Ninth Beatitude.

478. What is the Lord's ninth precept for blessedness?

They who would be blessed must be ready *to take with joy reproach, persecution, suffering, and death itself, for the name of Christ, and for the true orthodox faith.*

479. What is the name for the course required by this precept?

The course of *martyrdom.*

480. What does the Lord promise for this course?

A great reward in heaven; that is, a special and high degree of blessedness.

THE THIRD PART OF THE ORTHODOX CATECHISM.

ON LOVE.[1]

On the Union between Faith and Love.

481. What should be the effect and fruit of true faith in the Christian?

Love, and *good works* conformable thereto.

---

[1] [Blackmore uses *charity* in conformity with the English Bible (1 Cor. xiii. etc.); but *love* is the more correct rendering of ἀγάπη (*Liebe*), since it applies to God as well as man, while *charity* is now used in a more restricted sense.—Ed.]

In Jesus Christ, says the Apostle Paul, *neither circumcision avail-eth any thing, nor uncircumcision, but faith which worketh by love.* Gal. v. 6.

482. Is not faith alone enough for a Christian, *without love and good works?*

No; for faith without love and good works is inactive and dead, and so can not lead to eternal life.

He that loveth not his brother, abideth in death. 1 John iii. 14. *What doth it profit, my brethren, though a man say he hath faith, and have not works? can faith save him? For as the body without the spirit is dead, so faith without works is dead also.* James ii. 14, 26.

483. May not a man, on the other hand, be saved by love and good works, *without faith?*

It is impossible that a man who has not faith in God should really love him; besides, man, being ruined by sin, can not do really good works, unless he receive through faith in Jesus Christ spiritual strength, or grace from God.

Without faith it is impossible to please God: for he that cometh to God must believe that he is, and that he is a rewarder of them that diligently seek him. Heb. xi. 6.

For as many as are of the works of the law are under the curse: for it is written, Cursed is every one that continueth not in all things which are written in the book of the law to do them. Gal. iii. 10. *For we through the spirit wait for the hope of righteousness by faith.* Gal. v. 5.

For by grace are ye saved through faith; and that not of your-selves: it is the gift of God: not of works, lest any man should boast. Eph. ii. 8, 9.

484. What is to be thought of such love as *is not accompanied by good works?*

Such love is not real: for true love naturally shows itself by good works. Jesus Christ says: *He that hath my commandments, and keep-eth them, he it is that loveth me: if a man love me, he will keep my word.* John xiv. 21, 23.

The Apostle John writes: *For this is the love of God, that we keep his commandments.* 1 John v. 3. *Let us not love in word, neither in tongue, but in deed and in truth.* 1 John iii. 18.

On the Law of God and the Commandments.

485. What means have we to know good works from bad?

The *inward law of God*, or the witness of our conscience, and the *outward* law of God, or God's commandments.

486. Does holy Scripture speak of the inward law of God?

The Apostle Paul says of the heathen : *Which show the work of the law written in their hearts, their conscience also bearing witness, and their thoughts the mean while accusing or else excusing one another.* Rom. ii. 15.

487. If there is in man's heart an *inward* law, why was the *outward* given?

It was given because men obeyed not the inward law, but led carnal and sinful lives, and stifled within themselves the voice of the spiritual law, so that it was necessary to put them in mind of it outwardly through the Commandments. *Wherefore then serveth the law?* *It was added because of transgressions.* Gal. iii. 19.

488. When and how was God's outward law given to men?

When the Hebrew people, descended from Abraham, had been miraculously delivered from bondage in Egypt, on their way to the promised land, in the desert, on Mount Sinai, God manifested his presence in fire and clouds, and gave them the law, by the hand of Moses, their leader.

489. Which are the chief and general commandments of this law?

The following *ten*, which were written *on two tables of stone :*

1. *I am the Lord thy God : thou shalt have none other gods beside me.*

2. *Thou shalt not make unto thyself any graven image, nor the likeness of any thing that is in heaven above, or that is in the earth beneath, or that is in the waters under the earth : thou shalt not bow down to them, nor serve them.*

3. *Thou shalt not take the name of the Lord thy God in vain.*

4. *Remember the Sabbath day, to keep it holy : six days shalt thou labor, and do all thy work ; but the seventh day is the Sabbath to the Lord thy God.*

5. *Honor thy father and thy mother, that it may be well with thee, and that thy days may be long upon the earth.*

6. *Thou shalt not kill.*

7. *Thou shalt not commit adultery.*

8. *Thou shalt not steal.*

9. *Thou shalt not bear false witness against thy neighbor.*

10. *Thou shalt not covet thy neighbor's wife, thou shalt not covet thy neighbor's house, nor his land, nor his man-servant, nor his maid-servant, nor his ox, nor his ass, nor any of his cattle, nor any thing that is thy neighbor's.* Exod. xx. 1–17 ; Deut. v. 6–21.

490. You said that these Commandments were given to the people of Israel : must we, then, also walk by them ?

We must : for they are in substance the same law which, in the words of St. Paul, has been *written in the hearts* of all men, that all should walk by it.

491. Did Jesus Christ teach men to walk by the Ten Commandments ?

He bade men, if they would attain to everlasting life, to *keep the Commandments ;* and taught us to understand and fulfill them more perfectly than had been done before he came. Matt. xix. 17, and v.

On the Division of the Commandments into Two Tables.

492. What means the division of the Ten Commandments into *two tables ?*

This : that they contain *two kinds of love*—love to *God*, and love to *our neighbor ;* and prescribe two corresponding kinds of duties.

493. Has not Jesus Christ said something of this ?

When asked, *Which is the great commandment in the law ?* he replied : *Thou shalt love the Lord thy God with all thy heart, and with all thy soul, and with all thy mind. This is the first and great commandment. And the second is like unto it : Thou shalt love thy neighbor as thyself. On these two commandments hang all the law and the prophets.* Matt. xxii. 36–40.

494. Are all men our *neighbors ?*

Yes, all ; because all are the creation of one God, and have come from one man : but our neighbors in faith are doubly neighbors to us, as being children of one heavenly Father by faith in Jesus Christ.

495. But why is there no commandment of love *to ourselves ?*

Because we love ourselves naturally, and without any commandment. *No man ever yet hated his own flesh, but nourisheth and cherisheth it.* Eph. v. 29.

496. What relative order should there be in our love to *God*, our *neighbor*, and *ourselves ?*

We should love ourselves not for our own, but for God's sake, and

partly also for the sake of our neighbors; we should love our neighbor for the sake of God; but we should love God for himself, and above all. Love of self should be sacrificed to the love of our neighbor; but both should be sacrificed to the love of God.

Greater love hath no man than this, that a man lay down his life for his friends. John xv. 13.

He that loveth father or mother more than me, saith Jesus Christ, is not worthy of me; and he that loveth son or daughter more than me, is not worthy of me. Matt. x. 37.

497. If the whole law is contained in *two* commandments, why are they divided into ten *?*

In order the more clearly to set forth our duties towards God, and towards our neighbor.

498. In which of the Ten Commandments are we taught our *duties towards God?*

In the first four.

499. What are these duties?

In the first commandment we are taught to *know* and *worship* the true God.

In the second, to abstain from *false* worship.

In the third, not to sin against God's worship even by *word.*

In the fourth, to keep a certain order in the *time* and *acts* of God's worship.

500. In which of the Ten Commandments are we taught our *duties towards our neighbor ?*

In the last six.

501. What are these duties?

In the fifth commandment we are taught to love and *honor* those of our neighbors who are nearest to us, beginning with our parents.

In the sixth, not to hurt the *life* of our neighbor.

In the seventh, not to hurt the *purity* of his morals.

In the eighth, not to hurt his *property.*

In the ninth, not to hurt him by *word.*

In the tenth, not to *wish* to hurt him.

502. Do not the Ten Commandments include also *our duties towards ourselves?*

Yes; these duties are implied in the commandments of the second table relating to our neighbors; for our duty is to love our neighbor *as* ourselves.

On the First Commandment.

503. What mean these words, *I am the Lord thy God?*

By these words God, as it were, points himself out to man, and so commands him to *know* the Lord his God.

504. What particular duties may we deduce from the commandment to know God?

1. We must *seek to learn the knowledge of God*, as being the most essential of all knowledge.

2. We must listen attentively to *instructions* on God and on his works in church, and to *religious conversations* on the same at home.

3. We must read or hear read books of instruction in the knowledge of God; and in the first place, *holy Scripture;* secondly, *the writings of the holy Fathers.*

505. What are we taught in the words, *Thou shalt have none other gods but me?*

We are taught to turn and cleave to the one true God, or, in other words, devoutly *to worship* him.

506. What duties are there which refer to the *inward* worship of God?

1. *To believe* in God.

2. *To walk before* God; that is, to be ever mindful of him, and in all things to walk circumspectly, because he seeth not only our actions, but even our most secret thoughts.

3. *To fear* God, or stand in awe of him; that is, to think the anger of our heavenly Father the greatest ill that can befall us, and therefore strive not to offend him.

4. *To trust* in God.

5. *To love* God.

6. *To obey* God; that is, to be ever ready to do what he commands, and not to murmur when he deals with us otherwise than we could desire.

7. *To adore* God, as the Supreme Being.

8. *To glorify* God, as being all-perfect.

9. *To give thanks* to God, as our Creator, Provident Sustainer, and Saviour.

10. *To call upon* God, as our all-good and almighty helper, in every good work which we undertake.

507. What duties are there which refer to the *outward* worship of God?

1. *To confess* God; that is, to acknowledge that he is our God, and

not deny him, although for confessing him we may have to suffer, or even die.

2. To take part *in the public divine service* enjoined by God and appointed by the Orthodox Church.

508. In order the more exactly to understand and keep the first commandment, we must know further what sins there may be against it.

1. *Atheism;* when men, whom the Psalmist justly calls fools, wishing to rid themselves of the fear of God's judgment, *say in their heart, There is no God.* Psalm xiv. 1.

2. *Polytheism;* when, instead of the one true God, men acknowledge a number of false deities.

3. *Infidelity;* when men, who admit the existence of God, disbelieve his providence and his revelation.

4. *Heresy;* when people mix with the doctrine of the faith opinions contrary to divine truth.

5. *Schism;* that is, willful departure from the unity of divine worship, and from the Orthodox Catholic Church of God.

6. *Apostasy;* when any deny the true faith from fear of man, or for worldly advantage.

7. *Despair;* when men give up all hope of obtaining from God grace and salvation.

8. *Sorcery;* when men, leaving faith in the power of God, put their trust in secret and, for the most part, evil powers of creatures, especially of evil spirits, and seek to work by their means.

9. *Superstition;* when men put faith in any common thing as if it had divine power, and trust in it instead of trusting in God, or fear it instead of fearing God; as, for instance, when they put faith in an old book, and think they can be saved by none other, and must not use a new one, though the new book contain the very same doctrine, and the very same form of divine service.

10. *Sloth,* in respect of learning religion, or in respect of prayer, and the public service of God.

11. *Love of the creature more than of God.*

12. *Men-pleasing;* when they seek to please men, so as for this to be careless of pleasing God.

13. *Trusting in man;* when any one trusts in his own means and strength, or in the means and strength of others, and not in the mercy and help of God.

509. Why must we think that men-pleasing and trusting in man are against the first commandment?

Because the man, whom we please, or in whom we trust, so as to forget God, is in some sort to us *another god*, in place of the true God.

510. How does holy Scripture speak of men-pleasing?

The Apostle Paul says: *For if I yet pleased men, I should not be the servant of Christ.* Gal. i. 10.

511. How does holy Scripture speak of trusting in man?

Thus saith the Lord: Cursed be the man that trusteth in man, and maketh flesh his arm, and whose heart departeth from the Lord. Jer. xvii. 5.

512. In order to succeed the better in fulfilling his duties to God, how must a man act *by himself?*

He must deny himself.

Whosoever will come after me, says Jesus Christ, *let him deny himself.* Mark viii. 34.

513. What is it to *deny one's self?*

Basil the Great explains it thus: *He denies himself who puts off the old man with his deeds, which is corrupt, according to the deceitful lusts; who renounces also all worldly affections, which can hinder his intention of godliness. Perfect self-denial consists in this, that he cease to have any affection even for life itself, and bear the judgment of death in himself, that he may not trust in himself.* (Can. Long. Resp. 8.)

514. What consolation is there for him who, by denying himself, loses many natural gratifications?

The consolation of grace: a divine consolation, which even sufferings themselves can not impair.

For as the sufferings of Christ abound in us, so our consolation also aboundeth by Christ. 2 Cor. i. 5.

515. If the first commandment teaches us to worship religiously God alone, how does it agree with this commandment *to honor angels and holy men?*

To pay them due and rightful honor is altogether agreeable to this commandment; because in them we honor the grace of God, which dwells and works in them, and through them seek help from God.

On the Second Commandment.

516. What is a *graven image*, as spoken of in the second commandment?

The commandment itself explains that a graven image, or idol, is the likeness of some creature in heaven, or earth, or in the waters, which men bow down to and serve instead of God their Maker.

517. What is forbidden, then, by the second commandment?

We are forbidden to bow down to graven images or idols, as to supposed deities, or as to likenesses of false gods.

518. Are we not hereby forbidden to have any sacred representations whatever?

By no means. This very plainly appears from hence, that the same Moses through whom God gave the commandment against graven images, received at the same time from God an order to place in the tabernacle, or movable temple of the Israelites, sacred representations of Cherubim in gold, and to place them, too, in that inner part of the temple to which the people turned for the worship of God.

519. Why is this example worthy of remark for the Orthodox Christian Church?

Because it illustrates her use of holy icons.

520. What is an icon?

The word is Greek, and means an *image* or representation. In the Orthodox Church this name designates sacred representations of our Lord Jesus Christ, God incarnate, his immaculate Mother, and his saints.

521. Is the use of holy icons agreeable to the second commandment?

It would then, and then only, be otherwise, if any one were to make gods of them; but it is not in the least contrary to this commandment to honor icons as sacred representations, and to use them for the religious remembrance of God's works and of his saints; for when thus used icons are books, written with the forms of persons and things instead of letters. (See Greg. Magn. lib. ix. Ep. 9, ad Seren. Episc.)

522. What disposition of mind should we have when we reverence the icons?

While we look on them with our eyes, we should mentally look to God and to the saints, who are represented on them.

523. What general name is there for sin against the second commandment?

Idolatry.

524. Are there not also other sins against this commandment?

Besides gross idolatry there is yet another sort more subtle, to which belong—

1. *Covetousness*

2. *Belly-service* or *sensuality, gluttony*, and *drunkenness.*

3. *Pri 'e,* to which belongs likewise *vanity.*

525. Why is covetousness referred to idolatry?

The Apostle Paul expressly says that *covetousness is idolatry* (Col. iii. 5); because the covetous man serves riches rather than God.

526. If the second commandment forbid the love of gain, what contrary duties does it thereby necessarily enjoin?

Those of *contentedness* and *liberality.*

527. Why is belly-service referred to idolatry?

Because belly-servers set sensual gratification above every thing, and therefore the Apostle Paul says that *their god is their belly;* or, in other words, that the belly is their idol.   Phil. iii. 19.

528. If the second commandment forbid belly-service, what contrary duties does it thereby enjoin?

Those of *temperance* and *fasting.*

529. Why are pride and vanity referred to idolatry?

Because the proud man values above every thing his own abilities and excellences, and so they are his idol; the vain man wishes further that others also should worship the same idol.   These proud and vain dispositions were exemplified even sensibly in Nebuchadnezzar, king of Babylon, who first set up for himself a golden idol, and then ordered all to worship it.   Dan. iii.

530. Is there not still another vice which is near to idolatry?

Such a vice is *hypocrisy;* when a man uses the outward acts of religion, as fasting, and the strict observance of ceremonies, in order to obtain respect from the people, without thinking of the inward amendment of his heart.   Matt. vi. 5, 6, 7.

531. If the second commandment forbid pride, vanity, and hypocrisy, what contrary duties does it thereby enjoin?

Those of *humility*, and *doing good in secret.*

ON THE THIRD COMMANDMENT.

532. When is *God's name taken in vain?*

It is taken or uttered in vain when it is uttered in vain and unprofitable talk, and still more so when it is uttered *lyingly* or *irreverently.*

533. What sins are forbidden by the third commandment?

1. *Blasphemy,* or daring words against God.

2. *Murmuring*, or complaining against God's providence.

3. *Profaneness;* when holy things are jested on, or insulted.

4. *Inattention in prayer.*

5. *Perjury;* when men affirm with an oath what is false.

6. *Oath-breaking;* when men keep not just and lawful oaths.

7. *Breach of vows* made to God.

8. *Common swearing*, or thoughtless oaths in common talk.

534. Are not such oaths specially forbidden in holy Scripture?

The Saviour says: *I say unto you, Swear not at all, but let your communication be, Yea, yea; Nay, nay: for whatsoever is more than these cometh of evil.*   Matt. v. 34, 37.

535. Does not this go to forbid all *oaths in civil matters?*

The Apostle Paul says: *Men swear by the greater; and an oath for confirmation is to them an end of all strife.   Wherein God, willing more abundantly to show unto the heirs of promise the immutability of his counsel, confirmed it by an oath.*   Heb. vi. 16, 17.   Hence we must conclude, that if God himself for an immutable assurance used an oath, much more may we on grave and necessary occasions, when required by lawful authority, take an oath or vow religiously, with the firm intention of not breaking it.

ON THE FOURTH COMMANDMENT.

536. Why is it commanded to keep the *seventh*, rather than any other day, holy to God?

Because God in six days made the world, and on the seventh day rested from the work of creation.

537. Is the *Sabbath* kept in the Christian Church?

It is not kept, strictly speaking, as a holy day; but still in memory of the creation of the world, and in continuation of its original observance, it is distinguished from the other days of the week by a relaxation of the rule for fasting.

538. How, then, does the Christian Church obey the fourth commandment?

She still to every six days keeps a seventh, only not the last of the seven days, which is the Sabbath, but the first day in every week, which is the *Day of the Resurrection*, or *Lord's Day.*

539. Since when do we keep the Day of the Resurrection?

From the very time of Christ's resurrection.

540. Is there any mention in holy Scripture of keeping the day of the Resurrection ?

In the book of the Acts of the Apostles it is mentioned that the disciples—that is, the Christians—came together *on the first day after the Sabbath,* which was the first day of the week, or Day of the Resur-rection, *for the breaking of bread,* that is to say, for the celebration of the Sacrament of the Communion. Acts xx. 7. The Apostle and Evan-gelist John also in the Apocalypse mentions the *Lord's Day,* or the *Day of the Resurrection.*

541. Is there not yet something more to be understood under the name of the seventh day, or Sabbath ?

As in the Church of the Old Testament the name Sabbath was un-derstood to include divers other days appointed like the Sabbath for festivals or fasts, as *the festival of the Passover,* and *the day of Atone-ment,* so likewise are we now in the Christian Church bound to keep, besides the Lord's Day, certain others also, which have been appointed as *festivals* to the glory of God and the honor of the Blessed Virgin and other saints, or as *days of fasting.* (See Orthod. Confess. Pt. III. Q. 60 ; Pt. I. Q. 88.)

542. Which are the chief festivals ?

Those appointed in memory of the chief events relating to the Incar-nation of the Son of God for our salvation, and to the Manifestation of the Godhead ; after these, those appointed in honor of the Most Holy Mother of God, as the instrument of the mystery of the Incarnation. Such, in the order of the events, are the following :

1. The day of the birth of the Most Holy Mother of God.

2. The day of her being brought to the Temple to be dedicated to God.

3. The day of the Annunciation ; that is, when the angel announced to the Most Holy Virgin the Incarnation of the Son of God.

4. The day of the birth of Jesus Christ.

5. The day of the baptism of our Lord, and the Epiphany, or Mani-festation of the Most Holy Trinity.

6. The day of our Lord's being met in the Temple by Simeon.

7. The day of our Lord's Transfiguration.

8. The day of our Lord's entry into Jerusalem.

9. Pasch, or Easter : the feast of feasts, the anticipation of the ever-lasting feast of everlasting blessedness.

10. The day of our Lord's Ascension into heaven.

11. The feast of Pentecost; in memory of the Descent of the Holy Ghost, and in honor of the Most Holy Trinity.

12. The day of the Elevation of the Cross of our Lord, discovered by the Empress Helena.

13. The day of the Rest[1] of the Most Holy Mother of God.

543. What is the chief fast?

The *great fast;* that is, *Lent,* or *Quadragesima.*

544. Why is it called Quadragesima?

Because it continues forty days, besides the week of Christ's Passion.

545. Why has it been appointed that the great fast should continue forty days?

After the example of Jesus Christ himself, who fasted forty days. Matt. iv. 2.

546. Why has it been appointed to fast on the *Wednesday* and the *Friday?*

On Wednesday, in memory of the betrayal of our Lord Jesus Christ to suffer; and on Friday, in memory of his actual suffering and death.

547. For what cause are the fasts before the Nativity, the Rest of the Blessed Virgin, and the Day of the Holy Apostles?

The first two as preparatory exercises of abstinence, the better to honor the ensuing feasts of the Nativity, and of the Rest of the Mother of God; the last not only for like reason, but also in imitation of the Apostles, who fasted to prepare themselves for the work of preaching the Gospel. Acts xiii. 3.

548. How should we spend our time on Sundays, and the other greater holy days, in order to keep the fourth commandment?

First, on these days we should not *labor,* or do worldly and temporal business; secondly, we should keep them holy, that is, use them for holy and spiritual works, to the glory of God.

549. Why are we forbidden to work on holy days?

That we may with the less hindrance employ them in holy and godly works.

550. What particular things is it fit to do on holy days?

First, to go to *church,* for the public worship, and for instruction in the Word of God; secondly, when at home, to give ourselves to *prayer* and reading, or edifying conversation; thirdly, to dedicate to God a portion of our means, expending it on the necessities of the Church

---

[1] [Greek: Ἡ κοίμησις.   German: *Der Tag der Entschlafung.*—ED.]

and her ministers, and in *alms* to the poor, to visit the sick and prison-
ers, and to do other works of Christian charity.

551. But should we not do such things on work-days also?

It is well, if any can; but he whom business prevents should at any
rate devote holy days to such works.   But as regards prayer, it is certainly our bounden duty to use it every day, morning and evening, before and after both dinner and supper, and, as far as possible, at the
beginning and ending of every work.

552. What are we to think of those who on holy days allow themselves to indulge in
indecent plays and shows, vulgar songs, and intemperance in meat and drink?

Such people greatly desecrate holy days   For if even works inno
cent and useful for this present life are unfit for holy days, much more
such as these, which are unprofitable, carnal, and vicious.

553. When the fourth commandment speaks of working six days, does it not thereby
condemn those who do nothing?

Without doubt it condemns all who on common days do not give
themselves to works befitting their calling, but spend their time in idleness and dissipation.

On the Fifth Commandment.

554. What special duties are prescribed by the fifth commandment in regard to *parents*,
under the general phrase of honoring them?

1. *To behave respectfully* to them.

2. *To obey them.*

3. To *support* and comfort them in sickness and age.

4. After their death, as well as during their lives, *to pray* for the
salvation of their souls; and faithfully to fulfill their *last wills*, so far
as they are not contrary to law, divine or civil.   See 2 Macc. xii. 43, 44;
Jer. xxxv. 18, 19.   (J. Damasc. Serm. de Mort.)

555. What degree of sin is there in undutifulness to parents?

In proportion as it is easy and natural to love and honor parents, to
whom we owe our being, the more grievous is the sin of undutifulness
towards them: for this cause in the law of Moses he that cursed father
or mother was to be put to death.   Exod. xxi. 17.

556. Why has this particular commandment to honor parents a promise added to it of
prosperity and long life?

That men by a visible reward might be the more moved to fulfill a

commandment on which the good order first of families and afterwards of all social life depends.

557. How is this promise fulfilled?

The examples of the old Patriarchs or Fathers show that God gives special force to the blessing of parents. Gen. xxvii. *The blessing of the father establisheth the houses of the children.* Ecclus. iii. 9. God of his wise and just providence specially protects the life and promotes the prosperity of such as honor their parents upon earth; but for the perfect reward of the perfect virtue he gives everlasting life and blessedness in the heavenly country.

558. Why in those commandments which teach love to our neighbors is mention made first of all of parents?

Because parents are naturally nearer to us than all others.

559. Are there not others also to be understood in the fifth commandment under the name of parents?

Yes; all who in different relations stand to us in the place of parents.

560. Who stand to us in the place of parents?

1. Our *sovereign* and our *country;* for an empire is a great family, in which the sovereign is father, and the subjects children of the sovereign and their country.

2. Our *spiritual pastors* and *teachers;* for they by their doctrine and by the Sacraments beget us to spiritual life, and nurture us up in it.

3. Our *elders* in age.

4. Our *benefactors.*

5. Our *governors,* or superiors, in different relations.

561. How does holy Scripture speak of the honor due to the sovereign?

Let every soul be subject to the higher powers. For there is no power but of God: the powers that be are ordained of God. Whosoever therefore resisteth the power, resisteth the ordinance of God. Rom. xiii. 1, 2.

Wherefore ye must needs be subject, not only for wrath, but also for conscience' sake. Rom. xiii. 5.

My son, fear God and the king, and oppose neither of them. Prov xxiv. 21.

Render therefore unto Cæsar the things which are Cæsar's; and unto God the things that are God's. Matt. xxii. 21.

Fear God; honor the king. 1 Pet. ii. 17.

562. How far should love to our sovereign and country go?

So far as to make us ready to lay down our life for them.   John xv. 13.

563. How does holy Scripture speak of the duty of honoring spiritual pastors and teachers?

Obey them that have the rule over you, and submit yourselves: for they watch for your souls, as they that must give account, that they may do it with joy, and not with grief: for that is unprofitable for you.   Heb. xiii. 17.

564. Is there in holy Scripture any particular injunction to honor elders in age as parents?

The Apostle Paul writes to Timothy thus: *Rebuke not an elder, but entreat him as a father; younger men as brethren; elder women as mothers.*   1 Tim. v. 1, 2.

Thou shalt rise up before the hoary head, and honor the face of the old man, and fear the Lord thy God.   Lev. xix. 32.

565. How may we be assured that we ought to honor benefactors as parents?

By the example of Jesus Christ himself, who *was subject to Joseph;* although Joseph was not his father, but only his guardian.   Luke ii. 51.

566. Besides these, who are our superiors, whom we must honor after parents, and like them?

They who in place of parents take care of our education, as *governors in schools,* and *masters;* they who preserve us from irregularities and disorders in society, as *civil magistrates;* they who protect us from wrong by the power of the law, as *judges;* they to whom the sovereign intrusts the guardianship and defense of the public safety against enemies, as *military commanders;* and, lastly, *masters,* so far as relates to those who serve them, or belong to them.

567. What does holy Scripture prescribe as to our duty with respect to *authorities* generally?

Render therefore to all their dues: tribute to whom tribute is due; custom to whom custom; fear to whom fear; honor to whom honor.   Rom. xiii. 7.

568. How does holy Scripture speak of the obedience due from servants and serfs to their masters?

Servants, be obedient to them that are your masters according to the flesh, with fear and trembling, in singleness of your heart, as unto Christ; not with eye-service as men-pleasers, but as the servants of Christ, doing the will of God from the heart.   Eph. vi. 5, 6.

Servants, be subject to your masters with all fear, not only to the good and gentle, but also to the froward. 1 Peter ii. 18.

569. If holy Scripture prescribe duties towards parents, does it not likewise prescribe *duties towards children?*

It does.

Fathers, provoke not your children to wrath, but bring them up in the nurture and admonition of the Lord. Eph. vi. 4.

570. How does holy Scripture speak of the duty of pastors towards their spiritual flock?

Feed the flock of God which is among you, taking the oversight thereof not by constraint, but willingly, and according to God; not for filthy lucre, but of a ready mind; neither as being lords over God's heritage, but being ensamples to the flock. 1 Pet. v. 2, 3.

571. How does holy Scripture speak of the duty of them that are in *authority*, and of *masters?*

Masters, give unto your servants that which is just and equal, knowing that ye also have a Master in heaven. Coloss. iv. 1.

572. How ought we to act, if it fall out that our parents or governors require of us any thing contrary to the faith or to the law of God?

In that case we should say to them, as the Apostles said to the rulers of the Jews: *Whether it be right in the sight of God to hearken unto you more than unto God, judge ye;* and we should be ready, for the sake of the faith and the law of God, to endure the consequences, whatever they may be. Acts iv. 19.

573. What is the general name for that quality or virtue which is required by the fifth commandment?

Obedience.

ON THE SIXTH COMMANDMENT.

574. What is forbidden by the sixth commandment?

Murder; that is, taking away the life of our neighbor in any manner whatever.

575. Is it in all cases murder, and against this commandment, to kill?

No. It is not murder, nor against this commandment, when life is taken in the execution of duty; as, when a criminal *is punished* with death, by just judgment; nor, again, when an enemy is killed *in war*, in defense of our sovereign and country.

576. What is to be thought of involuntary homicide, when a man is killed accidentally and unintentionally?

The man who is guilty of involuntary homicide can not be reckoned blameless, unless he took all proper precautions against the accident; at any rate, he needs to have his conscience cleansed according to the Canons of the Church.

577. What cases must be reckoned as murder, and as breaches of this commandment?

Besides direct murder, by whatever means, the same sin may be committed in the following, and in similar cases:

1. When a judge *condemns* a prisoner whom he knows to be *innocent.*

2. When any one *conceals* or *sets free a murderer*, and so gives him opportunity for fresh crime.

3. When any one can save his neighbor from death, but does *not save* him; as, when a rich man suffers a poor man to die of hunger.

4. When any one by excessive burdens and cruel punishments *wears out* those under him, and so hastens their death.

5. When any one, through intemperance or other *vices, shortens his own life.*

578. What are we to think of *suicide?*

That it is the most criminal of all murders. For if it be contrary to nature to kill another man like unto ourselves, much more is it contrary to nature to kill our own selves. Our life is not our own, but God's who gave it.

579. What are we to think of *duels*, to decide private quarrels?

Since the decision of private quarrels belongs to government, while the duelist, instead of having recourse to law, willfully determines on an act which involves manifest danger of death both to himself and his opponent, it is evident that a duel implies three dreadful crimes— rebellion, murder, and suicide.

580. Besides murder of the body, is there not such a thing as *spiritual murder?*

A kind of spiritual murder is the *causing of offense:* when any one causes his neighbor to fall into infidelity or into sin, and so subjects his soul to spiritual death.

The Saviour says: *Whoso shall offend one of these little ones which believe in me, it were better for him that a millstone were hanged about his neck, and that he were drowned in the depth of the sea.* Matt. xviii. 6.

581. Are there not still some more subtle forms of murder?

To this sin are more or less referable all acts and words against charity; all which unjustly affect the peace and security of our neighbor; and, lastly, all inward *malice* against him, even though it be not shown openly.

Whosoever hateth his brother is a murderer.   1 John iii. 15.

582. When we are forbidden to hurt the life of our neighbor, what positive duty is thereby enjoined?

That of doing all we can to secure his life and well-being.

583. What duties follow from hence?

Those of—1. Helping the poor; 2. Ministering to the sick; 3. Comforting the afflicted; 4. Alleviating the distress of the unfortunate; 5. Behaving in a gentle, affectionate, and edifying manner to all; 6. Reconciling ourselves with those that are angry; 7. Forgiving injuries, and doing good to our enemies.

On the Seventh Commandment.

584. What is forbidden by the seventh commandment?

Adultery.

585. What forms of sin are forbidden under the name of adultery?

The Apostle Paul would have Christians not even to speak of such impurities.   Eph. v. 3.   It is only of necessity, to forewarn people against such sins, that we shall here name some of them.   Such are—

1. *Fornication;* or irregular carnal love between unmarried persons.   2. *Adultery;* when married persons unlawfully give that love which they owe each other to strangers.   3. *Incest;* when near relations enter into a union like that of matrimony.

586. What does our Saviour teach us to think of adultery?

He has said that *Whosoever looketh on a woman to lust after her hath committed adultery with her already in his heart.*   Matt. v. 28.

587. What should we do in order to guard against falling into this subtle *inward adultery?*

We should avoid every thing that may excite impure feelings in the heart; as wanton songs and dances, lewd conversation, immodest games and jokes, immodest sights, and the reading of books which contain descriptions of impure love.   We should strive, according to the Gospel, not even to look on that which may cause us to fall.

If thy right eye offend thee, pluck it out, and cast it from thee; for it is profitable for thee that one of thy members should perish, and not that thy whole body should be cast into hell. Matt. v. 29.

588. Must we, then, literally *pluck out the offending eye?*

We must pluck it out, not with the hand, but with the will. He who has firmly resolved not even to look upon that which causes him to offend hath already plucked out the offending eye.

589. When the sin of adultery is forbidden, what contrary virtues are thereby enjoined?

Those of *conjugal love* and *fidelity;* and, for such as can receive it, perfect *purity* and *chastity.*

590. How does holy Scripture speak of the *duties of man and wife?*

Husbands, love your wives, even as Christ also loved the Church, and gave himself for it. Eph. v. 25. *Wives, submit yourselves unto your own husbands, as unto the Lord; for the husband is the head of the wife, even as Christ is the head of the Church; and he is the Saviour of the body.* Eph. v. 22, 23.

591. What motives does holy Scripture set before us to make us flee fornication and live chastely?

It bids us keep our bodies in purity, because they are the *members of Christ,* and *temples of the Holy Ghost;* while, on the other hand, he who *committeth fornication sinneth against his own body;* that is, corrupts it, infects it with diseases, and, further, hurts his mental faculties, such as imagination and memory. See 1 Cor. vi. 15, 18, 19.

On the Eighth Commandment.

592. What is forbidden by the eighth commandment?

To steal, or in any way appropriate to ourselves that which belongs to another.

593. What particular sins are forbidden thereby?

The chief are—

1. *Robbery,* or the taking of any thing that belongs to another openly, by force.

2. *Theft,* or taking what belongs to another privily.

3. *Fraud,* or appropriating to ourselves any thing that is another's by artifice; as when men pass off counterfeit money for true, or bad wares for good; or use false weights and measures, to give less than

they have sold; or conceal their effects to avoid paying their debts; or do not honestly fulfill contracts, or execute wills; when they screen others guilty of dishonesty, and so defraud the injured of justice.

4. *Sacrilege,* or appropriating to ourselves what has been dedicated to God, or belongs to the Church.

5. *Spiritual sacrilege;*[1] when one sinfully gives and another fraudulently obtains any sacred office, not of desert, but for gain.

6. *Bribery;* when men receive a bribe from those under them in office or jurisdiction, and for gain promote the unworthy, acquit the guilty, or oppress the innocent.

7. *Eating the bread of idleness;* when men receive salary for duty, or pay for work, which they neglect, and so in fact steal both their pay and that profit which society, or he whom they served, should have had of their labor; in like manner when they who are able to support themselves by work, instead of so doing live upon alms.

8. *Extortion;* when, under the show of some right, but really against equity and humanity, men make their own advantage of the property, the labors, or even the misfortunes of others; as when creditors oppress their debtors by usury; when masters wear out their dependents by excessive imposts or tasks; when in time of famine men sell bread at an exorbitant price.

594. When these sins are forbidden, what contrary virtues are thereby enjoined?

Those of—1. *Disinterestedness;* 2. *Good faith in performing engagements;* 3. *Justice;* 4. *Mercy* to the poor.

595. Does he, then, who is not merciful to the poor sin against the eighth commandment?

Certainly he does, if he have the means of assisting them; for all that we have belongs properly to God, and our abundance is given us by his Providence for the assistance of the poor; wherefore, if we do not impart to them of our abundance, we do in fact thereby rob and defraud them of their right, and the gift of God.

596. Is there not yet a higher virtue contrary to sins against the eighth commandment?

Such a virtue is *absolute poverty,* or the renunciation of all property; which is proposed by the Gospel not as a duty for all, but as a counsel for them that would be perfect.

If thou wilt be perfect, go and sell that thou hast, and give to the poor; and thou shalt have treasure in heaven. Matt. xix. 21.

---

[1] Greek: πνευματικὴ ἱεροσυλία. German: *Simonie.*

On the Ninth Commandment.

597. What is forbidden by the ninth commandment?

False witness against our neighbor, and all lying.

598. What is forbidden under the words *false witness?*

1. *False witness in a court of justice;* when men bear witness, inform, or complain falsely against any one.

2. False witness out of court, when men *slander* any one behind his back, or *blame* him to his face unjustly.

599. But is it allowable to censure others when they are really to blame?

No; the Gospel does not allow us to judge even of the real vices or faults of our neighbors, unless we are called by any special office to do so, for their punishment or amendment.

Judge not, that ye be not judged. Matt. vii. 1.

600. Are not such lies allowable as involve no purpose of hurting our neighbor?

No; for they are inconsistent with love and respect for our neighbor, and unworthy of a man, much more of a Christian, who has been created for truth and love.

Wherefore putting away lying, speak every man truth with his neighbor; for we are members one of another. Eph. iv. 25.

601. If we would avoid sins against the ninth commandment, what rule must we follow?

We must *bridle our tongue. He that will love life, and see good days, let him refrain his tongue from evil, and his lips that they speak no guile.* 1 Pet. iii. 10. *If any man among you seem to be religious, and bridleth not his tongue, but deceiveth his own heart, this man's religion is vain.* James i. 26.

On the Tenth Commandment.

602. What is forbidden by the tenth commandment?

All *wishes* inconsistent with charity to our neighbor, and *thoughts* which are inseparable from such wishes.

603. Why are we forbidden not only evil deeds, but also evil wishes and thoughts?

First, because when the soul entertains any evil wishes or thoughts, it is already impure in God's sight, and unworthy of him; as Solomon says: *The unjust thought is an abomination to the Lord.* Prov. xv. 26. And therefore we must needs cleanse ourselves also from these inward impurities also, as the Apostle teaches: *Let us cleanse ourselves*

from all filthiness of the flesh and spirit, perfecting holiness in the fear of the Lord. 2 Cor. vii. 1.

Secondly, because, to prevent sinful acts, it is necessary to crush sinful wishes and thoughts, from which, as from seeds, such actions spring; as it is said: *For out of the heart proceed evil thoughts, murders, adulteries, fornications, thefts, false witness, blasphemies.* Matt. xv. 19. *Every man is tempted, when he is drawn away of his own lust, and enticed. Then, when lust hath conceived, it bringeth forth sin; and sin, when it is finished, bringeth forth death.* James i. 14, 15.

604. When we are forbidden to desire any thing of our neighbor's, what passion is thereby condemned?

Envy.

605. What is forbidden by the words, *Thou shalt not covet thy neighbor's wife?*

All lustful thoughts and wishes, or inward adultery.

606. What is forbidden by the words, *Thou shalt not covet thy neighbor's house, nor his land, nor his man-servant, nor his maid-servant, nor his ox, nor his ass, nor any of his cattle, nor any thing that is his?*

All thoughts of avarice and ambition.

607. What positive duties, corresponding to these prohibitions, are prescribed by the tenth commandment?

First, to keep *purity of heart;* and, secondly, to be *content with our lot.*

608. What is indispensable for the cleansing of the heart?

The frequent and earnest *invocation of the name of our Lord Jesus Christ.*

CONCLUSION.

APPLICATION OF THE DOCTRINE OF FAITH AND PIETY.

609. How must we apply the doctrine of faith and piety?

We must *act* according to our knowledge, and keep before our eyes the fearful judgment threatened for disobedience.

If ye know these things, happy are ye if ye do them. John xiii. 17. *That servant which knew his Lord's will, and prepared not himself, neither did according to his will, shall be beaten with many stripes.* Luke xii. 47.

610 What must a man do when he is conscious of any sin?

Not only should he immediately repent, and firmly resolve to avoid the same sin for the future, but also strive, as far as possible, to repair the scandal or injury that he has wrought by contrary good deeds.

Thus it was that Zaccheus the Publican acted, when he said to the Lord, *Behold, Lord, the half of my goods I give to the poor ; and if I have taken any thing away from any one by false accusation, I restore him fourfold.*   Luke xix. 8.

611. What caution do we need when we seem to ourselves to have fulfilled any commandment?

We must then dispose our hearts according to the words of Jesus Christ: *When ye shall have done all those things which are commanded you, say, We are unprofitable servants : we have done that which was our duty to do.*   Luke xvii. 10.

THE OLD CATHOLIC UNION CREEDS.

THE OLD CATHOLIC UNION CREEDS.

PAGE

THE FOURTEEN THESES OF THE OLD CATHOLIC UNION
CONFERENCE AT BONN. A.D. 1874.......................... 545

THE OLD CATHOLIC AGREEMENT ON THE FILIOQUE
CONTROVERSY. A.D. 1875.. 552

THE FOURTEEN THESES OF THE OLD CATHOLIC UNION CONFERENCE AT BONN. A.D. 1874.

[This interesting document deserves a place at the end of this volume as the first attempt to formularize the doctrinal consensus of Old Catholics, Greeks, and Anglo-Catholics, who acknowledge, besides the Holy Scriptures, the binding and perpetual authority of the ancient Catholic tradition before the separation between the East and the West. The object of this Consensus-Formula is to prepare the way, not for an absorptive or organic union, but for a confederation or intercommunion of Churches, on the basis of union in essentials and freedom in non-essentials. It involves a protest against some of the mediæval innovations of Romanism, and is so far an approach to Protestantism; but Protestantism goes beyond the œcumenical catholicity to the inspired fountain-head of the Apostolic Church.

A conference of divines friendly to the reunion of Christendom was called by Dr. Döllinger, of Munich (in behalf of a Christian Union Committee of the Old Catholic Congress), and held in the University at Bonn, Sept. 14–16, 1874. It consisted of about forty members—namely, 1. Old Catholics: Dr. DÖLLINGER (who presided with great ability), Bishop REINKENS, Drs. REUSCH, LANGEN, KNOODT, LUTTERBECK, MICHAUD, and others. 2. Orthodox Russians and Greeks: JOH. JANYSCHEW, Rector of the Ecclesiastical Academy of St. Petersburg, ALEXANDER KIREJEW, THEODOR VON SUKHOTIN, ARSENIUS TATCHALOFF, Professor RHOSSIS, of Athens. 3. English Episcopalians: Bishop EDWARD HAROLD BROWNE, of Winchester, Dean J. S. HOWSON, of Chester, Dr. HENRY PARRY LIDDON, Canon of St. Paul's, EDWARD S. TALBOT, Warden of Keble College, Oxford, Professor E. B. MAYOR, of Cambridge, Canon WM. CONWAY, of Westminster, G. E. BROADE, British Chaplain at Düsseldorf, and others. 4. American (High Church) Episcopalians: Bishop JOHN B. KERFOOT, of Pittsburg, Rev. Dr. WM. CHAUNCEY LANGDON, of Geneva, Rev. Dr. ROBERT J. NEVIN, Rector of the American Episcopal Church, Rome; Rev. H. F. HARTMANN, Rev. GEO. F. ARNOLD, and Rev. E. A. RENOUF. Besides, there were present as invited guests, without taking an active part in the transactions, several Lutheran and Evangelical theologians and ministers from Germany and Denmark, as Professors LANGE, KRAFFT, CAMPHAUSEN, of Bonn, Rev. VON GERLACH, of Frankfort-on-the-Main, Dr. WOLFF, of Rotweil, Rev. G. SCHMIDT, of Schlangen, Rev. J. V. BLOCH, of Copenhagen, and Rev. J. MCMILLAN, a Congregational minister from West Burton. The proceedings were held in English and German.

The text is taken from the official Report of the Conference, edited by Prof. Dr. REUSCH in the name of Dr. Döllinger.[1] The titles of the Articles we have supplied. The Theses were originally drawn up in English, and translated after the Conference by the editor, and revised and approved by Dr. Döllinger. The English text, therefore, is the authentic text.

The first and preliminary Thesis which was agreed upon, but not included in the fourteen, refers to the vexed question of the double procession of the Holy Spirit, which was the chief cause of the separation of the Greek and Latin Churches. It makes an important concession to the Greeks concerning the legal aspect of the question of the *filioque*, but leaves the dogmatic question to future conferences. It is as follows:

'We agree that the way in which the " Filioque" was inserted in the Nicene Creed was illegal, and that, with a view to future peace and unity, it is much to be desired that the whole Church should set itself seriously to consider whether the Creed could possibly be restored to its primitive form, without sacrifice of any true doctrine expressed in the present Western form.'

'*Wir geben zu, dass die Art und Weise, in welcher das Filioque in das Nicenische Glaubensbekenntniss eingeschoben wurde, ungesetzlich war, und dass es im Interesse des Friedens und der Einigkeit sehr wünschenswerth ist, dass die ganze Kirche es ernstlich in Erwägung ziehe, ob vielleicht die ursprüngliche Form des Glaubensbekenntnisses wiederhergestellt werden könne ohne Aufopferung irgend einer wahren in der gegenwärtigen westlichen Form ausgedrückten Lehre.*']

---

[1] *Bericht über die am 14, 15, und 16 September zu Bonn gehaltenen Unions-Conferenzen, im Auftrage des Vorsitzenden Dr. VON DÖLLINGER, herausgegeben von Dr. F. HEINRICH REUSCH, Prof. der Theologie.* Bonn, 1874. Compare also several communications on the Conference in the *Deutsche Merkur* (the organ of the Old Catholics) for 1874, No. 38–40; in the *Churchman* of Hartford, Conn. Oct. 10, 1874; and the *New York Observer*, Oct. 8, 1874.

Art. I.

[The Canon and the Apocrypha.]

We agree that the apocryphal or deutero-canonical books of the Old Testament are not of the same canonicity as the books contained in the Hebrew Canon.

Art. II.

[The Original Text and Translations of the Bible.]

We agree that no translation of Holy Scripture can claim an authority superior to that of the original text.

Art. III.

[Use of the Bible in the Vernacular Tongues.]

We agree that the reading of Holy Scripture in the vulgar tongue can not be lawfully forbidden.

Art. IV.

[Liturgy in the Vernacular Tongues.]

We agree that, *in general*, it is more fitting, and in accordance with the spirit of the Church, that the Liturgy should be in the tongue understood by the people.

Art. V.

[Justification by Faith working by Love.]

We agree that Faith working by Love, not Faith without Love,

Art. I.

[Der Canon und die Apokryphen.]

Wir stimmen überein, dass die apokryphischen oder deuterokanonischen Bücher des Alten Testaments nicht dieselbe Kanonicität haben, wie die im hebräischen Kanon enthaltenen Bücher.

Art. II.

[Der Urtext und die Uebersetzungen der Bibel.]

Wir stimmen überein, dass keine Uebersetzung der heil. Schrift eine höhere Auctorität beanspruchen kann, als der Grundtext.

Art. III.

[Gebrauch der Bibel in der Landessprache.

Wir stimmen überein, dass das Lesen der heil. Schrift in der Volkssprache nicht auf rechtmässige Weise verboten werden kann.

Art. IV.

[Gottesdienst in der Landessprache.]

Wir stimmen überein, dass es IM ALLGEMEINEN *angemessener und dem Geiste der Kirche entsprechender ist, dass die Liturgie in der von dem Volke verstandenen Sprache gebraucht werde.*

Art. V.

[Rechtfertigung durch den in der Liebe thätigen Glauben.]

Wir stimmen überein, dass der durch die Liebe wirksame Glaube

is the means and condition of man's justification before God.

nicht der Glaube ohne die Liebe, das Mittel und die Bedingung der Rechtfertigung des Menschen vor Gott ist.

Art. VI.

[*Salvation not by Merit.*]

Salvation can not be merited by 'merit of condignity,' because there is no proportion between the infinite worth of the salvation promised by God and the finite worth of man's works.

Art. VI.

[*Seligkeit ohne Verdienst.*]

Die Seligkeit kann nicht durch sogenannte 'merita de condigno' verdient werden, weil der unendliche Werth der von Gott verheissenen Seligkeit nicht im Verhältniss steht zu dem endlichen Werthe der Werke des Menschen.

Art. VII.

[*Works of Supererogation.*]

We agree that the doctrine of '*opera supererogationis*' and of a '*thesaurus meritorum sanctorum*,' i. e., that the overflowing merits of the Saints can be transferred to others, either by the rulers of the Church, or by the authors of the good works themselves, is untenable.

Art. VII.

[*Ueberverdienstliche Werke.*]

Wir stimmen überein, dass die Lehre von den ' opera supererogationis,' und von einem ' thesaurus meritorum sanctorum,' d. i. die Lehre, dass die überfliessenden Verdienste der Heiligen, sei es durch die kirchlichen Oberen, sei es durch die Vollbringer der guten Werke selbst, auf Andere übertragen werden können, unhaltbar ist.

Art. VIII.

[*Number of Sacraments.*]

1. We acknowledge that the number of sacraments was fixed at seven, first in the twelfth century, and then was received into the general teaching of the Church, not as a tradition coming down

Art. VIII.

[*Zahl der Sacramente.*]

1. *Wir erkennen an, dass die Zahl der Sacramente erst im zwölften Jahrhundert auf sieben festgesetzt und dann in die allgemeine Lehre der Kirche aufgenommen wurde, und zwar nicht als eine von den*

from the Apostles or from the earliest times, but as the result of theological speculation.

2. Catholic theologians (*e. g.* Bellarmin) acknowledge, and we acknowledge with them, that Baptism and the Eucharist are '*principalia, præcipua, eximia salutis nostræ sacramenta.*'

ART. IX.
[*Scripture and Tradition.*]

1. The Holy Scriptures being recognized as the primary rule of Faith, we agree that the genuine tradition, *i. e.* the unbroken transmission — partly oral, partly in writing — of the doctrine delivered by Christ and the Apostles, is an authoritative source of teaching for all successive generations of Christians. This tradition is partly to be found in the consensus of the great ecclesiastical bodies standing in historical continuity with the primitive Church, partly to be gathered by scientific method from the written documents of all centuries.

2. We acknowledge that the Church of England, and the Churches derived through her,

Aposteln oder von den ältesten Zeiten kommende Tradition, sondern als das Ergebniss theologischer Speculation.

2. *Katholische Theologen, z. B. Bellarmin erkennen an und wir mit ihnen, dass die Taufe und die Eucharistie '*principalia, præcipua, eximia salutis nostræ sacramenta*' sind.*

ART. IX.
[*Schrift und Ueberlieferung.*]

1. *Während die heilige Schrift anerkanntermassen die primäre Regel des Glaubens ist, erkennen wir an, dass die echte Tradition, d. i. die ununterbrochene, theils mündliche, theils schriftliche Ueberlieferung der von Christus und den Aposteln zuerst vorgetragenen Lehre eine autoritative (gottgewollte) Erkentnissquelle für alle auf einander folgenden Generationen von Christen ist. Diese Tradition wird theils erkannt aus dem Consensus der grossen in historischer Continuität mit der ursprünglichen Kirche stehenden Kirchenkörper, theils wird sie auf wissenschaftlichem Wege ermittelt aus den schriftlichen Denkmälern aller Jahrhunderte.*

2. *Wir erkennen an, dass die englische Kirche und die von ihr herstammenden Kirchen die*

have maintained unbroken the Episcopal succession.[1]

ART. X.

[*The Immaculate Conception of the Virgin Mary.*]

We reject the new Roman doctrine of the Immaculate Conception of the Blessed Virgin Mary, as being contrary to the tradition of the first thirteen centuries, according to which Christ alone is conceived without sin.[2]

ART. XI.

[*Public and Private Confession.*]

We agree that the practice of confession of sins before the congregation or a Priest, together with the exercise of the power of the keys, has come down to us from the primitive Church, and that, purged from abuses and free from constraint, it should be preserved in the Church.

ART. XII.

[*Indulgences.*]

We agree that 'indulgences' can only refer to penalties actually imposed by the Church herself.

---

ununterbrochene bischöfliche Succession bewahrt haben.

ART. X.

[*Unbefleckte Empfängniss der Jungfrau Maria.*]

Wir verwerfen die neue römische Lehre von der unbefleckten Empfängniss der h. Jungfrau Maria als in Widerspruch stehend mit der Tradition der ersten dreizehn Jahrhunderte, nach welcher Christus allein ohne Sünde empfangen ist.

ART. XI.

[*Öffentliche und Privat-Beichte.*]

Wir stimmen überein, dass die Praxis des Sündenbekenntnisses vor der Gemeinde oder einem Priester, verbunden mit der Ausübung der Schlüsselgewalt, von der ursprünglichen Kirche auf uns gekommen und, gereinigt von Missbräuchen und frei von Zwang, in der Kirche beizubehalten ist.

ART. XII.

[*Ablass.*]

Wir stimmen überein, dass 'Ablässe' nur auf wirklich von der Kirche selbst aufgelegte Bussen sich beziehen können.

---

[1] This article, which refers simply to an historical question, caused some discussion. Döllinger and Reinkens recognized the validity of the Anglican succession, to the gratification of the Anglican members of the Conference; but the Greek and Russian members expressed doubts, and withheld their consent till further investigation.

[2] It is remarkable that on this article Döllinger and the Old Catholics were more decided in their opposition to the papal dogma of 1854 than Canon Liddon, of St. Paul's, who was willing to tolerate the Immaculate Conception as a 'pious opinion.'

ART. XIII.

[*Commemoration of the Departed.*]

We acknowledge that the practice of the commemoration of the faithful departed, *i. e.* the calling down of a richer outpouring of Christ's grace upon them, has come down to us from the primitive Church, and is to be preserved in the Church.

ART. XIII.

[*Gebete für Verstorbene.*]

Wir erkennen an, dass der Gebrauch des Gebetes für die verstorbenen Gläubigen, d. h. die Erflehung einer reicheren Ausgiessung der Gnade Christi über sie, von der ältesten Kirche auf uns gekommen und in der Kirche beizubehalten ist.

ART. XIV.

[*The Mass.*]

1. The eucharistic celebration in the Church is not a continuous repetition or renewal of the propitiatory sacrifice offered once for ever by Christ upon the cross; but its sacrificial character consists in this, that it is the permanent memorial of it, and a representation and presentation on earth of that one oblation of Christ for the salvation of redeemed mankind, which, according to the Epistle to the Hebrews (ix. 11, 12), is continuously presented in heaven by Christ, who now appears in the presence of God for us (ix. 24).

ART. XIV.

[*Die Messe.*]

1. *Die eucharistische Feier in der Kirche ist nicht eine fortwährende Wiederholung oder Erneuerung des Sühnopfers, welches Christus ein für allemal am Kreuze dargebracht hat; aber ihr Opfercharakter besteht darin, dass sie das bleibende Gedächtniss desselben ist und eine auf Erden stattfindende Darstellung und Vergegenwärtigung jener Einen Darbringung Christi für das Heil der erlösten Menschheit, welche nach Hebr. ix. 11, 12 fortwährend im Himmel von Christus geleistet wird, indem er jetzt in der Gegenwart Gottes für uns erscheint* (Heb. ix. 24).

2. While this is the character of the Eucharist in reference to the sacrifice of Christ, it is also a sacred feast, wherein the faithful, receiving the Body and Blood of

2. *Indem dies der Charakter der Eucharistie bezüglich des Opfers Christi ist, ist sie zugleich ein geheiligtes Opfermahl, in welchem die den Leib und das Blut des Herrn*

our Lord, have communion one | *empfangenden Gläubigen Gemein-*
with another (1 Cor. x. 17). | *schaft mit einander haben* (1 Cor.
| x. 17).

NOTES.

1. Dr. Döllinger proposed also the following article concerning the Invocation of Saints, but withdrew it in consequence of the opposition of the Greek and Russian members, who maintained that such invocation was a duty, on the ground of the seventh œcumenical Council:

'We acknowledge that the Invocation of | '*Wir erkennen an, dass die Anrufung der*
Saints is not commanded as a duty necessary | *Heiligen nicht als eine Pflicht anzusehen ist,*
to salvation for every Christian.' | *deren Erfüllung für jeden Christen zur Selig-*
| *keit nothwendig wäre.*'

2. These theses have no official authority, and express simply the private convictions of the members of the Conference; but they may be regarded as the provisional creed of the Old Catholics until acted upon by their Synod, which is the official organ.

3. Art. XIV.—Dean Howson, of Chester, at the second Bonn Conference, held a year afterwards, entered, in behalf of some evangelical Anglicans, the following protest against a possible Romanizing interpretation of this Article:

'Some members of the Church of England, who earnestly desire success to the present efforts for reunion, having been made anxious and doubtful by that part of the Article on the eucharist, provisionally adopted last year, which speaks of the eucharistic celebration as a "representation and presentation on earth of the one oblation of Christ, which is continuously presented by him in heaven;" and those expressions being capable of different shades of interpretation, I beg leave respectfully to state the meanings which such persons, with myself, are disposed to attach to them. We view the eucharistic celebration as a "representation," because in it (according to 1 Cor. xi. 26) we show forth the Lord's death till he come; we speak of it as a "presentation," because those who receive, in the Holy Communion, the blessings procured by the sacrifice of Christ, do at the same time, as sinners, plead that sacrifice before God; and we conceive the sense assigned to Christ's "continuous oblation in heaven" must be limited by the revealed fact (Heb. vii. 27; ix. 12 and 25–28; x. 10 and 18) that his sacrifice for sin was made complete, once for all, before he ascended to heaven. I feel bound in conclusion to add that, on further reflection, I have less confidence than I had before as to the strict consistency of the language of this Article with the language of the English Book of Common Prayer.'

Dr. Liddon dissented from this protest, and expressed his agreement with the Article in the full sense of its language. Döllinger and the Old Catholics were silent. There is, however, no precise correspondence between the original 'representation and presentation' and the German translation, '*Darstellung und Vergegenwärtigung;*' and both terms are capable of different interpretations.

[NOTE.—Bishop Reinkens and Bishop Herzog, consecrated by Reinkens, Sept. 18, 1876, were excommunicated by Pius IX., Dec. 6, 1876, in these words: 'By the authority of Almighty God, we excommunicate and anathematize the sacrilegious consecration of Edward Herzog and all those assisting at the sacrilegious consecration,' etc., *Acta sed. sanc.* IX., 595. The Jansenist Abp. of Utrecht was excommunicated by Leo XIII., Feb. 28, 1893. An Old Catholic Confession of Faith was signed, Sept., 1889, by the Abp. of Utrecht and the Bishops of Haarlem and Deventer, and by Bishops Reinkens and Herzog. For the text, see Mirbt, 488, 574.—ED.]

THE OLD CATHOLIC AGREEMENT ON THE FILIOQUE CONTROVERSY. A.D. 1875.

[At the second Döllinger Union Conference between Old Catholics, Orientals, and Anglo-Catholics, held at Bonn, Prussia, Aug. 10–16, 1875, the following agreement on the old Filioque Controversy, essentially in favor of the Greek view, was adopted, but, like the agreement of the preceding Conference, it still waits for the official sanction of the Churches therein represented. The German text is the original, and is taken from the Secretary's *Bericht über die vom 10–16. Aug. 1875 zu Bonn gehaltenen Unions-Conferenzen, im Auftrage des Vorsitzenden Dr. von Döllinger herausgegeben von Dr. FR. HEINRICH REUSCH, Prof. der Theologie*, Bonn, 1875, pp. 80, 92, and 93. An English translation of this report by Rev. Dr. SAMUEL BUEL, Prof. of Divinity in the Gen. Theol. Sem. of the Prot. Episcopal Church at N.Y., with a Preface by Rev. Dr. Robert J. Nevin, Rector of the American Episcopal Church in Rome, was published in New York (1876), and another translation, with an Introduction by Canon Liddon, in London (1876).]

1. Wir stimmen überein in der Annahme der ökumenischen Symbole und der Glaubensentscheidungen der alten ungetheilten Kirche.

1. We agree in accepting the œcumenical symbols and the decisions in matters of faith of the ancient undivided Church.

2. Wir stimmen überein in der Anerkennung, daß der Zusatz des Filioque zum Symbolum nicht in kirchlich rechtmäßiger Weise erfolgt sei.

2. We agree in acknowledging that the addition *Filioque* to the symbol did not take place in an ecclesiastically regular manner.

3. Wir bekennen uns allerseits zu der Darstellung der Lehre vom heiligen Geiste, wie sie von den Vätern der ungetheilten Kirche vorgetragen wird.

3. We give our unanimous assent to the presentation of the doctrine of the Holy Spirit as taught by the Fathers of the undivided Church.

4. Wir verwerfen jede Vorstellung und jede Ausdrucksweise, in welcher etwa die Annahme zweier Principien oder ἀρχαί oder αἰτίαι in der Dreieinigkeit enthalten wäre.

4. We reject every representation and every form of expression in which is contained the acceptance of two principles, or beginnings, or causes, in the Trinity.

[The following additional Articles are explanatory of Art. 3, and were adopted at the request of the Greek and Russian delegates:]

Wir nehmen die Lehre des heiligen Johannes von Damaskus über den heiligen Geist, wie dieselbe in nachfolgenden Paragraphen ausgedrückt ist, im Sinne der Lehre der alten ungetrennten Kirche an.

We accept the teaching of St. John of Damascus concerning the Holy Spirit, as it is expressed in the following paragraphs, in the sense of the doctrine of the ancient undivided Church.

1. Der heilige Geist geht aus aus dem Vater (ἐκ τοῦ Πατρός)[1] als dem Anfang (ἀρχή), der Ursache (αἰτία), der Quelle (πηγή) der Gottheit.[2]

2. Der heilige Geist geht nicht aus aus dem Sohne (ἐκ τοῦ Υἱοῦ), weil es in der Gottheit nur Einen Anfang (ἀρχή), Eine Ursache (αἰτία) gibt, durch welche alles, was in der Gottheit ist, hervorgebracht wird.[3]

3. Der heilige Geist geht aus aus dem Vater durch den Sohn.[4]

4. Der heilige Geist ist das Bild des Sohnes, des Bildes des Vaters,[5] aus dem Vater ausgehend und im Sohne ruhend als dessen ausstrahlende Kraft.[6]

5. Der heilige Geist ist die persönliche Hervorbringung aus dem Vater, dem Sohne angehörig, aber nicht aus dem Sohne, weil er der Geist des Mundes der Gottheit ist, welcher das Wort ausspricht.[7]

---

1. The Holy Spirit proceeds from the Father as the beginning, the cause, the fountain of the Godhead.[2]

2. The Holy Spirit proceeds not from the Son, because in the Godhead there is only one beginning, one cause, by which all that is in the Godhead is produced.[3]

3. The Holy Spirit proceeds from the Father through the Son.[4]

4. The Holy Spirit is the image of the Son (as the Son is the image of the Father),[5] proceeding from the Father, and resting in the Son as the power shining forth from him.[6]

5. The Holy Spirit is the personal production out of the Father, belonging to the Son, but not out of the Son, because he is the Spirit of the mouth of the Godhead which pronounces the Word.[7]

---

[1] [Lit., *goes forth out of the Father.* The N. T., in John xv. 26, uses παρά, *from;* the Nicene Creed, ἐκ, *out of,* which, however. is implied in the compound verb ἐκπορεύεται.]

[2] *De recta sententia,* n. 1; *Contra Manich.* n. 4.

[3] *De fide orthod.* I. 8: ἐκ τοῦ Υἱοῦ δὲ τὸ Πνεῦμα οὐ λέγομεν, Πνεῦμα δὲ Υἱοῦ ὀνομάζομεν.

[4] *De fide orthod.* I. 12: τὸ δὲ Πνεῦμα τὸ ἅγιον ἐκφαντορικὴ τοῦ κρυφίου τῆς θεότητος δύναμις τοῦ Πατρός, ἐκ Πατρὸς μὲν δι' Υἱοῦ ἐκπορευομένη. *Ibidem:* Υἱοῦ δὲ Πνεῦμα οὐχ ὡς ἐξ αὐτοῦ, ἀλλ' ὡς δι' αὐτοῦ ἐκ τοῦ Πατρὸς ἐκπορευόμενον. *C. Manich.* n. 5: διὰ τοῦ Λόγου αὐτοῦ ἐξ αὐτοῦ τὸ Πνεῦμα αὐτοῦ ἐκπορευόμενον. *De hymno Trisag.* n. 28: Πνεῦμα τὸ ἅγιον ἐκ τοῦ Πατρὸς διὰ τοῦ Υἱοῦ καὶ Λόγου προϊόν. *Hom. in Sabb. s.* n. 4: τοῦτ' ἡμῖν ἐστι τὸ λατρευόμενον . . . Πνεῦμα ἅγιον τοῦ Θεοῦ καὶ Πατρός, ὡς ἐξ αὐτοῦ ἐκπορευόμενον, ὅπερ καὶ τοῦ Υἱοῦ λέγεται, ὡς δι' αὐτοῦ φανερούμενον καὶ τῇ κτίσει μεταδιδόμενον, ἀλλ' οὐκ ἐξ αὐτοῦ ἔχον τὴν ὕπαρξιν.

[5] *De fide orthod.* I. 13: εἰκὼν τοῦ Πατρὸς ὁ Υἱός, καὶ τοῦ Υἱοῦ τὸ Πνεῦμα.

[6] *De fide orthod.* I. 7: τοῦ Πατρὸς προερχομένην καὶ ἐν τῷ Λόγῳ ἀναπαυομένην καὶ αὐτοῦ οὖσαν ἐκφαντικὴν δύναμιν. *Ibidem,* I. 12: Πατήρ . . . διὰ Λόγου προβολεὺς ἐκφαντορικοῦ Πνεύματος.

[7] *De hymno Trisag.* n. 28: τὸ Πνεῦμα ἐνυπόστατον ἐκπόρευμα καὶ πρόβλημα ἐκ Πατρὸς μέν, Υἱοῦ δὲ, καὶ μὴ ἐξ Υἱοῦ, ὡς Πνεῦμα στόματος θεοῦ, Λόγου ἐξαγγελτικόν.

6. Der heilige Geist bildet die
Vermittlung zwischen dem Vater und
dem Sohne und ist durch den Sohn
mit dem Vater verbunden.[1]

6. The Holy Spirit forms the
mediation between the Father and
the Son, and is, through the Son,
united with the Father.[1]

NOTES.

1. The Filioque controversy, which is now a thousand years old, refers only to the meta-physical question of the *eternal procession* (ἐκπόρευσις) of the Holy Spirit (John xv. 26); the Greek Church, in the interest of the *monarchia* of the Father, maintains the single procession from the Father *alone;* the Latin Church, since Augustine, in the interest of the *homoousia* of the Son, the double procession from the Father *and the Son.* About the *temporal mission* (πέμψις) of the Spirit from the Father and the Son (John xiv. 26; xv. 26; xvi. 7), and the practical question of the *work* of the Spirit in the regeneration and sanctification of believers, there has been no controversy between the Greek and Latin Churches. See Vol. I. p. 26.

2. JOHN OF DAMASCUS, or JOANNES DAMASCENUS (surnamed CHRYSORRHOAS, gold-pouring; also called by the Arabs MANSUR, i. e., λελυτρωμένος), born at Damascus (then under Saracen rule), monk in the convent of St. Sabas near Jerusalem, died after 754, is the last of the Greek fathers, and the greatest and most authoritative of the divines of the Oriental Church. He may be called the Thomas Aquinas of the East. Inferior in productive genius and original-ity to Origen, Athanasius, Gregory Nazianzen, and Gregory of Nyssa, he is more compre-hensive in his range of teaching, and more uniformly orthodox in his dogmatic statements. His chief work is his 'Exposition of the Orthodox Faith' (ἔκδοσις ἀκριβὴς τῆς ὀρθοδόξου πίστεως), which sums up under a hundred heads the results of the theological labors of the Greek fathers and councils down to the seventh century. It was the first complete system of divinity, and by the use of Aristotelian dialectics ushered in the scholastic period. He distinguished himself also by his hymns, and by his eloquent defense of images against the iconoclasts, for which he was highly lauded by the second Council of Nicæa (787). The best edition of his works has been issued by Le Quien, Paris, 1712, two vols. folio, reproduced in Migne's *Patrologia Græca*, Vols. XCIV.–XCVI., Paris, 1857.

3. After reading this agreement, the aged Dr. Döllinger, who is the head of these Union conferences, added the following hopeful remarks: ' So far then are we agreed, and the theologians know that the question of the Holy Spirit is herewith properly exhausted. A dogmatic conflict concerning this question no longer exists between us. May God grant that what we have here adjusted be received by the Churches of the East in the spirit of peace and discrimination between dogma and theological opinion. What we have accom-plished furnishes a new ground of hope that our efforts are blessed by God, and that we shall succeed still further; while the history of former union transactions makes the impression that God's blessing did not rest on them. I think it no presumption to believe that here we per-ceive the blessing of God, there the absence of his blessing (*Gottes Unsegen*). Let us remember how much deception and fraud, what a tissue of falsifications, how much ambitious violence were employed at the Councils of Lyons and Florence, how both parties were always conscious of aiming at something else than agreement in the great truths of the Christian faith. I hope we shall be able to continue these international conferences next year. What a joy, if then the Orientals bring the glad tidings—Our Bishops, Synods, and Churches have approved our agreement.'

---

[1] *De fide orthod.* I. 13: μέσον τοῦ ἀγεννήτου καὶ γεννητοῦ καὶ δι' Υἱοῦ τῷ Πατρὶ συναπ-τόμενον.

APPENDIX I.

Encyclical Letter of our Most Holy Lord Leo XIII., by Divine Providence Pope, concerning the Christian Constitution of States. A.D. 1885.

[The Encyclical Letter of Pope Leo XIII., *De Civitatum Constitutione Christiana*, which is called from the first two words, *Immortale Dei*, was issued Nov. 1, 1885, during the Cultur-conflict (*Culturkampf*) in Germany, as a mild interpretation of the *Syllabus* of his predecessor, 1864 (pp. 213–233), which was understood to be an attack upon modern civilization and civil and religious liberty. The Encyclical is addressed "to all the Patriarchs, Primates, Archbishops, and Bishops of the Catholic World, in the grace and communion of the Apostolic See," and partakes of that infallibility which the Vatican Decree of 1870 claims for all the official or *ex cathedra* deliverances of the Pope on matters of faith and morals.

The Latin text of this document is taken from *Acta Leonis Papæ XIII.* (1879–1885), Parisiis, 1885, pp. 283–321, the translation from the "Tablet," London, Nov. 14, 1885, as revised by authority.]

Immortale Dei miserentis opus, quod est Ecclesia, quamquam per se et natura sua salutem spectat animarum adipiscendamque in cœlis felicitatem, tamen in ipso etiam rerum mortalium genere tot ac tantas ultro parit utilitates, ut plures majoresve non posset, si in primis et maxime esset ad tuendam hujus vitæ, quæ in terris agitur, prosperitatem institutum.

That imperishable work of a merciful God, the Church, though she looks essentially, and from the very nature of her being, to the salvation of souls and the winning for them of happiness in heaven, nevertheless she also secures even in the mere order of perishable things advantages so many and so great that she could not do more even if she had been founded primarily and specially to secure prosperity in this life which is spent upon earth.

Revera quacumque Ecclesia vestigium posuit, continuo rerum faciem immutavit, popularesque mores sicut virtutibus antea ignotis, ita et nova urbanitate imbuit; quam quotquot accepere populi, mansuetudine, æquitate, rerum gestarum gloria ex-

In truth wherever the Church has set her foot she has at once changed the aspect of affairs, colored the manners of the people as with new virtues so also with a refinement unknown before: and all nations who have received her have been distinguished for their

[Note.—For another translation with notes, Ryan and Millar, *Church and State*, pp. 1–61.—Ed.]

celluerunt. — Sed vetus tamen illa est atque antiqua vituperatio, quod Ecclesiam aiunt esse cum rationibus reipublicæ dissidentem, nec quicquam posse ad ea vel commoda vel ornamenta conferre, quæ suo jure suaque sponte omnis bene constituta civitas appetit. Sub ipsis Ecclesiæ primordiis non dissimili opinionis iniquitate agitari chrĭstianos, et in odium invidiamque vocari solitos hac etiam de caussa accepimus, quod hostes imperii dicerentur; quo tempore malorum culpam, quibus esset perculsa respublica, vulgo libebat in Christianum conferre nomen, cum revera ultor scelerum Deus pœnas a sontibus justas exigeret. Ejus atrocitas calumniæ non sine caussa ingenium armavit stilumque acuit Augustini: qui præsertim in Civitate Dei *virtutem christianæ sapientiæ, qua parte necessitudinem habet cum republica, tanto in lumine collocavit, ut non tam pro christianis sui temporis dixisse caussam quam de criminibus falsis perpetuum triumphum egisse videatur.*

Similium tamen querelarum

gentleness, their justice, and the glory of their deeds. But it is an old and time-worn accusation that the Church is incompatible with the welfare of the commonwealth, and incapable of contributing to those things, whether useful or ornamental, which every well constituted State rightly and naturally desires. We know that on this ground, in the very beginnings of the Church, Christians, from the same perversity of view, were persecuted and constantly held up to hatred and contempt, so that they were styled the enemies of the Empire. And at that time it was generally popular to attribute to Christianity the responsibility for the evils with which the State was stricken, when in reality God, the avenger of crimes, was requiring a just punishment from the guilty. The wickedness of this calumny, not without cause, armed the genius and sharpened the pen of Augustin, who, especially in his *De Civitate Dei*, set forth so clearly the efficacy of Christian wisdom and the way in which it is bound up with the well-being of States, that he seems not only to have pleaded the cause of the Christians in his own time, but to have triumphantly refuted these false charges forever.

But this unhappy inclination to

atque insimulationum funesta li-
bido non quievit, ac permultis
sane placuit civilem vivendi
disciplinam aliunde petere, quam
ex doctrinis quas Ecclesia ca-
tholica probat. Immo postremo
hoc tempore novum, *ut appel-*
lant, jus, *quod inquiunt esse*
velut quoddam adulti jam sæ-
culi incrementum, progrediente
libertate partum, valere ac do-
minari passim cœpit.—Sed quan-
tumvis multa multi periclitati
sunt, constat, repertam nunquam
esse præstantiorem constituendæ
temperandæque civitatis ratio-
nem, quam quæ ab evangeli-
ca doctrina sponte efflorescit.—
Maximi igitur momenti atque
admodum muneri nostro apo-
stolico consentaneum esse arbi-
tramur, novas de re publica
opiniones cum doctrina christia-
na conferre: quo modo erroris
dubitationisque caussas ereptum
iri, emergente veritate, confidi-
mus, ita ut videre quisque facile
queat summa illa præcepta vi-
vendi quæ sequi et quibus parere
debeat.

Non est magni negotii statuere,
qualem sit speciem formamque ha-
bitura civitas, gubernante christi-
ana philosophia rempublicam.—
Insitum homini natura est, ut in
civili societate vivat: is enim ne-

charges and false accusations was
not laid to rest, and many have
thought well to seek a system of
civil life apart from the doctrines
which the Church approves. And
now in these last times " *The new
Law*," as they call it, has begun
to prevail, which they describe as
the outcome of a world now fully
developed, and born of a grow-
ing liberty. But although many
hazardous schemes have been propounded by many, it is clear that
never has any better method been
found for establishing and ruling
the State than that which is the
natural result of the teaching of
the Gospel. We deem it therefore of the greatest moment, and
especially suitable to our apostolic
office, to compare the new opinions
concerning the State with Christian doctrine, by which method we
trust that, truth being thus presented, the causes of error and
doubt will be removed, so that every man may easily discern those
supreme commandments of conduct which he ought to follow and
obey.

It is not a very difficult matter
to set forth what form and appearance the State would have if Christian philosophy governed the commonwealth. Man has a natural
instinct for civil society; for since

cessarium vitæ cultum et paratum, itemque ingenii atque animi perfectionem cum in solitudine adipisci non possit, provisum divinitus est, ut ad conjunctionem congregationemque hominum nasceretur cum domesticam, tum etiam civilem, quæ suppeditare vitæ *sufficientiam perfectam solá potest. Quoniam vero non potest societas ulla consistere, nisi si aliquis omnibus præsit, efficaci similique movens singulos ad commune propositum impulsione, efficitur, civili hominum communitati necessariam esse auctoritatem, qua regatur : quæ, non secus ac societas, a natura proptereaque a Deo ipso oriatur auctore.*

Ex quo illud consequitur, potestatem publicam per se ipsam non esse nisi a Deo. Solus enim Deus est verissimus maximusque rerum dominus, cui subesse et servire omnia, quæcumque, necesse est : ita ut quicumque jus imperandi hàbent, non id aliunde accipiant, nisi ab illo summo omnium principe Deo. Non est potestas nisi a Deo.[1] *—Jus autem imperii per se non est cum ulla reipublicæ forma necessario copulatum aliam sibi vel aliam assumere recte potest, modo utilitatis bonique communis reapse efficientem. Sed in quolibet genere*

he cannot attain in solitude the necessary means of civilized life, it is a divine provision that he comes into existence adapted for taking part in that union and assembling of men, both in the Family and in the State, which alone can supply adequate facilities for the perfecting of life. But since no society can hold together unless some person is over all, impelling individuals by effectual and similar motives to pursue the common end, it results that an authority to rule is indispensable to a civilized community, which authority, no less than society itself, is based upon nature, and therefore has God himself for its author.

And thence it follows that by its very nature there can be no public power except from God alone. For God alone is the most true and supreme Lord of the world to whom all things whatsoever must necessarily be subservient and obey, so that whoever possesses the right of governing can receive it from no other source than from that Supreme Governor of all, God. *" There is no power except from God".*[1] But the right of ruling is not necessarily conjoined with any special form of commonwealth, but may rightly assume this or that

[1] Rom. xiii. 3.

reipublicæ omnino principes debent summum mundi gubernatorem Deum intueri, eumque sibimetipsis in administranda civitate tanquam exemplum legemque proponere.

Deus enim, sicut in rebus, quæ sunt quæque cernuntur, caussas genuit secundarias, in quibus perspici aliqua ratione posset natura actioque divina, quæque ad eum finem, quo hæc rerum spectat universitas, conducerent: ita in societate civili voluit esse principatum, quem qui gererent, in imaginem quamdam divinæ in genus humanum potestatis divinæque providentiæ referrent. Debet igitur imperium justum esse, neque herile, sed quasi paternum, quia Dei justissima in homines potestas est et cum paterna bonitate conjuncta: gerendum vero est ad utilitatem civium, quia qui præsunt cæteris, hac una de caussa præsunt, ut civitatis utilitatem tueantur. Neque ullo pacto committendum unius ut, vel paucorum commodo serviat civilis auctoritas, cum ad commune omnium bonum constituta sit. Quod si, qui præsunt, delabantur in dominatum injustum, si importunitate superbiave peccaverint, si male populo consu-

form, provided that it really promotes utility and the common good. But whatever be the kind of commonwealth, rulers ought to keep in view God, the Supreme Governor of the world, and to set him before themselves as an example and a law in the administration of the State.

For as God, in things which are and which are seen, has produced secondary causes, wherein the Divine nature and course of action can be perceived, and which conduce to that end to which the universe is directed, so he has willed that in civil society there should be a governing power, and that they who hold it should bear a certain resemblance to the power and providence of God over the human race. The rule of the government, therefore, should be just, and not that of a master but rather that of a father, because the power of God over men is most just and allied with a father's goodness. Moreover, it is to be carried on with a view to the advantage of the citizens, because they who are over others are over them for this cause alone, that they may see to the interests of the State. And in no way is it to be allowed that the civil authority should be subservient merely to the advantage of one or of a few, since it was established for the common

luerint, sciant sibi rationem ali- good of all. But if they who are
quando Deo esse reddendam, idque over the State should lapse into
tanto severius, quanto vel sanctiore unjust rule; if they should err
in munere versati sint, vel gradum through arrogance or pride; if
dignitatis altiorem obtinuerint. their measures should be injurious
Potentes potenter tormenta pati- to the people, let them know that
entur.[1] hereafter an account must be ren-
dered to God, and that with a strict-
ness proportioned to the sacredness
of their office or the eminence of
their dignity, " *The mighty shall be*
mightily tormented." [1]

Ita sane majestatem imperii re- Thus truly the majesty of rule
verentia civium honesta et libens will be attended with an honorable
comitabitur. Etenim cum semel and willing regard on the part of
in animum induxerint, pellere the citizens; for when once they
qui imperant auctoritate a Deo are assured that they who rule are
data, illa quidem officia justa strong only with the authority given
ac debita esse sentient, dicto au- by God, they will feel that it is
dientes esse principibus, eisdemque their just and proper duty to be
obsequium ac fidem præstare cum obedient to their rulers, and pay to
quadam similitudine pietatis, quæ them respect and fidelity with some-
liberorum est erga parentes. Om- what of the same affection as that
nis anima potestatibus sublimiori- of children to their parents. " *Let*
bus subdita sit.[2] *every soul be subject to higher*
powers." [2]

Spernere quippe potestatem legi- For to contemn lawful author-
timam, quavis eam in persona con- ity, in whatever person it is vested,
stiterit, non magis licet, quam divi- is as unlawful as it is to resist the
næ voluntati resistere : cui si qui Divine will; and whoever resists
resistant, in interitum ruunt vo- that, rushes voluntarily to his de-
luntarium. Qui resistit potestati struction. " *He who resists the*
Dei ordinationi resistit; qui autem *power, resists the ordinance of*
resistunt, ipsi sibi damnationem ac- *God; and they who resist purchase*
quirunt.[3] *Quapropter obedientiam* *to themselves judgment.*" [3] Where-

---

[1] Sap. (Wisd.) vi. 7.   [2] Rom. xiii. 1.   [3] Rom. xiii. 2.

abjicere, et, per vim multitudinis rem ad seditionem vocare est crimen majestatis, neque humanæ tantum, sed etiam divinæ.

Hac ratione constitutam civitatem, perspicuum est, omnino debere plurimis maximisque officiis, quæ ipsam jungunt Deo, religione publica satisfacere. — Natura et ratio, quæ jubet singulos sancte religioseque Deum colere, quod in ejus potestate sumus, et quod ab eo profecti ad eumdem reverti debemus, eadem lege adstringit civilem communitatem. Homines enim communi societate conjuncti nihilo sunt minus in Dei potestate, quam singuli; neque minorem quam singuli gratiam Deo societas debet, quo auctore coaluit, cujus nutu conservatur, cujus beneficio innumerabilem bonorum, quibus affluit, copiam accepit. Quapropter sicut nemini licet sua adversus Deum officia negligere, officiumque est maximum amplecti et animo et moribus religionem, nec quam quisque maluerit, sed quam Deus jusserit, quamque certis minimeque dubitandis indiciis unam ex omnibus veram esse constiterit: eodem modo civitates non possunt, citra scelus, gerere se tanquam si Deus omnino non esset, aut curam religionis velut alienam nihilque profuturam abjicere,

fore to cast away obedience, and by popular violence to incite to sedition, is treason, not only against man, but against God.

It is clear that a State constituted on this basis is altogether bound to satisfy, by the public profession of religion, the very many and great duties which bring it into relation with God. Nature and reason which commands every man individually to serve God holily and religiously, because we belong to him, and coming from him must return to him, binds by the same law the civil community. For men living together in society are no less under the power of God than are individuals; and society owes as much gratitude as individuals do to God, who is its author, its preserver, and the beneficent source of the innumerable blessings which it has received. And therefore as it is not lawful for anybody to neglect his duties towards God, and as it is the first duty to embrace religion in mind and in conduct — and that not the one that each may prefer, but that which God has enjoined, which he has proved to be the only true one by certain and indubitable evidence — in the same manner States cannot, without crime, act as though God did not exist, or cast off the

aut asciscere de pluribus generi-bus indifferenter quod libeat: om-ninoque debent eum in colendo numine morem usurpare modum-que, quo coli se Deus ipse demon-stravit velle.

Sanctum igitur oportet apud principes esse Dei nomen, ponen-dumque in præcipuis illorum of-ficiis religionem gratia complecti, benevolentia tueri, auctoritate nu-tuque legum tegere, nec quippiam instituere aut decernere quod sit ejus incolumitati contrarium. Id et civibus debent, quibus præsunt. Nati enim susceptique omnes ho-mines sumus ad summum quod-dam et ultimum bonorum, quo sunt omnia consilia referenda extra hanc fragilitatem brevita-temque vitæ in cœlis collocatum. Quoniam autem hinc pendet ho-minum undique expleta ac per-fecta felicitas, idcirco assequi eum, qui commemoratus est, finem tanti interest singulorum ut plu-ris interesse non possit. Civilem igitur societatem, communi utili-tati natam, in tuenda prosperi-tate reipublicæ necesse est sic con-sulere civibus, ut obtinendo adi-piscendoque summo illi atque incommutabili bono quod sponte appetunt, non modo nihil impor-

care of religion as alien to them or useless, or out of several kinds of religion adopt indifferently which they please; but they are absolute-ly bound, in the worship of the Deity, to adopt that use and man-ner in which God himself has shown that he wills to be adored.

Therefore among rulers the name of God must be holy, and it must be reckoned among the first of their duties to favor religion, pro-tect it, and cover it with the author-ity of the laws, and not to institute or decree anything which is incom-patible with its security. They owe this also to the citizens over whom they rule. For all of us men are born and brought up for a certain supreme and final good in heaven, beyond this frail and short life, and to this end every aim is to be re-ferred. And because upon it de-pends the full and perfect happi-ness of men, therefore, to attain this end which has been mentioned, is of as much interest as is conceiv-able to every individual man. Civil society, therefore, which came into existence only for the common good, must, in its defence of the State's well-being, so consult the good of its citizens as not only to offer no hindrance, but to afford every possible assistance to them in the winning and gaining of that

tet unquam incommodi, sed omnes quascumque possit, opportunitates afferat. Quarum præcipua est, ut detur opera religioni sancte inviolateque servandæ cujus officia hominem Deo conjungunt.

Vera autem religio quæ sit, non difficulter videt qui judicium prudens sincerumque adhibuerit: argumentis enim permultis atque illustribus, veritate nimirum vaticiniorum, prodigiorum frequentia, celerrima fidei vel per medios hostes hac maxima impedimenta propagatione, martyrum testimonio, aliisque similibus liquet, eam esse unice veram, quam Jesus Christus et instituit ipsemet et Ecclesiæ suæ tuendam propagandamque demandavit.

Nam unigenitus Dei filius societatem in terris constituit, quæ Ecclesia dicitur, cui excelsum divinumque munus in omnes sæculorum ætates continuandum transmisit, quod ipse a Patre acceperat. Sicut misit me Pater, et ego mitto vos.[1] *Ecce ego vobiscum sum omnibus diebus usque ad consummationem sæculi.*[2] *Igitur, sicut Jesus Christus in terras venit*

chief good which they naturally desire, and for which nothing can be taken in exchange. The chief assistance is, that attention should be paid to the holy and inviolate preservation of religion, by the duties of which man is united to God.

Now which is the true religion may be easily discovered by any one who will view the matter with a careful and unbiassed judgment; for there are proofs of great number and splendor, as, for example, the truth of prophecy, the abundance of miracles, the extremely rapid spread of the faith, even in the midst of its enemies and in spite of the greatest hindrances, the testimony of the martyrs, and the like, from which it is evident that that is the only true religion which Jesus Christ instituted himself and then intrusted to his Church to defend and to spread.

For the only-begotten Son of God set up a society on earth which is called the Church, and to it he transferred that most glorious and divine office, which he had received from his Father, to be perpetuated forever. "*As the Father hath sent me, even so I send you.*"[1] "*Behold I am with you all days even to the consummation of the world.*"[2] Therefore as Jesus Christ

---

[1] John xx. 21.

[2] Matt. xxviii. 20.

ut *homines* vitam habeant et abundantius habeant,[1] *eodem modo Ecclesia propositum habet, tanquam finem, salutem animarum sempiternam: ob eamque rem talis est natura sua, ut porrigat sese ad totius complexum gentis humanæ, nullis nec locorum nec temporum limitibus circumscripta.* Prædicate Evangelium omni creaturæ.[2]

Tam ingenti hominum multitudini Deus ipse magistratus assignavit qui cum potestate præessent: unumque omnium principem, et maximum certissimumque veritatis magistrum esse voluit, cui claves regni cœlorum commisit. Tibi dabo claves regni cœlorum.[3] — Pasce agnos ... pasce oves:[4]—ego rogavi pro te, ut non deficiat fides tua.[5] *Hæc societas, quamvis ex hominibus constet non secus ac civilis communitas, tamen propter finem sibi constitutum, atque instrumenta quibus ad finem contendii, supernaturalis est et spiritualis; atque idcirco distinguitur ac differt a societate civili: et, quod plurimum interest, societas est genere et jure perfecta, cum adjumenta ad incolumitatem actionemque suam necessaria, voluntate beneficioque conditoris sui, omnia in se et per se ipsa possideat. Sicut*

came into the world "*that men might have life and have it more abundantly*,"[1] so also the Church has for its aim and end the eternal salvation of souls: and for this cause it is so constituted as to embrace the whole human race without any limit or circumscription either of time or place. "*Preach ye the Gospel to every creature.*"[2]

Over this immense multitude of men God himself has set rulers with power to govern them; and he has willed that one should be head of them all, and the chief and unerring teacher of truth, and to him he has given the keys of the kingdom of heaven. "*To thee will I give the keys of the kingdom of heaven.*"[3] "*Feed my lambs, feed my sheep.*"[4] "*I have prayed for thee that thy faith may not fail.*"[5] This society, though it be composed of men just as civil society is, yet because of the end that it has in view, and the means by which it tends to it, it is supernatural and spiritual; and, therefore, is distinguished from civil society and differs from it; and —a fact of the highest moment— is a society perfect in its kind and in its rights, possessing in and by itself, by the will and beneficence of its founder, all the appliances

---

[1] John x. 10. [3] Matt. xvi. 19. [4] John xxi. 16, 17.
[2] Mark xvi. 15. [5] Luke xxii 32.

finis, quo tendit Ecclesia, longe nobilissimus est, ita ejus potestas est omnium præstantissima, neque imperio civili potest haberi inferior, aut eidem esse ullo modo obnoxia.

Revera Jesus Christus Apostolis suis libera mandata dedit in sacra, adjuncta tum ferendarum legum veri nominis facultate, tum gemina, quæ hinc consequitur, judicandi puniendique potestate: Data est mihi omnis potestas in cœlo et in terra: euntes ergo docete omnes gentes . . . docentes eos servare omnia quæcumque mandavi vobis.[1] *Et alibi:* Si non audierit eos, dic Ecclesiæ.[2] *Atque iterum:* In promptis habentes ulcisci omnem inobedientiam.[3] *Rursus:* Durius agam secundum potestatem, quam Dominus dedit mihi in ædificationem et non in destructionem.[4]

Itaque dux hominibus esse ad cœlestia non civitas, sed Ecclesia debet: eidemque hoc est munus assignatum a Deo, ut de iis, quæ religionem attingunt, videat ipsa et statuat: ut doceat omnes gentes: ut christiani nominis fines, quoad potest, late proferat; brevi ut rem

that are necessary for its preservation and action. Just as the end at which the Church aims is by far the noblest of ends, so its power is the most exalted of all powers, and cannot be held to be either inferior to the civil power or in any way subject to it.

In truth Jesus Christ gave his Apostles unfettered commissions over all sacred things, with the power of establishing laws properly so-called, and the double right of judging and punishing which follows from it: *"All power has been given to me in heaven and on earth; going therefore teach all nations . . . teaching them to keep whatsoever I have commanded you."*[1] And in another place he says: *"If he will not hear, tell it to the Church;"*[2] and again: *"Ready to punish all disobedience;"*[3] and once more: *"I shall act with more severity, according to the powers which our Lord has given me unto edification and not unto destruction."*[4]

So then it is not the State but the Church that ought to be men's guide to heaven; and it is to her that God has assigned the office of watching and legislating for all that concerns religion, of teaching all nations; of extending, as far as may be, the borders of Christian-

---

[1] Matt. xxviii. 18–20.   [2] Matt. xviii. 17.   [3] 2 Cor. x. 6.   [4] 2 Cor. xiii. 10.

christianam libere expediteque judicio suo administret.

ity; and, in a word, of administering its affairs without let or hindrance according to her own judgment.

Hanc vero auctoritatem in se ipsa absolutam planeque sui juris, quæ ab assentatrice principum philosophia jamdiu oppugnatur, Ecclesia sibi asserere itemque publice exercere numquam desiit, primis omnium pro ea propugnantibus Apostolis, qui cum disseminare Evangelium a principibus synagogæ prohiberentur, constanter respondebant: Obedire oportet Deo magis quam hominibus.[1] *Eamdem sancti Ecclesiæ Patres rationum momentis tueri pro opportunitate studuerunt: romanique pontificis invicta animi constantia adversus oppugnatores indicare nunquam prætermiserunt.*

Now this authority, which pertains absolutely to the Church herself, and is part of her manifest rights, and which has long been opposed by a philosophy subservient to princes, she has never ceased to claim for herself and to exercise publicly; the Apostles themselves being the first of all to maintain it, when, being forbidden by the leaders of the synagogue to preach the Gospel, they boldly answered, "*We must obey God rather than men.*"[1] This same authority the holy fathers of the Church have been careful to maintain by weighty reasonings as occasions have arisen; and the Roman pontiffs have never ceased to defend it with inflexible constancy.

Quin etiam et opinione et re eamdem probârunt ipsi viri principes rerumque publicarum gubernatôres, ut qui paciscendo transigendis negotiis, mittendis vicissimque accipiendis legatis, atque aliorum mutatione officiorum, agere cum Ecclesia tamquam cum suprema potestate legitima consueverunt. — Neque profecto sine singulari providentis Dei consilio

Nay, more, princes and civil governors themselves have approved it in theory and in fact; for in the making of compacts, in the transaction of business, in sending and receiving embassies, and in the interchange of other offices, it has been their custom to act with the Church as with a supreme and legitimate power. And we may be sure that it is not without the sin-

---

[1] Acts v. 29.

factum esse censendum est, ut hœc ipsa potestas principatu civili, velut optima libertatis suœ tutela muniretur.

Itaque Deus humani generis procurationem inter duas potestates partitus est; scilicet ecclesiasticam et civilem, alteram quidem divinis, alteram humanis rebus præpositam. Utraque est in suo genere maxima: habet utraque certos, quibus contineatur, terminos, eosque sua cujusque natura caussaque proxima definitos; unde aliquis velut orbis circumscribitur, in quo sua cujusque actio jure proprio versetur. Sed quia utriusque imperium est in eosdem, eum usu venire possit, ut res una atque eadem, quamquam aliter atque aliter, sed tamen eadem res ad utriusque jus judiciumque pertineat, debet providentissimus Deus, a quo sunt ambœ constituœ, utriusque itinera recto atque ordine composuisse. Quae autem sunt, a Deo ordinatæ sunt.[1]

Quod ni ita esset, funestarum sæpe contentionum concertationumque caussæ nascerentur; nec raro sollicitus animi, velut in via ancipiti, hærere homo deberet, anxius

gular providence of God that this power of the Church was defended by the civil power as the best defence of its own liberty.

God, then, has divided the charge of the human race between two powers, viz., the ecclesiastical and the civil, the one being set over divine, and the other over human things. Each is supreme in its own kind: each has certain limits within which it is restricted, and those limits defined by the nature and proximate cause of each: so that there is, as we may say, a world marked off as a field for the proper action of each. But forasmuch as each has dominion over the same subjects, since it might come to pass that one and the same thing, though in different ways, still one and the same, might pertain to the right and the tribunal of both, therefore God, who foreseeth all things, and who has established both powers, must needs have arranged the course of each in right relation to one another, and in due order, *"For the powers that are are ordained by God."*[1]

If this were not so, causes of rivalries and dangerous disputes would be constantly arising; and man would often have to stop in anxiety and doubt, like a traveller with

---

[1] Rom. xiii. 1.

quid facto opus esset, contraria ju-
bentibus binis potestatibus quarum
recusare imperium, salvo officio,
non potest. Atqui maxime istud
repugnat de sapientia cogitare et
bonitate Dei, qui vel in rebus phy-
sicis, quamquam sunt longe infe-
rioris ordinis, tamen naturales
vires caussasque invicem concilia-
vit moderata ratione et quodam
velut concentu mirabili, ita ut
nulla earum impediat cœteras,
cunctæque simul illæ, quo mundus
spectat, convenientur aptissimeque
conspirent.

Itaque inter utramque potesta-
tem quædam intercedat necesse est
ordinata colligatio: quæ quidem
conjunctioni non immerito compa-
ratur, per quam anima et corpus
in homine copulantur. Qualis
autem et quanta ea sit, aliter ju-
dicari non potest, nisi respiciendo,
uti diximus, ad utriusque natu-
ram, habendaque ratione excellen-
tiæ et nobilitatis caussarum ; cum
alteri proxime maximeque propo-
situm sit rerum mortalium curare
commoda, alteri cœlestia ac sempi-
terna bona comparare.—Quidquid
igitur est in rebus humanis quo-
quo modo sacrum, quidquid ad
salutem animorum cultumve Dei
pertinet, sive tale illud sit natura

two roads before him, not knowing
what he ought to do, with two powers commanding contrary things,
whose authority, however, he cannot refuse without neglect of duty.
But it would be most repugnant so
to think of the wisdom and goodness of God, who, even in physical
things, though they are of a far
lower order, has yet so attempered
and combined together the forces
and causes of nature in an orderly
manner and with a sort of wonderful harmony, that none of them is
a hindrance to the rest, and all of
them most fitly and aptly combine
for the great end of the universe.

So then there must needs be a
certain orderly connection between
these two powers, which may not
unfairly be compared to the union
with which soul and body are
united in man. What the nature of that union is, and what its
extent, cannot otherwise be determined than, as we have said, by
having regard to the nature of each
power, and by taking account of
the relative excellence and nobility
of their ends; for one of them has
for its proximate and chief aim the
care of the goods of this world, the
other the attainment of the goods
of heaven that are eternal. Whatsoever, therefore, in human affairs
is in any manner sacred ; whatso-

sua, sive rursus tale intelligatur propter caussam ad quam refertur, id est omne in potestate arbitrioque Ecclesiæ: cætera vero, quæ civile et politicum genus complectitur, rectum est civili auctoritati esse subjecta, cum Jesus Christus jusserit, quæ Cæsaris sint, reddi Cæsari, quæ Dei, Deo.[1]

ever pertains to the salvation of souls or the worship of God, whether it be so in its own nature, or on the other hand is held to be so for the sake of the end to which it is referred, all this is in the power and subject to the free disposition of the Church; but all other things which are embraced in the civil and political order are rightly subject to the civil authority, since Jesus Christ has commanded that what is Cæsar's is to be paid to Cæsar, and what is God's to God.[1]

Incidunt autem quandoque tempora, cum alius quoque concordiæ modus ad tranquillam libertatem valet, nimirum si qui principes rerum publicarum et Pontifex Romanus de re aliqua separata in idem placitum concenserint. Quibus Ecclesia temporibus maternæ pietatis eximia documenta præbet, cum facilitatis indulgentiæque tantum adhibere soleat, quantum maxime potest.

Ejusmodi est, quam summatim attigimus, civilis hominum societatis christiana temperatio, et hæc non temere neque ad libidinem ficta, sed ex maximis ducta verissimisque principiis, quæ ipsa naturali ratione confirmantur.

Talis autem conformatio reipublicæ nihil habet, quod possit aut

Sometimes, however, circumstances arise when another method of concord is available for peace and liberty; we mean when princes and the Roman Pontiff come to an understanding concerning any particular matter. In such circumstances the Church gives singular proof of her maternal good-will, and is accustomed to exhibit the highest possible degree of generosity and indulgence.

Such then, as we have indicated in brief, is the Christian order of civil society; no rash or merely fanciful fiction, but deduced from principles of the highest truth and moment, which are confirmed by the natural reason itself.

Now such a constitution of the State contains nothing that can be

---

[1] [Comp. Matt. xxii. 21.]

minus videri dignum amplitudine principum, aut parum decorum: tantumque abest, ut jura majestatis imminuat, ut potius stabiliora atque augustiora faciat. Immo, si altius consideretur, habet illa conformatio perfectionem quamdam magnam, qua carent cœteri rerum publicarum modi: ex eâque fructus essent sane excellentes et varii consecuturi, si modo suum partes singulœ gradum tenerent, atque illud integre efficerent cui unaquœque prœposita est, officium et munus.—Revera in ea, quam ante diximus, constitutione reipublicœ, sunt quidem divina atque humana convenienti ordine partita: incolumia civium jura, eademque divinarum, naturalium humanarumque legum patrocinio defensa: officiorum singulorum cum sapienter constituta descriptio, tum opportune sancita custodia. Singuli homines in hoc ad sempiternam illam civitatem dubio laboriosoque curriculo sibi sciunt prœsto esse, quos tuto sequantur ad ingrediendum duces, ad perveniendum adjutores: pariterque intelligunt, sibi alios esse ad securitatem, ad fortunas, ad commoda cœtera, quibus communis hœc vita constat, vel parienda vel conservanda datos.

thought either unworthy of the majesty of princes or unbecoming; and so far is it from lessening the imperial rights that it rather adds stability and grandeur to them. For, if it be more deeply considered, such a constitution has a great perfection which all others lack, and from it various excellent fruits would accrue if each party would only keep its own place and discharge with integrity that office and work to which it was appointed. For in truth in this constitution of the State, which we have above described, divine and human affairs are properly divided; the rights of citizens are completely defended by divine, natural, and human law; and the limitations of the several offices are at once wisely laid down, and the keeping of them most opportunely secured. All men know that in their doubtful and laborious journey to the everlasting city they have at hand guides to teach them how to set forth, helpers whom they may safely follow to show them how to reach their journey's end; and at the same time they know that they have others whose business it is to take care of their security and their fortunes, to obtain for them, or to secure to them, all those other goods which are essential to the life of a community.

Societas domestica eam, quam par est, firmitudinem adipiscitur ex unius atque individui sanctitate conjugii: jura officiaque inter conjuges sapienti justitia et æquitate reguntur: debitum conservatur mulieri decus: auctoritas viri ad exemplum est auctoritatis Dei conformata: temperata patria potestas convenienter dignitati uxoris prolisque: denique liberorum tuitioni, commodis, institutioni optime consulitur.

Domestic society obtains that firmness and solidity which it requires in the sanctity of marriage, one and indissoluble; the rights and duties of husband and wife are ordered with wise justice and equity; the due honor is secured to the woman; the authority of the man is conformed to the example of the authority of God; the authority of the father is tempered as becomes the dignity of the wife and offspring, and the best possible provision is made for the guardianship, the true good, and the education of the children.

In genere rerum politico et civili, leges spectant commune bonum, neque voluntati judicioque fallaci multitudinis, sed veritate justitiaque diriguntur: auctoritas principum sanctitudinem quamdam induit humana majorem, contineturque ne declinet a justitia, neu modum in imperando transiliat: obedientia civium habet honestatem dignitatemque comitem, quia non est hominis ad hominem servitus, sed obtemperatio voluntati Dei, regnum per homines exercentis. Quo cognito as persuaso, omnino ad justitiam pertinere illa intelliguntur, vereri majestatem principum, subesse constanter et fideliter protestati publicæ, nihil seditiose fa-

In the domain of political and civil affairs the laws aim at the common good, and are not guided by the deceptive wishes and judgments of the multitude, but by truth and justice. The authority of the rulers puts on a certain garb of sanctity greater than what pertains to man, and it is restrained from declining from justice, and passing over just limits in the exercise of power. The obedience of citizens is accompanied by honour and dignity because it is not the servitude of men to men, but obedience to the will of God exercising his sovereignty by means of men. And this being recognized and admitted, it is understood that it is a matter of justice to respect

cere, sanctam servare disciplinam civitatis.

the majesty of rulers, to obey public authority constantly and faithfully, to do nothing seditiously, and to keep the civil order of the State intact.

Similiter ponitur in officiis caritas mutua, benignitas, liberalitas: non distrahitur in contrarias partes, pugnantibus inter se praeceptis, civis idem et Christianus: denique amplissima bona, quibus mortalem quoque hominum vitam Christiana religio sua sponte explet, communitati societatique civili omnia quaeruntur: ita ut illud appareat verissime dictum: " Pendet a religione, qua Deus colitur, rei publicae status: multaque inter hunc et illam cognatio et familiaritas intercedit." [1]

In the same way mutual charity and kindness and liberality become public duties. The man who is at once a citizen and a Christian is no longer the victim of contending parties and incompatible obligations; and, finally, those very abundant good things with which the Christian religion of its own accord fills up even the mortal life of men, are all acquired for the community and civil society, so that it appears to be said with the fullest truth: " The state of the commonwealth depends on the religion with which God is worshipped, and between the one and the other there is a close relation and connection." [1]

Eorum vim bonorum mirabiliter, uti solet, persecutus est Augustinus pluribus locis, maxime vero ubi Ecclesiam Catholicam appellat iis verbis: " Tu pueriliter pueros, fortiter juvenes, quiete senes, prout cujusque non corporis tantum, sed et animi aetas est, exerces ac doces. Tu feminas viris suis non ad explendam libidinem, sed ad propagandam prolem, et ad rei fa-

Admirably, according to his wont, did Augustin in many places dilate on the power of those good things, but especially when he addresses the Catholic Church in these words: " Thou trainest and teachest children in childlike wise, the young with vigor, the old with gentleness, according as is not only the age of the body, but also of the mind of each. Women thou sub-

---

[1] *Sacr. Imp. ad Cyrillum Alexandr. et Episcopos. metrop. — Conf. Labbeum Collect. Conc.*, T. iii.

miliaris societatem, casta et fideli obedientia subjicis. Tu viros conjugibus, non ad illudendum imbeciliorum sexum, sed sinceri amoris legibus præficis. Tu parentibus filios libera quadam servitute subjungis, parentes filiis pia dominatione præponis. . . . Tu cives civibus, tu gentes gentibus, et prorsus homines primorum parentum recordatione, non societate tantum, sed quadam etiam fraternitate conjungis. Doces reges prospicere populis, mones populos se subdere regibus. Quibus honor debeatur, quibus affectus, quibus reverentia, quibus timor, quibus consolatio, quibus admonitio, quibus cohortatio, quibus disciplina, quibus objurgatio, quibus supplicium, sedulo doces; ostendens quemadmodum et non omnibus omnia, et omnibus caritas, et nulli debeatur injuria." [1]

jectest to their husbands in chaste and faithful obedience, not for the satisfaction of lust, but for the propagation of offspring and the formation of the family. Thou settest husbands over their spouses, not that they may trifle with the weaker sex, but in accordance with the laws of true affection. Thou subjectest sons to their parents in a kind of free servitude, and settest parents over their sons in a benignant rule. . . . Thou joinest together, not merely in society, but in a kind of fraternity, citizens with citizens, peoples with peoples, and in fact the whole race of men by a remembrance of their parentage. Thou teachest kings to look for the interests of their peoples. Thou admonishest peoples to submit themselves to their kings. With all care thou teachest to whom honor is due, to whom affection, to whom reverence, to whom fear, to whom consolation, to whom admonition, to whom exhortation, to whom discipline, to whom reproach, to whom punishment, showing how all things are not due to all, yet charity is, and wrong to none." [1]

Idemque alio loco male sapientes reprehendens politicos philosophos : " Qui doctrinam Christi adversam dicunt esse rei-

And in another place, speaking in blame of certain political pseudo-philosophers, he observes: "Let those who say that the doc-

---

[1] *De Moribus Cath.*, cap. xxx. n. 63.

publicæ, dent exercitum talem, quales doctrina Christi esse milites jussit, dent tales provinciales, tales maritos, tales conjuges, tales parentes, tales filios, tales dominos, tales servos, tales reges, tales judices, tales denique debitorum ipsius fisci redditores et exactores, quales esse præcipit doctrina Christiana, et audeant eam dicere adversam esse reipublicæ; immo vero non dubitent eam confitere magnam, si obtemperetur, salutem esse reipublicæ." [1]

trine of Christ is hurtful to the State produce an army of soldiers such as the doctrine of Christ has commanded them to be, such governors of provinces, such husbands, such wives, such parents, such sons, such masters, such slaves, such kings, such judges, and such payers and collectors of taxes due, as the Christian doctrine would have them. And then let them dare to say that such a state of things is hurtful to the State. Nay, they could not hesitate to confess that this doctrine, if it be obeyed, is a great safety to the State." [1]

Fuit aliquando tempus, cum evangelica philosophia gubernaret civitates: quo tempore Christianæ sapientiæ vis illa et divina virtus in leges, instituta, mores populorum, in omnes reipublicæ ordines rationesque penetraverat: cum religio per Jesum Christum instituta in eo, quo æquum erat, dignitatis gradu firmiter collocata, gratia principum legitimaque magistratuum tutela ubique floreret: cum sacerdotium atque imperium concordia et amica officiorum vicissitudo auspicato conjungeret. Eoque modo composita civitas fructus tulit omni opinione majores, quorum viget memoria et vigebit innumerabilibus re-

There was once a time when the philosophy of the Gospel governed States; when the power and divine virtue of Christian wisdom had penetrated into the laws, institutions, and manners of peoples — indeed into all the ranks and relations of the State; when the religion instituted by Jesus Christ, firmly established in that degree of dignity which was befitting, flourished everywhere, in the favor of rulers and under the due protection of magistrates; when the priesthood and the government were happily united by concord and a friendly interchange of offices. And the State composed in that fashion produced, in the opinion of all, more excellent fruits,

---

[1] *Epist.* cxxxviii (al. 5) *ad Marcellinum,* cap. ii. n. 51.

rum gestarum consignata monumentis, quæ nulla adversariorum arte corrumpi aut obscurari possunt.

Quod Europa Christiana barbaras gentes edomuit, easque a ferocitate ad mansuetudinem, a superstitione ad veritatem traduxit: quod Mahumetanorum incursiones victrix propulsavit: quod civilis cultus principatum retinuit, et ad omne decus humanitatis ducem se magistramque præbere cæteris consuevit: quod germanam libertatem eamque multiplicem gratificata populis est: quod complura ad miseriarum solatium sapientissime instituit, sine controversia magnam debet gratiam religioni, quam ad tantas res suscipiendas habuit auspicem, ad perficiendas adjutricem.

Mansissent profecto eadem bona, si utriusque potestatis concordia mansisset: majoraque expectari jure poterant, si auctoritati, si magisterio, si consiliis Ecclesiæ majore esset cum fide perseverantiaque obtemperatum. Illud enim perpetuæ legis instar habendum est, quod Ivo Carnutensis ad Paschalem II pontificem maximum præscripsit: " Cum regnum et sacerdotium inter se conveniunt, bene

the memory of which still flourishes, and will flourish, attested by innumerable monuments which can neither be destroyed nor obscured by any art of the adversary.

If Christian Europe subdued barbarous peoples, and transferred them from a savage to a civilized state, from superstition to the truth; if she victoriously repelled the invasions of the Mohammedans; if civilization retained the chief power, and accustomed herself to afford others a leader and mistress in everything that adorns humanity; if she has granted to the peoples true and manifold liberty; if she has most wisely established many institutions for the solace of wretchedness, beyond controversy it is very greatly due to religion, under whose auspices such great undertakings were commenced, and with whose aid they were perfected?

No doubt the same excellent state of things would have continued, if the agreement of the two powers had continued, and greater things might rightfully have been expected, if men had obeyed the authority, the teaching office, and the counsels of the Church with more fidelity and perseverance. For that is to be regarded as a perpetual law which Ivo of Chartres wrote to pope Paschal II.: "When kingship and

regitur mundus, floret et fructi-
ficat Ecclesia. Cum vero inter
se discordant, non tantum parvæ
res non crescunt, sed etiam mag-
næ res miserabiliter dilabuntur." [1]

Sed perniciosa illa ac deplo-
randa rerum novarum studia,
quæ sæculo xvi excitata sunt, cum
primum religionem Christianam
miscuissent, mox naturali quo-
dam itinere ad philosophiam, a
philosophia ad omnes civilis com-
munitatis ordines pervenerunt.
Ex hoc velut fonte repetenda illa
recentiora effrenatæ libertatis ca-
pita, nimirum in maximis per-
turbationibus superiore sæculo ex-
cogitata in medioque proposita,
perinde ac principia et funda-
menta novi juris, quod et fuit an-
tea ignotum, et a jure non solum
Christiano, sed etiam naturali
plus una ex parte discrepat.

Eorum principiorum illud est
maximum, omnes homines, quem-
admodum genere naturaque simi-
les intelliguntur, ita reapse esse
in actione vitæ inter se pares:
unumquemque ita esse sui juris,
ut nullo modo sit alterius aucto-
ritati obnoxius: cogitare de re
qualibet quæ velit, agere quod lu-
beat, libere posse: imperandi aliis

priesthood are agreed, the world is
well ruled, the Church flourishes
and bears fruit. But when they are
at variance, not only do little things
not grow, but even great things fall
into miserable ruin and decay." [1]

But that dreadful and deplorable
zeal for revolution which was
aroused in the sixteenth century,
after throwing the Christian religion into confusion, by a certain natural course proceeded to philosophy, and from philosophy pervaded
all ranks of the community. From
this spring, as it were, came those
more recent propositions of un-
bridled liberty which were first
thought out and then openly proclaimed in the terrible disturbances
in the present century as the principles and foundations of the new
law, which was unknown before,
and is out of harmony, not only
with Christian, but, in more than
one respect, with natural law.

Of those principles this is the
chief: that as all men are understood
to be alike in birth and nature, so
they are in reality equal throughout
the whole course of their lives: that
each is so completely his own master as not to be subject in any way
to the authority of another; that
he is free to think what he likes on
every subject, and to do what he

---

[1] Ep. ccxxxviii.

jus esse in nemine. His infor-
mata disciplinis societate, princi-
patus non est nisi populi volun-
tas, qui, ut in sui ipsius unice
est potestate, ita sibimetipsi solus
imperat: deligit autem, quibus se
committat, ita tamen ut imperii
non tam jus, quam munus in eos
transferat, idque suo nomine exer-
cendum. In silentio jacet domi-
natio divina, non secus ad vel
Deus aut nullus esset, aut humani
generis societatem nihil curaret:
vel homines sive singuli sive so-
cietati nihil Deo deberent, vel
principatus cogitari posset ullus,
cujus non in Deo ipso causa et
vis et auctoritas tota resideat.

Quo modo, ut perspicitur, est re-
publica nihil aliud nisi magistra
et gubernatrix sui multitudo:
cumque populus omnium jurium
omnisque potestatis fontem in se
ipso continere dicatur, consequens
erit, ut nulla ratione officii obli-
gatam Deo se civitas putet; ut
religionem publice profiteatur nul-
lam; nec debeat ex pluribus quæ
vera sola sit, quærere, nec unam
quamdam cæteris anteponere, nec
uni maxime favere, sed singulis
generibus æquabilitatem juris tri-
buere ad eum finem, dum disci-

pleases; and that the right of ruling over others exists in no one. In a society founded upon these principles, the ruling power is only the will of the people, which as it is under its own power alone, so it is alone its own proper sovereign, but chooses to whom it may intrust itself, only in such a way that it transfers, not so much the right, as the function of government, and that to be exercised in its name. God is passed over in silence, as if either there were no God, or as if he cared nothing for human society, or as if men, whether as individuals or in society, owed nothing to God, or as if there could be any government whose whole cause and power and authority did not reside in God himself.

In this way, as it is clear, a State is nothing else but a mob which is mistress and directress of itself. And since the people is said to contain in itself the fountain of all rights and all power, it will follow that the State deems itself bound by no kind of duty towards God; that no religion should be publicly professed; nor ought there to be an inquiry which of many is alone true; nor ought one to be preferred to the rest; nor ought one to be specially favored, but to each alike equal rights ought

plina reipublicæ ne quid ab illis detrimenti capiat.   Consentaneum erit, judicio singulorum permittere omnem de religione quæstionem ; licere cuique aut sequi quam ipse malit, aut omnino nullam, si nullam probet.

Hinc profecto illa nascuntur ; exlex uniuscujusque conscientiæ judicium ; liberrimæ de Deo colendo, de non colendo, sententiæ ; infinita tum cogitandi, tum cogitata publicandi licentia.

His autem positis, quæ maxime probantur hoc tempore, fundamentis reipublicæ, facile apparet, quem in locum quamque iniquum compellatur Ecclesia.   Nam ubi cum ejusmodi doctrinis actio rerum consentiat, nomini Catholico par cum societatibus ab eo alienis vel etiam inferior locus in civitate tribuitur : legum ecclesiasticarum nulla habetur ratio : Ecclesia, quæ jussu mandatoque Jesu Christi docere omnes gentes debet, publicam populi institutionem jubetur nihil attingere.

De ipsis rebus, quæ sunt mixti juris, per se statuunt gubernatores rei civilis arbitratu suo, in

to be assigned, provided only that the social order incurs no injury from them.   It is a part of this theory that all questions concerning religion are to be referred to private judgment; that every one is allowed to follow which he prefers, or none at all, if he approves of none.

Hence these consequences naturally arise; the judgment of every man's conscience is above law; opinions are as free as possible concerning worshipping or not worshipping God; and there is unbounded license of thinking and publishing the results of thought.

These foundations of the State being admitted, which at this time are in such general favor, it easily appears into how unfavorable a position the Church is driven.   For when the conduct of affairs is in accordance with the doctrines of this kind, to the Catholic name is assigned an equal position with, or even an inferior position to, that of alien societies in the State; no regard is paid to ecclesiastical laws; and the Church, which by the command and mandate of Jesus Christ ought to teach all nations, finds itself forbidden in any way to interfere in the instruction of the people.

Concerning those things which are of mixed jurisdiction, the rulers of the civil power lay down the law

eoque genere sanctissimas Eccle-
siæ leges superbe contemnunt.
Quare ad jurisdictionem suam
trahunt matrimonia Christiano-
rum, decernendo etiam de mari-
tali vinculo, de unitate, de stabi-
litate conjugii: movent possessio-
nes clericorum, quod res suas
Ecclesiam tenere posse negant.
Ad summam, sic agunt cum Ec-
clesia, ut societatis perfectæ genere
et juribus opinione detractis, plane
similem habeant cæterarum com-
munitatum, quas respublica con-
tinet: ob eamque rem si quid illa
juris, si quid possidet facultatis
ad agendum legitimæ, possidere
dicitur concessu beneficioque prin-
cipum civitatis.

Si qua vero in republica suum
Ecclesia jus, ipsis civilibus legi-
bus probantibus, teneat, publice-
que inter utramque potestatem
pactio aliqua facta sit, prin-
cipio clamant, dissociari Eccle-
siæ rationes a reipublicæ ratio-
nibus opportere; idque eo consi-
lio, ut facere contra interpositam
fidem impune liceat, omniumque
rerum habere, remotis impedimen-
tis, arbitrium.

at their own pleasure, and in this manner haughtily set aside the most sacred laws of the Church. Wherefore they bring under their own jurisdiction the marriages of Christians, deciding even concerning the marriage bond, concerning the unity, and the stability of marriage. They take possession of the goods of the clergy because they deny that the Church can hold property. To sum up, they so deal with the Church, that, having stripped her in their own opinion both of the nature and the rights of a perfect society, they clearly hold her to be like other associations which the State contains, and on that account, if she possesses any legitimate means of acting, she is said to possess it by the concession and gift of the rulers of the State.

But if in any State the Church retains her own right with the approval of the civil laws themselves, and any agreement has been publicly made between the two powers, they begin by crying out that the interests of the Church must be severed from those of the State, and they do this with the intent that it may be possible to act against their pledged faith with impunity, and have the disposal of everything without anything to stand in their way.

Id vero cum patienter ferre Ecclesia non possit, neque enim potest officia deserere sanctissima et maxima, omninoque postulet, ut obligata sibi fides integre religioseque salvatur, sæpe sacram inter ac civilem potestatem dimicationes nascuntur, quarum ille ferme est exitus, alteram, ut quæ minus est opibus humanis valida, alteri ut valiodori succumbere.

Ita Ecclesiam, in hoc rerum publicarum statu, qui nunc a plerisque adamatur, mos et voluntas est, aut prorsus de medio pellere, aut vinctam adstrictamque imperio tenere. Quæ publice aguntur, eo consilio magnam partem aguntur. Leges, administratio civitatum, expers religionis adolescentium institutio, spoliatio excidiumque ordinum religiosorum, eversio principatus civilis pontificum Romanorum, huc spectant omnia, incidere nervos institutorum Christianorum, Ecclesiæque Catholicæ et libertatem in angustum deducere, et jura cætera comminuere.

Ejusmodi de regenda civitate sententias ipsa naturalis ratio convincit, a veritate dissidere plurimum.—Quidquid enim potestatis usquam est, a Deo tanquam maximo augustissimoque fonte proficisci, ipsa natura testatur.

But when the Church cannot bear that patiently, nor indeed is able to desert its greatest and most sacred duties, and, above all, requires that faith be wholly and entirely observed with it, contests often arise between the sacred and the civil power, of which the result is commonly that the one which is the weaker in human resources yields to the stronger.

So it is the custom and the wish in constitutions of this kind, which are now admired by many, either to expel the Church altogether, or to keep it bound and restricted as to its rule. Public acts in a great measure are framed with this design. Laws, the administration of states, the teaching of youth unaccompanied by religion, the spoliation and destruction of religious orders, the overturning of the civil principality of the Roman pontiffs, all have regard to this end; to emasculate Christian institutes, to narrow the liberty of the Catholic Church, and to diminish her other rights.

Natural reason itself convinces us that such opinions about the ruling of a state are very widely removed from the truth. Nature herself bears witness that all power of whatever kind ultimately emanates from God as its greatest and most

Imperium autem populare, quod nullo ad Deum respectu, in multitudine inesse naturâ dicitur, si præclare ad suppeditandum valet blandimenta et flammas multarum cupiditatum, nulla quidem nititur ratione probabili, neque satis habere virium potest ad securitatem publicam quietamque ordinis constantiam. Revera his doctrinis res inclinavere usque eo, ut hæc a pluribus tamquam lex in civili prudentia sanciatur, seditiones posse jure conflari. Valet enim opinio, nihilo principes pluris esse, quam delectos quosdam qui voluntatem popularem exequantur: ex quo fit, quod necesse est ut omnia sint pariter cum populi arbitrio mutabilia, et timor aliquis turbarum semper impendeat.

De religione autem putare, nihil inter formas dispares et contrarias interesse, hunc plane habet exitum, nolle ullam probare judicio, nolle usu. Atqui istud ab atheismo, si nomine aliquid differt, re nihil differt. Quibus enim Deum esse persuasum est, ii, modo constare sibi, nec esse perabsurdi velint, necessario intelligunt, usitatas in cultu divino rationes, quarum tanta est differentia maximisque etiam de rebus

august fountain. Popular rule, however, which is said to be naturally in the multitude, without any regard to God, though it may excellently avail to supply the fire and attractiveness to many forms of covetousness, yet rests on no probable reason, nor can have sufficient strength to insure public security and the quiet permanence of order. Verily, things under the auspices of these doctrines have come to such a pass that many sanction this as a law in civil jurisprudence, that sedition may be raised lawfully. For the idea prevails that princes are really nothing but delegates to carry out the popular will; from which it follows of necessity that all things are equally liable to change at the people's will, and a certain fear of public disturbance is forever hanging over our heads.

But to think with regard to religion that there is no difference between unlike and contrary forms, clearly will have this issue—an unwillingness to test any one form in theory and practice. This, if it differs from atheism in name, is in fact the same thing. Men who really believe in the existence of God, if they are to be consistent and not supremely ridiculous, will of necessity understand that different methods of divine worship in-

dissimilitudo et pugna, æque pro-babiles, æque bonas, æque Deo ac-ceptas esse omnes non posse.

Sic illa quidlibet sentiendi lit-terarumque formis quidlibet ex-primendi facultas, omni modera-tione posthabita, non quoddam est propria vi sua bonum, quo socie-tas humana jure lætetur: sed multorum malorum fons et origo. — Libertas, ut quæ virtus est ho-minem perficiens, debet in eo quod verum sit, quodque bonum, ver-sari: boni autem verique ratio mutari ad hominis arbitrium non potest, sed manet semper eadem, neque minus est quam ipsa rerum natura, incommutabilis. Si mens adsentiatur opinionibus falsis, si malum voluntas adsumat et ad id se applicet, perfectionem sui neutra consequitur, sed excidunt dignitate naturali et in corrup-tum ambæ delabuntur. Quæcum-que sunt igitur virtuti veritatique contraria, ea in luce atque in oc-ulis hominum ponere non est æquum; gratia tutelave legum defendere, multo minus. Sola bene acta vita via est in cœlum, quo tendimus universi: ob eam-que rem aberrat civitas a regula et præscriptione naturæ, si licen-tiam opinionum praveque facto-

volving dissimilarity and conflict, even on the most important points, cannot be all equally probable, equally good, and equally accepted by God.

And thus that faculty of think-ing whatever you like and express-ing whatever you like to think in writing, without any thought of moderation, is not of its own nature a good in which human society can rightly rejoice, but on the contrary a fount and origin of many ills. Liberty, as being a virtue perfect-ing man, must have for its sphere the good and the true; but the true and the good cannot be changed at the pleasure of man, but remains ever the same, and is not less un-changeable than nature herself. If the mind assent to false opinions, if the will choose for itself evil, and apply itself thereto, neither attains its perfection, but both fall from their natural dignity, and both lapse by degrees into corruption. What-ever things, therefore, are contrary to virtue and truth, these it is no right to place in the light before the eyes of men, far less to defend by the favor and protection of the laws. A well-spent life is the only path to that heaven wither we all direct our steps; and on this account the State departs from the law and the ruling of nature if it allows license

rum in tantum lascivire sinat, in impuno liceat mentes a veritate, animos a virtute deducere. Ecclesiam vero, quam Deus ipse constituit ab actione vitæ excludere, a legibus, ab institutione adolescentium, a societate domestica, magnus et perniciosus est error.

Bene morata civitas esse, sublata religione, non potest: jamque plus fortasse quam oporteret, est cognitum, qualis in se sit et quorsum pertineat, illa de vita et moribus philosophia, quam civilem *nominant. Vera est magistra virtutis et morum custos Ecclesia Christi: ea est, quæ incolumia tuetur principia unde officia ducuntur, propositisque causis ad honesti vivendum efficacissimis, jubet non solum fugere prave facta, sed regere motus animi rationi contrarios etiam sine affectu.*

Ecclesiam vero in suorum officiorum munere potestati civili velle esse subjectam, magna quidem injuria, magna temeritas est. Hoc facto perturbatur ordo, quia quæ naturalia sunt præponuntur iis quæ sunt supra naturam: tollitur aut certe magnopere minuitur frequentia bonorum, quibus, si nulla re impediretur, commu-

of opinion and of evil doing to run riot to such a degree as to lead minds astray with impunity from the truth, and hearts from the practice of virtue. But to exclude the Church which God himself has constituted from the business of life, from the laws, from the teaching of youth, from domestic society, is a great and pernicious error.

A State cannot be well regulated when religion is taken away; and by this time more perhaps is known than need be of that philosophy of life and morals which men call *civil* —what its nature is, and what its results are. The Church of Christ is the true teacher of virtue and guardian of morals; it is she who keeps in safety the principles of duty, and by proposing most efficacious reasons for an honest life, bids us not only fly from wicked deeds, but rule the motions of the mind which are contrary to reason even though no act should follow.

To wish the Church in the discharge of her offices to be subject to the civil power is great rashness, great injustice. If this were done order would be disturbed, since things natural would thus be put before those which are above nature; a multitude of benefits, with which, if there were nothing to hinder her, the Church would enrich the life of

nem vitam Ecclesia compleret: præreaque via ad inimicitias munitur et certamina, quæ, quanquam utrique reipublicæ perniciem afferant, nimis sæpe eventus demonstravit.

Hujusmodi doctrinas, quæ nec humanæ rationi probantur, et plurimum habent in civilem disciplinam momenti, Romani pontifices decessores nostri, cum probe intelligerent quid a se postularet apostolicum munus, impune abire nequaquam passi sunt. Sic Gregorius XVI per Encyclicas litteras hoc initio Mirari vos, die xv Augusti anno MDCCCXXXII, magna sententiarum gravitate ea perculit, quæ jam prædicabantur, in cultu divino nullum adhibere delectum oportere: integrum singulis esse, quod malint, de religione judicare: solam cuique suam esse conscientiam judicem: præterea edere quæ quisque senserit, itemque res moliri novas in civitate licere. De rationibus rei sacræ reique civilis distrahendis sic idem pontifex: "Neque lætiora et religioni et principatui ominari possemus ex eorum votis, qui Ecclesiam a regno separari, mutuamque imperii cum sacerdotio

the community, either disappears or at all events is considerably diminished, and besides, a way is opened to enmities and conflicts—and how great the evils are that they have brought on both governments (the ecclesiastical and the civil) the course of history has too frequently shown.

Such doctrines, which are not approved by human reason, and are of the greatest gravity as regards civil discipline, the Roman pontiffs, our predecessors—well understanding what the apostolic office required of them—by no means suffered to go without condemnation. Thus Gregory XVI., by Encyclical Letter beginning *Mirari vos*, of August 15, 1832, inveighed with weighty words against those doctrines which were already being preached, namely, that in divine worship no preference should be made; and that it was left to individuals to judge of religion according to their personal preferences, that each man's conscience was to himself his sole sufficient guide, and that it was lawful to promulgate whatsoever each man might think, and to make a revolution in the State. Concerning the reasons for the separation of Church and State, the same pontiff speaks thus: "Nor can we hope happier results either

concordiam abrumpi discupiunt. Constat quippe pertimesci ab impudentissimæ libertatis amatoribus concordiam illam, quæ semper rei et sacræ et civili fausta, extitit et salutaris."

Non absimili modo Pius IX., ut sese opportunitas dedit, ex opinionibus falsis, quæ maxime valere cœpissent, plures notavit, easdemque postea in unum cogi jussit, ut scilicet in tanta errorum colluvione haberent Catholici homines, quod sine offensione sequerentur.[1]

Ex iis autem pontificum præscriptis illa omnino intelligi necesse est, ortum publicæ potestatis a Deo ipso, non a multitudine repeti oportere: seditionum licentiam cum ratione pugnare: officia

for religion or government from the wishes of those who are eagerly desirous that the Church should be separated from the State, and the mutual good understanding of the sovereign secular power and the sacerdotal authority be broken up. It is evident that these lovers of most shameless liberty dread that concord which has always been fortunate and wholesome, both for sacred and civil interests."

To the like effect Pius IX., as opportunity offered, noted many false opinions which had begun to be of great strength, and afterwards ordered them to be collected together in order that in so great a conflux of errors Catholics might have something which they might follow without stumbling.

From these decisions of the popes it is clearly to be understood that the origin of public power is to be sought from God himself and not from the multitude; that free play for sedition is repugnant to reason;

---

[1] *Earum nonnullas indicare sufficiat.*

Prop. XIX.—Ecclesia non est vera perfectaque societas plane libera, nec pollet suis propriis et constantibus juribus sibi a divino suo fundatore collatis, sed civilis potestatis est definire quæ sint Ecclesiæ jura ac limites, intra quos eadem jura exercere queat.

Prop. XXXIX.—Reipublicæ status utpote omnium jurium origo et fons, jure quodam pollet nullis circumscripto limitibus.

Prop. LV.—Ecclesia a statu, statusque ab Ecclesia sejungendus est.

Prop. LXXIX.— . . . Falsum est, civilem cujusque cultus libertatem, itemque plenam potestatem omnibus attributam quaslibet opioniones cogitationesque palam publiceque manifestandi, conducere ad populorum mores animosque facilius corrumpendos, ac indifferentismi pestem propagandam.

religionis nullo loco numerare, vel uno modo esse in disparibus generibus affectos, nefas esse privatis hominibus, nefas civitatibus: immoderatam sentiendi sensusque palam jactandi potestatem non esse in civium juribus neque in rebus gratia patrocinioque dignis ulla ratione ponendam. — Similiter intelligi debet, Ecclesiam societatem esse, non minus quam ipsum civitatem, genere et jure perfectam: neque debere, qui summam imperii teneant, committere ut sibi servire aut subesse Ecclesiam cogant, aut minus esse sinant ad suas res agendas liberam, aut quicquam de ceteris juribus detrahant, quæ in ipsam a Jesu Chrito collata sunt.

In negotiis autem mixti juris, maxime esse secundum naturam itemque secundum Dei consilia non secessionem alterius potestatis ab altera, multoque minus contentionem, sed plane concordiam, eamque cum caussis proximis cengruentem, quæ caussæ utramque societatem genuerunt.

Hæc quidem sunt, quæ de constituendis temperandisque civita-

that it is a crime for private individuals and a crime for States to make no account of the duties of religion, or to treat different kinds of religion in the same way; that the uncontrolled power of thinking and publicly proclaiming one's thoughts has no place among the rights of citizens, and cannot in any way be reckoned among those things which are worthy of favor or defense. Similarly it ought to be understood that the Church is a society, no less than the State itself, perfect in kind and right, and that those who exercise sovereignty ought not to act so as to compel the Church to be their slave or subject, or suffer her to have less than liberty to transact her own affairs, or detract aught from the other rights which have been conferred upon her by Jesus Christ.

That in matters, however, of mixed jurisdiction, it is in the highest degree in accordance with nature and also with the counsels of God—not that one power should secede from the other, still less come into conflict, but that that harmony and concord should be preserved which is most akin to the proximate cause and end of both societies.

These, then, are the things taught by the Catholic Church concerning

tibus ab Ecclesia Catholica prœ-cipiuntur.—Quibus tamen dictis decretisque si recte dijudicare velit, nulla per se reprehenditur ex variis reipublicœ formis, ut quœ nihil habent, quod doctrinœ Catholicœ repugnet, eœdemque possunt, si sapienter adhibeantur et juste, in optimo statu tueri civitatem.—Immo neque illud per se reprehenditur, participem plus minus esse pópulum reipublicœ: quod ipsum certis in temporibus certisque legibus potest non solum ad utilitatem, sed etiam ad officium pertinere civium.—Insuper neque caussa justa nascitur, ut Ecclesiam quisquam criminetur, aut esse in lenitate facilitateque plus œquo restrictam, aut ei, quœ germana et legitima sit, libertati inimicam.—Revera si divini cultus varia genera eodem jure esse quo veram religionem, Ecclesia judicat non licere, non ideo tamen eos damnat rerum publicarum moderatores, qui magni alicujus aut adipiscendi boni, aut prohibendi caussa mali, moribus atque usu patienter ferunt, ut ea habeant singula in civitatem locum.—Atque illud quoque magnopere cavere Ecclesia solet ut ad amplexandam fidem Catholicam nemo invitus cogatur, quia quod sapienter Augustinus monet, cre-

the constitution and government of States. Concerning these sayings and decrees, if a man will only judge dispassionately, no form of government is, *per se*, condemned so long as it has nothing repugnant to Catholic doctrine, and is able, if wisely and justly administered, to preserve the State in the best condition. Nor is it, *per se*, to be condemned whether the people have a greater or less share in the government; for at certain times and with the guarantee of certain laws, such participation may appertain, not only to the usefulness, but even to the duty of the citizens. Moreover, there is no just cause why any one should condemn the Church as being too restricted in gentleness, or inimical to that liberty which is natural and legitimate. In truth, though the Church judges it not lawful that the various kinds of divine worship should have the same right as the true religion, still it does not therefore condemn those governors of States who, for the sake of acquiring some great good, or preventing some great ill, patiently bear with manners and customs so that each kind of religion has its place in the State. Indeed, the Church is wont diligently to take heed that no one be compelled against his will to embrace the Cath-

dere non potest homo nisi volens.[1]

Simili ratione nec potest Ecclesia libertatem probare eam, quæ fastidium gignat sanctissimarum Dei legum, debitamque potestati legitimæ obedientiam exuat. Est enim licentia verius, quam libertas rectissimeque ab Augustino libertas perditionis,[2] *a Petro Apostolo* velamen malitiæ[3] *appellatur: immo, cum sit præter rationem, vera servitus est:* qui, *enim,* facit peccatum, servus est peccati.[4] *Contra illa germana est atque expetenda libertas quæ, si privatim spectetur, erroribus et cupiditatibus teterrimis dominis hominem servire non sinit: si publice, civibus sapienter præest, facultatem augendorum commodorum large ministrat: remque publicam ab alieno arbitrio defendit. — Atqui honestam hanc et homine dignam libertatem, Ecclesia probat omnium maxime, eamque ut tueretur in populis firmam atque integram eniti et contendere nunquam destitit.*

Revera quæ res in civitate plurimum ad communem salutem possunt: quæ sunt contra licen-

olic faith, for, as Augustin wisely observes, "no one can believe if he is not willing."[1]

For a similar reason the Church cannot approve of that liberty which generates a contempt of the most sacred laws of God and puts away the obedience due to legitimate power. For this is license rather than liberty, and is most correctly called by Augustin "the liberty of perdition;"[2] by the Apostle Peter, "*a cloak for malice*,"[3] indeed, since it is contrary to reason, it is a true servitude, for "*Whosoever committeth sin is the servant of sin.*"[4] On the other hand, that is the genuine and desirable liberty which, if it be considered in relation to the individual, suffers not men to be the slaves of errors and evil desires, the worst of masters; and, in relation to the State, presides wisely over the citizens, greatly facilitates the increase of public advantages, and defends the public interest from alien rule. This blameless liberty, worthy of man, the Church approves above all, and has never ceased striving and contending to keep sound and whole among the people.

In very truth whatever things in the State chiefly avail for the common safety; whatever have been

---

[1] Tract. xxvi., *in Joan.* n. 2.
[2] *Epist.* cv *ad Donatistas.* cap. ii. n. 9.

[3] 1 Peter ii. 16.
[4] John viii. 34.

tiam principum populo male consulentium utiliter institutæ: quæ summam rempublicam vetant in municipalem, vel domesticam rem importunius invadere: quæ valent ad decus, ad personam hominis, ad æquabilitatem juris in singulis civibus conservandam, earum rerum omnium Ecclesiam Catholicam vel inventricem, vel auspicem, vel custodem semper fuisse superiorum ætatum monumenta testantur.

Sibi igitur perpetuo consentiens, si ex altera parte libertatem respuit immodicam quæ et privatis et populis in licentiam vel in servitutem cadit, ex altera volens et libens amplectitur res meliores, quas dies afferat, si vere prosperitatem contineant hujus vitæ, quæ quoddam est velut stadium ad alteram eamque perpetuo mansuram.

Ergo quod inquiunt Ecclesiam recentiori civitatem invidere disciplinæ, et quæcumque horum temporum ingenium peperit, omnia promiscue repudiare, inanis est et jejuna calumnia. Insaniam quidem repudiat opinionum: improbat nefaria seditionum studia illumque nominatim habitum ani-

usefully instituted against the license of princes who have not their people's good at heart; whatever forbid the intervention of the supreme authority in municipal or domestic affairs; whatever avail to preserve the dignity of man and his personal rights, or to maintain the equality of rights in individual citizens, of all these things the monuments of former ages declare the Catholic Church to have been either the author, the promoter, or the perpetual guardian.

Ever therefore consistent with herself, if on the one hand she rejects immoderate liberty, which both in the case of individuals and peoples results in license or in servitude; on the other she willingly and with pleasure embraces those happier circumstances which the age brings if they truly contain the prosperity of this life, which is, as it were, a stage in the journey to that other which is to endure everlastingly.

Therefore when men say that the Church views with disfavor all modern state-craft, and repudiates without distinction all modern progress, it is an empty and contemptible calumny. She does, indeed, repudiate the madness of opinion; she reprobates the wicked plans of sedition, and especially that habit of

morum, in quo initia perspiciun-tur voluntarii discessus a Deo: sed quia omne, quod verum est, a Deo proficisci necesse est, quid-quid, indagando, veri attingatur, agnoscit Ecclesia velut quoddam divinœ mentis vestigium. Cum-que nihil sit i.i rerum natura veri, quod doctrinis divinitus tra-ditis fidem abroget, multa quœ adrogent, omnisque possit inven-tio veri ad Deum ipsum vel cog-noscendum vel laudandum impel-lere, idcirco quidquid accedat ad scientiarum fines proferendos, gau-dente et libente Ecclesia semper accedet: eademque studiose, ut so-let, sicut alias disciplinas, ita il-las etiam fovebit ac provehet, quœ positœ sunt in explicatione natu-rœ. Quibus in studiis, non ad-versatur Ecclesia si quid mens repererit novi: non repugnat quin plura quœrantur ad decus com-moditatemque vitœ: immo iner-tiœ desidiœque inimica, magnopere vult ut hominum ingenia uberes fe-rant exercitatione et cultura fruc-tus: incitamenta prœbet ad omne genus artium atque operam: om-niaque harum rerum studia ad honestatem salutemque virtute sua dirigens impedire nititur, quomi-nus a Deo bonisque cœlestibus sua hominem intelligentia atque indu-stria deflectat.

mind in which the beginnings of a voluntary departing from God are visible; but since every true thing must necessarily proceed from God, whatever of truth is by search at-tained, the Church acknowledges as a certain token of the divine mind. And since there is no truth in the world which can take away belief in the doctrines divinely handed down and many things which confirm it, and since every finding of truth may impel man to the knowledge or praise of God himself, therefore whatever may happen to extend the range of knowledge, the Church will always willingly and joyfully accept; and she will, as is her wont in the case of other studies, steadily encourage and promote those also which are concerned with the inves-tigation of nature. If the mind finds anything new in them, the Church offers no opposition; she fights, not against the search after more things for the grace and con-venience of life—nay, a very foe to inertness and sloth, she earnestly wishes that the talents of men should, by being cultivated and ex-ercised, bear still richer fruits; she offers inducements to every sort of art and craft, and directing by her own innate worth all the pursuits of these things to virtue and salvation, she strives to save man's own intel-

Sed hæc tametsi plena rationis et consilii, nimis probantur hoc tempore, cum civitates non modo recusant sese ad Christianæ sapientiæ referre formam, sed etiam videntur quotidie longius ab ea velle discedere.

Nihilominus quia in lucem prolata veritas solet sua sponte late fluere, hominumque mentes sensim pervadere, idcirco nos conscientia maximi sanctissimique officii, hoc est apostolica, qua fungimur ad gentes universas, legatione permoti, ea quæ vera sunt, libere, ut debemus, eloquimur; non quod non perspectam habeamus rationem temporum, aut repudianda ætatis nostræ honesta atque utilia incrementa putemus, sed quod rerum publicarum tutiora ab offensionibus itinera ac firmiora fundamenta vellemus: idque incolumi populorum germana libertate; in hominibus enim mater et custos optima libertatis veritas est: Veritas liberabit vos.[1]

Itaque in tam difficili rerum cursu Catholici homines, si nos, ut oportet, audierint, facile vide-

ligence and industry from turning him away from God and the good things of heaven.

But these things, although full of reasonableness and foresight, are not so well approved of in these days, when States not only refuse to defer to the laws of Christian wisdom, but seem even to wish to depart each day farther from them.

Nevertheless, because truth brought to light is wont of its own accord to spread widely, and by degrees to pervade the minds of men, we, therefore, moved by the consciousness of our exalted and most sacred office, that is our apostolic commission to all nations, speak the truth freely as we ought to speak: not that we have no perception of the spirit of the times, or that we think the honest and useful improvements of our age are to be repudiated, but because we would wish the highways of public affairs to be safer from attacks, and their foundations more stable, and that without detriment to the true freedom of the peoples; for amongst men the mother and best guardian of liberty is truth: "*The truth shall make you free.*"[1]

Therefore at so critical a juncture of events, Catholic men, if, as it behooves them, they will listen to us,

---

[1] John viii. 32.

bunt quæ sua cujusque sint tam in opinionibus, *quam in fåctis officia.—Et in opinando quidem, quæcumque pontifices Romani tradiderint vel tradituri sunt, singula necesse est et tenere judicio stabili comprehensa, et palam, quoties res postulaverit, profiteri, ac nominatim de iis, quas* libertates *vocant novissimo tempore quæsitas, oportet Apostolicæ Sedis stare judicio, et quod ipsa senserit, idem sentire singulos. Cavendum, ne quem fallat honesta illarum species: cogitandumque quibus ortæ initiis, et quibus passim sustententur atque alantur studiis. Satis jam est experiendo cognitum, quarum illæ rerum effectrices sint in civitate eos quippe passim genuere fructus, quorum probos viros et sapientes jure pœniteat.*

Si talis alicubi aut reapse sit, aut fingatur cogitatione civitas quæ Christianum nomen insectetur proferre et tyrannice, cum eaque conferatur genus id reipublicæ recens, de quo loquimur, poterit hoc videri tolerabilius. Principia tamen, quibus nititur, sunt profecto ejusmodi, sicut ante diximus, ut

will easily see what are their own and each other's duties in matters of opinion as well as of *action.* And as regards opinion, it is necessary both to hold all things whatsoever the Roman pontiffs have delivered, or shall hereafter deliver, with firm grasp and clear apprehension, and also as often as occasion demands openly to profess the same. And, to give an instance, concerning those things which are called recently acquired *liberties,* it is proper to stand by the judgment of the Apostolic See, and for every one to hold what she holds. Take care lest any man be deceived by the honest outward appearance of these things; and think of the beginnings from which they are sprung; and by what desires they are sustained and fed in divers places. It is now sufficiently known by experience what they produce in the State; for in many a place they have borne fruit, over which wise and good men justly grieve.

If there were in any place a State, either actual or hypothetical, that wantonly and tyrannically waged war upon the Christian name, and if such a modern kind of State as we are speaking of were compared with it, it is possible that this might be considered more tolerable; yet the princi-

per se ipsa probari nemini debeant.

Potest tamen aut in privatis domesticisque rebus, aut in publicis actio versari. Privatim quidem primum officium est, præceptis evangelicis diligentissime conformare vitam et mores, nec recusare si quid Christiana virtus exigat ad patiendum tolerandumque paulo difficilius. Debent præterea singuli Ecclesiam sic diligere, ut communem matrem: ejusque et jura salva velle: conarique ut ab iis in quos quisque aliquid auctoritate potest, pari pietate colatur atque ametur.

Illud etiam publicæ salutis interest, ad rerum urbanarum administrationem conferre sapienter operam: in eaque studere maxime et efficere, ut adolescentibus ad religionem, ad probos mores informandis ea ratione, qua æquum est Christianis, publice consultum sit: quibus ex rebus magnopere pendet singularum salus civitatum.

Item Catholicorum hominum operam ex hoc tanquam angustiore campo longius excurrere, ipsamque summam rempublicam com-

ples upon which it rests are absolutely such that, of themselves, they ought to be approved by no men.

Now the field of human conduct may lie either in private and domestic or in public affairs. In private life the first duty is to conform one's life and manners to the precepts of the Gospel, and not to refuse if Christian virtue requires of us to bear something more difficult than usual. Moreover, individuals are bound to love the Church as their common mother; to keep her laws obediently; to give her the service of due honor, and wish her rights respected, and endeavor to have her fostered and beloved with like piety by those over whom they may exercise authority.

It is also of great importance to the public welfare diligently and wisely to give attention to education and culture; to bestow careful attention upon them, and to take effectual care that public provision be made for the training of youth in religion and morality, as Christians are bound to provide; for upon these things depend very much the welfare of every State.

And further, to speak generally, it is useful and honorable for the attention of Catholic men to pass beyond this narrower field, and to em-

plecti, generatim utile est atque honestum. Generatim *eo dicimus quia hæc præcepta nostra gentes universas attingunt. Ceterim potest alicubi accidere, ut, maximis justissimisque de causis, rempublicam capessere, in muneribusque politicis versari, nequaquam expediat. Sed generatim, ut diximus, nullam velle rerum publicarum partem attingere tam esset in vitio, quam nihil ad communem utilitatem afferre studii, nihil operæ: eo vel magis quod Catholici homines ipsius, quam profitentur admonitione doctrinæ, ad rem integre et ex fide gerendam impelluntur. Contra ipsis otiosis, facile habenas accepturi suntii quorum opiniones spem salutis haud sane magnam afferant. Idque esset etiam cum pernicie conjunctum Christiani nominis: propterea quod plurimum possent qui male essent in Ecclesiam animati: minimum qui bene.*

Quamobrem perspicuum est, ad rempublicam adeundi causam esse justam Catholicis: non enim adeunt, neque adire debent ob eam causam, ut probent quod est hoc tempore in rerum publicarum rationibus non honestum; sed ut

brace every branch of public administration. *Generally,* we say, because these our precepts reach unto all the nations. But it may happen in some particular place, for the most urgent and just reasons, that it is by no means expedient to engage in public affairs, or to take an active part in political functions. But generally, as we have said, to wish to take no part in public affairs would be wrong in proportion as it contributed neither thought nor work to the common weal; and the more so on this account, because Catholic men are bound by the admonitions of the doctrine which they profess, to do what has to be done with integrity and with faith. If, on the contrary, they are idle, those whose opinions assuredly do not give any great hope of safety will easily get possession of the reins of government. This would be attended with danger to the Christian name, because they who are badly disposed towards the Church would become most powerful; and those least powerful who are well disposed.

Wherefore it is evident there is just cause for Catholics to undertake the conduct of public affairs; for they do not assume these responsibilities in order to approve of what is not lawful in the methods of government at this time; but in

has ipsas rationes, quoad fieri potest, in bonum publicum transferant sincerum atque verum, destinatum animo habentes, sapientiam virtutemque Catholicæ religionis, tanquam saluberrimum succum ac sanguinem, in omnes reipublicæ venas inducere.

Haud aliter actum in primis Ecclesiæ ætatibus. Mores enim et studia ethnicorum quam longissime a studiis abhorrebant moribusque evangelicis : Christianos tamen cernere erat in media superstitione incorruptos semperque sui similes animose, quacumque daretur aditus, inferre sese. Fideles in exemplum principibus, obedientesque, quoad fas esset, imperio legum, fundebant mirificum splendorem sanctitatis usquequaque, prodesse studebant fratribus, vocare ceteros ad sapientiam Christi, cedere tamen loco atque emori fortiter parati, si honores, si magistratus, si imperia retinere, incolumi virtute nequivissent.

Qua ratione celeriter instituta Christiana non modo in privatas domos, sed in castra, in curiam, in ipsam regiam invexere. " Hesterni sumus, et vestra omnia implevimus,

order that they may turn these very methods, as far as may be, to the unmixed and true public good, holding this purpose in their minds, to infuse into all the veins of the commonwealth the most healthy sap and blood as it were—the wisdom and virtue of the Catholic religion.

Such was the course adopted in the first ages of the Church. For the ways and aspirations of the heathen were as widely divergent as possible from the ways and aspirations of the Gospel; yet Christians were seen to be incorrupt in the midst of superstition, and always true to themselves, entering with spirit every walk in life which was open to them. Models of fidelity to their princes, obedient, where lawful, to the sovereign power, they exhibited the wonderful splendor of holiness everywhere; they sought the good of their neighbor, and to call others to the wisdom of Christ; bravely prepared to renounce public life, and even to die, if it was impossible for them to retain their offices, or magistracies, or commands with unsullied virtue.

And thus Christian customs soon found their way, not only into private houses, but into the camp, the senate, and even the imperial palace. "We are of yesterday

urbes, insulas, castella, municipia, conciliabula, castra ipsa, tribus, decurias, palatium, senatum, forum,"[1] ita ~ut fides Christiana, cum evangelium publice profiteri lege licuit, non in cunis vagiens, sed adulta et jam satis firma in magna civitatum parte apparuit.

Jamvero his temporibus consentaneum est, hæc majorum exempla renovari.—Catholicos quidem, quotquot digni sunt eo nomine, primum omnium necesse est amantissimos Ecclesiæ filios et esse et videri velle : quæ res nequeant cum hac laude consistere, eas sine cunctatione respuere : institutis populorum, quantum honeste fieri potest, ad veritatis justitiæque patrocinium uti : elaborare, ut constitutum naturæ Deique lege modum libertas agendi ne transiliat : dare operam ut ad eam, quam diximus, Christianam similitudinem et formam omnis respublica traducatur.

Harum rerum adipiscendarum ratio constitui uno certoque modo haud commode potest cum debeat singulis locis temporibusque, quæ

and we have filled all that you have, cities, great tenements, military stations, municipalities, councils, the very camps, the rank and file of the army, the officerships, the palace, the senate, the forum,"[1] so that the Christian faith, as soon as it was lawful to profess the Gospel publicly, was manifest at once in a great part of the empire, no longer as a babe crying in its cradle, but grown up to robust manhood.

Now in these times it is desirable to renew these examples of our forefathers. Catholics indeed, as many as are worthy of the name, must before all things be, and be willing to be seen to be, most loving sons of the Church ; whatsoever is inconsistent with this good report, they must without hesitation reject ; they must use popular institutions as far as honestly can be to the advantage of truth and justice ; they must take care that liberty of action shall not transgress the bounds ordained by the law of nature and God ; and so work that the whole of public life shall be transformed into what we have called a Christian image and likeness.

The means to these ends can scarcely be laid down upon one uniform plan, since they must suit places and times very different from

---

[1] Tertull. Apol. n. 37.

sunt multum inter se disparia, convenire. Nihilominus conservanda in primis est voluntatum concordia, quærendaque agendorum similitudo. Atque optime utrumque impetrabitur, si prescripta Sedis Apostolicæ legem vitæ singuli putent, atque Episcopis obtemperent, quos Spiritus Sanctus posuit regere Ecclesiam Dei.[1]

Defensio quidem Catholici nominis necessario postulat ut in profitendis doctrinis, quæ ab Ecclesia traduntur una sit omnium sententia, et summa constantia, et hac ex parte cavendum ne quis opinionibus falsis aut ullo modo conniveat, aut mollius resistat, quam veritas patiatur. De iis quæ sunt opinabilia, licebit cum moderatione studioque indagandæ veritatis disputare, procul tamen suspicionibus injuriosis, criminationibusque mutuis. — Quam ob rem ne animorum conjunctio criminandi temeritate dirimatur, sic intelligant universi: integritatem professionis Catholicæ consistere nequaquam posse cum opinionibus ad naturalismum *vel* rationalismum *accedentibus, quarum summa est tollere funditus instituta Christiana, hominisque stabilire in societate principatum posthabito Deo.*

each other. Nevertheless, in the first place, let concord of wills be preserved and unity of aim be maintained. And each will be best attained if all consider the admonitions of the Apostolic See a law of conduct, and obey the bishops whom *"the Holy Spirit has placed to rule the Church of God."* [1]

The defence of the Catholic name, indeed, of necessity demands that in the profession of doctrines which are handed down by the Church the opinion of all shall be one, and their constancy perfect, and under this head care must be taken that no one connives in any degree at false opinions or resists with less vigor than truth requires. Concerning those things which are matters of opinion, it will be lawful to hold different views with moderation and with a desire of investigating the truth, without injurious suspicions and mutual incriminations. For which purpose, lest unity of spirit be broken by temerity of accusation, let all understand that integrity of the Catholic profession can by no means be reconciled with any opinions approaching *naturalism* or *rationalism*, whose sum total is the uprooting of Christian institutions altogether, and the establishment of the

---

[1] Acts xx. 28.

supremacy of man upon the de-thronement of God.

Pariter non licere aliam offi-cii formam privatim sequi, aliam publice, ita scilicet ut Ecclesiæ auctoritas in vita privata obser-vetur, in publica respuatur. Hoc enim esset honesta et turpia con-jungere, hominemque secum fa-cere digladiantem, cum contra de-beat· sibi semper constare, neque ulla in re ullove in genere vitæ a virtute Christiana deficere.

Likewise it is unlawful to follow one line of duty in private and another in public, so that the au-thority of the Church shall be observed in private, and spurned in public. For this would be to join together things honest and disgraceful, and to make a man play a game of fence with himself, when on the contrary he ought al-ways to be consistent, and never in any the least thing or any rank of life decline from Christian virtue.

Verum si quæratur de rationi-bus mere politicis, de optimo ge-nere reipublicæ, de ordinandis alia vel alia ratione civitatibus, utique de his rebus potest honesta esse dissensio. Quorum igitur cognita ceteroqui pietas est, animusque de-creta Sedis Apostolicæ obedienter accipero paratus, iis vitio verti dissentaneum de rebus, quas dixi-mus sententiam, justitia non pa-titur: multoque est major injuria, si in crimen violatæ suspectæve fidei Catholicæ, quod non semel factum dolemus, adducantur.

But if it be a question of prin-ciples merely political, concerning the best form of government, of civil regulations of one kind or an-other, concerning these things, of course, there is room for disagree-ment without harm. Those whose piety, therefore, is known on other accounts, and whose minds are ready to accept the decrees of the Apos-tolic See, justice will not allow to be reproached because they differ on these subjects; and much great-er is the injury if they are charged with having violated the Catholic faith, or being of doubtful ortho-doxy—a thing we have had to de-plore more than once.

Omninoque istud præceptum te-neant qui cogitationes suas solent mandare litteris, maximeque ephe-

And let all hold this precept absolutely who are wont to com-mit their thoughts to writing, es-

meridum auctores. In hac quidem de rebus maximis contentione nihil est intestinis concertationibus, vel partium studiis relinquendum loci, sed conspirantibus animis studiisque id debent universi contendere, quod est commune omnium propositum, religionem remque publicam conservare. Si quid igitur dissidiorum antea fuit, oportet voluntaria quadam oblivione conterere: si quid temere, si quid injuria actum, ad quoscumque demum ea culpa pertineat, compensandum est caritate mutua, et praecipuo quodam omnium in Apostolicam Sedem obsequio redimendum.

Hac via duas res praeclarissimas Catholici consecuturi sunt: alteram, ut adjutores sese impertiant Ecclesiae in conservanda propagandaque sapientia Christiana: alteram ut beneficio maximo afficiant societatem civilem, cujus malarum doctrinarum cupiditatumque caussa, magnopere periclitatur salus.

Haec quidem, Venerabiles Fratres, habuimus, quae universis Catholici orbis gentibus traderemus de civitatum constitutione Christiana, officiisque civium singulorum.

Ceterum implorare summis pre-

pecially journalists and writers for the press. In this contention for the highest things no room should be left for intestine conflicts or the greed of parties, but let all, uniting together, seek the common object of all, the preservation of religion and the commonwealth. If, therefore, there have been dissensions, let them be obliterated in willing forgetfulness; if there has been anything rash, anything injurious, to whomsoever this fault belongs let reparation be made by mutual charity, and especially by obedience to the Apostolic See.

In this way Catholics will obtain two things that are most excellent: one that they will make themselves helps to the Church in preserving and propagating Christian knowledge; the other that they will benefit civil society, whose safety is gravely compromised by evil doctrines and inordinate cupidity.

These then, Venerable Brethren, are the teachings that we have had to transmit to all nations of the Catholic world concerning the Christian constitution of States and the duties of individual citizens.

But it behooves us to implore

cibus oportet cœleste præsidium, orandusque Deus, ut hæc, quæ ad ipsius gloriam communemque humani generis salutem cupimus et conamur, optatos ad exitus idem ipse perducat, cujus est illustrare hominum mentes, permovere voluntates. Divinorum autem beneficiorum auspicium, et paternæ benevolentiæ Nostræ testem vobis, Venerabiles Fratres, et clero populoque universo vestræ fidei vigilantiæque commisso apostolicam benedictionem peramanter in Domino impertimus.

Datum Romæ apud S. Petrum die 1 novembris anno MDCCCLXXXV, pontificatus nostri anno octavo.

LEO PP. XIII.

with most earnest prayers the protection of Heaven, and to beseech almighty God, whose alone it is to enlighten the minds of men and move their wills, himself to bring these our longing and efforts for his glory and for man's salvation to the issue that we hope for. As a pledge of the divine favors, and in witness of our paternal benevolence to you, Venerable Brethren, to the clergy, and to all the people committed to your faith and vigilance, we lovingly bestow in the Lord the apostolic benediction.

Given in Rome, at St. Peter's, on the first day of November, in the year of our Lord MDCCCLXXXV, of our pontificate the eight.

LEO PP. XIII.

NOTE.

THE ENCYCLICAL OF 1888.

IN a more recent Encyclical, " *Libertas præstantissimum naturæ donum,*" issued June 20, 1888, Leo XIII. — one of the wisest, most moderate, and most liberal popes of modern times—reiterates the same doctrine on civil government, liberty, and the relation of Church and State, even more strongly than in the bull of 1885. He begins by praising liberty as the most excellent gift of nature, which belongs only to intellectual or rational beings, but he makes true liberty to consist in submission to the will of God, as expressed in an infallible Church with an infallible head. He severely condemns what he calls

the modern liberties (1) of worship, (2) of speech and of the press, (3) of teaching, and (4) of conscience, because they tacitly assume the absence of truth as the law of our reason, and of authority as the law of our will. He first misstates the liberal theory, which he seems to know only in the form of infidel radicalism, and then denounces it.

In the same document the pope incidentally calls the separation of Church and State "a pernicious maxim."[1] And he concludes: "From what has been said, it follows that it is in no way lawful to demand to defend, or to grant, promiscuous freedom of thought, of speech, of writing, or of religion, as if they were so many rights which nature had given to man."

Cardinal Manning, in a preface to the English translation of this Encyclical,[2] fully approves of its sentiments, and predicts that "the pontificate of Leo XIII. will be known in history as the time when, upon a world torn and tossed by anti-Christian and anti-social revolutions, the abundant seeds of divine truths sown broadcast revived the conscience of Christendom." He also predicts that the two Encyclical letters of 1885 and 1888 "will be recorded as the pronouncements which have vindicated the political order of society from confusion, and the liberty of men from the license of liberalism."

But we venture to say that Pope Pius IX. (by the Syllabus of 1864) and Pope Leo XIII. (by these two Encyclicals) have seriously injured the cause of the Roman Church by placing her in open antagonism to the irresistible progress of history, which is a progress of liberty. By declaring the separation of Church and State "a pernicious maxim," Leo XIII. has unwisely as well as unjustly condemned the Constitution of the United States, which makes such separation the law of the land, not from indifference or hostility to religion, but from respect for religion, and which secures to the Roman Catholic Church

---

[1] "*Perniciosa sententia de rationibus ecclesiæ a republica disparandis.*"

[2] Published in London, Burns & Oates, and in New York by the Cath. Pub. Society. The Latin text is printed in *Acta Sanctæ Sedis,* ed. by Pennachi and Piazzesi, vol. **xx.**, Rom. (S. C. De Propaganda Fidei), pp. 593–613.

a greater amount of liberty and prosperity than she enjoys in Italy or Spain or Austria or France or Mexico or Brazil. American Roman Catholics generally are well satisfied with the freedom they enjoy. The highest American dignitary of that Church, Cardinal Gibbons, of Baltimore, who attended the centennial celebration of the Constitution at Philadelphia, September, 1887, said in his letter of acceptance: " The Constitution of the United States is worthy of being written in letters of gold. It is a charter by which the liberties of sixty millions of people are secured, and by which, under Providence, the temporal happiness of countless millions yet unborn will be perpetuated."

The crowning feature of the American Constitution is contained in the First Amendment, which forbids Congress to establish any Church as a state religion, and to prohibit *the free exercise of religion*. This is the magna charta of religious liberty within the jurisdiction of the United States.

APPENDIX II.

FAC-SIMILES OF THE OLDEST MANUSCRIPTS OF THE ATHANASIAN CREED
AND THE APOSTLES' CREED.

We present here a reproduction, on a small scale, of the Athanasian
Creed and the Apostles' Creed from the UTRECHT PSALTER, which
was brought prominently to light in 1873, in connection with the
Anglican controversy on the Athanasian Creed, and photographed in
London, 1875. See Vol. I., p. 37, note, and Vol. II., pp. 66–71. It is
the oldest copy known of these important documents. Between the
two is a rude picture of the last judgment, which could not be well
reproduced, and is unnecessary for our purpose.

The Athanasian Creed.

QINCIPITFIDESCATHO
UICUQUEUULT
SALUUSISSEANTEOMNIA
OPUSESTUTTENEATCATHO
LICAMFIDIM?
QUAMNISIQUISQUEINTE
GRAMINUIOLATAMQUE
SERUAUERITABSQUEDU
BIOINAETERNUMPERIBIT
FIDESAUTEMCATHOLICA.
HAECESTUTUNUMDMIN
TRINITATE ETTRINITA
TEMINUNITATEUENERE
MUR;
NEQUICONFUNDENTES
PERSONASNEQUISUBSTAN
TIAMSEPARANTES;
ALIAESTENIMPERSONA
PATRISALIAFILII ALIA
SPSSCI;
SEDPATRISETFILIIETSPSSCI

UNAESTDIUINITASAE
QUALISGLORIACOAET
NAMAIESTAS;
QUALISPATERTALISFILIUS
TALISETSPIRITUSSCS'
INCREATUSPATERINCRE
ATUSFILIUS INCREATUS
ETSPIRITUSSCS'
IMMENSUSPATERINMEN
SUSFILIUS IMMENSUS
ETSPIRITUSSCS;
AETERNUSPATERAETER
NUSFILIUSAETERNUS
ETSPIRITUSSCS;
ETTAMENNONTRESAETERNI'
SEDUNUSAETERNUS;
SICUTNONTRESINCREATI
NECTRESINMENSI SEDU
NUSINCREATUSETUNUS
INMENSUS)

SIMILITEROMNIPOTENS
PATER OMNIPOTENSFI
LIUSOMNIPOTENSETSPSSCS
ETTAMENNONTRESOMNI
POTENTISSEDUNUSOMPS/
ITADSPATERDSFILIUS
DSETSPIRITUSSCS;
ETTAMENNONTRESDII/
SEDUNUSESTDS;
ITADNSPATER ODNSFILIUS
DNSETSPIRITUSSCS;
ETTAMINNONTRESDNI/
SEDUNUSESTDNS/
QUIASICUTSINGILLATIM
UNAMQUAMQUEPERSONA
DMETDNMCONFITERILXPIA
NAUERITATICONPELLIMUR
ITATRESDEOSAUTTRES
DOMINOSDICERECATHO
LICARELIGIONEPROHIBE
MUR;

[Continuation of the Athanasian Creed.]

PATERANULLOESTFACTUS
NECCREATUSNECGENITUS
FILIUSAPATRESOLOEST
NONFACTUS NECCREATUS
SEDGENITUS
SPSSESAPATREETFILLIONON
FACTUSNECCREATUSNECCE
NITUSSIDPROCEDENS
UNUSERGOPATERNONTRES
PATRESUNUSFILIUSNON
TRESFILIIUNUSSPSSCS
NONTRESSPSSCI
ETINHACTRINITATENIHIL
PRIUSAUTPOSTERIUS NI
HILMAIUSAULMINUS
SEDTOTITRESPERSONAECO
AETERNAESIBISUNT ET
COAEQUALES
ITAUTPEROMNIASICUTIA
SUPRADICTUMESTETTRI
NITASINUNITATE ETU
NITASINTRINITATEUE
NERANDASIT
QUIUULTERGOSALUUS
ESSE ITADETRINITATE
SENTIAT
SEDNECESSARIUMEST
AD AETERNAMSALUTE
UTINCARNATIONEM
QUOQUEDNINOSTRI
IHUXPIFIDELITERCRE

DAT
ESTERGOFIDESRECTAUTCRE
DAMUSETCONFITEAMUR
QUIADNSNOSTERIHSXPS
DIFILIUS D ETHOMOEST
OSTESTIXSUBSTANTIAPATRIS
ANTESAECULAGENITUS
ETHOMOESTEXSUBSTAN
TIAMATRISINSAECULO
NATUS
PERFECTUSDSPERFECTUSHO
MOEXANIMARATIONALI
ETHUMANACARNESUB
SISTENS
AEQUALISPATRI SICUN
DUMDIUINITATEM
MINORPATRISECUNDU
HUMANITATEM
QUILICETDSSITETHOMO
NONDUOTAMENSEDU
NUSESTXPS
UNUSAUTEMNONCONUER
SIONEDIUINITATISIN
CARNE SEDADSUMPTIO
NEHUMANITATISINDO
UNUSOMNINONONCON
FUSIONESUBSTANTIAE
SEDUNITATEPERSONAE
NAMSICUTANIMARATIO
NALISETCAROUNUSESTHO
MO ITADSITHOMOUNUS

ESTXPS
QUIPASSUSESTPROSALUTA
NOSTRADESCENDITADIN
FEROSTERTIADIERISUR
REXITAMORTUIS
ASCENDITADCAELOSSEDIT
ADDEXTERAMDIPATRIS
OMNIPOTENTIS
INDEUENTURUSIUDICARE
UIUOSETMORTUOS
ADCUIUSADUENTUMOM
NESHOMINESRESURGERE
HABENTCUMCORPORIBUS
SUIS
ETREDDITURISUNTDEFAC
TISPROPRIISRATIONEM
ETQUIBONAEGERUNT
IBUNTINUITAMAETERNA
ETQUIMALAINIGNEM
AETERNUM
HAECESTFIDESCATHOLICA
QUAMNISIQUISQUEFIDE
LITERFIRMITERQUECREDI
DERITSALUUSESSENONPO
TERIT

The Apostles' Creed.

INCIPITSYMBOLU
CREDOINDMPA
PATREMOMNIPOTENTEM
CREATORECAELIETTERRAE
ETINIHMXPMFILIUMEIUS
UNICUMDNMNOSTRU
QUICONCEPTUSESTDESPU
SCO NATUSEXMARIAUIR

APOSTOLORUM
GINE AE PASSUSSUBPON
TIOPILATOCRUCIFIXUS
MORTUUSETSEPULTUS DES
CENDITADINFERNA TER
TIADIERESURREXITAMOR
TUIS ASCENDITADCAELUM
SEDITADDEXTERAMDIPA

TRIS OMNIPOTENTIS IN
DEUENTURUSIUDICARE
UIUOSETMORTUOS
CREDOETINSPM SCMSCAM
ECCLESIAMCATHOLICAM
SCORUM COMMUNIO
NEM REMISSIONEM

PECCATORUM CARNIS

RESURRECTIONEM

UITAMAETERNAM AMEN

APPENDIX III.

The Bull of Boniface VIII., *Unam Sanctam*, Nov. 18, 1302.

[Since the proclamation of the dogma of papal infallibility, 1870, deliverances issuing from the Vatican on biblical and theological subjects have assumed an importance, not definitely assigned to them previously by the canons of the Roman Church. Boniface's bull was called forth by the appeals against the exactions of Philip IV. on French ecclesiastical property for his wars against England In reprisal, Philip had the pope seized by French troops and imprisoned at Anagni. See Schaff: *Ch. Hist.*, V., Part I., pp. 15–29. The bull asserts (1) the supreme authority of the pope over the whole church; (2) the supremacy of the spiritual over the temporal power; (3) obedience to the Roman pontiff as the necessary condition of salvation. The translation is based upon the Latin text of W. Römer, *Die Bulle* unam sanctam, Schaffhausen, 1889. See also the text in Mirbt, p. 210.]

Boniface, Bishop, Servant of the servants of God. For perpetual remembrance. Urged on by our faith, we are compelled to believe and hold that there is One Holy Catholic and Apostolic Church and we firmly believe and clearly profess that outside of her there is neither salvation nor remission of sins as the bridegroom declares in the Canticles, my dove, my undefiled is one; she is the only one of her mother, the chosen one of her that bare her. And she represents the mystical body of Christ whose head is Christ and God the head of Christ. In her there is one Lord, one faith, one baptism. For, in the time of the flood there was the single ark of Noah which prefigures the one Church, and was finished according to the measurement of one cubit and had one Noah for pilot and captain, and outside of it every living creature on the earth, as we read, was destroyed. And this Church we revere as the only one even as the Lord said to the prophet, Deliver my soul from the sword, my darling from the power of the dog. Ps. xxii, 20. He prayed for his life that is for himself, head and body. And this body, that is the Church, he called one—*unicam*—on account of the one bridegroom; and the oneness of the faith, the sacraments and the love in the Church. She is that seamless shirt of the Lord which was not rent but was allotted by the casting of lots. Therefore, this one and only Church has one head and not two heads,—for had she two

heads, she would be a monster—that is, Christ and Christ's vicar, Peter and Peter's successor. For the Lord said to Peter himself, Feed my sheep. 'My,' he said (using the plural) that is all, not individuals, these and those; and by this he is understood to have committed to him all the sheep—*oves universas*. When, therefore, either the Greeks or others say that they were not committed to the care of Peter and his successors, they must confess that they are not of Christ's sheep, even as the Lord says in John, There is one fold and one shepherd, John x, 10.

That in this Church and within her power are the two swords, we are taught in the Gospels, namely, the spiritual sword and the temporal sword. For when the Apostle said, Lo here—that is in the Church— are two swords the Lord did not reply to the Apostles, It is too much, but It is enough. For, certainly, he who denies that the temporal sword is in Peter's power, listens badly to the Lord's words Put up thy sword into its sheath. Matthew xxvi, 52. Therefore, both are in the power of the Church, namely, the spiritual sword and the temporal sword,— the latter to be used for the Church, the former by the Church; the former by the hand of the priest, the latter by the hand of princes and kings, but at the nod and instance of the priest. The one sword must of necessity be subject to the other, and the temporal power to the spiritual power. For the Apostle said, There is no power but of God and the powers that be are ordained of God, Romans xiii, 1, but not ordained except as sword is subjected to sword and so the inferior is brought by the other to the highest end. For, according to St. Dionysius, it is a divine law that the lowest things are made by mediocre things to attain to the highest. Therefore, it is not according to the order of the universe that all things in an equal way and directly should reach their end, but the lowest through the mediocre and the lower through the higher; and, that the spiritual power excels the earthly power in dignity and worth, we will the more clearly acknowledge in the proportion that the spiritual is higher than the temporal. This we perceive quite distinctly from the donation of the tithe and the functions of benediction and sanctification, from the mode in which power itself is received and the government of things themselves. Truth being the witness, the spiritual power has the function of establishing the temporal power and sitting in judgment on it if it should prove not to be

good. And to the Church, and the Church's power, Jeremiah's prophecy, i, 9, applies: See I have set thee this day over the nations and the kingdoms to pluck up and to break down, to destroy and to overthrow, to build and to plant.

And, if the earthly power deviates from the right path, it is judged by the spiritual power, but if a minor spiritual power deviate from the right path, the minor is judged by the superior power, but if the supreme power [the papacy or the Church] deviate, it can be judged not by man but by God only. And so the Apostle testifies, He which is spiritual judges all things but he himself is judged of no man, I Cor., ii, 15. But this authority, although it is given to a man and exercised by a man, is not a human power, nay, much rather a divine power given by the divine lips to Peter, to Peter himself and to his successors in Christ, whom Peter confessed when the Rock was established—*petra firmata*—when the Lord said unto him, Whatsoever thou shalt bind, etc., Matt., xvi, 19.

Whoever, therefore, resists this power ordained by God, resists God's ordinance, unless perchance he imagines two principles to exist, as did Manichæus, a thing which we pronounce false and heretical because, as Moses testified, 'God created the heaven and the earth not in the beginnings, but "in the beginning".'

Further, we declare, say, define and pronounce it to be altogether necessary for salvation for every human creature that he be subject to the Roman pontiff.[1]

---

[1] The Roman Catholic historian, Funk, *Kirchengeschl. Abhandlungen,* I. 483–89, seeks to confine the application of the last words to princes and kings. But Hergenröther-Kirsch, Hefele-Knöpfler and other R. C. historians give to them their natural meaning. The passage of Jeremiah, 'See, I have this day set thee over the nations and over the kingdoms to root out and to pull down,' etc., was used at least eight times by Gregory VII. to prove the supremacy of the spiritual over the temporal power. Clement VII. applied it to himself in writing to Henry VIII. Pius V. used it in his letter deposing Elizabeth, as did also Bellarmine and, as late as 1910, Pius X.

APPENDIX IV.

LEO XIII.'S APOSTOLICÆ CURÆ, ON ANGLICAN ORDERS, SEPT. 13, 1896.

[It would seem as if the infallibility of this deliverance was not fairly open to question, as it concerns one of the sacraments of the Roman Church. Certainly papal language could scarcely be more vigorous and positive. See Leo's Works, Bruges ed., VI., 198–210; Roman ed., VI., 258–73; Mirbt, 401; Denzinger, 529; Trans. in Wynne: *The Great Encycl., Letters of Leo XIII.*, N. Y., 1903; *Answer of the Abpp. of England to the Apostol. Letter of Pope Leo XIII.*, London, 1877.

This papal deliverance pronounced Anglican orders invalid. Leo XIII., as the document states, appointed a commission of eight, with a cardinal at its head and including the historian Duchesne, to investigate the validity of Anglican orders. The members, so the rumor went, were, at the time of its appointment, equally divided on the question, but by study in the Vatican archives reached a unanimous decision. Leo's bull declares that Anglican ordination was 'vitiated at its origin' and 'under Edward VI. the true sacrament of orders as instituted by Christ lapsed.' This judgment, so the decision continues, had been given by Julius III. and Paul IV. in their dealings with the English Church during Mary Tudor's reign, as also later in the case of John Clement Gordon, Bishop of Galloway, who, passing over to Rome, was ordered by Clement XI., 1704, to be 'ordained to all orders from the beginning and unconditionally.' Moreover, the vitiated origin is evident from the 'animus of the Edwardean Ordinal against the Catholic Church. It is defective both in form and intention —the two equally essential to sacred orders.' The words 'Receive ye the Holy Ghost' were not followed in the Ordinal by the further words 'for the office of priest or bishop.' Additions made subsequently, 1662, were not sufficient to correct the alleged vitiated origin. Leo's sentence was announced in the following words]:

Itaque omnibus pontificum decessorum in hac ipsa causa decretis usque quaque assentientes eaque plenissime confirmantes ac veluti renovantes auctoritate nostra, motu proprio, certa scientia, pronunciamus et declaramus, ordinationes ritu anglicano actas, irritas prorsus fuisse et esse, omninoque nullas.	Strictly adhering in this matter to all the decrees of deceased pontiffs and most fully confirming them and of ourselves, as it were, reasserting them, we do of our own motion and with certain knowledge pronounce and declare ordinations performed according to the Anglican rite to have been and to be null and wholly void.

Then, after announcing the joy with which English clergymen returning to 'the bosom of the Catholic Church' would be welcomed, the pontiff further declared that his decision 'is and shall be perpetually valid and in force,' and observed 'without exception in law and other-

wise.' Two months later, writing to Richard, Cardinal-archbishop of Paris, Leo repeated himself when he pronounced the decision 'permanent, authoritative and irrevocable—*perpetuo firmam, ratum et irre vocabilem.'*[1]

---

[1] The Archbishops of Canterbury and York, Doctors Temple and Maclagan, in their reply addressed to 'the bishops of the Catholic Church' called for the documents on which the papal decision had been based, adduced the references in the Edwardean Ordinal to the sacrifice of thanksgiving and praise and the sacrifice on the cross, and laid stress on changes which the Roman rite itself had in the course of time undergone. To the humiliation of the larger part of the Protestant world, the reply, while parrying Leo's statements, laid no emphasis on the spiritual call to the ministry nor intimated the essential connection of the Anglican Church with the Reformation of the sixteenth century. Dr. C. A. Briggs, *Theol. Symbol.*, pp. 14, 226, 234; *Church Unity*, p. 121, reporting an audience he had with Pius X., represented Pius as having stated that 'Leo's decision was not a doctrinal but a disciplinary decision and cannot be classed as infallible and symbolical' and that Pius assured him 'in a private interview that Leo's decision does not belong to the catalogue of infallible decisions.' Dr. Briggs went on to say that 'Pius is certainly correct.' It is possible that the American professor misunderstood the language of the pontiff or put upon it an interpretation the pontiff did not intend. He has Roman Catholic writers on Canon Law against him. Leitner, *Handbuch d. kathol. Kirchenrechts*, p. 127, pronounces Leo's decision final, *'eine endgültige Entscheidung. Der Grund der Ungültigkeit ist der defectus formæ et intentionis.'*—'The cause of the invalidity is the defect in form and intention. It brings to a close an extensive and prolonged discussion.' So also Straub, *de ecclesia*, I, 325, and Eichmann, *Handbuch d. kathol. Kirchenrechts*, p. 295.

APPENDIX V.

AMERICANISM AND MODERNISM CONDEMNED.

The movement in the Roman Catholic Church, known by the names 'Americanism' and 'Modernism,' received a severe blow in encyclicals issued by Leo XIII.—see Leo's *Works*, Bruges ed., vii, 223–33. Denzinger, 530–32,—and Pius X. An official stamp was placed by these utterances on mediæval conditions as a state to which society and the Church of these modern times should return as to a model. Freedom of scholarly investigation and expression in religious matters was greatly limited if not forbidden.

'Americanism,' advocated by Father Isaac T. Hecker of the Paulist Fathers, New York City, and brought to Leo's attention in the Italian translation of Elliott's *Life of Hecker*, proposed a modified accommodation of certain Roman Catholic doctrinal statements and practices to modern Germanic and Anglo-Saxon views. The movement was denounced by the pontiff in a letter addressed to Cardinal Gibbons, January 22, 1899, as a defiance of the Church and the Apostolic see, whose function, so Leo declared, it is to define infallibly truth and error. He rebuked it as presumption 'for an individual to pretend to define what truth is.'[1] Forthwith, in a public address, Abp. Ireland, who with Bishop Keane and other leading Catholics had approved the movement, withdrew his approval, declaring that when the Roman pontiff speaks all good Catholics submit. Since Leo's encyclical was issued, nothing has been heard of 'Americanism' in the United States. January 13, 1897, Leo had shown his estimate of modern biblical studies by pronouncing genuine I John v, 7, 'There are three that bear witness in

---

[1] One of the closing clauses of Leo's letter runs, 'The Church is one by unity of doctrine as also by unity of government and at the same time Catholic; and, because God ordained her centre and foundation to be in the Chair of St. Peter, she is legally called Roman.'

heaven, the Father, the Son and the Holy Spirit,' a passage not found in the early manuscripts of the New Testament.

'Modernism,' a more liberal movement, has been advocated by scholars in Roman Catholic Europe and calls for the utilization of the results of modern biblical and historical study in a restatement of certain dogmas, such as the dates and authorship of the biblical books, the origin of the seven sacraments, the divine foundation of the Roman primacy and other non-Apostolic institutions In three encyclicals, 1907–1910, Pius X. made a vehement protest against the movement, threatening its supporters with the severest Church penalties, and outlawing freedom of thought and biblical scholarship so far as they are in any wise opposed to traditional Church views.   In 1908, he had a medal struck off representing the Roman pontiff as a sort of St. George, destroying the many-headed hydra of the new heresy.

In the first deliverance, *lamentabili*, July 3, 1907—called the new Syllabus—Pius in sixty-five propositions denounced the movement as 'changing Christianity into something like free Protestantism.'   In *pascendi gregis*, September 8, 1907, he reprobated 'the Modernists for daring to follow in the footsteps of Martin Luther' and for 'setting aside supernatural revelation for subjective opinions drawn from the religious consciousness, as they call it.'   In *sacrorum antistitum*, September 1, 1910, the pontiff stigmatized them as a most crafty set, *vaferrimum hominum genus*, forbade their writings being read and prescribed the oath, which follows, to be signed by all priests and Roman Catholic teachers, giving assent to Pius's two previous encyclicals and especially in so far as they concern 'what they call the history of dogma.'

The fulminations were met differently by the supporters of the movement.   Minocchi in Italy, as also Houtin and Duchesne in France, modified or recalled the free statements they had made in their writings. Loisy of Paris, distinguished for his biblical and historical studies, the eminent Church historians Schnitzer and Koch in Germany, and the brilliant English Jesuit, Tyrrell, persisted and were excommunicated. By papal order a movement to erect a monument to Professor Schell of Würzburg, one of the first advocates of the new method, was stopped. The erection of the monument had already been supported with subscriptions by the Archbishop of Bamberg and the Bishop of Passau.

In full agreement with the maledictions of Leo and Pius have been

the extravagant honors paid by recent pontiffs to the teachings and method of Thomas Aquinas, who died, 1274, a time when no one dreamed of biblical criticism and modern archæological discoveries. Thomas was elevated by Leo to the place of patron of Catholic schools and pronounced 'the safest guide in philosophy in the battle of faith and reason against unbelief and scepticism.' More recently Pius XI., June 29, 1923, on the 600th anniversary of Thomas's canonization, crowned him the chief teacher outside the Apostolic group.

Protestantism also came in for hard blows from Leo and Pius X. By Leo modern Protestant missions and missionaries in heathen lands were denounced. In his Borromeo encyclical of May 10, 1910, Pius repeated the old blast against 'the would-be reformers of the sixteenth century as having prepared the way for the revolutions of modern times' and characterized them as enemies of the cross—*inimici crucis Christi*—who 'mind earthly things and whose god is their belly.'

APPENDIX VI.

PIUS X.'S OATH AGAINST MODERNISM—JURIS JURANDI FORMULA.

[The original, which occurs in Pius X.'s encyclical, *sacrorum antistitum*, Sept. 1, 1910, is found in *Acta ap. sedis* for 1910, II., 655 sqq.; Mirbt, 515–17; Denzinger, 599 sqq.; Ayrinhac, Pres. St. Patrick's Sem., Menlo Park, Cal.: *General Code of the New Canon Law*, N. Y., 1923, 90–95. The oath was 'explicitly' reaffirmed by the Holy Office, March 22, 1918, as obligatory for Roman Catholic priests and teachers in addition to Pius IV.'s *professio catholicae fidei*—until otherwise decreed by papal authority.]

I firmly embrace and accept all and singly those articles which have been defined, set forth and declared by the Church's inerrant teaching-authority and especially those heads of doctrines which directly conflict with the errors of this age. And, 1., I confess that God, the beginning and end of all things, can with certainty be known and proved to be by the natural light of reason from those things which are made, that is by the visible works of creation, even as a cause may be certainly proved from its effects. 2. I accept and acknowledge the external arguments of revelation, that is the divine facts especially miracles and prophecy, and I also accept the most sure proofs of the divine origin of the Christian religion and hold that they are pre-eminently adapted to the intelligence of all ages and men and, in particular, of this age. 3. And with firm faith, I equally believe that the Church, the guardian and teacher of the revealed Word, was directly founded by the real and historical Christ himself, as he dwelt with us, and that she was built upon Peter, the prince of the Apostolic hierarchy and his successors forever. 4. I sincerely receive the teaching of the faith as it has been handed down to us from the Apostles and orthodox Fathers and handed down in the same sense and meaning; and furthermore, I utterly reject the heretical fiction—*commentum*—of the evolution of dogmas according to which they change from one meaning to another and a meaning contradictory to that meaning which the Church before had given; and equally do I condemn that entire error according to which philosophical dis-

covery suffices, although the divine deposit was given to Christ's bride
and given to be faithfully guarded by her, or according to which it [the
teaching] is little by little transformed in meaning by the creations of
the human consciousness and man's effort and brought to perfection in
the future by an indefinite progression. 5. I most surely hold and sincerely declare that faith is not a blind realization of religion drawn out
of the darkness of the subconscience, morally enlightened by the influence of the heart and the inflexions of the will, but that it is an honest
assent by the intellect, given to truth accepted through hearing of the
ear by the which we believe as true those things which have been revealed and confirmed by a personal God, our Creator and Lord, and on
the basis of the authority of God, who in the highest sense is trustworthy.

Likewise,—and this is equally important—I submit myself reverently
and with my whole mind to all the condemnations, declarations and commands contained in the encyclical *pascendi* and the decree *lamentabili*,
especially in regard to that which they call the history of dogmas—
historiam dogmatum. I also reprobate the error of those who assert that
the faith offered by the Church may by any possibility conflict with
history; and the error that it is not possible to harmonize, in the sense
in which they are now understood, the Catholic dogmas with the origins
of the Christian religion which are the more trustworthy.—I condemn
and reject the opinions of those who say that the more learned Christians
may represent at one and the same time two persons, the one a believer
the other a historian, as if it were possible to hold on as an historian to
things which are contradictory to the faith of the believer or lay down
premises according to which it follows that dogmas are either false or
dubious, just so they be not openly set aside.—Equally, do I reprobate
that principle of judging the holy Scriptures and interpreting them,
which, in defiance of the Church's tradition, the analogy of faith and
the rules of the Apostolic see, suits itself to the comments of rationalists
and, scarcely less lawlessly than rashly, accepts textual criticism as the
one only and supreme rule.—Further, I reject the theory of those who
hold that the teacher in the department of historic theology as well as
the writer on its subjects must place opinion above the principle of the
supernatural origin of Catholic tradition and the promise of divine aid
in the preservation of all truth and, further, that the writings of the

individual Fathers must be explained by the principles of science alone apart from any sacred authority and by the same free judgment that any profane document is studied or investigated.—Finally, I profess myself most averse to the error of the Modernists who hold that in sacred tradition there is not a divine element; or—what is far worse,— who reason in a pantheistic sense, so that nothing is left but the bare and naked historic occurrence like unto other occurrences of history which are left to men to carry on in subsequent periods by their industry, shrewdness and genius the teaching—*scholam*—begun by Christ and his Apostles. And I do most firmly hold to the faith of the Fathers and will continue so to do to the last breath of life, the faith concerning the unfailing charism of the truth which now inheres, has inhered and will always continue to inhere in the episcopal succession from the Apostles; that nothing is to be regarded as better or more opportune which the culture of this age or that age can suggest and that nothing is at any time to be otherwise believed or otherwise understood as the absolute and immutable truth preached from the beginning by the Apostles.

To all these things I promise to hold faithfully, sincerely, and wholly and I promise to keep them inviolably, never departing from them in teaching or by any words or writings. Thus I promise and swear, so help me God and these holy Gospels of God.

APPENDIX VII.

Pius XI.'s Encyclical on Church Union, *Mortalium animos*, Jan. 6, 1928.

[Pius XI.'s bull was intended to be the papal ultimatum on federation between the Protestant and Roman Catholic communions or their organic union. It explicitly reaffirms the distinctive dogmas which were fully developed in the Middle Ages and justified the split of Western Christendom in the sixteenth century. It repudiates the idea that there can be dealings between parts of the Christian family—so called—as between equals, insists that submission to the pope as Christ's vicar is the only method which can be tolerated by the Roman body, and demands from Protestants unconditional surrender and a confession of repentance for the so-called revolt from the 'Holy Father in Rome.' If they return, they must return as prodigal children. Such submission is the condition of being 'in the Church' and 'whosoever,' so the pronouncement runs, 'is outside the Catholic Church [meaning the R. C. Ch.] is a stranger to the hope of life and salvation.' The occasion of Pius's deliverance was the effort to bring the Church of England and the Roman Church into some accord, made in 'the conversations' held in Malines, Belgium, from 1921 to 1925 between Dr. Armitage Robinson, Bishops Frere and Gore, Dr. Kidd, and Lord Halifax, Anglicans, and Cardinal Mercier, and the invitation given to the Roman pontiff to join in the Christian conference in Lausanne, 1927. Card. Mercier died June 23, 1926. The temper of the Anglo-Catholics towards the conversations was shown by the message sent by a largely attended conference held in Albert Hall, July 13, 1923, through its chairman, the Bishop of Zanzibar, conveying 'the greetings of 16,000 Anglo-Catholics assembled in congress to the Holy Father, humbly praying that the day of peace may quickly break.' When, 1924, Cardinal Mercier in a letter to his clergy set forth the nature of the conversations, loud protests were made in England, and the Archbishop of Canterbury publicly stated, 1924, that 'the group' attending the meetings in Malines had 'no official standing. He had received the Anglican members and had proposed Drs. Gore and Kidd for the group, but had gone no further.' The conferences, he stated, were 'informal and private conversations with nothing of the nature of negotiations,' and that one of the first steps in the direction of the end proposed was to call for 'a repudiation of the Declaration against Anglican orders.' See *London Times*, February 7, 1924; *The Conversations at Malines, 1921–25*, Oxford, 1928; H. Wilson, *Life of Cardinal Mercier*, London, 1928, 391 pp.—Bell: *Documents on Christian Unity*, II., 32–64.

After referring to the extraordinary efforts being made among the nations to establish peace and fraternal relations among themselves, the document notes that 'a similar result was being aimed at by some in those matters which concern the New Law promulgated by Christ, our Lord,' large conventions being held to promote this object in which 'both infidels of every kind and true Christians—*Christifideles*—and even those who have fallen away from Christ or who with obstinacy deny his divine nature join in agreement.'[1] Such movements, the pontiff declared, may in no wise be approved by Catholics, based as they are on the false notion that all religions are more or less worthy. Catholics, in favoring such movements, abandon the divinely revealed religion, being easily deceived with the idea that by their actions outward good may come, inasmuch as the question concerned is unity among Christians. From this point the 'Encyclical Letter of our Most Holy Lord Pius XI. by divine Providence Pope' goes on:]

Is it not proper, so it is often repeated, yea even consonant with duty, that all who invoke Christ's name should abstain from mutual criminations and at last be joined in mutual love? Who would dare to say that he loves Christ who desires not to carry out with all his strength

---

[1] The Original in *Acta sed. s.*, XX., 1–9. Other trans. in *Cath. Hist. Rev.*, July, 1928; Bell: *Documents*, I., 32–44. The capitalizations are as in the original.

the wishes of him who begged his Father that his disciples might be one—John xvii, 21? And did not the same Christ will that his disciples should be stamped and distinguished from the rest by this that they love one another—'By this shall all men know that ye are my disciples, if ye have love one for another,' John xiii, 35. Indeed, they add that all Christians should be as 'one,' for if they were, they would be much more efficient in driving out the pest of irreligion which like a cancer daily creeps on and on and becomes more and more widely spread, weakening the Gospel. These things and others that class—*genus*—of men, who are called pan-Christians, continually and boastfully assert and these men unfortunately, far from being quite few and scattered, have grown to be veritable troops and have grouped themselves into societies widely diffused which, for the most part, are controlled by non-Catholics although among themselves they hold various opinions in the things of the faith. This movement is so actively promoted as in many places to win for itself the assent of the citizens and even to ensnare the minds of very many Catholics with the hope of bringing about such a union as might appear to be agreeable to the wish of Holy Mother Church who has nothing more fully at heart than to call back her erring sons and lead them to her bosom. However, in reality there lies hidden beneath these enticements and charms of words the gravest error, an error by which the very foundation of the Catholic faith is torn asunder.

Therefore, admonished by the obligation—*conscientia*—of our apostolic office, not to let the flock of the Lord be misled by pernicious fallacies, We invoke, Venerable Brethren, your zeal in guarding against this evil, for We are sure that by your writings and words the people will most easily get to know and understand those principles and considerations which we are about to lay down and from which Catholics will learn what they are to think and how to act when the question arises concerning those undertakings—*inceptis*—which look towards the coalescence in one body of all those who are properly called Christians.

We were created by God, the Creator of all things, in order that we might know and serve Him so that our Author has the full right to be served by us. God might have prescribed for man's government the law of nature alone which at creation He imprinted in man's soul and commanded additions to that same law by His ordinary providence, but

He preferred to offer precepts for us to obey, and as time went on, that
is from the beginnings of the human race to the advent and preaching
of Jesus Christ, He himself taught man duties which a rational creature
owes to him, the Creator,—'At sundry times and in divers manners,
God, who spoke in time past unto the Fathers in the prophets, hath in
these last days spoken unto us in His Son.' Heb. i, 1. From this it follows that there can be no true religion, other than that which is founded
on the revealed Word of God; which revelation, as begun at the beginning and continued under the Old Law, Christ Jesus himself under the
New Law perfected. Now, if God has spoken (and it is historically
certain that He has truly spoken), there is no one who does not see that
it is man's duty to believe absolutely God's revelation and to obey
implicitly His commands. And, that we might rightly do both, for the
glory of God and our own salvation, the only begotten Son of God
founded his Church on earth. Further, We believe that those who call
themselves Christians can do no other than believe that a Church—the
one Church—was established by Christ; but, if it is further asked what
must of necessity be its nature according to the will of its Author, there
all do not agree. A large number of these, for example, deny that the
Church of Christ must be visible and manifest,[1] at least to such a degree
that it appear as one body of the faithful, agreeing in one and the same
doctrine under one teaching authority—*magisterium*—and government;
on the contrary, they understand a visible Church as nothing else than
a Federation—*fœdus*—composed of various communities of Christians,
even though they hold different doctrines, which may even be in conflict one with the other. But Christ our Lord instituted his Church as
a perfect society, with external qualities and perceptible to the senses
which should carry on to later time the work of saving the human race,
under the leadership of one head,—Matt. xvi, 18; Luke xxii, 32; John
xxi, 15–17—with the authority of teaching by word of mouth,—Matt.
xvi, 15—and by the ministry of the sacraments, the fonts of heavenly
grace,—John iii, 5; vi, 48–50; xx, 22. Cp. Matt. xvi, 18, etc. For which

---

[1] *Adspectabilem et conspicuam.* Leo XIII., June 29, 1896, put the idea of the visibility
of Christ's kingdom and its identity with the Roman Church thus: 'As he willed that his
kingdom should be manifest—*conspicuam*—Christ was obliged to appoint a vice-regent
on earth in the person of Peter. He likewise determined that the authority given him
for the salvation of mankind should in perpetuity pass to Peter's successors.'

reason he asserted, by way of comparison, the similarity of the Church to a kingdom, a house, a sheepfold, and a flock—Cp. Matt. xvi, 18; John x, 16; xxi, 15–17. And the Church, after being so wonderfully instituted by its Founder and his Apostles,—who were the leaders in propagating it,—when they were being removed by death, could not be entirely extinguished and cease to be, for to it was given the commandment to lead all men without distinction of time or place to eternal salvation: Going, therefore, teach ye all nations, Matt. xxviii, 19. In the continual carrying-out of this task, will any element of strength and efficiency be wanting to the Church, when Christ himself is perpetually present with us, as he solemnly promised, Behold I am with you all days, even to the consummation of the world—Matt. xxviii, 20? It follows, then, that the Church of Christ not only exists today and has always existed, but is also exactly the same as it was in the Apostolic Age, unless we chose to say,—which God forbid,—either that Christ our Lord could not effect his purpose, or that he erred when he asserted that the gates of hell should never prevail against her. Matt. xvi, 18.

And, at this place, it seems opportune to explain and to remove that false opinion on which the whole case seems to hang and from which also that multiple action and combination—*actio et conspiratio multiplex* —of the non-Catholics seem to proceed which, as We have said, are designed to bring about the union of Christian churches into one society. For, it is to be noted, that the originators of this purpose—*consilii*— are forever accustomed to adduce Christ and his words: That they all may be one. . . . And there shall be one fold and one shepherd, John xvii, 21; x, 16, wishing to get from these words that they signify a desire and prayer of Christ Jesus which up to this time have not been fulfilled. For they are of the mind that the unity of faith and government—a note of the one true Church of Christ—has heretofore hardly ever existed and does not exist today; and that it is to be wished for and perchance some day will by a common bent of wills be secured but that in the meantime it is to be held as an ideal. They add that the Church of herself or by her very nature is divided into parts, that is, made up of a number of churches or separate communities which up to this have been distinct and which, although they have in common some articles of doctrine, are nevertheless at discord in regard to the rest. And, they are of the mind that each one of them properly enjoys the same

rights and that, at best, the Church was unique and one from the time of the Apostles down to the œcumenical councils. Therefore, so they say, controversies and ancient differences of opinion, which to this day have divided the Christian name, should be renounced and set aside and some common rule of belief concerning the other doctrines be wrought out and laid down so that in the profession of that faith, they will not only know themselves to be brothers but feel themselves such; and, that the many separate churches or associations—*communitates*—if joined as it were in one universal federation—*fœdus*—would then be in a condition to oppose vigorously and fruitfully the advances of irreligion. These things, Venerable Brethren, are what is said by them in common. There are indeed, some who affirm and acknowledge that Protestantism, as they call it, with much lack of consideration discarded certain articles of faith and a number of external rites of worship which are most pleasing and useful and which, on the other hand, to this day the Roman Church retains. But they go on to declare that this very Church showed herself rash in corrupting the original religion by adding certain doctrines not only foreign to the Gospel but repugnant to it and offering them to be believed. As the chief of these, they enumerate the jurisdiction of the Primacy appointed to Peter and his successors in the Roman See. Likewise, in their number,—although the number is not so large,—there are those who grant to the Roman Pontiff either a Primacy of honor and jurisdiction of a certain authority—*potestatem*—which, however, they assert comes not by divine right—*a jure divino*—but from a certain consent of the faithful. And others there are who even go so far as to wish the Pontiff himself to preside over their varicolored meetings—*conventibus*. And, further, although many non-Catholics may be found who preach loudly fraternal communion in Christ Jesus, you will find that none of them have reached down to the thought of subjecting themselves to the Vicar of Jesus Christ and obeying him either as teacher or ruler. At the same time, they affirm, that on common terms, that is freely as equals with equals, they would deal with the Roman Church; but, if they were to deal in this wise, it does not seem open to doubt that they would so treat the idea, that in the league—*pactem*—so vigorously entered into, they would not recede from those opinions which heretofore have been the cause that they have strayed and wandered outside Christ's only sheepfold—*unicum ovile*.

These things being as they are, it is evident that the Apostolic See can have no part in their meetings by any league—*pactum*—nor is it lawful for Catholics by any league to support such undertakings and give them aid. For, if they should do so, they would be giving countenance to a false Christian religion, quite alien to the one Church of Christ. Shall We suffer,—what would indeed be iniquitous—the truth, and that truth divinely revealed, to be drawn out by agreements? For here the question is one of defending revealed truth. Jesus Christ sent the Apostles into the whole world to imbue all nations with the Gospel faith and, lest they should err, he willed beforehand that they should be taught by the Holy Ghost—John xvi, 13. Has then this doctrine of the Apostles completely vanished away, or at times been corrupted in the Church whose ruler and guardian, God Himself is with us? If our Redeemer plainly taught that His Gospel was to hold not only during the times of the Apostles, but also to after ages, is it possible that the object of faith should in the process of time become so obscure and uncertain that it would be necessary today to tolerate opinions which are even contrary one to the other? If this were true, we should have also to say that the coming of the Holy Ghost on the Apostles and the perpetual indwelling of the same Spirit in the Church, yea the preaching of Jesus Christ itself a number of centuries ago, lost all their efficacy and use—to affirm which would be blasphemy. But the Only-begotten Son of God, when he commanded his representatives to teach all nations, bound all men to give credence to whatever was made known to them by the witnesses preordained by God, Acts x, 21, and he also confirmed his command with this sanction: He that believeth and is baptized shall be saved; but he that believeth not shall be condemned, Mk. xvi, 18. These two commands of Christ, which must be certainly fulfilled, the one, namely, to teach and the other to believe unto the reception of salvation, cannot be understood, unless the Church proposes a complete and easily understood teaching and is immune, when it thus teaches, from all danger of erring. In this matter, those also turn aside from the right path, who think that while the deposit of truth does indeed exist, it must be sought with such laborious trouble and with such daily study and reasonings that a man's term of life would hardly suffice to find it out and grasp it; as if the most merciful God has so spoken through the prophets and His only-begotten Son that only a few, and those stricken

in years, could learn what He had revealed through them, and not that
He might inculcate that doctrine of faith and morals, by which man is
to be guided through the whole course of his moral life.

These *pan-Christians* who turn their minds to uniting churches,—
consociandas ecclesias—seem indeed, to be pursuing the noblest plans
in promoting love among all Christians; nevertheless, how shall it
happen that this love inures to the injury of the faith? Certainly, no
one is ignorant that John himself, the Apostle of love, who seems to
reveal in his Gospel the secrets of the most Sacred Heart of Jesus, and
never ceased to impress on the memories of his followers the new commandment 'Love one another,' altogether forbade any intercourse with
those who professed a partial and corrupt version of Christ's teaching,
If any man come to you and bring not this doctrine, receive him not
into the house nor say to him: God speed you, II John x. For which
reason, since love is based on a complete and sincere faith, as its foundation, the disciples of Christ must be bound together by one faith
as the principal bond. Who then can conceive any Christian Federation—*fœdus*—members of which retain each his own opinions and private judgment, yea in matters which concern the object of faith, even
though their opinions be repugnant to the opinions of the rest? And
by what sort of league—*pacto*—We ask, can men who go off into opposing opinions, belong to one and the same Federation of the faithful?
For example, those who affirm, and those who deny that sacred Tradition is a true font of divine Revelation; those who hold that an ecclesiastical hierarchy, made up of bishops, priests and ministers, has been
divinely constituted, and those who assert that it has been brought in
little by little through the conditions of the time; those who adore
Christ really present in the Most Holy Eucharist by that marvellous
conversion of the bread and wine, called transubstantiation and adore
him really as present and those who affirm that Christ is present only
by faith, or symbolically and virtually in the Sacrament; those who in
the Eucharist recognize the nature both of a sacrament and of a sacrifice, and those who say that it is nothing more than the memorial or
commemoration of the Lord's Supper; those who believe it to be good
and useful to invoke by prayer the Saints reigning with Christ, especially Mary the Mother of God, and to venerate their images, and those
who urge that such worship is not to be employed since it is contrary

to the honour due to Jesus Christ, 'the one mediator of God and men.'
I Tim. ii, 5. How so great a discrepancy of opinions can make the way
clear to effect the unity of the Church, We know not; since that unity
can not arise except from one teaching authority, one law of belief and
one faith of Christians. But, We do know that from this, it is an easy
step to the neglect of religion or indifferentism and to modernism, as
they call it. For those who are unhappily infected with these errors
hold that dogmatic truth is not absolute but relative, that is, it adapts
itself to the varying necessities of time and place and to the varying
tendencies of the mind, since it is not contained in immutable revelation but is of such a nature that it accommodates itself to the life of
men. Besides this, in connection with things which must be believed,
it is nowise lawful to use that distinction which some have seen fit to
introduce between fundamental and non-fundamental articles of faith,
as they call them, as if the one are to be accepted by all while the other
may be left free to the assent of the faithful. For the supernatural
virtue of faith has a formal cause, namely the authority of God the
revealer, and this authority admits of no such distinction. For this
reason all who are truly Christ's believe, for example, the Conception
of the Mother of God without stain of original sin with the same faith
as they believe the mystery of the August Trinity and, likewise, the
Incarnation of the Lord no otherwise than they believe the infallible
teaching authority of the Roman Pontiff, according to the sense in which
it was defined by the Ecumenical Council of the Vatican. Are such
truths not equally certain or not equally to be believed, because the
Church has solemnly sanctioned and defined them, some in one age
and some in another, yea, even in those times immediately before our
own? Has not God revealed them all? For the teaching authority
of the Church, which in the divine plan was constituted on earth in
order that revealed doctrines might remain intact for ever and that
they might be brought easily and safely to the knowledge of men, as
that authority is exercised daily by the Roman Pontiff and the Bishops
in communion with him and has for its office—in case it is necessary to
resist more vigorously the errors and attacks of heretics or explain more
clearly and deeply the articles of the sacred doctrine and impress them
upon the minds of the faithful—to proceed at the proper times to make
definitions either by solemn rites or decrees. However, in the use of

this extraordinary teaching authority—*magisterium*—nothing newly discovered is introduced nor is anything new added to the sum of those truths which are at least implicitly—*saltem implicite*—contained in the deposit of Revelation, divinely handed down to the Church, but those things are declared which perhaps had seemed to many obscure or those things ordered to be held which by some had been regarded as matter of controversy.

Therefore, Venerable Brethren, it is evident why this Apostolic See has never allowed its own to take part in the meetings of non-Catholics, for the union of Christians can hardly be promoted otherwise than by promoting the return of the dissidents to Christ's one true Church, inasmuch as in the past they unhappily revolted—*descivere*—from her, yea Christ's one true Church,—We say,—which is clearly manifest—*conspicuam*—to all and by the will of her Author will so remain forever as He himself instituted it for our common salvation. For during the lapse of the centuries Christ's mystical Bride has never been contaminated nor can she be contaminated, as was said by Cyprian, 'Christ's Bride can never be adulterated; she is incorrupt and modest. She knows one dwelling and in chaste modesty guards the sanctity of one bed-chamber,' *de cath. eccl. unitate*, 6. And the same holy Martyr with good reason marvelled greatly that any one could possibly believe that 'this unity, proceeding from the divine foundation and knit together by the heavenly sacraments might be rent in the church and torn apart by divorce through wills in collision.' For, since Christ's mystical body, that is the Church, is one being compacted together and conjoined, Eph. iv, 16, as is for example the physical body, I Cor. xii, 12, one speaks indiscreetly and foolishly who says that the mystical body can be made up of disjoined and scattered members. Whosoever, therefore, is not integrally connected with it—*copulatur*—is not a member of it nor is he joined with Christ, the head. Cp. Eph. v, 30; i, 22.

And, indeed, in this one Church of Christ there is no one and no one will continue to be except that, by giving his obedience, he acknowledges and accepts the authority and power of Peter and his legitimate successors. Did the ancestors of those who are ensnared in the errors of Photius and the modernists—*novatorum*—obey the Bishop of Rome, the supreme Pastor of souls? Alas, the sons left the paternal house but it did not on that account fall to pieces and perish, for it was upheld

by God's perpetual and guardian care. Therefore, let them return to
the common Father who forgetting the unjust injuries done to the Apostolic See, will accept them most affectionately. For if, as they continually are saying, they wish to be with Us and with ours, why do they not
hasten to enter the Church, 'the mother and teacher of all Christ's
faithful,'—*Later. Counc.* IV, c 5. Let them also hear Lactantius crying
out, 'The Catholic Church is that alone which preserves the true worship. This is the font of truth, the house of the Faith, this the temple
of God. If any one enter not therein or if any one go out therefrom, he
is a stranger to the hope of life and salvation—*a spe vitae ac salutis
alienus.* No one should deceive himself with obstinate disputings. For
here it is a question of life and salvation which are hopelessly lost unless
they are dealt with advisedly and carefully.'—*Div. Instt.* lv, 30 11–12.

Let, therefore, the separated children draw nigh to the Apostolic See,
set up in the City which Peter and Paul, the Princes of the Apostles,
consecrated with their blood; to that See, We say, which is 'the root
and matrix of the Catholic Church,' S. Cyprian, *ep.* 48 *ad Cor.*, not
with the purpose and the hope that 'the Church of the living God, the
pillar and ground of the truth,' I Tim. iii, 15, will cast away the integrity
of the faith and tolerate their errors, but, on the contrary, that they
submit themselves to its teaching and government. Would that it were
Our happy lot to do that which so many of Our predecessors could not
do, namely, embrace with fatherly affection those whose lamentable
separation from Us We now bewail. Would that God Our Saviour,
'Who will have all men to be saved and to come to the knowledge of
the truth,' I Tim. ii, 4, would hear Us when We humbly beg that He
would deign to recall to the Unity of the Church all who stray. In
this most important undertaking We ask and wish that others should
ask the interceder, Blessed Mary the Virgin, Mother of divine grace,
Victor over all heresies and Help of Christians, that she may implore
for Us the speedy coming of the much hoped for day, when all men shall
hear the voice of her divine Son—'careful to keep the unity of the
Spirit in the bond of peace,' Eph. iv, 3.

You, Venerable Brethren, understand how much this question is on
Our mind and We desire that Our children should also know it, not only
those who belong to the Catholic world, but also those who are separated
from Us. If these latter will humbly beg light from heaven, there is no

doubt but that they will recognize the one true Church of Jesus Christ and will, at last, enter it and be united with Us in perfect love. Awaiting this event and as a sign of divine function and a pledge of Our paternal good will, We impart most affectionately to you, Venerable Brethren, and to your clergy and people, the apostolic benediction.

Given at Rome, at Saint Peter's, on the 6th day of January, on the Feast of the Epiphany of Jesus Christ Our Lord in the year 1928 and the sixth year of Our Pontificate.[1]

PIUS PP. XI.

NOTE

PIUS XI. AND THE RUSSIAN CHRISTIANS.

AN URGENT appeal was made by Pius XI., dated February 2, 1930, calling for prayer and relief for the oppressed Christians under the Soviet government. The document lacks, as it would seem, the marks commonly, if not always, regarded as essential for a papal utterance to be infallible. Nevertheless, the attitude taken by the Roman pontiff in the critical religious crisis in Russia and the claims he makes for the Roman Church render the document of more than usual importance.

After referring to Benedict XV.'s interest in the people of Russia and the commission on the Russian conditions which he had himself appointed, Pius appealed to the Russian government "to respect conscience, the freedom of worship and the goods of the Church." Again setting forth acts of "terrible persecution" going on to the extent of a formal demand on the part of the Soviet government that the people proceed to "apostasy and the hatred of God," he announced a "mass of expiation, propitiation and reparation in the basilica of St. Peter over the tomb of the Prince of the Apostles for Our most beloved Russian people—*Nostro dilettissimo popolo russo*." He called upon the Russians to return "to the one fold of Our one Saviour and Liberator, the Lord Jesus Christ," commended them anew to "the sweet thaumaturge of

---

[1] In his scarcely less important encyclical on the 'Christian Education of Youth' issued in Italian, Dec. 31, 1929, Pius XI. claimed as the Church's supreme right the authority to lay down the rules of education and conduct education. He also forbade anew training in mixed schools and also the coeducation of the sexes.

Lisieux, St. Thérèse of the Child Jesus," and implored further on their behalf the help of "the most holy and immaculate Virgin Mary, Mother of God, her most chaste spouse and patron of the Church Universal, St. Joseph, and the special protectors of the Russians, St. John the Baptist, St. Nicholas, St. Basil, St. Chrysostom and Saints Cyril and Methodius."

On the day appointed, March 19, 1930, which was the Feast of St. Joseph, the pontiff officiated at mass in the midst of an overflowing throng. A handbill, distributed to the worshippers and spectators as they passed from the portico of St. Peter's to the body of the church, contained on the one side the text of the papal appeal and the prayer to St. Thérèse which the pope had issued, with the promise of 300 days of indulgence for all repeating it for a month. Calling upon the saint to help "our brother Russians, the victims of a long and cruel persecution," the prayer further besought her to bring about "the return of the noble people to the one fold which Christ's most beloved heart intrusted to the care of St. Peter alone and his successors, that they might at last have the joy, in communion with the Catholic Church, of praising the Father, Son and Holy Ghost."

On the reverse side of the handbill under the caption, "The Catholic Church and Russian 'Orthodoxy'—*La Chiesa cattolica e la 'orthodossia' russa,*" it was affirmed that, while the National Russian Church "pretends to call itself orthodox, it is heterodox, the only orthodox Church being the Catholic Apostolic Roman Church."

INDEX TO VOL. II.

A.

Absolution, sacerdotal, 105, 113, 141, 143, 151, 153, 167, 387.

Adoption, 91.

Adoration, 131, 137, 138, 430.

"Americanism," 610.

Anathema, 27, 60, 73, 82, 85, 86, 87, 110, etc., etc., 169, 195, 205, 252, 253, 254, 260, 262, 266, 271.

Angels, 297, 323; functions of, 294; classes, 297; guardian, 463; intercession of, 295, 409, 435.

Anglican Orders, 608.

Anglo-Catholics, 616.

Antichrist, 337, 481.

Apocrypha, 82, 435, 451, 546. See *Scriptures.*

Apollinarianism, condemned, 36, 62, 64, 69.

Apostolic Constitutions, 39.

Apostles' Creed, 13, 40, 45, 46, 47, 604.

Apostolic Succession, 189, 263, 411, 412, 548, 615, 622.

Arius, Creed of, 28, 61.

Athanasian Creed, 25, 66, 350, 603.

Athanasius, 72, 285, 288, 350, 354, 451, etc.

Attributes of God, 239, 286 sqq., 288, 459.

Attrition, 145, 146.

Augustine, 48, etc.; on infant salvation, 424; on the state, 556; on the services of the "Catholic Church," 572 sqq., 588.

B.

"Bad Priests," confer grace, 122, 154, 167, 178.

Baptism, water only, 425; necessary, 122, 425; trine immersion, 376, 450, 491; once only, 124, 371, 376, 493; by laymen, 377, 425; into the Holy Ghost, 39; for remission of sins, 34, 58, 59, 374; of repentance, 32, 38; necessary to salvation, 123, 423; heretical, 123; infant, 124, 174, 424; indelible mark, 427; sacrament of, 122, 143, 373, 423, 491.

Baptismal formula, 5; regeneration, 86, 87, 88, 91, 92, 142, 143, 174, 375, 377, 392, 420, 425, 491.

Basil, 64, 301, 306, 448, 449, 486, etc.

Beatitudes, 514–519.

Bellarmin, 548.

Bible Societies condemned, 218.

Bishops, appointed of God, 257; set by the Holy Ghost, 263, 411, 596; and the pope, 193, 226, 264; and the state, 220, 415; the church committed to bishops, 413; elected by synods, 414; confer grace, 192, 415; functions, 126, 189, 375, 412, 414, 501; above priests, 189, 192; cases reserved to, 168. See *Apostolic Succession.*

Boniface VIII, 230, 608.

Bonn, Theses of, 545.

Borromeo Encyclical, 611.

Briggs and Pius X, 609.

C.

Caesarea, Creed of, 61.

Caesar's and God's, 569.

Calvinists denounced, 402, 411, 440, 441.

Capernaitically, 428, 429.

Catechism, defined, 445; Orthodox Eastern, 445.

Cathedra Petri, 238, 261, 269, etc.; *aedis Petri,* 351; *sedis Petri,* 261, 269, 592.

Catholic and Apostolic Church, 38, 58, 59, 200, 288, 359, 433, 444.

Catholic and Apostolic Oriental Church, 275.

Catholic and Orthodox Church, 271, 279, 350.

Catholic Church, 29, 60, 80, 88, etc., etc., 198, 208, 238, 359, 402, 433, 443, 488, etc.

Catholics, 158, 252, 254, 594, 599, etc.; to take part in government, 594.

Catholic, doctrine, 110, 118, 136, 587; faith, 66, 70, 83, 96, 118, 211, 395, 598; flock, 257; name, 597; profession, 597; religion, 67, 232, 266, 595; sense, 237; teachers, 219; truth, 190, 238, 246; unity, 245; writers, 146; world, 599.

Chalcedon, Statement of, 62.

character indelibilis, 121, 189.

Children and the eucharist, 174, 175.

"Christians," "Christian people," 83, 105, 109, 116, 121, 132, 133, 153, 155, 159, 195, 205, 231, 270, 365, 375, 383, 483, 556, 593, 595; not all priests, 189; in "the first ages of the Church incorrupt," etc., 595.

Christianity, Christendom, 234, 372, 378, 566, etc.

Christian character, 175; doctrine, 83, 242; Europe, 575; faith, 596; institutions, 597; life, 159; name, 135, 592, 593, 594, 620; order, 569; philosophy, 551, 557, 574; religion, 173, 200, 211, 217, 236, 270, 572, 576; virtue, 593, 599; world, 235.

Christian Constitution of States, 555, 599.

Church, 13, 21, 79, 96, etc., 371, 402, 403, 410, etc., 563, 572, 589, 591, 594, 599; attributes of, 20, 256, 359–362, 410, 483, 490; authority of, 269, 364, 443, etc.; inspiration of, 417, 555, 563; spouse of Christ, 177, 234; the pillar and ground of the truth, 127, 364, 402, 625; our mother, 498, 593; mother and teacher of the nations, 237; author and perpetual guardian of personal and equal rights, 589; guardian of morals, 583; guide to heaven, 565, 567, 569; perfect in kind and right, 586; founded on Peter, 259; services to the world, 555, 573, 575, 589, 592, 595 sqq.; and the state, 219–227, 231, 555–600.

Church, of God, 82, 84, 129, 130, 134, etc.; of Christ, 127, 499, etc.; the Christian, 488; the Christian and Catholic, 231; the true Church of Christ, 217, 483, 625; Holy Church, 20, 21, 47, 48, 49, 123, 255, 256, 402, etc.; the Holy Catholic, 32, 39, 50, 174, 175, etc.; the Holy Catholic and Apostolic, 410, etc.; the One Holy and Apostolic, 34, 58, 59, 359, etc.; the Holy Catholic Apostolic Roman, "mother and mistress of all Churches," 207, 209, 239, 263; the Holy Roman, 78, 117, 162, 169, 170, 183, "mother and mistress of all Churches," 207; the Holy Roman and Universal Church, 117; the Occidental Roman Church, 351; the Roman, 78, 122, 163, 186, 261, "the mother and mistress of all Churches," 209, 239, 263; Holy Mother, 138, 173, 181, 207, 237, 240, 250, etc.; the Occidental Roman, 351; the Oriental, 401, 411; the Oriental Catholic, 431; Orthodox and Catholic, 284; the Primitive, 162; the Universal—*universa*—, 132, 147, 151, 221, 258, 262, etc.; —*universalis*—, 194, 206, 262, 264; the

Universal Church of God, 258; the Militant, 234, 260, etc.; the Orthodox, 472, 485; the whole, 251, 258.

Churches, Catholic, 402, 403, 440; Oriental, 492; of the East, 489; of Jerusalem, "mother and first of all Churches," 361, 362; of Old and New Rome, 360, 362; of Russia, 489. See *Particular Churches.*

Clement of Rome, 413; VII, 608; XI, 608.

Communion, yearly, 138.

Concordats, 223, 566, 569.

Concupiscence, 38, 88.

Condignity, 547.

Confession, priestly, 133, 139, 143, 147, 163, 164, 165, 166, 368, 391, 549; yearly, 151.

Confirmation, 126, 378, 421, 494.

Conferring the sacraments, 121, 122.

Conscience, 578, 584.

Consensus, of the Catholic Church, 96; of the Church, 84, 271.

consensus patrum, 83, 184, 188, 200, 242.

Constantinople, Second council of falsified, 351; Creed of, 72.

Consubstantiality of the Son, 33, 36, 57, 66, 287, 312, 401; of the Spirit, 57, 66, 287, 348.

continere et conferre, 120, 422, etc.

Councils, 73, 84, 198, 200, 202, 204, 205, 209, 219, 222, 234, 239, 262, 265, 268, 277, 279, 293, 300, 364, 406, 463, 490; seven, 451; of Ephesus, 73; Florence, 262, 267; Lyons, 267; Constantinople, 351. See *Nice, Trent.*

Creation, 13, 15, 17, 19, 21, 26, 29, 32, 33, 35, 50, 57, 59, 239, 280, 291, 406 sq.

Cross, sign of, 332, 450, 493; venerated, 436.

Cup, 130, 175. See *sub utraque specie.*

Cyprian, 20, 624.

Cyril of Jerusalem, 31, 281, 322, 331, 438, 446, 451, 486, 493, etc.

D.

Damascus, John of, 291, 294, 305, 319, 330, 383, 413, 487, 498, 552, 554, etc.

Dead, prayers for. See *Suffrages.*

Decalogue, 521, 523, etc.

Deity of Christ, 23, 26, 28, 30, 31, 33, 35, 39, 47, 57, 60, 62, 63, 67, 282, 312, 317, etc. See *Consubstantial.*

Deposit of the Faith, 269, 614, 621, 624.

Descent into Hell, 46, 49, 69, 336, 347, 477.

Desire of the sacrament, 105.

Dionysius, 296, 297, etc.

Döllinger, 546, 551, 554.

Dositheus, Confession of, 401.
Dulia, 436.

E.

Ecclesiastical precepts, 198, 220, 365, 578.
Encyclicals of Boniface VIII, Gregory XVI,
584, 605; Leo XIII, 555, 610; Pius IX,
211, 213; Pius X, 610, 613; Pius XI, 616.
England, Church of, 548; orders of, 610.
Ephesus, Council of, 73.
Epiphanius, 33, 35.
Episcopate. See Bishops, Order.
Eucharist, 126, 129, 136, 350, 427, 495,
622; once yearly, 138; four times yearly
or every month, 498. See Sacraments,
Transubstantiation.
Eusebius of Caesarea, 29.
Eutyches, 62, 65, 67, 69.
ex cathedra, 270.
Evolution, 251, 613, 614, 615.
Exorcism, 492.
Extreme unction, 159, 169, 394, 414, 421,
502.

F.

Faith and the Faith, 113, 116, 242, 243,
253, 277, 417 sqq., 614, 615, 616, 621;
the gift of God, 243, 244; alone not sufficient, 101, 112, 113, 114, 416, 418, 445;
necessary to salvation, 410; and reason,
247, 254; the Christian, 245, 270, 496;
the Catholic, 210, 211, 214, 225, 234,
244, 254, 420; Catholic and Apostolic,
439. See Justification.
Faithful, the, 167, 194, 212, 249.
Fasting, Fast Days, 167, 365, 370, 391, 441,
530, 531.
Fathers, the, 63, 78, 79, 80, 84, 153, 157,
159, 162, 171, 174, 181, 183, 184, 188,
194, 198, 269, etc., 566.
filioque, 350, 351, 532, 545.
Flesh, Resurrection of the, 14, 17, 20, 29,
32, 39, 46, 47, 48, 49, 50, 69; of the body,
48, 69, 396, 503.
Florence, Council of, 262, 267.
Forgiveness, 39, 47, 48, 50, 58, 59, 87, 98,
105, 169, 187. See Absolution, Power of
the Keys, Priesthood.
Free Will, Liberty, 92, 111, 217, 307, 419,
576, 578, 582, 588, 589, 597.
Fundamental Articles, 623.

G.

Good Works, 96, 99, 100, 107, 112, 114,
115, 116, 117, 156, 168, 263, 275, 418,
445, 519 sqq., 547. See Justification.

Grace, prevenient, 92, 93, 110, 404; conferred, 120, 169, 192. See Sacrament.
Gregory, of Nazianzen, 288, 350, 487, etc.;
Thaumaturgus, 24; the Great, 264; VII,
607; XVI, 584.

H.

Hades, 477, 589, 597.
Head of the Church, the pope, 260, 261;
Christ, 363, 484, 485; "no mortal," 402,
404, 410, 411, 432, 443.
Hecker, 610.
Hell, 14, 15, 16, etc.; names of, 347, 477;
fear of, 112.
Heresies, Heretics, 27, 77, 78, 195, 196, 423,
439; heretical pravity, 255; books, 369.
Holy Mother Church, 83, 138, 242, 498.
Holy Roman Church, 78, 267. See Church.
Holy Spirit, 6, 13, 15, 18, 20, 21, 23, 27,
29, 30, 31, 32, 39, 47, 61, 79, 84, 119, etc.;
deity of, 23, 25, 27, 31, 33, 38, 57, 66
sqq., 211, 348 sqq., 461; spouse of Christ,
234, 250; charisms of, 352 sqq.; fruits of,
207, 358. See filioque.
homoousia, 60, 62, 72.
hyperdulia, 435 sq.

I.

Ignatius, 11.
Images, 201, 204, 435, 438, 527.
Immaculate Conception, 88, 115, 211, 408,
471, 549, 623. See Mary.
Immersion, time, 425, 491.
immortale Dei, 555 sq.
Incarnation, 12, 13, 15, 16, 18, 23, 26, 31,
33, 37, 57, 59, 60, 61, 62, 68, 86, 87, etc.,
319, 408, 471, etc.
Indulgences, 205, 206, 209, 220, 433, 549.
Infallibility, 266, 269, 270, 593, 605, 613,
621, 623.
Infants, baptism of necessary to salvation,
86, 87, 174, 423, 424, 492. Augustine
quoted on, 424.
Intention, 121.
Irenaeus, 12, 14, 448.

J.

James, bishop of Jerusalem, 413.
Jansenist bishops, excommunicated, 551.
Jeremiah I, 9, 607.
Jerusalem, creed of, 61; church of, 361,
362; synodical decrees, 401.
Justification, 89, 91, 94, 97, 110, 115, 275,
410, 418, etc.

K.

Keys, power of, 140, 142, 147, 151, 157,
164, 167, 169, 187, 260, 549, 564, 565.

L.

Lactantius on the Church, 625.
Lamentabili, 611, 614.
Last Judgment, 7, 15, 18, 20, 27, 38, 47, 69, 480.
Lateran Council, fourth, 151, 166.
latria, 131, 138, 430, 437, 438.
Leo III, 351.
Leo XIII, encyclical, 555–600; on Anglican orders, 608, 610,•619.
Liberties, 575, 587, 588, 592.
Lucian, 25.
Luther, Lutheranism, 374, 428, 611.
Lyons, Council of, 267.

M.

Magisterium of the Church, 236, 246, 254, 264, 618, 623, 624; of the Holy Spirit, 403.
Manning, Cardinal, 601.
Marriage, 193, 195, 196, 231, 293, 372, 393, 501, and the state, 231, 671.
Mary, 11; blessed, 115; virgin, 13, 15, 17, 18, 19, 23, 26, 34, 36, 46, 47, 50, 57, 63; holy, 39; *semper virgo*, 36, 320, 366, 408, 471; conceived without labor, 408; Immaculate Conception, 211; victor over heresies, 625. See *Mother of God*.
Mass, 176, sacrifice of, 177, 179, 430, 432; propitiatory, 179, 185, 385, 430, 496; for living and dead, 180, 199, 208, 429, 433, 550.
Materialism, 227.
Matthew, XVI, 18; 78, 258, 607.
Mercier, Cardinal, 616.
Merit, 104, 108, 116, 117. See *Good Works*.
Military service, 221.
Miracles, 19, 244, 253, 455, 483.
Mixed jurisdiction, 579, 586.
Modern progress, and the pope, 216, 233, 589.
"Modernism," 611, 613, 615.
Mogilas, Peter, 275.
Monothelites, 72.
Mopsvestia, Theodore of, 5.
Mortal and venial sins, 106, 116, 117, 128, 139, 140, 148, 167, etc.
Mother of God, 62, 63, 64, 88, 201, 209, 211, 320, 323, 366, 408, 435, 436, 472; of the divine Word, 407, 409, 435; worship of, 64, 320, 321, 409, 435.
Mysteries, 377 sqq., 490 sqq. See *Sacraments*.
Mystical body, 235.

N.

Nathaniel, confession of, 4.
Natural religion, 215, 227, 240, 252, 447, 561, 574.
Nestorianism, 62, 65, 67 sq.
Nicene Creed, 35, 57, 78, 79, 132, 202, 207, 279, 280 sqq., 312 sqq., 456 sqq. and the Holy Spirit, 350.
Novatian, 21, 141.

O.

Oath of priests, 207, 210, 229; against "Modernism," 613.
Old Catholics, 545; bishops of, excommunicated, 551.
Order, 42, 186; seven orders, 187; confers grace, 188, 191, 197; gives an indelible mark, 192; annuls marriage, 230; not conferred by the people, 192, 386, 421, 501. See *Apostolic Succession; Sacraments*.
ordines minores, 188, 386.
Original sin,.83, 85, 90, 301, 304, 375, 407, 419, 425; washed away by baptism, 85, 87, 308 sq., 375, 425.
Origen, 21, 345.
Orthodox Confession, 213.

P.

Pantheism, 213.
Particular Churches, 206, 222, 259, 261, 360, 365, 485.
pascendi gregis, 611, 614
Patriarchs, 364, 366, 369, 490.
Pelagians, 73, 92, 111.
Penance, 105, 113, 116, 140 sqq., 390, 421, 500; second plank, 163.
Perseverance of saints, 103, 114, 115, 116, 269.
Peter, confession of, 4; prince of the Apostles, 209, 257, 260, 266, 267; primacy, 261; visible head of the Church Militant, 260; Rock, 259, 260, 261, 607. See 363; pillar of the faith and foundation of the Catholic Church, 266; founder of the see of Rome, 261; his successors, 260 sqq., 413. See *cathedra Petri*.
Philosophy, 216, 566, 574, 583.
Pius IV, 210, 608, 613.
Pius V, 607.
Pius IX, 210, 213, 234, 585.
Pius X, 609, 611; XI, 612, 616, 626.
Polygamy, 195.
Pope, Peter's successor, 261, 267, etc.; vicar of Christ, 209, 262, 267, 620, etc.; authority, 77, 79, 209, 220, 231, 262, 263,

265, 266, 269, 292, 294, 597, 599; Head of the Church, 235, 258, 261, 262, 264, 265, 267, 287, 564, 566, 606. (See, 363, 410); father and teacher of all Christians, 262, 267; "supreme judge of the faithful,". 265; primacy of, 258, 260; over the "whole world," 262; above œcumenical councils, 265; announces no new doctrine, 269; faith and salvation lost by denying his jurisdiction, 263; anathema upon those denying his primacy or infallibility, 259, 262, 266, 271.

Popular rule condemned, 577, 581.

Prayer, 369, 506 sqq., 622.

Predestination, 103, 113, 114, 305, 307, 310, 403, 426, 464.

Priesthood, instituted by Christ, 187; all Christians not of, 189, 191; offers sacrifice, 177, 184, 186; a hierarchy, 189, 192, 387, 490. See *Order,* 191 sqq.

Protestantism, condemned, 217, 611, 612, 620, 624, 625, 626.

Protestant Reformation, the cause of revolutions, etc., 576.

Public schools, condemned, 224, 580.

Purgatory, 117, 198, 199, 209, 345, 432.

R.

Rationalism, 215, 597.

Reason and faith, 214, 215, 217, 247, 253.

Reformation of manners, 77.

Relics, 200, 209, 435 sqq., 527.

Religion, the first duty of, 561; the Catholic Church defines "the true religion," 219; it is easily understood; different forms of condemned, 232, 562, 587.

Reservation of the sacrament, 132, 138.

Reserved cases, 153, 168.

Rock, the, Peter, 260, 261, etc.; Christ, 363.

Roman Church, 610; primacy of, 267. See under *Church.*

Rufinus, 49, 50.

Rule of Faith, 13–19; of Truth, 21.

Ryan and Millar, 555.

S.

Sacraments, the seven instituted by Christ, 119, 207, 374, 420, 490; fixed in 12th century, 547; defined, 118, 374, 490; necessary to salvation, 120; contain and confer grace, 120–122, 375, 490.

Sacrarium, 132, 138.

Saints, invocation and worship of, 180, 184, 199, 200, 201, 211, 409, 436, 438, 622;

apparitions of, 486, 551; activity on earth, 487.

Salvation, wrought by the Incarnation, 30, 33, 36, 57, 62; to those who believe in Christ, 15; who believe "rightly," 68, 69; who are in the "true Church of Christ," 217, 605, 625; who keep the "rule of Faith," 266; to make known the chief end of the Church, 565; by obedience to the pope, 607, 624.

Scriptures, the, 15, 18, 21, 22, 27, 28, 34, 59; defined, 81, 238, 241, 435, 451; from God, 373, 412; dictated by Christ or the Holy Spirit, 80, 241, 242; and tradition, 80, 241, 244; in translation, 80, 546; interpretation of, 83, 207, 242, 402; reading of, 82, 434, 454; anathema on those not receiving all their parts, 253; and tradition, 80, 187, 241, 244, 448. See *Traditions.*

Second Coming 13, 17, 20, 31, 32, 33, 57, 60, 337, 479.

Seven orders, 187, 389.

Sirach, Book of quoted, 285, 302.

Sixtus IV, 88.

Socialism, 218.

Soul and body illustrates Church and State, 568.

State and Church, the State from God, 558; not exempt from the Church's jurisdiction, 227; its first duty, 562 sq.; different forms of government, 559, 581, 598; popular government, 577, 581; state only well regulated with religion, 574 sq., 583; may not suppress religious orders or annul concordats, 223, 226; should acknowledge the Church, 566 sq.; once did, 561 sq., 578 sq.; with signal blessings, 561 sq., 578, 579; proper interrelation, 557 sqq.; the state and marriage, ecclesiastical property, courts and schools, 220, 225, 231, 578, 580; the Church and insurrection, 228, 560; separation of Church and State, 218, 220, 224, 227, 579, 584, 607.

sub utraque specie, 130, 171, 173, 174, 208.

Suffrages, 198, 269, 343, 344, 370, 414, 429, 432, 433, 550.

Supererogation. See *Good Works.*

Swords, the two, 606.

Syllabus of Errors, 213, 595, 601.

T.

Temporal power, 219, 220, 225, 231, 232, 580, 606.

Tertullian, 16, 413.

Theophylact, 343.
thesaurus meritorum, 547.
Thomas Aquinas, 612.
Thomas, Confession of, 4.
Tradition, 14, 15, 82, 448, 449, 450, 548;
   Apostolic, 160, 180, 181, 188, 269, 614,
   615, 622; Apostolic and Ecclesiastical,
   207; of the Catholic Church, 187; of the
   universal Church, 194; unwritten, 80,
   241, etc.
Transubstantiation, 126, 129, 130, 136, 208,
   336, 380, 382, 427, 428, 431, 495, 497, 622.
Trent, Canons of, 77; œcumenical synod of,
   79; curse upon repudiating, 118; fathers
   of, 236, etc.
Trinity, 24, 25, 27, 30, 36, 66, 79, 280, 284,
   406, 461, etc.
Tritheism, 67.

U.

Unam sanctam, 608.
United States, 601.
Unity, Church, 616 sqq., 624.

V.

Vatican Decrees, 234; Council, 623.
Vows, 124, 226.
Vulgar tongue, and Bible, 82, 183, 186, 546,
   548.
Vulgate, authority of, 82, 241.

W.

Water and wine at the eucharist, 182, 186
Worship, 233, 365, 581; different kinds, 591
   non-Catholic patiently borne with by
   states, 581. See *Adoration, Saints*.